NATIVE WINE GRAPES of ITALY

The publisher gratefully acknowledges the generous support of the General Endowment Fund of the University of California Press Foundation.

The publisher also gratefully acknowledges the generous support of the Educated Palates Circle of the University of California Press Foundation, whose members are

Elizabeth and David Birka-White

Judith and Kim Maxwell

James and Carlin Naify

Ramsay Family Foundation

Patricia and David Schwartz

Meryl and Robert Selig

Peter and Chinami Stern

NATIVE WINE GRAPES of ITALY

Ian D'Agata

UNIVERSITY OF CALIFORNIA PRESS
Berkeley   Los Angeles   London

University of California Press, one of the most distinguished university presses in the United States, enriches lives around the world by advancing scholarship in the humanities, social sciences, and natural sciences. Its activities are supported by the UC Press Foundation and by philanthropic contributions from individuals and institutions. For more information, visit www.ucpress.edu.

University of California Press
Berkeley and Los Angeles, California

University of California Press, Ltd.
London, England

© 2014 by The Regents of the University of California

Library of Congress Cataloging-in-Publication Data

D'Agata, Ian.
 Native wine grapes of Italy / Ian D'Agata.
   p. cm.
 Includes bibliographical references and index.
 ISBN 978-0-520-27226-2 (cloth: alk. paper)
 ISBN 978-0-520-95705-3 (ebook)
  1. Grapes—Varieties—Italy. 2. Wine and wine making—Italy. I. Title.
 SB398.28.D34 2014
 634.80945—dc23

2013041569

Manufactured in the United States of America
23 22 21 20 19 18 17 16 15 14
10 9 8 7 6 5 4 3 2 1

The paper used in this publication meets the minimum requirements of ANSI/NISO Z39.48–1992 (R 2002) (*Permanence of Paper*).

CONTENTS

Preface   vii

Map of Italy's Wine Regions   xiii

Native Grapes by Region   xiv

Introduction: Understanding "Native" and Classifying Grape Varieties   1

PART I   Grape Varieties: What, Where, When, Why, and How

1   Ampelology: The Art and Science of Grape Variety Identification   15

2   The Origin of Viticulture and a Brief History of Italy's Grape Varieties   25

PART II   Italy's Native and Traditional Grape Varieties and Wines

3   Grape Groups and Families   49

4   Major Native and Traditional Grape Varieties   158

5   Little-Known Native and Traditional Grape Varieties   480

6   Crossings   538

Appendix   549

Glossary   567

Bibliography   571

General Index   593

Index of Grape Varieties   611

PREFACE

I hold a deep-rooted passion for the native grapes and wines of Italy. Though I am also a great fan of Riesling, Pinot Nero, Merlot, and proper Cabernet Franc (how can any wine lover not be?), it is wines made with Italy's native grapes I would want with me if banished to a desert island (given that Gwyneth Paltrow is already taken).

I have always been fascinated by the rich diversity of Italy's innumerable grape varieties. In 2001 I wrote the first series of detailed articles on a number of Italy's native grapes for *Porthos,* then a mainstream Italian wine magazine. I followed this up by doing the same for the *Gambero Rosso* magazine in 2002 and 2003, which led to the publication that year of the first guidebook ever specifically devoted to Italian native grapes and wines. Every time I catch up with Marco Sabellico, currently the elder curator of *Gambero Rosso*'s annual wine guide, our memories invariably drift back to what at the time seemed like an infinite string of late summer nights, a desperate and ultimately successful attempt at meeting our deadline. Whereas as recently as 2000 practically nobody in Italy ever wrote of wines in terms of native and international grapes, there are now myriad books and websites devoted to these subjects.

I now write about the world's many wonderful wines for Stephen Tanzer and his prestigious *International Wine Cellar,* and more recently, for the British wine magazine *Decanter.* However, I still champion native grapes and wines, and the people who have devoted their lives to them. I am enthralled with native grapes, each one's long-standing relationship with its local geology and climate, and how each one is expressed in unique wines. An added plus is the cultural bond these grapes have established with local people, territories, and traditions. Unfortunately, when I started out, little was known about these grapes and virtually nothing was being written about them; worse still, many were at risk of extinction. Given my love for drawing and my medical background (including a couple of years of bench research, spent doing western blots and learning polymerase chain reaction tests, the latter a technique also used for grapevine identification), I was naturally attracted to ampelology, the science that studies and identifies grape varieties. Over the years, I always paid more attention to the grapes people were using, and obsessed a great deal less than most about, for example, the type of oak or yeasts they used. Already then, I believed that understanding single grape varieties (as well as the relationships that different varieties have with each other) inevitably leads to a better understanding of the wines made from those varieties. Still today, I feel the need to broadcast and promote the as yet untapped potential of native grapes and wines: and not just Italy's, for that matter.

The book you hold in your hands is the summa of close to thirty years spent in the company of wine, and more pertinently, thirteen years of research, vineyard walks, and interviews especially devoted to the native grapes and wines of Italy. It is intended as both an academic text and a practical guide to the rich grape biodiversity that is Italy—and not just to the rich and famous jet set of Sangiovese or Nebbiolo, but also to Bellone, Centesimino, Rossese di Dolceacqua, and many others. This book is not for those who cannot manage without one-hundred-point scores, "inky-black hues," "sexy smokiness," "mouthcoating concentration," and all the rest of it. It will be appreciated even less by those who regard native grapes as a marketing ploy at best, or a nuisance at worst. No, this book is for all who realize that wine is not a soft drink, industrially made and replicable ad nauseam independently of its ties to the land, the history, the social context, and the people who live and make it. Most of all, it is for those who understand that wine cannot and should not be viewed independently of the grape varieties used to make it.

It is not my intention to give the impression that native grapes are better than international ones, or that traditionally made wines are more interesting than those made with an eye to modern tastes. There is no right or wrong way to enjoy wine, and each one of us will appreciate the aspect of wine that intrigues us most. Wine allows all of us to learn about new people and places, and I have always found that Italy's native grapes are a great way to gain a deeper understanding and appreciation of the sometimes crazy but always wonderful country that Italy is. Wine is nothing more and nothing less than a journey of discovery, and native grapes have always been one of my most trusted guides. To take the road less traveled does make all the difference: for me, it has been a long and at times trying experience, but mostly fun, and always instructive. While turning the pages of this book, my hope is you will enjoy the ride as much as I have.

HOW TO USE THIS BOOK

This book describes all the native varieties used to make wine in commercially significant volumes in Italy as of the date of writing. I will analyze why some grapes are better characterized than others. Historical, viticultural, and enological data illustrating the quality of the grapes and the wines (clones, rootstocks, soils, fermentation temperatures) and university studies documenting parentage and genetic makeup have been included. This is not possible for every grape, because of the paucity of scientific information on many of Italy's native varieties. In these cases, I have relied on my own years of observation and the experience and memory of older farmers and producers who have been the secret defenders of many an Italian native variety. Unburdened by the need to sell their wines—made mainly for personal consumption—their memories and comments are more useful than those of some consultant winemakers and producers plugging better known and easier to work with varieties.

There are two main sections to this book. Part I is an introduction to wine grapes: how they are classified and identified, their history, and why a variety-based approach to wine may not be a bad idea. The great potential of Italy's native grapes and wines and some worrisome trends are also analyzed, and a region by region list of varieties is provided.

Part II is devoted to describing about five hundred native grape varieties of Italy, all those for which either accurate DNA test results or, for less common cultivars, sufficient anecdotal, historic, viticultural, and enologic data are available. Truly monovarietal wines (not blends including other grapes) made from these varieties are listed and briefly described; many are on sale in and outside Italy. The best producers to look for are also listed.

Writing Grape and Wine Names: The Right Name for Each Variety

The 2004 International Code for Nomenclature of Cultivated Plants stipulates that grape variety names be written in normal block letters, with the first letter capitalized and the name placed between single quotation marks: for example, 'Chardonnay' or 'Vermentino' (Brickell, Baum, Hetterscheid, Leslie, McNeill, Trehane, et al. 2004). Writing wine grape names in this way is typical of academic journals, and some books too. However, in most—though not all—wine texts, authors capitalize grape variety names and omit quotation marks. Interestingly, José Vouillamoz and Giulio Moriondo, in their recent and thoroughly excellent book *Origine des cépages valaisans et valdôtains*, chose to use the more scholarly, and accurate, approach, and clearly state that this is the way grape names ought to be written. One of Italy's most famous grape wine scientists, Attilio Scienza of the University of Milan, confirms that the correct approach is to place grape variety names in quotation marks, or alternatively, to omit the marks but use italics. Nevertheless, as this approach is unfamiliar to the wine-loving public, and as it is never used by mainstream wine writers and wine magazines, I shall resort to writing grape variety names as most everyone else writing about wine today does.

Instead, names referring to general grape groups or families are written in italics, with the first initial capitalized, and without quotation marks: for example, the *Greco*s or the *Trebbiano* family. Wines that have the same name as the cultivar are written in normal block letters, but are not capitalized. Thus, sangiovese refers to the wine, while Sangiovese refers to the grape, though most of the time I'll just write Sangiovese wine. When the wine name is an official one, such as a *Denominazione di Origine Controllata* (DOC), then it will be capitalized: for example, Sangiovese di Romagna. As some Italian wines carry the name of a specific town or place, their names are capitalized. For example, Barolo or Soave, which are the names of two towns as well as of two wines.

I always call Italian native grape varieties by the name most commonly used in Italian; thus, names in dialects or other languages are listed among synonyms or aliases, even when the latter are more frequently used in local production zones. Therefore, I will always write Pinot Nero not Pinot Noir, and Scimiscia' not Cimixia. Variety entries are listed in alphabetical order. Similarly named varieties (for example, Greco Giallo or Greco Nero) are grouped together with all others sporting similar names (for example, the *Greco* group), though we now know some of these varieties to be unrelated. Whenever genetic tests have clarified that similarly named varieties are unrelated, I will make that explicit.

For wine producers, I use the simplest but most recognizable names. Though this may not be technically exact, it allows you to readily identify wines so that you may find and buy them. For instance, rather than list Fattoria di Felsina, I list Felsina; I list Frescobaldi, as opposed to Marchese de' Frescobaldi. Since people tend to fasten on the name most prominently visible on the label, these are very likely the names you and your wine store clerk will go by.

Finally, as some of the terms in this book can prove difficult for those who are neither wine experts nor have scientific backgrounds, a glossary of terms in the back of the book will, I hope, shed light on some of the issues discussed.

Traditional and International Varieties

This book does not discuss obvious international varieties such as Pinot Nero or Gewürztraminer, but it does tackle varieties that have been traditional to specific parts of Italy for hundreds of years and are integral to wines considered archetypal of a region's production. I offer more precise definitions of "international" and "traditional" grape varieties in the Introduction. Examples include Sardinia's Cannonao (called Alicante, Granaccia, Guarnaccia, and Tai or Tocai Rosso elsewhere in Italy), better known in the rest of the world as Grenache, and its Carignano, better known by English- and French-speaking wine lovers as Carignan. These two are traditional Italian grapes: indeed, there are hardly grapes and wines more traditional of Sardinia.

Gewürztraminer is most commonly associated with Alsace in France, where centuries ago the mutation turning the nonaromatic Traminer variety (native to the Alto Adige town of Termeno or Tramin that gave it its name) into the spicy variant called Gewürztraminer probably occurred. In fact, the German prefix "gewürz" means spicy or aromatic. Though a lot of Gewürztraminer is grown in Italy's Alto Adige (and to a much lesser extent in nearby Friuli Venezia Giulia and Trentino), it is neither native nor traditional to Italy; at best it is a traditional variety of Alto Adige, which only became part of Italy in 1917, after World War I. For the same reason, even though there are also significant plantings of Sylvaner, Kerner, and Müller-Thurgau in Alto Adige, we can neither consider them native nor traditional of Italy. At least, not yet.

Families and Groups, Major Varieties, Less-Known Varieties, and Crossings

To make the book easier to read, and to give readers a quick understanding of the relative importance of each native grape variety, I have broken down the rest of Italy's native and traditional cultivars into four chapters: families and groups, major varieties, less-known varieties, and crossings. All related grapes, or those sporting similar names, are placed in chapter 3; chapter 4 is devoted to Italy's most important grapes, such as Nebbiolo and Sangiovese; chapter 5 deals with the country's many less-known varieties (some of which are very important locally); and finally, chapter 6 is devoted to the topic of hybrids and especially crossings, as hybrid grapes are not common in Italy.

The "major" varieties not only account for many of Italy's best-known wines, but also are usually produced by more than one high-quality estate. In most cases the wines have a minimum total production of three thousand bottles a year. For each cultivar, a short list of estates making the best wines (and the name of each wine) is also included. I have listed those wines that are not only faithful to the variety, but may also, it is to be hoped, be easily found in stores outside Italy. Please note that in the context of this book, I will use the term "pure" wines only for "monovarietal" wines, made with 100 percent of the cultivar. I have gone to great lengths over the last thirteen years to ferret out truly monovarietal wines, and report only on those, for it is my belief that a wine made with 30 percent or 40 percent of a specific cultivar neither speaks of that variety nor should be used as an example of what that native grape variety is about. "Monovarietal" refers to a wine, while "variety" refers to a single kind of grape. So the Chardonnay grape is not a varietal, but a variety.

You will notice that the third category of grape is "less-known" varieties, rather than "minor" varieties: I believe that there are few truly minor varieties in Italy (or anywhere else), only less-studied and little-known ones. Undoubtedly in the future some will prove to have less potential for fine winemaking than others; but at our present state of knowledge, we simply don't know which. Descriptions of these varieties will be forcibly shorter, as less is known about them and most do not have any monovarietal wines of note made from them—yet. Nearly all the grape varieties described in this book are officially included in the *Registro Nazionale delle Varietà di Vite* (less often called the *Catalogo Istituzionale*), Italy's *National Registry of Grape Varieties,* which is controlled by Italy's Ministry of Agriculture and updated annually. Varieties in this book that are not yet included within the registry are indicated as "not registered." These as yet little-known varieties are either in the process of obtaining official certification (always a laborious and time-consuming endeavor in bureaucracy-happy Italy) or have enough supporting historical and anecdotal evidence that I believe them to be separate varieties.

In contrast, you will find that when I list recommended estates and wines for each variety, some well-known and award-winning wines supposedly made with specific native grapes are not included. This is because I am not comfortable with them for a variety of reasons, such as dubious winemaking or a lack of correspondence between the wine and what existing documentation, logic, and my experience (or that of locals) tells me the wine should taste like. After many years of researching these grapes, analyzing laboratory data, and tasting the wines, I have a good idea of what wines made with individual native and traditional grapes ought to taste like. Again, this book is the result of on-the-ground visits, tastings, and interviews and is not just a compendium of information gleaned from other sources.

I devote a small section to grapes derived from crossings: though they are certainly not native in the natural sense of that word, these are grapes that were created in Italian laboratories and are practically grown only in Italy.

Wine Ratings

Since this is not a wine guide, there is little need for scores, extensive tasting notes, and prices. However, as I have been tasting Italian wines in depth for close to thirty years, I do wish to offer you my impressions of the wines made with each specific grape variety. Each time I name an estate when discussing a grape variety, I address its ability to produce wine from that grape variety by using a three-star system. For the purposes of this book, the estates that perform best with a specific grape variety are scored three stars (***), the next most proficient estates earn two stars (**), and those making a reasonable product reflective of the grape variety are awarded one star (*). Please note: these scores reflect not which wines are most tasty or best made, but which are most archetypal of the native grape used. My goal is not to furnish yet another mind-numbing list of tasting notes and scores (for those who want tasting notes and scores for native wines, please allow me to suggest the in-depth wine articles and detailed tasting notes I write for the *International Wine Cellar* at www.internationalwinecellar.com), but to broadcast which estates produce wines that are typical of and faithful to specific grape varieties. For this reason, an estate may receive three stars for wines made with one grape variety and only two stars for wines from another grape they are less skilled with. This is a very important aspect of the book you are holding in your hands. To the best of my knowledge, there is no other text available to date in which most—if not all—the wines made with any given Italian native grape variety have been tasted by a professional wine writer with years of experience. Your guarantee in regard to the usefulness of the ratings and my impressions of the wines is that over these years I have actively researched and tasted the wines made from the grape varieties described in this book.

IN CONCLUSION . . .

The result of thirteen years of conducting interviews, walking vineyards, and tasting wines made from native Italian grapes is the book you hold in your hands. It details Italian native grapes and wines to a degree never attempted before, and it is as exhaustive as current knowledge allows it to be. Many of the Italian grape varieties named and described in this book have never been mentioned in any mainstream publication outside academic journals or scientific research. There may be native grapes and fine wines made in Italy that are not listed here, but there are not many, and I seize this opportunity to apologize to my readers and to producers whose fine wines and grapes I may have omitted. Also, I am greatly indebted to all those who were, over the years, generous and patient enough to allow me to taste from small experimental vats or to send me both finished wines and countless monovarietal samples. I realize the latter were never meant to see the light of day as such, their ultimate destination being estate blends, but they were absolutely invaluable in helping me form a "native grape and wine palate." I am sure some producers and winemakers never really believed I would one day write about what I learned and tasted thanks to them; in the end, I hope this book has made all the time spent with, or for, me worthwhile.

Clearly, thanks to modern genetic advances and new biotechnologies becoming available at breakneck speed, progress is rapid in the field of native grapes, and what is held true today may easily be confuted tomorrow. In some respects this book, once published, will already be old. However, it represents by far the most thoroughly researched, in-depth, and accurate book on Italy's native grapes and wines available today. I trust you will enjoy reading it as much as I did researching and writing it. Actually, as much as I did living it.

This book would not have been possible without wine producers and winemakers from all over Italy kindly sharing their knowledge, memories, time, and wines with me. I owe them all a huge thank-you. Special thanks go to my mom and dad, to Mark Ball, Bruce Levitt, John Macdonald, Stefano Polacchi, Orfeo Salvador, Attilio Scienza, Stephen Tanzer, and Gino Veronelli, some of whom were there in the beginning of my wine-tasting days, others who have led by example or helped me to become a better wine writer—in some respects, this book is their fault! A big thank-you to Caroline Knapp, my copyeditor, who has done an amazing job in correcting my text: at times I felt like I needed to go back to English writing class! A thank-you also to Julie Van Pelt, another copyeditor who stepped in briefly while Caroline was away on vacation, and Chalon Emmons, my production editor. Last but not least, a heartfelt thank-you to my sponsoring editor, Blake Edgar, for placing his faith and trust in me, and to everyone at the University of California Press who helped to make this book better and to let a young man's love of Italy's native grapes, history, and tradition live on long after him.

Italy's Wine Regions

NATIVE GRAPES BY REGION

VALLE D'AOSTA

Reds
Cornalin
Fumin
Mayolet
Nebbiolo (Picotener)
Petit Rouge
Prëmetta (Prié Rouge)
Vuillermin

Whites
Moscato Bianco
Prié

PIEDMONT

Reds
Barbera
Brachetto
Croatina
Dolcetto
Freisa
Grignolino
Malvasia di Casorzo
Malvasia di Schierano
Moscato Bianco
Moscato Nero
Nebbiolo
Pelaverga family
Ruché
Uva Rara
Vespolina

Whites
Arneis
Cortese
Erbaluce
Moscato Bianco
Nascetta
Timorasso
Vermentino (Favorita)

LOMBARDY

Reds
Barbera
Croatina
Groppello family
Moscato di Scanzo
Nebbiolo (Chiavennasca)
Uva Rara
Vespolina

Whites
Moscato Bianco
Verdea

TRENTINO-ALTO ADIGE

Reds
Enantio
Lagrein
Marzemino
Moscato Rosa
Schiava family
Teroldego

Whites
Moscato Giallo
Nosiola

VENETO

Reds
Casetta
Corvina
Corvinone
Croatina
Molinara
Raboso family
Rondinella

Whites
Durella
Garganega
Glera
Marzemina Bianca
Moscato family
Verdicchio (Trebbiano di Soave)
Verdiso
Vespaiola

FRIULI VENEZIA GIULIA

Reds
Pignolo
Refosco family
Schioppettino
Tazzelenghe

Whites
Malvasia Istriana
Picolit
Ribolla Gialla
Tocai Friulano
Verduzzo Friulano
Vitovska

LIGURIA

Reds
Dolcetto (Ormeasco)
Rossese

Whites
Albarola
Bosco
Pigato
Vermentino

EMILIA-ROMAGNA

Reds
Barbera
Centesimino
Lambrusco family
Sangiovese
Uva Longanesi

Whites
Albana
Pignoletto
Malvasia di Candia Aromatica
Trebbiano Romagnolo

TUSCANY

Reds
Aleatico
Canaiolo Nero
Ciliegiolo
Colorino family
Malvasia Nera family
Sangiovese

Whites
Ansonica
Biancone
Malvasia Bianca Lunga
Moscato Bianco

Trebbiano Toscano
Vernaccia di San Gimignano

UMBRIA

Reds
Cornetta
Sagrantino
Sangiovese

Whites
Grechetto
Trebbiano Spoletino

MARCHE

Reds
Lacrima
Montepulciano
Sangiovese
Vernaccia Nera

Whites
Biancame
Cococciola
Passerina
Pecorino
Verdicchio

LAZIO

Reds
Aleatico
Cesanese family
Montepulciano (Violone)
Nero Buono
Sangiovese

Whites
Bellone
Bombino Bianco
Malvasia Bianca di Candia
Malvasia del Lazio
Moscato di Terracina
Passerina
Trebbiano Toscano

ABRUZZO

Reds
Montepulciano
Sangiovese

Whites
Montonico Bianco
Pecorino
Trebbiano Abruzzese

CAMPANIA

Reds
Aglianico
Pallagrello Nero
Piedirosso

Whites
Asprinio
Biancolella
Coda di Volpe Bianca
Falanghina
Fiano
Forastera
Greco
Pallagrello Bianco

MOLISE

Reds
Montepulciano
Sangiovese
Tintilia

Whites
Cococciola

PUGLIA

Reds
Aleatico
Bombino Nero
Malvasia Nera family
Negro Amaro
Primitivo
Susumaniello
Uva di Troia

Whites
Bianco d'Alessano
Bombino Bianco
Malvasia Bianca
Moscato Bianco
Pampanuto
Verdeca

BASILICATA

Reds
Aglianico

Whites
Malvasia Bianca di Basilicata
Moscato Bianco

CALABRIA

Reds
Gaglioppo
Magliocco family

Whites
Malvasia di Lipari (Greco Bianco)
Mantonico Bianco

SARDINIA

Reds
Cagnulari
Cannonao (Grenache)
Carignano

Whites
Malvasia di Lipari (Malvasia di Sardegna)
Nuragus
Vermentino
Vernaccia di Oristano

SICILY

Reds
Frappato
Nerello Cappuccio
Nerello Mascalese
Nero d'Avola (Calabrese)
Nocera
Perricone

Whites
Ansonica (Inzolia)
Carricante
Catarratto Bianco
Grillo
Malvasia di Lipari
Moscato Bianco
Zibibbo (Moscato di Alessandria)

Introduction

UNDERSTANDING "NATIVE" AND CLASSIFYING GRAPE VARIETIES

ITALY HAS BY far the largest number of grape varieties from which to make wine. Even more than the blessing of ideal microclimates and geologically diverse soils, this rich biodiversity is the single greatest winemaking asset Italian producers share. Anna Schneider, one of Italy's most famous and best ampelologists, estimated that there were roughly two thousand native grape cultivars (that is, cultivated grape varieties) in Italy as recently as 2006, but that impressive number depends upon who's counting. Stoically attached to their grapes, Italians don't look kindly on foreigners (or even Italians) who tell them that one of their cherished local varieties might actually hail from elsewhere. Other experts have also suggested that roughly one thousand of Italy's cultivars had been genetically identified, more or less accurately (an important aspect I will broach in chapter 1), and that six hundred were being used to make wines in commercially significant numbers. More recent data suggests a somewhat lower number, identifying 377 (and possibly a few more) genetically distinct grape varieties that are used to make wine in commercially significant volumes (Robinson, Harding, and Vouillamoz 2012). However, the number of Italian native grapes is almost certainly much higher, as many of Italy's native grapes remain unidentified, growing in scattered, hard-to-reach vineyards, their existence known to only a few local farmers. My own count sits at over five hundred, and despite my walking the vineyards and speaking to farmers and producers incessantly, there are probably still more native grapes out there in old, forgotten Italian vineyards that I am not aware of. Then again, some of the varieties in my list may soon be proven to be just biotypes or synonyms of other, better-known varieties. To the best of my knowledge—current scientific knowledge—the list of wine grapes I present in this book is an accurate and up-to-date compendium of Italy's wine grape patrimony. But 377 is still an impressive number, and represents more native varieties than those of France, Spain, and Greece combined, the countries that boast the next largest numbers of native grapes. Considering that there are an estimated 1,368 vine varieties used to make wine in commercially significant numbers all over the world (Robinson, Harding, and

Vouillamoz 2012), even if Italy were to boast *only* 377 native grapes, it would mean that almost 28 percent of the world's varieties are native to Italy.

These grapes have called Italy their home for centuries, and Italians have been making wine from them for almost as long—wines not easily duplicated elsewhere. Speaking of them in terms of their "nativeness" reveals not an inferiority complex, but a justifiable pride: these grapes and wines speak of Italy to the world. In fact, the trump card for Italian wine producers is their potential to make world-class wines that exhibit aroma and flavor profiles altogether different from those well known to the wine-buying public. In other words, Italy's native grapes and wines offer jaded wine-loving consumers something new and interesting, at times even something wild and wacky. These wines are every sommelier's dream: delicious, food-friendly alternatives to the all-too-often overly alcoholic, oaky, tropical-fruit, or chocolate bombs that can be some chardonnays and cabernet sauvignons. And it's not just sommeliers having a jamboree with Italian native grapes and wines: others are getting into the act. Italian native varieties such as Sangiovese and Nebbiolo are allowed in numerous American Viticultural Areas (AVAs), and producers all over the world are trying their hand at local versions of Barbera and Fiano wines, admittedly, with varying degrees of success. Universities are paying attention too: American universities have set up seminars on Italy's native grapes and wines in their enology programs. With so many different grapes and wines to try, it is easy to understand why Italians have never felt the need to start "ABC clubs," those groups of wine lovers who get together and drink "Anything *But* *Chardonnay* or *Cabernet*." Italians may do a lot of foolish things, but drinking their own Chardonnay wines is not one of them.

Grape varieties can be divided into three categories: native (also called autochthonous or indigenous), international (also called allochthonous or foreign), and traditional.

Native or autochthonous grape varieties are those that were born in a specific place and have remained almost exclusively associated with that location. In fact, the word autochthonous is of Greek derivation: from *auto*, meaning own, and *khthôn*, meaning earth. Alternatively, a variety may be considered native to a country even when its true birthplace was elsewhere, provided that the grape has been associated with its new country for a very long time, usually thousands of years. In fact, many (but probably not as many as we once thought) of the so-called Italian native grapes are actually of Greek or Middle Eastern origin, imported by returning Roman legionnaires, seafaring Phoenician traders, and Greek colonists throughout ancient times. Strictly speaking, not all of Italy's grapes are therefore truly native: "local" might be a better term to describe those "native" varieties whose origin is not unequivocally Italian. However, many ancient grape varieties grown in Italy today bear minimal if any resemblance to grape varieties of their birthplaces, and can therefore be considered native to Italy for all intents and purposes.

At the opposite end of the grape spectrum, international grape varieties are those that have been planted everywhere within the last one hundred years, in hopes of duplicating the great wines of France. Grapes such as Chardonnay and Merlot are considered native to France but have become the ultimate international varieties. In fact, wines made with these grapes are so successful they have been planted extensively in Italy too.

Somewhere in the middle between native and international grapes are the traditional varieties: international varieties that have been grown in a specific place for three hundred to five hundred years (different experts favor different cut-offs; I would submit that three centuries is probably enough) and have become part of that land's tradition. This is why Cabernet Franc, Merlot, and Pinot Bianco, which have been grown in Italy's Veneto and Friuli Venezia Giulia regions since the eighteenth century at least, are traditional to those areas, while Chardonnay and Cabernet Sauvignon, much later arrivals, are not. For a grape variety to be considered native or traditional, and hence an integral part of an ecosystem, it has to have lived there for a very long time.

Grapes can also be classified in other manners: national (grown all over the country), interregional (grown in more than one region), and regional (grown in only one region or in even more restricted areas). Alternatively, they can be classified as diffusely cultivated (when the total surface under vine is greater than one thousand hectares or 2,470 acres), locally cultivated (between one hundred and one thousand hectares), scarcely cultivated (between ten and one hundred hectares), and at risk of extinction (less than ten hectares). These two, more specific classification systems are mainly used by scientific researchers and those who study grape varieties closely.

For a variety of reasons, native grapes travel poorly and generally have a hard time when confronted with new environments; few become traditional or international varieties, though many producers all over the world are trying Italian native grapes with increasing gusto. For example, in Australia in 1994, Fred and Katrina Pizzini decided to graft Brachetto onto Cabernet Sauvignon vines and their new wine met with public and private acclaim. Brachetto beating out the king of red grapes himself? Would anyone have imagined that David and Goliath tale only ten years before? All over the world, wine lovers can now indulge in and explore new wines made with Brazilian Ancellotta, California Dolcetto, Chilean Nebbiolo, Mexican Aglianico, New York State Friulano, New Zealand Arneis, and many more. In general however, it's tough to make fine wines from native grapes transported elsewhere. Unlike Cabernet Sauvignon and Chardonnay, which show great adaptive resources, native varieties often have low adaptability to external influences other than those typical of the habitats they have been exposed to over the centuries. Factors such as differences in soil and climate often significantly impact the behaviors of native varieties, and the resulting wines are almost always, at least initially, a far cry from the original Italian wines. Of course, we also know a lot less about Italy's native grapes than we do about Chardonnay or Cabernet Sauvignon, since for the greatest part of the twentieth century they weren't the focus of much academic study. I have no doubts that people outside Italy will eventually manage to harness the potential greatness of Nebbiolo or Brachetto; after all, we have seen this happen before (think Pinot Nero in California and Oregon). Slowly but surely, producers everywhere will get the hang of each Italian native grape's requirements, growth kinetics, and interactions with new *terroirs,* and great non-Italian wines made with Italy's native grapes will be much more common than they are today.

An example might be the famous Italian native variety Nebbiolo, the grape behind the world-renowned wines of Barolo and Barbaresco: outside Piedmont (and parts of Lombardy and Valle d'Aosta) it gives only moderately encouraging results. Not that foreign-produced Nebbiolo wines are bad—there are interesting Nebbiolo-wines made in California, Australia, and Chile—but currently they bear little resemblance to the Italian originals that made the grape variety famous. Witness the plight of Sangiovese in California and Washington: everyone's new darling in the 1990s, much has since been uprooted in favor of other varieties. As Steve Heimoff has written, "it turned out that Sangiovese by itself wasn't very interesting" and that "California supertuscans were a fad that fizzled." Of course, it might just have been a case of being ahead of their time. Even Piero Antinori of the world-famous Tuscan firm Antinori, one of the world's biggest Sangiovese experts, worried at first that his dream of making a great New World Sangiovese wine at Atlas Peak winery in Washington would never materialize. He recently told me that in the 1980s and 1990s, "Sangiovese in North America was plagued by poor clones and farming techniques: instead, heavy thinning, strict canopy control and properly-timed irrigation are key." His winemaker at Atlas Peak, Darren Procsal, remembers that Antinori originally felt that they were overplanting Sangiovese, because not enough was yet known about the new *terroir*. Fortunately, time has allowed for a better understanding of the needs of Sangiovese in the United States, leading to new vineyards and good monovarietal Sangiovese wines by Noceto, Duxoup, Kris Curran, and others (see SANGIOVESE, chapter 4). Indeed, Piero Antinori now believes he might yet make an American Sangiovese wine that will make him proud.

With more research and experience, some native varieties may one day become truly international varieties, and some seem already headed in that direction. This is not a surprising turn of events, as producers are always on the lookout for new wine grape varieties that might prove better suited to wine production areas characterized by increasingly hot and dry conditions, and that might offer reduced disease potential and produce better wines. As fewer than fifteen wine grape varieties account for 90 percent of the wine grapes grown in the United States and France, you realize why producers everywhere are looking at Italy's plethora of native grapes with increased interest. In many countries of the world, there are winemakers who hope to make great wines from native Italian varieties with a distinct, homegrown twist. Already in Australia, Argentina, Chile, and other countries, many wineries are making Nebbiolo and Barbera monovarietal wines or blends.

However, I want to stress that being "native" reaches far beyond mere semantics. Native grapes and wines hold cultural, financial, ecological, and social significance. In my view, native grapes are a part of the "cultural capital" theorized by French sociologist Pierre Bourdieu, those nonfinancial social assets which distinguish individuals and areas, propelling them beyond their economic means. Cultural capital allows entire areas to progress and prosper. Given recent market trends that show heightened consumer interest in native grapes and wines, defending and promoting native grapes and wines are a means to increase sales as well as defend the biodiversity of our environment.

Native grapes are also important from an ecological perspective. Evolution in winemaking over the centuries, and perceived consumer wishes for only the tried and true, have caused most present-day viticulture to be based on a limited number of cultivated varieties. This was not always so: farmers hang on to their crops proudly. Native grapes, by virtue of their long association with specific areas, are better able to cope with local microclimates and *terroirs*. In other words, each one is best adapted to its own particular habitat, allowing for more environmentally friendly viticulture.

Because they were not found anywhere else until only very recently, wines made with local grape varieties are special. To Italians, they represent Italy just as famous monuments, natural landmarks, or local recipes do. By virtue of the strong bond between these grapes and the people who have tended to them on a daily basis for centuries, they characterize specific areas of Italy. As French historian Fernand Braudel points out, it is not by chance that farmers view conservation as a social mission, since conserving these native grape varieties also conserves traditional ways of living (Giavedoni and Gily 2011).

As Italy only became a nation in 1861 when the Kingdom of Italy was officially born, people feel Lombard or Lazian before they feel Italian. To not understand this is to not understand Italy. It is therefore inevitable that native grapes, with their intimate links to specific areas, also speak of traditions and of identity: Friulians are Friulians not just because they were born in Udine or Gorizia but also because they prefer wines made with Friulano and Ribolla, instead of Sangiovese or Nebbiolo. This qualifies them as Friulian just as much as eating *cjalsons* or *gubana* rather than *panzanella* or *coda alla vaccinara*, dishes typical of other regions. Ultimately, wines made from native grapes remind us Italians of who we are and where we have come from: their roots dig deep within our collective memories. There is no future without a past.

NATIVE GRAPES: THE NUMBERS AND THE NAMES

The Numbers

Statistics are for losers, and never was this more evident than in trying to figure out how many of Italy's hectares under vine are planted with native grapes. Actually, in this country just understanding the total number of hectares under vine is difficult, as numbers change from source to source. Furthermore, collection of data is slow at best: Italians carry out vineyard surveys only once a decade. For example, relative to the 2002 vintage (hardly yesterday), data from Italy's National Institute for Statistics (ISTAT) cites 798,000 hectares under vine, while the UN Food and Agriculture Organization figure is 717,635 hectares; the discrepancies are due either to one source counting table grapes in addition to wine grapes, or confusing total hectares under vine with total hectares under vine in production. It follows that certainties on the exact diffusion of many native grapes in Italy are hard to come by.

Nevertheless, according to the most recent agricultural census performed by ISTAT in 2010, there are 652,000 hectares under vine in Italy. The latest data also shows the most common grape variety in Italy to be, by a large margin, Sangiovese. Of the top twenty planted grapes in Italy, sixteen are native and four are international varieties (Merlot, Chardonnay, Pinot Grigio, and Cabernet Sauvignon), and only two of these, Merlot and Chardonnay are in the top ten. (It should be noted that Merlot plantings fell by four thousand hectares, or 6 percent, between 2000 and 2010.) Of the sixteen Italian natives, fifteen are planted on ten thousand hectares or more. Three tables in the appendix reveal some patterns in the distribution of native grapes under cultivation in Italy.

Table 1 shows the breakdown of the one hundred most-planted grape varieties in Italy, by total hectares in Italy and per single region; table 2 shows the total hectares planted to each variety from 1970 to 2010, so that positive or negative trends can be examined with greater ease. This data reveals that roughly seventy of Italy's native grapes are grown on more than one thousand hectares, but close to two hundred are grown on less than one thousand hectares and for many others there are only a few dozen hectares under vine. Many of these native grapes have been neglected for the better part of the twentieth century, and are unfortunately now in danger of disappearing. Table 3 lists Italy's lesser-known and rare grape varieties, by total hectares planted. I caution readers that due to many identification errors (see chapter 1 for more on the hits and misses of ampelology) these numbers have to be taken with a good grain of salt, especially for varieties easily confused with others (for example, Aglianicone and Ciliegiolo). On a positive note, the resurgence in the last decade of interest in native grapes and wines has focused awareness and investments so that many cultivars no longer risk extinction. Much work is still needed before any "rediscovered" variety has a chance to break through, since by Italian law a grape variety has to be officially recognized for it to be legally cultivated and propagated, which makes things harder for less abundant native grapes.

The National Registry of Grape Varieties is the official document listing the varieties authorized for cultivation in Italy; if a grapevine is not registered, then no plant material from that variety can be made available for propagation in commercial nurseries. At this writing, the registry lists 461 official grape varieties, but private individuals and institutions are working furiously to have more varieties included all the time. Therefore, the number of cultivars on the list increases steadily every year. Unfortunately the registry contains a number of errors (or more accurately, what seem to be mistakes at our present state of knowledge), because grape variety identification has become increasingly rapid while government bodies react slowly to change at the best of times. Some grapes known today to be synonyms of other grapes are listed separately, which explains the high number of varieties in the registry. In fairness, it is true that some recent grape variety identifications were startling at best (I still shake my head when reading some new proposed identifications), and were subsequently proven to be erroneous, so this is one time politicians can wiggle off the hook. Still, these inaccuracies in the National Registry only add to the confusion. For example, Sangiovese, Grechetto Rosso, and Prugnolo are listed as separate entities (at numbers 218, 96, and 201 respectively) but they are in fact all Sangiovese, and all supposedly genetically identical. The same might apply to Biancame (number 25) and Trebbiano Toscano (number 244), which some believed to be genetically identical. Cataratto Comune (number 58) and Cataratto Lucido (number 59) are believed genetically the same, but Cataratto Lucido is a higher quality biotype, allowing for better wines. It therefore makes sense to keep the two separate, but for accuracy's sake there ought to be a provision in the classification indicating that the two seem to be genetically the same grape. A similar scenario plays out with Favorita (number 80), Pigato (number 190), and Vermentino (number 259), where the first two are reportedly just biotypes of the third; but differences between the three wines and the three grapevines are noteworthy enough that an argument can be made for listing the cultivars separately under one heading, specifying supposed genetic identity along with biotype-related differences. Of course, for some people it just doesn't matter: I know a number of farmers who steadfastly refuse to accept that their Pigato could be someone else's Vermentino. Though in reading those words you might think Italy really is a never-ending source of amusement, and that if the country hadn't existed, then someone would surely have invented it, things aren't quite that cut and dried. I can make a very good case for keeping separate some varieties said to be identical by scientists, and as I will explain in chapter 1, there is scientific method behind my madness.

The Names

More than one wine lover has confessed to feeling hapless in the face of the dizzying array of names of Italy's seemingly endless list of grape varieties, referring to sizes, shapes, growing characteristics, places of origin (or more exactly, supposed origin), animal names, and a rainbow of colors. According to Hohnerlein-Buchinger, the nomenclature used to name grape varieties was formed in the twelfth and thirteenth centuries, based on writings by Pliny and other Georgic Latin authors.

The names of Italian native cultivars derive from:

1. **A sensory attribute such as color, smell, or taste.** Color (of grape or wine) was most used, and popular already in ancient Rome, where grapes called *rubellae* (red) and *cinereae* (ashen) were legion. Just a few examples of color-coded grapes of today include Albana (from *albanus*, white); Bianchetta, Biancone, Bianco (from *bianco*, also white); Nerello, Nero, Neretto (from *nero*, black); Rossana, Rossese (from *rosso*, red); Verdello, Verdicchio, Verduzzo (from *verde*, green). In other cases, color was simply attached to the grape name: for example, Malvasia Bianca and Greco Bianco. The use of color to name grapes could also be more subtle, referring to a specific hue by its association with a physical state, animal, or fruit. Examples are Piedirosso, Palombina, and Piede di Colombo (all refer to the red legs of pigeons); Corvina and Corvinone (from *corvo*, raven), Ansonica (from *sauro*, the color of dry leaves), and my personal favorite, Erbaluce (from *alba* and *luce*, or the dawn's light, which is particularly bright and pale, just like this grape). Other varieties were named because of smell or

taste: Mammolo (from *viola mammola,* a specific type of perfumed violet), Dolcetto (from *dolce* or *douce,* sweet, in reference to the sweet grapes, not the wine).

2. **Physical attributes, especially of the grape bunch and the berries** (such as shape, size, and features of the pulp). Examples include Pignola and Pignolo (from *pigna,* or pine cone, due to small, compact grape bunches) or Olivella (from *oliva,* indicating olive-shaped berries).
3. **Viticultural behaviors, cultivation methods, productivity levels, and wine characteristics.** Examples include Canaiolo (from *dies caniculares,* the hot "dog days" of July and August, when the berries change color), Schiava (meaning slave, since the vines were tied to poles, or enslaved), Cataratto (from *cataratte* or *cascate,* waterfalls of wine, due to its copious productivity). My favorite is Pulcinculo: a zingy and peppery wine that gives you a kick, and supposedly gets you moving and shaking. Pulcinculo translates to "fleas up your rear end."
4. **Perceived origin of the varieties.** This was perhaps the most important means by which to name grapes in ancient Rome. Examples are Malvasia (from the Greek city of Monenvasia) and Vernaccia (from Vernazza, a town in Liguria, or, alternatively, from *vernaculum,* meaning local).
5. **Names of people, saints, or other religious references.** Examples include Santa Maria or Regina (queen).

Unfortunately, aliases—often erroneous ones—have always been plentiful. In Italy, the same name was often used for different varieties in very distant parts of the country, and even within the same region. For example, there are at least three different varieties named Greco Bianco in Calabria alone—and not to be outdone, there are at least five unrelated Greco Neros there as well. These are examples of homonyms, different varieties that have been erroneously attributed the same name. Another well-known example of homonymity is offered by the many unrelated *Malvasia* grapes found all over the world. Even larger is the problem posed by synonyms, identical varieties known under different names, such as Zibibbo and Moscato di Alessandria, which are one and the same. In Italy, where regionality has always ruled, synonymity can be taken to extremes: for example, Bianchetta Trevigiana has always had numerous and completely different names in various corners of Veneto, its home. Bianchetta is the name historically used for it around Treviso and Belluno; but it's Senese in the Breganze area, Vernanzina in the Colli Berici, and Vernassina in the Colli Euganei, all localities within an hour's drive (often less) from each other. Sometimes, there really can be too much of a good thing.

THE VARIETY-SPECIFIC APPROACH TO WINE

In today's world of *terroir*-obsessed wine lovers, it might strike the casual reader as curious to think of wines in terms of grape varieties first and foremost. In fact, many producers and winemakers decry the attention that a few (though in my view, not nearly enough) wine writers lavish on the cultivar with which the wine is supposedly made. For them, speaking of wine in terms of variety is too reductive—what counts most in their minds is not Sangiovese, but the Sangiovese of Montalcino or Montepulciano, not Pinot Nero that counts, but Musigny or Corton. The implication is that anyone can grow Sangiovese or Pinot Nero, but only a few blessed individuals in this world have Montalcino or Musigny to work with. This point of view has many merits, but it also has dangers. Undoubtedly, *terroir* is important: for example, a Riesling grown on slate soils in a cool climate will give a wine very different from one grown on clay in a warmer climate. What is even more fascinating, a Riesling grown in the same cool climate but on soils rich in red instead of blue slate will also give a different wine. Such diversities are the reason for *terroir*-based appellations such as those of Burgundy or the great rieslings made in different vineyards of the Mosel, whose amazing spectrum of aromas and flavors have historically been recognized by name on German wine labels.

This capacity to translate minute differences of *terroir* is typical of most grape varieties, though some, like Nebbiolo, Pinot Nero, and Riesling, seem better at it than others. However for most people who drink wine, the differences between wines made from grapes grown in different areas is minimal. Further, some grape varieties, such as Cabernet Sauvignon and Merlot, are remarkably capable of reproducing essentially the same wine no matter where they are planted. This is a gross generalization, of course: a Cabernet Franc wine from Napa *is* different than one from Sonoma, but few wine drinkers can really tell them apart.

Of course, a well-made Piedmontese Nebbiolo will always differ from a well-made Oregonian or Australian example. Though other places in the world might one day make Nebbiolo wines that are the envy of the Piedmontese, they will never be exactly alike, since each will reflect the *terroir* it comes from. That said, a significant problem with many appellations (in Italy, the United States, France, and everywhere else) is that only a small number produce wines really typical of a finite, well-established production area. This is because most appellations are far too broad, so that there is ultimately no connection between the land and the wine finally produced. Just as the characteristics of wines made in the large Sonoma Coast AVA are hard to pinpoint, even Italians don't know where DOCs such as Bianco Capena or Riesi are located, or what the wines made there should taste like. Famous DOCs are often particularly nonsensical: for example, there are two thousand hectares from which to make Brunello di Montalcino, a ridiculous figure no matter how you slice it (consider that all of France's Musigny *grand cru* is confined to less than eleven hectares). Whatever some people would like you to believe, it is impossible to make appellation-specific wine from an area as large as the one permitted to produce Brunello today, and given the myriad soil types, exposures, and altitudes, it follows that there is not one Brunello, but many different ones. In this case, *terroir* hardly speaks of one wine: Brunellos made in the northern parts of the Brunello zone are completely different from those made in the southern ones (and those made in the southwestern quadrant are different still from those made in the southeastern section of the zone, and it's actually a lot more complicated than that). In Alsace, where *terroir* is all-important, they have similar problems. For example, the famous Brand *grand cru* was originally three hectares large; today it is fifty hectares, and ought to be subdivided into one *grand cru* and at least three different *premiers crus*. I have been tasting Alsatian wines regularly for the past eighteen years and I find it difficult to speak of wines exhibiting a Brand "somewhereness," much as with Brunello. In fact, some Brand producers have resorted to bottling wines called Brand "K" and Brand "S," each made from specific subsections of the Brand, the Steinglitz and Kirchberg. In Bordeaux, wines are described as being "very Pomerol": but if one Pomerol wine is made with 90 percent Merlot (for example, Château Trotanoy) and the other with 53 percent Cabernet Franc (Château Lafleur) and on quite different soils (mainly clay for Trotanoy and mainly gravel for Lafleur), then it becomes objectively difficult for most people to recognize the two wines as being from Pomerol. However, a knowledgeable wine writer or expert will have no difficulty picking up that one of the two wines is top heavy with Cabernet Franc.

Varietal labeling is also easier to understand than geographic labeling, and many wine lovers like to know how a wine made with a given grape variety is supposed to taste. In fact, that's probably why they're buying the wine in the first place. Unfortunately, most wine-producing countries allow varietal labeling that is optimistic at best. While there *are* truly monovarietal (meaning 100 percent) wines made, Europe has passed legislation requiring that wines labeled with the name of a single grape variety contain at least 85 percent of that variety—and it's only 75 percent in the United States. This situation may yield short-term political and commercial benefits: farmers and producers are always happy to augment production of wines that sell, and blending in other grapes makes increasing the annual bottle production of a specific "monovarietal" wine easy, especially if grapevines of that native grape are still rare. But it does nothing to further the cause of the varieties and wines themselves, for a wine including 15 percent of another variety certainly will not taste exclusively of the main variety. The situation is worsened when highly aromatic or strongly flavorful varieties are used in the blend; for this reason there are many legal provisions specifying whether or not aromatic varieties such as Moscato Bianco may be added. It seems to me that producing a Picolit or Verdicchio wine that tastes of Chardonnay or Sauvignon Blanc is an exercise in futility, for the uniqueness of the grape and wine (and hence one of the reasons why someone might want to buy it) is hopelessly lost.

Colors, Aromas, and Flavors of Native Grapes and Wines

It is the grape variety that (in the absence of enological alchemy) will most dictate the aroma and flavor profile of a wine. I am not alone in believing this. In *Vines, Grapes, and Wines*, Jancis Robinson wrote that "the grape alone determines perhaps 90 percent of the flavor of a wine." In fact, this is intuitive: just as a green apple smells and tastes different from a yellow or a red apple, so do grapes. Taking this one step further, a Northern Spy apple has its own characteristics, different from those of Macintosh, Cortland, or Fuji apples, all of them red. Just as these apples obviously look, taste, and smell different, so do Sangiovese and Aglianico, and their respective wines. Wines are characterized by specific colors, aromas (primary, secondary, and tertiary), and flavors that are related to their grape varieties. Though winemaking and viticultural techniques can have an important effect on the final color, aroma, and flavor of wine, it must never be forgotten that the cultivar's genetics inevitably determines the wine's specific characteristics.

Color is a good example: you wouldn't normally expect pinkish berries to give black wines or vice versa, and you'd be right, more or less. Grape and wine color is due mainly to anthocyanins (anthocyanidins bound to a molecule of glucose), pigments located in the skins and to a lesser extent the pulp; co-pigmentation, the binding of anthocyanins with nonorganic molecules, is also important in the genesis of wine color. The combinations and ratios of the five different free anthocyanins and the presence or absence of stable, conjugated anthocyanin forms, such as acylated and dicumarilic anthocyanins, also dictate wine color. The five anthocyanins are malvin, petunin, delphin, cyanin, and peonin: the first two are most stable, while cyanin and peonin are easily broken down, or oxidized. Hence, wines made with grape varieties rich in these last two pigments tend to have lighter hues and less stable color; knowing that Nebbiolo is particularly rich in cyanin and peonin tells you that Barolo can never be pitch black, and that even super-dark ruby can be a stretch (though admittedly, new biotypes have managed to kick the shade up quite a notch). Same goes for Sangiovese, another variety rich in cyanin; Sangiovese's pigments have been the subject of extensive studies in recent years, with the goal of using its very characteristic anthocyanin profile as a marker for the variety in wines. Fulvio Mattivi of the Fondazione Edmund Mach, one of Italy's greatest anthocyanin experts, first described these pigments in depth in 1990, and his group has recently published a major and truly fascinating study detailing Sangiovese's anthocyanin profile as never before (Arapitsas, Perenzoni, Nicolini, and Mattivi 2012). More importantly, Sangiovese is known to be practically devoid (as Pinot Nero is) of acylated anthocyanins; by contrast, Merlot and Cabernet Sauvignon are loaded with them (Mangani, Buscioni, Collina,

Bocci, and Vincenzini 2011). Hence, a wine supposedly made with 100 percent Sangiovese (or Pinot Nero) that contains more than 1–2 percent acylated anthocyanins is not likely a monovarietal sangiovese or pinot nero. Of course winemaking techniques, climate, and viticultural methods can affect the intensity of a wine's hue: for example, thicker skins and smaller berries will give darker wines, as do oak-aging, and other techniques. However, there's a limit to how much color grapes can give before bitter tannins and other phenols leach out and wines taste unbalanced. Historically, specific varieties have been used to increase the color of anemic-looking wines: Italy is rich in *teinturiers* (coloring varieties) such as Colorino, Granoir, and many others. However, they cannot be added if the wine has to be monovarietal by law.

Just like color, the primary aromas and flavors of wine are also determined by the type of grape varieties used; it's not by chance that these aromas and flavors are known as varietal. Admittedly, secondary aromas and flavors, which are by-products of pre-fermentation and alcoholic fermentation, are of greater relevance to wine drinkers than primary ones—or, for that matter, than tertiary aromas, which develop with age and are responsible for wine bouquet. It is during alcoholic fermentation, the process by which yeasts turn grape sugar into alcohol and carbon dioxide, that new compounds are formed that smell of fruits, flowers, or spices and strongly characterize wines made with those grapes. Examples are the banana of chardonnay and the black pepper of syrah, or the red rose and violet aroma of wines made with Nebbiolo and Sangiovese respectively. However, these secondary aromas and flavors are also directly related to the grape variety used to make the wine, for they are only possible thanks to specific precursor molecules found in each. Obviously, grapes smell of neither banana nor black pepper, nor are these flavorings added to wine (at least, they are not usually supposed to be), so the aromas and flavors we characteristically associate with specific wines are the result of the winemaking process and materials (such as yeasts) interacting with the genetically predisposed core material of each grape variety.

Therefore, in the absence of specific selected yeasts (which can create new aromas and flavors on their own), flavored woodchips, faulty winemaking, specific soil or water regimens, and other confounding variables, wines taste and smell the way they do mainly as a result of the grape variety used to make them. For example, a wine can smell of peach if the grapes used to make it have precursor molecules that will allow the formation of gamma-undecalactone and jasmine lactone (for the joy of all those scientifically minded, the latter compound is more precisely known as Z-2-pentenylpentan-5-olide), two chemical molecules produced naturally that smell of peach—though other molecules can smell of peach as well. Likewise, for a wine to smell or taste of red cherries, it must contain among other compounds the worrisome-sounding benzaldehyde cyanhydrin, a molecule that smells of red cherries. Examples such as these clarify why wines made from native grapes smell and taste different from each other as well as from those made with Merlot or Chardonnay. There are countless studies dealing with this fascinating aspect not just of grapes and wines but of all foodstuffs (see Berger 2007; Krings and Berger 1998).

The above point is absolutely key in understanding wine. I firmly believe that each wine should be appreciated for more than just what it tastes of. I feel very strongly that it is neither useful nor correct to say, as many do, that "it doesn't matter what it tastes like as long as it's good." Often, the people who say this are the same ones who would be incensed if they learned that their expensive French dress or Italian shoes had been made elsewhere. Since wines are products of specific, individual grape varieties, each should taste relatively different from all others. Even better, they should taste of the grape variety used to make them. A failure to understand this inevitably leads to tragicomic situations such as black-as-ink Brunellos garnering impossibly high scores from less-than-knowledgeable wine critics: in the Brunellogate scandal a few years back, a number of Brunellos came under police scrutiny for abnormally dark colors. It is noteworthy that nowadays, molecular analysis is being increasingly used to analyze the exact composition of wines (and foods), relative not just to grapevine variety but also geographic origin and vintage, to determine possible adulterations. It's not just an intellectual need, but a matter of consumer safety and quality guarantees (see Brescia, Caldarola, De Gilio, Benedetti, Fanizzi, and Sacco 2002; Viggiani and Castiglione Morelli 2008, and Bigliazzi, Scali, Paolucci, Cresti, and Vignani 2012). For instance, while the total anthocyanin concentration of a wine can be altered by winemaking techniques, the chemical nature of the anthocyanins and their relative ratios cannot be changed, since the ratio in each variety is genetically determined. In this respect, the anthocyanin profile of a wine is very much like a fingerprint. Technology is increasingly coming to our aid; though it's costly and requires specific equipment, nuclear magnetic radioisotope imaging allows us to determine the specific patterns of trace elements that are characteristic of the geology of specific areas—and these can be evaluated in wine. Such a test proves whether the grapes used to make a given wine actually grew in the area the wine is said to be from. It's a technique that has also been used successfully to identify adulterated olive oil and buffalo mozzarella, the latter of which usually contains hefty percentages of cow's milk, and shouldn't (Mannina, Pattumi, Proietti, and Segre 2001; Brescia, Monfreda, Buccolieri, and Carrino 2005; and Mazzei and Piccolo 2012).

Encouragingly, there appears to be a progressively larger segment of grapevine-conscious wine consumers, who are genuinely interested in learning what, for example, authentic Passerina or Tazzelenghe wines really smell and taste of. In Italy, where sales of supertuscans and other blends containing international varieties are plummeting, awareness of what to expect from wines made from native grapes is increasing. Analogous to the locavore movement, there's a genuine desire to buy and drink wines made with local varieties that speak of specific places. In Italy at least, the future for these "new" wines made from "old" grape varieties looks very bright.

PART ONE

Grape Varieties

What, Where, When, Why, and How

ONE

Ampelology

THE ART AND SCIENCE OF GRAPE VARIETY IDENTIFICATION

AMPELOLOGY, NOT AMPELOGRAPHY

The first time I met one of the world's most famous wine experts, now many years ago, it took me all of two minutes to say something wrong. Jean-Claude Berrouet, for over forty years the head of winemaking at J. P. Moueix (the venerable French *négociant* firm that produces and sells legendary wines such as Petrus, Trotanoy, Magdelaine, and California's Dominus), stopped in mid-conversation, smiled, and pointed out I had used an incorrect term. That pernicious term was ampelography.

Ampelography is the science of vine description and classification based on observation and pictorial illustration of grapevines—and strictly speaking, nothing more. The term derives from the Greek *ampelos* (grape) and *grapho* (write) and literally means "vine description" or "writing about grapes." Historically, vine varieties and grapes have always been described and carefully reported via beautiful drawings, and later, photographs. Today, everyone uses the term ampelography to refer to the study of grape varieties in the broadest sense, including genetic studies, but such a broad use is a mistake. That fateful day now decades ago, I made that mistake, and Berrouet let me know it. I haven't stopped learning from the man since.

The fact is that modern grape scientists can count on so much more than their powers of observation in their search to identify grape varieties—and it's a good thing too, as we shall see. Modern advances in cellular and molecular biology have made it easier today to correctly identify grape varieties. Whereas grape cultivar characterization had been traditionally carried out using morphological and phenological observations, nowadays DNA analysis techniques based on molecular markers, when correctly performed, are able to provide objective information on the identity of a species. These techniques can also help clarify the origins of grapevine cultivars. Since grape identification no longer involves just the art of observation and graphic reproduction, but many other branches of science too, the correct name for grapevine science ought to be *ampelology*, not *ampelography*. Others besides Berrouet agree, yet wine writers and university experts have continued to use the older term out of habit. By analogy, consider whether, should you have a stomach problem or break an arm, you would prefer to go to a gastroenterology or orthopedic clinic, or to a gastoenterography (whatever that may be) or orthography clinic. In the latter they might teach you to write better, but it might prove hard to do with a broken arm.

"People can't speak to each other if they don't know if they're talking about the same grape variety," says Carole Meredith, a viticulturist and plant geneticist at the University of California at Davis in California, to whom we are all indebted for the great advances made in the past twenty years in identifying grape varieties accurately (Meredith 2002). Stella Grando, a professor at the Research and Innovation Center of the Applied Molecular Laboratory at the Fondazione Mach of the Istituto San Michele all'Adige and one of Italy's greatest (and nicest) grapevine scientists, told me that she feels exactly the same way: "A variety-oriented enology, aiming to obtain a distinct wine from a specific cultivar, requires complete knowledge of the cultivar itself."

HISTORY OF AMPELOGRAPHY IN ITALY AND EUROPE

Before modern biomolecular techniques became available, all we had to describe grape varieties was ampelography. The ancient Romans made the first attempts at classifying grape varieties in an orderly fashion. The simplest classification divided grape varieties into two broad categories, table grapes (e.g., *ad mensam, ad cibariae, ad suburbanae*) and wine grapes (e.g., *ad bibendum, ad vindemias*), and then by descriptors such as berry color and grapevine phenological characteristics.

The first true ampelographers were born in the nineteenth century. In Italy, Acerbi and Gallesio were the most famous, but there were other experts, such as Ciro Pollini, whose treatise in 1822 on the vines and grapes of the Verona province alone described roughly eighty different grape varieties (fifty-five red and twenty-seven white). In the nineteenth century, Italy saw the creation of its first varietal collections, and experts such as Gatta (1838), Agazzotti (1867), Mendola (1868), Incisa (1869), Di Rovasenda (1877), Gerini (1882), and Bianchi (1893) described accessions with ever greater accuracy. In 1872, the first International Commission of Ampelography was convened in Vienna: it coordinated European viticultural efforts and led to a catalogue listing the grape varieties of Europe. In Italy, the Comitato Centrale Ampelografico (Central Ampelographic Committee) and the Commissioni Ampelografiche Provinciali (Provincial Ampelographic Committees) were born: their mission was to study all of the nation's grape varieties, including their winemaking potential. Their work was summarized in the *Bollettini Ampelografici* (Ampelographic Bulletins) published mainly between 1876 to 1887 and still extremely useful today. Other countries developed varietal catalogues, containing either drawings or photographs of grapes: best known are those of France's Viala and Vermorel (1901, 1909). Italy's Molon (1906) was also among the Italian experts called upon to contribute to Viala and Vermorel's opus. In Italy, the Istituto Sperimentale per la Viticoltura di Conegliano Veneto (Research Institute for Viticulture), now called the CRA-VIT Centro Ricerche per la Viticoltura, was founded in 1923 as the Regia Stazione Sperimentale di Viticoltura ed Enologia, and has been the leader in the selection and conservation of Italy's grapevine genetic material over the years. From the beginning, grape variety collections were set up in the experimental vineyards of a farm in the town of Susegana (near Treviso). By 1967 the numbers of grape varieties grown had doubled, and since then many similar, world-class research institutions dedicated to grapevine study have been created.

AMPELOLOGY, OR THE IDENTIFICATION OF GRAPE VARIETIES

Ampelology is more of a science than the art form ampelography was (and is), and it includes diverse techniques and methods by which to identify grapes. These include:

- Ampelographic descriptions and ampelometrics: the former describe the morphological characteristics of grapevines; the latter consist in measurements of organs and are less subjective than ampelographic methods.
- Biochemical methods, such as isoenzyme analysis or aromatic molecule precursor analysis, that reveal the presence or absence of specific enzymes and of some metabolites in each variety.
- Biomolecular methods, which reveal DNA sequences specific to single varieties.

The use of all three methods together allows for more accurate variety identification. Ampelographers and geneticists cannot function to their full potential working alone; in fact, the identification of grape varieties is very much a team effort.

AMPELOGRAPHY

Ampelography is the first step toward characterization of a grape variety and of fundamental importance for subsequent genetic testing. Grapevines are classified based on the appearance of their leaves, shoots, berries, bunch appearance, and color, and by viticultural parameters such as date of flowering or harvest. The data compiled is tremendously specific and precise; for example, within the category of leaves, everything from single indentations to color of the veins is considered. Another example is the shoot tip, the color of which can be a very useful descriptor in the spring: for instance, the white tip of Merlot distinguishes it from Cabernet Franc or Cabernet Sauvignon, with which it is often confused. These ampelographic characteristics are classified by qualitative, quantitative, and alternative characteristics, and may be either present or absent. By compiling this data, a reasonably accurate but not infallible identification of a variety may be made. However, difficulties abound. For one, an immense level of experience is necessary to correctly identify cultivars on the basis of physical parameters alone (and not all researchers have that experience or the time and means to acquire it), and it is very easy to make mistakes. Furthermore, grapevine morphological features such as leaves and bunches can be greatly affected by the environment. For example, the size of grape bunches and berries can differ based on water access and the availability of minerals in the soil, as well as the yields of the grapevines.

Also, morphological identification can be applied only when berries and leaves are fully visible, so ampelographic recognition can take place only at certain times of the year. The onus is then on nursery personnel to work accurately and correctly: only several years after a vineyard is planted are mistakes noticed. Everyone knows of producers who thought they were growing Cabernet Franc or Merlot or Albariño only to realize their vines were Carmenère or Savagnin instead. Nursery mistakes such as these are more frequent than is commonly believed.

To increase precision, ampelometric methods were added to ampelographic observation. Ampelometric methods possess the advantage of being less subjective than ampelographic characteristics, as they are measurable. In 1983, the Office International de la Vigne et du Vin (OIV) published the *Code des caractéres descriptifs des variétés et espèces de Vitis* (Code of the Descriptive Characters of the Varieties and Species of *Vitis*) in French, English, Spanish, and German. In it, they presented the codification of 128 ampelographic descriptive characters (later reduced to a more manageable eighty-four), a method adopted by other international organizations, including the International Board for Plant Genetic Resource (IBPGR) and the International Union for the Protection of New Varieties of Plants (UPOV).

CHEMICAL ANALYSIS: ISOENZYMES, SECONDARY METABOLITES

Until DNA testing became routinely available in the twenty-first century, biochemical methods were most often used to bolster ampelographic information about varieties. Life is possible because of biochemical reactions catalyzed by enzymes (proteins composed of amino acid chains), the structure of which is determined by corresponding DNA sequences. Isoenzymes are different molecular forms (in size or electric charge) of enzymes that catalyze the same reactions. Since they are correlated to known specific gene loci, they behave as genetic markers. Isoenzymes can be differentiated by electrophoresis, which relies upon their different levels of mobility within a gel to which an electric current has been applied. The diverse positions reached by the different isoenzymes are called "profiles" or "patterns." Four enzymatic systems may be used, but two are most reliable: glucose phosphate isomerase (GPI) and phosphogluco mutase (PGM). Though useful, and in fact much employed once, isoenzyme analysis has limitations (Stavrakakis and Loukas 1983; Calò, Costacurta, Paludetti, Calò, Aruselsekar, and Parfitt 1989). While grapes with different isoenzyme patterns are certainly different varieties, it is not necessarily true that those with similar patterns are the same variety. However, over time numerous cases of synonyms and homonyms of grape varieties have been apparently resolved with this method (Calò, Costacurta, Cancellier, and Forti 1991; Moriondo 1999).

We know grape-derived secondary metabolites are the principal source of wine aroma, flavor, color, and taste and that they include polyphenols (like anthocyanins and flavonols) as well as aromatic compounds (like monoterpenes). Bate-Smith was the first to show, in 1948, the role of phenolic pigments as genetic markers, but Ribereau-Gayon was the first to apply them to grapevines, in 1953. Molecules like geraniol and linalool were used to identify grapes once. Unfortunately, concentrations of these compounds can be affected by a number of variables, including climate (Jackson and Lombard 1993), water supply (Hardie and Martin 1990), and canopy management (Smart and Robinson 1991). For example, wines made from aromatic varieties are immediately recognizable because of their spicy, floral, and very fruity aromas: these are the result of aromatic molecules such as terpenes, benzenoids, and norisoprenoids. All grapes contain these molecules in varying amounts, but grapes defined as "aromatic" have more. Wines made with *Moscato* varieties are especially rich in a terpene called linalool, while members of the *Malvasia* group have always been characterized by another terpene, geraniol. The two molecules are responsible for different aroma types, which once were used to distinguish *Moscato* wines from aromatic *Malvasia* wines: while linalool leaves a sweet, musky impression typical of all the *Moscato*s, geraniol recalls more refined rose-like aromas, typical of all the aromatic *Malvasia*s, white and red. For instance, Moscato Rosa's aromatic profile differs considerably from that of Moscato Bianco, and is more similar to that of Brachetto or Malvasia di Casorzo. For the same reason, Malvasia delle Lipari has an aroma profile that makes its wines more reminiscent of some *Moscato* varieties than of other *Malvasia*s. Unfortunately, though the aromatic expression of grapes is genetically predetermined, growing conditions and winemaking techniques can easily alter the aromatic profiles of wines to a significant degree.

CELLULAR AND MOLECULAR BIOLOGY TECHNIQUES

The genetic patrimony of each individual is mainly constituted by DNA (deoxyribonucleic acid) contained within the nucleus of cells, though DNA is not found just in nuclei, but also in other organelles within cells, such as mitochondria. For DNA's content to be actually useful, it needs to be copied and transported outside the nucleus to other structures called ribosomes, where its information is translated and transformed into proteins. This task is performed by two forms of RNA (ribonucleic acid): messenger RNA (mRNA) and translator RNA (tRNA). It is the mRNA that transports DNA information to the ribosomes where the tRNA then proceeds to have DNA's information translated.

Just like human beings, all grapevines have distinct DNA profiles. DNA testing was introduced by Jeffreys, Wilson, and Thein in 1985 and has been successfully used in the field of criminal law—it was first applied to vine research by Thomas and Scott in 1993. DNA testing represents the current state of the art for grape variety identification, as DNA is relatively easy to obtain with a little experience, testing can be carried out at any time of the year, and tests are not influenced by the environment. Initially, the molecular techniques used included restriction fragment length polymorphism (RFLP), amplified fragment length polymorphism (AFLP), and random amplified polymorphic DNA (RAPD), but these have been largely replaced by the use of microsatellite technology, which is characterized by high reproducibility and standardization. Microsatellite markers are the most commonly used DNA test for identification of grapevine cultivars today. There are two types of microsatellites most used at present: nuclear microsatellites (or nuclear simple sequence repeats, nSSR), which are the best known and most used to date, and chloroplast microsatellites (CpSSR), which may be more useful in parentage studies.

To genetically identify a vine, specific, small segments of DNA called alleles are targeted and the polymerase chain reaction (PCR) technique is used to make millions of copies of selected marker segments. The alleles in one marker site of a given variety are compared with those present in the same marker site of another variety. Though I am simplifying greatly, two vines are considered to belong to the same variety if they possess identical sequences of DNA in a sufficient number of these marker sites, called microsatellites and also known as single sequence repeats, or SSR. Microsatellites, found in all vegetal and animal species, including grapes, are simple sequence repetitions scattered randomly throughout an organism's DNA that were long believed not to be transcribed and translated. In other words, not to code for proteins. (However, as we shall see later in this chapter, it is becoming apparent that this view is increasingly obsolete.) As microsatellites are constant within each variety and differ from those of other varieties, they act as molecular fingerprints for varieties. The identification of unknown vines is done by comparing the SSR profiles obtained from the sample with reference SSR profiles of cultivars stored in internationally available databases, much as with fingerprints in criminology. A variety is considered "new" if the microsatellites do not match any in the database. Depending on the number of sites studied, the probability of different varieties having the same SSR pattern by chance is roughly one in eight billion.

While several sets of SSR markers have been proposed for grape research, the best known are the set of six suggested by the grape Genetic Resources (GENRES) projects. This project established the European Vitis Database (EVDB), which now includes data for more than 28,200 accessions, representing the *Vitis* collections of eighteen European contributors. The research group also selected six microsatellite loci allowing for the identification of grapevine cultivars (VVS2, VVMD5, VVMD7, VVMD27, VrZag62, and VrZag79). Though most researchers believe that six loci are enough to determine genetic identity between most species, at least nine are indicated for varieties that are close genetically. Statistically, the probability identity value increases by six powers of ten when nine, rather than six, SSR loci are studied. Analyzing more than ten loci of the grapevine genome further increases the accuracy of cultivar identification: the ten microsatellite loci internationally accepted are VVS2, VVMD5, VVMD7, VVMD25, VVM27, VVMD28, VVMD31, VVMD32, VrZAG62, and VrZAG79. Recently however, researchers have begun to think that even more loci might be necessary to increase the discrimination power of investigations performed.

Recently, another molecular DNA marker has come into use: single nucleotide polymorphisms, or SNPs (pronounced "snips"). Future genetic grapevine research will likely combine both SNP and SSR assessments. Lijavetszky, Cabezas, Ibanez, Rodriguez, and Martinez-Zapater (2007) found that SNPs provide a lower probability identity than microsatellites, so higher numbers of markers are needed to generate similar probability values. The advantage of SNPs is they are easier to work with than SSRs.

Chloroplast microsatellite studies are of particular interest, since the genetic material of chloroplasts (small chlorophyll-containing organelles that are the photosynthetic units of plants) is transmitted from mother to daughter without undergoing any variation. As a result of its perceived conservative rate of propagation, chloroplast DNA has proven extremely useful in plant population biology studies examining the migratory routes of species, as shown by Weising and Gardner (1999) and Avise (2000). Chloroplast-specific haplotypes, or chlorotypes, have been found in indigenous germplasm believed to be typical of the specific region. For chloroplast SSR analysis, as many as nine polymorphic chloroplast microsatellite loci have been used, such as cpSSR3, cpSSR5, and cpSSR10 (Arroyo-Garcia, Ruiz-García, Bolling, Ocete, López, Arnold, et al. 2006; Imazio, Labra, Grassi, Scienza, and Failla 2006).

HITS AND MISSES OF AMPELOLOGY

Through the combined efforts of the above methodologies, we have apparently been able to correctly identify many erroneously named cultivars. Examples include Pignoletto, which was proven identical to Grechetto di Todi (Filippetti, Intrieri, Silvestroni, and Thomas 1999), and Bonarda in Argentina, shown to be identical to Corbeau (known as Charbono in California) (Martínez, Cavagnaro, Boursiquot, and Aguero 2008). However, unless ampelographic and genetic studies are performed with utmost care, wrong attributions are common: well-known mistakes made in the past include misidentifying California *Refosco* as Mondeuse Noire, Cilegiolo as Aglianicone, and Casetta as Enantio. These pairs of cultivars are unrelated, and provide an example of how incorrect ampelographic identifications can nullify properly conducted genetic testing—and of course, the converse is also true. Accurately labeled vine samples in reference collections all over the world are a must, because genetic testing via microsatellite analysis can only confirm or rebuke the ampelographic identification proposed. Nowadays, better nurseries test new acquisitions, and offer to have the DNA of planting material of newer varieties tested, an increasingly interesting resource.

This rigor is necessary. Since genetic analysis is performed on vineyard collection grapevine samples (from a university or another source) that were originally identified by an ampelographer (and how experienced an ampelographer is anybody's guess) or by the farmer who originally planted it, subsequent genetic testing is at the mercy of that original identification. If grapevine samples are misidentified and mislabeled in varietal collections, then genetic test results will be hopelessly wrong and of no use. In the California *Refosco* example, a mistake was easy to make since the *Refoscos* and Mondeuse Noire resemble each other. The university collection sample had been identified ampelographically as a "Refosco" and when it was later found that its DNA matched that of Mondeuse Noire, it was logical to conclude that Mondeuse Noire and *Refosco* were one and the same. However, when DNA tests were performed on authentic *Refosco* varieties in Italy, the DNA of which is nothing like that of Mondeuse Noire, it became apparent that the California grapevine had been misidentified ampelographically, and had in fact been Mondeuse Noire all along. This example clearly demonstrates why tested, accurate ampelographic collections are a must. What's more, to refer to a generic "Refosco" is also incorrect: since there are at least four different *Refoscos* known, one needs to specify clearly which *Refosco* is being studied, for example, Refosco del Peduncolo Rosso or Refosco Nostrano. Clearly, Mondeuse Noire could not have been identical to both of those. It's either one or the other, and as it turns out, it's neither.

DNA PROFILING: POTENTIAL PROBLEMS AND PITFALLS

Several studies have shown that germplasm collections harbor many homonyms and synonyms (Ibanez, Andres, Molino, and Borrego 2003; Cipriani, Spadotto, Jurman, Di Gaspero, Crespan, Meneghetti, Frare, Vignani, et al. 2010; Laucou, Lacombe, Dechesne, Siret, Bruno, Dessup, Dessup, Ortigosa, et al. 2011). Emanuelli, Lorenzi, Grzeskowiak, Catalano, Stefanini, and Troggio (2013) concluded that "further studies of grapevine genetic data are required and that existing genetic databases may not be the useful reference standard" they were believed to be.

This is why some experts, such as Marisa Fontana and Roberto Bandinelli, believe that researchers might do better to visit areas where varieties naturally grow, verify that the grapevines under examination do have ampelographic characteristics typical of the variety they are studying, and then obtain genetic profiles of which they are certain, rather than relying simply and only on preexisting ampelographic databanks available in their home region or country, where the standard grapevines may have been misidentified. Clearly, this is an expensive proposition, and therefore leaves many cold. Still another problem with ampelographic identifications is that often too few accessions are examined. Most published studies report mind-numbing, long lists or tables of SSR microsatellite results performed on many different grape varieties, but often, carefully reading the results reveals that just a single accession or two has been studied for each grape variety, and that seems much too little.

An especially big problem in Italy is that most of the old vineyards are made up of promiscuously planted grapevines: even if farmers tell you that "this is an old vineyard of Aglianico," the chances are high there will be Piedirosso, Aglianicone, Tronto, and maybe even white grape varieties planted there. So unless quite a few of the vines in that vineyard are studied, mistakes are likely. One such problem variety is Verdello, grapevines of which apparently grow in different regions of Italy, alongside many cultivars named Verde-Something or Verde-like. It's quite likely that not all the "Verdello" grapevines in a given vineyard really are Verdello. Farmers often gave a "greenname" to any grapevine that generically fit the bill (and they still do so). Thus when sampling Verdello grapevines, the likelihood of picking up a vine that really isn't Verdello is high, and the skill of the ampelographer becomes of paramount importance. If the ampelographer mistakenly identifies one of the vines as Verdello (in a vineyard that likely contains many similar-looking but altogether different varieties), the DNA profile of that grapevine will be taken to be that of Verdello; this DNA profile will then be the reference DNA data for that research group's databank. Unfortunately, if the ampelographer mistakenly identified as Verdello a similar looking but actually altogether different grape, then future studies will inevitably conclude that Verdello (or what they wrongly believe to be Verdello) is identical to yet another grape that will be found to have the same DNA. This is how, perhaps years later, a researcher in another country might erroneously conclude that a local grapevine "X" is in fact Italy's Verdello, when in fact it is not, because the DNA considered to be that of Verdello wasn't Verdello's in the first place. Which leads to that nation's grape "X" being eliminated, and called Verdello from then on. Unfortunately, there are numerous examples of erroneous attributions, and these are a huge problem because they convey essentially wrong information as a certitude, thanks to the "end-all" that is genetic testing. Researchers always conclude in their studies that their findings require that the National Registry be changed or updated. Those changes might not take place immediately, but in the meantime everyone refers to the study that "determined" that two previously distinct varieties are identical. The risk is a restructuring of the Italian (and not just Italian, of course) ampelographic platform that rests on at times very sketchy data. In my opinion, there is currently a real danger of what I have defined as excessive revisionism of grape history, an attitude that privileges concluding that "this grape is not the grape you always thought it was."

WHEN IS IDENTICAL REALLY IDENTICAL?

Besides excessive revisionism, excessive reductionism ("These two, or three, or four, etc., grape varieties are all the same") is another potential problem. It is why some modern counts of Italy's native grapes list fewer than four hundred varieties, and why many local grape scientists believe that number to be much too low. As we have seen, genetic profiling involves analysis of DNA sequence repeats that scientist have always believed are not transcripted (copied) and transcribed (translated), or in other words, are not coded for anything. In fact, scientists are becoming increasingly aware that even the sequences of DNA that we once thought did not code for anything are in fact a lot more active than originally believed. Hence, even those portions of DNA that microsatellite testing uses to determine identity between varieties are not in fact quite as identical as we like to think they are.

One of the most interesting aspects in all of wine is the existence of biotypes or subvarieties (others use these two terms interchangeably with *clones*, but this is incorrect), meaning those varieties that are supposedly genetically "identical" but have obvious morphologic and physiological differences. Biotypes are members of a grape variety that exhibit phenotypic plasticity, by spreading out geographically and adapting to different environments over the centuries (see chapter 2). In so doing, they have built up mutations. These mutations, depending on where they affect the genome, may or may not have important consequences; clearly, the older the variety is, the more chances it has of undergoing mutations, thereby developing a slew of descendants that look and behave differently. In this sense, it's not that some varieties are more prone to mutation than others, just that they have been around longer. Pinot Nero and Nebbiolo come to mind: it's not that these two mutate more easily than others, as has always been believed, but rather that they are very old grape varieties.

Based on microsatellite analysis, Pinot Nero, Pinot Grigio, and Pinot Bianco have the same genetic profile, but all look obviously different: one has dark blue berries, another red-pink berries, and one white (actually yellow-green) berries. Yet microsatellite testing tells us they are. It's much more difficult to distinguish between, for example, Italy's many Verde-something varieties or between Cataratto Bianco Lucido, Cataratto Bianco Extralucido, and Cataratto Bianco Comune, because the morphologic differences present are a great deal more obscure, and limited mainly to differences in berry appearance. According to DNA microsatellite studies, all three are genetically identical: but in my experience, the *Cataratto*s not only look and exhibit viticultural behaviors that are different enough, but the wines are different too.

The world of Italian grapes is filled with many "different yet not so different-looking" grapes. Difficulties often arise because many completely different grapes are given the same name, such as the countless Montanaras, Montaneras, and others still. Pigato, Favorita, and Vermentino are another case in point. Pigato grows in Liguria, Vermentino in both Liguria and Sardinia, and Favorita in Piedmont. The three grapes have been deemed genetically identical based on DNA microsatellite results (as the three *Pinot*s have), but the vast majority of Ligurian producers (especially) refute this notion—and let me tell you, quite vociferously at times. In fact, you can't blame them, since there are obvious physical differences between the three grapes, but apparently their morphological differences are not considered sufficient to separate the three varieties as distinct. However, I am not so sure there are only minor consequences for the wines, because I find Pigato wines recognizably different from Vermentinos most of the time, and from Favorita even more often. Pigato and Vermentino in Liguria often share the same vineyard parcel, and yet, to my taste, their wines do smell and taste sufficiently different to warrant at least raising an eyebrow or two. Angelo Negro, one of the best producers of Roero in Piedmont, told me recently how years ago he planted both Pigato and Favorita side by side in a vineyard (because a university expert had told him the varieties were identical), but that both the grapevines and the wines made from them couldn't have turned out more different. Now there's food (er, wine) for thought.

Given how complicated the world of Italian native and traditional grapes is, with myriad slightly-different looking grapes that are said to be "genetically similar," this becomes a very important question. When we say—or are told—that varieties are "genetically identical," do we know exactly what that means? This is not at all a moot point, since we know that the different phenotype expressions of biotypes do have a genetic background: for example, analysis of up to one hundred DNA markers (which in practice is never done) showed that a few genetic variations can be observed among clones of *Pinot,* as with Chardonnay (Riaz, Garrison, Dangl, Boursiquot, and Meredith 2002). I don't think anyone knows for sure, but perhaps sequencing out the entire genome of the *Catarattos,* or of Pigato/Vermentino/Favorita might show that genetic differences between them are more widespread than we believe them to be.

In fact, even when DNA looks totally identical, it may function, or be made to function, in completely different manners, leading to completely different results. DNA is far more complex than scientists initially believed: in fact, over the last thirty years it has become increasingly apparent that we still don't know enough about the nucleic acids (both DNA and RNA) and their many intricate functions and interrelations. At the present state of genetic knowledge, when DNA profiling shows that two grapevines have the same microsatellite repeat sequences, scientists conclude that the two grapevines are identical. I wonder. For example, we have learned that those portions of DNA that supposedly don't code for anything, defined by scientists as "junk DNA" or "non-sense DNA," which DNA profiling using the microsatellite technique relies upon for its results, actually are not passive at all. They may all look the same, but they don't necessarily work the same way. Hence, it cannot be excluded that the end result of their activity may lead to altogether different results, in this case, what ultimately are distinct grape varieties. For example, even portions of junk DNA are transcribed (copied) into RNA molecules with different functions. RNA does a lot more than act only as a messenger and a translator. Rather it exerts an influence on DNA at many levels, regulating gene activity and expression: it can do so not just during transcription and translation, but at post-transcriptional and post-translational levels as well. In fact, while we tend to think of our world as governed by DNA, RNA is just as important, and perhaps even more. Besides the well-known mRNA and tRNA, other RNA molecules have been recently described, for example mRNA molecules that, despite their name, do not seem to transport any specific message. All these RNA molecules can exert control over what the DNA ultimately does, but they are themselves subject to various control mechanisms. How and why these RNA molecules interact with DNA is the subject of research studies in laboratories and universities all over the world.

Clearly, the genome is far more complex than we once thought: for instance, the present definition of *gene* as that portion of DNA which codes for a protein is undoubtedly limited. Using that definition, for example, only 2 percent of human DNA is made up of genes, and that's just not possible, for there are many more portions of DNA that are quasi-genes, which either do something or are made to do something by interaction with appropriate RNA molecules of various kinds. Returning to our grape varieties example, it follows that today we take microsatellite profiles at what might be described as only face value: when confronted with similar DNA microsatellite profiles, we conclude that similar sequences are in fact the same, and hence that the vines that share them are identical. But as we have seen, that is extremely unlikely, for though those DNA sequences all look the same, they may be transcribed and eventually translated in very different manners, leading to what are essentially different-looking and perhaps even distinct grape varieties. Therein may lie an explanation why, for example, Pigato, Vermentino, and Favorita, though genetically "identical" at our present state of knowledge, look different and produce different-tasting wines: because they are in fact distinct varieties. Which would also mean that many older farmers out there really do know best. In any case, Pelsy, Hocquigny, Moncada, Barbeau, Forget, Hinrichsen, and Merdinoglu (2010) have concluded that when clones of the same variety have phenotypes different enough to lead to the production of different wines, they are to be grouped into different cultivars. Furthermore, Emanuelli, Lorenzi, Grzeskowiak, Catalano, Stefanini, and Troggio (2013) have stated that accessions sharing the same SSR profile ought to be evaluated further before being eliminated from standard grapevine collections, because they might not be redundant at all.

Therefore, in my opinion, though at this time we cannot say that Pigato/Vermentino/Favorita or Cataratto Comune/Lucido/Extralucido are in fact distinct varieties, we should at least always stress that they are different biotypes and their resulting wines are different. This is true to greater or lesser degrees depending on the varieties involved.

TWO

The Origin of Viticulture and a Brief History of Italy's Grape Varieties

ROMANCING THE VINE

The grapevine, a climbing plant much like ivy, belongs to the botanical order Rhamnales, family Vitaceae, which is divided into two subfamilies, Leicodeae and Ampelideae. The latter is divided into five genera: *Ampelopsis, Cissus, Parthenocissus, Ampelocissus,* and *Vitis.* The first four include species of vines that are used mainly for ornamental purposes, and only the genus *Vitis,* which is further divided into the subgenera *Muscadinia* and *Euvites,* is relevant to wine drinkers. According to Fregoni, these two subgenera contain roughly seventy different species of grapevine (roughly forty of Eurasian origin, and thirty American), characterized by varying degrees of temperature, disease, and parasite resistance. However, recently some redundancies and synonyms have been eliminated, reducing the total to roughly thirty-two species. Of these, the most important is *vinifera,* the only one originating in Europe, Central Asia, and East Asia. It is divided into two subspecies: ssp. *silvestris,* which lives naturally in the wild, and ssp. *sativa,* the cultivated or domesticated variety of the grapevine, derived from the wild form. For the technically minded, the correct names of the two species are *Vitis vinifera* L. ssp. *silvestris* and *Vitis vinifera* L. ssp. *sativa*—the "L" is in honor of the naturalist Carl Linnaeus, who named the species. The likes of Nebbiolo, Sangiovese, and Chardonnay are all cultivated forms of *Vitis vinifera.*

Wine can be made from other *Vitis* species as well, such as *Vitis labrusca*'s Concord grape, but these wines often have a foxy taste (very grapey, and reminiscent of fruit syrups, bubble gum, and candied fruit) quite unlike that of those made with *Vitis vinifera.* Therefore, the other *Vitis* species are used mainly as progenitors of hybrids, or to provide rootstocks and table grapes. For example, the American *Vitis* species *labrusca, riparia, rupestris,* and *berlandieri* are important sources of phylloxera-resistant rootstocks.

Vitis vinifera is a perennial plant that lives in temperate climates. While ssp. *silvestris* has a greater resistance to cold weather than ssp. *sativa,* neither are particularly cold resistant; temperatures below −20°C can cause irreversible damage, as can excessive heat. This is why *vinifera* is limited to areas with an average annual temperature of 10°C and a vegetative cycle (the period from flowering to harvest) of at least two hundred days. Clearly, Italy's generally temperate, Mediterranean climate allows *vinifera* to thrive. While ssp. *sativa* performs best in relatively dry climates, ssp. *silvestris* can tolerate more humid conditions that mimic the woodland and marshy environments it calls home; both however are highly heliophilic, in that they need plenty of sunlight (and in fact wild vines prefer to live at the forest's edge or near clearings). The two subspecies differ considerably in a number of other aspects as well, such as the size and shape of their leaves, bunches, pips, and berries. The bunches and berries of ssp. *silvestris* are smaller and fewer, and their grapes are almost always darkly hued; there are very few white grapes in the wild. Wild grapes are also less sweet and higher in acidity, and have larger and rounder pips.

However, larger bunches and better-tasting berries are not the only advantages of the cultivated *vinifera* subspecies. Wild subspecies are dioecious, having male and female plants with unisexual flowers. Though there are functional exceptions, the domesticated *vinifera* is instead an hermaphroditic plant, bisexual, with sex organs that are both male (stamens that produce pollen) and female (pistils containing ovaries to be fertilized). Therefore, it can self-pollinate, and every plant can bear fruit: not a small advantage, and one that may explain why our farming ancestors might have preferred to cultivate vines rather than tend wild ones. Interestingly, a small percentage of ssp. *silvestris* vines are naturally hermaphroditic, paving the way for domestication of what was initially only a wild grapevine species.

Between 10,000 and 7,000 B.C.E. all *vinifera* grew wild, and the grape varieties we know today evolved from them. Grape varieties are the result of sexual reproduction between two parent varieties: a flower is pollinated or fertilized, leading to the formation of a berry and its seeds. The seeds are then propagated in a number of different ways and new vines are born. Self-pollination occurs when the pollen reaches the same flower it originated in, or a flower on the same vine, or a flower on a different plant of the same variety. Cross-pollination happens when the pollen from a flower from one variety reaches a flower from another variety. Clearly, the latter was a great deal more common in times past, when different varieties were planted in the same vineyard.

Most likely, the first grape varieties were wild vines that adapted over time to new *terroirs* via human efforts to cultivate them. In a phone interview with Attilio Scienza of the University of Milan, he told me that cross-pollination not just between cultivated varieties but also between wild vines and the earliest cultivated species also seems likely. Though some DNA-based studies reject the possible genetic relationships between cultivated and wild grapevine species (This, Lacombe, and Thomas 2006), others disagree and cite Italian native examples such as Sardinia's Bovale Piccolo and Veneto's Oseleta, which have been shown to have a high genetic affinity with local wild vines (Grassi, Labra, Imazio, Spada, Sgorbati, Scienza, and Sala 2003; Zecca, De Mattia, Lovicu, Labra, Sala, and Grassi 2009). According to a report by Di Vecchi Staraz, Bandinelli, Boselli, This, Boursiquot, Laucou, et al. (2007), seven Tuscan native varieties have important genetic relationships with wild grapevines. Due to the large differences observed between members of a few individual grapevine species (for example, Sangiovese), some experts have also postulated the existence of grapevine "variety-populations" via a mechanism of polyclonal inheritance, originating from several different grape seeds. The existence of these was hypothesized by Levadoux in the mid-twentieth century and again by Mullins and Meredith in 1989, and has been championed in Italy for Fortana and Glera (Silvestroni, Di Pietro, Intrieri, Vignani, Filippetti, Del Casino, et al. 1997; Calò, Costacurta, Cancellier, Crespan, Milani, Carraro, et al. 2000). This is currently a minority hypothesis, with most experts believing that every grape variety originates from a unique seed with just two parents (for example, a single seed is at the origin of Sangiovese).

CLONES AND BIOTYPES

Throughout the centuries, humans on the move transported cuttings or buds from individual grapevines they liked and replanted them in new, suitable habitats even in distant countries. In this manner there is no gene pool shuffling, and each new plant is a genetically identical copy of its parent, at least originally. However, grapevines transported via cuttings do not remain genetically identical to the progenitor grapevine over centuries. This is true of human beings too: according to Cavalli Sforza, migration represents nothing more than a flow of genes moving into or out of a gene pool to create new genetic entities or modify preexisting ones. Once reproductive cycles occur, there is a reshuffling of the parental genes, and the offspring will be genetically different from the parents. At each cell division, errors can happen and mutations are born. The ensuing grapevine may look and behave essentially the same or quite differently, exhibiting phenotypic plasticity, defined as the range of phenotypes a variety can exhibit due to its interactions with the environment and humans (larger or smaller berries, color differences, higher or lower yields, disease susceptibility, and so forth). Though we habitually describe these new and different grapevines as "clones," this is incorrect, as clones are by definition genetically identical to the mother plant. It is more accurate to refer to these new and different plants as biotypes. As we have seen, biotypes express intravarietal variability, the condition by which members of the same variety will look different from others, or from one area to another. These site-specific biotypes often draw even experienced observers into erroneous conclusions about their exact identity. Therefore, intravarietal variability is one of the biggest causes of synonymity in wine grapes, and of many erroneous ampelographic attributions. Clearly, the more ancient a variety, the more likely it is to have greater intravarietal variability—and hence many biotypes—simply because mutations have accumulated over time. As I stated in the previous chapter, biotypes are especially relevant to wine lovers, since many of these not only look and behave differently in the vineyards, but also give startlingly different wines, even with similar winemaking techniques.

Changes in genomes may occur via other mechanisms: when a plant is moved from one region to another, a modification of its genetic material takes place ("genetic drift"). Grapevines do not remain the same in their new or final destination because at each stop they undergo genetic introgression. Introgression is the introduction into a genome of small portions of the DNA of preexisting local species (cultivated or wild) or of grapevine species they traveled alongside (on a boat or a donkey, in a knapsack or a box) en route to their new home. The grapevine that finally "settles" for good in a new environment is no longer the same grapevine that left its original home. Further, over centuries in its new home the grapevine will undergo further changes to its genetic and phenotypic makeup, brought on by the environment, human selection pressures, and other causes. Humans notably prefer to propagate those grapevines with qualities valued at that moment: resistance to disease or copious productivity were most important in our poorer past, while in today's more hedonistic times better wine quality is the usual goal.

The end result of all this selecting, traveling, and shuffling is that there are an estimated eight thousand to ten thousand truly different grape varieties used to make wine all over the world today, though some report higher numbers of grape varieties when table grapes are included. Italy, for a variety of reasons, has more varieties than any other country: how this came to be is absolutely fascinating.

WHERE GRAPES GROW IN ITALY AND HOW THEY GOT THERE

How did *vinifera* arrive in Italy? It's an important question, for in the answer lies an explanation for the country's myriad native grapes. Thanks to the great body of work left us by the Russian botanists Vavilov and Negrul, who studied the evolution of wild vine species into the vines of today, we know that the distribution range of the wild vine from which the cultivated forms of grapevine developed originally included the Anatolian, Caucasus, and Caspian regions. These regions are widely considered to be primary centers of domestication of the grapevine. From there, the cultivated forms of *Vitis vinifera* moved westward into the Near East and the Mediterranean basin. Though the existence of secondary centers is still questioned by some experts, others agree there were six main secondary centers of domestication, where local grape varieties where born by naturally occurring crossings, first in Egypt, and then in Greece and Italy. These secondary centers of domestication therefore also doubled as centers of genetic diversity and accumulation. In this respect, it is interesting to notice that the majority of the better-known Sicilian native varieties, with the exception of Frappato, are closely related. This makes sense, since having been in the same place together for a very long time, they were subjected to introgression between themselves and interactions with the local environment and with other locally found grapes. Of course, this should also be true not only of Sicily, but also of other domestication centers and their grape varieties. Interestingly, secondary centers do not explain the births of all the new species: wine was being made in both Italy and France long before any Greek settlers or Phoenician traders arrived, from local wild and *vinifera* species. These local varieties were widely present throughout Europe and western Asia and were the subject of multiple domestications everywhere. According to Levadoux (1951), *vinifera* species also grew in southern Europe; Biagini has reported on fossils of *vinifera* dating back to the Quartenary period, found in archeological sites near Fiano Romano and Ascoli Piceno in central Italy.

In the Beginning: The Birthplaces of Italy's Native Varieties

Thanks to modern biotechnology techniques and DNA studies, researchers have made considerable progress in their quest to decipher the origin of specific grape varieties. Consequently it has become easier to distinguish which varieties are native to one area or another. When evaluated using DNA marker studies (especially using maternal haplotypes of chloroplast plasmid DNA), many varieties were clearly differentiated and structured by geographic subregions. Such studies make it clear that the genetic structures of many Italian native grapes are different from the germplasm types found in other countries. For example, according to experts such as Arroyo-Garcia and Scienza, all the varieties native to a specific territory share many haplotypes in common, different from those of varieties found in or native to other areas.

Debate continues, but it appears that some native cultivars descend at least in part from local wild species. Arroyo-García, Ruiz-García, Bolling, Ocete, López, Arnold, et al. (2006) published landmark results regarding chlorotype distribution along the geographical range of grapevines—1,201 accessions of *vinifera* and *silvestris* in all—and examined their genetic relationships. Eight different chlorotypes were identified; of these eight chlorotypes (A to H), type A is prevalent in European *silvestris* populations but is not found in the Near East, while chlorotypes E, D, and G are frequent in Near East populations but not found farther west. Interestingly, the study reports that about "70 percent of all Iberian cultivars display chlorotypes that are only compatible with the possibility of having derived from Western *silvestris* populations." Which makes Spanish and Portuguese grape cultivars also pretty native: just like most Italian native varieties, grapes such as Touriga Nacional grow nowhere else in the world.

Of the six secondary domestication centers, two are especially relevant to Italy and its native varieties. One covered an area that covered southern Italy (including Sicily and Sardinia) and northern Africa: grape pip fossils dating back to 1,500 B.C.E. have been found in the Eolian (Lipari) islands. Natives of this area appear to be Asprinio, Impigno, Nero d'Avola, Aglianico, Marsigliana, Carricante, Cataratto, and Grillo. Interestingly, Scienza (2004) analyzed four hundred Greek and southern Italian native varieties and found very little genetic affinity between the two groups, raising the doubts that many of southern Italy's native grapes, such as the *Malvasias* and Aglianico, are of Greek origin, as was once commonly believed. Of course, these results do not prove the "nativeness" of these cultivars beyond doubt, because genetic modifications may have been induced subsequently to their arrival on Italian shores. However, Scienza has explained to me that he believes that Aglianico to be not at all of Greek origin, but rather a natural crossing between a local species and an oriental one. To date however, its progenitors have not yet been identified. The other secondary domestication center relevant to Italy's natives covered an area akin to what is now Provence and northern Italy. According to Scienza, varieties such as Picolit, Pignolo, all the many different *Refoscos*, Oseleta, Abrostine, the many *Lambruscos*, Glera, and the *Groppellos* appear to be native to this part of Italy, though many were later brought elsewhere.

Back to the Twentieth Century

Although Italy's native grapes and wines are currently on a roll, the last 150 years or so have not been easy on Italy's many grape varieties: many became extinct and some are still at risk of disappearing. Though continued genetic erosion of Italy's native varietal base was a leading cause of concern up to fifteen years ago, the recent focus on native grapes has inverted that worrisome trend. So why did so many varieties, both high quality and not, run the risk of becoming endangered species? In general, most native varieties present one or more flaws—or qualities perceived as flaws—such as low yields, which were a big no-no for most of the twentieth century in Italy. Knowledge of these qualities led many a winemaker to pass up native grapes in favor of international varieties, which are much easier to work with. For varieties like Chardonnay and Merlot, there exist simple, highly researched winemaking protocols that allow just about anyone, given reasonably competent winemaking, to produce something palatable. Unfortunately, Italy's many native varieties were neither studied nor blessed with gifted winemaking; consequently, the wines they gave were more often than not unstable, dirty, and easily oxidized. It is easy to understand why few realized that grapes such as Malvasia Puntinata, Passerina, or Pecorino could yield high-quality wines.

Each one of the following events contributed to the loss of native varieties in Italy, or to their diminished distribution.

1850S–1900S: ADVENT OF OIDIUM, PERONOSPORA, AND PHYLLOXERA Practically all of Europe's vineyards are damaged by oidium and peronospora, and finally destroyed by phylloxera (an aphid that feeds on the roots of European grape varieties and kills them inexorably)—and Italy's were no exception. The only surviving vineyards are those planted at high mountain altitudes or in sandy soils, two habitats in which the aphid does not survive. Phylloxera is responsible for the disappearance of many varieties throughout Europe, though the exact number of the lost is not known.

1920–1930: POST-PHYLLOXERA WAVE OF PLANTINGS Replanting vineyards, farmers give preference to the most resistant and productive varieties, a selection process that limits the genetic variability and varietal diversity of grapes all over the country.

1950S–1970S: RENOVATION OF VITICULTURE PRODUCTION OBJECTIVES AND THE ROLE OF FEOGA The Common Agricultural Policy (CAP), a system of European Union agricultural subsidies and programs, is born with the 1957 Treaty of Rome. In the aftermath of the food shortage of post-WWII Europe, CAP is meant to guarantee adequate alimentary production, to ensure farmers a reasonable standard of living, and to preserve rural heritage. The European Fund for Agricultural Orientation and Guarantee (Fondo Europeo di Orientamento e Garanzia in Agricoltura, or FEOGA), since renamed the

European Fund for Agricultural Rural Development (Fondo Europeo Agricolo per lo Sviluppo Rurale, or FEASR), is the financial arm of the European Union's budget for agricultural support. Included among the original directives is a "rationalization" of agricultural vineyards that provides financial incentives for farmers to change to more modern, cost-effective, higher-yielding vineyards. As a consequence, old vines are ripped up and new plantings made all over Italy (if you hear something, that's me crying). Though it means well, CAP promotes a large increase in agricultural production that is not always quality-oriented.

1960–1970: BIRTH OF VQPRD, DOC, DOCG, AND OTHER LEGISLATION These laws, based on France's famous Appellation d'Origine Controlée (AOC), determine which wines can be made with which varieties. Though meant to help make better wines, these regulations also greatly damage Italy's native grape varieties because farmers abandon varieties that are no longer permitted.

LATE 1960–EARLY 1970S: CRISIS OF THE MEZZADRIA AND RURAL EXODUS The disappearance of crop sharing, or *mezzadria,* helps propel Italian wine into the realm of quality wine production. In the *mezzadria* system, farmers had been allowed to keep a percentage of what they grew; they had no reason to limit yields, a key for quality wine production, since they were interested in producing as much as possible. However, the rural exodus that ensues with the end of *mezzadria,* as people went looking for bank or office jobs, means vineyards are abandoned. Many local varieties already reduced in number no longer have anyone caring for them, and become extinct.

1960–1980: INTENSIFICATION OF CLONAL SELECTION The breeding of clones from carefully but misguidedly selected plants, designed for high yields and concomitant poor wine quality, causes diminished genetic biodiversity.

1999: THE EUROPEAN UNION REGULATES ITS WINE MARKET On May 17, 1999, the European Union passes Regulation 1493, which requires each member country to compile a list of the grape varieties from which wines for commercial sale may be made. Among other things, it decrees that only vines of the *Vitis* species and of crossings of *Vitis* species, may be used to make wine. Unfortunately, this legislation also specifies that all those vineyards planted with varieties *not* included in the official lists are to be uprooted, except in those cases where the wine is used for home consumption.

2006: ITALIAN LAW DEFINES NATIVE GRAPES Law 82, of February 20, 2006, defines a native grape as one that "is original to a zone or was introduced there at least fifty years ago and is traditionally integrated with the agriculture of that area." The fifty-year specification to define a cultivar as "native" is a joke, something only politicians could have concocted. The law is an obvious attempt to please potential voters by allowing them to use the word "native," which currently helps sell wine, to describe their wines.

EXTINCT AND FORGOTTEN VARIETIES: MAKING A COMEBACK?

Though it's true that university and research institutions are leading the way with genetics and field testing, oftentimes such testing has been spurred on by single wine estates. Passionate estate owners in Italy have always replanted and nurtured vines of rare varieties that they felt were capable of yielding good wines. Convinced the results were worth pursuing, many looked for help from universities to determine if such grapevines were in fact "new" varieties, or instead, old varieties that had long been consigned to the scrap heap.

In Calabria, the Librandi estate has long paid attention to local varieties (and the funding of appropriate research): thanks to them, Magliocco Dolce is no longer a forgotten blending grape. In Friuli, though many estates owned a few rows of Schioppettino vines, nobody ever bottled it on its own, until the Rapuzzi family of the Ronchi di Cialla estate chose to devote itself to Schioppettino and other native grapes. Their schioppettino had already started turning heads in the late 1970s, and today there are over thirty producers of a wine that only fifteen years ago had been reduced to a local curiosity. The estate is now actively studying (in collaboration with the University of Udine) Curvin and Cividin, two other forgotten varieties, hoping to make new monovarietal wines soon.

At other times, the relationship between estates and government institutions has evolved in a more creative manner. The world-famous house of Mastroberardino has entered into a long-term agreement with the Campanian regional government to cultivate vines at Pompei in the manner of the ancient Romans and to make wines from varieties used in those times. It is a thrilling experience to walk the little vineyard plots deep within the ruins of Pompei, your gaze falling on forgotten grapes such as the scrawny-looking "Coda di Volpe Rossa" and on marble ruins that, like the grape varieties, have reached us from across millennia.

In Sardinia, a consortium (Convisar or Consorzio Vino e Sardegna) was created in 2006 with the objective of gaining further knowledge about locally important varieties and improving the wines. In collaboration with local universities and the regional government, eleven different Sardinian natives, including Nuragus and Nasco, have been cultivated and compared using different viticultural techniques in standard and control conditions. Mariano Murru of the world-famous Argiolas estate, the consortium's technical director, told me that "over one hundred different wines have been produced to date, providing a better understanding of these native grapes. We have looked to improve the aroma expression of wines made with Monica and Carignano, to increase depth of color in those made with Cannonao, and to increase balance while diminishing alcohol levels in Bovale Sardo wines."

Back in 2000, practically no one ever mentioned the likes of Malvasia Puntinata or the wines that were made with it. Considered a blending variety at best, Puntinata came to my attention during my vineyard visits and cellar tastings: the variety was wildly better than the other *Malvasia*s used to make wines in Lazio. I began talking with vineyard managers and estate owners about the need to be more attentive not just to how their wines were labeled, but also to their exact makeup. For instance, I recall speaking with Pallavicini winemaker Carlo Roveda and marketing manager Giovanna Trisorio—now the marketing manager at the Cincinnato estate at Cori in Lazio but who held the same post at the Pallavicini winery near Rome for most of the first decade of the new century—about producing a pure Malvasia Puntinata sweet wine, and relabeling their dry wine to show it was specifically Malvasia del Lazio (also known as Malvasia Puntinata). Trisorio remembers:

> Up until 2000 we had planned to release our new sweet wine as a Frascati Cannellino, but after discussing and tasting together in the cellar with you, we started thinking that perhaps there was something to your idea. Certainly your enthusiasm for the variety got us thinking that we were missing out by not bottling a pure Malvasia Puntinata wine. Ultimately, we decided to name our sweet wine Stillato, with "Malvasia Puntinata" clearly written on the label. We redid the 2001 label of our dry Malvasia wine too: it was previously just called Malvasia La Giara, and we relabeled it Malvasia Puntinata La Giara.

At the time, these two were the first wines in Italy to be bottled, labeled, and sold as Malvasia Puntinata.

While visiting Basilicata to study the unique *terroir* of the Vulture volcano in 2001 and 2002 (back then I was on the Puglia and Basilicata wine panel for the *Gambero Rosso* guide), I realized that there was, despite what many had told me, still a great deal of Malvasia Bianca della Basilicata growing in the vineyards. Luigi Veronelli had always spoken highly to me about an unspecified Malvasia del Vulture and in Malvasia Bianca della Basilicata I thought I'd found it. Unfortunately nobody was producing any good wine with it, save for the Consorzio Viticultori Associati del Vulture, which was bottling a Bianco called Topazio. Though it was a very nice wine and supposedly mainly or all Malvasia Bianca della Basilicata, it wasn't labeled as such. I was left wondering what could be done to revive the wine. The problem was that most producers each owned only a few scattered vines of it; it was impossible to ask a small family-owned winery to make a pure Malvasia Bianca della Basilicata, as they wouldn't have enough grapevines to make wine in commercially significant numbers. So I turned to the people at the Cantina di Venosa, a social cooperative that was enjoying remarkable success at that time with their aromatic Dry Muscat wine, a bottling of Moscato Bianco. It stood to reason that if they were to scour all the vineyards owned by their members, they might be able to bottle a brand-new, monovarietal Malvasia della Basilicata wine. I distinctly remember my visit to the winery on the day I pointed out that they could resurrect a local wine that had been abandoned and that would place the winery at the forefront of regional innovation in winemaking. To their credit, the team, headed by winemaker Luigi Cantatore, was very gracious in its response and in 2005 the very first wine labeled as a Malvasia Bianca della Basilicata, called D'Avalos, saw the light of day. I was somewhat surprised to find that the finished wine was not at all aromatic (Malvasia Bianca della Basilicata is an aromatic variety), and was marked by oak (people at the winery explained they didn't wish to produce another aromatic fresh white wine, as it would only duplicate their Dry Muscat). Still, the die had been cast, and a wine that had not been heard of for decades was reborn. Today, on the heels of Cantina di Venosa's example, Eleano also bottles a monovarietal Malvasia Bianca della Basilicata wine; only ten years ago, there was none.

In the summer of 2003, while walking mile-high vineyards in the Valle d'Aosta with Gianluca Tellolli, then the winemaking director of the Cave du Vin Blanc de Morgex et La Salle, I came across a few scattered vines of Roussin de Morgex, a red grape traditional to the high alpine areas of the towns of Morgex and La Salle. Provided one knows what to look for, it is immediately recognizable due to the pale color of its berries and its highly indented, almost jagged leaves. It is found nowhere else in Italy, and to the best of my knowledge, nobody had made wine from it in commercially significant volumes for a century at least. Telloli had known of Roussin de Morgex's existence and had studied it a bit, but wasn't convinced of its winemaking potential and he soon left the winery to pursue other projects, so my hopes of seeing Roussin de Morgex wine resurrected were dashed. But you can't keep a good idea down, and in 2011, while talking wine with Nicola Del Negro, the new director of the Cave du Vin Blanc, I brought up the idea again. To his credit, Del Negro was very interested in the project. We first surveyed vineyards in the summer of 2011, and after identifying potential grape sources, Del Negro made a small volume of Roussin de Morgex wine (the equivalent of forty 750 milliliter bottles or so) in the 2012 vintage that we tasted together repeatedly following the harvest—Del Negro was kind enough to send small bottled samples to my home in Rome when I couldn't make it up to the Valle d'Aosta. Unfortunately the 2012 harvest was a difficult one and some of the grapes picked were not perfectly healthy, so that the wine showed a touch of excess volatile acidity. Still, the bright salmon-pink color and the aromas and flavors of red currant, rosehip, and sour cherries bode well for this wine's future. Furthermore, the extremely high acidity of both the berries and wine has led Del Negro to believe that Roussin de Morgex might be best used to make a sparkling red wine (his Cave du Vin Blanc de Morgex et La Salle is already adept at making very fine sparkling wines from Prié, a native white grape), which is the route he plans to go in 2013. Obviously, further studies and more work are needed, and the wine is predicted to go on sale (given the paltry volumes, it will be sold only at the winery) in 2015. In 2014 we also plan to have the putative Roussin de Morgex grapevines we have identified in scattered, small vineyard plots high in the mountains, subjected to university DNA profiling (but there is very little chance of our having misidentified the variety from an ampelographic point of view: it really is that easy to recognize).

I cannot begin to say how happy I am to have contributed to clearing the cobwebs of time from Roussin de Morgex. In fact, I consider this to be one of the highest points reached in my life devoted to wine, and it would have been impossible without someone as passionate and energetic as Nicola Del Negro, his president, Mauro Jacod, and as forward thinking an operation as the Cave du Vin Blanc de Morgex et La Salle: all deserve the highest praise possible and a heartfelt thank-you from every wine lover out there for providing their time and resources. I am currently helping wineries in two other regions, with the goal of bringing back to life two other forgotten varieties and, we hope, creating monovarietal wines.

Last but not least, in the winter of 2012–13, I helped unite six Friuli Venezia Giulia producers of the rare Tazzelenghe wine (made with the eponymous grape variety) into a group tentatively named the "Tazzelenghe Team." We met at the La Viarte winery of one of those Tazzelenghe producers to discuss the possibilities before us, and a series of tasting opportunities and conferences in different Italian cities have since been organized to promote the grape variety and the wine, including one in July 2013 at the American Embassy on via Veneto in Rome. The idea to do something on behalf of Tazzelenghe came to me during a visit to the region in the summer of 2012, when I was dumbfounded to hear a local, very well-known wine expert denigrate Tazzelenghe, stating not once but twice that one of Friuli's main problems was that farmers were bothering with unimportant varieties such as Tazzelenghe. In his view, Friuli didn't need to waste time with its last remaining six, maybe seven, hectares of Tazzelenghe. Though such opinions are no doubt made in good faith, I always shudder at such short-sightedness; and I immediately decided something needed to be done to help prevent Tazzelenghe from disappearing (which is what similar talk would no doubt lead to over time). Now, it will be wine lovers the world over who will decide if Tazzelenghe has a future or not: with the Tazzelenghe Team, my hope is that both grape and wine will become better known and understood, whatever their merits prove to be.

I should point out that I have participated and still participate in all these activities completely free of charge, and take care of all my own travel and hotel expenses. I will receive no percentages on sales or for promotional endeavors and tasting events concerning these wines. My only hope is that my efforts will be helpful in increasing awareness of forgotten grape varieties and wines. It's my way of giving something back to Italy's native grapes and their passionate producers, which together have contributed to making my life more interesting and happier.

WHAT THE FUTURE MIGHT HOLD: THE GOOD, THE BAD, AND THE UGLY

Though a great deal of excitement is being generated by Italy's rediscovered "new-old" native grapes, and wine lovers everywhere are thrilled to taste new and exciting wines, the truth is that not enough is yet known about them. When we consider that even an all-important native such as Sangiovese (the grape from which famous wines such as Chianti and Brunello are made) became the subject of university studies only in the 1960s, and of true in-depth analyses only in the 1980s, then the magnitude of the problem becomes evident. Long forgotten, these vines and wines still have their best days ahead. But not all is right in Italy's native grape and wine scene.

Jumping on the Bandwagon

Three true stories (I could tell you many more) from the last fifteen years will illustrate the attitudes and woeful ignorance of far too many of the people who talk, write, and deal with native grapes in Italy. (The names of grape varieties, estates, and people have been changed to protect the not-so innocent.) These anecdotes will give you more insight than anything else I could say or write.

STORY A   In 2003, while visiting a Tuscan estate and tasting the wines, I mention that they make a great Malvasia wine, called Night Passion. Everyone in the room beams: "We're happy you like it, Ian. We like it too, it really is a great wine. Unfortunately, we're having trouble selling it." I ask, "How come?" "We're not sure: It's bright, crisp. We think it's the name, it lacks appeal. So we plan to change it." I query, "Really? . . . but Night Passion is a cool name. What are you going to call your malvasia in the future?" The answer: "Vermentino."

STORY B   Back in 2002, a long article I'd written on Italy's native grapes had just hit newsstands, and promptly a producer called the wine magazine's office wanting to talk to me. "Ian, I know you wrote that there is no Grillo in Puglia, but I want you to know, it grows in my vineyard near Bari." "Really?" I asked uncomfortably, "my apologies, I must have been wrong. So how do you know it's Grillo? Who studied the vines? What tests did they do?" The quick reply—"No, no, you don't understand, my grandfather told me there's Grillo in that plot."

STORY C   On the back of a bottle of a Sicilian wine made with, among other grapes, Cabernet Sauvignon, I see the phrase "made from autochthonous soils," and wonder how the soil could be anything other than native, unless perhaps it were shipped from Algeria or Spain? Clearly, a wine made with Cabernet Sauvignon cannot be called autochthonous, but as the latter is an almost magical word in helping propel wine sales in Italy, everyone wants to use it—in any way they can!

The Problem with (Some) Consultant Winemakers

Consultant winemakers have undoubtedly played a major role in improving Italy's wines. Wine lovers everywhere, not just in Italy, owe them a huge thanks. That said, it is undoubtedly true that the many difficulties presented by native varieties—both in the field and in the cellar—make most winemakers wince in pain. Neither high-volume producers nor many well-known consultants really want to work with native varieties, though they state otherwise, of course. In fact, producers have told me countless times about how their famous winemaker insisted that the natives be uprooted in favor of planting Chardonnay and Merlot. This is not surprising: a consultant winemaker might have fifty or more estates, spread all over the world, in his or her portfolio. Consultants simply do not have the time to study local *terroirs* and the specifics of all those unknown local grapes. Furthermore, they are usually hired to deliver almost immediate results, and turning out so-so wines while attempting to understand the local variety is neither what they are paid for nor why they are so looked up to. In fairness, this attitude has begun to change, and some, such as Attilio Pagli and Alberto Antonini with their excellent Matura group (a team of viticulturalists and winemakers who work together), have devoted plenty of time and energy to little-known native grapes such as Tintilia and Molinara, launching new monovarietal bottlings.

Other winemakers in Italy have also always believed in the potential of native varieties. There is no bigger expert on Nerello Mascalese and all the Etna varieties than Salvo Foti. Arguably, nobody understands Sangiovese in Italy better than Maurizio Castelli or Franco Bernabei; both have a level of expertise achieved by working mainly with central Italian estates where Sangiovese is king. The aforementioned Attilio Pagli is the single biggest expert on Ciliegiolo, an extremely high-quality Italian native. To Pagli's credit, another estate he consults for produces a lovely 100 percent Corvina wine that is neither hugely tannic nor ridiculously black in hue, something a wine made solely with Corvina can never be. Lorenzo Landi works with Buriano and is making some of Italy's best Verdicchio wines, as Federico Staderini works with

Abrostine, Donato Lanati with Magliocco Dolce and Mantonico—and there are many other examples. Many of these native wines have met with both critical and commercial success. In wine, rather than uprooting and replanting, sometimes just settling down and playing the cards you've been dealt is the right move.

A Simple Question of Authenticity

Given the current trend toward authenticity in food and drink, native grapes and wines have become all the rage. Just as local produce holds immense appeal, and starred chefs pride—and sell—themselves on their use of locally sourced or even home-grown products, the same is true of wines. Therein lies many a problem. For example, many new bottles labeled Pecorino or Minutolo have miraculously appeared on store shelves. This is simply not possible. Many of Italy's natives are reduced to a few rows of vines dispersed here and there, and it is highly unlikely that, say, twenty estates can all of a sudden produce thousands of bottles. Many supposedly monovarietal bottlings made with native grapes taste nothing like they should. Unfortunately, too many "native" wines are made by unscrupulous people who aren't above—or rather below—blending unauthorized grape varieties into wines supposedly made solely with a native grape, in order to have something that sells well. The acreage of long-abandoned native grapes is small at best, so caveat emptor.

"Native Grapes Aren't Really that Good": Viticultural and Winemaking Difficulties

Given that they were forgotten (with very few exceptions) for almost all of the twentieth century, little is known about native grapes, both viticulturally and enologically. Problems with native grapes start in the vineyard, where most have been co-planted with more common varieties, regardless of soil and other differences. Many native plants are infected by viruses and don't grow particularly well, or give scrawny grape bunches from which only small volumes of wine can be made. The grapes themselves often show asynchronous maturation, meaning that the same bunch has green, unripe berries next to fully ripe ones. Unless the unripe berries are removed (an expensive, time-consuming process, since it usually needs to be done by hand, unless the estate is wealthy enough to own a very expensive optical sorting machine), the wine will have green, vegetal aromas and flavors. The hypothetical effect of an asynchronous mix on a wine's aroma and flavor profile has been well illustrated by Coombe and Iland (1987). Matters such as the best soils, rootstocks, and trellising systems for natives are still mainly a matter of conjecture. Another problem is the poor quality of nursery-propagated vine material. For instance, Tuscan producers will tell you that much of the Sangiovese replanted in the 1970s was a poor-quality biotype from Emilia-Romagna; for this reason, they prefer to call their truly Tuscan variety Sangioveto. Sardinia's Cannonao is not all one and the same, as the Tocai Rosso biotype from Veneto has been planted there in great quantity too; but, at least on Sardinia, Tocai Rosso produces wines of a quality inferior to those made from the island's original Cannonao vines.

Antiquated winemaking has threatened and damaged native grapes. In times past, grapes in a single vineyard were picked all at the same time, regardless of optimal maturity curves, and so musts of some varieties were completely oxidized and devoid of acidity; dull, flat wines were the norm. Lack of cellar hygiene also contributed to wine spoilage and consequently impeded our appreciation of what native grapes could really give. However, modern winemaking technology can also prove dangerous to Italy's natives. In this respect, the role of yeasts is illuminating. It is well known that different strains of *Saccharomyces cerevisiae*, the main yeast species used in alcoholic fermentation, can lead to very different enological results even when the same grape variety, grown in similar *terroirs*, is used. This is because each species of yeast leads to the formation of different secondary metabolites during fermentation, which influence a wine's final aroma and flavor profile. The total makeover that Grillo wines have undergone provides a good example (though there are others) of what yeasts and a highly reductive winemaking technique wherein oxidation is avoided at all costs can lead to. What used to be a big, almost meaty, white wine with earthy and lightly herbal notes is now almost always light, fresh, lemony, and crisp. It is, in fact, very sauvignonesque. It hardly resembles the grillo I remember; and though the new wines are excellent, some very well-respected winemakers such as Renato De Bartoli feel that the new wines have betrayed what Grillo is really all about. Asked to name a Grillo wine he liked today, besides his own excellent Terza Via rendition, De Bartoli smiled and promptly answered, "all the ones that don't taste like the majority made today." Whether today's wines are really exemplary of what these grapes are all about—rather than the winemaking technique employed—is still a matter of debate, and an issue that needs careful thought.

With that . . .

The Power of the Press

It's one thing to evaluate Merlot and Cabernet wines, given the prevalence of these varieties in the world's vineyards, but quite another to evaluate wines made with Oseleta, Quagliano, or Tintilia, varieties that hardly anyone ever tastes. Years ago, while tasting a Tintilia with winemaker Attilio Pagli, I mentioned that I really didn't know much about the grape or the wine. Pagli laughed and said, "nobody knows anything about Tintilia." Of course, it's a huge help if and when wine writers choose to write about such little-known grapes and wines; the promotional windfall for both grapes and wines is important. However, awarding scores to wines one knows next to nothing about is quite another matter—and some people *do* buy wines based on scores. It's hard for most people to taste wines made from little-known varieties, and made in very small volumes, with any regularity. Plus there simply isn't much written about native grapes, and what is written is often peppered with mistakes. For example, in a book devoted to Italy's native grapes, there are separate chapters for Sangiovese and Prugnolo: in fact, the latter is a biotype of the former and not a different variety. Another tome states that oaking Ribolla Gialla, "helps it express in a more important and fuller way," which must be news to about 98 percent of all Italian producers of ribolla, who choose not to oak it: the last thing Ribolla's delicate aromas and flavors need is oak. You might read that Rossese is resistant to oidium or mites, which it is not; and anyone who has seen Schioppettino's opulent, almost rubenesque berries would be surprised to read that the variety has "medium-small berries."

Italian Natives Set out to Conquer the World

I never cease to be amazed by the passion and dedication wine producers bring to their daily work. It's backbreaking labor, yet they are always thrilled to sit down with me or anyone else genuinely interested in their work. Many are fully devoted to native grapes, even though they could be making world-famous wines from international grapes too. Over the years, many producers in Italy have planted a few rows of little-known grapes to study their winemaking potential, or have started collaborations with university research institutions in an effort to know more about rare varieties they own already. Most produce 100 percent monovarietal wines, with only a few including 5–10 percent of another variety, an ideal situation.

However, the great news about Italy's native grapes is just how international they are slowly becoming. They have been around in small quantities for centuries, but now the numbers are starting to increase noticeably. For example, the arrival of Italian grape varieties in Sonoma dates back to the Italian Swiss Agricultural Colony, founded in 1881 by Andrea Sbarboro in Asti (not the one in Italy's Piedmont, the one in Sonoma's Alexander Valley). It cannot surprise anyone that when Italian immigrants bought land and planted grapes, Zinfandel (Italy's Primitivo) was one of the first grapes they decided to try, likely because it reminded at least some of them of home. Edoardo Seghesio joined in 1886 and planted his first Primitivo/Zinfandel/Tribidrag (apparently all synonyms) vines in 1895. He even renamed a local train station Chianti Station and planted other Tuscan varieties. Unless I am mistaken, the Sangiovese vines planted there are the oldest surviving Sangiovese vines in North America. Apparently, the Seghesio family was also the first to plant Arneis in California (in 1992) and Fiano (in 2003). Unti Vineyards in Sonoma is trying Dolcetto; VJB Vineyards is producing Primitivo Sangiovese, and even Aglianico. In Texas, New Mexico, Virginia, Oregon, Washington, and North Carolina, Italian native grapes are gracing the countryside. In Australia, New Zealand, Chile, Argentina, and other countries, the song remains the same. If you're an optimist, this means that consumers everywhere are bound to have an ever-increasing shot at tasting what monovarietal wines made with specific Italian native grape varieties are really all about. And if you're a pessimist? The same!

WHERE NATIVES TREAD: A QUICK SUMMARY OF ITALY'S NATIVE GRAPES BY REGION

At times, it really does seem like Italy has more grape varieties than it knows what to do with. Part of the reason is that Italy remained, for the longest time, a collection of different people speaking different languages, with different cultures and eating and drinking habits—some would say this is still very true today. Furthermore, the very mountainous landscape (roughly 70 percent of the country is made up of mountains and the hills leading up to those mountains) led to the geographic isolation of many areas. As we have seen, in Italy many varieties became entrenched in their local territories and thus were integral parts of their local cultures over centuries, as they still are today. Under the following regional headings I will briefly mention the most common varieties grown—please refer to grape variety entries in subsequent chapters for much more in-depth information on each cultivar.

Valle d'Aosta

Italy's smallest region but a giant when it comes to wine quality, Valle d'Aosta is Italy's least-known viticultural region, but has always been at the forefront of native variety research and conservation of its germplasm. Nestled high in the Alps on the border with France, this is the French-speaking part of Italy and a place where native grapes have thrived for centuries. Undoubtedly, the high alpine country and its geographic location far removed from major commercial routes helped the *valdostani* preserve their rich biodiversity. Alongside foreign varieties (mainly Chardonnay, Pinot Grigio, Pinot Nero, and Syrah), there are fourteen native cultivars ubiquitously grown today; a survey by Gatta dating from 1833 to 1838 mentions more than twenty supposedly native varieties known already then. The academic Institut Agricole Régional, a government-funded learning and research institution founded in 1951 as the Ecole d'Agriculture d'Aoste has contributed immensely over the years to the growth of a local workforce both proud and knowledgeable about its native cultivars. It set up the region's first experimental vineyards in the 1960s. In 2007, the Institut Agricole Régional further enlarged its varietal collection and created a germplasm bank of local native and traditional varieties. Today, it is also a leading producer of quality wines.

Until recently, Prié was the region's only native white grape, but in 2007 the Bianco Comune variety, long thought extinct, was rediscovered and identified in two old vineyards. Among the red grapes, Fumin is the most important native red variety, along with Petit Rouge; while the latter is more abundant, it is the former that yields the higher quality wines. Nebbiolo lovers might opt for Donnas, which is the only other Nebbiolo-based wine outside Piedmont and Lombardy's Valtellina that will actually remind you of the variety. Cornalin, Mayolet, and now Vuillermin are natives coming on like gangbusters: only ten years ago there was not a single pure bottling of these varieties, while there are many now. Primetta and Vien de Nus are rarer, and Ner d'Ala, Bonda, Roussin de Morgex, and Crovassa rarer still. Research on native grapes at the local Institut Agricole Régional, sometimes performed in collaboration with the University of Turin and the Regional Agriculture Department, has led to official acceptance of various clones of Petit Rouge and of biotypes of Moscato Bianco, Nebbiolo, and Vien de Nus. More recent studies have shed light on and permitted the propagation of both massal and clonal selections of Cornalin, Mayolet, Vuillermin, Bonda, Neret de Saint-Vincent, and other varieties.

Piedmont

Known the world over as the home of famous wines such as Barolo, Barbaresco, and Moscato d'Asti, Piedmont actually has many other great, if little-known, indigenous varieties. Look for the perfumed white wines made with Arneis; the high-acid, clean, and lemony Gavi wines made with the Cortese grape, or the minerally whites made with Timorasso. Favorita is another local white grape, but, as we have seen in the previous chapter, current knowledge states that it is a biotype of Liguria's Vermentino. Don't miss out on more or less obscure red varieties like Pelaverga Piccolo, Pelaverga Grosso, Ruchè, Grignolino, Malvasia di Casorzo, Freisa, Brachetto, Brachettone del Roero, Malvasia di Schierano, and Moscato Nero, all of which can, in the right hands, produce delightful wines (the latter four varieties are aromatic red grapes that produce wines not unlike the *Moscato*s). Lesser-known native red varieties are Croatina, Uva Rara, and Vespolina (these also grow in Lombardy) of which 100 percent pure versions can be found; by contrast, grapes such as Quagliano (and the lovely sparkling sweet wine of the same name), Neretto di Bairo, Avanà, and Avanengo are practically unknown outside their immediate production zones. Yet pure bottlings of the first three wines can easily be found locally.

Lombardy

Lombardy is where you'll find mainly international grape varieties, as most of the local varieties were abandoned long ago in favor of more famous foreign varieties, in part because this is one of Italy's most important sparkling wine production areas. Natives are there, though: Croatina and Barbera, as well as little-known varieties such as Invernenga, Pignola, Rossola, and others that are currently the subject of much study. In the Valtellina area, Nebbiolo thrives.

Trentino

Trentino is home to the native red grapes Marzemino and Teroldego, the first producing the lighter wines of the two. However, while Marzemino remains mainly a local variety, in recent years Teroldego has enjoyed a boom of sorts, and is increasingly planted elsewhere in the country, perhaps buoyed by wines that are no longer overly herbaceous, tannic, and bitter. When delicately herbal, Teroldego yields smoky, minerally, red-fruit-filled wines and makes some of Italy's most idiosyncratic reds—wines that can also age extremely well. Other very common Trentino natives are the members of the *Schiava* group (also typical of Alto Adige) with which delicious, fruity, light-bodied red wines, practically rosés, are produced. Other unknown Trentino natives that I think deserve more attention are Rossara, which has at least one pure bottling, and Enantio (also known as Lambrusco a Foglia Frastagliata), which has quite a few more. A very important native white grape is Nosiola. A study by Grando, Frisinghelli, and Stefanini (2000) showed that in Trentino's geographically narrow wine-producing areas, identical vine genotypes had received many different but similar denominations, for example, Biancaccia and Biancazza, or Schiava Grigia and Cenerina (these last two names both refer to the copious bloom of the berries, which gives the grapes a greyish look). However, some Trentino varieties believed to be local or indigenous were endowed with names completely unlike the names of what turned out to be the original varieties (such as a local Vernaccia Nera which was in reality Merlot and a Francesa Nera that was Carmenère). One variety studied, the practically unknown Nera dei Baisi, was even found to have alleles characteristic of non-*vinifera* species, resulting most likely from a naturally occurring cross between a European and an American grapevine. In testing, most of the local varieties still grown in Trentino were shown to have considerable genetic similarity, with 50–75 percent shared alleles. This is hardly unexpected given that the cultivars share a very limited alpine habitat not found on major human migration or commercial routes.

Alto Adige

Long famous for its white wines, Alto Adige also makes delicious reds, ranging from St. Magdalener (a light, easygoing red produced from the native *Schiava*s) to the much bigger, full-bodied lagrein (made from the native variety of the same name). Long a part of Austria, Alto Adige, which became Italian after World War I, is loaded with Germanic varieties such as Gewürztraminer and Riesling that, though traditional to this area, really cannot be considered native grapes of Italy. On the other hand, Moscato Rosa (pink muscat), which is not produced in great quantities elsewhere and is typical of the Alto Adige tradition and current wine production, can be.

Veneto

Veneto produces two of Italy's most famous red wines, the lighter Valpolicella and the massive Amarone. The latter wine, which often clocks in at 16 percent or even 17 percent alcohol, is by far Italy's biggest and most opulent red, and a real favorite of wine drinkers worldwide: sales of Amarone have never been better, despite ever-increasing annual output. Both are made with a blend of the native grapes Corvina, Corvinone, Rondinella, and Molinara, though the last of these, which gives light-pink, high-acid juice, is usually eliminated from Amarone by those who fear dilution. Corvina and Molinara are sometimes bottled on their own, though pitch-black Corvina wines are just as dubious as many inky-black Sangiovese wines of the past. Casetta (also called Fojatonda or Lambrusco Foja Tonda) is another red native that is coming on, and a fun wine to try. Oseleta, which gives extremely tannic monovarietal wines, has been increasingly added in small percentages to Amarone blends, providing color and body. By using Oseleta instead of the Cabernet Sauvignon and Cabernet Franc it replaces, producers hope to create wines more typical and traditional of the area.

Among white grapes, Garganega is well known (for instance, it is the basis of the wine called Soave), but Glera is just as famous, though readers may know it by its old name, Prosecco (now reserved only for the wine). Of course, this being Italy, there is a Glera Lunga variety as well; and the Bisol estate (of Prosecco fame) has recently produced the first modern wine made from Dorona, or Garganega Grossa. Verdiso and Vespaiola are lesser-known natives, but monovarietal renditions are not hard to find locally. Veneto is another region with a near-endless list of indigenous grapes that have only been recently studied in any depth. Whether some of them will yield interesting world-class wines is really a matter of conjecture, but many producers are giving these wines a try. I can personally vouch for the potential of wines made from Corbina, Turchetta, and Pomella. Corbinella is also very interesting; my guess is that it's a virus-affected variant of Corbina, but I have no hard scientific evidence to back up my impression.

Friuli Venezia Giulia

Few regions in Italy can match Friuli Venezia Giulia (FVG) for its sheer wealth of native red and white grape varieties. Schioppettino, the many

Refoscos, Pignolo, and Tazzelenghe are the best-known red natives. But there are countless other red native grapes in Friuli Venezia Giulia: some, like Curvin and Fumat (completely unknown even to Italians) appear to have quite the future. White grapes such as Ribolla Gialla, Malvasia Istriana, and Tocai Friulano make for wonderful dry white wines, while Verduzzo and Picolit produce two of Italy's best sweet wines. Little-known natives such as Ucelut, Sacrestana, and Siora also abound in the white grape category.

Manna Crespan and Massimo Gardiman of the Centro Ricerca per la Viticoltura of Conegliano (CRA-VIT) have conducted extensive research into the genetic variability of ancient Friuli varieties, recuperating and identifying old varieties that are essentially unknown today. From 2001 to 2008, they studied 178 varieties that reputedly were phenotypically different (based on supposedly expert field observation) from any other known Friuli native grape variety. The vines were subjected to DNA studies via eleven SSR markers for varietal identification. These molecular analyses revealed only ninety-three different genotypes, which were then compared with the CRAVIT database and with other published SSR data. Of these, thirty-eight (twenty-one red, seventeen white) were found to be unique to Friuli, including three that weren't even *vinifera*; only fifteen had been previously described in existing literature and ancient documents. The study also showed that forty-three of the vines studied were in fact known native varieties (identical to ones listed within the National Registry), and seven were actually well-known international varieties. These numbers show just how hard it is to recognize grape varieties on looks alone, and how unreliable phenotyping can be, even when performed by experts. Encouragingly, the fifteen as yet unknown varieties have been propagated and are now the subject of further study.

Liguria

The ribbon-shaped region of Liguria, immediately south of Piedmont, arches out from west to east like a sliver of moon. It is the home of some lovely white wines and a number of idiosyncratic reds. The wines of Liguria are among the easiest to get to know in all of Italy, since they are usually labeled with the variety name, such as Vermentino or Pigato, both native grapes. Current knowledge deems Pigato a biotype of Vermentino that mutated over the centuries. Not surprisingly, this being Italy, others feel differently and maintain it's not at all the same grape. In the bucolic Unesco World Heritage site known as the Cinque Terre, natives Albarola and Bosco are usually blended but pure bottlings of each can be found.

A recent study by Mannini, Schneider, Argamante, Moggia, and Tragni (2010) has greatly contributed to safeguarding the cultivation of the local, minor grape varieties of eastern Liguria. The Levante, or eastern portion of Liguria, is characterized by a mountain viticulture whose main varieties are Albarola, Bosco, and Vermentino, but it is also rich in little-known natives such as Frappelao Bianco, Ruzzese, Piccabòn, Rollo (not Rolle, which is Vermentino), Rossese Bianco, and Scimiscia'. The IVV-CNR (Istituto di Virologia Vegetale: Consiglio Nazionale delle Ricerche) has been conducting research on this local grape germplasm for years. In 2005, they set up an experimental vineyard in the Cinque Terre National Park at Riomaggiore and planted little-known local cultivars, with Albarola and Vernaccia di San Gimignano serving as controls. Vines were studied and collected in order to save them from extinction and were thus also introduced into the permanent collections of the IVV-CNR in Grinzane Cavour, and into a second genetic source collection of only Ligurian natives in Albenga, near Savona. So successful were the findings that Rossese Bianco, Ruzzese, and Scimiscia' were eventually registered in the National Registry. By 2008 and 2009, field observations and winemaking results indicated Ruzzese (also known as Rossese Bianco di Arcola), Rossese Bianco, and Piccabòn wines to be most promising. Furthermore, the study showed that Piccabòn is, it turns out, identical to Vernaccia di San Gimignano and to Berve-dino (the latter was previously believed identical to Vermentino, not Vernaccia di San Gimignano); Frappelao was shown to be identical to Scimiscia'.

Emilia-Romagna

Emilia-Romagna lies just above Tuscany and runs east-west across the country. This is the region often associated with Italy's finest regional cuisine (ravioli, tortellini, and ragù all share Emilia-Romagna as their birthplace) and is where world-famous gastronomic delights such as Parmigiano Reggiano, prosciutto di Parma, and *culatello* are produced. Although Emilia-Romagna is often described as a single entity, the eastern part, Emilia, and the western part, Romagna, couldn't be more different, and that goes for their wines as well. Though both feature considerable plantings of international grape varieties, the main players are natives: in Emilia, the white grapes are Pignoletto and Malvasia di Candia Aromatica and the main red grapes are *Lambrusco*s, while Romagna's main white and red varieties are Albana and Sangiovese respectively.

There are many other little-known indigenous varieties of Emilia-Romagna, such as the whites Ortrugo and Verdea, and the reds Malbo Gentile, Uva Longanesi, Fortana, and Centesimino. Monovarietal wines abound. Rarer finds are pure bottlings of Malvasia Rosa, Beverdino, Melara, and Santa Maria, all of them almost always blended with other grapes. Ervi, a recent crossing, is gaining popularity of late. Two little-known natives have been rediscovered: the red Uva del Fantini, located in an abandoned vineyard, and the white Forcella, found in the cloister of the church of Santa Maria in Regola. Both are the subject of ongoing research. Unfortunately, Silvestroni, Marangoni, and Faccioli reported in 1986 that local grape varieties in the Bologna countryside have been disappearing over the last fifty years, a trend that only recently has been reversed to a small degree, and researchers are having difficulty finding even those varieties that are supposedly still out there. In an important project spanning 2004–2010, sponsored by the Regione Emilia-Romagna and coordinated by Giovanni Nigro of the Centro Ricerche Produzioni Vegetali, in-depth field and laboratory studies (including ampelographic observations, isoenzymatic studies, DNA analysis, health status/virology workups, and microvinifications) were performed on little-known Emilia-Romagna grape cultivars. Of 157 accessions studied and ampelographically identified, fifty-eight DNA evaluations were performed and ultimately twelve microvinifications on the varieties that seemed most promising. Another interesting paper pertaining to the genetic characterization of endangered grape cultivars (Boccacci, Torello Marinoni, Gambino, Botta, and Schneider 2005) studied thirty-two indigenous varieties of Reggio Emilia, each at twelve microsatellite loci. Results showed a number of synonymous varieties (Bianca di Poviglio with Trebbiano Toscano, Balsamina with Marzemino, and Occhio di Gatto with Friulano).

Tuscany

The good news is that there are 127 officially recognized cultivars in Tuscany; the bad news is that 118 of them are planted in extremely small holdings and risk extinction. This is perhaps not surprising in a region so dominated by one grape: Sangiovese. Tuscany claims to be its rightful home, since the most famous and best Sangiovese wines are produced within its boundaries. Among the runners-up, Aleatico is a wonderful aromatic red variety, and Ansonica and Vernaccia di San Gimignano yield very good dry white wines. Canaiolo Nero, the *Colorino*s, and other natives are also being increasingly used to make monovarietal wines, and other natives are currently being studied, especially numerous Sangiovese-like varieties. Volpola is a completely unknown native white grape that has considerable potential in my view, and is not unlike Sauvignon Blanc. Not surprisingly, it is much better suited to the

Tuscan microclimate than its more famous "taste-alike," and initial vinification results have been more than encouraging. In 1981, the Dipartmento di Ortoflorifruttocoltura of the University of Florence established, in conjunction with other Tuscan institutions, a collection of 229 local and native grape varieties in specialized farms all over the region. Tuscany's best known experimental vineyard was set up in 1984 at the San Felice estate in Chianti (near Castelnuovo Berardenga). Two ancient varieties of the province of Siena, Gorgottesco and Tenerone, have been recently brought back from oblivion: well-described in ancient texts, and recently identified in old vineyards by researchers from the University of Siena, they were replanted in experimental vineyards in 2012. We can hope to see pure versions of wines made from these varieties in the not-too-distant future, though for right now knowledge about these two varieties is very thin.

Marche

The Marche's two best-known native varieties are Verdicchio and Sangiovese. The former can give what are arguably Italy's best white wines, while the latter is mainly used to make red blends such as Rosso Piceno and Rosso Conero, in wines where Montepulciano also plays an important role. However, two white varieties (both found in Abruzzo as well) are being increasingly talked about, and are causing people to look toward Marche with hope: Pecorino and Passerina. Cocucciola is another up-and-comer, and Maceratino has its fans. Lacrima and Vernaccia Nera are used to produce two aromatic red wines, made in both dry and sweet versions that are excellent.

Umbria

Umbria's most famous native red grape is Sagrantino (Sagrantino di Montefalco is probably Italy's most tannic red wine) but there are large plantings of Sangiovese too and what was once believed to be a unique strain of Umbrian Canaiolo Nero is now known to be in almost all cases Colorino del Valdarno. The main white grape is Grechetto, most often blended with other local natives such as Drupeggio (which is in reality Canaiolo Bianco), Verdello, and Procanico to make the famous wine of Orvieto and many deservedly less famous other blends. Unfortunately, this is one region where the lack of a quality winemaking history (Tuscany has always hovered over Umbria like a big brother) has allowed the unrestricted proliferation of international varieties. Consequently, Umbria is awash in a sea of mainly uninteresting Cabernet Sauvignon and Merlot wines that can't compete, in price or quality, with better examples from the rest of the world. Mercifully, the agriculture faculty at the University of Perugia has taken to studying the old local varieties.

Lazio

Shoddy winemaking and low-quality (but heavy-yielding) varieties such as Trebbiano Toscano and Malvasia Bianca di Candia have ruined the image of Lazio's wines and once-famous names like Frascati and Marino have deservedly bitten the dust. Cannellino, the sweet wine of Frascati, is also hampered by many truly lousy wines carrying its once-glorious name. Mercifully, over the last decade producers and legislators have realized that the future lies with high-quality natives such as Malvasia del Lazio (also called Malvasia Puntinata) and Bellone, and pure bottlings are on the increase. One caveat might be that some of the Malvasia del Lazio wines that sprang up almost overnight at the beginning of the twenty-first century really don't remind me of the variety at all. Among other natives, Moscato di Terracina is very similar to Moscato Bianco, but differs enough genetically to be considered a separate variety. Lazio's most important native red grape is Cesanese, of which there are two different varieties, Cesanese Comune and Cesanese d'Affile. The agriculture departments at the University of Viterbo, the enology school at Velletri, and passionate producers are studying many other local varieties: Maturano Bianco, Pampanaro, Capolongo, Uva Micella, Uva Molle, Lecinaro, and Tendòla, but accurate genetic characterization is a must, since these may be varieties grown elsewhere with better-known names. Then again, maybe not.

Abruzzo

Abruzzo is home to the famous Montepulciano red grape and the Trebbiano Abruzzese white variety, which together dominated the local wine scene to such an extent that other varieties were hardly looked at. That has changed with the recent success of Pecorino from the nearby Marche, leading producers in Abruzzo to bottle it separately rather than using it in blends, and Abruzzo has proven remarkably successful with it, to the point that its versions are outshining those of Marche. A few producers are also making wine from the little-known Montonico Bianco variety. Other natives need to be studied a great deal before we see any significant amounts of wine made from them.

Molise

Molise is an extremely small region: so small that its wine production is usually lumped together with that of Abruzzo. In fact, there weren't many Molise wine producers until recently, and chances are you haven't heard of the really good ones. The two main native grapes are the red Tintilia and white Cococciola. There are undoubtedly many others, given Molise's once forbidding mountain landscape, but people need to scour the old vineyards: elbow grease and research are indispensable.

Campania

Campania is perhaps the Italian region that has most resisted the temptation to plant foreign grape varieties: you'll have a hard time finding Sauvignon Blanc or Merlot here. Fiano and Greco are the best-known white grapes, but Falanghina, Forastera, Biancolella, and Coda di Volpe Bianca are delicious and deserve to be better known. The two main red grape varieties are Piedirosso and Aglianico, the latter the undisputed star red grape of southern Italy. The two recently discovered *Pallagrello* grapes (a white and a red) have become overnight successes, and there are many more Campanian natives to be discovered. Until recently, this incredible wealth of native varieties had hardly been studied at all: unbelievable as it may seem, as recently as in 2000, only ten varieties from Campania were listed in Italy's National Registry. Another ten have since been classified, but Luigi Moio has told me that most researchers estimate that there are over one hundred more varieties waiting to be discovered in Campania's bucolic countryside. Blessed with volcanic soils, the Vesuvio and Campi Flegrei areas immediately next to Naples are probably the richest in native biodiversity, if for no other reason than that phylloxera could not wreak havoc here. Olivella, Sciascinoso, Coda di Pecora, Marsigliana Nera, Catalanesca, and Coglionara are but a few of those being studied; 100 percent pure bottlings of some of them can be found. Bruno de Concillis, one of Campania's best producers, has recently set up an experimental vineyard in which he has planted a few thousand vines of four completely "new" varieties that were recently rediscovered. When I asked him about them, he smiled and answered, "We just planted them; let's talk about it ten years from now." On the island of Ischia, Andrea d'Ambra of the famous d'Ambra winery is working with Coglionara, Arilla, and San Lunardo, but he also says monovarietal versions of them are unlikely since they are especially sensitive to oidium. Still, some smaller producers are giving these wines a shot.

Why has Campania maintained such a wealth of native cultivars compared to other regions? Clearly, the volcanic origin of several soils averted the spread of phylloxera, thus preventing the extinction of ancient vineyards and the substitution of local cultivars by international ones. Poverty also played a role, as poor farmers and landowners were unlikely to engage in the expensive uprooting of their vines in order to plant the latest flavor of the month, as was done in many of Italy's wealthier regions.

In a very important study by Costantini, Monaco, Vouillamoz, Forlani, and Grando (2005), which I shall be quoting time and again in this book, a total of 114 accessions of sixty-nine local grape cultivars from Campania were analyzed with eight microsatellite markers (VVS2, VVMD5, VVMD7, VVMD25, VVMD27, VVMD31, VrZAG62, and VrZAG79) in order to evaluate their genetic diversity and relationships. The SSR analysis found fifty-six distinct varieties. These fifty-six varieties were compared to a database containing genetic data of cultivars from all over the world (including a large number from Italy): no case of synonymy was found, thus confirming the uniqueness of the Campanian genotypes.

Puglia

In Puglia, almost 40 percent of the regional acreage under vine was devoted to native grapes as of 2010. The main native red grape varieties in Puglia are Primitivo (better known to U.S. wine consumers as Zinfandel), Negro Amaro (correctly spelled as two separate words, despite the practice of nearly all wine books), and Uva di Troia. These three red grapes, along with the white grape Verdeca, another native, are in the top ten most cultivated grapes of the region. Slightly rarer but still noteworthy red natives include Susumaniello, still mainly used as a blending grape, and Ottavianello, a traditional variety of Puglia better known elsewhere as Cinsault. The best-known native white grapes of Puglia are Verdeca, Bianco d'Alessano, and Pampanuto, but most interesting is the aromatic Minutolo (originally but erroneously called Fiano Minutolo, as it is not a *Fiano*), which is not unlike a dry white muscat. Pure monovarietal wines made with Minutolo have been available for less than ten years. Other forgotten native grapes currently being reevaluated by university researchers and private individuals include Marchione, Uva della Scala, Palumbo, and Uva Attina. Antinello has just been inserted into the National Registry as of 2011, as has Somarello Rosso. The latter is an interesting attribution, since for the longest time Somarello was considered identical to Uva di Troia. Unfortunately, other ancient varieties have disappeared or perhaps turned out to be synonyms: the examples are too numerous to list, but include grapes such as Cuccipannelli, Pier Domenico, Tamiarello, and Maricchione. Then again, this being Italy, I wouldn't be surprised at all if someone someday discovers a rickety, centenary vine of one of those supposedly extinct varieties forgotten in the depths of a remote Puglian countryside or mountaintop. Nothing would make me happier.

Basilicata

This little region, tucked in between the heel (Puglia) and the toe (Calabria) of Italy's boot, makes only a few wines, but is blessed with some great native grapes. While Aglianico is known the world over, I wish people here would start paying more attention to the lightly aromatic Malvasia Bianca di Basilicata. Time and research money might also be well spent on studying Malvasia Nera di Basilicata, which is rarer than rare: even I have yet to see a vine, but this doesn't mean it's not out there, and I plan to meet up with it soon. Based on my last ten or twelve years of vineyard walks, I am also keenly aware that there is probably a bit more old vine Aglianicone growing in Basilicata than people realize. It's found in many of the Aglianico vineyards planted many decades ago, which helps explain differences between some Aglianico del Vulture wines that go well beyond anything *terroir* and winemaking might be responsible for.

Calabria

Even today, Calabria remains Italy's most fine-wine challenged region: the vast majority of its wines are rustic and uninteresting, an absolute shame considering this region's climate, soils, and grape varieties, which should instead enable it to do spectacularly well. Perhaps part of the problem lies with Gaglioppo, a native red variety that is probably not one of the world's great grapes: low in anthocyanins and high in rough tannins, its wines are often dusty and charmless. That said, some very well-made Gaglioppo wines have recently seen the light of day. There are however many promising varieties in Calabria, such as the red *Magliocco*s or the white Mantonico (not to be confused with the Montonico Bianco of Marche and Abruzzo) and Greco Bianco (not to be confused with the Greco of Campania, or other *Greco* varieties present all over Italy) that are finally being studied and cultivated. Then again, since Greco Bianco has been recently shown to be Malvasia delle Lipari, it really isn't a *Greco* at all (for more on it, see the entry for *Malvasia*). Calabria, and wine lovers everywhere, ought to be thankful for the superhuman efforts in time, energy, and money devoted by the Librandi estate to local Calabrian grape varieties. Indeed, almost all useful work and research on Calabria's native grapes in the last fifteen years has come thanks to this estate's involvement, something the Librandi family deserves great credit for.

Sicily

Sicily's native red grape varieties are dominated by Nero d'Avola, which is grown all over Sicily save for its northeastern corner, where Nerello Mascalese reigns instead. The latter is usually blended with Nerello Cappuccio, another native, which is low in tannins but rich in color (the opposite is true of Nerello Mascalese). Nonetheless, interesting pure versions of each are being produced. Other native red varieties are Frappato, Nocera, and Perricone; Corinto Nero (which some experts consider to be a seedless mutation of Sangiovese) is usually blended with other varieties, as is Acitana, of which very few vines are left in the wild. There are many more. Native Sicilian white grapes have, until recently, made neutral, lackluster wine but better winemaking techniques and vineyard care are behind the many crisp, minerally-scented, fresh white wines of today. Grillo holds real promise, as does Carricante: the latter grows well only in the high altitudes of the Etna volcano (at about 1,800 to 3,000 feet above sea level) in eastern Sicily. Inzolia (called Ansonica on Tuscany's coast) and Grecanico are increasingly used on their own as well. Malvasia delle Lipari and Moscato di Alessandria or Zibibbo (muscat of Alexandria) are the force behind monumentally good sweet wines. Unfortunately, back in the 1980s, many Sicilian producers opted for large plantings of Syrah, Cabernet Sauvignon, and Merlot, not to mention Chardonnay and Sauvignon Blanc. Besides the foolishness of trying to compete with the plethora of fine wines made from these varieties all over the world, these are towering examples of bad viticultural decisions, as it's just too hot on almost the entire island for the latter three varieties. Of course, you are welcome to believe the producer mantra that the high hillside vineyards offset this problem; I don't. Commendably, Sicily's regional governments have been among the leaders over the years in funding agricultural research programs; thus, Sicily's many little-known natives have been much better characterized than others. The Istituto della Vite e del Vino, now renamed Istituto Regionale del Vino e dell'Olio, is a model of efficiency and a helpful think tank for the island's many producers. Sicily, its producers, and the many different regional governments in place there over the last thirty years all deserve praise for having always been at the forefront of native grape variety research. Well done!

Sardinia

Sardinia, much like Campania, has long insisted on its native grape varieties, though most of Sardinia's grapes are actually recent arrivals, due to four centuries of Spanish domination. Hence the likes of Vermentino (better known as Malvosie à Petits Grains or Rolle in southern Spain and France), Cannonao (actually Grenache or Garnacha, the world's second most-planted wine grape), and Carignano (Carignan in France, or Mazuelo in Spain), the last of which does remarkably well in some parts of the island, including Sulcis in the southwest. White varieties original to Sardinia probably include Nuragus, Nasco, Semidano, and Vernaccia di Oristano. There are many more little-known varieties that await discovery, and others that deserve to be better characterized in all their viticultural and enologic potential. In a recent presentation at the Fourth National Congress on Viticulture, held in Asti on July 10–12, 2012, Graviano, Musa, Piras, Demelas, Piga, Aini, and Sgarangela estimated that there are 250 different grapevines living on the island (native, traditional, and international), only twenty-four of which have been listed in the National Registry to date. Undoubtedly, many of those varieties are synonymous with other, known varieties, but it still seems likely there are many more cultivars to be discovered on Sardinia. I don't know about you, but my glass is ready.

PART TWO

Italy's Native and Traditional Grape Varieties and Wines

THREE

Grape Groups and Families

THE FOLLOWING GROUPS and families include some of Italy's best-known grapes, hence its best-known wines. You will easily recognize the grapes within each group or family (for example Greco, Greco Giallo, and Greco Nero): these cultivars share the same basic name because they were thought to be related. In fact, these century-old assumptions are, more often than not, erroneous: thanks to ongoing advances in DNA profiling, we have very recently learned that some of these similarly named grapes are completely unrelated. However, for simplicity's sake I have chosen to leave them grouped together, so in this book you'll find all the various *Greco*s, *Lambrusco*s, *Malvasia*s, *Trebbiano*s, and others described in the same chapter.

What's more, because many of these grapes share essentially similar century-old histories and have been so traditionally and intimately attached to specific regions and viticultural areas, they are still referred to by their original names, out of habit and tradition. For example, nobody outside academic circles will ever refer to the Greco Bianco variety of Calabria as Malvasia di Lipari, the grape variety it has been recently proven to be. For locals and wine lovers everywhere, it's still Greco Bianco, and when in Calabria, you'll receive nothing but stern looks or condescending smiles should you refer to the variety by any other name. If you're lucky, that is: you may instead end up sitting through a good hour or more (sometimes, a lot more) of explanations as to why you, and the scientists, have it all wrong. Charmingly, these local, passionate grape growers and winemakers might also feel the need to call over relatives and friends who are "in the know" (this is Italy, after all, and everybody's got quite a few of those) to further reinforce their arguments. Trust me: been there, done that.

For the simple reason that some varieties included in this chapter may be more or less related, I use either the word *group* or the word *family* to unite them. When I speak of a grape group, it's because group members are so unrelated that speaking of a family is impossible, as for example in the case of the *Vernaccia*s, grape varieties that only have the name Vernaccia in common. Other times, there are enough similarly named grapes sharing close enough genetic ties (such as parent-offspring relationships) that I can speak of a family in the true sense of that word—as in the case of the *Rabosos*, since Raboso Veronese is an offspring of a Raboso Piave × Marzemina Bianca crossing.

THE COLORINO GROUP

WHERE IT'S FOUND: Tuscany, Liguria, Lazio, Marche, and Umbria. NATIONAL REGISTRY CODE NUMBER: 67 (though with all the subtypes and distinct varieties, it's hard to understand why there would be just one registry listing; officially, it refers to Colorino del Valdarno). GRAPE/WINE COLOR: red.

Colorino is a small name for a powerful grape: should you get carried away in bouts of overenthusiastic wine tasting, be warned that there are fewer varieties in Italy capable of making deeper stains on your clothes than the *Colorinos*. Despite its *–ino* ending (a diminutive meaning small), there is nothing smallish about the color imparted by *Colorinos* to the blends they are used in. In fact, this has always been their calling in life: usually lacking sufficient aroma and flavor complexity to make monovarietal wines, they have been historically used as coloring agents, hence their name. For example, *Colorinos* greatly augment the hue of wines made with Sangiovese, notoriously a light-colored variety, and, not surprisingly, have always been used by Chianti producers with this very purpose in mind. Paolo Masi of Fattoria di Basciano, believes that in this role, as part of the blend for his Sangiovese-based Chianti Rufina wines, *Colorinos* in general have three advantages over Canaiolo Nero (Chianti's more traditional blending grape): "First, *Colorino* is a low yielder, second it has a sparse bunch, and third, it's very disease resistant. It practically never succumbs to oidium, while Canaiolo Nero is too productive and is sickly." In fairness to Canaiolo Nero, I should point out that Masi is well known for liking bigger, blacker wines and that the degree of elegance that Canaiolo Nero brings to a Sangiovese blend is something the *Colorinos* can only dream of.

In this respect, *Colorinos* are very similar to France's Petit Verdot and other coloring agents, known there as *teinturiers*, from *teinture*, or dye. And just like the *teinturiers* (and many other groups of grapes, such as the *Grecos* and the *Trebbianos*), *Colorinos* are not a family, but very much a group of generally unrelated grapes: so much so that it is incorrect to speak or write of Colorino singly (without further specifications, such as "di Lucca" or "del Valdarno"). Just like *Grecos* and *Trebbianos*, *Colorinos* come in numerous Colorino-Something varieties. Color-wise, another important aspect of the *Colorino* varieties is that their leaves turn dark reddish when grapes are near optimal ripeness: in fact, it is extremely easy to recognize a *Colorino* vine from afar, as it will stick out amid a green sea of, say, Sangiovese and Canaiolo Nero.

Unfortunately for identification purposes, the *Colorinos* also share noticeable similarities with other less-common Tuscan varieties that are not part of the *Colorino* group, but are also coloring agents: among them, Giacchè, Granoir, Morone, Abrusco, and Abrostine are becoming increasingly known. Regrettably, many less-than-scrupulous nurseries, or simply inattentive ones, sell these and other grapes (including Alicante Bouschet, Ancellotta, Teinturie, and others) as *Colorinos*, though they are in fact distinct varieties. Therefore, when producers tell you they have *Colorino* in the vineyards and that they make a *Colorino* wine, it behooves you to find out exactly what is being grown (if the producer even knows, that is), since all these cultivars give wines that are completely different from one another.

There are four main varieties that include the *Colorino* name (the Colorino-Somethings) in Italy: Colorino del Valdarno (once referred to as Colorino Toscano), Colorino di Pisa, Colorino di Lucca, and Colorino Americano. Maurizio Castelli, the well-known consultant winemaker, believes that the *Colorinos* share at least some features, such as small bunches and very stable colors imparted to wines. Attilio Pagli, another very well-known consultant, points out that all the *Colorino*s are extremely resistant to disease. However, the varieties also present clear-cut genetic and morphological differences. The most important *Colorino* variety, and the one with the best fine winemaking potential, is Colorino del Valdarno; it is considered a true native grape of Italy, and many believe it derives from the domestication of an indigenous wild grapevine species over millennia.

Other *Colorino*s aren't necessarily even pure *Vinifera* species, but rather hybrids with native American grapevines. Pisani, Bandinelli, and Camussi (1997) showed that Colorino Americano is one such hybrid, most likely now gracing Italian vineyards by way of the United States, and is therefore genetically and enologically completely different from true Tuscan *Colorino*s. Experts such as consultant winemaker Lorenzo Landi believe that Colorino di Lucca and Colorino di Pisa are also related to American grapevines. Stefano Dini, one of Italy's most talented viticulturalists, goes one step further, cautioning that Colorino di Pisa is a misnomer: he believes (and he's not alone) that it's identical to a coloring variety called Alicante Bouschet, typically grown in Tuscany's coastal Maremma region, in France, and many other parts of the world. (In reality, Alicante Bouschet is not just one grape but rather a family of crossings, including Alicante Henri Bouschet and other similarly named grapes distinguished only by numbers, such as Alicante Bouschet number 1, number 2, and many others.) Dini also thinks that Colorino del Valdarno and Abrusco, another Tuscan coloring variety, are identical, but this time he's in the minority, and he admits that Abrusco has more orangey leaves come the fall than any other Colorino-Something variety he knows of. In fact, Giandomenico Gigante of the Tenuta La Traiana estate in Tuscany grows both a Colorino del Valdarno and an Abrusco del Valdarno, and views them as completely distinct. Still other experts, such as Giancarlo Scalabrelli of the University of Pisa, believe that Abrusco is identical not to Colorino del Valdarno but to Colorino di Pisa. As these questions are not resolved, I keep Abrusco separate from the *Colorino* group in this book, as does the National Registry, in which Abrusco is listed on its own, at number 347 (see ABRUSCO, chapter 4).

In any case, the most cogent difference among the four basic *Colorino*s is that Colorino Americano, Colorino di Lucca, and Colorino di Pisa all have colored pulps and juices, while Colorino del Valdarno's pulp and juice are clear. This is what really matters to wine lovers, for in general it is varieties with colorless pulps that make the best wines. Wines made with Nebbiolo, Merlot, or Pinot Nero—all varieties with colorless pulps—are red only because the juice is initially left in contact with the grape skins, which leach pigments, eventually turning what was a colorless juice into a red one. Colorino del Valdarno is therefore the highest quality of the Tuscan *Colorino*s, at least in terms of wine. In fact, this is the only point relative to the *Colorino*s that practically everyone agrees on. Given that this is Italy, that's no small feat, and so I'd be inclined to believe on the strength of this observation alone, even if I hadn't tasted wines made with each *Colorino* variety.

Castelli disagrees: he feels that Colorino del Valdarno is too productive, is a very late ripener, and often fails to reach full phenolic maturity. He is joined in his resistance to Colorino del Valdarno by a few outliers who prefer their own local *Colorino*s, or what they think are their own *Colorino*s. Enrico Lippi, the owner of the well-respected Frascole estate in Chianti Rufina (an area particularly rich in high-quality *Colorino*s), argues that "historically, the *Colorino*s of the Mugello area of Tuscany have always been of higher quality than those of the Valdisieve, Valdarno, and Aretino areas. Our area's *Colorino* looks very different from that of Valdarno, for example, characterized as it is by a much smaller, loosely-packed bunch and small berries." Of course, whether the grapevines Lippi is referring to look different because of viral diseases, or because they are different Colorino del Valdarno biotypes, or because they are distinct varieties altogether is anybody's guess.

Bernardo Gondi, a very well-respected viticulturalist and owner of the Marchese Gondi-Tenuta di Bossi estate in the Rufina area of Tuscany, cautions against planting Colorino del Valdarno in calcareous-rich soils, since in that case it fails to ripen properly and yields next to nothing. However, Elisabetta Fagiuoli of the Sono Montenidoli estate in San Gimignano points out that most estates in Tuscany don't rely exclusively on Colorino del Valdarno, but instead have a mix of *Colorinos* in their vineyards: "that was part of the imaginative way of life of farmers back in the sixties," she smiles. And countless nursery errors in the years that followed the end of *mezzadria*, I would add. In fairness, throughout history, farmers have always hedged their bets, preferring to plant different grape varieties in the same plots; for example, growing both cultivars that ripen early and others that ripen later puts them at an advantage relative to the diverse and fickle weather patterns of each vintage. Understandably, such habits have led to many different grape varieties being planted close to each other in the vineyards.

If you take a walk through the vineyards come harvest time, when the grapes are on the vine and are relatively ripe, you have some hope of distinguishing between the four Tuscan *Colorinos* by remembering just two facts. First, Colorino Americano is the easiest to spot, as its huge pentagonal, five lobed, reddish-tinged leaf is unmistakable. Second, both Colorino di Lucca and Colorino di Pisa have reddish stalks leading to the grape bunches, while those of Colorino del Valdarno and Colorino Americano remain green at all times.

Stefano Dini truly likes the *Colorinos*: "I think some unique wines can be made, as some old vintages of Colorino del Corno by Tenuta Il Corno have shown," he says. Dini has also taught me all I needed to know about *Colorino* clones but was afraid to ask:

> The most important thing to remember is that the only clones available are of Tuscan *Colorinos*, and all were selected from the higher quality Valdarno type. Of these, N6 is not very popular: the bunch and berries are too small and it's really not productive. Instead, US FI PI10 is the easiest to find everywhere, as it's the most productive; COLORO 2000/8 has only recently become available and it too seems a very stingy yielder. I have yet to use the new Vitis clones but I have tasted microvinifications of the 801 and it seems to me to be the richest in polyphenols. Of the VCR clones, I personally like to use the VCR64, which has better vegetative balance than the VCR2, which is hampered by bigger and more compact bunches.

I have been told more or less the same things by other consulting viticulture and winemaking experts. But Dini's particular affection for the *Colorinos* may spring from memories of his youth. "I remember that back in 2005, when I was working in Australia at the Chalmers nursery, I ran into a bunch of *Colorino* that had been sent to us by mistake along with a load of Sagrantino; I started working with it there, and haven't stopped since. Today I help make the wine Taffetà at the Poggiopiano estate and am very happy with the results." I have tasted many vintages of the wine he mentions, and I can vouch that it is excellent.

Which Wines to Choose and Why

Though *Colorinos* grow in Emilia-Romagna, Liguria, Lazio, Marche, and Umbria, the Colorino-Something varieties are essentially Tuscan. Historically, *Colorinos* have always been added to Sangiovese wines to increase their color; in this respect, *Colorinos* play the same role as do Cabernet Sauvignon, Merlot, or Syrah, but they are a more traditional, historically accurate choice. Therefore there is often anywhere from 1 to 10 percent of a *Colorino* variety included in any Chianti wine blend, especially those from Classico and Rufina. There are no 100 percent pure "Colorino" DOC wines, but producers have worked up the courage to bottle pure versions as Indicazione Geografica Tipica (IGTs) and some are really interesting and fun to try. In DOC wines—such as Tuscany's Montecarlo or Umbria's Lago di Corbara—*Colorinos* play a small part in the blends, and of course they also do so in better-known wines like Chianti Classico, Chianti Rufina, and Vino Nobile di Montepulciano.

In keeping with the notion that grapes with colored pulps give wines of inferior quality, Bernardo Gondi believes that wines made with *Colorino*s with colored pulps give wines that have more rustic tannins and age less well. However, as producers often own a mix of *Colorino*s in their vineyards, not all Colorino wines taste alike. Anyone who knows Italian wines even a little will never mistake, even tasting them blind, monovarietal wines or those made with heavy doses of Alicante Bouschet for wines containing mainly Abrusco or Colorino del Valdarno. Wines made with Alicante Bouschet are unabashed fruit bombs, while those made with Abrusco and Colorino del Valdarno are much more tannic and herbal. In the end, to say *sic et simpliciter* that there is *Colorino* in the blend means very little—particularly because sometimes people speak of *Colorino*s and really mean completely different varieties such as Granoir and Giacchè, which have aroma and flavor profiles even more far removed from the four basic Colorino varieties. That said, a wine containing any of the *Colorino*s (Colorino di Pisa and/or Alicante Bouschet excepted) will unfailingly remind you of Cabernet Sauvignon or Petit Verdot, though without the complexity of the former and the perfume of the latter. Attilio Pagli, star consultant winemaker and cofounder of the MATURA group of winemakers and viticulturalists, finds that *Colorino* wines remind him of those made with Ancellotta, another native coloring variety, with the difference that "*Colorino* wines, though they may lack complexity, are more elegant." Emiliano Falsini, a winemaker with the MATURA group, notes that "with their at times gamey and peppery aromas, wines made with Colorino del Valdarno can remind you of Syrah." However, he cautions that due to the *Colorino*s' wealth of polyphenols, wines made with it tend to reduce easily (reduction is what causes many wines to smell weedy or musty). For this reason, with *Colorino*s he likes to use winemaking techniques (such as rack and return or frequent pumping over) that favor plenty of air contact with the must. "If you aren't careful, the reduced aromas form quickly and once present they are very hard to remove," he warns. Since color is very easy to achieve with *Colorino*s, Falsini also believes that long skin-to-juice contact is not necessary with this variety: "Pigments leach out quickly, so seven- to ten-day macerations are all you need to get a fairly dark-hued wine; anything longer than that, and you risk pulling out green, hard tannins." Still, a well-made colorino from a good biotype can be a very interesting discovery for all those tired of the usual aromas and flavors of the cabernet-merlot-syrah set. Colorino wines rarely have profound complexity, but are full-bodied, structured, and match well with hearty foods. They all share inky colors, a big, structured, viscous mouthfeel, and aromas and flavors of small dark berries, licorice, blackberry jam and especially menthol and herbs, such as juniper berries and sage. A word of caution: since the *Colorino*s are usually late-ripening varieties, vintage really does count with *Colorino* wines. In rainy, cool years, the wines will almost always smell and taste green.

WINES TO TRY: Montenidoli*** (How owner Elisabetta Fagiuoli manages to make a smooth, velvety and even charming colorino is beyond me, but then, witness her outstanding Vernaccia di San Gimignano wines), Poggiopiano*** (Taffetà: The dynamic duo of Dini and Pagli never fail), Casabianca**, Fattoria di Piazzano**, Marchesi Pancrazi** (Casaglia), and Tenuta Il Corno** (Colorino del Corno). These very good, at times outstanding, wines really are more than the sum of their colorful parts.

THE GRECO GROUP

Along with the *Malvasia*s, the *Greco*s may be the most confusing of all grapes. That alone would seem to make them eminently Italian, but in reality, the *Greco*s are for the most part Greek imports. Which, given Greece's similarity to Italy where the love of organized chaos is concerned, is just as appropriate. Indeed, it has always been thought that many of these grapevines were first brought to southern Italy by Greek colonists, sometimes on the heels of wines imported from Greece. However, it's not so simple: many other grapes that never graced Greek soils were named "greco" too, because they were used to make wines in the "Greek style": sweet and resinous, made by concentrating the musts via cooking, adding resin, or air-drying the grapes. In fact, we know from modern genetic studies that many of southern Italy's grape varieties are not related to any found in Greece today (Scienza 2004; Crespan, Cabello, Giannetto, Ibanez, Karoglan Kontic, Maletic, et al. 2006b).

The individual *Greco*s were originally differentiated either by adding a reference to their color, hence Greco Giallo (Yellow Greco) or Greco Bianco (White Greco), or to their town of origin, hence Greco d'Ischia, di Tufo, di Napoli, del Vesuvio, della Torre. Of course, having witnessed the popularity and sales of Greco wines, producers and innkeepers weren't below endowing just about any grape and wine with the "greco" moniker; varieties could even be awarded Greco-sounding names like Grecanico and the various *Grechetto*s. The result was a proliferation of Greco wines and grapes: but most of these "Greco-Something" varieties are unrelated to one another. Rather than a family, the *Greco*s are a group of grapes sharing the same name and very little else; unlike other groups of grape varieties, such as the *Malvasia*s (members of which are found all over Europe), most *Greco*s are planted only in small pockets of the Italian countryside. Still, there are times when you'll feel like each pocket seems to hold its very own *Greco*. In Calabria alone there are at least four different so-called Greco Biancos and five Greco Neros; and though locals, in very Italian fashion, differentiate between these varieties by giving each a specific place name (Greco Nero di Sibari, Greco Nero di Scilla, etc ...), Italian law no longer allows place names for grape varieties, limiting their use for Italian wines. Besides, genetic analysis has proven many such grapes aren't *Greco*s at all.

The most famous and best-known of all Italian *Greco* varieties is simply called Greco, and it is the one with which the world-famous Greco di Tufo wine is made. (Note that contrary to some wine writers' practice, Greco di Tufo is the wine, and not the grape variety: the correct name of the grape with which this famous wine is made is simply Greco.) The other main white "*Greco*" variety in Italy is the outstanding Greco Bianco of Calabria, a grape used to make both greco di Gerace and, confusingly, greco di Bianco (Bianco and Gerace are towns in Calabria). Of course, wouldn't you know it: thanks to SSR profiling, Greco Bianco has been proven to be identical to Malvasia di Lipari, so it appears to be yet another variety named *Greco* that is not a true Greco either (Crespan, Cabello, Giannetto, Ibanez, Karoglan Kontic, Maletic, et al. 2006b; see MALVASIA DI LIPARI entry). However, since the "Greco Bianco" variety has been around for centuries (indeed, it's one of Italy's most ancient cultivars), use of this name has become so engrained it's hard to get people to give it up. Add to this that many don't even accept the study results that prove Greco Bianco to be Malvasia di Lipari, and it's all quite a mess. What's more, in Calabria there are many different varieties called Greco Bianco, depending on the part of the region, and most of these are quite distinct from one another.

Greco

WHERE IT'S FOUND: Campania, Lazio, Puglia, Tuscany. NATIONAL REGISTRY CODE NUMBER: 97. COLOR: white.

One of Italy's most famous wine grapes, given its association with the important Greco di Tufo wine, Greco is very recognizable, due to its extremely opulent, almost cascading appearance and bright yellow berries lightly speckled with brown dots. With at least one huge wing dripping down the side, the bunch looks as if it's been doubled, causing many experts (the first to go on record was Carlucci in 1909) to think Greco was Aminea Gemini Minor (according to Carlucci, the *major* was a cultivar called Grecula, now extinct), a variety the ancient Georgic Latin authors thought highly of. Its very generous, opulent bunch is such that in the 1960s and 1970s many believed Greco to be identical to Riesling Italico (Welschriesling), but the two varieties have since been proven to be distinct.

It behooves all those who write and speak about wine to be accurate when they broach this Greco variety and its wines. Simply put, it is incorrect to refer to Greco as Greco Bianco, as Greco and Greco Bianco are two distinct cultivars (not clones or biotypes), and are historically associated with completely different areas of Italy (Greco is typical of Campania, Greco Bianco of Calabria). And as we have seen, Greco Bianco is apparently Malvasia di Lipari, so it really cannot be used as a name by which to call Greco. Furthermore, it is also incorrect to refer to Greco as Greco di Tufo, as is all too often done (even in Italy), for greco di Tufo is not the name of a grape variety but the name of a wine made in a very specific, limited, area of Campania with the Greco variety. Historically, Greco in Campania was often identified with a place name, such as Greco di Napoli, Greco di Torre, and even Greco di Tufo, but the grape variety was in fact always Greco and that is the official name used for it today. Admittedly, the intricacies of the Italian language contribute to the general confusion. Many writers and even academics will at times mistakenly refer to Greco as "Greco Bianco" because the official name for it in the National Registry is "Greco B." where the "B." stands for *Bianco,* meaning this is a white grape. In fact all Italian grapes in the National Registry have either a large "B." a large "N." or an "Rs." attached to the end of their names: these abbreviations simply qualify the variety in question as either a white, red, or pink grape. Other examples might be "Sangiovese N." (Sangiovese is a red grape) or "Fiano B." (Fiano is a white grape). Unfortunately, without due attention to details such as these, many speak of a generic Greco Bianco variety, not realizing that there are two distinct cultivars, the more common and famous Greco of Campania and the rarer and less famous (but very high-quality grape, in my view perhaps better than Greco) Greco Bianco of Calabria. In fact, the official name of the Greco Bianco variety in the National Registry appears as "Greco Bianco B." so hilariously, if you were to read the whole thing out, the name of the grape would be Greco Bianco Bianco; however, the "B." and "N." are never read out. I point out that mistakes such as these are commonly made in the academic world as well. For example, in an otherwise interesting research paper (Caruso, Galgano, Castiglione Morelli, Viggiani, Lencioni, Giussani, and Favati 2012) analyzing wines made with Greco Bianco, there is no distinction made at any time between the study's wines from Campania and those from Calabria. As Greco Bianco is not commonly grown in Campania (which is the home of Greco, not Greco Bianco), it is highly unlikely that the Campanian wines in the study were produced with the Greco Bianco variety. Yet the study's title and discussion refer only to "Greco Bianco" wines.

The confusion between Greco and Greco Bianco is but one example confounding both those studying Greco for a living and those who wish to know more about what it is they are drinking. In 2005, Costantini, Monaco, Vouillamoz, Forlani, and Grando suggested a genetic identity between Greco and Asprinio (another grape variety of Campania) based on microsatellite analysis of four Asprinio accessions and eleven Greco accessions, but I wonder. Notwithstanding that drawing conclusions from a study of only four and eleven accessions seems a recipe for disaster, as the available data under examination is limited at best, over the years I've observed these two varieties in many different vineyards, and tasted wines made with each myriad times, and I'm not convinced at all. True, others have since confirmed their genetic identity, and morphologically the two cultivars can resemble each other, as documented by Boselli, Corso, and Monaco (2000), but they do not always, and the wines are too different for me to accept this proposed identity as likely. In this I am not alone: many local growers and winemakers feel exactly the same way. Granted, diverse growing conditions (Asprinio grapes are often grown in heavily shaded conditions, where the vines cling to natural supports such as trees, and are allowed to produce extremely high yields, so resulting wines are invariably thin, tart, and nothing at all like those made with Greco) and winemaking skills involved are such that the two wines taste very different, but Asprinio and Greco wines are more like vanilla and chocolate, rather than different chocolates made from Criollo and Trinitario beans. So it is very hard for me to believe that the two varieties are identical. This is one of the many cases of DNA profiling that makes me highly nervous. Now, I'll be the last to question properly obtained scientific data, but I wonder if the very few Asprinio or Greco accessions in this study really were true Asprinio or Greco; it wouldn't be the first case of a mistaken ampelographic observation leading to erroneous conclusions. Of course, I'm probably wrong, but still . . .

Greco is a difficult variety, both viticulturally and enologically. It ripens late, in October (not exactly a good thing in the cool and often rainy mountainous areas where Greco often grows), and is characterized by low vigor and productivity, as well as by sensitivity to grey rot, oidium, and peronospora; in this respect, it is less resistant than other Campanian varieties such as Coda di Volpe Bianca. Ferrante wrote in 1927 that Greco has been abandoned because of all the headaches it caused farmers, who replaced it with more prolific varieties. Greco is no easier for winemakers, as the variety is very rich in polyphenols that tend to oxidize, browning the wine and creating volatile acidity. It tends to be more productive in deep volcanic soils. There are different clones available: the VCR set (VCR 6, VCR 11, VCR 2, and VCR 5), all developed between 2001 and 2002, and Ampelos-TEA 25 and UNIMI-VITIS GRE VV31, available since 2008 and 2009. Of these, UNIMI-VITIS GRE VV31 gives the simplest wines, meant to offer early appeal, while VCR 11 tends to give more structured wines and its thick skins make it ideally suited for sweet wine production (of which there is however very little where Greco is concerned).

Greco is planted mainly in Campania; unlike Fiano, the other best-known Campanian white grape, it has not been "exported" to other regions in Italy, though pockets of it exist in neighboring regions such as Lazio, Abruzzo, Molise, Puglia, and even Tuscany. It has also been planted abroad, for example in Australia and the United States, but there too it usually takes a back seat to Fiano. Nevertheless, as it is both heat tolerant and drought resistant, Greco is potentially an extremely important "new" variety for the warmer viticultural areas in these countries. Greco also has little need for irrigation, making it even more ideally suited to these often water-challenged lands. In California, Noravine grapevine nursery acts as the importer of Italian budwood produced by Vivai Cooperativi Rauscedo (VCR), the world's largest producers of budwood. The Foundation Plant Services (FPS) have officially recognized Greco FPS clone 01, generated from the VCR 11 clone.

Which Wines to Choose and Why

Greco di Tufo is one of Italy's most famous wines, and the better versions are among Italy's best white wines. It usually shows much greater alcohol and structure than Fiano di Avellino, the other famous white wine of Campania, which is more minerally and refined. As of 2008, Greco di Tufo accounted for 14 percent of all DOC wines made in Campania (Fiano di Avellino represented only 8 percent) but can be made from grapes grown only in the countryside of eight small towns near Avellino. There are two true *grand crus* for Greco, Santa Paolina and Tufo, and one *premier cru*, Montefusco; and given similar winemaking techniques they yield very different wines. All three are located on the right side of the Sabato River, and are blessed with south to southeastern exposures, which are ideal to ensure proper ripening of this capricious grape. Tufo's is an extreme viticulture, at least in some sections of it, where slopes are extremely steep, impossible to work by machine, and vines can be found as high up as five hundred to six hundred meters above sea level; the volcanic soils are poor in nutrients, and rich in clay, limestone, and gravel, with a high presence of chalk and sulfur elements. Some of the lightest-colored, most mineral, and refined Greco di Tufo wines are made here. By contrast, vineyards in Santa Paolina and Montefusco, located at slightly lower altitudes and with less steep hillside gradients than Tufo's, are characterized by larger amounts of clay and organic matter, as well as a higher iron content. Hence, wines made in these areas are typically bigger and more structured. Elsewhere, in sandy soils rich in calcium carbonate, Greco tends to produce lighter, more perfumed wines. However, as Greco is grown almost everywhere in Campania, there are myriad wines made: Sannio Greco, Taburno Greco, Sant'Agata dei Goti Greco are just some of them. Greco is also found in many blends, for example Capri Bianco, in which it makes up to 50 percent of the total blend. Greco wines are usually very yellow in hue, big, fat, and rather high in alcohol; all share an almost oily, tannic texture (the exceptions are Mastroberardino's versions, which are remarkably delicate and herbal, but I find there is a house "signature" to their whites.) There really is a Greco mouthfeel, and Greco wines are easy to recognize when tasting blind. Typical aromas and flavors include yellow flowers, honey, peach, pear, and ripe tropical fruit. Unlike wines made with Fiano, which are always best with a few years of bottle age, Greco wines, in all their peachy-honeyed, opulent splendor are extremely enjoyable when young, though they too can age splendidly.

International versions of Greco include interesting examples from Australia, such as Beach Road in Langhorne Creek, Di Lusso Estate in Mudgee, and Chalmers in Murray Darling. The latter was long the largest vine nursery propagation business in Australia, but also had a winemaking arm: in 2005 they made an interesting Fiano-Greco blend as part of their Chalmers Wines Project series. Founders Bruce and Jenny Darling sold their Euston block in 2008 to the Macquarie Diversified Agriculture Fund, but have since purchased a new Murray Darling site at Merebin and branched out to the slightly cooler Heathcote region (where they have produced wines from other Italian varieties, such as Nero d'Avola, Vermentino, and Sangiovese). Interestingly, Beach Road used to label its Greco wine as Greco di Tufo (I distinctly remember seeing that name on the 2009 bottling) while now it is simply called Greco (witness the 2011 wine's label; however, as of mid-2013 their website still lists the wine as Greco di Tufo); a good thing too, since Greco di Tufo is an Italian DOCG wine and that name, much like Champagne, cannot appear on the wine labels of any other country. For this reason, Di Lusso Estate also stopped labeling its wine Greco di Tufo: the 2011 was still so labeled while their 2012 is simply, and correctly, labeled Greco. Nevertheless, these estates have a special touch with the grape; both the Beach Road and Di Lusso examples are very fine wines. In fact, Beach Road winemaker Briony Hoare won the Chairman's Award for the "Wines to Watch" category with her 2009 Greco di Tufo wine at the Australian Alternative Varieties Wine Show held in Mildura. In California, though there are only roughly forty hectares (about one hundred acres) planted to Greco, an increasing number of wineries are taking an interest in the variety. Route 3 Wines, in the Dunnigan Hills American Viticultural Area (AVA) has made a delightful 2012 Greco wine called GdT (get it?) that speaks of white flowers, minerals, peaches, and a trace of honey; I quite liked it, and at 11.5 percent alcohol, it is much lighter than Italian counterparts (not necessarily a bad thing). Rosa d'Oro Vineyards in Kelseyville has also produced a Greco wine (that I haven't yet tasted) and last I heard were still deciding what to call it. Apparently, a producer from Sonoma's Russian River area, Nico's Wines, has also started making a wine with Greco (that I have yet to taste). Clondaire Vineyard, just west of San Andreas in California's Calaveras County, has also planted Greco vines (as well as Fiano and Dolcetto). As perhaps the world's biggest lover of Italian grapes and wines, my hat goes off to these maverick producers, and I thank them all for their passion, energy, and desire to go where others have not yet gone before.

WINES TO TRY: For Greco di Tufo, try: Benito Ferrara*** (Vigna Cicogna is one of Italy's ten best whites; their entry-level Greco di Tufo is also exceptional), Di Prisco***, Mastroberadino*** (the vintage or library release: try the 2002 for an almost discreet, very unlike-Greco tasting experience), Pietracupa*** (both the "G" and entry level bottling; these may be the best Greco wines of all, along with Ferrara's), Quintodecimo*** (Giallo d'Arles), Vadiaperti*** (Tornante), Terredora** (Terre degli Angeli), Cantina Bambinuto**, Cantine dei Monaci**, Colle di San Domenico**, Feudi di San Gregorio** (Cutizzi), Macchialupa**, Salvatore Molettieri**, and Villa Diamante** (Vigna del Ciamillo). For Taburno Greco, try: La Rivolta**.

Greco Bianco

WHERE IT'S FOUND: Lazio. NATIONAL REGISTRY CODE NUMBER: 98. COLOR: white.

Now might be a good time to reach for an aspirin: there are few more confusing Italian grape varieties than Greco Bianco. The main difficulty lies in the habit of locals calling various different local grapes "Greco Bianco": for this reason, Calabria is awash with Greco Biancos of all sorts. The National Registry lists a Greco Bianco at number 98; however, research indicates that this grape (referred to as Greco di Gerace) is identical to Malvasia di Lipari, still listed separately in the National Registry at number 135 (Crespan, Cabello, Giannetto, Ibanez, Karoglan Kontic, Maletic, et al. 2006b). According to other research, another Greco Bianco, also called Greco Bianco di Cirò, is actually the variety known as Guardavalle (listed in the National Registry at number 105), while Greco Bianco di Rogliano (or Greco Bianco di Cosenza) is really Pecorello (Schneider, Raimondi, and De Santis 2008). Grapes locally known as Greco Bianco di Lamezia Terme and Greco Bianco di Donnici are also both Guardavalle, though locals will also often erroneously refer to them as Mantonico, yet another distinct Calabrian variety. Finally, Greco Bianco del Pollino is identical to Montonico Bianco (a variety much more common in central Italy), that Calabrians in parts of the region other than the Pollino will also call Mantonico Bianco Italico, but it is distinct and not to be confused with Calabria's high-quality Mantonico Bianco cultivar. You realize that in the world of Italian grapes and wines, just one vowel can make all the difference in the world. In an admirable attempt to clarify matters, Schneider, Raimondi, and De Santis call the Greco Bianco identical to Malvasia di Lipari Greco di Bianco, thereby only adding to the hilarity of the situation, since Greco di Bianco is actually the name of a DOC wine (just like Greco di Tufo is the name of a DOCG wine from Campania) and using it to identify a grape variety is really not a good idea. Have you reached for that aspirin yet?

All this might be irrelevant, if it weren't that the wine made with Greco Bianco (which is, once again, by most accounts and in most opinions the variety Crespan has identified with Malvasia di Lipari but that locals and the National Registry still refuse to recognize as such) is potentially, and often actually, one of Italy's very best, especially as a sweet dessert wine. So it seems to me that the grape variety responsible for its production really ought to be well characterized, once and for all.

While I believe that the folks running the National Registry do well to move slowly on new proposed identifications of grape varieties and their synonyms (see chapter 1), the research that identifies Malvasia di Lipari, Malvasia di Sardegna, Malvasìa di Sitges, Greco Bianco di Gerace, and Malvasia Dubrovačka as one and the same is impressive (Crespan, Cabello, Giannetto, Ibanez, Karoglan Kontic, Maletic, et al. 2006b). In this study, the accessions were studied at fifteen SSR loci and the ampelographic evaluations, carried out by different experts on different grapevines, yielded essentially the same results. Despite OIV descriptors, they concluded they could not exclude some subjectivity on the part of different experts from Italy, Spain, and Croatia, who made descriptions in the field. Whether these differences were due to diverse interactions between genotype and environment or were a consequence of mutations accumulated over centuries is unclear. In this respect, it is noteworthy that Galet (2000) classified Malvasia di Sardegna in a different group from the others only on the basis of the presence of hairs on the lower side of the leaf. Pastena (1993) also highlighted the great variability of some morphologic parameters in different Malvasia di Lipari grapevines, in particular bunch length (18–40 cm) and berry dimensions. A very interesting study by Barba, Di Lernia, Chiota, Carimi, Carra, and Abbate (2008) showed that all the Malvasia di Lipari accessions studied on the islands are affected either by fanleaf virus or leaf roll virus, which may go a long way in explaining the diverse phenotypes of this variety relative to Greco Bianco and other *Malvasia*s. That said, and not surprisingly, Calabrian producers like Ceratti do not believe their Greco Bianco is identical to Malvasia di Lipari. Currently, there are an estimated one hundred hectares of Greco Bianco growing in Calabria, though it can be planted in other Italian regions as well, such as Basilicata, Lazio, Puglia, and Umbria.

Which Wines to Choose and Why

In conclusion, current wisdom is that Malvasia di Lipari and Calabria's Greco Bianco are in fact the same variety, but caveat emptor, because the National Registry does not yet recognize this. It seems almost unfair to point out then that Italy's best *Greco* variety is in fact a *Malvasia*. I believe Greco Bianco to be the best *Greco* of all because just like Riesling, and unlike Chardonnay or Greco itself, Greco Bianco has the unique ability to give both fantastic sweet wines and very good dry ones. In this light, the proposed identity between Greco Bianco and Malvasia di Lipari seems logical, since the latter variety has always been associated with absolutely fantastic sweet wine production.

Greco di Bianco is the only air-dried wine to be granted DOC status in Calabria: it's typical of the lower Ionian (eastern) coast of the region. It should not to be confused with the wine labeled DOC Greco Bianco Cirò, which is made only as a dry white wine. In my mind, the *grand cru* areas for Greco di Bianco are undoubtedly Palazzi and Santa Anna at Bianco. Greco Bianco is also used to make the wine called Greco di Gerace, now essentially made by only a few locals for home consumption, though Veronelli (1989) cited it as one of Italy's greatest sweet wines. I last tried a Greco di Gerace roughly ten years ago, made by the only local farmer who still toiled at the craft; production has since ceased. Though the farmer clearly didn't believe in filters, the cloudy, sediment-rich wine was excellent, incredibly thick and textured, with lingering honeyed, tropical-fruit aromas and flavors. I hope this wine will soon make a comeback.

Greco Bianco can also be used as part of blends to make the DOCG Lazio wines of Frascati and Frascati Cannellino (a light-bodied, delicately sweet wine), Calabria's DOC wines Bivongi, Cirò, and Savuto (among others), as well as Lazio's Marino DOC wine; and many IGT wines such as Lazio's Frusinate; Puglia's Daunia, Murgia, and Valle d'Itria; and Umbria's Narni and Spello. With few exceptions, none of these are particularly exciting.

WINES TO TRY: Stelitano*** (their Greco di Bianco is a work of art), Ceratti**, Lucà**, and Lavorata*.

Greco Giallo

WHERE IT'S FOUND: Lazio. NATIONAL REGISTRY CODE NUMBER: not registered. COLOR: white.

Though there are historically many grape varieties that were referred to as Greco Giallo, sometimes interchangeably and erroneously with Trebbiano Giallo, the only true Greco

Giallo today appears to live in a few sporadic rows in the Lazio countryside around the town of Cori. These vines are mostly grown by Marco Carpineti, in my view Lazio's most talented and best wine producer. Carpineti's grapes have not yet been studied by a university-trained ampelographer, and DNA profiling has not been carried out either, so definitive conclusions cannot be drawn. Therefore, whether the grape he uses really is Greco Giallo, or even a true *Greco* for that matter, is a matter of conjecture; however, I can vouch for the fact that his Greco Giallo looks like no other grape variety I have ever seen. The grape bunch is small and downright scrawny, but most typical are the berries: small and round, a very bright, pale lemon yellow, so pale, they are practically translucent. In fact, you can see the pips right through the skins. It is not a particularly resistant variety and is a miserly producer, explaining why it was abandoned over the years by practical-minded farmers.

Which Wines to Choose and Why
Marco Carpineti uses this grape variety to make its famous, award-winning Moro wine, a blend of Greco Moro (90 percent) and Greco Giallo (10 percent) though just five years ago it contained as much as 20 percent Greco Giallo. Given that I liked Carpineti's Moro wine much more when it was made with larger percentages of Greco Giallo (which, in my opinion, gives a more refined wine than Greco Moro), I can only hope that he starts producing and using more of this grape.

WINES TO TRY: There are no monovarietal wines made with Greco Giallo. There is 10 percent Greco Giallo in the blend used by Marco Carpineti (Moro), but clearly, at only 10 percent of the total, this wine cannot speak of what Greco Giallo is about.

Greco Moro

WHERE IT'S FOUND: Lazio. NATIONAL REGISTRY CODE NUMBER: not registered. COLOR: white.

Greco Moro is another grape grown in the countryside of Cori in Lazio, and virtually only by Marco Carpineti, owner of the eponymous wine estate. Greco Moro takes its name from the dark coloration of the berries, which when ripe have a dark, rusty hue (*moro* meaning Moorish, or dark skinned). It's characterized by much larger, more tightly packed bunches and bigger, round berries with much thicker skins than the Greco Giallo.

Greco Moro is more susceptible to botrytis than Greco Giallo, but in fact both varieties virtually disappeared because of disease sensitivity and poor yields. When Greco Moro yields are allowed to creep up, botrytis goes rampant, something made easier by the variety's compact bunch (in this respect, Greco Giallo has an advantage); at 80 quintals per hectare Greco Moro performs well (a quintal is a commonly used measure of weight in Europe, equivalent to one hundred kilograms), but at 150 quintals per hectare the harvest is at risk because Greco Moro is easily overcome by botrytis from one day to the next, especially in rainy autumns. In any case, significant plantings of both Greco Moro and Greco Giallo, from massal selections, were reintroduced in 2009 at the very high-quality Cincinnato social cooperative winery in Cori. In fact, you still cannot buy either of these *Greco* (or believed to be *Greco*) varieties from nurseries. As with Greco Giallo, neither academic ampelographic studies nor DNA profiling have yet been carried out on Greco Moro. What studies have been performed, and my own observations compiled over the years, describe the leaves of Greco Moro as medium-sized, with five lobes and very jagged: they are quite obviously much bigger than those of the Greco of Campania. The grape bunch is conical-pyramidal in shape, and the medium-large berries round and tightly packed. Greco Moro is characterized by medium vigor and good fertility.

Which Wines to Choose and Why
The wine folks at Cincinnato believed in Greco Moro (and Greco Giallo); because of this, they

pushed politicians until the legislation determining how the local Cori Bianco wine could be made was changed. Now up to 30 percent Greco Moro and Greco Giallo may be included in the Cori Bianco blend (while they were at it, they also had the maximum allowed percentage of Bellone increased from 30 percent to 50 percent and allowed the inclusion of up to 15 percent Malvasia del Lazio). According to Carpineti, a light two-hour maceration on the skins at 5°C allows for a noteworthy increase in the wine's terpenic and thiol-derived aromas. The wine is always fairly full bodied, independently of oak aging, for like all *Greco* varieties, Greco Moro produces wines with plenty of structure. Greco Moro wines also age well thanks to their high polyphenol content: a monovarietal Greco Moro wine will remind you of white and yellow fruit, mint, and sage, and will have a very savory finish.

WINES TO TRY: There are no monovarietal Greco Moro wines made; the closest is by Marco Carpineti*** (Moro), a blend of 90 percent Greco Moro and 10 percent Greco Giallo.

Greco Nero

WHERE IT'S FOUND: Calabria, Sardinia. NATIONAL REGISTRY CODE NUMBER: 99. COLOR: red.

I wonder if Greco Nero suffers, Sybil-like, from split personalities. For "Greco Nero" is not just one Greco Nero: you will make the acquaintance of many different Greco Nero grapes throughout Italy. In fact, many obviously different Greco Neros can live side by side even within the same region. Throughout the years, I have been proudly shown similarly named grapes by farmers and producers all over the country: in Umbria, Lazio, Marche, Abruzzo, and Campania, and I may well be forgetting a region or two. Needless to say, all those grapevines looked different, at times incredibly different; and the wines were just as different, ranging from pink and light-bodied to deep red and structured. Hilariously, these similarly named grapes don't look anything alike even in vineyards located just a short drive from one another; ask their respective owners, and you get sheepish looks in return, for nobody has an answer as to why this might be. Sometimes, it really is all Greek to me.

Nevertheless, it is generally accepted that the "real" Greco Nero variety grows in Calabria: unlike Umbrian or Abruzzo namesakes, its presence has been documented in Calabria for thousands of years, where it is also called Maglioccone or Greca Niura. Indeed, calling it Magliocco or Marsigliana Nera (or at times Marcigliana) is wrong, as Calò, Scienza, and Costacurta (2001) proved these varieties to be distinct. Though Greco Nero is said to be Italy's most abundant *Greco* variety and is considered by some to be particularly abundant in Calabria, this too is controversial: while there were roughly three thousand hectares reportedly planted to Greco Nero in 2000, 2010 data documents only two hundred hectares in the region. Whether this large decrease is due to a real reduction in Greco Nero or just stricter grapevine identification, or is simply a mistake, is unclear.

This huge decrease in Greco Nero plantings might be explained by recent data determining that there are five different varieties named Greco Nero in Calabria (Raimondi, Schneider, De Santis, and Cavallo 2008). Until recently, all Greco Neros were thought to be one and the same. At the present state of Greco Nero knowledge (which admittedly, is not great) Calabria's "real" Greco Nero is taken to be Greco Nero di Cirò (also confusingly called Nerello in the Lamezia Terme area and synonymous with the well-known Nerello Mascalese of Sicily); according to Raimondi, Schneider, and De Santis (2008), it is distinct from both Greco Nero di Sibari and Greco Nero di Verbicaro (the latter is also called Mantonico Nero Italico by locals), two rare varieties requiring further studies. Meanwhile, Greco Nero di Lamezia Terme and Greco Nero di Scilla are not *Greco*s at all; the former is Magliocco Dolce, the latter is Castiglione, two other red-berried Calabrian cultivars.

Greco Nero di Sibari and Greco Nero di Verbicaro grow along the Thyrrenian and Ionian coasts of Calabria respectively. Greco Nero di Sibari is characterized by a medium-large, round, indented leaf that is completely different from that of Greco Nero di Verbicaro, whose leaf is much smaller (the exact ampelographic definition is medium-small) and usually cuneiform or triangular in shape. Greco Nero di Sibari also ripens in late September instead of mid-September, as Greco Nero di Verbicaro tends to do. The two have very obviously different bunches and berries too: Greco Nero di Sibari has medium-small and conical bunches, with small, oval, elongated berries, while Nero di Verbicaro has large, obviously cylindrical bunches and medium-large, oval berries.

In Sardinia, *Greco* varieties were not mentioned until the beginning of the twentieth century: the first description is of a white Gregu by Cara in 1909, who also mentioned an Aregu (most likely the same Uregu described by Cettolini). A Sardinian Greco Nero, apparently different from all others, does exist: Nieddu's SSR microsatellite analysis (2011) shows it to be a close relative of the little-known Vertura, and a distant relative of Pascale, both local Sardinian varieties. On the island, its presence is restricted to eight hectares around Oristano. I caution readers that I am not aware of this identification having yet been published in a peer-reviewed academic journal. In Umbria, a local Greco Nero variety has recently been identified as completely distinct from Calabria's Greco Nero di Cirò. It has been renamed Grero, and is listed in the National Registry at number 448 (see GRERO, chapter 5).

Which Wines to Choose and Why

Finding 100 percent pure Greco Nero wines takes a lot of work: anyone moved by curiosity and passion (and admittedly, with time on his or her hands) needs to visit those producers that have not immediately blended their Greco Nero with musts from other varieties. Otherwise, Calabrian DOC wines worth a search are Lamezia, Bivongi, Savuto, and Pollino—but these are all blends, and the role Greco Nero might play in any specific wine is hard to judge. Most Greco Nero vines grow interspersed with other local varieties (many of them also waiting to be "rediscovered") in rickety, old, promiscuously planted vineyards. Just imagine: years ago during one of my many vineyard walks in Calabria, I was able to taste, in only a small perimeter, a Greco Nero, a Castiglione, a Magliocco Dolce, a Gaglioppo, another Greco Nero that looked nothing like the first, a variety that looked suspiciously like Sicily's Nero d'Avola to me, a prickly pear, a never-before-seen (and for that matter, never seen again) type of plum, and a tangerine. You can understand why most small local producers just pick all the grapes together and make a single red wine blend.

On its own, Greco Nero di Cirò (or at least, what I was, during my tastings, told was Greco Nero di Cirò) is capable of yielding a lovely, medium-bodied wine that is fresh and vinous, high-acid and fragrant. Of the very few Greco Nero wines being bottled and sold commercially in quantities larger than a "drop in a bucket," some taste much richer and creamier than the artisanally made examples I have tried over the years. These commercial efforts are perfectly fine, even very good, wines, but perhaps a little Merlot has found its way in? In fairness, with all the very different Greco Neros available in the region, a certain variation in aromatic and taste profiles of wines has to be expected. And I am afraid that at the present time, the exact contributions Greco Nero might make to the world of wine still lie in the minds of each producer—and in the taste buds of the beholder.

WINES TO TRY: Statti makes a very good Lamezia Rosso that contains up to 40 percent Greco Nero. While visiting Calabria, I have tasted a couple of bottles from Azienda Agricola Cicchello (Zungri), who make a wine labeled Greco Nero (Vigneto Macroni) from organically grown grapes that is pleasant and enjoyable, with hints of tobacco and flint, and fresh dark-red cherry aromas and flavors; but I have yet to visit them, and so I couldn't possibly tell you which Greco Nero variety the wine is made with. I have not yet seen, let alone tasted, any monovarietal Greco Nero wines from Sardinia.

Greco Bianco del Pollino

See MONTONICO BIANCO, chapter 4.

Greco Bianco di Cirò

See GUARDAVALLE, chapter 4.

Greco Bianco di Cosenza

See PECORELLO BIANCO, chapter 4.

Greco Bianco di Donnici

See GUARDAVALLE, chapter 4.

Greco Bianco di Lamezia Terme

See GUARDAVALLE and MAGLIOCCO, chapter 4.

Greco Bianco di Rogliano

See PECORELLO BIANCO, chapter 4.

Grecomusc'

See ROVIELLO, chapter 4.

Greco Nero di Scilla

See CASTIGLIONE, chapter 5.

THE GROPPELLO GROUP

Groppello is the name that has been used since ancient times to describe grape varieties that have an extremely compact bunch, reminiscent of a closed fist or a knot (*grop*, in local dialect, means knot or fist). This aspect led some experts to refer to these varieties as *Pignole* (from *pigna*, pine cone, also referring to the compact nature of the grape bunch). This is unfortunate, as these two groups of grapes, *Pignola*s and *Groppello*s, are altogether different varieties.

Much like *Greco* and *Malvasia,* the term *Groppello* applies not to a single grape variety but to a collection of different but more or less related grapes. The main *Groppello* variety is called Groppello Gentile; the two others that make wines of note are Groppello di Mocasina (also called Groppello di Santo Stefano or Groppello Molinèr), which like Groppello Gentile is also typical of Lombardy's Garda area, though much harder to find, and Groppello di Revò, typical of the Val di Non in Trentino (and therefore sometimes called Groppello Nonesiano or Groppello Anaune). Groppellone is a biotype of Groppello Gentile with larger bunches and berries that is also grown in Lombardy. Finally, the variety confusingly called Groppello Ruperti and also found in parts of Lombardy is not a *Groppello* at all, but Lambrusco Viadanese, a distinct grape and, as the name implies, a member of the *Lambrusco* family (see LAMBRUSCO FAMILY entry).

The first to mention the *Groppello*s was Agostino Gallo (1565), and he included white grapes in the group as well, though we now know that what was then called Groppello Bianco is in fact Nosiola, another Trentino variety. In the *Bollettino Ampelografico* of 1884–87, cultivation of *Groppello*s was reported in thirty-nine of fifty-two townships in the province of Rovigo in Veneto; in the early 1900s, Viala and Vermorel state that a generalized *Groppello* was very common in Lombardy (Bergamo and Brescia), in Trentino (Val di Non and Tramin), and in Veneto (Verona, Vicenza, Belluno, and Rovigo). In 1964, Cosmo and Sardi expanded knowledge further by distinguishing between Groppello Gentile and Groppello di Santo Stefano (which we know today to be identical to Groppello di Mocasina), but many of their conclusions regarding the various *Groppello*s were wrong: Groppello di Revò and Groppello di Mocasina are not identical and Groppellone is not a biotype of Groppello di Revò.

It was only with the groundbreaking work of Costantini, Roncador, and Grando in 2001, in which nine SSR microsatellite loci of twenty-two accessions of *Groppellos* were analyzed, that a clear understanding of relationships and identities between these varieties was gained. It is now believed that Groppellone is a biotype of Groppello Gentile (this work confirmed results of previous studies by Villa, Milesi, and Scienza in 1997, who used isoenzymatic and electrophoretic methods only), that Groppello di Santo Stefano and Groppello di Mocasina are one and the same, and that Groppello di Revò is distinct, sharing only the Groppello moniker. The latter variety isn't closely related to Groppello Gentile, as the two only share seven out of eighteen alleles, and even less to Groppello di Mocasina, with which it shares only five of eighteen alleles. Groppello di Mocasina shares a somewhat closer relationship with Groppello Gentile (twelve of eighteen alleles in common), as might be imagined of cultivars that have long grown side by side in the same habitat. In defense of the many ampelographers of the past, who did not have the benefit of molecular biology techniques, their hypothesis that Groppello di Revò had been transported suitcase-style from Trentino to Lombardy (where they believed it morphed over time into Groppello di Mocasina or Groppello di Santo Stefano) has logic on its side. In 2007, Vouillamoz, Schneider, and Grando showed that both Groppello di Revò and Nosiola are offsprings of Rèze, a native variety of the Swiss Valais. This is not without interest, because some older Trentino farmers still occasionally refer to Nosiola as Groppello Bianco.

Today Groppello Gentile and Groppello di Mocasina are found only in Lombardy, mainly on the western, or Lombard, side of Lake Garda, reaching out eastward toward Brescia. Currently, there are an estimated five hundred hectares planted to the former and less than fifty to the latter. There are also some sporadic plantings of these two *Groppellos* (mainly Gentile) in Trentino, but this is believed to be due to nursery errors that caused the wrong *Groppellos* to be sold—probably during the time when everyone believed the three to be biotypes of each other, rather than distinct varieties. Groppello di Revò grows only in Trentino, mainly around the towns of Revò, Romallo, and Cagnò, as well as on the shores of Lake Cles. While it was once produced in large volumes, output decreased sharply in the twentieth century, and only began increasing again in the last decade: forty-seven thousand hectoliters of wine were reportedly made in the years 1910–14, as compared to four hundred hectoliters in 2000, three-quarters of which were grown around Revò.

Ampelographically, all *Groppellos* have cylindrical-conical bunches so compact that the berries are slightly flattened due to being squeezed together. Gentile is the only main *Groppello* to have a winged grape bunch and a tri-lobed leaf (all other *Groppellos* have a pentagonal leaf), while Groppello di Mocasina has the smallest bunch and berries. All *Groppellos* are disease resistant, though the compact nature of their bunch makes them sensitive to botrytis bunch rot. Clones are available only for Mocasina (MI-GROM-8 and LL-2) and Gentile (R3, the oldest and available since 1969, VCR 14, and VCR 11).

Which Wines to Choose and Why

A well-made *Groppello* wine will strike you with bright acidity, lively tannins, and intense aromas of red cherry, violet, tobacco, and plenty of spices (marjoram, olive wood, and especially black pepper). In general, all Groppello wines are best drunk within a year or so of the vintage, though *riserva* wines can age well longer. The DOC guidelines for production of Riviera del Garda Bresciano and Garda Bresciano Groppello (first established in 1990 and later updated in 1999) state that a minimum 85 percent *Groppello* (Gentile, Groppellone, and Mocasina) is required, plus another 15 percent of nonaromatic red grape varieties. I firmly believe that only 85 percent of any grape variety is too little for anybody to truly grasp what that variety is all about, but that's still a lot better than what the law allows for the DOC Garda and Riviera del Garda Bresciano Rosso or Chiaretto wines. Get ready: 30 to 60 percent *Groppello* (Gentile, Groppellone, and Mocasina), 10 to 25 percent Sangiovese, 5 to 30 percent Marzemino or Berzemino, 10 to 20 percent Barbera, plus up to 10 percent of any other nonaromatic red grape variety. They're only missing the kitchen sink.

Groppello dei Berici and Groppello di Breganze

Two more *Groppello*-named varieties have recently been discovered, grown respectively in Veneto's Colli Berici and Breganze areas, and called, appropriately enough, Groppello dei Berici and Groppello di Breganze. Though the two are distinct from the other three *Groppellos* (and the Groppellone biotype), genetic profiling by Cancellier, Giannetto, and Crespan (2009) has proved that what is routinely called Groppello di Breganze, which appeared to share considerable morphologic similarities with Groppello di Revò, is in fact identical to Pignola Nera. Groppello dei Berici, by contrast, is a true *Groppello* and has a pentagonal leaf; a small, winged, stocky bunch; and very small round berries. Its budbreak falls later in the season than that of all other *Groppellos*, and it apparently accumulates less sugar. Like all *Groppello* varieties, its very compact bunch makes it sensitive to botrytis.

Which Wines to Choose and Why

To the best of my knowledge there is nobody making a monovarietal wine from Groppello dei Berici. As for Groppello di Breganze, the wines to look for are those made with the Pignola variety, though Firmino Miotti bottles a monovarietal wine he calls "Groppello" and continues to call the grape variety used to make it Groppello di Breganze, not Pignola Nera (see PIGNOLA, chapter 4). Interestingly, Cantina Col Dovigo produces a wine named "Groppello," though it doesn't specify which Groppello variety is used, but they have told me it is in fact Groppello di Breganze. The wine is an IGT, but the word "Breganze" is printed in small lettering on the label below the words *Indicazione Geografica Tipica*. This is interesting, since Breganze is a DOC in Italy, not an IGT wine—I guess what they mean is that it is a Groppello di Breganze wine.

WINES TO TRY: For Groppello di Breganze (actually Pignola Nera), try: Firmino Miotti** and Col Dovigo**. For Groppello dei Berici, to the best of my knowledge, there is no monovarietal wine made yet with this variety.

Groppello di Mocasina

WHERE IT'S FOUND: Lombardy. NATIONAL REGISTRY CODE NUMBER: 102 (and, as Groppello di Santo Stefano, number 103 as well). COLOR: red.

Groppello di Mocasina is easily differentiated from all other *Groppellos* because of the downy undersurface of its leaves (hence the synonym Groppello Molinèr, from *mulinare*, in reference to mills and flour), and the fact that the cluster is almost never winged. Groppello di Mocasina is also easy to distinguish from the other *Groppellos* because it has the smallest bunches and berries of all. A rather vigorous variety, it can easily produce one hundred hectoliters per hectare, far too high for quality wine production, so its vigor needs to be reined in. For this reason, it does poorly with very vigorous rootstocks, such as the old Golia rootstock once commonly used in Italy. It is especially sensitive to magnesium and potassium deficiencies of the soil, as well as to botrytis bunch rot. It's best planted on hillsides on poor, rocky soils that allow for good water drainage.

Which Wines to Choose and Why

In my experience, wines that are pure Groppello di Mocasina tend to be more vegetal or herbal than monovarietal Groppello Gentile wines, but this may be a function of yields. Historically Groppello di Mocasina was always blended with other varieties such as Barbera, Sangiovese, and Marzemino (though not necessarily Groppello

Gentile, as around Mocasina the latter *Groppello* variety was rare). Groppello di Mocasina was always used in blends because its monovarietal wines are light in color and low in acid, while in blends it enhances perfume and provides smoothness. Currently, it is believed there are less than fifty hectares planted to Groppello di Mocasina in Lombardy, as well as a few sporadic vines in Trentino.

WINES TO TRY: Redaelli de Zinis** (roughly 15 percent of the grapes are late harvested), and Pasini-La Torre* (Garda Classico Mocasina; owner Pasini is a huge believer in Groppello di Mocasina's qualities). Cantine Turina produces a Garda Classico Groppello that is 50 percent Mocasina and 50 percent Gentile, but with these percentages, it's impossible to figure out what Groppello di Mocasina truly brings to the blend.

Groppello di Revò

WHERE IT'S FOUND: Lombardy. NATIONAL REGISTRY CODE NUMBER: 380. COLOR: red.

Groppello di Revò is believed to be the most ancient of the *Groppello*s: its cultivation was greatly helped by the propagation efforts of the noble Maffei family, who grew it on their estate in the Val di Non. Always an extremely important variety in Trentino (where supplying wine to the nearby Austro-Hungarian empire was a huge business), Groppello di Revò's importance to the local economy is also demonstrated by the fact that Trentino's third-oldest winemaking social cooperative was created in 1893 in Revò. After phylloxera, Groppello di Revò fell on hard times. It was probably saved from extinction only because it grew well on the steep shores of Lake Santa Giustina and apple trees (Trentino's main agricultural product and at that time, the more financially rewarding crop) did not, so that *Groppello* vines were mercifully left in peace. Local producers have since grouped together to form the Associazione del Groppello di Revò, an association of like-minded individuals who aim to publicize the qualities of their cultivar and wine.

Which Wines to Choose and Why

Monovarietal wines made with Groppello di Revò are characterized by a black pepper aroma and flavor. This is not surprising since researchers at the Istituto Agrario di San Michele all'Adige have recently discovered that the variety expresses high concentrations of rotundone in the wine. Rotundone smells of black pepper; a molecule also found in rosemary and marjoram, it is also present in noteworthy quantities in wines made with Vespolina, Schioppettino, and Austria's Grüner Veltliner.

WINES TO TRY: Augusto Zadra*** (I like his classic Groppello bottling more than the Groppello El Zeremia, which has more structure; this producer owns centenary vines, many ungrafted), Pravis** (El Filo'), Andrea Franch**, Valerio Rizzi**, Cantina Rotaliana**, Produttori di Montagna**, Marco Fellin* (aged in oak, so smoother than most), and Piero Pancheri* (Laste Rosse).

Groppello Gentile

WHERE IT'S FOUND: Lombardy, Trentino. NATIONAL REGISTRY CODE NUMBER: 104. COLOR: red.

Groppello Gentile is very easily distinguished from all other *Groppello*s due to its always winged grape bunch; when the bunch is particularly big, the grape is most likely the Groppellone biotype. Groppello Gentile is a remarkably delicate variety that is especially sensitive to water retention in soils. In waterlogged soils, Groppello Gentile greatly increases productivity—its berries enlarge and their skin becomes much thinner—making grey rot a huge problem. Not surprisingly, this variety prefers sandy or gravelly soils, which ensure excellent water drainage.

Which Wines to Choose and Why

Monovarietal examples of Groppello Gentile can be found among DOC wines, though it is almost always blended with Groppello di

Mocasina—honestly, I find many producers have no clue as to which *Groppello* they are growing. Costaripa makes a monovarietal Groppello Gentile with their excellent Castelline bottling. The *grand cru* for the Garda area, relative to Groppello Gentile, is Valtènesi (in the heart of Garda Classico) with light, sandy, gravelly soils that do not allow for water retention and therefore offer conditions in which Groppello Gentile can thrive. As Groppello Gentile has bigger berries than the other *Groppellos*, it is the one most often used for *rosato* and light red wine production.

WINES TO TRY: For Garda, try: Cantrina*** (Groppello Garda Classico), Costaripa*** (Castelline, light and fresh, a pure Groppello Gentile, and Maim, richer and velvety; this estate owns vines that are close to fifty years old and it shows), Comincioli**, Le Chiusure**, Zuliani**, Civielle*, and Pasini-San Giovanni* (Riserva Vigneto Arzane, a blend of Groppello Gentile and Groppello di Mocasina).

THE LAMBRUSCO FAMILY

The *Lambrusco* family of grapes and wines could do with better public relations, as their image is tarnished in most fine-wine drinking circles; fairly enough too, as these varieties are behind a collection of not very distinguished wines. On www.truelambrusco.com, Lidia Bastianich, the famous chef and restaurant owner, is quoted as saying that "Lambruscos have been misrepresented by industrial versions that have the soda pop flavors they think Americans might want." On the same site, one of the best food and wine writers in America, John Mariani, expresses a similar thought: "Prior to June 2012, I had never ordered a bottle of lambrusco in Italy; with memories of those sweet, fizzy, soda-like imports of the 1970s, I had no interest in revisiting such wines, even in Emilia-Romagna, where lambrusco is made." After all that, you couldn't be blamed for thinking that *Lambruscos* and lambruscos were best forgotten, but there are thrilling *Lambrusco* wines to be had too; and not just lip-smackingly delicious dry lambrusco *rosso* and *rosato*, but great sweet ones too. Wine snobs will sneer at the latter wines, but I don't see the problem: if some fetishists prize fruitiness and sweetness in their wines above all else, who am I to argue? And besides, I like those sweet wines too.

The *Lambruscos* may well be Italy's oldest family of native grape varieties, comprising many members that give similar yet ultimately distinct wines. *Lambruscos* have nothing to do with *Vitis labrusca*, which is a native North American grapevine; in fact, there exists evidence that the Etruscans were domesticating vines centuries before Rome was born, though more cogent documentation dates to centuries later, when Cato writes in *De agri cultura* that *labrusca* are those wild vine varieties that grow spontaneously from seeds. In relatively more modern times, Pier de' Crescenzi, in his thirteenth-century *Ruralium Commodorum Librim Duodecim* cites a wine made from *labrusca*. However, the first to mention "Lambrusco" as a specific grape variety instead of a generic domesticated wild grape was Bacci in 1596. In the seventeenth century records attest to as many as fifty *"labrusca"* varieties, a tally reduced to twenty-three by Molon in 1906 (one of which was a white grape). These were later reduced to ten red grapes by Cosmo and Polsinelli in 1962. The most recent studies by Calò, Costacurta, and Scienza (2001) speak of only eight closely related but different *Lambrusco* varieties, so the *Lambruscos* can be considered a family. According to Emilio Sereni in 1986, the term *Lambrusco* may stem from the paleoligurian prefix *lap-* or *lab-*, meaning rock or stone (as in *rupe*, in Italian, or *rupestris*). Another, less likely, derivation is from the Latin *labrum*, meaning lip or edge, as in the edge of the woods where wild grape varieties like to grow.

Lambrusco varieties are mainly grown in Emilia-Romagna, but are also found in Lombardy, Trentino, Veneto, and Puglia. However, they have always been, and are still today, mainly associated with Emilia-Romagna: in fact Molon (1906) proposed that the name

Lambrusco be reserved for varieties growing in this region and specifically in the countryside around the city of Modena. Nevertheless, though there are many so-called *Lambruscos* grown all over Italy, very few of these are related to the *Lambrusco* family of Emilia-Romagna. An extremely interesting study by Torello Marinoni, Raimondi, Boccacci, and Schneider (2006) recently provided ample proof: using twenty SSR loci for DNA typing, the genetic profiles of several grapes from Piedmont all named Lambrusco-Something were compared to those of other grapes from Piedmont and to well-known *Lambruscos* from Emilia-Romagna. Results showed that all the Piedmontese cultivars named *Lambrusca* or *Lambrusco* showed first-degree parentage relationships with Piedmontese varieties such as Lambrusca di Alessandria, Neretto di Marengo, and Malvasia di Casorzo, while the *Lambruscos* from Emilia-Romagna remained genetically distant.

Unfortunately, genetic erosion of the *Lambruscos* has led us to lose a number of species. However, there are still enough of these cultivars left to gain a glimpse of the complex and fascinating world that is the *Lambrusco* family. *Lambrusco* varieties share some ampelographic features such as medium-large, pyramidal-conical, longish bunches and round-to-oval berries characterized by thin but resistant skins of various depths of color (though the Grasparossa, Marani, and Maestri varieties have thick skins). With a little practice, it's very easy to recognize the various *Lambruscos* and to tell *Lambruscos* apart from other grapes in the vineyard. In contrast, the wines of individual *Lambruscos* are very different from one another and therein lies a great deal of their charm. Lambrusco di Sorbara gives the lightest, most floral wines, while Lambrusco Grasparossa produces bigger and more obviously structured wines. The latter is generally considered to be the best *Lambrusco* subvariety, and is the only one grown mainly on higher-quality hillside vineyards. Some local Italian experts are adamant that Lambrusco Grasparossa wines also show greater depth of flavor and complexity, but I wonder if they aren't being overly impressed by the much richer flesh and bigger tannins typical of wines made with the Grasparossa variety. Certainly, my experience is that wines made with the latter never exude the almost magical perfume of those made with Lambrusco di Sorbara, nor the creamy balance of wines made with Lambrusco Salamino, which are best described as a cross between those of Sorbara and Grasparossa, as they combine the perfume of the former with the structure and flavors of the latter. In my opinion, some Lambrusco Grasparossa wines also seem big but chunky, and could use a little more nuance and complexity. Again, those who write only *Lambrusco* when referring to just a single *Lambrusco* variety are being inaccurate, and offer little insight into what the grapes and wines are all about. For each *Lambrusco* is distinctive, and each has a story to tell.

Lambrusco wines are made most often in *secco* (dry), *semi-secco* (off-dry), or, more rarely, *dolce* (sweet) styles. There are also excellent *rosato* wines. Fewer wines, from Italy or anywhere else in the world for that matter, match better with fatty foods (for example, sausages and *charcuterie*) or staples such as tomato-based pizzas and pastas. Just match the right Lambrusco to the right food and you'll come away feeling like someone catapulted you into gastronomic nirvana.

Lambrusco di Sorbara

WHERE IT'S FOUND: Emilia-Romagna (like all *Lambruscos*, mainly in the Emilia portion of this region). NATIONAL REGISTRY CODE NUMBER: 115. COLOR: red.

Perhaps the most famous of all *Lambruscos*, Lambrusco di Sorbara is the easiest to find, the most abundantly produced, and also the closest in its characteristics to the wild grape, *Vitis vinifera silvestris*. It is also the most fragrant and lightest of all *Lambruscos*—which, in versions devoid of fruit, becomes an almost fatal flaw. When well made, its wines are characterized by an intense aroma of violet; in fact, this variety is also called Lambrusco della Viola. It is the oldest of all *Lambrusco*s, ripens earlier than most, and reaches its qualitative zenith when grown on sandy soils. Even though Sorbara's flower is hermaphrodite (as in all cultivated varieties), it behaves physiologically like a female organ; hence, Lambrusco di Sorbara needs to be cultivated with another *Lambrusco* variety (usually Lambrusco Salamino) that acts as a pollinator. This is of paramount importance, for otherwise, Sorbara does not ripen: in fact, it is common to find clusters of Lambrusco di Sorbara with both ripe red and small green unripe berries (*millerandage* or asynchronous maturation).

According to Cosmo and Polsinelli (1962), four different biotypes of Lambrusco di Sorbara were initially described, characterized by, respectively: spherical berries and red leaves; spherical berries and green leaves; sub-spherical or oval berries and red leaves; and olive shaped berries with green leaves. The fourth is now called Lambrusco Oliva and is no longer considered a biotype of Lambrusco di Sorbara, but rather a distinct *Lambrusco* variety, number 360 in the National Registry. First described in 1886, this *Lambrusco* has olive-shaped berries so different from those of other members of the *Lambrusco* group that some experts refused to accept it as a *Lambrusco* at the time of its discovery (Gozzi 2002; see OTHER LAMBRUSCO VARIETIES entry). Today, the other three biotypes of Lambrusco di Sorbara are believed to be expressions of specific habitats and growing conditions. Available clones of Lambrusco di Sorbara include the R4 (the first available, in 1969), CAB 2V, CAB 21G, and VCR 20 (perhaps the most interesting).

Which Wines to Choose and Why

Wines to look for are simply labeled Lambrusco di Sorbara, and the vine, which grows mainly in the province of Modena (and to a minor extent around Reggio Emilia) is especially found in the countryside around Comporto, Nonantola, and San Prospero. Its *grand cru* area is located between the Secchia and Panaro rivers near Modena, though good examples are also produced around the towns of Correggio, Rubiera, and San Martino in Rio in the province of Reggio Emilia. Other DOC wines that can be made mostly with this variety include Modena and Reggiano; IGT wines include Alto Mincio, Emilia (or dell'Emilia), Forlì, Quistello, Rubicone, and Sabbioneta, among others.

WINES TO TRY: Cavicchioli*** (Vigna del Cristo Secco and Vigna del Cristo Rosé), Cleto Chiarli*** (Antica Modena Premium), Francesco Bellei** (Rifermentazione Naturale), Paltrinieri*** (Frizzante Etichetta Bianca Fermentazione Naturale and Leclisse), Garuti Elio & Eredi Garuti Romeo** (Rosa lambrusco di Sorbara Rosato), and Francesco Vezzelli**. An archetypal Lambrusco di Sorbara wine is the Antica Modena Premium by Cleto Chiarli: delicate and lightly fizzy, with gorgeous redcurrant and wild strawberry aromas and flavors supported by bright acids, I guarantee it will change your mind about fizzy reds forever.

Lambrusco Grasparossa

WHERE IT'S FOUND: Emilia-Romagna. NATIONAL REGISTRY CODE NUMBER: 116. COLOR: red.

Lambrusco Grasparossa is also called Lambrusco di Castelvetro, or Lambrusco Grasparossa di Castelvetro, since its birthplace is the town of same name near Modena in Emilia-Romagna. The latter is also the name of the DOC wine made with this variety. It also grows in the countryside around the towns of Casalgrande, Quattro Castelle, and Scandiano near Reggio Emilia. Recent DNA results have shown it to be identical to the Scorzamara variety, so we now know this *Lambrusco* also grows around Coviolo (Boccacci, Torello Marinoni, Gambino, Botta, and Schneider 2005). It was first described by Agazzotti in 1867, who found the wine had a strong aroma of almond. Cosmo described four biotypes in 1965: green-stalked, red-stalked, sparse-clustered, and compact-clustered. The two biotypes most planted currently are the red-stalked and the sparse-clustered. All together, there are currently over 1,550 hectares of Grasparossa planted (slightly down from the 1,846 hectares reported in the 2000 census).

Considered by many in Italy to be the highest-quality *Lambrusco,* due to its ability to reach optimal ripeness even at cooler temperatures, Grasparossa is the only *Lambrusco* that grows mainly on hillsides rather than the plains of Emilia. Versatile in regard to the kind of soils it may be planted in, it probably does best in clay soils. The Grasparossa variety shows poor affinity to most rootstocks except Golia. It responds well to short pruning techniques. Available clones include R1 (an extremely old clone, available since 1969), CAB 7, and CAB 14 (which is the best at accumulating sugar and therefore potentially produces slightly more alcoholic, fuller-bodied wines).

Which Wines to Choose and Why

The Lambrusco Grasparossa di Castelvetro production zone is located in the provinces of Modena (especially) and Mantova, and can be essentially divided into the high hills and the lower hillside vineyards. The former are characterized by sandy-clay marl or clay-calcareous soils that are hard to till and don't offer great water drainage. The wine made from grapes grown here are particularly intense and concentrated. The latter are mainly sandy-loam soils with a noteworthy gravel content, allowing for better water drainage. Their wines are actually very similar to those made on the higher slopes, but are perhaps a little more graceful and lighter-bodied (always a very relative term with Lambrusco Grasparossa). In fact, the wine is more tannic than those made with other *Lambrusco*s, and though very deeply hued, it does not produce the darkest *Lambrusco* wine of all (that honor most likely goes to Lambrusco Maestri); however, its very deep purple-ruby hue is much darker than the medium-pale red of wines made with Lambrusco di Sorbara. As for the expert opinion that it is the best of all *Lambrusco* varieties, I find that arguable; size doesn't always matter. Certainly Lambrusco Grasparossa produces bigger, creamier and fuller-bodied wines than any other member of the family, redolent of ripe black cherry and dark plum aromas and flavors, but in my experience, also less intensely aromatic and complex ones. Certainly, you wouldn't match a Lambrusco Grasparossa wine to the same foods you would a Lambrusco di Sorbara; whereas the first is a sausages or stew-and-potatoes kind of guy, the latter is more at home in the company of a tomato-based pizza or tortellini in broth (for a match made in heaven, add a little of the Lambrusco di Sorbara into the broth before digging in).

The best DOC wine is the Lambrusco Grasparossa di Castelvetro (though the law states that Lambrusco di Grasparossa wines can be only 85 percent Grasparossa, there are many great monovarietal versions, and I will list some below); other DOC wines are Colli di Scandiano e Canossa and Modena. IGT wines include those labeled Alto Mincio, Emilia (or dell'Emilia), Forlì, Rubicone, and Sabbioneta, among others.

WINES TO TRY: Vittorio Graziano*** (Fontana dei Boschi), Fattoria Moretto*** (Monovitigno and Vigna Canova), Tenuta Pederzana*** (Canto Libero Semi Secco), Cleto Chiarli*** (Vigneto Enrico Cialdini), Corte Manzini*** (L'Acino), Villa di Corlo*** (Corleto), and Fiorini** (Becco Rosso).

Lambrusco Maestri

WHERE IT'S FOUND: Emilia-Romagna, Puglia.
NATIONAL REGISTRY CODE NUMBER: 117. **COLOR:** red.

The name derives from Villa Maestri, located near San Pancrazio in the territory of Parma in Emilia, which is where this variety is believed to have originated. It is one of the hardier and more adaptable *Lambrusco* varieties, and unlike the others, it is more abundant around Reggio Emilia than around Modena or Parma. What's more, Lambrusco Maestri is on a roll: plantings in Emilia-Romagna have essentially doubled in the last ten years, as producers are replacing Lambrusco Marani (which delivers less obviously creamy, full-bodied wines) with it. According to Zulini, this *Lambrusco* is also common in Puglia (though I'm there at least three or four times a year almost every year and have never heard anybody mention it) and there are reportedly roughly one hundred hectares planted in Argentina. Though Lambrusco Maestri was supposedly known in the nineteenth century, documentation on it is available only from the twentieth century. In 2005, Boccacci, Torello Marinoni, Gambino, Botta, and Schneider, studied its possible parentage relationships via molecular analysis and described a parent-offspring relationship between it and Fortana. This *Lambrusco* is characterized by a slightly more compact and smaller bunch, though the physical appearance depends on which clone or biotype is being examined. Clones available include CAB 6, CAB 16, and VCR 1, the last of which became available in 1995 and offers the largest production and usually the higher quality. This *Lambrusco* variety is characterized by bunches with a very obvious, opulent wing off to the side; Lambrusco Viadanese, for example, rarely has a wing. Generally speaking, Lambrusco Maestri is a very copious, dependable producer and ripens slightly earlier than other Lambrusco varieties. Due to its excessive vigor, excessively fertile soils are best avoided; short pruning is preferable.

While the *Lambrusco* varieties planted outside Italy are often not characterized fully, so that one is left wondering which type was planted, Lambrusco Maestri is one *Lambrusco* that seems to travel well. There are documented plantings of it in Argentina (Mendoza, San Juan) and Australia (Heathcote, Adelaide Hills).

Which Wines to Choose and Why

Lambrusco Maestri gives the fruitiest, creamiest, and most immediately appealing, if not the deepest and most complex, *Lambrusco* wines of all. When well made, the wine has extremely intense purple tones to its deep ruby hue and has an amazingly fruity, almost bubblegum-like quality to its aromas and flavors of dark plums, ripe black cherry, milk chocolate, and candied violets. It's effusively soft and creamy, but with a very fresh grapey quality. It is allowed in many DOC blends, such as Colli di Parma, Colli di Scandiano e Canossa, Emilia (or dell'Emilia), Lambrusco Mantovano, and Reggiano. IGT blends are numerous, and include Campania, delle Venezie, Forlì, Puglia, Rubicone, Salento, and Tarantino.

Outside Italy, try the very good Australian version by Chalmers, simply labeled Lambrusco but made with 100 percent Lambrusco Maestri. The 2012 is an excellent wine, atypically made by the traditional Champagne method of a secondary fermentation in the bottle; you'll love the heady vanilla, cinnamon, and strawberry aromas and flavors that seem to jump out of the glass. Parish Hill in the Adelaide Hills, also makes an outstanding lambrusco (simply labeled Lambrusco Frizzante) from this variety. From Argentina, try the versions by Tittarelli and the excellent one by Don Bosco.

WINES TO TRY: Cantine Ceci*** (Nero di Lambrusco Otello, guaranteed to change your mind about lambrusco forever and turn you into a believer), Dall'Asta*** (Mefistofele), Carra di Casatico** (Torcularia), and Monte delle Vigne** (Selezione Lambrusco dell'Emilia).

Lambrusco Marani

WHERE IT'S FOUND: Emilia-Romagna. NATIONAL REGISTRY CODE NUMBER: 118. COLOR: red.

Lambrusco Marani is (along with Grasparossa) a rare *Lambrusco* grown in hillside vineyards, though it is most often found on flatlands, where it proves resistant to relatively damp soils (it likes clay) but susceptible to winter cold. It prefers low-density cultivation systems with short pruning; yields are abundant and regular.

Little documentation exists of this variety's presence as recently as the twentieth century. It is a close relative of Fogarina, a variety native to Emilia-Romagna (Boccacci, Torello Marinoni, Gambino, Botta, and Schneider 2005). Nowadays, it grows mainly in the countryside around Reggio Emilio near towns such as Campagnola, Fabbrico, Novellara, Rolo, and Rio Saliceto, the same habitat as Lambrusco Maestri: the two are often planted together in the same vineyard. Today it is also grown around Bologna and Mantova: at over twenty-three hundred hectares planted as of 2000, it was a relatively abundant *Lambrusco* but things have changed greatly over the course of the last ten years, and its surface under vine has decreased by 41 percent. This is because modern producers prefer to plant (or replant) Lambrusco Maestri, which gives much fruitier and richer wines. Available clones include R2 and CAB 8A, and all are characterized by looser-packed bunches and smaller, almost elliptical berries than most other *Lambruscos*.

Which Wines to Choose and Why

The wines are fruity and tannic, and thanks to fairly high total acidity, come across as having a more floral quality (violet, iris, peony) and a little less sweetness and fruity flesh (black currant and red cherry, instead of ripe black cherry) than those made with Lambrusco Maestri. I find well-made Marani wines to be refined and not too tannic, with a bright, juicy personality. Marani is the mainstay variety of DOC Reggiano Lambrusco, but is also part of the DOC blends of Lombardy's Lambrusco Mantovano and Emilia-Romagna's Colli di Scandiano e Canosa wines (where it is usually blended with Lambrusco Montericco). It is present in such IGT blends as Emilia (or dell'Emilia), Forlì, Lambrusco Mantovano, Quistello, Ravenna, Reggiano, Rubicone, and Sabbioneta, and others.

WINES TO TRY: Rinaldini-Moro*** (Osè) and Cantine Riunite* (L'Olma, 85 percent Lambrusco Marani, 15 percent Lambrusco Salamino and Ancellotta, which they call Lambrusco Lancellotta).

Lambrusco Salamino

WHERE IT'S FOUND: Emilia-Romagna. NATIONAL REGISTRY CODE NUMBER: 120. COLOR: red.

Given Italy's love affair with *salame* (over two hundred and fifty varieties at last count, and you thought the country had too many grape varieties!), it's not surprising that a grapevine would be named after one of the country's favorite foods. Lambrusco Salamino is so called for its appearance: the short and cylindrical grape bunch will remind you, and everyone else, of a *salame*. Though also called Lambrusco Galassi and Lambruschino, the most commonly used synonym is Lambrusco Salamino di Santa Croce, as it originates from the area of Santa Croce di Carpi near Modena. Like other *Lambrusco* varieties it exhibits great intravarietal variability, with at least five different biotypes described: *tenero* (soft), *foglia rossa* (red leaf), *foglia verde* (green leaf), *graspo rosso* (red-stalked), and *graspo verde* (green-stalked). It has always been felt that the green-leafed biotype was the hardiest and most productive, but the wine made with the other varieties was usually higher in quality. At over four thousand hectares, it is the most abundantly planted of all *Lambruscos*, grown mainly in the provinces of Modena and Reggio Emilia (around Correggio, Fabbrico, Rio Saliceto, and San Martino in Rio, more or less where Lambrusco Marani grows), and more rarely around Bologna, Ferrara, and Mantova. Its abundance in the Modena countryside (Carpi is located in the northwestern sector of this province) is explained not just by its intrinsic qualities (in some respects, it's the best of all *Lambruscos*, as its wines combine the grace and fragrance of Lambrusco di Sorbara with the power and body of Lambrusco Grasparossa) but because it is also used as a pollinator for the Sorbara variety. Blessed by good vigor, it is a late ripener like all *Lambruscos* (on average, harvest occurs in mid-October), but guarantees steady, copious yields. It likes fresher soils and can stand up to humid conditions very well; botrytis is only a problem for those biotypes with more compact bunches.

In general, Lambrusco Salamino is characterized by a long but rather small grape bunch (around ten to twelve centimeters) and round berries of various sizes even within the same bunch. Available clones include R5 (the first to become available, in 1969), CAB 1, CAB 3, VCR 1, VCR 20, VCR 23, and Ampelos TEA 2D. Of these, VCR 20, available since 2006, has very high quality, giving wines with very intense red-cherry aromas and flavors. However it produces slightly less than the others and its compact bunch makes it best suited for slightly drier hillside environments where water drainage proves better. VCR 23 produces more and is less susceptible to botrytis, but in my view at least, allows for slightly less interesting wines.

Which Wines to Choose and Why

This is one lambrusco that is more often found in an off-dry (*semi-secco*) or frankly sweet (*dolce*) style, than in a dry one *(secco)*. It has aromas of violet, rose, and small, red, and dark berries, and though fairly tannic, can be almost creamy, especially when compared to Lambrusco di Sorbara wines. When well made, I think it delivers the most balanced lambrusco wines. I absolutely love its fruity exuberance and fleshy charms, as well as its dark purple-ruby hue. The soils it grows in have variable proportions of clay, sand, and silt, so the quality of the wine depends mostly on the yields and individual producer skill. DOC wines include Reggiano Lambrusco Salamino and Lambrusco Salamino di Santa Croce, but Lambrusco Salamino can also be included in the DOC blends of Lambrusco di Sorbara, Lambrusco Mantovano, and the Colli di Scandiano e Canossa. IGT wines in which it can be present are Alto Mincio, Emilia (or dell'Emilia), Rubicone, and Sabbioneta, among others.

WINES TO TRY: Cavicchioli*** (Tre Medaglie Semi Secco), Luciano Saetti*** (Vigneto Saetti), Medici Ermete*** (Concerto Granconcerto), and Pezzuoli*. Saetti makes a monovarietal, 100 percent Lambrusco Salamino di Santa Croce wine from forty-year-old vines with a paltry (by lambrusco standards) output of forty-one hectoliters per hectare. Medici Ermete's Granconcerto is a rare Lambrusco Salamino wine made by secondary refermentation in the bottle, in the manner of Champagne. Only three thousand bottles are made of what is a particularly elegant and refined version of this wine.

Lambrusco Viadanese

WHERE IT'S FOUND: Emilia-Romagna. NATIONAL REGISTRY CODE NUMBER: 121. COLOR: red.

The Viadanese name derives from the town of Viadana in the province of Mantova where this grape grows; some also call it Lambrusco Mantovano (though that name is best reserved for the wine) as it has historically been grown around that countryside as well. It owes its good fortunes to viticulturalist Ugo Ruperti, who greatly liked the wine made with it and encouraged locals to plant the variety as much as possible. Phenotypically, it looks a little like Lambrusco Salamino, though its cluster is even more compact, so much so that the berries are squeezed flat in parts of the bunch. For this reason, it is erroneously called Groppello Ruperti, but it is not a member of the *Groppello* family. Clones include VCR 15 (available since 2004, it adds the most perfume) and VCR 12 and VCR 13 (available since 2006, it adds the most structure), as well as the Ampelos series, CNT 3, CNT 14, and CNT 18, all of which have been available since 2009. The CNT 14 is the most promising, with both floral and fruity aromas and flavors; it also reaches higher potential alcohol levels most years.

Which Wines to Choose and Why

The wine can be made in two different subzones, Viadanese-Sabbiotano and Oltrepò Mantovano, and can be quite flavorful, with aromas and flavors of red cherry and sweet spices. Finding monovarietal Lambrusco Mantovano wines is hard, since the DOC legislation states the wine can include up to 85 percent of four different *Lambrusco* varieties (Salamino, Maestri, Marani, and Viadanese). Besides Lambrusco Mantovano, this variety can also be part of the DOC Reggiano Lambrusco. IGT blends include Emilia (or dell'Emilia), Forlì, Quistello, Ravenna, Rubicone, and Sabbioneta, and others.

WINES TO TRY: The following are essentially Lambrusco Mantovano wines that use a large quantity of Lambrusco Viadanese: Alberto and Giacomo Scaroni*** (Lambrusco Viadanese; an excellent wine that is almost entirely Lambrusco Viadanese, with only 7 percent Ancellotta added) and Pagliari Verdieri*** (Lambrusco Mantovano Viadanese Sabbioneta).

Other *Lambrusco* Varieties Worth Knowing (and Some Not)

A rare but high-quality Lambrusco variety is Lambrusco Barghi (National Registry code number 404), often called simply "Bardi" by locals, perhaps in honor of an ancient noble family that cultivated it. Until recently, it was thought to be synonymous with Lambrusco di Rivalta or Lambrusco Corbelli, and though you'll still read that in books and websites, it is not. In fact, these latter two varieties are distinct as well. It's easy to confuse the three since they look alike and share not just the same production zone but even the same vineyards—co-planting of the varieties was commonplace in the Canali di Reggio Emilia, Albinea, and Rivalta areas. Lambrusco Barghi is characterized by leaves that have reddish veins (Lambrusco di Rivalta does not), medium-large pyramidal bunches ranging from medium- to loosely-packed, and round berries. I find Lambrusco Barghi often has an almost overfull look compared to other *Lambrusco*s. Though it is rustic and adaptable (it used to grow all over the region), locals tell me that most people couldn't be bothered with this *Lambrusco* because its thick skin and juice-deficient berries meant less wine, always a no-no in the minds of quantity-oriented farmers—this despite the fact that it was a very botrytis-resistant grape. The monovarietal Lambrusco Barghi wines I have managed to taste were homemade for mainly personal consumption and were deeply colored, with a definite, aromatic, muscat-like quality on the nose, intense tannins, and saline flavors of black cherry, raspberry, licorice, and hints of roast coffee, with medium levels of acidity on the palate. Meglioraldi, Masini, Storchi, and Vingione (2008) found similar aromas in their research studies. Today the variety is mainly used in the DOC Reggiano Lambrusco and Colli di Scandiano blends and IGT wines such as Emilia and Ravenna; the only "official" monovarietal example I know of was made recently by the Cinque Campi estate (a five-hundred-bottle trial of a very interesting wine that I hope will continue to be made).

Recent genetic testing has shown that Lambrusco di Corbelli (not officially listed in the National Registry) is identical to neither Lambrusco Barghi nor Lambrusco di Rivalta (Pizzi was the first, in 1891, to consider it a synonym for the latter). This variety's name derives from that of the noble Corbelli family, and since, in the 1960s, it was cultivated mainly on their estates of Rivalta and Castelnovo di Sotto, this explains its mistaken identity as Lambrusco di Rivalta. Unlike Lambrusco Barghi, Lambrusco Corbelli's grape bunch is most often conical and loosely-packed, and unlike that variety, there is no reddish tinge to the leaf whatsoever; it also ripens early, around mid-September, while Lambrusco Barghi usually ripens at the end of September.

Another *Lambrusco* beauty is the little-known Lambrusco di Fiorano, so called because it grows abundantly around Fiorano near Modena. It's another rare *Lambrusco* that can be found growing on hillside vineyards. The cluster is medium-sized and the berries are quite large; it's susceptible to most vine pests. The wine is harmonic, complex, and altogether satisfying. It is most often used in blends with other *Lambrusco*s.

Lambrusco Montericco (National Registry code number 119), grown in the area around

Montericco near Reggio Emilia, is characterized by distinctive, very long, medium-large, pyramidal, loosely-packed clusters and elliptical blue-purple berries. Though susceptible to most grapevine diseases, it guarantees good, regular yields, and the wine is actually very interesting, balanced and fruity, with low alcohol and rather high acidity levels. It is used in DOC wines such as Colli di Scandiano e Canossa, Reggiano, and Modena, and IGT wines such as Emilia, Ravenna, and Rubicone. I would like to see more wines made with this variety. Boccacci, Torello Marinoni, Gambino, Botta, and Schneider (2005), who studied parentage relationships via molecular analysis, suggest a parent-offspring relationship between Uva Tosca and Lambrusco Montericco.

A very rare *Lambrusco* is Lambrusco Gonzaga (not listed in the National Registry), which is found only in old vineyards around Reggio Emilia and in the experimental vineyard of the Istituto A. Zanelli in Reggio Emilia. The Lambrusco Gonzaga wines I have tried are simple, light, and not complex, but I haven't tried enough pure Gonzaga wines (microvinifications included) to be sure. Perhaps this nobly named variety (the Gonzaga family was once almost as famous as the Medici of Florence and the Visconti of Milan) may yet have a story to tell.

Also found in the experimental vineyard at the Zanelli Institute is the curiously named Lambrusco Nobel (not listed in the National Registry), which locals tell me is so called because the wine is, wouldn't you know it, "so good it deserves a Nobel prize." My tastings of it (albeit in very artisanally made potions) have led me to question if said locals aren't perhaps imbibing way too much of the stuff, for I had trouble finding many redeeming features in it. I will say that it's a pretty enough grape, with medium to medium-large clusters and medium-small, intensely blue berries.

Lambrusco Benetti (National Registry code number 451) is a brand-new, or more precisely, recently rediscovered *Lambrusco* cultivar typical of the areas between Carpi and Campogalliano near Modena. With respect to other *Lambrusco* varieties, it is just as generous a producer, but its budbreak and flowering occur earlier, and it ripens later. It is of particular interest not just for the quality of its wines, but because of its considerable botrytis resistance, which makes it an ideal choice for estates that practice organic and biodynamic farming methods.

Lambrusco Oliva (National Registry code number 360) appears to be an extremely high-quality variety. It is sometimes also called Lambrusco Mazzone near Reggio Emilia and Olivone near Mantova. It was originally believed to be a biotype of Lambrusco di Sorbara, but was later demonstrated to be a separate variety. It ripens early in September, setting it apart from other *Lambruscos*, which usually ripen in the end of September and most often in early October. It also looks quite different from the other *Lambrusco* varieties: Lambrusco Oliva is characterized by medium-large, pyramidal, stocky bunches and medium-sized, thick-skinned, oval berries that are unlike those of any other *Lambrusco:* their olive-like appearance gives this variety its name. It offers good but irregular yields. Since 2012, one clone has been available, the Ampelos DGV 3. The wines are intensely colored, and have a richer, fruitier flavor than those made with Lambrusco di Sorbara; just as in the latter wines, there is an obvious saline quality accompanying the bright strawberry and raspberry flavors. Artisanally made wines I have tried were also more tannic than I am used to Lambrusco di Sorbara wines being.

Last but not least, Lambrusco Pjcol Ross is no longer classified, in academic circles at least, as a *Lambrusco,* as it's been proven identical to Terrano, a cultivar grown mainly in Friuli, Slovenia, and Croatia. Understandably, local producers (such as the standout estates of Rinaldini and La Piccola) prefer to continue speaking of it in terms of a local biotype that differs greatly from Friuli Venezia Giulia's Terrano.

If after all that you find you still haven't had enough *Lambrusco* information to last you a lifetime, reach for a bottle of Migliolungo, the truly unique red wine made in Emilia-Romagna by the Istituto A. Zanelli in cooperation with the Cantina di Arceto. The institute is a polytechnical teaching facility with a large grapevine collection of old local varieties that I have had the pleasure of visiting many times. Everyone on staff there is unfailingly kind and helpful, and I cannot begin to say just how much I have learned on my visits there. Migliolungo is made from forty different rare native varieties, of which fifteen are *Lambrusco*s.

Lambrusco a Foglia Frastagliata

See ENANTIO, chapter 4.

Lambrusco a Foglia Tonda

See CASETTA, chapter 4.

Lambrusco dei Vivi

See PERLA DEI VIVI, chapter 5.

Lambrusco Pjcol Ross

See TERRANO, chapter 4.

THE MALVASIA GROUP

Malvasia is my favorite group of wine grapes: simply put, I like them all, as well as the wines made from them. Though the *Malvasia*s are often referred to as a family of grapes, that is incorrect, as many Malvasia-Something grapes are genetically distinct. Still, some *Malvasia* members are related to a degree, and thus the *Malvasia*s (some of them, at least) are closer to being a family than the *Greco*s or the *Vernaccia*s. In Italy alone there are eighteen official varieties named *Malvasia* (listed as such in the National Registry) and almost as many wines; the latter are just as complicated as the grapes, since some are red wines, some white (and one pink); some dry, some sweet; some are still and some are bubbly. When buying a bottle of Malvasia wine, knowing what the individual grape variety offers is your best bet for happiness.

All this confusion arises because throughout history, *Malvasia* wines were famous and sought after. Their popularity was largely the result of Venice's domination of the Mediterranean sea and its trading routes—which essentially lasted from the eighth to the fifteenth centuries, so *Malvasia*s benefited from some pretty good promotion. *Malvasia* wines became so important throughout the ages that there are at least sixteen different sites I know of in Venice sporting the *Malvasia* moniker: the next time you take a walk in the world's most beautiful city, you'll find there's more than one street called Calle della Malvasia (for example, one in Sestriere Dorsoduro and one in Sestriere Castello, the latter not far from St. Mark's Square), a bridge called Ponte della Malvasia Vecchia, and a dock dubbed Fondamenta della Malvasia. Venetian wine bars were also called *malvasie*. You couldn't be blamed for thinking the city had a malvasia fetish, but it was, after all, the seafaring Venetians who broadcast the reputation of this variety and its wines. Between 1300 and 1600, malvasia was undoubtedly Europe's most famous wine, a direct descendant of famous wines of antiquity such as *capnios, tharrupia,* and *buconiates.*

Though there are other hypotheses, the prevailing opinion is that the name *Malvasia* derives from Monemvasia or Monemvaxia (it means "port with one entry"), a strategically located seaside town located in the Peloponnesian peninsula. Founded in 588, it was conquered by William de Villehardouin with help from the Venetians in 1248 and was annexed to the Venetian Maritime Republic in 1419. Monemvaxia was an important trading hub for malvasia and other wines of the Greek islands, and these were sold all over Europe—so successfully in fact that demand far outstripped supply, forcing Venetians to plant *Malvasia* vines on Crete, which had been under Venetian rule since 1204, after the Fourth Crusade. Throughout the centuries, Crete was a very important source of *Malvasia* wine production. Pillon (2005) mentions an official document of the Venetian government (dated 1342) in which both a "wine from Monembasia" as well as a "malvasia di Creta" (from the island of Crete) are mentioned, so the rabbit-style proliferation of *Malvasia* wines had already begun by then. Interestingly, Malvasia di Creta wine was apparently dry and was sold only in Italy, while other *Malvasia* wines were sweet (sweet malvasias were a specialty of the city of Retimno), made in the "Greek" fashion, either by concentrating the musts via cooking, by adding resin, or by air-drying the grapes, techniques that allowed the wines to travel well.

Thanks to modern genetic research, we know that most *Malvasias* are not just unrelated, but probably don't originate from Greece either (Crespan, Cabello, Giannetto, Ibanez, Karoglan Kontic, Maletic, Pejic, Rodriguez, and Antonacci 2006a). Given that the name "malvasia" helped propel sales, wines made from a *Malvasia* variety (or, more often, made in a style reminiscent of *Malvasia* wines), became common in all countries of the Mediterranean basin. Therefore, when you vacation in the Canary islands or Cyprus, you are likely to find *Malvasia* wines there just as you do in Italy. Nowadays, malvasias are made not just in Greece and Italy, but also in Cyprus, Slovenia (where it's called Malvezerec), Croatia (Malvasijie), southern France (Malvoisie), Spain (Malvagia or Malvasia), the Canary Islands, Portugal, and Madeira (Malmsey). Ironically, today there are no wine producers in Greece's Monemvasia: the producer of Monemvasia wines is G. Tsimpidis & Co. / Monemvasia Winery, actually situated in Velies, a small town ten kilometers away. Suffice it to say that Molon (1906) devoted sixteen pages to the *Malvasia* family alone in his landmark ampelography text. Unfortunately in most of those regions, you won't *really* be tasting a *Malvasia* wine, since homonyms were and are common. For example, the Malvoisie à Petit Grains of southern France is actually Rolle (called Vermentino in Italy) and Nus Malvoisie, a wine made around the pretty little town of Nus in Italy's landlocked, mountainous Valle d'Aosta, is made not with a *Malvasia*, but with Pinot Grigio.

Unlike their similarly well-nourished *Moscato* brethren, the *Malvasia* varieties are not characterized by a unifying trait such as the distinctive "muscaty" aroma; unlike *Moscatos*, they are not all aromatic. Based on this observation, Di Rovasenda in 1877 attempted a classification of *Malvasia* vines in two large groups, aromatic and nonaromatic, believing, not unreasonably in my view, that only the former should be named *Malvasia*. More recently, the *Malvasias* were classified into four major groups, with almost all the aromatic varieties included in one. Unfortunately, some members of one wine group will express aromas believed to be typical of varieties in other groups. For example, some *Moscato* varieties express aromas also typical of *Malvasias* and vice versa, and so classifying grape varieties as a Malvasia based on their aromatic profile is impossible.

Winemaking too can greatly alter how a *Malvasia* wine tastes. For example, yeasts metabolize linalool with great difficulty, but have an easier time with geraniol, in part transforming it into citronellol. Since Malvasia wines are characterized most often by a prominent geraniol content, it follows that alcoholic fermentation can have bigger consequences on the aromas of *Malvasia* than on *Moscato* wines: world-famous winemaker and university professor Donato Lanati told me that a good winemaker, when working with *Malvasia* grapes, will try to minimize the consumption of geraniol while maximizing production of citronellol, another potent aroma molecule. Therefore, a malvasia that smells strongly of roses (and it should) is in part also the result of the winemaker consciously avoiding the loss of that defining varietal aroma. The presence of these aromatic molecules explains why many *Malvasia* wines are both sweet and fizzy. Sugars diminish the solubility of aromas in liquids (wine, in this case) consequently increasing their concentration in the volatile (or gaseous) fraction, making the wine more aromatically intense and fragrant. Carbon dioxide also helps transport aroma molecules into the volatile fraction and this further intensifies the aromas of wine. Therefore a sugary and fizzy wine will be pushing the aromatic envelope to the fullest, and placing its variety's main selling point front and center.

Happily, advances in molecular biology allow us to tackle the classification of *Malvasia* varieties somewhat more accurately than in the past, and independently of aromatic profiles. Numerous university studies have recently broached the origin and parentage of *Malvasia* varieties, sometimes with truly surprising results. First, microsatellite studies performed by Crespan, Cabello, Giannetto, Ibanez, Karoglan Kontic, Maletic, Pejic, Rodriguez, and Antonacci (2006a) have demonstrated there is very little genetic affinity between the *Malvasia* vines of Italy and grapes of Greece, including Greek *Malvasias*. Crespan's group compared the information available from the Greek *Vitis* database (http://www.biology.uoc.gr/gvd) and from Lefort and Roubelakis-Angelakis (2000), which gave molecular profiles for four *Malvasia* cultivars they called Malvasia del Chianti, Malvazia di Candia, Malvazia Aromatica, and Malvazia Istriana. None of these was consistent with the genotype described by Crespan's group. A more general search in the Greek database by Crespan, Crespan, Giannetto, Meneghetto, and Costacurta (2007) also failed to show any similarities between their data compared to that published by Lefort and Roubelakis-Angelakis (2002) relative to Greek cultivars.

Therefore, the commonly held belief that many Italian varieties were brought over from Greece by seafaring traders and merchants does not appear to be correct! In fact, the *Malvasia* wines of Greece were made with varieties such as Athiri, Kydonitsa, Liatiko, Thrapsathiri, and Vilana, which to the best of my knowledge have never been grown (or only minimally so) in Italy. Of all the various Malvasia-Something grapes, most are completely unrelated, but those that are related to a degree include Malvasia Bianca Lunga, Malvasia Istriana (Malvazija Istarska), and Malvasia di Lipari (these three Malvasia varieties have been shown to have close genetic ties to each other by Lacombe, Boursiquot, Laoucou, Dechesne, Varès, and This in 2007), as well as Malvasia Nera di Brindisi, a red-berried *Malvasia* shown to be the result of a natural crossing between Malvasia Bianca Lunga and Negro Amaro (Crespan, Colleta, Crupi, Giannetto, and Antonacci 2008). At our current state of knowledge, these four make up something close to a Malvasia "family." However, there are simply too many different grapes named *Malvasia* to consider them all a family, extended or otherwise.

THE WHITE-BERRIED MALVASIAS

Malvasia Bianca

WHERE IT'S FOUND: Puglia, Campania, Calabria, Sicily. NATIONAL REGISTRY CODE NUMBER: 129. COLOR: white.

This is another confusing grape, as little is known about it. It's the typical white *Malvasia* associated with the wines of Puglia (the region is also home to two red *Malvasia* varieties), where historically a Malvasia Bianca di Trani was known to grow. Other experts have postulated that the Malvasia Bianca of Puglia is the same as Malvasia Moscata of Piedmont; the latter grape had virtually disappeared at the end of the nineteenth century due to its extreme sensitivity to oidium. The hypothesis was that Malvasia Moscata was packed away suitcase-style and transported to Puglia by people moving there. There is no documentation or research data to support his view, and I point out that in Italy almost all immigration flows were usually the other way around, from poorer south to richer north. Interestingly, the official description in the National Registry of Malvasia Bianca is from a Piedmontese source, but the variety is not officially listed for use in any Piedmontese DOC or IGT wines, and only appears in Puglian appellations. And yet, the ampelographic description of Malvasia Bianca in the National Registry is very similar, almost identical in fact, to that of Malvasia Moscata. However, while both the Malvasia Moscata typical of Piedmont and Puglia's Malvasia Bianca are deliciously musky and aromatic grapes that are wonderful to eat, the wines made in Puglia are not very aromatic (perhaps because of the warm climate, poor viticultural training systems, and excessively high yields). The main redeeming feature of Malvasia Bianca in the eyes of quantity-minded Puglian wine producers is that it produces large volumes of easy drinking, simple wines. Some experts believe that the *Malvasia* variety grown in Puglia is actually not that different from Malvasia Bianca di Candia or even Malvasia Bianca Lunga—but there is no genetic evidence to support this view. Just to add a little more confusion to this situation of general uncertainty, many Puglian producers have also chosen to plant Friuli Venezia Giulia's Malvasia Istriana, but of course just call the wine "malvasia."

Malvasia Bianca's grape bunch is fairly compact, medium-sized, and pyramidal-conical in shape, with medium to large, usually round, yellow-green berries that have very thick skins. The latter feature explains the variety's resistance to botrytis bunch rot: in this it has a huge advantage over Moscato Bianco (which is however more resistant to oidium), another aromatic grape grown both in Piedmont and Puglia that is much more botrytis sensitive. There is one clone of Malvasia Bianca, MC-1, available since 1990.

Which Wines to Choose and Why

Over the last fifteen years, quality-conscious Puglian producers have lowered yields, and the resulting wines appear to hold some promise. The best wines are those of the DOC Leverano (where 100 percent pure bottlings of Malvasia Bianca can be found), but there are IGT wines that can also be, should the producer so choose, 100 percent Malvasia Bianca. The variety is also included in DOC blends of Calabria, Campania, and Sicily, though it is almost never the main player. As many southern Italian producers have planted Friuli's Malvasia Istriana in their vineyards, some (many?) *Malvasia* wines from Italy's south might be made with that non-local variety, so these wines may not be reflective of the merits of Malvasia Bianca at all. I also believe that some of the white *Malvasia* wines in Puglia may be made with Malvasia Bianca Lunga, a completely different grape from Malvasia Bianca.

WINES TO TRY: Lomazzi & Sarli* (Imperium) and Conti Zecca* (Leverano Bianco Vigna del Saraceno and Terra). These both have a creamy texture and ripe tropical fruit flavors that are not usually associated with this variety, so I'm not sure what to think. Furthermore, both are only barely aromatic. That said, these wines are pretty good. Most likely, the encouraging results are due to lower yields and greater protection of the grape aromas and flavors during winemaking.

Malvasia Bianca di Basilicata

WHERE IT'S FOUND: Basilicata. NATIONAL REGISTRY CODE NUMBER: 130. COLOR: white.

In my personal gallery of native variety woes is the relative oblivion this very high-quality variety has fallen into over the last fifty years. Veronelli (1971) loved it (he often called it Malvasia del Vulture), and suggested pairing it with provolone cheese and even with octopus in chili-spiced tomato sauce.

Malvasia Bianca di Basilicata was once a very important cultivar in the Vulture area of the region, and it is therefore an error to consider Basilicata as a producer of only red wine. Historically, white *Malvasia* wines were made with grapes grown in many vineyards located above 500 meters of elevation, especially those on the mountain slopes past the Potenza-Foggia railway tracks. Over the years, during my walks on the rugged terrain of the Vulture volcano, it was obvious to me that the white *Malvasia* growing there was unlike any other I had seen. Not only did it look different (with its very long, scrawny bunch and smaller than average berries, it looks a little like Malvasia di Lipari), but the wine made by local farmers from it was different as well, spicily aromatic and complex.

In the past some experts believed it to be a biotype, or at least quite similar to Malvasia Bianca Lunga and Malvasia Bianca di Candia, but these three cultivars are distinct. Locals told me that in the past Malvasia Bianca di Basilicata was also blended into Aglianico wines to add freshness, while today it is most often blended with Moscato Bianco to make either dry or sweet wines. Apparently, it is hardy and resistant, though sensitive to potassium and magnesium deficiencies, as well as oidium.

Which Wines to Choose and Why

In 2000, there was only one major wine made mostly with Malvasia Bianca di Basilicata sold commercially, Topazio by Consorzio Viticultori Associati Vulture, simply labeled as a Basilicata Bianco. If memory serves me correctly, I remember tasting a few other wines that were said to be mainly or wholly made with this variety by other producers, but none reminded me of what a wine made mainly with the variety should have tasted like—for one, they ought to have been aromatic wines, and weren't. So just as I had done previously with Lazio producers, I began talking with those in the Vulture willing to listen, pointing out that it might be worthwhile to bring back their local variety, which historically had been found to have excellent winemaking potential. The problem was that Malvasia Bianca di Basilicata had been reduced to only a few scattered vines mixed in with other vines in often abandoned sites. Mercifully, the people at the Cantina Sociale di Venosa, a forward-thinking social cooperative led by winemaker Luigi Cantatore, were interested in the idea, and initiated a Malvasia Bianca di Basilicata recovery program. With over five hundred members scouring their vineyards, it was likely they'd succeed in producing a Malvasia Bianca di Basilicata wine again, and so D'Avalos was born with the 2005 vintage (its full name is D'Avalos di Gesualdo, but everyone uses the shorter name), a new, reportedly monovarietal Malvasia Bianca di Basilicata wine made in commercially significant numbers, so that people everywhere might try it.

That Basilicata is viewed by everyone as mainly red wine country is exemplified by the fact that if you want to taste wines made with Malvasia Bianca di Basilicata, you'll have to scavenge around the IGTs or Vino da Tavolas. Following on the heels of the Cantina di Venosa, Eleano, a small family-run winery, is now also making a Malvasia Bianca di Basilicata wine from extremely old vines. The wine tastes of slightly herbal aromas and flavors, with hints of dried apricot and peach, and does have a properly spicy, aromatic nose. The flinty finish will remind you of its volcanic origins. This is a big wine, usually sporting 14 percent alcohol, and can easily stand up to white meat dishes. Cantina di Venosa's version is not as delicately aromatic as I think the wine ought to be, and what's more, it's oak-aged—though I understand that since Cantina di Venosa already has one aromatic wine in portfolio, the extremely successful Dry Muscat, another might have been too much. The Cantina del Vulture (the former Cantina Viticultori Associati del Vulture) makes a very similar wine called Novalba. At the very least, these two add to the mix of wines made with a grape variety that had been forgotten. I would still like to see more of an aromatic quality to both these wines, if only a delicate one. Perhaps it's just a matter of yields. I have been made to taste other Malvasia Bianca di Basilicata wines over the years, but as they didn't taste anything like I thought they should, perhaps mistakenly, I have never pursued them further. Last but not least, Cantine del Notaio, the world-class Aglianico producer, makes a great sweet wine called l'Autentica, which is 30 percent Malvasia Bianca di Basilicata, but the strong percentage of Moscato Bianco causes the latter variety to dominate the wine's aroma and flavor profile.

WINES TO TRY: Eleano**, Cantina di Venosa* (D'Avalos di Gesualdo Malvasia), Cantina del Vulture* (Novalba), and Cantina del Notaio (l'Autentica, the best wine of the bunch, but only 30 percent Malvasia Bianca di Basilicata).

Malvasia Bianca di Candia

WHERE IT'S FOUND: Lazio, Campania, Emilia-Romagna, Marche, Puglia, Tuscany, Umbria.
NATIONAL REGISTRY CODE NUMBER: 131. COLOR: white.

Apparently the Venetians, looking for ways to increase the production volumes of a wine that sold extremely well, planted their generic *Malvasia* vines on the island of Crete (and many other islands as well: a document attests that *Malvasia* was planted near the town of Caiesa as early as 1363). Candia is the ancient Latin name for Crete, hence this variety's name. According to Lacombe, Boursiquot, Laoucou, Dechesne, Varès, and This (2007), Malvasia Bianca di Candia is a genetically distinct grape variety, unrelated to the similarly named Malvasia di Candia Aromatica (the latter is not simply the result of an aromatic mutation). Instead, Malvasia Bianca di Candia is closely related to the red-berried Malvasia di Casorzo. In a landmark work by Crespan, Crespan, Giannetto, Meneghetto, and Costacurta (2007), Malvasia Bianca di Candia has been shown to be a progeny of Garganega, the famous grape with which Soave is made. Though its other parent remains unknown, this finding also tells us that the variety is either a grandparent or half-sibling of Garganega's many progenies: Albana, Cataratto Bianco, Dorona, Marzemina Bianca, Montonico Bianco, Mostosa, Susumaniello, and Trebbiano Toscano.

At times, Malvasia Bianca di Candia is called Malvasia Rossa, not because of the color of its berries or wine, but because its apical buds (not its shoots, as has been erroneously written elsewhere) are intensely red. Of course, this wouldn't be Italy if wine producers and farmers of Lazio hadn't told me over the years that Malvasia Rossa is actually an altogether different variety (apparently reduced to only a few old vines in mainly abandoned vineyards). Were that true, using "Malvasia Rossa" as a synonym for Malvasia Bianca di Candia would be a mistake, but there's no genetic proof to back up such a statement. To me, some of the vines those enthusiastic locals believed were authentic Malvasia Rossa looked very similar to the Candia variety, and others very different, so I'm not sure what to think. Since I have been unable to find someone who makes a supposedly 100 percent Malvasia Rossa wine, I also can't say if it tastes different, better or worse, from a monovarietal Malvasia Bianca di Candia wine. Then again, it wouldn't take much for it to be better, so it might not be a bad thing if a distinct Malvasia Rossa existed after all. Though it's possible that there are rickety old vines of a true Malvasia Rossa surviving in the hodge-podge of promiscuous plantings that are many vineyards of the Castelli Romani, I am not sure they exist.

Ampelographically, the variety's appearance depends on which clone you look at, but in general Malvasia Bianca di Candia has a conical grape bunch, and both the bunch and the berries are large. The berries also have thin skins, unlike those of Malvasia di Candia Aromatica, which have thick skins. In an interesting recent study, four biotypes named AA, A, B, and AB were described thanks to ampelographic and ampelometric analysis (Meneghetti, Poljuha, Frare, Costacurta, Morreale, Bavaresco, and Calò 2012). All biotypes differed on the basis of berry and bunch sizes. AFLP, M-AFLP, and SAMPL molecular marker studies were performed to analyze intravarietal genetic variability. Interestingly, cluster analyses showed a correlation between molecular profile and morphological traits of bunches. For example, biotype B (smaller fruit size) was clearly differentiated from the remaining biotypes not just on ampelographic grounds but on a molecular basis as well.

Malvasia Bianca di Candia is most abundant in Lazio, though it is also found in Emilia-Romagna, Umbria, Tuscany, Marche, and Campania. At roughly 8,637 hectares it is in fact the most abundantly planted *Malvasia* in Italy, and is weathering the push for quality well, since plantings were reportedly down only 1.7 percent between 2000 and 2010. Actually, I would have thought that producers would have done away with more of it. Not so, apparently: perhaps this is because it's a dependable and generous yielder, susceptible only to humid conditions (rainy springs and excessively wet soils) especially when grafted on vigorous rootstocks; in similar conditions, berry shatter is common, and hence decreased production. Between 1969 and 2009, seven clones of Malvasia Bianca di Candia became available: R2, UBA 26/E, UBA 26/F, UNIMI-VITIS-MALB VV200, UNIMI-VITIS-MALB VV220, Ampelos TEA 20, and Ampelos TEA 22. The latter two produce slightly less and are considered high-quality clones; the two clones produced by the University of Milan (UNIMI) are complementary, in that clone 200 produces wines with a strong herbal aroma, while clone 220 gives wines that have a more tropical fruit flair (a very relative flair, in my opinion). In fact, the two are probably best used together, in order to obtain the most interesting wine possible.

Which Wines to Choose and Why

Wines that contain small or large percentages of Malvasia Bianca di Candia are produced mainly in Lazio, but also in Abruzzo, Molise, Tuscany, Umbria, Puglia, and Emilia-Romagna. However, though Malvasia Bianca di Candia is used in many blends (such as the DOCG wines Frascati and Frascati Cannellino; DOC wines as diverse as Castelli Romani, Colli Lanuvini, Colli Martani, Oltrepò Pavese, Sannio; IGT wines such as Colline Teatine, Colli Aprutini, Molise, and others, most not worth seeking out), monovarietal bottlings are extremely rare anywhere. A few producers have tried their hand at making a monovarietal wine from this variety over the years, but not many. These attempts are all characterized by weak aromas and flavors that can be described as reminiscent of white flowers and fresh citrus, with hints of green or yellow apple and herbs. The wines are very light bodied, almost thin, and notably acidic. They are best drunk within one year of the vintage.

WINES TO TRY: An example of monovarietal wine is from Banino* (Aureum) in Lombardy, which is oily, sweet, and a little acid-deficient. An outstanding Malvasia Bianca di Candia wine used to be made by the estate Fiorano***, owned by the Prince Ludovisi Boncompagni; though the wine is no longer made, old vintages are available here and there, and it would be worth your while to try one. Massa Vecchia in Tuscany produced a very interesting white wine that was totally Malvasia Bianca di Candia in 2005, and that can still be found in wine shops in Italy.

Malvasia Bianca Lunga

WHERE IT'S FOUND: Tuscany, Umbria, Lazio, Marche. NATIONAL REGISTRY CODE NUMBER: 132. COLOR: white.

As this variety has always called Tuscany its main home, it is not surprisingly also known as Malvasia del Chianti or Malvasia Bianca Lunga Toscana. Other infrequently used synonyms are Malvasia di Brolo, Malvasia di Arezzo, or Malvasia di San Nicandro. In 1877, Di Rovasenda cited rarer synonyms such as Sgranarella in the Marche and Silosder de Zara, which he believed were identical to Malvasia Bianca di Brolio. Studies show it to be synonymous with Prosecco Nostrano di Conegliano, also called Malvasia Trevigiana, which is grown in the Tre Venezie area of Italy, comprising Friuli Venezia Giulia, Veneto, and Trentino (Calò, Costacurta, Cancellier, Crespan, Milani, Carraro, et al. 2000).

In a landmark *Malvasia* study by Lacombe, Boursiquot, Laoucou, Dechesne, Varès, and This (2007), Malvasia Bianca Lunga was shown to be closely related to Malvasia Istriana (Malvazija Istarska) and Malvasia di Lipari. In 2007 and 2008, Crespan and his colleagues proved that Malvasia Bianca Lunga has at least two well-known offspring: Vitovska (a child of Malvasia Bianca Lunga and Glera Tondo) and Malvasia Nera di Brindisi (the result of a natural crossing between Malvasia Bianca Lunga and Negro Amaro). The variety is also one of the parents (the other is Garganega) of one of Italy's more successful laboratory crossings, Incrocio Bianco Fedit 51.

Ampelographically, the variety is very easy to recognize in vineyards, since it is characterized by large and long (twenty to twenty-five centimeters), compact, conical-cylindrical bunches (usually with two wings) and medium-small, round berries that though blessed with thick skins, are less thick and resistant than those of Trebbiano Toscano. Clearly, the morphology changes somewhat depending on the clones and biotypes observed: there are currently seven clones (R2, Cenaia 2, MBD F7-A2–11, FEDIT 26-CH, FEDIT 27-CH, VCR 10, and UBA-RA MV9) available to producers. Of these, the UBA-RA MV9 clone is the only non-Tuscan one: it was developed in Abruzzo and appears to have very high quality, but is very sensitive to botrytis. The FEDIT 26-CH clone is the best for *vin santo* production, since it has slightly less compact bunches than other clones and good botrytis resistance. In general, Malvasia Bianca Lunga is very susceptible to peronospora, and is none too resistant to other vine diseases either. It grows all over Tuscany, but is found in many other regions as well: Veneto, Marche, Lazio, Puglia, and especially in Umbria. Interestingly, five hundred hectares are planted to it in Croatia (where it's called Maraština) and it also grows in Greece (where it's called Pavlos).

Which Wines to Choose and Why

Malvasia Bianca Lunga is probably most famous because it was an important part of the Chianti blend as invented by Bettino Ricasoli, who felt that the best possible Chianti recipe was seven parts Sangiovese, two parts Canaiolo Nero, and one part Malvasia Bianca Lunga. It is rarely used nowadays to make Chianti (most of which is no longer made with any white grapes, save for the simplest, entry-level versions; Chianti Classico eliminated it altogether from the blend as of 2006), or even monovarietal dry whites. But Malvasia Bianca Lunga really produces something special in *vin santo,* on its own or more often with Trebbiano Toscano. Franco Bernabei, one of Italy's most famous winemakers, defines the variety as "delicately aromatic and gentle, slightly saline," and says that "its low acidity is why we blend it with Trebbiano Toscano." DOC wines in which it is prevalent (but practically never on its own) include Bianco della Valdinievole, Colli dell'Etruria Centrale, and Bianco dell'Empolese.

WINES TO TRY: Pietro Beconcini** (Antiche Vie) and I Selvatici** (Malvagia). *Vin santo* is even better: monovarietal ones are rare, as most producers like to add a little Trebbiano Toscano for added acidity, but try the *Malvasia* examples by Rocca di Montegrossi*** (they add a bit of Canaiolo Nero) and Castello di Cacchiano** (though they also add a bit of Canaiolo Nero from time to time).

Malvasia del Lazio

WHERE IT'S FOUND: Lazio. NATIONAL REGISTRY CODE NUMBER: 133. COLOR: white.

There are many reasons why the wines of Lazio have a poor reputation today: the most important is that quantity, rather than quality, was the goal for most of the twentieth century. Producers and some very short-sighted legislators insisted on using Malvasia Bianca di Candia (and to make matters worse, Trebbiano Toscano, a variety of *Trebbiano* not typical of Lazio) to make once-famous Frascati and Castelli Romani wines, instead of the higher-quality but lower yielding and less resistant Malvasia del Lazio (also called Malvasia Puntinata because its ripe berries are covered with rusty spots; *puntinata* means speckled in Italian). And so Malvasia del Lazio was gradually reduced to playing a marginal role to the not-so dynamic duo of Malvasia Bianca di Candia and Trebbiano Toscano. Until recently it was legally required that Frascati, Marino, and other wines of the Castelli Romani (the heartland of Malvasia del Lazio) had to be made with a minimum 70 percent of Trebbiano Toscano and Malvasia Bianca di Candia, possibly two of the worst grapes with which to try and make quality dry wine anywhere. The same nonsensical legislation limited the amount of Bellone and Bombino Bianco, two other quality varieties, to no more than 10 percent of the blend. Fortunately, legislators and producers have seen the error of their ways and the legal guidelines for making Frascati and Frascati Cannellino (the light-bodied, delicately sweet version of Frascati) were changed in 2011. Both these wines can now be made with a 70 percent minimum of Malvasia del Lazio and/or Malvasia Bianca di Candia and up to 30 percent Trebbiano Toscano, Trebbiano Giallo, Bombino Bianco, Bellone, and other varieties (of which up to 15 percent can be other varieties still, such as the international grapes). Though I think way too much Chardonnay and Sauvignon Blanc still find their way into Frascati wines, the current guidelines are a big improvement on the joke they once were.

So the wind has changed, and Malvasia del Lazio is now attracting considerable attention. In some cases too much, as for a while, in the middle of the first decade of the twenty-first century, when the grape got hot, it appeared that estates all over Lazio were making Malvasia del Lazio wines almost overnight. These considerations aside, I have always believed Malvasia del Lazio to be one of Italy's greatest white grape varieties. Back in 2001, I insisted to a few quality-minded Lazio producers (Pallavicini, Casale Pilozzo, Conte Zandotti) that it was a huge mistake to label their wines, which were much better than the regional average, simply as "malvasia": since both Malvasia Bianca di Candia and Malvasia del Lazio grow in the region, generically writing "malvasia" on the label wasn't telling consumers much. Furthermore, as Malvasia Bianca di Candia is also a Lazio inhabitant, writing "Malvasia del Lazio" on the label was not necessarily a solution either, since the potential for misunderstanding was great. And so a number of wines were either renamed "malvasia puntinata" (Pallavicini), or at least the latter name began appearing regularly on back labels, where an attempt was made to explain the uniqueness of the wine. Caveat emptor, though: not all the wines now sporting Malvasia del Lazio on the label remind me of the variety at all. In other words, if you want to taste the real thing, you need to know a little something about the producer.

The variety is a pretty grape to look at, with medium-large, pyramidal, stocky bunches with medium-small, round berries flattened at the extremities and covered with the brown dots that give the variety its name. When fully ripe, the grapes really do look like they have been hit by measles. Malvasia del Lazio can easily become overripe and drop its total acidity levels, so care must be taken to time the harvest right. It is also characterized by medium-low vigor and is prone to both oidium and botrytis bunch rot. Its low productivity was such that when I visited the enological school at Velletri back in 2001 or 2002, they where happy to show me their experimentations with training systems and pruning methods aimed at demonstrating that even Malvasia del Lazio, always thought to be a miserly producer, could have outputs of 180 hectoliters per hectare. And they were happy about this! Currently, there are no official clones available.

In Lacombe, Boursiquot, Laoucou, Dechesne, Varès, and This (2007), Malvasia Puntinata is shown to be the result of a natural crossing between Moscato d'Alessandria and Schiava Grossa, who are also the parents of Moscato d'Amburgo (a table grape, in Italy). This means Malvasia del Lazio and Moscato d'Amburgo are siblings, and it explains the lightly aromatic character of the Lazian *Malvasia*. Some producers insist the variety is not aromatic, but lack of aromatic character is most likely a function of their yields: when overcropped, this variety loses its delicately aromatic quality. Most of the best vineyards are located close to Rome, including Colle Mattia, the hills of Monteporzio Catone, and the slope along the via Anagnina at Grottaferrata. At close to three thousand hectares, Malvasia del Lazio is more abundant than was once believed.

Which Wines to Choose and Why
Wines made with Malvasia del Lazio include DOCG Frascati and Frascati Cannellino; DOC wines such as Castelli Romani, Colli Albani,

Marino, Colli Lanuvini, and others; as well as IGT Colline Frentane, Colline Pescaresi, Umbria, and Terre Aquilane, among others. Monovarietal wines are rare, but when you find a good one, it becomes apparent that Malvasia del Lazio is a potentially great cultivar. It yields bright, dry white wines that recall sage and ripe yellow fruit, and have a tell-tale, creamy, almost resiny fleshiness that wines made with Malvasia Bianca di Candia never have. Even better, it takes remarkably well to noble rot: indeed, there have been nobly rotten late harvest or air-dried Malvasia del Lazio wines that rank with some of Italy's greatest wines ever. Thick and creamy, with plenty of refreshing acidity, redolent with ripe peach, mango, banana, and passionfruit aromas and flavors, those were memorable wines: unfortunately the state of Lazio winemaking is such that wines such as these are few and far between. The problem here is the producers, not the grape. As for specific wines, either look for IGT efforts from reputable producers or DOC wines in which you know the producer uses a great deal of Malvasia del Lazio; when you taste a Frascati that is almost too good to be true, in particular fleshy and creamy-rich, and complex, you can be reasonably sure it's made with 80–90 percent Malvasia del Lazio. That such a blend is completely illegal is another matter—this is Italy after all.

WINES TO TRY: Pallavicini*** (especially the very sweet, complex Stillato; the dry Malvasia La Giara is refreshingly simple and crisp), Conte Zandotti*** (Rumon, but also an excellent Frascati containing a high proportion of Malvasia del Lazio), Le Quinte** (Virtù Romane, Orchidea), and Casale Pilozzo* (Villa Ari). I'm not so sure about other bottlings. Note that Le Quinte's Virtù Romane and Orchidea are blends of local Roman grapes, so they are an exception to my stringent monovarietals-only rule for this book, but are so good and inexpensive they deserve to be mentioned; Virtù Romane especially is one of Italy's best-value wines.

Malvasia di Candia Aromatica

WHERE IT'S FOUND: Emilia-Romagna, Lombardy, Lazio. NATIONAL REGISTRY CODE NUMBER: 279. COLOR: white.

An aromatic variety sometimes also called Malvasia Bianca di Candia Aromatica, this variety used to be, not surprisingly, also called Malvasia di Alessandria and/or Malvasia a Sapore di Moscato ("Malvasia that tastes like a Moscato"). It is completely distinct from the similarly named Malvasia Bianca di Candia, a nonaromatic variety. The many cuttings the Venetians picked up at the port of Monemvasia and then propagated elsewhere were not always necessarily of the same variety and some vines planted on Crete were later found to give aromatic wine. Hence the age-old distinction between an "aromatic" Malvasia di Candia and a regular, nonaromatic Malvasia di Candia. Ampelographically, the two look different: Malvasia di Candia Aromatica has a long, pyramidal, loosely-packed grape bunch, and both the bunch and the berries are medium-small. Its berries also have thick skins, while those of Malvasia Bianca di Candia have thin skins. There are four clones that became available between 1988 and 2002: PC MACA 62, PC MACA 66, PC MACA 68, and VCR 27. The first two produce wines characterized by higher total acidity levels and are often the choice for sparkling wine production; the VCR 27 is more useful for still aromatic white wines. Unlike the other three clones, VCR 27 does not suffer from dissection of the spine, and accumulates sugar easier. Malvasia di Candia Aromatica is typical of the Emilia portion of Emilia-Romagna, but is also grown in Lombardy and Lazio, for a total of close to two thousand hectares planted.

Which Wines to Choose and Why

DOC wines worth hunting out are the Colli Piacentini, Colli di Parma, and Colli di Scandiano e Canossa of Emilia-Romagna, where Malvasia di Candia Aromatica can be used to make 100 percent pure varietal wines. It is also used in Oltrepò Pavese blends from Lombardy and various IGT blends such as Rubicone and Terre degli Osci. Unlike Malvasia Bianca di Candia, this aromatic *Malvasia* is a high-quality grape: the wines are never as intense as a moscato bianco or gewürztraminer, but have lovely spicy and tropical fruit aromas, though dry versions are never particularly fleshy. Conversely, they are fresher and livelier than many wines made with aromatic grapes. However, in my experience, these wines often lack sufficient palate complexity for the variety to be considered truly noble. Probably best are the honeyed, sweet wines.

WINES TO TRY: Barattieri di San Pietro*** (Vin Santo Albarola Val di Nure, one of Italy's top five or six sweet wines), La Stoppa*** (Passito Vigna del Volta, a truly great dessert wine, though it can contain up to 20 percent Moscato Bianco), Luretta*** (Boccadirosa), and Vigneto delle Terre Rosse** (Malvasia di Candia Adriana Vallania). Pizzarotti* makes a sweet sparkling monovarietal version. Monte delle Vigne** (Callas) makes an excellent monovarietal dry version. For comparison's sake, readers may want to try the dry wine (Femina) and sweet wine (Malvazia Sweet, though the label reads Malvasia di Candia Aromatica) made with this variety by Nikos Doloufakis at his Doloufakis winery in Dafnes, Crete. The Femina is cask-aged (which rarely happens in Italy) and has delicate herbal aromas and flavors, while the Malvazia is redolent with orange and floral scents and flavors; of the two, the sweet is most similar to the Italian versions.

Malvasia di Lipari

WHERE IT'S FOUND: Sicily. NATIONAL REGISTRY CODE NUMBER: 135 (also listed at 98 as Greco Bianco and at 136 as Malvasia di Sardegna). COLOR: white.

Wine from the Malvasia di Lipari variety appears to have been produced since at least the first century B.C.E.; it was well described by Cupani already in 1696 (he called it *malvagia*). The modern notoriety of Malvasia di Lipari and its wine (called malvasia delle Lipari, differentiating it from Malvasia di Lipari, which is the grape) is largely the doing of Carlo Hauner, a Milanese painter and designer who first visited the Lipari (or Eolian) islands, off the northern coast of Sicily, in 1963. He turned them into his second home and was soon making the local wine. The results of his vinous efforts took Italy by storm in the 1980s and led to renewed interest in the wine (a good thing) and a sudden increase in the production of malvasia delle Lipari labels and very questionable wines (not a good thing). Allowing the wine to be bottled outside the islands (in Sicily, for instance) was probably not a good idea, though it probably couldn't be helped, given the logistical difficulties posed by the small islands. Also, while malvasia delle Lipari is made with the almost eponymous variety, many modern versions are disappointing. According to Francesco Fenech, one of the best producers of this wine, part of the problem is that on the wave of the wine's great popularity, increased demand for nursery material (of which there was little, as Malvasia di Lipari had been until then a completely forgotten variety) led to a great deal of, for example, Malvasia di Candia Aromatica finding its way onto the islands and the southern mainland. Clearly, everyone wanted a piece of the action, and the islands, amazingly beautiful but small, only had limited plantings of original old vines, and finite production capacities. Malvasia di Candia Aromatica is a fine variety, but less adapted to the island microclimate than the original Malvasia di Lipari; and anyway, in my view, the latter is the superior of the two, relative to fine-winemaking potential. Sweet malvasia delle Lipari wines especially offer greater depth and complexity.

In fact, the two varieties don't look anything alike. Malvasia di Lipari is immediately recognizable due to its very scrawny, elongated, cylindrical (rarely cylindrical-conical) grape bunch and small, round berries with thin skins. By contrast, Malvasia di Candia Aromatica has a large, pyramidal bunch with a large wing or two and medium-small, round berries with thick skins. There is only one official clone of Malvasia di Lipari available, the VM-4.

Crespan, Cabello, Giannetto, Ibanez, Karoglan Kontic, Maletic, Pejic, Rodriguez, and Antonacci (2006) published a landmark *Malvasia* study indicating that Malvasia di Lipari is identical to Sardinia's Malvasia di Sardegna, Calabria's Greco Bianco (which they called Greco Bianco di Gerace in their study), Croatia's Malvasia Dubrovačka, Madeira's Malvasia Cândida, and Spain's Malvasía de Sitges (Malvasía Rosada of the Canary Islands and Madeira's Malvasia Cândida Roxa are two red-berried mutations of this latter variety.) The researchers also showed this *Malvasia* to be different from Malvasia Istriana and Malvasia del Lazio, as the percentage of common alleles is low (33.3 percent and 27.6 percent, respectively).

Malvasia di Lipari looks and behaves very differently from most other *Malvasia*s. Early budding, it's susceptible to spring frosts and is oidium sensitive. It's a very irregular producer and worse, low-yielding; it thrives on volcanic soils, but is not very vigorous. The wine is also completely different than that made, for example, on Sardinia. I admit to being surprised by Crespan et al.'s conclusions, as I fail to see any resemblance between the Sardinian and the Eolian *Malvasia* cultivars, either as grapes or as wine, and the same applies to the Greco Bianco variety. Perhaps it is a matter of biotypes that have evolved over the centuries, changing their phenotypic aspect in response to different microclimates and soils: so-called ecotypes or site-specific biotypes. In this light, a study by Barba, Di Lernia, Chiota, Carimi, Carra, and Abbate (2008) is especially noteworthy, since it determined that all the accessions of Malvasia di Lipari from the islands they analyzed were affected either by leaf roll virus or fanleaf virus, diseases that can explain the great difference in morphologic appearance between the varieties. Furthermore, as Malvasia di Lipari is undoubtedly a very old cultivar, it seems reasonable to assume that it built up numerous mutations throughout the centuries leading to different phenotypes. Not surprisingly, Calabrian producers like Ceratti do not believe their Greco Bianco is identical to Malvasia di Lipari.

The study by Crespan's group (2006a) also showed that Malvasia di Lipari is identical to Malvasia di Sardegna. Given that the wines made from these two varieties smell and taste completely different, the proposed identity is surprising. In fairness, the grapes do look alike, and differences in the wines may just be the result of very diverse habitats and winemaking skills and methods. Somewhat disappointingly, in an extremely interesting study on Sardinian biodiversity and local grapevines (De Mattia, Imazio, Grassi, Lovicu, Tardaguila, Failla, et al. 2007), in which grapevine accessions were genotyped at thirteen microsatellite loci, Malvasia di Sardegna was, inexplicably, not among the Sardinian cultivars analyzed. A shame, as perhaps a little more light could have been shed on this variety and its relationships to other *Malvasia*s.

Locals in Sardinia have grown what they believed to be a specific Malvasia di Sardegna, also long known as Manusia and Marmaxia, at least since the sixteenth century, though according to Nieddu, two biotypes were described as early as 1877. Interestingly, the *Malvasia*s from Bosa and Cagliari were already renowned for their quality in 1933. Microsatellite testing at twelve SSR loci has confirmed the identity between the *Malvasia* vines grown around Bosa and Cagliari, so wines called Malvasia di Bosa and Malvasia di Cagliari are made with Malvasia di Sardegna, which in turn, is, as we have been told, Malvasia di Lipari. However, Malvasia di Sardegna still remains listed separately in the National Registry at number 136. There are as yet no clones available of Malvasia di Sardegna.

The curious thing is that Malvasia di Sardegna is, to the best of my knowledge, a nonaromatic or only very slightly aromatic variety, producing very mineral, powerful wines that can be either dry or sweet. This clashes a little with what I know of Malvasia di Lipari, which, though not the most aromatic of grapes, is more so than Malvasia di Sardegna, and it seems its wines are also more aromatic than any Malvasia di Sardegna or di Bosa wine I have ever tried. These differences in the wines may be the result of different winemaking or viticultural techniques, such as higher or lower yields, but still, I wonder. As of 2009 there were roughly 220 hectares planted to Malvasia di Sardegna on the island, especially in the central-eastern part, around the towns of Alghero, Bosa, Cagliari, and Sorso. The one true *grand cru* is Bosa, in the Planargia area of Sardinia.

Which Wines to Choose and Why

In Sicily there are fourteen estates, sixty grape growers, and sixty-five hectares under vine to Malvasia di Lipari, mainly on the island of Salina though the grapevine has recently reached Vulcano as well. Over two hundred thousand bottles of Malvasia delle Lipari wine are produced each year: 80 percent of those are sweet *passito* (or air-dried) and 20 percent are *naturale*. Island producers have also mentioned that the musts of other varieties find their way into some lesser examples of modern Malvasia di Lipari wines. Honeyed and long, with delicate dried apricot and fresh peach aromas and flavors, lifted by a lovely floral note and an extremely intense note of oranges, Malvasia di Lipari wines can be unforgettable. Over in Sardinia, the DOC wines are malvasia di Bosa and malvasia di Cagliari. The malvasia di Bosa is richer, deeper, and more alcoholic (it's also aged longer before being put up for sale) than the malvasia di Cagliari: both are available in dry and sweet styles, as well as fortified versions. These wines smell and taste very different from those made on the Eolian islands, and perhaps these differences are the consequence of different microclimates, soils and winemaking skills and techniques. Then again, many wine lovers won't be surprised if they are one day told that Malvasia di Lipari, Malvasia di Sardegna, and Greco Bianco were three distinct varieties after all.

WINES TO TRY: For Malvasia delle Lipari, try: Fenech***, Caffarella*** (super-expensive, if you can find it—the winemaker is, not by chance, also a jeweler), Giona**, Barone di Villagrande* (the lovely, large single-vineyard wine called Brigadiere), Caravaglio** (Passito), Mimmo Paone*, and Tasca d'Almerita* (Capofaro, also the name of a wonderful luxury hotel, Tenuta Capofaro). Hauner was once the most famous malvasia di Lipari producer (I love, and loved, their wines from the 1980s); today they produce wines from grapes grown on the islands of Salina and Vulcano. Punta dell'Ufala/Lantieri** now also makes a great wine on Vulcano. For Malvasia di Sardegna, try: Fratelli Porcu*** (dry or sweet), Battista Columbu***, and Meloni* (Donna Jolanda, sweet and inexpensive).

Malvasia Istriana

WHERE IT'S FOUND: FVG, Puglia, Veneto. NATIONAL REGISTRY CODE NUMBER: 138. COLOR: white.

Malvasia Istriana (called Malvazija Istarska in Istria) has been documented in Friuli Venezia Giulia (FVG) since the thirteenth century. It is usually considered to have an Istrian origin, as its name implies (Istria, a peninsula long a part of Italy, was lost in the aftermath of World War II). Interestingly, I have found no documents specifically mentioning this variety growing in Istria before 1891; Osterman (1940) writes that "malvagias" were among the most coveted wines of Friuli in the fourteenth century, but of course we have no way of knowing if it was Malvasia Istriana they were made with. A wildly interesting study by Pejić, Maletić, and Naslov (2005) demonstrated no genetic relationship between it and twenty-eight Greek varieties. According to the famous study by Lacombe, Boursiquot, Laoucou, Dechesne, Varès, and This (2007), Malvasia Istriana is instead genetically related to Malvasia di Lipari, Malvasia Bianca Lunga, and Malvasia Nera di Brindisi, and is one of the parents of the laboratory crossing Incrocio Dalmasso 2/26, also called Vega (the other parent is Furmint, a well-known Hungarian native variety). Crespan, Cabello, Giannetto, Ibanez, Karoglan Kontic,

Maletic, Pejic, Rodriguez, and Antonacci (2006a) also showed that Malvasia Istriana is distinct from Malvasia di Sardegna (Malvasia di Lipari) as the percentage of common alleles is low (33.3 percent).

Malvasia Istriana looks strikingly different from other *Malvasia*s grown in Italy, and the wines made with it differ as well. Usually the grape bunch is medium-sized, cylindrical, with one very small wing, and sparse; its round berries have thin but resistant, yellow-green skin. Of the clones available to producers (ISV 1, ISV F6, VCR 4, VCR 113, VCR 114, VCR 115, ERSA 120, ERSA 121, ERSA 122, ERSA 123, and ISV-VA 101) the most commonly used are VCR 4, VCR 120, VCR 121, and VCR 115 (they offer the best balance between vigor and aromatic personality), but many producers opt for massal selections, the best known of which is called "Mina." That said, Malvasia Istriana grapes have always looked quite different to me from producer to producer. According to Gianfranco Gallo, one of the best producers not just of Friuli Venezia Giulia but of Italy, huge intravarietal variability is characteristic of this specific grape. "In Friuli Venezia Giulia we have different biotypes of Malvasia Istriana, partly due to genetic differences and partly as the result of environmental and human selection pressures. This is why some of these grapevines have large, very compact bunches, with wings and without, but there are some very loosely packed biotypes too. What they all seem to have in common is a very well-developed stalk and rather large berries." The existence of site-specific Malvasia Istriana biotypes alluded to by Gallo has received scientific backing in a recent study that evaluated the morphological and genetic intra-varietal variability of Malvasia Istriana (Meneghetti, Bavaresco, Calò, and Costacurta 2013). Thirty Malvasia Istriana genotypes consisting of eight Italian clones and twenty-two accessions grown in the Istrian peninsula of Croatia were studied. Ampelographic characterizations of accessions were performed using twenty Office International de la Vigne et du Vin (OIV) descriptors. These and microsatellite analyses confirmed that the thirty genotypes were of Malvasia Istriana. The morphological analyses performed using the OIV ampelographic descriptors identified the Italian clones in accordance with their provenance: the two clones of the ISV (Veneto), the two clones of ERSA (FVG), and the four clones of VCR (Veneto). Not surprisingly, the Italian clones and Croatian accessions were easily distinguished by differing ampelographic characteristics. In order to study the intravarietal genetic variability of the thirty accessions, AFLP, SAMPL, and M-AFLP molecular analyses were also performed. Interestingly, results showed that the Istrian accessions were genetically more similar to each other than the Italian clones. However, the AFLP, SAMPL, and M-AFLP analysis results did not show a complete correlation with morphological observations. Furthermore, while the Croatian accessions were easily separated into ten subgroups in agreement with their geographic origins, such differences were not observed for the three Italian sub-groups. It appears these molecular approaches allow the identification of different biotypes within the Istrian *Malvasia* cultivar group and the characterization of accessions according to their geographic origins.

Overall, Malvasia Istriana is hardy and very resistant, though it's a little oidium sensitive. It does remarkably well in the flat, gravelly riverbed plains of Friuli Venezia Giulia's Isonzo River basin. Clay is a no-no, since the variety does not appreciate excessively water-retentive soils, a well-known property of clay. For this reason, many also plant Malvasia Istriana in the highest portions of hillside vineyards, where water drainage is facilitated. Hardships such as these help diminish the variety's natural vigor, an absolute necessity if high-quality wines are the goal. Gallo also believes that the best sites are those located on soils made of strata of Dolomia alpine rock, formed during the Wurm glaciation; these poor soils have more than 30 percent bedrock and the soil is never more than 150 centimeters deep. Giorgio

Badin, owner of Ronco del Gelso, another very fine Isonzo estate in Friuli, believes that "the keys are rocky, nutrient-poor soils that are low in clay, and the choice of rootstock. While you'd think less vigorous ones would prove best, not so with this grape: using somewhat vigorous rootstocks is better, as they handle water stress better in gravelly terrains."

Malvasia Istriana is actually most widespread in nearby Croatia, where, as of 2010, over three thousand hectares of it are planted (compared to the roughly two hundred hectares of Italy). Fine producers include Moreno Coronica, Kabola, Gianfranco Kozlević, and Bruno Trapan, but some producers such as Giorgio Clai and Roxanich employ long maceration techniques that result, in my view at least, in wines that taste (as almost all white wines do when made in this manner) like less than thrilling red wine wannabes. Malvasia Istriana has also been planted in Australia. There, the Vinea Marson estate in Heathcote makes a wine called Grazia (a blend of Sauvignon Blanc, Pinot Bianco, Malvasia Istriana, and Friulano, a take on some of Friuli Venezia Giulia's best-known white wine blends such as Vintage Tunina or Terre Alte) and the Chalmers Project in Murray Darling produced a lovely air-dried sweet-styled 2009 blend of Picolit and Malvasia Istriana.

Which Wines to Choose and Why

To my mind, the best dry white *Malvasia* wines in Italy are made with this variety, but I never cease to be amazed by the diversity of wines produced even within Friuli Venezia Giulia. Furthermore, I remain in awe of the extreme makeover these wines have undergone over the last fifteen years: whereas Malvasia Istriana wines of the 1980s were always mineral but neutral, today some can be remarkably aromatic—some wines remind me of gewürztraminer or moscato bianco. For anybody who was drinking Italian wines regularly twenty or thirty years ago, this new aspect of Friuli's Malvasia Istriana wines is obvious, and has puzzled me for years, as grapes are either aromatic or nonaromatic, never both. Initially, I wondered if the craze for aromatic wines that swept Italy in the first decade of the twenty-first century had led some producers to plant aromatic *Malvasia* grapevines instead of the Istriana variety—events such as these are not unheard of in Italy. But it's not so, according to Gianfranco Gallo. His Dessimis is, nowadays, a very aromatic *Malvasia* wine, and yet I distinctly remember much older vintages made in the family being anything but aromatic. So how could this be? I asked. "I think it's a matter of cultivation technique, soil fertility, pruning methods, and harvest timing," he told me matter-of-factly. "I remember the 1976 and 1981 vintages of my family's malvasia: as you say, they were wines devoid of truly aromatic character. But honestly, we had much higher yields then and the varietal expression of the wine was nullified by our wrongheaded viticulture choices." In other words, lowering yields allows the variety's true aromatic nature to shine through. (This may also be true, to a much lesser extent, of Malvasia del Lazio.)

Winemaking with Malvasia Istriana is not particularly complex. However, as a good deal of the variety's aromatic potential is the result of molecules located next to the cuticle of the grape skins, some producers opt for a short, cold maceration of the berries before fermentation. This can be tricky: over the years, more than one producer has told me that if the polyphenol-endowed Malvasia Istriana grape skins are not completely ripe, the resulting wine risks unpleasant aromas of cauliflower or chrysanthemum. When all goes well, Malvasia Istriana's wealth of norisoprenoids ensures that with bottle age (roughly three years, in my experience), wines develop aromas of apricot, peach, and wisteria; later still, with the formation of dihydronapthalene, the typical diesel fuel or hydrocarbon aroma characteristic of Riesling wines becomes pronounced.

Though it has also been planted elsewhere in Italy (Puglia and Veneto), Malvasia Istriana performs best in Friuli Venezia Giulia, where wines are generically labeled malvasia, with the appellation or DOC attached: Carso malvasia,

Collio malvasia, and Isonzo malvasia are most famous. Carso malvasia is usually spectacularly mineral and austere (indeed, it is probably the most minerally-tasting wine of Italy), Collio malvasia is the most refined and perfumed, while Isonzo malvasia, due to the much warmer microclimate, is rather high in alcohol (14.5–15 percent is not uncommon) and atypically full-bodied. The little-known DOC Friuli Annia has also recently produced promising Malvasia Istriana wines. Nearly always, a good Malvasia Istriana wine will offer aromas and flavors of honeyed peach, apricot, and pear, and mineral overlays of varying intensity. The aromatic ones have strong notes of ginger and white pepper. Unfortunately, some Friuli Venezia Giulia producers, mainly those of the Carso, have taken to making malvasias with long macerations on the skins, thereby producing wines that are orange in color and very tannic; all too often, wines made in this manner are also partly oxidized. Needless to say, many wine geeks and some fad-chasers have warmly embraced this style of wine, but my own experience is that the vast majority of wine lovers really don't like these wines and don't understand what all the fuss is about. Strange as it may seem to some wine intellectuals, most people out there actually want their white wine to be . . . well, white.

WINES TO TRY: For Collio malvasia, try: Borgo del Tiglio*** (this used to be very heavily marked by new oak, but no longer, and the wine is now even better), Alessandro Pascolo***, Doro Princic***, Dario Raccaro** (often with a little residual sugar), Paolo Caccese**, and Venica*. For Isonzo malvasia, try: Ronco del Gelso*** (Vigna della Permuta), Vie di Romans*** (Dessimis), and Drius**. For Carso malvasia, try: Castelvecchio**, Zidarich**, Skerk**, Castello di Rubbia*, and Kante*. For Annia malvasia, try: Le Favole*.

Malvasia Moscata

WHERE IT'S FOUND: Piedmont. NATIONAL REGISTRY CODE NUMBER: 462. COLOR: white.

Malvasia Moscata is the newest and the rarest of all the white-berried *Malvasia*s in Italy, but it's apparently the most abundant one in California, where it was planted by Piedmontese immigrants and is simply, but erroneously, called Malvasia Bianca. The latter is the name of another *Malvasia* variety, typical of Puglia and listed in the National Registry at number 129. Only recently rediscovered, Malvasia Moscata's presence was cited in Piedmont already in the early seventeenth century, as Malvasia Nostrale, by Croce (1606). An aromatic variety, Malvasia Moscata is (erroneously) called Malvasia Bianca in the province of Torino, where it is most common in the countryside around Albugnano and of the Pinerolese; it is also known as Malvasia Greca in the Alessandrino, as Moscato Greco in the Astigiano and in the Monferrato Casalese, and as Greco or Grec in the Roero (not to be confused with the Greco of the Novara area, which is Erbaluce, another native variety, or the Greco of Campania, which has nothing to do with this *Malvasia*). Just about everywhere in Piedmont it is also known as Moscatella, an obvious reference to its musky aroma and taste. In the ampelography texts of the late nineteenth century, when this *Malvasia* used to be locally very abundant and important, it was honored with the name of Malvasia Bianca del Piemonte. However, as the Italian Ministry of Agriculture does not allow place names by which to identify grape varieties, when this variety was finally officially listed in the National Registry on March 23, 2012, the name Malvasia Moscata was chosen.

In the late 1800s, cultivation of this variety was completely devastated by oidium, and farmers replanted with the more resistant Moscato Bianco instead. Though Malvasia Moscata is characterized by an obvious musky smell and taste (as is the wine), it's easy to distinguish from the much more common Moscato Bianco thanks to its leaf (with a rare seven lobes and far deeper indentations than those of Moscato Bianco) and especially its bunch, which has much bigger, round, thick-skinned berries.

Malvasia Moscata is also generally more vigorous and productive than Moscato Bianco, and less sensitive to botrytis.

Which Wines to Choose and Why

Malvasia Moscata vines are found only sporadically in old Piedmontese vineyards, so learning about the taste of a monovarietal wine made from it is not easy. Farmers and old timers have told me that dry wines made with this *Malvasia* variety reveal aromas and flavors of lemon, apricot, pear, tropical fruits, and aromatic herbs (sage, for instance). California versions by Bonny Doon (Ca' del Solo), Wild Horse, Ballentine, and Birichino have more or less similar organoleptic profiles to those just described, and often reveal a lightly aromatic nose and an almost oily, fleshy texture. One of Birichino's owner/winemakers, John Locke, worked for years with Bonny Doon's Randall Grahm and also with André Ostertag of Alsace, so he knows a thing or two about underappreciated and aromatic grapes, and his wines are excellent (the other Birichino owner is Alex Krause, who also worked with Grahm). The huge amount of confusion surrounding this cultivar (and Italian native grapes in general) is well evidenced by Birichino's user-friendly and well-thought-out website, where "Malvasia Bianca" is said to hail from Calabria (highly unlikely, unless they mean Greco Bianco), to grow in Puglia (unlikely, since it's distinct from Malvasia Bianca), and to be found in Piedmont in the Asti area (this is true, since it is commonly believed that the Malvasia Bianca grapevines present in California are in fact Malvasia Moscata). That said, I have tasted Birichino's wine, and found it excellent. However, since many very good U.S. wines made with Italian natives smell and taste different from the originals made in Italy (in fact, Birichino points out that their wine has far more intense aromas than do similarly named Italian wines), I cannot be sure of how it would compare to a Malvasia Moscata wine, if and when it were made in Italy. All we need to do now is wait and see if some Italian producer decides to give it a shot and produce a monovarietal wine with it, dry or sweet. I have no doubts this will happen some time soon, since by all accounts and testimonies, this is a very high-quality grape variety: its wines are in no way inferior to those made with Moscato Bianco.

WINES TO TRY: To the best of my knowledge, there are as yet no monovarietal wines made from this variety in Italy. So here you have it, the most international of all Italian native varieties: in fact, it couldn't be any more international, since the only wines currently made with it are produced outside Italy!

Malvasia Rosa

WHERE IT'S FOUND: Emilia-Romagna. NATIONAL REGISTRY CODE NUMBER: 318. COLOR: white.

Found only in Emilia-Romagna's province of Piacenza, Malvasia Rosa is used to make delicately fizzy and sweet light-bodied wines. In 1967, a farmer in Vigolzone found a Malvasia di Candia Aromatica grapevine producing pink grapes and called Mario Fregoni of the viticulture department at the University of Piacenza to come see. Fregoni understood the grapevine was a pink-berried mutation of Malvasia di Candia Aromatica, and selected and propagated the vine. It is a very productive variety, with a medium-large, pyramidal, elongated bunch (but smaller than that of Malvasia di Candia Aromatica) and large, round, pink berries with medium-thick skins. It ripens later in September than its parent, Malvasia di Candia Aromatica, and like its progenitor, it is an aromatic variety.

Which Wines to Choose and Why

WINES TO TRY: Tenuta Mossi** (Malvasia Rosa Passito Rosa di Vigna); Montesissa* (Rosa Malvasia Rosa Frizzante, a sparkling wine). Mossi's wine is made with air-dried grapes and the result is a delicately sweet, pink-hued, lovely wine reminiscent of raspberries and red currants.

THE DARK-BERRIED MALVASIAS

For me, and not just me, the *Malvasia Nera* varieties represent a conundrum. Of the numerous dark-berried *Malvasia* grapes in Italy, four share the "Malvasia Nera-Something" moniker: Malvasia Nera di Lecce, Malvasia Nera di Brindisi, Malvasia Nera Lunga, and Malvasia Nera di Basilicata (though the last of these is particularly rare). The first two, both typical of Puglia, have been the source of much confusion and myriad diatribes. Ampelographically, Malvasia Nera di Lecce and Malvasia Nera di Brindisi differ from each other: the Brindisi variety has smaller bunches and berries, though the bunches of both tend to become more loosely-packed with age. Furthermore, Malvasia Nera di Lecce ripens much later in the year (usually in the latter part of September and first ten days of October), compared to the Brindisi variety, which is early-ripening (usually in the first half of September). Last but not least, Malvasia Nera di Brindisi tends to produce wines that are lightly aromatic, while Malvasia Nera di Lecce, a neutral grape, does not. Both are excellent table grapes as well as wine grapes.

Despite these obvious differences, recent genetic studies seem to confirm the identity between the two. Coletta, Crespan, Costacurta, Caputo, Taurisano, Meneghetti, and Antonacci (2006) were the first to conclude that these two *Malvasia*s were the same cultivar, since they found them to have the same SSR profile. Studies analyzing more SSR markers, performed more recently on new samples from other vineyards in Puglia confirmed the previously published results (Gasparro, Caputo, Brini, Coletta, Crespan, Lapenna, and Antonacci 2008). Meneghetti, Bavaresco, Calò, and Costacurta (2013) also obtained similar results when they analyzed thirteen accessions of Malvasia Nera from Brindisi and thirteen accessions of Malvasia Nera from Lecce, finding that all the accessions showed the same SSR profile. Therefore, most researchers today view these two *Malvasia*s as a single variety, naming it in the process Malvasia Nera di Brindisi/Lecce, though this is not an officially recognized name and is not included as such in the National Registry. In keeping with the notion that these two are separate varieties, the official clones of these two black *Malvasia*s are also different, and the two varieties remain listed separately at numbers 140 and 141. As we shall see, this may not be a bad idea, in view of the arguments raised by what "genetic identity" really amounts to, at least at the present state of knowledge and technology available for genetic testing (see chapter 1). Crespan, Calò, Giannetto, Sparacio, Storchi, and Costacurta (2008) also established that Malvasia Nera Brindisi/Lecce is the result of a natural crossing between Malvasia Bianca Lunga and Negro Amaro. With the current drive to prove all *Malvasia Nera*s identical, it may well be that someone will soon enlighten all us Neanderthals that Malvasia Nera di Basilicata is also identical to the other two *Malvasia Nera*s, but genetic testing of the Basilicata variety thus far has not yet shown this to be the case, so the jury's out. Amid the never-ending confusion that is the *Malvasia Nera*s, recent research has shown that at least some of the so-called "Malvasia Nera" grown in Tuscany is in reality the well-known Spanish variety Tempranillo (Storchi, Armanni, Crespan, Frare, De Lorenzis, D'Onofrio, and Scalabrelli 2009; based on molecular studies first performed by D'Onofrio, De Lorenzis, Natali, and Scalabrelli 2008). Storchi's group focused on sixteen black *Malvasia*s of Tuscany (culled from different vineyards in the provinces of Grosseto, Pisa, and Arezzo, some with one-hundred-year-old vines), comparing accessions with four registered clones, at eleven microsatellite markers. Comparisons with databases confirmed that most of the Tuscan accessions, including registered clones, shared the molecular profile of Tempranillo. These results suggest that Tempranillo is in fact cultivated in Tuscany (where its presence has been documented since the nineteenth century) in vineyards, but most often under the erroneous alias of Malvasia Nera. Also, Giancarlo Scalabrelli of the University of Pisa has written as recently as 2012 that

Malvasia Nera di Lecce (and not Brindisi) is identical to Tempranillo. Clearly however, if it is Malvasia Nera di Lecce that is identical to Tempranillo and not Malvasia Nera di Brindisi, then the two *Malvasias* cannot be the same grape variety. I am tempted to speculate that it is Malvasia Nera di Lecce that is identical to Tempranillo, but that Malvasia Nera di Brindisi is a different variety.

For what it's worth, I'm not wholly convinced Malvasia Nera di Brindisi and Malvasia Nera di Lecce are one and the same, and a luminary such as Roberto Bandinelli of the University of Florence, probably Italy's best and most famous ampelographer, agrees. Bandinelli has told me flat out the two varieties cannot be the same, mainly on morphologic grounds but also on the basis of the viticultural behavior and aromatic nature of the *Malvasia* from Brindisi as compared to the one from Lecce. In fact, not only do the two *Malvasia Neras* look different (very different, to my eyes), but they ripen at different times in the year. More importantly, Malvasia Nera di Brindisi is a semi-aromatic variety while Malvasia Nera di Lecce is a neutral one. In some Tuscan wines where a "Malvasia Nera" is included in the blend (unfortunately most everyone in Italy outside Puglia still uses the Lecce and Brindisi qualifiers interchangeably), such as Capannelle's Solare, Castello di Ama's Vigneto Bellavista Chianti Classico, and Castellare's I Sodi di San Niccolò, there is an obviously light aromatic quality present which I think is brought on by the *Malvasia Nera* component. Clearly, many experts believe that the observed differences between Malvasia Nera di Brindisi and Malvasia Nera di Lecce are due to environmental influence on the same genotype rather than these two being distinct varieties. However, since both these varieties have long been grown in Puglia under similar viticultural circumstances, it seems unlikely that higher or lower yields or vastly different soils and exposures might explain, in this instance at least, grossly different aromatic expressions between the two. Furthermore, in the molecular studies performed by Lacombe, Boursiquot, Laoucou, Dechesne, Varès, and This (2007), comparing accessions present in the French grapevine collection of Vassal, the synonymity between Malvasia Nera di Brindisi and Malvasia Nera di Lecce was *not* confirmed. In this respect, recent results obtained by Meneghetti, Poljuha, Frare, Costacurta, Morreale, Bavaresco, and Calò (2012) are even more noteworthy. These researchers decided to perform more extensive molecular analyses aimed at investigating the differential molecular profiles between these two *Malvasia* cultivars. Thirteen accessions of Italian Malvasia Nera di Brindisi and thirteen accessions of Malvasia Nera di Lecce culled from old vineyards in the Salento area of Puglia were analyzed. All the accessions showed the same SSR profile and were identified as Malvasia Nera di Brindisi/Lecce. However, the intra-varietal variability was studied further by combining AFLP, SAMPL, M-AFLP, and ISSR analyses. Very interestingly, the authors found that the discrimination among the genotypes of Malvasia Nera di Brindisi/Lecce from the two different geographic origins of the Salento (Lecce and Brindisi) was possible using the four marker types. Genetic similarity as described by Dice (1945) estimated within and between the two origins confirmed that these two groups were not genetically identical. Whether these genetic differences are sufficient enough to consider the two *Malvasia Neras* in question as distinct varieties is unclear yet; but it is not without interest that two varieties with different geographic origin and that are not perfectly genetically identical look and behave differently, relative to wines that can be made with them.

My view (one that I have already illustrated along its general lines in chapter 1) is that, at the very least, these two *Malvasia Neras* are best considered biotypes (if they really are just biotypes) that produce very different wines. I can't help but wonder if genetic differences shown thus far, and others we may not yet be able to investigate with the biotechnology currently available, aren't enough to keep Malvasia Nera di Brindisi and Malvasia Nera di Lecce as distinct cultivars. I am not the only one who holds a similar view relative to biotypes that behave very differently in the vineyard and the cellar: in fact, Pelsy, Hocquigny, Moncada, Barbeau, Forget, Hinrichsen, and Merdinoglu (2010) have concluded that when clones of the same variety have different phenotypes and produce different wines, they should be considered different cultivars. Furthermore, Emanuelli, Lorenzi, Grzeskowiak, Catalano, Stefanini, and Troggio (2013) have stated that different-looking or -behaving accessions sharing the same SSR profile in standard grapevine collections ought to be studied further before being eliminated as duplicates. Nevertheless, Bandinelli told me in a 2012 interview that recent discussions between luminaries have gone as far as to conclude that the only true black *Malvasia* of Italy is Trentino Alto Adige's extremely rare Malvasia or Malvasier (the German name for all things *Malvasia*). In his always gracious and soft-spoken style, Bandinelli, who has spent many years of his life working with the *Malvasia Neras*, told me that he finds the suggestion "almost offensive."

Malvasia di Casorzo

WHERE IT'S FOUND: Piedmont. NATIONAL REGISTRY CODE NUMBER: 134. COLOR: red.

A red grape variety used to make the DOC wine of same name, the presence of Malvasia di Casorzo in Piedmont might date back to 1875, when De Maria and Leardi documented red-berried *Malvasia*s in the region. However, since there are three distinct red *Malvasia* varieties growing in Piedmont, we don't know which one of the three they were describing. In a recent microsatellite study by Torello Marinoni, Raimondi, Boccacci, and Schneider (2006) of several Piedmontese *Lambrusca* or *Lambrusco* varieties, there were parent-offspring relationships between Lambrusca di Alessandria, Neretto di Marengo, and Malvasia di Casorzo (while, not surprisingly, the *Lambrusco*s from Emilia-Romagna seemed to be genetically distant).

Malvasia di Casorzo is an aromatic grape (like the other two red-berried Piedmontese *Malvasia*s), blessed with thick skins and very fragrant, aromatic pulp rich in geraniol; I guarantee biting into the grape will make you immediately think of dark-red cherries and roses. In contrast to Malvasia di Schierano, it has a slightly larger and more cylindrical bunch with only one wing (the former has one or two wings and a smaller, conical bunch). The morphology also depends on the clone looked at: there are three available since 1992, the CVT AT 1, CVT AT 43, and CVT AT 159. Malvasia di Casorzo requires severe pruning to limit its vigor, and minerally, iron-rich, clay-loamy soils to avoid chlorosis and to maximize its aromatic potential. As it has a compact bunch, it can be affected by grey rot: otherwise, it's a resistant variety.

Which Wines to Choose and Why

The production zone of the DOC Malvasia di Casorzo is almost entirely limited to the countryside around the town of Casorzo, in the province of Asti, though there are vines in the province of Alessandria as well. These *Malvasia* vines grow especially prolifically near the towns of Casorzo, Vignale Monferrato, Altavilla, Ottiglio, Grazzano Badoglio, Olivola, and Grana, all in the Monferrato on mainly clay-calcareous soils at two hundred meters above sea level—there were an estimated 51.5 hectares there in 2007.

The grapes are best picked at night or early in the morning, since cool temperatures help to keep fermentation from starting on the way to the cellar, and potent refrigeration equipment is needed to lower the temperature of the grapes as quickly as possible once there. Cryomacerations of one to two weeks are employed to extract as much aromatic potential as possible from the skins, and the wine's fermentation is always interrupted so as to leave residual sugar, since Malvasia di Casorzo is either an off-dry or frankly sweet wine (it can also be made in a *passito* or air-dried style). It is a tannic wine, blessed with decent acidity, and so never seems cloying as some brachettos and moscatos can be. The fermentation process is at times performed in autoclaves so as to preserve the wine's natural carbon dioxide; this is why some versions are lightly fizzy. The wine is much less aromatic than that made with Malvasia di Schierano and a great deal more structured, with a tannic mouthfeel loaded with small blackberry and blackcurrant jam aromas and flavors (I find strawberry notes to be more typical of Malvasia di Schierano wines), at times with a chocolaty nuance.

WINES TO TRY: Accornero*** (Brigantino and the Passito Pico Conte Giovanni Pastrone), Bricco Mondalino*** (Molignano), Giorgio Cantamessa** (La Spigliata), Biletta** (Malvarossa Moncucchetto), Fracchia** (Voulet/ Antichi Giochi Piemontesi), La Sera** (Malvasia). The last two, especially, are charming examples of the lightly fizzy style. Montemagno** (Nectar) makes a good sweet version.

Malvasia di Schierano

WHERE IT'S FOUND: Piedmont. NATIONAL REGISTRY CODE NUMBER: 137. COLOR: red.

Malvasia di Schierano is another red-berried *Malvasia* that may have been first documented in Piedmont in the nineteenth century by Leardi and De Maria. In fact, *Malvasia* grapes (then called *Marvaxie*) were growing in Piedmont already in 1468: the statutes of the town of Mondonio (known today as Castelnuovo Don Bosco, the epicenter of Malvasia di Schierano cultivation) stated that stiff penalties would be imposed on all those caught stealing grapes of "*moscatelli, rinasii, vernace [. . .] et marvaxie.*"

Malvasia di Schierano gives, in my view, the best wines of the three red-berried *Malvasias* grown in the region. At times erroneously called Malvasia Rosa (see above), it has always been confused with Malvasia Nera Lunga (see below), with which it was often interplanted in vineyards. Malvasia Nera Lunga, which as the name implies has a much longer bunch, was preferentially propagated in the 1950s and 1960s due to its greater productivity, earlier ripening, and better resistance to diseases, relative to the higher-quality but more difficult Malvasia di Schierano, which is sensitive to leafhoppers and peronospora and though more vigorous is a less generous and irregularly yielding variety, being subject to *millerandage,* especially when yields are allowed to creep up. In fact, things got so out of hand that Chiara Martinotti of Cascina Gilli has told me that "most people aren't really sure of which variety, or how much of each, they have in their vineyards." The fact that Malvasia di Schierano usually ripens late (in the first week of October, though with climate change this may not be true for much longer) in its northern habitat didn't exactly endear it to producers either. There are no official clones available of the variety. According to Lacombe, Boursiquot, Laoucou, Dechesne, Varès, and This (2007), Malvasia di Schierano has close genetic ties to Moscato d'Alessandria and Malvasia del Lazio; this might explain why I find that its aromatic profile is more complex and interesting than that of the other two Piedmontese red-berried *Malvasias*, exuding some aromas similar to those of many *Moscatos* (that is, not just geraniol but also linalool derivations). For this reason, in the past, when SSR profiling had not yet become available and aromatic expression was still considered a defining characteristic of *Malvasias*, experts felt that Malvasia di Schierano was best considered a grape variety displaying characteristics in between those of the *Moscatos* and the *Malvasias*. Given its relationship to Moscato di Alessandria, they weren't that far off the mark. Gianni Vergnano, who produces the finest results with this grape at Gilli, points out that "the aromas are everything for this variety, since they are so intense, refined, and unique. And clay-calcareous soils are key to ensure more penetrating aromatics. The goal with this wine is to keep skin-to-must contact to a minimum, roughly at 2°C for a few hours only: the risk is tannin extraction that would make the wine unbalanced relative to its sugar content."

Which Wines to Choose and Why

Malvasia di Schierano grows in the countryside around Schierano, Castelnuovo Don Bosco, and Pino Torinese, all situated close to Turin. Though it can be used to make dry wines, it is most commonly used to make the sweet DOC wine called Malvasia di Castelnuovo Don Bosco, truly one of Italy's greatest and least-known wines. Named after the little town which is the epicenter of its production, Castelnuovo Don Bosco is also the birthplace of two famous saints, Giovanni Bosco and Giovanni Cafasso. The wine can be still or delicately fizzy, and is generally very light in alcohol (only 5.5–6 percent!); effusively fruity, it's like a red-berry fruit cocktail that is almost too delicious for words.

WINES TO TRY: Without doubt, the best producer of this wine is Gilli***. Also worth a try are Mario Mosso**, Alle Tre Colline*, and Terre dei Santi*.

Malvasia Nera di Basilicata

WHERE IT'S FOUND: Basilicata. NATIONAL REGISTRY CODE NUMBER: 139. COLOR: red.

Delicately aromatic, this now-rare variety differs from Malvasia Nera di Brindisi and Malvasia Nera di Lecce because it's more resistant to parasites and is more tolerant of inclement weather. It is found in the two Basilicata provinces of Matera and Potenza, and though no pure version of it is bottled, it is probably more common that is generally believed. Farmers have shown me the odd vine, always promiscuously mixed in with Aglianico vines (and there's often Aglianicone in those vineyards too, just to complicate matters). I have yet to meet someone who owns enough to make a monovarietal wine. In the past, researchers have also found Tempranillo grapevines in Basilicata locally called *Malvasia Nera,* so it may be that, as in Tuscany, at least some of Basilicata's *Malvasia Nera* is in fact Tempranillo. Of the two, this grape resembles Malvasia Nera di Brindisi more, mainly because both are aromatic varieties, which Malvasia Nera di Lecce is not. Morphologically, the three varieties resemble each other more than they differ. Malvasia Nera di Basilicata generally has medium-sized, compact bunches, and small, round berries. It is neither excessively vigorous nor a copious producer, but is more resistant to common grapevine diseases and pests than the other *Malvasia Nera*s. It ripens slightly later than Malvasia Nera di Brindisi, but before the Lecce variety.

Which Wines to Choose and Why

Malvasia Nera di Basilicata's winemaking potential is demonstrated by how well it accumulates sugars (fairly easily, and more so than Malvasia Nera di Lecce) while keeping very high acidity levels (pHs of 3.1 to 3.2 are not rare and total acidity levels can easily reach 8–9 grams per liter). These high acidity levels make it very unlikely that Malvasia Nera di Basilicata is identical to Malvasia Nera di Brindisi or Malvasia Nera di Lecce, since those two are known to be low-acid varieties. Over the years, older farmers and home winemakers have told me that they were always very happy to have Malvasia Nera di Basilicata to work with, for adding it to any wine blend meant three things, all positive: their wine would gain in aromatic complexity, potential alcohol, and total acidity levels. These observations are not without interest: they clearly tell us that Malvasia Nera di Basilicata may prove a variety of extreme interest in viticultural areas with warmer climates. Unfortunately, not nearly enough is known about it, and that's a shame, especially in times of rather worrisome climate change.

WINES TO TRY: To the best of my knowledge, there are no monovarietal wines made with Malvasia Nera di Basilicata.

Malvasia Nera di Brindisi

WHERE IT'S FOUND: Puglia, Tuscany, Calabria. NATIONAL REGISTRY CODE NUMBER: 140. COLOR: red.

As already mentioned in the introduction to the dark-berried *Malvasia* varieties, a great deal of confusion surrounds this variety's identity. Based on currently available SSR profiling, many experts consider Malvasia Nera di Brindisi to be identical to Malvasia Nera di Lecce and have come up with the unofficial name of Malvasia Nera di Brindisi/Lecce for this variety. However, not all agree and recent, more extensive, genetic testing by Meneghetti, Bavaresco, Calò, and Costacurta (2013) has shown that there exist some genetic differences between these two cultivars. Since the two *Malvasia Nera*s look and behave very differently (and not just relative to winemaking), some experts want to keep Malvasia Nera di Brindisi and Malvasia Nera di Lecce separate. To date, these two cultivars remain distinct in the National Registry.

Maurizo Castelli, the famous winemaker who consults for around twenty estates in Italy, says that "the problem with the *Malvasia Nera*s from Brindisi and Lecce is that they have unstable anthocyanins, and their wines tend to oxidize over time. For this reason, many producers don't want to use them in wines meant to age. Also, despite what you may think given its warm and sunny Puglian home, both these *Malvasia Nera*s also need to be grown in very cool places—if they aren't, in time, the wines tend to develop strong notes of burnt tobacco that aren't to everybody's liking." Castelli, who registered a few old biotypes of *Malvasia Nera* he selected in vineyards over time (he believes them to be most likely Malvasia Nera di Brindisi, given the characteristic lightly aromatic nature of some of his *Malvasia Nera*–containing wines), also feels that Malvasia Nera di Brindisi does best in soils that contain hefty doses of sand, which are more common in Puglia than Chianti. For the same reason, Leonardo Palumbo, one of Puglia's best-known winemakers, feels that Malvasia Nera di Brindisi does better in areas like Manduria, rather than around Locorotondo. The variety, a fairly early ripener usually harvested in the first half of September (neatly separating it from Malvasia Nera di Lecce, which ripens much later), is characterized by small bunches (recognizably smaller than those of the Lecce variety), but clearly the phenotype depends to an extent on the clone or biotype examined. There are three available clones: Santa Lucia 2, UBA 69/E and UBA 70/A. Interestingly, and in keeping with the notion that these two are separate varieties, these clones are different from the official clones of Malvasia Nera di Lecce. The variety is also characterized by high vigor and low fertility of the basal buds; its grapes tend to have low acidity and high pH. Pietro Colucci, owner of the Barsento estate in Noci near Bari, feels it's also a great variety with which to make *rosato*, but cautions that "the skins need to be thick to hold up to the winemaking process, or they break down easily and the wine develops off-putting smells." In fact, *Malvasia Nera*s, much like Sangiovese, are reductive varieties, and good winemaking is essential to bring out the best the variety has to offer.

Which Wines to Choose and Why

Malvasia Nera di Brindisi is also grown in Tuscany and Calabria, though its home is Puglia (mainly in the provinces of Bari, Brindisi, Lecce, and Taranto), where it's used for DOC wine blends Copertino, Lizzano, Squinzano, and others. It is apparently a great deal more common than Malvasia Nera di Lecce, with twice as many hectares planted to it in Italy compared to Malvasia Nera di Lecce. The fact that it is an early ripening variety compared to the latter variety may explain why Malvasia Nera di Brindisi is also the more common of the two in Tuscany, a generally cooler region than Puglia, and with much longer growing seasons. According to Sergio Botrugno of the Puglian estate Botrugno, the *crus* for this variety in Puglia are contrada Lobia, contrada Conella, and contrada Montenegro, all of them around Brindisi. In Tuscany, Malvasia Nera di Brindisi is added to Sangiovese in many wines such as Chianti, much as Canaiolo Nero might be, and though it is less used than other complementary varieties (both native and international) some of Tuscany's greatest wines are in fact made with 10–50 percent of what is most likely Malvasia Nera di Brindisi: Castello di Ama's Chianti Classico Vigna Bellavista, Castellare's I Sodi di San Niccolò, and Capannelle's Solare. However only those wines in which Malvasia di Brindisi plays a part will exude the delicately aromatic touch typical of the variety, which Malvasia Nera di Lecce does not supply. It's also an excellent table grape.

WINES TO TRY: To the best of my knowledge, and based on what the producers have told me, the following wines are made with Malvasia Nera di Brindisi, wholly or for the largest part. In Puglia, try: Duca Carlo Guarini** (Malia), Botrugno** (Nashi, a *novello-* or *nouveau*-style wine, and Botrus, a very interesting lightly sweet wine made from 50 percent late-harvested grapes), and Barsento* (Magilda, an excellent *rosato*). In Umbria, try I Girasoli di Sant'Andrea/Carlo Massimiliano Gritti**.

Malvasia Nera di Lecce

WHERE IT'S FOUND: Puglia. NATIONAL REGISTRY CODE NUMBER: 141. COLOR: red.

For more on the confusion surrounding this variety's relationship with Malvasia Nera di Brindisi, see the introduction to the dark-berried *Malvasia* varieties and the Malvasia Nera di Brindisi entry. Malvasia Nera di Lecce is grown in Puglia and does not appear to be found in other regions of Italy save for Tuscany, where the grape so called is most likely Tempranillo. Whether *all* Malvasia di Lecce is in fact Tempranillo is unclear. It should be noted that some Malvasia Nera di Lecce accessions from southern Italy have also been found to be Tempranillo; whether these originally grew there or were propagated from Tuscan Tempranillo vines mistakenly thought to be Malvasia Nera di Lecce remains unclear.

The variety, which ripens much later in the year than Malvasia Nera di Brindisi (usually in the latter part of September and first ten days of October), is also characterized by much larger bunches than those of the Brindisi variety, but clearly the phenotype depends to an extent on the clone or biotype examined (there are five available clones of Malvasia Nera di Lecce: M-N-6, U.S.FI-PI.3Np, U.S.FI-PI.4Np, U.S.FI-PI.1, and U.S.FI-PI.7). Interestingly, and in keeping with the notion that these two are separate varieties, these clones are different from the official clones of Malvasia Nera di Lecce.

In Puglia Malvasia Nera di Lecce is almost always blended with Negro Amaro, and there do not appear to be pure examples of it produced. At least, I have not yet met any producer who tells me his monovarietal Malvasia Nera wine is made wholly with Malvasia Nera di Lecce (because it's generally viewed as the lower quality variety of the two). It is part of the blend in DOC wines such as Squinzano, Alezio, Copertino, Leverano, and Salice Salentino.

WINES TO TRY: To the best of my knowledge, there are no 100 percent Malvasia Nera di Lecce wines made in Italy.

Malvasia Nera Lunga

WHERE IT'S FOUND: Piedmont. NATIONAL REGISTRY CODE NUMBER: 363. COLOR: red.

Also called Moscatella (a name more commonly used for the white-berried Malvasia Moscata) in the province of Alessandria and even Moscato Nero in the area between Asti and Turin, both of these are erroneous aliases. Malvasia Nera Lunga is an aromatic variety with a much greater ampelographic resemblance to Moscato di Scanzo than the other two red Piedmontese *Malvasias* have. It is clearly recognizable by its very long and medium-large bunch with one or two wings and medium-round berries. It is less vigorous than Malvasia di Schierano but a much more regular and generous yielding variety. Even better for farmers who make their living by tilling the land in Piedmont, a region known for its cool, rainy, and capricious fall weather, Malvasia Nera Lunga ripens at least a full two weeks before Malvasia di Schierano. No official clones are available as yet. Nowadays, Malvasia Nera Lunga is usually found in vineyards mixed in with Malvasia di Schierano in the townships of

Albugnano, Berzano, Castelnuovo Don Bosco, Moncucco, Passerano, Marmorito, and Pino d'Asti, and is sporadically present in the provinces of Asti, Alessandria, and Turin. It ripens earlier and is more disease resistant than Malvasia di Schierano, but it is also less acid and tends to overripen easily. From an aromatic perspective, while Malvasia di Schierano expresses aromas of both geraniol and linalool, Malvasia Nera Lunga expresses mainly geraniol. Interestingly, when high yields are produced, the berries are only lightly colored. Some local producers have told me that a blend of Malvasia di Schierano and Malvasia Nera Lunga produces the best wines, but they *would* say that, given that most own vineyards where the two cultivars are interplanted. That said, most Malvasia di Castelnuovo Don Bosco today probably is a blend of the two. However, when pressed, producers will admit that, wine-wise, Malvasia di Schierano is the superior of the two varieties, but as it's more delicate, later ripening, and less productive, use of Malvasia Nera Lunga was almost inevitable.

WINES TO TRY: To date, there are no monovarietal wines, or at least none that are admittedly so.

Malvasia

WHERE IT'S FOUND: Alto Adige, Trentino. NATIONAL REGISTRY CODE NUMBER: 128. COLOR: red.

The rarest Italian Malvasia, also called Malvasier or, more rarely, Malvasia Nera di Bolzano (there's yet another Italian *Malvasia Nera* grape!), grown only in Trentino and Alto Adige, Malvasia is hard to find, as there are only sporadic vines growing in old vineyards. At least, some light has been recently shed on the variety by Cipriani, Spadotto, Jurman, Di Gaspero, Crespan, Meneghetti, et al. (2010) who have documented that it is a cross of Perera and Schiava Gentile, two varieties typical of the northern parts of Italy. Possibly even harder than finding Malvasia grapevines is trying to locate wines made with it—and I should know,

after years spent trying. The few I have been able to try, courtesy of local farmers, were characterized by ruby-red and salmon-pink hues, with lively acidity and medium body, and faint strawberry aromas and flavors. But I'm not comfortable with the identity of the grapes used to make the wines I was given to try. It seems likely some of the wines may have been made, in perfectly good faith, with the locally more abundant Moscato Rosa; then again, a few of the wines didn't strike me as being particularly aromatic (which Moscato Rosa certainly is), and if yields weren't the issue, then maybe I did get to try a true Malvasier wine after all.

WINES TO TRY: To date there are no monovarietal wines in Italy made with this variety—that I know of.

THE MOSCATO FAMILY

The *Moscato*s (Muscat, in English) comprise one of the largest groups of grapes, and include a rainbow of fragrant and colorful varieties, from yellow to pink to red to almost black. Though there are some Moscato-named varieties that are unrelated to the others, the majority are; hence I have defined them a family, instead of a group. The list includes all the best-known ones: Moscato Bianco, Moscato di Alessandria (in Italy, its official name is Zibibbo, but that name is used almost exclusively in Sicily), Moscato Giallo, Moscato Rosso di Madera (also known as Moscato Violetto in Italy and Muscat Rouge de Madère in France), Moscato Giallo, Moscato Rosa, Moscatello Selvatico, and Moscato d'Amburgo (or Muscat of Hamburg). Actually, for the longest time experts believed that apart from the name and a muscaty aroma and flavor, *Moscato*s shared little else in common. Today we know this is not true: unlike the *Malvasia* group, which is plagued by synonyms and homonyms, the *Moscato*s are actually related (to a degree, at least) and are closer to being a family than any other large group of Italian wine grapes. True, *Moscato* grapes differ, at times considerably, on ampelographic grounds: color of the berries, size of the cluster, shape of the leaf, flowering dates, harvest dates, and degree of aromatic expression. This last characteristic was once believed to be a distinguishing feature of members of the group: varieties were classified into the family or not based on the presence or absence of the *moscato* aroma. However, this was incorrect, for the muscat aroma alone is not enough to qualify a variety as being a *Moscato*. Mutations allow the muscat quality to be expressed by neutral varieties such as Chardonnay and Chasselas: such biotypes, erroneously called "clones," are called *musqué*. The molecules responsible for the aromatic quality of these grapes are mainly terpenic in nature (linalool, geraniol, and nerol) and are responsible for the aromas and flavors of apple or pineapple, honey, sage, and rose that are typical of the group. In Moscato wines, linalool plays the biggest role, but importantly, it lacks staying power (concentrations drop considerably after roughly three years in the bottle), and this is one of the reasons why most of these wines are best consumed fairly young.

Emanuelli's research team in 2010 went searching for the candidate gene (VvDXS) that expresses the muscat aroma. Their control population included forty-eight neutral varieties and ninety-five aromatic ones, seventy-two of which expressed a *Moscato* aroma (Emanuelli, Battilana, Costantini, Le Cunff, Boursiquot, and This 2010). Relative to the muscat aroma and flavor, DXS-1 (that is, 1-deoxy-D-xylulose-5-phosphate synthase 1) was identified as a strong candidate gene for muscat flavor determination, as DXS is an important regulatory enzyme of the mevalonate-independent pathway involved in terpenoid biosynthesis. Most likely, what helped propel the cultivation of varieties expressing the muscat aroma is that human beings consider it a positive, likable trait. This has also led to the creation of not just myriad other *Moscato* varieties but also the *musqué* clones of Chardonnay and Chasselas.

The first in Italy to shed light on the subject of *Moscato* parentage and family ties were Crespan and Milani (2001) and Costacurta, Crespan, Milani, Carraro, Flamini, Aggio, et al. (2003); in particular, the latter team stated all *Moscato* varieties developed, either directly or indirectly, from one of three main *Moscatos*, each in a distinct center of origin: Moscato Bianco (Greece), Moscato Giallo (Middle East), and Moscato di Alessandria (Egypt). A more recent study has further clarified the situation, demonstrating that in fact the main *Moscato* variety is Moscato Bianco, from which practically all other *Moscatos* developed, including both Moscato Giallo and Moscato di Alessandria (Cipriani, Spadotto, Jurman, Di Gaspero, Crespan, Meneghetti, et al. 2010). In fact, Moscato di Alessandria is the result of a natural crossing between Moscato Bianco and Axina de Tres Bias, an ancient table grape grown in Sardinia and the Greek isles. At the present state of knowledge, there are at least fourteen progenies of Moscato di Alessandria and Moscato Bianco.

To give just a few branches of this family tree, Moscato Giallo, Moscato di Scanzo, Moscato Rosa, and Moscato Violetto (not grown in Italy) all are direct descendants of Moscato Bianco, while its indirect descendants include (all of them also directly related to Moscato d'Alessandria) Moscato d'Amburgo, Moscatello Selvatico, and Moscatel Amarillo (not grown in Italy). It is unclear where Moscato di Terracina, a white-berried *Moscato* typical of the coast south of Rome fits in all of this; once thought to be related to Moscato Bianco (even though it has a greater morphological resemblance to Moscato d'Alessandria), it appears to be genetically distinct from both of these.

Some *Moscato* cultivars are among the oldest varieties known: Moscato Bianco was likely known in ancient Rome, if not earlier. The famous Uve Apiane of antiquity described by Pliny and other Roman men of letters are believed to have been for the most part *Moscatos* (Bianco, in particular) and not Fiano, as once believed. Apparently, the Uve Apiane were the same as the high-quality Anathelicon Moschaton described by the Greeks. Interestingly, though the word *moscato* is generally believed to descend from the Latin *muscus* or *muscatum*, and in turn, from *moschos* in Greek and *muchk* in Persian (experts postulate that in the beginning, the word *moscato* was used to describe the musky aroma produced by the male musk deer of Southeast Asia), that etymology has been questioned. In fact, the Latins referred to aromatic qualities as *suavitis* rather than *muscatum;* and Berta and Mainardi wrote in 1997 that the word *muscatum* was first used only in the 1200s, and was derived from the medieval Greek term *moscheuo,* meaning vine.

Today, Italy grows at least eight different *Moscato* varieties (at least, eight are officially recognized in the National Registry thus far), the most abundant of which is Moscato Bianco. Wine lovers would do well to become acquainted with this family of grapes, as some of their wines are among Italy's most interesting, and greatest.

THE WHITE-BERRIED MOSCATOS

Moscato Bianco

WHERE IT'S FOUND: Piedmont; throughout Italy. NATIONAL REGISTRY CODE NUMBER: 153. COLOR: white.

The most common of all *Moscato*s, not just in Italy but all over the world, Moscato Bianco (also rarely called Moscato di Canelli in Italy) is better known as Muscat Blanc à Petit Grains in France (though Muscat de Frontignan, Muscat de Lunel, and Muscat d'Alsace are locally important names); Moscatel de Grano Menudo, Moscatel de Grano Pequeno, Moscatel Morisco, Moscatel Castellano, and Moscatel Fino in Spain; Moscatel Branco, Moscatel Galego Branco, and Moscatel do Douro in Portugal; Moscato Mazas, Moschato Lefko, Moschato Spinas, Moschato Kerkyras, and Moschato Samou in Greece (the latter especially on the island of Samos); Gelber Muskateller or just Muskateller in Austria and Germany; Frontignan in Australia; and Muscatel in South Africa. Though it is a white grape, mutations can turn its berries pink to light-red, into a so-called Moscato Rosa (not to be confused with the true Moscato Rosa, a related but different variety that grows mainly in Trentino and Alto Adige), Muscat d'Alsace Rouge, Muscat à Petits Grains Roses, Muscat à Petits Grains Rouge (what Australians refer to as Brown Muscat, which therefore is a term that should not be used as a general synonym of Moscato Bianco), or Moscatel Galego Roxo (a Portuguese mutation of Moscato Bianco). Clearly, so many countries, people, color mutations, and *Moscato* relatives all contribute to a great deal of confusion about this grape, so wine lovers need to be careful about exactly what they are drinking. All over the world (and in most websites and books) there are myriad examples of wines called Muscat Blanc (when they are in fact made with Moscato di Alessandria) or Moscato Giallo (made with Moscato Bianco). I remember the incredibly hard time I had once in getting an Austrian wine producer to understand that his Gelber Muskateller was actually Moscato Bianco and not Moscato Giallo. Years later, he sent a lovely email telling me that he had proceeded with SSR profiling of his vines and was shocked to learn that his grandfather had gotten it wrong: they really had been growing Moscato Bianco, and not Moscato Giallo, all along. That said, it is still common to hear southern Italian wine producers refer to their Moscato Bianco grapes as Moscato Giallo, mainly because in sunny and warm climates this variety's grapes can turn a deep yellow color. Moscato Bianco is also characterized by relatively small berries, especially when compared to other members of the Muscat family: this explains its many aliases referring to this feature *("grano menudo," "grano pequeno," "à petits grains").*

Moscato Bianco is the progenitor of most known *Moscato* varieties. As strange as it may seem, practically all the red varieties of *Moscato,* including Moscato di Scanzo and Moscato Nero, are directly related to Moscato Bianco. Indeed, Moscato Bianco shares parent-offspring relationships with at least five other *Moscato* grapes (Moscato di Alessandria, Moscato di Scanzo, Moscato Violetto or Moscato

Rosso di Madera, Moscato Giallo, and the authentic Moscato Rosa) as well as Aleatico, all of which originated in Italy. This, plus the huge volumes of Moscato Bianco wine produced annually, and the almost twelve thousand hectares (11,729 hectares, to be precise) planted to it throughout Italy, make it unlikely that Moscato Bianco is anything but an Italian native grape, though some experts still favor a Greek origin. For this reason, I strongly disagree with those who continue to refer to this variety by its French name, Muscat à Petit Grains, as it is neither an original nor a particularly important grape variety of France. When writing about wine grapes, it behooves those in the know to call the variety either by its Italian name, Moscato Bianco, or by a Greek one.

Moscato Bianco and its wines have long and very strong associations with almost every Italian region. In Piedmont, Moscato Bianco has been grown since at least the 1300s, but its cultivation became especially important in the fifteenth century, when Duke Emanuele Filiberto di Savoia (Savoia was the reigning noble house of Piedmont, and later became Italy's first and only royal family) passed legislation limiting imports, in an effort to advance the cause of local wine production. Though it is truly grown all over Italy (I do not believe it is missing from any Italian region), Moscato Bianco is thus mainly associated with Piedmont, where it was highly popular in the sixteenth century, especially in the provinces of Asti, Alessandria, and Cuneo. A statute of La Morra (dated 1511) cites that any new vineyard had to be planted to at least one-fifth *muscatellum*. The most important centers of production were Canelli (thus the wine's alias) and Santo Stefano Belbo. From these towns, Moscato Bianco vines were shipped everywhere: a document from 1593 tells of an order for "vines of Moscatello" to be sent to the Duke of Mantua. Moscato Bianco became so important for the local Piedmontese economy that the Consortium of Moscato d'Asti was formed in 1932, two years before Barolo's.

Moscato Bianco has long made two of the country's most famous and best loved wines, Piedmont's Asti Spumante and Moscato d'Asti. Asti production was well described by Croce in 1606, when his Moscato wine proved so successful that he was forced to write the procedure down for all to use—or accept that people he didn't know would continue to pop by his home asking how to go about it. Croce made his sweet wine by stopping fermentation with repeated filtrations and rackings; though it's likely he didn't mean for the result to be a sparkling wine, it probably was, given his artisanal winemaking process. In 1865, Carlo Gancia imported the techniques he had learned in Champagne for performing secondary refermentation in the bottle and so, for a while, a Moscato "Champagne" wine was produced in Piedmont.

In Tuscany, Moscato Bianco was long at the heart of Montalcino's most prized wine, which was not Brunello, but moscadello di Montalcino (the wine's name is written *moscadello* not *moscatello*). A letter from Piero Aretino to a friend, dated 1540, thanks the missive's recipient for the gift of "delicate moscadello, round and light." At the beginning of the seventeenth century, Pope Urban VIII was known to be quite the fan of moscadello. At this time, it was already habitual for Montalcino's producers to make two versions of moscadello, one sparkling and another still, the latter from late-harvested grapes. However, moscadello was always a very expensive wine to make, and over time, Montalcino's producers preferred to concentrate on red wine production.

In Puglia, Moscato di Trani was always highly prized, such that the Moscato Bianco grape was locally referred to as Moscato Reale. Historically famous, the wine was already being sold by the Venetians in the thirteenth century, and it became so popular that in the fourteenth century Roberto d'Angiò, Count of Trani, had to limit exports from local and distant ports. Moscato di Trani's importance and prestige were officially recognized when it became Puglia's first DOC wine in 1974. In Sicily, Moscato Bianco grapes have always been grown amid all the Moscato di Alessandria, and wines made with it, such as Moscato di Noto and Moscato Siracusa, have a long and distinguished history. In fact, some experts believe Moscato di Siracusa to be the most ancient wine made in Italy, a direct descendant of Pollio or Biblino, a wine named in honor of King Tracio Pollio, who governed Syracuse in the seventh century B.C.E.

In Sardinia, Moscato Bianco was first documented in the sixteenth century as Moscadeddu, but there was also a Moscatellone grown on the island, most likely Moscato di Alessandria, which was felt to be better as a table grape or raisin. Studies are under way to select biotypes of Sardinian Moscato Bianco for propagation. Recently, Anna Schneider and her team at the Istituto di Virologia Vegetale in Grugliasco also studied Liguria's Moscatello di Taggia, likely a biotype of Moscato Bianco. The wine made from this variety was popular in the fifteenth century, and Carassale describes it being traded in most western Mediterranean ports, Britain, and Flanders. That history helps explain interest in both the variety and the wine; the Mammoliti, Barucchi, and Rodi estates have all worked closely with the Fratelli Obice nursery in Santo Stefano Belbo, who specialize in the reproduction and propagation of *Moscato* vines.

Moscato Bianco is also hugely popular nowadays, and its wines sell extremely well. Garoglio believed the best soils for Moscato Bianco were those formed from the breakdown of ancient marine deposits from the Quartenary period, as these increase the wine's musky, aromatic qualities. According to star producers Aldo Vajra, Paolo Saracco, and Pietro Ratti (whose father Renato wrote about Moscato Bianco) Moscato Bianco does best on marly-clay soils, specifically those formed in the Middle and Late Miocene eras (especially the former), a fact apparently known to our ancestors, according to Strucchi and Zecchini. Not by chance, the areas of Canelli, Santo Stefano, and Loazzolo are true *grand crus* for Moscato Bianco and all boast soils formed during the Middle Miocene, very lightly chalky and limestone-rich. Similar soils are also found in the provinces of Alessandria and Cuneo though not to the same extent, due to a higher presence of clay, but Moscato Bianco thrives there too.

For all its popularity today, Moscato Bianco was never a huge favorite of growers, as it's a difficult variety to work with. In fact, the latest agricultural census data shows an 11.7 percent decrease in Moscato Bianco plantings from 2000 to 2010. There are reasons. First, Moscato Bianco is a late ripener, and in northern regions such as Piedmont this leads to problems come fall. It is also prone to most common grapevine pests, including hymenoptera and mites, and its thin-skinned berries mean more difficulties when grapes are near optimal ripeness. Furthermore, it likes well-exposed sites with plenty of sunlight: such sites help defend against peronospora, which Moscato Bianco is very sensitive to, but they are less helpful against oidium, to which the variety is also sensitive. Botrytis bunch rot can also have a field day with this variety, but the fact that its clusters are often loosely packed makes this less of a problem. To its favor, while Moscato Bianco prefers cooler temperatures, it is remarkably adaptable, and thrives even in warmer conditions provided the heat is not excessive and is tempered by winds and breezes. Moscato Bianco's ability to stand the heat is well exemplified by how it thrives in warmer parts not just of Italy (such as Puglia, Sicily, and Sardinia), but also of France, Greece, Portugal, and Spain, though quite often the best vineyard sites in these warmer lands are found at higher elevations (three hundred meters above sea level and up) or have northern exposures. Still, with such disease sensitivity, and smaller berries than most other *Moscato*s, it's clear why this cultivar was not the darling of our farming ancestors. Due to the difficulties Moscato Bianco presents in the field, it's not surprising that nurseries have worked long and hard at selecting and propagating the more resistant, perfumed, and productive varieties, which explains the large number of clones available to estates looking to plant it. Most commonly used are R 2, Fedit 6, MB 25 Bis, CN 4 (small bunch), CVT CN 16 (a very interesting clone that provides plenty of terpenes and structure), CVT AT 57 (medium-small, moderately compact bunches), AL-MOS-30, VCR 3 (medium bunch and very thick skins), and CVT 190 (medium-small, moderately compact bunches).

Moscatello di Castiglione is a recently rediscovered grapevine that is a site-specific biotype or ecotype of Moscato Bianco typical of the Casauria area of Abruzzo, where it was first described in the 1400s. Together with the Regione Abruzzo and the University of Bari, the Angelucci estate had the variety studied ampelologically (that is, with both ampelographic and genetic tests), and determined it to be a biotype of Moscato Bianco, improperly called "clone." The variety is now available for propagation from certified nurseries and has been labeled Moscato Bianco "clone Casauriense" or UBA-RA-MO 16.

According to Angelucci, Moscato Bianco and Moscatello di Castiglione differ considerably ampelographically; the latter is distinguished by slightly longer internodes, a more stocky, compact bunch, and a rounder and thicker-skinned, smaller berry. They also point out the variety is especially rich in linalool, rather than geraniol. Domenico Pasetti of the Pasetti estate also makes a Moscatello di Castiglione wine and thinks the variety shares features with Moscato Giallo and Moscato Bianco, though the variety is clearly a biotype of Moscato Bianco. "From a viticultural perspective," he says, "its ampelographic characteristics and kinetics of air-drying make it similar to Moscato Giallo, while its enological behavior and aromatic profile are more typical of Moscato Bianco." It seems to grow best on clay soils that are not too humid, such as the soils of the townships of Castiglione a Casauria, Pescosansonesco, and parts of the townships of Pietranico and Tocco Casauria. Compared to the Moscato Bianco grown elsewhere in Italy, it is always characterized by lower productivity.

Which Wines to Choose and Why

Moscato Bianco is a real chameleon when it comes to wine: several different wine styles are produced from it not just in Italy but all over the world—from light-bodied, perfumed dry and off-dry whites, to rich and sweet late-harvest table wines, to the unique fortified styles Australia is famous for. When not shriveled to raisiny extremes, Moscato Bianco is remarkable in that it delivers a wine that actually tastes of grapes: its intense and highly characteristic aroma and flavor profiles are such that the grape variety used to make the wine is virtually unmistakable. In contrast to Moscato Giallo and Moscato di Alessandria, the other two most important white-berried *Moscato* varieties, it is capable of producing both dry and off-dry wines with real finesse and an extremely pure, hauntingly refined floral aroma that though highly aromatic, is less obviously spicy. If there is one weakness to Moscato Bianco, it is its relatively low acid levels; therefore, most of the wines made from it are best enjoyed young, though this is by no means an all-encompassing rule.

Given the positives about its wines, it cannot be a surprise that Moscato Bianco plays a dominant role in at least thirteen Italian DOC and DOCG wines. It is used to make wines in Italy's extreme north (the Valle d'Aosta) and its deep south (Puglia, Sicily, and Sardinia). Therefore, not all of southern Italy's Moscato wines are made with the heat-resistant Moscato di Alessandria. Italy's best-known Moscato Bianco wines are those of Piedmont, such as the DOCG Moscato d'Asti, usually bubbly and delicately sweet, but also available in an air-dried, very sweet dessert-style version. Moscato d'Asti is made by keeping freshly pressed Moscato Bianco juice at about 0°C in autoclaves, where about half the residual sugar present is fermented to alcohol and the rest is left as natural sweetness. Asti Spumante, a less-important DOCG wine, is obtained by refermentating moscato wine in autoclaves; the wine is then bottled under isobaric conditions so that the foam is very minute and intense. This means that the wine is bottled at a higher pressure, usually around 4.5 or 5 Bar. compared to Moscato d'Asti's maximum of 1.7 Bar.; hence the latter is a softer, creamier, less-sparkling wine.

Other wines of note are Tuscany's moscadello di Montalcino, a name that harkens back to the medieval moscatellum with which Moscato Bianco is identified, though it also has an unfortunate association with Moscatello Selvatico, a related but different variety. However, according to no less an expert than Franco Biondi-Santi of the world-famous Montalcino estate, Moscadello di Montalcino used to be made with a local variant that differed substantially from the typical Moscato Bianco. Was it an altogether different variety or just a site-specific biotype? We don't know, yet, though all the producers I have talked to over the years agree that modern nursery plantings have been of the Moscato Bianco grown everywhere else. In an effort to recuperate the original variety that was at the heart of Montalcino's famous wine, the well-known Montalcino Col d'Orcia estate performed massal selections a decade ago by literally sending their people (clearly, with permission) into other estates' vineyards, looking for the original Montalcino *Moscato* variant. Franco Biondi-Santi believed the original biotype (or is it an altogether separate variety?) produced richer, deeper, and more fragrant wines. Moscadello di Montalcino is usually made in a late-harvest or air-dried style, and is frankly sweet; very few producers still make it in the sparkling version that was once also made.

In Valle d'Aosta, the wonderful Chambave Moscato is 100 percent Moscato Bianco, grown in the countryside around the pretty little town of Chambave in the middle part of the region. It is available in dry and sweet styles, the latter made from air-dried, or *flétri* grapes.

There are four very interesting Moscato Bianco wines made in southern Italy. Puglia's moscato di Trani, once famous but forgotten in the latter part of the twentieth century, is now starting to make a comeback, thanks to a handful of small, quality-conscious producers such as Franco di Filippo and Villa Schinosa. The former is a young seventy-something who one year saw his grapes refused by the big outfit he had annually sold them to, because of its economic difficulties. He decided to make and bottle the wine on his own, and met with such success that he hasn't had to look back since. I have visited his old, canopied vineyards even in July and can vouch for the fact that the Moscato Bianco bunches look healthy and well under their copious leaf canopy, an ideal training system considering Puglia's stifling summer heat—I was just as happy as the grapes to be standing under those leaves.

In Calabria, moscatello (or moscato) di Saracena has seen a notable increase in production over the last ten years, thanks mainly to the success enjoyed by the Cantine Viola estate. It is made mainly with the Moscatello di Saracena variety (and small percentages of a few other local varieties), also called Zibibbeddu in the area around Ferruzzano; Moscatello di Saracena is considered to be a local biotype of Moscato Bianco. By contrast, Calabria's moscato bianco di Scalea is not made with Moscato Bianco at all, but rather Moscato Giallo. Unfortunately, while in Italy's south it is an old habit to refer to Moscato Bianco as Moscato Giallo, there actually are a few, rare plantings of true Moscato Giallo down south as well. Sicily's moscato di Noto and moscato di Siracusa are excellent wines, though some recently successful wines from Noto tasted to me as if they had been made with a good dollop of Moscato di Alessandria. Moscato di Noto can also be made as a very sweet *passito*, and is typical of eastern Sicily, near Noto, Pachino, Rosolino, and Avola (close to Syracuse). Good, authentic moscato di Noto speaks of white muscat grown in warmer climates, and is a perfumed, lightly sweet wine full of grapefruit and rose aromas and flavors, but with a creamier, lower-acid mouthfeel and obvious saline tang compared to Moscato Bianco dessert wines made in Piedmont or in cooler Italian regions. In contrast to Noto's recent success, production of moscato di Siracusa has tailed off in recent decades, and risked disappearing altogether with the demise of the Cappello winery. Thankfully, the Pupillo estate produced five thousand bottles of the 1997 vintage and so this wine, though not the easiest to find, continues to exist. As a general rule, moscato di Siracusa is always less thick and sweet than moscato di Noto, and this is true even when comparing the *passito* versions of both. Certainly, its aroma profile is closer to a lighter, fresher moscato than to moscato di Noto.

In Sardinia, Moscato Bianco is used to make three DOC wines: moscato di Sardegna, moscato di Cagliari, and moscato di Sorso-Sennori. The last of these, produced only in those two townships, is made in a naturally sweet and fortified style called Liquoroso Dolce Naturale; its production guidelines demand lower yields. Moscato di Cagliari can be made only in Oristano and Cagliari and exists in both a Liquoroso Naturale and a Liquoroso Naturale Riserva, while the sparkling version *(spumante)* can be made anywhere on the island. In Abruzzo, the Moscatello di Castiglione subvariety gives honeyed and lightly aromatic wines, with floral and grapefruit aromas and flavors. I find there is a hint of lavender on the finish, as well as an intriguing saline tang; the wine has a viscous mouthfeel but not the highest possible acidity.

There are many interesting Moscato Bianco wines made outside Italy. In Australia, De Bortoli produce a slew of good Italian-like sparkling wines under different brand names such as Emeri, in both white and pink versions. The latter are called Pink Moscato wines and are not made with the true Moscato Rosa but are rather Moscato Bianco wines to which about three percent Shiraz is thrown in for a little added color. Of course, the most famous Australian Moscato Bianco wines are those of Rutherglen and Glenrowan in northeast Victoria, such as those made by Chambers Rosewood (an estate that has garnered extremely high critical praise and scores for its Rare and Grand Muscat wine bottlings over the decades) and Morris. These fortified, extremely sweet wines are wood-aged in often hot tin sheds and are really a must-try for anyone in love with wine; but as great as they are (and they are), they don't even vaguely resemble wine made with Moscato Bianco in Italy.

Of course, there are numerous fine examples of Moscato Bianco wines made in France, many of which are fortified, such as those labeled Vin Doux Naturel: Muscat du Cap Corse by Domaine Antoine Arena and the Muscat de St. Jean de Minervois by Domaine de Montahuc immediately come to mind but these are just a few among a very impressive list of wines. The best non-fortified French examples are those of Alsace, but beware that wines labeled Muscat in Alsace are almost always a blend of Moscato Bianco with Muscat Ottonel, a very popular, intensely aromatic variety that isn't grown much in Italy. Alsatian Muscat wines can be anywhere from half to as much as 95 percent blends of these two grapes, usually in favor of the more popular, easier to grow Ottonel variety. In Greece, the island of Samos has historically been associated with very fine and much sought-after Moscato Bianco production. The Union of Winemaking Cooperative of Samos makes a series of splendid wines, such as the fortified Samos Anthemis (also good: Samos Nectar and Samos Grand Cru). Over on mainland Greece, Moscato Bianco grows in Patras and Cephalonia, most often planted higher up and in north-exposed vineyards. Try the Muscat de Rio Patras by Paraparoussis, made from grapes grown on the northern coast of the Peloponnese, just east of Patras. This is not a fortified wine, but made from air-dried grapes (at least, the 2006 vintage I tried recently was so made). In Austria, very good examples of Gelber Muskateller wines are made by the extremely talented folks at Wenzel or Heiss Tschida.

Another non-fortified Moscato Bianco wine, and perhaps the most famous of all, is made in South Africa: Vin de Constance by Klein Constantia. A wine loved by Frederick the Great and Bismarck, it was also mentioned regularly in famous works of literature. In *The Mystery of Edwin Drood,* Charles Dickens tells of "the support embodied in a glass of Constantia and a home-made biscuit," and in *Sense and*

Sensibility, Jane Austen recommended Constantia for "its healing powers on a disappointed heart." The wine is a late-harvest gem that after years of oblivion was back in production at the estate with the 1986 vintage from vines planted in 1982. Nedeburg Private Bin Eminence is also a potential standout South African Moscato Bianco.

In the United States, Moscato Bianco has long been popular: in 2012, domestic sales by volume of Muscat wines overtook those of Sauvignon Blanc wines and now sit in third place after those of Chardonnay and Pinot Grigio, though Muscat wines sell at much lower retail prices. Wines are labeled either as Muscat Blanc or Muscat Canelli; the once-common Muscat Frontignan name was ruled inadmissible by the U.S. Bureau of Alcohol, Tobacco and Firearms in 1996, and was disallowed from labels after 1999. Excellent examples of California Moscato Bianco wines include those by Callaway Vineyard and Winery, Wilson Creek Winery and Vineyard, Cougar Cellars, and Bolero Cellars in Temecula Valley (the sweet Muscat Canelli by Bolero Cellars won Best Dessert Wine at the 2012 Temecula Valley Balloon and Wine Festival), Navarro Vineyards, Eberle Winery, St. Supery, Vino Noceto (they use Moscato Bianco on the label, but it's actually a blend of Moscato Bianco and what they call Orange Muscat), Lange Twins Winery and Vineyards, Wattle Creek Winery, Tobin James, and Husch Vineyards (I particularly like their version). Merryvale makes a wine called Antigua that is 100 percent Moscato Bianco (still named Muscat de Frontignan on their website, though not on the wine's label) fortified with fine pot-still brandy. California's Treatch Cellars makes a sparkling Moscato wine called Cuve'e de Frontignan (Cuve'e is their spelling), but that is made with Moscato di Alessandria grapes.

Moscato Bianco is also popular in Washington, where Inland Desert Nursery, Washington's largest commercial grape nursery, sold out their *Moscato* planting material (only a small portion of which was Moscato Bianco) in 2011 and 2012. In Washington, Moscato Bianco is mainly a blending grape. There are some old vineyards of Moscato Bianco (usually referred to as Muscat Canelli), such as the one at Phil Church Vineyards in the Yakima Valley, planted in the late 1970s and still in production. Now sold to Precept Wines, the contract for those grapes was first held with Covey Run, which made Muscat Canelli wine with the grapes, then with Ste. Michelle Wine Estates. Moscato Bianco wines are also made in many other U.S. states such as Indiana (Chateau Thomas) and New Mexico (Blue Teal Winery); I visited the latter winery (associated with other wine labels such as St. Clair, all under the same ownership) just a few years ago and found it to have a pretty and very large tasting room. Not all the wines are successful, and there's plenty of room for improvement, but it's great to see Italian varieties thriving in lands as far removed from the mother country as is beautiful New Mexico, and that people there wish to try their hand at making wine from them.

WINES TO TRY: For Moscato d'Asti, try: Paolo Saracco***, La Spinetta*** (Bricco Quaglia and Biancospino), Borgo Maragliano** (La Caliera), Ca' d' Gal** (Vigna Vecchia), Ca' du Sindic-Sergio Grimaldi** (Capsula Argento), Elio Perrone** (Clarté), and GD Vajra**; for Piemonte Moscato, try: Paolo Saracco*** (Moscato d'Autunno), Marchesi di Gresy*** (L'Altro Moscato); for Loazzolo, try: Forteto della Luja*** (Piana Rischei Vendemmia Tardiva) and Borgo Maragliano** (Vendemmia Tardiva). For Asti, try: Contratto*** (De Miranda Metodo Classico), Cascina Fonda*** (Bel Piasi), and Caudrina** (Dolce La Selvatica). For Moscadello di Montalcino, try: Col d'Orcia*** (Pascena), La Poderina***, Capanna**, Caprili**, Il Poggione**, Silvio Nardi**, Banfi* (Florus), and Camigliano* (L'Aura). For Moscato di Noto and Noto Passito, try: Planeta*** (Noto Passito, an outstanding wine) and Marabino** (Moscato di Noto Passito Moscato della Torre). Other producers, whose wines I have not tried lately, include Rio-Favara** (Notissimo), Orazio Candido*, and

Feudo Rudini*. For Moscato di Siracusa, try: Pupillo** (Solacium, late harvested and sweet, and Pollio, less sweet), Fausto Consiglio*, Barone Beneventano*, and Laganelli*. For Moscatello di Castiglione, try: Angelucci***, Galassi**, Zaccagnini**, and Pasetti*. Moscatello di Saracena: Cantine Viola**, Feudi di San Severino**.

Moscato di Terracina

WHERE IT'S FOUND: Lazio. NATIONAL REGISTRY CODE NUMBER: 281. COLOR: white.

Moscato di Terracina, previously thought to be very similar to and related to Moscato Bianco, though it actually resembles Moscato di Alessandria more, is apparently genetically distinct from all the known *Moscatos*. The vineyards are located close to the Lazio seashore in the province of Latina, about an hour south of Rome. Hence the grapes are subjected to warm winds, marine breezes, and plenty of salt in the soil, but have adapted remarkably well over the decades to what are fairly extreme living conditions. Depending on the biotype, the grapes are characterized by compact or loosely-packed but always fairly large, pyramidal-conical bunches and medium-large, round, yellow-green grapes. It ripens early, in late August or early September. There are no official clones available yet.

Which Wines to Choose and Why

Both the variety and wine have been a remarkable success story. In 2002 there was only one producer of Moscato di Terracina wine; today there are six producers and over one hundred vine growers. The variety has always been important for the local economy: in the 1820s, cultivation of Moscato di Terracina was the prime source of income for the area of Terracina, and wines were regularly exported to northern Italy and Germany. The wine can be made in a variety of styles, including sparkling (these have to be 100 percent monovarietal), *secco* (dry), *amabile* (off-dry), and *passito* (sweet).

WINES TO TRY: Sant'Andrea*** (Oppidum Secco, Templum Amabile, Capitolium Passito), and now a sparkling wine (Spumante Secco Oppidum and Spumante Amabile Templum), Terra delle Ginestre**, and Villa Gianna.

Moscato Giallo

WHERE IT'S FOUND: Alto Adige, Trentino, FVG, Veneto. NATIONAL REGISTRY CODE NUMBER: 154. COLOR: white.

Moscato Giallo is also called by its German name, Goldenmuskateller, in Alto Adige, and is not to be confused with the Gelber Muskateller of Germany and Austria, which is Moscato Bianco. Less often, one hears it referred to as Moscato Sirio or Moscato di Siria—it was once thought to originate in the Near East. In reality, there is no proof that Moscato Giallo hails from Syria, and the fact that it has been proven to be either a grandchild or half-sibling to four other *Moscatos* (Moscato di Scanzo, Moscato Rosa, Moscato di Alessandria, and Moscato Violetto or Muscat Rouge de Madèire) and one *Moscato*-like variety (Aleatico), all of which originated in Italy, makes its oriental origin very unlikely. Furthermore, it is an offspring of Moscato Bianco, most likely also an Italian native. For all these reasons, while some experts still argue about the possible Greek origins of Moscato Bianco and Moscato di Alessandria, there are no such doubts about Moscato Giallo, which is considered a true Italian native.

Moscato Giallo is generally characterized by rather large and elongated, pyramidal, sparse bunches with one to two wings and round, thick-skinned, bright-yellow berries. Appearance and viticultural behavior depend on the clone or biotype observed; there are seven officially certified clones (R 1, VCR 5, VCR 102, ISV-V-5, ISV-V-13, VCR 100, and CRSA-Puglia-F 38). A vigorous variety, it's also a fairly early ripener (harvest ranges from late August to mid-September), it's very susceptible to *millerandage* in rainy springs and to phomopsis, but has good disease resistance overall. In fact, its grey rot resistance differentiates it considerably from Moscato Bianco. Moscato Giallo is very sensitive to iron-deficient soils (chlorosis is a problem), and performs best on calcareous or volcanic slopes. It prefers generally cooler temperatures: therefore its presence in Italy is limited to northern regions such as Trentino and Alto Adige, with very small plantings in Friuli Venezia Giulia, Veneto, Lombardy, and Emilia-Romagna. At times, you will hear or read of a Moscato Giallo grape or wine from Sicily, but that is an incorrect use of the name, since the variety planted there is Moscato Bianco. In Veneto, there has always been a wine called Moscato Fior d'Arancio, made, confusingly, with Moscato Giallo, rather than the rare *Moscato* variety Moscato Fior d'Arancio, which is uncommon in Veneto (including that of the Padova countryside, mistakenly believed by many to be Moscato Fior d'Arancio, but it too is Moscato Giallo). True Moscato Fior d'Arancio (the Orange Muscat of California) is instead sparsely cultivated in Trentino: according to Crespan and Milani (2001), it is related to little-known *Moscato* varieties such as Moscato Jesus and Moscato Bianco Grosso. Though I imagine vines of true Moscato Fior d'Arancio may be found in the Colli Euganei, vineyards there are planted almost exclusively to Moscato Giallo and Moscato Bianco. The former is the *Moscato* used to make the DOC wine Colli Euganei Moscato Fior d'Arancio, while the latter is the main player in Colli Euganei Moscato.

As Moscato Giallo prefers cooler environments, it is not surprising that this grapevine is also found, albeit in limited numbers, in Switzerland (where it is also called Muscat du Pays), Austria, Germany, and Hungary. Determining just how common Moscato Giallo grapevines really are remains a difficult chore since the variety is confused with Moscato Bianco grapevines everywhere.

Which Wines to Choose and Why

Moscato Giallo wines are very different from those made with the other white-berried *Moscatos*. In fact, with a little practice, it is virtually impossible to confuse them with any other *Moscato* wines. Just as with the other members of this large family, both dry and sweet wines are made. In contrast to Moscato Bianco wines, those made with Moscato Giallo have aromas that are more reminiscent of yellow flowers and of sweet spices (cinnamon, nutmeg). Orange blossom is typical in moscato giallo too, but overall the nose is more herbal and spicier and has neither the penetrating grapey quality of moscato bianco nor the figgy, date, and saline quality of moscato di Alessandria. Moscato giallo smells and tastes less of fresh grapes than does moscato bianco and less of raisins than does moscato di Alessandria. Furthermore, moscato giallo is usually even lower in acidity, and therefore always seems sweeter (even when dry) than moscato bianco. Last but not least, Moscato Giallo wines are rarely made as sparkling wines. The most important and best monovarietal Moscato Giallo wines are the DOC Trentino Moscato Giallo and the Alto Adige Moscato Giallo (labels may read Goldenmuskateller). Moscato Giallo gives an amazingly wonderful dry wine that exudes almost intoxicatingly intense floral and spicy aromas and flavors (grapefruit, mango, lychee, orange blossom, broom, cinnamon, nutmeg, and white pepper), the best examples of which you will not easily forget. The very sweet late-harvest or air-dried style labeled *passito* has thick honeyed tropical fruit and sweet spice aromas and flavors. These wines are among Italy's best, thick and voluptuously sweet, though they can at times seem a little low in acidity, given the extremely high residual sugars.

WINES TO TRY: For Alto Adige Passito, try: Caldaro*** (Serenade Castel Giovanelli), Merano*** (Sissi Graf von Meran), and Nalles Magré*** (Baronesse). For Alto Adige Moscato Giallo, try: Manincor***, Burggrafler** (Privat), and Castel Sallegg**. For Trentino's Moscato Giallo, try: Riccardo Battistotti**, Bolognani**, Gaierhof** (Dolce; this is a rather sweet wine). For Veneto's Colli Euganei Moscato Fior d'Arancio, try: Il Mottolo** (Passito Vigna del Pozzo), Conte Emo Capodilista** (Passito Donna Daria), and Monte Fasolo** (Passito Solone).

Zibibbo (Moscato di Alessandria)

WHERE IT'S FOUND: Sicily. NATIONAL REGISTRY CODE NUMBER: 343. COLOR: white.

Moscato di Alessandria is listed in the National Registry as Zibibbo, a name derived from the Arabic *zabīb*, which probably refers to a dried grape or raisin, though not all experts are in agreement. Zibibbo is the oldest name for this variety: a *zibibo* wine was documented in Sicily by Pietro Andrea Mattioli in 1563. By contrast, the name Moscato di Alessandria first appears only in 1713, in the catalogue of the Certosini Frères in Paris. According to Schneider, Mainardi, and Raimondi (2011), the Abbot Rozier provided a rather complete description of the variety in his 1793 *Dictionnaire d'agriculture*. Interestingly, Moscato di Alessandria or Zibibbo was already known by several synonyms at that time. The name Moscato di Alessandria is reasonable, because the variety was believed to originate in the Egyptian city of Alexandria, though it is far more likely that it was born either in southern Italy (Sicily, most likely) or Greece. Cipriani, Spadotto, Jurman, Di Gaspero, Crespan, Meneghetti, et al. (2010) have shown that Moscato di Alessandria was born of a natural crossing between Moscato Bianco and Axina de Tres Bias. The latter is also known as Trifera, Uva di Tre Volte, and Tre Volte l'Anno, names which refer to its ability to flower and crop three times a year. Dismayingly, a 2011 study by Myles, Boyko, Owens, Brown, Grassi, Aradhya, et al. came to a different conclusion than Cipriani's work, saying that Moscato di Alessandria is instead a progeny of Moscato Bianco and Black Morocco. The likely answer to the riddle is that Black Morocco and Axina de Tres Bias are synonymous, though I do not believe there is any hard genetic evidence detailing this yet (though the French name Marocain Noir for Axina de Tres Bias is very encouraging).

In any case, Moscato di Alessandria, along with Moscato Bianco, with which it shares a parent-offspring relationship, is the progenitor of at least fourteen different cultivars, some of which, like Grillo (Moscato di Alessandria × Cataratto Bianco) and Malvasia del Lazio (Moscato di Alessandria × Schiava Grossa) are extremely important varieties. The less abundant Moscatello Selvatico is also the result of a Moscato di Alessandria × Bombino Bianco natural crossing. Therefore, despite its name recalling Egypt and the city of Alexandria, the fact that the name Zibibbo is antecedent to that of Moscato di Alessandria (or Muscat of Alexandria) and that so many of these progeny also originated in Italy makes it likely that Moscato di Alessandria is a native Italian grape (or perhaps Greek). Current knowledge dictates that it is identical to several Spanish *Moscatos*—Moscatel de Jerez, Moscatel de Malaga, and Moscato Gordo Blanco—as well as to the Portuguese cultivar Moscatel de Setúbal (Lopes, Sefc, Eiras-Dias, Steinkellner, Laimer, and da Câmara Machado 1999) and to Greece's Moschato Alexandreias (Lefort, Anzidei, Roubelakis-Angelakis, and Vendramin 2000). The variety is known by many other synonyms in the Mediterranean countries where it grows: Angliko, Apostoliatiko, Limnos, and Moschato Limnos in Greece; Iskendiriye Misketi in Turkey; Moscatel Graúdo in Portugal; and an almost endless list in Spain, including, besides those already mentioned, Gordo, Moscatel de Chipiona, Moscatel de Grano Garda, and Salamanca. It is also called Lexia in Australia (derived from the word Alexandria); Muscat Berkain, Muscat El Adda, and Muscat de Fandouk in Algeria; and Muscat Raf-Raf in Tunisia. Last but not least, there are red-berried mutations of Moscato di Alessandria: Black Muscat of Alexandria (grown in the United Kingdom), Red Hanepoot (South Africa), and Flame Muscat (California). There are no official clones available of Moscato di Alessandria, so descriptions depend on the biotype you look at. Antonio Rallo of the Donnafugata estate in Sicily has told me that there still exist very rare plantings on the island of many different smaller-berried variants that are thought to be even better for fine wine production.

The vast majority of Moscato di Alessandria grapevines are characterized by large, compact bunches that are conical-pyramidal and slightly elongated in shape, with medium-large oval or round berries that have yellow-green, thick skins. The berries are noticeably bigger and juicier looking than those of Moscato Bianco. Moscato di Alessandria is susceptible to oidium and zinc deficiency. It is one of the most heat- and drought-resistant *Moscato*s, and also tolerates hot seaside breezes and windy conditions well. This explains its distribution in countries hugging the Mediterranean sea. In fact, it was once also known as Moscato Romano. It's still grown in large areas in Lower Egypt and there are documents attesting to its cultivation there in antiquity.

When you drink a "Muscat" wine from Sicily, Greece, Cyprus, or the Canary Islands, you are most likely drinking a wine made with Moscato di Alessandria, though Moscato Bianco also grows in the same areas. In fact, Moscato di Alessandria is the most common *Moscato* of the eastern Mediterranean. In France it is much less common than Moscato Bianco; quite the opposite instead in northern African countries (Egypt, Tunisia, Algeria), in California, Washington, South Africa (where it is the most common *Moscato* variety), Australia and South America, where it has given rise to a number of different crossings such as Cereza, Moscatel Amarillo, Torrontés Mendocino, and Torrontés Sanjuanino. In California, it grows mainly in the Central Valley, most notably around Fresno where I lived roughly two decades ago and was always surprised by just how well the variety seemed to thrive there. Interestingly, Washington's oldest *Moscato* vineyard, planted in 1917, is of Moscato di Alessandria and is still producing today: these 95-year-old vines are located on Snipes Mountain near Sunnyside.

Which Wines to Choose and Why

Perhaps because of its larger bunch and berries and some very thick, sweet wines it is associated with, Moscato di Alessandria is often unfairly described as a coarser member of the Moscato family, but that's an unfair description. In the hands of skilled producers, both dry and sweet wines made with Moscato di Alessandria can be a thing of beauty. The wine is always richer than those made with Moscato Bianco and Moscato Giallo, and usually have a more saline and raisiny quality, even in the dry versions. The sweet wines, rather than win you over with floral aromas of orange blossom (fairly typical of wines made with the other two *Moscato*s), are more about orange jam, caramel, sweet figs in sugar syrup, and raisins.

Moscato di Alessandria is typical of Sicily and especially the island of Pantelleria, a volcanic island jutting out into the sea and believed by some to be a vestige of Atlantis. The wines made here are archetypal of what the cultivar can deliver in the dry and sweet styles: the DOC Moscato di Pantelleria wine is fresh, dry, and aromatic, with aromas and flavors of dried herbs, lily of the valley, ginger, and apricot; the Passito di Pantelleria, made from air-dried grapes, is sticky-sweet and lusciously creamy, with obvious honey and orange marmalade aromas and flavors.

As Moscato and Passito di Pantelleria are two of Italy's best-known and most-loved wines, everyone wants to cash in on a supposedly easy payday, so there are countless truly horrible versions available. By that I mean they generally lack meaningful acidity so as to make them nothing more than just sweet "one sip at most" type failures. Therefore, knowing the better producers is absolutely key. Unfortunately, the difficulties tied to viticulture on Pantelleria (80 percent of which is a national park, so that planting new vineyards is difficult), the extreme working conditions (harvesting on hot volcanic rock is no picnic), and the impossibility of mechanical harvesting have greatly lowered wine production on the island over the last twenty years. Whereas there were 450,000 quintals (one quintal is equivalent to 100 kilograms) of grapes picked in 1973, there were only 240,000 in 1990, and a steep decline to the 28,000 picked in 2009. Fortunately, there are estates that believe in the variety and the wine, and are doing marvelous things with both. Donnafugata deserves much credit for having invested heavily in Pantelleria and the wine. Thanks to their efforts, differences in subzones are becoming clear: Moscato and Passito di Pantelleria made with grapes grown in different sectors of the island differ appreciably in aroma and flavor profiles. Areas (*contrade,* in Sicily) in the southern half of the island—such as Dietro Isola, Bukkuram, Martingana, and Coste di Barone—tend to have earlier ripening grapes that are best suited to air-drying. But even in those southern areas, wines made with grapes from Barone, which is located at four hundred meters above sea level tend to be lighter and more fragrant than those from Martingana, a warmer microclimate. The estate has also recuperated a seven-hectare vineyard in Khamma that is largely made up of pre-phylloxeric vines. Furthermore, in March 2010, Donnafugata set up an experimental vineyard planted to thirty-three different biotypes of Moscato di Alessandria (ten from Italy and twenty-three from Spain, Greece, and France), and is participating in a research project with Attilio Scienza of the University of Milan, to study this cultivar's biodiversity.

Not much Moscato di Alessandria is grown in Italy outside Sicily, so monovarietal wines are not to be found elsewhere. Instead, interesting wines are made with this variety in other countries. Look for the wines of Telmo Rodriguez (both dry Moscatel and sweet Moscatel de Malaga wines) and Jorge Ordoñez in Spain and those of Horácio Simões and Venâncio da Costa Lima in Portugal. Perhaps the most famous French wine made with Moscato di Alessandria is Muscat de Rivesaltes, but the wine is almost always a blend of both *Moscato* varieties.

Lenora Winery in California's Ramona valley makes a lightly sweet estate Muscat of Alexandria wine; Treatch Cellars makes two different wines with Moscato di Alessandria (my preference goes to the one labeled Muscat of Alexandria); I also remember liking Martinelli's 2002 Jackass Hill bottling quite a bit. Australia's Brown Brothers makes numerous wines called Zibibbo or Moscato (and one called Lexia), all made with Moscato di Alessandria. They also make pink versions of both Muscat-labeled wines: the pink color is obtained via the addition of small percentages of Cienna (a crossing of Sumoll, a grape variety from Spain, with Cabernet Sauvignon). In South Africa, look for Boplaas Family Vineyards, Lillypilly Estate, Sittella, and Stellar Organic Winery; Constantia Uitsig Winery makes a thrilling sweet version from Red Hanepoot (the rare red-berried mutation of Moscato di Alessandria found in South Africa but not in Italy) from the oldest vines on their estate.

WINES TO TRY: For Passito di Pantelleria, try: Donnafugata*** (Ben Ryè), Ferrandes***, Marco De Bartoli*** (Bukkuram), Coste Ghirlanda (L'Alcova), and Salvatore Murana* (famous thanks to some Italian wine guides, but I'm less impressed). For Moscato di Pantelleria, try: Donnafugata*** (Kebir), Coste Ghirlanda (Jardinu), Terzavia**, and Serragghia-Gabrio Vini*.

THE RED-BERRIED MOSCATOS

Moscato di Scanzo

WHERE IT'S FOUND: Lombardy. NATIONAL REGISTRY CODE NUMBER: 308. COLOR: red.

All those who grow up in Bergamo and love wine as I do cannot help but fall in love with Moscato di Scanzo. Luigi Veronelli, Italy's greatest wine expert ever (to whom I will always be indebted for much of what I know about Italian wines), used to live in Bergamo and extolled the virtues of Moscato di Scanzo at any chance he had. However, Moscato di Scanzo's many charms go far beyond halcyon memories of a gilded childhood or a soft spot for the local darling: the variety is rare and unique, the wine is great, and it's produced in the bucolic but steep hillsides around Bergamo, one of Italy's prettiest if least-known countrysides. For those who don't yet grasp the power of native grapes, business boomed once the DOCG was established in 2009: in the years following, one hotel, a couple of restaurants, and six bed-and-breakfasts and country inns have opened for business, "and all because of this wine," says Paolo Bendinelli, past president of the local consortium and a well-known producer of Moscato di Scanzo wine. Considering the only other noteworthy wines of the area are Valcalepio Bianco and Rosso, sorry Cabernet Sauvignon– or Chardonnay-based blends nobody clamors for, you understand the significance of having a truly good native grape and wine to promote.

The wine's name is that of the grape, and neither should ever be referred to as "Moscato Rosso" or "Moscato Nero," both names that refer to other varieties. The name Moscato di Scanzo derives from the town of Scanzorosciate, itself a combination of Scanzo, a centurion in Julius Caesar's army, and Rosciate, from *ros*, Greek for cluster of grapes. They have been making wine in Scanzorosciate since at least 1340 (the date of the oldest document attesting to the grape growing locally), but many historians and wine experts believe the grape and wine were known already to the ancient Romans. For all its current lack of notoriety, Moscato di Scanzo wine (then simply called moscato rosso) was long one of Italy's most famous wines, sought after by tsars, princes, and notables of sixteenth- and seventeenth-century Europe. Giacomo Quarenghi, an architect native to Bergamo (who designed many of St. Petersburg's most beautiful buildings, including the Winter Palace), is credited with starting the craze when he donated the wine to Catherine the Great, who was known to have been quite the fan (as a letter from December 15, 1784, documents). In 1820, author Giovanni Maironi Da Ponte wrote that the wine was famous all over Europe; prices of Moscato di Scanzo were even quoted on the London exchange in the eighteenth century (at one gold guinea a barrel) and the English were especially fond of it. It is believed they were among the first to suggest air-drying the grapes, and the result must have been to their liking, since the wine's price had increased to fifty guineas a barrel by 1850.

Moscato di Scanzo is the progeny of Moscato Bianco and another still-unknown parent, making it a direct relative of at least five other *Moscato*s or *Moscato*-like varieties. Researchers once suggested that it originated via a natural crossing of Moscato Bianco and Aleatico, but this seems less likely now (see Cipriani, Spadotto, Jurman, Di Gaspero, Crespan, Meneghetti, et al. 2010). However, both Moscato Bianco and Aleatico were varieties that Roman legionnaires were known to travel with when conquering new lands, and to plant once they settled down. In fact, according to the Moscato di Scanzo Consortium, Celso Lotteri wrote in 1852 that in the first century B.C.E., the Roman founders of the towns of Villa, Scanzo, and Rosciate, realized that local grapes were special and began production of a *Moscato* wine that soon was fetching higher prices than many of the wines then sold in Rome. However, we cannot be sure that the grapevine they used was in fact Moscato di Scanzo; perhaps the viticulture and enology department of the University of Milan and the Consorzio di Tutela, currently studying the genetic makeup of this *Moscato*, will shed light on the issue. Current Consorzio president Angelica Cuni says, "We wish to safeguard and shed light on Moscato di Scanzo's unique past, but to also improve the wine for future generations of wine lovers. In this respect, having identified as many as twenty-three possible clones is very important."

Moscato di Scanzo is an aromatic red grape that resembles but is different from Moscato Nero or Aleatico, red-berried varieties it is often confused with. Its pyramidal, elongated, and sparse bunch is medium-sized, just like its blue-black berries that are covered in copious bloom, giving them a velvety look. It has good disease resistance, but is susceptible to grey rot. It ripens in late September or early October, later than both Moscato Nero and most Aleatico except Elba's. It is also an excellent table grape, but the wine made is too scarce and expensive for the grapes to be used that way anymore.

Which Wines to Choose and Why

Moscato di Scanzo is Italy's smallest DOCG, at roughly six hectares, which produce only sixty thousand bottles, 20 percent of which are exported. Only wines made from Moscato di Scanzo grown in the countryside surrounding the towns of Scanzorosciate on Bergamo's doorstep can be labeled as Moscato di Scanzo. However, a very similar (and often just as good) wine named Valcalepio Moscato Passito is also made near Scanzorosciate, in the hills of the Valcalepio area (between the Seriana and Cavallina valleys, on the left side of the Serio River). In the past, these other *Moscato* wines carried the label of the town the grapes grew near, so there were, for example, also a Moscato Passito di Gandosso and a Moscato Passito di Castello di Grumello, all made a stone's throw from Scanzorosciate. Even considering the extended production area, with twenty-two producers in all and thirty hectares in total, estates here are Lilliputian, most producing between one thousand and four thousand bottles each year. Moscato di Scanzo is planted at relatively high altitudes (usually around 350 meters above sea level, though it can go quite a bit higher). The best wines are made from grapes grown in the marly-calcareous, whitish soils known locally as *"sass de luna,"* very friable, nutrient-poor soil in which the vines grow slowly and poorly, as there is very little topsoil; due to its grey-rot sensitivity, its grapes are trained high off the ground to increase air circulation.

Moscato di Scanzo is among the very few sweet red wines in the world that combine laser-like precision of spicy red berry and violet aromas and flavors and high but harmonious acidity. When they are not the product of excessively air-dried grapes, these wines have a lightness and fragrance to the wine that is truly rare. These wonderful wines—admittedly, a minority of those produced—won't strike you as having 15 percent or more alcohol (though they do) or as the result of air-drying grapes (though by law, air-drying proceeds for a minimum of twenty-one days, and most producers choose thirty to forty days). All the wines are fairly sweet and luscious; by law, they must have fifty to one hundred grams of residual sugar per liter and 4.5 grams per liter of total acidity. I have learned over the years that Moscato di Scanzo wines show obvious *terroir*-related differences, and that there are at least three *terroirs*. Spicy, red berry aromas and rich flavors are the norm in wines made in the classic zone around Monte Bastia, while those from the eastern part of the DOCG are fruitier and mineral, and those from the central part richer and thicker, with more black fruit (prunes even) and hints of cocoa.

WINES TO TRY: In the eastern section, try: La Brugherata*** (Doge), La Rodola*** (Passito, located just outside Scanzorosciate, in Trebulina), Il Frances*, and Savoldi*. For the most classic part of the production area, try: Pagnoncelli Folcieri*** and La Belèndesa*. For the central region, try: Il Cipresso*, La Bionda*, and Cerri*. Interestingly, producers have recently made dry wines with this variety: the Vermiglio di Roxia is a dry red wine made with 85 percent Moscato di Scanzo (and 15 percent Merlot or Cabernet Sauvignon). The inclusion of these latter two grapes might seem like cause for wonder, but in fairness, the international varieties have long been traditional to the Bergamo area and provide the dry wines with added backbone and aging potential.

Moscato Nero di Acqui

WHERE IT'S FOUND: Piedmont. NATIONAL REGISTRY CODE NUMBER: 155. COLOR: red.

Moscato Nero di Acqui is one of the many Moscato Neros that seem to colorfully dot many of the world's vineyards. In fact, most often these are completely unrelated varieties that only share the dark color of their berries. More often than not they are table grapes, rather than wine grapes, and are found growing all over Italy. Though a color mutation of Moscato Bianco may always be possible, true Moscato Nero di Acqui is a distinct variety; according to the 2001 study by Crespan and Milani, the two share a parent-offspring relationship. That study also identified Moscato Nero with Aleatico, another variety, but this is wrong: genetic profiling in that same study demonstrated that two Moscato Nero samples, obtained from two different ampelographic collections, were not the same variety. In 2009, Scalabrelli, D'Onofrio, Ferroni, and Vignai showed that Aleatico has a different molecular profile from Tuscan accessions of a Moscato Nero variety (or varieties). Last but not least, Moscato Nero di Acqui is not synonymous with Moscato d'Amburgo (Muscat of Hamburg), which in Italy is considered a table grape and is listed as such in the National Registry, at number 517.

Moscato Nero di Acqui is a lightly aromatic red variety (much less aromatic than Moscato di Scanzo, another red-berried *Moscato*) grown in Piedmont and described in detail by Di Stefano and Corino in 1984. It takes its name from Acqui, the town at the center of its production zone, but it is also sporadically found in the provinces of Asti and Alessandria. Though the grape is rare, incorrect synonyms abound: in Liguria it might be called Malvasia Nera, while in Piedmont it's occasionally called Aleatico or simply Moscato Nero (which creates confusion with Moscato di Scanzo, also improperly called Moscato Nero). Furthermore, the National Registry neither lists any synonyms of Moscato Nero di Acqui, nor lists it as a synonym of Moscato d'Amburgo. In 2006, Raimondi, Valota, and Schneider also reported failing to see any similarities between the two.

Historically, Moscato Nero di Acqui was always confused by farmers with Brachetto, another red-berried aromatic variety typical of the same Piedmontese area: generally speaking, many who believed they were growing Brachetto actually owned vines of Moscato Nero di Acqui. My belief is that, though undoubtedly rare, there is currently more Moscato Nero di Acqui planted in the vineyards than is commonly believed. In my experience, even those producers who were aware they were growing two different varieties usually just blended them together, since Moscato Nero di Acqui added much-needed tannic backbone to wines made with Brachetto. In fairness, and for accuracy's sake, not everyone did so. Carlo Daglio, of the Daglio estate, recalls that his family has been growing this variety at least since the 1800s, but that they never blended it in Brachetto wines, since they liked Moscato Nero di Acqui's specific aromatics. Over the years, other producers have told me the variety was also used to improve wines made with Malvasia di Casorzo.

It's characterized by medium-small, cylindrical-conical, and loosely packed bunches with one long wing and medium-large berries that have very little bloom, thereby appearing particularly shiny. This latter feature makes the variety extremely easy to recognize in my opinion, since it differentiates it completely from other dark-berried *Moscato*s and *Moscato*-like varieties such as Moscato di Scanzo or Brachetto. It's a vigorous variety that ripens relatively early (usually in the first half of September) but not a particularly generous producer due to its small bunch size; it is resistant to most common grapevine diseases. There are no officially certified clones available.

There are many reasons why Moscato Nero di Acqui fell out of favor with farmers and wine producers: since it's a poor to moderate producer, does not accumulate large amounts of sugar, and its typical *Moscato* aroma tends to degrade rapidly once the berries are ripe. On the positive side, Daglio believes it to be a hardy variety that adapts well to different soils. As it is an excellent table grape, it is also grown by local farmers with that purpose in mind.

Which Wines to Choose and Why

A good moscato nero is pinkish-red in hue, light and refreshing, and very delicately aromatic, with aromas of roses and geraniums (the grape has high concentrations of nerol, a molecule that smells strongly of roses), and of small red and black berries. Its aromas are gentler and lack the penetrating, intense quality of wines made with Moscato di Scanzo. It's however a very pleasant, delicious, light-bodied wine. Today most of the Moscato Nero di Acqui still present in old vineyards gets blended into Brachetto wines.

Elsewhere in the world, it is unlikely there are any Moscato Nero di Acqui vines to be found, unless some Piedmontese immigrants of centuries past decided to pack some away amid their suitcases. The black muscat wines made everywhere are usually made with the Muscat of Hamburg grape, though many times producers never bother to specify this, limiting themselves at a generic "Black Muscat" designation.

WINES TO TRY: Daglio** (Negher, a *rosato*) makes probably the only currently commercially available and monovarietal Moscato Nero di Acqui wine in Italy. Marco Gaudio at Bricco Mondalino owns a small vineyard of Moscato Nero di Acqui and the La Capetta estate is also replanting the cultivar. These producers have worked closely with Anna Schneider and Stefano Raimondi to provide virus-free grapevine material.

Moscato Rosa

WHERE IT'S FOUND: Alto Adige, Trentino, FVG.
NATIONAL REGISTRY CODE NUMBER: 156. COLOR: red.

This variety's name (Rosenmuskateller in Alto Adige) is not due to its berries or wine being pink (in fact the wine is a very deep crimson) but because the wine smells intensely of red roses. Moscato Rosa might have been first brought to Italy in the nineteenth century from Dalmatia as a wedding gift for a local young lady, though there have been many farfetched theories in this respect (even Peruvian and Oriental origins have been postulated). However, in a study comparing genotypes obtained from Croatian cultivars with those obtained from grapevines of neighboring regions, the Croatian grape Muškat Ruža Porečki (previously called Muškat Ruža Omiški) was proved identical to Rosenmuskateller, and this finding lends credence to a possible Dalmatian origin of the grape (Maletic, Sefc, Steinkellner, Karoglan Kontic, and Pejic 1999).

However, it's not so simple (and this being Italy, I'm not surprised): in the landmark 2001 study of the *Moscato* family by Crespan and Milani, three different Moscato Rosa accessions were analyzed (one originally from the countryside near Belgrade but growing in an Italian grapevine collection, one from Breganze in Veneto, and one from Trentino) and found to be completely distinct varieties. Actually, the Belgrade sample was a color mutation of Moscato Bianco, while the Breganze Moscato Rosa and the Trentino Moscato Rosa were truly different varieties. The Trentino Moscato Rosa is considered traditional to Italy and to be the true Moscato Rosa, and the variety's official name in the National Registry is, simply enough, Moscato Rosa (though this engenders confusion with the similarly named but rarer pink mutation of Moscato Bianco) and not Moscato Rosa del Trentino, a name that for accuracy's sake should therefore not be used. The Breganze Moscato Rosa is yet another Italian cultivar practically nothing is known about, more indication that limiting Italy's native grape count to less than four hundred varieties is a gross underestimation. In the past, researchers such as Calò, Scienza, and Costacurta (2001) believed Moscato Rosa should not be considered a *Moscato* at all; in those earlier times, when microsatellite testing was not quite as commonplace as it is today, the variety's high geraniol content (an aromatic molecule more commonly found in members of the *Malvasias*) was considered proof of a lack of "Moscatoness." However, in their study, Crespan and Milan carried out parentage analysis showing that Moscato Rosa has a parent-offspring relationship with Moscato Bianco, which therefore means that it is also either a half-sibling or grandchild of four other Moscato varieties: Moscato di Scanzo, Moscato Giallo, Moscato di Alessandria, and Moscato Violetto (very rare in Italy and perhaps better known elsewhere as Muscat Rouge de Madère).

Like other red-berried *Moscatos*, this variety also has an elongated, pyramidal, medium-large bunch and ripens in late September or early October; its berries are smaller than most, and have very thin skins, making them susceptible to botrytis. The flowers are physiologically female only, and so Moscato Rosa needs another pollinating variety present in the vineyards to avoid poor fruit set. Furthermore, it's affected by *millerandage,* making for very scrawny-looking bunches and often very low productivity. According to Willi Sturz, the winemaker at the excellent Tramin estate in Italy, Moscato Rosa is great for air-drying, as it dehydrates easily and quickly, "but it's miserly and I can attest it's a very irregular producer, due to poor fruit set—and its thin skins mean it's very susceptible to flowering issues should it rain. In some vintages, half of the potential production can be lost." Wally Plattner of the Waldgries estate points out that its difficult flowering often causes bunches to have berries of different sizes and ripeness levels, never a good thing, as unripe berries have to be manually removed in order to avoid making wines with green or vegetal flavors.

Which Wines to Choose and Why
Most common in Alto Adige, DOC wines labeled Alto Adige Moscato Rosa (or Rosenmuskateller) are best. Also worth a look are Trentino Moscato Rosa (though Moscato Rosa comprises only a minimum of 80 percent of the wine, as opposed to Alto Adige's 85 percent) and the Moscato Rosa made in DOC Friuli Isonzo of Friuli Venezia Giulia. There are sporadic plantings in Piedmont, Emilia-Romagna, and even Lazio, while I am tempted to speculate that Lombardy's old vines of Moscato Rosa might be of the Breganze variety. There are some mainly experimental and limited plantings in Austria, Germany, and Croatia.

Moscato Rosa wine is made in both a rare, lighter-styled but still sweet wine and as a thick, creamy, and very sweet *passito*. Plattner feels that sandy soils are ideal for sweet wine production with this variety since the grapes tend to dehydrate faster. For this reason, he points out that the area of Santa Maddalena, loaded with sandy soils, is ideal. On clay it tends to be very vigorous, but the water retention capacity of such soils appears to heighten the aromatics in the final wine. Sturz believes the best results are obtained by harvesting the grapes late instead of air-drying them, since the former technique maintains freshness and preserves the typical aromas and flavors of the variety, which tend to become jammy and less refined when the grapes are air-dried. A good moscato rosa is a thing of beauty for its extremely floral yet fruity aromas and flavors of rose, red cherry, strawberry jelly, and raspberry, together with notes of cinnamon, cloves, and nutmeg. Over the years, I have found that Moscato Rosa is the perfect wine to have people try when they say wine is not to their liking. Even those reluctant imbibers usually succumb to this beautifully colored, intensely perfumed sweet wine. The only high-quality non-Italian wine made with Moscato Rosa I know of is made in Austria: the Rosenmuskateller Trockenbereenauslese by Kracher is an extremely luscious and sweet wine that is utterly irresistible. Just beware that many "Pink Muscat" wines made outside Italy are in reality, almost always, wines made with Moscato Bianco to which a small percentage of juice or wine from red-berried varieties (Syrah, Durif, and more) is added. These are often made in a sparkling mode as well. They are therefore not, in any way, to be taken as typical of what Moscato Rosa and its wines are all about.

WINES TO TRY: For Alto Adige Passito, try: Schloss Sallegg*** , Tramin*** (Terminum), Waldgries*** (Passito), Franz Haas**, Muri Gries**, Abbazia di Novacella* (Praepositus), Bolzano* (Rosis), Colterenzio* (Rosatum), Girlan* (Pasithea Rosa), and Kettmeier* (Athesis). For Trentino, try: Zeni*** (Rosa; once light and fragrant, now very rich and sweet), Maso Martis**, Gaierhof*, Maso Bergamini*, Letrari*, and Battistotti*. For Friuli Venezia Giulia, try: Emilio Bulfon*.

Moscatello Selvatico

WHERE IT'S FOUND: Puglia. NATIONAL REGISTRY CODE NUMBER: 307. COLOR: white.

Fewer Italian grape varieties cause more errors among wine writers than this one. First, Moscatello Selvatico is a distinct cultivar, but *moscatello* has always been the generic name for varieties characterized by a delicate muscaty aroma and flavor, even though known not to be true *Moscato*s. Second, to further confuse matters, some wine producers have unfortunately chosen to name their wine moscatello even when it is made with known *Moscato*s, such as Moscato Bianco or Moscato di Alessandria. Perhaps the best example is Montalcino's famous moscadello (with a *d*) wine, which more than one writer has written is made with Moscatello Selvatico, fooled by the wine's name: in fact, moscadello di Montalcino is made, by law, with Moscato Bianco (though in Siena Province, up to 15 percent other cultivars is permitted for viticulture, and apparently Moscatello Selvatico is one of them). There are also Moscatello wines made in Calabria and Sicily that are *not* made with Moscatello Selvatico, so the word *moscatello* on a label guarantees nothing. Which of course in Italy is par for the course.

The beautiful Gargano (a tourist heaven) was already known in the 1700s due to its production of Moscatello wine though there is no way of knowing if the wines were made with Moscato Bianco, Moscatello Selvatico, or some other variety. In the landmark study of the *Moscato*s by Crespan and Milani (2001), Moscatello Selvatico is shown to be the offspring of Moscato di Alessandria and Bombino Bianco, a finding confirmed by Cipriani, Spadotto, Jurman, Di Gaspero, Crespan, Meneghetti, et al. (2010). Therefore, Moscatello Selvatico must be a grandchild of Moscato Bianco and Axina de Tres Bias (a rare variety still found in Sardinia that flowers and crops up to three times a year). Clearly, if Moscatello Selvatico really is the result of a natural crossing between two such well-known southern varieties, it seems less likely that it was brought to Italy by Greek colonists (a past assumption).

Historically, the famous Moscato di Novoli, known locally as Muscateddhra (or Moscatella) was believed to be produced from a biotype of Moscatello Selvatico, known today to be identical to Moscato di Barletta. Moscatello Selvatico's scarce modern-day diffusion can be partially explained by compatibility problems with the area's chosen rootstock, Berlandieri × Riparia 157. While Primitivo and Negro Amaro encountered no difficulties being grafted to 157, Moscatello Selvatico behaved miserly, with only two or three small bunches per vine. However, the aromas of the grapes and wines were spectacularly intense, and so, even though farmers were not thrilled at the volume of grapes and wines produced, they continued to grow a few vines. For this reason, Moscatello Selvatico survived in the Gargano area; another reason is that the locals appreciated it as a table grape and raisin. Moscatello wine was the typical quaff on the day of Santo Antonio's feast. Most often, Moscatello Selvatico is characterized by medium-large bunches and berries; the former are conical, the latter round. The grapes ripen relatively early in September, and are resistant to most pests. Productivity is good on the right rootstock and the usually large berries release copious amounts of juice. There are no official clones.

Antonio Guerrieri of Cantine Guerrieri in Puglia, whose family has done much to save and bring back Moscatello Selvatico, points out that the IGT Salento denomination only allows the word Moscato on the label, and not Moscatello, which is a shame. Antonio and his brother decided to plant the old grapevines grown by their uncle, against the wishes and suggestions of their father, who was completely unimpressed by the variety's poor productivity, and they are very happy with the results.

Which Wines to Choose and Why

True Moscatello Selvatico wines are not easy to find. The Centro Ricerca e Sperimentazione in Agricoltura (CRSA), the experimental research station in Locorotondo, produces excellent microvinifications every year and a number of producers do so as well. A good Moscatello wine is recognizably lighter in body and less intense in its aromas than a wine made from Moscato Bianco or Moscato Giallo; it is also less sweet and viscous than anything made with Moscato di Alessandria. It is a fresh, crisp, delicately muscaty wine that works wonderfully as an aperitif or with shellfish dishes or delicate ethnic cuisines. It is included in many IGT blends such as Daunia, Murgia, Salento, Tarantino, and Valle d'Itria; some of these wines are reportedly 100 percent Moscatello Selvatico.

WINES TO TRY: Guerrieri** (a ridiculously small number of bottles—two hundred for the 2010 vintage—so your only hope for a bottle is to visit Puglia), Speziale 1855* (Ualani Moscatello Selvatico, from organically farmed grapes), and CRIFO* (Augustale Oro).

THE NEGRARA GROUP

Negrara Trentina is currently the most important of what is one of Italy's smaller groups of grapes, the *Negrara*s. Like other Italian grape groups, the *Negrara* grapevines have highly diverse morphological and phenological characteristics as well as geographic origins. They were all lumped together because of a generic dark or black (*negro*) hue to their bloom-covered berries (hence another synonym, Farinella, recalling the Italian word *farina*, or flour), and they were once most commonly found in Trentino and Veneto. In fact, it is estimated that 20 percent of the varieties grown in the province of Verona in the 1930s belonged to this large family. Pollini in 1824 mentions a Negrara Bastarda (probably the Negrara Veronese of today), a generic Negrara or Negronz (most likely today's Negrara Trentina), and a Negronza Rizza (probably the result of an infection with grapevine fanleaf virus or one of the grapevine leaf-roll associated viruses 1, 2, 3, or 7) that disappeared from its home in the Val d'Illasi in Veneto in the nineteenth century. Over the years, I have been told by many a local that Negronza was actually a rarer, distinct variety, and I am inclined to believe this, given the depth of collective memories I have been privy to. Interestingly, this Negronza variety was reportedly identical to a Negrera di Gattinara, a now extinct variety. Acerbi (1825) wrote of a *Negrara* that was grown mainly around Schio in Trentino, describing it as resistant to hot weather and used to make excellent, deeply colored wines.

By the early twentieth century, it became apparent to experts that there were many *Negrara*s that differed on the basis of their leaves, bunches, and berries, and that a precise classification was needed. For example, one of the *Negrara*s was being confused not just with obscure, rare cultivars, but also with Raboso Veronese (Molon 1906). Marzotto (1925) provided the lengthiest list of *Negrara* varieties, which remained the definitive one until more recent times: Negrara Cenerente or Farinente (also called Gambujana); Negrara Comune, typical of the countryside of Vicenza, Verona, and Trentino; Negrara Femmina (of Calvene); Negrara Friulana, synonymous with Negruzzo; Negrara Dal Picciuolo Duro (of Arcugnano); Negrara Dal Picciuolo Rosso; Negrara di Monte, synonymous with Doveana; Negrara Farinella (del Friuli), identical to Farinella; Negrara di Gattinara, believed to be synonymous with Negretta di Gattinara; and Negrara Modenese, believed to be identical to Negretta Modenese.

However, unlike other better-known Italian grape groups or families, such as the *Malvasia*s and *Trebbiano*s, almost all the members of the *Negrara* group have fallen into oblivion, deservedly or not; and almost all are limited to sporadic rows in the countryside of Italy's north, used in very small percentages in various wine blends. Though Negrara Veronese is currently the more abundant of the two, it is Negrara Trentina that is making a sort of comeback and the only one currently used to make a monovarietal wine.

Negrara Trentina

WHERE IT'S FOUND: Trentino, Alto Adige, Veneto. NATIONAL REGISTRY CODE NUMBER: 161. COLOR: red.

Over the years, researchers, winemakers, and wine cellar personnel I have interviewed at the Istituto Agrario San Michel dell'Adige (now renamed Fondazione Edmund Mach) and elsewhere have always seemed convinced that Negrara Trentina is the original Negrara. It is generally considered a high-quality cultivar traditionally used to make the best wine of the house by the local farmers. By the end of the 1800s, more than eighty-five thousand hectoliters of *Negrara* wine were being made annually in Trentino, and Negrara Trentina was the most commonly used grape to blend into Schiava wines (though I'm not sure there is any way of knowing how much of that *Negrara* wine was Negrara Trentina and how much Negronza or other *Negrara* varieties).

What appears to have hurt Negrara Trentina the most was the advent of phylloxera, which proved even more disastrous than usual; and grafting of Negrara Trentina onto American rootstocks was not as helpful as with most other varieties, for it greatly increased the variety's vegetative vigor while diminishing wine quality. The lack of rootstock-grapevine synergy was such that the grapes were unable to ripen fully, and resulting wines were green and thin, an unfortunate turn of events reminiscent of the fate befalling Malbec in Cahors, another variety that had great difficulty adapting to new rootstocks. In time, Negrara Trentina managed to adapt somewhat and today the problem is not as dire.

Also called Doleara, Dovenzana, and Zoveana (and there were many more routinely used synonyms depending on where in Trentino the variety grew), Negrara Trentina apparently has a parent-offspring relationship with Enantio (Grando, Stefanini, Zambanini, and Vouillamoz 2006). It is easy to spot in the vineyards, since its leaf is pentagonal and has five lobes (while Negrara Veronese, for example, only has three lobes), and its bunch is cylindrical, very compact, with one or two wings at most (Negrara Veronese's bunch is larger, pyramidal, and has two or three wings); otherwise the two *Negrara*s are very similar. Negrara Trentina is very sensitive to peronospora, less so to oidium; the compact bunch makes it prone to botrytis.

Which Wines to Choose and Why

Negrara Trentina is still grown all over Trentino, albeit in small quantities, though it is less abundant than Negrara Veronese. It's usually included as a blending grape in the Valle dei Laghi wines, but some monovarietal IGT wines are made. The wine is medium-dark red, with grapey, herbal, and red currant aromas. It tastes bright and fresh, with delicate sour red fruit and herbal, underbrush notes. It's a very good, light- to medium-bodied, low-alcohol, high-acid, everyday table wine ideal for uncomplicated drinking and early consumption, guaranteed to leave your taste buds tingling and your mouth fresh. There's a hint of herbal bitterness at the back that contributes to leaving the palate feeling clean and lively.

WINES TO TRY: Pravis** (a great wine for Sunday brunch or BBQs).

Negrara Veronese

WHERE IT'S FOUND: Trentino, Alto Adige, Veneto. NATIONAL REGISTRY CODE NUMBER: 161. COLOR: red.

Sometimes also called Terodola, Negrara Veronese is an ancient variety first described by Pollini in 1824 that has recently been shown to have close genetic ties with another rare Veneto variety called Gruaja (Salmaso, Dalla Valle, and Lucchin 2008). Though in Trentino they like to say that Negrara Trentina is the better of the two varieties, the truth is, in Veneto they are pretty happy with their version of Negrara. In fact, along with Oseleta, it is one of the lesser-known native varieties that has made a resurgence in the last twenty years, and numerous producers are evaluating whether the variety is best used in dry wine blends or air-dried and added to sweet *recioto* blends.

I know of nobody seriously considering a monovarietal wine at present, if for no other reason than that no single estate owns enough grapevines to make a monovarietal version in sufficient commercial volumes. In fact, Negrara Veronese's diffusion is limited to a few sporadic rows in Valpolicella near Verona and in the provinces of Padova and Vicenza. It is listed as one of the blending grapes in DOCs Bardolino, Breganze Rosso, Valdadige, and Valpolicella. Most often, it is used in the wines of Bardolino, but the percentage is too low to draw any conclusions about the variety (if anything, Bardolino is also where greater than usual percentages of Molinara are used). I have yet to try a monovarietal Negrara Veronese: producers have told me the wine has good acid-tannic balance but is a little neutral.

THE PALLAGRELLO GROUP

Perhaps more than any variety, the *Pallagrellos* (of which there are currently two, a white-berried Pallagrello Bianco and a red-berried Pallagrello Nero, though in the past there were many supposedly different grapes referred to as *Uve Pallarelle*, or *Pallagrelle*) embody the plight of native Italian grapes. Completely forgotten by everyone until the early twenty-first century, these *Pallagrellos* are now on an absolute roll and are considered two of Italy's most exciting varieties. As recently as 2003, a state-of-the-art book on the wines of Campania, by Attilio Scienza and Maurizio Boselli, made no mention of either *Pallagrello*. Indeed, in 1995 there was not a single producer of a pure *Pallagrello* wine. Today there are more than a dozen good ones, and some of the wines rank with Italy's best. Not coincidentally, as reported by the British wine magazine *Decanter* in May 2011, a panel tasting of southern Italian wines bestowed its top two awards on *Pallagrello Nero* wines, not wines made with the more famous Aglianico or Primitivo. Though these results were partly skewed because some of the best Aglianico producers were not represented, the *Pallagrello* wines were the only two of two hundred wines evaluated that scored five stars, or 18.5/20.

Some experts believe the name Pallagrello derives from *paglia* (hay), because the grapes used to be air-dried on straw and eaten like raisins; others insist that the *Pallagrellos* are direct descendants of the *Pallarelle* varieties of the eighteenth and nineteenth centuries. Others go back even further, to the ancient Roman Pilleolata, so called because of its very small, round berries (*pilleola*, or small ball). The Borboni dynasty held *Pallagrello* wines in high esteem and offered them to visiting notables as gifts or at royal dinners. They referred to them as Piedimonte, the area where the wines were made (Piedimonte Matese). In fact, Ferdinando IV Borbone (1751–1825) included the two *Pallagrello* grapevines in his famous *vigna del ventaglio* (or vineyard of the fan) near the magnificent royal building at Caserta. This vineyard contained the ten grape varieties the sybaritic king claimed were the best in his kingdom, planted in rows that jutted out like the rays of a fan (*ventaglio*).

The varieties have come back to national prominence thanks to the passion of Peppe Mancini and Alberto Barletta, who created the Vestini Campagnano estate and began production of Pallagrello Bianco and Nero wines in commercially significant numbers (and in the process also resurrected a third wine-worthy native, Casavecchia). The two friends have since parted ways, with Mancini setting up the Terre del Principe estate, another high-quality Pallagrello and Casavecchia wine producer. True Pallagrello Bianco and Pallagrello Nero are those grown in the province of Caserta, whereas another variety grown in the province of Avellino and also called Pallagrello in the past, is a distinct variety according to Costantini, Monaco, Vouillamoz, Forlani, and Grando (2005). In any case, these and other homonyms probably date back to the end of the nineteenth century, when the name was used to indicate several distinct vines now known to be Coda di Volpe Bianca, Trebbiano Giallo, or Malvasia Bianca.

Pallagrello Bianco

WHERE IT'S FOUND: Campania. NATIONAL REGISTRY CODE NUMBER: 381. COLOR: white.

Long confused with Coda di Volpe Bianca, Pallagrello Bianco is a distinct variety characterized by higher acidity. Froio, one of the great experts in Campanian grape varieties, noted in 1876 that Coda di Volpe Bianca and Pallagrello Bianco (which he called Pallagrella) were not the same. Ampelographically, Pallagrello Bianco shares many of the features of Pallagrello Nero (small, cylindrical bunch and small, round berries), but it almost always has a wing (and better botrytis resistance). There are no official clones yet. Pallagrello Bianco's distribution is limited to northwestern Campania, in the area above Caserta, grown especially around the towns of Caiazzo, Castel Campagnano, and Castel di Sasso.

Which Wines to Choose and Why

There are some wonderful pure bottlings of this variety, a real star in my eyes, though some versions are too clever for their own good and have excess residual sugar, so the wines don't taste dry, a turnoff for experienced tasters. In fairness, the wine tends to be alcoholic, as the variety accumulates sugar easily. Pallagrello Bianco wines smell and taste a little like Viognier (though some believe that it is more reminiscent of Chardonnay) but have better acidity (though this tends to drop very quickly as the grapes reach full maturity, usually between the second and third weeks of September), and less exuberant perfume: it gives aromas of yellow apple, lemon, and minerals; and, in warmer climates, pineapple, peach, and vanilla. They therefore differ from wines made with Coda di Volpe Bianca (though a lot depends on where the grapes of the latter are grown); Pallagrello Bianco wines have higher acidities, while Coda di Volpe Bianca wines tend to be softer and less tropical-fruit accented. According to Luigi Moio of the University of Naples Agriculture Department, probably the most recognized expert on *Pallagrello* varieties today (also the consultant winemaker at Vestini Campagnano, first, and now at Terre del Principe), Pallagrello Bianco is not endowed with terpenes, so it is never too aromatic or floral, but consumers love its tropical fruit exuberance. The best ones to try are the IGTs Terre del Volturno and Campania.

WINES TO TRY: Vestini Campagnano***, Masseria Piccirillo**, Le Cantine di Hesperia**, Terre del Principe**, and Castelloducale** (Vigna del Ventaglio).

Pallagrello Nero

WHERE IT'S FOUND: Campania. NATIONAL REGISTRY CODE NUMBER: 382. COLOR: red.

Like Pallagrello Bianco, Pallagrello Nero was also thought to be related to Coda di Volpe Bianca, which explains its synonyms: Coda di Volpe Nera, Oliorpa, Due Code, Mangiaguerra, and Coda di Volpe Rossa (the last two erroneous, as these are names of completely distinct varieties). In my experience, Coda di Volpe Rossa has a much scrawnier bunch and even smaller berries (clearly a fox, or *volpe*, whose hunting fortunes were on the decline) than Pallagrello Nero, which by comparison looks positively Rubenesque, though it has a small bunch and berries too. Its tightly packed bunch is more compact than Pallagrello Bianco's and is never winged (while Bianco's is). Pallagrello Nero has decent tolerance to drought but is susceptible to most diseases (more so than Pallagrello Bianco), especially botrytis bunch rot. It tends to ripen about a week before Aglianico when the two are grown in the same vineyards, but still relatively late (in early October; Pallagrello Bianco is usually harvested in September). It has been described by Rasetti (1904), Carlucci (1909), and Violante and Bordignon (1960) with some accuracy, while today's recognized expert is Luigi Moio.

Which Wines to Choose and Why

Pallagrello Nero was once grown all over Campania, a significant difference from Pallagrello Bianco, which has always been limited to the countryside of Caserta Province. Nero was even grown in nearby regions such as Molise and Calabria. But today its habitat is restricted to the same Caserta countryside that's home to Pallagrello Bianco. A close relationship to Casavecchia has been postulated (Masi, Vignani, Di Giovannantonio, Mancuso, and Boselli 2001), which doesn't seem far-fetched, given that the two varieties have lived in the same finite area of Campania for centuries—specifically, the small towns of Alife, Alvignano, Caiazzo, and Castel Campagnano. The best wines exhibit aromas and flavors of red cherry, black currant, tobacco, black pepper, and blackberry jam typical of the variety; the wines are usually characterized by soft tannins and low levels of acidity. Some excellent IGT Terre del Volturno wines are made with Pallagrello Nero.

WINES TO TRY: Vestini Campagnano*** and Terre del Principe*** (Ambruco) are stellar, though there are now many other fine producers, such as Fattoria Selvanova**.

THE RABOSO FAMILY

The *Raboso*s are distinct varieties but Raboso Piave and Raboso Veronese are closely related in that the latter is an offspring of a cross between Raboso Piave and Marzemina Bianca. Hence, it is correct to consider the *Raboso*s as a family of grapes, albeit a small one. The oldest of the two is therefore not surprisingly, Raboso Piave, first mentioned in the literature in 1679, while Raboso Veronese only begins to be described in the nineteenth century. The name Raboso is believed to stem from a similarly named tributary of the Piave River, which flows through the wine's production area, but others believe it is a derivation of *rabbioso* (angry, in Italian), a reference to the incredibly harsh tannins and high acidity of wines made with these varieties.

Crespan, Cancellier, Chies, Giannetto, Meneghetti, and Costacurta (2009) showed that there is no relationship between Grapariol, a white variety often called Rabosina Bianco locally, and the two *Raboso*s. Studies also suggest a parent-offspring relationship between Raboso Piave and Fogarina (Myles, Boyko, Owens, Brown, Grassi, Aradhya, et al. 2011), and that Raboso Piave is one of the two parents (the other is Moscato d'Amburgo) of Manzoni Moscato. Interestingly, Friularo is a synonym of Raboso Piave, while Raboso Friularo, is actually synonymous with Raboso Veronese (Salmaso, Dalla Valle, and Lucchin 2008). This can be the source of much confusion since everyone, so-called experts and real ones included, talks and writes about a generic Friularo or Friularo Raboso variety as synonymous with Raboso Piave only. Finally, the laboratory crossing of Merlot and Raboso Veronese has produced a new variety called Fertilia.

Though the two *Raboso* varieties look alike, they show clear differences in morphology and viticultural behavior. Furthermore, they can be easily separated on the basis of isoenzyme analysis and by anthocyanin profile. The latter was analyzed in detail by De Rosso in his brilliant doctoral thesis presented at the university of Padua in 2010. According to these results, though both *Raboso*s are characterized by high anthocyanin levels in general (comparable to those of Cabernet Sauvignon and Barbera, two of the world's most darkly pigmented grapes), Raboso Piave is characterized by a larger concentration of peonin-3-monoglucoside and of malvin-3-monoglucoside (confirming previous results published by Mattivi, Cova, Dalla Serra, and Soligo in 2004), while Raboso Veronese is characterized by a higher level of cyanin-3-monoglucoside and delphin-3-monoglucoside, and a lower concentration of peonin-3-monoglucoside. And though both *Raboso* varieties present very low levels of acylated anthocyanins, Raboso Veronese has a slightly higher concentration of these than Raboso Piave.

Raboso Piave

WHERE IT'S FOUND: Veneto, FVG. NATIONAL REGISTRY CODE NUMBER: 203. COLOR: red.

Still often called Friularo because it was believed to be a native of the Friuli Venezia Giulia region, Raboso Piave is one of Italy's oldest varieties: the first historical information we have relative to the wine is from the thirteenth century, when it was called *vinum plavense* according to Calò, Paronetto, and Rorato (1996), though it's not clear to me how anyone could be really sure that wine was made with Raboso Piave. For much of the nineteenth and twentieth centuries, Raboso Piave was thought to be different variety from Friularo; descriptions of a Friularo a Pecol Ros (with a red stalk), thought to be Raboso Piave, and a Friularo a Pecol Vert (green stalked), believed to be the true Friularo, abound in the scientific and popular literature of those times. Subsequently, it was shown that the stalk-related color differences are only the result of the different environments the grapevines grow in. Therefore, Friularo and Raboso Piave are one and the same. The difficulty with this is that Friularo and Raboso Friularo are not one and the same, though these two names are used interchangeably to mean Raboso Piave. However, according to Salmaso, Dalla Valle, and Lucchin (2008), who analyzed nineteen grapevines at thirty nuclear and three chloroplast microsatellite loci, Friularo is synonymous with Raboso Piave, while Raboso Friularo is a synonym of Raboso Veronese. Further studies on this issue are probably required.

In any case, an 1868 document attests that a family called De Vindimian (or Widmann) transported Raboso Piave to Veneto from Friuli Venezia Giulia, though it seems likely others had done so before. However, in those times the boundaries of Friuli Venezia Giulia were much larger than today, stretching as far as the Piave's left bank; therefore it seems likely that *Raboso* was at that time in fact growing in what is today Veneto. According to Carpenè and Vianello, by 1874 *Raboso* was cultivated in thirty different townships around Treviso and over fourteen thousand hectoliters of wine were produced yearly (so it seems unlikely that so much raboso could be made if the vines had been brought over from Friuli Venezia Giulia just six years earlier). *Raboso*'s popularity increased further in the early twentieth century: it is estimated that by 1930, almost 90 percent of the wine made around Treviso involved Raboso Piave.

Raboso Piave's popularity might be puzzling at first glance, since it has always been associated with the production of high-acid, tannic, and deeply colored wines that were thought of mainly as ideal blending agents for more anemic wines made elsewhere. In past centuries, Raboso wine was referred to as a *vin sgarboso*, meaning a rude, tough wine (*sgarbato* is impolite or rude). Alas, those were poorer and simpler times, in which high-acid, tannic wines were much in demand not just as blending agents but as a source of calories, while after the 1960s that same wine style was tragically out of fashion. This very high acidity also made Raboso Piave wines better suited to hot weather and to lengthy travels made in perilous conditions (for example, poor storage and extreme temperature variations), and this explains why *Raboso* wines were locally nicknamed *vin da viaio* (*vin da viaggio* in Italian) meaning that they could be taken on voyages. This extreme, harsh acidity also explains why the grape fell out of favor and was largely replaced by French imports such as Cabernet Sauvignon and Merlot. In fact, it was customary centuries ago to blend raboso with gentler wine made from Pinot Nero, in an effort to tame both tannins and acidity. Given the acid and tannic nature of Raboso Piave, Giacomo Agostinetti di Cimadolmo (1679) recommended using—or blending with—biotypes Rabosina and Rabosazza, which also performed better when late harvested but were intrinsically "garbe di natura," of a gentler nature.

In more modern times, different viticultural and winemaking techniques (such as extensive deleafing and air-drying) have been studied and employed to decrease the grape's naturally occurring high malic and tartaric acidities and tannins. Clonal selection has also been aimed at developing less acid, less tannic grapevines.

Different officially certified clones are available: RII gives a high-acid wine, ISV V2 accumulates higher levels of sugars; and more recent clones such as VCR 19, 20, and 43 are characterized by smaller, less compact bunches. For example, the newer VCR clones are characterized by musts that have acidity levels three times lower than those from older clones, such as ISV-V2. In general, Raboso Piave is very vigorous and shows good adaptability to different soils. It has a very long vegetative cycle, with early budbreak and late ripening, which means it is highly sensitive to bad weather (both spring frosts due to its early flowering and rainy autumns due its late ripening).

Morphologically, Raboso Piave resembles Raboso Veronese, but there are differences. Veronese has much more jagged leaves than Raboso Piave, and the grape bunch is also more cylindrical and less compact; Piave's is shaped like a truncated cone and is tightly packed. Viticulturally, Raboso Piave usually reaches optimal ripeness about two weeks after Raboso Veronese, and it prefers heavier clay soils than does Veronese.

Resurgent interest in the Raboso Piave variety, finally recognized as a potentially high-quality source of unique red wines, has led to the formation of the Confraternity of Raboso (www.confraternitarabosopiave.it), founded in 1996 in Vazzola di Piave with the commendable aim of promoting the knowledge, the awareness, and the diffusion of the Raboso Piave variety and its wines.

Which Wines to Choose and Why

Raboso Piave is found mainly in Veneto, in the countryside around Treviso, and to a much smaller extent, in Friuli Venezia Giulia. The best wines are the DOC Piave Raboso: these have to be aged a minimum of three years in oak before release, and some estates, such as Ornella Molon Traverso, age them longer still (in their case, for two years more) in an effort to smoothen the high total acidity. The DOC Vicenza Raboso and the Friularo wines of the area around Bagnoli can be good too. Some wines are labeled *vendemmia tardiva* (late harvest), meaning that at least 60 percent of the grapes used to make the wine were harvested on or after the day of Santo Martino, November 11.

Late harvesting or air-drying the grapes has always been a technique by which to reduce raboso's acid ferocity. An interesting study on gene expression relative to transcription products compared Raboso Piave grapes subjected either to late harvest or to air-drying directly on the vine, where grapes are left on the vine but cut off from the rest of the plant by severing or twisting the stalk feeding the grape bunch (Bonghi, Cargnello, Ziliotto, Rizzini, Teo, Veilleux, et al. 2006). It was found that 80 percent of the genes were differentially expressed in the air-drying group compared to 10 percent in the late-harvest group. The genes most affected in the air-dried grapes were those responsible for polyphenol synthesis (especially the reduction of leucoanthocyanin reductase), for higher concentrations of acid phenols, and for lower levels of polyphenols overall; the few genes affected in the late-harvest group were essentially unrelated. The wines made from the air-dried grapes were much smoother and softer, with 40 percent less total acidity than the control, and 20 percent less than the late-harvest group. The lower acidity levels were due to reductions in both malic and tartaric acid. This biochemical result is due to the induction of transcription by the genes that code for the enzymes malate dehydrogenase and ATP-citrate lyase. In practical terms, these results provide a scientific basis for why air-dried Raboso wines tend to taste more velvety and luscious than those made from late-harvested grapes, which are however characterized by greater freshness and, in my view, refinement.

Raboso Piave may be used alone or in blends in a number of different DOCG (Piave Malanotte and Bagnoli Friularo), DOC (Bagnoli di Sopra, Piave), and IGT wines (Alto Livenza, Colli Trevigiani, delle Venezie, Marca Trevigiana, and more). Interestingly, relative to the question of whether air-drying is the future of *Raboso* wines, the Piave Malanotte DOCG, recently created in 2010, demands there be a minimum of 70 percent Raboso Piave and up to 30 percent Raboso Veronese in the blend, but 15 to 30 percent of the grapes have to be air-dried. By contrast, the Bagnoli Friularo DOCG requires 90 percent Raboso Piave grapes.

Good dry wines made with Raboso Piave are intensely perfumed and can be quite a revelation, given the wine's less-than-stellar reputation. More often than not, these wines are mean and tough, but well-made ones are brightly fruity (strawberry, black cherry) and floral (violet) with hints of tobacco and black pepper. I never cease to be amazed at just how intensely perfumed they are; the lively acidity is refreshing and not at all bothersome when supported by enough extract and sweetness. Air-dried wines are smooth and opulent, and resemble a lighter-styled Amarone, though red-fruit aromas and flavors are more common in wines made with the Raboso Piave variety than in Amarone. In my experience, monovarietal Raboso Piave wines made with the VCR 19 clone are more intense, those with VCR 20 more refined, and those with the VCR 43 more complex, but more tasting experience needs to be accumulated before passing definitive judgments. As is often the case, a blend of the three may offer the best results of all. It is only fair to recognize that this is one of Italy's most improved wines of the last twenty years, and there are now many different and very fine bottlings available that testify that the variety deserves more than its so-so reputation.

WINES TO TRY: Giorgio Cecchetto*** (Raboso is the name of the traditional bottling, Gelsaia is the air-dried version; both are excellent, but I prefer the Raboso), Bellussi** (L'Autentico), Ornella Molon Traverso**, Bonotto delle Tezze* (Potestà, but truly noteworthy is the Passito), and Tenuta Santomè* (also a very good Raboso Passito). Italo Cescon* is a famous local and very traditionally minded producer who makes both a Raboso (Il Tralcetto) and a Raboso Rosé; unfortunately he fails to specify which Raboso variety he uses, though it's certainly Raboso Piave. Barbaran* is another good producer who also makes a Raboso Veronese wine, so it's very interesting to drink his two different raboso wines side by side and catch the differences between them (partially due to winemaking however, as they macerate the Raboso Piave must on the skins for a longer period of time, thereby obtaining a more structured wine). La Montecchia is an outstanding producer of *Raboso* wine (Forzatè) but it is a blend of the Piave and Veronese varieties, and so cannot be taken as an example of either variety (and hence no asterisk rating).

Raboso Veronese

WHERE IT'S FOUND: Veneto, Emilia-Romagna.
NATIONAL REGISTRY CODE NUMBER: 204.
COLOR: red.

Raboso Veronese was long misidentified not just with the other *Raboso*s but with *Refosco*s (Mas and Pulliat 1874–79) and with Fortana (Di Rovasenda 1877); the fact that it was sometimes called Negron or Negrar also caused confusion with Negrara Veronese, another cultivar. Morphologically, Raboso Veronese is very similar to Raboso Piave, but the two are distinct isoenzymatically and genetically, and as I mentioned in the introduction to the *Raboso* family, both *Raboso* varieties can easily be distinguished on the basis of their respective anthocyanin profiles.

It's a good thing those tests exist, for though I have walked Veneto's vineyards countless times, I still get the two regularly mixed up, even when the grapes are visible and fully ripe. Looking at the leaves helps, as Veronese's are much more indented than those of Raboso Piave; the grape bunch is also more cylindrical and less compact, and its berries are more spherical. The grapes also taste less acidic and astringent than those of Raboso Piave. In general, Raboso Veronese ripens as much as two weeks earlier than Raboso Piave, a direct consequence of its genetic link to Marzemina Bianca, an early to mid-ripening variety; Raboso Veronese is also oidium sensitive but drought-resistant. Other differences are that Raboso Veronese seems better suited to sandy soils and is resistant to cold weather; therefore it is planted more in the flat vineyards of the Veneto plain, where cool winds and frost are not uncommon. There are four official clones available of Raboso Veronese: Fedit 2 CSG, ISV-V1, ISV-V2, and VCR 3; the latter has slightly smaller bunches, is slightly more productive and less sensitive to botrytis than the other clones. The ISV-V2 has the advantage of ripening a little earlier than the others.

Despite its Veronese name, Raboso Veronese is not found in the countryside around Verona (something already pointed out by Molon in 1906: he wrote that "in Verona it is almost unknown, and the name was given by those who first brought it to Noventa di Piave"); like Raboso Piave, according to Zava (1901), it has long been linked to the countryside around Treviso and Bagnoli di Sopra. Maybe the "Veronese" is in reference to the farmer (perhaps a Veronese or Veronesi) who first brought Raboso Veronese to the Treviso area. Another possible explanation for the "Veronese" attribute is that the natural crossing that gave rise to the grape variety occurred in the 1800s near Verona and was then transported to the Treviso area, later disappearing from the Verona region. The ampelographer Norberto Marzotto declared that Raboso Veronese was first brought to the Veronese area by Count Papadopoli of San Polo di Piave and Cologna Veneta, in the province of Verona. According to Crespan, Cancellier, Chies, Giannetto, and Meneghetti (2006), it is most likely here that the cross between Raboso Piave and Marzemina Bianca took place. *General Ampelography of the Province of Treviso* (1870) states that Rabosa Veronese was grown in the Treviso area along with Rabosa Nostrana (or Trevisana, in other words Raboso Piave), and eventually became more widely used than Raboso Piave. In 1931, the viticultural indications for the provinces of Veneto drawn up by the Experimental Institute of Viticulture and Enology of Conegliano recommended Rabosa Veronese as an ideal grape for the provinces of Treviso (lowlands), Venice, Padua, Vicenza, and Rovigo. Today, Raboso Veronese grows everywhere Raboso Piave does, but unlike the latter it is also found in the countryside around Vicenza and in Emilia-Romagna, near Ferrara and Ravenna.

Which Wines to Choose and Why

Experimental monovarietal Raboso Veronese wines I have tried, prior to their being blended with Raboso Piave, seem less acid and tannic than those made with the latter, but "less" with any *Raboso* is a very relative term. Commercially available wines also strike me as being routinely gentler and softer than those made with Raboso Piave. Raboso Veronese wines also exude a more delicate, floral raspberry and Morello cherry aroma. Some experts do believe that wine made with Raboso Veronese is more refined than wine made with Raboso Piave—though producers of Raboso Piave wines strongly disagree. There are fewer truly monovarietal Raboso Veronese wines made compared to Raboso Piave wines. Of course, if we take Raboso Friularo to be Raboso Veronese (Salmaso, Dalla Valle, and Lucchin 2008), then the myriad "friularo"-labeled wines produced today are Raboso Veronese; but I'm not sure we can be certain they are all monovarietal. In any case, Raboso Veronese can be used in many DOCG (Piave Malanotte), DOC (Bagnoli di Sopra, Piave, and others) and IGT (Alto Livenza, delle Venezie, Marca Trevigiana, and others) blends, most of which overlap with those of Raboso Piave.

WINES TO TRY: Barbaran* (a good producer making both a Raboso Veronese wine and a Raboso Piave wine—it's very interesting to drink the two different raboso wines made at the estate and note the differences, some of which are due to winemaking, as the Veronese receives shorter maceration time, thereby obtaining a gentler wine) and Moletto* (a "Raboso Piave" wine that is all Raboso Veronese). For sparkling versions, try: Villa Almè* (I Gai Raboso Veronese Rosato), Luigino Molon*, and Montegrande* (Frizzante).

THE REFOSCO GROUP

Few other Italian grapes and wines cause bigger headaches than the *Refosco* group: and that's without drinking the wines. This is because this so-called family of grapes comprises a group of genetically heterogeneous varieties with little in common besides a few physical characteristics, viticultural behaviors, and their limited area of cultivation. Not that this situation is all that different from that of many other Italian indigenous cultivars (consider the *Greco*s and the *Malvasia*s), but in the case of the *Refosco*s, confusion reaches levels absurd even by Italian standards and mistaken attributions throughout the centuries have been raised to the level of an art form. Suffice to say that when I asked Paolo Sivilotti, formerly lead researcher at Friuli Venezia Giulia's Regional Institute for the Development and Promotion of Agriculture for a clarification on the *Refosco*s (after having received completely different answers from many other local university experts), his immediate reply was, "listen, nobody understands anything about *Refosco*s."

As usual, genetic studies using microsatellite methodologies have helped shed light on the intricate parentage and relationships of the various *Refosco*s, but as the words *refosco* and *refošk* are used in Italy, Slovenia, and Croatia to name what are in effect distinct varieties, for now much remains to be clarified and verified. Mercifully, Carlo Petrussi, perhaps the single greatest living expert on Friuli Venezia Giulia native varieties, has completed years of research (published in 2013 in a new book by Sivilotti and Stocco) and clarified matters somewhat. Even more important to wine drinkers, experts have always agreed upon the potential high quality of *Refosco* wines, though this is strictly correlated to their habitat, as in general the *Refosco* varieties are not a particularly adaptable bunch. Nonetheless, at the 1891 Austrian Enological Congress, the most famous *Refosco* of our day, Refosco del Peduncolo Rosso, was deemed the "queen of all Friuli grapes." And it wasn't even the most common or best-known *Refosco* of the time.

An almost-endless list of synonyms, a problem typical of all grape varieties that have been around for a very long time, has always plagued the *Refosco*s. Since a *Refosco* wine made in Friuli Venezia Giulia was documented as early as 1390, at least one of these varieties is very old, though perhaps not old enough to have been (as some experts have written) the variety used to make pucinum, the famous wine of ancient Rome, which was reportedly a favorite of Livia, wife of Octavian Augustus, first emperor of Rome. Besides, the lineup of grape pretenders to pucinum is lengthy, and the *Refosco*s are complicated enough as it is.

In the early nineteenth century, Di Maniago listed three different *Refosco*s: Refosc Dolz (with large, loosely-packed berries), Refosc (which gave a lighter wine), and Refoschin (with large, very round berries, grown in both flatlands and hillsides). Obviously, in this case the diminutive *refoschin* referred to the light-bodied wine, and not the grape variety. However, during the same century, many other *Refosco*s were mentioned, such as Refosco dal Pecol Vert (or del Peduncolo Verde, both referencing its green stalk), Refosco dal Pecol Rosso (del Peduncolo Rosso, red stalk), Refosco d'Istria, Refosco di Rauscedo, Refosco di Faedis, Refosco del Boton, Refosco di Vicenza, Refosco di Pagnacco, Refosco di Pozzuolo, Refosco di Roncus, Refosco Ungherese, Uva di Guarnieri (later renamed, you guessed it, Refosco Guarnieri), with a couple of white-berried *Refosco*s thrown in for good measure. You couldn't be blamed for thinking that every town in the area had its own specific *Refosco* growing in its vineyards.

A landmark research study made the single biggest inroads toward shining a light on the starless night that is all things *Refosco*, suggesting that the members of the *Refosco* family are best divided into two subgroups (Costacurta, Calò, Carraro, Giust, Aggio, Borsa, et al. 2005). The first includes two distinct varieties, Refosco del Peduncolo Rosso and Refosco d'Istria, better known as Terrano; the second includes the five other *Refoscos*, which were at that time thought to be Refosco Gentile (also called Refosco di Rauscedo), Refoschin (also called Refosco degli Uccelli), Refoscone (also called Refosco Nostrano, Refosco di Faedis, and Refosco di Ronchis), Refosco Guarnieri, and Refosco del Boton. However it was already apparent then that some members of the second group, especially the last three, differed enough from members of the first group that they were likely distinct species and not true *Refoscos*. In fact, the genetic research performed by Costacurta's group showed that Refosco del Boton is identical to Tazzelenghe (another red-berried Friuli native), and a study identified Refosco Guarneri with Trevisana Nera, a rare variety of Veneto (Crespan, Calò, Giannetto, Sparacio, Storchi, and Costacurta 2008).

Thanks to Petrussi's recent work (presented in Sivilotti and Stocco 2013) which refutes previous conclusions drawn not just by Costacurta et al. but other researchers as well (see Cipriani, Frazza, Peterlunger, and Testolin 1994), we have acquired new knowledge about the *Refosco* group. First, Refosco Nostrano (though producers prefer the name of Refosco di Faedis as it ties the grape to their local territory) is not a biotype of Refoscone, but a distinct variety; instead, it is Refosco di Ronchis that is most likely a biotype of Refosco Nostrano. In fact, ampelographical differences between Refoscone and Refosco Nostrano are obvious even to the uninitiated, as the former has much bigger leaves and bunches. Refoscone's leaves are heavily indented and have at least five lobes, while Refosco Nostrano's characteristically vary (even on the same grapevine): some are circular, others pentagonal and marginally indented. The bunches are also very different: those of Refoscone weigh 800 grams or more, while Refosco Nostrano bunches weigh only 150–200 grams. Unfortunately, both varieties are often planted together in the same vineyard, as Petrussi showed me during a walk through an old vineyard last fall; over and over again, I saw a vine of Refoscone standing right next to one of Refosco Nostrano, though the vineyard was supposedly planted entirely to the Refosco Nostrano variety. Second, Refoschin (or Refosco degli Uccelli) is apparently identical to Refosco del Peduncolo Rosso, and therefore not a distinct variety: it's different morphologic appearance is the result of the latter variety being planted in poor, nutrient-deficient soils. Third, there still exists a very small population of Refosco Bianco, a white-berried variety that carries the same name as the red-berried *Refoscos* though it is completely unrelated to the others. Last but not least, there appears to be no truth to the hypothesis that yet another Friuli native, Piculit Neri, is a biotype of Refosco Nostrano or of Refosco del Peduncolo Rosso, as some experts have stated over the years. Interestingly, Petrussi had already pointed out to me in an interview years ago that it was highly unlikely that Piculit Neri and Refosco Nostrano were one and the same, as in over fifty years of speaking with farmers, he had never heard anyone refer to Piculit Neri as a *Refosco*. That men of science might do well to listen more thoroughly to what old-timers with decades of experience have to say about their local grapes is well demonstrated by the fact that many farmers have always used the name Refosco del Peduncolo Rosso interchangeably with Refoschin (as was done in localized areas of Friuli Venezia Giulia centuries ago), despite the fact that university studies of the last few decades had stated that the two varieties were genetically distinct. With better research tools, it appears they are not.

Sticking with relative certainties, at the present state of knowledge we can include four distinct varieties in a *Refosco* group: Refosco del Peduncolo Rosso, Refosco Nostrano (Refosco di Faedis), Refoscone, and Refosco Bianco. Wine is made in commercially significant volumes with the first two only; and though Refosco del Peduncolo Rosso is the most important and best-known *Refosco*, now that more is finally being learned about Refosco Nostrano (Refosco di Faedis) it appears it may actually be the better of the two. Of course, sometimes wine producers are handcuffed by legal requirements. Producers of Refosco Nostrano have had to label their wine as a generic *Refosco* up until now, but since Refosco Nostrano has finally been inserted in the National Registry, they will now be able to use the correct variety's name on their wine labels. That the Italian legal system and laws have allowed many such escape hatches over the years is another (sad) matter altogether, and gives a very clear-cut idea of just how much (or little) attention politicians used to pay to their local native grapes only a decade ago.

Refosco Bianco

WHERE IT'S FOUND: FVG. NATIONAL REGISTRY CODE NUMBER: not registered. COLOR: white.

Identified ampelographically and genetically only in 2004, in an old vineyard at Coia di Tarcento in the Colli Orientali DOC zone of Friuli Venezia Giulia, Refosco Bianco was first mentioned in the nineteenth century by Di Maniago. The leaf is medium-sized, triangular, with five lobes; the bunch is cylindrical, loosely packed, and has one or two wings; the berries are round, yellow-green, and spotted. Late ripening and highly productive, this variety has been shown to have good aromatic potential, as Refosco Bianco grapes contain high concentrations of benzenoids (45 percent) and terpenes (32 percent), with interesting levels of both linalool and geraniol.

Despite its name, Refosco Bianco is completely unrelated to any of the other *Refosco*s, but Petrussi feels it is appropriate to continue calling it so since locals have historically referred to this variety as a *Refosco* grape. There are a very few, sporadic old vines left of Refosco Bianco, but ERSA and local growers are trying to bring Refosco Bianco back from the brink of oblivion.

Which Wines to Choose and Why

Clearly, given the extremely limited plantings of Refosco Bianco, there are no monovarietal wines made with it. Microvinifications have offered lovely aromas and flavors of citrus, dried fruits, and aromatic herbs, with hints of tropical fruit. Not a blockbuster wine, but bright and lively, thanks to its harmonious, fresh acidity.

Refosco dal Peduncolo Rosso

WHERE IT'S FOUND: FVG, Veneto. NATIONAL REGISTRY CODE NUMBER: 205. COLOR: red.

Probably Friuli Venezia Giulia's best-known red grape variety, its name appears as such in the literature only in 1877, when it was differentiated from myriad *Refosco*s because it ripens one to two weeks earlier and especially because of its stalk, which reddens once the grapes are fully ripe. Poggi (1939) stated that this *Refosco* was the only one worth concentrating efforts on, because of the superior quality of its wine.

Refosco del Peduncolo Rosso has always sparked controversy and the Refosco-Mondeuse Noire fiasco of the last half of the twentieth century shows why ampelogical identification is rife with traps. Simply put, a so-called *Refosco* accession sampled by the University of California Berkeley, from Jackson Vineyard in Amador County, was later identified via genetic testing as Mondeuse Noire. Fortunately, no *Refosco* variety growing in Italy matched the American "Refosco-Mondeuse Noire" in DNA profile, and so it was clear to all that the original U.S. grapevine sample had been misidentified ampelographically from the beginning, sparing wine lovers and producers alike any further worry that Refosco del Peduncolo Rosso and Mondeuse Noire were one and the same.

Fortunately, recent research has shed considerable light on the Refosco del Peduncolo Rosso family tree, revealing that Teroldego, a Trentino native grape, spontaneously crossed at least twice with the same unknown variety to give birth to Lagrein in Trentino and Alto Adige and to Marzemino in Trentino and Lombardy (Grando, Stefanini, Zambanini, and Vouillamoz 2006). The latter and an unknown other parent then gave birth to Refosco dal Peduncolo Rosso, most likely in Friuli. Therefore,

Teroldego is a grandfather and Lagrein either an uncle or an aunt of Refosco del Peduncolo Rosso. Furthermore, Refosco del Peduncolo Rosso is a parent of Corvina and a grandparent of Rondinella, two famous Veneto varieties used to make Valpolicella and Amarone wines, so it turns out that Refosco del Peduncolo Rosso is a pretty noble grape. Last but not least, this study also confirms that Piculit Neri is unrelated to Refosco del Peduncolo Rosso.

Refosco del Peduncolo Rosso has a medium-large, pyramidal bunch with one small wing, and medium-small, very dark blue berries with thin but resistant skins (a good thing, in view of it being a late ripener). A strong differentiating factor between it and all other Refosco-named varieties is that the underside of its leaves is milky-white, covered in a downy sheen that is absent from the greenish underside of leaves of all other *Refoscos*. Refosco del Peduncolo Rosso adapts well to just about any soil type but does best in nutrient-poor, calcareous-clay soils and hillside locations, as it's very vigorous. Above all, it needs to ripen well in order to avoid green, vegetal aromas and flavors; and as ripeness is everything, nurseries and research personnel have strived to develop better clones. The best of these are ISV-F1, ISV-F4 Toppani (one of the most widely planted, as it's less vigorous than most, producing more complex and ageworthy wines), VCR 14 (the least sensitive to botrytis), ERSA FVG 400 (slightly less productive than the rest, giving complex wines), and ERSA FVG 401 Villa Chiozza.

Which Wines to Choose and Why

I find that Refosco del Peduncolo Rosso wines are by far the most complex of any made with *Refosco* varieties, hinting at dried red cherries, fresh herbs, almonds, and flowers (lavender, geranium, violet). However, they are often short, with aromas and flavors that though very intense, even seductive on entry, fail to linger much. The tannins can also be quite tough, certainly much more aggressive and astringent than those of wines made with Refosco Nostrano. Furthermore, Refosco del Peduncolo Rosso is a reductive variety and according to Collavini estate winemaker Walter Bergnach "stainless steel can be used, but care has to be taken to provide lots of air in the immediate post-fermentation phase, for if off-odors develop, they're very hard to get rid of. Small barrels also serve to smoothen the variety's somewhat angular tannins, but they don't have to be new oak." Clearly, when Refosco del Peduncolo Rosso grapes fail to reach optimal maturity, the wines display varying degrees of greenness and vegetal aromas and flavors, something true of all the *Refosco* varieties. In this respect, *Refoscos* have plenty in common with the *Cabernets*.

Refosco del Peduncolo Rosso is by far most common in Friuli Venezia Giulia, though it is also grown in Veneto. The best wines to try are those of the DOC Colli Orientali del Friuli of Friuli Venezia Giulia; Friuli Grave, Friuli Annia, and Friuli Latisana can also be good, but it is often too rainy, especially in central and western Grave, or yields are too high, to achieve truly great wines. However, potential for very fine wines made with this variety is considerable in DOCs such as Latisana, Annia, and Aquilea, as Refosco del Peduncolo Rosso is a variety that likes very loamy soils rich in red clay; in that light, the combination of strongly gravel soils and high rainfall typical of some parts of the Grave makes it unlikely, in my opinion, that truly great Refosco wines will ever be made there. Unsurprisingly, Refosco wines from these DOCs have noticeably improved over the last decade or so. Veneto's DOC Lison Pramaggiore also grows this variety, but those wines fail to excite.

Outside Italy, besides very rare examples from Greece and Croatia (Terrano is far more common in the latter country), Refosco del Peduncolo Rosso is grown in Argentina's Mendoza and Chile's Colchagua viticultural areas; and it has sparked interest in the United States, especially in New Mexico and California. Though a great deal of so-called *Refosco* in the latter state is Mondeuse Noire, in the last twenty years there have been many new plantings of Refosco del Peduncolo Rosso (though most everyone just refers to it simply as "Refosco"), and many very good wines made. Examples include Tobin James (James Gang), Bianchi San Juan Vineyards, Oreana, and Napa Valley's Mathiasson. You know the grape must be drumming up considerable interest if even Trader Joe's is getting in on the act: witness their rather good Petite Reserve wine, a one-time offering that carries the very successful grocery chain's label but is produced and bottled by Familia Nueva, owned by Ancient Peaks Winery.

In New Mexico, I was thrilled to find Refosco del Peduncolo Rosso vineyards in fine shape: Estrella del Norte (they source their grapes from southern New Mexico) and Amaro are just some of the wineries to watch. There are others making refosco in this state, but the results left me underwhelmed.

WINES TO TRY: Miani*** (Calvari), Ronchi di Cialla***, Alberice**, Gigante**, Iole Grillo**, La Viarte**, Moschioni** (his version is partially air-dried, so the wine is rounder and creamier), Jacuss**, Le Favole**, Scarbolo**, Tenuta Tomasella**, Marinig*, and Vigna Petrussa**.

Refosco Gentile

WHERE IT'S FOUND: FVG. NATIONAL REGISTRY CODE NUMBER: not registered. COLOR: red.

Refosco Gentile has the smallest bunch of all the *Refosco* family members, and the berries are small too: this makes it the least productive of all *Refoscos*, which explains why its cultivation was abandoned. It is also marked by an inability to accumulate high sugar concentrations, and maintains high total acidity levels even when optimally ripe. Whether this is just a consequence of nonideal rootstocks, sites, or pruning methods is not yet clear to me—or to anyone I've asked, for that matter. Microvinifications have shown a darker wine than that obtained with other *Refoscos*, and delicate floral and black fruit aromas and flavors that don't seem to be particularly complex. However, I have been told by more than one producer and local viticulture expert that Refosco Gentile appears to have considerable winemaking potential, and the University of Udine has been busy studying it, so we are likely to learn more about Refosco Gentile in the near future.

Refoscone

WHERE IT'S FOUND: FVG. NATIONAL REGISTRY CODE NUMBER: not registered. COLOR: red.

Refoscone is mainly if not only found in the Colli Orientali DOC zone of Friuli Venezia Giulia. Sporadic Refoscone grapevines can be located in the old vineyards of towns such as Cividale, Prepotto, Buttrio, Manzano, Corno di Rosazzo, and San Giovanni al Natisone, but the variety is most common (though still rare) in the countryside near Nimis, Faedis, and Torreano, where it's called Berzamino. Unlike what you'll read in even recently published books, it is not to be confused with Refosco Nostrano (Refosco di Faedis), which though similar to Refoscone, has a much smaller bunch and very differently shaped leaves. I guarantee that with a few minutes practice you will also be able to pick them out in vineyards every time. Refoscone is characterized by very large pentagonal leaves with three to five lobes that are often superimposed. Its bunch is conical and very large (easily reaching eight hundred grams or more), and is medium to tightly packed, with anywhere from one to four wings. The dark-blue, round berries are also large. Refoscone ripens late in the year, at the end of October, exposing it to the risks of Friuli's very rainy late season weather (see, for example, the 2010 vintage, when the rain basically never let up). However, its basal buds are more fertile than those of other *Refoscos*: this, combined with bigger bunches and berries, explains its much higher productivity compared to other *Refoscos*. Despite this, Refoscone failed to become a huge hit with farmers over the centuries because the large berries have very thin skins; this, combined with the very compact bunch, makes

Refoscone susceptible to botrytis. Also, it succumbs easily to oidium, and unlike the other *Refosco* varieties, suffers greatly from magnesium deficiency. It prefers dry, clay-alluvial sites, but suffers water stress easily.

Which Wines to Choose and Why

Describing a wine made solely with Refoscone is difficult, for there aren't any pure examples that I know of. In fact, having visited Friuli vineyards an average of ten times a year for the last thirteen years, I can state there is no 100 percent Refoscone wine being made by anyone in significant commercial quantities. Even a pure Refoscone wine made for home use is unlikely, as this variety is almost always found in only small numbers, haphazardly planted among other grapevines in old vineyards. That should not be taken to mean that the wine is without potential merits. Microvinifications of 100 percent Refoscone wines I have tried offered lovely violet and delicately vegetal notes, with tough but not unpleasant tannins, though all seemed to lack flesh to me, which makes the tannins stand out more. Research at the University of Udine has shown that such wines have good concentrations of benzenoids (50 percent) and norisoprenoids (more than 30 percent). The dark color of both grapes and wines is explained by high total anthocyanin concentration, especially malvin and delphin, which are two of the darker and more stable pigments in grapes.

WINES TO TRY: To the best of my knowledge, there are no monovarietal wines made with Refoscone—yet. Forchir labels a wine as "Refoscone" and though some people have written that it is 100 percent Refoscone, it is mainly Refosco Nostrano. Ten years ago, the wine was said to be made with Refoscso del Peduncolo Rosso, since Refoscone wasn't even a legally recognized variety.

Refosco Nostrano (Refosco di Faedis)

WHERE IT'S FOUND: FVG. NATIONAL REGISTRY CODE NUMBER: 206. COLOR: red.

The official and correct name of this variety, as recorded the National Registry, is Refosco Nostrano, though local wine producers would prefer to have it called Refosco di Faedis, after the town that is considered the epicenter of production of this grape. According to Carlo Petrussi, the region's best and most experienced ampelographer, Refosco Ronchis is most likely a biotype of Refosco Nostrano, as the two differ slightly, both ampelographically and behaviorally, but to the best of my knowledge, this view is not yet supported by extensive and accurate ampelographic and SSR profiling data. Costacurta's team of researchers showed that parent-offspring relationships exist between Refosco Nostrano and Tazzelenghe (or Refosco del Boton) and the very rare Refosco Gentile (or di Rauscedo) which survives only as scattered vines in very old vineyards. Though Refosco Nostrano and Refoscone were identified as one and the same by Calò, Scienza, and Costacurta in 2001, recent ampelographic and genetic evidence disproves this notion. Morphologically, Refosco Nostrano is characterized by leaves of very variable appearance even within the same plant, a rarity in the grapevine kingdom: some are round, others pentagonal, some indented, others not.

According to Poggi, Refosco Nostrano was considered a potentially high-quality if little-known variety already three centuries ago; in fact, wine made with it was referred to as the "master's wine," for nobles and landowners, who chose first between the wines made by their farmers, always picked Refosco Nostrano wines for themselves. Poggi also wrote that it was the most planted of all *Refoscos* since it was the one that, in light of its bigger berries, yielded the largest amount of must. More recently, Calò and Costacurta have also considered the wine to be potentially very fine. Apparently a native of the countryside around Torreano and Faedis, its very strong vigor, large berries, and copious yields logically endeared it to farmers everywhere in the region. Its only Achilles' heel is that it suffers from dissection of the spine. There are five official clones available to producers: VCR 2, VCR 470, VCR 471, VCR 472, and CRA-VIT-ERSA FVG 390. The original VCR clone (available since 1999) was actually a very good clone that, in my opinion, the subsequent VCR clones (available since 2007) have not really improved upon; the very recent ERSA clone (available since 2010) produces some excellent, very refined wines, though it's characterized by much lower productivity than all the other clones.

Which Wines to Choose and Why

Many *Refosco* wines made around Torreano are made with Refosco Nostrano, and recently producers around Faedis have formed the Associazione Volontaria Viticoltori del Refosco di Faedis (there are roughly twenty members, though there only are about twenty-five Refosco di Faedis producers in total), to promote their wines accordingly. In late 2012, they contacted me about helping their Refosco di Faedis gain some visibility and notoriety. In a rare example of team spirit in a country where individual creativity reigns supreme and where century-old bitter feuds still exist between neighboring towns, the producers of Refosco di Faedis wines have even taken to producing their *riserva* wines, which require a minimum two years of aging, eighteen months of it in five-hundred-liter barrels or large oak casks. Since production volumes of this wine are forcibly small (the variety and its vines has only recently been rediscovered, and each producer makes one thousand to two thousand bottles at most), they have agreed on general guidelines by which to make the *riserva* wine and as to what it should taste like. These *riserva* bottles of the Associazione Volontaria Viticoltori del Refosco di Faedis all carry the same black label with a gold eagle: for those who wish to select Refosco Nostrano wines by the many different local producers (at last count, roughly thirty), the name of the specific producer is written in freehand (in admittedly very small writing) on the front label and in bolder block type on the back label. Since there is nothing worse in the world of wine (besides making bad wines) than making small quantities of wines that are all completely different from each other (nothing confuses and turns off potential customers more), this is a novel idea with some merit. I am sure that as the *denominazione* grows and the wine becomes more popular things will change, but for now, refosco di Faedis is truly a unique wine in Italy.

Interestingly, as legal permission to rename their wine "Refosco di Faedis" was only given by the government in 2011, until very recently wines were labeled simply "Refosco," with a majority of estates even going as far as to state that they were using the better-known Refosco del Peduncolo Rosso. That situation didn't make sense, given that they are located in the birthplace of Refosco Nostrano, and mercifully the absurdity of the situation has finally been rectified. However, due to the aforementioned aging requirement, bottles with the "Refosco di Faedis" title will only come to market in 2014; until then labels will continue to read "Refosco."

A positive quality about Refosco Nostrano is that it is less reductive than Refosco del Peduncolo Rosso, and so is less difficult to work with in the cellar. In my view, however, while Refosco Nostrano wines are fruitier than those made with Refosco del Peduncolo Rosso, the aromas and flavors also tend to be less persistent and complex, with a more pronounced floral (lavender, iris, rose), fruity, and delicately spicy quality (cardamom, cinnamon, marjoram). A note of red licorice is almost always present; some versions can also be slightly mineral, though this really isn't a usual trait of these wines. They also tend to be more acidic and less tannic than wines made with Refosco del Peduncolo Rosso (this is not surprising, given the higher pulp-to-skin ratio). In fact, it is the quality of their tannins that is Refosco Nostrano's trump card. Without doubt, they are far more silky and refined than those of any other *Refosco*, and the wines, though never as full-bodied and structured as those made with Refosco del Peduncolo Rosso, are more graceful, with a smoother, less aggressive tactile presence on the palate. Emilio Del Medico, a very well-respected winemaker (best known for working with star consultant winemaker Maurizio Castelli at the Bastianich's wine estate in Friuli) helps out the producers in the association when they have a question or a problem from time to time. A native of Tarcento (a town close by Faedis), Del Medico also believes that wines made with Refosco Nostrano age spectacularly well; he especially likes the tertiary aromas that develop in time. "Every time I try a ten- or twelve-year-old wine," he says, "I am amazed by the complexity of the floral and spicy notes; they have a really unique bouquet among wines made with other Italian red grape varieties."

WINES TO TRY: Gianni Comar***, Flavia De Gaspero**, Elvio Zani**, Ronc dal Luchis**, Vigna delle Beccacce*, Maurizio Perabò*.

Refosco del Boton

See TAZZELENGHE, chapter 4.

Refosco di Faedis

See REFOSCO NOSTRANO entry.

Refosco di Guarnieri

See TREVISANA NERA, chapter 5.

Refosco di Ronchis

See REFOSCO NOSTRANO entry.

Refosco d'Istria

See TERRANO, chapter 4.

THE SCHIAVA GROUP

The *Schiava*s are a group of unrelated grape varieties typically found in Europe's alpine countries, all characterized by a rugged disposition and potentially very good, light-bodied, light-colored wines. Though grapes of this group are better known as Trollinger in Austria and Germany (save in Württemberg, where the name used is Urban) and as Vernatsch or more rarely Geschlafene in Alto Adige, the *Schiava* group of grapes was already well known by that name in ancient Rome, where vineyards *cum vineis sclavis* ("with vines enslaved," that is, tied to poles as opposed to running free around trees or other natural supports) fetched four times more than others. Already in Roman times, people were aware that providing some sort of non-natural support (such as poles or wires, for example, instead of trees) for the vines improved the quality of the wines. This is because trees, though pretty and capable of providing another crop (for example, olives) also caused the grapes to sit in the shade, and therefore made it rare for them to achieve full maturity. Other experts believe the name *Schiava* derives from "Slavic," implying an Eastern European origin for the variety (thanks to the Huns or the Longobards; in the late Middle Ages the grape was referred to as Hunnisch). Though a stimulating hypothesis, this interpretation seems unlikely: *Schiava* varieties appear to be unrelated to grapes of Hungary, Romania, Armenia, or Georgia.

The *Schiava*s are undoubtedly the most frequently mentioned family of grapes in the Middle Ages, both in agricultural treatises and official documents. A plot of *Schiava* in Trentino is mentioned in a 1311 document from the monastery of Santa Margherita in Ala. *Schiava* wine must have been well regarded, since it was bequeathed in wills, such as William di Castelbarco's, who in 1319 left his heirs *"urnas uvae sclavae grapulae."* In 1536, country wine in Trentino sold for two *quattrini a moiolo*, while schiava sold for three *quattrini*. The vines may have been called "slaves," but they were well paid. In the Middle Ages and later, the *Schiava* group included many cultivars that were probably not even distantly related. However, some of the varieties did have features in common: all were hardy, early ripening, very fertile and productive, and generally gave light-colored wines (and tended to suffer from dissection of the spine). They also shared ampelographic characteristics such as pyramidal, winged bunches and round berries, with only minor differences between varieties: Schiava Grigia's and Schiava Piccola's bunches are more loosely packed than most, and Schiava Grigia's bunches are longer than Schiava Grossa's; the latter also has darker-colored berries. Strangely enough, in medieval Italy, most of the *Schiava*s cultivated were white-berried, while there is no single white *Schiava* in Italy today. Instead, the dark-berried *Schiava*s became common only much later.

The first to have tried classifying the many *Schiava* varieties was Tamaro in 1902, who, clever chap, greatly simplified matters for himself by listing only two: a large-bunched cultivar called Schiava Margellana (or Schiava Patriarca), and a medium-small one named Schiava Gentile (or Schiava Piccola). Marzotto in 1925 was a little more detailed and also took geographic origin into account, but he considered that only large-berried grapes could be *Schiavas*. At that time experts believed, as did others before them, that the Rossara grape of Trentino was also a *Schiava*, a hypothesis refuted by experts such as Rigotti (1932) and which we now know to be wrong. Research by Grando, Frisinghelli, and Stefanini (2000) and Fossati, Labra, Castiglione, Scienza, and Failla (2001) attempted to shed light on possible genetic relationships linking these varieties and distinguished between the Lombardy (Schiava Nera or Schiava Lombarda) and Trentino (Schiava Grigia, Schiava Grossa, Schiava Piccola) groups of *Schiava*s. Fossati's team also showed that Rossara shares a similarity only to the Lombard *Schiava*s, while Grando's team demonstrated that all the main Schiava grapes known today (Schiava Gentile, Schiava Grossa, Schiava Grigia, and Schiava Nera) are unrelated, so this is not a family of grapes, though they tend to look similar. The fact that a grape variety grown in Lombardy is distinct from others carrying a similar name but grown in Trentino and Alto Adige, is further evidence that the term *schiava* referred to a common grapevine training system, rather than to a specific set of related grapes.

Today, *Schiava* varieties are grown almost exclusively in Trentino and Alto Adige (though they were once also common in Lombardy) and are often called (in Alto Adige, at least) by their German name, *Vernatsch*. It is a group of grapes with at least three well described subvarieties: Schiava Gentile, Schiava Grossa, and Schiava Grigia (or Grauvernatsch). These three are quite similar to one another, but being distinct cultivars, they are listed separately in the National Registry. Schiava Nera, a grape found only in Lombardy, is also registered, though some feel it is identical to Schiava Grossa.

According to Harald Schraffl, the talented young winemaker at the Cantina Produttori Nalles Magré, the *Schiava* that is most popular with producers nowadays is Schiava Grossa, with few people planting the Gentile or Grigia subvarieties anymore. This is quite a turnaround, since only ten years ago almost every producer I talked to used to say that Schiava Grigia was the best *Schiava* of all. Shraffl notes that *"grossa* is a very relative term, since the new clones of Schiava Grossa—LB40 and LB56, which are planted by everyone nowadays—actually have much smaller berries than Schiava Grossa used to. These clones are definitely superior to any clone of Grigia or Gentile available. But the main difference is the wine—the wine we can make from these new clones is richer and ages better." *Prost!*

The main problem in choosing schiavas is that DOC regulations don't always specify which *Schiava* can be used to make which wine, so most of the time, unless otherwise specified, it's safe to assume that *Schiava* wines are made with a blend of the three main *Schiava* varieties (Gentile, Grossa, and Grigia). *Schiava*s are used to make DOC wines called St. Magdalener (Santa Maddalena), Lago di Caldaro, Casteller, Botticino, Cellatica, and more, but only the first two are well known and easy to find. They are also the best wines made with these varieties; in fact, some Santa Maddalena and Lago di Caldaro wines are among Italy's very best light-to-midweight red wines. The Santa Maddalena wines can include up to 15 percent Lagrein, a grape giving very dark, structured wines, but that's too high a percentage, for in that case the delicate nature of *Schiava* is completely overwhelmed. Intensely perfumed of strawberry, almond, and violets, light- to medium-bodied, and high in acids, schiavas ought to be very fresh, uncomplicated wines with sneaky concentration and complexity, especially when they come from very old vines.

Schiava Gentile

WHERE IT'S FOUND: Trentino, Alto Adige, Lombardy. NATIONAL REGISTRY CODE NUMBER: 222. COLOR: red.

Also known as Schiava Piccola or Rothervernatsch, due to its small bunch, Schiava Gentile was well drawn and described by Molon in 1906 and Rigotti in 1932. According to Cosmo and Polsinelli (1962), growers believed there was also a Schiava Media variety, characterized by grapes of a size in between those of Schiava Gentile and Schiava Grossa. However, as Schiava Gentile can often have slightly bigger berries mixed in with typically smaller ones even in the same bunch, it is now clear that Schiava Media does not exist. Schiava Gentile appears to be genetically similar to some *Moscato*s (surprisingly, since it is not at all aromatic) and seems to have some features in common with little-known varieties of Veneto such as Turchetta and Pavana. In 2010, Cipriani, Spadotto, Jurman, Di Gaspero, Crespan, Meneghetti, et al. wrote that Schiava Gentile is a parent of Lagrein (the result of a Schiava Gentile × Teroldego crossing), but this finding is disputed by Vouillamoz because in Cipriani's study the proposed parentage was not verified at two of the thirty-nine markers analyzed, a level of discrepancy that Vouillamoz reports has also been found in nonoffspring-offspring pairs. Furthermore, Vouillamoz and Grando (2006) refute this conclusion because, according to their results based on the analysis of sixty DNA markers, Marzemino, a sibling of Lagrein, cannot be a progeny of Schiava Gentile.

The easiest way by which to tell Schiava Gentile apart from the other *Schiava* varieties is by looking at the grape bunch, as the medium-large, roughly circular or at most three-lobed leaf is similar in all three. In Schiava Gentile, the bunch is medium in size (roughly fifteen centimeters long), loosely-packed, pyramidal, with one obvious wing. Berries are medium-sized too, generally round, but irregularly so, in both size and shape, even within the same bunch. It's a late-ripening, vigorous variety that is only mildly susceptible to oidium. To date, there is still only one officially certified clone available, R-1, developed in 1969. As Schiava Gentile is a low yielding, small-berried variety many producers believe it capable of giving quality must, but they are less than thrilled with its lack of generosity.

Which Wines to Choose and Why

Unfortunately, truly monovarietal Schiava Gentile wines are rare, as most often these are made with blends of the three varieties. Supposedly monovarietal wines I have tried over the years are all characterized by pale red to dark pink colors, fresh red fruit (redcurrant, sour red cherry, strawberry) and floral (buttercup, violet) aromas and flavors. Schiava Gentile's delivery of perfumed, light-bodied, and high-acid wines makes it an ideal candidate for *rosato* wine production and indeed many producers choose to grow it with this purpose in mind.

WINES TO TRY: Grigoletti** (Schiava Gentile), Pravis** (Sort Magré), Cantina Aldeno*, Niedermayer*, and Zanoncelli*.

Schiava Grigia

WHERE IT'S FOUND: Trentino, Alto Adige. NATIONAL REGISTRY CODE NUMBER: 223. COLOR: red.

Also called Grauvernatsch, the *grigio* in this variety's name refers to the copious bloom that gives a grey look to its dark-blue berries. According to Grando, Frisinghelli, and Stefanini (2000), Schiava Grigia is identical to the rare Cenerina variety of Trentino ("cenerina" stems from *cenere*, or ash, underlining the grey [*grigio*] look of the berries). It was once felt by many to be the best of all the *Schiavas*, producing the most interesting wines. Currently, views seem to differ. In my opinion, the quality of *Schiava* wines has more to do with vine age, since the best *Schiava* wines regardless of subvariety are made from very old vines. It differs from Schiava Gentile due to its larger, pentagonal leaf, higher vigor, and a less compact, pyramid-shaped bunch that is much longer (over twenty centimeters on average). Like Schiava Gentile, it is subject to dissection of the spine and presents *millerandage* in cold rainy springs. Of all the *Schiavas*, Schiava Grigia is the most sensitive to oidium. It is as late ripening and as vigorous as Schiava Gentile and Schiava Grossa (the latter usually ripens a little earlier). There are no official certified clones available.

Which Wines to Choose and Why

Monovarietal Schiava Grigia wines can be found in Alto Adige. The wine is always a bright pink and exudes aromas of violet, red currant, pomegranate, and marzipan, delivering a slightly salty-sour tang on the usually bright finish. I find its wines to be the most refined of all those made with the various *Schiavas*.

WINES TO TRY: San Michele Appiano** (Schiava Grigia or Grauvernatsch), Terlan** (Grauvernatsch), and Cantina Bolzano** (Grauvernatsch).

Schiava Grossa

WHERE IT'S FOUND: Trentino, Alto Adige, Lombardy. NATIONAL REGISTRY CODE NUMBER: 289. COLOR: red.

Schiava Grossa is also called Edel-Vernatsch, Gross Vernatsch, and Trollinger in Alto Adige, Austria, and Germany; Black Hamburg or Black Tripoli in the United Kingdom; and Bressana around the city of Brescia. The related, high-quality wine grape, Tschaggele, is a biotype of this *Schiava*. As the name implies, it has a big bunch and big berries, though winemakers like Harald Schraffl of Nalles-Magré maintain that modern clones actually have smaller berries than most field samples. Schiava Grossa is also the highest-yielding *Schiava*. Compared to wines made with Schiava Gentile, wines made with Schiava Grossa are characterized by more delicate aromas and flavors and, usually, by higher acidity. According to Crespan (2003), the white Malvasia del Lazio and the black table grape Moscato d'Amburgo are both progenies of Schiava Grossa × Moscato d'Alessandria, so this is another *Schiava* variety that has family ties to the *Moscatos*. According to Vouillamoz and Arnold (2010), Schiava Grossa is one of the parents of Madeleine Royale (no longer cultivated), and so is a grandparent of Müller-Thurgau, one of the world's best-known deliberate laboratory grape crossings. Others have also suggested that it is a parent of Uva Tosca, and possibly Lagrein, but this is more controversial (Cipriani, Spadotto, Jurman, Di Gaspero, Crespan, Meneghetti, et al. 2010). It is the parent of at least one extremely important crossing, Kerner (which is the result of Schiava Grossa × Riesling); Rotberger, another Schiava Grossa × Riesling crossing that is not grown in Italy, has proven decidedly less successful and interesting. The also forgettable Bukettraube, a Sylvaner × Schiava Grossa crossing, is not grown in Italy either.

Schiava Grossa grows mainly in Trentino and Alto Adige, but can also be found in Lombardy (around Brescia, Bergamo, and Pavia) and Veneto (around Verona). It is characterized by larger but otherwise similar leaves to those of Schiava Gentile, while the also larger grape bunch is a truncated cone in shape and more compact. The berries are irregular in shape and size, but are usually round and larger than those of any other *Schiava*. Unlike the other *Schiavas*, Schiava Grossa has been the subject of much clonal selection research, and there are a rather amazing nineteen officially certified clones available for planting. Though the commercial importance of the *Schiava*s may not be anywhere near what it used to be in the past century, so many clones are a clear-cut indication that at least this *Schiava* was deemed to be of significance.

Which Wines to Choose and Why

As I explain above, DOC regulations make it difficult to find schiavas that are not a blend of varieties. Still, some producers reportedly use only or mainly (that is, 90 percent or more) Schiava Grossa.

WINES TO TRY: In Trentino, try Soini Quinto (Schiava Grossa La Laita). In Alto Adige, try: Produttori Nalles-Magré*** (Galea, a thing of beauty; some vines are over one hundred years old), Produttori Merano*** (Meranese St. Valentin; also made mainly from fifty-plus-year-old vines), Ramoser** (Santa Maddalena; a very good example, with only 2 percent Lagrein, so you get to taste the *Schiava*), Franz Gojer** (Santa Maddalena), Cantina Girlan* (Schiava fass n. 9), and Josephus Mayr* (Santa Maddalena).

Schiava Nera

WHERE IT'S FOUND: Lombardy. NATIONAL REGISTRY CODE NUMBER: 224. COLOR: red.

Also called Sciava, Sciava Peloseta, and Sciava Spinarola, today Schiava Nera grows mainly in Lombardy, especially around the shores of Lake Garda, so many in that region refer to it as Schiava Lombarda. In the late 1800s it was cultivated everywhere in Trentino especially, with roughly eighty thousand hectoliters per year produced, not a small amount. The variety is characterized by large, pentagonal leaves (much larger than those of the other three *Schiava*s) with three lobes and a lightly downy undersurface (a feature the other three *Schiava*s lack), and large, long bunches (twenty-five to thirty centimeters; again, larger than the other three *Schiava*s) that are conical-cylindrical in shape and winged. The round berries are also quite large. It is vigorous and late ripening like all the *Schiava*s, and there are two officially certified clones (BS-S10 and BS-S12).

Which Wines to Choose and Why

Today, it's not easy to find a monovarietal Schiava Nera wine, though in Lombardy DOC Colleoni (or Terre del Colleoni) must be made with a minimum 85 percent Schiava Nera (a sparkling version is also possible). It hardly helps when a well-known, excellent producer such as Gino Pedrotti (his Trentino Vino Santo made with Nosiola is one of Italy's greatest wines) labels a wine "Schiava Nera" when it is in fact made with Schiava Grossa.

WINES TO TRY: Cantina Bergamasca (Rosato is the only monovarietal Schiava Nera I know that is easy to find, and a wine that has managed to win awards in well-known international wine competitions).

THE TREBBIANO GROUP

Naming members of the *Trebbiano* group often involved adding an adjective that referred to their place of origin, the place where they were most abundant, or their color. Thus there are countless different Trebbiano-Something varieties, from *verde* to *giallo* and from *Romagnolo* to *Toscano*. According to Labra, Winfield, Ghiani, Grassi, Sala, Scienza, and Failla (2001), these varieties lack a common progenitor, deriving either from domesticated local Italian varieties or crossings between these and new grapevine arrivals. Labra's study (still the most-cited research paper detailing the *Trebbiano* group), illustrated how the *Trebbiano*s share some morphologic and behavioral features like white berries (there are no red-berried *Trebbiano*s), large and generally long bunches, high vigor, late ripening, and very good adaptability to diverse *terroirs*, but are, for the most part, unrelated. In fact, a dendrogram charting shared bands, based on the SSR data, suggested that Trebbiano Abruzzese and Trebbiano Spoletino are the only two *Trebbiano*s with probable family ties; it also showed that Trebbiano di Soave, Trebbiano di Lugana, and Verdicchio have a high proportion of bands sharing similarity, which is not surprising, as the first two are synonyms of Verdicchio, rather than true *Trebbiano*s.

The origin of the name *Trebbiano* itself is unclear. Pliny writes of a *Vinum tribulanum* produced in the Agro Tribulanis near Capua in his *Naturalis Historia,* but *tribulanum* wines from Umbria and Tuscany were also known then. Others have hypothesized the name derives from the locality of the same name near Luni, while still others have suggested the Trebbia River in Emilia-Romagna, where a *Trebbiano* grows. Hohnerlein-Buchinger (1996) has noted a phonetic similarity with the Frankish term *drajbo* (meaning vigorous shoots or inner strength), and the Franks and Longobards did play an important role in rebuilding medieval Italy's vineyards. Interestingly, in the thirteenth and fourteenth centuries, *Trebbiano* wines were considered luxury items, which may help explain why the name became so common and attributed to so many diverse cultivars.

In 1925, Marzotto differentiated and classified fifteen different *Trebbiano* varieties in Italy, some of which (such as Trebbiano Romagnolo and Trebbiano Toscano) are still grown today.

Trebbianina

WHERE IT'S FOUND: Emilia-Romagna, Marche. NATIONAL REGISTRY CODE NUMBER: 434. COLOR: white.

In Italy, Trebbianina is also known as Trebbiano di Spagna, a correct synonym; calling it Trebbiano Giallo is a mistake, as the two are distinct varieties. Trebbianina is mainly associated with Aceto Balsamico Tradizionale production, rather than wines, but this is not entirely correct. The Trebbiano di Spagna grapes associated with balsamic vinegar production grow on heavy yielding flatland vineyards around Modena; by contrast, small artisanal producers who work higher-quality hillside vineyards near Modena are able to turn out delicious, fruit-forward wines with plenty of early appeal though admittedly they are hard to find outside the immediate production area.

Trebbiano di Spagna is characterized by medium-sized leaves that are roughly triangular or cuneiform in shape, very long cylindrical-conical winged bunches, and medium-sized, round to oval berries. It is resistant to pathogens like all *Trebbiano*s but ripens a little earlier in the fall than most other members of this group. There are no official clones of this variety.

Which Wines to Choose and Why

Trebbiano di Spagna is mainly grown around Modena in Emilia-Romagna, and is part of four IGT wine blends in Italy: Emilia, Forlì, Ravenna, and Rubicone. It is not included in the guidelines of any DOCG or DOC wine. And yet, there are some truly delicious monovarietal examples for wine lovers to try, for example Claudio Plessi's Tarbianen, with only nine hundred bottles made ... for the world! Tarbianen is a unique wine, one taste of which will have you thinking of curry, cinnamon, green tea, and ripe citrus fruits. Admittedly, it is hard to find, though you might look for it near Castelnuovo Rangone; in the past, the brilliant Beppe Palmieri, chief sommelier of the Michelin three star Osteria Francescana in Modena, arguably Italy's best restaurant, had a few bottles to offer the lucky gastronomic traveler. Made from organic grapes, the wine tastes as much of the way it is made as of the grape variety. Restaurants prove a good source for Trebbiano di Spagna wines: at the Osteria di Rubbiara restaurant, owned by the Pedron family, you'll be able to taste another sparkling, deliciously fruity wine made with Trebbiano di Spagna served directly at the restaurant, though it's on sale elsewhere.

WINES TO TRY: Venturelli** (Spumante Metodo Classico, a sparkling wine made by refermentation in the bottle just like Champagne; I tasted the excellent 2006 recently, and it was still holding up beautifully), Pedroni* (Bianca Pedroni Spumante di Spagna), Cantina Formigine

Pedemontana* (Vino della Luna Trebbiano di Modena Amabile; not just bubbly but also sweet, with roughly forty grams per liter of residual sugar).

Trebbiano Abruzzese

WHERE IT'S FOUND: Abruzzo. NATIONAL REGISTRY CODE NUMBER: 322. COLOR: white.

To be clear, the correct, official name of the variety is Trebbiano Abruzzese, not Trebbiano d'Abruzzo: the latter is the name of the wine made with this cultivar, though people have taken to calling the grape and the wine by the same name. The earliest reference to Trebbiano Abbruzzese is by Molon (1906), who noted that it was different from Trebbiano Campolese, which had larger berries. However, Trebbiano Abruzzese has always been confused with other varieties, most notably Bombino Bianco, from which it has been clearly distinguished only recently. In fact, the National Registry currently lists both Bombino Bianco and Empibotte (another name commonly used by locals to refer to Trebbiano Abruzzese) as erroneous synonyms. According to Domenico Pasetti of the Pasetti estate, Trebbiano Abruzzese derives from Biancame, itself derived from Trebbiano Toscano; a link between Biancame and Trebbiano Abruzzese was first mentioned by Calò, Scienza, and Costacurta (2006). Others, like Luigi Cataldi Madonna of the Cataldi Madonna estate, believe there isn't that much true Trebbiano Abruzzese in the vineyards, as over the years a great deal of Bombino Bianco and Trebbiano Toscano were planted instead. "It is likely that only 20 percent of all the *Trebbiano*s grown in Abruzzo are really of the Abruzzese variety, though of course, once turned into wine everything gets labeled as Trebbiano d'Abruzzo," he told me. His winemaker, Lorenzo Landi, takes a less dire view, saying that there is still quite a bit of this high-quality *Trebbiano* in the countryside. Francesco Valentini of the world-famous Valentini estate, who makes an outstanding wine labeled Trebbiano d'Abruzzo, believes his vines are, for the most part, true Trebbiano Abruzzese, and not Bombino Bianco, as has been erroneously written elsewhere. Cristiana Tiberio, owner of one of Italy's truly up-and-coming estates, told me that Trebbiano Abruzzese is her favorite grape variety of those she grows. In fact, her father, who has been working in wine all his life, quit his job as export manager at another Abruzzo winery to found his own estate (called Tiberio) after coming upon an old forgotten vineyard of beautiful, healthy-looking, fifty-year-old Trebbiano Abruzzese vines. "There is no way you can confuse it with Bombino Bianco, Trebbiano Toscano, or any other such variety," says Tiberio "because they really look completely different. If anything, I think it's Passerina that people most often mistakenly identify as Trebbiano Abruzzese." For example, the excellent producer of Abruzzo wines called Faraone makes a white wine labeled trebbiano d'Abruzzo that is actually made with Passerina instead.

In my opinion, Trebbiano Abruzzese is characterized by large leaves with five lobes, and large, long, pyramid-shaped bunches with medium-large berries that have little bloom. The vine is vigorous, oidium sensitive, and dislikes excessively windy sites; acidity drops very quickly if the grapes overripen. The large leaves protect the berries very well from the sunlight, and for this reason, the grapes rarely become darker than a deep straw-green in color when fully ripe; so unlike other *Trebbiano*s, Trebbiano Abruzzese's berries almost never become yellow-gold or reddish and this is true even when the producer decides to deleaf in order to maximize ripeness. There are two officially certified clones of Trebbiano Abruzzese (VCR 3 and UBA-RA TR27), but numerous biotypes also exist, which has only added to the difficulties in accurately recognizing Trebbiano Abruzzese in the vineyards (provided that those showing you the grapevines aren't getting them confused with Bombino Bianco or Passerina). There appear to be at least two biotypes of Trebbiano Abruzzese: Sbaganina, typical of the area of Vasto, characterized by a medium-large bunch, very thin-skinned berries, and as many as three wings, and Svagarina, more typical of the Marruccina area, with a larger bunch, thicker skins, and usually two wings. Pasetti believes it is the latter biotype that is more reminiscent of Bombino Bianco, and most often confused with it.

Which Wines to Choose and Why

Trebbiano Abruzzese is certainly a higher quality grape than Trebbiano Toscano, and the wine made with it is too. Therefore, it would be a real shame if Trebbiano Abruzzese were as rare as some producers think it might be. Trebbiano d'Abruzzo offers an interesting white wine alternative to Abruzzo's other white wine offerings, such as those made with Pecorino wines, which are more structured and saline. Good Trebbiano d'Abruzzo has just a hint of white flowers and stone fruit on the nose, a creamy mouthfeel, and plenty of acidity with a citrusy minerality. Cristiana Tiberio believes that this variety is better picked sooner rather than later, for late harvesting Trebbiano Abruzzese means making wines that are dull and devoid of perfume. Harvesting a few days in advance, or at the point of optimal ripeness, allows wines that are far better than once believed. In past decades, since Trebbiano Abruzzese was confused with other varieties, it is likely the cultivar was never harvested at the best possible time, a situation that did not allow Trebbiano Abruzzese to show off its potential. Another difficulty posed by this variety (especially so in Italy's winemaking-challenged, not-so-distant past) is that due to its high polyphenol content, Trebbiano Abruzzese's must oxidizes easily, so flat, dull, and overly-dark white wines were common. Nowadays, in order to avoid oxidating and losing aromas, many producers have turned to hyperreductive winemaking techniques when making trebbiano d'Abruzzo, such as using presses with inert gas.

WINES TO TRY: Cataldi Madonna***, Tiberio*** (both the Trebbiano d'Abruzzo and the Fonte Canale, a *cru* bottling), Valentini***, Barba**, Castello di Semivicoli*, Pasetti*, Jasci & Marchesani*, Nicodemi*, and Zaccagnini* (Chronicon and San Clemente).

Trebbiano Giallo

WHERE IT'S FOUND: Lazio, Umbria, Lombardy, Veneto, Puglia. NATIONAL REGISTRY CODE NUMBER: 240. COLOR: white.

This variety is particularly confusing due to many synonyms that are commonly used but most likely erroneous, such as Rossetto (likely a distinct variety) and Trebbiano di Spagna (which is actually Trebbianina). The true Trebbiano Giallo is historically associated with the Castelli Romani in Lazio, where it is also known as Trebbiano Giallo di Velletri (as well as, incorrectly, Greco Giallo and Greco Giallo di Velletri). It was an important part of the blend of wines made in the Roman countryside, in contrast to Trebbiano Toscano, which is only a recent arrival in the region and is not native to Lazio. Therefore, the *Trebbiano* variety historically associated with the wines of Frascati, Marino, and the Colli Albani was Trebbiano Giallo, not the Trebbiano Toscano you read and hear about today. Trebbiano Giallo takes its name from the golden hue of its berries when fully ripe. Acerbi was the first to describe the golden look of this variety in 1825, and also correctly pointed out that the variety was anything but a generous producer. Molon started getting things wrong in 1906 by considering Greco Giallo and Trebbiano Giallo identical. Then Prosperi in 1939 compounded the problem by writing that Rossetto, another variety typically associated with the countryside of Montefiascone in Lazio's northeast, was a synonym for Castelli Romani's Trebbiano Giallo, since he believed the golden-yellow berries of the latter variety could turn pinkish-red when fully ripe. However, according to the local Castelli Romani and Cori farmers I have talked to over the years, such a color change is not characteristic of the grapes they know as Trebbiano Giallo, so in my opinion, it's very likely Prosperi just confused the two varieties, because Rossetto and

Trebbiano Giallo are probably not the same variety (though the National Registry currently lists the two as synonymous). Things plummeted when, about ten years ago, world-famous winemaker Riccardo Cotarella (owner of the Falesco estate at the border between Umbria and Lazio) began making a very successful wine with a local variety called Roscetto, also known in the area as Rossetto (its official name in the National Registry; see ROSSETTO, chapter 4) or as ... Trebbiano Giallo. So everyone has begun referring to Trebbiano Giallo, Rossetto, and Roscetto as the same variety. To complicate matters even further, there is a so-called Trebbiano Giallo variety growing in sporadic rows in Lombardy's Garda Colli Mantovani area, and according to Calò, Scienza, and Costacurta (2006), the same is also found in Umbria, Veneto, and Puglia.

It's not a very clear situation. For one, Rossetto and Roscetto might not be identical varieties: at least, grey-haired locals have told me—and old documents confirm—that Roscetto and Rossetto were once considered distinct (if they actually were is a different matter). Since hard evidence of any kind is lacking to back up this specific observation, it may also be that Roscetto is simply another term for Rossetto in the local dialect. Second, Cotarella believes that the Roscetto grape is not a *Trebbiano* at all, but rather a *Greco*: "I think it's a *Greco* for sure," he's told me, "since the grape looks and behaves like one. Plus, the wine is very tannic and rich, and the skin is loaded with polyphenols, just like the Greco of Campania." In other words, Cotarella believes that Rossetto should not be identified with Trebbiano Giallo, and that to refer to it with the latter name is a mistake. Though I agree with Cotarella that Trebbiano Giallo and Rossetto are not one and the same, and while I also understand his very logical observation (which would seem to be backed up by the outstanding wine called Ferentano he produces with Rossetto, which is big and tannic, just like those made with the *Greco* varieties, and quite unlike those made with any *Trebbiano* variety), Roscetto/Rossetto is not a *Greco*, or at least, DNA studies show that it is neither Greco nor Greco Bianco (Muganu, Dangl, Aradhya, Frediani, Scossa, and Stover 2009). I add that Cotarella's Roscetto or Rossetto looks nothing, at least to me, like the Greco Giallo found in the Castelli Romani and Cori areas of Lazio, but this does not mean it isn't a *Greco* after all. That all is not well in the world of Trebbiano Giallo is also shown by the fact that the National Registry describes the variety as an "abundant and regular" producer, which doesn't sound anything like the Trebbiano Giallo variety described to me by Marco Carpineti. Based on these numerous considerations, it follows that further accurate ampelographic studies and DNA analysis are needed to fully resolve the question of Rossetto versus Roscetto versus Trebbiano Giallo versus Greco Giallo.

Last but not least, Trebbiano Giallo was once also identified with Trebbiano di Spagna, but this is incorrect. Trebbiano di Spagna is a variety more accurately called Trebbianina, the name with which it appears in the National Registry at number 434. Trebbianina's role as a wine grape has only been recently appreciated; up until now, it was considered at best a blending grape used to make Aceto Balsamico Tradizionale (traditional balsamic vinegar) in Emilia-Romagna. Trebbianina has been recently studied by Pastore and Allegro (2007), and described as having cuneiform leaves, grape bunches that are pyramid-shaped, long, and winged, with medium-small berries. It clearly does not look anything like the real Trebbiano Giallo, based on my observations and those of Carpineti, nor does it resemble the description of Trebbiano Giallo in the National Registry.

Generally speaking, Trebbiano Giallo is characterized by large pentagonal leaves, medium to large, cylindrical-conical bunches, with medium-round berries that turn yellow-gold when fully ripe, dotted with brown flecks. Though there are no officially recognized clones, there are at least three different biotypes of Trebbiano Giallo that have been described in old Lazio vineyards, differentiated by the size of the bunch and the wings (medium-small with two wings, medium with one or two wings, and large with one large wing or two); some have described even a fourth biotype. One of these may yet be proven to be related to the *Greco*s, to Roscetto, or to Rosseto.

Marco Carpineti, Cori's best wine producer, who knows both Trebbiano Giallo and Greco Giallo well (and owns vines of the latter), says that Greco Giallo, with its superior disease resistance, has taken Trebbiano Giallo's place in the vineyards: "Trebbiano Giallo is too susceptible to diseases, is small-bunched, and produces little; the wine is always of great quality but ultimately the grape has virtually disappeared because of its limited productivity." In the absence of genetic testing, we do not know if Greco Giallo and Trebbiano Giallo are truly distinct, as Carpineti believes, though it seems likely. Complicating matters is that Carpineti's so-called Greco Giallo variety looks a lot more like a *Trebbiano* to me than it does a *Greco*: Carpineti's Greco Giallo has a long, scrawny bunch, small berries, and thin skin, all morphologic features more typical of the *Trebbiano*s than the *Greco*s. Last but not least, to the best of my knowledge, nobody really knows the identity of the variety—or varieties—growing in Lombardy and Veneto.

Which Wines to Choose and Why

True Trebbiano Giallo only grows in the Lazio area of the Castelli Romani and Cori. In my opinion, it should not be confused with the Rossetto variety typical of northeastern Lazio. Therefore, there is no monovarietal wine made with Trebbiano Giallo, and the few grapes still grown around Rome are used in blends such as Castelli Romani and other wines of the area. Marco Carpineti told me he tasted some trebbiano giallo wine made for home use when he was much younger. Though the wines were never truly monovarietal (locals tended to vineyards that were promiscuously planted with many different varieties, as was commonly done in those times), he remembers the wine as intensely flavored and glyceral, with aromas and flavors of fresh herbs and ripe peach.

Trebbiano Modenese

WHERE IT'S FOUND: Emilia-Romagna. NATIONAL REGISTRY CODE NUMBER: 241. COLOR: white.

Also known as Trebianella, Trebbiano di Modena, and Trebbiano Comune, this *Trebbiano* variety really comes into its own not so much for the wine that can be made from it (though there are decent dry white and especially sparkling wines) but because it is the main ingredient of the wonderful Aceto Balsamico Tradizionale di Modena (which is different from the much cheaper, industrially made Aceto Balsamico *tout court*). It is characterized by fairly large leaves, bunches that are medium-large, pyramid-shaped, and fairly compact with one or two wings, and medium-sized, round berries covered with bloom. A clone called CAB-1 became available in 2011; it accumulates more sugar and is less productive than the average grapevines of Trebbiano Modenese. As far as *Trebbiano*s go, this variety is a fairly early ripener, as it is usually picked already by the end of September or in the early part of October.

Which Wines to Choose and Why

Trebbiano Modenese grows in Emilia-Romagna, mainly in the provinces of Modena and Reggio Emilia, where many old vines still exist. There is no DOC wine specifically devoted to it, but it is used in IGT blends such as Bianco di Castelfranco Emilia, Rubicone, Forlì, and Ravenna. The wine made with Trebbiano Modenese is usually light and fresh with delicate herbal and lemony aromas and flavors, sometimes with a hint of honey on the finish. Even though it's not the last word in complexity or depth, it's pleasant enough and will match well with light vegetable and fish dishes. However, Vittorio Graziano believes Trebbiano Modenese can offer so much more than that. Graziano, a recognized leading light in Italy's fledgling natural wines movement, makes wines that may not be for everyone due to their tannic nature and slightly oxidized aromas and flavors. Nevertheless, he is a big believer in Trebbiano Modenese and feels it has been unfairly banished to a "light everyday wine" or balsamic vinegar context only. In his opinion, Trebbiano Modenese is instead capable of delivering big, structured wines unlike any commonly associated with the *Trebbiano* varieties; the wines are always high in acidity and show best after three years or so of bottle age.

WINES TO TRY: Vittorio Graziano** (Tarbianaz), Corte Manzini* (Il Gherlo, sparkling), Il Monte, and Celso Vandelli.

Trebbiano Romagnolo

WHERE IT'S FOUND: Emilia-Romagna. NATIONAL REGISTRY CODE NUMBER: 242. COLOR: white.

Trebbiano Romagnolo is an ancient variety, documented in Romagna by Pier de' Crescenzi in 1303—or at least, he documented a *Trebbiano* variety that was then grown in Romagna. In the countryside around Lugo, in the province of Ravenna, it is also known as Trebbiano della Fiamma, "of the flame," as its berries tend to a bright golden-bronze when fully ripe. However, the latter is actually a very high-quality biotype of Trebbiano Romagnolo; not all biotypes share the same reddish hue of the berries or the penchant for making high-quality wine. Unfortunately, there is so much Trebbiano Toscano grown in Emilia-Romagna that Romagnolo and Toscano grapevines often grow next to each other right in the same row of vines; and I've often seen producers who believe theirs is the Romagnolo variety but actually have Toscano.

Trebbiano Romagnolo is characterized by pentagonal, medium-sized leaves, medium-sized, pyramid-shaped bunches that have one or two wings, and round berries. It's very resistant to peronospora and botrytis, less to oidium; like all *Trebbiano*s it's a vigorous variety that guarantees regular and abundant crops. Ten official clones exist (R5, TR 3 T, TR 5 T, TR 8 T, TR 12 T, VCR 424, VCR 429, VCR 436, Ampelos DGV 4, and Ampelos DVG 6); the TR 8 T is particularly high quality, earlier ripening, and less vigorous than the others, used to produce more complex, deeper wines. Of the numerous biotypes of Trebbiano Romagnolo, two are most common: one located especially in flatland vineyards, and one found high in the hills. The former can produce as much as four hundred quintals per hectare (a ridiculously large amount) and has a medium-small, compact cluster with medium-large, round berries. The second biotype is the one that most often looks like a Trebbiano della Fiamma, and is reddish in hue, very rich in acids, and gives more complex wines. It has a very long compact bunch with a large leaf (larger than the other biotype of Trebbiano Romagnolo), and likes clay-loamy soils. Though it presents few problems to farmers, it began disappearing nonetheless in the 1960s and 1970s because it produces very little. At 16,285 hectares, in 2010 Trebbiano Romagnolo was Italy's tenth most-planted variety (actually eighth, if we remove Merlot and Chardonnay from the list), but I wonder just how many of those supposed Trebbiano Romagnolo grapevines really aren't Trebbiano Toscano instead.

Which Wines to Choose and Why

Trebbiano Romagnolo is found in Emilia-Romagna, especially in the provinces of Ravenna and Forlì. In my view, the authentic Trebbiano Romagnolo has plenty to say in the realm of everyday, light, easy-going wines, but it's hard to come across a truly pure version of it. The wine seems to me to be richer and more complex than those made with even old vine Trebbiano Toscano, hinting at riper yellow fruit, chlorophyll, and aniseed, and with a richer texture. That said, many wines labeled trebbiano romagnolo are insipid and neutral, which may just be a matter of the biotype used; this is why Trebbiano Romagnolo is often made as an inexpensive, uncomplicated sparkling wine meant for drinking in the very near term (at most within one year from the vintage).

Wines made with the better biotypes have the acidity, the flesh, and the ability to age and improve. I caution readers that just because a label reads "Trebbiano di Romagna," that does not necessarily mean it is a wine made wholly with Trebbiano Romagnolo, as the DOC guidelines only require that a minimum 85 percent Trebbiano Romagnolo be used.

WINES TO TRY: Leone Conti**, Fattoria Zerbina**, Tre Monti** (Vigna Rio), Battistini*, La Berta* (they simply write the wine is made with 100 percent "Trebbiano," which is incorrect), and Celli*.

Trebbiano Spoletino

WHERE IT'S FOUND: Umbria. NATIONAL REGISTRY CODE NUMBER: 243. COLOR: white.

Though Trebbiano Spoletino was known already in the nineteenth century, it is not clear if this variety is native to the countryside of Perugia, where it grows today, or if it was brought to Umbria from elsewhere. This variety has met with huge popularity in Umbria in the last ten years, and as is all too often the case, suddenly many estates started churning out their own version of Trebbiano Spoletino wine, or drastically increased their existing production to large numbers of bottles. Though farmers in Umbria have always owned a row or two of Trebbiano Spoletino in their vineyards, nobody made a monovarietal wine with it; only when Cantina Novelli, at the beginning of the twenty-first century, began paying attention to the variety and started making crisp, citrusy wines very reminiscent of those made with Sauvignon Blanc, did Trebbiano Spoletino's popularity take off. However, many trebbiano spoletino wines don't taste anything alike, something that may have to do with the grapevine that's actually growing in people's vineyards. Having walked the Umbrian vineyards over the years, I can safely say that no two Trebbiano Spoletino producers have grapes that look alike—or to be kind, there seems to be a very large intravarietal variability with this grape, especially among the older vines. I have tasted some grapes (and wines) that are downright aromatic, almost Gewürztraminer-like, while most others are neutral, so my feeling is that a lot of homework still needs to be done on the subject.

The description of Trebbiano Spoletino in the National Registry is of a grapevine with medium-large leaves that have a downy undersurface, cylindrical or cylindrical-conical, medium-sized, very compact bunches, and medium-sized, round berries. It behaves like all other *Trebbianos*, in that it is a late ripener and is resistant to peronospora and botrytis, but slightly less to oidium. There is one official clone of Trebbiano Spoletino, named 1 ISV-ICA PG. According to Borgo, Cartechini, Lovat, and Moretti (2004), this clone is more resistant to oidium and botrytis than the standard populations and also has more total acidity at similar levels of ripeness.

Which Wines to Choose and Why

Trebbiano Spoletino is found only in Umbria, especially in the townships of Spoleto, Montefalco, and the many small towns in the area. For all the phenotypic differences presented by the grape, the wines are uniformly quite good, thereby explaining why so many estates in the area want to try their hand at producing this wine. So far, wines have ranged from fresh and lemony, with sauvignonesque characters, to unctuous and alcoholic, with a few even sporting aromatic notes, much like a moscato bianco. In my view, these aromatic wines are most likely not made with Trebbiano Spoletino, but rather with a local aromatic variety; of course, there may well be a "Trebbiano Spoletino Aromatico," as with Malvasia Bianca di Candia and Malvasia di Candia Aromatica, but in my view Trebbiano Spoletino is not an aromatic variety. Those wines that are intensely lemony, figgy, and herbal are most likely the product of hyperreductive winemaking techniques, but in this manner they become less interesting, losing in personality, since they smell and taste like a Sauvignon Blanc.

WINES TO TRY: Tabarrini** (Adarmando), Antonelli-San Marco**, Perticaia**, and Celesti*. Others, even well-known names, are too reminiscent of sauvignon blanc for my taste.

Trebbiano Toscano

WHERE IT'S FOUND: everywhere in Italy. NATIONAL REGISTRY CODE NUMBER: 244. COLOR: white.

Trebbiano Toscano is known by a huge variety of synonyms in Tuscany, some acceptable (Procanico, Brucanico, Santoro) and others erroneous, in that they refer to different varieties or specific biotypes of Trebbiano Toscano (for example Coda di Cavallo is an altogether different variety from Campania and Biancone is another Tuscan variety or perhaps a specific biotype of Trebbiano Toscano typical of Elba). Biancame is no longer recognized, by most experts, as a Trebbiano Toscano biotype (see BIANCAME, chapter 4).

In any case, there are few cultivars in Italy with deservedly poorer reputations than Trebbiano Toscano, which has always been associated with the production of neutral, insipid white wines that won't age, or with lackluster Chiantis. However, the original Chianti blend invented by Bettino Ricasoli called for seven parts Sangiovese, two parts Canaiolo Nero, and one part Malvasia Bianca Lunga. Ricasoli did not want Trebbiano Toscano in the blend, while he liked Malvasia Bianca Lunga, which he felt added a nice aromatic, refreshing touch. Trebbiano Toscano was included when the official guidelines for Chianti production were drawn up only because it is both a very abundant variety in Tuscany and because it allows for more wine to be made. In France, where they know better, it is distilled to make Cognac: ironically, Ugni Blanc, the French name of the variety, derives from the *Eugenias*, a group of noble varieties described by Pliny. The first mention of it with a name resembling Ugni Blanc dates back to 1514 when it was called Uniers in areas of Vaucluse and Pernes (Rézeau 1997). Trebbiano Toscano is however an unmistakably Italian grape variety since it has been proven to have a parent-offspring relationship with Garganega, the grape most associated with the Soave wine (Di Vecchi Staraz, Bandinelli, Boselli, This, Boursiquot, Laucou, et al. 2007). Since Garganega also has parent-offspring relationships with eight other varieties (Albana, Cataratto Bianco, Malvasia Bianca di Candia, Dorona, Marzemina Bianca, Montonico Bianco, Mostosa, and Susumaniello), Trebbiano Toscano is also either their grandparent or their half-sibling. According to Boccacci, Torello Marinoni, Gambino, Botta, and Schneider (2005), the variety known as Bianca di Poviglio is identical to Trebbiano Toscano. Filipetti, Silvestroni, Thomas, and Intrieri (2001) have indicated that Alionza, another variety typical of Emilia-Romagna may be closely related to this *Trebbiano*. Finally, Garofanata, recently added to the National Registry, is an offspring of Trebbiano Toscano (Cipriani, Spadotto, Jurman, Di Gaspero, Crespan, Meneghetti, et al. 2010).

Trebbiano Toscano has been used to achieve a number of crossings; some are of very limited wine interest (Chenel, Folignan, and Nouvelle) while others are decidedly more promising, such as Fubiano and Manzoni Rosa. Most importantly, Trebbiano Toscano has been used to create one of the world's few truly successful hybrid grapes, Vidal (a cross of Trebbiano Toscano × Seibel 4986, also known as Rayon d'Or). Developed in the 1930s by grape breeder Jean-Louis Vidal, his namesake grape is one of the world's most important sources of ice wine.

Though Trebbiano Toscano is not associated with world-famous or outstanding dry white wines in Italy (or anywhere else for that matter), there are some biotypes of Trebbiano Toscano, most likely the result of viral infections, that strike me as possibly being higher quality. For example, old vines of a Trebbiano Toscano characterized by pinkish, almost red berries (when fully ripe) yield a much deeper, more flavorful wine (mind you, deep and flavorful with Trebbiano Toscano are relative terms).

Field studies on different training systems, bud loads, yields, and dates of harvest have all helped in shifting Trebbiano Toscano cultivation to a more quality-oriented direction. For example, a three-year comparison by Di Vaio, Pasquarella, Scaglione, Boselli, and Forlani (1998) between two bud loads (eleven and twenty-two) and two different training systems (long and short) of Trebbiano Toscano in Campania gave interesting results. Reduction in bud load gave rise to longer shoots and an increase in the soluble solid content of the must at harvest, while reducing yield per plant. With the same bud load, short pruning led to greater vigor, less productivity, and a reduction in must sugar content. Comparative analysis showed that long pruning combined with the lower bud load provided the best balance between vegetative and productive activity.

In general, Trebbiano Toscano is characterized by abundant and regular productivity due to the high bunch weight and good fertility. Trebbiano Toscano has good tolerance for spring frost since it has a late budding, and though it needs plenty of sunlight and heat and long growing seasons to ripen fully, it can adapt to many conditions due to its rusticity. It's very easy to recognize this variety in vineyards, as its bunch is medium-large, cylindrical (at times cylindrical-conical), and quite long. It can be more or less compact and winged, and very often has a bifurcated tip. There are officially fifteen recognized clones of Trebbiano Toscano (R4, Santa Lucia 30, I-T-N 8, CSV-AP TR1, CSV-AP TR2, Fedit 28-CH, Fedit 29-CH, S. Lucia 12, T34 ICA-PG, VCR 8, CRA 437, CRA 546, UBA-RA TRT 8, TRE VISP, and CRA Vic BC SF7).

Trebbiano Toscano is Italy's most commonly planted white grape (and is the seventh most-planted grape in the world). In Italy it grows practically everywhere, but mainly in Tuscany, Marche, Umbria, Lazio, and Emilia-Romagna. Due to its productivity, it was planted to the detriment of local, higher-quality *Trebbiano*s, such as Trebbiano Giallo and Trebbiano Romagnolo, both of which give more interesting wines than does the Toscano variety. Unfortunately, confusion is such that many producers don't know exactly which of the *Trebbiano*s they own, which is why in Emilia-Romagna or Abruzzo, for example, there are estate owners who have wildly different opinions on the merits of their *Trebbiano* vines.

Besides France, Trebbiano Toscano has been planted in many other countries in the world, such as Greece, Argentina, Australia, Canada, and the United States. In Australia, Trebbiano Toscano, along with Colombard, has always been popular as a source of good bulk wine. The variety seems to grow well in the hot Riverina region of southwestern New South Wales. In Argentina it's grown in Mendoza, San Juan, and Río Negro, while in California there are small plantings in Paso Robles and the Central Valley.

Which Wines to Choose and Why

Planted everywhere in Italy, Trebbiano Toscano plays an important part in the blends of many admittedly not so famous DOC wines: for example, Bianco Colline Lucchesi, Bianco della Valdinievole, Bianco dell'Empolese, Bianco Pisano di San Torpè, Elba Bianco, Val d'Arbia, Bianco di Pitigliano, Montecucco, Montescudaio, Sant' Antimo in Tuscany; and Bagnoli, Bianco di Custoza, Breganze, Colli Euganei, Gambellara, Garda Orientale, Lugana, and Valdadige in other regions. The list is much longer, however. Some of these wines are much better than others; witness Bianco di Pitigliano or Elba Bianco. Trebbiano Toscano also plays a role in the production of many Tuscan IGT wines and it is important for *vin santo*, traditionally produced in Tuscany (Chianti, Chianti Classico, Carmignano, Montepulciano, Elba, Capalbio, Montescudaio, and other denominations), as well as in Umbria and Emilia-Romagna. As Trebbiano Toscano is blessed with high acidity even when harvested late, it's a useful addition to many white wine blends that can benefit from the extra lift. There are some worthwhile monovarietal dry white wines, always from very old vines, but such wines are made in very small quantities and are hard to find. Even then, though these wines will have more intense aromas and flavors, the aromatic spectrum and depth of flavor is, in my experience, always limited in Trebbiano Toscano wines. In fact, I find while that monovarietal Trebbiano Toscano wine is delicately herbal, lemony, and fresh, even very good ones will never be rich, dense, or mouthcoating. It can act as a very good, if simple, aperitif or pasta wine.

The one product for which this variety is unquestionably a standout is *vin santo*, the best examples of which are some of Italy's greatest wines. But even there, most producers will tell you that a very large dollop of Malvasia Bianca Lunga is necessary to make the best wines possible. Trebbiano Toscano plays an important role in this blend, adding acidity and allowing for slightly bigger production volumes, but Malvasia Bianca Lunga is necessary for flesh and texture.

Foreign versions of Trebbiano Toscano can be interesting and quite different from the Italian ones. Taminick Cellars in Australia makes three versions of a trebbiano wine (one of these is a sweet wine), from vines that were planted in 1919. Bella Ridge Estate in the Swan district also makes a good trebbiano wine.

WINES TO TRY: Baroncini/Fattoria Sovesto** (La Faina Vendemmia Tardiva) and Acquaviva** (Tutti Santi Vendemmia Tardiva, which includes 10 percent other local grapes), Ambra**, and Capezzana** (this used to be a little too oaky, but thankfully the use of oak has been scaled back). The first two wines are particularly interesting: they are both made with late-harvested *Trebbiano*s, which seems like a very good idea to me, as the technique helps increase texture and depth of aromas and flavors. Certainly, this hardy, high-acid grape can take late harvests smiling.

Trebbiano di Lugana

See VERDICCHIO, chapter 4.

Trebbiano di Soave

See VERDICCHIO, chapter 4.

Trebbiano Valtenesi

See VERDICCHIO, chapter 4.

THE VERNACCIA GROUP

Over the centuries, the term *Vernaccia* (first used to describe a grape variety in Liguria in 1276) was attributed to many Italian varieties with completely different ampelographic characteristics, from both the northern and southern parts of the country. In fact, of the many "families" of Italian native varieties, there are few with members more unrelated than the *Vernaccia* group. The only thing that Vernaccia di Oristano, Vernaccia di San Gimignano, and Vernaccia Nera have in common is the first part of their name. Vernaccia Nera is not the same as Grenache or Garnacha—though Vernaccia Nera is listed as a synonym of Garnacha by some experts, I couldn't find any ampelographic or genetic evidence to support this. Admittedly, it is easy to understand the association between *garnacha* and *vernaccia* since both descend from the same linguistic root, the Latin word *vernaculum*. However, it appears that many of the Vernaccia Nera vines dispersed in the countryside of central Italy are in fact different from one another. Though some of these grapevines may have been originally misidentified as Vernaccia Nera and really are Grenache, there do exist distinct Vernaccia Nera varieties; for example, Vernaccia Nera Grossa Cerretana is distinct from Vernaccia Nera, and neither is identical with Spain's Garnacha. Apparently, Vernaccia Bianca, which used to grow in Trentino, is no longer cultivated. To make matters even more interesting, there is a Vernaccia Rossa too; however, it is not a *Vernaccia* at all, but a biotype of Aleatico. However, little things like these hardly faze Italians, who blithely continue referring to it by its *Vernaccia* moniker; and it wouldn't be Italy if there didn't exist a

Vernaccina variety as well, also apparently completely unrelated to all the others.

It only gets better when you consider that there are many wines named Vernaccia-of-Somewhere that are not made with any known *Vernaccia* grape: a very good one is Umbria's Vernaccia di Cannara, which is made with the Cornetta grape, also referred to as Vernaccia Nera, but apparently distinct from the two other, better-known Vernaccia Neras. Luigi Veronelli used to talk to me about many other once-famous Vernaccia wines such as Vernaccia delle Cinque Terre, Vernaccia di Quiliano, Vernaccia di Serra Meccaglie, and Vernaccia di Villasor, all made with unspecified *Vernaccia* grapes, or with altogether differently named grapes. All are nearly forgotten today, save for Vernaccia di Quiliano.

Most likely, the reason *Vernaccia* was such a common name for grape varieties is that it is a linguistic corruption of the late-Latin term *vernaculum*, which means local. Hence the name has always been attributed by farmers to locally grown varieties in just about every corner of the country, which explains the proliferation of a rainbow's worth, and more, of so-called *Vernaccia* grapes. Other experts believe that the word derives from *Helvenacia* or *Helvenaca*, a variety that Pliny considered foreign, so in this case the name would indicate varieties that were not local at all. Still other experts mention a place-related origin of the *Vernaccia* name, for example Vernazza, a charming Ligurian town in the Cinque Terre, famous for its white wine; Gallesio was the first to promote this idea, in the nineteenth century, but it is a minority view today. Fewer still believe that the name might stem from *verrus* ("a grape liked by wild boars"), *ibernum* ("winter," or dried grapes consumed during that season), *vernum* ("springtime"), or *vernaceus* ("wine made from grapes destined for slaves", a derivation from *vernus,* or "a slave born in that house"). Interestingly, Vernatsch, the German name for Schiava Grossa, also derives from *Vernaccia*, as does *Grenache*.

I don't know about you, but I like the "local" theory. In fact, one might think that the word *vernaccia* was once used, when speaking of grapes, as frequently as the words *indigenous* and *native* are today. So maybe I could have called this book *Vernacular Wine Grapes of Italy* . . . or then again, maybe not.

Vernaccia di Oristano

WHERE IT'S FOUND: Sardinia. NATIONAL REGISTRY CODE NUMBER: 260. COLOR: white.

Vernaccia di Oristano is the name of the grape variety, but the wine is also called Vernaccia di Oristano. Also known locally as Garnaccia, Moranina, or simply Vernaccia, Vernaccia di Oristano goes a long way back in Sardinia. It is first mentioned in a law passed on June 8, 1327 (and cited in the book *Breve di Villa di Chiesa*) by Philip IV the Conqueror, who forbade tavern keepers from placing water on tables and obligated them to display signs listing the various wines served (including vernaccia). Manca dell'Arca mentions a "Garnaccia" or "Granazza" with large, long berries; Gallesio (1839) wrote that it was one of Sardinia's best wines, as did Molon (1906). In 1966, Bruni, Breviglieri, and Casini showed that Vernaccia and Vernaccina were not identical—though they also stated, erroneously, that the latter was Vernaccia di San Gimignano. Recent ampelographic and molecular characterization has shown Vernaccia di Oristano to be distinct from Vernaccia di San Gimignano (Nieddu, Nieddu, Cocco, Erre, and Chessa 2007); other study results have proved it distinct from Spain's Garnacha (De Mattia, Imazio, Grassi, Lovicu, Tardaguila, Failla, et al. 2007; Zecca, De Mattia, Lovicu, Labra, Sala, and Grassi 2010). Further, and very interestingly, Nieddu (2011) reports that the *Vernaccia* variety grown in the Ogliastra zone of Sardinia is different from the majority of the Vernaccia di Oristano grown on the island. De Mattia's group found that while some Sardinian varieties with local *Vernaccia*-like names (such as Vernaccia Santa Rosalia, Vernaccia, and Granaccia) are identical and are in fact all Vernaccia di Oristano, others, such as the *Vernaccia*s grown in the countrysides of Solarussa and near Escalaplano, have different SSR profiles.

In any case, Vernaccia di Oristano is a beautiful grape, and quite recognizable because of its very round leaf. It also has medium-small, conical bunches, usually winged and compact (these clearly differentiate it from Vernaccia di San Gimignano, which has large, pyramidal bunches). The berry is small and round, with thin, yellow-gold skin. The harvest usually occurs at the beginning of October. It is very sensitive to late spring frosts and to both oidium and peronospora. There are three officially recognized clones (CAPVS 1, CAVPS 2, and CAPVS 3). These three clones are fairly similar in their morphology, viticultural behavior, and the wines made from them; perhaps CAPVS 1 produces wines that are a bit more graceful than the others.

Nieddu's interesting and very informative 2007 study tells us that only 9 percent of Sardinia's Vernaccia di Oristano vineyards are larger than five hectares, with 48 percent less than one hectare (Nieddu, Nieddu, Cocco, Erre, and Chessa 2007). Also, the majority of these vineyards are quite old: only 6 percent have been planted within the last six years, while 28 percent are between thirty and fifty years old and 28 percent are over fifty years old. This sort of information is invaluable: on the one hand, it tells us that wines made with Vernaccia di Oristano are made mainly with old vines, which gives the wine lover hope they will be complex and deep. On the other, it also means that not much Vernaccia di Oristano is being planted of late, a sure sign the wine is falling out of favor with the masses. In fact, while most Vernaccia di Oristano is planted in the lower valley of the Tirso River, there isn't that much Vernaccia di Oristano planted around Oristano itself; most plantings are located close to the nearby towns of Riola Sardo, Cabras, and San Vero Milis. While there used to be close to 1,500 hectares planted to this variety in the 1970s, as of 2010 there were only 435 hectares (a further decrease from the 582 hectares recorded in 2000) planted to Vernaccia di Oristano in Sardinia.

The area near Sinis is particularly noteworthy, since many old vines still exist there, planted in highly sandy soils. Actually, the variety has always been cultivated in two different soils: the *gregori,* which are higher, drier, very low in limestone content, and not very fertile, and the *bennaxi,* which are fertile soils of alluvial nature, rich in loamy clay, and located at lower altitudes (they were once marshes). These two are believed to give the best wines; there is also a third soil type in which Vernaccia di Oristano is grown (for example, near San Vero Milis, Riolo, and Zeddiani), reddish-brown in color, containing more limestone and iron.

Which Wines to Choose and Why

DOC wines are Vernaccia di Oristano, which can also be made in a fortified style (DOC Vernaccia di Oristano Liquoroso) that may be either dry *(secco)* or sweet *(dolce).* All have minimum ageing requirements; *superiore* means the wine has more alcohol. This wine is traditionally aged in chestnut or oak barrels in a *solera* system (an aging system that consists in progressively topping up barrels filled with older wine—a part of which is removed for bottling—with slightly younger wine; the same process is used in the making of fine Sherry). Therefore, most vernacccia di Oristanos are blends of wines of different age, made in a slightly oxidized style reminiscent (after roughly two years) of a Fino or Amontillado Sherry. The best vernaccia di Oristanos are not fortified. Due to the specific microclimate and the specific local yeast population, a thin coating of powdery white *flor* develops on the wine's surface—usually, roughly 20 percent of the barrels are left open to air, for up to ten years, allowing for a slow, controlled oxidation and the development of *flor.* The *flor* doesn't always develop in all wines, and those without it are simple, herbal-lemony whites meant for early drinking. A good vernaccia di Oristano can be a thing of beauty, exuding aromas and flavors of dried apricots, hazelnut, almond paste, orange rind, fresh aromatic herbs, white chocolate, and faded flowers. Though vernaccia di

Oristano is traditionally dry, there are slightly sweeter versions offering nuances of caramel and chestnut honey as well. Somewhat unfashionable today, these can all be unbelievably good wines, right up there with the best in their category worldwide.

WINES TO TRY: Contini*** (Antico Gregori, which contains one-hundred-year-old wine, is a benchmark: it's not just the best vernaccia di Oristano of all, but one of Italy's greatest wines; and the other two vernaccias Contini makes are great too), Josto Puddu** (Riserva, available at an unbeatably low price), and Fratelli Serra**.

Vernaccia di San Gimignano

WHERE IT'S FOUND: Tuscany. NATIONAL REGISTRY CODE NUMBER: 261. COLOR: white.

Vernaccia di San Gimignano is the name of both grape and wine produced in the countryside around San Gimignano in Tuscany, one of Italy's top twenty or so most beautiful (and beautifully kept) medieval towns. Renowned since the Middle Ages, Vernaccia di San Gimignano was Italy's first wine (white or red) to be awarded the DOC appellation nearly fifty years ago, in 1966, before Barolo, Amarone, or Brunello; it earned DOCG status in 1993.

Considering how old the variety is, it is strange that it doesn't have more synonyms. In the early nineteenth century, Gallesio reported that the Vernaccia di San Gimignano was cultivated in Liguria, where Piccabon grapes were grown (he mistakenly believed that Piccabon was Vermentino); instead, we know today that it is Vernaccia di San Gimignano and Piccabon that are identical (Torello Marinoni, Raimondi, Ruffa, Lacombe, and Schneider 2009). Vernaccia di San Gimignano was also believed to be identical to Canaiolo Bianco, also planted in Tuscany, but we now know this to be erroneous: these two varieties are distinct (Storchi, Armanni, Randellini, Giannetto, Meneghetti, and Crespan 2011), and are registered separately in Italy. In 2009, Torello Marinoni, Raimondi, Ruffa, Lacombe, and Schneider (and not Storchi et al., as reported elsewhere) reported that Vernaccia di San Gimignano is identical to Bervedino, a variety typical of Emilia-Romagna, but I wonder; in any case, Bervedino continues to be listed separately from Vernaccia di San Gimignano in the National Registry. Commendably, in 2010, the Consorzio della Denominazione di San Gimignano began a collaboration with the Siena provincial council and the University of Siena to identify the DNA of the Vernaccia di San Gimignano variety and to guarantee the traceability of the wines made with this variety. In 2011, results showing the standard genetic profile of the variety were presented, and in 2012 preliminary results regarding the application of a molecular wine tracing method for vernaccia di San Gimignano were also presented. Interestingly, the genetic makeup of the majority of the Vernaccia di San Gimignano vines studied was similar, a consequence of the fact that most of the modern vineyards of this variety in San Gimignano were planted with grapevines issued from the same massal selections.

Both the Vernaccia di San Gimignano grape and wine have a noble history. First mentioned as such in 1276 in tax documents *(ordinamenti di gabella)* in San Gimignano's town archives, the wine was also a favorite of Lorenzo de Medici (who apparently routinely asked the San Gimignano authorities to send wine to Florence), with the church, and generally, with those who counted most. Ludovico il Moro had two hundred flasks delivered for his son's wedding to Isabella, daughter of King Alfonso II of Naples; he must have been quite a fan, because he then also asked the town of San Gimignano for five hundred vines to plant in his home region of Lombardy. Sante Lancerio, cellar master of Pope Paul III, also had words of praise for the wine. In his *Divine Comedy,* Dante banishes Pope Martino IV to purgatory for his gluttonous habit of drowning eels in vernaccia: however, an analysis of Dante's text reveals that he only wrote of vernaccia, and not specifically that of San Gimignano. Wines from the Cinque Terre (Vernazza, Monterosso, Corniglia, Manarola, and Riomaggiore) had a solid reputation in the fifteenth century, and a *Vernaccia* from Corniglia was mentioned by Sacchetti (1332–1400), who wrote that grapevines of this variety were introduced into Tuscany from the Cinque Terre (Tellini 2007). Clearly, if grapevines really were brought into Tuscany from Liguria, this would mean that Tuscany's most famous white wine and grape is actually a Ligurian native. This is possible, given that we now know the Ligurian variety Piccabon is actually Vernaccia di San Gimignano (Torello Marinoni, Raimondi, Ruffa, Lacombe, and Schneider 2009). De Astis, in 1937, was the first to describe the variety in detail and how it was unrelated to the other *Vernaccia* varieties, though, according to Scalabrelli and D'Onofrio, Fregola had already mentioned this briefly in 1932.

Vernaccia di San Gimignano has large, pyramidal, fairly compact bunches (usually winged), and medium, oval or elliptical berries with medium-thick skins. In other words, it couldn't look anymore different from Vernaccia di Oristano. The harvest usually occurs in late September or early October. It prefers marly-clay soils but does well in tufa-sandy ones too, both of which are common around San Gimignano. There are eleven official clones of Vernaccia di San Gimignano (V-P-6, U.S. FI-PI 8, UFI RC S 414, VCR 435, and the UFI RC S. Gimignano clones 3, 5, 13, 15, 16, 17, 19).

Which Wines to Choose and Why

The best and most famous wine made with the Vernaccia di San Gimignano grape is DOCG vernaccia di San Gimignano, but the variety can also be used to make DOC Gimignano wines and many IGT wines (for example, Bettona, Cannara, Colli Cimini, Narni, and Planargia). Of course, by far the best of all is vernaccia di San Gimignano, of which there are numerous interpretations, some oaky (the *riserva* wines usually are too much so, as they receive a minimum of one year of oak aging), some citrusy (and to my taste, far too reminiscent of Sauvignon Blanc wines), some exceptional. As the requirement is for a minimum of 90 percent Vernaccia di San Gimignano and 10 percent other (nonaromatic) white grapes, some wines can be marked by too much Chardonnay at times, or even by the delicate pepper of Manzoni Bianco.

There is probably no white wine that has improved more in Italy over the last ten years; there are now a bevy of wonderfully crisp wines of sneaky concentration that, most of the time, actually remind you of the Vernaccia di San Gimignano variety. Non-*riservas* are usually very good examples of wines made in a modern unoaked, crisp, fruit-driven style, though be warned that the aromas and flavors of vernaccia di San Gimignano are never of mind-obfuscating intensity or penetration. On the other hand, *riserva* wines are suitably beefed up by the intelligent use of oak, and I admit to always being surprised by just how well vernaccia di San Gimignano can tolerate, and be improved by, a gentle judicious oaking. Given its somewhat neutral aromas, a hint of vanilla spice is a welcome addition, but in the hands of wannabe woodcutters, the wines can turn out hopelessly overoaked, beyond boring and undrinkable. Fortunately, such wines are now very much in the minority. Due to its tannic nature, vernaccia di San Gimignano was once considered by locals as a red wine in white clothing, but modern versions tend to be fresher and lighter. The wines are not only very good now, but clear-cut differences between production sub-areas are becoming apparent, always an added value in the realm of fine wine. For instance, with wines from the Pancole zone taste meaty and thick and those from Santa Maria lighter and more perfumed. Overall, there are at least four different sub-areas yielding rather different wines, in my opinion. If things are now looking up, it's thanks in part to the hard work of the Consorzio della Denominazione San Gimignano and Giovanni Panizzi, its past president and owner of the (excellent) eponymous winery, who sadly passed away a few years ago. He will be missed.

WINES TO TRY: Fontaleoni*** (Vigna Casanuova and the entry-level wine), Guicciardini

Strozzi/Fattoria di Cusona*** (1933), Giovanni Panizzi***, La Lastra*** (the entry-level vernaccia), Sono Montenidoli*** (Fiore and the entry-level wine; the Carato is a little too oaky for me), Casa alle Vacche**, Casale-Falchini**, Pietrafitta**, Rampa di Fugnano**, Signano**, and Simone Santini**. I recommend the entry-level, non-Riserva wines from all these producers. The wines of Sono Montenidoli harken back to the traditional wine made in the area decades ago, rich, nutty, almost oxidized and very satisfying, by all accounts the best of the whole *denominazione*. Mattia Barzaghi, who in my view shares with Sono Montenidoli's owner Elisabetta Fagiuoli the honors as most talented winemakers in all of San Gimignano, has run into some financial difficulties that will hopefully be resolved soon so that he can get back to making his wines out of his own estate; in the meantime, he is making them while working at Mormoraia.

Vernaccia Nera

WHERE IT'S FOUND: Marche, Umbria. NATIONAL REGISTRY CODE NUMBER: 262. COLOR: red.

Completely unrelated to the previous two, this *Vernaccia* was just as famous in centuries past as it is today: already in the 1800s it was believed to give one of the best wines of the Ancona area in the Marche. There is also a Vernaccia Nera grown in the province of Arezzo, but the plants I have seen bear no resemblance whatsoever to the Vernaccia Nera of the Marche, so my guess is (at least until genetic tests tell us otherwise) that the Arezzo variety, whatever it maybe, was so named with the aim of cashing in on *Vernaccia*'s popularity. Other synonyms for Vernaccia Nera are Vernaccia di Teramo and Vernaccia Selvatica; we know today that Vernaccia Nera is not the same grape as Vernaccia Nera Grossa Cerretana. Clearly, as the latter two are different from one another, they both can't be Grenache (or Garnacha) either, as some have suggested. By 1893 the grape was believed by authorities to be practically extinct, and by the end of the twentieth century there were less than fifty hectares planted to it. Fortunately, things have improved somewhat, and the latest estimates are that there are about ninety hectares under vine in Italy to date. Generally, it likes marly-sandy soils, and is usually vigorous and capable of hefty but high-quality yields. It both flowers and ripens late in the season. Morphologically, Vernaccia Nera is characterized by medium-large leaves that are almost circular, but usually have five lobes; the bunches are medium-sized, cylindrical-conical, compact, and often winged, with dark round berries. There is only one official clone available (I-ISV CSV).

Which Wines to Choose and Why

Throughout the centuries the very aromatic Vernaccia Nera wines have been considered of exceptional quality, but were always scarce. Even today, production is limited to small pockets of the Marche, and even smaller ones in Umbria. Historically very good vernaccia di Serrapetrona was made by Franci (the wines of this producer were famous already in the 1920s), followed later by the also very good wines made by Umberto Francioni and Quacquarini. However, there is more than one wine that can be made with the Vernaccia Nera grape. Clearly, the best wine is the DOCG vernaccia di Serrapetrona (by law, made with a minimum 85 percent of Vernaccia Nera grapes, 40 percent of which have to be air-dried), a delicious sparkling wine made by secondary fermentation in the bottle that is not unlike a much richer, fuller-bodied lambrusco. I guarantee you'll find this wine's intense red rose, violet, black cherry, and inky aromas and flavors absolutely thrilling. It can be made in a sweet *(passito)* style, as this grape takes to air-drying very well. For those who prefer nonsparkling red wines, the DOC Serrapetrona wines are full-bodied and rich still wines made with at least 85 percent Vernaccia Nera grapes. To my taste, these wines can at times be a little too tannic and oaky, but the better examples are certainly very impressive, structured wines of real breeding and depth. All told, Vernaccia

Nera grown in this remote and small corner of the Marche can produce some of Italy's greatest wines, but sadly, also some of the least known.

Besides Serrapetrona, Vernaccia Nera also grows well in the countryside of the nearby towns of Belforte del Chienti, Caldarola, and San Severino Marche, the last of which has a promising new DOC Terreni di San Severino Marche. Wines such as Colli Maceratesi Rosso can have as much as 50 percent Vernaccia Nera, but that's too small a percentage for one to truly understand what the variety is all about.

WINES TO TRY: For vernaccia di Serrapetrona, try: Alberto Quaquarini*** (both the Secca and the Dolce), Colli di Serrapetrona** (especially their *passito*, Sommo Rosso), Cantine Claudi**, Fabrini**, and Lanfranco Quacquarini**. For Serrapetrona Rosso, try: Colli di Serrapetrona** (Robbione).

Vernaccia Nera Grossa

WHERE IT'S FOUND: Marche. NATIONAL REGISTRY CODE NUMBER: 415. COLOR: red.

The existence of Vernaccia Nera Grossa, also called Vernaccia Nera Cerretana (as it grew mainly around Cerreto d'Esi in the Marche), was first documented in 1877 by Carlo Morbelli, a professor of industrial chemistry who wrote about it in the *Ampelographic Bulletin* briefly published by the Ministry of Agriculture, Industry, and Commerce (1876–81). Vernaccia Nera Grossa was moderately common at that time in the area around Fabriano, and today it is mostly grown in the higher reaches of the Esino River basin. Though you will find the name Vernaccia Nera Grossa often used as a synonym of Vernaccia Nera, the two are not identical (this has been confirmed by ampelographic and microsatellite studies) and the former variety was given its own National Registry code number. In fact, morphologic differences between the two varieties were apparent long before DNA testing became the norm in ampelologic circles, and in 1962 Bruni had already hypothesized that the former was a biotype of the latter (though he erroneously used the word "clone"). It is characterized by large pentagonal leaves with five lobes; the bunch is medium-large (it averages 330 grams), with medium-sized, round, thin-skinned, blue-black berries. Though not a particularly vigorous variety, it is a decent and regular yielder that ripens by mid-October and that shows good resistance to grapevine pests and diseases. Currently, there are no officially certified clones.

Which Wines to Choose and Why

The wines tend to be saline, refreshing, and bright but only medium-dark red due to low anthocyanin concentrations. They are also usually quite refreshing and vibrant, due to high levels of malic acid. The aromas and flavors are of flowers, strawberry, and raspberry.

WINES TO TRY: There are no monovarietal wines that I am aware of, though I am sure some local grower makes some for home consumption. I just haven't found him—yet.

Vernaccina

WHERE IT'S FOUND: Emilia-Romagna. NATIONAL REGISTRY CODE NUMBER: 437. COLOR: white.

Also known as Ribolla Piccola and typical of the area around Rimini, Vernaccina was first described and studied accurately by De Bosis in 1879. Isoenzymatic analysis has shown it to be different from all known *Vernaccia* grapes in Italy, and genetic microsatellite studies are under way. In the early part of the past century, the variety fell out of favor because it gave poor quality wine, but this was probably the result of poor viticultural techniques: Vernaccina is a very early ripener, but in times past farmers used to harvest all the grapes together, thereby condemning Vernaccina, picked much too late, to give must that would invariably be oxidized and flat. It is characterized by medium-small, triangular leaves with seven lobes, while the bunch is medium-small to small, compact, cylindrical, with a big wing; the berries are medium-small and yellow-green. It is vigorous and fertile, and ripens early. Clearly, there are no officially certified clones yet.

Which Wines to Choose and Why

Vernaccina may be included in IGT wine blends Emilia, Forlì, Ravenna, and Rubicone. There are no DOC or DOCG wines that currently contemplate its presence.

WINES TO TRY: There are no monovarietal wines made, to the best of my knowledge.

Vernaccina Riminese

Thanks to the early twenty-first-century project Vitigni Minori of the Regione Emilia-Romagna, we have new research studies on over one hundred different accessions of unknown or rare grape varieties of the region. Some of its results have been truly fantastic, including the identification of the Famoso and Ruggine varieties, but less trumpeted was the identification of Vernaccina Riminese, which appears to be different from any other currently known Italian *Vernaccia* variety (some believe that it's identical to Vernaccina, but this is currently a minority view). Vernaccina Riminese has a very large leaf with seven lobes (a rarity, in ampelographic circles), a medium-sized, compact, cylindrical-conical bunch, with medium-small, round, yellow-green berries covered in bloom. There have been roughly ten different biotypes identified.

Which Wines to Choose and Why

The wines thus far appear to be balanced and straightforward, with fragrant if simple yellow fruit and delicately floral aromas and flavors. The wine is medium-bodied, but has more structure and palate weight than the aromas would lead you to expect.

WINES TO TRY: I am not aware of any monovarietal Vernaccina Riminese wines being yet produced.

FOUR

Major Native and Traditional Grape Varieties

FOR THE PURPOSES of this book, I have defined Italy's major native and traditional grapes as those that are generally recognized as the country's best known. For the most part, these grapes have been well studied and described for centuries, are characterized genetically, and are turned into monovarietal wine and sold to the public by at least one estate. Practically all are listed in the National Registry. Since having fun with wine and tasting the many different offerings Italy has in store for us is our ultimate goal, these grape varieties are common enough for you to find their wines more or less easily, either in stores near you or while on vacation in Italy. All the Italian grapes you might already know (for example, Nebbiolo, Sangiovese, Fiano) are described in this chapter, but there are many other less-famous varieties that also give rise to wonderful wines and are worth getting to know. For the same reasons, you will not find a famous cultivar like Rondinella (an important part of the Valpolicella and Amarone wine blends) in this chapter, as nobody uses it to make a monovarietal wine in Italy—but you can read about it in chapter 5. Details such as these aside, my hope is you will have as much fun reading about all the grapes that have called Italy home for centuries (and sometimes for much longer than that) as you will drinking the wines. Cheers!

Abrostine

WHERE IT'S FOUND: Tuscany. NATIONAL REGISTRY CODE NUMBER: not registered. COLOR: red.

Also referred to as Abrostolo, Abrostine is an example of the difficulties facing anyone interested in Italy's native grapes, and in ampelology in general. An ancient Tuscan native grape first described, in the fifteenth century, as growing on the edge of forests (much like wild grapevines), little information is available on it today, and that is contradictory and inaccurate. For example, in the otherwise informative book on Italy's native grapes edited by Slow Food, under the heading Abrusco, the text states that it is a variety closely related to Abrostine, while under the heading Abrostine, the text states that the two are identical. Clearly, if they are closely related then it follows that they are not identical; and if the varieties aren't identical, then their wines won't be either. I posed the same question to three of Italy's best-known winemakers: two answered that the grapes were identical, and one that they were very different. To make matters worse, Abrostine has always been confused with the members of the *Colorino* group, from which it is distinct. So it goes for Italy's natives.

The scientists aren't in agreement either: Mancuso (2001) wrote that Abrostine is a synonym of Abrusco, a finding apparently recently confirmed in a private communication by Rita Vignani (Robinson, Harding, and Vouillamoz 2012), though this would contradict her own previously published data (Vignani, Scali, Masi, Milanelli, Scalabrelli, Wang, et al. 2008). However, until scientific data is published in peer-reviewed academic journals of note (and preferably, confirmed by other research groups) it is of doubtful use and cannot be taken at face value. As things stand now, this is exactly where we are with the question of the relationship between Abrusco and Abrostine.

Abrostine is most likely a direct descendant of an ancient Tuscan native wild grapevine, or the result of a crossing between a wild and a cultivated species. Abrostine's wild, rustic appearance and wine once led some experts to consider it a member of the *Lambrusco* family, which we know today not to be the case. A look at an Italian dictionary under the word *abrostine* will reveal "an American vine species (*Vitis labrusca*)" or "grapes produced from an American grapevine," both of which are incorrect. According to a report by Di Vecchi Staraz, Lacombe, Laucou, This, and Boselli (2009), Abrostine shares alleles with local Tuscan wild grapevine species, as do six other native Tuscan grapevines, including Sangiovese. As we have seen, Abrostine has always been thought to be related to wild grapevines, so this finding is not surprising.

Abrostine belongs to the class of grape varieties known as *teinturiers* (*tintori*, in Italian): examples include France's Petit Verdot and Italy's Giacchè, Grand Noir, and the various *Colorinos* (for the last of these, see chapter 3). In the vast majority of cases, wines made from the *teinturier* grapes are not interesting or complex enough to stand alone, though of course that hasn't stopped producers everywhere in the world, Italy included, from trying. But very rarely, *teinturiers* can do more than contribute color and size to a wine: they can pleasantly surprise on their own. Abrostine, together with a few *Colorino* varieties and even Abrusco, is among these rare *teinturiers*. It is noteworthy that the best *teinturier* wine grapes are characterized by colorless pulps, a trait shared by all of the world's great wine grapes, from Pinot Nero to Nebbiolo to Chardonnay; tellingly, Abrostine's pulp is as colorless as they come.

Abrostine performs best on clay-calcareous soils, though little is known about its potential on other soil types. It has a medium-sized, pyramidal, loosely packed bunch (always bigger than that of Abrusco), with one or two wings, and very small, thick-skinned, blue-black berries; the leaf stalk is red tinged. This variety ripens late, usually at October's end. Unfortunately, with no proper studies of it under way, this variety remains cloaked in darkness.

Which Wines to Choose and Why

Given the paucity of trustworthy information available on Abrostine, I am indebted to Federico Staderini, a consultant winemaker responsible for some of Italy's greatest wines (the Brunello di Montalcino Poggio di Sotto springs to mind), who has been a gold mine of knowledge over the years. Staderini developed an interest in Abrostine thanks to his association with Roberto Bandinelli of the University of Florence, Italy's greatest expert in Tuscan native grape varieties, and currently Italy's greatest ampelographer. Over at the San Felice estate, where the beautiful experimental vineyard Vitarium has been developed, Bandinelli has gone as far as cross-pollinating Abrostine with Sangiovese to create a new variety (that he did so with Abrusco as well clearly tells you that he believes the two varieties to be distinct).

Inspired, Staderini decided to plant Abrostine in his ex-wife's Podere Santa Felicità estate in Pratovecchio near Arezzo. He chose a massal selection (no clones are available for this little-known variety) obtained from the San Felice estate in Castelnuovo Berardenga; 2006 was the first vintage of his wine.

Staderini's techniques are designed to bring out the best in Abrostine, admittedly a difficult variety to work with. For one, he believes that "given Abrostine's color intensity and wealth of polyphenols, it never needs to macerate for more than three or four days. I use new, small oak barrels [for the malolactic transformation], since I believe the wine needs oxygen contact to smoothen and avoid developing strongly reductive odors, which are always present with Abrostine." The wine stays in barrels for roughly two years, "but I add about three kilos of white grape lees during the first and second years in barrel, to help increase mouthfeel, looking for greater unctuousness in a wine that's otherwise too tannic and rigid. Without this addition, I'd need to age the wine at least another year in bottle prior to releasing it for sale, and that's a long time to go without selling a single bottle." In normal to excellent vintages, the cultivar ripens well with good sugar accumulation (musts go into barrel with as much as 150 grams per liter of sugar); however, since it is a late ripener, Abrostine must be planted due south for maximal sunlight exposure to achieve full ripeness and the softest tannins.

Currently, Abrostine is grown only in Tuscany (most likely, there are farmers growing Abrostine elsewhere in Italy without knowing it), and its most common destiny is to be added in small percentages to red wine blends. With one exception, there are no monovarietal Abrostine wines, DOC or IGT. The one exception is made by Staderini: the wine is fairly rich and creamy, with vanilla, black pepper, juniper, dried prune, and dark cherry aromas and flavors complicated by hints of underbrush and tobacco. On the palate, it's actually much lighter bodied and less complex than the nose implies, and is blessed with lovely acidity and decently smooth tannins. Abrostine may not be the second coming of Pinot Nero, but it's not Concord either.

WINES TO TRY: Podere Santa Felicità** (Sempremai).

Abrusco

WHERE IT'S FOUND: Tuscany. NATIONAL REGISTRY CODE NUMBER: 347. COLOR: red.

All but forgotten today, Abrusco (rarely called Raverusto) is an ancient variety that was described by Soderini in 1600 and by Di Rovasenda in 1877, and more recently, by Pisani, Bandinelli, and Camussi in 1997. Beyond that there is little or no information available on this variety. The cultivar may be related to the *Lambrusco* family (the name Abrusco is believed to derive from Lambrusco) though not to the *Colorino*s, as was initially believed. It also appears to be closely related to Abrostine, another *teinturier* variety and Tuscan native; in fact, some experts believe that the two are identical, but this is controversial (see ABROSTINE entry). Unfortunately, many of the *Colorino*s, Abrostine, and Abrusco look alike, so confusing them is easy. In this respect, it is not the least bit surprising that Ducci, Fausto, D'Onofrio, Ferroni, and Scalabrelli (2012) have recently shown that many Abrusco accessions they investigated in the Tuscan countryside around Pisa are in fact Colorino del Valdarno. This doesn't necessarily mean that Abrusco and Colorino del Valdarno are one and the same, as is reported in the Italian vitis database (www.vitisdb.it), but rather that some Colorino del Valdarno grapevines were originally misidentified as Abrusco. As we have seen in chapter 1, similar mistaken identifications are unfortunately common in ampelology. By contrast, according to Stefano Dini—a viticulture expert who works for the Matura group of winemakers and viticulturalists, set up years ago by Attilio Pagli and Alberto Antonini—these two varieties are extremely similar but show definite genetic differences.

I have tried countless times over the last fifteen years to gain precise, consistent information regarding this variety, but the goal has been elusive to say the least. Even talking to producers who were supposedly making an Abrusco wine proved of limited use, though Giandomenico Gigante of Tuscany's Fattoria La Traiana estate has been a pleasant exception. He believes that Abrusco is a distinct variety, which he calls Abrusco del Valdarno (though he prefers to write it as Val d'Arno, in honor of the spelling in Cosimo Medici's time and of the new DOC that now encompasses all of the Valdarno di Sopra production zone). Further, he says it is in no way related to Colorino del Valdarno, which he also grows; he points out that his estate has been visited numerous times both by government inspectors and by researchers from the nearby Istituto Sperimentale di Viticoltura di Arezzo, and nobody has ever found Colorino del Valdarno and Abrusco del Valdarno to be the same variety. He also remembers that the old-timers working in the vineyards when he was a child called this variety Raverusto or even Colore, but never Colorino, and always distinguished it from the Colorino del Valdarno that also grew there. At the Tre Stelle estate near San Gimignano, Donatella and Antonella Rubicini (who are, along with their mother Maria, the three stars the estate's name refers to: the label depicts the profiles of three women and stars) own twenty vines of Abrusco interplanted with other varieties, and they too feel the grapevine is different from any other they know (their plantings were originally identified by Giancarlo Scalabrelli, one of Italy's most famous academic viticulture experts and professor at the University of Pisa).

In conclusion, according to our current knowledge, Abrusco is characterized by medium-small, pyramidal, winged bunches (much smaller than Abrostine's) with medium-small, blue-black, thick-skinned berries. It's both vigorous and very resistant to disease. Most important, for it speaks of Abrusco's winemaking potential, the variety has, like Colorino del Valdarno and all the best wine grapes, a colorless pulp. Matters such as the most suitable rootstocks, pruning techniques, training systems, and soils for Abrusco are still a matter of conjecture. There are apparently less than ten hectares planted in all of Italy.

Which Wines to Choose and Why

Abrusco grows mainly around Florence and Pisa, and no DOC wine exists. It is used primarily as a blending variety (in IGT wines such as Alta Valle del Greve, Val di Magra, or Costa Toscana) though there are a few pure IGT versions of note. Abrusco's well-pigmented skins result in wines of deep color, though aromas and flavors are somewhat more limited in their complexity and range. According to Gigante, Abrusco wines are even more deeply colored and more tannic than those of Colorino del Valdarno, and he finds the tannins slightly more rough and bitter. Abrusco wines also have lower alcohol levels and higher acidities than those made with Colorino del Valdarno.

Based on my tastings over the years of what I was told (sigh . . .) were monovarietal Abrusco wines, delicate notes of spicy red and chewy tannins seem the norm with Abrusco, as well as limited potential for aging and limited depth. Gigante agrees that red-fruit aromas and flavors (red currant, dark red cherry, and strawberry) are the norm. Gigante does not believe Abrusco makes a good monovarietal wine (too astringent, too hard tasting), but likes it as a blending agent, because it adds color and structure without altering the wine's basic aroma and flavor profile, provided that not more than 5–6 percent of Abrusco is added. Clearly, the Rubicini sisters have a different view, as they have been making a 100 percent Abrusco wine (called Agino) for the past decade, dedicating it to the memories of their father and of Luigi ("Gino") Veronelli, Italy's most famous and first professional wine writer.

WINES TO TRY: The only reportedly 100 percent Abrusco wine worth reporting is by Le Tre Stelle** (Agino), made near San Gimignano. The wine is dedicated to Italy's greatest wine writer of all time, Luigi (Gino) Veronelli—"Agino" reads "A Gino," meaning "To Gino." Fattoria La Traiana's Campo Arsiccio wine is made with 4 percent Abrusco del Valdarno.

Aglianico

WHERE IT'S FOUND: Campania, Basilicata, Puglia, Abruzzo, Lazio, Molise. NATIONAL REGISTRY CODE NUMBER: 2 (note that Aglianico del Vulture is still listed separately at 266). COLOR: red.

Aglianico is one of the world's great red grapes, one that is finally carving a place in mainstream wine-drinking consciousness. Along with Nebbiolo and Sangiovese, it is generally believed to be one of Italy's three best wine grapes, but in my opinion, it is far more: at the very least, it's one of the world's dozen or so best wine grapes. After all, Aglianico wines can be highly reminiscent of those made with Nebbiolo, and nobody disputes the notion that Nebbiolo is one of the world's greatest cultivars. In fact, Italian wine insiders are well aware that one of Italy's twenty greatest red wines of all time is Mastroberardino's 1968 Taurasi, made with Aglianico. Furthermore, like very few other cultivars, Aglianico has a knack for turning out a full range of potentially stellar wines, from fragrant, juicy light-bodied versions to deep, rich, very ageworthy and complex behemoths. These and other characteristics have always ensured Aglianico immense popularity, at least in Italian winemaking and wine-drinking circles.

Aglianico's many virtues have been obvious to all for centuries, and consequently locals weren't shy about attaching the name Aglianico to any other grape variety they might be growing, regardless of whether those grapes had anything at all in common with the more famous cultivar. This is one reason that Aglianico has always been plagued by a litany of erroneous synonyms and homonyms. In 1906, Molon described almost thirty Aglianico or Aglianico-Something grapes, but other experts compiled even more plethoric, and inaccurate, lists. Another reason for Aglianico's many synonyms and homonyms is that it has always expressed many different biotypes, grapevines which looked so different to nonexpert eyes that they were considered distinct varieties. In 2005, Costantini, Monaco, Vouillamoz, Forlani, and Grando showed that a number of differently named Aglianicos previously thought to be distinct varieties were really all just Aglianico: for example, Aglianichello (an Aglianico characterized by small grape bunches) and Aglianico Pannarano (a toponym referring to the place of origin) are both Aglianico. By contrast, Aglianico di Napoli (preferably now called Tronto to avoid confusion), shows a different SSR profile from Aglianico and is therefore a homonym, though it was long thought to also be an Aglianico biotype. Of course, there are no more famous Aglianico biotypes than Taurasi, Taburno, and Vulture, long believed to be different varieties, and each one responsible for the unique characteristics of an eponymous wine. In fact, Aglianico del Vulture is still listed separately in the National Registry.

Curiously, given that Aglianico is believed to be one of Italy's oldest grape varieties, present on Italian soil at least since the days of the Roman Empire (if not earlier), there is little written documentation of it as a cultivar or as a wine. In fact, we don't really know if Aglianico made any part of famous blends such as *falernum, gauranum, faustianum,* and *caecubum,* Campanian wines famous in antiquity with which Aglianico has been associated at one time or another. The name Aglianico first appears in print in a 1520 document attesting to the Count of Conversano's ownership of vineyards planted with *Aglianiche* (the feminine plural of Aglianico) and in a mid-sixteenth century reference to Aglianico wines produced on Monte Somma. In more modern times, Acerbi mentions Aglianico in 1825, and Viala and Vermorel in 1909.

As it has always been accepted that Aglianico first arrived on Campania's shores around the eighth century B.C.E., courtesy of colonizing

Eubean or Thessalian Greeks, the popular consensus at one time was that the variety's name harkened back to its Greek origins, deriving from the word *ellanico* (or Hellenic). The first to draw upon Greek etymology for this purpose was della Porta, who found a similarity between the Helveola grapes described by Pliny the Elder (though these were most likely white grapes) and an admittedly not well-characterized Hellanico grape. As the story goes, when Campania fell under the rule of the Bourbon royal family, of Spanish origin, the name gradually changed from Ellanico to Aglianico, since in Spanish the double "ll" is pronounced "gl." Unfortunately, most linguists do not find that *aglianico* can derive from *ellanico*. In fact, the exact origin of Aglianico and of its name remains unclear. Attilio Scienza of the University of Milan (one of Italy's most important grape variety experts) believes that Aglianico stems from the Spanish word *llano* (or plain), making it a "grape of the plains." He supports this by pointing out that there was no record of Aglianico existing prior to the sixteenth century, after the Spanish domination of southern Italy began in the fifteenth century.

According to Scienza, this is not to be taken to mean that Aglianico vines were once grown in the plains of Campania (in fact, the variety does best in volcanic soils and steep mountainous slopes) but rather that the grape derives from the domestication of native, wild grapevines that grew at the edge of forests, on the plains and elsewhere. To date, his team has been unable to identify either of the two parents, though they have been hard at work on this for the last ten years (private communication). Furthermore, Scienza believes that Aglianico originated from one of the six secondary domestication centers (the one in southern Italy and northern Africa), in which many of the cultivars we know today were supposedly born. DNA profiling studies (Scienza and Boselli 2003, Scienza 2004) support that thesis, finding no major genetic links between Greek varieties and Aglianico, or indeed between Greek varieties and other southern Italian native varieties as groups, suggesting that many of Italy's southern native grapes, including the *Malvasia*s and Aglianico, are not of Greek origin as has always been commonly believed. Clearly, these results do not prove the "nativeness" of Aglianico beyond doubt, because genetic modifications may have been induced subsequent to this variety's arrival on Italian shores.

The greatness of Aglianico starts with the grape itself. Generally speaking, Aglianico has medium-small, pyramidal, usually winged, compact bunches (150–200 grams of average weight) and small, round, dark blue-black berries equipped with thick skins, but the phenotypic expression depends on which biotype is being observed. There are three main biotypes: Taurasi, Taburno, and del Vulture. The Taurasi biotype has a more cylindrical bunch and smaller berries than the del Vulture and Taburno biotypes, suffers from *millerandage*, and is also less vigorous. The Taburno biotype is also called Aglianico Amaro, not because the grapes or wines are bitter (as could be inferred from the translation of the word *amaro*) but because of the high natural acidity this grape is famous for (*amaro* actually means acidic in the local dialect). This biotype is also affected by *millerandage*, mostly in reaction to non-ideal rootstock choices and boron deficiency in the soil. It is less fertile than the other two biotypes, but its bunch is the largest; the berries change color later than Taurasi or del Vulture, but Taburno ripens sooner, and usually with higher sugar and acid concentrations. The del Vulture variety usually expresses the most intense fruit aromas and flavors. New biotypes are on the way: the venerable Mastroberadino estate, now in its tenth generation, is currently studying a new Taurasi Aglianico biotype called Redimore that they hope to have officially certified soon.

Besides the many different biotypes, there are also many Aglianico clones available: VCR 11, VCR 14, UNIMI-VITIS-AGV VV401, UNIMI-VITIS-AGV VV404, and Ampelos VCP-VL5 (these five are all Aglianico del Vulture selections developed between 1997 and 2012); VCR 7, VCR 2, VCR 13, AV 02, AV 05, AV 09, VCR

23, VCR 111, VCR 106, VCR 109, VCR 103, UNIMI-VITIS-AGT VV 421, UNIMI-VITIS-AGT VV 411, BN 2.09.014, BN 2.09.025, Ampelos TEA 22, and Ampelos TEA 23 (these are all Campanian Aglianico selections developed between 1997 and 2008). Recently two clones have been developed from Aglianico grown in Puglia: CRSA Puglia D382 and CRSA Puglia D386. Interestingly, it is plantings of the VCR 2 clone, which yields bigger, blacker wines, that have increased greatly in the last ten years, especially in the Irpinia portion of Campania. This long list of clones, and the monumental clonal selection research behind it, tells you just how important Aglianico is in Italy.

Aglianico is blessed with thick skins that enable it to resist botrytis, allowing for late harvesting of this slowly ripening variety. In fact, Aglianico grapes are perhaps the latest of all great red wine grapes to be picked: for example, in the Vulture area of mountainous Basilicata, starting the harvest in late November is not unheard of. Long and slow growing seasons blessed by relatively warm autumns are a panacea for this variety, since its naturally high acidity and strong tannins need the softening effect of fully ripe berries. These late-season harvests expose Aglianico to the vagaries of autumn weather; though it's a generally resistant variety, in wet years peronospora can be a problem, while in hot and dry ones Aglianico can also suffer. Aglianico grows very well even at altitudes (six hundred to seven hundred meters above sea level) where most red grapes never manage to reach optimal ripeness. Yet Aglianico doesn't just get by in these marginal climates: it manages to produce some of the world's greatest, richest, most ageworthy wines there. What's more, while Aglianico is very capable of translating site-specific nuances into the glass, it always preserves its identity wherever it is grown. In other words, Aglianico seems able to dominate its *terroir,* much as Cabernet Sauvignon and Merlot do, and in contrast to Nebbiolo or Pinot Nero.

Today, Aglianico grows mainly in Campania and Basilicata, though there are also small holdings in Puglia, Abruzzo, Molise, Lazio, and Calabria. The Taurasi production area in Campania is made up of seventeen different communes, while Basilicata's Vulture area essentially revolves around the many small towns in the province of Potenza. But Aglianico is beginning to attract increasing attention outside Italy too: as climate change is all too obvious globally, producers everywhere are hitting panic buttons and asking for ever-later-ripening varieties. Aglianico plantings now dot the world map. In Australia, Aglianico has been planted in regions as diverse as Adelaide Hills, Barossa Valley, Langhorne Creek, King Valley, Mudgee, McLaren Vale, Riverina, and even Northern Tasmania (the Grey Sands estate owns Aglianico vines)—not just the drought-plagued inland wine regions. In California, there are plantings in various AVAs such as Alexander Valley and Paso Robles, but the variety has also been planted in less-famous wine-producing states, such as Texas and New Mexico. In the United States, the first Aglianico vineyard planted was in 1988 by Dave Caparone of the Caparone winery in Paso Robles; their San Marcos Road vineyard was planted with cuttings identified by Harold Olmo of the University of California at Davis, and later by Anna Schneider, one of Italy's most distinguished wine grape scientists. Aglianico has also been planted in Argentina and Mexico. Given the grape variety's many strengths and few weaknesses, it will likely be planted more widely in years to come.

Which Wines to Choose and Why

The three most famous wines made from Aglianico are Campania's DOCG Taurasi (near Avellino, in the mountainous Irpinia section of the region) and DOCG Taburno Aglianico (around Benevento, to the southeast), and Basilicata's DOC Aglianico del Vulture. However, there are many very good, even excellent, wines made in other DOCs, such as Cilento, Sannio, and Gallucio, all in Campania; the grape can also be included in IGT wine blends such as Colli Cimini, Colline Pescaresi, and Daunia. Though Aglianico is more than good enough to stand on its own, it is often blended with other local varieties that play a softening role. In Taurasi, producers are allowed to add up to 15 percent of grapes other than Aglianico, and throughout Campania tradition calls for blending Aglianico with the fresher and more aromatic Piedirosso. In Puglia, the choice falls on Primitivo (Zinfandel) to make faster-maturing, fruitier wines, while in Abruzzo or Molise it's Montepulciano. By contrast, Aglianico del Vulture legislation demands 100 percent Aglianico grapes, as does that for Taburno Aglianico.

No matter where Aglianico wines are made, they always share certain features. They will always be firm, savory red wines with real mineral rather than animal or vegetable nuance, and plenty of underlying fruit to go along with their great structure and depth of flavor—and the promise of a long and generally happy cellar-life. If the grapes aren't allowed to overripen, the wines invariably express a lovely floral note, most often recalling red roses, another similarity to Nebbiolo. Aglianico's floral perfume, high tannins and acidity, and obvious ageworthiness have given it its reputation as the "Barolo of the south." And just like Nebbiolo wines, those made with Aglianico can be downright ornery when young. Unless the wine is specifically made to be easygoing and fresh, young Aglianico wines will prove tough, tannic, and tarry, with at times eye-tearing acidity.

It is noteworthy that most of the *terroirs* where great Aglianico wines are made have in common a volcanic origin: Taurasi, Taburno, and Vulture are all extinct volcanic sites. The complex geology of the soils and the generally cool microclimates of these three areas allow for the development of smoky and spicy notes of amazing complexity, complicating the typical red rose and sour cherry of wines from Taurasi, the leather and herbs of Taburno, and the rich plum and highly mineral nuances of wines from the Vulture.

Taurasi is prized not just for its volcanic soils, but for its altitude as well. The vineyards climb to more than five hundred meters, providing hot, sunny days and cool nights; these day-night temperature differentials (often more than 10°C difference) help develop the penetrating aromas of the better Taurasi wines and the cool mountain weather allows the grapes to ripen slowly. The aromas and flavors of Taurasi can be remarkably similar to Nebbiolo-based wines at times, though Taurasi wines made with the VCR 2 clone need a lot of aeration for the typical floral note of Taurasi to emerge. This similarity is one reason why, in the early parts of the twentieth century, Aglianico wine was shipped to northern Italy (and Bordeaux as well) to reinforce weak vintages of more famous wines made in those weather-challenged areas. In Taurasi, the "wine railroad" is still famous, a train loaded with vats of wine sent off to more northern locations to "correct" their low alcohol, meager reds. (In the Vulture area you can still see the ruins of the Macchi building, where old-timers have told me that vats of Aglianico wine were stored before their journey north.)

The Taburno area of Campania is much less famous than Taurasi, as up until the 1980s, wine production here was mainly oriented to quantity, not quality: Trebbiano Toscano and *Lambrusco* varieties were being planted and the most common training system was the very high-yielding *pergola*. However, all that changed in the 1990s, and today, in Italy at least, wine lovers are quite aware of the very good and at times outstanding wines made there. Even better, the wines are very inexpensive given the quality in the bottle. The Taburno area is made up of fourteen townships located mainly on the eastern side of the Taburno mountain, where soils are heavily clay-calcareous and where there can be day-night temperature differentials even more brutal than in Taurasi. Furthermore, the Taburno area has considerable summer rainfall, and a generally cooler microclimate, so Aglianico wines born here are marked by particularly high total acidity levels, relatively lighter frames, and delectable fragrance.

However, as great as the wines of Taurasi and Taburno can be, they are often bested in blind tastings by the superstars coming out of the Vulture area in Basilicata. Basilicata (at times called Lucania) is the country's smallest region, tucked away between the heel (Puglia) and toe (Calabria) of Italy's boot-shaped geography. There is hardly a better habitat for the Aglianico variety than the volcanic soils of the Vulture ("almost too mineral," insinuates Antonio Mastroberardino, but then, he's from Campania, so you understand his position), the extinct volcano that dominates northern Basilicata. The Vulture is so named because it's shape is said to be reminiscent of that large scavenger, but this likeness is undoubtedly much easier to appreciate after having imbibed very large amounts of the red wine in question. Otherwise, I can't imagine anyone seeing any resemblance to a vulture or any other bird, for that matter. And I'm an animal lover. In theory, these wines ought to be fairly different from one another, given that they are made in different *terroirs* and with biotypes specific to each individual area; however, many producers have planted all three biotypes (a huge shame, in my opinion) in their vineyards and therefore nuances are lost in many modern wines.

The sine qua non of all Aglianico wines is an extremely high acidity (mainly due to high natural concentrations of tartaric acid) that makes the wine capable of aging magnificently, as well as a wonderfully nuanced minerality. This natural acidity is also responsible for the wine's light-on-its-feet personality—despite its being usually very full bodied and structured—while the mineral, almost flinty touch adds further minerality, freshness, complexity, and depth. The gracefulness and minerality of Aglianico wines offer considerable refinement while eschewing gamey or leathery notes, a combination that sets the Aglianico grape and wine apart from all other central and southern Italian red wine grapes, including Montepulciano, Nero d'Avola, Primitivo, or Negro Amaro. For this reason, it was a shame to see more and more producers—especially in Taurasi, but this was true of many wines from Basilicata as well—in the early part of the twenty-first century attempting to join the arms race by making always bigger, chocolaty-sweet, very ripe, low pH, and overly alcoholic wines. Whether this was out of a heartfelt conviction (misguided, in my view) that such wines represented an improvement over past efforts, or the secret hope of winning over less-than-expert wine critics with soft, approachable wines, I don't know. It doesn't matter really: mercifully, producers have been scaling back, giving us wine lovers the Aglianico wines we have always known and loved. Last but not least, the astute wine buyer will take note of the fact that Aglianico's wines are grossly underpriced relative to their quality; except for a few examples, most cost a good 30 percent less than Barolo, Brunello, and the other great reds from around the world.

Beyond Italy's borders, Aglianico wines of note are being made in Australia, usually in a more accessible, less acid and tannic style than in Italy. Many are garnering critical acclaim and awards: in the Australian Alternative Varieties Wine Show 2010, Westend Estate of Griffith, in New South Wales, won a best red wine trophy with a 2008 Aglianico. Australian Aglianico producers of merit include Amadio, Beach Road, Brown Brothers, Chalmers Murray, Di Lusso Estate, Karanto Vineyards, Pertaringa, and Westend Estate (in their Calabria series of wines). Many are excellent wines: for example, Chalmers bottled a 2005 that was big and almost pruney, while their 2009 was lighter and more refined. I find the Aglianico by Amadio, made from Barossa Valley grapes, also noteworthy.

In California, Seghesio and Kenneth Volk are producing Aglianico wines, but less well-known and very interesting wines are being made by Caparone in Paso Robles, Sutter Creek Vineyard (the 2006 Domenico Aglianico was a blend, while the 2007 was monovarietal), Villa Creek (Luna Matta Vineyard; I tasted the 2008 bottling, a well-made wine), Jacuzzi Family Vineyards, Ryme Wine Cellars (this estate is devoted to many Italian cultivars and first started out with Aglianico in 2007), and Terra d'Oro. Caparone made in 1992 what is, to the best of my knowledge, the first Aglianico wine born on American soil, but there are some other places in the United States making good Aglianico wines that will surprise you: Witch Creek, which uses Mexican fruit but makes the wine in California, and Mandola from Duchman Family Winery in Texas (a very light-bodied, almost pinot noir–like aglianico made from grapes grown in the Reddy Vineyard in the Texas high plains). I have tried promising versions made in New Mexico too, by Bellanzi and Luna Rossa winery; to date, the latter's barrel sample is the single best wine I have ever tried from New Mexico.

WINES TO TRY: For Taurasi, try: Antonio Caggiano*** (Macchia dei Goti), Mastroberardino*** (Radici Riserva; they also make a rare but ultra-delicious air-dried, sweet aglianico called Anthares), Quintodecimo***, Salvatore Molettieri*** (Vigna Cinque Querce Riserva), Contrade di Taurasi** (Riserva), Donnachiara**, Di Prisco**, Perillo**, Ponte**, Luigi Tecce** (Poliphemo), Terredora** (Fatica Contadina), and Urciolo**. For Taburno, try: Cantina del Taburno*** (Bue Apis, from one-hundred-year-old vines), Cantine Tora** (Riserva), and La Rivolta**. For the Pestum IGT, try D'Orta-De Conciliis*** (Zero, humorously refers to it on the label as a "supercampan"). For Vulture, try: Cantine del Notaio*** (La Firma and Il Sigillo), Elena Fucci***, Paternoster*** (Rotondo and Don Anselmo), Basilisco**, Cantina di Venosa** (Carato Venusio), Eubea** (Roinos), and Macarico**. For Puglia, try: Tormaresca** (Tordilupo) and Rivera* (Cappellaccio).

Aglianicone

WHERE IT'S FOUND: Campania, Basilicata. NATIONAL REGISTRY CODE NUMBER: 3. COLOR: red.

With Aglianico always hovering in the vicinity, poor Aglianicone has always had to fight for attention. And yet this variety has always been cultivated in Campania: it represents a striking estimated 90 percent of all red grapes grown in the Val Calore, in the southern province of Salerno. First mentioned by Acerbi in 1825, and long thought to be a subvariety of Aglianico, at times it was called Aglianico Femmina or Aglianichello (a name that should be reserved for another grape, a biotype of Aglianico). Semmola documented an Aglianicone near Naples in 1848, as did Froio (1878) and Carusi (1879); reading carefully and comparing the descriptions given by these last two researchers shows clearly that there are two Aglianicone subvarieties, one near Benevento (oval, reddish berries) and another found near Avellino, Caserta, and Salerno (round, dark-blue berries). These morphologic differences explain why in the Avellino and Salerno areas Aglianicone used to be called Aglianico Bastardo, while in the province of Caserta it was thought to be a different variety, and referred to as Aglianico di Caiazzo. Things didn't get any easier when, following Monaco and Manzo's study documenting Aglianicone's relationship to Aglianico (2001), Calò and Costacurta found Aglianicone identical to Ciliegiolo and not related to Aglianico at all (Calò, Costacurta, Carraro, and Crespan 2004). The fun never stops when identifying Italian native grapes.

The Aglianicone / Ciliegiolo fiasco is but one of many well-known, headache-inducing, not-so scientific capers, among them the Californian Mondeuse Noire / Refosco and the Australian Savagnin / Albariño misidentifications. As in those other instances, the erroneous conclusions were arrived at via genetic testing performed on incorrectly identified grapevines (in this case, likely an atypical-looking Ciliegiolo that had been believed to be Aglianicone). Clearly, if vineyards are sampled poorly and DNA profiles are performed on the wrong grapevines, then wrong results are predictable. These two varieties *do* look alike—though their wines couldn't be more different—and local producers have told me that in the past, careless nurseries sometimes sold Ciliegiolo to producers looking for Aglianicone.

There is no doubt that not all the Aglianicone vines dotting the countryside in Campania are in fact Aglianicone. Given the huge popularity of Aglianico in the region, and its huge economic importance, any half-witted farmer who found bigger-than-usual, Aglianico-like grape bunches and berries in the vineyards would undoubtedly have started referring to them as "big Aglianico," or Aglianicone. In fact, some experts believe that a good deal of the vines identified as the Tronto variety of Aglianico (also called Aglianico di Napoli) are in fact Aglianicone, especially those grown in the Val Calore of Salerno, and perhaps in the provinces of Avellino and Caserta as well. By contrast, true Aglianicone is most likely to be found in the Beneventano area; those Aglianicone grapevines present clear-cut morphologic differences from Aglianico biotypes. Of course, I have seen other Aglianicone vines that I feel certain actually *are* Aglianicone that look like Aglianico, albeit with bunches that are more loosely packed and bigger berries.

Aglianicone has medium-large, conical-pyramidal bunches and medium-sized, round berries. Never too vigorous, Aglianicone has reduced fertility and yields because of *millerandage;* so though it produces many bunches, Aglianicone's yields are low. All its phenologic phases occur earlier than those of Aglianico, and its resistance to oidium and botrytis is good. The berries usually present lower sugar and higher acid concentrations than those of Aglianico. There are no officially certified clones of Aglianicone available.

Things are looking up for Aglianicone. In 2003, Michele Clavelli, mayor of Sant'Angelo a Fasanella, set up the Tenute del Fasanella estate, which devotes attention to local natives, especially Aglianicone. Bruno De Conciliis, one of Campania's most famous producers, is also now producing a 100 percent Aglianicone, though he told me that he suspects his grapevines may be a different variety altogether, since the genetic analysis performed on them by the University of Potenza failed to show a match with the Aglianicone genetic fingerprint in the database. Then again, as we've seen, it's anybody's guess what variety was originally studied to create that database. "They are sixty-year-old vines owned by one of my employees," De Conciliis told me. "His grandfather was sure it was Aglianicone, but we're not." I can't say I'm surprised.

Which Wines to Choose and Why

In Campania, though more accurate verifications are necessary, Aglianicone appears at present to be limited to the countryside around Salerno and Benevento; by contrast, in Basilicata it is probably more common than is widely believed. No pure DOC wines exist (the sole DOC Aglianicone wine is Castel San Lorenzo), though there are a number of supposedly pure Aglianicone IGT wines. In Basilicata, an Aglianicone Rosato Frizzante, a sparkling rosé, is being made. Though the pH and total acidity of wines made with Aglianicone (or what I was told was Aglianicone) are similar to those of Aglianico wines on paper, well-made Aglianicone wines I have tried over the years strike me as fruitier and less spicy than Aglianico wines, though almost as full bodied and tannic.

A very interesting grape of uncommon potential, Aglianicone deserves to be better known—that is, once we all agree upon exactly what it is we are tasting. Aglianicone's undeserved reputation as a generally low-quality variety is most likely due to its frequent confusion with Tronto, as almost everyone gets the two cultivars, and hence the wines, completely mixed up. Though Aglianicone will never cause anyone to rip up his or her Aglianico vineyards, it is by no means a low-quality variety.

WINES TO TRY: De Conciliis** (Monteforte Aglianicone Pestum), Canto delle Vigne** (Aglianicone Pestum) with a whopping forty-one grams per liter dry extract in 2006, and Tenute del Fasanella**.

Albana

WHERE IT'S FOUND: Emilia-Romagna. NATIONAL REGISTRY CODE NUMBER: 4. COLOR: white.

Albana's name most likely derives from Colli Albani, where Roman legionnaires apparently first culled the variety before planting it around the Rubicon in Emilia-Romagna, the variety's main home to this day. However, since grape variety names referring to colors were very common in ancient Rome (see the introduction), it is very possible that *albana* may be a derivation of *alba*, meaning white. A less likely hypothesis is that the name derives from *albuele*, though it is true that there are many similarities between Albana and Germany's Elbling grape, which many in Germany believe was imported by Romans in the fourth century C.E.

While Albana's presence has long been documented in Italy, beginning with Pier de' Crescenzi (1303), and then Tanara (1644) and Molon (1906), a walk in the vineyards easily confirms the existence of what is likely more than one Albana variety. I never cease to be amazed by the myriad appearances of Albana clusters: long and scrawny, fat and compact, long and compact, and intermediate forms all abound. Historically, many unrelated varieties were named Albana-Something (Nera, Gialla, etc.), but today there are five recognized biotypes of Albana: Albana della Bagarona (medium-large cluster), Albana della Compadrona (large bunch), Albana della Gaiana (small bunch), Albana della Serra (also known as Albana della Forcella; very long, scrawny, often bifid cluster and very small, reddish berries), and Albana Gentile di Bertinoro (large bunch). Over the years I have seen another biotype, Albana Pizzigatti, which is not yet officially recognized but is considered ideal for sweet wine production. Its clusters are less compact than those of other biotypes; it also has two large wings, larger berries, and ripens about ten days later than the others. Later ripening, it holds its acidity better, but I find the berries have a simpler taste. Local growers have always told me that Albana della Serra and Albana Gentile di Bertinoro are the best biotypes; the latter is also most common of all the biotypes. Albana della Serra, which is also known as Albana della Forcella and is limited in its distribution to the countryside around Imola and Faenza, should not be confused with a distinct local variety called Forcella. Both these cultivars carry the *forcella* moniker because they are characterized by a bifid, or two-pronged, cluster: *forcella* means "fork."

To the best of my knowledge, DNA profiling has not yet been applied to Albana subvarieties or biotypes, so it is possible that some or all of them are not biotypes but altogether different cultivars. Instead, recent genetic studies by two different research groups (Di Vecchi Staraz, Bandinelli, Boselli, This, Boursiquot, Laucou, Lacombe, and Varès 2007; Crespan, Calò, Giannetto, Sparacio, Storchi, and Costacurta 2008) have confirmed a parent-offspring relationship between Albana and Garganega, the latter of which is one of Italy's oldest varieties; therefore, Albana is either a grandparent or half-sibling of Cataratto Bianco, Dorona, Malvasia Bianca di Candia, Marzemina Bianca, Montonico Bianco, Mostosa, Susumaniello, and Trebbiano Toscano. According to the world-famous French ampelographer Pierre Galet, Albana might be identical to a now-rare Corsican variety called Riminèse (Galet 2000). However, this is still a matter of conjecture: to the best of my knowledge, no SSR profiling evidence or other hard scientific data supporting this proposed identity is available; furthermore, Fontana and Filippetti (2005) have identified a Riminese di San Rocco variety in Emilia-Romagna that is distinct from Albana as well as ten other very common Italian white cultivars, though it might be related to Vernaccina. So there appears to be another grape variety out there with a claim to the Riminese name.

The size and shape of Albana's bunch, leaf, and berry depend not only on which biotype is under discussion, but also which clone, of which there are many: Rauscedo 4 (Serra), 002-AL 7 T, 003-AL 14 T, 004-AL 18 T, 005-AL

19 T, 006-AL 17 T, and 007–VCR 21. It flowers late and ripens in mid-September. Its thick skins and ability to accumulate sugar make it ideally suited for production of sweet wines, but over-ripeness can be problematic in humid conditions, which prevail in many parts of Emilia-Romagna, as they cause Albana's skin to break easily. Albana is enormously vigorous, but its large lymphatic canals mean that it suffers heat shock easily; this variety hates water deprivation.

Which Wines to Choose and Why

Albana grows in the provinces of Bologna, Modena, Rimini, Ravenna, and Forlì, but is most abundant in the latter two. Soils that allow Albana to show its best are often characterized by the presence of the *spungone romagnolo*, a geologic formation dating back to the Pliocene epoch (roughly three and one-half million years ago). *Spungone romagnolo* is a calcareous-sandy soil extremely rich in fossils, and is found mainly between the Marzeno stream near Brisighella up to Capocolle, between Forlimpopoli and Cesena. Excellent Albana wines can be made elsewhere, but they are usually less refined and more structured; choosing between them is a matter of individual tastes. The *grand* and *premier cru* areas for Albana appear to be Dozza (Imola), Riolo, Santa Lucia delle Spianate (Faenza), Terra del Sole e Castrocaro, Bertinoro, Longiano, and Montiano; these areas were first documented in the fourteenth century by Pier de' Crescenzi and Mariano Savelli, of the Regio Laboratorio Autonomo di Chimica Agraria di Forlì (the Royal Autonomous Laboratory of Agricultural Chemistry). In particular, the area around Bertinoro, with its calcareous-clay soils, has always been considered a true *grand cru* for the variety. Not all these areas are good for both dry and sweet wines: around Faenza, with its dry, windy conditions, noble rot is rare. Unfortunately plantings of Albana have steadily decreased since the beginning of the twenty-first century, when there were a noteworthy twenty-eight hundred hectares under vine; to combat this, the city of Imola is collaborating with university structures CRPV and CATEV to actively select old vines and different biotypes for new plantings. Albana can also be found in other parts of Italy, such as in Tuscany (near Pisa or La Spezia), though in limited numbers.

It's often said that Albana is a red wine in a white's clothing: chunky (when not overcropped), full bodied, and tannic, with a typical taste of pear, but also of acacia honey, aromatic herbs, and exotic fruits. However, most dry Albana wines on sale are usually very simple and citrusy. It can be painful in the cellar, because it oxidizes very easily: I have seen grapes picked and pressed the same day whose juice was already obviously golden-brown from incipient oxidation. Therefore, some producers hyperoxigenate the must; others try to obtain the same result by using *barriques* (small 225-liter oak barrels used around the world to age wine, as opposed to much larger oak casks). "But it's difficult," Giovanna Madonia, one of Emilia-Romagna's better producers, says simply.

Albana wines can be dry (DOCG Albana di Romagna) or sweet (Albana Passito, which is air-dried). The Albana *passitos* are probably more worthy of the honor bestowed upon Albana in 1966, when to general surprise, the dry Albana di Romagna was named Italy's first DOCG white: the dry whites, though not bad (lemony-floral, and on the thin side), are at times so nondescript that you wonder just what those legislators were drinking prior to making their historic decision. The *passito* wines are immensely sweet and thick, and can be remarkable (Albana takes very well to noble rot), though I prefer some of the slightly less massive, late-harvest wines (harvested directly from the vine) that are increasingly being produced, as they usually show better sugar-acid balance. Albana *passito riserva* has to be much sweeter still. Not to deprive themselves of anything, producers have also turned to making sparkling versions of albana, though I'm not sure Prosecco or any other decent sparkler need quake in its boots at the thought of possible competition.

WINES TO TRY: Fattoria Zerbina*** (outstanding *sélection de grains nobles* wines such as the 2006 AR Albana di Romagna Riserva Passito and the dry wine Secco As), Podere Morini** (excellent dry albana, and sweet Cuore Matto Albana di Romagna Riserva Passito; the 2006 had 230 grams per liter of residual sugar and 8 grams per liter of total acidity, and only 8.5 percent alcohol), Giovanna Madonia** (excellent dry Neblina), Raffaella Bissoni** (Passito), Villa Papiano** (Passito Riserva), and Tre Monti* (both the dry Vigna Rocca and the sweet Casa Lola, though I think this producer does even better with Trebbiano Romagnolo). To the best of my knowledge, there are no pure Riminèse wines made on Corsica; a shame, as it would be interesting to compare them to Italian versions.

Albana Nera

WHERE IT'S FOUND: Emilia-Romagna. NATIONAL REGISTRY CODE NUMBER: not registered. COLOR: red.

Albana Nera is a virtually unknown cultivar that I believe might have fine-wine potential—but I am not sure it is an Albana. In the fourteenth century, Pier de' Crescenzi wrote of the *Albatichi* group, grape varieties that all looked like Albana, but (contrary to popular opinion) he did not specifically write about an Albana Nera (Cavazza 1904). According to de' Crescenzi, the dark-berried Albana was also called Albanina and was considered a good table grape. For their part, Tanara (1644) and Acerbi (1825) clearly describe, in vineyards around Cesena, a dark-berried Albana named Albana Rossa, and distinguish it from Albana Nera. It is more likely however, as other experts have written, that Albana Rossa was the name used to describe Albana Nera in the area of Forlì and Cesena, but that the two grapes were the same.

Farmers have always liked Albana Nera because it tolerates higher altitudes and cooler weather. It appears to have gradually moved from hillsides to plains and from Emilia into Romagna in the seventeenth century; in these early days, it was often made into a lightly sparkling wine. Unfortunately, Albana Nera is quite rare today. Fontana and Filippetti (2006) have tried to rediscover old vines in the areas around Forlì and Riolo that Cavazza believed were the variety's home.

It appears that Paolo Babini, owner of the Fondo San Giuseppe estate near Brisighella, where the variety was reportedly cultivated in the past, owns twenty-five-year-old Albana Nera vines he selected from a local farmer's vineyard. Given how forgotten this area of Romagna is, and the altitude and steep hillside location of the vineyards where he found the vines, a grapevine discovery of this sort is plausible. I can personally vouch for the altitude and the steepness of the slopes: walking those hills with Babini on a hot summer day last year, I was left panting after only ten minutes into a much longer walk (being out of shape doesn't help). For what it's worth, the vines certainly looked to me like a black-hued Albana. Further, there are some fairly different-looking bunches among Babini's vines, so it seems likely that, as with Albana, there are different biotypes of Albana Nera. However, some grapevines I saw that day were clearly Centesimino, so I'm not sure all twenty-five hectares owned by Babini are Albana Nera.

Even more interesting is that amid the normal-looking Albana Nera bunches peppering Babini's vines, perhaps a quarter of the total were actually white-berried. Since entire bunches were made up of nothing but white grapes, it cannot be a case of asynchronous ripening—as it was Babini who selected the grapevines to replant, it is highly unlikely that these are different Albana vines planted promiscuously or erroneously in the same vineyard. All this leads me to postulate that Albana Nera may be a colorful mutation of Albana. In any case, Albana Nera and Albana wouldn't be the first examples of varieties that obligingly mutate at the slightest provocation; the fact that Albana is a very old variety makes color mutations particularly likely, as in Pinot Nero. Of course, Albana Nera may just be a different variety altogether, completely unrelated to the white-berried Albana. I hope Paolo decides to have genetic testing performed on his vines soon, and then we'll know exactly what he owns.

In any case, research conducted in 2004 in Tebano proved that Albana Nera is distinct from all other grapes currently listed in the National Registry, though the differentiation between it and Abrusco (though the two don't look even remotely alike to me) was arrived at in 2005 only via ampelographic measures (Fontana and Filippetti 2006). Molecular genetic testing by the same research group confirmed a relationship between Albana Nera and Marzemino: these two varieties apparently share one allele in each of the ten loci examined. Originally, it was believed there were two different Albana Nera biotypes: Albana Nera Balducci (growing in the area around Forlì) and Albana Nera Vignoli (found in the countryside around Ravenna). However, results from this study showed that the Vignoli biotype is identical to Ciliegiolo, so it's not an Albana Nera at all.

Which Wines to Choose and Why

Albana Nera grows only around Faenza, Brisighella, and the hills of Imola, especially in Santagata sul Santerno in Emilia-Romagna. There are no DOC wines, and I only know of the IGT wine made by Babini. It's not an easy grape to make wine from: like Dolcetto, it produces a lot of solids and therefore needs pumping or racking in order to ward off the development of unpleasant odors. When well made, these wines have deep purple-ruby hues, grapey aromas, and flavors of dark berries and herbs, and is very bright and fresh with sneaky concentration.

WINES TO TRY: Babini's Fondo San Giuseppe** (Collanima, it also contains 10 percent Centesimino, planted haphazardly among the Albana Nera vines).

Albanella

WHERE IT'S FOUND: Marche. NATIONAL REGISTRY CODE NUMBER: not registered. COLOR: white.

Another fine bureaucratic mess. Albanella was long considered a synonym of the much less valid Trebbiano Toscano, and the lawmakers who crafted the DOC regulations for the Colline Pesaresi in Marche outlawed the use of the name Albanella until 2000. In their misguided belief that Trebbiano Toscano was locally called Albanella, they effectively wiped the true Albanella off the map. If it hadn't been for the Mancini family of Pesaro, we might not be speaking of Albanella today; but Ettore and Luigi knew that their Albanella grapes looked and behaved nothing like the lowly Tuscan *Trebbiano*. Better still, the wine made with Albanella was more interesting. Consequently, they have been bottling it since 1992.

Thanks to the Mancinis getting Attilio Scienza of the University of Milan involved, we know that Albanella is related to Elbling and Albariño, and unrelated to Trebbiano Toscano, though, to the best of my knowledge, these research results have yet to be published in a peer-reviewed academic journal. Apparently, Albanella also bears a morphologic resemblance to the rare Sardinian variety Albaranzeuli Bianco. There appear to be three biotypes: large, intermediate, and small bunches and berries; the intermediate biotype also has a downy underside to its leaves, while in the other two this is smooth. Precious little historical information is available on it: the first mention is in a nineteenth-century document kept in the Biblioteca Oliveriana in Pesaro. It should not be confused with Albanello, which is a Sicilian grape.

Which Wines to Choose and Why

Reduced to only a few rows of vines here and there, Albanella is a variety on the rebound, and an increasing number of local producers are setting down rows of it. It is grown almost exclusively near Pesaro, in subzones such as Roncaglia and Montebacchino. The DOC wines are Colline Pesaresi, but they have to include 25 percent Pinot Nero (removed immediately off the skins, as for a white wine), so monovarietal versions are available only as IGT. The presence of Pinot Nero may seem strange, but it was brought to the area during the Napoleonic wars. Mancini claims that "Pinot Nero doesn't change the wine much," but one wonders. Albanella is a high-acid variety that never accumulates much sugar, so it is best as a light, lively wine offering pleasant citrusy and mineral notes. It ages remarkably well, and I have had bottles from the first years of this century that are still in top shape.

WINES TO TRY: Fattoria Mancini** (Roncaglia).

Albanello

WHERE IT'S FOUND: Sicily. NATIONAL REGISTRY CODE NUMBER: 5. COLOR: white.

Albanello is a largely unknown variety that was never cultivated extensively, though its winemaking potential has always been highly thought of. It was mentioned as early as 1700 as a high-quality variety and represents one of the historical cultivars of the Syracuse area. The wines, both dry and sweet styles, were praised by Viala and Vermorel (1909). In the 1960s, Italy's greatest wine writer, Luigi Veronelli, described Albanello wines as excellent, alcoholic (up to 19 percent alcohol, nonfortified) and expensive (unbelievable as it may seem, in those days a bottle of albanello fetched as much as a fine Barolo). The first known albanello producer was the noble Landolina family, who began blending it with grillo in 1712. Another longtime producer was the Cantina Aretusa, and until the 1950s albanello was still being bottled regularly by the Cantina Sperimentale di Noto. In the nineteenth and early twentieth centuries, Albanello's production zone was once limited to the southeastern corner of Sicily, in Ragusa and Syracuse (the best were from Noto, Syracuse, and Avola), but by the 1970s, Pastena attested that it was grown and wine made with it near Catania as well (1976). Salvo Foti, Sicily's greatest winemaker and certainly the greatest expert on the varieties of Etna, told me that years ago a DOC was proposed for Albanello wine but was refused, probably due to its very limited and inconsistent productivity. In 2010, Carimi, Mercati, Abbate, and Sunseri showed that a rare local variety called Fumisi is synonymous with Albanello.

Today, Albanello is limited to sporadic vines in the province of Syracuse and Ragusa. Arianna Occhipinti of the eponymous winery planted Albanello in 2005 in selected old vineyards around the town of Chiaramonte Gulfi, near Ragusa, in what has always been the heart of Albanello's production zone. She is very happy with the variety, finding it easy to work with and resistant to common diseases. Gulfi also grows a few vines of Albanello.

Which Wines to Choose and Why

There is no DOC wine. Albanello can be part of IGT blends Avola, Camarro, Salina, Terre Siciliane, and Valle Belice, none of them exactly household names even in Italy. The wine is still made locally in both a dry and a much better air-dried version, for which the grapes are left to dry eight days.

Sebastiano Gulino, who is an otolaryngologist in addition to a winemaker, deserves the highest possible praise for having had the courage to make a monovarietal Albanello wine, and it may be hoped that Occhipinti will soon follow suit. She says: "Even though it's not an aromatic variety, Albanello tends to develop complex floral and austere notes with age." Frankly, since her Albanello wine, SP68, has a hefty dose of Moscato di Alessandria, organic winemaking that results in low sulfur, and ten to fifteen days of maceration on the skins, I'm not sure how anyone tasting her wine can grasp what Albanello can and cannot give. Though it's a very fine wine (Occhipinti is a tremendously talented winemaker and one of the up-and-coming stars of Italy) and the Italian wine guides have been very generous in their praise, I think more credit is due to the little-known Cantine Gulino for truly pioneering work: their Pretiosa is bright and crisp, with pretty floral and herbally white stone-fruit aromas and flavors. Salvo Foti has planted a small vineyard of old-vine Albanello massal selections taken from Gulfi's

Vignamare vineyard (in fact Gulfi's wine called Carjcanti, which is mainly Carricante, does contain a little Albanello), and hopes to make a monovarietal wine someday soon. I hope so too.

WINES TO TRY: Cantine Gulino** (Pretiosa; pure Albanello, though it used to include 20 percent Chardonnay), Arianna Occhipinti* (SP68; 85 percent Albanello and 15 percent Moscato di Alessandria).

Albarola

WHERE IT'S FOUND: Liguria, Tuscany. NATIONAL REGISTRY CODE NUMBER: 8 (also at number 26 as Bianchetta Genovese). COLOR: white.

Near Genoa, Albarola is also known as Bianchetta Genovese (or Bianchetta *tout court*), though the latter was until recently believed to be a separate variety. In fact, Bianchetta Genovese is still listed as a separate variety at number 26 in the National Registry. In 1965, Dell'Olio and Macaluso wrote that it was highly unlikely that Albarola and Bianchetta Genovese were identical, since what they believed to be the true Albarola was historically grown only in the Cinque Terre and near La Spezia. According to them, it became common elsewhere in Liguria only in the wake of post-phylloxeric replanting. No surprise then that Albarola is the name more commonly used from La Spezia and Sarzana into Tuscany (where it is also named Erbarola or Erbarola Trebbiana), while Bianchetta is still used in Liguria's Val Polcèvera and Riviera di Levante (areas west and east of Genova). However, Dell'Olio and Macaluso's view is in contrast with Gallesio's identification of Albarola with a so-called Bianchetta del Genovesato in the early nineteenth century; in 1993, Schneider, Mannini, and Argamante confirmed that Albarola and Bianchetta Genovese are identical. Furthermore, the morphological descriptions of Albarola and Bianchetta Genovese by Dall'Olio and Macaluso differ only mildly. In any case, both names clearly refer to the grape's whitish-green, almost translucent berries. In the past, Albarola was also confused with Trebbiano Toscano (explaining the Trebbiano Erbarolo or even Albarola Trebbiana synonyms), especially near Liguria's border area with Tuscany. This should come as no big surprise, because at one point or other, almost every Italian white grape variety has been taken to be Trebbiano Toscano (probably due to the latter variety being grown all over the country).

If today we know more about Albarola and its wines, credit must go to Daniele Lugano, owner of the Bisson estate, who, at the end of the 1970s, decided to try making a pure Albarola wine. There are four known clones of Albarola (VCR 3, VCR 14, VCR 17, and CVT Kihlgren). Of these, the first three are of more or less equal value. The Kihlgren clone, officially available since 2012, was named in honor of the owner of the vineyard where it was found, in Sarzana (Torello Marinoni, Raimondi, Ruffa, Lacombe, and Schneider 2009; Mannini, Schneider, Argamante, Moggia, and Tragni 2010). Its looser and smaller bunches are useful characteristics in inclement weather, as Albarola's tightly squeezed berries have a tendency to break, and are easy prey to molds and other pests. Recently, research has suggested that Albarola di Lavagna, listed everywhere as a synonym of Albarola, is neither identical nor even a biotype, but an altogether different grape (Botta, Scott, Eynard, and Thomas 1995; recently duplicated by the previously mentioned 2009 study by Torello Marinoni et al.). Albarola di Lavagna differs because of its habitat too, since it only grows in Liguria's Val Graveglia and near Chiavari, in the eastern part of the region. Whether Dell'Olio and Macaluso inadvertently studied Albarola di Lavagna instead of true Albarola, thereby generating confusion relative to the Albarola / Bianchetta Genovese question, is a matter of conjecture.

Albarola is a very pretty grape and remarkably easy to spot in the vineyards, given its nearly round, indentation-free leaves and translucent, pale berries (I don't wish to add fuel to the controversy, but I will point out that while Bianchetta Genovese grapevines look very much like

Albarola, the former's leaves are more pentagonal and have clearer indentations and only mildly downy undersides, while Albarola's are hairier). In an interesting study comparing monovarietal wines made with Albarola and Bosco grown at different altitudes (240 and 430 meters above sea level) in the 2007 vintage, results showed that wines grown at the lowest altitude had higher contents of isoamyl acetate (responsible for banana and exotic fruit aromas) and 2-phenylethylacetate (floral sensations), probably as a result of higher average temperatures that allow for development of riper, tropical notes (Cravero, Bonello, Piano, Chiusano, Borsa, Tsolakis, and Lale Demoz 2010). The low *pergola* (canopy) training system commonly used in the Cinque Terre allows for greater protection from sunlight and heat, more even ripening, and better wines. According to Pierluigi Lugano, owner of the Bisson estate in Chiavari, Liguria, Albarola wants fresh and well-exposed sites; for such a thin-skinned variety, it has good resistance to marine winds but is sensitive to excessively humid conditions. It does best in *tarso*, very friable, dry, rocky, hillside soils typical of the Chiavari-Sestri Levante area (note that *tarso* should be distinguished from other local, much harder soils such as *pietra dolce* and *colombina*). It's a very consistent producer, but poorly resistant to fungi and oidium.

Which Wines to Choose and Why

Grown in Liguria and Tuscany (as far down as Massa Carrara and even Pisa), Albarola is also found in the Cinque Terre, where it is used in blends with Bosco and Vermentino to give not only delicious, dry white wines, but also noteworthy, if rare, sweet, air-dried ones. It's very useful in blends, since it adds alcoholic strength and body. The only 100 percent albarolas are the DOC Golfo del Tigullio and Val Polcèvera (and its subzone Coronata); there is a rare Golfo del Tigullio DOC Passito (air-dried) sweet wine. Albarola is also included in many better-known Ligurian blends, including those of Colli di Luni and Cinque Terre, and even in Tuscany's Montescudaio. The one *grand cru* for Albarola is Liguria's Missano area, where the grape probably originated.

I think albarola is an underrated wine that deserves to be better known. The grape is naturally high in malic acid, and its wines exude fresh citrus and delicate almondy aromas and flavors, with a clean, minty-saline edge. Though not everybody appreciates its high acidity, I do: it makes for an excellent food wine, and given its dainty personality, producers mercifully do not oak it. When the vine is overcropped, the wine is thin and tart. When sipping a well-made Albarola wine, paying at least a little attention to what you are drinking will ensure that the wine's discreet but very present charms won't be lost on you. In my experience, wine made from the Kihlgren biotype is smoother and richer, with a more obvious tropical fruit presence. Keep in mind that these wines have never shown any cellaring potential, rather the reverse: drink them up soon after the vintage.

WINES TO TRY: Bisson*** (Bianchetta Genovese U Pastine Golfo del Tigullio), Pino Gino*** (their Bianchetta Genovese Golfo del Tigullio is mouth-puckeringly tart with lovely hints of pear and melon), Santa Caterina*** (Bianco; this is the estate owned by Andrea Kihlgren). Cantina Bregante* and Daniele Parma* are also worth a look, as is AeP Tenimenti, where Sara Arrigoni is making a very good monovarietal albarola, among other wines. Lunae Bosoni* makes a highly aromatic, fuller version that is a little atypical and too glyceral for me, but it's an impressive wine that has many admirers. Cantine Segesta* (Sole della Costa) makes a sweet wine from air-dried grapes, 80 percent Albarola and 20 percent Vermentino. Bisson* (Acinirari) also makes a sweet, air-dried Albarola and Vermentino blend.

Aleatico

WHERE IT'S FOUND: Tuscany, Lazio, Marche, Puglia, Sicily, and Umbria. NATIONAL REGISTRY CODE NUMBER: 9. COLOR: red.

Among the wine world's most undervalued treasures, wines made with Aleatico can demonstrate a thrilling combination of raciness and richness. Aleatico is a delicious, lightly aromatic red that will have you thinking of a black muscat wine. It is also one of Italy's most ancient grapes, appreciated by the Romans, though the exact origins of the cultivar are debated. Some experts believe it was brought to Puglia by the Greeks, and note that the name Aleatico is very similar to Liatika, a Greek grape (though the two could not be more different, and most importantly, Liatika is not an aromatic variety). Others believe Aleatico's name refers to July (*lugliaticum,* in Latin), the month in which the ripening grapes change color. Molon traces the Aleatico name to another ancient name, *livatica.* In his *Liber Ruralium Commodorum,* Pier de' Crescenzi writes of a Tuscan grape called Livatica, but described it as white, while Aleatico is red. In any case, a red Aleatico was well known in Tuscany in the seventeenth century: Bartolomeo del Bimbo, painter of the Medici court, depicted a red grape called *liatico della Villa de' Biadori,* and Trinci describes a red wine made from Aleatico in 1726.

Synonyms, erroneous and not, have long plagued Aleatico. In the nineteenth century, three different Aleatico varieties (Nero, Bianco, and Rosso) were believed to exist. In their major work of 1909, Viala and Vermorel name at least ten varieties, and the list of names and synonyms by which Aleatico is known throughout Italy today is virtually endless: Aleatica, Aleatica di Firenze, Aleatichina, Aleatico de Corse, Aleatico dell'Elba, Aleatico de Portoferraio, Aleatico di Altamura, Aleatico di Beneventoare, et cetera. Some of its synonyms (Moscato Nero, Moscatello Nero, Moscato Rosso) are flat-out wrong, and should be avoided at all costs.

DNA profiling of the *Moscato* grapes has demonstrated Aleatico's parent-offspring relationship with Moscato Bianco, and also identified Aleatico with Moscatello Nero (Crespan and Milani 2001; Filipetti, Ramazzotti, Intrieri, Silvestroni, and Thomas 2002), but distinguished it from Moscato Nero (Scalabrelli, D'Onofrio, Ferroni, and Vignai 2009). According to Filipetti, Silvestroni, Thomas, and Intrieri (2001), Aleatico also shares close genetic ties to Lacrima di Morro d'Alba (that's easy enough to imagine), as well as to Sangiovese and Gaglioppo (that's a lot harder, given the three grapes have very little in common). Though it is reported in Robinson, Harding, and Vouillamoz (2012) that the Hungarian variety Halápi is also identical to Aleatico, I have found no scientific study in which this conclusion has been accepted for publication, but it's hopefully just a matter of time. Last but not least, in 2003, Crespan, Cancellier, Costacurta, Giust, Carraro, Di Stefano, and Santangelo showed that Vernaccia Rossa, a variety grown in the Marche and used to make the Vernaccia di Pergola wine, is actually a biotype of Aleatico. In fact, in 1876, De Bosis writes that a very good aleatico was already being produced on the hillsides of Jesi in the Marche.

Aleatico is a vigorous variety that has good drought tolerance, and prefers well-ventilated, dry, and not too fertile soils. It suffers from potassium deficiency in the soil and for optimal ripeness it needs plenty of deleafing in order to guarantee maximum ventilation and exposure of the berries. This is especially true for tightly packed bunches, as the variety is prone to fungal diseases. The most common training systems are the spur cordon and Guyot, while *alberello* (a grapevine training system also known as gobelet or bushvine in English) is typical of older vineyards. Aleatico is sensitive to wet springs, when poor fruit set (due to berry shatter or to *millerandage*) can be problematic. Today, though there are six clones available from mainland Italy (AL-PA 1, VCR 438, ARSIAL-CRA 489, AL-VAL 1, CRA VIC BC SF3, and AL-FI.PI-1) and eight from Corsica, with two more from Elba awaiting certification. As the grapes are almost always subjected to dehydration techniques, developing less compact clones of moderate vigor with thick-skinned berries is of paramount importance. New, virus-free grapevine material is also necessary, as many Aleatico vines in the field are virus infested, particularly with fanleaf virus. Given that Aleatico often lives in hot and dry microclimates, it does best with rootstocks such as 110 R that allow its roots to dig deep for water. It's also sensitive to magnesium and potassium deficiency in the soil. Due to the many different areas it grows in, harvest dates vary, but the grapes are usually ripe by the end of September.

Aleatico is found in numerous Italian regions, and is most common in Tuscany, Puglia, Lazio, and Marche. The area under vine is unfortunately declining: in 1991, Aleatico represented only 0.18 percent of the total hectares devoted to red varieties in Tuscany; these have been further reduced to the current sixty hectares, though there are a little less than two hundred in all of Italy. In Tuscany, Aleatico grows on the coast (in Livorno and Grosseto), and on the islands of Elba and Capraia. These two islands represent true *grand crus* for the variety and their aleaticos are some of Italy's greatest wines. The two *terroirs* are quite different, however: according to winemaker Leonardo Conti, who works with the La Piana estate on Capraia, Capraia is drier and fresher than Elba, with better drainage. All the phenological phases occur later on Capraia, so the harvest also occurs later.

In the Marche, the confusingly named wine Vernaccia di Pergola is also made with Aleatico, which was brought to the town in 1234 by its founders, former citizens of Gubbio. The efforts of passionate farmers and producers of today and times past—including Guido Bruschi, Giovanni Orfei, Giulio Fulvi, and Francesco Tonelli—led to the DOC Vernaccia di Pergola in 2005. Today this Aleatico biotype is also grown in other small towns around Pergola: San Lorenzo in Campo, Fratterosa, Frontone, and Serra Sant'Abbondio. A *grand cru* for Vernaccia di Pergola is Grifoleto.

Aleatico is also grown in France (Corsica), Kazakhstan, Uzbekistan, California, and Australia. In Australia, Aleatico is not a recent arrival: it was first planted in the Mudgee area roughly one hundred years ago by Thomas Fiaschi.

Which Wines to Choose and Why

The best Aleatico wines are those of Elba, but the area around Lazio's Lake Bolsena is quickly gaining a reputation, as a new generation of Lazio winemakers turn heads with many lovely sweet wines. Ludovico Botti of the Tre Botti estate even devoted his enology school thesis to Aleatico, and shares with his close friend Andrea Occhipinti of the Occhipinti estate a passion for Aleatico that dates back to their school days. Occhipinti has taken his experimentation with Aleatico to the point where he now produces an excellent, if rather full-bodied and pinkish-tinged, white wine (appropriately enough called Alter Ego) from this red-berried grape. In the Marche, winemaker Alberto Mazzoni believes the Pergola biotype of Aleatico gives a much more intense, richer wine than those of the other regions.

Aleatico can be either dry or sweet, and it makes outstanding *rosati*; the wines have strong aromas and flavors reminiscent of a red-berried Muscat. They are also always very deeply hued, thanks to a high percentage of malvin in the skins—and since this is the most stable of the five main grape pigments, the wines tend to remain dark over time. Dry and *rosato* wines are delicately floral, with spicy aromas reminiscent of wild strawberry, raspberry, cinnamon, and rose (mainly thanks to geraniol, though Aleatico wines have high levels of citronellol and nerol too). Don't make the mistake of thinking that Aleatico *rosatos* are among the overly sweet and simple rosé or blush wines; nothing could be further from the truth. Aleatico *rosatos* are splendid wines, with abundant aromas and flavors, a crisp texture and bright acids; fruity and floral, they deliver a touch of spice that makes them crowd pleasers and very versatile with food.

Clearly, though both *rosato* and dry *rosso* wines are increasingly made with Aleatico, it's the sweet wines that first grabbed the attention of wine lovers everywhere. The aromatic intensity of the wines appears to increase if the grapes are subjected briefly to high temperatures just before harvest, causing a mild increase in free volatile terpenes such as geraniol and nerol. While late harvesting decreases the total terpenic concentration, it increases free specific fractions, through dehydration and the dissolution of skin terpenes into the pulp. However, true late harvesting is not possible on Elba and Capraia due to the risk of autumn showers, and so those sweet wines are made via the traditional method of air-drying on shelves. There are two schools of thought about air-drying Aleatico grapes: traditionally, on Elba, the grapes air-dried directly in the sun, but more modern winemakers prefer to air-dry the grapes in the shade so as to produce wines that express fully the unique and very intense aromas and flavors Aleatico is capable of delivering. In both methods, the grapes are almost always picked by the end of August, because after that point Aleatico's leaves stop working and the grapes tend to dehydrate directly on the vine. Different estates champion different sources and methods: for example the Tuscan estate La Fazenda has planted clonal selections of Aleatico, while Terre del Sillabo has chosen to work with massal selections; La Fazenda air-dries the grapes in the shade, while Terre del Sillabo does not. Therefore, tasting the Aleaticos by these two producers allows you to decide which winemaking method is more to your liking. Both methods produce sweet wines that are some of the world's very best: the intense, concentrated aromas and flavors of spicy red and black cherries, red roses, violet, lavender, cinnamon, nutmeg, and cloves are absolutely unforgettable. Keep in mind that, in my opinion, the best aleaticos are made by small, passionate producers, while bigger outfits have, at least until now, mainly gone through the motions. Unfortunately, sweet Aleatico wine is very expensive to make, since the bunches carry few grapes (because of *millerandage*), and so few producers really want to devote much time and effort to it. That's another reason why, in Italy at least, small, artisanal producers are your best bet for a memorable Aleatico wine experience.

Outside Italy, Aleatico's island affinity is further shown by its presence on Corsica, where it's traditionally used to make Rappu, a highly alcoholic aperitif wine. There are some lovely Aleatico wines being made much farther away. In California, Aleatico is grown at Serres Ranch in Sonoma, where the grapes are dry farmed on mainly loamy soils. These grapes have been used by many wineries to make standout Aleatico wines. Imagery Estate Winery in Glen Ellen and Viansa in Sonoma are two such estates; their Aleatico rosés are excellent. La Piazza di Sonoma and Jacuzzi Family Vineyards have also made thicker, sweeter, late-harvest Aleatico wines. In Australia, Aleatico is made by Di Lusso Estate in Mudgee (a lovely wine in a very pretty bottle simply labeled "Aleatico") and Tizzana in the South Coast Zone (Ambrose, a rosé; Tizzana also used to make a blend of 80 percent Syrah and 20 percent Aleatico called Tomasso). In Hilltops, Freeman Vineyards grows Aleatico, and includes just a small splash of it in a rather wild blend of Pinot Grigio, Chardonnay, Riesling, and Sauvignon Blanc called Freeman Fortuna. In Darling Downs, Rimfire Vineyards used to make an Aleatico *vin gris* (it even won a bronze medal at the Australian Alternative Varieties Show in Mildura in 2003) but I haven't seen any bottles of the wine in a long time. Queenland's Riversands Vineyards made a wine I never managed to get a hold of, once intriguingly called Dr. Seidel's Soft Red Aleatico Moscato Rosso, now just Dr. Seidel's Soft Red Muscat said to be made with "Black Muscat" grapes.

WINES TO TRY: For Elba, try: Acquabona*** (Aleatico Passito Riserva; the best producer of sweet aleatico in Italy), Tenuta delle Ripalte*** (Alea Ludendo), and Mola**. For Capraia, try: La Piana*** (Rosa della Piana, a head-turning, delightful dry *rosato*), La Fazenda* (Passito), and Terre del Granito* (Passito). For the Tuscan mainland, try: Piandibugnano* and Bulichella*. For Puglia, try: Lomazzi & Sarli** (Dimastrodonato, intensely air-dried Aleatico, very thick and sweet) and Francesco Candido* (Aleatico di Puglia). For Lazio, try: La Carcaia**, Occhipinti** (Montemaggiore Rosso, Alea Viva, Alter Ego), Tre Botti** (Bludom Passito). For Marche (Vernaccia di Pergola), try: Fattoria Villa Ligi*, Terracruda*, and Michele Massaioli*.

Ancellotta

WHERE IT'S FOUND: Emilia-Romagna. NATIONAL REGISTRY CODE NUMBER: 12. COLOR: red.

One of the rare Italian grapes for which there is scanty historical documentation, Ancellotta may take its name from the Lancellotti (or Lancellotto) family: there is documentation that a Tommassino Lancellotti, who worked in the wine business, propagated Ancellotta in the fourteenth and fifteenth centuries. Alternatively, its name may derive from the lanceolated (spear-like) middle lobe of its leaf, though of course many other varieties have spear-like leaves, including Fogarina, long cultivated in the same areas of Emilia-Romagna as Ancellotta, and the much rarer Lanzesa. One of its synonyms is Ancellotta di Massenzatico, named after a small town that is a hotbed of Ancellotta cultivation.

Ancellotta is grown mainly in flatland vineyards of Emilia-Romagna, especially around Reggio Emilia (where it represents half of the provincial grape production) and to a lesser degree, Modena. Apparently, there exists a Trentino subvariety I have yet to see, with smaller bunches and berries, that tends to give higher alcohol wines. It also grows in Brazil (where they use it to make monovarietal wines) and in Switzerland's Valais region, where it adds color to anemic reds, which is exactly the role it has always been famous for in Italy as well. There are four clones available: Fedit 18 C.S.G., R 2, VCR 540, and CAB 1. In general, Ancellotta has a medium-sized, pyramidal bunch with dark, thick-skinned, spherical berries. It's sensitive to spring frosts and to oidium, but has good resistance to wind and drought. It likes clay-rich soils of alluvial origin, and is characterized by medium-high vigor, and large, regular production; it flowers relatively early and ripens in very late September or early October. Ancellotta was apparently used to breed Galotta, a laboratory Ancellotta × Gamay Noir crossing grown in Switzerland's Canton Ticino but not found under any guise in Italy (not even as a table grape or grape "for special purposes").

Which Wines to Choose and Why

Traditionally, little bottled wine is made with this variety, its production being directed toward concentrated musts or bulk wines used to increase the color of anemic red wines made all over Italy. That Ancellotta is viewed as a very important and useful variety is well illustrated by the fact it is included in two DOC blends (Colli di Faenza and Reggiano) and an almost ridiculous forty-two IGT blends (one of the largest numbers of any Italian grape variety), including well-known ones such as Tuscany's Costa Toscana and Sardinia's Isola dei Nuraghi. The name of Ancellotta's main by-product, Rossissimo ("extremely red"), illustrates Ancellotta's main appeal. However, the intensity of Ancellotta's red coloration and its wealth of polyphenols have also found uses in the pharmaceutical, food, and cosmetic industries. An important natural coloring agent called enocyanin is obtained from its skins, and is used to color fruit juice and sauces. Villiam Friggeri, talented winemaker and director of the Cantina di Santa Croce in Carpi, makes a Lancellotta dell'Emilia Filtrato Dolce that is 100 percent Ancellotta, a lightly alcoholic, sparkling, fermented grape juice best paired with sweet fruit pies and cookies, as well as a Mosto di Uva Ancellotta, used to flavor sauces. Ancellotta is also used in blends of DOC Lambrusco Reggiano and Lambrusco Salamino di Santa Croce.

A good ancellotta is not just about almost impenetrably deep ruby-purple looks; it exudes plenty of fruity charm, with almost sweet, low pH, and soft, tactile ripe blackberry and cherry aromas and flavors. Those who prize fruit in their wines, or who fantasize about alcoholic fruit juices, will simply love anything involving Ancellotta.

From Brazil, I have tried Don Guerino's monovarietal version, which resembles richer versions made in Italy, as well as the Don Laurindo Reserva, from that country's Serra Gaucha wine region. Dal Pizzol made a very good Ancellotta wine in 2008. In Switzerland's Canton Ticino, the Cantina Sociale di Mendrisio and Enrico Trapletti both grow Galotta.

WINES TO TRY: For rare examples of almost monovarietal wines, try: Coste Archi**, Cantina Puianello* (Ancellotta dell'Emilia Bondamatt, a delicately sweet, fizzy red wine with only 6.5 percent alcohol, containing 15 percent *Lambrusco* varieties); La Girolda* (Lancellotta della Girolda and Riserva, both with no more than 5 percent Lambrusco Salamino), and Rota* (Nero di Castellazzo). The new Rubicone IGT contemplates an Ancellotta wine, but few producers bottle it on its own, as the legislative guidelines allow up to 15 percent other grapes. Otherwise, Ancellotta is used mainly in *Lambrusco* blends, such as the excellent Lambrusco Scuro by the Luni 910 estate or the Lambrusco La Fojeta by Fratelli Caprari, a blend of Lambrusco Salamino and Ancellotta.

Ansonica

WHERE IT'S FOUND: Tuscany, Sicily. NATIONAL REGISTRY CODE NUMBER: 13. COLOR: white.

The correct name of this grape variety is Ansonica, which derives from the French *sorie* (dark, gold), because Ansonica grapes turn golden when very ripe; it goes by Inzolia in Sicily, but this is not the variety's official name, and should not be used. In the past, it was postulated that Ansonica was the same as the Irziola variety mentioned by Pliny the Elder, but clearly we have no evidence to support this view. Instead, a 1999 study by Labra, Failla, Fossati, Castiglione, Scienza, and Sala suggested considerable genetic similarity between Ansonica and Greek varieties such as Rhoditis and Sideritis; this group believes the Ansonica of Giglio to be in fact Rhoditis, but this remains controversial. Furthermore, Carimi, Mercati, Abbate, and Sunseri (2010) showed that Ansonica is closely related to other Sicilian varieties such as Grillo, Frappato, and Nerello Mascalese, which would seem to confirm the Sicilian rather than Greek origin of the variety, since those three varieties are all clearly of Italian origin (and are in turn, either the offspring or siblings of other eminently Italian varieties such as Sangiovese and Gaglioppo).

Ansonica has always been common in Sicily, where it was also much appreciated as a table grape. Many different Inzolia grapes have been documented in Sicily throughout the centuries, beginning with Cupani in 1696, who described both a white- and a red-berried Inzolia. It has long been unclear if once common grapes Inzolia Nera, Inzolia Moscatella, Inzolia di Lipari, and Inzolia Imperiale (some of which, like the last of these, are actually black grapes, rarely if ever used to make wine), were members of the same family or not. Carimi's group (2010) showed that Inzolia, Inzolia Imperiale, and Inzolia Nera have different SSR profiles; therefore, based on these study results, these three grape varieties are not identical. Instead, Inzolia Imperiale was shown to be synonymous with a rare local variety called Primintia or Giugnettina. It may well be that in Sicily farmers named many different grapes with an Inzolia-like moniker, given that Inzolia was a well-regarded grape. Though Ansonica is very abundant there, Sicily is, in the words of Roberto Zironi of the University of Udine, the wrong place for it: "Inzolia is a low-acid variety, so Sicily's naturally warm climate is not ideal for it, though the variety is very drought resistant." In Tuscany it has taken particularly well to two other island *terroirs*, Elba and Giglio (where they write its name Ansonico and pronounce it Ansonaco). It appears that the acid soils derived from granite desegregation in these island *terroirs* suit it particularly well.

Ansonica is characterized by large, pyramidal bunches and oval berries. It prefers medium- or low-expansion training systems (Guyot and *alberello*) with short or mixed pruning, and ripens early, in late August or early September. It adapts well to the hot and arid environments typical of central and southern Italy. However, though it tolerates drought, it is sensitive to high summer temperatures; it shows a moderate sensitivity to *Plasmopara viticola* and oidium.

Which Wines to Choose and Why

In Sicily, most Ansonica wines are from Caltanissetta, Palermo, and Agrigento, but it is included in the varietal makeup of almost every Sicilian DOC—examples include Alcamo, Contessa Entellina, and Delia Nivolelli. From the Tuscan coast, DOC wines such as Elba and Costa dell'Argentario are good. Giglio, a small but beautiful island that is also a national park, has only fifteen hundred inhabitants, so quantities of its wine are limited. Ansonica is also part of the Calabria Bivongi Bianco blend.

Ansonica is the rare example of a naturally tannic white wine. Furthermore, it has low natural acidity, which tends to drop very quickly upon approaching full ripeness. "Wines with natural total acidities of six grams per liter are unheard of," says Marilena Barbera of Cantina Barbera, a high-quality producer in Sicily. In the past, especially in Sicily, Ansonica was always picked too ripe, but as it was rarely made into a fresh, monovarietal wine but rather used in the Marsala blend (the oxidative character of which suits Ansonica well), this didn't matter much. However, modern viticultural practices and a better understanding of the variety's strength and weaknesses have recently led to a slew of bright, crisp Sicilian Ansonica wines. On Giglio's twenty-one square kilometers of beautiful but barren rock, Ansonica wine production risked extinction as recently as fifteen years ago. In 1987, Nunzio Danei effectively resurrected Giglio's wine scene when he bottled a Giglio Ansonica wine in his cellar in Orbetello, a coastal town on mainland Italy (at the time the wine was bottled under the Coste dell'Argentario DOC). In 1999, Francesco Carfagna also bought vineyards and invested heavily in a winery, in the process renewing over twelve kilometers of dry stone walls. Ansonica on Giglio has become so successful that it is rarely sold in bottles there, but rather as bulk wine, in demijohns or similarly large formats; because of supply and demand, the wine fetches high price regardless (six euros per liter) and so producers have little incentive to waste money on bottles, fancy labels, corks, and capsules, as all they produce literally flies out the door.

For me, best of all is Elba Ansonica, a medium- to full-bodied white wine of deep golden hue and delicately herbal, yellow apple, and dried apricot aromas and flavors, with a saline personality and plenty of chewy extract. When the grapes are air-dried, Elba makes an interesting, at times outstanding, *passito* version, though I usually prefer the dry wines. I find the wines of Elba and Giglio to be more concentrated, saline, and alcoholic than Sicilian versions, which are more citrusy and much lighter-bodied. Nowadays, Ansonica is such a popular grape and wine that many producers have started making it along the Tuscan coast, as an alternative to Vermentino. Interestingly, the well-known Moris Farm estate once produced an Ansonica wine called Sinfonia in the late 1980s on the Tuscan coast: production was stopped because it didn't sell. Back then, thin, tart white wines like Galestro were all the rage, and so a tannic, medium-bodied white wine with plenty of character like Ansonica stood no chance. How times change.

WINES TO TRY: For Giglio try: La Fontuccia*** (Senti, a truly excellent dry white; Nantropò, a mesmerizing sweet wine made from Ansonica grapes air-dried for forty days), Altura estate** (Ansonaco Carfagna), and the two wines from Greppe del Giglio. For Elba, try: Acquabona***, La Chiusa** (Ansonica Passito), Acquacalda* (an ansonica that has 15 percent Vermentino), and Cecilia* (an ansonica that has 10 percent "other grapes"). For Sicily, try: Barbera**, Valle dell'Acate**, and Duca di Salaparuta* (Bianca di Valguarnera).

Arneis

WHERE IT'S FOUND: Piedmont. NATIONAL REGISTRY CODE NUMBER: 14. COLOR: white.

In the 1980s, Arneis made Italy's most popular dry white wine, mainly on the strength of Ceretto's iconic, beautifully labeled and bottled Blangé bottling. Though detractors doubted that this almost-too-good-to-be-true wine was ever 100 percent Arneis—as Federico and Alessandro Ceretto have told me time and again it is—the fact remains that Arneis, thanks mainly to that wine, took the country by storm. A singular turn of events for a grape that had up until then almost always been made into a sweet wine, and when made into a dry wine, was considered nothing more than an afterthought. Even when the arneis craze set in, Arneis was still thought of and used as a workhorse grape, though it has become clear in time that the cultivar has thoroughbred potential.

The name *Arneis* derives from Renexij, the ancient name of the locality Renesio di Canale: in time this morphed into *Arnesio* (used at the beginning of the twentieth century), and finally, *Arneis*. It's not by chance that a high-quality *cru* for this variety is Bric Renesio, a specific site first described in 1478. Interestingly, in Piedmontese dialect, the word *arneis* is also used to describe rascally individuals, those who tend to get on everybody's nerves: "Just like the older clones of Arneis, which yielded poorly and irregularly and were a pain to work with," laughs Giovanni Almondo, one of the best producers of Arneis today.

By the 1960s, Arneis had been reduced to only a few rows of vines in the Langhe, and it was only thanks to two producers, Alfredo Currado of the Vietti estate in Castiglione Falletto and Bruno Giacosa of the eponymous estate in Neive, that it didn't disappear altogether. How ironic that a Piedmontese white wine would be saved by two of the region's most famous Barolo producers! In reality, Arneis was at the same time also being replanted and studied by Giovanni Negro in the Roero region. Interestingly though, Arneis has always had ties to Piedmont's most famous wine: in fact, it used to be called Nebbiolo Bianco, as it grows tall and erect just like Nebbiolo. In centuries past it was also very common to add a little arneis to Barolo and even to barbera, both high-acid wines, to soften things up. It was also planted in the vineyards along with red varieties, so that birds would be attracted to the sweeter, earlier ripening but less pricey Arneis grapes, before turning their voracious attentions to Nebbiolo. Sweet and low in acid, it's also an excellent table grape. Unfortunately, the variety is not easy to work with, as it is disease-prone; it is particularly sensitive to pests of the *Lepidoptera* genus, which perforate the berries and allow grey rot to fester, though lately, *Scaphoideus titanus* and the resulting esca disease have become a big problem. These pest-related difficulties are also due to the cultivar's geographic home: the Roero, located on the left bank of the Tanaro River, has been particularly hit by insect problems in recent years.

The first academic studies on Arneis date back to the 1970s and were performed at the enology school of Alba, led by Albino Morandi. Morandi was one of the teachers of Roberto Damonte, winemaker and owner (along with his brother Massimo) of Malvirà, in my view the best producer of Arneis wines, along with Negro and Giovanni Almondo. Damonte thinks Arneis is a fairly easy variety to work with except for its sensitivity to diseases (among which he numbers oidium) and a tendency to oxidize. For this reason, Damonte believes that extra care must be taken to avoid excessive oxygen contact when working in the cellar, for example, excessive stirring of the lees. Bruno Giacosa, who despite being Italy's single greatest red wine producer is also remarkably adept at churning out delicious Arneis wines, vintage after vintage, told me that "in reality, there was never that much Arneis planted in the Roero, or anywhere for that matter, because it's small-bunched, small-berried, and drops its acidity very quickly once it nears optimal ripeness. Understandably, farmers weren't keen on maintaining vigilant surveillance of the vines and having to drop everything else on a moment's notice just because the Arneis was ready to go."

Arneis is characterized by medium-sized bunches and berries; its pyramidal-conical bunches are so compact that the tightly squeezed round berries can look almost oval. There are six clones available (CVT CN 15, CVT CN 19, CVT CN 32, VCR 1, VCR 2, and VCR 4); the VCR 1 and 2, and the CVT CN 19 and 32 clones tend to be less vigorous than the others, though that's still quite vigorous. More importantly, CVT CN 15 and 19, as well as VCR 1 and VCR 2, have less tightly packed bunches. Compared to massal selections, these new clones are also more resistant to diseases such as oidium.

Roero, on the left side of the Tanaro River in the province of Cuneo, has always been the home of Arneis, though today Arneis is grown throughout the region. It is especially common around the towns of Canale, Corneliano d'Alba, Piobesi d'Alba, and Vezza d'Alba, but also appears near Monteu Roero and Castagnito. Arneis is also grown in small quantities in Sardinia, and has attracted increasing attention abroad. In the United States it has been planted in California and Oregon, while in Australia plantings in King Valley of North East Victoria, the Mornington peninsula, and the Riverland wine region of South Australia have been in production for a few years, though the grape now grows in countless regions, from the Adelaide Hills to Hunter Valley.

Which Wines to Choose and Why

There is not just one Arneis wine, but many. Despite this wine's reputation as a simple, everyday tipple, there is more to arneis: complex, site-specific arneis is there to be found, especially in the Roero. There, geological differences can translate into huge differences between wines. A very adaptable grape, Arneis seems at its best in the Roero's white, friable, porous soils where layers of sand and chalk are intertwined with small amounts of marl, typically found near the town of Monteu Roero. On clay-rich soils, such as those near Castellinaldo, wines tend to have more body and extract, though lesser examples have less interesting aromas, coarser flavors, and are generally shorter lived. Wines from Canale, though generally similar to those from Monteu Roero, actually strike me as exhibiting elements of the wines of Castellinaldo as well, so are best thought of as representing a version of arneis that sits between the two.

Making wine with Arneis is not just a matter of geology; it is also very much a matter of picking the grapes at exactly the right time. Angelo Negro of the famous Negro estate tells me that "one day you taste the grapes and they don't seem ready—and two days later they have dropped all their acidity and you are stuck with what will inevitably be a flat wine. This is why excessive deleafing is a real no-no with this variety." Lorenzo Negro, a distant relative of Angelo Negro and his family, runs his own eponymous estate but believes that some deleafing is necessary: "Otherwise, you cannot make a truly complex wine with Arneis; the variety needs to see sunlight to some extent, and the degree of solar irradiation you allow the berries to have will determine the success or failure of your wine." For this reason, Angelo Negro's top Arneis wine, called Perdaudin, is the result of three different pickings, ensuring a mixture of levels of total acidity. Roberto Damonte believes that what you do in the cellar with Arneis is just as important as what you do in the vineyards: "Arneis tends to oxidize very easily, so it's always best to work with reductive winemaking techniques, so as to avoid oxidizing aroma molecules." These techniques, aimed at reducing the must's oxygen contact to the utmost, have been taken to extremes in some parts of Italy (producing a bevy of all-too-similar lemony and figgy wines), but estates in the Roero have applied them more judiciously. Hence, Arneis wines have retained their aromas and freshness and remain true to their aroma and flavor profile.

Arneis can be one of Italy's most delicious white wines, exhibiting a thrilling range of aromas and flavors of surprising if subtle complexity. The wines are delicately straw-green, with aromas of white flowers, chamomile, white peach, and apricot and flavors of citrus, ripe pear, apricot, and sweet almond. Softly scented and surprisingly creamy on the palate, a good arneis can be utterly irresistible; versions that lack this creaminess and are more herbal are not as thrilling. Usually produced in a fresh, crisp style, some estates produce gently oaked versions, though oak can be overpowering for the delicate aromas and flavors of arneis. Though rare, there are also sparkling and sweet arneis. These two wine styles are risky with Arneis, a cultivar notoriously low in acid.

In Italy, Arneis is used to make one DOCG wine (Roero Arneis), two DOC wines (Langhe and Terre d'Alfieri), and fifteen different IGT wines (all in Sardinia, such as Isola dei Nuraghi, Planargia, and Valle del Tirso).

Beyond Italy's borders, Arneis is enjoying a wave of popularity. In the United States, good wines are being made by Cougar Vineyards in Temecula, and Ponzi in Oregon has championed the variety for decades; there have been countless very good Arneis wines from this esteemed Oregon producer over the years. In Australia, almost fifty different estates work with Arneis: for example, Amadio, Box Stallion, Catherine Vale Vineyard, Chrismont (in their La Zona lineup), Gary Crittenden (Pinocchio Arneis), Dromana Estate, Mac Forbes, Parish Hill, Patritti, Pizzini, Rutherglen, and Thick as Thieves (The Aloof Alpaca, a very good wine). I have liked the version by Mac Forbes, which I recently tried in a London restaurant: at only 12.5 percent alcohol and delicate white flower aromas and flavors, it reminded me of an arneis from Piedmont. Dromana Estate makes both dry and late-harvest Arneis in their "i" line of wines made from Italian grapes. In fact, Arneis has become popular enough in Australia that it has been planted even in less-than-likely places such as the hot Riverina district, where the wines have lowish acidity and may require acid correction. By contrast, the cool Mornington peninsula (blessed with the maritime influences of Port Philip Bay to the north and west and Bass Strait to the south) seems like a suitable habitat for this variety. Port Philip Estate's Quartier Arneis bottling is a case in point. In New Zealand, Coopers Creek makes a very good arneis, but the one I tried most recently (the 2008 vintage) was surprisingly full bodied, alcoholic (14.5 percent), and generally much richer than the Italian versions.

WINES TO TRY: Giovanni Almondo*** (Bricco delle Ciliegie, one of Italy's fifteen or twenty best white wines), Malvirà*** (Trinità, one of the few oaked arneis worth trying; also Renesio, which is unoaked), Negro*** (Perdaudin, perhaps the most typical arneis of all; and the Sparkling Extra Brut, refermented in the bottle in the manner of Champagne), Matteo Correggia***, Bruno Giacosa***, La Granera**, Marsaglia** (Serramiana), Lorenzo Negro**, Pace**, Fratelli Rabini**, Paola Sordo**, Vietti**, Baracco de Baracho*, Ca' du Russ* (Costa delle Rose), and Deltetto*. Cornarea* is worth hunting out for a unique, very interesting sweet version (Tarasco), but I am less thrilled by their dry versions. Another good sweet version is by Cascina Chicco** (Arcass Vendemmia Tardiva).

Asprinio Bianco

WHERE IT'S FOUND: Campania, Puglia, Basilicata. NATIONAL REGISTRY CODE NUMBER: 16. COLOR: white.

Is asprinio the best wine in the world to drink with pizza? Yes, according to Luigi Veronelli, to whom I owe all my initial, salad-days Italian wine knowledge, but only provided it's the simplest pizza of all: tomato, garlic, and oregano. The name (officially Asprinio Bianco, but everyone just calls the variety Asprinio) might suggest otherwise, as *asprinio* derives from the Italian *aspro,* or the Latin term *asper,* meaning tart. In fact, this grape will never be accused of low acidity; not surprisingly, asprinio has been sold throughout the centuries to producers from Italy and abroad who enlist its help in making sparkling wines.

The exact origin of the grape has been clarified recently by Attilio Scienza and his team at the University of Milan. It was once thought that Asprinio was related to the *Pinot* family and imported into Italy by the French at the beginning of the eighteenth century, but it is now clear the variety is truly native, most likely deriving from the domestication of wild, local vines thousands of years ago. Asprinio looks and behaves like a wild vine species, with extremely long creepers growing high above the ground between trees such as poplars, and is able to thrive even in very shaded environments. Even today, it's common to see vines running free as much as twenty meters above the ground, wrapped around and hanging between poplars and oaks that act as live supports. This training system of vines is called *alberate* (from *albero,* tree, and not to be confused with *alberello,* which is a different grapevine training system), and it is beautiful, creating a barrier of leaves and grapes in a jungle-like environment. Asprinio is an extremely vigorous variety: producers once culled up to two hundred kilos of grapes per vine, which is unheard of for any other quality wine grape variety.

Always abundant in the area north of Naples, Asprinio's potential for fine wine was much appreciated throughout history. In a rental agreement signed by a notary in 1495, the owner was to receive two containers of wine, one of them asprinio (the other was *verdesca,* but we don't know which modern variety that name refers to, or if is now extinct); the new tenant also had to replace all the dark grapes on the property with vines of Asprinio and Verdesca. In the beginning of the twentieth century, Asprinio was commonly grown in Puglia too, where it was known as Olivese or Ragusano.

Between 2009 and 2011, the Adolfo Spada estate sponsored and led a series of research studies on Asprinio, in collaboration with the agriculture department at Portici in Naples, the Istituto Sperimentale per la Patologia Vegetale (Institute of Plant Pathology Research) in Rome, la Fondazione Edmund Mach of Santo Michele all'Adige in Trento, and the Istituto per la Virologia Vegetale (Institute of Plant Virology) of CNR in Grugliasco. Forever to his credit, Enrico Spada wished to "rediscover" asprinio, a wine that in his view was not only rare, but also was no longer made in the manner it once had been. Historically, asprinio was always a very light, high-acid wine, averaging alcohol levels of 10 percent and total acidity of 7.5 grams per liter (most wines hover below 6 grams per liter), figures which are admittedly very different from the numbers sported by some alcoholic fruit bombs sold as "asprinio" in these recent, rather degenerate, times.

Research (Monaco, Nasi, Paparelli, and Spada 2011) has confirmed Asprinio's general morphologic similarity to Greco (in fairness, a similarity noted already by Nicola Columella Onorati in 1804), as both have compound clusters and a noteworthy sensitivity to viral diseases. A few experts (I am not among them) believe that the wines of the two also share similar aromatic profiles, though Monaco's latest research results do indicate that there are more similarities between the wines than was once believed. These similarities have led some researchers to investigate further, and in 2005 Costantini, Monaco, Vouillamoz, Forlani, and Grando wrote that Greco and Asprinio were identical. A similar finding was reported by Cipriani, Spadotto, Jurman, Di Gaspero, Crespan, Meneghetti, et al. (2010), though it is disputed by others (Scienza 2011). I have a hard time believing the two are identical, and therefore have kept Asprinio separate from Greco in this book; the National Registry also distinguishes between them (see GRECO GROUP, chapter 3). In any case, Asprinio has a remarkably homogenous population, with very few, if any, biotypes. There are few Asprinio clones, and it's unlikely that will change in the near future, since the currently available grapevine populations are almost entirely virus affected, especially by fanleaf virus.

Which Wines to Choose and Why

Asprinio grows mainly in the area north of Naples, around the city of Caserta, in the countryside surrounding the twenty-two communes included in the DOC Asprinio d'Aversa. The latter has long enjoyed *grand cru* status for asprinio. The wine is light and lively, a perfect summertime beverage, ideal for uncomplicated sipping. Due to its high natural acidity, it is also used to make the sparkling DOC Asprinio d'Aversa Spumante, though the still version remains my favorite. The wine always exudes a crisp lemony zing, and is characterized by pretty if very delicate citrusy, spicy, and almondy notes. Asprinio is rich in monoterpene and norisoprenoid molecules, particularly linalool and limonene, which helps explain the wine's usually marked citrusy aromas. However, these molecules reach significant concentrations only with grapes grown at certain heights off the ground, as heavily shaded grapes, grapes growing low to the ground, and those in excessively humid environments fail to accumulate enough of these molecules to sufficiently characterize the wine.

WINES TO TRY: Magliulo**, Cantina Cicala**, I Borboni** (two versions, one oak-aged, which doesn't strike me as a great idea), Tenuta Adolfo Spada** (they also make a *spumante brut*), Caputo* (their Fescine is named after the baskets traditionally used to carry the grapes), Grotta del Sole*, and Vestini Campagnano*.

Avanà

WHERE IT'S FOUND: Piedmont. NATIONAL REGISTRY CODE NUMBER: 17. COLOR: red.

It is safe to say that the great majority of talented, elbow-lifting wine aficionados—Italian and otherwise—have never heard of this variety. Documented as Avanato in 1606 by Croce, and not to be confused with Avarengo, another Italian native grape, Avanà may have been imported into Italy from France when Piedmont and Savoy were part of the same kingdom, but of course, it is also quite possible that Avanà moved in the other direction, from Italy to France. As the grape is more common today in Italy than France, Avanà is considered to be an Italian native. In this respect, a wildly interesting study by Schneider, Carrà, Akkak, This, Laucou, and Botta (2001) using molecular markers that analyzed synonymies between French and Italian border grape varieties apparently confirmed that Avanà is identical to France's Hibou Noir and Hibou Rouge. These results were in accordance with a previous observation by Rougier (in Viala and Vermorel 1901–10) but are in contrast with those reported by Galet (1990). Furthermore, in the eastern part of Switzerland's Valais region (especially in the Mattertal valley) grows yet another variety called Eyholtzer Rote or Eyholzer Rote that is locally known as Hibou Rouge, but I have been unable to find any scientific data in support of this synonym. In fact, a careful review of the 2001 study reveals that the presumed identity between Avanà and the two *Hibou*s was determined only by RAPD analysis, and not by SSR profiling, which was performed on only eleven other varieties. Since RAPD testing is not the state-of-the-art method by which to identify cultivars (results are too dependent on, and affected by, the reaction conditions, such as DNA extraction and purification techniques), we do not as yet have conclusive evidence as to the synonymity of Avanà with the *Hibou*s. Finally, according to DNA parentage analysis, it appears that Avanà is related to Amigne, another Valais grape, and either a parent or offspring of Cacaboué, a practically extinct variety of France's Savoie region (Vouillamoz and Moriondo 2011).

The word *avanà* derives from the Latin term *abante*, meaning forward, probably in reference to the variety's precocious ripening phase. Recently Mannini, Cavallo, Rolle, Ferrandino, and Mollo (2008) have studied Avanà's genetic profile and overall health, important steps in making the variety more available for future plantings—and hopefully, more wines. Since 1990, two experimental vineyards were set up, at Chianocco (in the Lower Susa valley) and at Chiomonte (in the Upper Susa Valley). The Chianocco vineyard was planted in 1993 with thirty-three different presumed clones and biotypes of Avanà, and their characteristics were studied. Of these, two potentially higher-quality biotypes were selected (pre-clones 1 and 35) and replanted in the Chiomonte vineyard in 2000; thus far, one officially certified clone has become available, CVT 1, which is apparently less fertile, vigorous, and productive than others. Wines made with it are more structured and higher in alcohol.

Avanà has medium-sized, pyramidal-conical bunches and very large, round, dark berries; the latter often show asynchronous ripening and need plenty of sunlight. It's a fragile variety, prone to disease—it is very sensitive to peronospora, oidium, and grey rot—that does poorly in windy conditions (the berries fall easily to the ground) or environments of late-season rains, both of which are rather typical of its Piedmontese home. At least, it ripens relatively early, usually in late September. It also needs drought-resistant rootstocks. Avanà is typical of the Valle di Susa (where it is the most important local variety) and the Pinerolese, cool, mountain territories to the west of Turin in Piedmont, on the border with France. On their next foray in this very beautiful neck of the Italian woods, wine lovers passionate about art might want to take in, besides the splendid mountain panorama and a drink or two, the well-kept Arch of Augustus (13–8 B.C.E.) in the town of Susa. Though Barbera, Freisa, and Bonarda are more famous, less well-known natives like Avanà are actually quite abundant in these parts, and I find people are always amazed at the many delightful wines made with little-known cultivars such as Avanà.

Which Wines to Choose and Why

Despite its sorry viticultural characteristics, Avanà delivers not only interesting red wines, but also much rarer examples of Italian ice wine. Despite the country's wealth of mountainous, snow-capped slopes, ice wine is neither traditional nor a specialty of Italy; for this reason alone, little Avanà stands very tall indeed in the panorama of native Italian cultivars. In Italy, ice wine is labeled *vino del ghiaccio* and is most often blended from frozen native grapes, roughly 60 percent Avanà, picked at −6°C or colder still.

The most traditional wine of the area is the DOC Ramìe (named after the *ramìe,* or stacks of branches once piled up when trees were cut down to make room for vineyards), a blend of roughly 30 percent Avanà and roughly 70 percent other native local varieties, such as Avarengo and Neretta Cuneese. The Avanà supplies fragrance, the other two varieties provide tannins and body. There are 100 percent Avanà wines to be found in the area, as many local producers—who often employ artisanal winemaking techniques besides running bed-and-breakfasts or similar activities to make ends meet—produce small lots of bottles for their clients, friends, and home consumption. They go to the trouble because good avanà is very enjoyable: almost garnet in color, with fresh red-berry and floral aromas, and low in alcohol (usually around 12 percent). Not surprisingly, it is almost never aged in oak, and should be drunk young. Avanà is also used to produce an eau-de-vie called Eigovitto.

WINES TO TRY: Casa Ronsil* (the Ronsil family has been linked to viticulture since 1342; after a brief hiatus, they're back at winemaking with Pierino Ronsil and his son-in-law Franck Thollet at the helm), Martina*, and Sibille*. Besides dry wines, Casa Ronsil and La Clarea also make good *vino del ghiaccio.* These are very charming wines made in one of the most bucolic, charming areas of Italy, and the wines will add to memories of halcyon vacation days.

Barbera

WHERE IT'S FOUND: Nearly everywhere in Italy.
NATIONAL REGISTRY CODE NUMBER: 19. COLOR: red.

Barbera is one of Italy's five most-planted native grapes, and the third most-common red grape, found in almost every region of the country. It is also one of the fifteen most-planted grape varieties in the world. The origin of its name is unclear: Pietro Ratti of Renato Ratti feels it's a derivation of *barbaro* (barbarian) due to its deep red color, while others believe the origin is *vinum berberis*, an astringent, acidic, and deeply hued medieval drink. *Vinum berberis* is different from the *vitibus berbexinis* referred to in a 1249 document located in the archives of Casale Monferrato, which was most likely another variety, Barbesino or Berbesino, better known today as Grignolino.

For all its abundance and the loyalty it breeds (the people of Piedmont and Lombardy grow up in barbera's company: drinking it characterizes a Milanese almost as much as the Duomo, via Montenapoleone, and *risotto alla Milanese*), the grape variety does not have a long and distinguished history. Most Italian experts believe it to be original not of Asti or Alba, but of the Monferrato area of Piedmont, near Alessandria, where documents mention its presence in the seventeenth century; luminaries such as Gallesio called it *Vitis vinifera montisferratensis* (though that name could refer to any number of local grapes). Others feel the grape was known centuries before, as Uva Grisa or Grisola (de' Crescenzi 1495), and was the result of the domestication of local wild vines. However, given Barbera's very dark berries and wine, I find it hard to understand why it would have been called *grisa*, as that refers to a reddish-grey color. At the end of the eighteenth century, Conte Nuvolone Pergamo mentions Barbera under that name, citing the grapevine grown in Asti as identical to the Ughetta of Vercelli and the Vespolina of Novara (though we know that the latter is a completely different variety).

Though Barbera is viewed as an archetypal Piedmontese variety, the lack of historical information on Barbera's presence in the region prior to the eighteenth century makes it hard to believe the grape has always resided there, or that it really derives from domesticated wild vines growing in Piedmont. In fact, DNA profiling (Schneider, Boccacci, and Botta 2003) has shown that Barbera does not share close genetic ties to any other Piedmontese cultivar, which would be highly unlikely had Barbera truly been on Piedmontese soil for millennia. Barbera is also unrelated to another, similarly named Piedmontese native, Barbera d'Davi: the two have in common only oval berries. Also distinct are the very rare, similarly named Piedmontese cultivars Barbera Ciarìa, Barbrassa, and Barbera Dou Ciorniou. According to Schneider and Mannini (2006), Barbera also appears, tentatively, to be distinct from the local *Barberùn* family of grapes, while it is certainly distinct from Barbera del Sannio and the white-berried Barbera Bianca (Sefc, Lopes, Lefort, Botta, Roubelakis-Angelakis, Ibanez, et al. 2000; Costantini, Monaco, Vouillamoz, Forlani, and Grando 2005). The latter is neither a mutation nor an albino variant of Barbera. Most likely, it was so named because it is also high in acid (for added fun, Barbera Bianca is also called Carica L'asino, though that's a quite distinct variety).

Barbera has been witness to some of the most important moments in Italy's wine history, good, bad, and ugly. Among the bad was the methanol scandal of 1986, when a number of lesser names were caught fraudulently adding methanol to their finished barbera wines in an effort to add richness and strength—and save costs. It was a tragically criminal idea, for a number of people died in the process (methanol is highly toxic, and can cause blindness and death); the only positive spin-off was the backlash, which forcibly improved Italy's wine scene, resulting in stricter attention to quality control at all levels. Among the good was the birth of Barbera Bricco dell'Uccellone, made by Giacomo Bologna (one of Italy's great names in wine) in the late 1970s; Bologna was the first to age high-quality barbera in new oak *barriques*. Thanks to him and his insight, everyone finally realized that barbera could be rich, complex, and ageworthy, and not just a joyous everyday trattoria-style, high-acid potable. Until then nobody had thought it in the same class of Italian greats Barolo or Brunello. Some might argue barbera still isn't considered by most experts to be in that league, but there's no denying that it's hard to keep a good grape like Barbera down: its chameleon-like properties relative to wine styles are a very endearing trait.

Barbera is characterized by medium-large, pyramidal (rarely cylindrical) bunches and medium-sized, oval, very dark blue berries covered in bloom. Barbera is the darkest of all the major Piedmontese varieties: there's almost twice as much malvin in Barbera skins as there is in those of Nebbiolo (Gerbi, Rolle, Zeppa, Guidoni, and Schneider 2005). One biotype, Barbera Grossa, is, not surprisingly, characterized by much bigger berries, but also more tightly packed bunches that make it more susceptible to botrytis. Due to its importance in local economies and the large volumes of wine made, Barbera has been the subject of much clonal research. Today's most commonly used clones are R4, Fedit 3 C.S.G., AL 115, Mi-B-12, Mi-B-34, PC-Ba-9, PC-Ba-26, AT 84, CVT-ALL 115, CVT AT 171 (the last three clones are characterized by slightly lower total acidity levels, not a bad thing with Barbera), CVT AT 424, BA-AL-128, BA-AL-132 (the latter two are from the Alessandria province and are generally characterized by higher average acidities and slightly bigger bunches), 17-BA, CVT 83, VCR 19, VCR 101, VCR 433, VCR 207, VCR 223, CVT OB66, and CVT CJ1. It is a very vigorous, drought-resistant grape that ripens in late September or early October, but is susceptible to spring frosts and is very sensitive to fanleaf virus. It's highly productive and capable of very large yields, so strict pruning to prevent overcropping is generally required for quality wines.

Barbera is grown mainly in Piedmont, Lombardy (in the Oltrepò Pavese near Pavia), Emilia-Romagna (Colli Bolognesei, Piacentini, and di Parma), and Sardinia, but nobody disputes the notion that the best examples hail from Piedmont. In this region it performs especially well near Alba, Asti, and near Alessandria in the Monferrato. In the Asti area it has basically replaced most of the other varieties. Barbera is an adaptable variety and produces copiously everywhere it is planted; better still, wine quality is never horrid even at high yields, though it too shows site-specificity. For these reasons, it's a favorite of farmers everywhere; countless people have told me over the years that they wished all their grapes were as easy to work with. Sergio Germano of the Ettore Germano estate in Serralunga d'Alba in Piedmont makes a very good point when he talks about Barbera and *terroir*: "A site like Paiagallo, which has a dark, rich, heavily organic clay is a much better site for Barbera than Sarmassa, which has more white calcareous-clay." The lesson to learn here is that the greater name is not always the solution: Sarmassa is a much more famous vineyard than Paiagallo, mainly because it has always been associated with excellent Barolo production; yet its soils, so good for Nebbiolo, are not ideal for high-quality Barbera production. Besides, in lighter soils, Barbera becomes extremely sensitive to boron and potassium deficiencies, and its acidity tends to remain high: the last thing barbera needs is even more acidity.

Barbera has become less popular than in previous times, with its total planted area decreasing by roughly 25 percent in the first decade of the new century. Instead, it seems to be doing very well in other countries. In the United States, Barbera was first planted in California near Cupertino in the 1880s; today it grows in Lodi, Napa, Paso Robles, Santa Barbara, Santa Cruz, the Sierra foothills, and Sonoma, just to name a few AVAs. Barbera is also found in Arizona, New Mexico, Oregon, Texas, and Washington. Barbera vineyards have also been established in Greece, Croatia, Romania, Slovenia, Mexico, Brazil, Chile, Argentina, Uruguay, South Africa, and Australia (there are almost one hundred different Australian wineries growing Barbera vines). This isn't a surprising turn of events: though Barbera, a generous yielder, was first planted in most of these countries by Italian immigrants, the fact that it does well in dry climates and poor soils makes it particularly suited to Australia and other warmer viticultural zones. Given its popularity, it's not surprising that Barbera was also chosen to breed new varieties: it is one of the parents of Albarossa, Cornarea, Ervi, and Incrocio Terzi 1, all of which are successful wine grapes (some, like Albarossa, very successful); while Nebbiera, Nigra, Prodest, San Michele, and Soperga have yet to prove their worth.

Which Wines to Choose and Why

Like many who have decided to consult plastic surgeons in these appearance-dominated modern times, Barbera wines have also undergone a remarkable makeover. Out with old tart, eye-watering wines of unbelievable shrillness (well, some of those are still around), and in with richer, softer, small-barrel, oak-aged wines of remarkable finesse and tactile charm. Of course, like everything else, even good ideas can go too far, and more often than not when I drink a barbera today I find myself wondering why I bother. Notes of chocolate and vanilla are everywhere, and frankly, all that gets old quickly. Mercifully, there are still many more traditional, bright, and fruity Barbera wines made: when it comes to this grape and its wines, you might say that the good, the bad, and the downright ugly are always at your doorstep. It really is best—and certainly less depressing—to consider only the best wines made with this variety. It is these that are absolutely world-class wines, with high acidities and brightly fruity aromas and flavors that make them very food-friendly and flexible. These characteristics of low tannins, high acidities, and very concentrated color also explain why Barbera has always been considered an excellent blending grape, and many wine blends of Barbera and other varieties are produced all over Italy. In fact, a little Barbera must or wine has historically always been added to wines made with Nebbiolo, in an effort to spike the latter's color. Angelo Gaja, one of Italy's more famous producers, says he pulled his *cru* wines out of DOCG Barbaresco with the 1996 vintage because the law does not allow the addition of a little barbera to deepen Barbaresco's hue. "That this practice was once common is shown by the fact that when we bought our parcel of Nebbiolo vines in the Cerequio vineyard, we found that the previous owner had co-planted a few Barbera vines as well," his talented daughter Gaia told me. For this reason, Gaja's Conteisa Langhe Nebbiolo wine is a blend of 92 percent Nebbiolo and 8 percent Barbera. The grapes are picked and fermented together.

The best DOCG Barbera wines in Piedmont are those labeled Barbera d'Asti (generally made from the oldest Barbera vines in the region) and Barbera del Monferrato Superiore. These are always made with at least 85 percent Barbera and often more. A higher-quality Barbera d'Asti is Barbera d'Asti Superiore Nizza (or more simply, Nizza), which is made from 100 percent Barbera grapes grown in a small subzone of the Monferrato, under stricter production and viticultural guidelines. These producers have created the Nizza consortium and are to be commended for the very strict production guidelines they have adopted. Another DOCG wine that can be made with small percentages of Barbera is Lombardy's Curtefranca. There are many DOC Barbera wines, the most famous of which is Barbera d'Alba (mostly made from younger vines planted at higher densities than elsewhere), and even more IGT wines (that there are 106 IGTs that allow Barbera tells you just how popular this grape is all over Italy). Generally speaking, Barbera d'Alba is bigger, richer, and more velvety than Barbera d'Asti and Barbera del Monferrato, which are lighter and fruitier, have sharper tannins, and are more acidic. The d'Alba versions usually benefit from better winemaking, but as the best spots in that subzone are reserved for Nebbiolo, well-made Barbera d'Asti wines can be just as good. Oltrepò Pavese in Lombardy also makes a lovely barbera, fresh and vinous, ideal with hearty fare and winter nights; those of Emilia-Romagna are just as fresh but a little coarser (their Barbera is usually used in blends such as Gutturnio).

A good, authentic barbera is distinguished by numerous features: high acidity, intensely purple hues (even when aged), a recognizable, grapey aroma of red fruits, underbrush, and delicate spices, plus a very dry finish (increased by the high acidity). As this variety is very rich in color and low in tannins, some producers extend the maceration time to increase complexity and depth of flavor and oak it more or less gently, though some oak-fetishists have gone much too far, in my opinion. Barbera has historically been made in a sparkling version (referred to as *mossa* or *vivace*) that is ideal with sandwiches, charcuterie, and any fatty fare that appreciates the company of high acidity.

Thanks to Italian immigrants and open-minded producers of other nationalities, Barbera wines are made all over the world in a variety of styles. The best I've tried are those by California's BellaGrace (their 2010 barbera won top honors in the 2012 California State Fair Commercial Wine Competition), Boeger (this estate owns several Barbera vineyards planted to different clones ideally matched to different soils and microclimates; I especially like their Vineyard Select bottling), Cooper Vineyards, Macchia (big, high-alcohol wines; their Righteous and Infamous barbera is made with grapes grown in Amador County vineyards, while their Delicious barbera is made from Lodi grapes), Renwood (another very rich, Amarone-like wine I used to drink regularly during my days in the United States), Sierra Ridge Winery (at the foot of the Sierra foothills at Sutter Creek), Yorba, and Jeff Rundquist—but there are countless excellent examples to choose from. VJB Vineyards and Cellars even makes a Barbera Port. The fact that there is an annual Barbera Festival in California's Amador County, with as many as ninety different Barbera wines poured, tells you just how popular the grape and the wine have become in California. Not all these wines remind me of barbera made in Italy (which is usually less soft and more austere in its crisp fruit delivery), but they are very well-made wines, exuberantly fruity and delicious. Personally, I love to try them any chance I get; in fact, of all the American wines now being made with Italian native grapes, it is the barberas that I enjoy the most.

In Australia, Barbera wines are made by Brown Brothers, Chain of Ponds (called The Stopover Barbera), Coriole, Gary Crittenden, Dal Zotto, Robert Oatley Vineyards (their Montrose Omaggio Barbera bottling is excellent and benefits from some old vines; Barbera was planted in the Montrose vineyard in 1972), and Michelini. Apparently, there are good Barbera wines made in Greece, Israel, and Uruguay, none of which I've tasted yet. In South Africa, Altydgedacht in Durbanville has been making a monovarietal barbera since 1992 (but this estate has always been a believer, planting Barbera in the early 1900s; it also makes the Ralph Parker bottling for Cape Wine Cellars); Fairview (from grapes planted in 2000 and 2001) also reportedly makes a good barbera. I also remember drinking a decent Brazilian example once, the name of which I can't remember—one glass too many, obviously.

WINES TO TRY: For Piedmont, try: Braida*** (Barbera d'Asti Bricco dell'Uccellone, Bricco della Bigotta, and Ai Suma; the La Monella is a wonderful example of barbera vivace), Dacapo*** (Nizza), Vietti*** (Luca Currado is more famous for his Barolos, but the Barbera d'Alba Scarrone and the Barbera Nizza La Crena are the best wines he makes), Giacomo Conterno*** (Cascina Francia and Ceretta, both Barbera d'Alba), Marchesi Gresy*** (Barbera d'Asti Monte Colombo), Iuli*** (Superiore Barabba), Accornero** (Cima Riserva della Casa Barbera del Monferrato), La Barbatella*. For Lombardy, try: Riccardo Albani**, Castello di Luzzano**, Bruno Verdi* (Campo del Marrone), Gradizzolo* (Riserva Garò), Marchesi di Montalto* (Bandera). For Emilia-Romagna, try: La Stoppa**; La Berta* (Floresco), La Colombina*, Poderi Morini* (Estroverso Frizzante), Pandolfa*.

Barsaglina

WHERE IT'S FOUND: Tuscany. NATIONAL REGISTRY CODE NUMBER: 22. COLOR: white.

Long burdened by a bad rap (wines made from it supposedly had less-than-impressive, even musty aromas), Barsaglina (at times, incorrectly spelled Bersaglina) is a rare variety originally of the Massa Carrara territory in Tuscany. Not surprisingly then, a very commonly used synonym is Massaretta. Di Rovasenda (1877) mentioned Barsaglina without describing it; the first to do so accurately was Marzotto (1925), followed by Breviglieri and Casini (1964). Barsaglina is very easily recognizable in the vineyard; like the *Colorinos*, it's characterized by large leaves that turn red in the fall.

The variety was essentially saved from extinction by the Lorieri family, owners of Podere Scurtarola in Tuscany, who were helped by Paolo Storchi, a well-known Italian grape scientist. Lorieri and Storchi set up a unique collection of local grapevines, including Barsaglina, in an experimental and research vineyard at Podere Scurtarola in 1996 thereby ensuring the survival of this and other varieties. According to Valerio Brighi, the owner of the small estate Mocine in Asciano (Tuscany), who works with Attilio Pagli and Stefano Dini and has plenty of experience with Barsaglina, the cultivar likely fell out of favor with farmers due to its thin skin, which make it easy prey to botrytis (Barsaglina's tightly packed bunch only compounds this problem); its poor adaptability to environmental stressors, such as drought, probably didn't win it admirers either. Roberto Bandinelli, one of Italy's leading grape variety experts and professor of viticulture at the University of Florence, also points out that Barsaglina hates excessive sunlight exposure; it's prone to oidium and sunburn and tends to drop its leaves. Furthermore, though vigorous, it has poor fertility and therefore production volumes are low. This is why Stefano Dini suggests using vigorous rootstocks. Another common problem is posed by yellow and red spiders: as the underside of Barsaglina's leaf is very downy, it offers a wonderful habitat for these pests, making Barsaglina a difficult cultivar to grow organically. Stefano Dini told me once he has tried just about everything in the organic viticulturalist's armory in his battle with Barsaglina against spiders, but so far he's only met defeat. On the positive side, Barsaglina is a beautiful variety, characterized by erect growth and long internodes on its branches, so rows of Barsaglina vines have an airy, refined look to them. There is one certified clone, BARSA-FI.PI-1.

Barsaglina is rare, limited to no more than fifty known hectares: there are scattered vines in the Colline Lucchesi (in my view, probably an environment that's too cold for it), in Chianti Classico, and the Tuscan coast (given the heat, these wines tend to be high in pH and low in total acidity). It is most abundant in the Massa Carrara / La Spezia area of Tuscany, where it is part of the DOCs Colli di Luni Rosso and Candia dei Colli Apuani, and IGT wines (some famous such as Costa Toscana, others unknown even to most Italians, including the Colline del Genovesato, Montecastelli and Val di Magra blends).

Which Wines to Choose and Why

"By itself, Barsaglina wine is extremely dark, almost impenetrable, with ripe, dark-berry and black-plum aromas. In cold years however, it can be green," says Brighi. "In the old days, people thought the wines had off odors, but we know today this happened because the thin skins tend to break down easily. Without proper enologic care, these skins cause reductive, foul-smelling odors." Nonetheless, Barsaglina has won admirers and is now coming on strong, with more producers giving it a try. Both reds and *rosati* are made, and Barsaglina's delicate aromas and flavors are well suited to the latter. The red wines are very dark (plenty of anthocyanins) with good structure. They are noteworthy for a savory, delicately herbal quality and small blackberry aromas and flavors, usually lifted by decent acidity. The wines may not be the most complex you'll ever taste, but they are a welcome change from the tried and true.

WINES TO TRY: Cima** (Massaretta) and Mannucci Droandi* (Barsaglina). Mocine is growing quite a bit of Barsaglina but currently prefers to blend 20–40 percent Barsaglina into its only two wine blends, Ottorintocchi and Mocine Rosso. Podere Scurtarola makes a Scurtarola Rosso blend that contains 15 percent Barsaglina.

Becuet

WHERE IT'S FOUND: Piedmont. NATIONAL REGISTRY CODE NUMBER: 373. COLOR: red.

When I first visited the area where Becuet (rarely spelled Becuèt, Becuét, or Biquét) grows, years ago, I learned what animals at the zoo feel like, with everyone gazing at them. Becuet is hardly one of Italy's better-known cultivars, and when I arrived, there obviously hadn't been too many grape variety–watchers (or wine journalists, for that matter) visiting the area in recent times. People were tickled pink that a wine writer from Rome was visiting asking questions about rootstocks, wanting to taste from barrels, and trying even the older vintages. In this very remote, bucolic, and folksy part of northern Italy, all I needed was a DeLorean and a flux capacitor and I would have been ready for a Michael J. Fox turn in my very own *Back to the Future*.

According to Schneider, Carrà, Akkak, This, Laucou, and Botta (2001), Becuet is identical to the French grape Persan from *princens*, a combination of *prim*, meaning prime, and *cens*, meaning fee, in reference to the high value of Princens vineyard land and to the fact the variety was once believed to make the best wines of the Savoy. Not surprisingly, some in Italy beg to disagree. In fact, though the study used molecular markers to analyze the grape varieties, the synonymity between Persan and Becuet was confirmed only by RAPD analysis; SSR profiling in the study was not applied to these two cultivars, and RAPD is no longer considered the state-of-the-art method for grape variety identification, as reproducibility among different laboratories is often poor. However, it is also noteworthy that there is very little historical documentation of Becuet's presence in Italy, while Persan has been described in France since the seventeenth century (Gros 1930). According to Rézeau (1997), the first to mention Persan was Albin Gras in 1846, then secretary of the Statistical Society of Isère and a board member for the Agricultural Society of Grenoble. Gras documented the existence of Persan vines in the countryside of the Isère (further specifying that the name Persan was used locally only on the left bank of the Isère River, while on the right bank farmers mistakenly called it Etraire, which is a different, possibly related, variety). Tochon in 1868 also wrote that Persan was one of the most cultivated grapes in France's Savoie region. The absence of similarly detailed documentation of Becuet's presence in Italy makes it more than likely that it was first brought over to Piedmont from France; hence, Becuet is more correctly viewed as a traditional rather than a native grape of Italy. However, Frankie Thonet of the Casa Ronsil estate in Chiomonte is unconvinced, and argues that Persan is most likely only a "very distant cousin of Becuet," or at least a very different biotype, and perhaps even a different variety. According to him, the only phenotypic trait the two cultivars share is the shape of the berries, while leaves and other ampelographic characteristics are markedly different.

Though you won't find it anywhere else in Italy, finding Becuet is easy when you arrive in its native part of Piedmont, a mountainous cool-weather zone east of Turin that hugs the border with France. The berry is oval and fairly small, explaining why this variety is also humorously called Berla 'd Crava Cita, which in Piedmontese dialect means "in the shape of goat's dung." Becuet, though sensitive to oidium and peronospora, is generally a resistant and very vigorous variety, and seems to grow better on Paulsen rootstocks, which help the vines handle drought. It was crossed with

Peloursin to breed Joubertin, but the latter is no longer cultivated (and never was in Italy, to the best of my knowledge).

Which Wines to Choose and Why

Becuet is grown mainly in the Valle di Susa and Pinerolese areas of Piedmont; it has essentially the same stomping grounds as Avanà. In fact, Becuet is almost always blended in with the latter (generally as the DOC wine Ramiè), where it adds structure and depth of color. For example, according to Gerbi, Rolle, Zeppa, Guidoni, and Schneider (2005), there is almost three times as much malvin in Becuet grape skins compared to Avanà's. On its own, Becuet is a very tannic wine, with light, floral, red-berry aromas and flavors; in my experience (admittedly only with wines made in a rather artisanal manner in both vineyard and cellar), the tannins don't smooth out much in time, so the wine remains hard and rigid. It is always very dark in color, and not by chance: Thonet refers to it as a "concentrate of polyphenols." Late-harvested grapes and small oak barrels may help create a more velvety mouthfeel, and some producers are in fact experimenting with these ideas. Recent wines have been encouraging, and becuet's slightly austere mouthfeel is a welcome asset when digging into hearty stews or saucy meat dishes. Furthermore, the two mountain valleys Becuet calls home are characterized by very pretty panoramas, and are ideal summer vacation destinations. I therefore exhort wine lovers to try a pure becuet with a hearty meat dish when next in the area, because it really is likely to be the only place and time you'll ever get to taste a monovarietal Becuet wine. The cultivar has not yet spread in any quantity to new vine regions, though some good wines made with it show that Becuet deserves to be better known.

WINES TO TRY: Martina** (Malliolo, a monovarietal made from grapes grown in the Malliolo, Rocchetto, and Signou vineyards; you can try the wine at the adjacent, lovely Crè Seren bed-and-breakfast) and Sibille*. Casa Ronsil does not yet make an unblended wine.

Bellone

WHERE IT'S FOUND: Lazio. NATIONAL REGISTRY CODE NUMBER: 23. COLOR: white.

Bellone is a magical grape but I believe that very few of the producers who make wine with it realize that. In fairness, the realization may be hard to come by because they have only a limited number of Bellone grapevines at their disposal and just mingle it with all the other varieties they own. Though most producers in the area of the Castelli Romani (where the variety was once very abundant) still own a few sporadic rows of it, they simply don't have enough Bellone to try making a monovarietal wine. Instead, in historically poorer parts of the Lazio such as Cori, where local growers didn't have the time or money to uproot old vines in favor of more productive but lousier varieties, Bellone survived to tell its tale of quality.

Bellone's ancestor is believed to be Uva Pantastica, described by Pliny in the *Naturalis Historia* as a particularly high-quality grape. Another possible synonym, Uva Pane (from the common belief that this grape was as good as bread) is more controversial—a minority believe that Uva Pane is a different variety, but all the examples of supposed Uva Pane I have seen over the years looked identical to Bellone. In ancient Rome, there was already a family of grapes known as *Belli,* due to the particularly opulent, generous look of their bunches. In comparing vines designated Bello Romanesco, Di Rovasenda (1877) revealed several accessions with different morphological and productive characteristics, and Bellone, noteworthy for its vigor, was included among them (Mengarini 1888). Due to its vigor, Bellone was also referred to as Pagadebito, one of the many high-yielding varieties given this name in Italy; Muganu, Dangl, Aradhya, Frediani, Scossa, and Stover (2009) showed that Tuscia's Pagadebito VT5 has the same microsatellite profile as Bellone (this Pagadebito variety should not be confused with the Pagadebit variety of Emilia-Romagna). We also know from Mancini (1893) that grapevines then called Romanesco and Bello Velletrano were considered synonymous varieties. Whether Bellone was one of those *Belli* or is a direct descendent, it is certainly a good-looking, downright Rubenesque variety with large, round berries and portly bunches; not by chance another of its synonym is Paciocone, meaning fatso. It is also known as Cacchione, Pampanaro, and Arciprete, though the last of these is not exact. There is, of course, more than one Arciprete: according to Marco Carpineti (owner of the eponymous winery and probably the most important living expert on the variety), Bellone is identical to one Arciprete biotype, Arciprete Bianco Liscio, and different from another, the rarer Arciprete Bianco Peloso. The latter has a fuzzy underside to its leaf (*peloso* means hairy), while both Bellone and Arciprete Liscio are smooth (that is, *liscio*). Peloso's grape bunch is also more sparse than Liscio's. These morphologic differences may be virus-induced, but nobody knows for sure. In any case, microvinifications (very micro) of the Peloso variety I have tasted over the years yield wine similar to Bellone's, perhaps less refined and less acid, but similar nonetheless. The VCR 2 clone was selected from vines in Cori owned by a local grower named Giupponi, who supplies his grapes to the local cooperative; another recently available clone is ARSIAL-CRA 618. Though it's too early to tell, the ARSIAL clone gives lighter-bodied, less glyceral wines that seem to not represent Bellone at its best.

Both biotypes are characterized by very low basal fertility, so Bellone cannot be grown with the spur cordon system. Nazzareno Milita, president of the extremely high-quality Cincinnato cooperative in Cori (they control thirteen hectares under vine, three of them Bellone and five Nero Buono, another local, up-and-coming native variety) explains that "budding is precocious but there is no frost risk in these parts of Lazio, though it would be a problem in cooler parts of the region or the country. Like all vigorous grape varieties, Bellone rises to the sky quickly. Then the growth cycle slows and the berries ripen in the first ten days of September. It's not sensitive to oidium, but botrytis and peronospora are problems; especially botrytis bunch rot, because Liscio's bunch is especially compact, and has trouble drying in wet conditions."

The best soils for Bellone are volcanic, but limestone is good too (it's always good, a Frenchman would say); Carpineti believes that Bellone prefers volcanic and even *pozzolana* (sandy-clay) soils where humidity is managed quickly. "It doesn't like wet soils and that's why historically Bellone was planted on hills, aiming at better drainage." Most of the vines are now grafted to SO4 rootstocks, as a 420A is not ideal, due to Cori's volcanic soils. Bellone's natural vigor has to be kept under control or the vine tends to produce a great deal of foliage and very little fruit. Milita noted that using an SO4 rootstock decreases total sugar concentration by an average of 0.5 grams per liter, "which may be an advantage in today's increasingly hot weather. The greater sugar buildup with the Kober rootstock is probably due to a more developed leaf canopy allowing more photosynthesis, thus, more sugar in the grapes and ultimately more alcohol in the wines."

Bellone is an outstanding grape variety, one of the best in Italy today. Like few other grapes, it is capable of producing both dry and sweet wines (it likes noble rot) of real depth and complexity. The history of Bellone provides ample insight about why the wines of the Castelli Romani have fallen (deservedly) on hard times. Bellone (like Malvasia Puntinata) was basically forgotten in the twentieth century by the region's farmers, who were interested only in quantity and replanted in favor of lesser grapes such as Trebbiano Toscano and Malvasia Bianca di Candia. The resulting wines could only be neutral and thin. This state of affairs led to another casualty: Frascati Cannellino, the delicately off-dry dessert wine typical of the Castelli Romani that used to be made with Bellone. Today, there are no worthwhile examples of Cannellino, now one of Italy's most disappointing wines; this mainly because the wine isn't made with Bellone anymore. Castel De Paolis is the only estate that still makes a good Cannellino, though it isn't produced every year. Its owner, Giulio Santarelli, believes that noble rot also played an important role in Cannellinos of the past: "The grapes for Cannellino were traditionally laid on straw mats in grottos and caverns, which have specific microclimates, and noble rot was common there. Today nobody bothers with that anymore." Bellone loves noble rot so much that older farmers in the Cori area like to say that "it needs to be picked as soon as it smokes," because the bunches are attacked very quickly by the *Botrytis cinerea,* and consequently look dusty or smoky on windy days.

Which Wines to Choose and Why

Bellone is unfortunately rare today. It can still be found in the vineyards of the Castelli Romani, where it constitutes up to 10 percent of the Frascati and Marino wine blends, though rules for the Marino and Nettuno DOCs allow the theoretical possibility of making a 100 percent Bellone wine. It is also found in the seaside around Anzio and Nettuno, and especially around Cori, where it is most common. Cori is a small town located about forty-five minutes southwest of Rome, and is one of the up-and-coming, truly exciting wine production areas of Italy. The best Bellone wines, and the only ones made with 100 percent Bellone, are IGT Cori, an area already famous for high-quality tobacco, the Moro di Cori.

The wine has a telltale luscious texture and juicy acidity (wines without this creaminess or resiny mouthfeel are poorly made), and delightful honeyed, citrus, and tropical fruit aromas and flavors. Bellone's large berries are very thin skinned but rich in pectin and polyphenols, so grapes need to be pressed slowly and vinification is reductive; despite its polyphenol content, Bellone wine's oxidize easily. The variety is also blessed with high natural acidity (values of 8.5 grams per liter are not rare), which allows the production of good sparkling wines. When made from late-harvested grapes, the resulting sweet wine is thick, unctuous, amazingly complex, and never cloying because of its high acidity; I think it's on par with the greatest sweet wines in the world. The stalk is twisted in September and the grapes are left on the vine until November, to lose about 50 percent of their water content. A good late-harvested or air-dried bellone resembles high-quality Sauternes, with differences: more honey, sweet spice, and peach aromas and flavors, less saffron and tropical fruit. Without doubt, it is—or can be—one of Italy's three or four greatest sweet wines.

WINES TO TRY: Must-tries are by Marco Carpineti*** (the dry Collesanti, which is all Bellone; Capolemole Bianco, which is 60 percent Bellone and 40 percent other local varieties, and though much improved, far inferior to Collesanti; and the remarkable Ludum, which is 100 percent late-harvested Bellone) and Cincinnato*** (their Castore is aged in stainless steel, and has aromas of yellow peach and green apple; their Bellone, with hazelnut, honey, and tropical fruit flavors, undergoes a gentle oaking in large, used barrels). These wines are not just delicious, but remarkably inexpensive. Also worth trying are Alfredo Mastropietro* (Uvapane) in San Vito Romano, and Terre delle Ginestre* (Lentisco, aged in used chestnut barrels in an effort to smoothen out the wine's strong personality).

Biancame

WHERE IT'S FOUND: Marche, Emilia-Romagna. NATIONAL REGISTRY CODE NUMBER: 25. COLOR: white.

While books and websites, many local growers, winemakers, and even expert academicians (Fontana 2001) report that Biancame is synonymous with Trebbiano Toscano, there are, to the best of my knowledge, no recently reported SSR microsatellite studies, or even accurate ampelographic verifications, confirming this. A careful review of all the most important literature of the last decade detailing parentage studies and identities of grape varieties reveals that the question of a possible Biancame/Trebbiano Toscano identity remains unanswered. Furthermore, Biancame remains separate from Trebbiano Toscano in the National Registry. Not that things are all that free of confusion there either: while the two varieties are listed among the synonyms of each, the names of the officially certified clones for each of these two cultivars are different. In any case, I will also list them separately in this book. I can add that in my own experience, the two varieties look and behave differently enough to warrant their being viewed as distinct cultivars.

Biancame is also known as Bianchello (which is the name of the best-known wine made from it, Bianchello del Metauro), Balsamina Bianca, and Biancone. However the last of these is incorrect, as Biancone is likely another variety entirely (typical of Elba and long confused with Trebbiano Toscano, hence the erroneous identification with Biancame). Experts once believed Biancame to be a relative of Greco, but this is wrong too. Last but not least, there is some evidence that Biancame and Morbidella might be identical as well, but more research is required on this matter.

Biancame is a historically famous variety: the Carthaginian troops of Asdrubal (Hannibal's much less clever cousin) got carried away in their libations while campaigning in Metauro, and ended up on the wrong end of a horrific defeat at the hands of the Romans, the battle of Metauro. Were this story proven true beyond doubt, we could then say that Biancame contributed to creating the world as we know it today; for had Rome lost that battle, historians are in agreement that Carthage would have ultimately won the Punic wars. Biancame is generally described as having medium-large, pentagonal leaves with a lightly downy undersurface (Trebbiano Toscano's is much more hairy), large, cylindrical-conical bunches that often have a bifid tip, and medium-size yellow-green berries with very little bloom. In fact, this is for me one of the distinguishing features of Biancame: even when fully mature, its berries never turn golden-yellow or reddish as do those of Trebbiano Toscano (or at least, some biotypes of it) and of many other *Trebbiano* varieties. In this respect, Biancame lives up to its name, obviously derived from *bianco*, which means white. The variety is vigorous and very resistant to pathogens, even more than other *Trebbianos*; only botrytis can cause problems in rainy years. Biancame takes well to rootstocks K5BB and 41B on fresher soils, while 140 is the rootstock of choice on dry ones. There are six official clones (CSV-AP PS-2, CSV-AP PS-3, CSV-AP PS-7, CSV-AP PS-8, CAB 19, and CAB 20).

Which Wines to Choose and Why

Biancame is grown in the Marche, mainly around the cities of Urbino and Pesaro. The three most important DOCs are the aforementioned Bianchello del Metauro, Colli di Rimini Biancame, and Colli di Rimini Bianco (though in this last, the preponderant variety is Trebbiano Romagnolo). A good monovarietal Biancame wine is fresh and crisp, with delicate herbal nuances, white fruit, and citrus notes. It is lemony fresh and light-bodied.

WINES TO TRY: For Bianchello del Metauro, try: Guerrieri** (reputedly 100 percent Biancame), Claudio Morelli** (Borgo Torre), Roberto Lucarelli* (Rocho), and Valentino Fiorini* (Tenuta Campioli).

Bianchetta Trevigiana

WHERE IT'S FOUND: Veneto. NATIONAL REGISTRY CODE NUMBER: 27. COLOR: white.

It was Italo Cosmo who added "Trevigiana" (in reference to the pretty city of Treviso, located in the center of Bianchetta's historic growing zone) to this variety's name in 1964, in an effort to avoid confusion with the many other Bianchettas: not a bad idea. Bianchetta is one of many Italian natives named on the basis of skin color, which means there are many unrelated "Bianchetta" varieties all over Italy that have only a pale hue in common. To further complicate matters, Bianchetta Trevigiana has always been known by a variety of other names, including Bianca Gentile di Fonzaso, Biancara,

Bianchetta, Bianchetta Gentile, Pavana Bianca, and Pignola Bianca. Other names were used only in specific areas: Senese in Breganze, Vernanzina in the Colli Berici, Vernassina in the Colli Euganei, and Vernaccia, Vernazza, or Vernaccia Trentina in the Trentino and Alto Adige regions. This is because local farmers were always convinced their grape was different from that of others. We know today that many of these synonyms are wrong, as they refer to varieties such as Pavana which are distinct from Bianchetta Trevigiana. A recent DNA study has also suggested that Bianchetta Trevigiana is the result of a natural crossing of Brambana (a red-berried grape) and Durella, another Veneto native, but this is controversial (Cipriani, Spadotto, Jurman, Di Gaspero, Crespan, Meneghetti, et al. 2010).

Though Bianchetta Trevigiana is somewhat forgotten today and reduced to the role of a minor blending grape, I believe it is noteworthy that Bianchetta Trevigiana has always been appreciated for making high-quality wines. It was probably first mentioned in 1679 by Giacomo Agostinetti di Cimadolmo, who called it Bianchetta Gentile and believed it made the best wines of the Trevigiano area. Bianchetta's fortunes took a turn for the worse at the beginning of the eighteenth century, when a severe frost killed off many of the more delicate varieties; farmers preferred to replant with more resistant and fertile varieties. In 1864, Semenzi described the wine as "super-delicious" and tells us that Bianchetta wines from the Colli di Conegliano were exported to Austria and Germany. By 1874, according to Carpené, Bianchetta Trevigiana was cultivated in thirty-nine townships. Ampelographically, it was described only in 1901 by Zava, who mentioned that it was abundant in many areas of Veneto, including Padova, Venezia, Verona, Vicenza, Treviso, and Belluno. Bianchetta Trevigiana is characterized by medium-large, pyramidal, stocky bunches with one very large wing, so that it looks as if there are two bunches in one. The berries are medium-sized, round, and covered with average amounts of bloom; unfortunately, though the berries have very thick skins (an important winemaking feature for Bianchetta Trevigiana), the fairly tightly packed bunch makes the variety an easy prey of botrytis. Bianchetta Trevigiana ripens in late September or in the first ten days of October. There are as yet no official clones available.

In Italy, Bianchetta Trevigiana is most commonly found in the Prosecco production area, around Conegliano and Valdobbiadene, especially near Maser, Cornuda, Asolo, Castelcucco, and Monfumo; it is also grown, more rarely, in Trentino. It has been planted outside Italy as well, most notably North America. In California, in field trials to evaluate varieties for planting in the San Joaquin Valley, Bianchetta Trevigiana was found to rot too easily in that particular microclimate. Bianchetta Trevigiana is instead being looked at in cooler American microclimates. A Colorado State University project is aimed at testing wine grapes (including Bianchetta Trevigiana) in various wine grape growing areas in more than twenty states.

Which Wines to Choose and Why
Bianchetta Trevigiana is almost always used in blends, in variable percentages: DOC wines are Colli di Conegliano, Garda, Lugana, Montello, Colli Asolani, Valdadige, and Trentino's Vigneti delle Dolomiti Bianco. A maximum of 10 percent Bianchetta Trevigiana can be used to make the Veneto sweet wine Torchiato di Fregona. Often, it is blended with Glera to add acidity and especially structure to many proseccos. Desiderio Bisol, of the famous Prosecco Bisol estate, feels that monovarietal Bianchetta Trevigiana wines are light and fresh, but lack complexity and depth, though a number of local producers still make small quantities of 100 percent Bianchetta wines. Eighteenth- and nineteenth-century documents reveal that Bianchetta Trevigiana was often made in two ways: by cold fermentation off the skins for maximum freshness and fruit expression, and by macerating on the skins to create richer, more complex wines. Clearly, winemakers of

centuries past had more faith in Bianchetta Trevigiana's potential. That Bianchetta Trevigiana is not just another simple white grape was demonstrated in 2009 by Lomolino, Zocca, Spettoli, Zanin, and Lante who recorded high flavanol (polyphenol) concentrations in wine made with the variety; in fact, higher than those of some red wines. In this light, recent research by Lomolino and Lante (2012) is extremely interesting: reducing agents such as β-mercaptoethanol, threo-1,4-dimercapto-2,3-butanediol (DTT) and $K_2S_2O_5$, used in winemaking, were found to reduce grape skin esterase activity. Since esterase is important for the hydrolysis and synthesis of esters, which in turn characterize the wine's aroma and flavor profile, over-enthusiastic use of reducing agents in vinification of Bianchetta Trevigiana grapes may alter the wine's typical aromatic profile. Relative to the expression of native grape variety characteristics in wine, excessively reductive winemaking is a problem I have broached before in this book (see chapter 1). I know of no estate-bottled monovarietal Bianchetta Trevigiano wine made outside Italy, but a 2012 Bianchetta Trevigiana bulk wine has been sold in Paso Robles, California, at ten dollars a gallon. Also from California, a wine named Cameo made by Laraneta Vineyards in Templeton is supposedly monovarietal "Vernaccia," which the producers also refer to as "Bianchetta Trevigiano," which they describe as an ancient grape known in the Veneto region of Italy since the 1500s and associated with the town of San Gimignano in Tuscany. There seems to be a little confusion here: though the grape used to make this wine might be Bianchetta Trevigiana, this variety has nothing to do with San Gimignano or with the Vernaccia di San Gimignano grape; still, I hope to visit them soon. It's thrilling for me to see someone so far from Italy trying their hand at making a wine with what is still a very rare variety in the United States. Laraneta has apparently been very successful too: the 2007 Cameo won bronze at the 2010 Central Coast Valley Wine Competition.

WINES TO TRY: Pure examples made in commercially significant numbers are hard to come by, but try Fratelli Collavo**. Another excellent example is by De Bacco** (Saca), an extra dry sparkling wine made from grapes culled in very old vineyards growing in the hinterland of Mugnai di Feltre and Fonzaso.

Bianco d'Alessano

WHERE IT'S FOUND: Puglia. NATIONAL REGISTRY CODE NUMBER: 28. COLOR: white.

It's unlikely that anyone will ever mistake a wine made with Bianco d'Alessano as the second coming of Riesling. That said, the grape and wines deserve better—if only Italian producers would lower yields and give this a grape a chance.

Also known as Acchiappapalmento, Bianco di Lessame, and Verdurino, Bianco d'Alessano has recently been proven identical to the Calabrian variety Iuvarello (Schneider, Raimondi, De Santis 2008). The history of Bianco d'Alessano is not particularly well documented. There's little or no information prior to 1870, when it was mentioned for the first time. It is probably original to the Valle d'Itria in Puglia and has always been planted promiscuously with Verdeca, a more popular white Puglian variety, because of the delicate aromatic quality, higher productivity, and vibrant green color of the Verdeca wines. On its own, Bianco d'Alessano has less to offer; its nonaromatic wines can be watery and neutral. The variety has conical-cylindrical bunches and round berries; it ripens between late September and early October. Two clones that became available in 2010 and seem promising are CRSA-Regione Puglia C2 (more productive, medium-compact bunch) and CRSA-Regione Puglia C5 (loosely packed, more productive, and more disease resistant). Viticulturally, it is characterized by its relatively early budding and flowering, which exposes it to the double whammy of spring frosts and *coulure,* or berry shatter, a viticultural condition arising in cool, rainy, or abnormally hot springtime weather conditions in which flowers fail to fertilize and fall off, thereby reducing yields. However, Bianco d'Alessano is not particularly demanding and is fairly hardy. In fact, it is likely that besides the oceans of wine it generates, Bianco d'Alessano owes its popularity to its ability to withstand very hot, arid conditions, which are always more than likely in Puglia. This is precisely why it is a grape variety that is being looked at with increasing interest in warm-weather wine producing areas, such as in parts of California and Australia.

In Italy, Bianco d'Alessano has always been linked to Puglia, and grows mainly in the provinces of Brindisi, Bari, and Taranto. Otherwise, it grows around the Valle d'Itria towns of Cisternino, Locorotondo, Martina Franca, and Ceglie Messapica and in the high, barren, windswept plains of the Murgia on the border between Puglia and Basilicata. The long-recognized *grand cru* area is the Gallinajo subzone of Locorotondo, a pretty town close to Bari. Bianco d'Alessano also grows in Calabria, where it has been cultivated for centuries, but under different names: Iuvarello, Vuiune, Iuvino, and Buino. Still, this is a variety that is falling out of favor. Unless new producers can show others how to make wine (monovarietal, let us hope) that will be both critically acclaimed and financially rewarding, the future looks dim for this variety, at least in Italy. However, it is also true that there has been no better time in the last fifty years of Italy's wine history for a forgotten or poorly regarded variety to break through. The longest yard is just ahead for Bianco d'Alessano.

Which Wines to Choose and Why

The most important wines are the DOC Locorotondo (in which Bianco d'Alessano is blended with Verdeca) though it's part of the more rare DOC wines Gravina, Ostuni, and Lizzano, as well as IGT wines Daunia, Murgia, Salento, and Valle d'Itria. Livio Carparelli, the longtime director of the Locorotondo Social Cooperative and also the winemaker at the Torrevento estate, knows this area of Puglia and its varieties intimately. His eponymous estate produces wines made from 100 percent Verdeca and Minutolo, as well as a monovarietal Bianco d'Alessano. A pure Bianco d'Alessano wine is delicately herbal, with nuances of green apple, bitter orange, and white flowers. Carparelli's is by far the best example made in Italy, but in my view, tasting his three monovarietal wines side by side proves that Bianco d'Alessano wine is inferior to the other two, lacking their complexity and depth. Still, Bianco d'Alessano is not the loser many people thought it was, and it would be nice to see what might happen with further reduction of yields.

In California, Sonoma's Viansa Winery made a 2007 and 2008 Bianco d'Alessano called Anatra, but I haven't seen this wine in a long time. In Australia, the Salena Estate (Ink Series Bianco d'Alessano) has won critical acclaim, prizes, and consumer devotion with its now monovarietal Bianco d'Alessano wines. Perhaps the warmer inland areas of Australia (such as the Riverlands region, where Salena Estate is located) may be a new, ideal home for it, seeing as its fortunes in Italy are somewhat on the decline. Winemaker Melanie Kargas finds that her wine exudes "apple, pear, and loquat aromas and flavors, hints of citrus and underlying minerality."

WINES TO TRY: I Pastini / Livio Carparelli*** (Cupa, floral, herbal, apricot- and lychee-marked, is the benchmark by which all others are measured) and Apollonio** (Elfo Bianco d'Alessano, also 100 percent monovarietal). The Locorotondo Social Cooperative** (Locorotondo Vigneti in Gallinajo) does not yet make make a monovarietal Bianco d'Alessano wine, but rather fresh and light Locorotondo wines with an agreeable crisp lemony zing and admixture of Verdeca, as is traditional in the area.

Biancolella

WHERE IT'S FOUND: Campania. NATIONAL REGISTRY CODE NUMBER: 29. COLOR: white.

Also known as Jancolella, Janculilla, and similar, very rarely used names, Biancolella has long been associated with the island of Ischia:

experts believe it arrived courtesy of emigrating Euboean Greeks as early as 770 B.C.E., though there is no real documentation of this. Likely enough perhaps, but the first official recognition of Biancolella dates back only to 1867, when it is mentioned by D'Ascia in his book on Ischia, *Storia dell'isola d'Ischia*. According to Bordignon, Biancolella is likely the variety that always flourished on the island, though a usually trustworthy source such as Acerbi does not mention it at all in his writings. Froio (1875) also identified the presence of Biancolella in the area around Caserta, on the Campanian mainland. Foëx (1909), who wrote the Biancolella heading for Viala and Vermorel in their ampelographic opus, believed that Biancolella was the variety called Petite Blanche in Corsica; however, his description differs considerably from that of Salvatore d'Ambra, of the D'Ambra estate, the most important winery on the island, generally considered to have been the greatest expert on Ischia grape varieties.

Biancolella is called San Nicola (or simply Bianco) on Capri, and Teneddu on Procida; on these nearby islands, it is likely that the same genotype was named differently over the centuries. Unfortunately, its island habitat has limited the data available relative to Biancolella: other Campanian varieties have been the subject of much closer scientific scrutiny. Only recently have researchers (Cipriani, Spadotto, Jurman, Di Gaspero, Crespan, Meneghetti, et al. 2010) shown that Biancolella is probably a parent of Sanlunardo, while earlier studies (Costantini, Monaco, Vouillamoz, Forlani, and Grando 2005) had suggested it was closely related to Falanghina Beneventana. Biancolella has medium-sized, cylindrical bunches that may look pyramidal because of the presence of small wings; there are no official clones available, but there are two biotypes, Verace and Selvatica. In the vineyard, Biancolella is characterized by ripening in late September, but also by early budding and flowering, which exposes it to the risk of spring frosts and *coulure*. It's very sensitive to peronospora, which has contributed to limiting its distribution in Italy and abroad.

In Italy, Biancolella grows almost exclusively in Campania, mainly on the islands off the coast of Naples but it also grows along the Amalfi and Sorrento coast and farther north toward Caserta. Outside Italy, Biancolella has been the subject of field trials, such as those conducted in the United States by the Department of Viticulture and Enology at the University of California at Davis's Kearney Agricultural Research and Extension Center in Fresno County.

Which Wines to Choose and Why

The sight of Ischia's vineyards is a beautiful one: due to the island's strong tourist industry and resultant hotels and homes, the vines have been pushed uphill, onto the rugged slopes of Mount Epomeo, six hundred meters of green rock jutting out into the Mediterranean that essentially divides the island into two halves. The slopes are green because of the unique composition of this volcanic tufa, rich in sulfur, manganese, and iron. The high mountain vineyards and the extremely rich mineral content of the soils doubtless contribute to the considerable potential for complexity of flavor and perfume in Biancolella wines. These wines, though not blessed with palate-burning levels of acidity, can age remarkably well. I have tried numerous bottles of biancolella from the 1960s and 1970s over the last three decades that have held up spectacularly, with wines from the 1970s presenting a petrol note not unlike that of Riesling. Unfortunately, it used to be a lot easier to find these wines fifteen or twenty years ago, when estates still had many old bottles available.

Wines that are 100 percent Biancolella are DOC Ischia Biancolella, but Ischia Bianco blends exist too (usually with Forastera, as well as small percentages of other local natives such as Coglionara and Sanlunardo). Biancolella wines are always golden tinged, with strong white flower and thyme aromas, flavors of fresh herbs, spearmint, grapefruit, oregano, and a noticeable saline quality. In warmer years, notes of pineapple and grilled plantain are not uncommon. However, wine lovers ought to take note of the fact that Biancolella wines will taste remarkably different depending on where the grapes are grown on the island. Wines made from Biancolella grown on the southern part of the island are usually richer and softer, as the vines are sheltered from rains and winds, but even wines made in the island's southern half can differ considerably. For example, the low-lying, high-quality Calitto vineyard produces grapes used to make fruit-forward wines of early accessibility, while the wine made from Vigna del Lume grapes, a vineyard that literally grows next to the sea, is remarkably more herbal and saline; meanwhile, wine made from grapes grown in the Frassitelli vineyard is more refined and elegant. Frassitelli is possibly the island's one true *grand cru*. Located at six hundred meters above sea level, it is also one of the most beautiful vineyards in the world, offering a vantage point from which you can gaze out over the Mediterranean and watch Capri, Procida, and Vesuvius in the distance. Frassitelli's slopes are so steep it is virtually impossible to stand there, so the grapes are brought down via a monorail train system. These richer, more structured wines stand up to weightier fish dishes; otherwise biancolella is ideal as an aperitif or with simply prepared fish dishes. All Biancolella wines have the potential to be delicious, with complexity and depth of flavor uncommon in many Italian white wines, but you do have to like a saline note in your wines.

WINES TO TRY: The best producer is D'Ambra*** (especially his Frassitelli, but the regular bottling is also very good), Cenatiempo**, Antonio Mazzella** (Vigna del Lume; a seaside vineyard, where the only way to bring the grapes to the cellar is by boat), Tomasone*, and Pietratorcia*.

Bombino Bianco

WHERE IT'S FOUND: Puglia, Emilia-Romagna, Marche, Campania, Lazio, Sardinia, Umbria.

NATIONAL REGISTRY CODE NUMBER: 32. COLOR: white.

Bombino Bianco has always been grown mainly in Puglia, but only recently has its potential to make very high-quality wine become apparent. It is unrelated to the other Puglian Bombino variety, Bombino Nero, a red-berried variety with which it appears to share only a name. Instead, recent research suggests that Bombino Bianco is most likely a parent of two other Puglian cultivars, Impigno and Moscatello Selvatico (Cipriani, Spadotto, Jurman, Di Gaspero, Crespan, Meneghetti, et al. 2010). The cultivar's origin is unknown: some experts believe Bombino Bianco was brought to Italy by the Templar knights during the Crusades, others that it's of Spanish origin, but there is no convincing documentation to support either hypothesis. Its name probably derives from the unique shape of the bunch, which resembles that of a cuddling infant and has nothing to do with bombs (fruit, small, or otherwise); in fact, it is also called Bambino. Another hypothesis is that the name is a corruption of *bonvino,* or good wine.

There are many reasons why Bombino Bianco's merits have long gone unrecognized, not the least of which is a great deal of confusion regarding its exact identity. In fact, Puglia's Bombino Bianco has long been misidentified with Emilia-Romagna's Mostosa (another variety typical of that region, which many believe to be a synonym of Pagadebit), with Abruzzo's Trebbiano Abruzzese, and more recently with Lazio's Ottonese. In Lazio's Castelli Romani area, the presence of Bombino Bianco has been documented for centuries, but recent research implied that it is also identical to Ottonese, a variety typical of the more southern reaches of the region. Following these misidentifications, a long sequence of planting errors ensued; in the belief that Bombino Bianco is identical to Mostosa (or Pagadebit), it was planted extensively in Emilia-Romagna, and for the same reason, it was also much planted in Abruzzo, because producers wishing to plant Pagadebit or Trebbiano Abruzzese were told they were identical varieties. However, the converse is also true: when nurseries were asked for Bombino Bianco, they were just as likely to send one of the other varieties. For example, most of the producers in Emilia-Romagna I have talked to over the years have told me that the nursery grapevines available over the last twenty or thirty years in Emilia-Romagna were undoubtedly of Bombino Bianco and not of true Pagadebit (or Mostosa). Unfortunately, situations such as these further compounded problems and added to the confusion, because all these varieties behave differently in the field and do not produce wines of similar quality. So while many farmers and scientists believed they were dealing with Bombino Bianco, it is likely they were actually growing or studying mixtures of distinct if similar-looking varieties: older vines of the original variety were interplanted with newer vines of another variety right in the same vineyard. This explains why, over the years, I have never ceased to be amazed at how many producers told me *their* Bombino Bianco grapevines behaved differently—and their wines tasted different—from those of other estates in other regions of Italy.

So today we have a situation in which farmers and producers in Puglia, Lazio, Abruzzo, and Emilia-Romagna are all supposedly growing Bombino Bianco and making wine with it, when in fact some are using the true Bombino Bianco, others Trebbiano Abruzzese or Mostosa or Ottonese, and many a mix of all of these. Under these conditions, to draw conclusions about the characteristics of the grapevine and the wine becomes next to impossible. This is why there is disagreement over Bombino Bianco's true merits: some think it's a high-quality cultivar, others are less impressed. Currently, Bombino Bianco, Trebbiano Abruzzese, and Mostosa are all listed separately in Italy's National Registry, mainly on ampelographic grounds; and in the absence of definitive SSR profiling results that tell us otherwise, I also treat them as distinct varieties in this book.

For example, there are two schools of thought about Bombino Bianco's productivity.

One says that it produces high yields. Indeed, many of its synonyms—Caricalasino (one of many "load up the donkey" varieties), Stracciacambiale ("rip up the promissory note"), Buttapalmento ("fill up the tank"), and Schiacciapalmento ("crush the tank")—attest to large yields that endear it to farmers everywhere. But a second school says it's far from being a generous producer: Girolamo d'Amico, Louis Rapini, and Ulrico Priore (owners of the D'Arapri estate in Puglia: the name is an acronym of their initials) certainly agree that it is not. Sebastiano De Corato of the Rivera estate in Puglia says that Bombino Bianco is "a great variety, easy to work with: sparse bunch, thick skin . . . but it's a rather miserly cultivar, and that is precisely one of the reasons why it went into decline in the twentieth century." And it's true that for the greater part of the twentieth century, the Bombino Bianco vines in Puglia suffered the same plight as other varieties that are high on quality but short on productivity: it was gradually replaced by Trebbiano Toscano, Malvasia Bianca Lunga, and even Cococciola. Whereas it represented 90 percent of the surface under vine in the province of Foggia (Puglia) in the 1900s, this had been reduced to 40 percent by the 1950s. Angelo Paradiso, who helps run the large social cooperative in Cerignola founded by his grandfather, says that "at the beginning of the new century we wished to make a 100 percent Bombino Bianco wine but had great difficulty in finding decent grapes—and the farmers didn't want to plant it." This contradiction—that Bombino Bianco's many synonyms hint at copious yields, while at least in Puglia it appears to be a low-yielding cultivar—coupled to different morphological characteristics, makes it apparent that at least some of the Bombino Bianco vines of one region are not the Bombino Bianco of another. Or at the very least that the variety behaves very differently in diverse habitats.

True Bombino Bianco is characterized by conical, sometimes conical-cylindrical bunches that are medium-large; the round berries are also fairly large. All of its phenological phases occur late, so while spring frosts pose no threat whatsoever, autumn rains are a potential problem, though given its southern Italian habitat, true downpours aren't likely to occur. Bombino Bianco is both vigorous and resistant to most grapevine pests. There are three official clones available (ARSIAL-CRA 231, CRSA-Regione Puglia 191, and CRSA-Regione Puglia 197); most of the grapevines labeled as Bombino Bianco available from nurseries today derive from clonal research performed in Abruzzo and Puglia between 1973 and 1974. The research work done in the field originally focused on twenty-eight accessions obtained from five different estates (four in northern Puglia, near San Severo; and one from Abruzzo, near Ortona). Clones CRSA-Regione Puglia C191 and CRSA-Regione Puglia C197 descend from two old San Severo vineyards. Today, Bombino Bianco is most typical of Puglia (in the areas around Foggia in the north, but also near Bari and even Lecce), but also grows in Abruzzo, Marche (around Macerata and Ascoli Piceno), Campania (Avellino), Lazio (Rome and Frosinone), and Emilia-Romagna. Sporadic plots of Bombino Bianco are also found in Umbria and Sardinia.

Which Wines to Choose and Why

Bombino Bianco is included in the blend of two DOCG wines, both from Lazio: Frascati and Frascati Cannellino. It is also allowed in DOC blends such as Puglia's Cacc'e' Mmitte di Lucera, Castel del Monte, and San Severo, Lazio's Marino and Frascati, Abruzzo's Trebbiano d'Abruzzo, Emilia-Romagna's Colli della Romagna Centrale and Pagadebit di Romagna, and Abruzzo's Trebbiano d'Abruzzo. Hilariously, and a reflection of all the problems mentioned above relative to the exact identity of Bombino Bianco, more than one of these DOC wines is produced under guidelines that border on the schizophrenic. For example, the DOC wine Pagadebit di Romagna has to be made by law with 85 percent Bombino Bianco, but in fact it is often made—as it should be—at least in part with Mostosa; of course, many local producers believe that there is a separate Pagadebit variety, and that it should be the only one used to make this wine (see MOSTOSA, chapter 5). Hard as it maybe to believe, the Trebbiano d'Abruzzo DOC is even worse: it requires the wine to be made with a minimum 85 percent of either Trebbiano Abruzzese and/or Bombino Bianco and/or Trebbiano Toscano. It's enough to drive one to drink. Bombino Bianco is also allowed in roughly forty IGT wines, including Puglia's Daunia, Murgia, Puglia, Salento, Tarantino, and Valle d'Itria, Abruzzo's Terre di Chieti and Terre Aquilane, Umbria's Narni and Spello, Molise's Terre degli Osci, Campania's Pompeiano, and Emilia-Romagna's Ravenna and Rubicone. This large presence in many regional wines is a testament to Bombino Bianco's importance.

In my opinion, based on years of tasting the various Bombino Bianco wines all over Italy, wines made with true Bombino Bianco in Puglia are creamier (with aromas and flavors of minerals, almonds, and aniseed, and hints of apricot and tropical fruit) than those of Lazio or Emilia-Romagna, which are thinner, more herbal, and lemony, but I think many of the former were made with quantity in mind rather than quality, while the latter were almost always blends of Bombino Bianco with Pagadebit and/or Mostosa and probably Trebbiano Toscano, which are lesser varieties. In Lazio, Bombino Bianco has always made up a small percentage in the blended wines made around Rome; though it was always highly thought of, nobody ever thought to make a monovarietal wine from it. Most producers in the Castelli Romani area didn't own enough Bombino Bianco grapevines to make wine in any commercially significant volumes; Donnardea is the first estate to have gone the monovarietal route with this cultivar, in the early 2000s. In southwestern Lazio, monovarietal bombino is easier to come by, but it is labeled ottonese, as that is the name the variety is known by there. Ottonese wines are very high acid, lemony, and mineral, and for this reason many producers prefer to blend in a little Bellone or one of the local *Malvasias* to soften their edge somewhat. Though most of these wines are simple, they make refreshing, uncomplicated aperitifs and some have considerable potential to be a whole lot more. However, Puglia remains the place for high-quality Bombino Bianco wines, though for the longest time, Puglian versions were nothing to write home about either. This is because Puglia was long a backwater of enological knowledge, with people limiting themselves to churning out bulk wine, the majority of which was at best neutral and uninspired. Even today, most of Puglia's Bombino Bianco grows in old canopied vineyards where the variety can never ripen fully, giving thin, extremely tart, tasteless wines. At the beginning of the new century, Nicholas Belfrage, in his *Brunello to Zibibbo* book, wrote that "Bombino Bianco can make as dull and tasteless a wine as you could hope to find." You can't blame him: most likely he had tasted either the product of those canopied vineyards yielding copious quantities of unripe berries or perhaps wines that weren't really made with true Bombino Bianco.

At the time Belfrage's book came out, most wines made with Bombino Bianco probably were just as bad as he described, but happily this is no longer case. De Corato believes that Bombino Bianco wines are "fresh and complex, much like good Chardonnay wines and we have very high hopes for it," but adds that "the problem is its naturally high acidity: if picked unripe, the wine is undrinkable. That's why traditionally it was blended with the lower-acid Pampanuto, which softened it." D'Alfonso del Sordo's Catapanus wine has become a resounding success. "It was my father who, in the mid-1980s, decided to give Bombino Bianco a serious try," recalls Gianfelice d'Alfonso del Sordo di San Severo. "Selecting plant material from old forgotten local vineyards, in 1999 he laid down our first three hectares, and we've never looked back." Spagnoletti Zeuli, another Puglian producer thinks that Bombino Bianco is "a pretty variety with big berries and we're making increasingly promising wines." In fact, Bombino Bianco's naturally high acidity has been turned to advantage by at least one estate: the D'Arapri estate in Puglia makes truly excellent sparkling wines from the variety. It was the first to think of this possibility, and produced a trial of sixty bottles in 1979 by using empty Champagne bottles obtained from friends at local restaurants. The success of the wines has been nothing short of phenomenal, and the rest, as they say, is history.

WINES TO TRY: For Puglia, try: D'Alfonso del Sordo*** (Catapanus), D'Arapri*** (Brut, Brut Nobile Riserva), Rivera*** (Marese), Cantina Ariano* (Sogno di Volpe), and Cantina Paradiso* (Bombino). The sparklers by D'Arapri, mostly made in the manner of Champagne with refermentation in the bottle, are excellent, but make sure you try the monovarietal Bombino Bianco wine, without Pinot Nero additions. For Lazio, try: Rosalba Vendrame** (Ottonese Gocce Preziose) and Donnardea* (Bombino). The very good Cibele by Compagnia di Ermes, which used to be a pure Ottonese, is unfortunately no longer (now half Ottonese and half Bellone).

Bombino Nero

WHERE IT'S FOUND: Puglia. NATIONAL REGISTRY CODE NUMBER: 33. COLOR: red.

Unlike Bombino Bianco, which is grown in many different regions, Bombino Nero is essentially limited to Puglia. Like its white counterpart, its name is also believed to result from the particular shape of the cluster, which resembles a cuddling infant, but the two varieties are unrelated. To the best of my knowledge, it has nothing to do with a small bomb, as you'll find written elsewhere—in fact, it is also referred to as Bambino in Puglia, reinforcing the analogy with a small child, and as Buonvino (good wine). Farmers in Northern and Central Puglia used to prefer it to the other local red grape, Uva di Troia, because it is a more generous producer, but Bombino Nero's role was always to play second fiddle to Negro Amaro. Just like Canaiolo Nero in Chianti, Bombino Nero is used to make Negro Amaro–based wines more genteel.

There is only one official clone of Bombino Nero, CRSA-Regione Puglia D205. Old farmers have told me there also exist two biotypes of Bombino Nero, but they swear the wines are indistinguishable: the biotype Bombino Nero dal Peduncolo Corto is short stalked and the biotype Forcella takes its name from *forced* (meaning pronged or forked in local dialect). In both cases the bunch is conical and medium-sized (Forcella's is usually the larger of the two) but Forcella's is much more compact. Due to the latter characteristic, the Forcella biotype is more prone to rot and diseases and it suffers in excessively humid or wet conditions. The berries of both biotypes are similarly blue and round, with thin skins. Both biotypes are late-ripening and are characterized by asynchronous bunch maturation, meaning that Bombino Nero rarely reaches optimal ripeness of its berries, so the variety tends to have high acidity and poor sugar accumulation. Along with the delicate thin skins, this explains why Bombino Nero rarely gives important, full-bodied red wines but is excellent for *rosato* production. Due to its tendency to produce light- to medium-bodied wines of high acidity, the cultivar differs considerably from most other southern Italian varieties, as practically all these red grapes give full-bodied, bold wines almost too heavy and too alcoholic. This explains why many southern Italian producers look at Bombino Nero with interest. "It is very atypical in this respect," concludes Carlo De Corato of the famous Rivera estate, "these lighter, more fragrant wines marked by high acidity and crisp berry aromas and flavors—it's a northern grape in Italy's south." I couldn't have said it better myself.

Bombino Nero is grown around Foggia, Bari, and Taranto, though it is mostly found in the Castel del Monte area near Bari; this is where wine lovers can hope to snag a wine made with 100 percent Bombino Nero. The *grand cru* sites for it are around Ruvo and Corato, especially in old vineyards trained with the *alberello* system; according to Leonardo Palumbo, long the winemaker at the famous Rivera estate, "there is no better *terroir* for Bombino Nero, though it also does well in the rocky, calcareous soils of the Murgia. The reason is that the black soils of the Murgia are thin but rich in humus and organic debris; beneath is stratified marly-calcareous rock, the so-called *chiancarelle,* but thanks to the humidity of the soils, Bombino Nero can weather the frequent droughts well." Interestingly, the variety does not do well in irrigated, highly productive vineyards, where it produces a wine that is nondescript. For this reason, low-vigor rootstocks such as 140 Ruggeri and 157.11 are best. Bombino Nero is also grown in Basilicata near Potenza and Matera, but is not an important variety there.

Which Wines to Choose and Why

Bombino Nero is rarely bottled on its own. It is almost always added to Negro Amaro wines, as 10–20 percent of the blend. There is one DOCG wine made, Castel del Monte Bombino Nero, which is a good example of how highly regarded the variety is. DOC wines such as Castel del Monte and Lizzano are good examples, and there are roughly thirty IGT wines as well, made in regions like Sardinia, Lazio, and Basilicata (examples include Basilicata, Colli Cimini, Daunia, Planargia, and Tharros).

Though Bombino Nero was once very popular, times and tastes have changed so much that the acreage of Bombino Nero around Bari has been reduced by half in the last fifty years. This is because the lighter, simpler, fresher wines made with Bombino Nero fell out of favor in a popular culture that is dominated by scores and obsessed with inky behemoth wines. By contrast, red wines made with Bombino Nero are tasty and medium-bodied, with mineral and inky red-berry aromas and flavors. They usually have lovely balance and I think their quality goes unrecognized. Their light texture and freshness makes them ideal with simple tomato pasta and pizzas, or white meat dishes.

Where Bombino Nero is unbeatable is in some of Italy's best *rosato*. In Puglia (which is, along with Abruzzo, Italy's most important source of *rosato*), these are made either with Negro Amaro (in the Salento area of southern Puglia) or Bombino Nero (in northern and central Puglia). I think Bombino Nero *rosato* wines are fresh, fruity, and have lovely red-berry, floral, and citrus notes; they are lighter and fruitier than those made with Negro Amaro. And I'm not the only one who thinks the difference between *rosati* made with Bombino Nero and Negro Amaro is striking. De Corato says that "with Negro Amaro, *rosato* is really a by-product, as it's made via the *saignée* process; those *rosati* have the same alcohol level as the red wines made from Negro Amaro. They are also bigger, richer wines, and I'm not sure that's what people are looking for in their *rosato*." Palumbo adds that not only the *rosati*, but also the red wines are much better than people realize: "Bombino Nero wines used to be too delicate and low in dry extract, but with better viticultural practices that is no longer a problem."

WINES TO TRY: Rivera*** (Pungirosa and Rosé), Terranostra* (Alterium, which also makes a Bombino Nero red wine in their Piano Mangeri line), and Cantina Vignuolo (Manieri di Federico Rosato). Rivera's two *rosati* are very different wines: while Pungirosa is paler and delicate and not unlike a blush wine from Provence, Rosé is meatier and richer though still bright and fresh. Pungirosa is macerated and fermented at lower temperatures (5–10°C), but with longer skin contact; Rosé is a more traditional wine, where the maceration only lasts twelve hours at temperatures of 10–15°C. Different strokes for different folks, but equally good.

Bosco

WHERE IT'S FOUND: Liguria. NATIONAL REGISTRY CODE NUMBER: 36. COLOR: white.

Bosco is the lone cultivar typical of Liguria's Cinque Terre to be cultivated right next to the sea, in contrast to other local natives Albarola and Vermentino. It also produces the fullest-bodied, richest wine of the three: locals refer to it as a "red grape in a white grape's clothing." In fact, it is the grape used to provide body and structure to typical local Ligurian wines, which are often blends of the three varieties. Bosco's name derives from that of the villa of the Marchesi Durazzo of Genoa, from where the first Bosco vines were supposedly brought to the Cinque Terre, though there is no hard proof of this. Very rarely is it also called Madea, and then only around Genoa. In any case, it's clear that the variety was described in 1833 in ampelographic bulletins and deemed appropriate for planting all over Liguria. Bosco, just like Albarola and Vermentino, all but disappeared from the Cinque Terre in the wake of phylloxera, and the local economy took a hard hit, surviving only by commercial fishing. According to Giacomo Forlini Cappellini, one of Liguria's best producers, Bosco and the other varieties were brought back to life thanks to local priests who replanted with material obtained from the Vatican nurseries located in the Colli Romani.

In a study comparing monovarietal wines made with Albarola and Bosco at different altitudes (240 and 430 meters above sea level), bosco made from grapes grown at 430 meters had lower color intensity and was less agreeable to tasters (Cravero, Bonello, Piano, Chiusano, Borsa, Tsolakis, and Lale Demoz 2010). Grapes grown closer to the sea, on the other hand, gave wines with higher sugar content, lower acidity, and greater body (apparently, no relevant differences were observed in the aromatic profiles). If nothing else, this study confirms that Bosco seems to thrive in the marine environment. Interesting research (Romano, Capece, Serafino, Romaniello, and Poeta 2008) has been trying to genetically and technologically characterize yeast strains of *Saccharomyces cerevisiae* isolated from Bosco grapes, hoping to isolate specific yeast ecotypes that are potentially more suited for the vinification of Bosco wines.

Bosco is characterized by medium-large, loosely packed bunches and medium-large, oval berries. It buds early and ripens in the second half of September; it is vigorous and productive, and adapts readily even to difficult environmental conditions, making it a favorite of farmers. It has good resistance to most common grapevine pests. There are three official clones available: CVT 3 and CVT 101 were developed in 2002, and CVT 18 has been available since 2008. Today, Bosco is most common on Liguria's eastern side, while in the Cinque Terre it is especially abundant in Manarola and Riomaggiore. It is essentially unheard of anywhere else in Italy.

Which Wines to Choose and Why

Few people have ever tried a monovarietal bosco, since the variety is always blended in with Albarola, in DOC wines Cinque Terre, Val Polcevera, Colline di Levanto, and Sciacchetrà, as well as IGT blends such as Colline del Genovesato and Golfo dei Poeti. However Walter De Batté has been consulting for a few estates and is now making two different monovarietal boscos, a rarity. The wine is mineral and high acid, with much bigger structure than anything made with pure Albarola or Vermentino, and hints of herbally, ripe yellow fruit that will remind you of some dry Austrian Rieslings. Clearly, Bosco is most important in the production of the sweet wine Sciacchetrà (made from air-dried grapes), characterized by thick, honeyed, apricot jam, dried fig, and herbal aromas and flavors, with hazelnut and toffee notes. When good, Sciacchetrà can be a memorable experience.

WINES TO TRY: For monovarietal Bosco, try: De Batté***. For Sciacchetrà, try: Buranco*** (unmissable) and Possa**. Sciacchetrà is never a monovarietal wine, so these are not examples of pure Bosco wine.

Bovale Grande

WHERE IT'S FOUND: Sardinia. NATIONAL REGISTRY CODE NUMBER: 37. COLOR: red.

At only twenty-seven hectares under vine, almost all located around Cagliari, Bovale Grande (also called Bovale di Spagna or Bovale Mannu) is much rarer than Bovale Sardo. But like Bovale Sardo, Bovale Grande has multiple biotypes, characterized by small, long, and even compound bunches. Its leaf is remarkably different from that of Bovale Sardo: the lateral sinuses are small and subtle and the petiolar sinus (the indentation between the leaf margin and the leaf's main stalk) is large and U-shaped as opposed to Sardo's very large, lyre-shaped lateral sinuses and tighter, U- or V-shaped petiolar sinus. The berries of Bovale Grande I have observed are lighter colored and usually taste sweeter and less tannic than those of Bovale Sardo, and are far bigger; the grape bunch is also much bigger, but stockier. Not surprisingly, the anthocyanin concentration in the skin is much less than that of the obviously darker Bovale Sardo.

These and other differences between the two *Bovale* varieties were apparent to Cettolini already in 1897, who distinguished the two and wrote that Bovale Grande was also known as Cagnulari, Nieddera, Moristeddu, Cadinissa, and Mostaia: we now know that the first two are erroneous synonyms. Modern genetic analysis (Nieddu, Nieddu, Cocco, Erre, and Chessa 2007) has found that Bovale Grande is identical to the Spanish variety Mazuelo, better known as Carignano in Italy. Recent SSR profiling at twelve microsatellite loci on a grapevine collection in Oristano speaks of a strong similarity between Mazuelo and Bovale Grande. Bovale Grande and Carignano do look alike and so this synonym may be correct. Fabio Angius, director of the highly respected Pala estate, told me flat out that most of the Bovale Grande growing on the island (the little that there is) is probably Carignano: "In the 1970s, the commercial grapevine nursery of the Sardinia regional government simply delivered Carignano to all those looking for Bovale Grande, because they already thought the two were identical."

Therefore, it appears that Bovale Grande (like many other Sardinian varieties) is of Spanish origin, a logical enough conclusion, given Spain's four-hundred-year domination of the island—and perhaps, its synonym Bovale di Spagna. Older Bovale Grande might be a specific biotype of Carignano (Mazuelo) that has adapted to Sardinian *terroirs* over the course of centuries, but more recently planted grapevines are liable to be Carignano. It follows that Bovale Grande is probably more correctly viewed as a traditional grape variety of Italy, rather than a truly native one.

WINES TO TRY: I know of no monovarietal Bovale Grande wines commercially for sale, but of course, if Bovale Grande really is Carignano, then monovarietal Bovale Grande wines are far more common than was previously known (see CARIGNANO entry): a far cry from most of the twentieth century, when Bovale Grande was mainly used to spice up weak Monica or Cannonao wines.

Bovale Sardo

WHERE IT'S FOUND: Sardinia. NATIONAL REGISTRY CODE NUMBER: 38. COLOR: red.

We know today that Bovale, which used to be considered one grape, is in fact two different varieties sharing almost the same name. Though it was thought Bovale might have, over the centuries, adapted to Sardinian *terroir* by forming two different biotypes, called Bovale Sardo and Bovale Grande, the two are in fact unrelated (Reale, Pilla, and Angiolillo 2006; Nieddu, Nieddu, Cocco, Erre, and Chessa 2007). Taking a walk through the vineyards clearly shows the two don't look anything alike: Bovale Sardo has smaller berries and a longer, winged, usually very tightly packed bunch (some biotypes are so tightly packed that in humid vintages rot becomes a major problem), while Bovale Grande has a short, stocky bunch with very large, also tightly packed berries. As if that weren't enough, the leaves look completely different too. Recent genetic testing at twelve SSR loci has shown that Bovale Sardo has more in common with Cagnulari and the Spanish variety Graciano (please note I do not write "identical", as others have; for more, see CAGNULARI entry), while Bovale Grande is a close relative (perhaps identical) of Carignano (more correctly called by its Spanish names Cariñena and, even better, Mazuelo; see CARIGNANO entry). Finally, the most recent research reported upon by Nieddu (2011) confirms a previous report by Reale's group (2006) and other data demonstrating that Bovale is not identical to Nieddera, to Molise's Tintilia, nor to Spain's Bobal, as previously believed.

Bovale Sardo is also called Bovaleddu, Cardinissia, Moraiola Minora, Muristellu (or Muristeddu), and an almost endless list of other dialect names that I'll spare you; some of these may actually be different biotypes of Bovale Sardo. Bovaleddu and Muristellu especially are considered biotypes of Bovale Sardo by some Italian experts. The Muristellu synonym deserves further analysis. Manca dell'Arca first mentioned a Muristellu in 1780, while Moris (a professor of botany at Turin University and the director of its botanical gardens, who published the first major work on the flora of Sardinia and adjacent islands) first described the *Bovale* family only in 1837, so it is only logical to wonder if these two luminaries meant different grapes. In this respect, a very interesting study using both ampelographic and microsatellite analysis concluded that Muristellu might not be just one variety but rather a group of distinct grapes sharing morphologic and genetic features (Lovicu, Farci, Sedda, Labra, De Mattia, Grassi, et al. 2010). These results indicate that Muristellu (or Muristeddu) is actually synonymous with a variety called Bovaleddu Antigu, localized in the Marmilla region of Sardinia, and distinct from the *Bovale*s, as well as from Bovaleddu (which other experts believe to be most likely Bovale Sardo) and Bovaleddu Mannu (according to some experts, most likely Bovale Grande). Of course, one might object that this study only analyzed six microsatellite loci, and the general consensus is that more are needed to effectively study closely related grape varieties. This study raises the issue that Muristellu deserves to be better characterized and that further research is needed before drawing conclusions relative to a synonymity between it, Bovale Sardo, Graciano, or any other Sardinian variety. In any case, use of the name Muristellu over the years has been especially confusing, because locals and experts alike have also associated this name with another grape variety, Monastrell (better known as France's Mourvèdre), to which Bovale Sardo can show a morphologic resemblance. However, Monastrell and Bovale Sardo are distinct varieties: besides some ampelographic similarities, the similarity between the Monastrell and Muristellu names likely also contributed to the general confusion.

The main point of contention concerning Bovale Sardo's identity today is whether it is identical to Spain's Graciano, as some experts believe. Analysis of the *Bovale* family of grapes on Sardinia found that Bovale Sardo was identical to Graciano and to another Sardinian grape called Cagnulari, but these results were presented at a conference and published in the proceedings, *Acta Horticulturae*, rather than in a peer-reviewed journal (Nieddu, Nieddu, Cocco, Erre, and Chessa 2007). That said, genetic testing performed on a grapevine collection in Oristano partially confirmed the earlier results, finding that Bovale Sardo is similar to Cagnulari (twenty-three shared alleles out of twenty-four and at least one common allele in all twelve SSR loci analyzed) and Graciano (nineteen alleles out of twenty-four) (Nieddu 2011). However, similar does not mean identical. Furthermore, in an earlier study published in a peer-reviewed journal, researchers found no relationship between either *Bovale* and Graciano or any of the other varieties studied, establishing that each was a separate cultivar (Reale, Pilla, and Angiolillo 2006). However, a careful read reveals that the two samples of Bovale Sardo and two of Bovale Grande they took all had different DNA profiles. In my opinion, given all these observations, it's hard to draw any hard conclusions about what Bovale Sardo and Bovale Grande really are identical to. Cipriani, Spadotto, Jurman, Di Gaspero, Crespan, Meneghetti, et al. (2010) conclude in their study that synonyms can differ from each other in a number of aspects that may be important relative to the wines produced with each. As such differences originate in mutation (not through sexual reproduction), these synonyms maintain a common genetic origin, but ought to be considered singly, because each produces a wine different from the others.

These considerations aside, given the Spanish domination of Sardinia for close to four hundred years (1327–1720), it's likely that Bovale Sardo arrived on Sardinian shores by way of Spain (perhaps of Rioja, should its identity to Graciano prove correct). Therefore, just like Bovale Grande, Bovale Sardo is more correctly viewed as a traditional grape variety of Italy rather than a truly native one. Of course, not even that is simple: other evidence has linked it and other Sardinian cultivars to an island origin, as the result of natural crossings with or mutations of local wild vines (Grassi, Labra, Imazio, Spada, Sgorbati, Scienza, and Sala 2003; partially confounded by Zecca, De Mattia, Lovicu, Labra, Sala, and Grassi 2009). In this respect, Bovale Sardo *would* qualify as a true native of the island. However, while it once seemed that Bovale Sardo was strongly related to the wild grapevines that are still abundant on Sardinia, the most recent data available makes this possibility seem less likely.

Bovale Sardo is a very miserly producer, and for this reason locals call it Baovabi Mascu ("Male Bovale"). There are no official clones of Bovale Sardo available. Old vines are so abundant that estates choose massal selections whenever they need to replant. As of 2009, Bovale Sardo was grown on 784 hectares on Sardinia, mainly in the area around Cagliari, Sardinia's biggest city, but also in the Campidano and Terralba production zones, and distributed diffusely on the island. It does remarkably well on sandy soils like those of Terralba (*terralba* means white earth, because of its high white-sand content), Uras, and San Nicolò d'Arcidano, all *grand crus* for the variety. Due to the high sand content of these soils, most of the vines, many of which are roughly one hundred years old, are all ungrafted. Serdiana is another high-quality island area for Bovale Sardo.

Which Wines to Choose and Why

On Sardinia, Bovale Sardo is generally viewed as having the better fine-wine potential of the two *Bovales*; much Bovale Sardo wine is made from ungrafted vines planted in very sandy soils. The best DOC wines are Campidano di Terralba (occasionally 100 percent Bovale Sardo) and Mandrolisai (Bovale Sardo blended with Cannonau and Monica). Stefano Casadei, a much sought-after viticulture expert (also owner of the Castello del Trebbio estate in Chianti Rufina) finds that Bovale Sardo reminds him a bit of Canaiolo Nero, as both give up color with difficulty: Bovale Sardo "has a ton of color to give, but getting it to do so isn't always easy. I find it needs to be worked at about 30°C for fifteen days to finally get it to release pigments, but it's a very good variety for Sardinia since it tolerates the heat well." Fabio Angius, director of the high-quality Pala estate, agrees and points out that "wine made from Bovale Sardo can be so tannic and brutal that in the Terralbese district the habit was always to add small percentages of lighter wines made from a variety of local, little-known grapes, some of them even table grapes, such as Niedda Pedra Serra, Arramungiau Arrubiu, Arramungiau Biancu, Gregu Nieddu, Greco Nero, Monica, and Pascale." According to Mariano Murru, winemaker at Argiolas, the best-known estate of Sardinia, Bovale Sardo wines are so tannic that sometimes even blending with low-acid, lightly tannic varieties doesn't soften them. He finds that "the best approach is to slightly air-dry it directly on the vine, and use short and light macerations only, or the resulting wines will be too astringent." Angius also adds that it's a difficult variety in the cellar because it tends to be highly reductive, and off odors are always possible: "For example, though we have tried many times over, using indigenous yeasts is just not a good idea with Bovale Sardo; the wine invariably smells too strong and almost sweaty." Everyone I have talked to over the years believes it's a great variety; Angius goes as far as to say that it in his opinion it's the best Sardinian variety of all, especially when aged five or six years. Furthermore, its strong color, tannins, and acid concentrations make it ideal as a blending grape, and it is used to add acidity to wines made with Cannonau and Carignano, structure to those made with Monica, and color to them all. I also point out that Bovale Sardo wines don't taste anything like those made with Cagnulari, even when made by the same producer from grapes grown in the same area. Bovale Sardo is an up-and-coming Sardinian variety that an increasing number of producers are taking a long look at as a possible monovarietal wine; thus, purer Bovale Sardo wines are becoming easier to find all the time.

WINES TO TRY: Pala*** (Essentija, from sixty-year-old and ninety-year-old vines planted on white sandy soil) and Argiolas** (Is Solinas).

Brachetto

WHERE IT'S FOUND: Piedmont. NATIONAL REGISTRY CODE NUMBER: 40. COLOR: red.

Brachetto is an aromatic red grape and yet another Italian native variety that belongs to a group of similarly named grapes whose closely related members are nonetheless distinct from each other. Since none of the other members of the group are known outside their immediate production area and have never been commercially important, I have chosen not to speak of a Brachetto group, for there are only two Brachetto varieties of any consequence. True *Brachetto*s are aromatic, and include Brachetto (its correct name, not Brachetto del Piemonte), Brachetto a Grappolo Grande (also known as Brachettone or Birbet or Brachetto Lungo del Roero, typical of the Roero area in Piedmont), Brachetto Migliardi (or Brachetto di Montabone, grown mainly between Acqui and Nizza Monferrato), a very rare as yet not better defined Brachetto sporadically found in vineyards around Nizza Monferrato in the province of Alessandria, and perhaps a few more still. In the nineteenth century, a very high-quality Brachetto was described by both Gallesio and Di Rovasenda in the coastal Nizza area, but we have no way of knowing if it wasn't just regular Brachetto. Nonaromatic *Brachetto*s (hence not true *Brachetto*s at all, but rather other varieties erroneously called Brachetto) include Brachèt (Canavese area), Brachetto Valsusino (actually Lambrusca di Alessandria), and, across the border in France near Nice, Brachet, a now very rare variety (also spelled Braquet or Braquet Noir). Brachetto is an ancient variety the exact origin of which is unclear, and as we have seen, the many different cultivars also called Brachetto do not simplify matters for grape historians and ampelographers. Furthermore, Moscato Nero, which grows in the same areas of Piedmont as the various *Brachetto*s, was historically called Brachetto too, a mistake still made today.

Brachetto's popularity was boosted immensely by Arturo Bersano's late nineteenth-century decision to make a sparkling version of brachetto using the Charmat method, a wine that met with resounding success—the house of Bersano is still a very important producer of sparkling brachetto today. Brachetto then fell on hard times due to phylloxera and essentially disappeared from production, only to reappear in full force in the 1980s.

Brachetto has a very large bunch, conical (occasionally cylindrical), very long, and loosely packed toward the tip, which is often forked; Brachetto is easy to recognize in Piedmontese vineyards because of its very round leaf. There are three clones of Brachetto (AL-BRA 33, AL-BRA 34, and CVT 20): of these, the CVT 20 is characterized by higher sugar concentrations when ripe and higher levels of aromatic molecules such as geraniol, nerol, and citronellol. Brachetto likes marly-calcareous soils with plenty of clay, as in these sites the variety unleashes all of its considerable aromatic potential (note that wines made on the left side of the Tanaro River, in the Roero area of Piedmont, are not produced with Brachetto, but with the Brachettone variety). Brachetto Migliardi (another related variety, well characterized by Schneider, Soster, and Ricci 1994) is usually mixed in with Brachetto in vineyards around Acqui. It is not as rare as once believed; in fact a good deal of brachetto may be made with large doses of grapes from this variety rather than Brachetto tout court. Brachetto Migliardi ripens a little later than Brachetto and is more productive and vigorous. The general consensus is that it is not as high quality as Brachetto.

Brachetto's home in Italy is the vineyards around Asti and Alessandria, but the recognized *grand cru* for it is Acqui Terme, a delightful spa town that is well worth a visit. There are actually rows grown in Emilia-Romagna too. Elsewhere, Brachetto has been planted in California, Argentina, and Australia.

Which Wines to Choose and Why

The best wines made with Brachetto are labeled Brachetto d'Acqui and made in the vineyards of eighteen towns in the Asti area and eight more towns in the area around Alessandria, but Brachetto d'Asti is often very good too. Brachetto d'Acqui became a DOCG wine in 1996, while the DOC wine Piemonte Brachetto was created in 1994, allowing the wines made in and around eighty-nine towns to be so labeled. That an area so vast and so geologically and climatically different could qualify to produce the same wine tells you two things: first, just how popular Brachetto and its wine are with locals (and politicians are never at a loss when it comes to keeping potential voters happy) and second, the uselessness of some DOC and DOCG labels. Though these rules giving everyone everywhere a chance to make brachetto may have considerable short-term appeal, they may not be in the best interests of the variety, the wine, or ultimately, the producers themselves, who are inevitably going to be faced with falling sales when people tire of yet another lousy wine.

Brachetto can be made both as a still wine and as a sparkler. The latter is delicately sweet and not unlike a red version of Prosecco, though many sparkling brachettos are nothing to write home about. I prefer the still version of brachetto, but if the sparkling success of some brachettos has helped the variety survive and gain a stronger foothold, then I'm all for it. If you get a good sparkling version, chances are you'll like it just as much as everyone else, but the problem is just that: you have to find a good one. Many of these wines, though inexpensive, are not particularly deep or interesting, and they risk alienating an ever-more discerning wine-loving public. I think that if producers want to keep making sparkling Brachetto wines, and to continue to enjoy strong sales, then the onus is on the more serious among them to gradually improve the quality of the bubbly in the bottle.

No such problems beset still versions of Brachetto, most of which are downright delightful. They are wonderfully aromatic and light bodied, with lovely aromas and flavors of sour red cherries, sweet raspberries, cinnamon, and nutmeg: I always find it hard to put the glass back down (in my defense, I find all my friends do the same). Often, the Brachetto experience is akin to sipping on lightly alcoholic red-berry juice (with or without bubbles, depending on the producer). Its characteristics are such that it matches well with fruit cocktails, red-berry tarts, cherry pie, and simple cookies. It also stands up very well to light chocolate desserts. I have met very few people who don't like brachetto once they've tried it; and its bubbly, sweet, perfumed qualities are so different from those of most other wines that your friends will be not just pleasantly surprised, but enthusiastic, when you choose to serve it.

According to popular tradition, brachetto was the preferred beverage of one of the most famous characters of the Italian commedia dell'arte, Gianduja da Gioan d'laduja, or Giovanni of the Jug. The figure drew inspiration for his bubbly high spirits from brachetto: unsurprisingly, the character had the reputation of being a heavy drinker and was just as bubbly as the wine. Having his priorities straight, Giovanni viewed brachetto the ideal wine with which to fill the jug he always carried. In that respect at least, I have a lot in common with Gianduja: there can never be too much good brachetto in my glass (or jug, or thermos, or . . .). I'm not alone: in Piedmontese dialect, brachetto is known as *brachet per cantè*, brachetto to sing with, or a wine so good it makes you sing out of happiness. A glass of the good stuff, and I guarantee you'll be singing too.

In Australia, Fred and Katrina Pizzini make their brachetto from ten-year-old vines. They refer to it at times as "their Pink Moscato," which makes the native grapes purist in me cringe, but hey, they're the current Brachetto pioneers Down Under, so I'm with them. In California, Cougar Vineyards in Temecula Valley also makes a Brachetto (which they call Brachetto Bubbly), and to the best of my knowledge it is the only commercial grower of this variety in the United States.

WINES TO TRY: Forteto della Luja*** (Piemonte Brachetto Passito Pian dei Sogni, made from air-dried grapes), Braida** (Brachetto d'Acqui), Piero Gatti** (Piemonte Brachetto), Marenco** (Pineto Brachetto d'Acqui), Isolabella della Croce* (Brachetto d'Acqui Trentasei), and Fratelli Rovero* (Piemonte Brachetto). Also try Barattieri di Santo Pietro**, an estate in Emilia-Romagna that strangely enough makes an outstanding brachetto (Il Faggio) in very small quantities far away from its Piedmont habitat.

Brachettone del Roero

WHERE IT'S FOUND: Piedmont. NATIONAL REGISTRY CODE NUMBER: not registered. COLOR: red.

All Brachettone's names—it is also called Brachetto a Grappolo Grande or Brachetto Lungo del Roero—clearly indicate it has bigger bunches and berries than Brachetto: the *-one* ending in Italy always implies "bigger." Its grapes are also more aromatic than Brachetto's, with aromas so intense that *Moscatos* will spring to mind. Brachettone grows best on well-exposed sites with soils that are not excessively humid, and is a vigorous, rustic variety with good productivity and disease resistance, though it is prone to red spider infestation. It is very recognizable come fall because its leaves turn a beautiful red-orange. Historically, it was also considered a good table grape.

Brachettone is not yet listed in the National Registry, as its proposed inclusion a few years ago met with refusal. I have been told that authorities did not wish to allow another Brachetto-like name, which seems silly: Brachettone has been documented in Piedmont for at least three hundred years and an alternative name such as Brachetto Lungo would have been no different than Glera Lungo and the like. Besides, Brachettone works just fine, in my view. The fact is, many producers don't like the name Brachettone, and resist using it. If you consider that brachettone is also the name of a very good *salume* made in Emilia-Romagna near Bobbio, you can understand why some producers are miffed at having to use the same name for their grape. Some producers have taken to calling the variety Birbet, which is the name of the wine made with it, but others don't like that name much either, and so still refer to the variety simply as Brachetto, which is not a good idea, as that does nothing to further the cause of their specific grape variety and wine, and only engenders confusion. Local producers tell me that Brachettone will be listed soon, though I'm not sure anybody knows under which name.

In Italy, Brachettone del Roero grows on the left bank of the Tanaro River, in the Roero production zone and has been doing so for over four hundred years. Very fine Brachettone vineyards can be found near the towns of Monteu Roero, Canale, and Montà.

Which Wines to Choose and Why

Due to the nomenclature difficulties, the official name of the wine made with Brachettone is birbet, a *vino rosso da tavola* that is also often labeled *mosto parzialmente fermentato*, meaning it is an only partially fermented grape must. For this reason, birbets usually sport a catchy 6 percent alcohol content, or less, on the label. Though it can also be made as a dry wine, most producers prefer it as a sparkling and a delicately sweet version. In general, I find birbets to be a little more rustic and wilder in their aroma and flavor profile than sparkling wines made with Brachetto. I also find birbet to be more saline and tannic, and to give an impression of higher overall acidity. Though birbet is loaded with rose and red-cherry aromas and flavors, wines made with Brachetto seem to have more balance and gentler aromatics, with more floral notes compared to birbet's herbal, fruity, and spicy (nutmeg, cinnamon, marjoram, bay leaf) nuances. Rarer air-dried wines are also made.

WINES TO TRY: Giovanni Almondo*** (Fosso della Rosa), Malvirà***, Cascina Chicco***, Filippo Gallino***, Cantine Rolfo**, Michele Taliano**, Giacomo Vico**, and Malabaila di Canale**.

Cagnulari

WHERE IT'S FOUND: Sardinia. NATIONAL REGISTRY CODE NUMBER: 45. COLOR: red.

Cagnulari is also known as Bastardo Nero, Cada Reio, Caldareddu, and Cagliunari; the first synonym creates confusion since historically there was another grape (perhaps a biotype of Cagnulari) called Bastardo Nero in Sardinia, perhaps related to the grape known as Bastardo in Spain or Trousseau in France. Cagnulari was first described by Di Rovasenda in 1877, but its diffusion was so limited that Manca dell'Arca (1780), who focused mainly on varieties grown around Cagliari, didn't mention it. Cettolini in 1897 found, not unreasonably, that Cagnulari resembled the *Bovales*, while Cara (1909) erroneously thought it had more in common with Cannonau. In 1962, Bruni, Breviglieri, and Casini reiterated Cagnulari's resemblance to the *Bovales*.

I have reviewed past impressions of important grape scientists with regard to Cagnulari because today many believe that Cagnulari is identical to Bovale Sardo (but not Bovale

Grande) and to Graciano. The reason for this is the oft-cited study by Nieddu, Nieddu, Cocco, Erre, and Chessa (2007) that established via microsatellite analysis an identity between these varieties, two Italian and one Spanish. If this were true, then Cagnulari would not be a native Italian grape, but rather a traditional one, probably brought over from Spain during roughly four centuries of Spanish domination (1323–1720) of Sardinia. Though I have no objections to this proposed scenario, which actually makes a great deal of sense, I do have issues with the identification process itself. First, to the best of my knowledge, Nieddu's study is to date the only one attesting to the exclusive relationship of Graciano, Bovale Sardo, and Cagnulari. However, these results were not published in a peer-reviewed journal, but as the proceedings of a conference (Acta Horticulturae). Also, an earlier study established that the Bovales of Sardinia were distinct varieties (Reale, Pilla, and Angiolillo 2006). What's more, in this same study of the two pairs of Bovale Grande and Bovale Sardo accessions, the members of each pair had different genetic profiles, meaning that the Bovales under study were in fact, at least in part, different varieties. So the question immediately springs to mind: if this research group can collect grapevine accessions that are not what they are supposed to be, then is it not also possible that the Nieddu, Nieddu, Cocco, Erre, and Chessa study (2007) compared apples and oranges?

As noted before, mistakes such as these are always possible in ampelology: researchers draw their conclusions based on the grapevines sampled for the study, but if accessions are wrongly identified from the start then results are inevitably going to be inexact, and grapes will be believed identical when in fact they are not.

So it's not surprising then that genetic profiling done very recently on Cagnulari accessions in an Oristano field collection (Nieddu 2011) showed that though Cagnulari and Bovale Sardo share twenty-three of twenty-four alleles, they are distinguishable by one allele on locus VVMD31. Hence, Cagnulari and Bovale Sardo would appear to be very similar indeed, but not identical. The same study showed that Bovale Sardo and Graciano share nineteen of twenty-four alleles, so these two cultivars aren't identical either. It follows that Graciano, Cagnulari, and Bovale Sardo cannot all be the same grape. Another recent study also failed to show synonymity between the Bovales and Cagnulari (Lovicu, Farci, Sedda, Labra, De Mattia, Grassi, et al. 2010). However, given that Cagnulari shares numerous morphologic features with Bovale Sardo, and that the two share alleles in common, it appears Cagnulari is at least closely related to Bovale Sardo. It is possible that Cagnulari is a biotype of Bovale Sardo that has slowly adapted to its island habitat over the centuries. Cipriani, Spadotto, Jurman, Di Gaspero, Crespan, Meneghetti, et al. (2010) conclude in their study that "genetically identical" members of a cultivar can express different morphologic and behavioral traits that are important to wine production and are, according to the authors "often worthy of being individually considered."

Cagnulari has medium-large, conical-cylindrical bunches, as Bovale Sardo does; its berries are usually a little more oval than Bovale Sardo's. Also, Cagnulari's leaves tend to be rounder and most often only have three lobes, while Bovale Sardo's usually have five. Both varieties ripen late, in October, and have good resistance to most common vineyard pests except botrytis (and perhaps slightly to oidium). There are no official clones of Cagnulari available. Though once common in Sardinia, Cagnulari plantings decreased greatly in the twentieth century (cultivation declined from 1,800 hectares in 1963 to 266 hectares in 2009) and the wine was no longer being made in any significant commercial volumes. Salvatore Cherchi, owner of the Giovanni Maria Cherchi estate, which has singlehandedly done the most to save the variety and bring it back to everyone's attention, believes that Cagnulari's extreme rot sensitivity is the main reason why the cultivar risked extinction on Sardinia—though low fertility and yields didn't endear it to farmers either. Today, its diffusion is limited to the area around the Sardinian city of Sassari (where it represents roughly 13 percent of the area under vine), and in the countryside around Issiri, Ossi, Tissi, Sorso, Usini, and Usi. According to Cherchi, the countryside around Usini is potentially Cagnulari's one *grand cru;* the variety seems to prefer its calcareous-clay soils. More than other Sardinian cultivars, Cagnulari maintains a snobby, aloof disposition in its remote northeastern Sardinian home.

Which Wines to Choose and Why

Everyone has favorite grape varieties and wines, and I'll admit Cagnulari is one of mine. It is most often used in blends (usually with Cannonao and Pascale), but 100 percent Cagnulari wines can be made, for example in the DOC Alghero. Cherchi's version is a joy: lovely pinkish-red hue, fragrant red-berry aromas, refreshing midweight body, and plenty of vinosity and fruity-floral charm. I find that Cagnulari wines are a great deal more perfumed and lighter in body than those made with Bovale Sardo, which are far more herbal and tarry in their aroma and flavor profile, and more tannic and tougher in texture. The two wines really don't taste anything alike to me.

WINES TO TRY: Giovanni Maria Cherchi***, Chessa**, Cantina Santa Maria La Palma*, Carpante, Poderi Parpinello.

Calabrese

WHERE IT'S FOUND: Sicily, Calabria. NATIONAL REGISTRY CODE NUMBER: 46 (where Nero d'Avola is listed as a synonym). COLOR: red.

For centuries, Nero d'Avola has also been called Calabrese in all regions of Italy, from Calabria to Sicily to Tuscany, and Calabrese is the official name listed in Italy's National Registry of grape varieties. However, Calabrese is a name used to describe other varieties in Italy (usually erroneously) and everyone in Italy and the world knows this grape variety much better as Nero d'Avola. For that reason, I'll refer to it as Nero d'Avola in the rest of this discussion.

In fact, the name Nero d'Avola derives from the Sicilian dialect name Calau Avulisi, which, given its spelling and pronunciation, you'd be excused for thinking meant "Calabrese," but you'd be wrong. Calau Avulisi means "coming down from Avola," the little town near Ragusa from which this feisty grape set out to conquer the rest of the island, and the world. So Nero d'Avola's nickname, Calabrese, was arrived at via a series of modifications: from Calau Avulisi, to Calaurisi, Calavrisi, Calabrisi, and Calabrese. Others have suggested that *Calavrisi* is simply a word in dialect meaning "from Calabria," thereby hinting at a possible Calabrian origin of the variety, but this seems a simplistic interpretation of the name's genesis, and few experts endorse it. The Nero d'Avola moniker is a more modern evolution, due to the typically Italian habit of calling dark grapes Nero-Something; the place from where the variety supposedly hails is one of the "Somethings" most often attached. Hence, the dark-berried grape from Avola became Nero d'Avola in popular winespeak, but the official name remains Calabrese, for now. Already in the early seventeenth century, Cupani wrote of a round-berried Calavrisi (while Nero d'Avola's is more elongated, almost elliptical) but only in the nineteenth century did the Calabrese name become again associated with Avola and the black color descriptor.

Ampelographically, Nero d'Avola has medium-large, conical, compact, winged bunches, with medium-large oval berries. There are four official clones of Nero d'Avola (AM 28, AM 39, Ampelos VCP 2, and Regione Sicilia 64), but according to Alessio Planeta of the world-famous Planeta estate, which has done so much to bring Nero d'Avola into the limelight, a large number of very different biotypes exist, born out of adaptation to Sicily's many different *terroirs* over the centuries. "There must be at least one hundred different Nero d'Avolas out there," he shakes his head smiling, "I say this because in our trials with Nero d'Avola grown in different parts of the island, even using similar winemaking and viticultural techniques, the wines could not have been more different; to my mind, the soil and climate alone cannot explain the amazing diversity of the wines." Four such biotypes, simply named A through D, have recently been the subject of study by the University of Milan, and two are apparently of very high quality, one with round and the other with oval berries (the latter is believed to be the better of the two). Nero d'Avola is very vigorous, so canopy management is essential, but despite its vigor, difficulties with flowering impact yields greatly. Nero d'Avola generally flowers early in the season and ripens by mid-September. It is blended with Frappato in wines like Cerasuolo di Vittoria. But it ripens two weeks earlier than Frappato, and manages well even in damper, cooler soils (Frappato does not, preferring dry and hot conditions) and so is planted in areas where its complementary variety cannot grow well. However, Nero d'Avola also likes heat and this is why it is often trained close to the ground.

At over eighteen thousand hectares in 2010 data, Nero d'Avola is Sicily's second most-common cultivar, almost three times more abundant than Ansonica (Inzolia), the third most-planted Sicilian variety. Nero d'Avola's popularity is well exemplified by what happened between 2000 and 2008, when a 33 percent increase in plantings was recorded on the island, mainly in its southeastern corner, Nero d'Avola's original home and where the best vineyards are located. Other data, from 2008, reports that there were over 19,000 hectares planted to Nero d'Avola, but it's not clear if this number referred to Italy as a whole or just Sicily; were the latter true, then it could mean that some of the wind is sagging out of Nero d'Avola's sails (and sales). Still, the only part of Sicily where Nero d'Avola is not prevalent is in the northeastern corner, the domain of the *Nerello* varieties. Nonetheless, Nero d'Avola is now the seventh most-common wine grape variety in Italy as a whole, and is starting to attract interest outside Italy too. The grape's ability to tolerate highly saline soils and heat without dropping its acidity has garnered it increasing interest by producers in the world's warmer wine production areas. In Australia for example, there are numerous plantings in Adelaide Hills, McLaren Vale, Geelong, Heathcote (in the ancient, red, rocky volcanic soils of the driest, most northern part of Heathcote), Riverina, Riverland (another suitably hot area), and Margaret River and a number of estates are making Nero d'Avola wines. In California, it is planted in Sonoma County, Tracy Hills, and Ukiah Valley, among other regions. Since Nero d'Avola buds relatively early and ripens late (and in these lands, apparently later than it does in Sicily), there is a potential frost risk at both the start and finish of the growing season in cooler areas such as the Ukiah Valley.

Which Wines to Choose and Why

Any Sicilian red wine is likely to include Nero d'Avola; of the blends, I strongly recommend Cerasuolo di Vittoria, now a DOCG, in which Nero d'Avola is blended with Frappato, a match seemingly made in heaven, as the floral fragrance and light body of Frappato marry well with Nero d'Avola's richer texture. Those Cerasuolo di Vittoria wines that are made with larger amounts of Nero d'Avola (wines can have as much as 40 percent Frappato) are easily recognized, invariably richer and deeper, but less perfumed. DOC wines of note include Delia Nivolelli and Contea di Sclafani, but the list is virtually endless (and includes Alcamo, Marsala, Noto, and Eloro), as is the list of IGT wines in which Nero d'Avola can be used (at last count, close to sixty different IGTs).

Nero d'Avola is by far Sicily's most important red wine, and is being increasingly bottled on its own as a monovarietal. Crazy blends still exist though, such as those with large percentages of Merlot, Syrah, or Cabernet Sauvignon, declared up front or not (and in my opinion, far too many "important" and highly scored Nero d'Avola wines reek of these other varieties). Such blends do absolutely nothing for the variety, camouflaging its characteristic aromas and flavors, replacing them with the tried and true and instantly recognizable black pepper, graphite, chocolate, and coffee notes now common to wines made all over the world. Very small percentages of similar international varieties added to Nero d'Avola wines might be another story, but I still greatly prefer the monovarietal bottlings.

Variable quality levels is still the biggest problem with Nero d'Avola wines. The variety is used to make wines ranging from absolutely horrible to downright memorable. In truth, this has always been the problem with Nero d'Avola; as the poor wines far outnumber the good ones, it's no wonder that the variety didn't excite imaginations for the better part of the twentieth century. Still, if you were to ask a local producer's grandfather about his youth, the gentleman would be quick to say that one of his big childhood amusements (in an age when there was no TV, video, or Internet) was to go to the local port with *his* grandfather and watch the tankers filled with wine leave for distant shores. Those tankers would have been full of Nero d'Avola, on their way to Tuscan, Ligurian, and French ports, aimed at increasing the color and alcohol of anemic red wines made in those colder, less sunlight-blessed northern lands. That all began to change with the renaissance of Sicilian wine in the 1980s: better winemaking and viticulture allowed Nero d'Avola and its wines to surge to the top of the heap. There was a moment in the late 1990s in which Nero d'Avola was *the* wine to drink at home and in restaurants in Italy: much like Argentinean Malbec today, people everywhere just couldn't get, or drink, enough. However, just as it was quick to rise, Nero d'Avola was quick to fall: a victim of its own success, and the greed of some who churned out too many rustic, unpleasant, and nonsensical wines. So today, while still an important variety and wine, Nero d'Avola wines have become a slightly harder sell, at least in Italy: "going out of stock" bins in large wineshops in Rome or Milan will reveal plenty of Nero d'Avola wines. Another big problem has always been off-island bottlers and the suspect quality of their "Nero d'Avola" wines, which have done much to damage the cultivar's reputation. Recent government steps to curb this practice has been welcome news for all those who love Nero d'Avola wines.

In fairness, Nero d'Avola's great moment of popularity did serve an important purpose: it made clear, once and for all, that the variety is capable of making at least very good wines (and sometimes great ones, in the right hands), and can take its place among Italy's noble (or almost noble) varieties. Its bright dark-red cherry and spicy, aromatic herb aromas and flavors are appreciated by wine drinkers everywhere, as are its low astringency and high but usually harmonious acidity. In my view, Nero d'Avola's potential greatness is best harnessed in Sicily's southeastern corner around the city of Ragusa, but monovarietal Nero d'Avola wines differ greatly in their expression depending on *terroirs*. This has been clearly shown over the years by Vito and Matteo Catania of the famous Gulfi estate, who along with their winemaker Salvo Foti, have done more than anyone else to showcase what Nero d'Avola can do in different *terroirs*. To their credit, theirs is the only estate bottling many different single-vineyard Nero d'Avola wines. That Nero d'Avola can express site sensitivity admirably was already well known to many winemakers and Sicilian producers at the end of the twentieth century, but only Gulfi has bothered to take advantage of this feature. Nero d'Avola from different vineyard sites in the manner of Burgundy and Pinot Nero, or Piedmont and Barolo is essentially unheard of. Most Sicilian producers are quite happy in making an entry-level bottling and perhaps a more complex reserve-type bottling (usually christened with a fancy, fantastical name), but I really believe this limits what Nero d'Avola might be capable of expressing, and amounts to a missed opportunity.

For example, when made from grapes grown at higher altitudes in the central part of the island, Nero d'Avola wines tend to have paler colors and more mineral personalities; in central Sicilian vineyards at lower altitudes and warmer climates, they are richer and more structured. Nero d'Avola wines from Agrigento and Riesi, farther south, can be astringent yet fruity. Around Noto, wines have great ripeness, with herbal and saline notes (almost anchovy-like), while those made in nearby Vittoria are lighter and more floral, almost gentle, and actually resemble wines made with Frappato. I point that out not to insinuate that Frappato is blended into supposedly monovarietal wines, but to highlight how Nero d'Avola grown here seems dominated by the area's unique *terroir*, exuding some of the floral-fruity charm of the area's monovarietal Frappato wines and seeming less "Nero d'Avolesque" than monovarietal Nero d'Avola wines made elsewhere. Wines from Pachino, perhaps the single greatest *grand cru* of all for Nero d'Avola (another *grand cru* is the triangle formed between Butera, Mazara and Riesi) can be almost pungent, with aromas and flavors reminiscent of ripe tomato sauce, aromatic herbs, dark cherries, and tar, with saline nuances. In short, they are Nero d'Avola wines at their most complex, a characteristic that monovarietal wines made with this grape don't always exude in spades. To generalize, Nero d'Avola wines from old vines (of which there is no shortage in Sicily) can be remarkably good, but finding the best wines means doing some homework, and knowing not just a little bit about the respective Sicilian *terroirs*, but also what the producer believes in, and does.

Australia makes a number of very good, interesting Nero d'Avola wines that seem to me generally fruitier and brighter than Sicilian versions, which are usually more herbal and tarry: try Bassham, Brash Higgins (NDV Amphora Project), Chalmers, Ducks in a Row, Golden Grove Estate (their Nero d'Avola won a gold medal and Top of Class honors at the 2012 Australian Small Winemakers Show), Montevecchio (estate grown and made by the Chalmers family), and Staffordshire Lane. Other estates such as Politini, Kay Brothers Amery, and Pertaringa have planted Nero d'Avola but I haven't tried their wines or don't know of any bottled by them with this variety yet. In California, Chiarito Vineyards (in Mendocino) and Sonoma's Jacuzzi Family Vineyards and VJB Wines are good sources of Nero d'Avola. I find it interesting that in California, Nero d'Avola seems to have been planted in what are generally thought of as cooler microclimates. In Texas, Brennan Vineyards has made a very good, even complex Nero D'Avola called Dark Horse.

WINES TO TRY: Gulfi*** (the best producer of Nero d'Avola wines, and by a long shot. Their Nerojbleo, a blend of Nero d'Avola grapes from different sites, is a standout, but my two favorite wines by this estate are Nerobufaleffj and Nerosanlorè; the entry-level Rossojbleo, which is not pure nero d'Avola, is almost Pinot Neroesque in its charm and lightness, and Nerobaronj and Nero Maccarj are also good), Feudo Montoni*** (the old-vine Selezione Vrucara is a must, but the entry-level Nero d'Avola is a thing of beauty), Donnafugata** (Mille e una Notte), Planeta* (Santa Cecilia), and Tasca d'Almerita's (Rosso del Conte: very famous but I find vintages of the last fifteen years too often marred by strongly herbal and cedary aromas and other very spicy flavors). For Cerasuolo di Vittoria, a Nero d'Avola–Frappato blend, try: Cos***, Planeta***, and Valle dell'Acate** (Il Moro). Barone la Lumia** (Nikao) makes a very rare sweet Nero d'Avola Passito, from air-dried grapes.

Canaiolo Nero

WHERE IT'S FOUND: Tuscany, Umbria, Lazio, Marche, Liguria. NATIONAL REGISTRY CODE NUMBER: 49. COLOR: red.

You know a variety is problematic when its name most likely derives from the Latin *dies caniculares*, literally the dog days of August, because this variety changes color between the end of July and mid-August. Another hypothesis links the name to the dog rose *(rosa canina)*, the fragrance of which is evoked by good examples of Canaiolo Nero wines.

Also called Merla in parts of the region, Canaiolo Nero is a very ancient Tuscan variety, mentioned in documents dating back to the early fourteenth century, when it was referred to as Uva Canaijuola (de' Crescenzi 1303); later it was called Canaiolo Colore by Villifranchi (1773) and Acerbi (1825). Gallesio in his *Pomona Italiana* describes it as a great match for Sangiovese, softening wines made with the latter variety while Sangiovese allowed Canaiolo Nero wines to age better (and I couldn't agree more). Prior to the sixteenth century, most of the wine made in Chianti was largely Canaiolo Nero and not Sangiovese. Nevertheless, in 1873 Bettino Ricasoli, inventor of the original Chianti blend, decided that the best Chianti possible was seven-tenths Sangiovese, two-tenths Canaiolo Nero, and one-tenth Malvasia Bianca Toscana Lunga—no Cabernet Sauvignon or Merlot in sight, though Ricasoli knew those grapevines too.

Things have since changed immensely in Tuscan wine (not always for the better), and Canaiolo Nero today has only a marginal role. Many factors contributed to Canaiolo Nero being forgotten, if not abandoned. After the phylloxera onslaught, Canaiolo Nero, like Malbec in Cahors, showed a very poor adaptation to American rootstocks: it is difficult to graft. "For that reason, in Tuscany it had long been cultivated by letting it run free around trees, right up until recent times, though this didn't do much for the ripeness level of the grapes," says Maurizio Castelli, arguably the modern winemaker who knows Tuscan grape varieties best. According to Roberto Bandinelli of the University of Florence, another huge problem posed by Canaiolo Nero is the almost complete lack of virus-free grapevine material, making for rickety, slowly growing, irregularly yielding grapevines, never a thrilling sight for wine producers. The fact that it's a late ripener with thin-skinned berries never helped endear it to farmers either. Bandinelli continues: "It can be very productive at times, though it's not especially vigorous—but unless many bunches per vine are thinned, the final wine will have an unstable, light color." Canaiolo Nero is also susceptible to problems with spiders, since its leaf has a downy underside, a perfect habitat for these critters. (Canaiolo Bianco, now known to be a distinct variety also called Drupeggio, shares this downy characteristic, making it resemble Canaiolo Nero.) It buds later than Sangiovese, but usually ripens earlier, in late September or the first ten days of October.

Thus far, Canaiolo Nero hasn't been much helped by clonal research to improve on the original. Lamberto Frescobaldi recalls that "back in the 1980s, Professor Pisani and his then-assistant Roberto Bandinelli came to the Castello di Nipozzano and selected what eventually became two commercially available clones, clone 6 and clone 8; the latter was the less productive of the two." Of the clones commercially available today (Rauscedo 6, Nipozzano 8, Mugello 30, CAN-N-6, CAN-N-8, Fedit 23 CH, Fedit 24 CH, Fedit 25 CH, VCR 10, VCR 109), the most interesting from an enological perspective, according to a study by Giannetti, Epifani, Perria, and Valentini (2012) presented at the Fourth National Viticulture Congress held in Asti July 10–12, 2012 (and not yet been subjected to the peer-review process of a major journal), are Fedit 24 CH and Fedit 25 CH, which have better color, more intense aromas, and flavors of balsamic and spicy red fruits. The same study showed that Canaiolo Nero, though low in overall anthocyanins (which explains the wine's usually light color) is nonetheless rich in malvin (a darker, more stable anthocyanin), and in particular, has ten to fifteen acylated anthocyanins, mainly of the p-cumarate form, differentiating it neatly from Sangiovese, which has virtually no acylated anthocyanins.

Nevertheless, Bandinelli points out that Canaiolo Nero's reputation as viticulturally difficult and enologically uninspiring is partly undeserved, the result of careless nursery practices. More often than not, when estates asked for Canaiolo Nero grapevines in the 1970s and 1980s, nurseries would send vines of Bonamico, Canaiolo Nero Pratese (a biotype), and other high-yielding varieties, all of which resemble Canaiolo Nero phenotypically but have far poorer winemaking potential. In this way, Canaiolo Nero's reputation was greatly tarnished with producers everywhere. Even today, Canaiolo Nero is mistaken for other varieties, particularly *Colorino*s, grape varieties that add color to wines but often little else. In fact, in northern coastal Tuscany, growers believe that two different biotypes of Canaiolo Nero exist in the area, Merla and Tintoretto. Clearly the latter is a coloring variety, given its name. This situation is not uncommon: at the world-famous Lungarotti estate in Umbria, where for decades the famous Rubesco wine has been labeled as 70 percent Sangiovese and 30 percent Canaiolo Nero, they are now aware that their supposed Canaiolo Nero is Colorino del Valdarno instead. In fact, much of the Umbrian so-called Canaiolo Nero used in blends such as Rosso Orvietano is one of the many *Colorino*s instead, though as this is a fairly recent discovery that even most Italians aren't aware of, you'll still find it written everywhere that Canaiolo Nero is quite abundant in Umbria as well as in Tuscany. Winemaker Lorenzo Landi confirms that this was a mistake made all over Umbria, and he also believes that much of the Canaiolo Nero planted in Umbria is in fact one of the *Colorino*s. Now that I know this, I can't say I am at all surprised: over the years, I tasted many Umbrian "Canaiolo Nero" wines that struck me as being very unlike Canaiolo Nero, though I thought it was due to a specific, different tasting Umbrian biotype. Landi's hypothesis makes sense, since the aroma and flavor profiles of those Umbrian wines (namely an obvious green streak that in my experience canaiolo nero wines rarely show) really do resemble those of the *Colorino*s.

Problems aside, most producers and winemakers admit that Canaiolo Nero has qualities that have gone unappreciated. "There just isn't enough good Canaiolo Nero to go around," says Castelli, "so people never get the chance to see what the grape can really deliver. I use it whenever I can. Normally at Badia di Coltibuono we include 3–4 percent in the regular Chianti Classico, but sometimes that percentage creeps upwards, like 10 percent in 2004." Filippo Rocchi of Castelvecchio, a high-quality estate in the Chianti Colli Fiorentini with another star winemaker, Luca D'Attoma, is a believer: "It's an underrated variety that gives wines that surprise for their elegance and drinkability." Rocchi owns forty-year-old vines that look different from most other Canaiolo Nero: the bunches and berries are smaller and more loosely packed. Perhaps he's just fortunate to own a higher-quality biotype. "I think that some of the viticultural Darth Vader reputation is exaggerated," jokes Sebastiano Capponi, owner of the high-quality Villa Calcinaia estate in Greve in Chianti, another individual who thinks Canaiolo Nero is a great variety. He explains that "Canaiolo Nero is easy to spot in the vineyards because it grows erect, straight up in the air: if it were up to my vineyard workers, I'd be growing only Canaiolo Nero." Canaiolo Nero does very well in light-red sandy soils such as those of Barberino Val d'Elsa in Chianti Classico, where Castello della Paneretta owns some of the best Canaiolo vines of Italy, though Rocchi thinks it does best in soils containing at least a bit of gravel mixed with a little clay. As Bandinelli, whose name is more usually associated with Sangiovese, told me while we walked through vineyards together one day, "I believe Canaiolo Nero is a major grape variety in all respects."

Canaiolo Nero is not the only colorful member of the family. Of course, Canaiolo Bianco is not a true *Canaiolo* at all, but Drupeggio, a distinct native Umbrian variety, and is therefore discussed separately (see CANAIOLO BIANCO, chapter 5). For its part, Canaiolo Rosa is a mutation of Canaiolo Nero, though strangely enough, it is listed as a separate variety in the National Registry, at number 314. Its exact birthplace is unknown, but is thought to be either the Montecarlo or Rignano sull'Arno (near Florence) areas. Today its presence is limited to only a few vines in the provinces of Florence and Lucca, usually interspersed with Canaiolo Nero, and usually blended with the latter, though some farmers have told me they think it makes, perhaps not surprisingly given the variety's name, a good *rosato*. A likely biotype of Canaiolo Nero is Cannaiola, used to make the wine Cannaiola di Marta, and grown in Lazio's Tuscia region on the shores of Lake Bolsena, its historic and natural habitat. It was first described by Cinelli in 1884 and though he felt it was a different variety from Canaiolo Nero, most experts today believe Cannaiola is a biotype of the former that differs noticeably in some vitricultural aspects, such as the period of the year when the berries turn color or when they are harvested, and vigor. Differences between the two varieties were recently illustrated by Bignami and Filippetti (2002) and again by Muganu, Dangl, Aradhya, Frediani, Scossa, and Stover (2009). In the latter study, noteworthy ampelographic differences were found between Cannaiola and Canaiolo Nero: the former was characterized by a later budbreak, while the latter presented a different color of shoots and young leaves, a greater density of hair on the underside of mature leaves, more loosely-packed bunches, and more (but smaller) seeds per berry. The study also described two distinct biotypes of Cannaiola in Tuscia: Cannaiola di Marta (CM VT 1) and Cannaiola Macchie di Marta (CMM VT 2). SSR profiling at sixteen loci proved that these two biotypes and Canaiolo Nero were genetically identical. According to Biasi, Brunori, Ceccariglia, and Botti who presented data relative to Cannaiola at a conference on *terroir* in 2010, it seems to perform best in well exposed, sandy-rich soils at higher hillside altitudes; productivity falls off in soils that are rich in clay, probably because good water drainage is a necessity for Cannaiola. In Tuscia's *terroir*, Cannaiola performs better than Canaiolo Nero, accumulating higher sugar concentrations and total polyphenols. I find this to be yet another example of the potential importance of using locally adapted biotypes in the production of wines that are meant to be typical of a specific area.

Outside Italy, Canaiolo Nero has been planted in California's Temecula, Shenandoah, and Napa Valleys.

Which Wines to Choose and Why

Canaiolo Nero is unmistakably associated with Tuscany, where it is the ultimate blending agent for Sangiovese in the many DOC or DOCGs where the latter variety is king. Thus, Canaiolo Nero is an important part of Chianti, Vino Nobile di Montepulciano, Carmignano, and many other wines, including less-famous names such as Montecarlo and Colli dell'Etruria Centrale. Monovarietal Canaiolo Nero wines are available, often but not always as *rosati*. These wines can be excellent and are worth a search. A DOC that comes close to monovarietal Canaiolo Nero wines is Tuscany's Pietraviva Canaiolo (minimum 85 percent Canaiolo Nero), but tellingly, no producers of note engage in its production. Winemaking prowess is needed: the wine tends to undergo very strong reduction from the moment the malolactic transformation has been completed to the following spring, but then opens up in pretty floral and sour red-cherry aromas and flavors.

I love Canaiolo Nero, one of Italy's most misunderstood and less appreciated varieties; and in my opinion, the consequences of this nihilistic attitude have been dire. The fact is, there is simply no better partner for Sangiovese in the world; and therein lies Canaiolo Nero's greatness. More than any other variety—even Merlot—Canaiolo Nero blends with Sangiovese in an absolutely magical way. Merlot can soften Sangiovese's tannins and acidity, making it Sangiovese's best partner among the international varieties: certainly far better than Cabernet Sauvignon, the tannins and acidity of which are the last thing Sangiovese needs, or Syrah, which adds a spiciness and superripe fruit notes of no benefit to Sangiovese. In contrast, Canaiolo Nero supports and improves Sangiovese and never takes over the wine as Merlot will tend to do. With a healthy dollop of

Canaiolo Nero (I would say at least 10–15 percent) Sangiovese's bright floral and red-berry notes gain in power and clarity, resulting in a refined mouthfeel and a lightness of being that can be wondrous. By contrast, wines containing internationals are marked by black fruit, tar, and inky notes that have less appeal than the refined fruity charm of the Sangiovese–Canaiolo Nero combination. In this respect, Canaiolo Nero acts much like a co-factor with Sangiovese: co-factors are those molecules that help reactions catalyzed by enzymes run smoother, by improving enzyme efficiency. Only Malvasia Nera comes as close to being Sangiovese's ideal sparring partner. Over the years, I have tasted countless well-kept Chiantis from the 1960s and 1970s (brimming not just with Canaiolo Nero, but with white varieties too) and they are all infinitely more delicious and drinkable today than some very thick and rich Cabernet- and Merlot-laced wines from the 1980s and 1990s.

When good, a Canaiolo Nero wine offers a light-to-medium body, and refreshing, lightly tannic experience, with pretty red-berry and delicate floral notes and plenty of saline tang. Le Terrine by Castello della Paneretta, a reportedly 50 percent Canaiolo Nero and 50 percent Sangiovese blend, is truly amazing, one of Italy's best but least-known red wines. Stefano Casadei of the Castello del Trebbio estate in Chianti Rufina points out that the wonderful fruitiness and drinkability of these wines explain why Canaiolo Nero was the Tuscan grape of choice to make *nouveau*-style wines (*novelli* in Italian) thirty years ago when these wines were more in demand. Rocca di Castagnoli, another excellent Chianti estate, also owns very high-quality Canaiolo Nero vines, but does not bottle a monovarietal Canaiolo Nero either. The Lazio wine Cannaiola di Marta from the shores of Lake Bolsena is made from lightly air-dried grapes and is delicately sweet and rich.

WINES TO TRY: Castelvecchio*** (Numero Otto), Flli Grati*** (Mondo Canaiolo), Podere Lavandaro** (Vigna Nera, made in very small quantities), and Podere Terenzuola** (Merla della Miniera, where they also make a *rosato*). For *rosati*, try: Sono Montenidoli*** (Canaiuolo, by the famed Vernaccia di San Gimignano producer) and Villa Calcinaia*** (Rosato). For Umbria, try: Le Poggiette* (though it tastes more like a *Colorino* to me; I could be wrong). For Liguria, try Possa** (U Neigru Rosso di Possaitaru). For Lazio's Cannaiola di Marta, try: Castelli**, San Savino**, and San Lazzaro**. If there exist any monovarietal bottlings outside Italy, I have not yet been fortunate enough to taste them.

Canina Nera

WHERE IT'S FOUND: Emilia-Romagna. NATIONAL REGISTRY CODE NUMBER: 50. COLOR: red.

Canina Nera probably represents yet another case of ampelographic misidentification leading to erroneous genetic conclusions, in the vein of previous mistaken identities such as Mondeuse Noire / Refosco and Albariño / Savagnin. As we shall see, Canina Nera is most likely not identical to Fortana (another variety typical of Emilia-Romagna), despite what has been written elsewhere.

Also known as Canèna, Canina Nera was less commonly called Canaiola, Canucula, and Canica, while Canina *tout court* was reserved for an unrelated white-berried variety. According to Breviglieri and Casini (1964) it was once confused with Canaiolo Nero, which I have no trouble believing, given the similarity of the two names. In the past, Canina Nera was believed it to be a very low-quality grape that gave a very light red wine of little interest. Fortunately, not everyone agreed with this view and the grape wasn't abandoned; in fact it was the most abundantly planted grape in the Romagna area in the late 1800s, so it had to have merits. Canina Nera has been grown in Romagna since at least the 1800s; it's a protagonist in the 1836 poem *"Brindisi ad un esimio bevitore"* ("A Toast to a Noble Drinker") written by Jacopo Landoni. In 1839, Gallesio describes in his *I giornali dei viaggi*, two different types of Canina Nera, one green stalked and another red stalked. Marzotto (1925) and Dotti (1927) also confirm the two subvarieties; the former finds the resulting wine pleasant and renowned, while the latter appears to have been less impressed. Dotti also clearly states that Canina Nera differs from Fortana (then often called Uva d'Oro) because it ripens earlier and its leaves turn reddish in the fall. Luigi Veronelli, in his 1961 guide to Italy's wines, describes Canina Nera as a "charming wine that pairs well with local foods": if you ask me, that's a pretty good compliment from Italy's first, best, and most knowledgeable wine writer.

Some authors have stated that Canina Nera is identical to Fortana, an assertion largely based on the study published by Boccacci, Torello Marinoni, Gambino, Botta, and Schneider (2005), which also hinted at a possible parent-offspring relationship between it and Lambrusco Maestri and at close genetic ties to Malbo Gentile. Robinson, Harding, and Vouillamoz (2012) also equate the two varieties to one, Fortana. However, this is a minority view in Italy. In fact, in the fourteenth official bulletin of the Emilia-Romagna region, dated January 29, 2008 (hence well after Boccacci's study) describing the species of agricultural interest in the region, there is no mention anywhere of Canina Nera and Fortana being identical. In fact, all the historical references cited in the bulletin describe Canina Nera as distinct from Uva d'Oro, the name for Fortana that was used in centuries past. Nor is Fortana listed among Canina Nera's synonyms. Marisa Fontana, Emilia-Romagna's best-known and most respected ampelographer, who worked for years at the Tebano Research station, told me flat-out recently that to consider Fortana and Canina Nera identical is nonsense: "the Emilia-Romagna region has never once had the slightest inclination to officially recognize the two varieties as synonymous because they are very obviously not. They don't even remotely look like each other." Admittedly, Fontana's assertion that visually the two grapes don't look anything alike is hard to argue with: their leaves couldn't be more different, and while Fortana's berry is round, Canina Nera's is oblong, almost oval. Furthermore, Boccacci's article is very rarely quoted anywhere and is hard to find; other references to Lambrusco Maestri being related to Fortana or Canina Nera are likewise hard to come by, but perhaps I am wrong.

Interestingly, in a presentation at the Fourth International Viticultural Congress held on July 10–12, 2012, in Asti, Giancarlo Scalabrelli of the University of Pisa presented data relative to rare grape varieties in the Colline Pisane, in which he mentions that local varieties Canina Nera, Oliva, and Uva Vecchia are all synonymous with Fortana and distinguishes them from the Canina Nera listed in the National Registry. Other erroneous identities plague Canina Nera: for example, the grape has always been mistakenly associated with cagnina, a sweet red wine also made in Emilia-Romagna though with a completely different grape, Terrano.

Canina Nera is characterized by medium-large, pyramidal, long bunches and round berries of varying sizes within the same bunch. It ripens in late September or early October. There are no clones available. Vineyard data (2000) shows that there are fifty-three hectares of Canina Nera in the province of Ravenna, and another thirteen in the rest of Emilia-Romagna. Unfortunately, given the limited financial benefits of growing Canina Nera (at least until recently), it is very likely that a number of those hectares have been since uprooted in favor of other varieties, if they were replanted at all. So Canina Nera is not abundant. But interest in the variety in the early twenty-first century is such that the city of Russi near Ravenna in Romagna actively sponsored research led by Francesco Donati at the Centro Ricerche Produzioni Vegetali (CRPV) in Tebano (an important grapevine research institution located in this town) in an effort to safeguard local wine production. We can hope that the Russi township's decision to study and to increase awareness of the local grape variety and wine will increase new plantings. Currently, Canina Nera is grown only in Emilia-Romagna mainly around the towns of Russi, Santo Alberto, Bagnacavallo, Faenza, Cotignola, Lugo, and Castel Bolognese. It is essentially a local phenomenon and the wine is rarely seen outside its production zone.

Which Wines to Choose and Why

Canina Nera is a little-studied variety that yields bright fresh wines that have a vivid tannic streak and plenty of acidity, the exact merits of which are being rediscovered. It is included among the authorized varieties in a number of IGT wines such as Emilia, Ravenna, and Rubicone. It's not easy to taste a pure example, as Canina Nera is almost always blended with other varieties such as Ancellotta and Marzemino. Furthermore, as it is a mainly local, artisanally made product, each farmer tends to make it following his or her own recipe. For this reason, the researchers have established that to make a proper canina nera wine, the blend should be as follows: Canina Nera (minimum) 50 percent, Barzamé (Marzemino) 25 percent; Cornacchia 10 percent; Ancellotta 5 percent; Tinturie Romagnole and/or Colorino 8 percent; Pignolo Nero 1 percent; and Romanino (Corinto Nero) 1 percent. That complicated blend may seem strange, but Tebano's Marisa Fontana, one of the leading grapevine scientists in Italy, believes that canina nera was once made using even more grape varieties. Legend has it that canina nera was a favorite wine of Stefano Pelloni, a highway robber nicknamed Il Passatore and his band of outlaws, who used to drink copious amounts of it from the traditional mugs of terracotta used in and around the town of Cotignola. Historically, this wine flowed copiously during Russi's Fiera dei Sette Dolori (a religious feast for Our Lady of Sorrows), which has been held in the third week of September since 1876. Producers come to the festival to show off their canèna nova (a term in local dialect meaning "new canina," akin to Beaujolais Nouveau), a fresh young Canina Nera wine that is still finishing alcoholic fermentation and is often cloudy and lightly sweet; the more mature canèna wine is classically dry and can age a few years.

Wines I have tried by local farmers reveal a pale red hue, almost like a *rosato*, with lovely aromas of pomegranate, black fruits, and wet earth. It's a very acid, almost tart wine (though this may be more a result of how the farmer grew the grapes and when they were harvested) with lively tannins, generally slightly off-dry and low in alcohol (9–11.5 percent). Locals enjoy it matched to the typical dish *bel e cot*, a *cotechino* (that is, a very fatty sausage) that greatly benefits from canina nera's high acidity. The estate on which I am pinning my hopes is Tenuta Uccellina near Russi, which has planted Canina Nera grapevines and is actively studying the grape and its potential to make a monovarietal wine to be sold commercially.

WINES TO TRY: Tenuta Uccellina**.

Cannonau

WHERE IT'S FOUND: Sardinia. NATIONAL REGISTRY CODE NUMBER: 51 (also listed at number 10 as Alicante and at number 236 as Tocai Rosso). COLOR: red.

Many years ago, I realized that studying Cannonau was going to be difficult: producers couldn't even agree (in fact, still can't) on its spelling, never mind all the rest. Some want it called Cannonao, others Cannonau; still others maintain that Cannonao is the variety's correct name, while cannonau (with a final "u" instead of an "o") is the name of the wine. The National Registry lists the grape as Cannonau, so that is the spelling I use in this book.

Nevertheless, Cannonau has tales to tell that we can all learn from. First, it offers a good example of the difficulties involved in writing a book on Italy's native grapes: simply put, for historical, sentimental, and financial reasons, nobody in Italy wants to accept that a locally important grape variety may not be a native. Hence, people from all walks of the wine world trip all over themselves trying to find historical documentation (that almost always amounts to nothing more than anecdotal evidence) of the variety's existence on Sardinian soil since the dawn of time. And not only with Cannonau, but with Vermentino as well, and many other grapes (not just in Sardinia), and so it becomes harder to separate fact from fiction. Second, Cannonau allows an opportunity to think about what "identical" really means in ampelological terms, a subject that fascinates me (see chapter 1).

Calò, Costacurta, Cancellier, and Forti (1990) first confirmed that Cannonau is identical to Grenache (Spain's Garnacha, a name deriving from the Italian *Vernaccia*), the world's most abundantly planted high-quality grape, to Sicily's and Tuscany's Alicante (not to be confused with Alicante Bouschet, a different group of varieties), Umbria's Gamay Perugino, and Veneto's Tocai Rosso. However, more recent studies have provided contradictory findings (De Mattia, Lovicu, Tardaguila, Grassi, Imazio, Scienza, and Labra 2009; Meneghetti, Costacurta, Frare, Da Rold, Migliaro, Morreale, et al. 2011). Identification of Garnacha and its synonyms is difficult because of the vast ampelographic variability (such as differences in berry color) found in many similarly named grapevines (Cabezas, Cervera, Arroyo-García, Ibáñez, Rodríguez-Torres, Borrego, et al. 2003). The previously mentioned 2009 study by De Mattia's team suggested that the Spanish *Garnacha* group consists of cultivars displaying different morphologies and genetics because of somatic mutations or crossings between grapevines over centuries. Cannonau grapevines grown in Sardinia and in other parts of Italy also show great ampelographic diversity. It follows that the relationship between Garnacha and Cannonau grapevines depends greatly on the specific accessions being analyzed. Meneghetti's team demonstrated that fifty-three accessions of Garnacha from Spain, Alicante from Sicily, Tocai Rosso from Veneto, Cannonau from Sardinia, and Gamay Perugino from Umbria all had the same genetic profile (fourteen SSR sites studied), but data collected by De Mattia, Imazio, Grassi, Lovicu, Tardaguila, Failla, et al. (2007) does not allow the same conclusion. While this group's results suggest that the four Cannonau varieties (collected at different sites in Sardinia) were genetically identical, only some Spanish accessions of Garnacha Tinta (also from different areas of Spain) showed the same SSR profile as the Cannonau in the study. Therefore, we can conclude that while these results confirm that Cannonau and several Spanish accessions of Garnacha Tinta are identical, at the same time not all Garnacha Tinta cultivars have the same genetic makeup as Cannonau.

Actually, ampelographers first began to identify the two varieties as synonymous in 1877 due to obvious ampelographic similarities. The name Cannonau is considered a deformation of the Spanish Canoñazo; it first appears as Canonat in notary acts of the sixteenth century. Manca dell'Arca (1780) describes both a white- and a red-berried Cannonau: curiously, he believed the red one to be mediocre. In contrast, Moris (1837) believed it excellent, and synonymous with *Vitis praestans*. Furthermore, in the seventeenth century, Sardinians took to calling it Guarnaccia or Granaccia, names still used today in other Italian regions where the variety grows. It seems likely that Cannonau first arrived on Sardinian shores with the conquest of the island town of Alghero by Peter IV of Aragon in 1354. A rare white-berried Cannonau Bianco has also been described (just as there are a Grenache Blanc and Garnacha Blanca), which means it would be more accurate to refer to the red-berried varieties as Cannonau Nero, Grenache Noir, and Garnacha Tinta. For simplicity's sake, I will reserve and use the shorter name for the red-berried varieties, which are much more common than the white-colored ones.

However, while few still dispute that Garnacha is (more or less) identical to Cannonau, the variety's birthplace is still a matter of heated debate. The presumed Spanish origin of Cannonau has been recently questioned by Italian experts such as Lovicu (2006), though written references to Garnacha (Grenache) and Cannonau appeared in the literature at more or less the same time. However, Lovicu believes that the Garnacha mentioned in the early Spanish literature refers to a white grape and wine, and that a red garnacha wine is not mentioned in that country until the eighteenth century (in a dictionary published in 1734). By contrast, other researchers believe that Garnacha was present on Spanish soil long before the eighteenth century but was called Aragones, a red-berried variety from the area around Madrid (where this synonym is still used for Garnacha), and was first mentioned in Alonso de Herrera's *Agricultura General* (1513). However, Alonso de Herrera's description is reportedly insufficient to support the conclusion that he was in fact describing Garnacha / Cannonau. The first reliable mention of Garnacha in Spain would appear to be Estevan de Corvera's 1678 *Cataluña Illustrada*, in which a list of grape varieties dotting the countryside (including *Garnachas*) is given; but I fail to understand how anybody could conclude that the *Garnachas* the book alludes to were really Garnacha / Cannonau instead of some other *Vernaccia* variety. After all, in light of the proliferation of spurious *Malvasia*-named grapes and wines that occurred all over Europe only as a result of the fame of the original malvasia wine, the likelihood of something similar happening with the almost as famous *Vernaccia* grapes and wines is high. Italy's first mention of a Canonat variety dates to 1549, in a notary act written by Bernardino Coni. Therefore, Italian experts hold that Cannonau was present on Sardinian soil long before the Spanish domination of the island began, and that as a result of translation and printing mistakes, the name Cannonau was derived from a later reference to a different Spanish cultivar, Canonazo. In one of the editions of Di Rovasenda's ampelographies (1877), just such a Canonazo variety from Seville is described. However, no such Spanish variety exists: the correct spelling ought to have been Cañocazo, and it is a white variety first mentioned by Spanish ampelographer Simon de Rojas Clemente y Rubio in 1807, almost extinct today.

Still, given Spain's long domination of Sardinia, it is hard to imagine Cannonau as a native Sardinian variety rather than native to Spain. Though there exist many biotypes of Cannonau on the island, the various color mutations of Garnacha that are frequent in Spain are found not at all or only very rarely in Sardinia. I do not know of much grey or pink Cannonau on Sardinia. In fact, even the white mutation of Cannonau may not grow in Sardinia, for the island's Cannonau Bianco was proven to be an only distant relative; Cannonau Bianco and Cannonau only share fifty percent of alleles (De Mattia, Imaz, Grassi, Lovicu, Tardaguila, Failla, et al. 2007). Therefore, it would appear that in the absence of abundant color mutations of Sardinian Cannonau, it is more likely that Cannonao/ Grenache is Spanish, rather than Sardinian, as in the former country the color mutations are more common. However, recent study results have added more food for thought (Meneghetti, Costacurta, Frare, Da Rold, Migliaro, Morreale, et al. 2011). While the accessions of Garnacha from Spain, Alicante from Sicily, Tocai Rosso from Veneto, Cannonau from Sardinia, and Gamay Perugino from Umbria all had the same genetic profile, the Italian samples were characterized by a strong genetic variability, in contrast to the Spanish samples, which showed great genetic similarity. Clearly, as discussed at length in chapter 1, genetic variability is linked to morphologic, viticultural, and enological differences perhaps resulting from mutations occurring over time. Since Cannonau has lived in Sardinia for centuries, the grapevine has likely undergone more than its share of mutations over time, induced both by man and the environment. Meneghetti's group draws the conclusion that the genetic diversity of the Italian accessions, by contrast to the high genetic similarity present among Spanish samples, would appear to support the hypothesis that Cannonau's birthplace may be Italian after all. In any case, Cannonau has been living on the island for a very long time indeed.

Available clones of Cannonau are CAP VS 5, CFC-13, CAP VS 1, CAP VS2, and VCR 23, but most high-quality Sardinian estates prefer to use massal selections of very old vines, which are still plentiful on the island. Commonly used synonyms for Cannonau in Italy are Alicante, Gamay Perugino, and Tocai Rosso. Each is used to make a wine highly associated with a specific region and area: for example Gamay Perugino in Umbria is used to make Trasimeno Gamay and Tocai Rosso is used in Veneto to make Tai (since the word *tocai* can no longer be used to designate wines made outside Hungary). However, Cannonau and Tocai Rosso are not identical; there is one allele that helps discriminate between Tocai Rosso and Cannonau (and Garnacha). Therefore, it is more correct to consider Tocai Rosso a biotype of Cannonau, since it has adapted over the decades to a completely different environment (Veneto instead of Sardinia). Tocai Rosso seems a relative newcomer to Veneto, but perhaps earlier experts simply failed to recognize it. In fairness, the two grapevines look slightly different: Tocai Rosso has slightly bigger, more compact bunches and berries with thicker skins. Certainly producers in Sardinia feel that there is a night-and-day difference in quality between the two—but then, one *would* expect them to believe that. It may not be a matter of one biotype being much higher quality than the other, but rather of the variety adapting over the centuries to a specific habitat and becoming more successful in producing interesting wines there.

Recent study results suggest there is a genetic basis to growers' long-held belief that the various Cannonau biotypes aren't at all alike, despite their presumed genetic identity. In the 2011 study by Meneghetti's group, molecular tests were able to separate samples into distinct groups based on their respective origin (Sardinia, Sicily, Umbria, Vicenza province, Spain, and France). In the study, Cannonau accessions fell in the first group while all the remaining accessions clustered into three different subgroups of a second group. It follows that if genetic tests can separate between grapevines on the basis of their place of origin, and that these cultivars exhibit a spectrum of morphologic and viticultural diversity, then it is likely that such differences are reflected in the characteristics of the wines made in each specific region. Therefore, the impression that growers have about there being noteworthy differences between Cannonau and Tocai Rosso, for example, and the wines made with them, may not be a figment of their imagination.

In fact, Cannonau is a textbook example of the damage that can be wreaked by careless nursery practices. In the 1980s, when Italy's wine boom was beginning to take shape, growers turned to nurseries in order to increase their plantings of Cannonau, which was fast becoming a hot commodity. Unfortunately, in the words of well-respected producer Alessandro Dettori "probably because of a sense of urgency that did nothing for attention to detail, varieties other than Cannonau (or at best, low-quality biotypes) were shipped to Sardinia. The University of Sassari has estimated that 80 percent of the Cannonau vines planted on the island are of the low-quality Tocai Rosso biotype. I don't know if this is true. I know my vines are almost one hundred years old and don't come from nursery selections, and that's what really matters to me." At the Alberto Loi estate, where the grandfather of the present owners first planted Cannonau vines at the turn of the twentieth century, they believe that "studies have shown genetic diversity between populations of Cannonau grown in different parts of the island, so it is important to avoid bringing in plant material from outside the island. At Loi, we'd even go further, and veto the mixing of Cannonau biotypes from within different areas of the island itself. Each should remain planted in its own *terroir,* for the varieties behave differently and so do the wines." Slightly different-looking Cannonau grapevines are found in vineyards located near Alghero, Barisardo, Quartu Santa Elena, Sennori, and Cagliari: all show the same genetic profile at fourteen SSR loci. Studies of the exact characterization of the organoleptic features of wines made in similar manner but from what might be different biotypes is currently under way (Nieddu 2011).

Cannonau also grows in the volcanic Colli Berici near Vicenza and in the Colli Euganei near Padova in Veneto. In Umbria it grows near the shores of Lake Trasimeno, in the countryside surrounding the pretty towns of Castiglione del Lago, Magione, Paciano, Panicale, Passignano, Tuoro, Città della Pieve, and Corciano. In Tuscany it is called Alicante (not to be confused with Alicante Bouschet, a group of different varieties) and in Sicily it is grown only sporadically and has never been associated with specific zones.

Which Wines to Choose and Why

Cannonau is by far the most important red variety of Sardinia, and its wine is emblematic of the island's wine production. It has been the most commonly grown variety in Sardinia since the 1950s, and today there are an estimated eight thousand hectares under vine to Cannonau. It is most planted in the province of Nuoro (roughly five thousand hectares), followed by those of Sassari (one thousand hectares), Cagliari (one thousand hectares), and Oristano (five hundred hectares). The most important DOC is Cannonau di Sardegna (in my view, much too large a DOC, extended to the entire island) with three high-quality subzones: Oliena (or Nepente di Oliena) in central Sardinia, Jerzu in east-central Sardinia, and Capo Ferrato in southeastern Sardinia. There are clear-cut differences between these wines, even when they are similarly made. According to Loi, Cannonau prefers "sandy soils with granite breakdown products. Unfortunately when the DOC legislation was revised in the mid-1980s, quality controls were diminished, allowing cannonau to be made in a multitude of styles, from light and simple to the complex wines of the subzones, and this has been very damaging to what used to be a unique wine." Another important fact about cannonau is that historically it always included small amounts of wine made with Pascale, another native grape.

Tonino Arcadu, of the well-respected Gostolai estate believes that "it's a real shame that the use of other grapes, especially international ones, has changed the authentic expression of Sardinian cannonau; many wines today are only shortcuts meant to pander to international tastes looking for Cabernet Sauvignon or Merlot aromas and flavors." I would add that, much as with sangiovese, adding a brute of a grape such as Cabernet Sauvignon to cannonau makes very little sense.

A good cannonau made with nothing but Cannonau cannot be black, for the variety is not rich in anthocyanins (190–500 milligrams per kilo of catechin). Its lack of high polyphenol concentrations also means that it is not a good idea for producers to age it in small new oak barrels—but there are those who try anyway. Dettori likes to say that proper cannonau doesn't need to age in oak at all, while wines made from the Tocai Rosso biotype do need the benefit of the barrel. Young wines are characterized by both fresh and faded red floral aromas, and depending on the subzone, dry field herbs. With age, it picks up volume, becoming creamier and spicy, with hints of underbrush and a definite nuttiness. Veneto's DOC Barbarano offers many good examples of Tai wines, light, appealing reds that are ideal as an aperitif or with simpler fare. These wines match particularly well with moderately rich pasta and rice dishes and are perfect with Sopressa Vicentina and Prosciutto Veneto Berico-Euganeo (a local, high-quality cured ham). There is also a more intensely colored and structured style of Tai Rosso, called Tocai Rosso Riserva, that is aged in oak. The tai of the Colli Euganei is very similar to the wines of the Colli Berici. Good Umbrian wines made with Gamay Perugino include the DOC Trasimeno Gamay (which can be monovarietal) or the DOC Colli del Trasimeno or IGT wines, in which Gamay Perugino is blended with other grape varieties. These wines have typical bitter-almond, herbal, and underbrush notes, and are best drunk in the first three to five years from the vintage, with hearty pasta and meat dishes. I find them less fruity than the Veneto and Sardinian versions, but a lot depends on what the producer does in the cellar. In Liguria, some wines labeled Granaccia or Guarnaccia are made with a local Cannonau variety.

WINES TO TRY: For Cannonau, try: Dettori***, Alberto Loi***, Gostolai***, Ferruccio Deiana***, Argiolas***, Cantina Santadi***, and Pala***. For Barbarano/Tai Rosso Riserva, try: Costalunga**, Torengo** (Le Pignole), Piovene Porto Godi**, Dal Maso*, Lidio Pretti*, and Pialli*. For Umbria, try: Duca della Corgna** (Trasimeno Gamay Divina Villa Etichetta Bianca), Madrevite** (Bisbetica Rosé, a *rosato*), and La Querciolana** (Gamay Rosso dell'Umbria). All are 100 percent Gamay Perugino wines.

Caprettone

WHERE IT'S FOUND: Campania. NATIONAL REGISTRY CODE NUMBER: not registered. COLOR: white.

Wine lovers with unconfessed masochistic tendencies will revel in the knowledge that fewer Italian grape varieties will provide a headache faster than Caprettone. Trouble is, nobody seems to agree on this cultivar's identity, with everyone holding steadfastly to his or her view. For many experts, Caprettone is exactly the same as Coda di Volpe Bianca, another native white grape of Campania, but don't try telling that to anyone farming the volcanic soils of the Vesuvius (where, wouldn't you know it, Coda di Volpe Bianca is also grown, though it is not common), unless you're a sucker for an eruption of a different kind. Folks in Italy are viscerally attached to their local varieties, and so nobody in this neck of the woods wants to hear that their beloved Caprettone is the same as someone else's variety. The latest in genetic analysis by Costantini, Monaco, Vouillamoz, Forlani, and Grando (2005) confirms that the two grape varieties are different, and that Caprettone is closely related to Ginestra (a white grape) and Piedirosso (a red variety). Still, the century-old habit of referring to Caprettone as a local Vesuvian "Coda di Volpe" persists and many people making wine on and around the volcano will tell you that the grape they use is "Caprettone, or Coda di Volpe."

For what it's worth, Caprettone looks very different from Coda di Volpe Bianca to me. The names themselves would seem to point this out: Coda di Volpe Bianca is so called for its opulent cluster, which resembles the bushy tail of a fox, while Caprettone, a much scrawnier cultivar, is named after the small "beard" of goats (or perhaps because the first to farm Caprettone where local goat herders). Caprettone's berries are also smaller than those of Coda di Volpe Bianca, though I have been shown supposed Caprettone bunches that were so big and round they seemed to have more in common with fat turkeys than true Caprettone. These phenotypic differences were once thought to be the result of local *terroir* diversity—the poorer volcanic soils where Caprettone grows were believed to play a role in causing scrawny bunches and small berries. Interestingly, while Antonio Mastroberadino has told me in the past that he is not convinced there is much difference between Coda di Volpe Bianca and Caprettone, the majority of Campanian wine producers and winemakers I have talked to are. In fact, it's more than likely that the majority of growers on the volcano own Caprettone, but many took to calling their grapes Coda di Volpe Bianca, as the latter is a better-known and hence better-selling grape. Nevertheless, I think Caprettone is a very interesting variety and its wines potentially exciting. Chances are high that we shall hear a lot more about it in the future. Currently, Caprettone is typically grown on volcanic soils, which might explain the wine's bubbly personality. Vineyards are mainly located on the slopes of fifteen towns near—and even on—the Vesuvius volcano (especially the southeastern slope, where soils are more fertile than in the almost barren northern sector). Look for vineyards around Boscotrecase, Trecase, San

Sebastiano al Vesuvio, Torre del Greco, Terzigno, Sant'Anastasia, Somma Vesuviana, and Viuli. It is also grown on the Monte Somma, a lower portion of the ancient volcano, where the colorful landscape of black lava, brownish tufa, red *pomodorini del piennolo*, and green trees loaded with orange apricots of a local, high-quality biotype makes a beautiful sight.

Which Wines to Choose and Why

Though few people outside the locals know the good news, there are a number of monovarietal wines made with Caprettone to choose from. In fact the variety's naturally decent acidity levels (that's another difference between it and Coda di Volpe Bianca) are the reason that some producers have chosen to make sparkling wines with Caprettone, though its tartaric acid levels are much lower than those of Fiano and Greco, for example. These sparkling wine versions are not unlike a slightly bigger-bodied, more mineral, and less fruity Prosecco. The best known DOC wine is Lacryma Christi del Vesuvio Bianco, but Caprettone plays only a small role in those blends. To try pure Caprettone wines (lemon, minerals, white flowers, unripe apricot), just look for IGT wines labeled caprettone. Grotte del Sole makes a rare sweet caprettone, in honor of traditions of the past.

WINES TO TRY: Cantine Olivella** (Lacryma Christi del Vesuvio Bianco L'Emblema), Casa Barone**, Sorrentino** (Natì), Fuocomorto** (Lacryma Christi del Vesuvio Bianco, with bright straw-yellow color, aromas of magnolia and broom, and a saline bent to the crunchy white stone-fruit and citrus flavors; Pompeiano Caprettone, partly aged in chestnut barrels, with aromas and flavors of dried apricots, resin, and fresh white flowers). For sparkling wine, try Casa Setaro* (Caprettone Spumante Metodo Classico). For sweet caprettone, try Grotta del Sole* (Lacryma Christi del Vesuvio Dolce). All these wines are 100 percent Caprettone.

Carica L'asino

WHERE IT'S FOUND: Piedmont. NATIONAL REGISTRY CODE NUMBER: 53. COLOR: white.

Also known as Barbassese in Italian, and Barbassìs or Barbassé in the Piedmontese dialect, this grape is more commonly known as Carica L'asino, probably due to its highly productive and regular yields (*carica l'asino* means "load up the donkey"). Another theory holds that it acquired its name from the steep slopes and tightly spaced rows of its vineyards, where the only way to harvest and carry grapes was by donkeys, since neither carts nor wagons would fit. Incidentally, this is the version preferred by Bruna Ferro, owner of the Carussin estate, one of the very few estates to make a monovarietal carica l'asino. Ferro has a soft spot for donkeys—at last count, she owns eleven of them—and thinks it an amazing coincidence that she bought a vineyard in an area called Valle Asinari ("valley of the donkeys"), partly planted to Carica L'asino by the previous owners, who retrieved the cuttings in the Acqui area, where Carica L'asino once thrived. Unfortunately Carica L'asino is a common name, used to describe grape varieties all over Italy (including Barbera Bianca in Piedmont, though the latter has a much more compact bunch and no wings), and so confusion abounds. In fact, it runs so deep that the variety included in the National Registry as Carica L'asino appears to have more in common with Vermentino than with the variety I describe here. For this reason, it is probably best to refer to this cultivar by the name Barbassese, but as the latter has not yet been officially accepted, I will continue to use Carica L'asino instead. The variety is characterized by medium-large, pyramidal-conical bunches and medium-large, round berries. It appears to be sensitive to spring frosts (though budbreak does not occur particularly early in the season) and to oidium; old timers have told me these are the two features that led to the variety's decline in popularity and plantings. Though Carica L'asino reportedly ripens late in September, Ferro tells me that in her neck of the woods it's always harvested in the first two weeks of the month. In the past, its large sweet berries made this variety a much sought-after table grape.

Which Wines to Choose and Why

It's rare but not impossible to find a monovarietal Carica L'asino, as the variety is usually blended with Cortese, Timorasso, or Favorita. However, Patrizia Marenco decided it was time to bring the variety back to everyone's attention, and after having identified a local farmer who grew Carica L'asino in the Valle Bagnario near Strevi (Alessandria), she propagated three thousand vines with the help of a local nurseryman. However, I know that Marenco has a low-yielding, not very productive Carica L'asino, which flies in the face of what we know about the variety and its tendency to be generous in its yields; furthermore, her wine is delicately aromatic, which other supposedly monovarietal Carica L'asino wines I have tried are not. Still, the wine is excellent. Marenco's example was followed by Luigi and Bruna Ferro of the Carussin estate: their wine is mineral and fresh, with aromas and flavors of dried herbs, pear, and apricot, but it contains 20 percent Cortese because, as Bruna says, "as a monovarietal, we find it too mineral and saline, a consequence of the clay-rich soils in our area, while the variety does better in drier, less water-retentive soils." It is less aromatic than Marenco's, though this may have more to do with the organic winemaking Ferro employs, and her use of very low doses of sulfur dioxide (a technique which, in my experience, can "flatten" aromas somewhat). Until the vines owned by Marenco and Ferro are genetically profiled, we won't know if these are different biotypes of Carica L'asino (more and less aromatic), or if the grapevines grown by these two pioneering estates are even the same variety.

WINES TO TRY: Marenco** (Carialoso) and Carussin** (Caricalasino).

Carignano

WHERE IT'S FOUND: Sardinia. NATIONAL REGISTRY CODE NUMBER: 54. COLOR: red.

Better known as Carignan in France and Cariñena in Spain, where it is an important part of many wines, this is one grape variety that is almost certainly traditional and not truly native to Italy. Its cradle seems to be the Aragonese city of Cariñena, hence the grape's Italian name of Carignano; though its other moniker, Mazuelo (from Mazuelo de Muñó, a village in the province of Burgos in Castilla y León), is probably a more accurate name. This is because Cariñena in Spain is also the name of a Denominación de Origen, which engenders confusion. In any case, it seems Carignano was transplanted mainly to the French departments of Aude and Hérault as well as to Pyrénées-Orientales, Gard, and Provence.

Of course, not everyone agrees with the Spanish origin. Some hypothesize that Carignano was brought to Sardinia by the ancient Phoenicians during their trading travels, but admittedly, this is very hard to prove. Furthermore, while there exist color mutations of Carignano (Cariñena Blanca grows in Spain and France, while a very rare Carignano Gris is found in France), I am not aware of their existence in Sardinia. The lack of these color mutations makes it even less likely that Sardinia is the birthplace of Carignano, as the richest amount of biodiversity (according to the teachings of Vavilov) is found in a variety's original home. Therefore, it seems more likely that Carignano arrived courtesy of the Spanish, who ruled Sardinia for centuries. Its synonyms in Sardinia, Uva di Spagna ("grape of Spain") and the less-frequent Axina de Spagna, also suggest a Spanish origin; certainly De Astis believed so. Thanks to Martin, Borrego, Cabello, and Ortiz (2003) we know Cariñena and Mazuelo to be identical, but surprisingly, more recent data published by Nieddu, Nieddu, Cocco, Erre, and Chessa (2007) has also suggested the identity between Carignano and Bovale Grande, while distinguishing it from Nieddera, another island grape variety. As I have illustrated earlier, I think the presumed Bovale Grande / Carignano synonym is not a cut-and-dried issue, though this is one instance in which the proposed synonymity between two cultivars is easier to accept (see BOVALE GRANDE entry). The two varieties look very much alike, but similar does not mean identical, and wines made from even similar-looking biotypes can be different. It's possible that sixty- or seventy-year-old Bovale Grande vines might look and behave differently enough from Carignano to give a recognizably different wine, but this is not clear, given the scarcity of Bovale Grande planted on the island and the absence of known monovarietal wines made with it. Such biotypes can produce very different tasting wines and a number of experts believe that they ought to be viewed as separate cultivars, for example (see CANNONAU and CAGNULARI entries). Last but not least, the National Registry still lists Carignano and Bovale Grande separately. According to Reale, Pilla, Angiolillo (2006), Carignano is also distinct from Tintilia, another Italian variety typical of Molise.

Carignano's basal buds are very fertile, so long pruning is unnecessary for large harvests, but spurs should be left no longer than the two buds, since long pruning greatly weakens Carignano and, if repeated, may even lead to grapevine death. Furthermore, as its grapes cling to the vine, it is not an ideal variety for mechanical harvesting. Late budding and late ripening, Carignano needs heat to reach optimal ripeness and is therefore perfectly suited to Sardinia's warm and dry climate—it doesn't do well in damp climates. Apparently, the combination of the island's marine environment and coastal vineyards encourages more thorough ripening, though I'm not sure anyone has ever furnished me with a physiologically plausible explanation for this (Carignano is wind resistant and even more drought resistant). It does especially well in extreme conditions that tame its natural vigor: shallow sandy soils or clay-sandy soils are best. Stefano Cova, winemaker of the world-class Mesa estate, believes that some areas in Sardinia's interior can also yield noteworthy wines: these are more fertile and have a larger presence of schists and clay. While old vines in Sardinia planted on sandy soils are all ungrafted, younger vineyards planted on soils with higher clay content benefit from specific rootstocks like 110 Richter and 140 Ruggeri that will reduce the variety's naturally high vigor. Unfortunately, Carignano is very susceptible to oidium, but given its success on the island (plantings have increased steadily throughout much of the twentieth century) I imagine that its exceptional vigor and very high yields (two hundred hectoliters per hectares, though old Sardinian vines produce much less) probably made farmers grin and bear the problem. The only noteworthy clone is CFC-8 and few producers count on it, as there are plenty of old vineyards from which more interesting and usually higher quality massal selections can be obtained.

Though grown all over the island, Carignano is found mainly in the countryside and seaside of the Sulcis Iglesiente (around the towns of Giba, Santa Anna Arresi, Santa Giovanni Suergiu, Santadi, Masanais, Carbonia, Santo Antioco, and Calasetta) where 89 percent of the almost two thousand hectares on Sardinia are located. It is also grown near Sarrabus, Santa Margherita di Pula, and Terralba. Cova believes that the true *grand crus* for the variety are Calasetta and Sant'Antioco, the coastal vineyards from Porto Pino (near Sant'Anna Arresi) that stretch toward Is Solinas (near Masainas). These are all characterized by mainly sandy and sandy-clay soils. The vineyards that surround the small pond of Porto Pino are also exceptional in his view, and they grow on mainly sandy soils. Of course, if one accepts the identity between Carignano and Bovale Grande, as seems likely, then there are over twenty-five hundred hectares planted to Carignano on Sardinia alone. The cultivar is also planted, in far smaller amounts, in Lazio, Marche, Sicily, and Umbria. Producers have also told me over the years that Carignano is grown in Tuscany too, though officially it's not supposed to be.

Which Wines to Choose and Why

Carignano is a traditional rather than a native grape of Italy, but Italians can take solace in the knowledge that Italy's Carignano wines (or a few of them at least) are probably the world's best. The most famous wine is the DOC Carignano del Sulcis, where Carignano represents roughly 80 percent of grape varieties cultivated. Vineyards here are often one hundred years old, and this is in large measure the secret behind the exceptionally high quality of Sardinia's Carignano. The most famous wine is Sardinia's DOC Carignano del Sulcis, but the variety can be included in DOC Sicilia wine blends. Close to thirty IGT wine blends may also include Carignano (a short list includes Colli Cimini, Frusinate, Narni, and Terre Siciliane). However, outside Sardinia, Carignano grown in Lazio, Marche, Umbria, and Tuscany is only of anecdotal significance. That said, in Tuscany more than one producer has told me off the record that Carignano must was (or is?) often added (shall we say via involuntary mistakes?) to many anemic Tuscan musts. Of course Italian producers, thoroughly scared by the tough controls exercised by the local authorities and the iron will of their local politicians to do what's right and best for the country and its wine loving consumers, would never dream of doing such a thing.

For those weaned on less than impressive Spanish and French versions, old-vine Carignano wines can be one of Italy's most interesting and sensual offerings, with a velvety-fleshy, almost sweet, and softly tannic personality. Therein lies the greatness of Sardinia's Carignanos, for nowhere else—not even under the best conditions of old vines and low yields—is "creamy" a word associated with what are most often very high-acid, roughly tannic wines. In truth, creamy personalities are typical only of Sardinian wines made from old seaside vineyards planted on mainly sandy soil: by contrast, wines produced from inland vines, on soils with a much higher clay content, are brawnier and more austere, and greatly repay cellaring. So doing a little homework before you buy will go a long way in guaranteeing how much you'll like the Italian Carignano wine you buy.

WINES TO TRY: Agricola Punica*** (Barrua and Montessu, made from younger vines), Cantina Santadi*** (both the Terre Brune and Rocca Rubia Riserva), 6Mura*** (Giba, Carignanoo del Sulcis), Mesa*** (Buio, Buio Buio), Cantina Calasetta** (Piedefranco, Maccorì).

Carricante

WHERE IT'S FOUND: Sicily. NATIONAL REGISTRY CODE NUMBER: 55. COLOR: white.

Carricante's name (it's also very rarely called Carricanti, Nocera Bianca, or confusingly, Cataratto, which is a distinct variety) tells you a lot about its productivity: the word Carricante refers "to loading up" the cart or the donkey with the copious grapes this variety can produce when left to its own devices. Which is strange, considering that Carricante, a hermit that loves mountainous altitudes, is potentially one of Italy's greatest cultivars, white or red; when properly tended to, it yields wines of great longevity and very intense mineral character. It grows well on the volcanic slopes of Etna, clasping crooked crags where little else thrives; attempts starting in at least the nineteenth century to transplant it elsewhere on the island have not fared well.

Carricante is really a one-zone variety, as it is found only on the slopes of the Etna volcano, in the countryside around towns such as Viagrande, Randazzo, and others. It grows at extremely high altitudes (where Nerello Mascalese has trouble ripening), on both the eastern and the southern slopes of the volcano, at altitudes of 950 meters above sea level and 1,050 meters above sea level respectively. Alessio Planeta of the world-famous Planeta estate shook his head while telling me that he had been thinking of working with Carricante on Etna, "but when I actually saw where it lives, I said, 'You know what, I think we'll just leave it here and let the eastern Sicilians work with it. I'll find another, more reasonable variety, to deal with! Either that, or plant it at more reasonable heights.'" Planeta is too smart and knowledgeable a winemaker not to recognize Carricante's qualities, and in fact Planeta now makes a Carricante wine.

Carricante used to grow all over Sicily in centuries past, when it was in fact not confined just to the volcano. Today all that has changed, and Carricante, at roughly 146 hectares in 2009, is only the thirty-first most-planted variety in Sicily (representing 0.12 percent of the region's surface under vine), though over one third of those vines are more than fifty years old. Even more interestingly, though it accounts for roughly 95 percent of the white varieties grown on Etna, it makes up only 10 percent of those grown around Catania, a city less than an hour's drive away. Again, paucity of diffusion is not a reflection on Carricante's quality, which is inordinately high, but rather a consequence of the limited areas the variety can be effectively cultivated in. Or rather, farmers in other parts of Sicily never appreciated its tendency to give wines that were both very low in alcohol and very high in total acidity. That is a shame, since Sicily could stand to have a lot less Viognier and Sauvignon Blanc (of which there are more than five thousand and one thousand hectares, respectively), which give, for the most part, truly lousy Sicilian wines.

Carricante's bunch is usually medium-large, cylindrical-conical, and long, with elliptical berries covered with little bloom. There are at least two clones (CR-7 and Regione Siciliana 2) and at least two known biotypes (simply called A and B) that have been studied ampelographically and from which microvinifications have been obtained, but at least to me it seems that neither the two vines nor the two wines differ that much. Neither one is particularly resistant to common vine diseases, the Achilles's heel of Carricante. In any case, most producers try planting massal selections of old vines whenever possible. The berries have thick, yellow-green skins with slashes of white, but are easily sunburned.

Which Wines to Choose and Why
Carricante is the main player in DOC wines Etna Bianco and Etna Bianco Superiore (in which it can be blended with small percentages of other local white grapes such as Minella), though there are also pure versions labeled with the name of the cultivar. The wine is characterized by low potassium concentrations, very high total acidity, and very low pH (values of 2.9–3 are common) due to high malic acid concentrations. For this reason, it is necessary to ensure malolactic transformation, something that Sicilians already knew in the eighteenth century (Sestini 1774); Etna vintners used to barrel-age Carricante wines on their lees so that malolactic fermentation would kick in and soften the wines' sharp acidic edge. This is also why many producers chose to harvest it as late as possible.

A great carricante is best described as a dry Riesling look-alike (when five to ten years old, it expresses very obvious flinty, diesel-fuel aromas just as Riesling does), very refined and pure in its graceful mineral aromas and racy, lemony flavors, complicated by aniseed, green apple, orange flower, chamomile, and unripe apricot. I caution readers that not all Carricante wines made today share the same degree of depth and complexity, possibly as a result of grapevines planted only recently (at roughly ten years old, the variety's boom in popularity is a relatively recent one). It is one of only a handful of Italian white wines that age well, benefiting from ten years or even more. Its penetrating aromas, saline flavors, and extremely high acidity are something not everyone gets used to, but those who do are usually hooked for the rest of their lives.

A number of carricantes are blended with small or large amounts of Chardonnay, which helps soften Carricante's angular profile but greatly changes the unique experience that Carricante can deliver. I believe that quality producers should realize they have a unique grape and wine on their hands and should know better than to go mixing it up with Chardonnay. Mercifully, high-quality Etna Bianco wines are blends (a minimum 60 percent Carricante, or 80 percent for Etna Bianco Superiore) with Cataratto and other local varieties, including Minnella.

WINES TO TRY: For Etna Bianco Superiore, try: Benanti*** (Pietramarina) and Barone di Villagrande**. For Etna Bianco, try: Fessina*** (Bianco A' Puddara), Vivera** (Bianco Salisire), Graci* (Quota 600 Bianco, 30 percent Cataratto), and Girolamo Russo* (Bianco Nerina, which contains a percentage of Coda di Volpe Bianca—it never ceases to amaze me how a truly local Campanian cultivar like Coda di Volpe can find its way elsewhere in Italy in time!). For Sicilia, try: Gulfi*** (Carjcanti).

Casavecchia

WHERE IT'S FOUND: Campania. NATIONAL REGISTRY CODE NUMBER: 365. COLOR: red.

Casavecchia owes its name ("old house") to the discovery of a unknown centenary vine by a farmer, Prisco Scirocco, at the end of the nineteenth century, outside the ruins of an ancient Roman home near the town of Pontelatone, in northern Campania's province of Caserta. At first nobody could have cared less, and even the first attempts at winemaking went unnoticed; but eventually, the variety was taken to heart by local farmers who propagated it, often ungrafted, and continued to make wine for local consumption. Around the turn of the twenty-first century, Peppe Mancini and Alberto Barletta of the estate Vestini Campagnano (assisted by the infinite talents of professor and winemaker Luigi Moio) brought Casavecchia to national attention, thanks mainly to a string of vintages that really impressed. Unfortunately, Barletta and Mancini later had a falling out, and Mancini moved on, founding the Terre del Principe estate; today, these two are the estates leading the pack in terms of quality Casavecchia wines.

Not much is yet known about the variety, though in the past there have been suggestions that Casavecchia might be related to the *trebulanum* cited by Pliny; besides the fact that an almost endless list of other grapes and wines have been linked to *trebulanum*, as there is no manner by which to determine the synonymity of the two, similar statements are inaccurate at best, and also very unhelpful for those who want to learn about Italy's native grapes and wines. A study by Costantini, Monaco, Vouillamoz, Forlani, and Grando (2005) suggested that Casavecchia may be related to Summariello (though it's not clear which Summariello they mean, as this is a synonym of both Uva di Troia and another Puglian variety called Sommarello), Catalanesca, and Barbera del Sannio. The authors conclude that as all these varieties are genetically distant from other Campanian cultivars, they may all be only relatively recent introductions to Campania. Obviously, this is not the only conclusion that can be drawn, and in fact the same authors write that other varieties, restricted in their diffusion to interior niche habitats, share a lower percentage of SSR markers with other Campanian varieties. It seems to me this line of reasoning could also apply to Casavecchia, which also has a limited distribution, and living in isolation is also likely to have maintained a specific and uncontaminated genetic makeup. Hence, it doesn't have to be a "recent" introduction to Campania at all. To date, the study by Masi, Vignani, Di Giovannantonio, Mancuso, and Boselli (2001) remains the one specifically devoted to Casavecchia, with ampelographic and DNA analysis (at eight SSR loci) performed. Their results show that Casavecchia is related to Pallagrello Nero (another local variety typical of the Caserta area) but is distinct from all other Campanian varieties, as well as from Sangiovese. The most recent study broaching Casavecchia parentage somewhat confusingly states that Casavecchia is the result of a natural cross of Malvasia Bianca di Candia and Cecubo (not Abbuoto, as erroneously reported elsewhere; these researchers consider Cecubo a synonym of a variety called Tintoria or Tintiglia), yet also provides evidence that Cecubo is the result of a natural crossing of Casavecchia and Piedirosso (Cipriani, Spadotto, Jurman, Di Gaspero, Crespan, Meneghetti, et al. 2010). I spoke about this apparent contradiction directly with Raffaele Testolin, senior author of the Cipriani research paper and professor of agricultural sciences at the University of Udine. As he explained it: "The two pedigrees are certainly in conflict, yet both have a very high LOD (logarithm of odds) scores, which is a statistical measure that compares the likelihood of events happening if they are linked, instead of happening by chance. The scores for both pedigree possibilities are similarly high in this specific case because the four grape varieties (Casavecchia, Malvasia Bianca di Candia, Cecubo, and Piedirosso) are certainly related to a degree, but more SSR loci need to be analyzed in order to determine the exact relationships present. This is typical of all those ancient varieties that have undergone many crossings over the centuries and have complex family relationships: Malvasia Bianca di Candia, Piedirosso, Cecubo, and Casavecchia are among Italy's oldest known cultivars. For cultivars such as these, at least fifty to sixty loci need to be analyzed." Clearly, further research on Casavecchia's parentage is needed.

Casavecchia only grows in the countryside north of Caserta, in the areas surrounding the towns of Castel di Sasso, Formicola, Liberi, and Pontelatone, but plantings are increasing. Its return from the brink of extinction, and the quality of its wines, have won it media attention and a slew of new admirers. Despite its poor productivity and low vigor, Casavecchia is here to stay.

Which Wines to Choose and Why

Casavecchia's fairy tale teaches a useful lesson: a wine that was literally nonexistent in any significant numbers in the mid-1990s, and of which there were only a couple of producers as recently as 2000, is now being made by at least a dozen quality Campanian estates, all located around the city of Caserta, the vine's birthplace. I could not be more happy about this, considering all those experts who insisted, not so long ago, that the future in this part of Campania was in making merlots and cabernets and that Casavecchia and other natives were best ripped out. Of course they all deny this now, but the producers remember only too well.

The biggest expert on Casavecchia wines is Luigi Moio, who has undertaken research studies on the variety at the University at Portici in Campania. Initial results show Casavecchia to be particularly rich in anthocyanins and to be blessed with short-chain tannins that taste smooth and supple when properly ripe. In fact the wine is always soft and smooth, unlike that made with Pallagrello Nero, the other recently rediscovered local variety. The total acidity is usually so low in Casavecchia wines that performing a malolactic transformation is unnecessary. This supple nature of the wines make them somewhat similar to those made with Merlot, according to Moio. In my opinion, casavecchia also has a very discreet aromatic quality that is evident in pure, well-made wines, neatly separating this cultivar from other local red varieties like Pallagrello Nero or the better-known Aglianico. The aromas of delicate field herbs, bay leaf, rosemary, dried mushrooms, green peppercorns, and oregano are typical, though hard to find in many wines. However, it's this delicate but discernible aromatic note that sets Casavecchia wines apart from most other reds of Campania.

Casavecchia di Pontelatone is a recently created DOC for Casavecchia, covering the entire area of the townships of Formicola and Liberi and parts of those of Caiazzo, Castel Campagnano, Castel di Sasso, Piana di Monte Verna, Pontelatone, and Ruviano. Casavecchia has to make up at least 85 percent of the total blend. Wine lovers can however taste reputedly 100 percent monovarietal casavecchia, depending on what the producer chooses to do. A good IGT is Terre del Volturno.

WINES TO TRY: Vestini Campagnano*** (winemaker Paolo Caciorgna has effortlessly stepped into Moio's shoes), Terre del Principe** (Centomoggia, some past vintages had a little too much residual sugar for my taste), Alois* (Trebulanum, too oaky for me), Tenuta di Castel Campagnano*, Fattoria di Selvanova*, and Viticoltori Casavecchia* (Vigna Prea and Futo, the latter a rare and compelling Casavecchia Passito from air-dried grapes).

Casetta

WHERE IT'S FOUND: Trentino, Veneto. NATIONAL REGISTRY CODE NUMBER: 369. COLOR: red.

Casetta's name, which means little house, probably derives from the typically human endeavor of growing wild grapes near one's home in an attempt at domestication. It also goes, rarely, by Maranela, a name probably stemming from the eighteenth-century noble family called Marani, hailing from Ala, who were the first to try growing it in their vineyards. Casetta is also known in the local dialect as Foja Tonda, not to be confused with Foglia Tonda, a distinct variety that grows in Tuscany. Other less common synonyms include Ambroasi, Lambrusco a Foglia Tonda, and Lambrusc'Avio. Though it was long been considered one of the many *Lambrusco* varieties, it has been proven genetically distinct from other members of that family. Phenotypically, it resembles Enantio, also known as Lambrusco a Foglia Frastagliata, a similarity remarked upon by Acerbi in 1825.

Casetta has medium-small bunches and small, almost oval berries; clearly, its distinguishing feature is its round leaves, which present little in the way of indentations or sinuses. There are no official clones available. The variety is characterized by good vigor and productivity. Budbreak is early, subjecting Casetta to the vagaries of spring frosts, though it's very resistant to cold weather; it's also sensitive to grey rot, but is resistant to peronospora and oidium. It is an interesting cultivar in that it manages to accumulate high sugar concentrations in combination with high total acidity levels, and because its wines have a pretty, deep hue. Once very common in Trentino's Vallagarina, south of the city of Trento (by the end of the 1800s, annual production was roughly five thousand hectoliters), its susceptibility to grey rot and the late twentieth-century craze for all things international saw the old vineyards uprooted in favor of Cabernet Sauvignon, Carmenère, and even Syrah. As irony would have it, none of those varieties ripens especially well in Trentino's cooler northern habitat, so producers would have done much better, in my opinion, to stick with their local native, a high-quality variety. Today there are less than fifteen hectares planted, but I am happy to report that interest is mounting among local producers. Most of the Casetta plantings belong to the Albino Armani estate, as Armani was the first to believe in the variety and to do something to help save it. In 2003, he created the Conservatoria, a small experimental vineyard at Dolcè, planted to a number of typical Vallagarina cultivars that risked extinction (among them Casetta, of which he had discovered a few one-hundred-year-old vines). In the 1990s, Armani worked successfully with the Istituto di San Michele all'Adige and with Tiziano Tomasi, winemaker and owner of the Cadalora estate (who was then doing research at the Istituto Agrario di San Michele all'Adige) to bring this variety and wine back from the dead.

Casetta was finally allowed for cultivation only in 2002, and is grown mainly on the right bank of the Adige River, around the towns of Avio, Ala, and Rovereto. It also grows in Veneto, near Verona, and in the countryside around Brentino and Belluno.

Which Wines to Choose and Why

The wine has always been highly thought of; recent examples I have tasted are impressive, characterized by high, very juicy acidity and bright red fruit, with vinous and grapey flavors and aromas. With two or three years of age it picks up increased notes of tobacco and minerals, though it is a wine not meant to age. Though there's plenty of tannin and structure, the wine seems medium-bodied and fresh, lighter than it really is, because of copious amounts of vibrant acids. It can stand up to judicious amounts of oak to give a smoother, richer wine. Without that extra touch of buttery oak, whether you'll appreciate what casetta has to offer depends on how you feel about high-acid red wines. My only question is the depth of complexity the wine can develop. Time will tell, as commercially available wines age: their success, or lack thereof, will ultimately be the deciding factor relative to Casetta's potential as a noble wine grape. Currently, only Albino Armani produces a monovarietal casetta for commercial sale. His first vintage dates to 1994 and I have never had a wine that is less than excellent. The wines to try are the DOC Terre dei Forti (created only in 2006) and IGT blends such as Delle Venezie, Vallagarina, and Vigneti delle Dolomiti.

WINES TO TRY: Albino Armani***.

Catalanesca

WHERE IT'S FOUND: Campania. NATIONAL REGISTRY CODE NUMBER: 398 (also listed as Catalanesca Bianca at number 508, as a table grape). COLOR: white.

For a variety that has always been viewed as an excellent table grape, it's surprising that almost every ampelographer describing Catalanesca in centuries past was convinced of its fine winemaking potential. Yet, it was officially recognized as a cultivar from which to make wine only in 2006; prior to this date, Catalanesca in Italy was thought of primarily as a table grape. Presently it is listed as a wine grape and a table grape in the National Registry. Most likely of Spanish origin, as its name clearly implies (it is also known as Catalana or Uva Catalana), local lore would have it that Catalanesca arrived in Campania in the mid-1400s along with Alfonso I of Aragon, the king of the Kingdom of the Two Sicilies. At that time it was planted on the slopes of the Monte Somma, at altitudes ranging between 150 and 500 meters above sea level; it appears to have taken extremely well to the volcanic soils, and was soon planted everywhere on and around the volcano. Catalanesca was already well known in and around Naples in the fifteenth century, and in fact was of great significance to the Vesuvian economy up until the 1950s, as it was the main variety used to make the wine Lacryma Christi Bianco, though it later lost out to Caprettone. Interestingly, because of the volcanic soils (clearly, phylloxera was never a problem on Vesuvius) and the advanced age of most of the remaining vineyards, most Catalanesca vines are still on their original rootstocks.

A Catalanesca Nera grows in the province of Caserta, but it is not clear whether it is related to Catalanesca or is a distinct variety. Costantini, Monaco, Vouillamoz, Forlani, and Grando (2005) suggested that Catalanesca may be related to Casavecchia, Summariello (that is, either Uva di Troia or the Puglian Sommarello), and Barbera del Sannio. Interestingly, another local variety called Gianniello (with which Catalanesca used to be blended to make Vesuvius white wines) is now considered a biotype of Catalanesca. According to Benny Sorrentino, the young and talented winemaker of the family estate of the same name, there are two biotypes of Catalanesca, one of which may correspond to Gianniello (or not): one biotype is characterized by a cylindrical bunch with elongated, loosely packed, oval berries; the other has bunches that are more conical and compact, because the ramifications from the main stalk are shorter and hence the berries are packed closer together. There are also differences between Catalanesca populations in Campania today: the Catalanesca studied by the University of Turin in 2008 presented noteworthy genetic differences from the Catalanesca reported on by the University of Naples in 2005. This raises the question whether both were true Catalanesca varieties to begin with. Clearly, more research is needed for what is essentially a recently rediscovered variety. Antonio Mastroberardino perhaps summed it up best when I asked him about this cultivar: instinctively throwing his hands up in the air, he smiled, "We just don't know enough about it yet . . . and anyway, for me, it's just too weird and aromatic!"

As Catalanesca's cluster is very sparse, and the berries thick skinned, it can stand being left on the vine to achieve degrees of *surmaturité*; it also keeps very well once picked, explaining why it makes such a great table grape (the sweet, large berries are another plus, of course). A late ripener (it's typically harvested at the end of October), it needs plenty of sunlight, and so greatly benefits from good exposures; however, when grown in areas such as Ercolano and Torre del Greco, it ripens extremely early, even in late August, but I don't think this is an ideal situation for Catalanesca. It's a rustic, productive variety but it is exquisitely sensitive to oidium and care has to be taken especially in warm summer months.

Which Wines to Choose and Why
Catalanesca del Monte Somma is the main IGT wine, and can be produced in the townships of San Sebastiano al Vesuvio, Massa di Somma, Cercola, Pollena Trocchia, Sant'Anastasia, Somma Vesuviana, Ottaviano, San Giuseppe Vesuviano, and Terzigno. The guidelines also allow for a *passito,* or air-dried, version to be made, as was once common in the area. Catalanesca can give potentially very good wines, all of which seem to have an obvious mineral bent with a little bottle age, but start out life soft and fruity, with hints of pineapple, apricot, and apple.

According to Luigi Moio, whose team studied the variety at the University in Naples, Catalanesca is characterized by high total acidity and this should make it less prone to oxidation than wines made with other Campanian white varieties. Hence, he also expects well-made wines to be able to age for at least four or five years after the vintage. Benny Sorrentino goes one step further, pointing out that thus far, given the still recent revival in interest in Catalanesca, "nobody really knows what it could do if planted on different soils." Vesuvius is characterized by two different *terroirs:* the southwest slope that looks to the sea, where the towns of Boscotrecase and Terzigno are located, and the northern slope, Monte Somma, where towns such as Sant'Anastasia and Somma Vesuviana are found. The former is characterized by a geologically younger, more fertile soil, resulting from multiple volcanic eruptions, and richer in sand and minerals; grapes grown here are picked sooner, and the wines seem to have lower acidities. In the latter, there is more clay in the soil, and the wines seem to have bigger structures and higher acidities—and this is where Catalanesca is usually harvested in late October. For what it's worth, I think that the better examples of this wine are produced on the northern slopes. And though Mastroberadino believes it to be aromatic, I think Catalanesca is a neutral variety (though of course there may be an aromatic biotype, or a *musqué* clone, or the aromatic catalanesca may be a distinct variety altogether), and so it is important to extract as much of the aromatic potential from its skin as possible. Sorrentino says that she likes to "cryomacerate a part of my grapes, though not all, because that could extract too much potassium, thereby lowering the overall acidity by precipitating tartrate crystals, giving my wine a higher pH and a softer mouthfeel that is not so typical of the variety."

WINES TO TRY: Sorrentino*** (Katalò), Casa Barone**, Cantine Olivella** (Katà and VO, the latter an air-dried wine where VO stands for Verso Ovest, in reference to the western exposure of the vineyards).

Catarratto Bianco

WHERE IT'S FOUND: Sicily. NATIONAL REGISTRY CODE NUMBER: 58 (Catarratto Bianco Comune) and 59 (Catarratto Bianco Lucido). COLOR: white.

If you love waterfalls as I do, then you must have a soft spot for the ultimate waterfall in wine grape varieties: the name Cataratto refers to the cataracts of wine the variety is very capable of producing. One understands why the *Cataratto*s have always been looked upon as charming fellows in Sicilian farming circles, where quantity not quality was the password for most of the last couple centuries. There, the *Cataratto*s were both the base for everyday quaffing wines and an integral part of the wines of Marsala (though the best Marsala are made with high percentages of Grillo). It was only with the wine revolution of the 1980s that people started looking at the *Cataratto*s as something more than workhorse grapes, and different subvarieties began to be distinguished with an eye to quality.

Historic Sicilian varieties, first described by Cupani in 1696, the *Cataratto*s are also called Catarattu Vrancu, Catarratteddu, Catarrattu Lu Nostrum, and very confusingly, Carricante, in areas other than Etna (where the real Carricante is historically grown). The *Cataratto* name covers many similar-looking biotypes that give different enological results. Therefore it is best to write *Cataratto*s, or to refer to the variety as Cataratto Bianco *tout court* (Di Vecchi Staraz, Bandinelli, Boselli, This, Boursiquot, Laucou, Lacombe, and Varès 2007) and then specify which biotype one is discussing. The most insightful classification of *Cataratto* biotypes was that of Pastena (1971), who characterized them on the basis of the appearance of the grape cluster and the berries into Comune, Lucido (further subdivided into Serrato [compact] and Lucido Spargolo [sparse]), and Extra-Lucido or Lucidissimo. *Lucido* refers to the brightness of the berry, with *lucidissimo* or *extra-lucido* indicating a virtual lack of bloom. The most important of these biotypes are Comune and Lucido, and the first to distinguish between them was Macagno in 1883. These *Cataratto Bianco*s have been determined to be identical, first on ampelographic grounds (Di Vecchi Staraz, Bandinelli, Boselli, This, Boursiquot, Laucou, Lacombe, and Varès 2007) and by SSR profiling (Crespan, Calò, Giannetto, Sparacio, Storchi, and Costacurta 2008; Carimi, Mercati, Abbate, and Sunseri 2010). There appear to be many other less-common biotypes such as Cataratto Ammantiddatu, Cataratto Bagascedda, Cataratto Fimminedda, and Catareddu Mattu, though in the absence of accurate ampelographic descriptions accompanied by genetic testing, it's impossible to know if there are distinct varieties among them. Most often, all these grapevines are interplanted together in the same vineyard, making their study especially difficult. Recent parentage analyses have determined that the natural crossing of Cataratto Bianco Lucido and Moscato di Alessandria gave birth to Grillo, a very important and high-quality Sicilian native. Furthermore, the *Cataratto Bianco*s share a parent-offspring relationship with Garganega, making Cataratto Bianco either a grandparent or half-sibling of eight other varieties (see GARGANEGA entry).

Not surprisingly, not everyone is convinced that Cataratto Bianco Comune and Cataratto Bianco Lucido ought to be considered interchangeably; though they are synonymous, they exhibit enough different traits (morphological, behavioral, and enological) that an argument can be made to keep the two varieties separate, as they are in the National Registry. Other experts believe that the National Registry hasn't gone far enough, and ought to list Extra-Lucido separately as well. Those who support the latter view suggest that Lucido and Extra-Lucido give the most refined wines (in particular Extra-Lucido). Of these biotypes, Comune tends to have higher sugar and lower acidity levels (and therefore is prized for Marsala production); Extra-Lucido has even higher acidity and lower sugar levels than Lucido. Comune has better oidium resistance than Cataratto Bianco Lucido, which has more compact bunches. All are very regular, dependable yielders. Official Cataratto Bianco Comune clones are CS 1, VCR 7, VCR 8, Regione Siciliana 60, and VFP 31, while there are none listed for Cataratto Bianco Lucido.

The *Cataratto*s are grown everywhere in Sicily, most abundantly around Trapani and Palermo; only in the island's northeastern corner are they less common. At over thirty-three thousand hectares in 2010, or roughly 29 percent of the island's total vineyard surface, Cataratto Bianco Comune is still Sicily's number-one grape variety. In fact, it's Italy's second most-common white grape variety, after Trebbiano Toscano. Cataratto Bianco Lucido is planted on more than six thousand hectares (or 5.3 percent of the total surface area under vine) which means that by themselves, the *Cataratto* varieties account for close to 35 percent of the land devoted to grapevines in Sicily. Though that's an impressive figure, it is noteworthy that it is a huge decrease from the 75 percent of only fifteen years ago. Interestingly, the *Cataratto*s are also planted in California, but acreage is decreasing there as well.

Which Wines to Choose and Why

The main DOC wines that can be 100 percent *Cataratto* are Alcamo, Contea di Sclafani, Monreale, and Santa Margherita di Belice (the latter two will be harder to find). Both *Cataratto*s are used in the white-wine blends of DOC Contessa Entellina, Menfi, and Sambuca di Sicilia. However, the variety's long association with low-quality wines with a penchant for facile oxidation (which explains its time-honored use in the production of Marsala) has caused the *Cataratto*s to be planted in significant numbers in regions other than Sicily. A good cataratto is medium- to full-bodied and not unlike a chardonnay, though I always wonder if that's because more than a little of that international has been added to the Cataratto wine. Certainly, Cataratto wines are best when made from grapes grown on higher hillsides, so that the variety may conserve its acidity and deliver more penetrating aromas and flavors. Aromas and flavors of sage, thyme, banana, pineapple, butter, and ripe citrus are common, with a slightly buttery, bitter twinge at the back.

WINES TO TRY: BioViola*** (Yule), Centopassi** (Terre Rosse di Giabbascio), Feudo Montoni**, Calatrasi-Accademia del Sole*, and Gambino* (Meridiano).

Centesimino

WHERE IT'S FOUND: Emilia-Romagna. NATIONAL REGISTRY CODE NUMBER: 378. COLOR: red.

Centesimino is also known in Emilia-Romagna's Faenza area as Sauvignôn Rosso or Savignôn Rosso, though nobody seems to know why or how the latter names were born—and I've asked! The name is really a curious choice, for Centesimino is certainly unrelated to Sauvignon Blanc or any other Sauvignon color permutation. Not very well known outside its immediate production zone, Centesimino is a lightly aromatic red variety that has been grown in Romagna in ever-increasing quantities since World War II. All the grapevines planted in the countryside around Oriolo (the epicenter of Centesimino wine production) derive from the Terbato estate owned by Pietro Pianori, nicknamed Centesimino (literally "small cent," or tightwad). Apparently, it was Pianori who decided to propagate cuttings from a centenary vine he had found in the garden of a noble family's villa in the heart of Faenza's downtown, the likes of which he had never seen before. Centesimino's very large, indented leaf is a striking sight, but only in Italy can someone hope to find a long-lost native grape variety in the middle of a bustling city! Thanks to his efforts, Centesimino and its wines are now on their way to a comeback; and so, since the 1960s, the variety has been called Centesimino in his honor. A good idea, since without his efforts it is likely the variety would have gone extinct.

Going unrecognized has been a common fate for this variety. Alessandro Morini of the Podere Morini estate had a story similar to Pianori's to tell: "When I bought the estate in 1998, among the many parcels of Sangiovese I also found this group of roughly forty-year-old, really weird-looking vines, unlike anything I had ever seen before. I thought it might have been Sangiovese that had been really manhandled by viruses, but by asking around I learned it was Centesimino, a variety the local old-timers knew well, but not us newcomers." Morini recalls that even Veronelli, Italy's greatest wine writer, didn't know Centesimino when he visited the estate in 2003; Veronelli actually recommended asking the high-quality Capovilla distillery about distilling Centesimino for grappa production. The variety was included in the National Registry only in 2004, after ampelographic studies had been completed by the nearby Centro Ricerche Produzioni Vegetali (CRPV) in Tebano, isoenzymatic analysis at the Istituto Sperimentale di Viticoltura of Conegliano (interestingly, Centesimino shares an isoenzymatic profile with Aglianicone, Barsaglina, Cesanese Comune, Ciliegiolo, Franconia, Montepulciano, and Moscato di Scanzo), and finally DNA profiling at the Istituto di Viticoltura in San Michele all'Adige.

Centesimino is an early-ripening variety, often harvested in August, as it tends to build up sugar levels easily. You might read that it's picked in late September, but that's the theory: in practice that doesn't happen. Leone Conti, one of Emilia-Romagna's best wine producers, says "it's a very vegetative variety: two weeks before harvest it's still pushing out new leaves, and it produces very little in the way of grapes." The grapes it does produce have a tendency to shrivel on the vine, so the variety thrives only in climates that are not particularly hot, partly explaining why it hasn't moved into other wine regions over time. However, its tendency to dehydrate on the vine does make it an ideal candidate for sweet wine production, and in fact some of the best Centesimino wines are *passiti*, or sweet wines made from air-dried grapes.

In the past, Centesimino was often confused with Grenache, but genetic studies from the CRPV of Faenza and isoenzymatic studies performed at Conegliano have disproved this notion. In fact, we now know that the so-called Alicante del Faentino is actually a biotype of Centesimino; there is something vaguely satisfying in seeing the lesser-known of the two varieties gain the upper hand.

Though it can be found around Forlì and in the valley of Brisighella, Centesimino is grown mainly in Oriolo dei Fichi, a pretty town in a small valley near Faenza, famous for its high-quality ceramics and named after the more than one hundred fig trees planted courtesy of the town's mayor decades ago.

Which Wines to Choose and Why

Centesimino wine can be labeled as an IGT with the Centesimino name in full view, or more often than not as Savignôn Rosso, or Savignôn; lately there are increased bottlings of IGT wines such as Ravenna Rosso, but there are also Emilia, Forlì, and Rubicone IGT bottlings available.

The wine will taste of red berries and sweet spices, with telltale fresh acidity and lively tannins packed on a light- to medium-bodied frame. In my experience, the centesimino made from grapes grown in the Val Camone (at higher altitudes) is lighter, fresher, and more refined in its aroma profile than the heavier, more structured wines from Oriolo. Neither is better, but they are certainly different. Due to its lightly aromatic nature, some experts believe that centesimino resembles lacrima di Morro d'Alba (a wine from the Marche made with the similarly aromatic red native grape Lacrima), but this is a mistake: the aromatic profiles of the two wines are completely different, at least to a trained "nose" (that of lacrima is more floral, that of centesimino more fruity). Still, due to the aromatic component (lavender, geranium, bay leaf, rosemary, cinnamon, nutmeg) centesimino does very well in a late-harvest, air-dried style. Though not every producer in the area makes a sweet version (for example, Paolo Baini of Vigne dei Boschi doesn't like his wine sweet), others maintain that as the wine is quite tannic, a little sweetness goes a long way. In my mind, it can also be a rather alcoholic wine, because the grape packs in sugar easily. According to Morini, "the wine oxidizes very easily and doesn't age particularly well: it offers the greatest pleasure when still young because of its penetrating, spicy, fruity charm."

In 1995 local producers united and formed the Associazione Produttori della Torre di Oriolo, including Claudio Ancarani, Andrea Balducci, Mauro Altini of La Sabbiona estate, Paolo Zoli, Quintan, Leone Conti, and Luciano Menti of La Spinetta estate, aimed at promoting local foodstuffs and centesimino.

WINES TO TRY: Podere Morini*** (Savignone, Traicolli Ravenna Centesimino Riserva, NV Rubacuori Passito; the latter is a sweet red wine not unlike a good Porto), Vigna dei Boschi** (Rosso per te Rosso Ravenna), Ancarani**, Leone Conti** (Arcolaio), Paolo Francesconi**

(D'Incanto Vino Passito, a sweet wine), and all the producers of the Associazione, who work remarkably well and in unity.

Cesanese

WHERE IT'S FOUND: Lazio. NATIONAL REGISTRY CODE NUMBER: 60 (Cesanese Comune) and 61 (Cesanese d'Affile). COLOR: red.

Cesanese, of which there are two main varieties, Cesanese Comune and Cesanese d'Affile, recently shot to prominence when it was learned that porn star Savanna Samson's first wine, the 2004 Sogno Uno, was a blend of 70 percent *Cesanese*, 20 percent Sangiovese, and 10 percent Montepulciano. The wine actually earned favorable scores from some American wine critics (it never hurts with some wine critics to have the talented Roberto Cipresso as your winemaker), a testament to the many qualities of cesanese. In fact, it's a shame that the cultivar used to make it needed publicity of this sort just to earn its due. For *Cesanese*s are great, if little-known, Italian native varieties.

In fact, porn stars and famous winemakers aren't the only believers: *Cesanese* wines have been highly sought for centuries. The Roman Emperor Nerva was apparently so smitten by the wines made around Piglio that he had a palace built there (now there was a man who had his priorities admirably straight). *Cesanese* experts like Prosperi believed the *Cesanese*s were the ancient *Alveole,* a high-quality family of grapes described by Pliny, though I'm not sure there is any way Prosperi could have been certain of that. In fact, the first documentation we have of a Cesanese grape or wine is from Acerbi (1825), even though Soderini had written of a Cesenese (with an *e*) grown around Florence in the 1600s. Despite the slight difference in spelling, it is likely that *Cesenese* was the modern *Cesanese*. *Cesanese* was a favorite of princes and popes in papal Rome (Popes Innocent III and Bonifacius VIII were known fans), but these grapes have had their share of admirers in modern times too. For example, the esteemed Andrea Franchetti of the high-quality, world-famous Tenuta di Trinoro estate in Tuscany produced a wine called Cincinnato from Cesanese Comune grapes. Though he eventually gave up on the variety because of its well-known difficulties in ripening fully, the vintages that Franchetti did make are among Italy's all-time great red wines, not a small compliment in the land of many memorable Barolos, Barbarescos, Brunellos, and Amarones. Franchetti has planted some on Etna as well (where he makes his excellent Passopisciaro wines), admittedly a curious place to put a variety renowned for not ripening easily.

Also known by the very rarely used names Bonvino Nero, Cesanese Rosso, Cesanese Nero, Nero Ferrigno, and Sanguinella, *Cesanese* is, much like Sangiovese in Tuscany and Montepulciano in Abruzzo, the most famous and important grape variety of its region, in this case Lazio. The variety's name derives from Cesano, a small town just south of Rome.

It is commonly accepted that there are two distinct *Cesanese* varieties, Cesanese Comune, found all over Lazio (though mainly in its southern reaches), and Cesanese d'Affile, which is native to the area around the small town of the same name just outside Rome. In reality, there is a third, recently discovered *Cesanese* variety that few are aware of: Cesanese di Castelfranco, localized in sporadic plots in the northeastern section of Lazio, in the hinterland around Rieti. This variety is at high risk of genetic erosion and needs to be studied further; presently its relevance is still only anecdotal. All these *Cesanese*s are neither clones nor biotypes, but rather distinct varieties sharing a similar name, with different isoenzymatic and SSR profiles. The first to correctly recognize the main two varieties as separate was Mengarini (1888), though Mancini (1893) was the one who described the fundamental difference in berry size, and Prosperi (1939) was the first to furnish truly detailed descriptions of each. The d'Affile variety is considered to be the higher-quality one, but as it prefers very high altitudes it usually has trouble ripening, which is something of a chore even for Cesanese Comune. However, as Comune is easier to work with, it is, appropriately enough, the more common of the two. Of course, were you to listen to what producers say, you couldn't be blamed for concluding that Cesanese Comune has gone the way of the dodo, since everyone and their sister seem to be growing, perhaps not surprisingly, only the higher-quality d'Affile variant. A simple walk in the vineyards will reveal to all those who know a little bit of the variety that this is in fact not so: Cesanese d'Affile's much smaller berries are a clear giveaway to its presence—or not—in the vineyards. Yet another variety called Cesanese Velletrano has been described to me by local farmers, but has never been studied on a genetic level. If it really is separate from the other two (Mancini in 1893 wrote that it was synonymous with Cesanese Comune), then my guess is that it's just another *Cesanese* biotype. Certainly it's rare to find anyone talking about it anymore, and the last time a producer showed me some Cesanese Velletrano was in 2001 or 2002—though it really didn't look all that different to me from Cesanese Comune, he poetically went on and on, about biodiversity in the vineyards and all the usual suspects.

Cesanese Comune is morphologically different from Cesanese d'Affile: though both have winged, compact bunches, Comune's are cylindrical or conical in shape, while d'Affile's are pyramidal, and medium-sized (280 grams on average, to d'Affile's average of 220 grams). Comune's round berries are also medium-large (average weight 2.25 grams) compared to d'Affile's medium-small ones (1.8 grams). Further, there are three different biotypes of Cesanese Comune: biotype 1 has a five-lobed leaf, a large, compact bunch, and large berries, while biotype 2 has a leaf with three lobes, and small, compact bunches and berries; the leaves of both have shiny smooth undersides. In contrast, biotype 3 not only has leaves with a downy underside, but also has larger berries and more loosely packed bunches. Due to the quality that the *Cesaneses* are undoubtedly capable of, improving available clonal selections is a recent objective. In the early twenty-first century, Ciolfi and Garofalo at the Istituto Sperimentale per l'Enologia at Velletri developed a series of new Cesanese d'Affile clones, labeled A5, A8, A9, A10, A19, A20, and A21; of these, A9 and A20 seem best suited for making wines of early appeal, while A8, A19, and A21 are the choice for slightly more ageworthy wines. The list of Cesanese d'Affile clones is completed by the more recently developed ARSIAL-CRA 228 and ARSIAL-CRA 232. The ARSIAL clones have the advantage of ripening earlier (in the last part of September, as opposed to October like all the other clones), which is a big advantage; but their wines are said to have a slightly more obvious bitter note on the finish. The 232 clone is characterized by darker color and lower total acidity levels. The only official clone of Cesanese Comune available is ARSIAL-CRA 838; it's not very productive, which is strange considering it's a Cesanese Comune. Usually, Cesanese Comune is both vigorous and productive, while Cesanese d'Affile is neither vigorous nor a regular producer. Both Cesanese Comune and d'Affile are peronospora sensitive. All *Cesanese* biotypes are characterized by anthocyanin concentrations of roughly 25–30 percent peonin and cyanin, with acylated forms hovering below 8 percent, meaning that, despite what some people may tell you, the wines aren't going to be the darkest around.

Which Wines to Choose and Why

Cesaneses are found mainly in Lazio, though they have also been planted in Tuscany, Umbria, and Sicily. With few exceptions, the most important wines are those of Lazio, where one DOCG and two DOC wines are made; the former is Cesanese del Piglio, the latter are Cesanese di Olevano Romano and the somewhat confusingly named Cesanese d'Affile, a wine theoretically made only from Cesanese d'Affile. Cesanese del Piglio is made in the southern province of Frosinone (around the hilltop towns of Acuto, Anagni, Paliano, Piglio, and Serrone) and Cesanese d'Affile around Affile (and a small amount around Serrone), while Cesanese di Olevano Romano is made around the town of the same name and Genazzano, just south of Rome. Other wines of note that are made with the *Cesanese*s include DOC Velletri and IGT Colli Cimini, Colli di Saleno, Narni, and Spello.

Cesanese Comune is also grown southeast of Rome in the Cori area, which may come as a surprise, yet the local Cori DOC has called for 20 percent *Cesanese* since it was created in 1971, implying the variety had always lived there (since *Cesanese* really wasn't famous enough in the 1970s for local growers to have desired pushing it in the blend). Differences in the *Cesanese* wines of Cori with respect to those of d'Affile or Olevano Romano are mainly due to diversities in the *terroir*. At Cori, since there is not much limestone, the wine has less structure, but nice freshness and minerality. The microclimates are very different too: Cori has one of the highest sunlight hour totals in Italy, rather like northern Puglia, and is much warmer and sunnier than Olevano Romano, even though the two towns are less than an hour's drive apart. This is important because the *Cesanese*s don't ripen well in general, but at Cori, they do, and the lighter soils guarantee the wine will be considerably perfumed. Also, there are no problems obtaining darkly colored wines in Cori, as there are in Olevano, Piglio, and Affile. But remember that a black-as-ink cesanese is just as absurd as a sepia or ebony sangiovese or nebbiolo. Some creative producers might insist otherwise, but you know better.

In fact, with a more quality-focused approach to winemaking, and with greatly reduced average yields, cesanese might have returned to fame much earlier in the twentieth century. Historically, *Cesanese*s were used to make all types of wine, from sparkling to dry to late harvest, but these wines were always plagued by shoddy winemaking and unhygienic cellars. Today things have changed for the better, and *Cesanese* wines are definitely something to get excited about. These days, cesanese is almost entirely produced as dry wine, though *passito*s, sweet air-dried wines, have recently begun to appear again. Even better, there are many new, exciting young producers who have stopped turning their grapes over to lowly local co-ops; and though rustic and nondescript wines still abound, there really are many fine cesaneses made today. The better wines are ripe red-cherry fruit bombs, with aromas of delicate sweet spices (a hint of cinnamon and of white pepper) and red rose petals, and come across as luscious and creamy. I can't stress enough the wonderful, delicately aromatic nose that a well-made cesanese is endowed with: one whiff and you'll be hooked for life. The variety is not massively tannic, so anything tasting astringent and behemoth-like is probably the result of overgenerous use of oak, which is a real shame, since balance is what makes cesanese such a great red wine. When good, these really are some of Italy's best and most fairly priced reds. In fact, cesanese has to be considered one of the big success stories of Italian winemaking in the last ten years.

WINES TO TRY: For Cesanese del Piglio, try: Casale della Ioria*** (especially the top wine Torre del Piano, but they're all good here), Coletti Conti** (Hernicus, Romanicum, at times oaky), La Visciola** (Ju Quarto, Vicinale), and Terenzi** (Velobra). For Cesanese di Olevano Romano, try: Damiano Ciolli*** (the entry-level Silene and the stellar Cirsium, made from eighty-year-old vines), Buttarelli* (I Colli), Migrante* (Consilium), and Proietti* (Corte alla Luna, Vignalibus). For Cesanese d'Affile, try: Colline di Affile*** (Le Cese) and Formiconi** (Capozzano). For Cori, try Cincinnato** (Arcatura, a monovarietal cesanese). The Cesanese del Piglio wines of Marcella Giuliani have been praised in the past by others, but though well made, they are very dark and creamy-sweet: apparently, the wine's deep color is the result of very strong bleeding in the cellar.

Chatus

WHERE IT'S FOUND: Piedmont. NATIONAL REGISTRY CODE NUMBER: 379. COLOR: red.

Usually also known as Bournin (in Piedmontese dialect) or as Nebbiolo di Dronero,

Chatus has still other synonyms depending on where it grows in the region. It goes by Brunetta and Scarlattinin in Val di Susa, and Brachet in the Canavese (though the latter is a mistake: Brachet is a different variety). It is unrelated to the better-known Nebbiolo, and for this reason the variety is increasingly being called Chatus, in order to avoid confusion with the more famous cultivar of the Langhe.

As this book is devoted to Italy's native and traditional grapes, the question before us is whether Chatus is a native of France's Ardèche and Isère regions (where it is also called Chatus), and therefore only traditional to Piedmont, or if it traveled in the opposite direction, making it a traditional, not native, variety of France. On Italy's behalf, Rovera (1981) found documents dating 1268 and 1399 attesting to a Nebiolus grown around Dronero. While it's possible that the grape being described was Nebbiolo, that variety was never grown much in this neck of the Piedmontese woods, so more than likely, it was Chatus being described. Relative to France, the oldest mention of a Chatus dates only to the 1600s, when Olivier de Serres described it as one of the best varieties of Ardèche (then called Vivarais). Apparently, DNA parentage analysis has implied that a crossing of Chatus and Gouais Blanc gave birth to Sérénèze de Voreppe, an abandoned variety in France, admitted into the official French catalogue of grape varieties in 2012. Were it proven true that Sérénèze is a natural progeny of Chatus and Gouais Blanc, that would make a French origin more likely, since the latter is a very rare variety in Italy (if it's present at all). Nowadays, Chatus is almost extinct in France, while it hangs on, albeit in small amounts, in Italy; and it is also one of the parents of many Italian laboratory crossings. For all these reasons, I view Chatus as an Italian, rather than French, grape.

Confusion and Chatus have always gone hand in hand. One fine mess was caused (or is it endured?) by Italy's esteemed Giovanni Dalmasso, the academic responsible for the creation of some of Italy's best laboratory grapevine crossings, among them his crossing of Chatus with Barbera to create Albarossa, one of Italy's most successful crossings ever. However, the researcher believed it was the real Nebbiolo that he was crossing with Barbera, not the Nebbiolo of Dronero, which is of course Chatus. In fact, the poor professor was fooled more than once: Torello Marinoni, Raimondi, Mannini, and Rolle (2009) have shown that practically all Dalmasso's crossings are offspring of Chatus instead of Nebbiolo. Consequently, Chatus is a parent of the following laboratory crossings: Albarossa, Cornarea, Nebbiera, Passau, San Martino, San Michele, Soperga, and Valentino Nero (see chapter 6). Stories such as these are common outside Italy as well (remember Müller-Thurgau, long believed to be a crossing of Riesling and Sylvaner, which it isn't) and confirm that identifying grape varieties on the basis of inaccurate ampelography is fraught with peril.

A mutation of Chatus is known as Nebbiolo Pairolé or Pirolé, the berries of which are characterized by so little bloom that they look black as the bottom of a dark pot, or *paiolo,* in Italian. Interestingly, this mutation has been observed in France too, where it is known as Noir de Maure. Chatus is very sensitive to hail and slightly sensitive to oidium, but it's an easy variety to grow and is resistant to grey rot. As it is very vigorous and productive (but with poor basal bud fertility), green harvests are a necessity, especially on fertile flatland soils where the quality of wines produced with Chatus is average at best. Once very common, Chatus is found today only in the lower Val Maira, mainly on the hills around Saluzzo and Pinerolo. Save for some grapevines still found in Ardèche, it had virtually disappeared from France, but has been the subject of some plantings recently around the villages of Largentière and Rozière, in an effort to revive both the variety and the wine.

Which Wines to Choose and Why

Chatus is often blended with other local varieties, such as Barbera or Neretta Cuneese, providing such blends with body and structure.

Though Chatus does not accumulate huge amounts of sugar (its wines are never too alcoholic, not a bad thing in these days of climate change), the variety's small berries have plenty of polyphenols (both anthocyanins and tannins), making the wines both deeply hued and structured. As the anthocyanins are very stable, the wines are characterized not only by deep hues but by long-lasting ones. The deep ruby-red, almost purple-black color of wines blended with Chatus is very different than that of Barolo or Barbaresco, which are made solely with Nebbiolo. In fact, Pelizza and many other local experts believe that Nebbiolo is an ideal blending partner for Chatus, especially since in the Salluzese area Nebbiolo gives wines that are even lighter colored than in the Langhe.

Pure Chatus wines are characterized by deep purple-black hues and delicately spicy, herbal aromas complicated by hints of blueberry and prunes. Chatus has a spicier and more savory quality than does wine made with Nebbiolo, and also lacks the perfume of red roses that makes the Langhe variety so unique. Try it with the local *salam 'd patata,* a salami typical of the Canevesano area.

WINES TO TRY: Caretto Loris** (one of the first estates to have believed in Chatus), Podere del Palas** (Desmentià), and Tomatis* (Neirantich); the Cantina Sperimentale Bonafus has also produced pure examples of this wine.

Ciliegiolo

WHERE IT'S FOUND: Tuscany, Lazio, Liguria, Puglia, Umbria. NATIONAL REGISTRY CODE NUMBER: 62. COLOR: red.

In my view, Ciliegiolo is one of the country's greatest but most underappreciated grape varieties, allowing for wines of mesmerizingly pure aromas and flavors. Ciliegiolo was most likely first described in the 1600s by Soderini, whose description of a Ciriegiuolo grapevine resembles the Ciliegiolo we know today. It does not appear to be of Spanish origin as was once believed (legend had it that it was brought back to Italy by pilgrims returning from Santiago de Compostela). Its name means small cherry, as both its berries and its wine smell of cherries.

When discussing Ciliegiolo, it is necessary to also refer to Sangiovese, for a number of reasons. First, Ciliegiolo's greatness has gone unnoticed partly because it has always been confused with Sangiovese (and a long list of other varieties): tasting a monovarietal Ciliegiolo wine will reveal a striking similarity to better monovarietal Sangiovese wines. In fact, I believe that many of Tuscany's greatest Sangiovese wines have been made over the years, unknowingly, with more or less large percentages of Ciliegiolo, erroneously mistaken for the more-famous cultivar. This is because wines made with Ciliegiolo can exude very pure, extremely refined and vibrant aromas and flavors of red berries and red cherries—just the profile found in many reportedly 100 percent Sangiovese wines. Second, the two varieties have also shared cultivation areas for a long time. It will be no surprise then that the two have morphological similarities that have often been the cause of incorrect attributions. In fact, in Montalcino there has always been a good deal of Ciliegiolo grown, and star winemaker and Sangiovese expert Maurizio Castelli states that growers there always referred to it as Brunellone (though there also exists a separate Brunellone variety). Castelli has also told me that "wines made with Ciliegiolo can be unstable, with a very high pH, but it was always a favorite of Montalcino growers because it increased color and perfume. For this reason, they also called it Sangiovese Forte, but that's another mistake, since the latter is a distinct variety." Third, it now appears likely that Ciliegiolo is a progeny of Sangiovese.

At times it seems as though Ciliegiolo has been confused with just about every other variety besides Sangiovese. It has been mistaken for Garnacha (Grenache), as its erroneous synonym Alicante di Spagna implies, and for Aleatico, as can be inferred from the just as erroneous synonym Aleatico di Spagna. It has also been considered synonymous with Riminese

Nero, Mazzese, and Sangiovese Polveroso, but the last two synonyms are erroneous, as Mazzese and Sangiovese Polveroso are different varieties (see SANGIOVESE entry; see MAZZESE, chapter 5). It's not surprising then that Ciliegiolo has also been the subject of a famous scientific misattribution in Italy, on a similar level as the California Refosco / Mondeuse Noire and Australia Albariño / Savagnin capers. In 2004, Calò, Costacurta, Carraro, and Crespan, analyzing data from Crespan, Calò, Costacurta, Milani, Giust, Carraro, and Di Stefano (2002), mistakenly identified Aglianicone with Ciliegiolo. This happened when a Ciliegiolo grapevine mislabeled as Aglianicone in the varietal collection was used for the genetic profiling. As Ciliegiolo and Aglianicone resemble each other (wouldn't you know it, Ciliegiolo can look like Aglianico too!), erroneous ampelographic recognitions and sampling errors are easy to make. It may be that some—but not all—of the many grapevines called Aglianicone basking in the Campanian countryside are in fact Ciliegiolo (see AGLIANICONE entry). But experts, including Luigi Moio (professor of enology and winemaker) and Castelli, do not believe that Aglianicone and Ciliegiolo are identical. Others have suggested that Emilia-Romagna's Albana Nera and Ciliegiolo may be the same cultivar, but I believe this to be impossible: I have seen numerous Albana Nera and Ciliegiolo grapevines and they look nothing like each other. Which doesn't mean that some so-called Albana Nera vines growing in Emilia-Romagna aren't actually Ciliegiolo, but certainly not all Albana Nera is Ciliegiolo, or vice versa.

Apparently, recognizing Ciliegiolo is difficult enough: however, Ciliegiolo's parentage is just as complex. DNA parentage analysis has shown that Ciliegiolo and Sangiovese have a parent-offspring relationship (Crespan, Calò, Costacurta, Milani, Giust, Carraro, and Di Stefano 2002), while later research showed Sangiovese to be the natural progeny of Ciliegiolo and an almost-unknown variety called Calabrese di Montenuovo that's not listed in the National Registry (Vouillamoz, Imazio, Stefanini, Scienza, and Grando 2004; Vouillamoz, Monaco, Costantini, Stefanini, Scienza, and Grando 2007). Unfortunately, this last conclusion does not jell with a DNA parentage study in which Ciliegiolo was shown to be a natural cross of Sangiovese and Moscato Violetto, also known as Muscat Rouge de Madère (Di Vecchi Staraz, Bandinelli, Boselli, This, Boursiquot, Laucou, Lacombe, and Varès 2007). This would mean Sangiovese cannot be a progeny of Ciliegiolo but rather that the opposite is true. The finding that Ciliegiolo is the offspring of a Sangiovese × Moscato Violetto cross was also confirmed in another study (Cipriani, Spadotto, Jurman, Di Gaspero, Crespan, Meneghetti, et al. 2010). Another recent study has concluded that Sangiovese is the result of a Ciliegiolo and Negrodolce cross, the latter a little-known Italian cultivar (Bergamini, Caputo, Gasparro, Perniola, Cardone, and Antonacci 2012). Clearly, this is a matter that needs to be studied in more detail.

Ciliegiolo's bunch is large and long (average weight 350–460 grams), pyramidal, and compact with one or two wings; it has medium-large round berries. It's sensitive to grey rot, strong wind, and spring frosts, but drought resistant. Its budbreak occurs after that of Sangiovese but before that of Canaiolo Nero; it ripens early, often by the end of August, and it is both a very vigorous and a reliable producer. Available clones include U.S. PI FI Pec. 21, VCR 1, CL CAB 8, ARSIAL-CRA 223, and UBA-RA CI 3. Its large, round berries pose potential problems with bloating and busting. The key is to plant Ciliegiolo in soils that have excellent water drainage (therefore never in flatland vineyards); hillside positions are also best because mildly windy conditions are ideal for Ciliegiolo's large, botrytis-prone bunch. Ciliegiolo's vigor makes for difficult times in the vineyard, producing excessive foliage that must be removed or thinned to ward off the risk of rot in excessively humid conditions. Viticulture expert Stefano Dini told me that for this reason, people have always selected Ciliegiolo grapevines with the loosest-packed bunches of all. With Ciliegiolo, he likes to perform a careful deleafing very early in the season, to allow easier penetration of breezes, but also so that the berries may develop thicker skins in response to the sunlight. "It's almost too generous and vigorous," adds Castelli. "Even more than with other varieties, the best wines are invariably made with older vines with deep root systems." Not surprisingly, given that Ciliegiolo has lived in the hottest parts of Tuscany for centuries, it tolerates heat and drought very well (old vines certainly help in this respect): unlike Sangiovese, the metabolism of which tends to shut off in extreme conditions, so that grapes cook rather than ripen, Ciliegiolo's does not. You might say that Ciliegiolo is an excellent example of how specific grape varieties are, or become, particularly suited to their habitat over centuries: there's a reason why grapes are native or local.

The estate most intimately associated with Ciliegiolo in recent years has been Tuscany's Sassotondo, where owners Carla Benini and Edoardo Ventimiglia have worked closely with their winemaker, Attilio Pagli, to promote the variety. Pagli is a highly respected winemaker who has had starring roles in wineries in and out of Italy (witness his great Argentinean Malbecs) and fell in love with Ciliegiolo in 1988, just by looking at the bunches and big red berries. "I first encountered Ciliegiolo in an estate bought by Rascioni and Ceconello, who wanted to uproot it," he says. "But since the grapes were juicy and sweet, I thought that trying Ciliegiolo on its own was worth a shot. Time proved us right, though the start wasn't easy. We had to replant many vines and perform numerous microvinifications to get it just right. Luck played a role too: the 1988 vintage was a stellar one in Tuscany and so our first-ever Ciliegiolo wine was very impressive, setting our resolve for future vintages. However, we hadn't grasped Ciliegiolo's full potential at the time. We still thought it was good only for simple, everyday wines." When Pagli first met Edoardo and Carla at Sassotondo nine years ago, he realized they owned an old Ciliegiolo vineyard, and he suggested running with it. Given the amazing success of Sassotondo's Ciliegiolo wines, it's fair to say they've never looked back.

In Italy, Ciliegiolo is mainly grown in Tuscany, though there is probably more than commonly believed in Umbria and Lazio, with small plantings in Liguria and Puglia. In fact, it's likely to be found all over central Italy. In Tuscany, its growth is concentrated in the southeastern coastal area known as Maremma, around the beautiful town of Lucca, and, of course, in both Chianti and Montalcino, as well as in the Colline Lucchesi and Montecarlo. Importantly, though there is a lot of Ciliegiolo in Chianti, Ciliegiolo doesn't ripen well in this cooler part of Tuscany; it's only in Maremma's sunny, hot, dry climate that it comes into its own. That said, excessive heat can be too much of a good thing, as low acidity is a potential Achilles's heel for Ciliegiolo. The variety performs better in the inland areas of Maremma, around Pitigliano or Scansano, where summer days are on average five degrees Celsius cooler than in coastal Maremma, and where the volcanic, mineral soils offer excellent drainage (Ciliegiolo likes tufa soils).

Outside Italy, Ciliegiolo has been planted in the United States and Argentina, but given the variety's heat tolerance and drought resistance, it seems to me like it would be a very good match for many viticultural areas in the New World. Therefore, it's not surprising to see that University of California at Davis viticulture specialists are conducting field trials to evaluate Ciliegiolo (among other varieties) for quality and economic suitability in California's hot and dry San Joaquin Valley.

Which Wines to Choose and Why

Though Ciliegiolo is recommended in about twenty different DOC wines and twice as many IGT blends, monovarietal wines are rare, though on the increase. DOC wines outside Tuscany include Rosso Orvietano Ciliegiolo from Umbria (though the most interesting Umbrian wines are still IGTs) and Golfo del Tigullio and Colli di Luni from Liguria.

Ciliegiolo, at its best, is an amazingly fruity wine with a very graceful, refined mouthfeel: it really will remind you of a sour red-cherry fruit cocktail with alcohol. Its acidity can be lacking at times (especially when made from grapes grown in warmer microclimates), but well-made wines are medium-bodied, bright, and juicy, the red-cherry and berry flavors crisp and sweet, with smooth tannins. It takes very well to carbonic maceration and for this reason can make wonderful *novello* or *nouveau*) wines, but very few Italian producers take *novellos* seriously, so beware. The best Ciliegiolo wines are from Tuscany's Maremma region, while those from Liguria are more herbal and those from Umbria simpler and a little neutral, but still embody ciliegiolo's fresh, fruity appeal.

WINES TO TRY: For Tuscany, try: Sassotondo*** (Sanlorenzo, a great Italian red), Antonio Camilli*** (Principio), La Selva***, Poggio Argentiera** (Vallerana Alta), Rascioni & Cecconello** (Rotulaia, the fresh entry-level version, and Poggio Ciliegio), Cesani** (Serrise), La Busattina*, and Roccaccia* (Poggiocavalluccio). For Liguria, try: Bisson**, Pino Gino**, and Il Monticello (Serasuolo, a good *rosato*); many other locals use Ciliegiolo in red blends with Sangiovese or Granaccia. For Umbria, try: Zanchi** (Carmìno), Vallantica*, Cantine Colli Amerini, and San Lorenzo (Cleos).

Cividin

WHERE IT'S FOUND: FVG. NATIONAL REGISTRY CODE NUMBER: 388. COLOR: white.

The name Cividin derives from the town of Cividale, the ancient Forum Julii founded by Julius Caesar, later the first capital of the Longobard kingdom, the ancient tribe from which the Lombardy region takes its name. It is not known if Caesar liked wines made with this variety (though he was a known fan of Sicily's mamertino), but given its birthplace, Cividin certainly qualifies as a grape of the Caesars. Despite the variety's name, Marzotto (1923) wrote that Cividin is not original to Cividale but rather to the San Pietro al Natisone Valley, where it used to be common. However Ivan Rapuzzi of the Ronchi di Cialla estate, who has recently been experimenting with Cividin, believes that Cividin is the grape of Cividale.

The first accurate description of the variety is that of Maniago in his nineteenth-century *Catalogue of the Grape Varieties of the Veneto Kingdom* (Bulfon, Forti, and Zuliani 1987). In any case, Cividin was apparently once highly thought of. In the seventeenth and eighteenth centuries its wines were particularly sought after, curiously enough, for wedding banquets. Today, Cividin seems to be on a comeback course, with a number of different estates working with the University of Udine to set up experimental vineyards and microvinifications.

Cividin has medium-sized, pentagonal leaves with five obvious lobes and jagged teeth. The grape bunch is also medium-sized, cylindrical, and very tightly packed, with one to two wings. Berries are spherical tending toward an almost oval shape. Very sensitive to oidium, Cividin needs well-exposed sites, otherwise it fails to ripen properly, as it's also a very late ripener (it some vintages, late October harvests are not unheard of). There are no official clones. It grows only in small vineyard plots of Friuli Venezia Giulia. Cividin is most planted around Pinzano al Tagliamento, though recently vines have been located near the upper reaches of the Vipacco River and even in the Carso, near Trieste.

Which Wines to Choose and Why

Given its only very recent rediscovery, Cividin wines are still a work in progress. Microvinifications show dry extracts of medium concentration, generally high alcohol (Cividin grapes have no trouble accumulating sugar), and high total acidity levels. The latter characteristic suggests Cividin might be particularly suited for sparkling wine production. Wines I have tried over the years all exude aromas of citrus and tropical fruits, plus a terpenic note that recalls the white-berried *Moscatos*. They are almost always somewhat more austere and straightforward in the mouth, expressing nuanced saline and mineral notes. The only current cividin produced for commercial sale is made by Emilio Bulfon, about whom I can't say enough good things, seeing as he almost single-handedly saved about six or seven grape local varieties that were otherwise most likely headed for extinction. That said, I don't think cividin is Bulfon's most successful or interesting wine. Over the years (and I have tasted every vintage time and again) I have found his cividin to be a little neutral, with only delicate aromas and flavors of tangerine, pineapple, and white flowers. It does offer some structure and palate presence, perhaps explaining its appeal to others. I must be missing something, since Pierpaolo and Ivan Rapuzzi of Ronchi di Cialla, a leading Friuli Venezia Giulia estate, who know a lot more about Cividin than I ever will, have faith in the variety and have planted it—who am I to argue?

WINES TO TRY: Emilio Bulfon**, though I am a much bigger fan of Bulfon's Sciaglin.

Cjanorie

WHERE IT'S FOUND: FVG. NATIONAL REGISTRY CODE NUMBER: 390. COLOR: red.

Also known as Canòre, Canòrie, Chianòrie, Cianòria, Rossàrie, and Vinosa, the correct spelling of this variety's name is with a "j," as in Cjanorie and not Cianorie. Cjanorie was never intensely cultivated in Friuli Venezia Giulia (its only Italian home), but was described in the hinterland of the provinces of Pordenone and Udine: this despite its having being sought after by local eighteenth-century nobles, who appreciated the delicate, almost pink, lightly alcoholic wines it made (though some experts dispute this, believing that Cjanorie was first reliably documented by Marzotto only in 1923). Cjanorie's name derives from *cjane* ("canes" in Friulian), possibly because the vines were tied to canes or the grapes were once partially air-dried prior to being pressed. Another possibility is that the name is related to *canuto*, in reference to the pale color of the variety's leaves, or its small bunches. According to Orfeo Salvador, Carlo Petrussi, and Emilio Bulfon, three of the biggest experts in matters pertaining to Friuli wines, it is less likely that the name stems from *bere a canna*, meaning to drink copiously, as this is a relatively recent colloquialism.

Cjanorie is a very vigorous, fertile, and disease-resistant variety. We know today that there are at least two biotypes of this variety, one typical of the Spilimbergo area and the other of Nimis. Though both have fairly large circular or pentagonal leaves, the former's are obviously much larger than the latter's. Both biotypes are characterized by medium-sized, cylindrical, loosely packed bunches with one to two wings; the berries of the Spilimbergo biotype are round, while those of the Nimis variant are oval. All the phenologic phases of Cjanorie's growth cycle occur late (budbreak, flowering, and *veraison* or the start of ripening) except for ripening, which occurs by mid-September (Spilimbergo biotype) and in late September or early October (Nimis biotype). There are no official clones of this variety.

Marzotto wrote that Cjanorie used to be especially cultivated in the area around Gemona; today it is limited to the hillsides of the Spilimbergo area, near Artegna, Peonis, Venzone, and Pinzano in the province of Pordenone, but also Maniago, Meduno, Navarons, and the area of Vito d'Asio, with scattered vines farther east, near Nimis. Emilio Bulfon is the person we have to thank that today we can speak of Cjanorie. He started out in 1972 and "it didn't take me long to realize that all the grapevines I saw around my house were completely different than any I had ever seen previously. Deciding I wanted to know more about them was easy—setting out to select, propagate and save them was a lot more difficult." In this, Bulfon acknowledges the help of Enrico Murador, past director of the agriculture department of the province of Pordenone and former president of the province. Thanks to these enlightened men, we know a little bit about and can drink cjanorie today.

Which Wines to Choose and Why

Monovarietal wines are rare, as very few estates own enough Cjanorie vines to make wine in commercially significant volumes. Also, due to their very pale red hue (the prevalent anthocyanin is peonin, so the wine's color is anything but dark and stable) and light body, these were wines that, twenty or thirty years ago, had apparently nothing to offer, since big, inky, chocolaty, high-pH wines were all the rage. Consequently, growers had little incentive to invest in the variety; as a result, Cjanorie's return from oblivion is a very recent phenomenon. Some believe the aroma profile is neutral and bland, but I don't agree at all. Rather, I think Cjanorie makes an ideal light, delicately aromatic red wine, even a *rosato*, with pretty if delicate aromas and flavors of red berries and roses. In fact, microvinifications have revealed high benzenoid and norisoprenoid concentrations, and slightly lower terpene levels; these findings explain why wines made with Cjanorie can exhibit a fragrant, delicately aromatic nose.

WINES TO TRY: Bulfon* and Florutis (Ricciul, a blend of Refosco Nostrano, Piculit Neri, and Cjanorie).

Cococciola

WHERE IT'S FOUND: Abruzzo, Molise, Puglia.
NATIONAL REGISTRY CODE NUMBER: 64. COLOR: white.

Also known as Cocacciara and Cacciola, Cococciola was essentially unknown outside its immediate production zone as recently as the 1990s. In many respects, Cococciola is another example of the upside of the craze for all things native, especially since it is now obvious to all that the wine deserved better than oblivion. Prior to this surge in interest, the variety had always been blended into Trebbiano d'Abruzzo, the region's most important white wine. There is not much available historical documentation on Cococciola, though it does appear in Viala and Vermorel (1909). Cococciola's highly localized distribution suggests it was most likely the result of either a spontaneous mutation in a preexisting grapevine, or of a natural crossing, perhaps even with a local wild grapevine.

For some time, Cococciola was believed to be a biotype of Trebbiano Toscano, but we now know that not to be the case. Instead, recent DNA studies seem to indicate it might be a relative of Bombino Bianco (the authentic one, from Puglia). According to Fontana and Filippetti, there exist at least three biotypes of Cococciola (2006).

An accommodating variety, ripening early and adaptable to even less amenable sites, the vine is delightfully easy to grow and to harvest and a favorite of farmers due to its high yields. Its only difficulty is a slightly higher than normal sensitivity to peronospora. Cococciola is characterized by a bunch that is generally described as cylindrical-conical, but that in my experience can take many and various shapes. Available clones are UBA-RA CC 6, UBA-RA CC 31, and 8 ISV; that there are so many clones, and an estimated eight hundred hectares of the variety in Italy as of 2009 tells us that locals really care about the variety.

Cococciola is found mainly in Abruzzo, in the area of Chieti (the townships of Ari, Rocca San Giovanni, and Vacri, in particular), though it is also grown in Molise and the northern parts of Puglia, where many experts believe the variety originated.

Which Wines to Choose and Why

There are DOC wines made with Cococciola in Abruzzo and Puglia, and over a dozen IGT wines that also allow Cococciola. There are now some interesting well-made IGT wines that are reportedly nothing but Cococciola. There's a real, if delicate, personality to Cococciola wines: pale straw-green, with menthol and lemony aromas and flavors buoyed by vibrant acidity, and a saline, tactile, and herbal quality that those accustomed to simpler, straightforward white wines often don't find to their liking. Anna Giovanna Di Ludodico, owner with Augusto Tano of the Coste di Brenta estate, arguably the best cocacciola producer today, likes to pair it with oysters and even white meat casseroles. The one caveat with Cocacciola wines is that now that the variety has become popular, all of a sudden there seem to be many new bottlings available. I suggest you stick closely to the names of producers I recommend below.

WINES TO TRY: Coste di Brenta** (Elisio), Cantina Frentana* (Costa del Mulino), Martello* (Brado), Ulisse* (Unico).

Coda di Volpe Bianca

WHERE IT'S FOUND: Campania, Puglia, Sicily. NATIONAL REGISTRY CODE NUMBER: 65. COLOR: white.

Though teachers will never admit it, they almost always have a favorite student in their class, much as writers tend to favor one of their characters over another. So I feel entitled to state unabashedly that Coda di Volpe Bianca is one of my favorite Italian native grapes.

There are many reasons why. First, it has long been an underdog, with most so-called experts poetically waxing on about the merits of Fiano and Greco, even Falanghina of all grapes (granted, wines made from the real stuff certainly are interesting, but many so labeled have only seen Falanghina with a telescope), scarcely giving Coda di Volpe Bianca a second thought. Second, it is a very pretty grape: its cluster is Rubenesque and opulent, bushy and plump, with a terminal curvature rendering it very reminiscent of the tail of a fox (or *coda di volpe*). According to Pliny the Elder's *Naturalis Historia* (though not all translates are accurate on this point), the Latin name of the variety, Cauda Vulpium or Alopecis, stems from the shape of the bunch. Third, Coda di Volpe Bianca is remarkable in its ability to give wines that are distinctly different depending on the *terroir* it is grown in; in this respect, it is a true translator of *terroir*, much like Riesling, Pinot Nero, and Nebbiolo. Last but not least, Coda di Volpe Bianca is an archetypal native Italian grape: apparently known and appreciated in ancient Rome, it tends to perform well only in its original habitat, seemingly unable to appreciate the merits of travel.

Though it is commonly called simply Coda di Volpe, precision requires that the "Bianca" adjective not be forgotten; this being Italy, it won't surprise you to know there is also a Coda di Volpe Rossa and even a Coda di Volpe di Lapio. The latter is most likely a biotype of Coda di Volpe Bianca that adapted over the centuries to Lapio's mountainous territory, though it could be a different variety altogether. Coda di Volpe di Lapio was first described in 1909 by Carlucci, but I have not been able to find any vines to look at, or at least none that could be trusted. Fortunately, few people still talk of a Coda di Volpe Nera, a synonym of Pallagrello Nero best unused as it only engenders confusion.

In centuries past, Coda di Volpe Bianca has often also been confused with Caprettone (in the province of Naples, on Vesuvius) and with Pallagrello Bianco (in the province of Caserta), but recent genetic studies have differentiated the three. Carlucci, in the 1909 Viala and Vermorel opus, wrote that it was identical to Coda di Pecora, a mistake that is hard to understand, since the two varieties don't look or behave at all alike. Porta, in 1584, was the first expert to draw attention to the similarity between the "fox-tailed" variety described by Pliny and Coda di Volpe Bianca.

This cultivar is characterized by medium-large, pyramidal bunches that taper in cylindrical fashion to a curve; the berries are medium to medium-small in size and round. Relatively easy to grow, it adapts to myriad soils and microclimates, but is not especially vigorous or productive. All the phenological phases of its growth cycle occur late, and flowering, a somewhat slowly-occurring and delicate process with this variety, can be an issue in wet springs. Coda di Volpe Bianca is generally low in acidity, a problem that is fixed by harvesting the grapes at different times, so as to obtain a mix of berries with higher and lower acidities. Its polyphenolic content can be a problem too: it can give musts with plenty of extract and color, but that can oxidize easily. It grows in Campania, in the provinces of Benevento, Avellino, Napoli, and Caserta, though it is most abundant in the first two. There are also sporadic plantings in Puglia. That said, the well-known American importer Marc de Grazia, now also a wine producer in Sicily, has found what he believes are old Coda di Volpe Bianca vines on his Etna estate. Given the penchant Italians (of all epochs, as we have seen) have for traveling with grapevines in their suitcases, he may well be right. Outside Italy, Coda di Volpe Bianca has been planted in California's Temecula Valley and in the San Joaquin Valley.

Which Wines to Choose and Why

The main DOC wines are the Sannio Coda di Volpe and the Taburno Coda di Volpe, both produced in the Benevento area, the latter the better of the two. Around Avellino it is almost always used in blends with Fiano and especially with Greco where it adds a softer touch, so Coda di Volpe Bianca can also be used to make DOCG wines such as Fiano di Avellino and Greco di Tufo; but there it has only a very minor role. On the slopes of Vesuvius, in Naples, it is included in the DOCs Lacryma Christi and Vesuvio Bianco, but more often than not it is confused with Caprettone, the predominant variety on those volcanic grounds.

Coda di Volpe Bianca has a sensitivity to soil differences that means it can produce a diversity of wines. In Irpinia the wines are very fruity, almost opulently so, while on mineral, lava soils they are austere. On the cold mountain slopes of the Taburno, an extinct volcano, Coda di Volpe Bianca wines can be intensely mineral and steely, almost like dry Riesling, while in richer soils and warmer climates, it tends to become remarkably softer and riper, resembling a rich, tropical-fruit-infused Chardonnay. Antonio Mastroberardino, who doesn't believe that Caprettone and Coda di Volpe Bianca are two distinct varieties, remembers that the Coda di Volpe Bianca wines born on mineral soils were once so austere they were almost bitter. Overall, the wine has always been highly regarded, and rightfully so. When the product of normal yields and vineyard care, on soils that aren't exceedingly mineral, wines can show prodigious richness and above-average complexity, with a honeyed, creamy texture and bright yellow and tropical fruit flavors (ripe peach, pineapple, papaya) that are hard to forget. Coda di Volpe Bianca is a wine that has something for everyone, matching well with simple vegetable dishes or more complex fish preparations, and even white meats. It's usually inexpensive too, another plus.

WINES TO TRY: Cantina del Taburno*** (Amineo, an outstanding buy), Vadiaperti*** (the longest-lived Coda di Volpe Bianca wines, and very Riesling-like in their intense minerality), La Rivolta***, Ciabrelli**, Cantine degli Astroni*, Cavalier Pepe*, Casa dell'Orco*, Ocone*, and Renna* (Lammicato, a rare air-dried version that is sweet and perfect with almond cookies).

Colorinos

See COLORINO GROUP, chapter 3.

Cordenossa

WHERE IT'S FOUND: FVG. NATIONAL REGISTRY CODE NUMBER: not registered. COLOR: red.

Also called Cordenos, Cordenossa is a rediscovered variety that until recently was no longer used to make wine; at most, the grapes from sporadically grown vines were blended with other red varieties growing in the area. Only recently has Cordenossa begun to attract attention again, thanks to the work of Emilio Bulfon, who was helped by Antonio Calò and Ruggero Forti in saving the variety from extinction. For Bulfon, who had previously saved and begun making wines from other similarly unknown varieties Forgiarin, Cjanorie, and Cividin, cordenossa wine was the last addition to his portfolio of Friuli rarities.

A reliable, large producer, Cordenossa was always held in high esteem by locals who distinguished between two biotypes: Cordenossa Grande, the more common and more highly regarded of the two, and Cordenossa Piccolo, with smaller berries and a more compact bunch. I wonder about this evaluation, as back in the nineteenth century a compact bunch and small berries meant problems with botrytis and less juice, two factors that would have held little appeal for quantity-minded growers. The Cordenossa present in today's vineyards has a very large, pentagonal leaf with essentially no indentations, so that it appears to have no lobes. The grape bunch is medium-sized and conical, with one to two wings; the small, round berries are characterized by thin but resistant dark-blue skins. It ripens very late in the season: the grapes are usually picked in October.

Cordenossa is only grown in Friuli Venezia Giulia and even there only in sporadic vineyard plots of the Pordenone province; it is most typically found in the Spilimbergo hills around San Vito al Tagliamento, San Giorgio della Rinchivelda, and Pinzano al Tagliamento.

Which Wines to Choose and Why

Recently, the Regional Institute for the Development of Agriculture in Friuli Venezia Giulia, in collaboration with the town of San Giorgio della Rinchivelda and the Tondat estate, re-created vin di uchi, a historic blend of three varieties (Palomba or Piedirosso, Refosco Gentile, and Cordenossa) that were commonly grown in the flatland vineyards near San Giorgio della Rinchivelda. The wine was an assembly of varieties, with the very rare Refosco Gentile, of which few vines remain, comprising roughly 50 percent of the blend and providing aromas and spices, the Palomba drinkability, and the Cordenossa tannins. In fact Cordenossa microvinifications reveal medium-dark hue (the variety has good concentrations of acylated, or stable, anthocyanins), aromas of red berries and fresh herbs, and strong tannic structure, heightened by high total acidity (with especially high levels of tartaric acid). The wine is uncomplicated and easygoing: local authorities hope it might become a symbol of the town and its local wine production. Emilio Bulfon makes a tremendously enjoyable, light-bodied monovarietal Cordenossa wine. It's the only monovarietal cordenossa I know of, and very good, in the typical soft and fruity Bulfon style, with strong aromas and flavors of black currant and violet, and less tannic vehemence than I might have expected given what I know about the variety. Biochemical exams performed on microvinifications of Cordenossa I have tasted show the wine to have a good concentration of both norisoprenoids and benzenoids, explaining its perfumed aromas.

WINES TO TRY: Bulfon**.

Cornalin

WHERE IT'S FOUND: Valle d'Aosta. NATIONAL REGISTRY CODE NUMBER: 304. COLOR: red.

While visiting the Anselmet estate in Valle d'Aosta in 2001 or 2002 (memory fails me), I was told I was one of the first nonlocal wine writers to taste the first commercial release of the estate's Cornalin wine—the variety had never been available as a monovarietal bottling until then. This means that Cornalin has only been available as wine for twelve years or so. That I was the first or one of the first didn't matter much to me, but getting to taste the wine did: I had driven nine hours from Rome just for that opportunity! What made Anselmet's bottling really special was that it apparently was the first-ever bottling of a rare Cornalin biotype called Broblanc, which I had previously only read about.

Cornalin is believed by some to take its name from *corniola,* or carnelian, the semiprecious mountain gemstone, while others think it stems from the town of Colignola, one of the epicenters of initial Cornalin cultivation. Another possibility is that the name derives from the cornelian cherry tree, which is renowned for its extremely hard wood. However, confusion regarding the origin of its name is not the only complicated aspect of Cornalin. The first written documentation of Cornalin's existence in Valle d'Aosta is by Lorenzo Francesco Gatta, the father of Valle d'Aosta ampelology. In his seminal 1838 *Essay on the Vines and Wines of the Valle d'Aosta,* he describes (with remarkable accuracy and detail) all of the region's native grape varieties and mentions both a Corniola and a Cornalin variety. Though his descriptions of the two share obvious ampelographic similarities, Gatta describes the former as one of the three most-cultivated varieties in the central part of the region (where most of Valle d'Aosta's viticulture has always been concentrated); he states that the latter is rare. However, thanks to recent work done by Moriondo (1999), we know that Cornalin and Corniola are in fact identical. Therefore, it appears that in the eighteenth century Cornalin was a very common cultivar in Valle d'Aosta. This changed in the nineteenth century, when all ampelographers, from Tibaldi (1886) to Louis Napoléon Bich (1896), record a huge reduction in both Cornalin and Corniola cultivation. By the time the twentieth century rolled around, Cornalin had been reduced to only a few sporadic vines and risked extinction.

Ironically, what probably saved it was its strong phenotypic resemblance to Petit Rouge, another highly productive local variety, with which it was interplanted. When nursery people had to collect vines for reproduction and propagation of Petit Rouge, many Cornalin grapevines were selected by mistake. In so doing, farmers and nursery personnel effectively ensured Cornalin's survival. Some farmers also continued to look after their old vines of Corniola, while others in the towns of Aymavilles, Jovençan, and Gressan cultivated Broblanc (a biotype of Cornalin), a variety they realized was different from Petit Rouge. The name Broblanc means white stalk in the local patois language, as Broblanc and Cornalin have this in common at the time of winter pruning; in this respect it is noteworthy that cornelian cherrywood is reddish on the outside but sandy-brown on the inside.

Why Cornalin's cultivation diminished so abruptly in a short period of time is not clear, for all the existing documentation attests that it gave wines of the highest quality. Furthermore, unlike Petit Rouge, it doesn't suffer sunburn, accumulates high levels of sugar, and yields reliably every year. Perhaps it was for these reasons that at the beginning of the twentieth century, Cornalin was exported to the Swiss Valais, where the wine quickly earned a good reputation. In Switzerland, Cornalin was renamed Humagne Rouge (nobody knows why, as the only Humagne is a white grape that looks nothing like Cornalin—the irony is that with Humagne Rouge making a name for itself, the authentic Humagne variety had to be renamed Humagne Blanc). Gotten a headache yet? Wait, it gets much better. In 1972, Nicollier, an eminent Swiss ampelographer, wrote a paper in which he lobbied to have the name of the local Swiss cultivar Rouge du Pays (or Rouge du Valais) changed to the much better-sounding Cornalin, a variety he and others believed to be extinct. Nicollier's idea must have been well received, since today there are 128 hectares of so-called Cornalin (formerly Rouge du Pays) in the Valais, which are more than the ten or so (though the count is rapidly growing) hectares of the real Cornalin in Valle d'Aosta (2010 data).

To simplify matters, Vouillamoz, Maigre, and Meredith proposed in 2003 that the Cornalin of Valle d'Aosta be renamed Cornalin d'Aoste, and the Swiss Cornalin impostor renamed Cornalin du Valais. This seems sensible, but unfortunately clashes with the International Code of Nomenclature for Cultivated Plants (ICNCP), which decrees that varieties be named in order of precedence. The result is that the Cornalin of Valle d'Aosta is to be named Cornalin *tout court,* while Cornalin du Valais has to revert back to its original name, Rouge du Pays. Ampelographic and isoenzymatic tests (Moriondo 1999) and DNA testing (Labra, Imazio, Grassi, Rossoni, Citterio, Sgorbati, Scienza, and Failla 2002; Vouillamoz, Maigre, and Meredith 2003) have confirmed the identity between Humagne Rouge and the real Cornalin. Furthermore, via recent DNA analysis, the study by Vouillamoz et al. has established that Cornalin is an offspring of Rouge du Pays and an unknown parent; in turn, Rouge du Pays is the son of Mayolet and Petit Rouge, two other Valle d'Aosta native grapes. Therefore, Petit Rouge and Mayolet are the grandparents of Cornalin.

All these semantic gymnastics would have very little meaning if Cornalin weren't an excellent grape with which to make wine. Thus in 1997 the Institut Agricole Régional, after localizing a number of old Cornalin vines in the central valley, initiated a program of massal selection. The mother plants were evaluated for presence of viral diseases via ELISA laboratory tests, reliability of yields, and quality of the wines. In 2000, vines deemed most suitable for quality wine production were multiplied and planted in the experimental vineyards of the institute, for an unbelievable total of fifty-nine different biotypes. The result of all this work is that in the past ten years, there has been no other native variety in Valle d'Aosta that has grown faster in number of hectares planted or new wines produced than Cornalin.

Cornalin is characterized by a medium-small, pyramidal or cylindrical bunch, more or less tightly packed depending on the biotype, with medium-small, dark-blue, round berries. It ripens in October, and is both vigorous and a dependable producer. Today, Cornalin in Italy grows only in Valle d'Aosta, over a very large area ranging from Arnad to Arvier, with vineyards planted up to seven hundred meters above sea level. Higher altitudes are dangerous for Cornalin as it fails to ripen in cold microclimates; but it cannot be planted in lowland warmer microclimates either, since it drops acidity too fast and then gives flabby, uninteresting wines.

Which Wines to Choose and Why

In addition to being used in Valle d'Aosta DOC blends such as Torrette, this grape has been awarded its own subdenomination, Valle d'Aosta cornalin. The sine qua non of cornalin, a point I cannot stress enough, is that this wine really needs to age to show off all of its considerable potential; it is not a wine to buy and open the same night, but rather to cellar for four to five years from the vintage. The color is pretty, usually medium purple-red with garnet highlights; intense redcurrant and delicately smoky-spicy aromas and flavors (pepper, vanilla, thyme, tobacco) are typical, as are medium-low acidity, and a very strong finishing tannic kick. When young, the wine seems a little dull and monolithic, with little in the way of nuance and complexity to boast about. It stands up very well to oak aging, but this needs to be done judiciously, as the wine risks becoming too tannic and chunky. Any cornalin worth its name on the label will always have an austere mouthfeel to it; charming is not how I would describe this wine, but its refined, delicately smoky, red berried and peppery elegance is hard to resist.

WINES TO TRY: Grosjean*** (Vigne Rovettaz), Renato Anselmet*** (Broblan), Feudo di San Maurizio***, La Vrille**, Le Clocher**, Les Granges**, IAR**, Rosset** (a rare unoaked example).

Cornetta

WHERE IT'S FOUND: Umbria. NATIONAL REGISTRY CODE NUMBER: not registered. COLOR: red.

Cornetta takes its name from its berries, which are horn-shaped (*corno* means "horn") when not yet fully ripe but ultimately elongate and become oval in shape. As this grape is also called Vernaccia Nera, is Cornetta a distinct Umbrian variety or is it a Vernaccia Nera biotype? (Of course, I am referring to the true Italian native Vernaccia Nera, which I can't believe is related to Grenache or Garnacha, despite what has been written elsewhere—see VERNACCIA GROUP, chapter 3.) In the absence of carefully matched ampelographic observation and corresponding genetic analysis no one can be sure. Initial studies performed at the University of Perugia did rule out any similarity with other major and local Italian varieties. Unfortunately, provincial funds allocated in 2009 for the study of the Cornetta grape were diverted to another project before reaching their destination and so we curious folks were left in the lurch.

Over at the Di Filippo estate, which has kept up production of vernaccia di Cannara, a historic wine of the Cannara area near Perugia, they believe the two varieties are different. Emma and Roberto di Filippo have told me over the years that in their area, vernaccia was the name used for this variety, not because of a relationship to other *Vernaccia* cultivars, but because the grapes were air-dried through the winter to make a sweet wine (hence, at least in this specific case, *vernaccia* from the Latin *vernum*). Furthermore, as local producers wished to call their wine vernaccia di Cannara, the only way to do so was to rename the Cornetta grape Vernaccia Nera, otherwise the "Vernaccia" name would have been legally off limits. In the words of Emma di Filippo, "What we did, incorrectly I know, was to use a technical paradox to resolve a bureaucratic paradox. The latter was a real impediment to any commercial success the wine might have: it's one thing to sell a famous wine such as Vernaccia di Cannara, and quite another to try and sell a Cornetta wine nobody has ever heard of." You know, Italy wouldn't really be Italy without this sort of clever initiative and ingenuity.

Cornetta is characterized by a conical-pyramidal bunch, with crescent or oval berries. It is very susceptible to oidium, less so to botrytis, and is very vigorous; therefore, both deleafing and green harvests in the spring and summer are necessary to ensure proper ripening of the grapes. There are no official clones available and quality-minded producers opt for old massal selections when they need to replant their vineyards. Cornetta grows only near Cannara in the province of Perugia (between Torgiano and Montefalco, two very well-known wine towns).

Which Wines to Choose and Why

Vernaccia di Cannara has to be made with at least 85 percent Cornetta, with the other 15 percent made up of red varieties authorized for cultivation in the province, but most examples are monovarietal or close to it.

The wine is always made from air-dried grapes, and is bright deep red, redolent of sweet red- and black-cherry aromas and flavors, complicated by notes of blackberry jam and cinnamon and other sweet aromatic spices. It finishes long and fresh, and is usually blessed with high acidity (roughly 6–6.5 grams per liter) and residual sugars of about 120 grams per liter. It is not unlike a less massive, less sweet Recioto della Valpolicella or a more tannic, richer California black muscat wine. For what it's worth, I don't think it tastes at all like a sweet wine made with Vernaccia Nera, as these are usually more aromatic and floral. Wines from different producers can differ greatly: since Vernaccia di Cannara is the product of air-dried grapes, left on straw mats (or more hygienic, EU-approved plastic shelves) for three to four months, the individual length of air-drying greatly affects wine taste profiles.

WINES TO TRY: Di Filippo*** (really lovely, and the only monovarietal Cornetta wine I know—don't miss it).

Cortese

WHERE IT'S FOUND: Piedmont. NATIONAL REGISTRY CODE NUMBER: 69. COLOR: white.

Cortese is a grape variety that has seen the ups and downs of life. Back in the 1960s and 1970s, it was desired by all, invited everywhere, admired, and imitated. This was because Gavi, then Italy's most famous white wine, is made with Cortese. Then the 1980s arrived, and so did the first few wrinkles on Cortese's image: too many wines made with Cortese, Gavi included, were neutral, tart, and meager, and wine lovers turned their fickle attention to other varieties and other wines. Today, Cortese is back, a little like an older lady or gentleman with enough class and experience to once again be a topic of conversation and desire.

In fact, Gavi has probably never been better, with a plethora of young up-and-coming producers now churning out one good wine after another. Cortese wines, when well made, have many selling points: high acidity (such that excellent sparkling wines, as well as great food wines, can be made), real minerality, and even ageworthiness. The problem resides in the yields: produce too many grapes, something that Cortese has no problem doing, and the resulting wine will be insipid and devoid of interest. In all honesty, the aroma of even the best Cortese wines does not exactly burn the nostril with laser-like intensity, and thus careless and greedy producers can be left holding the bag.

Cortese, also known locally as Courteis and Corteis (and as Bianca Fernanda in Veneto), has always been an important variety in the Piedmont because it is also a very good table grape. One romantic legend has it that the name of Cortese's most famous wine, Gavi, derives from the golden-haired, beautiful, and gentle-natured Princess Gavia, daughter of Clodomiro, King of the Franks, who eloped to get married against the wishes of her family. The whereabouts of the two lovebirds were discovered thanks to an overly talkative innkeeper (I dare say not a first, in the history of innkeepers and taverners); once caught, the two youngsters were not only pardoned, but received the modern territory of Gavi as a wedding gift from Amalasunta, Queen of the Goths. Alas, while many have tied the name of the territory and of the wine to that of the princess (Gavi/Gavia), in reality Gavi derives from the Latin term *cavatum*, meaning cavern, which later evolved into Gavio and finally Gavi.

Cortese has been documented in Piedmont since at least the seventeenth century, first in 1614 in an inventory of the cellars of the castle of Casale Monferrato and then in 1659 in Montaldeo by the farmer in charge of the vineyards at Castello di Montaldeo, who in writing to the Marquis Doria mentions "vines of Cortese."

However, the first ampelographic description of Cortese is by Count Nuvolone in 1799, for the Turin Agricultural Society. In 1856 the Marquis Cambiaso planted the first large holdings of Cortese at his estates of Toledana and Centuriona, and in 1870 Leardi and De Maria wrote that Cortese was the most-planted variety in the province of Alessandria. Cortese appears to have been always appreciated by farmers for its resistance to cold weather and good productivity, as well as the high-quality wine that could be made with it. However its thin-skinned berries make it liable to attacks of grey rot in humid or rainy autumns. The variety is characterized by wide biodiversity: an almost unbelievable seventy-five different biotypes have been described, which are currently being evaluated in their agricultural and enological aspects. Studies such as these have led to over thirty different Cortese clones being certified and available for sale. In general, Cortese has medium-large, pyramidal-conical bunches and medium-large berries. It has good vigor and productivity, and usually ripens in the middle of September. Nowadays Cortese grows in Piedmont, Lombardy (Oltrepo' Pavese), and Veneto (region). In Piedmont it is found mainly in the provinces of Asti and Alessandria (where Gavi is located), in the southeastern corner of the region. Gavi can only be made from Cortese vineyards located in the countryside around the ten pretty towns of Bosio, Capriata d'Orba, Carrosio, Francavilla Bisio, Novi Ligure, Parodi Ligure, Pasturana, Gavi, San Cristoforo, Serravalle Scrivia, and Tassarolo. The last four are by far the most famous for wine production, in particular Gavi (especially the Rovereto subzone) and Tassarolo: these two are reputedly where the best Cortese wines are made. Cortese is also grown in the Alto Monferrato and Tortonese areas of Piedmont. as well as in the province of Cuneo.

In Australia, Lost Valley Winery in the Upper Goulburn region of the Central Highlands in Victoria is making a good Cortese wine. Their 2011 won a silver medal at the Concours du Vin de Victoria, organized by the

French-Australian Chamber of Commerce and Industry. In California, I have also tried impressive wines, such as the Castelletto from Mount Palomar Winery in Temecula, and wines by Enotria from Mendocino and Fatto a Mano from Napa.

Which Wines to Choose and Why

The best wines made with the Cortese grape are labeled Gavi di Gavi or Gavi di Tassarolo. Unfortunately, there's an almost disheartening number of disappointing, neutral Gavi di Gavi wines made, and even more such wines simply labeled Piemonte Cortese. So I suggest you concentrate your attention on producers you know or wines also carrying the Rovereto designation, which means the grapes were culled from this specific subzone, known for powerful, more concentrated wines. Bigger structure is key for Gavi, as counterbalance to its naturally high acidity. In and around Rovereto, and to an extent in and around all of Gavi, soils contain chalk, guaranteeing wines with a level of finesse and depth unattainable elsewhere. By contrast, the nearby area of Tassarolo contains higher percentages of clay, and its wines have a richer, less mineral structure, though they can also be excellent.

In fact, the *terroir* of the Gavi area is far more complex than I have suggested. Even within the boundaries of Rovereto, there are notably different soil structures. Those vineyards located on the Rovereto area sloping toward Tassarolo grow on gravel-rich, clay-marl soils loaded with a high iron content, while the Rovereto portion sloping toward San Cristoforo is less rocky and has looser, much less compact soils. Therefore, the wines of Rovereto, always the most intensely perfumed of all the *Gavis*, will (given similar winemaking techniques) differ depending on which slope the grapes grow on: where those on the more compact iron-rich soils will be piercingly mineral and floral, those from the San Cristoforo side will be more structured and closed when young, and feature power rather than finesse. Stefano Massone makes an excellent example of Gavi from San Cristoforo, and that's how he labels the wine.

Piemonte Cortese wines of the Alto Monferrato and Tortonese areas, as well as those made in the province of Cuneo, are lighter and meant to be consumed young. DOC wines to look for include Cortese dell'Alto Monferrato, Cortese di Monferrato Casalese, Cortese dell'Oltrepo Pavese, and Piemonte Cortese. There also exists some Cortese in Lombardy's Oltrepò Pavese and in western Veneto, in the area of Custoza, with DOC Garda Cortese, Bianco di Custoza, Bianco Collina del Milanese, and Oltrepò Pavese. In Veneto, either as Cortese or as Bianca Fernanda, it is allowed in blends of DOC wines and IGTs.

A good cortese, or even better, a Gavi, is a lemony, truly mineral wine that features delicate white flower and herbal nuances, more or less marked depending on the ripeness of the grapes and the yields. The sine qua non of Gavi and all Cortese wines is the bitingly high acidity, which in cold vintages can reach enamel-stripping dimensions. The wine is almost always made in a crisp dry style, but some producers have taken to oaking in an effort to tame the acidity: the trouble is that most of these wines then end up smelling and tasting only of vanilla and caramel, for Cortese is a variety of gentle aromas and flavors and easily overpowered. Of course, because of all that acidity, sparkling wines are de rigueur with Cortese.

WINES TO TRY: Castellari Bergaglio*** (Rovereto Vignavecchia and Rolona are excellent; the entry-level Salluvii is a steal given its quality and price; the Fornaci is the best Gavi di Tassarolo made by anyone today; Pilin is their oaked Gavi, but too oaked for me); Bruno Broglia / La Meirana*** (Bruno Broglia and entry-level Gavi); Castello di Tassarolo** (La Spinola, Vigneto Alborina, both are Gavi di Tassarolo), Chiarlo** (Rovereto), La Giustiniana** (Montessore, Lugarara), La Raia** (Pisé), Le Marne** (Marne Bianche), Morgassi Superiore**, Stefano Massone** (Masera, San Cristoforo, both excellent), Franco Martinetti*

(Minaia, an oaked Gavi, too oaky for me), La Toledana* (Raccolto Tardivo), Nicola Bergaglio*, Villa Sparina* (Monte Rotondo).

Corvina

WHERE IT'S FOUND: Veneto, Lombardy. NATIONAL REGISTRY CODE NUMBER: 70. COLOR: red.

One of the many "bird-grapes" of Italy, Corvina's name means little raven (*corvo* is raven). Whether this stems from the fact that the ripe grapes have always been an attraction for the gourmet birds, or whether the dark Corvina berries reminded people of the birds' dark plumage is not known (in any case, though the grape's name may refer to a dark color, the wine should never be inky or especially deep in hue). The name *corvina/corbina* can also derive from *crova/croà* (dark berries), from *corba/corbera* (*corba*, or large basket, indicating large quantities of grapes), or from *cruina* (unripe, a reference to it being a late ripening variety usually harvested in early October).

Corvina is the most important variety in the blend of the world-famous wines Valpolicella and Amarone; however, for such an important variety, there is surprisingly little historical documentation available. Some believe that Corvina has been used to make wines in Veneto since 1627, when Alessandro Peccana wrote of *vini corvini* in his curiously titled opus, *The Problem with Drinking Cold Beverages* (a medical doctor, Peccana believed that drinking cold wine, perhaps with a little snow added for good measure, helped facilitate digestion). In truth, we don't know if Corvina was the variety he was recommending, as these *corvini* could have been any number of similarly named *Corvine* varieties (there are numerous, not necessarily synonymous cultivars with Corvina-like names). In 1755, Guglielmo Marani wrote that planting Corvina in less-fertile soils would give the best results (Calò, Paronetto, and Rorato 1996), while in 1810 Moro mentioned that the *Corvine Gentili* were among the best red grapes of the Veronese area. Corvina itself was probably first described in detail only in 1824 by Pollini; the fact there were (and are) many *Corvine* grapes believed to be distinct varieties only made things more difficult. Among the first to distinguish between the many varieties sporting similar names was Bertani (1886), who listed a Corvina Comune (which he also called Corba and Corva, but we know today that the latter is most likely a distinct variety), Corvina Rizza, and Corvinon, while Sormani Moretti (1904) cites a Corvina Gentile, Corvina Nera, Corvina Nostrana, Corvina Pelosa, Corvinella, Corvinetta, and Corvina Rizza. A probably more accurate list was drawn up by Cosmo and Polsinelli (1960) that mentioned only Corvina Veronese, Corvina Gentile, Corvina Rizza and Corvinone. Many of these *Corvinas* were either biotypes or distinct varieties, and not all are blessed with high fine-wine potential. For example, while Corvinella (or Corbinella) was considered a low-quality wine grape grown in flatland vineyards around Padova, Corvina was instead always grown on hillsides. It is worth noting that a profound connoisseur of Veneto grapevines, Leonildo Pieopan (of the world-famous Pieropan estate in Soave) believes Corbinella to be nothing more than a virus-affected Corvina. Corvina Rizza is another, now rare, Corvina biotype, the morphology of which is most likely the result of a viral infection. Corvina Gentile is still another biotype, apparently unaffected by viruses, that has considerable winemaking potential according to many old-timers I have talked to over the years; unfortunately its presence is now limited to old vineyards planted at higher altitudes. Calò, Costacurta, Cancellier, and Forti (1991) also described Corvina biotypes Piccola, Media, and Grossa, distinguished by the size of their berries and bunches.

Of all these *Corvine* grapes, Corvinone is especially important: long considered either a mutation or biotype of Corvina, Cancellier and Angelini (1993) proved it a separate variety by isoenzymatic studies, findings later confirmed by Vantini, Tacconi, Gastaldelli, Govoni, Tosi, Malacrinò, Bassi, and Cattivelli (2003). This same study also proved that Oseleta, Rondinella, and even Dindarella are closer relatives of Corvina than Corvinone. In 2007, Cancellier, Coletti, Coletti, Soligo, and Michelet also showed that Corvina is distinct from the much rarer but similarly named Corbina, a cultivar that is also believed to have outstanding winemaking potential. It is noteworthy that despite the absence of accurate modern investigative technology in centuries past, the distinction between the *Corbine* and *Corvine* varieties was quite clear to our ancestors, as documented by Marzotto in 1925, who stated that the *Corvine veronesi* were distinct from the *Corbine*. Furthermore, Friuli Venezia Giulia's almost extinct and little-known Curvin variety (currently being studied by the prestigious Ronchi di Cialla estate in conjunction with the University of Udine) is also distinct from both Corvina and Corbina: the three really don't look alike at all, and Curvin has a distinct SSR profile (Crespan, Fabbro, Giannetto, Meneghetti, Petrussi, Del Zan, and Sivilotti 2011). Finally, an important study (Grando, Stefanini, Zambanini, and Vouillamoz 2006) revealed that Corvina has parent-offspring relationships with Refosco del Peduncolo Rosso and Rondinella (the latter another Veneto cultivar used in making the wine blends of the Valpolicella area). What is fascinating is that since we know that Refosco del Peduncolo Rosso is a progeny of Marzemino, then Corvina must be an offspring of Refosco del Peduncolo Rosso and a parent of Rondinella, which also means that Corvina is likely a grandchild of Marzemino (see MARZEMINO entry; see REFOSCO GROUP, chapter 3).

Corvina is characterized by medium-sized, long, cylindrical-pyramidal bunches that often have a long wing dripping down the side; in these cases, it almost looks as if there are two bunches in one (local farmers still refer to this as Corvina Doppia, thinking it's a distinct variety, but it's not); the medium-sized berries are oval shaped and have plenty of bloom. It prefers dry, well-exposed sites. Though vigorous and dependably productive, ensuring large yields, it tends to be disease-prone (compact subvarieties are especially botrytis sensitive), is very sensitive to water stress, and its berries are prone to sunburn. It can also undergo dissection of the spine, and care is needed so that mechanical harvesting does not damage the stalks. It is still often trained with the *pergola veronese* system, where the grapes grow high above ground horizontally, a different setup from the better-known *pergola trentina,* in which the grapes grow lower to the ground but are trained diagonally upwards. The pergola training systems are ideal for Corvina, since it does not fruit on the first few buds of the cane and therefore needs plenty of space, and since it is disease sensitive and therefore benefits from additional air currents and distance from the ground's humidity.

Thanks to a thick, resistant skin, Corvina takes extremely well to air-drying, explaining its use for Amarone and Recioto della Valpolicella, the latter Veneto's sweet red wine. In fact, air-drying is an absolute necessity with Corvina, as it has trouble reaching adequate sugar concentrations and alcohol potential. To help it reach optimal ripeness, some winemakers, like the talented Laura Zuddas, who consults at the Giovanna Tantini estate, also harvest late and directly on the vine, weather permitting, and perform strong green harvests, removing up to 50 percent of the bunches at the time of the berry color change.

Corvina grows practically only in Italy's Veneto region, especially in the province of Verona in the Valpolicella area and in the Bardolino area, the latter hugging Lake Garda, on the border with Lombardy. It is also grown in Lombardy, in the province of Sondrio, where it is called Corvino. It is currently enjoying remarkable success, and the surface area planted to Corvina in Italy increased 27 percent from 2000 to 2010. It is also grown in Australia and in Argentina, where the famous Masi estate of Veneto has led the way.

Which Wines to Choose and Why

The best DOCG and DOC wines in which to taste Corvina are Valpolicella (up to 80 percent

Corvina), Amarone della Valpolicella (up to 80 percent Corvina), and Bardolino Superiore (up to 80 percent Corvina). In order to taste a pure Corvina wine, look for IGT wines such as Rosso Veronese. What should never be forgotten is that, paradoxically enough, the wine made from Corvina is never ultra-dark. This is a situation analogous to that of Pinot Nero, Sangiovese, or Nebbiolo: though the grape's name may imply a dark hue, the wine is rarely deeper than bright red. Wine writers tasting a supposedly 100 percent corvina need to keep this in mind. True, over the last decade, much as with Sangiovese and similarly light-colored wines, efforts have been directed to obtaining new clones that guarantee deeper hues; in this respect, the ISV 48 clone is increasingly being planted, but not all producers are convinced it has any worthwhile qualities beyond its deep hue. Also important is that Corvina wines are blessed with very fine tannins, but not a huge abundance of them, so while monovarietal corvinas can be lightly tannic, they cannot, and should not, remind you of a Sagrantino or a similarly tannic behemoth.

A good corvina will remind you of violet, blackberry, and red cherry, with a delicately aromatic touch of herbs. Some producers like to age corvina at least partly in cherrywood barrels, as this heightens their sweet red-cherry note, adding an almost resiny quality that may however prove too sweet for some palates. Giovanna Tantini tells me that "since with Corvina there aren't many tannins to worry about and the anthocyanin content is low, longer macerations (in excess of ten days) and higher fermentation temperatures (26–30°C) are fine, to help extract as much color as possible. Bitterness from excessive tannin extraction isn't really a concern." The most famous Corvina wine of all is Allegrini's La Poja, now a Rosso Veronese IGT wine that has the distinction of being the first monovarietal corvina to gain media attention and critical acclaim, winning numerous awards over the years. An impressive wine, I find it a little too dark and tannic for my taste.

Successful Corvina wines are being made in Argentina and Australia. I know of no monovarietal corvina examples from the latter country, but Freeman Vineyards in New South Wales blends it with Rondinella to make an Amarone-styled wine (the grapes are harvested up to three months later than their other grapes and are air-dried for roughly ten days). In Argentina, Masi has planted it at their Masi Tupungato estate, where it gives highly perfumed wines benefiting greatly from day-night temperature differences that heighten the aromatics. Masi even blends Corvina with Malbec to make two wines called Corbec and Passo Doble. Raffaele Boscaini of Masi jokes that pretty soon his Argentinean corvina will start challenging the one from Veneto for "best in show."

WINES TO TRY: Giovanna Tantini*** (Rosso Veronese Greta, my favorite corvina, a wine that is respectful of what the variety can give), Luigi Brunelli** (Corte Cariano), Allegrini* (Rosso Veronese La Poja), Davide Sterza*, and Le Vigne di San Pietro* (CordeRosa, dedicated by the owner to his wife, Rosa).

Corvinone

WHERE IT'S FOUND: Veneto, Lombardy. NATIONAL REGISTRY CODE NUMBER: 328. COLOR: red.

Its name seems to say it all: Corvinone is "big Corvina." But even though Corvinone's clusters are twice the size of Corvina's, it isn't always easy to tell the two apart. Also called Cruinon and Corvinon, this variety has always been surrounded by confusion: for centuries, it was simply considered a larger-than-usual Corvina, and there is a paucity of historical references to it. The association with Corvina is an easy enough mistake to make because there is a large-berried biotype of Corvina, Corvina Grossa, that looks almost exactly like Corvinone. For this reason, it's hard to be sure about prior opinions about this variety: Acerbi (1825) and Bertani (1886) were both enthusiastic (Bertani especially liked Corvinone's ability to perform well both in hillside and flatland vineyards) but I wonder if they weren't all just describing a Corvina biotype. It was only with the isoenzymatic analysis by Cancellier and Angelini (1993) that Corvinone and Corvina were finally distinguished as two distinct cultivars. For this reason, Corvinone is a relatively late addition to the National Registry, listed at number 328 only in 1993 (for comparison's sake, Corvina is number 70, and was included in 1970). I distinctly remember that in the decade following Cancellier and Angelini's study, every producer I talked with believed that Corvina and Corvinone, though separate varieties, were closely tied, possibly by a parent-offspring relationship. Only with a 2003 study by Vantini, Tacconi, Gastaldelli, Govoni, Tosi, Malacrinò, Bassi, and Cattivelli did everyone's understanding of Corvinone deepen: it turns out that the two varieties are not even closely related and that Corvinone is not related to any other Veronese variety.

Corvinone grows well in both flatland and hillside vineyards: in the latter sites it produces very little due to the development of more-loosely packed bunches. It's typically characterized by asynchronous maturation of berries, both within the same bunch as well as in different bunches growing on the same grapevine. This means that Corvinone is a lot of work come harvesttime because the green berries have to be picked out by hand and discarded. In what is a testament to Corvinone's burgeoning popularity among growers, there are seven different clones to choose from, all developed in a relatively short period of time.

Which Wines to Choose and Why

There are no pure Corvinone wines, since it is always blended with small to large percentages of Corvina: the two varieties are planted together in vineyards. This is not surprising, since the two varieties really do complement each other: Corvinone supplies Corvina with the tannins it is missing, and the end result is really much better than the single components on their own. If I have one quibble about Corvinone's modern success, it's that the variety's increased popularity means Valpolicella and Amarone are less and less characterized by the presence of Molinara, another grape that was historically an important part of these blends, to which it contributed acidity and a certain lightness of being. By reducing Molinara's role and increasing Corvinone's, these wines have all become much meatier and structured, which is a shame; at least, I do not believe that Amarone should be reduced to a wine drunk out of a liqueur glass, or that Valpolicella should be yet another bodybuilder-wannabe wine. In those rare cases where there is enough Corvinone harvested to make small, usually experimental batches of monovarietal wines, I have found it reveals a very intense red-cherry flavor, even stronger than that of Corvina wines, and of course much more obvious tannins. Given the "bigger is better" mantra that has often accompanied fine wine, I am actually surprised that no one has yet tried to make a monovarietal corvinone.

Croatina

WHERE IT'S FOUND: Lombardy, Piedmont, Emilia-Romagna, Veneto, Sardinia. NATIONAL REGISTRY CODE NUMBER: 71. COLOR: red.

Looking for a headache? Here goes, Italian style, and without drinking any wine. Croatina is the name of a grape and also a wine. Croatina is the main variety used to make a DOC wine called Bonarda in the Oltrepò Pavese of Lombardy, but there is a Bonarda grape variety too (different than Croatina; actually, there are at least six grapes in Italy all sporting a Bonarda-Something moniker), which is used to make a wine also called bonarda (but note the lowercase "b"!). To simplify matters, the grape name Bonarda has now been changed to Bonarda Piemontese but the wine is—wouldn't you know it—still called just bonarda (see BONARDA PIEMONTESE, chapter 5). Don't look now, but there is a Bonarda Novarese as well, though that's a synonym of Uva Rara, another distinct grape variety. And then there is also the matter of a particularly high-quality biotype of Croatina, charmingly called Bonarda di Rovescala and also known as Bonarda Pignola. And let's not forget two other synonyms for Croatina, Nebbiolo di Gattinara and Spanna di Ghemme: you won't be surprised to know that the real, world-famous Nebbiolo does grow in both the areas of Gattinara and Ghemme, where it is usually called Spanna, and that it has nothing to do with Croatina, which is however also planted in the same areas and included in the blends of most wines made in Gattinara and Ghemme. It's enough to drive one to drink ... a good Croatina wine, perhaps.

Well known since medieval times, Croatina is probably a native of the Rovescala area of Lombardy, though Di Rovasenda believed it to be originally from northern Piedmont. The first official descriptions of Croatina date to 1831 by Gallesio—an oft-cited notary's document from 1192 attests to wine production in the Rovescala area, but not necessarily to the presence of Croatina. However, in the late nineteenth century Croatina increasingly became a subject of study, as shown by the writings of De Maria and Leardi in 1875 and Di Rovasenda in 1877. Though not the easiest variety to grow (an irregular producer, it's also sensitive to drought and peronospora), Croatina's resistance to oidium endeared it to farmers and so local acreage increased over time at the expense of Moradella (see MORADELLA, chapter 5) and Nebbiolo. While it is one and the same as variously named local grapes such as Uva Vermiglia, Uga del Zio, Crovattina, and Neretto, it should not be confused with Crova (better known as Lambrusca di Alessandria), a similarly named but different and lower-quality grape as far as wine is concerned.

One reason for the many different names attributed to Croatina is its high intravarietal variability, which has led to the existence of many biotypes even in limited areas. The most important and highest quality of these is typical of Rovescala and is called Croatina Pignola (or Bonarda Pignola, though that is a mistake), but it remains unclear whether it is a true natural biotype, a variant affected by viruses, or a different variety altogether. Generally, Croatina is characterized by medium-sized, pyramidal or conical bunches and round berries. There are eight different clones available. Croatina's qualities are such that it has been the subject of crossings: Fregoni created Incrocio Fregoni 108, better known as Ervi, by crossing Croatina with Barbera (see chapter 6). This new variety, officially recognized in 1999, is the source of some good, if little-known, wines. Croatina is common in northern Italy (as its budbreak is late, spring frosts are not a problem), especially in Lombardy and Piedmont, but it can be found in Veneto, Emilia-Romagna, and Sardinia too.

Which Wines to Choose and Why

Croatina is a high-quality variety that deserves to be better known; wines made with it are fleshy and creamy sweet, and it's a useful softening agent in blends such as Amarone. It is likely that producers will use it increasingly and that we shall see more wines made with 100 percent Croatina in the future. Currently, it is usually used to make IGT Croatina wines (that are often monovarietal) or DOC wines such as Oltrepo' Pavese Bonarda that are blends of Croatina and other varieties like Barbera and Uva Rara. In Lombardy it is especially abundant in Oltrepò Pavese, where it is the most important native variety, while in Piedmont it is grown mainly in the provinces of Alessandria, Novara, Vercelli, and Cuneo (and more rarely, in the Colli Tortonesi). In Emilia-Romagna there is a DOC called Colli Piacentini Bonarda (the wines are made with Croatina mainly), but in this region Croatina is most valued for its role in the DOC wine Gutturnio, blended with Barbera. For good-quality examples of croatina, try the DOC wines of Collina Torinese Bonarda (made with a minimum of a not-otherwise-specified "Bonarda"), Colline Novaresi Croatina, Cisterna d'Asti, and Coste della Sesia Croatina. In Veneto, Croatina is increasingly being used to make Amarone (especially those made outside the Classico zone), as Croatina's soft tannins and fleshy, fruity personality are considered a better match for the wine than the more tannic and herbal Oseleta or Rondinella—more tannin is the last thing Amarone needs, of course.

Of course, Croatina also has plenty of tannins, and they are slightly rustic; for this reason, producers like Christoph Kunzli of the outstanding Le Piane estate in Boca like to perform very short fermentations (roughly four days) before the wine becomes completely dry and then pump over once a day. Oak aging, even 25 percent new oak, also helps, further smoothening the tannins, but five hundred liter barrels are better than smaller *barriques*, which impart too much oakiness. The wines are always fleshy and creamy and though dry, seem to have a pleasant sweetness about them. They are very deeply hued and fruity (featuring red fruits especially) and are high in polyphenol content. Croatina's very specific anthocyanin profile is characterized by a large percentage of malvin (an anthocyanin that doesn't oxidize easily), guaranteeing the wine's deep color will hold over time; its high tannin concentrations mean that care is needed to avoid over-extraction and the resulting astringent wines. Croatina's potentially tannic personality explains why farmers have historically made Croatina wines with a little residual sugar. Finally, as it is a very reductive variety (like Dolcetto and Sangiovese), attentive winemaking with plenty of rackings and air contact is a must in order to avoid off odors. Likewise, I suggest decanting or opening the bottle at least two hours before drinking.

Last but not least, remember that most often Argentinean and Californian wines made with, or labeled, "Bonarda" are not made with Croatina, but a completely different variety, France's Corbeau, called Charbono in the United States. In reality neither name is correct, as the variety should be known as Douce Noire (Martínez, Cavagnaro, Boursiquot, and Aguero 2008).

WINES TO TRY: For Lombardy, try: Alziati Annibale / Tenuta San Francesco*** (Bonarda Gagiarone, an Amarone-like wine), Anteo*** (Possessione del Console: an example of a wine made with Croatina Pignola subvariety), Bruno Verdi** (Bonarda Possessione di Vergombera Frizzante), and Conte Vistarino* (Sorbe). For Emilia-Romagna, try: Lamoretti*** (Vino del Campo Passito) and Lusenti*** (Pistamota Passito), both outstanding sweet, air-dried monovarietal Croatina wines—called, of course, bonarda.

Dindarella

WHERE IT'S FOUND: Veneto. NATIONAL REGISTRY CODE NUMBER: 316. COLOR: red.

For centuries, Dindarella and Pelara were thought to be different varieties, but genetic studies (Vantini, Tacconi, Gastaldelli, Govoni, Tosi, Malacrinò, Bassi, and Cattivelli 2003) have proven their identity. Pelara (from *pelato*, or bald) is a biotype of Dindarella that has been hit with floral abortion and so its grape cluster looks very sparse and scrawny, or bald. There's a real morphologic difference to the two: Dindarella is a positively pretty grape, and makes you hungry just looking at it, while Pelara looks sickly and ugly. First mentioned by Pollini in 1824, Dindarella and Pelara were described separately by other experts (Acerbi 1825; Zantedeschi 1862; Zava 1901), though most seem to have limited themselves to simply reproducing Pollini's information. Vantini's study also showed that Dindarella is related to Oseleta and Rossetta di Montagna, all rare native varieties that have grown over the centuries in limited areas where contamination with other grape varieties was less likely to happen. Another Dindarella biotype, rare nowadays, has also been described: Dindarella Rizza, most likely resulting from a viral contamination.

Dindarella is characterized by large, pyramidal, winged bunches, with irregularly sized berries; the Rizza biotype has a smaller bunch and very jagged leaves (a typical manifestation of virus-affected grape varieties). Pelara is scrawny looking with few berries. Dindarella has good vigor, productivity (not surprisingly,

Pelara less so), and disease resistance, but it is unfortunately very subject to *coulure*, which can greatly reduce yields. The thick-skinned berries have a characteristic, faint *Muscat*-like flavor; the thick skins and large, loosely packed bunches make Dindarella ideal for air-drying, though it tends to drop acids quickly when ripe. There are no clones available.

Stefano Cesari of the world-class Brigaldara estate in Veneto, who planted his own Dindarella vineyard in a collaboration with the University of Verona, has no illusions about why Dindarella started falling out of favor: "It's all about money. Since the markets didn't care for light red wines, everybody got rid of Dindarella, since the grape can never yield anything even remotely dark, given its anthocyanins. Only those who couldn't care less about wines being deep ruby in color held out." This is an interesting observation, since Dindarella's reddish-blue grapes do not look particularly pale, a telling example of how wine and grape color do not necessarily match.

Which Wines to Choose and Why
Typical of Veneto, where plantings were recently on the decline, Dindarella is making something of a comeback thanks to today's appreciation for lighter-bodied, lower alcohol red and *rosato* wines that marry better with food. It is also particularly suited to air-drying, making it interesting for producers in Valpolicella, where air-drying is a way of life. You are most likely to come across it as part of the blends of DOCs Valpolicella, Amarone, Recioto, Valdadige, and Garda Orientale. Cesari produces a lovely monovarietal Dindarella Rosato at his Brigaldara estate: "I used to use it as part of my Recioto blend, because I feel it adds a lovely spicy aroma. Then my Italian distributor asked me to make a *rosato*, which we didn't have in our portfolio, and Dindarella, with its penchant for giving lightly hued wines, seemed an ideal candidate." Interestingly, Cesari feels that Pelara makes an even spicier contribution to wines it's blended into, but he only has a few vines of it.

While pure dindarella is hard to come by, its wines are still easier to find than many made with other rare Italian natives. Made as a *rosato*, something Dindarella has a real calling for given its generally high total acidity levels, it is a lovely, dainty wine exuding a delicately aromatic nose reminiscent of cinnamon, bay leaves, and red currant. The wines are usually labeled as IGT Rosso Veronese, Vallagarina or delle Venezie, or as Vino da Tavola.

WINES TO TRY: Brigaldara*** (Dindarella) and Aldegheri* (a reportedly monovarietal Dindarella wine that depending on the vintage sports roughly eight grams per liter of residual sugar and is big, dark, and tannic; very fine and enjoyable, but different from other wines made with the variety).

Dolcetto

WHERE IT'S FOUND: Piedmont, Liguria, Sardinia. NATIONAL REGISTRY CODE NUMBER: 73. COLOR: red.

Decades ago the Langhe, a beautiful area of Piedmont situated around the Tanaro River and most famous for its production of Barolo and Barbaresco, was a kaleidoscope of colors at harvesttime, alive with an entire spectrum of leafy reds, yellows, and greens. Dolcetto, which ripens earlier in the season than Nebbiolo or Barbera, was a big contributor to the panorama, along with varieties such as Grignolino and Barbera. Alas, thanks to human nature (and the high prices Barolo and Barbaresco fetch nowadays), producers have taken to planting Nebbiolo just about everywhere, even in sites that are not especially suited to that late-ripening variety. The end result is that Dolcetto and other varieties (Freisa and Grignolino have fared even worse) have been planted less and less, and that much of the Barolo and Barbaresco made today is from lower-quality sites. I'm not being needlessly poetic or intellectual here: the latest Italian agricultural census (2010 data) reveals that the total hectares planted to Dolcetto in Italy have decreased

18 percent since 2000. And of course, we have lost that beautiful kaleidoscope of colors, not to mention biodiversity.

While the wine made with Dolcetto is resolutely dry, never sweet, the grapes are quite sweet and low in acidity (which explains its name, "little sweet one"). Dolcetto, or Dosset in Piedmontese dialect, was always much in favor as a table grape. However, it is a difficult variety to work with, and that is one reason why it has slowly been falling out of favor with those who have to tend the vines and makes the wines. For one of Italy's best-loved and most-planted varieties, Dolcetto's history and origins aren't well known. It is believed to be a native of the Monferrato area of Piedmont, in the province of Alessandria. Ligurians will object, as they believe the variety to be original to their region, where they have grown and produced Dolcetto for centuries, often calling it Ormeasco (though most often this name was reserved for the wine). However, the word Ormeasco derives from the city of Ormea, which is in Piedmont, where the grape was also known as Uva Ormeasca; there is evidence that it was brought into Liguria by the Marchesi del Carretto, a Piedmontese noble. In fact, written descriptions of Dolcetto go back only as far as the sixteenth century, though it's hard to believe the variety was not found on Italian soil before then. Interestingly, there have never been many synonyms for Dolcetto, nor confusion with other varieties. We know two of Italy's most important political figures loved Dolcetto and cultivated it extensively: Luigi Einaudi, Italy's first president, planted thousands of Dolcetto vines on his Piedmontese estate; and at the Castello di Grinzane Cavour, owner Camillo Benso, Count of Cavour and an Italian prime minister, left many handwritten letters documenting his amazement at how much earlier Dolcetto ripened compared to other Piedmontese cultivars, and at the very interesting prices Dosset grapes fetched at the nearby Alba market.

Dolcetto is a variety with many biotypes: not only do they look slightly different from one another, but they behave differently too. The most important phenotypic difference is the color of the stalk: most have a green-tinged stalk leading to the grape bunch, but at least one biotype's stalk becomes fiery red when the grapes are fully ripe. Found in the area around Tassarolo near Alessandria, it is called Nibiò (Nibieu in local dialect) or Dolcetto dal Peduncolo Rosso ("Dolcetto of the red stalk"). Despite what *Nibieu* might imply, it is not a Nebbiolo at all, though locals will refer to it as one. There is apparently even a very rare white-berried Dolcetto (I haven't seen it yet), whose grapes are blended with all the others by locals who make wines for family consumption; it's not an albino Dolcetto but a distinct cultivar (Schneider and Mannini 2006). Dolcetto must not be confused with the rare Dolcetto di Boca, a native typical of the Boca area, nor with the Douce Noire of France (called Charbono in California), which was once erroneously believed to be synonymous with Dolcetto.

Some Dolcetto biotypes are very fertile and highly productive, others produce only a few berries per plant. Available clones are many: R3, CN 69, CVT CN 22 (which gives very refined dolcetto wines), CVT CN 275, AL-DO 67, AL-DO 100, CVT 8 (characterized by strong sugar buildup and potentially high alcohol levels, it gives high-quality, complex wines; it's also a rare short or stocky-bunched Dolcetto, as most have elongated bunches), CVT 237 (with CVT 8, two of the few clones to have pyramidal bunches, as most are conical), CVT 167, UNIMI-VITIS DOL VV901, UNIMI-VITIS DOL VV910, VCR 464, VCR 466, and CVT 4. Expert producers such as Michele Chiarlo and Pio Boffa have told me the most interesting clones are CN 69, CVT CN 22, and CVT 8.

No matter which Dolcetto clone one chooses, it remains a difficult variety to grow as its buds are fragile and break easily. What's more, it grows low to the ground, requiring backbreaking vineyard work. It has poor vigor, and tends to give scrawny vines. Close to harvesttime, Dolcetto becomes very weather sensitive and excessive swings in maximum and minimum temperature values can cause dissection of the spine. While it usually ripens earlier than other Piedmontese varieties (up to three weeks earlier than Barbera and four earlier than Nebbiolo), something that ought to endear it to farmers, given Piedmont's notoriously fickle and cold autumn weather, prolonged cold snaps cause a physiological blockage that Dolcetto recovers from with difficulty. Excessive humidity is a major no-no, as Dolcetto rots easily. Another characteristic of the grape is that the berries cling very loosely to the vine; you'll find it takes practically no effort to nab a few grapes and eat them during your next vineyard walk. In fact, it tends to drop its berries when ripe, another problem. All this is true even for massal selections, so the grapevine's problems do not result from poor clonal selections. The fully ripe berries really are sweet, just as you'd expect given Dolcetto's name, but ironically, I find they're less sweet than those of Barbera, and certainly less sweet than those of the red-berried *Malvasias* of Piedmont. Dolcetto has been crossed with Chatus to give the Passau, San Martino, and Valentino Nero laboratory crossings, all of which are only rarely, if ever, used to make wine in Italy.

Dolcetto del Peduncolo Rosso is a very specific biotype of Dolcetto that I will address separately from the rest of the Dolcetto discussion in an effort to avoid confusion. This is because, while not yet proven to be a distinct variety (preferentially called Nibiò by those who produce it), it looks, behaves, and produces wines that are sufficiently different from those made with regular Dolcetto that a separate analysis is warranted. Over the years, I have found that the chances are good not much is known about a grape when people cannot even agree on how to spell its name: such is the fate of Dolcetto del Peduncolo Rosso or Nibiò or Nibiö or Nibieu, depending on whom you ask. And I'm probably forgetting a few more possible permutations. Though most agree it is an ancient biotype of Dolcetto, the genetic studies that would confirm that are currently under way; for now, researchers at the Regione Piemonte have told me Nibiò is a biotype of Dolcetto. What is sure is that it's not a Nebbiolo, though that is how *nibiò* in Piedmontese dialect might translate in Italian. Apparently, Nibiò is the variety historically used to make the red wines of Tassarolo and Gavi in Piedmont, and has been documented in those areas for at least one thousand years—given that it was so highly renowned, locals honored it with the Nebbiolo moniker.

Nibiò is characterized by very small bunches and berries, and a red stalk, all of which distinguish it from Dolcetto and explain its other name, Dolcetto del Peduncolo Rosso. It seems to perform best on calcareous-clay soils (many varieties do) and gives a smoothly tannic wine (not something Dolcetto is known for) that is rich in red-fruit notes and spices (bay leaf, marjoram, nutmeg). However, it apparently doesn't always ripen fully in Piedmont's cold autumns.

Dolcetto is mainly found in Piedmont and Liguria, though it grows in small amounts in many other Italian regions, including Lombardy and Sardinia. Dolcetto has been planted outside Italy too, for example in California, Oregon, Texas, New Mexico, Australia, and New Zealand. It seems to me like the latter country's cooler microclimate ought to be ideal for a perfumed variety such as Dolcetto, but to my surprise I have found the variety does very well in slightly warmer New World microclimates too (the key is large day-night temperature differentials).

Which Wines to Choose and Why

Dolcetto does best on calcareous-clay and sandy-calcareous soils. In Piedmont, there are eleven DOC wines made and they can differ considerably: the best known are Dolcetto d'Alba, Dolcetto d'Ovada, Dolcetto di Dogliani, Dolcetto di Diano d'Alba, Dolcetto delle Langhe Monregalesi, Dolcetto di Acqui, and Dolcetto d'Asti. The Dolcetto d'Alba is the fullest bodied, while the Dolcetto di Dogliani is floral and fresher, and more perfumed. It can also be the most powerful. This is because in the Dogliani area Dolcetto has always been viewed as the most important grape and the best sites have been reserved for it. Diano d'Alba is another town that takes Dolcetto very seriously and in 1974 had a very detailed and extensive zonation study performed in which geological and other important differences were analyzed within the DOC boundaries. This commendable effort was one of the first times a viticultural area in Italy actually mapped out its own *terroirs* and performed geological studies. In style, Dolcetto di Diano d'Alba falls somewhere between the richer Dolcetto wines of Alba and Dogliani and the lighter Monferrato and Langhe Monregalesi wines, but this depends on the producer. Historically, some believed that the best Dolcetto wines were those of Acqui, but today these wines are not very well known or easy to find, as they're made only in small quantities by mainly local producers. The Dolcetto of the Langhe Monregalesi is usually austere and lighter in tannin content and perfume: it's a classic example of a "mountain" wine, made at higher altitudes and cooler climates. Liguria's Dolcetto wines tend to be more herbal and saline than the fruitier ones of Piedmont. DOC Riviera Ligure di Ponente Ormeasco di Pornassio are the best Ligurian examples of Dolcetto wines; Pornassio is the recognized *grand cru* for the variety in Liguria. In Liguria they often make a Ormeasco sciac-trà *rosato,* an unfortunate name given that it closely resembles that of schiacchetrà, which is the name of a famous Ligurian sweet wine.

At times, I find that Dolcetto wines bear little resemblance to what I know a Dolcetto wine should taste of, leaving me to wonder if a small amount of Merlot hasn't somehow found its way in. Given that Dolcetto wines are a joy to drink in all their fresh, fruity exuberance, to make a wine with Dolcetto that tastes of Merlot (with chocolate and coffee notes and soft creamy textures that are completely atypical of Dolcetto wines) seems to defeat a Dolcetto's purpose in life. Unfortunately, such wines are often scored highly in guides and reports written by people who apparently don't pay much attention to, or don't care about, how that wine should really taste. The point is that if producers turn dolcetto into another merlot, cabernet, or syrah look-alike, they might enjoy short-term success, but will inevitably lose customers in the long run, as cabernet or merlot wines are made all over the world, while dolcetto is a unique, fresh, medium-bodied red wine. It would seem more logical to try and improve on their wine, stressing and promoting its qualities and uniqueness. Recently, the DOCG Dogliani was created to allow producers to make bigger-bodied dolcettos, no doubt in the hopes of capitalizing on the fashion for bigger, full-bodied wines. However, what must have seemed like a good idea at the time, has not quite worked out in terms of sales. So let's give wine-loving consumers their due: the charms of well-made Dolcetto wines reside in bright personalities, very grapey aromas and flavors, and brightly acid, mouthcleansing finishes. To oak and camouflage all that, or to increase the concentration and alcohol of the wines, would seem to be at the very least counterintuitive, though some very successful bigger-boned Dolcetto wines are certainly made.

Dolcetto is difficult not just viticulturally, but also enologically. A highly reductive variety (like Sangiovese), it easily acquires off odors, so winemakers need to use frequent pumpings over or rack-and-return techniques to air the wine out. Its low acidity and high tannins also require winemakers to use softer extraction methods and shorter fermentation times; cooler temperatures are also indicated to avoid extracting drying tannins and to preserve the variety's fresh, vibrant aromas.

Non-Italian examples of dolcetto are legion; to the best of my knowledge, there are no wines made from Nibiò outside Italy. I distinctly remember trying my first-ever non-Italian Dolcetto wine back in the 1990s: I was extremely impressed by just how good the wine, made by Monte Volpe in Mendocino, was—successfully fusing the Italian perfumed, earthy minerality with an American fruity charm all its own. In the United States, famous estates are giving Dolcetto a try: Ponzi in Oregon, Duxoup and Palmina in California, and even Texan wineries such as Duchman Family Winery and Mandola. Texas isn't often thought of as an important wine production area, but the wines deserve attention and credit: the 2008 Dolcetto by Duchman Family Winery was named one of the ten best Texas wines in 2010, but also won double gold at the 2010 San Francisco International Wine Competition. There's plenty of dolcetto to choose from in New Mexico; though the level of winemaking in this state stands to improve, I am fascinated and thoroughly enthusiastic about the efforts made by many wineries I visited on a trip a few years back. Black Mesa, Luna Rossa, and Vivác all make dolcettos from New Mexico–grown grapes, and I plan on following their progress.

There are also many fine examples of dolcetto made in Australia, though it's fair to say the wines have encountered less success there than Nebbiolo and especially Barbera. Very interesting wines by Box Stallion, Catherine Vale Vineyard (where they make a *dolcetto rosato* called Dolcetto Rosé with a small addition of semillon), Grant Burge (they make a sparkling version blended with a little shiraz), and Parish Hill. Last but not least, an unlikely source for high-quality, thoroughly excellent dolcettos is Heron's Flight in New Zealand's Matakana Coast wine country, less than an hour north of Auckland. They make as many as four different wines from Dolcetto: three monovarietals (Reserve, Unplugged, and a *rosato*) and a blend with Sangiovese.

WINES TO TRY: For Dolcetto d'Acqui, try Paolo Pizzorno Vini** (Il Commensale). For Dolcetto d'Alba, try: Marcarini*** (Boschi di Berri; made from centenary ungrafted vines, this is a great Dolcetto wine) and Vajra***. For Dolcetto di Diano d'Alba, try: Gigi Rosso** (Moncolombetto), Giovanni Veglio**, and Fratelli Savigliano**. For Dolcetto di Dogliani, try: Quinto Chionetti*** (Briccolero), Einaudi**, Osvaldo Barberis** (Valdibà), Pecchennino** (San Luigi), San Fereolo* (Valdibà), and San Romano* (Bricco delle Lepri). For Dolcetto di Ovada, try Luigi Tacchino**. For Dogliani, try: Einaudi*** (Tecc, from vines planted in 1937; one taste tells you old vines are at work here), Marziano Abbona** (Papà Celso), Francesco Boschis** (Sorì San Martino), and Pecchennino** (Siri d'Jermu). For Ormeasco, try: Lorenzo Ramò*** (many different versions: try the Sciac-trà and the Passito, a rare air-dried version), Lupi** (Sciac-trà, a *rosato*), Cascina Nirasca, Fontanacota (both the Ormeasco and the Sciattrà are simple and fresh), Case Rosse** (Sciac-trà), and Depero* (Sciac-trà). Colle Sereno** makes an excellent *passito*. For Nibiò, try: Daglio** (Nibiö), La Colombera** (Suciaja, a word derived from the local dialect meaning "droughty"; these vines were planted in the 1930s by owner Elisa Semino's grandfather), Rugrà* (Picùla Rùsa), Cascina degli Ulivi* (Terre Rosse; made biodynamically, it can be marred by excessive volatile acidity in some vintages), and Forti del Vento* (Ventipassi).

Dorona

WHERE IT'S FOUND: Veneto. NATIONAL REGISTRY CODE NUMBER: 460. COLOR: white.

Dorona was almost always viewed in the past as a table grape, probably because of the big, round, juicy berries that also caused it to be called Garganega dall'Oro (in the Colli Euganei), Garganega Piramidale, Garganegona, and Garganega Grossa. In fact, the variety is distinct from Garganega though closely related to it; its official name, Dorona, is that typically used on the islands of the Venetian lagoon. Apparently, Dorona was well known and described in fourteenth-century Venice, and there are good descriptions of it both by Acerbi (1825) and in the *Ampelografia della Provincia di Treviso* (1870). However, given Garganega's immense intravarietal variability, it may be that some of those supposed Dorona sightings were instead of one of the many different Garganega biotypes, especially the large-berried ones. In this light, results by Di Vecchi Staraz, Bandinelli, Boselli, This, Boursiquot, Laucou, Lacombe, and Varès (2007) defining Dorona as the result of a natural cross between

Garganega and Bermestia Bianca, a table grape from Emilia-Romagna, might mean that Dorona is not as old as is commonly believed. However, Bermestia Bianca is not officially listed among Italy's table grapes in the National Registry, and references from the early twentieth century also speak of a Piedmontese Bermestia, as well as of a red-berried Bermestia, so I'm not sure what to think.

In any case, in time Dorona seemed to slowly disappear, or more likely, was just confused with the more famous and abundant Garganega. Nowadays, though Dorona vines are liberally sprinkled throughout Veneto, the cultivar is rare. Researchers from the University of Verona have located it in persuasive numbers on the Sordato estate in Selva di Montebello, and have pinpointed a similar but different variety on the estate of Ca' Piovene in Toara. The Bisol family has also traced its presence on the islands of the Venetian lagoon, notably Torcello and Sant'Erasmo, and planted it on nearby Mazzorbo, literally across a bridge from pretty Burano, famous for its colorful homes (the *buranelli*) and lace of exquisite manufacture. "Ten years ago," recalls Gianluca Bisol, "while visiting the basilica on beautiful Torcello with an American client, I noticed a few vines dispersed among other plants in the walled garden of the house close by the basilica, so I asked the owner if I could have a look. I was surprised to find three vines of Dorona, which I had never heard of or seen before anywhere in the area." Bisol contacted Venetian researcher Carla Coco to study the vines, began searching for more Dorona until another ninety vines were identified elsewhere in the lagoon, and the rest is history. It is safe to say that prior to Bisol's interest, few knew or had heard about Dorona. In fact, Dorona is such a recently rediscovered grape that its official listing in the National Registry dates back to only 2012.

Morphologically, Dorona looks to me very much like an opulent Garganega, with bigger berries and bunches (typically long and somewhat cylindrical like Garganega's), though I've noticed considerable ampelographic variation between accessions within the same vineyard. The variety is vigorous and produces constant and abundant yields: a long-cane pruning system is best. Dorona has demonstrated low sensitivity to fungal diseases, in particular botrytis, with a long conservation capacity both on the vine and once harvested, which explains its past use as a table grape.

Which Wines to Choose and Why

Due to Dorona being interplanted in Veneto vineyards with Garganega, I find it likely that many Soave and Gambellara wines have, unknowingly, always been made with a small proportion of Dorona. However, the only important Dorona vineyard I know of today is currently found on Mazzorbo on the ancient ScarpaVolo estate, where the Bisol family planted grapevines and makes the wine called Venissa (near their stunningly beautiful country hotel, which shares a name with the wine). Desiderio, Gianluca, and all of the Bisol family deserve the highest credit and much applause for their passion and desire to preserve the rich but endangered biodiversity of the Venetian lagoon (their estate is also home to rare native varieties of other fruits and vegetables). As Dorona produces a light, crisp white wine not so different from that made with Garganega, the Bisol family and their consultant winemaker Roberto Cipresso feared a Dorona wine might go unnoticed. Therefore, they decided to ferment on the skins and leave the must in contact with air, then to age the wine in oak. The final result is certainly interesting and fine, but I'm not sure the character traits of Dorona are shown to their fullest effect. However, the most recent vintage of Venissa, just released in 2013, is light years better than any Venissa I tasted previously, revealing a much fresher, easier-to-drink wine with recognizable garganega-like aroma and flavors. Gianluca Bisol told me "I'm not sure that using Dorona to make just another white wine would have added much—there are already many fresh, linear white wines made in Veneto and Italy today. With Venissa we are trying to produce a wine that typifies the production of the island of Mazzorbo." Desiderio Bisol added that "back in 2002, when we started searching for Dorona grapevines in the other islands, we weren't sure we'd get anywhere, so you can imagine how happy we are to have produced our first wine with the 2010 vintage." Almost as happy as I was to taste a sip of history, a wine made from a grape that, if it hadn't been for Bisol, none of us would know much about. And though I wish they'd make a "normal" bottling of Dorona too, I am very thankful for their efforts and passion.

WINES TO TRY: Venissa/Bisol** (Dorona Venissa).

Doux d'Henry

WHERE IT'S FOUND: Piedmont. NATIONAL REGISTRY CODE NUMBER: 75. COLOR: red.

The origins of the peculiarly named Doux d'Henry, a rare native variety, are unclear, but despite its French name, the majority of experts now believe it to be a true native of the Pinerolese area of Piedmont. It wasn't always so: earlier luminaries such as Incisa and Di Rovasenda were in complete disagreement, the former believing it was of French origin, while the latter held out for a Pinerolese origin. The variety's name is believed to have been coined in 1600, when King Henri IV of France, in Italy to sign a treaty with Piedmont's King Carlo Emanuele I of Savoy, tasted and liked a sweet wine reportedly made with the grape. It is likely these wines sported residual sugar, either purposefully or as a result of stuck fermentations (not an unlikely event in Piedmont's cold weather and cellars)—this explains the *doux*, or sweet, in its name.

In the 1800s Doux d'Henry was considered an excellent wine grape, but was also appreciated as a table grape due to its large, sweet berries. Unfortunately, many of Doux d'Henry's berries do not reach full poyphenolic ripeness even at full technological maturity (when grapes reach technological maturity, it means that they have ripened enough to accumulate plenty of sugar so that they are technically ripe, but their polyphenols—namely the tannins—may not be ripe yet), so even ripe-looking grapes may taste tough and astringent. Worse, there may be asynchronous maturation, so that the grape bunch often has a speckled look, with dark berries alongside obviously green ones. The variety was greatly damaged by the arrival of phylloxera, and its diffusion in Piedmont has been limited ever since.

Though some believe the grape can be confused with other varieties such as Ciliegiolo, I don't see how, given how different the two cultivars look—but then Ciliegiolo has often been the source of misidentifications. Doux d'Henry is affected by *millerandage* and berry shatter, and when its bunches are compact, botrytis bunch rot becomes a problem too. However, being both an early ripener and very frost resistant, it is an ideal variety for the cold Piedmont areas it inhabits. Doux d'Henry has functionally female flowers, and so requires the presence of other pollinating varieties in the vineyard to be fertilized.

Though Doux d'Henry is especially typical of—and most likely native to—the countryside stretching from the town of Pinerolo right up to the entry of the Val Pellice, nowadays its diffusion is limited to small pockets on the outskirts of Torino, to Piedmont's Pinerolese area (around Prarostino), and to the Valle Chisone and the Valle Germanasca.

Which Wines to Choose and Why

Doux d'Henry has always been used in blends, adding perfume to wines, though there are a number of very good, refreshing monovarietal red wines made. However, today it is being studied as a potential source of very good *rosato* and even late-harvest or air-dried monovarietal wines. Microvinifications have revealed it as a light and fragrant, delicately fruity wine with flavors and aromas of sour red cherry and red berries. The DOC Pinerolese Doux d'Henry wines are probably best, but the variety is also included in DOC Rosso Pinerolese wine blends.

WINES TO TRY: Dora Renato* (a white sparkling wine made by avoiding skin contact with the must), Fratelli Berger* (a *rosato*), La Rivà*, Terre del Pinerolese* (formerly Il Tralcio; they used to also make an air-dried version called Curbaran, but I haven't seen or tasted it in years), and Daniela Bruno*.

Durella

WHERE IT'S FOUND: Veneto, Tuscany, Lombardy. NATIONAL REGISTRY CODE NUMBER: 77. COLOR: white.

Durella takes its name from its rather tough skin (*durella* means hard or angry), something that older synonyms no longer much in use, like Cagnina, Duroncino, Durello, and Rabbiosa also point to. However, since Durella is also a very high-acid variety, some experts believe its name refers to this feature, which can make for some tough drinking moments. That same acidity explains why Durella is often used to make sparkling wines. According to Guerrino Fongaro of the excellent Fongaro estate, Durella is an ancient variety native to the Monti Lessini, where it was known as Uva Durasena starting in the thirteenth century. Others believe it is the Duracina variety described by the ancient Romans. In 1825 Acerbi described a Durella grown near Vicenza, while Di Rovasenda (1877) and Perez (1900) described a Durella growing near Verona. In fact, Durella was so well thought of that Montanari and Ceccarelli (1950) recall that it was recommended for replanting and cultivation in the post-phylloxeric period by the Consiglio Provinciale di Economia di Vicenza (specifically in the areas of Arzignano and the lower Chiampo Valley), and that later other luminaries recommended it for cultivation in many other areas of Veneto as well. Durella was once confused with Nosiola (a variety that produces lovely, fragrant white wines), though Cosmo stated the two varieties were distinct as early as 1960. Cipriani, Spadotto, Jurman, Di Gaspero, Crespan, Meneghetti, et al. (2010) have recently suggested that Durella is one of the parents of another Veneto native, Bianchetta Trevigiana.

Durella grows mainly in Veneto, between Verona and Vicenza, but is also found in northwestern Tuscany near Massa Carrara (where it is called Durella Gentile) and in Lombardy.

Which Wines to Choose and Why

The name of the grape is Durella, the name of the wine is Durello—more precisely, the DOC wine is Lessini Durello (from the region between Verona and Vicenza). For the greater part of the last thirty years, Durella wines were an afterthought on the Italian fine white wine scene, when the race was on to see who could make the biggest and oakiest wines around. In those sorry times, there was little place for a high-acid wine blessed with delicate aromas and flavors, so Durella and its wines survived mainly as local phenomena. Things are very different nowadays, with crisp, low-alcohol wines all the rage—admittedly, they match better with most foods and are easier in today's hectic, work-intensive lifestyle. Recent Italian sales figures have shown that consumers outside Durella's immediate production areas are once again paying attention. After a period of difficulty, it looks as though Durella and its wines happen to find themselves in the right spot at the right time. The Lessini-Durello DOC requires no more than 85 percent Durella in this blend, but there are producers making 100 percent Durella wines. Other DOC wines that include small percentages of Durella are Monti Lessini, Breganze, and Gambellara; there are numerous IGT wines to choose from too, but Durella often plays only a marginal role.

Durella can be used to produce sparkling, still, and sweet wines, and most producers will have at least still and sparkling versions, so you have a spectrum of possibilities to choose from. The aroma and flavor profile speaks of minerals, white flowers, and fresh fruit (especially green apple and lemon), coupled with low alcohol concentrations (rarely exceeding 12 percent, and most 10.5–11 percent). Its very high acidity makes sparkling wines an ideal vehicle for Durella's charms, and usually precludes the sweet wines from tasting cloying. Of course, in the hands of less-than-talented producers or those who let yields creep too high, these wines can make for some rather tough going, with tear-inducing acidity. One problem is that the wines have a tendency to oxidize easily, quickly turning an unpleasant orange color, and so utmost care is needed to avoid unnecessary oxygen contact during the winemaking process.

WINES TO TRY: Fongaro*** (Etichetta Viola and Etichetta Nera Riserva; this estate has been growing Durella since its founding in 1975, so it is blessed with old vines), Marcato*** (Etichetta Gialla and A.R. Brut), and Corte Moschina*. For *passito,* try Casa Cecchin** (Il Montebello, excellent).

Enantio

WHERE IT'S FOUND: Trentino, Veneto. NATIONAL REGISTRY CODE NUMBER: 114 (listed as Lambrusco a Foglia Frastagliata). COLOR: red.

In Trentino and Veneto, Enantio is still most often called Lambrusco a Foglia Frastagliata, while Sbeccàa, Zicolada, and Nostram de Avi are less commonly used synonyms. Though I am told that Enantio has recently become the official name for this variety (hence this is the name I use in this book), in the most recent update of the National Registry (March 23, 2012), it is still listed as Lambrusco a Foglia Frastagliata, so the change is slow in coming. The fact is that, though most producers want the variety called Enantio to help differentiate it from the many *Lambruscos* from which it is genetically distinct, the name (first suggested by Mario Fregoni, professor of viticulture at the Università Cattolica del Sacro Cuore of Piacenza, who chose it in reference to a variety named by Pliny the Elder) really hasn't caught on and many just view it as a marketing gimmick.

Enantio has been grown for centuries in the countryside of the low Vallagarina in Trentino, specifically in the Terra dei Forti, an area located between Monte Baldo and the Lessinia, along the river Adige. At the end of the 1800s, there were over thirteen thousand hectoliters produced annually in Trentino, mainly around the towns of Ala and Avio. It is also commonly found in the countryside around Verona. Some vines also grow in Emilia-Romagna: a token appearance there is only fair, I guess, since that region is the recognized home of *Lambruscos* and lambrusco. In the 1950s, Enantio and Casetta, another local variety, together accounted for more than 60 percent of the grape varieties planted along the Adige valley, stretching from Avio in Trentino to Rivoli in Veneto.

But the decline that confronted many other native varieties also affected Enantio. It was not until Luigi Spagnolli of the Vilar estate took matters in his own hands that the fate of Enantio began to improve. With a group of winemaking friends, Spagnolli created the I Dolomitici association, comprising eleven small wineries among the very best of the region: Castel Noarna, Cesconi, Elisabetta Dalzocchio, Elisabetta Foradori, Eugenio Rosi, Maso Furli, Gino Pedrotti, Francesco Poli, Giuseppe Fanti, and Vilar. I Dolomitici recently saved a small vineyard of centenary Enantio vines by renting it from the new owners, who intended to rip out the old vines and plant other varieties in their place. Saving this vineyard is especially noteworthy, not just because of the age of its vines, but also because the vines are still ungrafted; the high sand content of the vineyard's soil (near the shores of the Adige River at Avio) never allowed the phylloxera louse to set up shop. The association has begun bottling a wine made from these old vines, naming it after the old owner's nickname, Ciso. To its credit, the association is also sponsoring a study aimed at saving the intravarietal variability typical of Enantio.

As its original name, Lambrusco a Foglia Frastagliata, implies, this variety is easily recognized by the heavy indentations of its leaves (*frastagliato* means jagged). The first to clearly differentiate Enantio from other *Lambrusco* varieties was Acerbi in 1825—it must have been no small measure of work, since recent studies have shown that there are at least 107 other varieties phenotypically very similar to Enantio. According to early work done by Grando and Frisinghelli (1998), Enantio is related to Marzemino, Teroldego, and other local Trentino varieties; subsequent work by Grando, Stefanini, Zambanini, and Vouillamoz (2006) related that Enantio is either a parent or progeny of Negrara Trentina. It is possible that a *Lambrusco* variety brought to this part of Italy from Emilia-Romagna eventually mutated and changed into what is now Enantio, but the relationship to Negrara Trentina makes this hypothesis very unlikely. Scienza, Failla, Anziani, Mattivi, Villa, Giannazza, Tedesco, and Benetti (1990) believe that Enantio resulted from the domestication of local wild grapevines, but further proof is probably needed, particularly given research showing it did not originate from Veneto (Vantini, Tacconi, Gastaldelli, Govoni, Tosi, Malacrinò, Bassi, and Cattivelli 2003).

Enantio has medium-sized berries and bunches; the latter usually have one or two wings and are not very tightly-packed. It is a vigorous and reliable producer that does best in gravelly-sandy soils and in drier microclimates, and is very disease and frost resistant. There is one official clone available, SMA-ISV 317.

Which Wines to Choose and Why

DOC wines are Valdadige-Terre dei Forti Enantio and Valdadige-Terre dei Forti Rosso; in the latter, it is blended with other varieties. The wine is bright and juicy, with sneaky concentration to the red-berry and delicately herbal aromas and flavors. It has very good acidity and a richer mouthfeel than most Lambrusco wines, with a slightly herbal back end.

WINES TO TRY: I Dolomitici*** (Ciso), Vallarom*** (blessed with vines planted in the early 1970s, they label their wine Lambrusco a Foglia Frastagliata), Lorenzo Bongiovanni* (who air-dries a portion of his grapes to achieve a richer mouthfeel), Letrari*, and the Cantina Sociale di Avio*.

Erbaluce

WHERE IT'S FOUND: Piedmont. NATIONAL REGISTRY CODE NUMBER: 78. COLOR: white.

Legend has it that the fairy Albaluce blessed the townspeople of Caluso with Erbaluce as her gift, hence the variety's name. An ancient cultivar already known in the seventeenth century (as Elbalus, first described by Croce), its pale hue as well as that of its wine explains why Erbaluce is also called Bianchera, Albaluce and Ambra; the pale yellow-green color of this variety's berries when not fully ripe recalls pale dawn light. In the local dialect, Erbaluce is called Bian Roustì and Uva Rustìa, a reference to the color of the berries when ripe (*roustì* and *rustìa* are akin to *arrostito* or *arrosto*, meaning roasted or to roast)—when ripe its grapes become amber-pink. Locally, it is still also called Greco (especially in the area around Novara), or Greco di Caluso, but this is a mistake: though today we know there are some genetic similarities between Erbaluce and the Greco of Campania, the two are distinct varieties. On a less scientific note, a taste of the two wines will clearly tell you the varieties are only distantly related. Labra, Winfield, Ghiani, Grassi, Sala, Scienza, and Failla (2001) postulated a relationship with France's Clairette variety but nobody appears to have taken this up, leading me to think more research is needed. In the nineteenth century, Erbaluce was also confused with Arneis and Trebbiano Toscano, though this is hard to fathom, given how different the varieties look. Despite the confusion, Erbaluce and Caluso have a distinguished history. Winemaker Piero Genta won a gold medal for his Caluso wine at the Paris Exhibition of 1855, and reportedly had the honor of seeing his wine served at the court of Napoleon III (Gnavi 1973). In 1896, Chiei-Gamacchio, the manager of the Royal Agriculture School in Caluso, wrote that the wines of Caluso were considered among the best of the region. Throughout the centuries, Erbaluce wines were also traditionally used by families to greet important guests (Nuvolone 1798; De Maria and Leardi 1875).

Even though it's a high-acid variety, Erbaluce is usually trained in canopy systems (called *topia* in the Canavese region where Erbaluce grows), so as to have a thick wall of leaves protecting the hanging grape bunches from hail, always a risk in this northern part of Italy. Clearly, grapes trained in this manner see less sunlight too, so proper vineyard work has to be done, with selective deleafing in order to allow enough sunlight. From a viticultural perspective, and for a variety of reasons, Erbaluce is not the easiest variety to work with. Budbreak occurs early, so spring frosts, which are not uncommon in northerly Piedmont, are a threat. Despite high vigor, Erbaluce is not the most obliging producer, due to the double whammy of susceptibility to common grapevine diseases and poor fertility, which makes for yields that are both low and irregular. Walking through the vineyards, you'll notice that Erbaluce leaves are often marked by white borders, a characteristic sign of magnesium deficiency, not uncommon in the calcareous soils where Erbaluce grows.

Erbaluce's leaf is highly recognizable, with a bulbous upper surface, very pronounced sinus indentations, and a round shape. Usually, Erbaluce's grape bunch is medium-sized, elongated, and cylindrical, with medium-large, round, thick-skinned berries. However, its appearance will depend on which clone or biotype is observed. Tedeschini described two biotypes of Erbaluce in 1930: of these, the higher-quality pink-stalked one was sicklier and poorly productive, and essentially disappeared by the mid-twentieth century. Today there are four clones of Erbaluce available: the CVT 29 has berries that tend to become amber-pink when ripe, CVT 30 yields the most typical wines, while clone 71 is very compact and subject to rot (so is rarely used to make sweet wines), and CVT 55 is characterized by the highest acidity, which is already high in all Erbaluce clones.

Today Erbaluce is planted on roughly 250 hectares in Piedmont, mainly immediately outside Turin, as well as in the provinces of Biella and Novara. It has also been sporadically planted in Lombardy in the past, but Erbaluce is one Italian native grape variety that really hasn't traveled much outside its main production zone.

Which Wines to Choose and Why

The most famous wine is the DOC Erbaluce di Caluso (Piedmont's first white DOC wine, named in 1967), right around the bucolic hamlet of Caluso, but Colline Novaresi Erbaluce (or Bianco) and Coste della Sesia Erbaluce, also DOC wines, can be just as good—note that these Erbaluce wines, produced outside the official Caluso DOC zone, cannot be labeled *di Caluso*. Caluso is a uniquely blessed area for Erbaluce because of its nutrient-deficient, sandy-gravel soils, rich in potassium and phosphates. The best sites are all located in an amphitheater roughly four kilometers long and include true *crus* such as Baiarda, Barbetta, Castellazzo, Feralda, Macello, Montasso, Sant'Andrea, Sant'Antonino, and Santa Croce. Other noteworthy sites, located at slightly lower altitudes in more fertile soils, include Cose, Madonna, Pero, Quaro, and Viassola.

Erbaluce wines can be still or sparkling, but all are dry wines, though an excellent DOCG dessert wine, Caluso Passito, is also made with Erbaluce; there are also wonderful, sweet Erbaluce wines that are not DOCGs. Sweet wines would seem to be a logical choice for Erbaluce, as the berry's thick skins are ideal for air-drying: in fact, Mas and Pulliat documented that this part of Italy once used to make *vins de paille* in the French manner. Today, sweet wines from late-harvested grapes are made (with pleasant if delicate aromas and flavors of apricots, peach, and acacia honey) but are rarer, given the region's climate. The air-dried sweet wines, with their resiny, tannic quality and bittersweet chestnut honey, almond, dried fig, and saffron flavors that linger on the long sweet, tropical-fruit aftertaste, hark back to the Campanian Greco, though this is where similarities end. Erbaluce dry wines are dainty and fresh, very floral and loaded with green apple and lemony aromas and flavors that are nothing like those of Greco. Given the delicate nature of their aromas and flavors and the high, refreshing acidity, I don't think that oak aging is at all necessary with Erbaluce wines, though of course that hasn't stopped producers from trying.

Though nobody will ever mistake a wine made with Erbaluce for a blockbuster, when well made these wines are a marvel of balance, with minerally, crisp, white flower and fruit aromas and flavors combining hints of chlorophyll and apricots. It's true that poor examples can be marred by eye-watering acidity, but this same high natural acidity has given us sparkling wines in increasing numbers. Made either by refermentation in the bottle in the manner of Champagne or by the Charmat method like Prosecco, these can be marvelous wines, and are underrated in my view.

Since Erbaluce's thick skin releases its polyphenols with difficulty, in order to augment the tactile sensation and the aromas and flavors of wines, many producers employ cold temperature pre-fermentation soak techniques, that also reduce total acidity by precipitating tartrate salts. With the aim of reducing total acidity levels, some producers also perform a partial malolactic transformation, something I am not too keen on, as I believe it lessens the bright acidic impact of a good Erbaluce wine.

WINES TO TRY: Cieck*** (Misobolo, Brut San Giorgio sparkler, and Alladium Passito; the latter made from air-dried grapes but less sweet than you might expect), Ferrando*** (especially the two sweet wines: Cariola, a lighter-styled late harvest, and the Passito, thick and rich, from air-dried grapes; their La Torrazza sparkler is also good), Proprietà Sperino***, Tenuta Roletto***, Favaro-Le Chiusure** (13 Mesi, a rare erbaluce aged in *barrique,* and Passito Sole d'Inverno), and Orsolani** (Erbaluce di Caluso, Brut Tradizione). For Colline Novaresi, try Rovellotti** (Bianco, Passito Valdenrico). For Coste della Sesia, try Antoniolo** (Erbaluce).

Falanghina

WHERE IT'S FOUND: Campania, Puglia, Lazio. NATIONAL REGISTRY CODE NUMBER: 79 (with unfortunately no distinction between biotypes). COLOR: white.

Along with Aglianico this is believed to be Campania's oldest variety. Its name derives from the Latin *falangae* (phalanx), from the resemblance of the poles used to support the vines in the vineyard to the typical military formation of the Roman legions, made up of many phalanxes of men (who were known to take vine cuttings with them to plant on their long journeys of military conquest). Considering the meteoric rise to fame and success of the *Falanghina* grapes in the last thirty years, the analogy with the conquering Roman armies is more than apt. *Falanghina* is also sufficiently close enough to falernum, antiquity's greatest and most sought-after wine, that local luminaries such as Froio (1876) and Fiorito (1954) hypothesized that this was the variety (tellingly also called Uva Falerna) used to make falernum—but of course they *would* say that. In reality, we have no hard proof that falernum was made with Falanghina, and over the centuries many other grapes have been suggested as the key ingredient of that wine.

Thanks to the work of Costacurta, Calò, Carraro, Giust, Aggio, Borsa, Di Stefano, De Zan, Fabbro, and Crespan (2005), today we know there are at least two genetically distinct *Falanghinas*, Falanghina Flegrea and Falanghina Beneventana. According to these same researchers, the former appears to be closely related to Suppezza, while the latter is more closely related to Biancolella. In fact, there are probably more different *Falanghinas* out there just awaiting discovery, but in the absence of accurate ampelographic descriptions and genetic profiling, which grapevines are biotypes of Flegrea and Beneventana and which are altogether distinct *Falanghina* varieties is anybody's guess. For instance, though the *Falanghina* grapevines from Naples, Vesuvius, Campi Flegrei, and Caserta are believed to be

Falanghina Flegrea, they are not likely to be all the same variety; experts such as Froio have been pointing out differences between them since the 1870s. For example, Froio described a Falanghina Bianca typical of the countryside of Naples, and a Falanghina Bastarda in the Campi Flegrei; Bordignon named the latter Falanghina Mascolina or Falanghina Piccola. Again, while it is agreed that the Falanghina variety original of the hinterland of Benevento and that of the Campi Flegrei are distinct varieties, when I look at the *Falanghinas* grown around Caserta and compare them to those found in the Campi Flegrei, I see clear-cut differences between them as well, though there is as yet no genetic evidence to support the existence of a third clearly distinct *Falanghina*. Presently, these *Falanghinas* showing slight morphologic differences are thought to be the result of the natural adaptation of Falanghina Flegrea to very different and specific *terroirs* over time, that is, different phenotypic expressions rather than distinct genotypes. This explains the existence of small-berried *Falanghina* cultivars in many vineyards, such as the Falanghina Pigna Piccola (a biotype of Falanghina Flegrea), which may be the Falanghina Bastarda or Falanghina Piccola described in the past. Characterized by smaller berries and naturally smaller yields, it has almost disappeared because of its limited production capacity.

Given this multiplicity of *Falanghinas*—and their popularity—we should perhaps not be surprised that not all the grapes finding their way into *Falanghina* wines belong there. In spite of the millions of bottles of wine sporting the *Falanghina* name and now being sold all over the world, I have never found that *Falanghina* grapevines were so abundant during my journeys through the Campanian countryside. Of course, I probably don't know what to look for. Then again, this wouldn't be Italy if charming stuff like this weren't going on all the time.

Leonardo Mustilli, of the high-quality Mustilli estate in the Sant'Agata dei Goti area of Campania, was the first to actively differentiate between his *Falanghina* and that grown in the area around Naples, choosing and propagating old vines of a *Falanghina* he believed was typical of the Sant'Agata dei Goti production zone. Beginning in the 1970s, he and a few other local producers and growers actively sought out vines in older and abandoned vineyards to reproduce and propagate. In the end, they identified eighteen different native or local varieties that risked extinction, and used them to make experimental wines. The resulting *Falanghina* wines were most impressive, and the local varieties Mustilli and his companions had isolated were later identified as Falanghina Beneventana. It is to Mustilli's credit that he was the first producer to ever bottle a monovarietal *Falanghina* wine—his first vintage was the 1979. I distinctly remember the evening in 1981 (or was it 1982? Well, maybe not so distinctly) in Rome when I and the owner of what was then the city's best wine shop tried a *Falanghina* wine for the first time. Neither one of us was overwhelmed, but the wine was interesting and well made, and we were thrilled that an ancient variety had made a comeback. Since then, Mustilli, who has since planted both the Flegrea and Benevantana varieties, has identified and selected a third biotype or variety, with which he makes his best wine, called Vigna Segreta. Genetic studies are planned in order to differentiate this either as a *Falanghina* biotype or new *Falanghina* variety. The best compliment I can make is that Mustilli's *Falanghina* wines always speak of their *terroir,* for over the years winemakers have changed at the estate, and yet the wine has always remained more or less the same.

The Beneventana variety is the most recently identified *Falanghina* and ought therefore to be the least abundant of the two, though this is unclear from agricultural census data. Morphologically, Falanghina Beneventana has a conical grape cluster, with oval, yellow-green berries, in contrast to Falanghina Flegrea's cylindrical bunch, with round, yellow-green marked by a recognizable grey tinge, due to this variety's greater presence of bloom. The Beneventana variety is thought to have originated in Bonea, which is not far from Benevento. In the past, *Falanghina* was thought identical to the Biancazita variety of the Campanian coast; the first to suggest this identity was Goethe in 1887, an observation later repeated by many other experts such as Bordignon (1965). Today we know that Biancazita (and its synonym Biancatenera) are instead identical to Ginestra, another local native grape.

Prior to genetic analysis confirming Falanghina Beneventana as a distinct grapevine, all descriptions of *Falanghina* and its wines were included under the umbrella heading of *Falanghina* or Falanghina Flegrea. The true Falanghina Flegrea, now grown mainly around Naples and Caserta (in fact, it is now the most abundantly grown white variety in those two provinces), can be grown anywhere in Campania, and is also allowed in the region of Molise, Lazio, and the northern Puglian province of Foggia. Almost extinct due to phylloxera, it was brought back to general attention by the Avallone family of the Villa Matilde estate near Caserta, and by the Martusciello family who propagated it in the Campi Flegrei production zone.

Which Wines to Choose and Why

You can taste the *Falanghina*s in DOC wines such as Falerno del Massico, Campi Flegrei Bianco, Capri Bianco, Costa d'Amalfi Bianco, Lacryma Christi del Vesuvio Bianco, and Penisola Sorrentina but it's almost always blended. In theory, Falanghina Beneventana should be used to make the DOC wines Taburno Falanghina, Falanghina Sant'Agata dei Goti, Falanghina Guardiolo (also called Guardia Saframondi), and Falanghina Solopaca, all four of which are now subdenominations—thanks to legislative changes made in October 2011—of the Benevento DOC, and should also be used to make the wines labeled Sannio Falanghina. There are about fifty different IGT wines that can also include the *Falanghina*s in the blend, such as Beneventano Falanghina.

Any way you slice it, falanghina is one of the greatest success stories in Italian wine of the last thirty years. People immediately recognize the name and the wine's style (more or less). In short, it's a wine that has brilliantly managed to break through barriers in Italy, as experts and beginners alike look for it in stores and on restaurant wine lists, generally quite liking it, though some less-well-made bottles might strain both goodwill and patience. Just consider this: we know that in 2010 there were 4,800,000 bottles of falanghina bottled in the province of Benevento alone, with another 400,000 from the other two DOCs. That's a lot of bottles from a relatively small area, and they are neither all of the same quality nor all reminiscent of the variety, in my opinion.

In general, wines made with Falanghina Beneventana have more structure and alcohol than those made with Falanghina Flegrea, though such differences are not readily apparent nowadays, with most producers planting both varieties in new vineyards. In my view, the best *Falanghina* wines are made from grapes grown in packed soils rich in clay-tufa. I also find that Falanghina Beneventana wines tend to be more floral, while Falanghina Flegrea wines (especially those of the Sannio, where Falanghina Flegrea will ripen up to three weeks earlier), tend to be less complex but more fruity, with flavors and aromas of unripe peach, Golden Delicious apple, apricot kernel, and cherry pit. All *Falanghina* wines have a leafy, chlorophyll note that is typical; those of the Sant'Agata dei Goti area (and Mustilli's in particular) are notably mineral and aromatically pungent.

Both *Falanghina*s have excellent naturally high acidity and can be used to make decent sparkling wines, but I don't find them to be complex enough to warrant much interest, unless they are priced at the level of an easy-going, inexpensive sparkler (and then why not just stick to a delightful Prosecco?). Even *Falanghina* sparkling wines made with secondary fermentation in the bottle don't hold much appeal to me, but since producers have started making these wines only recently, everyone's learning curve is still growing, mine included.

Given that an important estate such as Feudi di San Gregorio has enlisted the consultation of Champagne luminary Anselme Selosse, my belief that *Falanghina* sparklers are so-so may soon be proven wrong, and nothing would make me happier.

WINES TO TRY: Cantina del Taburno*** (Falanghina Taburno: rich, expressive wine and very inexpensive), Mustilli*** (a very personal style, mineral and pungent and typical of the Falanghina of Sant'Agata dei Goti; the Vigna Segreta bottling is fruitier and richer), Contrada Salandra** (Falanghina Campi Flegrei), Fontanavecchia** (Falanghina Taburno), Grotta del Sole** (Falanghina Campi Flegrei Coste di Cuma), Vesevo** (Falanghina Sannio), Viticoltore Moccia/Agnanum** (Falanghina Campi Flegrei Aganum; the Vigna del Pino bottling is also impressive), Astroni* (Falanghina Campi Flegrei Colle Imperatrice), Quintodecimo* (Via del Campo, in a richer creamier style than most but typical of Luigi Moio's white wines), Mastroberadino* (Falanghina Irpinia Morabianca, in a creamy international style, but you won't want to put the glass down), Nifo Sarrapochiello* (Falanghina Alenta, which is slightly late harvested and a good value), Ciabrelli* (Falanghina Alexia Sannio), Colle di San Domenico* (Falanghina Vendemmia Tardiva), Corte Normanna*, De Lucia*, Ponte*, Terra dei Briganti*, Torre del Pagus*, and Villa Matilde (Falerno del Massico and Carracci; the latter, a creamy rich, gently oaked version, is a very impressive, excellent wine made in an international, buttery style that has garnered numerous awards through the years, but doesn't taste anything like I expect *Falanghina* to).

Famoso

WHERE IT'S FOUND: Emilia-Romagna. NATIONAL REGISTRY CODE NUMBER: 420. COLOR: white.

There is not one Famoso variety in Italy but two: the Famoso of Cesena and Famoso di Pesaro/Rimini (see FAMOSO DI PESARO/RIMINI entry). The former is the variety recently listed in the National Registry (in 2009) simply as Famoso, while the latter requires further study and has yet to be officially recognized and named as a separate variety. I will keep them separate in this book while waiting for the second Famoso to also be inserted into Italy's National Registry—and I will show that there is enough historical, ampelographic, and anecdotal data to do so. Though in the future one Famoso may be proven to be just a biotype of the other, I don't think that's very likely.

Famoso, whose synonyms include Rambella, Rambela, Uva Rambella, Valdoppiese (or Valdupies, in dialect), and Bianca di Spinello is a white aromatic grape variety that will remind you of Moscato Bianco. It is yet another Italian grape variety with a very interesting if complex history. Cultivated for centuries in the Romagna portion of Emilia-Romagna, mainly in the countryside around Cesena, Faenza, Bertinoro, Lugo, Forlì, Ravenna, and throughout most of the Savio River valley (hence the "di Cesena" descriptor still used today by many locals), it was known to be distinct from another, rarer Famoso variety that also grew in Emilia-Romagna, farther south and west, near Pesaro and Rimini. In any case, Famoso di Cesena virtually disappeared in the twentieth century. And yet, the variety had always been described favorably by experts, including at the 1876 Forlì ampelographic fair (Comizio Agrario di Folì 1877) and in the tenth volume of the ampelographic bulletin (Ministero Agricoltura, Industria e Commercio 1879). The fall in Famoso di Cesena's total acreage was most likely a consequence of phylloxera, but perhaps the reduction was also due to difficulty in recognizing Famoso di Cesena without confusing it with another similar-looking local native variety called Cargarello (currently only grown in the experimental vineyards of the Centro Ricerche Produzioni Vegetali in Tebano, though it appears to have promise as a wine grape).

In any case, Famoso di Cesena was believed by locals and experts alike to be virtually extinct when in 2000, two rows of very old vines of grapes the owner called Famoso were discovered near Mercato Saraceno, in the province of Forlì-Cesena. Ampelographic analysis subsequently confirmed that the newly discovered grapes were indeed Famoso di Cesena, but it was found that the variety was also remarkably similar to another local cultivar known as Rambella (or Rambela), and more rarely as Valdoppiese or Valdupies. In any case, just like Famoso di Cesena, Rambella had always been highly thought of, as described by experts such as such as Pasqualini and Pasqui (1875), De Bosis in the *Bollettini Ampelografici Provinciali* (1876), and Marzotto (1925b). Not surprisingly, and just as with Famoso di Cesena, Rambella's fortunes turned for the worse with the advent of phylloxera: by 1923, Bazzocchi wrote that it was "a good-quality but not much cultivated variety typical of the Cesenate area."

Winemaker Giancarlo Soverchia of the Santa Lucia Vinery (yes, with a "V"), who also consults at other local estates and is perhaps the single biggest expert on the *Famoso* varieties in Italy today, told me that "Famoso is a hard variety to identify correctly: not just the grapevine, but its wines can be a pain to recognize as well. It's very easy to come away with a mistaken impression. For example, Famoso wines made on the hillsides of Cesena are different from those of the flatlands of nearby Faenza, even when the wines are made in the same way and the grape variety used is exactly the same. Actually, though I am among those who think that the Rambella of Cesena really is a different biotype of Famoso (and its wines will differ accordingly), I also wonder how much of these differences are man-made. For example, in the flatland vineyards around Faenza yields are invariably higher, so the wines can seem more diluted and less intense in their aroma and flavor."

Soverchia points out minor ampelographic differences between Rambella and Famoso too, such as Rambella's conical, winged cluster and large oval berries and Famoso's pyramidal, loosely packed bunch. However, despite these minor differences, Famoso is generally characterized by large bunches and berries; so much so that it is also appreciated as a table grape. The variety usually ripens by early September and tends to drop its acidity quickly at that time; it is both vigorous and productive. There are as yet no official clones available. The defining characteristic of Famoso and one that has attracted plenty of attention is that it is intensely aromatic, especially the Ercolani biotype—so much so that comparisons have been drawn to Moscato Bianco, though all tests performed to date have shown this variety to be distinct from known *Moscato*s (Crespan and Milani 2001; Fontana, Filippetti, Pastore, and Intrieri 2007).

In fact, it is thanks to researchers at Tebano and the University of Bologna that Famoso got a second lease on life. The Vitigni Minori project, launched at the beginning of 2000 and financed with regional funds, was aimed at characterizing the less-known native grapes of Emilia-Romagna and evaluating their fine-wine potential. The project involved both the Centro Interdipartimentale di Ricerche Viticole ed Enologiche (Interdepartmental Center for Viticultural and Enologic Research) of the University of Bologna and the Centro Ricerche Produzioni Vegetali (CRPV) in Tebano. Over one hundred different accessions of then-unknown or rare grape varieties were studied using ampelographic, isoenzymatic, and DNA analysis. This body of work has led to the characterization of many now important cultivars such as Famoso and Ruggine, as well as other local varieties. Producers such as Leone Conti and others (unfortunately, still only a handful) who are now actively producing Famoso wines credit a scientific presentation and tasting held roughly ten years ago of wines made from those little-known but finally studied varieties for getting them turned onto Famoso and other previously forgotten cultivars.

In any case, it all adds up to quite a turn of fortune for Famoso, a variety and wine that was off all radars only a decade ago. Leone Conti really believes in the variety: "I can't figure out why Famoso was abandoned by our ancestors: it's productive and not sickly, though it's so vigorous that to make good wines you have to work very hard in the vineyards with it." Claudio Ancarani of the Ancarani estate tends to worry about acidity levels: "My estate is up in the hills, so budbreak occurs earlier and I can harvest a little earlier than most, thereby preserving total acidity levels in the grapes. Clearly, with Famoso there is no deleafing whatsoever, for the variety accumulates sugar easily, and the last thing it needs is to see more sunlight." Plantings of Famoso have slowly but surely increased in Emilia-Romagna over the last ten years and it's currently found in the countryside around Bertinoro, Brisighella, Castrocaro, Cesena, Faenza, Forlì, and Riolo (especially toward the Marche).

Which Wines to Choose and Why

Most Famoso wines are bottled as IGT Ravenna Bianco or Forlì Bianco; other IGT wines are labeled Rubicone and Emilia. In my experience (I have tasted every Famoso wine made in numerous if not all vintages) the best are characterized by an obvious aromatic note of rose petals, talcum powder, lychee, and peach, with hints of white pepper; that laundry list may lead you to think otherwise, but the nose is less aromatic than most Moscato Bianco or Malvasia di Candia Aromatica wines. Unfortunately, I haven't tasted any wines made with the Ercolani biotype so I cannot describe those at the present time.

Leone Conti, whose first vintage dates to 2006, loves the wine but tries not to let the aromatic side take over: "I think this is the most French of all my wines, and by that I mean a truly great wine of breeding and depth. I especially love its mineral, almost saline bent, but it can be almost overwhelmingly aromatic at times." At the Santa Lucia Vinery they also try to tame Famoso's innate aromaticity (though I can't figure out why: I find this a delicious and fascinating aspect of Famoso wines) by aging 50 percent of the wine in oak barrels. Reportedly they make their Famoso Cru Artigianale wine by harvesting grapes in October, though that seems to fly in the face of what I know about this variety: acid levels in Famoso grapes drop precipitously as they near optimal ripeness, and most people harvest Famoso either in early or mid-September. Not every local producer is convinced of Famoso's uniqueness. For instance, Alessandro Morini of Podere Morini told me that "I like it, but find the wine too similar to Moscato Bianco, though I know the grapevines are genetically different. I just don't see enough of a special character to Famoso wine to want to invest heavily in it. Who knows, I may yet change my mind." And Ancarani cautions that "the real risk, now that Famoso is becoming famous, is of a huge number of Famoso wine bottlings springing up overnight, which isn't possible given the current very limited grapevine availability. My fear is that less-than-scrupulous producers may try to cut it with Malvasia di Candia Aromatica, which is very easy to obtain, in order to make more wine. However, the latter variety is much more aromatic and dominating, so it gives people the wrong impression as to what Famoso wines are really all about."

WINES TO TRY: Leone Conti*** (LeOne), Ancarani*** (Signore, an unoaked Famoso: a good thing in my view), Santa Lucia Vinery**, Tenuta Uccellina** (Rambèla), and Villa Venti** (Serenaro).

Famoso di Pesaro/Rimini

WHERE IT'S FOUND: Emilia-Romagna. NATIONAL REGISTRY CODE NUMBER: not registered. COLOR: white.

I may be going out on a limb in giving this variety a separate heading in this book, as it's not an officially recognized cultivar and not much wine is made with it (yet?). In fact, even its name is bound to change, if and when the variety is finally included in the Registry, as the use of place names such as "di Pesaro" or "di Rimini" to qualify grape varieties is now avoided by legislators in Italy. After all, I could have just briefly discussed this variety in the Famoso section above, as I have done with the two *Falanghinas*, which are genetically distinct. However, unlike those two grapes, the two *Famosos* give such radically different wines that I will keep them separate in this book.

There is historical evidence that the *Famoso* growing in the Pesaro and Rimini countrysides is different from that of Cesena (the grape we know as Famoso today). These differences were clearly remarked upon at the 1876 Forlì ampelographic fair (Comizio Agrario di Folì 1877) and in the tenth volume of the 1879 ampelographic bulletin (Ministero Agricoltura, Industria e Commercio 1879a). Already at that time, the Famoso of Cesena was considered to look and behave more like an Albana, while the Famoso of Pesaro and Rimini was likened to Biancame or Trebbiano Toscano. Pastore and Allegro (2007) distinguish clearly between Famoso and Famoso di Pesaro/Rimini, on ampelographic and genetic grounds. Ampelographically, Famoso di Pesaro/Rimini has a much smaller, conical bunch and its berries are also smaller and have thinner skins. Genetically, Famoso has been analyzed at eight SSR microsatellite loci and it is distinct from Famoso di Pesaro/Rimini. Last but not least, but perhaps of greatest relevance to wine drinkers, Famoso di Pesaro/Rimini is a nonaromatic variety.

Which Wines to Choose and Why

Given that the variety is not yet officially recognized, the wines made with it can only be labeled as *vino da tavola*. Famoso di Pesaro/Rimini wines are undoubtedly *Trebbiano*-like, in that they have a delicate white-flower, lemony-herbal aroma and flavor profile, are light bodied, and high in acid. Unlike Famoso wines, Famoso di Pesaro/Rimini wines do not express any spicy or pungent qualities typically associated with the *Moscatos* and other aromatic grapes. The Terracruda estate in Fratte Rosa deserves the utmost credit for having launched a program aimed at preserving local grapevine biodiversity and has recently started producing monovarietal wines from little-known cultivars such as Famoso di Pesaro/Rimini in collaboration with the University of Ancona. They are greatly helped in this project by the fact that Giancarlo Soverchia is their winemaker: there's probably nobody who knows the *Famoso* grapes better than he.

WINES TO TRY: Terracruda**, Il Conventino** (Il Famoso nel Convento).

Fiano

WHERE IT'S FOUND: Campania. NATIONAL REGISTRY CODE NUMBER: 81. COLOR: white.

I think Fiano may well be Italy's greatest native white grape: only Verdicchio can lay a similar claim to that title (though if we consider sweet wines, then Picolit has a shot too). Like few other white cultivars in Italy, Fiano can make a range of wines, from light- to full-bodied, dry to sweet, easygoing to very ageworthy; the latter examples easily last and improve for ten or more years, a rarity with Italian white wines.

Fiano is also one of Italy's oldest cultivars, once believed to be one of the *viti apiane* cited by Pliny and Columella, though most experts today argue these were Moscato Bianco. Carlucci (1907) hypothesized that Fiano was cultivated in ancient Roman times because of Fiano's common synonym, Latino. Documentation of a wine called fiano is available starting in the twelfth century, when records show that King Federico II, during his stay in Foggia (Puglia), bought Greco, Grecisco, and Fiano wines for private consumption (we still have no idea with what cultivar Grecisco may have been). Most likely, Fiano is a native of the area of Lapio (the variety's name may in fact derive from Appia, then Apiano, finally Lapio and Fiano), a small town located east of Avellino at roughly 590 meters above sea level and one of the real *grand cru* areas for the variety. In 1661, a publication written by Brother Scipione Bella Bona mentions the town and its production of the wine apiano. In 1861 Fusco cited records kept by Guglielmo De Fisoni indicating that in the thirteenth century King Carlo d'Angiò II bought sixteen thousand Fiano vines and had them planted in the royal vineyard at Manfredonia (Scienza and Boselli 2003).

Synonyms of Fiano rarely used nowadays include Santa Sofia (erroneous, since this is a distinct cultivar), Fiore Mendillo, and Latino. Fiano should not be confused with Puglia's Fiano Minutolo, an unrelated variety (and aromatic, which Fiano is not) the name of which has since been officially changed to Minutolo. There are also records of a Fiano Rosa in Puglia; documentation on it is scarce, though a study by Caputo, Brini, Gasparro, Milella, Forleo, Pepe, and Antonacci (2008) attempted to differentiate between it and the other two Fiano-named varieties.

The real Fiano was an extremely rare, altogether forgotten variety as recently as the 1970s, a fact that might surprise those walking into any Italian wine shop or restaurant today, where seemingly endless lists of Fiano wines await. In the early twentieth century, Fiano was hardly mentioned in texts (an exception is Cavazza in 1914) and by the 1940s the cultivar was reduced to sporadic wines grown haphazardly in the Campanian countryside, the grapes thrown among others to make local wine blends. It was Antonio Mastroberardino of the venerable Mastroberardino estate of Campania who brought Fiano back from oblivion. By searching out grapes in old vineyards around Avellino, he was able to produce his first vintage in 1945, a grand total of thirty bottles. From there production slowly grew, though it remained small and little known right into the 1970s. Things began turning for the better in the early 1980s: I remember attending a tasting in 1981 organized by the Rome branch of the International Food and Wine Society (sadly no longer active) at a via Veneto hotel, where Mastroberardino presented unfamiliar wines made with Greco and Fiano. The wine made with Fiano especially elicited positive responses, and while I thought then that the variety and the wine might have a bright future, I admit I never envisioned the rock star–like success Fiano would meet with over the next three decades.

In fact, only ten years before, things still looked glum. In an address given by Mastroberardino in 1968 at the Accademia della Vite e del Vino, he stated that the grapevine was grown only sporadically near Avellino, and that old vines yielded very low volumes of grapes and wine—which is normal enough, considering the cultivar's small bunch and berries. He concluded by saying that the wine was of such noteworthy quality, he hoped to see its production increase. I am sure he had no idea at the time just how prophetic he would turn out to be.

Fiano is a remarkable success story and an example of what could be lost by not paying proper attention to native varieties. In fact, Fiano is so clearly a great wine grape that it is now being actively planted in other regions including Marche, Basilicata, Puglia, and Sicily, as well as outside Italy in California and Australia, for example.

Ampelographically, Fiano has medium-small (150–220 grams), pyramidal bunches, winged and compact; and medium-sized, oval berries with thick, yellow-green skins that show brown spots when ripe. A late ripener (it's usually harvested in October), Fiano is very sensitive to oidium and less so to peronospora; its thick skins render it botrytis resistant. It is this feature that allows late harvests in cold, rainy parts of Campania. In the past, Fiano was also a table grape, often made into raisins for winter storage. Available clones include VCR 3, VCR 107 (very common and not all that different from the previous), Ampelos TEA 24, Ampelos EVA 2, UNIMI-VITIS FIA VV 21, and UNIMI-VITIS FIA VV 29.

In Italy Fiano grows in Campania especially, but is also found in Puglia, Basilicata, and Sicily. Internationally, it has found welcome homes in California, Oregon, and Australia, where it has been planted everywhere from the Barossa Valley to Heathcote, Margaret River, Adelaide Hills, and Riverland.

Which Wines to Choose and Why

The best-known wine is DOCG Fiano di Avellino, made in close to thirty townships around

Avellino. Sannio Fiano and Cilento Bianco can be good too, either as monovarietal fianos or as blends. In Sicily, at least one extraordinarily successful wine is being made by Planeta, and some Puglian wines are compelling. Interestingly, an analysis of the viticultural and enological characteristics of Fiano and other varieties planted in Tuscany found that the wine was not characterized by features noteworthy enough (at least from those vines planted near Arezzo, Grosseto, and Pisa) to recommend planting it in Tuscany (Bucelli, Egger, Faviere, Giannetti, Pierucci, Piracci, and Storchi 1999).

In my view, volcanic soils are best for Fiano, as they allow the formation of penetratingly pure mineral and delicately fruity aromas, archetypal of great Fiano wines. In fact, even more than with many cultivars, soils are all important, for there are marked differences in wines from the various sites where Fiano is grown in Campania. In my view there are at least three specific subzones of quality Fiano production: one famous area (Lapio, Montefalcone) is heavy and clay-dominated; most others (Cesinali, Santo Stefano del Sole) are very loosely packed and rich in sand, yielding fruity, lighter wines of early appeal; finally areas such as Montevergine, Sant'Angelo a Scala, Summonte, and Capriglia, all at about four hundred meters above sea level, give fruitier wines marked by smoky or *fumé* notes, due to soils rich in calcareous conglomerates and a thin layer of volcanic ash. That said, Antonio Mastroberardino believes that true Fiano never gives smoky wines: therefore, he suspects some might be unknowingly using a similar but distinct variety.

In fact, part of Fiano's appeal is that, depending on growing conditions, it can give either a steely-mineral or decadently lush and rich wine. The most typical Fiano wines are the former, offering very refined aromas of hazelnut, green apple, pear, and honey. This is especially true of those wines made in the manner of Mastroberardino (two-week maceration/fermentation at 18°C maximum, more usually at 15–16°C). Other vinification techniques can increase the size and weight of wines, giving surprisingly smoky, almost muscat-like aromas. Most likely, Mastroberardino is correct in his assumption that some estates may be unwittingly growing a different, aromatic biotype of Fiano (or a distinct variety altogether); but my experience also tells me that some of those smoky, almost burnt-rubber notes (in wines really made with nothing but true Fiano) may result either from fermentation temperatures that are too high (estates without temperature-control in the cellars), grapes grown in excessively hot conditions or picked overripe, or from grapevines planted in northern exposed, cold, loose soils. I could very easily be wrong.

According to Luigi Moio, one of Italy's greatest winemakers and perhaps the single greatest expert on the cultivars of Campania, concentrations of geraniol and linalool (which give Fiano a floral note) allow easy sensorial discrimination between wines made with Fiano, the *Falanghina*s, and Greco (2012). According to Moio, Fiano wines develop a toasty, slightly herbal note with age that is most likely due to the presence of free alkyl-2-metoxypyrazines and volatile phenols. His research team at the University of Naples has also found that while concentrations of geraniol and linalool are linked to specific yeast metabolic activity, concentrations of molecules such as terpin-4-ol, β-damascenone, 1,1,6-trimethyl-1,2-dihydronaphthalene (TDN, a molecule usually associated with riesling's diesel-fuel aromas), and 1-(2,3,6-trimentilfenil)buta-1,3-diene (TPB) are influenced by acid-catalyzed reactions, and are most likely responsible for aromas of wild fennel, broom, and acacia sometimes described in Fiano wines. Interestingly, the Fiano variety appears to be rich in glycosilated aromatic precursors, an important finding because these act as a "deposit" of aroma and flavor molecules that can be freed via specific viticultural and winemaking decisions. This also means that, more than with other Campanian varieties, varying the time of harvest, length of must to skin contact, or length of air-drying will greatly affect the characteristics of Fiano wine.

There are also late-harvest or air-dried sweet Fiano wines, though I don't particularly like them, finding the grape does best as a dry wine. In a study by Genovese, Gambuti, Piombino, and Moio (2007), the sensory descriptors of sweet fiano wine (citrus jam, dried apricot, dried figs, prune, honey, and coconut) were evaluated biochemically; the researchers found higher concentrations of thirty-five free volatile compounds (mostly terpenes, lactones, aldehydes) in the sweet Fiano wines than in the dry wines. The main odor-impacting compounds in sweet Fiano wines were terpenes such as nerol, geraniol, and linalool (orange flowers); and lactones such as γ-nonalactone (coconut), δ-decalactone and γ-decalactone (apricot), and 1-octen-3-ol (mushroom). Apparently, these differences are due to the drying process, which allows concentration of varietal aromatic compounds already present in the Fiano grape, as well as an easier transfer of these from skins to must during vinification.

In California, Scribner's Bend (Novantina), Solis Winery (their 2011 Estate Fiano bottling won gold and best of region at the California State Fair Wine competition and silver at the Los Angeles International Wine Competition), Giannelli, and Seghesio all make noteworthy Fiano wines. In Australia, Barossa Valley's Saltram (Winemaker's Selection) and Jacob's Creek, Riverland's Bassham, Margaret River's Seven Ochres (a cool climate area allowing for perfumed, pungent fiano that is excellent), Ducks in a Row (an interesting fiano from northern Heathcote's red soils), McLaren Vale's Coriole, Oliver's Taranga, and Fox Gordon (Princess), Victoria's Rutherglen Estate, Granite Belt's Witches Falls Winery, and Back Pocket all make Fiano wines of note, but there are close to thirty producers now doing very interesting things with the grape. Sure, they're often quite different from the Fiano wines I am accustomed to, but I think this is one Italian white variety where a New World twist is welcome. In the end, what we get is a different but just as interesting rendition of fiano. Wine is a voyage, and the great encounters you make—bottles of Fiano wine included—are what memories are made of.

WINES TO TRY: For Fiano di Avellino, try: Ciro Picariello***, Colli di Lapio-Romana Clelio*** (this is arguably Italy's single best white wine), Mastroberardino*** (especially the library or vintage bottlings that are released from time to time), Pietracupa***, Tenuta Sarno 1860***, Vadiaperti*** (Aiperti), Villa Diamante*** (Vigna della Congregazione), Di Prisco**, Quintodecimo** (Exultet), Rocca del Principe**, Terredora** (CampoRe), and Urciolo**. For Paestum, try Luigi Maffini*** (both the non-oaked Kratos, my favorite, and the oaked Pietraincatenata). For Sicily, try Planeta*** (Cometa, a very personal interpretation of Fiano but utterly irresistible). For Basilicata, there are no monovarietal fianos of note, but there are good blends, such as Paternoster's Bianco di Corte. For Puglia, try: Conti Zecca*, Guttarola* (Amphora), Morella* (Mezzogiorno), and Valle dell'Asso*.

Fogarina

WHERE IT'S FOUND: Emilia-Romagna. NATIONAL REGISTRY CODE NUMBER: 393. COLOR: white.

Talk about getting no respect: try an Internet search for the words "Uva Fogarina," and ten of the first fifteen citations refer not to a grape variety but to an Italian folk song *"Com'è bella l'uva fogarina,"* very popular in the 1930s. I guess that if a grape variety was famous and loved enough to have a song written about it, it got plenty of respect—but still. Fogarina is also known as Fogarina di Gualtieri (the name of the town it is most associated with) and Uva Fogarina, though this last may be an erroneous synonym, as some experts believe Uva Fogarina to be a distinct variety typical of Bologna. According to some reports, Fogarina was discovered by Carlo Simonazzo (or Simonazzi), who, while fishing the Crostolina River on a November day in 1820, found grapevines close to the river's edge that were unlike anything he had ever seen before.

Others believe Fogarina was found in a forest called Fogarin near Guastalla, hence its name. Another theory believes the name is derived from *fugare,* or to run away, from the inundations of the Po River—apparently, the grape variety was historically grown close to the riverbanks. Recent DNA tests have shown it might be related to Lambrusco Marani and possibly to Raboso Piave.

Centuries ago Fogarina thrived in the alluvial soils of the Po and lower Enza rivers, and it was, along with Ancellotta, still the most abundantly cultivated variety in Emilia in the first half of the nineteenth century, when it began to lose ground to Lambrusco Maestri and Fortana. According to Zini and Caleffi, the first Fogarina monovarietal bottling, produced by Ettore Pecorini, dates to 1900. As recently as the early twentieth century, 80 percent of all the grapes grown in the Reggiana part of the region were Fogarina and there was even a wine producer named in its honor, Cantina della Fogarina. Today Fogarina grows mainly around the hamlets of Guastalla and Gualtieri, around Modena. The Cantina Sociale di Gualtieri (a modern reincarnation of the original Cantina della Fogarina) is currently involved in a very meritorious safeguarding of the variety, encouraging the cooperative's members to plant it. Its first wines were presented to the public only in 2009, so this is a very recent revival of a native grape and wine. Carlo Simonazzi has also devoted time and energy to this variety, planting sixty-two hundred vines in 2001 propagated from an original ungrafted grapevine he found near Pieve di Gualtieri, near an old farmhouse. Simonazzi thinks the grape is not ideally suited for winemaking, but thanks to its high acidity, it can also be made into Aceto Balsamico Tradizionale, though the variety has not yet been officially registered for this purpose by the Italian government. According to Simonazzi at least two biotypes of Fogarina exist; the green-stalked, which usually gives better wines but is very variable in quality from year to year, and the red-stalked, which apparently produces wines of more regular quality levels. It's also a very vigorous variety, easily producing in excess of 150 hectoliters per hectare. Apparently there is one clone available, Fedit 7 C.S.G.

Which Wines to Choose and Why

Fogarina wines are characterized by good color and extremely high acidities and so were historically used in blends to add color, lower pH values, and increase aroma. The variety can be included in such IGT wines as Ravenna Rosso, Forlì, and Rubicone.

WINES TO TRY: Cantina Sociale di Gualtieri** (Demi Sec Rosé, a sparkling wine that is fresh and enjoyable, redolent of wild strawberry and raspberry aromas and flavors, with a little bit of residual sugar; Passito di Fogarina di Gualtieri, a light and enjoyable sweet wine that is rich yet lively, with syrupy red-cherry and strawberry jam notes).

Foglia Tonda

WHERE IT'S FOUND: Tuscany. NATIONAL REGISTRY CODE NUMBER: 82. COLOR: red.

The name of this variety derives from the shape of its leaf, which can be almost perfectly round (*foglia tonda* means round leaf). However, it is not to be confused with another round-leafed variety called Foja Tonda (which is not a synonym of Enantio, like you are liable to read elsewhere) and Lambrusco a Foglia Tonda (better known as Casetta), a cultivar native to Trentino. Instead, Foglia Tonda is an ancient variety related to Sangiovese and apparently native to Chianti Classico. It was first described in the vineyards of the Castello di Brolio in Gaiole in Chianti by Di Rovasenda in 1877; later, Breviglieri and Casini (1964) described in detail grapevines found near Arceno. Recently, Crespan, Calò, Giannetto, Sparacio, Storchi, and Costacurta have suggested a parent-offspring relationship between Foglia Tonda and Sangiovese (2008).

Though Foglia Tonda is still a relatively unknown variety, everyone seems to agree that it has huge winemaking potential—in fact, it's considered to be second only to Sangiovese Forte among the most recently rediscovered Tuscan natives. It's characterized by medium-sized, pyramidal bunches and round berries with plenty of bloom. It has shoots with a large distance between internodes, so there aren't many leaves; for this reason, deleafing has to be done with extreme care, for the berries are prone to sunburn. Viticulturalist Stefano Dini is enthusiastic and says its only problem is that "rain in the fall can make the berries rupture easily. Otherwise, the real problem is finding grapevine material: there just isn't that much of it around for us to plant." There is an officially certified clone available, the FT-BRO-1; unfortunately, Dini reports, there appear to be some doubts over the health status of the clone, and that's why not much has been heard about it. According to Dini, the Vivai Cooperativi Rauscedo (VCR) nursery in Friuli Venezia Giulia (the world's largest producer of nursery grapevine material) is currently working on certifying two clones of Foglia Tonda that ought to be available soon. Without doubt, a very desirable trait of future clones would be slightly looser-packed bunches: Foglia Tonda has an extremely compact bunch and botrytis is a real problem in wet autumns.

The two estates that have most worked with Foglia Tonda over the years are Donatella Cinelli Colombini (the source of the plants VCR used to perform its clonal selections) and Mannucci Droandi; the latter was part of a research project in the mid-1990s, spearheaded by the Istituto Sperimentale per la Viticoltura di Arezzo (Research Institute of Enology in Arezzo), in which an experimental vineyard was set up and over forty native varieties and biotypes were planted. The results showed that Foglia Tonda had real fine-winemaking potential, encouraging even famous winemakers such as Maurizio Castelli to give it a try. "Unfortunately," he says, "we still don't know much about it, and so we are moving ahead by trial and error." For example, it is generally believed—and written—that Foglia Tonda is very vigorous, and therefore poor soils and use of low-vigor rootstocks are a must. "Not so," says Castelli, "it's more correct to say that it's characterized by very irregular productivity: for example, it doesn't produce much when spur cordon trained." Castelli prefers the Guyot training system for Foglia Tonda, as does Dini, who feels it allows for better balance of this cultivar's vegetative and productive aspects. But according to Cinelli Colombini, with Guyot training Foglia Tonda produces too much, and the ensuing wine quality is very poor—he prefers the spur cordon system. Time and further experience will soon cure our present lack of knowledge.

Though a little Foglia Tonda grows everywhere in Tuscany, it's most common in Chianti, where it tends to ripen a little later than Sangiovese. It is believed to be quite rare, though just how rare is debatable. Foglia Tonda is officially allowed in the provinces of Pisa, Firenze, and Siena, and over the years I have been told or have heard that Foglia Tonda grows in the vineyards of many estates, sometimes in just a couple of rows here and there. Official data regarding total hectares of Foglia Tonda in Italy is of little help: relative to 2000, I have found numbers ranging from 3.1 to 42 hectares, and in the most recent 2010 census, there were no numbers given for Foglia Tonda. However, the numbers of Foglia Tonda grapevine cuttings sold by nurseries in Italy between 1998 and 2004 show an increase from less than three thousand per year to over twenty-two thousand, so plantings are certainly on the way up.

Which Wines to Choose and Why

Producers are impressed with Foglia Tonda's fine-wine potential, as its wines are characterized by softer acidity and tannins than those made with Sangiovese. For this reason, Foglia Tonda is viewed favorably not just as a possible source of monovarietal wines, but also as a useful partner for Sangiovese in blends, where it adds body. According to Giancarlo Scalabrelli of the University of Pisa, monovarietal Foglia Tonda wines are excellent for drinking in the medium term, but are not as ageworthy as Sangiovese wines. I find monovarietal wines recall red currant, dried plums, and cinnamon, with nuances of tobacco, and are blessed with strong but smooth tannins and overall high acidities; like Sangiovese, they have dark ruby-red hues tinged with garnet, though they are deeper in color than those made with Sangiovese alone.

WINES TO TRY: Mocine*** (s'Indora), Mannucci Droandi**, Guido Galassi** (wines vinified in open-topped wooden fermentation tanks before aging for ten months in oak casks of various sizes and ages, rolled continuously to keep the lees moving). Other estates that have considerable plantings of Foglia Tonda are Donatella Cinelli Colombini, but the wine produced (the very good Cenerentola) is a blend (65 percent Sangiovese and 35 percent Foglia Tonda).

Forastera

WHERE IT'S FOUND: Campania. NATIONAL REGISTRY CODE NUMBER: 83. COLOR: white.

The name tells the story: *forastera* (or *forestiera*, in Italian) means foreigner and this grape variety, one of the two really important white grapes of the island of Ischia (the other is Biancolella), was a late arrival to the island. According to d'Ambra (1962), Forastera arrived on Ischian shores only in the mid-1800s, though the island has a millenary tradition of fine winemaking dating back to ancient Roman times. Though D'Ascia doesn't mention its presence in his detailed 1867 treatise on the history of the island, Froio mentions it a few years later, in 1878. Very curiously, and probably erroneously, Di Rovasenda in 1877 considered this cultivar to be abundant in the province of Bergamo in northern Lombardy, which seems highly unlikely to me. For reasons that escape me (and everyone else I have asked), on the island of Procida it is called Uva dell'Isola. It's characterized by only modest sugar accumulation and total acidity levels, even when grown in highly different *terroirs,* according to Andrea D'Ambra, certainly the most important producer on the island of Ischia and the one who currently knows the most about the cultivars that hug Ischia's mountain slopes.

Which Wines to Choose and Why

Forastera is grown almost exclusively on the island of Ischia, though there are some vines located on the island of Procida, and on the Penisola Sorrentina and the Campi Flegrei on mainland Campania. The best wine is DOC Ischia Forastera, though DOC Ischia Bianco wines, in which Forastera is part of a blend, are excellent too. A good forastera is herbal (wild fennel, oregano, mint) and saline, with hints of ripe Golden Delicious apple and dried apricot. It has a richer mouthfeel than Biancolella wines, which are always brighter and fresher.

WINES TO TRY: D'Ambra*** (Euposia), Antonio Mazzella**, Cenatiempo**, Pietratorcia**.

Forgiarin

WHERE IT'S FOUND: FVG. NATIONAL REGISTRY CODE NUMBER: 321. COLOR: red.

Forgiarin's name derives from the town of Forgaria (Forjarie), where this cultivar originates. Not much is known of its history. At the Regional Grape Exhibition organized in 1863 by the Udine chapter of the Associazione Agraria Friulana (Friuli Agricultural Association), the San Daniele hills were indicated as the typical production area for Forgiarin. Pirona (1871) wrote that in time the production area expanded to Spilimbergo and Maniago.

Also called Forzarin or Forgiarina, Forgiarin is not to be confused with other similarly named varieties such as Uva Fogarina. Forgiarin's extreme oidium sensitivity led farmers to turn their backs on it, and it was only rediscovered roughly twenty years ago and brought back to life as a monovarietal wine by Emilio Bulfon from Pinzano al Tagliamento in Friuli Venezia Giulia. So though it is not a totally "new" variety and wine, Forgiarin is so limited in its availability today that it is about as obscure a grape and wine as there are in Italy today.

Which Wines to Choose and Why

Today, Forgiarin is grown only in the Pordenone province, around Pinzano al Tagliamento and Castelnovo del Friuli. With little production volume, there is clearly no DOC available. Emilio Bulfon's example has spurred other local growers to try their hand at making and bottling monovarietal Forgiarin. I love a good forgiarin: in fact, there are few Italian wines I enjoy drinking more during a hot summer day than these lightly colored, fresh, floral, almond- and blackcurrant-accented medium-bodied reds. Forgiarin wines remind me of well-made Schiava (Lago di Caldaro, Santa Maddalena) or light-bodied Pinot Nero wines.

WINES TO TRY: Bulfon** (though some recent versions have been marked by excessive residual sugar) and Ronco Cliona**.

Fortana

WHERE IT'S FOUND: Emilia-Romagna. NATIONAL REGISTRY CODE NUMBER: 84. COLOR: red.

In the 1980s, there was a perceptible diminution in popularity of Fortana and many other native varieties as more fashionable cultivars took hold everywhere in Italy. The ensuing glut of extremely mediocre Chardonnay and Cabernet Sauvignon wines has thankfully dried up since then, and varieties such as Fortana are jumping back onto the stage, and onto dining tables. And deservedly, since Fortana always enjoyed good press and its wines have been met with considerable favor through the ages.

Up until the twentieth century, Fortana was known as Uva d'Oro ("golden grape"). Both this name and another commonly used synonym, Fruttana ("plenty of fruit" or "very fruity") refer to Fortana's copious yields, something that, understandably, was always much appreciated by farmers who had to survive with what their fields produced. Another theory is that Uva d'Oro refers to the variety's origin in Burgundy's Côte d'Or, though there is no hard evidence of this. Fortana's cultivation was documented in Emilia-Romagna in the sixteenth century by Agostino Gallo; in 1825 Acerbi wrote that it also grew in Lombardy's Oltrepò Pavese and the Veneto. However, others believe that Fortana was cultivated by the Benedictine monks of the abbey of Pomposa starting in the eleventh century.

Fortana is characterized by very high intravarietal variability, so that there are numerous biotypes phenotypically quite different from each other. One important biotype found today is called Fortanina or Fortanella, characterized by smaller berries and much darker skins, richer in polyphenols. Roberto Miravalle, viticulturalist of the Corte Pallavicina estate, has apparently planted both Fortana and Fortanella in his vineyards and makes wines from both—he is trying to determine the major differences between the two wines, so I guess we just need to wait and see.

Fortana is a rustic variety that behaves like wild grapevines, and in this it resembles the *Lambruscos* to an extent. This connection is supported by analysis (Boccacci, Torello Marinoni, Gambino, Botta, and Schneider 2005) of the genetic characterization of endangered grape cultivars of the Reggio Emilia province, with eight SSR microsatellite loci used to investigate possible parentage relationships, which suggested a parent-offspring relationship between Fortana and Lambrusco Maestri. Unfortunately, the same authors advance the notion that Fortana is identical to Canina Nera, another native of Emilia-Romagna, and this is most likely wrong (see CANINA NERA entry). Romagna's best-known and respected ampelographer, Marisa Fontana, does not believe the two varieties are at all synonymous. Both their leaves and their berries are very different (Fortana's berry is round, Canina Nera's oblong, almost oval). Interestingly, in a presentation at the fourth International Viticultural Congress held on July 10–12, 2012, in Asti, Giancarlo Scalabrelli of the University of Pisa presented data relative to rare grape varieties in the Colline Pisane, in which he mentions the existence of local varieties called Canina Nera, Oliva, and

Uva Vecchia, all synonymous to Fortana and different from the Canina Nera variety listed in the National Registry.

Brugnola, typical of Valtellina and used there in blends with other local varieties to make wines such as Sassella and Inferno, was long considered a biotype of Fortana, but as the two are not genetically identical, Brugnola is now viewed as a distinct variety. Schneider, Torello Marinoni, Boccacci, and Botta have determined that Brugnola is instead closely related to Nebbiolo (2005–6).

Fortana grows mainly in the coastal countryside that extends from the mouth of the Po River at Goro to the source of the Reno River, and around the towns of Alfonsine, Bagnacavallo, Lugo, and Russi near Ravenna, in the provinces of Parma and Reggio Emilia. It is usually harvested in the first two weeks of October and there are two clones available, CAB 1 and CAB 13.

Which Wines to Choose and Why

The wine is most interesting when the grapes are grown near Ferrara, in the Bosco Eliceo, which is the one *grand cru* for the variety and the only DOC that allows for up to 100 percent Fortana (with a minimum 85 percent). The Bosco Eliceo is so called because there used to be large quantities of oaks (*eliseti*, in Italian, or *Quercus ilex*). It is a truly unique habitat, characterized by its location close to the sea, with salt-rich, extremely sandy soils, marine breezes, plenty of fog, and very high humidity. Furthermore, due to the sand content of the soils (in fact in Italy these are known as *vini delle sabbie* or wines of the sands), most of the vines are ungrafted, as phylloxera was unable to survive in this environment. The IGT Fortana del Taro is also a source of good wines, made more often than not with Fortanella. A good fortana is characterized by bright red-cherry and raspberry aromas and flavors, complicated by notes of cocoa, black pepper, quinine, and licorice. The sparkling versions are characterized by more fragrant floral aromas, and there are good *rosato* versions as well. The wine can be both dry or sweet: the dry sparkling version is the most typical.

WINES TO TRY: Corte Madonnina***, Mattarelli*** (Emanuele Mattarelli's sweet fortana is probably the best of all), Antica Corte Pallavicina** (Fortana del Taro, Tamburén Rosé, and Fortanella), Ca' Nova**, La Romanina**, Mariotti** (Duna della Puia, a very interesting non-sparkling version of fortana), Cantine Bergamaschi* (Fortana del Taro Podere Rosa).

Frappato

WHERE IT'S FOUND: Sicily. NATIONAL REGISTRY CODE NUMBER: 87. COLOR: red.

Also known in the past as Surra or Nero Capitano, Frappato is the variety responsible for some of Sicily's most delicious unknown wines. Once rarely used to make monovarietal wines, Frappato's role was always that of second fiddle to Nero d'Avola, with which it is blended to make Cerasuolo di Vittoria, an important wine from the southeastern corner of the island. In blends such as this one, Frappato has much the same softening role that Canaiolo Nero has with Sangiovese in Tuscany or Malvasia Nera with Negro Amaro in Puglia. Frappato is most likely a native of southeastern Sicily, where it has a long history (its presence documented there since at least the seventeenth century). However, the first detailed description dates to 1760 (Sestini 1991). Recent DNA studies (Di Vecchi Staraz, Bandinelli, Boselli, This, Boursiquot, Laucou, Lacombe, and Varès 2007) have suggested a parent-offspring relationship between Frappato and Sangiovese, and that Frappato is a sibling of the Gaglioppo variety of Calabria. Interestingly, while Frappato is one of Sicily's oldest grape varieties, it is essentially unrelated, or far removed, from most of them.

Most often, Frappato has medium-sized, pyramidal, compact bunches and round-oval, medium-sized berries, but a huge amount of intravarietal variability exists. At least two Frappato biotypes have been described, with type B characterized by a slightly smaller, more compact grape bunch and a tendency to produce wines that are slightly lower in total acidity and pH. Two clones available (FC 26, FC 31) are not so different. Frappato likes hot and dry conditions, so it is ideally suited as a companion to Nero d'Avola, which does well in cooler, moist soils. Another difference between the two is that Frappato grows erect, while Nero d'Avola tends to spread out radially. At Cos, one of the two best producers of Frappato wines (the other is Valle dell'Acate), they believe Frappato, which is neither vigorous nor especially fertile, is best pruned by the Guyot system as this pushes the grapevine to produce more, and more loosely packed, bunches.

Frappato is a variety characterized by the light color of its wines, and so it behooves the wine lover to know something of its anthocyanin profile. Anthocyanin analysis reveals that the most abundant pigment is malvin, but peonin concentration is also relevant, while acylated anthocyanins (stable anthocyanin forms) are scarce: the latter two findings explain the wine's lighter, unstable color.

As of 2011 there were 803 hectares planted to Frappato in Sicily, down slightly from 833 hectares in 2010: though not a small amount, this acreage is still less than 1 percent of the land planted to vineyards in Sicily, making Frappato only the seventeenth most-planted variety in Sicily. Frappato's home is the province of Ragusa, especially in the countryside around Vittoria (a pretty baroque city very much worth a visit), and around Syracuse, though it also grows in the province of Trapani. It seems to perform best when grown on red sandy-calcareous soils such as those of the Vittoria area; it doesn't do as well on clay-rich soils, where it produces wines that are less fragrant and refined. I think one *grand cru* area for Frappato is between Pedalino and Acate; another is Bastonaca.

Which Wines to Choose and Why

Though it's difficult in the vineyards, Frappato is a relatively easy variety to work with in the cellar, as the low tannin and sugar concentrations mean shorter fermentation times and low alcohol levels that are easier to manage. However, it is a reductive variety, so frequent pumpings over or rack and returns meant to increase oxygen delivery are necessary in order to avoid the development of off odors. Michele Bean, viticulturalist and consulting winemaker at Cos, likes to say that "with Frappato, you can't ask for the color of merlot, because it's an altogether different wine, but it's pleasant and smooth, with lively acidity and wonderful fragrances. It's meant to be drunk young. And for bigger taste sensations, there's always Cerasuolo di Vittoria."

The most famous Frappato wine is the DOC wine Cerasuolo di Vittoria (in this case, "Cerasuolo" does not imply the wine is a rosé, as it would in Abruzzo where Cerasuolo is the name of the local *rosato*); Eloro is another DOC. However neither is monovarietal: for example, the Cerasuolo di Vittoria DOC legislation allows no more than 40 percent Frappato in the blend (the rest is Nero d'Avola), so in order to see what Frappato wines are all about, try one of the many excellent IGT wines. In fact, Frappato wines have improved by leaps and bounds over the last decade (I certainly didn't think highly of it in the past), and are now delicious, light, refreshing red wines that match well with many different dishes, including complex fish preparations. Its delicately tannic personality means you can also lightly chill it. A good monovarietal Frappato will therefore be pale red, explosively fragrant (strawberry, violet, broom, dried herbs), medium bodied at most, and very fresh and juicy. In fact, with a little experience it becomes very easy to pick out those Cerasuolo di Vittoria wines that are made with significant percentages of Frappato. Those with closer to 40 percent Frappato are lighter and more fragrant, with a very recognizable herbal-floral nose that wines containing high proportions of Nero d'Avola do not have.

WINES TO TRY: Cos***, Valle dell'Acate***, Paolo Calì*** (Rosato Osà, Mandragola), Arianna Occhipinti**, La Moresca*, Poggio di Bertolone*, Terre del Gattopardo*.

Freisa

WHERE IT'S FOUND: Piedmont (Veneto). NATIONAL REGISTRY CODE NUMBER: 88. COLOR: red.

This variety's name derives from the Latin *fresia* meaning strawberry: a whiff of Freisa wine will immediately explain why. Freisa's existence was first documented as Fresearum in 1517 when, customs tariffs exercised by the town of Pancalieri reveal that this wine was twice as expensive as any other made in that area at the time. Vineyards of Freisa have been documented around Neive (today it is one of the most important centers for Barbaresco production) since 1692, though the name Freisa first appears only in 1799 in the writings of Nuvolone, when he cites it as a "first quality grape." In the eighteenth century there was a distinction made between a Freisa Piccola and Freisa Grossa di Nizza: but this was a mistake, as the latter variety is in fact Neretta Cuneese, also called Freisone. In modern times, some (Schneider, Boccacci, Torello Marinoni, Botta, Akkak, and Vouillamoz 2004) have suggested that Freisa may be closely related to Viognier, while others (Vouillamoz, Monaco, Costantini, Stefanini, Scienza, and Grando 2007) have shown it might also share close genetic ties to the Valais variety called Rèze. However, by far the most important and interesting revelation has been that Freisa is a very close relative of Nebbiolo, universally considered one of the world's greatest cultivars. Genetic studies (Schneider, Boccacci, Torello Marinoni, Botta, Akkak, and Vouillamoz 2004) have shown that Freisa and Nebbiolo share alleles on a whopping fifty-four microsatellite loci, and the two have a parent-offspring relationship. Either Nebbiolo derives from Freisa, or more likely, Freisa is the child of a naturally occurring cross between Nebbiolo and another as yet unknown parent. This explains the many ampelographic and viticultural similarities between the two cultivars, right down to their anthocyanin profiles. For instance, both varieties are characterized by a profile strong in cyanin and peonin, which explains the light or unstable color of their wines (Cravero and Di Stefano 1992). The two can be easily differentiated because Nebbiolo's cluster is usually bigger and more compact, with a much shorter stalk leading to the grape bunch, and a leaf that is slightly hairy on both sides, while in Freisa only the underside is downy.

Freisa was once much more popular than it is today. By 1861 it was apparently included in almost all Piedmontese red wine blends, and in 1875 De Maria and Leardi documented that Freisa often represented one third to one half of all the acreage devoted to vines in properties in the Asti and Alessandria provinces. Farmers liked it because of its rustic, easy to grow, very productive nature and its disease resistance. Unfortunately, due to these positive attributes, Freisa was often planted in the poorest sites (where less hardy varieties wouldn't fare well) and made to produce huge amounts of grapes that were often underripe; the ensuing wines were easy targets for criticism. This explains why throughout history there were both fervent supporters and disdainful detractors of Freisa and its wines. Still, Freisa di Chieri, a wine made from the best-known Freisa biotype, must have had its supporters: Goffredo Casalis, a nineteenth-century writer from Chieri, mentions a "sacred tincture" as a remedy against the plague, the key ingredient of which was *"vino di Chieri"* made with the locally grown Freisa. In *A Farewell to Arms*, Ernest Hemingway mentions being curious about Freisa di Chieri. Certainly, the queens of the royal house of Savoy enjoyed the vineyards of Chieri. Ludovica of Savoy, Elisabetta Teresa of Lorraine, Polissena d'Assia, and other queens all preferred to live at the Villa Reale, a magnificent country retreat on the outskirts of Turin near Chieri where a vineyard, called the *vigna reale*, was located. Though it is not clear from old documents what varieties were grown there, Freisa seems a logical choice, since it has always been associated with the wines of Turin. In an interesting and intelligent move, the Italian Ministry of Culture and the Piedmont and

Turin provincial governments have worked together with the estate of Franco Balbiano to resurrect the wine made at the royal retreat; they call it Villa della Regina (Queen's Villa) and its first harvest was in 2008.

Freisa has medium-large, cylindrical bunches, with very long stalks and medium-sized, oval-round berries. However, intravarietal variability is common with Freisa: I remember Aldo Conterno, one of the great men of Barolo (who sadly passed away in June 2012), liked to call Freisa a "polymorphous" grape, the bunches of which often look different even on the same vine. Therefore numerous biotypes of Freisa exist, the best known of which is the Freisa grown around the city of Chieri, near Turin, which has smaller clusters and berries. Producers have always told me that these phenotypic expressions result from differences in soil and microclimates, rather than genetic differences. For example, Chieri has plenty of ventilation and especially clay-sandy soils, while the soils of Asti are generally more calcareous and loamy; it's the presence of sand that allows Freisa to best express its truly remarkable aromas. Because of the great morphologic variability and unreliable behavior of Freisa grapevines, Conterno actually didn't mind clones, which also have greater resistance to viral diseases (though his estate owns mainly massal selections, some fifty years old). Two of the best clones available today are CVT 15 and CVT 20; others are CVT 154, VCR 1, VCR 3, VCR 208, CVT 157, and CVT 177.

Different clones and biotypes aside, all Freisa grapevines are very resistant to disease, excessive sun, and inclement weather. Conterno held a deep-rooted love for the grape, greatly appreciating its rusticity and disease resistance: "not only can we harvest it late, even after Nebbiolo, but it also does well in humid, northeastern exposed sites that would be untenable for Nebbiolo, Barbera, or other varieties." Gianni Voerzio, whose Bastioni Sotto La Morra Freisa wine may be the best freisa of all (tragically, he is likely to rip up the vineyard, as the wine doesn't sell), thinks Freisa is problematic in that it yields very little naturally, a characteristic that is worsened by its tendency to undergo floral abortion in the springtime. On the other hand, he agrees that the variety is remarkably disease resistant: "You know, in fifty years of winemaking, I have yet to see a Freisa cluster affected by botrytis." Chiara Martinotti, of the high-quality Gilli estate in Piedmont, well known for excellent Freisa wines, has a slightly different view: "For reasons I can't explain, floral abortion is not a problem for us, and it's actually very productive: if we left Freisa to her own devices, we'd be covered in grapes here . . . I love it!"

Unfortunately, modern wine drinkers don't seem similarly smitten, and Freisa's lack of fashion is causing many growers to replant with other varieties: 2010 agricultural census data shows a 30 percent decrease in total hectares planted to Freisa in Italy since 2000. In my view, as I love both the grape and the wine, this is nothing short of a tragedy. Once grown in Lombardy and Veneto, where it is still found in sporadic rows of vines (especially around Vicenza in Veneto), Freisa is essentially found only in Piedmont today (where it makes up only 2 percent of the total grapevine surface), mainly around Chieri, the Langhe, the Astigiano, Monferrato, Canavese, and Salluzzese. Freisa seems to have its share of admirers in the United States: in California, Bonny Doon, Viansa, Lucas & Lewellen, and Mandolina have all planted it at one time or another.

Which Wines to Choose and Why

The best DOC wines are Freisa d'Asti, but also good are Langhe Freisa and Piemonte Freisa. It can also be used in blends such as Langhe Rosso, or DOC wines from Valle d'Aosta, Veneto (Breganze Rosso), and Tuscany (San Colombano). It is most often either a still or a sparkling wine, though there is also a lovely, but hard to find, Chiaretto di Freisa, a rosé.

I believe Freisa can give magnificent wines, which shouldn't be surprising, considering it is a very close relative of Nebbiolo. However, the wine is neither pitch black nor soft and fleshy; it's often made in a fizzy style, and fizzy red wines are anathema to many modern wine drinkers. Its perfume, though, is haunting and complex, its crisp strawberry and sour red-cherry flavors memorable. In fact, Freisa wines have fragrances and freshness that other varieties can't match, and locals appreciate its high acidity and tannic bite, both useful when matching wines to foods in need of robust palate-cleansing acidity. Thanks to its wealth in tannins, Freisa wines actually age well, though few wine lovers ever think of cellaring them.

If Freisa wines have a problem, it is that they can be bitter, as the grape variety packs potentially brutal tannins. For this reason, producers got into the habit of leaving some residual sugar to counterbalance this bitterness. But some (including Aldo Conterno) don't care for this solution, preferring to make slightly sparkling versions, in the belief that the carbon dioxide helps neutralize, to a degree, the wine's tannic mouthfeel. Most importantly, recent studies by Caudana, Rolle, and Gerbi (2009) have shown that to make the best possible wine with Freisa very ripe grapes are key, so that the polyphenols in the pips (Freisa's are particularly bitter) are maximally ripe. Leaving Freisa on the vine a little longer than expected is less of a risk with this variety than it might be with other varieties due to its thick skin; furthermore, slightly late harvests help decrease the malic acid concentration, which in Freisa is always high and responsible for the high-acid mouthfeel (not always appreciated by consumers). These same researchers have shown that the finished wine has especially high concentrations of geraniol (which explains the strong rose aroma), 3-oxo-alpha-ionol (tobacco), and dihydro-beta-ionone (violet). Luca Balbiano of the Balbiano estate (producer of excellent Freisa di Chieri) is bullish about the wine's future prospects: "Undoubtedly, production volumes are down, and almost all the wine guides and magazines have ignored our sparkling and dry wines, but we persevere, in the knowledge that we have an excellent product to sell." Enrica Gastaldi of La Borgarella adds: "I think similarities between Freisa and Nebbiolo are not stressed enough, and they should be, since the two are relatives. It might help people focus on our grape and wine more."

WINES TO TRY: For Langhe Freisa and Freisa d'Asti, try: Cavallotto*** (Bricco Boschis), Gianni Voerzio*** (Bastioni Sotto La Morra), La Montagnetta*** (Bugianen, perhaps my favorite Freisa of all; I Ronchi Vivace; and Il Ciaret, which is a chiaretto), GD Vajra*** (the very structured, serious Kyè), Brezza** (Santa Rosalia), Gilli** (Vivace, Vivace Luna di Maggio, Vigna del Forno, Arvelé), and Scarpa** (La Selva di Moirano). For Freisa di Chieri, try: Balbiano**, La Borgarella** (Barlèt, aged in oak barrels), and Terre dei Santi* (La Torrigiana; made by the former Cantina Sociale del Freisa, now merged with the Cantina Sociale di San Damiano d'Asti).

Fumin

WHERE IT'S FOUND: Valle d'Aosta. NATIONAL REGISTRY CODE NUMBER: 89. COLOR: red.

Perhaps more than any other grape variety, Fumin has demonstrated to wine lovers everywhere the virtues of stubborn people. In the 1960s, famous viticulture experts and university professors such as Giovanni Dalmasso and Giuseppe dell'Olio, then Italo Cosmo, recommended that Fumin be abandoned, for in their view it was not a variety that could make wines of any merit. Unfortunately, this led to Fumin almost disappearing from its original home, the slopes of the central valley that plunge down toward the Dora Baltea River in Italy's bucolic Valle d'Aosta. Fortunately though, not all vine growers and farmers paid heed to those "expert" words; a good thing too, since today Fumin is universally recognized as being the highest-quality native red grape variety Valle d'Aosta has.

There's a lesson to be learned here, one that applies to modern society too, as it is not rare nowadays to hear media-darling winemakers denigrating the potential of some native grapes: wine lovers can find some measure of solace in

Fumin's proof that absolutely brilliant individuals can at times be totally without a clue. At the same time, had it not been for those farmers and wine producers who were fiercely loyal to their neighborhood grape variety, Fumin might well have gone the way of other now-extinct grape varieties of the Valle d'Aosta.

Many years removed, it's not always easy to fathom why esteemed luminaries would decide to pan a grape variety. Clearly, the people of the Valle d'Aosta had always thought highly of Fumin, and records attest to its prevalence and economic importance in the region's viticulture. Though monovarietal wines were not made with it, Fumin was always added to local red wine blends to increase their color and body (D'Agata 2001a). The first mention of a Fumin grape variety is that of Lorenzo Francesco Gatta, one of Italy's great grape historians, who described it in 1838. Back then Fumin was one of the most abundant grape varieties grown in both the high and central portions (the Alta and Media Valle) of the Valle d'Aosta. He even described two different Fumin varieties: one had leaves which were heavily indented and characterized by red streaks, the other had smaller leaves lacking any red hue. Gatta mistakenly believed that this second Fumin variety was identical to Freisa (a native variety of Piedmont), an opinion shared by another expert, Napoleon Bich; we now know that Freisa and Fumin are unrelated. Bich also left us descriptions of two Fumins, which he referred to as *maclo* (male) and *femella* (female); the latter was believed to give better wines. My female readers might revel in the knowledge that it appears the *maclo* subtype was characterized as a "lazy" variety, growing poorly and unreliably, and it thus lost out in time to the more levelheaded, consistently productive female subtype, which is the more common one today. The fact that Fumin was once very abundant in the Valle d'Aosta vineyards is also documented by a report in an 1877 Central Government Ampelology Committee survey that found over 30 percent of the vines grown around the towns of Gressan, Aymavilles, and Jovençan to be Fumin. Much as Gatta and Bich before him, Di Rovasenda (1877) describes fumin as a darkly colored, satisfying wine that reaches good alcohol levels and requires bottle age. In more modern times, DNA testing by Vouillamoz and Moriondo (2011) have shown Fumin to have a parent-offspring relationship with Vuillermin, another native Valle d'Aosta grape that is on the rise. Most likely, Fumin is the parent, in part because all historical documentation of its presence precedes that of Vuillermin (Fumin is first documented in 1785, Vuillermin only in 1890). What's more, a fraternal relationship has been established between Fumin and Petit Rouge (Vouillamoz, Maigre, and Meredith 2003); the latter discovery tells us that Fumin cannot be the offspring of Vuillermin, since that would make Vuillermin one of the parents of Petit Rouge, which recent DNA analysis excludes.

Viticulturally, Fumin also proves popular, as it is a hardy, disease-resistant variety; and as if that weren't enough good news for perennially weather-challenged farmers, it also happens to be right at home in cold weather, a quality whose importance was, and is, not lost on those farming in an alpine landscape. Blessedly, Fumin is not an early budding or early flowering variety, which means it is not susceptible to the double whammy of spring frosts and berry shot. It is also characterized by good vigor and productivity, though both can be unreliable, depending on the subtype. Fumin's resistance to the cold explains why it was historically planted in the north-exposed vineyard sites of the valley, and on the colder right bank of the Dora Baltea, while more delicate varieties were planted in warmer sites with southern exposure. Though the global warming scenario may change things (and to some extent it already has), vineyards with northern exposures are rare in viticulture, as historically the goal for farmers everywhere has been to maximize ripeness, and hence sugar levels in the grapes, so as to make wines of decent alcoholic strength. Yet there is also another reason why Fumin is, much like Merlot in Bordeaux, very much a right bank variety: its thin skins are especially prone to sunburn. In fact, of all native grapes of the Valle d'Aosta, only Petit Rouge is more susceptible to the effects of excessive sunlight. Today, in an effort to maximize ripeness and produce wines that show all of Fumin's considerable potential, it receives the benefits of full southern exposures (with adequate leaf canopy protection, no doubt) and is never planted above six hundred meters above sea level. The only other real problem Fumin presents is "that its shoots break easily," says Costantino Charrère of Les Cretes.

Fumin bunches are medium-small (160–200 grams on average), pyramidal, and compact; its berries are medium-small, round, and covered in bloom. In fact, Fumin's name derives from this thick white bloom, which gives it an ash-like, smoky appearance (*fumin* refers to *fumo*, or smoky). There are currently no commercial clones of Fumin available, but the Institut Agricole Régional, having conducted a massal selection in 1998, is currently completing clonal selection work. A suitable clone appears to have been identified for propagation (private communication). Due to the lack of nursery material and of in-depth university studies and information regarding it, Fumin is currently planted only on the SO4 rootstock, usually a rather sorry excuse of a rootstock, given its superficial root system. SO4 does offer the advantage of adaptability and good productivity, however, and therefore represents an adequate choice for a variety we have only empiric knowledge of.

Fumin has rebounded brilliantly from initial academic-inspired setbacks and is today the most cultivated red variety of the central third of Valle d'Aosta (where most of the region's grape cultivation takes place). Though this amounts to just slightly over 20 hectares, it's still a considerable amount given that the variety had almost completely disappeared and that the whole region only has about 480 hectares under vine. Sales of nursery cuttings show that while slightly more than five thousand Fumin vines were produced in 1998, over twenty thousand were in 2004, indicating increased interest in the variety. I really believe that Fumin is an exciting native Italian grape variety, capable of producing wines that can be quite special. It grows nowhere else in the world, and nowhere else in Italy.

Which Wines to Choose and Why

At its best, a Fumin wine is perfumed and spicy, with a good combination of red-fruit flavors, extract, acid, and tannins. It is also a wine that has demonstrated an uncanny ability to age well and improve over time. It does not have the seemingly endless capacity for aging of a Barolo or Brunello, but in my experience, the better wines improve and last for seven to ten years—surely longevity of this sort is a component of greatness in wine. More and more producers have a fumin in their estate portfolio; whereas there were no monovarietal fumin bottlings as recently as the 1990s, there are at least eight very valid ones on the market today. Once little thought of, Fumin is now here with us to stay.

Textural toughness can be a problem in Fumin wines: hence, fermentations are kept short and extended skin contact is avoided, as color is never a problem with Fumin. For the same reason (a wealth of polyphenols), small oak barrels are preferred for the aging process to smooth the final wine. Costantino Charrère, owner of Les Cretes, Valle d'Aosta's most famous estate, knows Fumin better than anyone else and deserves credit for having been the first to bring monovarietal fumin to everyone's attention. He has tried air-drying a portion of the grapes in an effort to obtain a smoother, creamier wine, and was happy with the result but cautions that too high a percentage of air-dried grapes makes the wine less typical. Well-made fumin has a lovely, intense aroma of black pepper, red fruits, and sweet spices, with a green, herbal, peppery undercurrent never too far away. It can be fleshy and smooth, but the generally high acidity keeps it light and lively on the palate, leaving one with the impression of a vibrant, medium-bodied, perfumed wine. When the grapes are picked unripe, or at less than ideal physiological maturity, fumins are always marred by an excessively green, vegetal, almost weedy streak.

WINES TO TRY: Les Cretes*** (Vigne La Tour, the most balanced wine of the lot, with fine tannins and depth of flavor), Elio Ottin**, Grosjean** (Vigne Rovettaz), IAR**, La Crotte de Vegneron** (Esprit Follet), Lo Triolet** (always a sure bet), Anselmet* (Fumin, a rather oaky version from one of the region's best producers), Chateau Feuillet*, D&D*, Feudo di San Maurizio** (another sure bet), La Vrille*, and Les Granges*. Di Barrò makes a Fumin much lauded by other critics, but I find it usually too ripe and soft in its aromas and flavors.

Gaglioppo

WHERE IT'S FOUND: Calabria, Campania, Marche, Sicily. NATIONAL REGISTRY CODE NUMBER: 90. COLOR: red.

Gaglioppo's name is derived from a Greek word meaning "beautiful foot," and in fact, ripe grape bunches of Gaglioppo (also known as Cirotana in the Bivongi area of Calabria) are florid, plump, and very appealing. Unfortunately, the wines made from it have long been a different matter: its most famous wine, Cirò, has rarely been a head turner, though due to its low cost it has always sold well. But this lowly variety actually appears to have very noble origins. It is one of Italy's oldest varieties: a wine that some maintain was made with Gaglioppo, called Krimisa, was the reward for winners of the Olympic games. Krimisa took its name from Cremissa, the ancient name for the city of Cirò, one of three very important Greek cities in what is now Calabria and famous in antiquity for a temple devoted to wine. The appeal and availability of this wine were also assisted by Sibari, an important trading town with a very busy port that played a role not unlike that played by the port of Bordeaux in France. De Bonis (2002) wrote of sales of a *galoppo* wine between Sicily and Campania as early as 1239, but it is unclear what the exact grape variety was.

Recent DNA studies (Cipriani, Spadotto, Jurman, Di Gaspero, Crespan, Meneghetti, et al. 2010) have clarified that Gaglioppo is a natural crossing of Sangiovese and Mantonico, the latter a very typical grape of Calabria, also Gaglioppo's home. This means that Gaglioppo and Frappato are most likely siblings, which is not unlikely in my view given the characteristics of the two varieties and their wines. By contrast, I find the posited relationship with Aleatico (Filippetti, Silvestroni, Thomas, and Intrieri 2001) impossible, as I find that neither grapes nor wines have anything in common. For the same reason, I cannot see Gaglioppo and Morellino Pizzuto as identical varieties (Scalabrelli, D'Onofrio, Ferroni, DeLorenzis, Giannetti, and Baldi 2008): I think it would be more correct to state that the grapevines labeled as Morellino Pizzuto in that study were in fact Gaglioppo but I do not take this to mean that all Morellino Pizzuto grapevines in Tuscany are in fact Gaglioppo. They're simply too different. Gaglioppo has also been proven distinct from a recently rediscovered native, Galliopo delle Marche.

Gaglioppo has medium-large to large (470 grams on average), pyramidal-conical, compact bunches and medium-large, oval berries. Multiple biotypes of Gaglioppo exist: Caparra described a Gaglioppo Paesano and a Gaglioppo Napoletano in 1921, the latter the more vigorous and larger bunched of the two. Sesto and Rissone also described a Gaglioppo di Cosenza in 1988 that had a completely different anthocyanin profile from Gaglioppo, but as they did not provide a precise ampelographic description, it is difficult to say if it is truly a different Gaglioppo. Gaglioppo is also called at times Magliocco, Magliocco Dolce, and Magliocco Canino, but these names properly refer to different varieties and so should never be used for Gaglioppo. It is sensitive to most common vine diseases, but shows good resistance to frost, and a little less to drought.

Gaglioppo wines have historically been plagued by reddish, orangey colors and the grape's anthocyanin profile explains why. Cyanin and peonin, unstable anthocyanins that oxidize easily (so that wines loaded with these two pigments tend to drop their color over time) represent over 60 percent of the total anthocyanins of Gaglioppo, with malvin, one of the more stable pigments, barely over 15 percent of the total (note that these percentages do not change much even in the case of very ripe grapes). There are no measurable acylated anthocyanins (stable anthocyanin forms).

Which Wines to Choose and Why

Gaglioppo is confined mainly to Calabria and reaches its potentially greatest heights in the area around Cirò, on the Ionian coast, which includes the towns of Cirò Marina, Crucoli, and Melissa. However, it is an integral part of Calabrian DOC wines such as Bivongi, Donnici, Lamezia, Pollino, and Savuto, among others. In my experience, the wines of the last three are best, especially Savuto, though Gaglioppo is almost always blended with other varieties in these wines. When Gaglioppo is blended with one of the *Maglioccos*, the wines can be interesting, while when Cabernet Sauvignon is used, the wine becomes to my taste almost undrinkable. Though I understand that a producer might want to increase Gaglioppo wine's weak color by adding Cabernet, the last thing Gaglioppo needs is more tannin. Think about it: what sense does it make to join a high-acid, tannic, and potentially herbal variety such as Cabernet Sauvignon to Gaglioppo, which has more or less the same characteristics?

The best examples of Cirò, or of any monovarietal Gaglioppo wine, exude aromas of small red berries and citrus zest, with mineral and delicate underbrush notes that are not unlike a lighter, more saline Nebbiolo wine. When poorly made however, it's astringent and completely devoid of fruit, and then vies for the title of Italy's worst grape variety. Severino Garofano, one of Puglia's most famous winemakers and the man behind the rise of Negro Amaro from workhorse grape to star material, also consulted with many Calabrian wineries in an effort to improve their Gaglioppo wines. Garofano greatly improved matters by suggesting that they extend maceration times, but at low temperatures in order to obtain better polymerization of the tannins and more stable color.

The aromatic profile of Gaglioppo is interesting, with high levels of benzenoids and norisoprenoids; terpenes are low, but this is typical of most neutral red grapes. Well-made wines are rich in ethyl-hexanoate, ethyl-octanoate, and β-damascenone, which explain the red-fruit aromas and flavors of the wine (Marchi and Lanati 2008). Unfortunately, Gaglioppo's combination of low anthocyanins, high acidity, and rough tannins (though its tannins aren't prevalent, neither are they particularly smooth) is not endearing to modern consumers, and this, coupled with what used to be very rustic winemaking, pretty well sealed Cirò's fate (and that of other Gaglioppo wines) in fine-wine circles. Fortunately, recent research and better winemaking have brightened Gaglioppo's outlook.

WINES TO TRY: Caparra & Siciliani*** (Rosso Classico, Superiore Riserva), Ceraudo*** (Dattilo, Grayasusi), Librandi*** (Duca Sanfelice Riserva), San Francesco*** (Ronco dei Quattro Venti, Ronco dei Quattro Venti Rosato, an outstanding wine), Vigna de Franco*** ('A Vita, my favorite Cirò of all; the F36-p27 is also very good), Ippolito** (Riserva Ripe del Falco), Santa Venere**, and Vinicola Zito** (Classico Riserva).

Gamba Rossa

WHERE IT'S FOUND: Piedmont. NATIONAL REGISTRY CODE NUMBER: 403. COLOR: red.

There are three main partridges in Europe that people love to hunt: the chukar, which lives high up on mountainous cliffs of Sicily; the Barbary partridge, typical of North Africa and Sardinia (called in fact "Sardinian partridge" in Italy); and the red-legged partridge, common in Spain and Mediterranean Europe, if for no other reason than that it is easily bred and used to repopulate countrysides. The third bird's main characteristic, besides being excellent on the dinner table, is the bright red legs that give it its name, and provide the name for this grape variety as well. Gamba Rossa (red leg), better known as Gamba di Pernice (leg of partridge) is just one of the many grape cultivars named after their red stalks (for example, Piedirosso and Refosco del Peduncolo Rosso), which are reminiscent of the red legs of partridges, pigeons, and other birds. I find that Gamba di Pernice is characterized not only by its red stalk but also by its yellowish leaves in the fall. Though similarly named, Gamba di Pernice (or Gamba Rossa) is a distinct variety from the others, and is also different from Malbec, which in France is also called Pied de Perdrix or Oeil de Perdrix.

Gamba Rossa was only recently chosen by the powers that be as the official name of the cultivar, and it now appears under this name in the National Registry of grape varieties. This is surprising, since the grape has always been better known, in academic and local circles, as Gamba di Pernice. It is also called Pernicine and, in the Salluzzese area of Piedmont, Neretto di Alteno, where *"alteno"* means trained to living supporting structures such as trees. According to Berta and Mainardi (1997), this system of cultivation was surprisingly common around Alba, Pinerolo, Saluzzo, and Turin in Piedmont between the sixteenth and eighteenth centuries. Perhaps for this reason Gamba di Pernice was never considered a premier variety, as it could hardly have ripened properly with trees hiding it from necessary sunlight. In 1798 Nuvolone even wrote that Gamba di Pernice belonged to what he called second-tier grapes, those best blended with the better, first-tier wine grapes.

The cultivar is characterized by moderate anthocyanin concentrations: malvin accounts for 25 percent of the total anthocyanins and the acylated forms are low too. The fact that these two very stable forms of anthocyanins are low compared to cyanin and delphinin, which are much less stable, accounts for the only medium hues of the wines. As a late ripening variety with a compact bunch, Gamba di Pernice is easily subject to botrytis bunch rot, especially in rainy autumns: airing out the bunches earlier in the season is key to producing better, cleaner wines. Currently, the few specialized Gamba di Pernice vineyards are planted with massal selections, but Valter Bosticardo of Tenuta dei Fiori (one of the two most important producers of Gamba di Pernice wine), has selected ten different clones over the years that are now being evaluated for viticultural characteristics and winemaking potential. Today, the variety grows mainly in the Asti province, especially around the towns of Calosso and Costigliole d'Asti, and in small quantities in the countryside of Costigliole Saluzzo, in the Salluzese part of Piedmont.

Which Wines to Choose and Why

Young wines have a pretty, bright, medium-ruby color, very fresh floral and red-berry aromas, and are medium bodied; wines five years and older have amber-red hues, and more spicy-peppery, tarry, and balsamic aromas and flavors. All well-made Gamba di Pernice wines are medium bodied, balanced, and refined; never blockbusters, they match well to most foods, from lighter white meat preparations to slow-cooked, concentrated beef stews. The wine has an uncanny knack for aging: for example, the 1990 Tenuta di Fiori gamba di pernice is still splendid today. In general, as Gamba di Pernice is a variety high in malic and low in tartaric acids, malolactic transformation risks leaving a wine low in acidity, though locals welcome gamba di pernice's softer mouthfeel in contrast to barbera's almost eye-watering shrillness. The wine made by Tenuta dei Fiori and other producers in the Calosso area is called Calosso, rather than gamba di pernice, in an effort to shore up a link with this variety's historic zone of cultivation (and because these producers understandably were miffed at the choice of Gamba Rossa as the official name of the variety).

WINES TO TRY: Carlo Benotto**, Tenuta dei Fiori**, Collina d'Oro / Tenute Baldovino* (Gamba d'Pernis), La Canova*, Fea*, Villa Giada*, all excellent monovarietal wines.

Garganega

WHERE IT'S FOUND: Veneto. NATIONAL REGISTRY CODE NUMBER: 92 (listed at number 94 as Grecanico Dorato). COLOR: white.

The grape variety with which Italy's world-famous Soave wine is made, Garganega has long had a good reputation, even though wines made from it are not always something to write home about due to excessively high yields. In fact, locals have always appreciated Garganega's dependable and generous productivity, especially in times past, when wine quantity was more important than quality. Limiting yields and advances in winemaking have revealed Garganega's true potential.

Described at length by numerous experts over the centuries, from Pollini (1824) to Molon (1906), wines made in the area of Soave are among the oldest documented in Italy. Apparently, in 500 B.C.E., Flavius Magnus Aurelius Cassiodorus, a minister in the Lombard government of King Teodorico, described the process by which sweet wines were made in Soave (via the air-drying of grapes), though there isn't any way to be sure that Garganega was the grape being used. Cassiodorus is also credited with having described the wine as "so white and pure it seems born from lilies." The name Soave does not derive from "suave" in the modern-day sense of that word, but rather from Svevia and then Suavia, the name of the Longobard Germanic tribe that invaded and settled in this part of Italy after the fall of the western Roman Empire. Garganega was mentioned as early as the fourteenth century, though, by Pier de' Crescenzi, who described it in the regions of Bologna and Padova. In the nineteenth century, as Garganega had also always been cultivated around Vicenza and Verona, the grape was commonly called Garganega di Gambellara (Gambellara, like Soave, is a famous Veneto white wine).

Garganega is, like Sangiovese and Nebbiolo, one of Italy's oldest and most important grapes and has therefore played a key role in the evolution of Italy's ampelographic base. According to Di Vecchi Staraz, Bandinelli, Boselli, This, Boursiquot, Laucou, Lacombe, and Varès (2007) and to Crespan, Calò, Giannetto, Sparacio, Storchi, and Costacurta (2008), it holds first-degree relationships with numerous other cultivars: Trebbiano Toscano, Albana, Empibotte (now called Mostosa), Malvasia Bianca di Candia, Marzemina Bianca, Catarratto Comune, and Greco del Pollino (now known to be identical to Montonico Bianco). All share at least one allele at each of the thirty-six SSR loci used in the study. Crespan's study also showed that, at least in the four accessions of Garganega and Grecanico Dorato they profiled, the two are identical (confirming the findings in Vantini, Tacconi, Gastaldelli, Govoni, Tosi, Malacrinò, Bassi, and Cattivelli 2003, who analyzed only two samples of each), though these two grapes are still listed separately in the National Registry. Since Garganega is known to exhibit great morphologic variability, it is believed that Grecanico Dorato is a local biotype adapted over the centuries to its specific Sicilian *terroirs*. Pastena (1969) dates the presence of Grecanico Dorato in Sicily back to the end of the seventeenth century, when different phenotypes were described. In light of Grecanico's name, which hints at a possible Greek origin, Crespan, Calò, Giannetto, Sparacio, Storchi, and Costacurta (2008) compared the Grecanico Dorato SSR profile to those in preexisting microsatellite databases of the Centro di Ricerca per la Viticoltura of Conegliano, the University of California at Davis, and University of Crete in Heraklion. Grecanico Dorato's profile was found to be distinct from that of any sample in those collections, including all the Greek varieties. Studies also tell us that Garganega is identical to Spain's no longer commercially cultivated Malvasía di Manresa (Di Vecchi Staraz, Bandinelli, Boselli, This, Boursiquot, Laucou, Lacombe, and Varès 2007; Crespan, Calò, Giannetto, Sparacio, Storchi, and Costacurta 2008), most likely yet another example of a grape being attributed the *Malvasia* moniker just to help improve its sales (see MALVASIA GROUP, chapter 3). Though Garganega is most likely native to Italy's north and may have genetic similarities to typical Veronese cultivars such as Corvina and Rondinella (Vantini, Tacconi, Gastaldelli, Govoni, Tosi, Malacrinò, Bassi, and Cattivelli 2003), it has always been popular enough to have ties to Italy's south, even besides Grecanico Dorato. In fact, Garganega is also a parent of Puglia's Susumaniello, which is a natural Garganega × Uva Sogra crossing. The latter is a rare variety no longer cultivated in Italy that Zulini, Russo, and Peterlunger (2002) believe to be identical to the variety called Uva Sacra.

Two distinct Garganega-named cultivars exist: Garganega Comune and Garganega Grossa or Garganegona, the official name of which is now Dorona (see DORONA entry). The former is the best known and the true Garganega variety used in production of wines such as Soave and Gambellara. A very late ripener (even in this era of climate change, October harvests are common), Garganega has a large, very long grape bunch (reaching 25 centimeters and 500 grams, 185 grams on average), usually pyramidal-conical in shape. The round, at times slightly flattened berries have yellow-green, thin skin that can turn slightly amber when the grapes are fully ripe. Garganega also has myriad biotypes, the result of strong intravarietal variability; as many as twenty-four different biotypes have been described to me by Emanuele Tosi, who is in charge of the Centro per la Sperimentazione in Vitivinicoltura della Provincia di Verona. These biotypes have been well described throughout history. According to producers I have talked with over the years, the Garganega biotypes commonly found in vineyards nowadays are Garganega Tipica (the standard and most common Garganega that everyone knows and loves); Garganega di Dario (mostly located around Brognoligo near Monteforte d'Alpone, but stretching as far as Vicenza and characterized by larger berries and by ripening earlier than all other Garganega biotypes; because of its larger berries it was also called Garganega Grossa, thereby confusing it with Dorona); Garganega Verde (characterized by small and sparse berries, and a sparse bunch; found mainly on the hillsides west of Soave, around Costeggiola); and Garganega Agostega (a poorer-quality, large-berried biotype that is the earliest ripening of all, hence its name, which harkens back to August; characterized by low acidity and a tendency to rot easily, so it's being phased out, it is still found occasionally in old vineyards between Soave and Monteforte d'Alpone). The Garganega biotypes Biforcuta, Frastagliata, and Rossa are now rare. Of course, probably the best-known Garganega biotype of all is Grecanico Dorato of Sicily. Grecanico Dorato was so named because it was believed to be a grape of Greek origin and because of its golden berries. It was probably first described by Geremia (1835), who distinguished between two biotypes: Grecanico a Giramoli, with very sparse grape bunches; and Grecanico a Croce, with a more compact cluster and two long wings that make it look almost cross-like (*croce* means cross). Two modern-day biotypes of Grecanico Dorato appear to have been found in Mazara del Vallo and in Belice, but the two look very similar to me (the wines, tasted from microvinifications, also do not differ sharply). The typical Grecanico Dorato bunch is large (average weight three hundred grams), long, cylindrical, and loosely packed, with one to two wings. It produces dependably and abundantly.

There are fourteen clones of Garganega available: Fedit 9 has larger berries and higher sugar accumulation. ISV-CV 84 (a selection of the Verde biotype) appears to give more balanced wines and its loosely packed bunch makes it suitable for air-drying. ISV-CV 11 and 18 have loosely packed bunches and are ideal for air-drying and sweet wine production, while ISV-CV 69 (a selection of the di Dario biotype) is not suitable for either of those objectives, due to its larger berries and compact bunch. Garganega has also been the subject of laboratory crossings; Incrocio Bianco Fedit 51 is an example. In general, Garganega is very vigorous (yields need to be reigned in) but is sensitive to winter cold and common grapevine diseases and suffers desiccation of the stalk. It's usually harvested in September. There are also two registered clones of Grecanico Dorato: VCR 13 and Regione Sicilia 94.

At more than twelve thousand hectares, this variety is the twelfth most commonly grown wine grape in Italy (based on 2010 data); it's almost ubiquitous in the western part of Veneto, around the towns of Soave and Gambellara, but is also grown in Lombardy, Emilia-Romagna, Lazio, Umbria, and Sicily. As Grecanico Dorato it is found all over Sicily and not in small quantities. There were roughly five thousand hectares planted as of 2010, making it the ninth most-planted variety in Sicily (slightly more than 4 percent of all land on the island devoted to grapevine cultivation), mainly around Trapani and Marsala. Interestingly, for such a common grape in Italy, and one that has obviously been around for centuries (given its complex relationships to many other Italian varieties), Garganega has not been planted much outside the country. A little is grown in Australia.

Which Wines to Choose and Why

Today, 100 percent pure Garganega wines are among the best white wines Italy produces; indeed, for some experts, the best of all. Most famous are DOCGs Soave and Gambellara, but DOC Bianco di Custoza wines are also noteworthy. Clearly, Soave is the most famous wine. It is made east of Verona, its DOCG territory spanning an area from San Martino Buon Albergo to San Bonifacio; the Soave Classico zone, centered around the towns of Soave and Monteforte d'Alpone, is north of San Bonifacio. Garganega is often blended with 10–20 percent other varieties, such as Trebbiano di Soave (which is Verdicchio) and even (perish the thought) Chardonnay and Sauvignon Blanc, which only masks Garganega's delicate qualities and charms. Almost all Garganega clones produce wines with good concentrations of norisoprenoids (bright aromas of ripe fruit and hay) and terpenes (floral aromas). A well-made non-oaked Garganega wine is steely and mineral, with bright white flower, apricot, fresh citrus, and Golden Delicious apple aromas and flavors.

Angelo Sabbadin, the sommelier at the famous three-Michelin-star restaurant Le Calandre near Padua in Veneto, is amazed at how well pure Garganega wines age: "I find that after eight to twelve years the wines resemble some of the great Loire wines made with Chenin Blanc and have a delicacy and complexity that are truly rare." Alessandro Pipero, another longtime sommelier of Michelin-starred restaurants who has worked mainly in and around Rome and now at the one-Michelin-star restaurant in Rome that carries his name, agrees: "I think a couple of non-oaked pure Garganega wines are among Italy's ten best white wines, and by a wide margin."

Sweet whites called Recioto di Soave and Recioto di Gambellara are also good. The former is rich, honeyed, and floral; the latter mineral and often made in a more oxidative style; when well made, these are among Italy's half dozen best sweet wines. True Recioto is never marked by noble rot, though some producers have recently tended to make it from *Botrytis cinerea*–affected grapes, banking perhaps on a more international appeal and greater complexity. Wine lovers ought to know that such wines are very good indeed but are not traditional for the area.

In Sicily, Grecanico Dorato is produced either as a monovarietal wine or, more commonly, as a blending grape with other Sicilian varieties. Your best bet for good Grecanico wines is the Alcamo DOC, though DOCs Delia Nivolelli, Contessa Entellina, and Contea di Scalafani can be good too. It can be blended with any number of varieties, such as Inzolia (adds acidity) and Chardonnay (inevitably overpowers the more delicate Grecanico Dorato, so this is a usually pointless blend). You'll need to read back labels to see if what you have chosen is 100 percent Grecanico. Of course, this being Italy, there may not even be a back label, or if there is it may be of limited usefulness. A large measure of good faith in what that back label says will also help, though you can get around that by buying the wines of producers you know and trust.

In Australia, Domaine Day is making a Garganega wine and was reportedly the first to do so in Australia; more recently, Politini has started bottling a Grecanico wine. The Domain Day 2009 I tasted last year was simple and fresh, with aromas and flavors of pear, winter melon, and almonds, and wouldn't have looked out of place in a lineup of Soave wines from Italy. The 2010 Grecanico by Politini was more citrusy and had more grapefruit and tangerine rather than the pear and almond nuances of the Domain Day wine, but both are very enjoyable, easy-drinking wines. I am told that Domain Day also makes a very good sweet wine called Dolcezza from late-harvested Garganega grapes, but I have yet to try it.

WINES TO TRY: For Soave, try: Pieropan*** (Calvarino and the oak-aged La Rocca), Inama*** (Foscarino and du Lot), Prà*** (Staforte and Monte Grande), Anselmi** (Capitel Croce), Gini** (Salvarenza Vecchie Vigne), Ca' Rugate* (Monte Fiorentine), Coffele*, Filippi*, Nardello*, Suavia*, Tamellini*, and Vicentini Agostini*. For Recioto di Soave, try: Anselmi*** (I Capiteli) (though it can lack acidity), Pieropan** (Le Colombare), and Tamellini** (outstanding, but made in a botrytis-affected, atypical style). For Gambellara, try: Domenico Cavazza*** (Creari), Cristiana Meggiolaro** (Gambellara Classico and Gambellara Classico Ceneri delle Taibane), and Luigino Dal Maso** (Fischele). For Recioto di Gambellara, try: La Biancara***, Domenico Cavazza** (Capitel Santa Libera), Zonin** (Podere il Giangio Aristos), and Virgilio Vignato*** (makes an extraordinary Vin Santo di Gambellara). For Grecanico Dorato, try: Caruso & Minini* (Terre di Giumara) and Settesoli* (Mandrarossa Grecanico).

Garganega Grossa

See DORONA.

Giacchè

WHERE IT'S FOUND: Lazio, Tuscany, Umbria. NATIONAL REGISTRY CODE NUMBER: not registered. COLOR: white.

Giacchè is a *teinturier* grape variety, a coloring agent just like the members of the *Colorino*s. It has one of the highest concentrations of polyphenols of any variety in Italy: in fact, locals joke that overenthusiastic imbibers find it virtually impossible to remove Giacchè stains from their clothes. Historically Giacchè was always used to deepen the hue of wines made elsewhere, especially in Tuscany, but was never too popular otherwise, for it's a very late-ripening variety, producing very small wine volumes (mainly because of extremely small berries). Therefore, it was slowly abandoned and risked extinction. Researchers believe it to be a descendant of a wild grapevine species that mutated over the centuries, and in fact its other name in Lazio is Ciambrusca, a generic term also used to describe wild grapevines. There has been no genetic study of Giacchè accessions to date, so we do not yet know if this is a truly separate variety or just a biotype of one of the many coloring agents Italy has, such as Grand Noir and Abrostine. However, an early genetic study using inverse sequence tagged repeat fingerprinting (ISTR) and amplified fragment polymorphism length analysis (AFLP), the molecular marker technology available at that time, compared Sangiovese varieties and biotypes with coloring varieties such as Colorino del Valdarno, Colorino di Pisa, and Giacchè (by Sensi, Vignaniz, Rohde, and Biricolti 1996). A careful review of the results reveals that the ISTR profile of Giacchè differs from those of the other *Colorino* varieties (and of course, from Sangiovese) and that the AFLP analysis also showed genotypic diversity within the *Colorino* group. Therefore, though further studies on the subject are certainly needed, it appears that Giacchè is a distinct coloring variety.

Giacchè grows in central Italy in sporadic plots of vines and is probably most abundant in Lazio.

Which Wines to Choose and Why

Recently, with interest in all things local and native perking up, estates have taken to producing a monovarietal wine with Giacchè, in both dry and sweet versions. The Lazio Casale Cento Corvi estate is the best-known producer. The Collacciani family selected and propagated old Giacchè vines they found in the countryside around Cerveteri in northwestern Lazio and created a line-up of very interesting varietal wines. Dry wines are fully saturated, deep purple in color, with aromas and somewhat chunky flavors of prunes, cocoa, and herbs, and they almost always have a weedy, floral edge. In my opinion, the weedy, vegetal streak is common to many *Colorino* and *teinturier* varieties in general, and not just because they all have trouble ripening fully. On a positive side, Giacchè wines offer real structure but relatively smooth tannins, and many wine lovers looking for something novel to try will love the mouthcoating texture these wines offer. The air-dried version, which I prefer, made from grapes left on the vine but with the stalks severed or twisted, is also rich and intense, with heady aromas and flavors of chocolate syrup, roasted coffee beans, dried aromatic herbs, and red cherries macerated in alcohol. Compared to the dry version, I find it offers greater depth and complexity of flavor.

WINES TO TRY: Casale Cento Corvi** (Giacchè, a dry red, and Passito).

Girò

WHERE IT'S FOUND: Sardinia. NATIONAL REGISTRY CODE NUMBER: 93. COLOR: red.

Girò is unique in the panorama of Sardinian enologic offerings, and Italy's overall, for that matter. The cultivar and wine have almost the same name (the wines indicate place, for example, noting "di Sardegna"), and like many other Sardinian varieties, Girò is most likely a traditional rather than native grape of Italy, probably a Spanish import, arriving on Sardinian shores during Spain's domination of the island. That explains the grape's many Spanish-related synonyms, such as Girone (or Zirone) di Spagna, though in the Sardinian dialect it is referred to as Nieddu Alzu or Aghina Bar-ja. Interestingly, at the end of the eighteenth century, Manca dell'Arca wrote of three different Girò varieties grown around Sassari: Zirone (round berried, early ripening), Zirone di Spagna (larger berries), and Zirone Barzu (similar to another variety, Negro, but less dark). Whether these three were in fact all Girò biotypes or different grapes altogether is unknown, but it is noteworthy that later documents also distinguished at least two Girò grapes, Girone and Girone di Spagna. According to recent DNA analysis, Girò may be one of the two parents of Albaranzeuli Bianco, a rare Sardinian variety (Cipriani, Spadotto, Jurman, Di Gaspero, Crespan, Meneghetti, et al. 2010). A comparison of the data obtained by De Mattia, Imazio, Grassi, Lovicu, Tardaguila, Failla, et al. (2007) and Ibañez, Andres, Molino, and Borrego (2003) also shows that Girò and Girò Blanco (a white-berried variety from Spain) are distinct, and not color mutations of the same grape. In fact, many colored versions of Girò have been described on Sardinia as well: Girò Nigro (or Arzu, in dialect), Girò Rosso (generally used as a synonym of Girone di Spagna), Girò Chiaro (or Braghiu), and Girò Bianco. In Nieddu (2011), Girò grapevines were genetically profiled at twelve SSR loci and apparently shown to be similar but not identical to Girone di Spagna (also called Zirone Alzu), which must be considered a biotype of Girò and not a different variety. In a very interesting recent study in which 196 different Sardinian grapevines were analyzed at six SSR markers, four different Girò varieties were identified: one called Girò Morbido from the island's Sarcidana area, and three genetically different varieties all called Girò, respectively from the island's Campidano di Sanluri, Campidano di Cagliari, and Planargia areas (Lovicu, Farci, Sedda, Labra, De Mattia, Grassi, Bacchetta, and Orrù 2010).

Obviously, further studies are required, possibly with more SSR loci investigated, but apparently there may be a healthy number of distinct Girò-Something varieties growing on the island. As these varieties have lived for centuries in remote inland, mountainous areas of the island, genetic contamination was very unlikely, and this helped maintain the island's biodiversity. Whether these Girò varieties are truly distinct and what they might provide to the world of wine drinkers will require a great deal more work and time, but I for one am happy to know these vines have survived. Who knows, their story might yet hold more interesting twists for all of us.

Girò's cultivation was encouraged by the Piedmontese, who also briefly dominated Sardinia, and especially the Marquis di Rivarolo. Unfortunately, Girò was another casualty of phylloxera (or rather, the post-phylloxera period) when farmers took to planting other varieties that were easier to grow and promised larger yields. Girò has medium to medium-large bunches and medium-sized berries; the former are usually pyramidal or conical, while the latter are round. It wants relatively warm and dry microclimates and deep, marly-clay soils; its grapes are robustly resistant to the vagaries of weather, while they have a harder time with most common diseases and grapevine pests. It usually ripens in September. It grows around Sassari and the Basso Campidano, in the province of Cagliari, and to a lesser extent near Oristano. Unfortunately, Girò's cultivation is on the decline: whereas roughly 500 hectares were under vine in 1990, only 121 remained in 2009. Of course, statistics such as these might just be the result of more accurate ampelographic reconnaissance, but given that Girò is used to make mainly sweet wines and that such wines have trouble selling nowadays, it might be that Girò really is falling by the wayside. A shame, given the grape's and wine's unique charms.

Which Wines to Choose and Why

Girò is used to make a rare example of a sweet red wine that is not particularly aromatic (aromatic sweet reds like Aleatico and many different *Malvasia*s abound in Italy); it is easy to drink, light, and refreshing. In this style, the wine to try is DOC Girò di Cagliari, which demands that no less than 100 percent Girò be used. Girò is available in a dry, sweet, *liquoroso secco* (fortified dry) and *liquoroso dolce* (fortified sweet) but is almost always found in the sweet version. The latter two can also be made as *riserva*. Girò can also be used in roughly fifteen different IGT blends such as Barbagia, Isola dei Nuraghi, Planargia, Romangia, Trexenta, and Valle del Tirso.

Girò is a lovely wine and deserves to be better known, exuding lovely aromas of candied red cherries, milk chocolate, and plums macerated in alcohol. On the palate it is delicately sweet and spicy, with abundant notes of very ripe red fruit. It generally strikes me as a great deal more refined than other sweet red wines made all over the world. It is not a dark wine, as the variety has possibly the lowest anthocyanin concentrations of any Sardinian red grape (130–250 milligrams per kilogram of catechin). The sweet versions are especially noteworthy and age well.

WINES TO TRY: Panevino*** (Giròtondo; a very powerful, alcoholic rendition) and Meloni Vini** (Donna Jolanda; a more typical, well-made girò).

Glera

WHERE IT'S FOUND: Veneto, FVG. NATIONAL REGISTRY CODE NUMBER: 200. COLOR: white.

The exact origin of Glera, once better known as Prosecco (a name now used only to describe the wine, though this is the subject of some debate), remains unclear. According to Villifranchi (1773) and other experts, Glera is native to the Carso Triestino in Friuli Venezia Giulia (where the town of Prosecco is found); from there it moved into Veneto's Treviso area (where Prosecco wines are made) and then farther east to the region's volcanic Colli Euganei, where the grape is called Serprina (some view Serprina as a specific local biotype yielding slightly different wines). Other experts believe the exact opposite is true: that Glera's birthplace is the Colli Euganei. Still other experts believe that Glera's home is Slovenia or Croatia, and that the variety may have arrived in Prosecco while in transit from outside Italy. The birthplace diatribe aside, what nearly everyone agrees upon is that the variety and its wines were always highly thought of. Marescalchi and Dalmasso (1937) agreed with Villifranchi that this grape was used to make pucinum, the famous wine of the Roman Empire and apparently a favorite of Empress Livia Drusilla, wife of Octavian Augustus, Rome's first emperor (Pliny the Elder localized its production near Duino Aurisina, which is in fact located in the Carso Triestino). Clearly, it's hard to verify that pucinum, made thousands of years ago, was really the product of Glera, so I'm not sure how past and modern luminaries come to be so sure about this. But as many other grape varieties have been claimed to be the basis of pucinum, Glera may not be the source of that historic wine at all. Interestingly, the first mention of the word *Prosecco* associated with Veneto is found in the dithyramb "Il roccolo" by Aureliano Acanti (1754), which describes the *"melaromatico Prosecco"* produced near Monte Berico (Vicenza) by Count Jacopo Ghellini. Experts such as Villifranchi (1773) and Semenzi (1864) all sung the praises of both grape and variety; in 1772 Malvolti also spoke of Prosecco in glowing terms (Calò, Paronetto, and Rorato 1996). In fact, when the Società Enologica Trevigiana was founded in 1868 in Veneto by Carpenè and Benedetti, the grape and wine were specifically targeted for study and promotion. Interestingly, a few years later, Carpenè and Vianello (1874) documented Prosecco's cultivation in only four towns around Conegliano, Valdobbiadene, and Asolo. Part of the reason for its lack of appeal, despite the perceived quality of the wine, was its lack of resistance to common vine pests.

While these scientists and experts often referred for simplicity's sake to a single "Prosecco" or "Glera," in reality this is a group of varieties and biotypes long cultivated in Veneto and in Friuli Venezia Giulia, as well as in Slovenia and Croatia. Though the list of grapes named Prosecco or Glera-Something was almost endless for the better part of three centuries, until recently the general consensus was that there was just one main variety which could be subdivided into three "clones": Prosecco Tondo (so called because of its round berries), Prosecco Lungo (because of its more oblong, almost oval berries) and Prosecco Nostrano ("local" or "our" Prosecco); the first was selected in the seventeenth century by Count Marco Giulio Balbi Valier, who tirelessly championed the qualities of both grape and wine, and the other two in the 1980s at the Istituto Sperimentale per la Viticoltura at Conegliano. Subsequent DNA profiling has shown the three to be distinct varieties; in fact Prosecco Nostrano, first described by Sannino (1904) as Prosecco Nostrano di Conegliano, isn't a Prosecco at all, but rather Malvasia Bianca Lunga (Costacurta, Crespan, Milani, Carraro, Flamini, Aggio, et al. 2003; Crespan, Cancellier, Costacurta, Giust, Carraro, Di Stefano, and Santangelo 2003). Though Prosecco Tondo and Prosecco Lungo are distinct varieties, they are related to a degree (Crespan, Cancellier, Chies, Giannetto, Meneghetti, and Costacurta 2009) and perhaps this is what induced scientists and experts into thinking that the two were just clonal variants.

In light of this revelation and the variety's recent name change, there would seem to be two varieties left: Prosecco Tondo, now renamed Glera Tondo and usually called simply Glera, and Prosecco Lungo, renamed Glera Lungo. But in reality, there are many different varieties still called Glera-Something in Italy's Carso and the bordering Karst region of Slovenia; and there are also many biotypes of each. For example, it is noteworthy that Balbi Valier selected not just the Tondo variety, but also a Tondo biotype that was especially perfumed and aromatic and characterized by a loosely packed bunch, now known as the Balbi biotype or Prosecco Bianco. Another Prosecco biotype still common today, Cosmo, is less aromatic and has a more compact bunch. In the past there were an almost endless list of other Prosecco biotypes, which either were more common than they are today or were erroneous synonyms. One such grape was Prosecco di Piave: whether it was a true Prosecco or not, it was characterized by uneven flowering and therefore low yields, and so disappeared (or rather, was made to disappear) quickly. In the *Ampelografia italiana* (1887), another Prosecco variety appears: Prosecco dal Pecol Rosso (red stalked). Not to be outdone, Zava (1901) indicates the existence of a Proséco and a Proséco Piccolo. I am sure all this may seem moot to some readers, but it is actually a helpful reminder of just how difficult the ampelographer's work is (not to mention that of the wine lover who would just like to know exactly what he or she may be drinking). By 1913, the *Bollettino dell'Associazione Agraria Friulana* listed a veritable Noah's ark of *Prosecco* varieties: Prosecco Tondo Bianco (also called Proséco, Prosecco Balbi, Proseccon), Prosecco Tenero Bianco (also called Proséco, Prosecco Lungo, Prosecco Tenero), Prosecco Gentile Bianco (also called Proséco, Prosecco Piccolo, Prosecco del Pecol Rosso, Prosecco Schittolin, and Prosecco Zentil, these last two names only used around Asolo), *and* Prosecco Nero. Of course, Friuli Venezia Giulia had its own populations of Prosecco subvarieties: Prosec, Resecco, Glera Secca, Glera Grossa, and Glera Rossa (Calò and Costacurta 2004). Many of these were in fact Prosecco Lungo. Between the end of the nineteenth and the beginning of the twentieth centuries, the repeated vineyard selections made by growers, scientists, and wine producers from the existing populations of Prosecco biotypes and varieties led to the establishment of the two main Prosecco, rather Glera, varieties we know today: Glera Tondo or Glera (with its two main biotypes, Balbi and Cosmo) and Glera Lungo.

Which brings us to the controversy about the recent change of the variety's name from Prosecco to Glera. Beginning in 2009, a series of events led to a sizable increase in the size of Italy's Prosecco DOC to include portions of Friuli Venezia Giulia. In the course of that extension, Proseccco di Conegliano-Valdobbiadene was raised to DOCG status, and Prosecco's name was changed to Glera. As we have seen, Glera varieties were grown in Friuli Venezia Giulia, where the name was used as a synonym for Prosecco; therefore, authorities wished to differentiate the grape variety (Glera), which can be grown anywhere, from the wine (prosecco), which in theory at least, is the expression of a specific place's *terroir,* history, and tradition. However, cynics have cried foul, viewing this decision as nothing more than a protectionist attempt to safeguard the commercial value of a local Italian product. Since "prosecco" is now linked to a specific Denominazione di Origine, producers elsewhere in the world can no longer use it to label their sparkling wines. Understandably, many are not happy with this turn of events; however, while most Italian authorities and prosecco producers say that commercial protectionism was not their original intention, some will also mumble that given the centuries of history that both the wine and the grape can boast on Italian soil, it hardly seemed fair that anyone anywhere could suddenly start planting Prosecco vines and then call their wine with that same name. When you realize that a U.S. wine producer, for example, advertises his sparkling wine as "Prosecco-style" and that the wine is said to be made with "Gewürztraminer, Riesling, Chardonnay, Sauvignon Blanc and Muscat," you can understand why some might worry about indiscriminate use of the word "Prosecco." That said, it's only honest to admit that many Italians also use the name "Prosecco" haphazardly, and will ask the wine waiter or sommelier at their favorite watering hole for a glass of "Prosecco" or a "Prosecchino" and, perish the thought, quite often any sparkling wine will do.

In any case, recent studies have helped increase our understanding of Glera and its relationships to other varieties. Crespan, Cancellier, Chies, Giannetto, Meneghetti, and Costacurta (2009) have shown that the majority of

Glera varieties growing in Slovenia's Karst next to the Italian border are actually Glera Lungo, and that very few are Glera or other Italian varieties. Štajner, Korosec-Koruzam, Ruzjan, and Javornik (2008) also showed that not all Slovenian Glera varieties are identical to Italy's, though Bela Glera has been shown to be identical to Pienel (Crespan, Fabbro, Giannetto, Meneghetti, Petrussi, Del Zan, and Sivilotti 2011). Furthermore, Maletić, Sefc, Steinkellner, Karoglan Kontic, and Pejic (1999) demonstrated that Glera is identical to Croatia's Teran Bijeli, once thought rare but now known to be growing in Istria; apparently, the variety is also identical to Slovenia's Briška Glera and Števerjana (Štajner, Korosec-Koruzam, Ruzjan, and Javornik 2008). Finally, recent genetic profiling by Crespan, Crespan, Giannetto, Meneghetto, and Costacurta (2007) has shown that Glera and Malvasia Bianca Lunga are the parents of Vitovska, a grape common in Friuli Venezia Giulia. Glera was also crossed with Cabernet Sauvignon to obtain Incrocio Manzoni 2.15.

Glera grows mainly in Veneto, most famously in the Conegliano and Valdobbiadene zones, as well as in the Colli Asolani. It is also extensively planted in Friuli Venezia Giulia, where it is forcing out other natives such as Friulano, and there's a little growing in Lombardy too, around Bergamo. It has also been planted in Argentina and many different wine regions of Australia, from Adelaide Hills to Upper Goulburn and Murray Darling.

Which Wines to Choose and Why

The most important wine is clearly the DOCG Conegliano-Valdobbiadene Prosecco (minimum 85 percent Glera and 15 percent other varieties such as local natives Bianchetta Trevigiana and Verdiso, though unfortunately some producers use Chardonnay, which in my view is too overpowering for Glera). High hillside vineyards with full southern exposure allow Glera to develop unusually complex and refined fragrances and flavors, especially compared to those found in many wines made in flatland vineyards or other *terroirs*. Interestingly, the traditional recipe for Prosecco called for one-third each of Glera, Bianchetta Trevigiana, and Verdiso: much as with the original blend invented by Ricasoli for Chianti, each of these grapes was felt to contribute something important to the final wine. Modern-day Prosecco allows only a maximum 15 percent of Bianchetta Trevigiana and Verdiso combined, and the wine is none the better for it. In any case, great Prosecco reminds you of buttercups, green apples, and white peaches (and for this reason, the famous Bellini cocktail ought to be made with Prosecco and white, not yellow, peach juice).

Even better Glera wines are made in the DOCG Cartizze, from grapes grown on the specific hill of Cartizze that allows for fuller-bodied wines that always carry a little residual sugar. Therefore, Cartizze is always a little sweet, but acidities are such that the wine tastes off-dry. Caveat emptor: given the ludicrous number of Cartizze bottlings sold all over the world, and the small size of the Cartizze hill (and hence the limited number of vines that grow there), it's better to stick with known producers to be assured of authenticity. Like all other sparkling wines, Prosecco can come in different levels of sweetness, labeled extra brut (the driest), brut, extra dry (off-dry), and dry (the sweetest; though, thanks to the carbon dioxide and the acidity, the wine never seems sweet). Other DOC wines of interest are the Colli Euganei Serprino (100 percent Glera) and Colli Asolani Prosecco. Prosecco remains a specialty of the Treviso area, where roughly 6,500 of the 7,000 total hectares planted to Glera are found. For comparison, there are only one hundred hectares of Glera in the DOC Colli Euganei. Glera is also an important part of the blend used to make the sweet *passito* called Torchiato di Fregona; and one producer, Bisol, makes a sweet dessert-style wine even in the heart of the Prosecco production zone.

In Australia, Glera wines of note are being produced by Box Grove Vineyard, Boyntons Feathertop, Brown Brothers, Chrismont (in the

La Zona series of wines), Coriole, Dal Zotto Estate, Mount Towrong, Parish Hill Wines, Sam Miranda Wines, Terra Felix, and Vinea Marson. In the United States, Trinchero Family Estates sells a wine called Avissi Prosecco, but it's made with grapes grown in Veneto.

WINES TO TRY: Bisol*** (Brut Crede, Extra Dry Del Fol), Adami*** (Dry Giardino), Frozza***, Ruggeri**, Fratelli Bortolin**, Bortolomiol**, La Jara**, Le Case Bianche**, Silvano Follador**, Sorelle Bronca** (Particella 47), Zucchetto**, Andreola*, Drusian*, and Le Bertole*. For Cartizze, try: Col Vetoraz*** (by far the best), Bisol**, and Bortolomiol**.

Glera Lungo

WHERE IT'S FOUND: Veneto. NATIONAL REGISTRY CODE NUMBER: 359. COLOR: white.

Based on the conventions I follow in this book, I shouldn't include Glera Lungo as a "major variety," since I don't known of any monovarietal wines made with it (or none that is so declared). However, as Glera Lungo is interplanted with Glera in almost all vineyards, chances are good that we may all be tasting Glera Lungo wines (all or in part) at least some of the time we devote to serious Prosecco imbibing (which means often, in my case). As discussed in the Glera entry, Glera and Glera Lungo are distinct varieties (Crespan, Cancellier, Costacurta, Giust, Carraro, Di Stefano, and Santangelo 2003); however, they are related (Crespan, Cancellier, Chies, Giannetto, Meneghetti, and Costacurta 2009). Also called Serprino, Glera Lungo is apparently much less common than Glera; nearly every prosecco producer I have ever spoken with says he or she has very little of it in the vineyards. According to Dalmasso and Dall'Olio (1936–37), Glera Lungo was common around Valdobbiadene and Farra di Soligo in pre-phylloxera times but was abandoned due to uneven yields. As recently as the latter part of the twentieth century, it was considered virtually extinct (Cosmo and Polsinelli 1960). However, it was rediscovered at the beginning of the twenty-first century when grapevines called Prosecco di Refrontolo (found near Treviso) and Tocai Nostrano (near Breganze) were confirmed to be Glera Lungo by Cancellier, Giacobbi, Coletti, Soligo, Michelet, Coletti, and Stocco (2003). According to the previously mentioned 2009 study by Crespan's group, it is also identical to the Ribolla Spizade variety found in Friuli Venezia Giulia. These studies led to Glera Lungo being included (as Prosecco Lungo) in the National Registry in 2000; its name in the registry later changed to Glera Lungo. Nowadays the variety seems rare even in the hills of Col San Martino (where it's believed to be native); I usually find it with much greater ease in the hills around Breganze, where it's called Tocai Nostrano. Near Padua and Bagnoli, in the western part of Veneto, there are roughly one hundred hectares cultivated to Serprina. Crespan's group (2009) also showed that Glera Lungo is surprisingly common in the Slovenian Karst.

Which Wines to Choose and Why

Anecdotal evidence culled from recollections of farmers and growers tells us that wines made with Glera Lungo are different from those made with Glera. Supposedly, these wines are more spicy and less floral than those made with Glera. Since I'm not sure I've ever tasted a monovarietal, well-made Glera Lungo wine, I have no firsthand evidence of this. Locals tell me Varaschin at San Pietro in Barbozza, in the heart of the prosecco production zone, makes a monovarietal Glera Lungo wine, but I am not sure.

Grecanico Dorato

See GARGANEGA.

Grechetto

WHERE IT'S FOUND: Umbria, Emilia-Romagna, Lazio, Marche. NATIONAL REGISTRY CODE NUMBER: 95 (also listed as Pignoletto at number 300). COLOR: white.

The name Grechetto clearly denotes this variety's presumed Greek origin. But due to the popularity of "Greek" wines in ancient Rome, many different, unrelated grapes were called Grechetto and Greco. Grechetto has always been an extremely important variety in Umbria and has long been the subject of studies there. In 1975, the University of Perugia's Department of Plant Cultures (Istituto di Coltivazioni Arboree) tackled the issue of what Grechetto is and determined there to be two varieties: Grechetto di Orvieto (or Grechetto G109) and the Grechetto di Todi (or Grechetto G5). Both are occasionally and improperly referred to as "clones" (for example, Grechetto di Todi clone G5). But the two are not clones at all. In fact, they're not even related. Filippetti, Intrieri, Silvestroni, and Thomas (1999) and others have shown that Grechetto di Todi, which some would prefer to call Grechetto Gentile (more correctly reserved for a specific clone of Grechetto di Todi, I G5 ICA-PG), is in fact Pignoletto (a native variety of the Emilia portion of Emilia-Romagna; it's also called Rébola in the Romagna portion of the region; see PIGNOLETTO entry). Other research has indicated that some of the Grechetto grapevines of northeastern Lazio are also identical to Grechetto di Todi, that is, Pignoletto, while Grechetto di Orvieto is most likely related to the *Trebbiano* family. For what it's worth, when I look at Grechetto di Orvieto, with its long bunch and small berries, I think of the *Trebbiano*s right away, while Grechetto di Todi, with its stocky, short bunch and fat round berries, does not call to mind any *Trebbiano* variety I can think of. The *Grechetto* varieties also have numerous synonyms, such as Pulcinculo, Strozzavolpe, Occhietto, and Montanarino Bianco (some experts believe all of these to be Grechetto di Todi only).

When we speak of "Grechetto" today, it is Grechetto of Orvieto we mean: ampelographic and viticultural descriptions should not be contaminated with observations more pertinent to Pignoletto. Still, there are a number of other interesting and vexing issues concerning the correct identification of *Grechetto*s. First, the National Registry contains numerous redundancies pertaining to clones of the *Grechetto*s and Pignoletto (clones listed for the two varieties have different labels but are the same grape: Grechetto G5 ICA PG is identical to Pignoletto ICAB 5, while Grechetto VCR 2 is identical to Pignoletto VCR 3, yet these are all listed separately under the respective Grechetto and Pignoletto headings). In the past a Grechetto clone R3 was known as biotype Ribolla, a silly situation, since it is not related to Ribolla Gialla at all, and so allowing this name for the clone only led to more confusion. In any case, the ICA PG clone is especially resistant to oidium and botrytis, though according to Borgo, Cartechini, Lovat, and Moretti (2004) it drops acidity quickly when overripe (notably tartaric acid), especially in hot, humid years.

Sergio Mottura's estate in Lazio is blessed with some very old vines of many different Grechetto biotypes (some planted as early as the 1930s), differences now believed to be due to the different *terroir* of northeastern Lazio compared to that of nearby Orvieto in Umbria, though some of the vines there are most likely of Pignoletto. The different Mottura biotypes include Grechetto Grappolo Piccolo and Grechetto Perazzeta, resembling Grechetto Caciolla (reportedly identical to Grechetto Mecone) and different from Bianchetta Castelli, which presently remains an unknown variety of this corner of Lazio. Sergio Mottura told me that they are apparently all genetically identical to Grechetto di Todi, hence to Pignoletto, but I have not yet seen any published study confirming this.

Grechetto di Orvieto is most abundant in Umbria (especially in the countryside around Orvieto, in the western part of Perugia, and Terni) and Lazio.

Which Wines to Choose and Why

Of DOC wines that can be supposedly 100 percent *Grechetto* (though producers are not obligated to specify the variety present: the wines are usually a mixture of the Orvieto and Todi varieties) worth a look are Assisi Bianco, Colli Perugini, and Colli del Trasimeno—the best of these, Colli Martani is in my experience most often pure Grechetto di Todi, that is, Pignoletto. Of course there are IGT wines simply labeled grechetto that might be quite good too. The most famous supposedly Grechetto wine is Orvieto, but it too is almost always a blend not just of the two varieties previously thought to be *Grechetto*s, but of Procanico (a Trebbiano Toscano biotype), Verdello, Drupeggio, and others. In fact, the law states that Orvieto must contain 60 percent Procanico *and/or* Grechetto: Grechetto component can be as little as 1 percent. Therefore, it is impossible to speak of Orvieto as a monovarietal Grechetto wine; furthermore the majority of Orvietos are thin, tart, and lack any real interest. When there are roughly eighteen million bottles of any wine produced a year—and in the case of Orvieto, produced by 120,000 different bottlers, 95,000 of which are located outside the DOC zone—then a large variation in quality, with many nonsensical products, is to be expected.

Grechetto di Orvieto makes uncomplicated, light-bodied, lemony wines that are easygoing, with hints of white flowers, chamomile, lime, and yellow apples, with generally high acidity. When the product of high yields, wines are tart and neutral and hold little interest. Grechetto di Orvieto's thick skins and loosely packed, sparse bunches mean it can be used to make the late-harvest, noble-rot-affected wines that Orvieto was once particularly famous for. Finding a monovarietal Grechetto di Orvieto wine is not easy but may well be the way of the future now that more is known about the grape's lineage and genetics. If nothing else, now that the identity between Grechetto di Todi and Pignoletto has been established, there is hope that people who want to make a Grechetto in Umbria will be more likely to plant only the real Grechetto, rather than a Grechetto-Pignoletto mix or even just Pignoletto, as was done in the past.

However, not everyone is a big fan of Grechetto. Giovanni Dubini, owner of Palazzone, is one of the two or three best Orvieto producers; with thirty-seven vintages in Umbria under his belt, he should know what he's talking about when it comes to Grechetto, and he has told me repeatedly over the years that "Grechetto marks the blend considerably; even just 2 to 3 percent, depending on the vintage characteristics, will have a deep impact. In a vintage like 2010, the Grechetto really shows up in the wine and I don't like the rusticity it supplies." Neither is Dubini especially keen on sweet wines made with Grechetto: "True, some very good late harvests are possible, but at least in my opinion, the wine is never especially deep or rich: late harvests are difficult with Grechetto, and a big risk, because it needs to ripen long, late into the season, and it always starts raining in this part of Umbria in the fall. Grechetto picked in late October would still need about a month to produce a truly interesting sweet wine; on the other hand, Sauvignon Blanc grapes would be just perfect by then and ready to go. So I don't know of anyone who's willing to risk the crop just to make a monovarietal grechetto late-harvest wine, when using Sauvignon Blanc and other varieties will allow them to make a wine that's just as good if not better."

WINES TO TRY: For Grechetto di Todi/Orvieto mixtures, try: Barberani***, Antonelli/San Marco** (Colli Martani), Podere Marella** (Godot; from organic grapes, not always a good thing in Italy, as the wines often smell horrible and taste worse, but not in this case), Palazzone**, Roccafiore**, San Rocco**, Franco Todini**, Tudernum**, and Argillae*. For Grechetto (Lazio), try: Sergio Mottura*** (Poggio della Costa and Latour a Civitella, which is oak-aged).

Grignolino

WHERE IT'S FOUND: Piedmont. NATIONAL REGISTRY CODE NUMBER: 100. COLOR: red.

One evening in Rome in 1980, on a date with a wonderful young French lady who liked wine, I tasted my first ever Grignolino wine and we both fell in love. Not with each other, but the wine. We all have favorite wines, and one of mine is made with this misunderstood but lovely variety, one of the prettiest in Italy. No less than world-renowned winemaker Donato Lanati also loves it (he dedicated his enology school thesis to Grignolino), so I'm not alone. And the fact that an educated French wine palate such as that of my never-forgotten girlfriend was also enthralled by Grignolino's charms speaks volumes of what the cultivar can deliver, in the right hands.

A native to the Monferrato Hills of Piedmont between the two towns of Asti and Casale, Grignolino was once also called Balestra, Verbesino, Arlandino, Rossetto, and especially Barbesino in Piedmont and Lombardy. It is very rare in the latter region today, whereas centuries back, in the countryside around the town of Bobbio, even a white-berried Grignolino Bianco could be found, though the red and white Grignolino cultivars are believed to unrelated.

Grignolino was abundant and highly thought of as early as the thirteenth century: from legal documents dated between 1246 and 1287 (preserved in the capitulary archives of the cathedral at Casale Monferrato), we know that property rentals were regulated by contracts that also strictly forbade tampering with Barbesino vines. The wine was especially appreciated for its use in making *chiaretti*, light red wines that were widely diffused in Piedmont in the sixteenth century. Di Rovasenda (1877) thought the wine was "extremely fine" and was also aware that the variety needed specific soils to show its best. No less a bon vivant than Carlo Gonzaga of Spain appreciated Barbesino wines. In fact, Grignolino wines were very popular with the noblemen of Piedmont, who prized the wine's light hue and refined mouthfeel. Back then, people appreciated the stark contrast of Grignolino wines with the deep hues and in-your-face aromas and flavors of wines made with Barbera, viewed not just as peasant wines, but *for* peasants. How times change: in those days, Grignolino wines fetched the same prices as Barolos, and Grignolino sparkling wines (rare nowadays) were especially popular. Eventually, the name Barbesino gave way to Grignolino: not surprisingly, since the latter was commonly used in Asti (where rich bankers did much to promote the wine's merits), and because the word *grignolino* is linked to Piedmontese dialect, in which the word *grignolè* refers to the grimaces (or grating of one's teeth) made when biting into the high acid and tannic Grignolino berries. Another hypothesis is that the word means "pips," a reference to the fact that Grignolino has, on average, more pips per berry than other cultivars (Grignolino has at least three while most others have two).

In light of Grignolino's delicate aromas, reminiscent of white wines, and the pale hue of the berries, some researchers and producers have told me that they believe Grignolino may be a centuries-long mutation of what was originally a white grape, but I know of no hard evidence of this.

The variety demands well-exposed sites with plenty of sunlight, and such top-quality spots, at least in the Langhe, are usually reserved for varieties that bring better financial returns, such as Nebbiolo (this is why Grignolino has virtually disappeared there). It also needs well-ventilated sites, to ward off the risk of rot due to its compact bunch. The irony is that in the nineteenth century, the majority of Grignolino wines were produced in the Langhe by estates that bought the grapes grown in the Astigiano and Monferrato.

Grignolino has medium to large pyramid-shaped, very long, compact bunches, with up to three wings; the berries themselves are medium-small, and the thin skins have a pretty blue-red hue. However, Grignolino has a huge amount of intravarietal variability, which can lead to wildly different-looking vines (and wines) across producers and areas. In addition to many biotypes, there is also a series of clones: R1, CVT AT 261, CVT AT 275, AL-GRI-79, AL-GRI-87, and CVT 113. Many of the older grapevines are also virus affected, and the cultivar suffers from *millerandage*. As if that wasn't enough, Grignolino succumbs easily to common grapevine diseases and yields generally very little juice (remember, small berries and plenty of pips). Most important, asynchronous maturation is frequent in Grignolino, so bunches sporting green berries right next to pinkish-red ones are common: therefore, reducing the variety's inherent vegetative vigor is paramount, for otherwise the grapes don't ripen properly and evenly. On a positive note, Grignolino is an excellent translator of soil types, and so wines express a huge diversity of aromas and flavors, depending on soil type and microclimates (as well as biotype).

While still found sporadically in old vineyards of the Langhe, Grignolino is mainly grown in the provinces of Alessandria and Asti. Recent interest in the variety and its light wines has led to cultivation expanding westward toward Tortona, but the highest-quality areas for Grignolino are on the right bank of the Tanaro River and in the Monferrato area located between Asti and Casale Monferrato. Unfortunately, Grignolino covers only about 1 percent of the total vineyard surface in Piedmont, but my hope is that in these modern, fast paced times, the charms of Grignolino's delicate wines will lead producers to replant the variety. Incidentally, American readers might like to know that there is a little Grignolino planted in Napa Valley, less than fifty hectares. Heitz Cellars continues to make a lovely wine from its small plot of vines, at times even a delicious Port-styled wine, which is unheard of in Italy. The grape is also grown in Santa Clara Valley, where Guglielmo makes its Private Reserve Grignolino.

Which Wines to Choose and Why

Admittedly, Grignolino wines are an acquired taste many people have failed to acquire. That might change now that the new Pope Francis, Jorge Bergoglio, has publicly voiced his appreciation of grignolino; both Beppe Bologna of Braida and Franco Morando of Montalbera reported to me that their grignolino sales took off after the pope's admission. Maybe this will get other people to appreciate grignolino's many charms. Most tasters usually forgive the high tannins and acidity if the wine also has enough fruit flavors to beat these into submission, but Grignolino, well . . . Simply put, Grignolino was, until recently, a tragically unfashionable wine because of its pale red-pink color, lack of obvious sweet, ripe, soft fruit flavors, and very high acidities and tannins. In short, a recipe for wine disaster. "But things are changing," smiles Lanati. "People are turning away from monstrous wines of a recent past that were all alcohol, chocolate and vanilla, with very low acid levels and plenty of residual sugar. And with our improved understanding of Grignolino and how to bring it to show its best, there's hope yet." Then he adds quickly, "But it's not easy."

Well-made Grignolino wines are magical: the wine resembles a big *rosato* more than a *vino rosso* and often has an orange or garnet tinge from birth; the garnet edge is not a sign of premature age but rather is a typical characteristic of the wine. Actually, it's the dark-red Grignolino wines that should worry you, for that's not normal, despite what you might be told, so caveat emptor. The wines exude a lovely aroma of fresh flowers, small red berries (strawberry, raspberry, sour red cherries), and spices such as white pepper (not the black pepper more typical of syrah, for example), and they are blessed with high, refreshing acidity and crisp tannins that leave the palate feeling fresh and clean. As Grignolino doesn't need any more tannins than it already has, oak aging is a no-no, as the delicate aromas and flavors would be completely overwhelmed. The wines are classically dry and have blessedly low alcohol levels (12 or 12.5 percent is the norm, and only with recent global warming have some uncharacteristic 14 percent wines appeared), which make them both wonderful aperitifs and splendid with vegetable and white-meat dishes (rabbit, chicken, veal). The wine's high acidity and tannic bite make it ideal with fatty foods, and its delicate spiciness matches perfectly with soy-sauce-enhanced dishes. Grignolino's perfume and light frame ensure that it's the perfect red wine for those who mainly drink white wines, a selling point that producers are increasingly aware of. Last but not least, there is absolutely no better match in the world than grignolinos for archetypal Piedmontese dishes such as *vitello tonnato, lingua in salsa verde*, and *agnolotti alla Piemontese* or *al sugo di carne*. Luigi Veronelli believed these two last dishes were perfect with grignolinos, and I am not about to argue with Italy's greatest wine and food expert.

The best wines are DOC Grignolino d'Asti of Asti Province and Grignolino del Monferrato Casalese of Alessandria Province, though Piemonte Grignolino (an umbrella denomination for Grignolino wines made anywhere else in the region) can also be very good. There are many monovarietal wines, though all can contain up to 10 percent Freisa and/or Barbera. However, Grignolino's soil and site sensitivity are such that the wines can show remarkable diversity, and this can double the fun for wine lovers. Besides choosing the finest and most reliable producers, insiders know to specifically look for the Grignolino wines of Portacomaro, Castello di Annone, and Costigliole d'Asti (Asti Province) and those made near Moncalvo, Vignale Monferrato, and Casale Monferrato (Alessandria Province), all of which are true *grand cru* areas for the variety. All Grignolino wines tend to be tannic and high in acidity, but as the soils in the best Asti areas can be quite sandy, the wines are very fragrant and perfumed; in contrast, soils around Alessandria are richer in calcareous clay (they look very whitish in color, what the Piedmontese refer to *terre bianche*), and wines are relatively bigger (this being a relative term with Grignolino wines). Places such as Vignale Monferrato are also linked to high-quality grignolino: producers there are applying for a DOC "Vignale" especially created for their Grignolino wines. In general, the best wines are made from grapes grown on relatively sunny sites, and this is why I always thought the Grignolino wines made in the Langhe could be truly magnificent. One of the greatest was made by Bartolo Mascarello, of Barolo fame: when he stopped making it (replacing his Grignolino vines with Barbera), I mourned for days.

Working with Grignolino can be an exercise in frustration. Veronelli defined it "anarchist and individualistic," and he was right. Not only are Grignolino's anthocyanins of the easily oxidized kind (peonin, cyanin) but they are also hard to extract. Therefore, it's not a matter of simply macerating the must on the skins for longer periods of time, for highly astringent, bitter tannins leach out quickly. Beppe Bologna of the Braida estate, world famous for Barbera wines of great class, has devoted much energy to this wine and has tried different techniques—such as late harvesting the grapes and even using a small percentage of carbonic maceration—in an effort to increase overall fruitiness. Mauro Gaudio of Bricco Mondalino, one of the quality producers of grignolino, cautions, "You really can't macerate the skins for more than four–five days, because the wine turns bitter; and you can't get carried away with sulfites, for they tarnish the vivacity of the wine's hue."

When well made from grapes grown on quality sites, the wine is remarkably perfumed and crisp, almost cloudlike in its breezy lightness, refreshing like few other wines in the world. Much like Pinot Nero, Grignolino is a very difficult grape variety that represents a challenge to every skilled grape grower and winemaker out there. Provided one has the talent and wits to match with it, Grignolino can bring something special to the table, and therein lies its unique magic.

WINES TO TRY: For Grignolino d'Asti, try: Braida***, Cascina Tavijin***, Crivelli***, Spertino***, Incisa della Rocchetta***, and Montalbera***. For Grignolino del Monferrato Casalese, try: Accornero*** (Bricco Battista), Bricco Mondalino***, Pio Cesare***, Il Mongetto**, Isabella** (Monte Castello), La Casaccia** (Poggetto), Canato** (Celio), and Tenuta Migliavacca**. For Piemonte Grignolino, try: Cavallotto*** and Francesco Boschis***.

Grillo

WHERE IT'S FOUND: Sicily. NATIONAL REGISTRY CODE NUMBER: 101. COLOR: white.

Why is Grillo (locally also called Ariddu or Riddu) named after a cricket *(grillo)* you ask?

Actually, it's not: the word *grillo* in this context refers to *grilli*, another word in Sicilian for "pips." Interestingly, though Grillo is universally considered one of Sicily's highest-quality cultivars, its existence on the island seems only relatively recent, after the eighteenth century. There is no mention of a Grillo variety anywhere in Italy prior to this, which is strange considering how common it was to use similar names for different cultivars. Pier de' Crescenzi (1304) wrote of a red-berried Grilla grown in central Italy that was "horrible to eat but good for winemaking." Clearly, that can't have been the same as Sicily's Grillo, a white grape. In the *Horthus catholicus* (1696), Cupani listed all the Sicilian cultivars known at the time, but not Grillo. Neither was it mentioned in 1853 by Minà Palumbo, an important nineteenth-century Sicilian naturalist; nor was it included in the *Bollettini delle Commissioni Ampelografiche* of the Sicilian provinces of Caltanissetta, Agrigento, and Palermo (Mendola 1881, Mendola 1884). Curiously enough, just one year later, in 1882, Grillo was included in the list of grapes grown around Trapani that was sent to Abele Damiani by Baron Mendola, president of the Ampelography Commission. Grillo finally makes an appearance in the context of Marsala wine production in an 1892 session of the Circolo Enofilo di Conegliano (a wine club). However, other important documents around the same time omit Grillo in reference to Marsala production, and so the exact date of Grillo's appearance on Sicilian soil is destined to remain unresolved—strange, given that all the other Sicilian varieties, such as Cataratto, Inzolia, and even lesser-known ones such as Nave, were all mentioned time and again.

This lack of documentation lends strength to the argument that Grillo may be Puglian in origin: 1884 documents show that it was used to improve the white wine blends of San Severo in northern Puglia, and up to the 1970s it was grown in the Castel del Monte area of central Puglia. Nevertheless, Grillo met with success in Sicily and by the 1930s represented roughly 60 percent of all the land under vine around Trapani and Marsala (where it's still most common today). At that time, the variety was very popular in the aftermath of phylloxera devastation (Grillo is more resistant than Sicilian varieties such as Cataratto Bianco) but fell out of favor in the latter half of the twentieth century, when quantity and not quality was the password in Sicilian wine. Grillo, not the most generous cultivar, was replaced by Inzolia and other more productive grapes. However, over the last twenty years Grillo has been making a resounding comeback, its intrinsic qualities apparent to all. Grillo acreage doubled between 2000 and 2007, and another 486 acres were planted between 2007 and 2008.

The origins of Grillo have also recently been clarified. Microsatellite testing of twelve SSR loci by researchers at the University of Milan shows Grillo to be the result of a natural crossing of Cataratto and Moscato di Alessandria, also called Zibibbo. Del Zan, Failla, and Scienza (2004) have also proposed that Grillo is identical to Malagouzia, a variety native to the western Greek region of Aitoloakarnania, but this has yet to be confirmed. In a 2009 study by Torello Marinoni, Raimondi, Ruffa, Lacombe, and Schneider, one of the Ligurian grapevines called Rossese Bianco (the Rossese Bianco di Riomaggiore) was identified by DNA profiling as Grillo. But I have tried Rossese Bianco wines from Liguria and Piedmont (where there exist at least three distinct but similarly named varieties) and they taste absolutely nothing like Grillo, so I am quite sure that not all Rossese Bianco, if any, is Grillo (see ROSSESE BIANCO entry). The authors of the study conclude themselves that this finding must have been the result of an "evident misnaming"; I point out that the misnaming in question is not that Rossese Bianco (or more precisely, one variety of those so named) is in fact Grillo, but rather that the local grapevine (which was Grillo all along) had been given, over time, a locally "more appropriate" name. To conclude from this that one of the Rossese Bianco varieties is Grillo, given what we know of those varieties, would seem to make little sense.

There are four official Grillo clones: Regione Sicilia 297, VFP 91, VFP 92, and VFP 93. In general, Grillo has medium-sized bunches and medium or medium-large, round berries. It's a vigorous variety and a dependable producer that is very heat and drought tolerant, a good thing when its main habitat is Sicily. In any case, Grillo's confinement over the centuries to a specific part of Sicily and its apparent lack of cultivation elsewhere in Italy (except Puglia) explains the scant intravarietal variability and lack of biotypes, of which there are only two: Grillo Vecchio and Grillo Nuovo. The latter is much less susceptible to shot berries and *millerandage* and is therefore the one most cultivated today. These problems can be reduced by using the 420A or 110R rootstocks; the SO4 rootstock is best avoided with Grillo as it does not guarantee regular yields.

In Italy Grillo is almost exclusively found in Sicily, though there are sporadic plantings in Puglia; some has been planted in Australia.

Which Wines to Choose and Why

Modern winemaking has had an amazing impact on Grillo wines. Precise timing of the simple action of deleafing has significant repercussions on the wine's final aroma profile: because Grillo is sensitive to sunburn, deleafing too early in the season or excessively decreases the aromatic components (benzenoids, terpenes, and norisoprenoids), making the resulting wine less perfumed. Grillo's aroma molecules are also easily oxidized, and so winemakers are increasingly using reductive winemaking techniques. In particular, winemakers are careful to preserve thiols (molecules once called mercaptans due to their tendency to precipitate in contact with mercury salts), alcohols in which an oxygen atom has been replaced by a sulfur atom, which greatly influence wine aroma. At high concentrations and depending on which volatile thiols are present, their presence is revealed by a very unpleasant odor.

However, Vermeulen, Gijs, and Collin (2005) and many other researchers have shown that thiols are also responsible for pleasant aromas that we recognize as cassis, grapefruit, and passion fruit, among others, all aromas we normally associate with Sauvignon Blanc wines. Wines made with Sauvignon Blanc are particularly rich in volatile thiols, particularly 4-mercapto-4-methylpentan-2-one (4MMP); using yeast strains that free it from larger, odorless precursor molecules greatly increases its concentration. Thiols are, however, very sensitive to copper and oxygen: the former causes the formation of insoluble sulfur compounds, while the latter leads to aldehyde production, which also makes the characteristic thiol-associated aromas disappear. In short, by adopting specific viticultural practices, yeast strains, and reductive winemaking techniques, producers can now make Grillo wines that are lemony, herbal, and crisp and that share more than a passing resemblance to wines made with Sauvignon Blanc. Therefore, modern-day Grillo wines are completely different, generally cleaner and fresher, than the somewhat earthy, fatter wines made decades ago.

This has led some to question whether modern-day Grillo wines reflect characteristics of the variety itself or simply winemaking alchemy. Some see today's wines as un-Grillo-like or almost "unauthentic," while others insist that Grillo grapes have precursor molecules that allow Sauvignon Blanc–like aroma formation, and so the new techniques only allow Grillo to finally reveal its true self. Ivo Basile, commercial director of the famous Tasca d'Almerita estate, says, "I'm not sure we really know what true Grillo wines should be like. Was it earthy and overly alcoholic before only because poorly made? Or maybe now we can at last see what the variety can really give?" Renato De Bartoli, who makes the excellent Terzavia wines, feels otherwise: "I don't believe these new wines taste anything like Grillo wines should." It doesn't look like the debate will be resolved anytime soon.

The best DOC wines made with 100 percent Grillo are Contea di Sclafani, Alcamo, Delia Nivolelli, and Monreale, but there are also monovarietal IGT wines worth a taste. Since most of those DOCs are meaningless, as there is little sense of place or type attached to any of them, your best bet is to remember the name of the producer whose wines you like. In Australia, Adelaide Hill's By Jingo Wines has made a very interesting first vintage of Grillo wine, with grapes from Riverina.

WINES TO TRY: Terzavia***, Marco De Bartoli*** (Grappoli del Grillo), Tasca d'Almerita*** (Grillo Mozia; but it won't be made for the next few years because voracious rabbits recently wreaked havoc on the Mozia vineyard), Baglio Hopps**, Feudo Montoni**, and Feudo Arancio*.

Gropellos

See GROPELLO GROUP, chapter 3.

Guardavalle

WHERE IT'S FOUND: Calabria. NATIONAL REGISTRY CODE NUMBER: 105. COLOR: white.

Guardavalle is named for a little town located between Locri and Noverato in Calabria, the toe of Italy's boot-shaped peninsula (though this cultivar is occasionally called Vardavalli). It is also likely that the name at least in part derives from this variety's penchant for hillside vineyards, as *guardavalle* in Italian means "to look at or over the valley" (De Bonis 2002). It's not a particularly vigorous variety and is characterized by relatively late phases in all its vegetative cycles, with late-season budbreak and harvest dates, though flowering occurs early. Studies have shown that Guardavalle is identical to Greco Bianco di Cirò (Costacurta, Calò, Antonacci, Catalano, Crespan, Carraro, et al. 2004) and that Montonico di Rogliano, Uva da Passito, and Uva Greca are also synonyms (Schneider, Raimondi, and De Santis, 2008a).

Guardavalle is characterized by medium-sized, conical bunches and medium-sized berries. Budbreak occurs late, so that spring frosts are not a concern with this variety, but it tends to ripen late as well; fortunately, autumn weather in Calabria is not as fickle and cold as in more northern parts of Italy. Guardavalle is a rare variety, grown mainly around the city of Reggio Calabria, especially in the eastern vineyards of the region in the viticultural zones of the Kalipera, Locride, and Bivongi on the side of Calabria that looks toward the Ionian sea.

Which Wines to Choose and Why

One doesn't hear much about Guardavalle and monovarietal wines, but it has been recently recovered and re-evaluated by local viticulturists and producers. Having only recently emerged from decades of indifference, hopefully it will be studied more, such that there will be more monovarietal wines to choose. What I have tasted in monovarietal versions has left me suitably impressed: Guardavalle can make good wine, with a complex nose that will remind you of hazelnuts, red fruit, and tobacco, finishing long and with an almost tannic mouthfeel. It may be that many "greco bianco" wines I have been given to taste over the years were in reality made with Guardavalle, which would mean the variety has a lot of potential, since many of those wines were either already quite good or showed enormous potential. Furthermore, given that this variety's synonyms hint at its ability to withstand air-drying and to make *passito* wines, I think it would be wise if estates tried making Guardavalle sweet wines too.

WINES TO TRY: Santa Venere* (Vescovado; the estate deserves credit for reportedly producing a monovarietal Guardavalle from organic grapes), Cantina di Bova* (Feingas; contains up to 40 percent "Greco Bianco," which could be Greco Bianco or Greco Bianco di Cirò, so it's difficult to understand what Guardavalle is all about in this specific bottling).

Invernenga

WHERE IT'S FOUND: Lombardy. NATIONAL REGISTRY CODE NUMBER: 277. COLOR: white.

First mentioned in 1826 when it was supposedly a common variety planted around Brescia, an affluent northern Italian town known as the "Lioness of Italy," Invernenga is also known as Invernesca, Brunesta, Bernestia, and Pergola. Its main name derives from the century-old habit of letting the grapes air-dry and then enjoying them as table grapes or raisins (hence Invernenga, in reference to winter, or *inverno*). Another synonym, Imbrunesta, refers to the variety's late harvest season, when fog (from *nebbia* or *bruma*) are common among the vines. It's not surprising therefore that locals also used to make a highly thought of sweet wine with this cultivar.

Invernenga's greatest claim to fame today is that it is planted in Europe's biggest functioning urban vineyard, in the heart of Brescia. The vineyard is located near via Pusterla, via Turati, and via San Rocchino at the foot of the castle in the middle of the city's downtown and at about four hectares is much larger than, for example, the Clos de Montmartre in Paris (which is only 1.556 square meters). The vineyard, which was once even larger, is planted almost entirely to the rare white, lightly aromatic Invernenga variety, though there is also a variety of red grapes, reportedly Marzemino, Uccellina, and Corva plus unspecified *Groppellos* and *Schiavas*, planted in its lowest section.

The vineyard has had a long and checkered history. In the 1800s, it belonged to the Riccardi brothers, who won a number of awards for their wines (for example, a gold medal at the 1904 Esposizione Bresciana). The winery and vineyard were later inherited by the Capretti family, and in 1940, Mario Capretti registered the name "Pusterla" for his winery and vineyard ("Vigneto Pusterla"): Pusterla is the name the wines have been known by until recently. With the ownership change, the wines proved none the worse for wear: the estate won a gold and two bronze medals at the 1953 Concorso Enologico dell'Italia Settentrionale and another of the estate's wines won a gold medal at the 1966 Concorso Enologico di Asti. All this indicates that Invernenga is capable of producing a wine that will win accolades. With Mario Capretti's death the winery and vineyard fell on very hard times and it was only in 1996, with the advent of Pierluigi Villa and Piero Bonomi, who agreed to rent the vineyard, that the Pusterla vineyard's wine was reborn. Villa, a viticulturalist from the University of Milan, and Piero Bonomi, a winemaker of the Bellavista estate, also changed the vineyard's name to Ronco Capretti. In 2011, the rental agreement expired and the vineyard returned to the control of the Capretti family.

Invernenga is characterized by medium to medium-large bunches and berries; the latter are round and have little bloom. Budbreak occurs early, and the grapes usually ripen in September. Two different clones became available in 1999, MI-BRIXIA 98–313 and MI-BRIXIA 98–377.

Though the single-biggest Invernenga vineyard is in downtown Brescia, I have been told the grape is also planted sporadically in the countryside surrounding the city.

Which Wines to Choose and Why

It's not easy finding an Invernenga wine to try. The IGT wine to look for is Ronchi di Brescia Bianco, but Invernenga can also be included in the IGT Sebino blend. I recall that the 2006 Ronchi di Brescia Bianco by the Pusterla estate was bottled in a pretty Rhine-style bottle with a white label and that the wine was a delicate yellow-green in hue, with aromas of honey and apples and a noticeable almond flavor with a floral-spicy edge at the back. It was also fairly saline. I once also tried a 2007, the most recent vintage I have seen, but I don't have any specific recollections of it. If I have ever had the red wine, I don't remember it at all.

WINES TO TRY: Pusterla* (Ronchi Bianco).

Lacrima

WHERE IT'S FOUND: Marche, Emilia-Romagna, Tuscany, Puglia. NATIONAL REGISTRY CODE NUMBER: 111. COLOR: red.

Lacrima in Italian means tear, and one look at the berry of this unique Italian native grape tells you why it is so named: the berries are in fact tear shaped. But the wine, though little-known, is so good that the only tears it will bring are of joy. Another hypothesis is that the name comes from the fact that the ripe grape's thin skin breaks easily, therefore tearing on the vine and in your hands (Lacrima is also a delicious table grape). Stefano Mancinelli, perhaps the most famous producer of Lacrima di Morro d'Alba wine supports the latter hypothesis, and I am not about to argue.

The variety is an aromatic red grape and apparently closely related to Aleatico (Filippetti, Silvestroni, Thomas, Intrieri 2001), while it has nothing to do with Lacryma Christi, a wine from Campania made with different grapes. Many different grape varieties have been named Lacrima throughout the centuries, all more or less unrelated, the only point in common being berries shaped somewhat like tears or kidney beans. The bunch is medium-large and pyramidal, and the berries are round to tear-shaped. This is obvious even in the writings of two of Italy's greatest ampelographers, Di Rovasenda (1877) and Molon (1906). the true Lacrima variety is nowadays considered the one grown in the Marche, where the wine was a favorite of Emperor Federico Barbarossa in 1167. That didn't stop the cultivar from risking extinction, as the thin skin that breaks easily is a magnet for all sorts of pests and diseases (otherwise, it's a very resistant variety). Another problem for Lacrima is its limited affinity with all American rootstocks, with a callus formation at the site of grapevine-rootstock insertion. The callus tends to increase in size over time, strangling the grapevine trunk and blocking off lymphatic flow, ultimately killing the vine. According to Mancinelli, the most successful Lacrima-rootstock combination is with 1103 Paulsen. There are no official clones available.

Once plentiful in the Marche, Emilia-Romagna, Tuscany, Umbria, Campania, and Puglia, today it is common only in the first region. Even in the Marche it is limited mainly to the province of Ancona, where the DOC wine Lacrima di Morro d'Alba (258 hectares under vine) is produced. Still, this is quite an increase from only twenty-five years ago: in 1985, when the first DOC for Lacrima di Morro d'Alba was created, there were only seven known hectares of Lacrima under vine, surviving thanks to the dedication and passion of producers such as Stefano Mancinelli. He and his colleagues have been amazingly successful, as those initial scant seven hectares became twenty-eight in 1994–95, sixty-five in 1999–2000, and more than two hundred today. Don't confuse this Lacrima with another distinct variety in Tuscany, called Lacrima del Valdarno, which is extremely rare nowadays.

The best *crus* are those around Senigallia, where the soils are rich in clay and have southern exposures. The name Morro d'Alba often confuses people, who believe it is in Piedmont, home to the other famous town called simply Alba, in the center of Barolo and Barbaresco production. Morro d'Alba is instead in the province of Ancona, and its name derives from the terms *mur* (rock, cliff) and *alba* (high hill).

Which Wines to Choose and Why
Though legislation states that Lacrima di Morro d'Alba need contain as little as 85 percent Lacrima, the best wines are made with nothing else. The 85 percent requirement has been in place since the very first DOC was instituted, and back then (1985) the inclusion of white grapes such as Verdicchio was allowed too. This enabled producers to make a slightly lighter-colored wine (Lacrima gives extremely dark, deep-hued wines, almost blackish). In the 1999 revision of the DOC legislation, the non-Lacrima 15 percent was limited to nonaromatic red grapes. Nonaromatic grapes is a *conditio sine qua non,* for Lacrima di Morro d'Alba is an aromatic wine, guaranteed to turn heads especially of those who have never tried it before. The intense aroma of lavender, red rose, cinnamon, and nutmeg is unforgettable, coupled with strongly saline and floral dark berry and black cherry flavors. Think of it as similar to a

black muscat, though the aroma profile is very different, more floral and less spicy, less sweet. Due to its wonderful aromatics, Lacrima di Morro d'Alba rarely sees a lot of oak in its aging process, which would mute the bright fruit flavors, a shame. Also good is Lacrima di Morro d'Alba Passito, an air-dried, sweet version. These are very tannic sweet wines that match marvelously with thick chocolate desserts. Unfortunately, some Lacrima wines are much less aromatic than you'd expect and a lot more tannic: some producers, such as Mancinelli, imply that since Lacrima di Morro d'Alba has become a popular sales-worthy wine, there are an ever-increasing number of atypical wines made with a good dollop of, for example, Montepulciano. Needless to say, such wines are best avoided as they do not reflect what a wine made with the Lacrima variety is about.

WINES TO TRY: Luigi Giusti*** (Luigino Vecchie Vigne), Stefano Mancinelli*** (Superiore, Sensazioni di Frutto and S. Maria del Fiore), Conti di Buscareto** (Compagnia della Rosa), Mario Lucchetti** (Superiore Guardengo), and Marotti Campi** (Superiore Orgiolo and Rubico). For Lacrima Passito, try: Lucchetti**, Stefano Mancinelli** (Re Sole), and Vicari* (Amaranto del Pozzo Buono).

Lagrein

WHERE IT'S FOUND: Alto Adige, Trentino.
NATIONAL REGISTRY CODE NUMBER: 112. COLOR: red.

It tells you something about wine (and human beings) that one of the main reasons why, centuries ago, people got into a war was because they wanted the right to drink the good stuff. Hard to believe? During the popular insurgence of 1526 in what is modern-day Alto Adige in Italy, hero Michael Gasmayr led local farmers in revolt against the nobles and their troops, demanding (among other things) the right to also drink Lagrein wine, previously reserved for the nobility, the courts, and the church. I can't say how moved I am every time I think about men and women who had their priorities so straight.

Lagrein seems to have found its ideal home in the countryside around Bolzano in Alto Adige, where it's the region's most important red variety. It's intimately linked to this part of Italy, where the grapevine was so highly thought of that already in 1097 local government edicts determined the official annual harvest dates; at that time the monks of the abbey at Gries were the most famous local producers of the wine—not surprising, considering that the *terroir* of Gries is the one true *grand cru* for this variety. In 1370, Emperor Charles IV passed a law forbidding Lagrein wine among his troops, allowing soldiers to drink only the lighter, less alcoholic wines made with the *Schiava*s.

Lagrein's name probably derives from the Val Lagarina or Vallagarina in Trentino, though some experts have suggested a Greek origin, linking the grape to the variety used to make the wine called *lagaritanos* around the city of Lagaria on the Ionian seacoast of Basilicata. However, recent DNA profiling studies have shed light on Lagrein's complex origins. In 2006, Vouillamoz and Grando demonstrated that Marzemino and Lagrein are offspring of Teroldego and another as yet unidentified parent, a now probably extinct grapevine species. This extinct variety is a likely progeny of Pinot Nero, which makes the latter a grandparent of both Lagrein and Marzemino. This recently discovered pedigree therefore appears to disprove Lagrein's supposed Greek origin, establishing it as an ancient native variety of Alto Adige. However, the conclusions reached by Vouillamoz and Grando appear to conflict with Cipriani, Spadotto, Jurman, Di Gaspero, Crespan, Meneghetti, et al. (2010), who proposed that Lagrein is a natural crossing between Teroldego and Schiava Gentile from Alto Adige. But evidence of this parentage is not consistent at two out of the thirty-nine SSR markers they analyzed, "a discrepancy level also observed in non-parent-offspring pairs" (Robinson, Harding, and Vouillamoz 2012). Also, the Teroldego and Schiava Gentile proposed parentage also clashes with the pedigree illustrated by Vouillamoz and Grando based on sixty DNA markers, as Marzemino, a sibling of Lagrein, cannot be a progeny of Schiava Gentile. Of course, the missing parent of Lagrein and Marzemino could be a relative of Schiava Gentile. If we accept the DNA parentage analysis and pedigree reconstruction that have established Lagrein as a natural cross between Teroldego from Trentino and an unknown variety possibly related to Schiava Gentile and a progeny of Pinot Nero, we then know that Lagrein is a sibling of Marzemino, a nephew of Dureza from Ardèche, a grandchild of Pinot Nero from Burgundy, and a cousin of Syrah from the Rhône Valley.

While Lagrein's family tree is more than a little difficult to pin down, it's a difficult variety from a viticultural standpoint as well; and this helps partly explain why it hasn't spread significantly outside Trentino and Alto Adige. The main problem is the conformation of its flower: not only is there very little pollen but many of the female flowers are morphologically imperfect with ensuing fertility problems and reduced annual productivity. These negative effects on yields are further amplified by rainy springs causing *coulure* and variable annual production output. So you can understand why, in the eyes of always practical farmers, this cantankerous beast is hardly worth planting elsewhere.

Christian Werth, the longtime *kellarmeister* (winemaker/technical director) of Cantina Convento Muri-Gries, told me that there are more than one hundred different Lagrein biotypes, and at Cantina Convento they have selected and propagated about twenty, currently still under observation. For the most part, lagrein producers work with two main biotypes of Lagrein, short bunched and a long bunched (it's actually the stalk that's short or long, hence the grape bunch). For the longest time, local producers preferred to plant clones (all derived from the main two biotypes) characterized by lower sugar buildup capacity (the pyramid-shaped SMA 63, SMA 65, LB 511, and LB 523) rather than the smaller, cylindrically shaped LB 509 and SMA 66 clones (the two short-stalked ones), which were less generous producers. Clone SMA 66 especially differs from the others, a miserly producer averaging roughly half the berry production of other clones (so the aversion shown it by farmers is understandable), resulting from less heavy and numerous bunches (30 percent less). On the positive side, Lagrein (and clone SMA 66 in particular) has one of the highest total anthocyanin concentrations of all Italian grape varieties (and so wines are very deeply colored). The good news is that recently developed short-stalked Lagrein clones ISMA 261 and ISMA 265 seem to embody the best of both worlds: higher productivity and sugar accumulation.

Besides the two biotypes, Scartezzini (2005) has written that a white-berried Lagrein, or Lagrein Bianco, was described as early as 1379 in the countryside around the city of Termeno, and again in 1497 around Appiano and in 1532 near Terlano. However, the exact nature of Lagrein Bianco is unclear, and many experts believe it to be either Sauvignon Blanc, Lagarino Bianco (once common in Trentino's Val di Cembra, Faver, and Grumes), or even a name used to indicate a local white blend. I have never seen it. In Italy, there are significant plantings of Lagrein only in Trentino and Alto Adige (though it's been experimentally planted in other regions, such as Tuscany); elsewhere, there are important plantings in the United States and Australia.

Which Wines to Choose and Why

Grown everywhere in Alto Adige and Trentino, monovarietal Lagrein wines are found in DOC Alto Adige Lagrein and Trentino Lagrein. Of course, the variety is also included in many other local DOC red wine blends. The best wines come from grapes grown on calcareous, gravelly soils that heat up, as Lagrein likes warm temperatures that allow it to ripen effectively (a late ripener, Lagrein needs all the sun it can get).

Wines made with Lagrein have an almost impenetrable color and can be characterized by harsh tannins, making them bitter and unpleasant. Over the last decade, this aspect has been corralled (mainly via a combination of shorter maceration times, lower fermentation temperature, and use of small oak barrels), though a tinge of bitterness at the back is a characteristic of the wine. Lagrein wine is big and full-bodied, offering an excellent alternative to Cabernet Sauvignon or Merlot wines, though in my experience it is best within its first ten years of life, rarely improving after that. Wines can be red (Lagrein Dunkel: *dunkel,* meaning dark in German) or *rosato* (Lagrein Krtezer: *kretzer,* meaning pink or light). *Rosato* efforts can be especially good.

In California, Arbios/Praxis Cellars is probably the largest U.S. Lagrein producer and makes a very good wine (2007 was their first vintage). Also try Tobin James (Silver Reserve), Tre Anelli, and Belvino. Australian efforts include excellent examples by Chalmers (the 2009 is fresher than some past vintages; though they haven't always been the last word in complexity, all the lagreins made here strike me as very successful, pleasant wines characterized by silky tannins and a chocolaty note on the finish), and Cobaw Ridge (which I believe produced Australia's first commercial release of Lagrein wine in 1997). The version from Hand Crafted by Geoff Hardy includes 15 percent Cabernet Sauvignon, and Heartland's Langhorne Creek is a rare blend of Lagrein with Dolcetto. Seppeltsfield also makes a lagrein in Barossa, which might strike one as an interesting choice, given Alto Adige's cool climate, but this is not such a strange choice at all. First because there are cooler parts to Barossa, but also because it is easy to forget that in Alto Adige the vineyards are planted in south-facing valleys which have summer daytime temperatures in the mid- to high 30s. In fact, Italians know that Bolzano is, along with Palermo in Sicily, one of Italy's hottest cities in the summer.

WINES TO TRY: Cantina Convento Muri-Gries*** (Abtei Muri Riserva), Cantina Produttori Santa Maddalena/Cantina di Bolzano*** (Taber Riserva; maybe the most classic, best all-around lagrein, every vintage), Cantina Terlano*** (Porphyr Riserva; from grapes not solely from the classic zone of Bolzano but from Egna, so this is a more elegant, suave Lagrein wine), Josephus Mayr*** (Lagrein Dunkel Riserva, a very idiosyncratic red that you can recognize blind every time; thick, rich, viscous, and very intense spicy, inky, and fruity flavors), Lageder*** (Lindenburg), Abbazia di Novacella** (Praepositus Riserva; always dependable and satisfying—I'm not sure these guys could make a bad wine even if they tried), and Georg Ramoser** (Riserva).

*Lambrusco*s

See LAMBRUSCO FAMILY, chapter 3.

Lanzesa

WHERE IT'S FOUND: Emilia-Romagna. NATIONAL REGISTRY CODE NUMBER: 452. COLOR: white.

An ancient variety that has been known in Romagna since 1400, but a very recent addition to the National Registry: Lanzesa was officially recognized only in 2011. Lanzesa is so named for its spear-shaped berry (spear in Italian is *lancia,* hence *lanzesa* in the *romagnolo* dialect). This is a remarkably interesting grapevine to look at and an even more interesting wine to taste: you can just see Lanzesa descending lineage-wise from local wild grapevines. It has tellingly characteristic long shoots with well-distanced internodes and large leaves. In some respects it looks a little like Trebbiano Romagnolo, but Lanzesa's tiny, conical bunch and pointy, spear-shaped, medium-small berry differentiate the two clearly. Lanzesa does very poorly with vigorous training systems such as the *pergola* (canopy) and needs to be pruned Guyot-style to be capable of producing ripe berries and a decent wine. Part of the problem is

Lanzesa's physiologically female flower, and therefore its penchant for *millerandage* (the failure of some grapes in the bunch to develop fully, resulting in berries of uneven sizes) and so annual productions can be irregular. As a result, even though Lanzesa is vigorous, productivity is low. There are no official clones. In the past, it was used as a table grape.

There are few, sporadic vines in the province of Ravenna, around Bagnocavallo, Brisighella, Castel Bolognese, Faenza, and Fisignano, with many vines close to or over one hundred years of age.

Which Wines to Choose and Why

The wines I have tasted are certainly off the beaten track, even strange: pale yellow-green hue, pungent (really pungent) aromas of white flowers (acacia and buttercups), green apples, and unripe citrus (with a touch of volatile acidity almost always present), and then herbal and riper apple and honeyed, tropical fruit flavors with a sharp acid finish. The wine also has a richer mouthfeel than the fresh nose would lead you to expect, with a slightly saline finish. I think Lanzesa has potential for air-dried wines, since the skins are quite thick and resistant and the berries large and juicy; to date, though, I have only tasted dry wines made with the variety. A wine made with Lanzesa is unique, hitting all the right chords, maybe because it plays chords no other grape variety does.

WINES TO TRY: Tenuta Uccellina** (Alma Luna; medium-bodied, saline, lovely) and Istituto Professionale di Stato per l'Agricoltura e l'Ambiente-Persolino* (drink up soon after bottled).

Lumassina

WHERE IT'S FOUND: Liguria. NATIONAL REGISTRY CODE NUMBER: 123. COLOR: white.

Lumassina is also called Acerbina, Lumassa Bianca, Lumaca, Buzzetto (in the area of Quiliano), and more commonly Mataossu (when produced around Finale, Noli, and Spontorno), though some believe the latter to be an unrelated variety. The variety's best-known name, Lumassina, derives from the Italian *lumasse*, meaning "snails," and also from an area of Liguria where locals drink copious volumes of this light, refreshing white wine while eating snails, a local delicacy. Other synonyms, such as Acerbina and Buzzetto, refer to the typically high acidity that wines made with Lumassina are famous for. Documented in Liguria as early as the 1300s, Lumassina was first accurately described by Di Rovasenda in 1877 and then in the *Bollettino ampelografico* of 1883. Once more common in the countryside around Genoa and later Savona, it has always been blended with other local varieties to produce simple everyday wines called *vini nostralini*.

Lumassina is characterized by medium-large, pyramidal, rather long bunches with two or three wings and medium-small, round berries that are very green in color. There are no official clones. It's a late-ripening variety that is found only in Liguria, with sporadic rows in the neighboring part of Tuscany. In Liguria, Lumassina grows mainly in the Savona countryside, around the towns of Noli, Spontorno, and Varigotti, but also around Quiliano and Finale Ligure. Excellent hillside vineyards are found in Cappuccini, Montagna, Roviasca, Viarzo, Garzi, Rive, Molini, Tecci, and Treponti. Unfortunately, as it ripens about two weeks later than most local varieties, farmers were never keen to devote much vineyard space to it.

Which Wines to Choose and Why

Lumassina gives a delicious, lightly alcoholic (often only 11 percent alcohol) floral white wine. Trouble is, Lumassina's hauntingly fresh, pure aromas are much less obvious than those of wines made with Vermentino, and therefore producers choose to put most if not all of their eggs in the latter's basket. While everybody in Liguria produces a monovarietal Vermentino, the same can't be said for Lumassina. But there are monovarietals available, and they are especially easy to find when you spend some time in the area. The wine to look for is IGT Colline Savonesi. Lumassina wines can be extremely crisp, reminiscent of white flowers, marine sea breezes, with hints of pear, green apple, and thyme. They are remarkably good with simply prepared fish and shellfish dishes typical of coastal towns.

WINES TO TRY: Cascina delle Terre Rosse*** (L'Acerbina), Punta Crena*** (Mattaossu, and also a sparkling Mataossu Brut; the Lumassina Brut, also sparkling, is less effervescent and closer to a still wine), Sancio***, Durin*** (Mataosso), Viticultori Ingauni*, Giuseppe Sacone*, Cascina Praié* (Zefiro, a sparkling version), and Cooperativa Viticoltori Coronata (another sparkling lumassina).

Maceratino Bianco

WHERE IT'S FOUND: Marche. NATIONAL REGISTRY CODE NUMBER: 124. COLOR: white.

Also known as Ribona, this variety may be related to Verdicchio, though it presents notable morphological and phenological differences. It's an ancient variety, which explains the many synonyms it is known by: Bianchetta Montecchiese and Uva Stretta are accurate; and there are some improper ones such a Greco delle Marche or Verdicchio Marino. The official name is Maceratino Bianco, in honor of the city of Macerata, which is in the middle of the main production zone. Maceratino has garnered considerable interest from local producers, and many estates are applying different agricultural and enological techniques as they busily learn about the variety. Maceratino does not appear to be very adaptable and needs well-exposed, ventilated sites, and nutrient-poor soils for best results.

Maceratino is characterized by medium-large to large, usually conical bunches that are tightly packed; the berries are round and medium in size. It buds and ripens relatively late. There are five official clones (CSV-AP MC1, CSV-AP MC4, MC-MM 1, MC-MM 3, and MC-VPD). The MC4 clone is a little less tightly packed than the MC1. Maceratino is planted only in the Marche (there's also a little in Umbria), mainly in the province of Macerata and in the countryside around Loreto, in the province of Ancona, preferably in hillside vineyards at altitudes less than 450 meters.

Which Wines to Choose and Why

The DOC Colli Maceratesi is 244 hectares (with various varieties planted). The DOC Colli Maceratesi Bianco wine has to be at least 70 percent Maceratino; Colli Maceratesi Ribona can instead be monovarietal (though the law requires only a minimum of 80 percent Maceratino, which is a shame). The DOC also allows a Ribona Spumante (a sparkling wine). In the Marche, there are only about one hundred hectares planted to Maceratino. There are also some IGT wines from Umbria such as Cannara, Narni, and Spello that allow Maceratino in the blend, but in these wines the variety has only a minor role. I'm not sure it's presently easy to define what a good Maceratino wine is like, because the wine has exploded onto the scene only recently and everyone is still learning. In general, Maceratino wines seem lighter than those made with Verdicchio (especially di Matelica); but because Maceratino is a highly reductive variety, off odors are frequent in poorly made examples. The wines also seem like they have the potential to age and to have a very nice mineral edge, something I have found in all the maceratinos I have tried. Overall, I would say there are a number of interesting wines made with this variety, but as for every native that has been the subject of almost overnight success, there are also several far less distinguished wines.

WINES TO TRY: Fattoria Forano*** (Colli Maceratesi Bianco Monteferro, a monovarietal Maceratino wine), La Muròla** (Andrea Baccius and Le Jole, the fresher and lighter of the two and the one I prefer), Saputi* (Castru Vecchiu, soft and creamy), and Capinera* (Murrano, slightly herbal).

Magliocco

WHERE IT'S FOUND: Calabria. NATIONAL REGISTRY CODE NUMBER: not registered. COLOR: red.

This variety grows mainly in the Bivongi area of Calabria and is also known as Magliocco Dolce and Magliocco Tondo (to differentiate it from Magliocco Canino, which has oval berries instead of this cultivar's typically round berries). Magliocco has many synonyms, most of them erroneous. A correct synonym appears to be Arvino, a name likely derived from Lake Arvo in la Sila. Erroneous synonyms include Guarnaccia Nera and Greco Nero. It appears that Magliocco may be synonymous with the Greco Nero grown around Lamezia Terme, while it is different from the Greco Nero di Sibari and the Greco Nero di Verbicaro. According to Schneider, Raimondi, and De Santis (2008), Magliocco is synonymous with Marsigliana Nera, but I have found no other evidence in support of this finding; Magliocco is likely to be more common in Calabria than commonly believed, and it may be that some Marsigliana Nera grapevines were misidentified by locals and are in reality Magliocco. However, Marsigliana Nera is officially listed in the National Registry while Magliocco is not; further studies are probably warranted in order to confirm this synonym. This is not a matter of being overly cautious: in Pellerone, Edwards, and Thomas (2001), Marsigliana Nera was found to be identical to Castiglione, but the authors conclude that this finding was due to a misidentified Castiglione sample (an easy error to make, since Castiglione and Marsigliana Nera have similar ampelographic features). In any case, that study showed that Marsigliana Nera is distinct from Magliocco Canino, but no Magliocco accessions were analyzed. Unbelievably enough, Magliocco is also an official synonym for Gaglioppo, which is crazy, since the two varieties have little in common and are genetically distinct. I also have trouble understanding Lacrima as a supposed synonym for Magliocco, because the former should have tear-shaped berries by definition (*lacrima* means tear) while Magliocco is also known as Magliocco Tondo because of its round berries. Most often, Magliocco has medium to medium-small bunches that are tightly packed and roughly conical in shape, without the large wings exhibited by Magliocco Canino.

According to Marchi and Lanati (2008), Magliocco is characterized by high levels of acylated anthocyanins and malvin (76 percent of the total anthocyanin profile). Terpenic concentrations (geraniol, nerol) increase greatly with late harvests. When Magliocco yields too generously it produces unripe, herbal wines of little charm. Late harvesting in ideal weather conditions is a technique by which to obtain polished tannins and sweeter fruit flavors. Fortunately, Magliocco is a late ripener, so in sunny autumns the grapes can be left long enough on the vine, allowing them to ripen fully, which smooths out the tannins that can remain hard years after the vintage. In this light, warmer soils that may help bring about faster ripening of the berries also help. In contrast to Magliocco Canino, Magliocco has a noticeably smaller bunch (at an average of 260 grams, it's roughly half the size), is much more drought resistant, and is both strongly vigorous and fertile.

Which Wines to Choose and Why

In the provinces of Crotone, Catanzaro, and Cosenza, Magliocco is used for DOC Donnici or IGT Val di Neto blends or monovarietal wines that are classically dry. The monovarietal wines are hard to come by because of the old habit of planting Magliocco Dolce promiscuously with other cultivars in the same vineyard; but some monovarietal vineyards are found in the province of Cosenza. A very good Magliocco wine will have surprisingly smooth tannins and sweet black cherry, exotic fruit, with notes of tobacco (aromas can be very floral, even pungent, in young wines but soften over time) and underbrush on the finish, with just a hint of herbs. According to Pineau, Barbe, Van Leeuwen, and Dubourdieu (2007), Magliocco wines are almost always characterized by exotic fruit aromas of β-damascenone (which also enhances those due to ethyl cinnamate and caproate while reducing the herbal ones of 3-isobutyl-2-methoxypyrazine (IBMP), and the wines have a low olfactory perception threshold. They can be surprisingly good and far removed from the sometimes tough and angular tannins of wines made with Gaglioppo or Magliocco Canino.

WINES TO TRY: Librandi*** (Magno Megonio) is always a sure bet. If we are to believe that Lacrima and Magliocco Dolce are identical, then try: Feudi di Sanseverino*** (Lacrima Nero), Cantine Gallicchio**, and Tenute Ferrocinto**.

Magliocco Canino

WHERE IT'S FOUND: Calabria. NATIONAL REGISTRY CODE NUMBER: 125. COLOR: red.

According to De Bonis (2002), the first official mention of a Magliocca variety (with a terminal *a*) in Calabria dates back to the 1500s, though there is no way to know which cultivar was really being described. Trouble is, there are many *Magliocco* varieties in Calabria, most of which are not closely related. Magliocco Canino is also called Magliocco Ovale (due to the characteristic oval shape of its berries, different from all the other *Magliocco*s) and at times Nocera, a mistake, since the latter is a distinct variety more typical of Sicily (morphologically, it resembles Magliocco more than it does Magliocco Canino). Magliocco Canino should not be confused with the other *Magliocco*s, for only Magliocco (also called Magliocco Tondo or Magliocco Dolce) is qualitatively valid as a wine grape. Confusion is such that Marchi and Lanati (2008) determined that what was being called Magliocco Dolce in the Lamezia area of Calabria was in fact a biotype of Magliocco Canino. It has been suggested that Magliocco Canino could have a parent-offspring relationship with an extremely rare variety called Calabrese di Montenuovo, which according to Vouillamoz, Monaco, Costantini, Stefanini, Scienza, and Grando (2007) is one of the two parents of Sangiovese (according to this study, the other is Ciliegiolo). Were this true, then Magliocco Canino would be either a half-sibling or a grandparent of Sangiovese. I caution readers though that the Ciliegiolo × Calabrese di Montenuovo crossing that is presumed to have given birth to Sangiovese is not supported by other data; actually there are two studies that have reached different conclusions. It might be more prudent to wait until further analysis of the complex relationships of Sangiovese, Magliocco Canino, and other varieties has been performed. Furthermore, Pellerone, Edwards and Thomas (2001) have shown that Magliocco Canino may be distantly related to Sicily's Perricone.

The name Magliocco Canino derives from two different sources. *Magliocco* indicates a knot or closed fist and thus a small and compact bunch (much like the *Groppellos*). However, since Magliocco Canino's bunch is anything but small (it's medium-large, on average 450 grams) with long wings dripping down the sides and is also very loosely packed, I wonder. Other *Magliocco*s are characterized by small bunches, but not this one. The *canino* part of the name is believed to come from the fact that the sweet grapes were enthusiastically eaten by dogs (or *canini*). Of course, this being Italy, there are many who completely disagree. In any case, Magliocco Canino is characterized by very dark blue-black skins, and the grape's anthocyanin profile shows high concentrations of malvin (a whopping 78 percent of the total five monomeric anthocyanins) and 16 percent acylated anthocyanins. The wealth of similarly stable pigments explains why Magliocco Canino wines have deep, long-lasting colors. The variety is particularly rich in benzenoids and alcohols, especially benzilic acid, 4-vinilguaiacole, and hexanol. The grape has strong vigor but poor fertility and productivity and is sensitive to droughty conditions (yet another noteworthy difference between this cultivar and Magliocco, which is strongly vigorous *and* fertile). Magliocco Canino is grown all over

Calabria (only in limited quantity in the province of Reggio Calabria), mainly on the western side of the region, facing the Tyrrhenian Sea.

Which Wines to Choose and Why

Savuto and Terre di Cosenza are the DOCs that specifically mention Magliocco Canino as one of the allowed grape varieties. There are also numerous IGT wines that allow Magliocco Canino in the blend such as Locride, Pellaro, Scilla, Valle dei Crati, and Val di Neto.

WINES TO TRY: Casalnuovo del Duca** and Tenuta Terre Nobili* (Cariglio, reportedly a blend of 80 percent Magliocco Canino and 20 percent Magliocco Dolce). Many so-called Magliocco wines contain Cabernet Sauvignon: recognizing Magliocco Canino's contribution in such wines becomes impossible, or close to it. This is true even when less than 20 percent of a similarly powerful grape is said to have been added; to make matters worse, in Italy such percentages are most often aspirations, rather than exact figures.

Malbo Gentile

WHERE IT'S FOUND: Emilia-Romagna. NATIONAL REGISTRY CODE NUMBER: 333. COLOR: red.

Malbo Gentile looks and behaves very much like a wild grapevine and its exact origin is unknown. It is also known as Amabile di Genova, which has led some in the past to postulate a Ligurian origin. Today's majority view is that the variety hails from Emilia-Romagna, the result of either a domesticated native wild grapevine or of natural cross-pollination between a wild species and a cultivated one, though specific evidence in support of this hypothesis is lacking. The variety has been documented in the Emilia part of the Emilia-Romagna region since at least 1800, where it was used to add power and sweetness to the various *Lambrusco* wines made there. Centuries ago, going the monovarietal route had not been considered.

If we can talk about Malbo Gentile today, and taste wines made from it, it is thanks to the efforts of, among others, the Istituto di Stato per l'Agricoltora e l'Ambiente-Persolino, a state-run and -funded teaching and winemaking facility in Faenza with its own experimental vineyard. In the 1960s, researchers noticed three very different-looking and lonely vines from all the others planted; a dirty old tag indicated they were Amabile di Genova. Little else was known about the cultivar. Nothing was made of the vines for a long time, but researchers became impressed with the cultivar's loosely packed but large bunches and noteworthy sugar concentrations. The logical next step was to attempt experimental microvinifications, and so plantings were increased in 1988 by grafting Malbo Gentile onto thirty-nine Sangiovese vines. In 1990 roughly 140 kilograms of grapes were harvested and air-dried for thirty days; the wine went on sale in 1992, meeting with resounding success. This led to a genetic workup in collaboration with the Experimental Viticultural and Winemaking Station (ESAVE) in Tebano that determined the cultivar to be Malbo Gentile. Interestingly, Emilia's Malbo Gentile behaves and looks morphologically different than Romagna's, ostensibly a consequence of the former region's more fertile soils in which the variety becomes overproductive and assumes a different phenotype. Therefore, different biotypes of Malbo Gentile exist. For example, the Brisighella biotype of Romagna (Brisighella is a town near Faenza) is loosely packed and almost rachitic looking; though a high-quality subvariety, it was disappearing due to its low production. Because its morphologic aspect was so different from that of the Malbo Gentile of Emilia no one at the state institute realized that Amabile di Genova was in fact Malbo Gentile. Instead, the most common Malbo Gentile biotype grown in Emilia resembles Ancellotta and some *Lambruscos*. In a 2005 study that I find controversial, Boccacci, Torello Marinoni, Gambino, Botta, and Schneider claimed that Malbo Gentile has close genetic ties to Fortana and is identical to Foglia

Tonda. I don't know of anybody else who has published similar results; the same study also stated that Fortana and Canina Nera are identical, which is also refuted by many experts.

In general, Malbo Gentile is characterized by large, loosely packed, pyramidal bunches with one or two wings, and medium-small, round, dark berries. There are three clones: VCR 68, VCR 69, and VCR 70. The first of these is characterized by the particularly thick skin of the berries; therefore this is the clone most suited to air-drying and the one often used to make sweet, *passito* wines. Independent of clone or biotype, Malbo Gentile is a very interesting, if difficult, variety to work with. Eraldo Tura, the viticulturalist at the Istituto di Stato per l'Agricoltura e l'Ambiente-Persolino, believes that "it's a hardy grape; for instance, in 2002 when it rained practically nonstop from August to October, Malbo Gentile was the only variety producers in the area were able to pick and use." From a viticultural perspective, Malbo Gentile seems to grow better at or above four hundred meters above sea level, in *terroirs* that allow it to better preserve its natural acidity. It flowers early, but this is not a problem in this relatively warmer part of Italy where spring frosts are rare; instead, it tends to drop its leaves immediately in droughty conditions, and so deleafing requires care. Malbo Gentile can also suffer from floral abortion and reduced productivity, since the male flower has downturned, curved stamens and is therefore unable to self-pollinate (unlike cultivated varieties that are hermaphroditic). It follows that Malbo Gentile requires a pollinating species (just as Lambrusco di Sorbara does); the best co-planting varieties are Lambrusco Salamino, Lambrusco Maestri, Ancellotta, and even Marzemino, but these vines must be planted within three to five rows of the Malbo Gentile vines, or the efficacy of cross-pollination efforts is greatly diminished.

Malbo Gentile grows almost everywhere in Emilia-Romagna, if in sporadic plots: it can be found in the provinces of Piacenza, Modena, Reggio Emilia, and Forlì-Cesena. In total, there are about ten hectares in the region.

Which Wines to Choose and Why

Historically, in Emilia, Malbo Gentile wines were never produced as monovarietals but were used as blending agents, while 100 percent pure efforts were, and are, more common in Romagna. Today, DOC or IGT wines to look for are Colli di Scandiano e Canossa (a sparkling version is allowed) and Ravenna Rosso, but Malbo Gentile is also used in various *Lambrusco* blends, such as in some Lambrusco Grasparossa and Reggiano Lambrusco wines. Importantly, there are a preponderance of old Malbo Gentile grapevines that produce extremely dark and tannic wines: indeed, these are some of the most tannic wines you'll ever taste, and so some producers have taken to leaving a little residual sugar behind to buffer the palate sensation of brutal tannic strength. In my view, if whoever named this grape *gentile* was thinking of the wine it made, then he or she had a well-developed sense of humor.

The sine qua non of a good Malbo Gentile is an intense note of blackberry on both nose and palate, turning to a blackberry syrup when the grapes have been late harvested or air-dried. I'm not sure that wines made with Malbo Gentile are complex enough to ever rival the world's best, but they certainly are different and unique, and when well made have smooth, magically mouthcoating textures. The sweet versions are perfect with chocolate desserts and aged blue cheeses.

Malbo Gentile doesn't just pose problems in the vineyard but presents enological challenges as well. The grape is naturally rich in polyphenols, and so shorter maceration times and avoiding high fermentation temperatures are necessities: for example, skin to juice contact today is typically twenty days instead of the forty of decades past (and even twenty seems too much to me); pumping over and rack and returns have to be performed judiciously, for these techniques risk pushing the overextraction envelope. Not surprisingly, new oak is used quite a bit to try and smoothen the wine further via controlled oxygenation; usually most producers will let the wine mature for fifteen to eighteen months in oak barrels. Both dry and sweet wines are made with Malbo Gentile. A late ripener (late September or most often early October), it's blessed with thick skins and so is suited to air-drying and sweet wine production, a local tradition. "Picking the grapes late and then hanging them to dry rather than laying them on straw mats or plastic shelves is even better," says Tura. "But it's a technique that takes up too much space. It's usually air-dried for twenty-five to thirty days." Nowadays, with dry wines being in vogue, producers have turned to harvesting Malbo Gentile earlier, so as to make dry red wines.

WINES TO TRY: Vigne dei Boschi** (Borgo Stignani; the Settepievi is not monovarietal), Casali Viticoltori** (Sanmartein, a *novello* wine, and the Passito Passione di Rosa), Istituto di Stato per l'Agricoltura e l'Ambiente-Persolino** (L'Amabile Persolino, the best wine made by this research station), La Piccola** (Mitis, air-dried and sweet), Bonluigi** (Bucamante, a dry red; Apice Rosso, a late-harvest selection of the best grapes; and La Pinona, a *passito*), and Reggiana* (Vigna dei Gelsi, a sparkling wine).

*Malvasia*s

See MALVASIA GROUP, chapter 3.

Mammolo

WHERE IT'S FOUND: Tuscany. NATIONAL REGISTRY CODE NUMBER: 142. COLOR: red.

Nomen omen, the ancient Romans used to say, or "truth lies within the name." So it is with this smile-inducing grape variety (every time I see Mammolo's stocky, almost fat bunch with its big, round juicy berries I think it looks like one happy grape), which takes its name from the flower *viola mammola*, or violet. No other red wine I know of, made from any other cultivar, exudes aromas that are so intensely violet and so instantly recognizable.

Mammolo is a Tuscan native, historically described only by Tuscan researchers, from Soderini in 1600 to Di Rovasenda in 1877. Actually, those luminaries described various *Mammolo*s, which are not easy to find in contemporary vineyards (and I have gone looking over the years). Even when I have found them, the amount of time producers spent talking about the likes of Mammolo Grosso, Mammolo Asciutto, Mammolo Tondo, or the many other anciently described *Mammolo*s (Rosso, Serrato, and a few more I am surely forgetting) was measurable in nano- or femtoseconds. In fact, Cipriani, Spadotto, Jurman, Di Gaspero, Crespan, Meneghetti, et al. (2010) point out that there are five genetically distinct varieties called Mammolo in the literature, and so it appears the *Mammolo*s are best viewed as a group of grapes, rather than one single variety. All of the other various *Mammolo*s described are likely just biotypes of one or two main *Mammolo* varieties; today it is widely believed that all others descend from Mammolo Nero and Mammolone di Lucca. Since Mammolo is an ancient variety, it is only reasonable to expect it to have many biotypes, as well as genetic ties with numerous other Tuscan varieties. Di Vecchi Staraz, Bandinelli, Boselli, This, Boursiquot, Laucou, Lacombe, and Varès (2007) showed that it is related to Biancone, Caloria, Colombana Nera, and Pollera Nera, plus two Corsican varieties, Sciaccarellu (or Sciaccarello in Italian) and Malvasia Montanaccio. It is likely that Mammolo was brought to Corsica during the island's Italian days, when it was ruled first by the powerful Repubbliche Marinare of Pisa and then by Genoa, from the eleventh through eighteenth centuries. Very interestingly, the study by the Cipriani group showed that Moscato Violetto (also known as Muscat Rouge de Madeire) is a natural crossing of Moscato Bianco and Duraguzza, a little-known variety. However, the 2007 Di Vecchi Staraz group's study found that Duraguzza was synonymous with Mammolo; this is especially noteworthy because their data also shows that Ciliegiolo, another important Tuscan cultivar, is the offspring of Moscato Violetto and Sangiovese. Therefore, Mammolo would be a grandparent of Ciliegiolo, not an unlikely possibility given Mammolo's centuries in the Tuscan countryside. However, the exact family relationships of Sangiovese and Ciliegiolo are currently the subject of some controversy, so these results need further verification (see CILIEGIOLO and SANGIOVESE entries).

Unfortunately, Mammolo started falling out of favor with winemakers in the 1960s, mostly because its wines oxidize rapidly, a real no-no for important red wines that are meant to be ageworthy. Still, star winemaker Maurizio Castelli especially likes the variety, and has given a great deal of thought to the environments that are best for it. "Mammolo is truly fantastic when faced with extreme conditions," he says, "but it demands clay-rich soils: overly fertile ones are not ideal, as those wines are diluted and uninteresting. On clay-dominated, sodium-rich, alkaline soils, with traces of sand, the variety is exceptional and gives memorable wines that will keep a couple of years. On these soils, Mammolo expresses an almost aromatic nose, with a note of black pepper so strong that puts Syrah to shame."

Mammolo is a beautiful grape variety to look at. Its round leaves are instantly recognizable for they curve sharply inwards, giving the petiolar sinus a narrow lyre-like shape and an appearance of overlapping edges. The bunch is medium-large, pyramidal, and chubby, with large, round, red-blue berries. The grapevine grows erect and is both vigorous and reliable, so farmers like to work with it. Its budbreak is after that of Sangiovese but Mammolo is usually the earlier ripener of the two, and is picked either in late September or early October. Due to the fact that Mammolo is a very ancient variety, morphologic variations are common, and you can find more than one Mammolo grapevine that has long, cylindrical bunches, though this is not Mammolo's most typical look. There are also two available clones of Mammolo (MAM-PA-1, VCR 432), and Roberto Bandinelli of the University of Florence was at the forefront of the first studies needed to certify clonal selections. He and his team set out to select those biotypes of Mammolo characterized by smaller bunches and berries, with thicker skins. Clonal selection holds promise because the grape has unstable anthocyanins and so tends to drop its color over time. Mammolo is a hardy, rustic variety characterized by good, regular productivity, though it can be sensitive to botrytis bunch rot depending on how compact the bunch is. According to Attilio Pagli, choice of rootstock is essential with Mammolo, otherwise the variety doesn't behave the way you expect it to; he likes to use the Paulsen series, of course taking into account the characteristics of the soil.

Mammolo is found nowhere else in Italy but Tuscany, and even in this region less than one hundred hectares are planted (based on 2010 data), though I imagine there is more, hidden away in promiscuously planted old vineyards. Mammolo grows in vineyards in the provinces of Arezzo, Grosseto, Lucca, Pistoia, and Siena but also grows in places as diverse as Corsica, the United States, and Australia. In the latter country, Chalmers Nursery grows a Mammolo clone labeled Mudgee HT. In the United States, Mammolo is one of the varieties that has been studied for planting and winemaking suitability in the San Joaquin Valley by the University of Davis Cooperative Extension Services.

Which Wines to Choose and Why

Though Mammolo is easily found playing bit parts in many wine blends, it rarely gets top billing, which, in my opinion at least, is a shame. Look for Mammolo in DOC blends such as Carmignano, Chianti (all denominations), Morellino di Scansano, Monteregio di Massa Maritimma, Colli di Luni, Montecucco, and others, but especially Rosso and Vino Nobile di Montepulciano. Monovarietal IGT wines also exist, but are few and far between. I guarantee that anyone, with a little practice and attention, can and will recognize Mammolo's presence in blend with Sangiovese if the percentage of Mammolo is 10 percent or above. For Mammolo's signature really is expressive and unique. Best of all, it doesn't beat Sangiovese into submission (like additions of Syrah or Cabernet Sauvignon do); instead, it has the uncanny knack of bringing out the best that Sangiovese has to offer.

Many readers might not know that Mammolo has always been the defining feature of the wines of Montepulciano: or so it should be, if foolish producers hadn't started adding Cabernet Sauvignon or Merlot to their Sangiovese, instead of Mammolo. Not because these two great wine grapes don't have anything to add, but because they inevitably take over the wine: Sangiovese gets lost in the mix, and the wine loses any sense of place or uniqueness it may have had. The end result is that many of the wines of Montepulciano no longer taste like the unique wine that a Mammolo-enhanced Sangiovese can be; in other words, wines that don't remind anyone of Montepulciano and its surrounding countryside. In my view, Nobile di Montepulciano is perhaps Italy's most famous wine with the biggest identity crisis and poor sales, and the decision to abandon Mammolo is one of the main reasons why.

Mammolo's main problem is that its wines tend to oxidize sooner than those made with varieties like Sangiovese, and a red wine that can't be cellared automatically becomes a second-tier player. However, some winemakers disagree with these prevailing views. For example, Federico Staderini believes too much has been made of Mammolo's tendency to oxidize quickly and correctly points out that the excellent monovarietal Mammolo wine he helps make at Villa Calcinaia in Chianti Classico ages well for two to three years. Another problem (or rather, a perceived problem) is that pure Mammolo wines aren't especially deep in hue, and light color has been a big no-no with the wine buying public (and many wine critics) for the better part of the last thirty years.

Monovarietal Mammolo wines are characterized by an archetypal floral pungency that is truly unforgettable; the smell of violets is much more intense than in Sangiovese, not itself a shy variety when it comes to expressing that aroma. In the mouth, I find well-made examples of mammolo to be graceful, with very juicy fruit (black cherry, raspberry) and floral (violet, lavender) flavors that last and last. Mammolo wines may not be blockbusters, but they have a sense of balance that is rarely in red wines.

Elsewhere, Clos Ornasca makes a reportedly pure Sciaccarello Rosé in Corsica; monovarietal or not, it's a very good *rosato;* their red wine has about 20 percent Nielluccio (Sangiovese) added. Comte Abbatucci makes both red and rosé wines in Corsica; I greatly prefer the former (Faustine), which is roughly 70 percent Sciaccarello and 30 percent Nielluccio. Clos Canarelli makes a very good Figari Rosé wine that is 50 percent Sciaccarello. In the United States, Acorn Winery/Alegria Vineyards in Sonoma County has planted Mammolo but does not make a monovarietal wine with it (though it does do other Cal-Italian wines, such as dolcetto and sangiovese). In Australia, several estates have planted Mammolo but they use it in only very small percentages, in blends with their other Italian varieties to add a little more in the way of perfume.

WINES TO TRY: Villa Calcinaia*** (a light-bodied, fragrant work of art; not meant to age, but it doesn't fall apart quickly either, belying the notion that Mammolo always causes wines to oxidize and age faster). I Balzini produces a Sangiovese-Mammolo wine called Green Label with roughly 25 percent Mammolo, and the wine is remarkably perfumed and enticing. The owner, Antonella d'Isanto, has guaranteed that she will go "Mammolo alone" as soon as she has enough massal selections of Mammolo grapevines to make wine in commercially feasible numbers. Given the quality of her mammolo, I am eagerly awaiting that wine. On the other hand, I caution readers that Cennatoio's very good wine called Mammolo di Toscana is 100 percent Merlot. Only in Italy, I guess.

Mantonico Bianco

WHERE IT'S FOUND: Calabria. NATIONAL REGISTRY CODE NUMBER: not registered. COLOR: white.

Typical of Calabria, this is a naturally tannic white grape variety that has been confused with

Abruzzo's similarly named Montonico Bianco; unlike the latter, Mantonico Bianco makes not only good dry white wines but also very good sweet wines. The variety is also called Mantonico Viru in the Locride area in southeastern Calabria (*viru* means "real" in the local dialect). A biotype called Mantonico Pizzutella (first shown to be identical to Mantonico Bianco by Pellerone, Edwards, and Thomas in 2001), characterized by slightly more pointy berries (in this case, *pizzo* refers to something pointy), is also grown along the Ionian coast. Though genetically identical to Mantonico Bianco, this biotype differs from the standard variety not just because of its obvious morphologic differences but also because of lower sugar accumulation (Zappia, Gullo, Mafrica, and Di Lorenzo 2007). Cipriani, Spadotto, Jurman, Di Gaspero, Crespan, Meneghetti, et al. (2010) have also suggested that Mantonico Bianco is a relative of Gaglioppo, Marchione, and Nerello Mascalese, all southern Italian red-berried natives. Mantonico Bianco is unrelated to any of the Mantonico Nero varieties (of which there appear to be at least four in Calabria alone) and Mantonico Russeda, yet another *Mantonico,* a few vines of which grow near Bivongi (in the province of Reggio Calabria). All of these dark-berried varieties need to be studied via microsatellite analysis for clear-cut identification, for they may not be *Mantonicos* at all. In an unfortunate turn of events that only confuses things more, Montonico Bianco (with an "o" instead of Mantonico Bianco's "a"), a white-berried cultivar that lives mainly in central Italy but of which there is also a little growing in southern Italy, is called Mantonico Bianco Italico (or Greco Bianco del Pollino) everywhere in Calabria except in the Pollino area. Finally, Mantonico Bianco should not be confused with Guardavalle, another Calabrian grape, which is usually called Mantonico in the area around Cosenza. Surprisingly, Mantonico Bianco is not listed in Italy's National Registry, where only Montonico Bianco is included, and though I could certainly be mistaken, I think this is an error that ought to be rectified.

Mantonico Bianco has been grown in Calabria since the eighth century B.C.E. and its name (according to the Ceratti family, which produces the best mantonico bianco in Italy today) derives from the Greek *mantis-eos* (meaning prophet, because the wine was apparently used by sorcerers and offered to those who predicted the future). Mantonico Bianco is both a high-acid and tannic variety, and though it's not generally viewed as an aromatic cultivar, careful analysis of its aroma molecules suggests that it's very close to being just that. In particular, grapes are especially rich in benzenoids (especially benzyl alcohol, 2-phenylethanol, and 4-vinylguaiacol) and terpenes (geraniol and 8-OH linalool), which are responsible for spicy, gamey, rose-like aromas, but these latter molecules are less evident in the wines, where norisoprenoids are more frequent (Lanati and Marchi 2008).

Mantonico Bianco is mainly grown along the lower Ionian (or eastern) coast of Calabria, where in 2010 there were an estimated forty-five hectares. It is especially found around the towns of Bianco, Casignana, Locri, Monasterace, and Palazzi, the classic areas where it has always been cultivated, all in the province of Reggio Calabria. Without doubt, the *grand crus* are found around Bianco and Casignana. However, interest in Mantonico Bianco is resurgent, and it is being increasingly planted in the areas of Cirò and Lamezia as well. Though I do not have any data regarding its presence in New World countries, I have no doubts that this variety would be well suited to warmer, drier climates as it tolerates heat and drought well; more importantly, Mantonico Bianco maintains high total acidity levels in its grapes even in the face of high temperatures.

Which Wines to Choose and Why

There is increasing interest in mantonico bianco wines. Mantonico Bianco has historically been famous for its sweet wines, but encouraging attempts are being made at producing successful dry whites with it too. Especially around Cirò and Lamezia Terme it is made as a dry wine, unlike the air-dried, sweet version typical of its classic distribution area. Officially, the variety is confused with Abruzzo's very similarly named Montonico Bianco, which is in varying percentages in the DOC and IGT wines of Lamezia, Savuto, and Terre di Cosenza, but I think the authorities are really referring to a different grape variety, Montonico, not Montonico, Bianco.

Mantonico Bianco wines are characterized by strong acid and tannin contents. Studies have shown them to be especially endowed with vanillin-reactive flavans that account for the very tannic mouthfeel. The high acidities and tannins explain why the grape can make a spectrum of wines, ranging from full-bodied dry whites to sweet and sparkling ones. The sweet wines are (by far) the best, redolent with honeyed tropical-fruit aromas and flavors (dried apricot, papaya, candied ginger, figs), with a slightly more rustic, less complex character than wines made with Greco Bianco (better known as Malvasia delle Lipari). Mantonico wines also share a typical tartness at the back. At Ceratti they age the wine for roughly four months in old *barriques*, which they tell me is a return to the tradition of aging in old oak barrels; mantonico is thick and rich enough to stand up to oak very well.

WINES TO TRY: For dry mantonico, try: L'Acino** (Mantonicoz), Librandi** (Efeso; its first vintage, in 2002, was very oaky and chardonnay-like, but it has improved greatly over the years, becoming less oaky), and Statti**. For sweet mantonico, try: Ceratti***, Librandi** (Le Passule), and Lento.

Marsigliana Nera

WHERE IT'S FOUND: Calabria. NATIONAL REGISTRY CODE NUMBER: 143. COLOR: red.

This variety is also known as Marcigliana or Marcigliano, but the extent of our knowledge essentially stops here, as the grape has often been confused with other varieties such as the many *Greco Nero*s and even the Sicilian table grape of the same name. Pellerone, Edwards and Thomas (2001) analyzed seventeen Calabrian and Sicilian cultivars at thirteen SSR loci and found that Marsigliana Nera was synonymous with Castiglione, but they concluded that there had been an error made in the sampling of the former variety, either at the planting, propagation, or documentation stage. Research by Schneider, Raimondi, and De Santis (2008) implies that Marsigliana Nera is identical to Greco Nero di Sibari as well as to Magliocco Dolce, but this is unclear. Producers and growers are adamant that the two varieties are not one and the same, and the situation isn't helped by the fact the cultivar is characterized by great intravarietal variability, which is why we need more research done on many different accessions before reaching a final verdict.

Federico Scala of the organically farmed Santa Venere estate in Cirò produces a reportedly monovarietal wine called Speziale: "We selected vines from old vineyards about five years ago and planted it in an amphitheater-shaped vineyard that gives the name to the project, Anfiteatro. From what I have seen so far, [Marsigliana Nera] appears very resistant to diseases and is not very vigorous, though that may be due to our vineyard, high in the hills and on very poor nutrient-deficient soil." Ampelographically speaking, I don't think Marsigliana Nera looks anything like the *Maglioccos*: its loosely packed bunch is medium-small and conical-cylindrical, with medium-large round berries, compared to the usually bigger Magliocco Dolce bunch, which appears to me to have a conical-compound shape, with one to two small wings, and packed, medium-small, round berries. It looks even more different from Magliocco Canino, which has a loosely packed, much bigger bunch with wings dripping down the sides and oval berries. Of course, the differences I have seen may just be due to different biotypes with different phenotypic aspects, and the Marsigliana Nera bunches and the Magliocco varieties may in fact be the same. There are no official clones of Marsigliana Nera. Marsigliana Nera is typical of Calabria, though it has also been described in Sicily (or at least, a grapevine also called Marsigliana Nera, or Marcigliana was described there). In its native Calabrian home, Marsigliana Nera grows mainly along the Tyrrhenean (western) side of the region, especially near Lamezia Terme, as well as around Pianopoli, Belmonte Calabro, and San Pietro a Maida.

Which Wines to Choose and Why

DOC Lamezia is the DOC wine containing various percentages of Marsigliana Nera, but the variety can be included in DOC Scavigna blends too. IGT wines in which it can be found as part of the blend are Costa Viola, Locride, Palizzi, and Scilla. Historically, Marsigliana Nera has been used as a coloring agent for blends of sorry-looking red wines, as it is endowed with anthocyanins and a small dose goes a long way in spiking color. According to Scala, the problems with Marsigliana Nera begin in the cellar: "It's a very tannic and dark wine: we have decided to macerate it on the skins for only sixty hours, treating it almost like a *rosato*. Still, it comes out tannic and structured, a red wine in *rosato* clothing." He has also recently been experimenting with an air-dried, sweet version. I'm happy to see this dedication to a native grape from a winery that has been in the same family since the 1600s (they also breed of racehorses and Charolais cattle). I have already told Federico that my glass is ready and waiting for their new wine.

You could also ask to try the monovarietal wines that local farmers and growers make for home use (many just blend all their grapes together, often picked at different levels of ripeness). You might discover a deep red wine with bright red berry and tobacco flavors that is ideal for short-term drinking, though tannic clout is such that one could imagine Marsigliana Nera giving ageworthy wines too. However, there are too few producers of monovarietal wines to draw any clear-cut conclusions.

WINES TO TRY: Santa Venere ** (Speziale; fresh, bright yet chewy, with lovely small red-berry aromas and flavors, and slightly herbal at the back).

Marzemina Bianca

WHERE IT'S FOUND: Veneto, Lombardy. NATIONAL REGISTRY CODE NUMBER: 329. COLOR: white.

Also known as Sciampagna, Marzemina Bianca is a native of Veneto, though it is also grown in and around Pordenone, in western Friuli Venezia Giulia. It is mentioned for the first time in 1679 by Giacomo Agostinetti and subsequently by other authors such as Piero Caronetti, all of whom thought it was a high-quality variety. The modern-day importance of Marzemina Bianca as a wine grape is inversely proportional to its historical importance: being a very old variety, it has close genetic ties with a number of famous grapes. Molon (1906) believed it to be identical to Switzerland's Chasselas, but we have no modern evidence of this. Instead, in 2008 Salmaso, Dalla Valle, and Lucchin reported that Marzemina Bianca has a parent-offspring relationship with Marzemino (the latter is most likely one of Marzemina Bianca's parents), and Crespan, Calò, Giannetto, Sparacio, Storchi, and Costacurta (2008) found the same between it and Garganega. Therefore, the relationship with Garganega (see GARGANEGA entry) makes it a half sibling or grandparent of Albana, Cataratto Bianco, Dorona, Malvasia Bianca di Candia, Marzemina Bianca, Montonico Bianco, Susumaniello, and Trebbiano Toscano. Furthermore, thanks to the 2008 study by Salmaso's group we know that Raboso Veronese is the product of a natural crossing between Marzemina Bianca and Raboso Piave. Despite this, Marzemina Bianca eventually fell out of favor due to low productivity.

Marzemina Bianca has a large, pyramidal, usually winged bunch with medium-large berries and a good amount of bloom. Obviously, it cannot be confused with Marzemina Grossa or one of the many other *Marzemina*s, which are dark-berried varieties.

Today Marzemina Bianca is found around the cities of Padova, Treviso, and Vicenza in Veneto and near Brescia in Lombardy, but there are less than one hundred hectares planted to it (based on 2010 data).

Which Wines to Choose and Why

Marzemina Bianca is used in the DOC blends Colli Euganei, Colli di Conegliano, and Bagnoli, as well as in Prosecco. Small percentages are also employed in local sweet wines such as Torchiato di Fregona and Breganze's Torcolato. Monovarietal examples can be found among IGT wines such as Marca Trevigiana, Delle Venezie, and Colli Trevigiani. In the past it was also used to improve the oceans of mediocre, or at best ordinary, table wine made in the region, but I think Marzemina Bianca is capable of producing wines of much greater interest; it would be fascinating to see what would result from limiting yields and going the monovarietal route. Of course, some monovarietal examples exist, and with such good acidity levels that many use Marzemina Bianca for sparkling wine production. The delicate aromas and flavors recall buttercups, lilies, fresh herbs, lime, and green apples. It's a very nice wine that doubles as an aperitif and as a sparring partner for simply prepared fish and vegetable dishes. Due to the wine's intrinsic qualities and the interest in all things native, more producers have started bottling monovarietal versions or are thinking about it.

WINES TO TRY: Firmino Miotti*** (Sampagna) and Casa Roma**.

Marzemino

WHERE IT'S FOUND: Trentino, Veneto, Emilia-Romagna. NATIONAL REGISTRY CODE NUMBER: 144. COLOR: red.

The origin of Marzemino's name is unclear: most experts believe it derives from the town of Merzifon in Asia Minor or from Marzemin in Austria, as postulated by Odart in 1874, or from Marzèmini, a port in Sicily, but there is no definitive proof. Also known as Barzamino and Berzemino, this variety's origins are complex, only recently becoming better understood. Initially, researchers postulated that Marzemino originated in the Middle East, moving along the trade routes from Asia Minor to ancient Greece, brought there by the Euboeans from Cyprus, where it was known as Lefkas (Labra, Imazio, Grassi, Rossoni, Citterio, Sgorbati, et al. 2003). In Greece it was renamed, depending on where it was grown, as Barzavi, Marzavi, Mavro, and Vartzami (apparently, the latter name is still used on the island of Corfù). From Corfù, it was transported along the Adriatic coast to Dalmatia and finally into northeastern and central Italy. Eventually, Venetian dominance extended west and Marzemino arrived in Trentino and Lombardy (visitors to the beautiful city of Bergamo, north of Milan, will have noted statues and emblems of Saint Mark's lion all over the Città Vecchia).

However, this erudite theory has been upset by recent genetic work shedding light on the history of Lagrein, a very close relative of Marzemino. In 2006, Vouillamoz and Grando demonstrated that Marzemino and Lagrein are offspring of Teroldego and another as yet unidentified parent, perhaps a progeny of Pinot Nero. It seems therefore unlikely, given this parentage, that Marzemino could hail from the Middle East. Marzemino is also a parent of Marzemina Bianca and Refosco del Peduncolo Rosso.

In Italy, Marzemino's presence is first acknowledged in fourteenth-century documents that call it Marcenium, along with the easier to recognize Sclavum and Garganicum. Professor Enrico Peterluger of the University of Udine cites a 1409 banquet held in Cividale in honor of Pope Gregory XII at which marzemino (made near the Friuli Venezia Giulia town of Gradiscutta) was one of the wines served. This in itself tells us that Marzemino was already held in high esteem: by 1412 it was considered one of the best varieties grown in the province of Vicenza (Varanini 1988). By the sixteenth, seventeenth, and eighteenth centuries, Gallo

([1595] 1937) and Agostinetti ([1679] 1988) write that locals considered Marzemino a native variety of northeastern Italy. Mozart appears to have been quite the fan; he had his libretto writer, Lorenzo Da Ponte, pen a well-known reference to it in the opera *Don Giovanni*. Lando writes in 1553 that Marzemino was also being air-dried to produce a sweet red wine, most likely the ancestor of Passito di Refrontolo, an excellent if little-known wine today. Unfortunately, after a few cold winters at the beginning of the eighteenth century, Marzemino's fortunes began to decline, as local growers bypassed it in favor of hardier if less noble varieties such as Verdise.

By 1825, Acerbi distinguished between seven different biotypes of *Marzemino* (at least one of which was a white variety), based on ampelographic differences. Of these, research has shown the real Marzemino to be Marzemino Gentile Comune, found in Trentino and Lombardy (where it is called Berzemino; most experts consider Marzemino Gentile and Marzemino Comune to be the same), closely related to the Marzemino Bianco of Brescia (most likely a chromatic mutation of Marzemino, not to be confused with Marzemina Bianca) (Labra, Imazio, Grassi, Rossoni, Citterio, Sgorbati, et al. 2003). Marzemino is also different from Marzeminone, another variety sporadically grown near Bergamo. It is still unclear whether Balsamina, an important and well-known medieval variety long considered a synonym of Marzemino, is a distinct cultivar or not. In the minds of some experts, the high intravarietal variability of old-vine *Marzemino*s accounts for some of the different characteristics observed, but there is no conclusive proof. Certainly, the various *Balsamina*s grown in Emilia-Romagna differ morphologically from each other and can be easily distinguished from *Marzemino*s, though this might just be the result of different phenotypic expressions owing to centuries-long adaptation to different *terroirs*.

Today producers can choose from many clones, all with redeeming features. Older vineyards (for example, planted in the 1970s) are often characterized by clone SMA 14 (very vigorous and ideal for the old *pergola Trentina* training system); newer vineyards (for example, planted in the twenty-first century) often have a prevalence of less generous clones such as MIDA 172/49 that can be trained and pruned with spur cordon systems. Clone VCR 3 also allows good sugar accumulation and acceptable productivity levels. Overall, Marzemino performs best in alluvial soils and well-ventilated sites, which ensure optimal ripeness. It's susceptible to viral diseases.

In Italy, Marzemino is grown mainly in Trentino and also in Lombardy, though small plantings are likely to be found in Emilia-Romagna, Abruzzo, and Sardinia too. In Trentino, Marzemino has found an ideal home, especially in the Vallagarina in the countryside around picturesque towns such as Rovereto and Isera. Marzemino has also been planted in Australia's King Valley, New Zealand's Hawkes Bay, and California's Lodi AVA.

Which Wines to Choose and Why

In Trentino there are two recognized Marzemino *crus*: the first is on the right bank of the Adige River, a swath of land that cuts from Mori to in front of Rovereto and the hills of Isera, Nomi, and Aldeno. This is the home of marzemino di Isera DOC wine (Isera is a subzone allowed in the DOC Trentino Marzemino Superiore wines), born from grapes grown on soils of disaggregated tufa and basaltic rocks, where manganese concentrations are responsible for a specific, refined aroma in the wines. The second area is located on the opposite side of the valley, extending from Calliano to Volano, rich in calcareous clay and alluvial deposits that yield generous, richer marzeminos. It is here, near Volano, where the one true *grand cru* for Marzemino is found: the Ziresi (a term that refers to "cherry trees," which dot the countryside). Here the Adige River makes a right-angle turn, catching the sun's rays at full force, and on these well-exposed plots Marzemino achieves a degree of finesse and ripeness unattained elsewhere, thanks to the microclimate created by the interaction of water, sunlight, and soil.

In Lombardy, the DOC Garda includes a monovarietal Marzemino wine, while other DOCs (Botticcino, Cellatica, Riviera del Garda Bresciano) include the grape in blends. The Emilia-Romagna DOC Colli di Scandiano e Canossa also includes Marzemino in its blend. According to Filippo Scienza of the excellent Vallarom estate, Marzemino is a very reductive variety, so it's important to expose it to oxygen during the winemaking process, with frequent rack and returns in order to avoid the development of off odors. A good wine will recall sour red berries, violets, and delicate fresh herbs, with high acids, a midweight body, and a wild, herbal quality, finishing with a characteristic slightly bitter touch. Some producers have taken to air-drying in order to obtain a softer wine with sweeter aromas and flavors.

WINES TO TRY: Riccardo Battistotti***, Conti Bossi Fredrigotti***, Bruno Grigoletti***, Eugenio Rosi*** (Poiema, made from lightly air-dried grapes, is excellent, if in a slightly atypical style), De Tarczal**, Enrico Spagnolli**, Longariva**, Vallarom**, Vallis Agri** (Vigna Fornas), Vilàr**, Letrari*, Cantina d'Isera*, Cantina di Nomi*, Gaierhof*, Lavis and Val di Cembra*, and Armando Simoncelli* (a very good expression from basaltic-tufa soils).

Mayolet

WHERE IT'S FOUND: Valle d'Aosta. NATIONAL REGISTRY CODE NUMBER: 306. COLOR: red.

I love the Valle d'Aosta, and I love Mayolet, truly a great native grape variety. By that I mean it delivers everything you'd expect from a native cultivar: unique and pretty aromas and flavors that better-known varieties such as Syrah or Merlot do not (though they have other virtues), as well as countless headaches in the vineyard and the cellar, which of course explains why Mayolet faces trouble while the two noble internationals do not.

Mayolet's name may stem either from *mayola*, meaning "young vine," or from the Mayolet family surname, still common in much of Valle d'Aosta. The earliest mention of Mayolet is in the *Cahiers de la cave* of the Passerin d'Entrèves in 1787 and probably not, as reported elsewhere, the 1822 presumed reference by Arguettaz, the curate of Valpelline. The Passerin wrote of the 1783–87 vintages, the latter an apparently very good year for Mayolet, as this was the one he deemed suitable "to age." Not surprisingly, the best and most accurate historical description of Mayolet is Gatta's in 1838, which said the variety was especially abundant in vineyards of Aymavilles, Sarre, and especially Saint-Pierre. Bich (1896) also wrote that Mayolet was one of the region's oldest known cultivars. It constituted at the time an important part of the high-quality Torrette wine, made locally from partially dehydrated grapes. Berget (1904) wrote that there were more than 100 hectares planted to Mayolet between Charvensod and Saint-Pierre, a remarkable amount given that today there are only 480 hectares devoted to grapevines in the whole of the Valle d'Aosta. Recent DNA analysis has shown Mayolet to be, along with Petit Rouge, one of the parents of Rouge du Pays or Rouge du Valais, considered a Swiss native grape. Mayolet also shares a parent-progeny relationship with Prié and Vuillermin, as determined by Vouillamoz, Maigre, and Meredith (2003).

Unfortunately Mayolet quickly fell out of favor with growers after an initial moment of excitement. Eleonora Charrère of the prestigious Les Cretes estate muses, "It's a grape that produces a remarkably refined, lovely wine, but in the vineyard it's a nightmare; the bunch is too compact, making it a botrytis smorgasbord, and the skin's very thin." Michel Vallée, the extraordinarily talented force behind the I Feudo di San Maurizio estate, adds, "Just imagine that people who had planted Mayolet only six or so years ago are already ripping it out in order to replant other local, easier to work with cultivars." A real shame, I'd like to add. Today Mayolet grows on both sides of the Dora Baltea River, from Saint-Vincent to Avise (but especially from Nus to Arvier), up to eight hundred meters above sea level. There are currently more than ten hectares planted to Mayolet.

Which Wines to Choose and Why

There are numerous excellent DOC Valle d'Aosta Mayolet wines made, plus the variety is a bit player in the Torrette blend (which is at least 70 percent Petit Rouge, so differently from centuries ago, there's usually little Mayolet included in modern versions). Monovarietal Mayolet wine is exceptional and completely different from the fuller-bodied Torrette: light to medium bodied, it has extremely refined aromas of black currant and mountain flowers, with a lovely hint of cinnamon and white pepper. I am firmly convinced that everyone who tries a well-made Mayolet wine for the first time will fall easy prey to its many very aromatic charms. Unfortunately, due to the viticultural difficulties it presents, Mayolet risks disappearing again, having already once come back from the dead. Fortunately, there are a few quality-minded, passionate, and dedicated producers who will likely not allow a remake of that horror movie.

WINES TO TRY: Feudo di San Maurizio*** (perfumed and graceful, simply irresistible), Cave des Onzes Communes** (a fantastic source of inexpensive, well-made wines in general, but they are apparently giving up on the variety), Di Barrò** (Vigne de la Toule; also good, but less perfumed), Cooperativa de Enfer* (Vin des Seigneurs), and IAR*.

Minutolo

WHERE IT'S FOUND: Puglia. NATIONAL REGISTRY CODE NUMBER: 455. COLOR: white.

Minutolo is an aromatic white variety grown in Puglia since 1200, where it was believed to be an aromatic Fiano subvariety. For this reason, they called it Fiano Aromatico, Fiano Minutolo, Moscatellina, or Fianello (Fonseca, who coined the latter name in 1892, is believed to be the first to have described the variety). Lino Carparelli had heard of the variety and its fine wine potential and had always wanted to make wine with it. A longtime director of the Cantina Sociale Locorotondo and then head winemaker of the Torrevento estate, he knows the vineyards and varieties of his native region like few others. In 2000, he set out with local old-timers and farmers to search for remaining, forgotten vines of Minutolo and then spurred researchers to better characterize an aromatic variety that he realized could not be a Fiano (which is a nonaromatic variety). In 2001, Calò, Costacurta, Crespan, Milani, Aggio, Carraro, and Di Stefano established (via ampelographic, isoenzymatic, and DNA analysis) that Fiano and this aromatic variety were distinct. In 2006, the name Fiano Minutolo was agreed upon officially, as Minutola was a synonym of Fiano used in the 1800s. However, in 2009 an official name change was proposed, from Fiano Minutolo to either Minutolo or Moscato Minutolo di Puglia (previous work by Costacurta had shown a close family relationship between Fiano Minutolo, Moscato di Alessandria, and Moscato Bianco). Ultimately, Minutolo was chosen as the new and official name of the variety.

Research performed at the Institute Basile Caramia in Puglia has allowed the development of two clones, CRSA-Regione Puglia B7 and B11. The first has loosely packed bunches and is not very productive, but the wine is reportedly of better quality. Nowadays Minutolo is found mainly in the Valle d'Itria in the province of Bari. The success of this variety has been such that plantings are on the increase all over the region: Minutolo is now grown in the provinces of Brindisi and Taranto too.

Which Wines to Choose and Why

There are monovarietal IGT Minutolo wines made, and Minutolo can also be included in the DOC blends Locorotondo and Martina Franca, in which it is used to spice up more neutral white wines. Minutolo wines are more reminiscent of those made with Moscato Bianco, rather than Moscato di Alessandria, as they are fresh and light bodied like the former, with white flower, ginger, and yellow fruit aromas and flavors. They never have the oily richness or body of wines made with Moscato di Alessandria. Not knowing this puts wine lovers at risk of drinking just about anything poured that's said to be Minutolo, a currently hot commodity. Honestly, you may want to exercise caution: too many wildly different wines sport the name Minutolo on the label (some of which bear no resemblance to what Minutolo wine should taste like), and said differences are too marked for my taste. True, wines may differ on the basis of clones used. Apparently the B7 clone gives wines that have intensely ripe apricot and peach aromas, while clone B11 wines have stronger herbal accents and acidity. For these reasons, the first may be used to produce air-dried wines, while the second may have a future in sparkling wine production, should any producer be so inclined. Any Minutolo wine currently made is dry. It makes an excellent aperitif but matches well with shellfish, spicy fish dishes, and simple pastas.

WINES TO TRY: I Pastini-Lino Carparelli*** (Rampone), Tenuta Chiaramonte* (Kimìa; curiously, the 2012 was labeled only Fiano, which is, with all due respect, unhelpful and misleading), and Candido* (Tenuta Marino). Carparelli has set up his own estate where he now makes what are, in my view, Puglia's best white wines.

Molinara

WHERE IT'S FOUND: Veneto. NATIONAL REGISTRY CODE NUMBER: 148. COLOR: red.

Though well described and much appreciated by Pollini in 1824 and Di Rovasenda in 1877, today Molinara risks being the forgotten variety in Valpolicella and Amarone, where it has always been grown and used to make the world-famous wines named for those regions.

Molinara belongs to a high-yielding group of formerly widespread varieties that have practically all disappeared in the Veneto-Adige geographical area, producing light-colored wines greatly appreciated by consumers especially north of the Alps. Alas, modern-day tastes veered sharply away from that style of wine in the last two decades of the twentieth century, and so Molinara, but for a few tradition-respectful and passionate producers, has almost joined its relatives on the extinct list.

Molinara is a very pretty grape: its name derives from *mulinara* or *mulino* (mill), where bread was once made by milling flour; since Molinara's berries are covered in an especially thick, powdery white bloom, they look dusted with flour. The grape is also called Rossanella and Rossara in the Lake Garda zone (the latter is an erroneous synonym, since there is a true Rossara variety grown in Trentino) or Brepon (especially in Valpantena) and Uva Salà (referring to the obvious saline quality of its wines). The Serego Alighieri estate, owned by Count Pieralvise Serego Alighieri, direct descendant of Dante Alighieri, owns a biotype of Molinara (named biotype Serego Alighieri) that is characterized by a smaller and more compact bunch. A monovarietal wine made with it is very interesting and they used to sell it directly at the estate. It's a slightly richer, spicier, high-quality molinara, but paradoxically even lighter in color than usual (hence called Molinara Ciara, in the local dialect). The biotype has been studied by Attilio Scienza of the University of Milan, who characterized it ampelologically; apparently it's more sensitive to botrytis than regular Molinara.

There are different clones of Molinara available (R 2, ISV-CV 87, ISV-CV 100, ISV-CV 3, VCR 12), but they do not seem to give high-quality results. In general, Molinara has medium-sized bunches and berries, the former slightly pyramidal and the latter round-oval. It is very sensitive to excessively humid conditions and to potassium deficiency, while it is resistant to most diseases except grey rot. It needs lots of space to grow (another factor limiting its interest for farmers). Today it is grown mainly in the province of Verona (the home of Valpolicella, Amarone, and Bardolino in Veneto), but plantings are on the decline (in 2010, less than thirteen hundred hectares were planted to Molinara).

Which Wines to Choose and Why

Molinara is mainly used in blends such as Valpolicella, Amarone, and Bardolino, the latter located close to Lake Garda (Italy's biggest lake, which straddles the Lombardy-Veneto border). All these wines are blends of Corvina, Corvinone, Rondinella, and Molinara, with possible smaller additions of Oseleta, Croatina, and/or even Cabernet Sauvignon and Merlot. However, Molinara is being increasingly phased out in Valpolicella and especially Amarone wines, for its rosy, light color wine strikes fear in the hearts of producers looking to make the biggest, blackest wines possible. Nowadays it plays a much more important role in Bardolino, where it can make up even 40 percent of the blend, providing Bardolino wines with lovely freshness, lightness, and a strong saline note.

Rare Molinara monovarietal IGT wines can be found, but monovarietals are rare: the wine is always pink in hue, redolent in aromas and flavors of small red berries, citrus, and delicate herbs and spices; it also has mouth-watering acidity. In fact, a wine made with Molinara alone is very similar to a *rosato*, so you understand why Amarone producers, especially, worry about diluting their superconcentrated (and expensive) juice by including Molinara. Not everybody is so fearful: Sandro Boscaini of the world-famous Masi estate adamantly defends Molinara's virtue: "Are we looking to turn Amarone into a liqueur?" he asks rhetorically. "If so, fine: but if we want people to keep drinking our wines, then I think Molinara is a very important part of Amarone's makeup." Diego Bertoni, winemaker of Cantine Buglioni (another high-quality estate in the heart of the Valpolicella production zone), signed an agreement with the University of Verona's Department of Science, Technologies and Markets of Vine and Wine to collaborate on studying and promoting Molinara's exact winemaking potential. He believes that "we tried a *rosato* in the past and really liked it; it appeals to all those looking for something younger and fresher." Owner Mariano Buglioni also confirms that "our primary objective is to create a safety net for Molinara; I have come to understand that as a wine producer, I am not just a businessman, but one who has to also act as a defender of traditions and local history. Planting a vineyard is not just about harvesting grapes and selling a wine; it is also about maintaining and propagating an area's specific culture and way of life; and here in Valpolicella, Molinara is very much a part of that." Attilio Pagli sums it up very well: "Listen, Molinara is essential in this part of Italy, where all the red wines are now running the risk of being very structured and in need of time in the cellar."

I can't say I disagree with any of them; for instance, Amarone wines are now tipping the scales at 17 percent alcohol and often have textures you need a knife to slice through. So I don't think that recent vintages of Amarone and Valpolicella (especially) have been better than those made decades ago, with more Molinara in the blend. If anything, all those wines had better balance and easy-drinking charm. Unfortunately, since Amarone sells like hotcakes, producers have either not paid much attention to Valpolicella (of which there are an alarming number of horrific examples) or have tried to beef it up, turning it into a baby Amarone (especially the *ripasso* versions), and that of course means yanking away even more Molinara. The end result is that Valpolicella sales are dropping precipitously, as it is no longer the wine it is supposed to be and that people ask for. Therein lies a small measure of revenge for Molinara.

Perhaps the most famous Molinara wine is by Giuseppe Quintarelli, who sadly passed away recently and whose wines are cult items. The greatness of Quintarelli is exemplified by the fact that his rendition was always "normal": pale in color, light and refreshing, with a nice saline edge. In other words, the master did not churn out a massive, caricatured, and completely unrealistic molinara just because it was a Quintarelli wine. Interestingly, the Amarone Vajo Armaron from the Serego Alighieri estate from the 1970s and early 1980s contained as much as 30 percent Molinara and was always characterized by a lighter mouthfeel and wonderful drinkability (it was also aged partly in cherrywood, adding a sweet, soft quality). Many modern-day wine critics who aren't aware of these two facts complain that the Serego Alighieri wines are less concentrated than other Amarone wines tasted alongside, which they always invariably score higher. It's not that one wine is better than the other: rather, they are different, and should be so, given the different varietal makeup of each. There's more than one lesson to learn there.

WINES TO TRY: Quintarelli***, Buglioni** (Il Vigliacco, lightly sparkling), Carlo Boscaini**, La Dama * (L'Aura Rosato), Monte Saline* (also a sparkler), and Secondo Marco* (owned by Marco Speri and where the world-famous Attilio Pagli consults; the wine, Solo Tu, was sold for the first time in late 2012, a very light, high-acid *rosato*-like wine).

Monica

WHERE IT'S FOUND: Sardinia. NATIONAL REGISTRY CODE NUMBER: 149. COLOR: red.

Once called Monaca, Monica's other synonyms include Niedda Mora and Mora di Spagna; the latter names attest to a possible Spanish origin. Cettolini and Mameli (1933) hypothesized that Monica was identical to Spain's Morillo variety, but this is not so. Genetic characterization at twelve SSR loci has demonstrated a close affinity with Nieddu Mannu, with which Monica shares one allele in each of the twelve loci, and with another little-known variety called Carenisca, typical of the Sulcis area of Sardinia. I have seen Carenisca during my wine travels (there's not much of it), but it looks like Monica to me: most likely, the former is a biotype of the latter.

The fact is that there are multiple varieties named *Monica* growing on the island, but most are completely unrelated. For years, nurseries selected *Monica* grapevines growing in the southern reaches of Sardinia, thinking that any *Monica* was the same as all the other *Monicas*, but we now know this not to be the case. A study by De Mattia, Imazio, Grassi, Lovicu, Tardaguila, Failla, et al. (2007) described how many of the differently named *Monicas* in Sardinia (where the term "Monica" is usually followed by a name indicating the cultivation area, or the place of supposed origin, or the color) had identical SSR profiles, implying they were all the same variety. The only *Monica* that was truly distinct in the group of accessions studied was the *Monica* from the Sorgono area, which was found to be ampelographically and genetically identical to the Nieddu Mannu accession grown in the Padria area. Some have therefore taken this to mean that Monica and Nieddu Mannu are identical, which besides constituting a considerable leap of faith (given the low number of accessions in the study), is also fraught with danger of broadcasting wrong information. Seeing that there are almost too many *Monicas* to count on the island, it is more than likely that many will prove genetically distinct from the others. As was precisely shown by a more recent study. When Lovicu, Farci, Sedda, Labra, De Mattia, Grassi, Bacchetta, and Orrù (2010) studied Sardinian grapevine biodiversity, they collected seven dark-berried *Monicas* (Monica Nera), two white-berried *Monicas* (Monica Bianca), and one that had lighter colored, almost pink berries (Monica Rosa). Their work showed that the white-berried and dark-berried *Monicas* are not mutations but distinct cultivars. The Monica Bianca of the Campidano area was synonymous with another rare island white grape called Pansale (not Pascale, which is a red grape) and distinct from the Monica Bianca growing in the Marmilla area; the "Monica" from the Sarcidano countryside was identical to Manzesu, a little-studied local grape but distinct from all the other *Monica* accessions, so one cannot conclude that Manzesu is a synonym of all *Monica*s, but rather a synonym of that one specific *Monica* variety. Another *Monica*, from the Mandrolisai part of Sardinia, was found to be synonymous with Nieddu Mannu, Medrulinu (another very rare local grape), and Falso Manzesu (no surprise: this being Italy, it was almost certain that there would be yet another apparently distinct but similarly named Manzesu grape).

The grape that is usually regarded to be the "real" Monica and that has been described in the National Registry is usually characterized by large leaves, loosely packed, large bunches (average weight 450 grams) of various shapes (conical, pyramidal, and even cylindrical) and medium-sized, round, dark blue-black berries. I point out that the large and almost always loosely-packed bunch is highly typical of all the *Monica*s, and has likely contributed to more than one ampelographic misidentification throughout the centuries. Though there are likely also many *Monica* biotypes (besides many homonyms), there is only one official clone of Monica, developed by Consorzio Interprovinciale per la Frutticoltura di Cagliari in 1993, though the University of Sassari has selected an abundance of virus-free plant material from which to hopefully develop new clones. Monica grows erect, so it's not hard on the back, hence farmers love it; it's also very vigorous and a dependable, abundant producer, ripening by mid-September. The quality of its wine notwithstanding, now you know why it's the third most-planted variety on Sardinia.

Which Wines to Choose and Why

Monica is one of the most abundant varieties on Sardinia, with almost three thousand hectares planted (based on 2009 data). The Pala estate has been growing it since the mid-1850s. It's used as a blending grape along with Cannonao and both *Bovale* types in DOC Mandrolisai wines, or it's used to produce the DOC wines Monica di Sardegna and Monica di Cagliari, where it can be 100 percent pure. The former wine can be produced everywhere on the island, the latter only in the townships of Cagliari and Oristano, in different styles: dry, fortified dry, and fortified *riserva*. Monica, a gently tannic wine, is meant to be drunk young, a simple, easy-drinking pleasure. It offers delicate red-berry aromas and flavors complicated by fresh herbs and hints of tar and tobacco: it's an excellent everyday table wine, much like a fresh young Chianti, but needs to be the product of low yields; otherwise the wine is neutral and uninteresting. That it's a wine with some potential is shown by the fact that a Cannonao specialist such as Alberto Loi grows it in many satellite estates of the main one in Cardedu.

WINES TO TRY: Contini***, Dettori *** (Chimbanta & Dettori), Argiolas** (Perdera), Cantina Santadi** (Antigua), Ferruccio Deiana** (Karel), Josto Puddu** (Torremora), and Cantina Trexenta* (Bingias).

Montepulciano

WHERE IT'S FOUND: Abruzzo, Marche, Molise, Lazio, Tuscany, Puglia, Umbria. **NATIONAL REGISTRY CODE NUMBER:** 150. **COLOR:** red.

If I had a hundred dollars for every time in the last thirty years I've had to explain that Montepulciano is a grape while Vino Nobile di Montepulciano a wine made with Sangiovese, not Montepulciano, I really would be a wealthy man. This confusion is a strange twist of fate for a cultivar, Montepulciano, that is linked to its territory in Abruzzo like few others in Italy. Montepulciano is a beloved grape variety in Italy, and its wines run the gamut from the cheap and cheerful (and at times horrid) to the extremely fleshy and fruity and hopelessly overoaked and undrinkable. So though generally a workhorse grape, Montepulciano has thoroughbred potential: the problem is harnessing that potential and turning it into great wine.

The first historical mention of Montepulciano in Abruzzo is in the travel diary of Michele Torcia, archivist of King Ferdinand IV, who saw the vines and tasted the wine while traveling around Sulmona in 1792. How Montepulciano arrived in Abruzzo has long been a matter of conjecture: many believe it arrived from Tuscany (though there is no early record of a Montepulciano grapevine grown in that region) with the Medici family, who created the Baronia di Carapelle and the Marchesato di Capestrana in Abruzzo between 1549 and 1743. What is certain is that Montepulciano, wherever it originated from, quickly spread to other regions of central and even southern Italy. Unfortunately, Montepulciano has always been confused with Sangiovese: as recently as the beginning of the twentieth century, all of Italy's most important ampelographers failed to distinguish between the two varieties. Which is strange, because Michele Torcia (1793) wrote of the grape as clearly different from Sangiovese, describing its presence in Abruzzo more than two centuries ago; furthermore, Serafini in 1853 also separated an earlier ripening Montepulciano Primaticcio from a Montepulciano Cordisco, the latter being the true Montepulciano. Part of the difficulty lies in the ancient habit of renaming grapes for the name of the town or region they came from. For this reason some experts believe that Prugnolo Gentile, typical of the town of Montepulciano and the surrounding area in Tuscany, upon arriving in Abruzzo was renamed Montepulciano. Nevertheless, current thinking is that the variety originated in the Val Peligna area of Abruzzo and that the Mazzara (or Mezzara) and the Tabassi families were the first to replant Montepulciano vines in nearby areas such as Torre dei Passeri, Tocco de Casauria, and Musellaro (Cercone 2000). In fact, Bruni wrote in 1962 that a common synonym of Montepulciano was Torre dei Passeri, a fact he had already noted in 1955 while taking part in a national ampelographic commission.

Federico Staderini, a well-known Tuscan winemaker, points out that Montepulciano is a difficult variety in that, like many other native grapes, its berries experience asynchronous maturation: "Right in the same bunch you see grapes of different hues; if you add to that, that the must has a tendency to pick up off odors, it's no picnic." Fausto Albanesi of the excellent Torre dei Beati estate mentions that for such a hearty, big wine, the variety itself isn't that disease resistant: "We find our Pecorino vines can stand up to disease much better than Montepulciano, at least in our experience." Concezio Marulli of the Zaccagnini estate loves the variety's color and flexibility, both in the vineyard and the cellar. The color is due to Montepulciano's rich endowment of anthocyanins, a wealth that allows Abruzzo producers to make their *rosato* wines (called Cerasuolo) with little or no maceration of the skins.

Water stress is also a concern with Montepulciano (though not as much as with Sangiovese), and so deleafing has to be done cautiously. Many cheap, neutral, and uninteresting wines are made using the high-yielding tendon trellising system (*tenda* means tent; a *tendone* is a big tent), since the raised canopy of leaves covers the grapes hanging below. You'd never expect grapes to ripen properly or fully with such a high-yielding production system, yet Italy's best Montepulciano wine, actually one of Italy's ten or twelve best reds, is made by Valentini with nothing but big tents in sight. Clearly, the canopy has to be thinned somewhat to allow a certain amount of sunlight through. Still, so much for theory in wine. Cristiana Tiberio of the up-and-coming high-quality Tiberio estate, helps put this into perspective: "Personally, I view climate as the most important factor for quality Montepulciano production: being a late-ripening variety, it needs a long growing season, so as to ripen slowly and fully; otherwise, the pips don't ripen properly and wines will be bitter. Plus it's very susceptible to oidium, which is more likely to hit in warmer climates."

A sure sign of Montepulciano's importance is the almost endless number of clones available, among which are different series: AP-MP (1 and 3), VCR series (7, 100, 453 through 456, 462, 496, 498), UBA-RA MP (11 through 14), Ampelos-TEA (5 and 21), and UNIMI-ASSAM

MTP VV (301, 312, 321). Some clones have given much better results than others, but not surprisingly, opinions are not uniform. For example, R7 was once the most-planted clone, but some producers, such as Fausto Albanesi, are no longer using it, finding the wines too marked by pyrazine notes when the grapes are not perfectly ripe. On the other hand, Cristiana Tiberio believes the R7 to be the best possible compromise, because the R100, originally created as the ultimate high-quality clone, is too subject to *millerandage*, hence its productivity is too low and the risk of green flavors too high, given all the small, unripe green berries, even with careful selection of berries and bunches. The VCR 456 is nicknamed the Casauria clone because it apparently performs well in the Casauriense area of Abruzzo. A Montepulciano biotype specific to the northeastern corner of Lazio is called Violone.

Montepulciano bears an uncanny resemblance to another grape, Pugnitello. In fact, for the longest time, it was believed that the two were one and the same; today the prevailing opinion holds that the two are not even biotypes but altogether different varieties. Maurizo Castelli still believes the two varieties are closely related. "They certainly look very similar, so it's easy to get fooled," he says. "Every time I visit an estate where I consult that has planted Pugnitello, I hear the vineyard workers talking among themselves saying that the two are identical." "You'd ask for one and the nurseries would just send you the other," adds winemaker Laura Zuddas of the Matura group, "so many people are growing both side by side, but don't know it. The two grapes are not the same however: only those who don't know them that well believe that. And Pugnitello tends to be less reductive during vinification than Montepulciano: the latter requires a lot more work, and there are times when you think all you do is rack and return."

Montepulciano's popularity is persistently high. In the first decade of the twenty-first century, plantings increased by another 4 percent, firmly entrenching the grape as Italy's fourth most-planted variety. It has been planted elsewhere in the world too. California has roughly eighty hectares planted in, for example, Lodi, Paso Robles, and Temecula Valley, but it grows in North Carolina and Texas too. Not surprisingly, it's also found in Valle de Guadalupe in Mexico's Baja California. Australia's Adelaide Hills and New Zealand also grow Montepulciano.

Which Wines to Choose and Why

Montepulciano is so associated with Abruzzo (where it represents over 50 percent of the region's surface under vine) that the DOC Montepulciano d'Abruzzo was the first all-region DOC of Italy, later fine-tuned by allowing subdenominations such as Colline Teramane, now a DOCG, and the DOC Controguerra. Particularly interesting are wines from Val Peligna, where mountain viticulture allows for more vibrant wines. The variety also likes clay, and this is why the Colline Teramane, a district heavily laden with clay, is a rare DOCG that actually makes sense (though, allow me, most of the wines don't). Fausto Albanesi also believes that the vineyards with west–northwest exposure, in the Passo Cordone area near Loreto Aprutino at roughly three hundred meters above sea level, are good quality.

Montepulciano grows well all along the Adriatic coast, unbothered by the marine environment (what a difference from Sangiovese!), and there are large areas devoted to its cultivation in Molise, Marche, and Puglia, and even in more inland regions such as Tuscany, Umbria, and Lazio. In fact, it is the most important red variety of the Marche, used to make DOC Rosso Conero and DOCG Conero near Ancona and DOC Offida Rosso and Rosso Piceno near Ascoli Piceno. It is also included in many wine blends, such as Molise's Biferno Rosso, Puglia's Castel del Monte, and Lazio's Castelli Romani Rosso. In Tuscany, though Montepulciano is not as clearly associated with any one production area, there is probably more present than currently believed.

As Montepulciano is a real jack-of-all-trades, it can be used to make sparkling, dry, and sweet (air-dried) red wines, as well as outstanding *rosato*. The latter can be labeled either Rosato or Cerasuolo d'Abruzzo: the latter are bigger, more tannic and acid, and more complex, with remarkable ageworthiness—a good five- or six-year Cerasuolo is not uncommon. Issued from longer macerations on the skins, these are the best *rosato* wines of Italy, along with those of the Salento in Puglia and the Chiarettos of the Garda in northern Italy. But the Cerasuolo wines are usually more mineral, deep, and complex and fleshier than most other *rosati*, and not just Italy's. Furthermore, they are rarely marked by residual sugar as many blush or rosé wines often are.

In the dry red wine version, Montepulciano d'Abruzzo, can be either light and easygoing or massive and rich, loaded with ripe red-cherry fruit and more delicate herb nuances, with very soft, thick tannins. My own impression is that Montepulciano rarely delivers, even in the most important and expensive bottlings, wines of mind-blowing complexity—save for a few examples—and rarely improves much after ten years in the bottle. Also, far too many of the top-of-the-line Montepulciano wines are over-oaked. Though in theory, longer maceration times and high-quality oak should bless us with Montepulciano wines of great breeding, structure, and complexity, this seems rarely the case. Off odors are always a possibility with Montepulciano and so *délestage* and pumping over, or any technique that helps maximize air contact with the wine and the lees, is very helpful, though too much early racking may cause the release of harsher tannins.

There are an impressive number of New Zealand wineries churning out noteworthy Montepulciano wines from grapes grown in Nelson (Blackenbrook Vineyard makes a powerful rendition), Marlborough (Framingham makes a good one), and Waiheke Island (for example, Obsidian's excellent Weeping Sands bottling). Given Montepulciano's renowned difficulty in ripening fully and properly, cool climate New Zealand is an interesting if potentially difficult place in which to make montepulciano: but if Syrah and Cabernet Sauvignon can be successful in the country's warmer zones, so can Montepulciano.

In Australia, notable Montepulciano wines are being made by Banrock Station, Bassham, Brown Brothers (Cellar Door Release), By Jingo Wines, Cirami Estate, First Drop (Minchia), Galvanized Wine Group, Kimbolton (Special Release Bard's Block Langhorne Vineyard), Mr. Riggs Wine Company, Oak Works, Springton Hills (a cabernet-grenache-montepulciano blend), Staffordshire Lane, and Whistling Kite. The warm and dry Riverland area seems to be very well suited to this grape. In the United States, Duchman Family Winery in Texas or Riffaldini Winery in North Carolina will ward off any "same as usual" wine blues you might be having. Another "I can't believe they're making it there," 100 percent Montepulciano wine worth getting to know, and not just for its novelty factor, is by Witch Creek, which is made in San Diego using Mexican fruit. Seven Artisans in Suisun Valley is another good example, while Mahoney Vineyards in Carneros is making a Montepulciano blend. I've also had an excellent Montepulciano from the cask in New Mexico (Luna Rossa Winery), one of the two best New Mexican wines I have had made from an Italian variety. Also, Cougar Vineyards in California makes a lovely dry Blush. Pardon me, I meant *rosato* or *Cerasuolo!*

WINES TO TRY: Valentini*** (the best of all, extremely ageworthy), Marina Cvetic*** (S. Martino Rosso, rare in that everyone seems to like it), Torre dei Beati*** (Cocciapazza especially, but Mazzamurello is great too), Cataldi Madonna*** (Toni especially, but Malandrino is a good example of a lighter-styled montepulciano), Emidio Pepe* (give it plenty of air by decanting at least three hours ahead), Italo Pietrantonj** (Arboreo and Cerano), Tiberio**, Zaccagnini** (San Clemente; a thicker, richer style that has recently seemed tough and bitter), Fratelli Barba*, Masciarelli* (Villa Gemma, slightly overoaked; I prefer the Marina

Cvetic, a line of wines in the Masciarelli estate portfolio), Nicodemi* (Notàri; I find the top of the line Neromoro too oaky), Praesidium* (especially the Riserva), Barone Cornacchia*, Filomusi Guelfi*, Camillo Montor (Fonte Cupa)*, Orlandi Contucci Ponno/Colle Funaro*. For Cerasuolo d'Abruzzo, try: Valentini***, Tiberio***, Cataldi Madonna** (Piè delle Vigne, a *rosato*), Emidio Pepe**, Praesidium**, and Pasetti*. With few exceptions, beware the many award-winning Montepulciano wines (in Italian wine guides), the names of which you don't see here; they are disappointing at best.

Montonico Bianco

WHERE IT'S FOUND: Abruzzo, Marche, Puglia. NATIONAL REGISTRY CODE NUMBER: 151. COLOR: white.

This historically important variety is saddled with a confusing name, as there are many different *Mantonico*s (with an *a* as the second letter instead of an *o*) and other *Montonico*s as well. Montonico Bianco has always been grown in central Italy (Abruzzo, Marche, Emilia-Romagna), where it is also known as Chiapparone, Chiapparù, Ciapparuto, Fermana Bianca, Firman, Rappenollo, and Uva Regno. It is apparently rarer in southern Italy, but grows there too. In Puglia it is known as Uva della Scala and Pagadebiti (an unfortunate and incorrect synonym, since Pagadebit is a different variety typical of Emilia-Romagna and because all over Italy there are legions of generously yielding grapes that have been so named throughout the centuries). Montonico Bianco apparently also grows in Calabria where it's usually referred to either as Greco Bianco del Pollino or (outside the Pollino area) as Mantonico Bianco Italico. This has proven a mess, because most people tend to use the words *montonico* and *mantonico* almost interchangeably. So you'll read often of Montonico grapes and wines from Calabria, but what is practically always meant is Mantonico Bianco, a similarly named but unrelated variety native to Calabria. In this respect, Montonico Bianco is also not to be confused with Montonico di Rogliano, which Schneider, Raimondi and De Santis (2008d) have identified in Guardavalle. Most important, however, is that Montonico Bianco has a parent-offspring relationship with Garganega, as shown by Crespan, Calò, Giannetto, Sparacio, Storchi, and Costacurta (2008). This means that Montonico Bianco is either the sibling or the grandparent of the other eight varieties with which Garganega has parent-offspring relations (Albana, Cataratto Bianco, Dorona, Malvasia Bianca di Candia, Marzemina Bianca, Mostosa, Susumaniello, and Trebbiano Toscano).

Montonico Bianco has always been associated mainly with Abruzzo, where it was well described by Acerbi in 1825, though some documents attest to its being diffusely cultivated in the early seventeenth century. Unfortunately, Montonico Bianco almost wholly succumbed to phylloxera, with very few old vines saved from extinction. Marchi and Lanati (2008) analyzed samples of grapes (grown in Calabria) from the 2007 vintage and found significant terpene concentrations of geraniol and linalool, but the grapes needed to be at full, optimal ripeness for interesting wines to be made. This is because this highly productive variety is characterized by extremely large bunches (on average 450 grams, but 650-gram bunches are frequent, 1-kilogram not uncommon), and getting all those medium-sized berries to ripen properly isn't easy. There exists one clone (I-UBA-RA MT32 UBA) of reportedly good winemaking potential. However, La Quercia, the best producer of monovarietal Montonico (and they deserve great credit for believing in the variety: the estate has planted a whole vineyard to the cultivar), has relied thus far on old vines obtained via massal selections.

Montonico Bianco grows mainly around Bisenti near Teramo (Montonico di Bisenti and Poggio delle Rose of Abruzzo), in Foggia, in Bari (Puglia), and in the southeastern part of Calabria. In these areas it has always been appreciated as a table grape too.

Which Wines to Choose and Why

Montonico Bianco yields a high-acid fresh, floral white wine, though monovarietal versions are rare because it usually just gets blended into other wines. Better examples I have tried are also delicately spicy and fruity, with hints of acacia flowers, anise seed, and fresh herbs, with a slightly tannic, astringent mouthfeel and always plenty of refreshing acidity. It is fair to say this wine is not the last word in palate presence or textural richness, though I admire its fragrance and easy-drinking charm. In my opinion at least, it really tastes nothing like wines made with Mantonico Bianco, which are richer, more structured and tannic (Mantonico Bianco strikes me as a rare tannic white grape, while Montonico Bianco does not).

Apparently, Cantina Frentana used to make a Montonico Bianco wine in its Costa del Mulino lineup, but to the best of my knowledge no longer produces it (it now makes a Cococciola wine from the native cultivar of that name). Though Robinson, Harding, and Vouillamoz (2012) report in the Montonico Bianco entry that Librandi's well-known Efeso bottling is made with Montonico Bianco, they also write in the Mantonico Bianco entry that the same wine is made with Mantonico Bianco; clearly, the wine is either made with one variety or the other. I have always known Efeso to be made with Mantonico Bianco (not the Montonico Bianco typical of Abruzzo), a logical scenario given the wealth of Mantonico Bianco in Calabria. And they confirm this at Librandi.

WINES TO TRY: La Quercia** (Santapupa) and Cantine Torri* (both monovarietal wines).

Montù

WHERE IT'S FOUND: Emilia-Romagna. NATIONAL REGISTRY CODE NUMBER: 152. COLOR: white.

Also known as Montuni, Montù has always grown on the plains of Emilia-Romagna, where it was also called Bianchino or Bianchetto, because wines made from it had a very pale hue. Montoncello is another but rarer synonym used in centuries past, when it was also believed, erroneously, to be identical to Montonico Bianco. Cavazza wrote in 1904 that the Marchese Bevilacqua believed the variety's name to derive from *molt' ù* in the local dialect, meaning "plenty of grapes." Cavazza himself described a Montenego variety identical to today's Montù, which might also have been identical to the Montonego Bianco variety described by Acerbi (1825).

Montù is recognizable by its long, cylindrical, compact medium-sized bunches and medium-small round, yellow-green berries covered in bloom and brown dots. It is disease resistant overall (especially to oidium and less so to botrytis bunch rot) and grows easily, ripening in early October. It seems to grow best in clay-calcareous soils. There is one official clone available, CAB 14. Interestingly, Filippetti and Fontana (2006) hypothesize that Montù was abandoned because it is much less productive than most *Trebbiano*s. Though Montù is not a household name, at six hundred hectares planted in the province of Bologna alone and about one thousand in Italy overall (2010 data), the variety is more common than many realize. In fact the cultivar does well even in flatland vineyards that are easily worked with cost-effective mechanical harvesters, so it's a native that's not likely to disappear anytime soon. Though typical of the Emilia portion of Emilia-Romagna (especially the flatlands along the Reno River, north of Bologna up to Pieve di Cento), it was once common in Romagna (where it is more commonly called Bianchino); today it is hard to find past Ravenna. However, there are other Bianchino grapes grown in Romagna, and they are not all identical to Montù; there is most likely a distinct Bianchino variety after all.

Which Wines to Choose and Why

The best wines are usually found in the IGTs Castelfranco dell'Emilia, Ravenna, Forlì, and Rubicone and in the DOC Reno Montuni (a minimum 85 percent Montù is required, but monovarietal wines exist). The wine is high in acid (the grape is mainly used to make sparkling wines) and the wines are very light bodied with aromas of fresh flowers and unripe citrus fruits.

WINES TO TRY: Cantina Barone**, Luigi Bassi**, and Cantina Sociale di Faenza** (Frizzante).

Moscatos

See MOSCATO FAMILY, chapter 3.

Nascetta

WHERE IT'S FOUND: Piedmont. NATIONAL REGISTRY CODE NUMBER: 362. COLOR: white.

There are native grapes that are found in only one country. Then there are native cultivars that are found only in one region of that country. And there are even natives found in only a few areas of that one region. Now meet Nascetta, which takes the meaning of locally grown to a whole new level: it is a one-town native. For the longest time, it was only found around the hamlet of Novello, better known for Barolo production. The earliest document I have been able to find that specifically mentions Nascetta is Fantini's seminal 1880 book on the enology and viticulture of the Cuneo province; otherwise not much has been written about the variety in past centuries and the local producers themselves don't seem to know much about it or its history. Ten years ago, a book on Italy's native grapes would have only mentioned Nascetta (also called Anascetta or Nas-cëtta') in passing, if at all. Today there are a dozen producers of this wine, which has come to characterize Novello even more than Barolo does. Credit for this must go to Elvio Cogno, one of the historic figures of the Langhe, and to the Danieli brothers of the Le Strette estate (winemakers at Ceretto for roughly twenty-five years) who were the first to believe in the variety. Not that Nascetta had disappeared: it was always there, but forgotten, if not ignored. In the 1980s, when I used to visit Barolo producers, I rarely ventured as far as Novello, but already back then, when I asked old-timers in Castiglione Falletto or Barolo about local native varieties other than Nebbiolo, more than one mentioned an "aromatic or herbal" white wine made by friends of theirs in Novello. In fact, Nascetta is a semi-aromatic grape, and that tells you a lot about the wine.

Today Nascetta is on a roll and it has been planted in many other parts of the Langhe besides Novello. Efforts are under way by an impressively large and ever-increasing number of producers to restore the variety, in the hopes of yielding better wines of increased structure and softness. Enrico Rivetto of the Rivetto winery in Serralunga d'Alba admits that Nascetta isn't the easiest variety to work with: "Genetically, it just doesn't produce much, maybe one bunch per cane. Plus, its tight bunch is a grey-rot magnet, especially in humid or wet years; and so it causes a lot of extra work in the vineyards, where deleafing is a necessity. Cryomaceration in the cellar also means more work, and all this added work means higher costs." Savio Danieli of Le Strette agrees: "Canopy management with Nascetta is a ton of work, as the grapevine will grow all over the place, in all directions; but the real problem is that some years the grapevines are devastated by *millerandage*. Those who keep saying it's a good, regular producer simply don't know Nascetta: it's a very irregularly yielding grape." At least Nascetta grows erect, making it slightly easier time on the backs of those working in the vineyards. No clones are currently available: generally it has medium-large cylindrical, compact bunches with two wings and medium round-oval berries. It ripens in early September.

By and large, Nascetta is still grown mainly around Novello, in the southwestern corner of the Barolo production zone, but it's being increasingly planted elsewhere in the area, for example around Serralunga d'Alba.

Which Wines to Choose and Why

Rivetto began producing a Nascetta wine a few years ago, attracted by the new challenge. "It's the only true white grape native of the Langhe," he says, "and in my view, one with untapped potential. Most examples of this wine are meant to be drunk young, but with the marly-clay and sandy soil of Serralunga and cryomaceration, I think Nascetta could give complex, ageworthy wines." Danieli is happy that others are finally making the wine too, but points out that there are huge differences between wines labeled simply "Langhe Nascetta" and those carrying the words "Langhe Nascetta del Comune di Novello." This is because the latter wines have to be 100 percent Nascetta, with lower yields (ninety quintals per hectoliter), while the former wines can be made with a minimum of 85 percent Nascetta and are allowed yields up to one hundred hectoliters per hectare. Last but not least, Nascetta del Comune di Novello has to be made with grapes grown in the variety's original home, not just grown anywhere.

Elvio Cogno, his daughter Nadia, and son-in-law Walter Fissore of the Elvio Cogno estate are deeply attached to Nascetta and believe in its qualities. The wine they make reminds me of one made with Vermentino or Sauvignon Blanc (a little more fruity than the former and a little more minty-balsamic than the latter), and in fact, I think Nascetta looks like Vermentino too (or at least, those vines of Nascetta I have seen in vineyards of Novello). Perhaps the best analogy is to say that Nascetta wines are an ideal mix of Sauvignon Blanc and Vermentino, but with a touch of Riesling. If young Nascetta wines have a fruity and herbal pungency reminiscent of Sauvignon Blanc, with age they pick up honeyed notes more reminiscent of the latter, and they always exude a balsamic mintiness that brings Vermentino to mind. I find this balsamic minty note is really the main feature of any nascetta, and with a little practice, makes the wine instantly recognizable, even in blind tastings. Another characteristic is that nascettas are always extremely saline, a salinity that gives the wine a strong savory quality and leaves the taster with a huge impression of acidity, though total acidity levels really aren't that high (rarely more than five-and-a-half grams per liter). Studies show Nascetta to have above average concentrations of terpenes and norisoprenoids and this explains its mildly aromatic personality. The wine is delicious, straw yellow–golden, with aromas of aromatic herbs, orange, ginger, and star fruit, complicated by sage, rosemary, and balsamic mint. Honey and vanilla emerge as the wine ages, which it does well; I have tasted many nascettas that were five years old and were still vibrantly fresh. It is quite unlike any other white wine of Piedmont, and therein lies part of its charm.

WINES TO TRY: For Nascetta del Comune di Novello, try: Cogno*** (Nas-cëtta, 30 percent oak-aged) and Le Strette*** (less famous than the former but the most faithful representative of the variety because it's not oak-aged). For Langhe Nascetta, try Rivetto** and Ettore Germano**.

Nasco

WHERE IT'S FOUND: Sardinia. NATIONAL REGISTRY CODE NUMBER: 159. COLOR: white.

Locally called Nuscu, Nascu, and Resu, this variety's name may derive from the Latin *muscus*, and the Sardinian *nuscu*, both meaning "musky," a recognizable aromatic characteristic of the wine. Nasco was highly thought of in the nineteenth century, when it was considered one of the best varieties grown around Cagliari; it was also believed to be Sardinia's most ancient cultivar. Nasco has always been highly prized and its qualities as a wine grape recognized: of the two hundred producers showing wines at the 1861 Florence Exhibition, Pietro Marini was one of the few to win a medal, with his Nasco wine. Given its high quality as a wine grape, Cettolini and Mameli (1933) regretted it wasn't more diffuse. Though dark-berried varieties called Nasco Nero have been described, ampelographic and SSR profiling at six loci confirmed its identity to Aregu Giallo or Barberone (Lovicu, Farci, Sedda, Labra, De Mattia, Grassi, Bacchetta, and Orrù 2010). Clearly, Nasco Nero is unrelated to true Nasco, which is a white grape that Sardinia's better estates, such as Pala and Argiolas, have records of cultivating since the nineteenth century. Fabio Angius, technical director at Pala says, "We only wish we had more of it!"

It is not clear whether Nasco is a true native or if it was brought to Sardinia by Greek colonists or, much later, by the Spanish. It is genetically distinct from all other Sardinian varieties, and that includes the little-known Ogu de Arrana variety, erroneously believed to be identical to Nasco (the two only share an allele in nine of twelve SSR loci studied). Unfortunately, Nasco was uprooted for the better part of the twentieth century so that more productive and parasite-resistant varieties could be planted in its place. In modern times, things have changed considerably, and local universities are busy trying to develop clones (as yet unavailable), proof positive that the variety is attracting attention and that it has numerous supporters.

For what it's worth, I find Nasco to be one of Italy's prettier grapes and a joy to look at. The cylindrical-conical medium-large bunches have two wings and medium-large round-oval berries. Not that vigorous, it's disease-resistant (except to oidium) and tends to produce a lot of foliage; however, as it grows erect, it's easy on the back during vineyard work. Nasco's budbreak is relatively early in the season, but this does not pose much of a problem in Sardinia's warm island climate, where spring frosts are practically unheard of.

Nasco grows mainly east of Cagliari (75 percent of the 105 total hectares planted to Nasco are in Cagliari's Campidano area) and to a lesser extent around Oristano; however, the quality of the wines is such that plantings are increasing, and so Nasco is now found around Nuoro too. The best sites for Nasco are the calcareous-marly hillsides near Cagliari (Parteolla and Sibiola in the townships of Serdiana and Dolianova, and around Settimo Ninnai and Quartu). Therefore, rootstocks such as 140 Ruggeri are a good choice, or 1130 Paulsen in less calcareous and droughty zones.

Which Wines to Choose and Why

Local farmers believe Nasco is one of the oldest grape varieties of Sardinia and potentially the best. They get no argument from me, if for no other reason than that Nasco is one of those rare grapes that yields mesmerizingly good dry and sweet wines.

In cooler areas and on more fertile soils, the dry wines tend to be more vegetal and less interesting. Of course, Nasco wines are always characterized by a strong herbal note, with rosemary and thyme sticking out, and a muskiness that recalls the variety's name. The wine is DOC Nasco di Cagliari, available in sweet, dry, fortified dry, and fortified sweet *riserva* versions, though there are also about fifteen IGT wines that allow use of Nasco. The best Nasco wine by far is the sweet one; Nasco tends to dehydrate easily on the vine and accumulates sugar quickly but without dropping its already rather low acidity too fast, so sweet wines can be thrilling. Care needs to be taken with Nasco's pips, particularly rich in potentially bitter polyphenols, while the compounds are in surprisingly low concentrations in the skin. I find it interesting that Nasco is able to deliver wines of above average complexity even though it's an early ripener: usually, complexity stems from long, slow ripening in cooler areas, but Nasco is an exception to this rule.

WINES TO TRY: Gigi Picciau***, Argiolas*** (Iselis, which has a little Vermentino added. Their Angialis is the best sweet version, though not 100 percent Nasco; they believe that a little Malvasia di Cagliari turns the monovarietal into a more genteel wine, as the variety's strong personality may not suit everybody), and Meloni Vini** (Donna Jolanda, another sweet nasco).

Nebbiolo

WHERE IT'S FOUND: Piedmont, Lombardy, Valle d'Aosta. NATIONAL REGISTRY CODE NUMBER: 160. COLOR: red.

Nebbiolo is Italy's greatest native grape and, by most expert accounts, one of the world's five or six great cultivars. Barolo and Barbaresco are the two best-known wines made from Nebbiolo grapes—internationally famous monovarietal Nebbiolo wines that are extremely ageworthy (a good, well-kept Barolo from 1947 or 1961 is still a thing of beauty). But Nebbiolo is also at the core of other fantastic Italian wines such as Gattinara, Lessona, Ghemme, Boca, Sfursat, and many more. In these wines, Nebbiolo is usually blended with small percentages of local varieties (such as Croatina, Pignola, Vespolina, or Brugnola).

Nebbiolo, one of Italy's oldest cultivars, is a native variety for which we have some of the earliest available documentation. Apparently Pliny the Elder referred to it as *nubiola*, the Latin word for "fog" *(nebbia)*, as Nebbiolo ripens late in the fall season, when fog in the vineyards of Piedmont is common. Another theory holds that Nebbiolo's name derives from the abundant bloom of its grapes, making them look like they're bathed in fog. The name *nibiol* first appears in the literature in the mid-thirteenth century (according to one producer, as early as 1268), after which the variety was increasingly mentioned: in 1292, *"filagnos di vitibus neblorii"*; in 1295, *"nebiolo"*; in 1340, *"nebiolus"*; and many more instances after that. That Nebbiolo was held in high esteem by our ancestors is well exemplified by the town of La Morra passing laws in 1402 handing out stiff penalties to all those caught damaging Nebbiolo vines. In 1799, Count Nuvolone described and addressed the many subtypes of Nebbiolo. After this, the greatness of Nebbiolo and the excellence of its wines are lauded by all of Italy's greatest "grape minds," from Incisa della Rocchetta to Di Rovasenda. Already by the nineteenth century, there was no doubt that Nebbiolo was truly a Piedmontese grape asset.

Phenotypic and Genotypic Variability of Nebbiolo
Nebbiolo has always lived in a very circumscribed area of Italy, and practically nowhere else. Much like Pinot Nero, it is a servant of its environment and has not spread in any quantity to new vine regions, though Nebbiolo plantings outside Italy have been increasing of late. Not that it, or Pinot Nero, can't adapt elsewhere: it's just that the resulting wines are almost nothing like those made in Italy. Even in Italy Nebbiolo's diffusion is limited to the Valle d'Aosta, Lombardy, and Piedmont (and in fact, only in specific parts of these regions). As Nebbiolo is, and has been, intimately linked to only a few viticultural zones over the centuries, locals have strongly identified with the variety and its wines, which explains the variety's many synonyms, specific to its areas of cultivation. In centuries past, many different *Nebbiolos* were described: for example, Nebbiolo Maschio, Nebbiolo Femmina, Nebbiolo Fino, Nebbiolo Gentile, Nebbiolo Piccolo, and Nebbiolo Grosso, though these synonyms were neither commonly used nor of particular importance. However, three synonyms were and are still important today: Spanna, Picotener, and Chiavennasca. In northeastern Piedmont, toward Novara and Vercelli, Nebbiolo has always been called Spanna. Farther north, in Valle d'Aosta, Nebbiolo has always been known as Picot Tendre (this region's French roots are obvious), modified over time to the modern Picotener or Picotendro. Finally, in Lombardy, Nebbiolo has historically been called Chiavennasca, not to be confused with Chiavennaschino (which is not Grignolino, as you'll read elsewhere, but Nebbiolo Rosé, distinct from Nebbiolo). These three synonyms have been used by locals for centuries, another sign that Nebbiolo has been hanging around Italian soil for a very long time; use of the word Spanna was first documented in 1466, that of Chiavennasca dates to 1595, and of Picotendro to the nineteenth century. According to Berta and Mainardi (1997) all three are predated by Prünent (from *pruina*, or bloom), another Nebbiolo synonym used in Piedmont's Val d'Ossola since 1309. Still other Nebbiolo synonyms include the Canavese's Pugnet, because the Nebbiolo there is often characterized by a very small cylindrical bunch (rather than the more typical pyramidal shape) resembling a small closed fist (*pugno* in Italian and *pugnet* in local dia-

lect); Pignolo is yet another name, from Barbaresco, now rarely used (and rightly so, since Pignolo is a distinct variety native to Friuli Venezia Giulia). In Piedmont, care must be taken not to confuse true Nebbiolo with Nebbiolo di Dronero, a different variety typical of alpine areas, nowadays most usually referred to by its other name, Chatus (see CHATUS entry).

This plethora of synonyms reflects not only Nebbiolo's age and intimate links to specific pockets of the Italian countryside, but also the fact that there are many Nebbiolo biotypes. Nebbiolo is marked by high intravarietal variability, and its ability to adapt to new environments by mutating its phenotype is well known to growers. Such intravarietal variability does not necessarily result from a relative disposition to mutate, but can also result from a long history of cultivation (not surprisingly, Aglianico and many other varieties growing in Italy seemingly since the dawn of time, also have many biotypes). These morphologic and phenologic differences have led to at least thirty different Nebbiolo biotypes being described and grown, of which four in particular have always been considered the most important (Nebbiolo Bolla, Nebbiolo Lampia, Nebbiolo Michet, and Nebbiolo Rosé, but the latter is now known to be a distinct cultivar). As recently as the 1990s, you couldn't find a wine producer in Piedmont who would talk about Nebbiolo without mentioning the subtype he grew. Nebbiolo Michet was reputed to be the best: wouldn't you know it, every time I visited a wine estate in the Langhe, they always seemed to grow this biotype only. Nebbiolo Lampia was the most dependable, Nebbiolo Rosé the most perfumed but also the lightest in color and body, a virtual kiss of death in those "wine bodybuilder" fixated times. Nebbiolo Bolla was considered a high-yielding, poor-quality biotype and was eliminated. Legislation even went so far as to specify which subtype could be grown to make wines like Barolo. This was not surprising, given Nebbiolo's unique soil and microclimate sensitivity and its ability to translate *terroir* into the glass. It was only with the new century, thanks to brilliant research results obtained mainly by Anna Schneider and her colleagues, that we have finally gained a better understanding of Nebbiolo's intravarietal variability and complex family relationships.

Schneider, Boccacci, and Botta (2003) and Schneider, Boccacci, Torello Marinoni, Botta, Akkak, and Vouillamoz (2004) studied ampelographic and ampelometric characteristics as well as nuclear microsatellite markers of the various Nebbiolo biotypes. The focus was initially on thirty-three descriptors following known Organization Internationale de la Vigne et du Vin (OIV) guidelines, with SSR microsatellites (twenty-three to fifty-eight loci) studied. These landmark results confirmed the existence of only two *Nebbiolo* genotypes: Nebbiolo Lampia and Nebbiolo Rosé. The studies further showed that biotypes Bolla, Picotendro, and Chiavennasca all originate from Lampia. While there are two genotypes, there are three main phenotypes: Nebbiolo Michet, Nebbiolo Rosé, and Nebbiolo Lampia. Nebbiolo Michet is a virus-affected form of Nebbiolo Lampia, and therefore the two look different, though they are genetically one and the same: all the morpho-physiologic differences exhibited by Nebbiolo Michet (small compact bunch, short internodes, highly indented leaves, reduced fertility and vigor) result from grapevine fanleaf virus infection. It is named *michet* because the small compact bunch makes it resemble a *mica* (loaf of bread, in Piedmontese dialect). In other words, Nebbiolo Lampia, at the current state of knowledge, has to be considered the main or "real" Nebbiolo variety. Nebbiolo Rosé is instead distinct from Nebbiolo (and hence I treat it separately in this book, as should every other wine writer), but it has a first-degree relationship with Nebbiolo, because the two have at least one allele in common in twenty-three loci (see NEBBIOLO ROSÉ entry).

Also, Schneider, Boccacci, Torello Marinoni, Botta, Akkak, and Vouillamoz (2004) confirmed that Freisa is very closely linked to Nebbiolo Lampia, as the two cultivars share a common allele in at least fifty-eight loci; a first-degree relationship exists between these two varieties as well. Clearly, just tasting the wines (when made by similarly minded and competent producers) demonstrates this as well. The two varieties also look alike and exhibit similar viticultural behaviors.

In this same study, and in Schneider, Torello Marinoni, Boccacci, and Botta (2005–6) important results were presented on the genetic relationships between Nebbiolo and other varieties (local and not), analyzing the proportion of shared alleles between the varieties (Bowcock, Ruiz-Linares, Tomfohrde, Minch, Kidd, and Cavalli-Sforza 1994). Results showed the ten closest relatives of Nebbiolo to be Negrera (a little-known and rare variety from Valtellina in Lombardy), Freisa, Nebbiolo Rosé, Vespolina, Bubbierasco (a now extremely rare native of the Salluzese area of Piedmont), Pignola, Rossolino Nero (another extremely rare variety), Neretto di San Giorgio, Brugnola, and Rossola. Based on an analysis of twelve microsatellite markers and twenty-three to fifty-eight SSR loci, these varieties all appear to have a first-degree relationship with Nebbiolo (meaning they could be either parents or offspring of the main variety). The study authors believe any major phenotypic difference present to be the result of sporadic mutations. Of these varieties, Bubbierasco is an offspring of Nebbiolo and Bianchetto, but we don't yet know the status of the other varieties relative to Nebbiolo. Interestingly, eight of these related grapes grow and live only in northern Lombardy's Valtellina area (where Nebbiolo remains the major variety and is the main player in important wines such as Sfursat, Sassella, and Inferno).

The fact that all these cultivars are present only in this part of Italy indicates that Nebbiolo is most likely a true native of northwestern Italy, where it mainly lives to this day. In particular, given the strong link of these varieties with Lombardy's Valtellina, and Nebbiolo's presence there, it is tempting, if somewhat disheartening for the Piedmontese, to speculate that Nebbiolo's original home is in fact Valtellina, not Piedmont; but of course, all the related cultivars of Nebbiolo could turn out to be just the progeny of Nebbiolo and not its ancestors. In noteworthy, if somewhat strange, results of the same studies, varieties as wildly different as Bressana, Ortrugo (a white grape from Emilia-Romagna), and Chasselas (a white grape typical of Switzerland famously used to make the delicious wine called Fendant du Valais) also seem to show genetic proximity to Nebbiolo. Mercifully, the results also show that other varieties such as Barbera, Dolcetto, and Cabernet Sauvignon are far removed genetically from Nebbiolo (the genetic distance is estimated at between 0.65 and 0.7, with a value of 1.00 being the maximum distance possible). I don't know about you, but I find immense solace in the knowledge that Cabernet Sauvignon and Nebbiolo are no relation at all.

Not All Nebbiolo Clones Are Created Equal

Much like with Sangiovese, clonal selection has been extremely important for Nebbiolo, especially as the cultivar's anthocyanin endowment is nothing to write home about. Furthermore, though vigorous, Nebbiolo is characterized by only medium fertility, especially in the basal buds, and so productivity is very clone dependent. However, for a good chunk of the 1990s and into the twenty-first century, the crux of the (perceived) problem was Nebbiolo's bright but lightly hued wines, with strong orangey tinges even when young (with Nebbiolo wines, garnet is not necessarily a sign of age), far removed from the deep, almost black-ruby color all the rage for "important" (or so deemed) wines. Not surprisingly, producers clamored for Nebbiolo's color to be kicked up a notch (or two or three); and so the race was on to develop the biggest, blackest (and meanest, to my way of wine thinking) Nebbiolo clone possible. Unfortunately, as is always the case and any parent can tell you, when you go looking for trouble you usually find it, and so it was with this particular well meaning but very misguided quest.

Generally speaking, clones available to producers in the 1970s and 1980s ranged from unspecified plants of Lampia and Michet, moving on into the early 1990s with the CVT 142 and 230 clones (Lampia biotype). Beginning with the new century, CVT 71, 66 (Michet biotype), 180, and 185 (Lampia biotype) became trendy. After these Nebbiolo clones were developed (in general, a rather civilized bunch), many newer clones (certified between 2001 and 2005) diverged sharply from pre-existing clonal populations. The new clones were CVT 4, 63, 66, and 71, all derived from the Michet biotype, and CVT 308, 415, and 423, all derived from the Picotener biotype of Valle d'Aosta (though CVT 308 was actually originally grown in Piedmont's Carema area, so even though it's a Picotener, it's not correct to qualify it as a Nebbiolo *valdostano*).

The main differences between these and previously available clones (all from the Lampia biotype, save for CN 111, which had been developed from Nebbiolo Rosé) were much smaller bunches, smaller and darker berries ("they've tried turning Nebbiolo into a Pinot Noir look-alike," quips Domenico Clerico, one of the area's best producers), lower yields, and theoretical (very theoretical, as we would discover) higher enological potential for fine wine production. A further note of merit (this one true) was that these clones were virus-free (the Michet had been subjected to thermotherapy and the Picotener to meristematic therapy, two methods by which to free grapevines of viruses), thereby eliminating all presence of GFLV in Nebbiolo Michet and grapevine leafroll-associated virus (GLRaV) and grapevine virus A (GVA) in the Nebbiolo from Valle d'Aosta. However, while the Michet CVT 71 clone proved reliable and seriously wine-worthy (so much so that it's what you'll most likely encounter in today's Nebbiolo vineyards), this was not the case with the Picotener clones, in my humble view an absolute disaster. In short, all Barolos or Barbarescos made with the latter clones are very dark (though never black, they are extremely dark ruby), but are all devoid (or have very muted) Nebbiolo aromas: an amazingly huge shortcoming, considering the fact that what makes Nebbiolo one of the world's greatest grape varieties is its ability to produce wines of mesmerizingly wonderful and unique perfume.

About seven or eight years ago, I began systematically noting the absence of aromatic complexity in wines made from Picotener clones. After compiling enough tasting data, I mustered up the courage to broach the subject with some producers I knew to be honest and candid enough to tell me what they really thought. I will never forget the look on Aldo Vajra's face when I raised the issue with him in 2007 or 2008. Looking like he wanted to be anywhere else (or asking himself why I had been inflicted on the human race), he set his jaw and straightforwardly replied that, yes, Picotener produced very aromatically monolithic wines and that he and many other producers were either uprooting them or not planting them at all anymore. There is no small measure of irony in the knowledge that clone CN 111 (the Nebbiolo Rosé clone), deemed a poor-quality clone back in the last decade of the twentieth century, is one that produces thinner wines, but with amazing perfume.

Clearly, as with every other cultivar, massal selections are very important with Nebbiolo. Angelo Gaja, the world-famous Italian winemaker who has done so much for the image and quality of Italian wines at home and abroad, told me that "it was my grandfather, Angelo Gaja (1876–1944) who began massal selections in 1937, searching out those grapevines with characteristics that are still valid today: lack of vigor, loosely packed bunches, small berries. We've never stopped, and at Gaja, all our vineyards are planted with 50 percent massal and 50 percent clonal selections." Most producers in the Langhe always plant their vineyards with large percentages of grapevines issued from massal selections—a good idea, because monoclonal vineyards, besides yielding potentially boring wines, are also at greater risk of being completely wiped out by a specific disease.

In general, Nebbiolo wines are only medium-dark: in fact, it's a specific characteristic of theirs. If you know something about grapes in general and Nebbiolo in particular, this won't come as a surprise. Nebbiolo is characterized by a large proportion of peonin and cyanin in its anthocyanin profile, determining the lighter hue of its wines and relatively unstable coloration over time, with a tendency to turn garnet sooner (and the wines are usually born with a strong garnet tinge). Despite its lack of deep hue, wines made from Nebbiolo grapes age amazingly well, thanks to a combination of dry extract, total acidity, tannins, and alcohol. Nebbiolo is very sensitive to spring frosts (it buds very early) and to autumn rains (it ripens very late); due to their rapid growth and considerable length, the buds risk breakage in excessively windy conditions. Nebbiolo's plentiful leaf canopy grows vigorously, but good growers reduce the foliage to encourage just the right amount of photosynthesis, while creating open space for airflow and optimal sunlight to the berries. Clusters are thinned either by removing the lower half of all clusters, or by removing half of all the clusters on each vine. In Piemonte this cluster management typically occurs in two moments: once in July, at the time of the *vendemmia verde* (or green harvest), and then again during the last weeks of ripening. Cluster management with Nebbiolo is necessary but time consuming and it must be done over and over in order to yield excellent grapes. Furthermore, Nebbiolo needs plenty of sunlight and warmer sites to ripen fully and historically has been planted in southern-exposed sites in Italy: *sorì della sera,* vineyards exposed southwest (so the grapes catch the afternoon sun), and *sorì del mattino* (characterized by southeast exposures so grapes see more of the morning sun), as well in the *bricco,* the very top part of the hill, so that the exposure is 360 degrees. Unfortunately, such is the hunger for great Barolo and Barbaresco that in the Langhe many producers have taken to planting Nebbiolo in less than ideal sites just to have more wine to sell—not exactly a stellar idea with a variety that is so site sensitive. It follows that many Barolos and Barbarescos are less than they should be, and the world is being deprived of excellent Freisa or Grignolino wines. I'm not joking: it's time someone told Langhe producers that enough is enough and instead of another less than stellar (but always expensive) Barolo or Barbaresco, we would all be grateful for some less expensive, everyday table wine to have at lunch or dinner. Of course, nebbiolo fits that bill very nicely too.

In Italy Nebbiolo only grows in Piedmont, Valle d'Aosta, and Lombardy, and while the Nebbiolo of Sardinia has been identified mainly as Dolcetto, Nebbiolo grapevines can also be found on the island. Italy has roughly 6,500 hectares planted to Nebbiolo, of which 5,500 are in Piedmont. Outside Italy, it grows in Argentina, in the United States (in Oregon, California, Washington, and in less famous wine states such as New Mexico, Idaho, Pennsylvania, Tennessee, and Virginia), in Australia, in Mexico (especially in Baja California), in South Africa, in New Zealand, and in Chile. In each one of these countries there are undoubtedly some viticultural areas that offer reasonable chances for success with Nebbiolo. For example, as Nebbiolo wants less-fertile soil rich in clay and limestone with some sand, it follows that California's coastal regions ought to prove very suitable, since these soil types are found there. In Australia, cool climate districts such as the Mornington Peninsula in Victoria and the Margaret River area of Western Australia have been shown to have weather patterns similar to those of the Langhe region of Piedmont, so Nebbiolo ought to thrive there too. And there is no reason to think that New Zealand, which has already managed to successfully corral Pinot Noir and the difficulties it presents, can't do the same with Nebbiolo.

Which Wines to Choose and Why

Nebbiolo seems to be perfectly happy growing on the clay-limestone soils of the Albese; at least the best Nebbiolo wines are all made there. Obviously a homebody, it doesn't seem to mind this area's hail, floods, fog, and cold weather. The difficulty with Nebbiolo grown elsewhere in Italy or abroad is that the resulting wines, though at times truly outstanding and always interesting, never combine structure with perfumed, fruity charm, which is a major selling point of great Barolo or Barbaresco. Though most people tend to think of wines such as Barolo and Barbaresco as tannic, ageworthy brutes, in reality great Nebbiolo wines are paragons of grace and perfumed refinement. True, they are always marked by high acidity and assertive tannins, though I think their structure and size have always been excessively characterized. Certainly any wine made with Cabernet Sauvignon—a great grape variety—isn't any less tannic than one made with Nebbiolo, but I find wines made with the latter have a gracefulness and refinement that the former can only dream of. One whiff of a great Barolo's or Barbaresco's intense aromas of red rose and sour red cherry and you're hooked for life; but the same degree of depth and substance is inevitably lacking in wines born from the sandier soils of the Roero, and elegance is *desaparecido* in hot places like Sardinia or some areas of California.

As most wine lovers know, there are many other great, if different, Nebbiolo wines, made in the Roero, a viticultural zone hugging the left side of the Tanaro River, opposite the Langhe. Though there is geological variability in the Roero, a good portion of its soils are far sandier than those of the Langhe, and so these Nebbiolo wines will offer more perfume and less size. The best Roeros also have enough creamy fruit to avoid tasting excessively austere, which is a flaw I find in a number of Roero bottlings. Roero is a much cooler and wilder area than the Langhe: most of the vineyards are still surrounded by forests (hardly the case in the Langhe, where entire wooded areas have been eliminated over the years in order to plant more vineyards). Further complicating matters, Roero vineyards are planted on steeper slopes and therefore late-ripening Nebbiolo doesn't ripen fully every year. Even in the Roero though doing a little homework will greatly increase your chances of buying a wine you'll like. For example, generally the soils of Monteu Roero are richer in sand and those around Castagnito richer in clay, while the Canale area has soils that combine elements of both. It follows that similarly made wines from similarly grown grapes from these three subzones are bound to be very different.

In these times of climate change the less well-known Nebbiolo wines of Piedmont's cooler northeastern sector are becoming increasingly sought after. Wines to look for from the northeast are Bramaterra, Gattinara, Boca, Lessona, Ghemme, and Fara, though most of the time they contain various percentages of other local grapes such as Croatina, Vespolina, Uva Rara, and others (though pure versions do exist, and they are outstanding). In Valle d'Aosta, don't miss out on Donnas, perhaps the least known of all the great Nebbiolo-based wines (here also local varieties may be included in the blend), while in Lombardy the best and richest is Sfursat, made from air-dried Nebbiolo grapes in the manner of Amarone. Sfursat is smooth and velvety just like the famous Amarone; because of Nebbiolo's presence it is also more refined and lighter styled, though "light" is a very relative term with Sfursat and all Nebbiolo wines. A well-made Barolo or Barbaresco is one of the world's greatest wines, characterized by an amazingly intense and penetrating aroma of red roses and sour red cherries, complicated by light sweet spices and especially tar with bottle age. Even nebbiolos, the entry-level version of Barolo or Barbaresco, are unbelievably wonderful food wines. Nebbiolos are wines made from grapes that often are grown in an area that would allow the producer to make a Barolo or a Barbaresco, but instead are used to make a simpler, inexpensive wine (most often because the vines are still young). Other times a vintage isn't particularly great and so producers prefer to downgrade their Roero, Lessona, Gattinara, Barolo, or Barbaresco to simple nebbiolo status in an effort to protect the image of their best-known wines.

There are many *grand crus* for Nebbiolo, and given the variety's penchant for site specificity and capacity to translate even minute soil differences into the glass, Nebbiolo's location is a complex but fascinating discussion that deserves an entire book to itself. Names such as Brunate, Bussia, Cannubi, Cerequio (which no less an expert than Lorenzo Fantini described as *sceltissimo,* or top choice), Rocche dell'Annunziata, Rocche di Castiglione Falletto, and Vigna Rionda are just some of the names most worth remembering, though there are others. I will limit myself here to saying that the best *terroirs* for Barolo can be loosely defined as those to the left and right of a diagonal line drawn through the city of Barolo from northwest to southeast. On the left side, the soils are of Tortonian origin (a geologic era), characterized by blue-grey marl, while to the right the soils are of another geologic era, the Helvetian (or more accurately, Serravalian), and are characterized by yellow-grey compacted sand and clay. In reality, the situation is much more complex, with nine different geological formations identified, four of which are especially capable of producing stellar wines. The wines born on the left, or Tortonian, are lighter and develop sooner (but still have forty-plus years of ageworthiness), while those of the right, or Serravalian, are hard as nails when young (these Barolos start being somewhat ready to drink ten to fifteen years after the vintage) and last even longer.

Wine styles don't differ that much anymore, though in the 1980s the modernist and traditionalist winemakers nearly came to blows. The former believed in shorter maceration times (using rotofermentor machines), lower fermentation temperatures, tighter spacing of the vines and lower yields, and aging in small oak barrels (often new) called *barriques;* the latter thought nothing of fermenting for forty-plus days at temperatures well in excess of 30°C and only used old, large oak barrels (and often not French but Slavonian oak). Today, most producers walk a common ground, and though some staunch traditionalists remain, most true modernists have gone the way of the dodo (rightfully so, as those wines didn't age well and failed to develop aromatic complexity, witness the very disappointing 1990 wines of many a modernist). Today, there are almost too many great producers of monovarietal Nebbiolo and mainly Nebbiolo-based wines to name, but I've tried to compile a short list of some good ones.

Outside Italy there are many thrilling Nebbiolo wines worth trying. They may not always remind you of Barolo and Barbaresco, but the quality they express can be eye-opening. Granted, much like Pinot Noir, Nebbiolo undergoes a complete personality change once it leaves its homeland, and so wines made elsewhere are necessarily different from those made in the grape's native home.

Whereas twenty years ago I would have had difficulty advocating for the merits of Nebbiolo wines made outside Italy, this is no longer true today, with many at least interesting Nebbiolo wines to choose from. In California, Nebbiolo was likely introduced in the nineteenth century by Italian immigrants. However, Nebbiolo was often planted in areas like the upper San Joaquin Valley, where the hot climate is not ideal for Nebbiolo; in fact a lot of California Nebbiolo still grows in the too-hot Central Valley, where a lot of jug wine is made. Around 1972, Montevina Winery in California's Amador County planted Nebbiolo and produced several vintages until about 1980; the wines weren't about to make anybody forget Barolo or Barbaresco, but they showed that Nebbiolo could have a future outside its native home. Unless I am mistaken, Dave Caparone was the first to identify the coastal vineyards of Paso Robles as potential high-quality sites for Nebbiolo: this is where much of California's highest quality Nebbiolo wines are made nowadays. He planted his first Nebbiolo vineyard in 1980 and made his first wine in 1985. Today California Nebbiolo wines of note are also made by Castelli Vineyards, Harrington, Karmère Vineyards and Winery, Mahoney Vineyards, Madrona Estate, Palmina (an especially dedicated New World nebbiolo producer, with five different bottlings, all excellent), Renwood (very rich and high in alcohol, given the Lodi climate), Toccata, Urban Legend Cellars, and Wind Gap. Randall Grahm used to make a good Nebbiolo wine at Ca' del Solo, the certified biodynamic vineyard in Soledad he sold in 2009. Zonin has made a successful, if lightish, Nebbiolo wine in Virginia. Barolo and Barbaresco, for example, are some of the world's longest-lived wines, but I am afraid we don't yet know just how well New World Nebbiolo will age. However, Montevina certainly made wines that have aged well.

In Australia, Coriole, Di Lusso, Longview Vineyard (both an excellent Boat Shed Rosé and a Nebbiolo Riserva), Mount Surmon, Parish Hill, Pizzini (both a Nebbiolo and a Coronamento Nebbiolo bottling), and Sandhurst Ridge are just some of the many sure bets. Curiously enough, some of the most Nebbiolo-like Nebbiolo wines I have tasted recently are made in Chile.

WINES TO TRY: Bruno Giacosa*** (Barolo Le Rocche del Falletto Riserva, Barbaresco Asili Riserva, Barbaresco Rabajà Riserva, Nebbiolo d'Alba), Giacomo Conterno*** (Barolo Cascina Francia and Monfortino), Gaja*** (Barbaresco), Bartolo Mascarello** (Barolo), Giuseppe (Mauro) Mascarello** (Barolo Monprivato, Barolo Villero), Giuseppe Rinaldi** (Barolo Brunate-Le Coste), Luciano Sandrone (Barolo Cannubi Boschis and Barolo Le Vigne), Paolo Scavino (Barolo Bric del Fiasc and Rocche dell'Annunziata Riserva), Pio Cesare** (Barolo and Barolo Ornato), Renato Ratti (Barolo Rocche), Elvio Cogno** (Barolo Bricco Pernice), Ceretto** (Barolo Bricco Rocche Bricco Rocche and Barolo Bricco Rocche Prapò), Marchese de Gresy** (Barbaresco Camp Gros and Barbaresco Martinenga), Bruno Rocca** (Barbaresco Maria Adelaide and Rabajà), Giacomo Fenocchio** (Barolo Villero), GD Vajra** (Barolo Bricco delle Viole), Antoniolo** (Gattinara Osso San Grato and San Francesco), Proprietà Sperino** (Lessona), Antichi Vigneti di Cantalupo** (Ghemme Collis Breclamae), Produttori Donnas** (Donnas Napoléon), Sandro Fay** (Sfursat), Mamete Prevostini** (Sfursat), and Triacca** (Sfursat).

Nebbiolo Rosé

WHERE IT'S FOUND: Piedmont, Lombardy, Valle d'Aosta. NATIONAL REGISTRY CODE NUMBER: not registered. COLOR: red.

I love this grape: sure, wines made with Nebbiolo are more complete and balanced, but wines born from Nebbiolo Rosé have an utterly compelling, mesmerizing perfume that is truly unforgettable. However, it appears that perfume will only carry you so far, unfortunately. It is telling of the difficult times Nebbiolo Rosé has faced that when I asked Pio Boffa, one of the nicest and better wine producers you are liable to meet anywhere in the world, if he owned any Nebbiolo Rosé vines, he vigorously shook his head (in typical Pio Boffa style), saying, "No, I hated it, and when I was younger I used to rip it out every time I found a vine." This sentiment was shared by many other producers, who weren't interested in a Nebbiolo biotype (or so it was thought to be) characterized by slightly less acidity and very light hue and tannic structure. Michele Chiarlo adds more fuel to the fire in noting that "we never used it, because besides low color, it delivers high alcohol." Winemaker Luca Veglio of Oddero adds: "I view Nebbiolo Rosé and its clone CN 111 as a remnant of a viticulture of the past: today nobody is interested in a similar grape." You can forgive Luca: a very talented winemaker, he is also a young man who has grown up on modern behemoth-like wines, in a climate that until recently, systematically penalized nuance and grace in all kinds of tastings. Another extremely talented and passionate young winemaker, Francesco Versio of Bruno Giacosa, has a different point of view: "We have a little Nebbiolo Rosé, and are happy to use it. In fact, I really like the Marchesi di Gresy's entry-level Barbaresco bottling, where 20 to 30 percent Nebbiolo Rosé is used: sure, it's lightly colored and not hugely structured, but it's a wine of amazing grace and refinement."

Of course, as Angelo Gaja points out in his humorous, piercing style, there isn't that much Nebbiolo Rosé around anyway: "Listen, I bought the famed Podere del Pajoré vineyard from Giovannino Moresco back in the seventies, said to be planted to Nebbiolo Rosé. Though we still have a large parcel of those old vines, we don't think it's Nebbiolo Rosé at all; but if you come up and show us around, maybe we'll learn something new." There's nothing like a world-class winemaker/producer who doubles effectively as a comedian, but Angelo, a man of uncanny intelligence, can get away with it, for his ideas and impressions are always worth listening to. Besides, I've seen reports of the Podere del Pajoré having been planted mostly or all to Nebbiolo Rosé, so finding out otherwise from the man who now owns it is a wine writing scoop.

In any case, all of the above negativity is enough to make a Nebbiolo Rosé lover like yours truly start to have doubts. Well... almost. Thanks to work by Botta, Schneider, Akkak, Scott, and Thomas (2000), we now know that Nebbiolo Rosé is a variety genetically distinct from Nebbiolo, though the two are closely related (first-degree parentage), according to studies by Anna Schneider and her colleagues (2004). In this respect, the situation between Nebbiolo Rosé and Nebbiolo is not unlike that of Glera, of which there is a Glera (or Glera Tondo) and a Glera Lungo, differentiated mainly by the characteristics of the berry (Calò, Costacurta, Cancellier, Crespan, Milani, Carraro, et al. 2000).

Surveys carried out in diverse viticulture areas such as Valtellina also confirmed Nebbiolo Rosé to be synonymous with Chiavennaschino, previously held to be Grignolino. In Valtellina, Nebbiolo Rosé has always been welcome, for in potentially hot summertime viticultural areas such as Inferno (the name says it all) and especially Sassella, Nebbiolo Rosé holds the advantage of greater drought resistance over Nebbiolo. Documents such as those of the Ampelography Commission of the province of Sondrio (Gerini 1882) mention a Chiavenasca Piccola (Nebbiolo Rosé) cultivated over a not small surface of five hundred hectares, compared to the only one thousand hectares of Chiavenasca Comune (Nebbiolo) and the two hundred hectares of Chiavenasca Intagliata (Nebbiolo Michet). Note that *chiavenasca* is correctly spelled in these two cases; this was the spelling (with only one *n*) used back then, while it's *chiavennasca* today.

It's not clear if Nebbiolo Rosé is the result of a natural crossing between Nebbiolo Lampia with an as yet unknown other variety, or if Nebbiolo Rosé is one of the two parents of Nebbiolo; and though the latter hypothesis seems less likely given that Nebbiolo has always been more abundant than Nebbiolo Rosé, the possibility can't be excluded. Nebbiolo Rosé ripens slightly earlier than Nebbiolo, so much so that it's also called Nebbiolo Matiné by local producers (as in *mattino*, or morning, the early part of the day), but it also differs from Nebbiolo due to its greater vigor, a larger leaf with a characteristically bulbous upper surface and deeper lateral sinuses, a slightly smaller and more compact bunch, with a lighter, more violet (rather than dark-blue) tinge to its berries. The berries are certainly less endowed with anthocyanins and polyphenols, almost translucent when held up to the light; say what you will, but I think their pinkish-red color is utterly beautiful. It is a very vigorous and fertile cultivar, less affected by *millerandage* and berry shatter, and has fewer flowering problems during cold and rainy springs than Nebbiolo.

Which Wines to Choose and Why

Everywhere Nebbiolo grows, Nebbiolo Rosé is also present and diffusely cultivated, though never abundant. Clone CN III was one of the first Nebbiolo clones to be made available, and growers planted it. It is also found in the Astigiano area of Piedmont, where Nebbiolo is very rare. Pure Nebbiolo Rosé wines have always been exceptionally rare, and this is even more true today. Historically, Nebbiolo Rosé was always planted alongside the other Nebbiolo biotypes, but usually in smaller numbers; producers liked to include 10 to 20 percent Nebbiolo Rosé in their Nebbiolo wine blends in order to increase their wine's perfume, but few ventured further. One noteworthy exception is Elvio Cogno's Barolo Bricco Elena Riserva, a pure Nebbiolo Rosé made from clone CN III. It is archetypal for the variety: pale ruby in hue, penetratingly perfumed (rose petal, red currant, sour red cherry, marzipan, white pepper, violet, iris), austere, and mineral; years of patience are required for it to smoothen out completely, but even then it never displays the creamy charm and power of other Nebbiolo Lampia–dominated Barolos and Barbarescos. Trying to choose between Nebbiolo Rosé's perfumed steely resolve, or Nebbiolo's fleshier, sweeter mouthcoating texture is really tantamount to deciding who is first among equals.

The best (and only producer) of pure Nebbiolo Rosé is Elvio Cogno. The Barbaresco Martinenga of Marchese di Gresy contains at least 20 percent Nebbiolo Rosé (which explains its much lighter hue). Brovia owns two small parcels of vines entirely planted to this variety but, alas, makes no monovarietal wine. In the 1970s, Vietti used to make a Barolo Briacca that was reportedly entirely Nebbiolo Rosé and I can vouch that it was a thing of beauty. Reportedly, the famous Barbaresco Podere del Pajoré by Giovannino Moresco (now owned by Gaja; those grapes are blended into his regular Barbaresco bottling), another of the truly great Italian wines of the past, was also monovarietal Nebbiolo Rosé, but, as I mentioned earlier in, Gaja disputes this, and has told me repeatedly that when he bought the vineyard there was no more than 30 percent Nebbiolo Rosé present.

WINES TO TRY: Elvio Cogno*** (Barolo Riserva Bricco Elena).

Negretto

WHERE IT'S FOUND: Emilia-Romagna. NATIONAL REGISTRY CODE NUMBER: 162. COLOR: red.

Negretto is also known as Maiolo or Morina and by the less accurate name of Neretta (best avoided, as there are many other *Neretta* varieties in Italy; also, while the grape is darkly hued, the wine isn't, or shouldn't be). Some still use the old name of Negrettino and label their wines thus (which is actually illegal, as the registered name of the variety is Negretto). Negretto was first mentioned by Pier de' Crescenzi in 1495 (who called it Maiolus). Centuries later, the twelfth volume of the ampelographic bulletin of 1879 listed it as an oidium resistant variety and therefore very popular in Emilia-Romagna, and according to Marzotto (1925), Cavazza wrote that it was the most abundantly planted variety in the province of Bologna (of twenty thousand total hectares, fourteen thousand were Negrettino). Still, it risked extinction in the latter half of the twentieth century. A big problem in grasping just how cultivated this variety really was at any point in time is that Negretto was always confused with other varieties such as Negratto, Negrettino, Moretto, Maiolo, and a Negretto Dal Raspo Rosso. As recently as 2000, it was misidentified as Uva Longanesi (Marangoni, Venturi, and Fontana 2000). Credit for its resurgence is due both to large estates such as Consorzio Vini Colli Bolognesi that have actively worked to save the variety and promote its merits, and to small producers such as Erioli that searched out old vineyards and selected the best-looking grapevines worthy of propagation. Giorgio Erioli sourced vineyards planted before World War II and some even in 1915–18; this material, and vines from Tenuta Bonzara and Vallona too, were then used by the large nursery Rauscedo to multiply and propagate Negretto, making it available to any other interested producers.

Ampelographically, Negretto has medium-large bunches and berries, the former cylindrical-conical (with one to two wings) and the latter round-oval in shape (with thin blue-black skins). However, Negretto's morphology can vary substantially, not because of clonal variations (no clones are available to date), but because of some intravarietal variability (at least seven biotypes are recognized, and based on the many weird-looking Negretto vines I have seen, there are probably many more). This variability reaches its zenith with the biotype Erioli, once believed to be identical to Uva del Fantini (also known as Pianoro 350), but research has shown this to be untrue. Overall, Negretto is a very regular, dependable producer. It is very resistant to oidium, while botrytis bunch rot and spring frosts are a risk (even though it doesn't budbreak or flower particularly early in the season). Giorgio Erioli told me recently that "Negretto grows particularly well on hillsides, where it was always traditionally grown in the area of Bologna. In contrast to Albana, Montuni, and other varieties relegated to poor-quality flatland vineyards, Negretto was always given the choicest positions." Today, Negretto grows all over Emilia-Romagna, especially in the provinces of Bologna and Ravenna (mainly around Forlì and Faenza), though only in sporadically planted vineyard plots.

Which Wines to Choose and Why

In the past, Negretto was always made as a fresh, lightly sweet wine best drunk soon after harvest; locals matched it with fruit tarts, dry cookies, ravioli with *saba* (a sweet syrup made from grape must), and cakes made with chestnut flour. Unfortunately, for most of the twentieth century it went missing, reduced to a curiosity only good for local consumption. In 2004, the Centro Ricerche Produzioni Vegetali in Tebano proceeded with the first-known experimental microvinifications of monovarietal Negretto, after identifying at least seven biotypes of the grapevine. The wine was appreciated for its color and complex aromas but less on the palate, where it was found to be slightly bitter. Since then, greater care in fermentation temperatures and length of macerations have ensured better rather than bitter wines. Giorgio Erioli explains: "Negretto's real problem is its irregular buildup of sugars, which is highly variable year to year, and so wines vary in extract and alcohol. The latter can range anywhere from 10.5 percent to 13 percent or more, depending on the vintage." In my view, the wine, though not exactly the last word in complexity, is absolutely delightful, light red in hue, with delicate aromas and flavors of small red berries and sweet spices, usually with low alcohol (rarely more than 11 percent), high acidity, and vibrant but civilized tannins. It matches extremely well with red-berried tarts, sweet pancakes, and desserts made with chestnut flour.

WINES TO TRY: Erioli-Laura Malaguti*** (Maiolus; also makes a critically acclaimed sparkling rosé in the Champagne tradition, with secondary fermentation in the bottle, and a lovely sweet Passito di Negretto) and Ognibene Luigi** (Naigar Tèn; the estate practices biodynamic agriculture and its wines hark back to past traditions, featuring long macerations on the skins and aging in wood barrels).

Negro Amaro

WHERE IT'S FOUND: Puglia, Basilicata, Campania. NATIONAL REGISTRY CODE NUMBER: 163. COLOR: red.

Though experts and novices alike believe the *amaro* in this variety's name refers to the tannic structure or a bitter quality in the wine, in reality Negro Amaro derives from the Greek and Latin words *mavros* and *niger,* both of which mean "black" and refer to the dark color of the berries rather than to the color of the wine (which is actually not that somber, usually). I also need to clarify the variety's correct spelling, as people everywhere get it wrong (in Italy too): Negro Amaro is two words, with a space between them, as you see written in this book.

Perhaps because of its importance and diffusion within Puglia, Negro Amaro has long been written about and saddled with many different spellings. Montefiore (1916) wrote about Negramaro and *Moscato* infected by fanleaf virus. Vitagliano (1980) preferred the Negroamaro spelling, while Bianchi spelled the variety Nero Amaro in his 1893 book describing the grape in Basilicata. Still, Negro Amaro it is, and this is not just a moot point: a few years ago, a Puglian wine producer was fined for having the wrong spelling of the variety's name on his label. A trivial matter? Sure. But the law requires exact information on labels, which also function as consumer guarantees.

Erroneous synonyms for Negro Amaro include Lacrima (due to Negro Amaro's at times tear-like or more usually oval-shaped berries); this synonym is best avoided, as there are many true Lacrima varieties in Italy), Uva Olivella (around Pozzuoli, in Campania), Jonico (typically the name used around Galatina in Puglia), and others that are rarely used anymore. Negro Amaro is believed to be a Greek import (what is now the Puglia part of Italy was colonized by the Greeks as early as the seventh century B.C.E.), but official documentation of its presence only dates to 1872. In that year, in a letter written to Professor Apelle Dei, Achille Bruni complains of a parasite that was damaging the vines of Negro Amaro. Furthermore, Negro Amaro appears to be unrelated to most Greek varieties.

Ampelographically, Negro Amaro is characterized by short, compact medium-large bunches shaped as truncated cones, with medium-small oval, blue-black berries. However, morphology can vary considerably, given the huge number of clones available. The list includes VCR 10, ISV sn-Cle 56, ISV sn-Cle 64, ISV sn-Cle 71, UNIMI-VITIS-NEG VV 606 (characterized by higher concentrations of polyphenols, with resulting wines that are more structured and full-bodied, ideal for long-term aging), UNIMI-VITIS-NEG VV 688 (characterized by smaller bunches and berries, yielding wines that are less structured but finer, ideal for *rosato* production), VCR 23, and ISV sn-Cle 87. This long list also speaks to the importance this variety holds in Italian circles (or Puglian ones, at least).

Viticulturally, Negro Amaro is characterized by abundant and dependable production, by being very adaptable to most soils (though it prefers those that are calcareous clay), and good disease and drought resistance. Its skins are especially rich in polyphenols such as resveratrol (a much studied antioxidant), phenolic acids, and anthocyanins (of which the very stable malvin represents 38 percent). Most important, Negro Amaro weathers heat extremely well and doesn't drop its acidity easily, which is one reason why producers in warmer wine-production regions are increasingly interested in it. Recently, another Negro Amaro variety, Negro Amaro Precoce or Negro Amaro Cannellino, has been discovered. Though genetically identical to Negro Amaro, and therefore most likely just a biotype of Negro Amaro, its viticultural behavior is so different that it has been listed separately in the National Registry (see NEGRO AMARO PRECOCE, chapter 5).

Today, Negro Amaro grows all over Puglia, though more in the central and especially southern third of the region, known as Salento. There it grows mainly in the countrysides of Lecce and Brindisi, where it is the most abundant variety, and to a lesser extent in the more central Puglian provinces of Bari and Taranto. A small number of vines are also found in Basilicata and Campania. It is also grown in the United States, where Montoliva Vineyards and Cougar Winery both produce monovarietal wines. In Australia, it's grown in Adelaide Hills, Murray Darling, Eden Valley, and Hunter Valley (producers include By Jingo Wines, Chalmers, Tallavera Grove, Parish Hills, and Torzi Matthews).

Which Wines to Choose and Why

A number of very good DOC wines feature Negro Amaro (Copertino, Lizzano, Salice Salentino, Squinzano, Leverano, and more). Of these, Salice Salentino is most famous and sold all over the world. Negro Amaro makes a lovely medium bodied, refreshing red wine, though *riservas* can be more corpulent; most people can't tell it apart from a well-made Lizzano or Squinzano. Negro Amaro is, however, seldom a monovarietal wine: this is because on its own, with few exceptions, it can yield somewhat tough, monolithic, uninteresting wines. For this reason, it is usually softened by a small addition of one of the local *Malvasia Neras*, which have historically been to Negro Amaro what Canaiolo Nero was and is to Sangiovese. A jack-of-all-trades, Negro Amaro makes a range of wines, from inexpensive and uncomplicated to rich and full-bodied, plus some of Italy's best *rosato* wines. The latter are among the best *rosatos* of Italy, along with Cerasuolo d'Abruzzo and Chiaretto del Garda.

When well made, Negro Amaro wines have typical aromas of black fruit, tobacco, and a characteristic note of shoe polish. On the palate the wine can be rich and suave or light and refreshing. The wine has always been used to add alcohol and size to many anemic wines made in central and northern Italy, because at high yields Negro Amaro has plenty of alcohol but little in the way of distractingly floral or fruity aromas. It is therefore an ideal complementary grape, though sometimes, and some would write many times, its presence in the blend is only as an alcoholic support. Word has it that Negro Amaro is often added to famous Italian wines outside Puglia too, though it's not officially allowed in famous non-Puglian DOC blends. Still, producers whisper that there is a veritable lake of Negro Amaro–filled cisterns traveling up and down the country.

The *rosato* wines can be delicious, though a number are plagued by unclean aromas and faulty winemaking, and others have a little too much residual sugar for my taste. When good, they're very good, with aromas and flavors of almond flowers, wild strawberries, and fresh citrus; they're also much darker in color than the *rosato* wines of the Garda or France's Provence; and though some wine lovers might wince at the cherry-ade color of Puglian *rosatos*, these wines can be remarkably interesting and delightful. Piernicola Leone de Castris, of the famous family estate in Puglia that was the first to bottle a *rosato* in Italy, says that "Puglian *rosato* wines are bright, medium-pale red: it's tradition, not just a marketing ploy, and what our customers want. Lighter and salmon-toned as they do elsewhere is not necessarily better." Damiano Calò of Rosa del Golfo (another of Italy's best *rosato* producers) adds, "Problem is, Provence rosés are so famous that wine lovers have come to expect all rosés or *rosato* wines to be of that very pale *oeil de perdrix* color, while ours are redder and fruitier. My point being that pale colors and intensity of sweet fruit don't always go together." When all is said and done, with Negro Amaro the best of all possible worlds is at your lips: *rosso* and *rosato* wines that are extremely refined and interesting. Just beware the collection of much less distinguished wines.

WINES TO TRY: Agricole Vallone*** (Graticciaia, from lightly air-dried grapes, featuring a unique creamy texture and bright rich red-cherry and sweet spice flavors; not unlike an Amarone, but with less tannins and the higher drinkability of Negro Amaro), Taurino*** (Patriglione, also made from lightly air-dried grapes), Candido** (Duca D'Aragona, but there's Montepulciano mixed in), Conti Zecca* (Negramaro; a good, simple, everyday wine). For Salice Salentino, try: Agricole Vallone** (Vereto Riserva), Leone de Castris** (Riserva), Mocavero*, Cantele*, and Due Palme*. For *rosato*, try: Rosa del Golfo*** (both the oak-aged Vigna Mazzì and the more traditional Rosa del Golfo), Leone de Castris*** (Five Roses, Five Roses Anniversario), Candido** (Le Pozzelle Rosato), Alessandro Bonsegna** (Nardò Danza della Contessa), Felline** (Vigna Rosa), and Racemi** (Anarkos; used to be made with Ottavianello—France's Cinsault—but its makeup has since changed to mainly Negro Amaro).

Nerello Cappuccio

WHERE IT'S FOUND: Sicily, Calabria. NATIONAL REGISTRY CODE NUMBER: 164. COLOR: red.

Surprisingly little is known about this variety, though it has always been an important part of the viticulture of Etna's volcano and the immediate surroundings. Geremia (1834) was the first to describe its presence in the areas of Trescagni and Viagrande near Catania. Then in 1878, the *Bollettini ampelografici* noted a Nerello Ammantellato in the province of Catania and a Niureddu Ammantiddatu in the province of

Palermo. Both these names, just like Nerello Cappuccio, derive from the cultivar's appearance, characterized by an opulent, bushy canopy that resembles a cowl or cap *(cappuccio)* and that hides the grapes from view. It is much rarer than its Etna soul mate Nerello Mascalese, with which it is usually blended: though Nerello Cappuccio can be used to make an interesting wine on its own, it is generally viewed as lacking the tannins necessary to stand alone. However, it provides color and softens acidity, the main reasons why it's blended into weakly hued and more acidic wines made with Nerello Mascalese. The high concentrations of malvin and acylated anthocyanins (which are less subject to oxidation) means the deep hue of Nerello Cappuccio wines will last longer. I believe Nerello Cappuccio should be allowed to fly solo more often: over the years, I have tasted many fine wines made of mainly if not all Cappuccio, and though they undoubtedly shared a certain lightness of being and a rustic quality, they were pleasant and refreshing.

Another controversial aspect of this variety is its synonymity with Nerello Mantellato (or Mantiddatu Niur, in local dialect), which the majority of experts believe to be identical to Nerello Cappuccio. Salvo Foti, who used to be the winemaker at the Benanti estate and knows Etna varieties like nobody else, believes they are. But Marc de Grazia, the famous American importer of Italian wines and now owner of the high-quality Tenuta delle Terre Nere estate on Etna, believes otherwise: "Despite what some ampelographic studies have documented, the two vines look different and the wines also taste different." To prove his point, in 2011 he separately vinified lots of Nerello Cappuccio, Nerello Mascalese, and what he believes to be Nerello Mantellato. These discordant views have been common over the decades. Di Rovasenda (1877) believed these two *Nerellos* to be identical (and identical to Nerello di Sant'Antonio, a variety practically nobody seems to know anything about, and I've asked); but Mazzei and Zappalà (1964) as well as Cavazza (1914) disagree. Clearly, the jury will be out until genetic testing is performed on the vines perceived to be Mantellato, but it's fun to try a wine supposedly made from a different variety. In fairness, Foti also points out that "in western Sicily, much as in Calabria, Nerello Cappuccio is a name attributed to many other red varieties, even Sangiovese."

In this respect, a recent study on the genotypic and phenotypic characterization of Nerello Mascalese and Nerello Cappuccio is enlightening (Branzanti, Brancadoro, Scienza, Fichera, and Raiti 2010). Of 156 accessions (115 of Nerello Mascalese and 41 of Nerello Cappuccio) from eastern Sicily evaluated for both phenotypic and genotypic variability, false synonymies were rampant. The results were of the utmost interest, for the study showed that 70 percent of the accessions initially reported to be Nerello Cappuccio were in fact Carignano, and another 10 percent were a mix of Sangiovese and Ciliegiolo. Therefore, only the remaining 20 percent were truly Nerello Cappuccio, and among these grapevines many phenotypes were found, and five distinct varieties. So not only is Nerello Cappuccio less common than previously thought, there are plenty of biotypes and the grape is interplanted with other as yet unknown grape varieties all of which have been given the same name.

In this light, and to my way of thinking, the discovery of different varieties in vineyards believed to be of Nerello Cappuccio makes the existence of Nerello Mantellato all the more likely. Clearly, the grape varieties in the Branzanti study looked like each other, or were "cowled," and so the likelihood of Mantellato existing seems to make sense. Of note, the forty-one reported Nerello Cappuccio vines were sourced from fourteen different townships around Etna, making the likelihood of truly gross errors in field cultivar recognitions less likely—this is the only part of Sicily in which Nerello Cappuccio thrives, so people ought to recognize it. However, if the varieties planted had been misnamed from the start, then locals might believe them to be Nerello Cappuccio even though they are not. I wonder if this isn't what has happened to Nerello

Mantellato in relation to Nerello Cappuccio, and vice versa. Nevertheless, this study's results lead to two possible conclusions: either Nerello Cappuccio and Carignano are identical, which is not the case (though there is a resemblance between them); or, more likely, the real Nerello Cappuccio was slowly replaced, over time, by Carignano in many, but not all, Etna vineyards because of grower preference for the latter variety. Clearly, even though Carignano replaced much of Nerello Cappuccio, locals continued to erroneously refer to it as Nerello Cappuccio.

Ampelographically, Nerello Cappuccio differs considerably from Nerello Mascalese. Its medium-sized bunches are pyramidal, compact, and short; Mascalese's are medium-small, long, winged, and conical-cylindrical. The berries differ too: Cappuccio's are medium-large, round, and dark blue, while Mascalese's are medium-small, oval, and light blue. Cappuccio's early budbreak and flowering expose it to the vagaries of weather, and spring frosts and *coulure* can be problems. Otherwise, the variety is easy to grow and not particularly demanding, with good vigor and production levels, usually ripening a couple of weeks before Mascalese.

Nerello Cappuccio, just like Nerello Mascalese, can be found in small quantities in Calabria (around Reggio Calabria and Catanzaro), but it is more easily found in the northeastern corner of Sicily, around Catania and Messina (where, as recently as the 1950s, Nerello Cappuccio, or more precisely, what was thought to be Nerello Cappuccio, represented more than 30 percent of the area under vine). It is also present in the southern provinces of Agrigento, Enna, and Caltanissetta, but I wonder how much is really planted there. At roughly 720 hectares (based on 2010 data), it is only the eighteenth most commonly planted variety in Sicily (representing about 0.62 percent of the surface under vine on the island).

Which Wines to Choose and Why

Nerello Cappuccio, just like Nerello Mascalese, is included in the Calabria DOC blends Lamezia, Savuto, and Scavigna (often blended with Gaglioppo; but complementary colors aside, uniting two varieties whose monovarietal wines are each endowed with coarse or rustic mouthfeels makes little sense to me). Of course, Nerello Cappuccio is more easily found in Sicilian wines such as DOC Etna Rosso (where it can make up to 20 percent of the final blend) and Faro (with Nerello Mascalese and Nocera, another local variety) near Messina.

The wine is wonderful and different from all other Sicilian wines. A monovarietal Nerello Cappuccio is medium-dark red in hue and offers aromas and soft flavors reminiscent of ripe red cherry (not surprising given the wine's benzaldehyde content), vanilla, minerals, and light coffee; it is not particularly floral, just like wines made with Nerello Mascalese, but is certainly more floral than its stablemate. Nerello Cappuccio wines usually have tougher tannins too and a slightly coarser quality to them, which has people thinking, saying, and writing that it is the lesser of the two Sicilian *Nerello*s, but I shudder at such oversimplifications. Monovarietal wines from Cappuccio have been made for roughly ten years or less (and then by the only producer easily available to those who don't live in Italy or who visit the country for short trips once a year or so), the grape has always been confused with other varieties such as Carignano and Sangiovese, and there is little knowledge of what the best exposures, altitudes, soils, and rootstocks might be; yet experts are pontificating away. Perhaps waiting a little until we have more data from wines made appropriately and accurately, for longer than just a decade, might be a good idea.

WINES TO TRY: Benanti*** (who has made a practically pure version since 1998, in his I Monovitigni series, thanks to the talented winemaker Salvo Foti, unfortunately no longer with the estate; it was Foti who performed the first massal selection of Nerello Cappuccio in a vineyard located one thousand meters above sea level on the southern slope of Etna, and Benanti then replanted the selected vines on the northern side), Fessina** (owner Silvia

Maestrelli sources fruit from the same vineyard as Benanti), and Cummo* (1908).

Nerello Mascalese

WHERE IT'S FOUND: Sicily, Calabria. NATIONAL REGISTRY CODE NUMBER: 165. COLOR: red.

One of my life-defining moments in wine happened in 1980 or 1981. Having endured countless so-so wines brought to Sunday lunch by my Sicilian grandfather, and having given up hope on his wine knowledge, one fateful day he finally brought something spectacular: a wine he simply called *vino nero* (black wine). I had never tasted a wine from Sicily that was even a tenth as good as that one, and believe me, I still remember every drop: it was then that I finally understood the magic that Nerello Mascalese was capable of, in the right hands. And I suddenly understood why my grandfather, who had lived in the foothills of the Etna volcano most of his life (our family owned small holdings in Randazzo and Linguaglossa, prime Nerello Mascalese sites today), had always waxed poetic about the wines made in his area. At last, I had seen Nerello Mascalese's light, and I became a believer.

Also locally called Niureddu, Nerello Mascalese's name derives from Mascali, the plain northeast of the city of Catania that separates it from the sea, as well as from the name of a township north of Riposto near Catania, from where ships full of Nerello wine left for other shores. Sestini described the variety in 1760, placing it in the family of the *Nigrelli* varieties, and Geremia wrote about it in 1835. But Nerello Mascalese and its wines only surged to prominence at the turn of the most recent century. Prior to 2000, nobody talked about this variety (or of Nerello Cappuccio, its stablemate in most wines made in the northeastern corner of Sicily). Today, things couldn't be more different, and the Etna area has become, without question, Italy's single hottest wine-production zone—shades of Chianti-shire and Tuscany, in fact, with many new and moneyed owners moving into the area and new estates springing up.

The cultivar has therefore become the subject of numerous studies. According to Cipriani, Spadotto, Jurman, Di Gaspero, Crespan, Meneghetti, et al. (2010), Nerello Mascalese is a natural crossing of Sangiovese and Mantonico Bianco, which would also make it a sibling of Gaglioppo. These findings confirmed previous results obtained by Di Vecchi Staraz, Bandinelli, Boselli, This, Boursiquot, Laucou, Lacombe, and Varès (2007), who had observed that Nerello Mascalese and Gaglioppo were both members of the extended Sangiovese family. A relationship between Nerello Mascalese and Carricante has also been suggested recently, which is hardly surprising, given that the two varieties have coexisted in the same finite space (Etna) for centuries. Last but not least, just as with Nerello Cappuccio, a study by Branzanti, Brancadoro, Scienza, Fichera, and Raiti (2010) showed that many genetically distinct varieties are planted in what were thought to be vineyards of nothing but Nerello Mascalese, highlighting the difficulties inherent in ampelographic study and genetic confirmation. Importantly, studying Nerello Mascalese's anthocyanin profile reveals a concentration of peonin and cyanin greater than 50 percent, with a very low presence of acylated pigments, clearly explaining why Nerello Mascalese wines are generally light in color (or should be). However, a few biotypes appear to have slightly higher levels of acylated anthocyanins; therefore some wines could have slightly deeper hues, depending on the winemaking and viticultural techniques employed. Of note, anthocyanin concentrations can vary noticeably in Nerello Mascalese depending on growing conditions, as noted by Foti (1991).

Nerello Mascalese displays considerable intravarietal variability. Smaller-berried individuals might be optimal choices for obtaining greater polyphenol (especially anthocyanin) synthesis. Despite the many biotypes, though, Nerello Mascalese is obviously very different from Nerello Cappuccio: it has smaller, conical-cylindrical, long, winged bunches compared to Cappuccio's medium-large, pyramidal, compact ones. Berries also differ: Mascalese's are oval, medium-small (though many biotypes have large ones), and light blue, Cappuccio's are medium-large, round, and dark blue. Nerello Mascalese is very vigorous but strongly influenced by vintage characteristics, the area of cultivation, training method, and density of planting; it's an abundant but irregular producer, and it's not particularly resistant to common vine diseases, especially botrytis bunch rot and oidium.

The grape is a late ripener, and Etna is a cold place: winemaker Francesco Bartoletti cautions that choosing the right moment to deleaf is key: "[Mascalese is] large berried and thin skinned, [so] proper ripening and botrytis are always two concerns. If you deleaf too soon, the berries will sunburn, so best to go ahead in mid-September. You can't do without it, though, for if the berries don't ripen fully, this variety's tannins are green and astringent. They remain so to a degree even when grapes are fully ripe. For this reason, macerations have to be short and fermentation temperatures can't get too high." Personally, I would add that short pruning is an absolute must with this variety, in order to decrease yields and increase concentration.

Grown on both sides of the Messina Strait, Nerello Mascalese is also found in Calabria, though it is far less common there. Its real home is Sicily's northeast corner, around the cities of Messina and Catania (especially on the northern, eastern, and southern slopes of the Etna volcano, where vines grow even at one thousand meters above sea level). Due to its vigor and the excellent wines it makes, it has also been planted extensively in the provinces of Palermo and Agrigento, where producers use intensive training methods to yield truly ridiculous amounts of grapes (350–400 quintals per hectare). At roughly thirty-eight hundred hectares, it is the eleventh most commonly cultivated variety in Sicily (about 3.5 percent of the island's surface under vine) and is roughly five times as common as Nerello Cappuccio. Given the rampant cultivar misidentification in vineyards concerning both varieties, all these statistics are somewhat suspect. But there can be no doubt that Nerello Mascalese is on a roll, while Cappuccio is not, and so an increasing difference in total hectares planted to each is likely.

Which Wines to Choose and Why

One of the reasons that Etna's wines can be so good is that many vines of Nerello Mascalese are old and pre-phylloxeric. The grape is usually blended with Nerello Cappuccio, a good match because the Mascalese is low in anthocyanins (color) while the Cappuccio is low in tannins. The best wines are the DOC Etna Rosso blends, but up-and-coming Faro wines are good too. Nerello Mascalese can also be part of the DOC blends Contea di Sclafani and Sambuca di Sicilia, or in Calabrian DOCs such as Lamezia; however, it is not typical of these areas.

Etna Rosso is one of Italy's most exciting wines today: the penetratingly pure aromas and flavors of sour red cherry (unlike the riper cherry of Nerello Cappuccio wines), tobacco, aromatic herbs, and minerals will make a believer of you. Nerello Mascalese wines express more herbs and tobacco than those made with Nerello Cappuccio, which tend to be slightly more floral (though flowers aren't a typical descriptor of the wines made with either variety). Many find a Pinot Nero–like quality in Nerello Mascalese wines, and both grapes have a remarkable ability to translate even minute differences in *terroir*; not by chance is the Etna zone referred to as Italy's Burgundy, with the many *contrade,* or sectors, of the volcano yielding remarkably different wines.

WINES TO TRY: Benanti*** (I monovitigni Nerello Mascalese, a standout monovarietal). For stellar examples of Etna Rosso (essentially 90 percent Nerello Mascalese), try: Tenuta delle Terre Nere*** (Calderara Sottana, La Vigna di Don Peppino, Guardiola, Feudo delle Rose), Girolamo Russo*** (Feudo), Passopisciaro*** (Porcaria, Rampante, Sciaranuova), Calcagno** (Arcuria), Graci** (Quota 600), Cottanera**, and Tasca d'Almerita** (Tascante).

Neretto di Bairo

WHERE IT'S FOUND: Piedmont. NATIONAL REGISTRY CODE NUMBER: 167. COLOR: red.

Also known as Neretto di San Giorgio, Nerét, Nerét Gros, Nerét a Cuceglia, and Valperga, Neretto di Bairo is but one of many *Neretto* varieties, most of which are completely unrelated but all so named because of the berries' dark hue. In this respect, Neretto di Bairo resembles Neretto Gentile but is different from Neretto Duro, Neretto di Salto, and Neretto Nostrano, extremely rare local varieties. Well known already in the nineteenth century, it was described by Gallesio ([1817] 1839). Studies indicate that Neretto di Bairo is a likely progeny of Nebbiolo and another, perhaps extinct local variety (Schneider, Boccacci, Torello Marinoni, Botta, Akkak, and Vouillamoz 2004). A 2007 study by Di Vecchi Staraz, Bandinelli, Boselli, This, Boursiquot, Laucou, Lacombe, et al. also suggested a parent-offspring relationship between Neretto di Bairo and Mammolo. If these results are true, it would mean that either Neretto di Bairo or Mammolo had to have been grown, at one point in time, either in Tuscany or Piedmont, respectively, but I don't think I've ever seen documentation to that effect.

Ampelographically, Neretto di Bairo has a large, pyramidal compact bunch and small oval dark-blue berries. It's a resistant variety, but spring frosts and showers are a problem due to early flowering, and it's susceptible to *millerandage*. Many growers have told me it does very well with old pergola canopy training systems, while results are less impressive with the Guyot system. In the past, a little Avarengo was added to Neretto di Bairo: the very sweet Avarengo grapes would induce a secondary fermentation in the wine, turning it into a delicately frothy, fruity sparkler. Unfortunately, Neretto di Bairo's ripening period coincides with that of Erbaluce, placing it at a disadvantage; the latter is the area's most important grape variety and so most estates pay little attention to a *Neretto* that is rare and therefore less important for their economic survival.

Neretto di Bairo is grown mainly in the province of Turin, though it is also found in the provinces of Vercelli and Novara (where, wouldn't you know it, locals call it by a different name, Vermiglia, though Vermiglia is a synonym more correctly used for a different variety, Neretto Gentile). This is why *Neretto* vines such as Neretto di Bairo can be seen in many vineyards of Gattinara, where the world-famous wine of the same name is made.

Which Wines to Choose and Why

DOC wines are Pinerolese or Valsusa Neretto (where it is blended in with Barbera, Nebbiolo, and others), but monovarietal wines are hard to find. The best wine of all is the Canavese Rosso Neretto by Cieck (also one of the star producers of Erbaluce). Owner Domenico Caretto, whose wines are the benchmark for the variety and that seem less tannic to me than they used to be (the 2010 seems about half as tannic as the 2004 and 2005), told me, "We have purposely worked on our winemaking to create a wine that is a little more fruit-forward and less tannic than before. Now we macerate only ten days and it has made all the difference." No temperature control, but the wine is pure and precise, with lovely red fruit and grapey aromas and a nice sweet fleshiness on the long, almondy finish. You'd never guess it sat in *tonneaux* for more than nine months. Think of this as a richer Bourgogne Villages.

WINES TO TRY: Cieck*** (Canavese Rosso Neretto).

Nero Buono

WHERE IT'S FOUND: Lazio. NATIONAL REGISTRY CODE NUMBER: 168. COLOR: red.

Nero Buono is one of Italy's least-known native grape varieties, but as is often the case, one that has a lot to say. No, the wines of Musigny or Petrus need not quiver in their boots, but the fact is that Nero Buono (which means "good black grape") can be the source of excellent, midweight red wines. Legend holds that it was brought to the area of Cori, immediately southwest of Rome, by Cincinnato, the ancient Roman statesman and farmer who settled in the area in the fifth century B.C.E., after defeating the Equi tribe, and propagated the variety. There is no hard proof of this to the best of my knowledge, though they beg to differ at the local, very high-quality wine cooperative named after Cincinnato. The variety was once called Nero Buono di Cori, but the latest European Union rules and regulations do not allow place names to be attached to grape varieties, and so the cultivar is now just Nero Buono, much to the chagrin of fuming locals. According to Marco Carpineti, Cori's best producer, genetic analysis of Nero Buono has been carried out at the Istituto Agrario di San Michele all'Adige (recently renamed Fondazione Edmund Mach), and though results are pending, the variety appears unrelated to any of the major known cultivars.

Nero Buono's name is a clear reference to its dark grapes, and analyzing its anthocyanin profile reveals a preponderance of malvin: the grapes also have very low percentages of easily oxidized pigments such as peonin and cyanin and high levels of acylated anthocyanins, which explains the potentially dark color of Nero Buono wines. The variety likes higher altitudes and volcanic soils; in Cori, where the vineyards are as high up as five hundred meters above sea level, it finds both. The vines are a striking sight: Nero Buono grows erect and there are obvious differences, even to an untrained eye, between the basal and apical leaves, the basal ones trilobed and enormous, fig leaf–like. Nero Buono is very vigorous, but with low basal fertility, so only the Guyot training system works well. Almost all the recently planted vineyards were selected from one specific site owned by a grower called Corradini; later vines were also selected from the parcel owned by Nazareno Milita, president of the Cori cooperative. To date there are no clones available, but a walk in the Nero Buono vineyards will show many morphologically different vines or biotypes. Therefore, massal selection is the method by which to identify plants that grow well and produce better wine. Interestingly, if you observe different Nero Buono vines you'll notice they often have different-sized bunches but vigor is apparently more or less the same (on the same soils and rootstocks). A big problem is Nero Buono's variable production, because it vegetates continuously; growers need to remove the leaves even four or five times a year. Marco Carpineti, Cori's best wine producer and one of the truly up-and-coming names in Italy, says it best: "After you've done all that work deleafing, only twenty days later you look at the vineyard and you'd think nothing had been done, they've all grown back."

The cultivar does well on both calcareous and volcanic soils: on the former it tends to give more structure and body, while on the latter the wines have more elegance. Of late, the preferred rootstocks are Kober 5BB and SO4, but choosing the most appropriate rootstock is vital in this Lazio corner, where there isn't much summer rainfall, so vigor can't be curtailed too much. Excessively long hang times are also not recommended because Nero Buono's thin skins tend to rip.

Which Wines to Choose and Why

In one of Italy's many complex bureaucratic intrigues, the DOC Cori wine calls surprisingly for only a maximum of 40 percent Nero Buono; in the nearby Castelli Romani DOC Rosso, where the variety has always been historically less important than in Cori, it can be used for up to 100 percent. Go figure. Of course IGT wines can be 100 percent Nero Buono. Though the grapes are characterized by low proanthocyanin levels, these are easily extracted, and so the wines have higher total anthocyanin levels than those made with many other red grape varieties (Morassut and Cecchini 1995). A good Nero Buono wine is grapey and vinous, light to medium bodied, with juicy black fruit and pleasant fresh herb aromas and flavors. As it ages, I have found it develops notes of quinine, ink, and rhubarb. In an effort to increase structure and texture, producers attempt to dehydrate the berries somewhat, most often directly on the vine. Cincinnato has tried air-drying for three months, but the wine becomes too sweet, so they prefer late harvests (about twenty days longer, to gain more concentration). Carpineti prefers to harvest late only for his *riserva* wines.

WINES TO TRY: Cincinnato*** (three bottlings: Nero Buono, Ercole, and Polluce; the Ercole is made from a selection of the best grapes, but the entry-level wine is excellent too, and all are remarkably inexpensive) and Marco Carpineti** (Os Rosae, a very good *rosato*). The latter also makes an impressive wine called Dythirambus, but it's not monovarietal, containing large doses of Montepulciano. Because Nero Buono is an up-and-coming variety, expect an increase in such wines (to some extent, it's already happening). My advice for wine writers and wine lovers alike is to please pay attention to the name of the producer for wines labeled Nero Buono, as not everyone's heart is in the right place.

Nero d'Avola

See CALABRESE.

Nieddera

WHERE IT'S FOUND: Sardinia. NATIONAL REGISTRY CODE NUMBER: 170. COLOR: red.

One of the oldest varieties on the island, Nieddera is thought to have arrived either via Greek or Phoenician traders or by way of the almost six hundred years of Spanish domination. No conclusive evidence exists one way or the other. Contini, the best producer of Nieddera wine, who deserves great credit and everyone's admiration for essentially saving the variety from extinction, believes that Nieddera was already on Sardinia between the eighth and seventh centuries B.C.E. Also called Niedda Vera, Nieddaera, Nireddie, or Nigra Vera, the grape was first accurately described by Cettolini (1897) and Cara (1909). Genetic testing at twelve SSR loci confirmed Nieddera as a different variety unrelated to the *Bovale* family and to Nieddu Mannu, as others had suggested (these results were published by Nieddu in 2011 in an extremely well written and interesting book on Sardinian varieties, but not yet in a peer-reviewed journal). That ampelographic recognition of varieties was never easy is demonstrated by past luminaries such as Vialà and Vermorel (1909) believing Nieddera to be identical to Perricone, a completely unrelated Sicilian variety. Contini also told me that in 2010 Vouillamoz, the Swiss researcher who has done so much for the identification of wine grapes, had told him about a genetic analysis comparing Nieddera to two thousand grape varieties (a quarter of them Italian), in which he found that Nieddera might be identical to Mantilaria (or Mandilaria), a Greek grape from Rhodes and Crete. But as the Swiss makes no mention of this finding in the recent *Wine Grapes* book, I imagine further testing excluded this possibility after all. Nieddu, Nieddu, Cocco, Erre, and Chessa (2007) wrote that Nieddera is closely related to Nieddu Mannu, which Vouillamoz believes to be identical to Pascale; therefore, logically, Nieddera and Pascale would be closely related too. In reality, and a clear-cut example of why some study results have to be taken with a large grain of salt, things are most likely not so straightforward. I have no doubts that some so-called Nieddera grapevines on Sardinia are in fact Nieddu Mannu, while others are probably Pascale; but the fact is that Nieddera is a commonly attributed name to many distinct grapevines on the island. In the 2007 study by Nieddu's group, a number of such similar-looking but differently named grapevines (Picciolo Rosso, Primidivu Nieddu, Nera Tomentosa, Falso Gregu, Nieddu Pedra Serra, and Nieddu Mannu from the Pattada area; Pascale from the Padria area; Pascale from the Oliena area; and Pascale from the Cagliari area) were compared morphologically and by SSR analysis and found to be identical. So the logical conclusion is that Pascale and the other varieties analyzed in this study, such as Nieddu Mannu are all one and the same, but this conclusion is most likely applicable only to the specific accessions studied. Pascale is also said to be identical to Nieddera: however, recent findings by Nieddu (2011) show that Nieddera and Nieddu Mannu are not one and the same.

Nieddera is characterized by medium-large, conical, winged bunches and medium-large berries. It's vigorous, grows erect, and so is easy to work with in the vineyard. And while budbreak is late, it's usually an early ripener (September). Found mainly in the Sinis area, on the western side of the island, Nieddera grows in the countryside around Cagliari, Nuoro, and especially Oristano, on the right bank of the Tirso River, where most of the 113 hectares under cultivation are located.

Which Wines to Choose and Why

Nieddera is usually a lightly tannic wine that matches well with most foods; it does not benefit from long maceration times (eight to ten days are usually sufficient). Wines are delicately floral (notes of rose, buttercup, and iris are common) and fruity (red currant and red cherry), with an obvious saline element that makes them seem more acid than they really are. Nieddera is usually blended with other varieties in IGT wines such as Barbagia, Ogliastra, Trexenta, and Valle del Tirso.

Contini is one of the few producers of monovarietal (or very close to it) Nieddera wines and by far the largest and best. Granted, at close to 30 grams per liter of dry extract, it's difficult to think of his version as a light wine, and yet it comes across just so, with medium levels of acidity (usually around 5.5 grams per liter) and despite aging in once- and twice-used small oak barrels. Due to the variety's penchant for yielding light-bodied, fruity wines, it is excellent for making *rosato* wines, indeed some of the least known but most interesting *rosati* in Italy.

WINES TO TRY: Contini*** (IGT Niedderra Valle del Tirso, Rosso and Rosato, both made with 90–95 percent Nieddera and other local varieties depending on the vintage; the Rosato is absolutely outstanding) and Cantina Sociale di Oristano** (Rosato Seu and Montiprama).

Nocera

WHERE IT'S FOUND: Sicily. NATIONAL REGISTRY CODE NUMBER: 172. COLOR: red.

Nocera is originally from northeastern Sicily but nowadays is also found in Calabria. According to Mas and Puillat (1874–79), it was brought to France (Provence and Beaujolais) as well, where it is called Suquet and Barbe du Sultan. Some experts believe it may have been the main grape of mamertino, the famous wine of antiquity produced as early as 289 B.C.E. and known to be a favorite of Julius Caesar. Pliny the Elder considered it the fourth best wine in his classification of 195 wines. In more recent times, Nocera was an important cultivar of northeastern Sicily: in fact, it used to be the main ingredient of Faro wine blends, while it plays only a minor role in this wine today. Nocera-based wines were also sought after as *vini da taglio*, bulk wines used to perk up anemic red wines made elsewhere, due to Nocera wines' astringency, color, and acidity. The most famous such wine was Milazzo, named after the northeastern Sicilian town where the wine was produced. Curiously, there's not much in the way of documented references to this grape: the first mention I was able to find dates back only to 1896, in the *Notizie e studi intorno ai vini ed alle uve d'Italia*, published by the Italian Ministry of Agriculture, Industry, and Commerce. Modern-day producers are looking at Nocera with interest.

Morphologically, Nocera is characterized by medium-sized (up to 320 grams in weight on average), cylindrical-conical or more often pyramid shaped, and loosely packed bunches, with one to two very large wings and often a two-pronged appearance. The berries are large and blue-black. There is one clone (I-NV1), but there are at least two biotypes, Nocera Milazzo and Nocera Vulcanica. Nocera is rich in malvin and stable acylated anthocyanins, explaining the wine's deep and stable color. Though it is most often reported to be a vigorous and disease resistant (but at times affected by *millerandage* and berry shatter) variety, Emiliano

Falsini believes it's not resistant at all to any of the major common grapevine diseases. The berries are very sweet when ripe but don't drop their acidity, making Nocera ideal for warmer climates.

Nocera was once much more common, and easily found in northeastern Sicily at least until the 1960s (Pastena 1973). Nowadays, cultivation is mostly limited to the countryside around Messina, at the northeastern tip of Sicily, especially between Furnari and Castanea. It is also grown sporadically in Calabria (in every province except for Cosenza).

Which Wines to Choose and Why

Nocera is another local variety that has largely disappeared. In fact, it is not even listed among Sicily's thirty most-planted vines. I find this sad because Nocera seems perfectly capable of giving full-bodied, rich, satisfying wines blessed with acidity and ageworthiness, given the appropriate cellars. If you consider that there are almost five thousand hectares of *Merlot* in Sicily (the tenth most-planted variety on the island), a variety that due to the region's hot microclimate really should not be planted there at all, you realize the silliness of not having more of an indigenous variety like Nocera, a quality if little-known wine grape.

The good news is that some producers are taking notice: for example, the Cambria winery believes in Nocera as few others do, though even Alessio Planeta told me he thinks more could be done with Nocera, if only more was known about it. He even foresees making a monovarietal wine one day.

You are most likely to taste Nocera in Sicilian DOC wines such as Faro or Mamertino and Calabria's Sant'Anna Isola di Capo Rizzuto (blends of small amounts of Nocera with the two *Nerello* grapes) and IGT wines such as Avola, Costa Viola, Locride, Palizzi, Pellaro, and Valle Belice. Monovarietal Nocera wines are hard to find. The Cambria estate is thinking of making a sweet wine with Nocera, but it's planned as a Nero d'Avola–Nocera blend. Enza La Fauci of the eponymous estate is studying the variety and I am trying to convince both her and her winemaker Emiliano Falsini to take the plunge.

WINES TO TRY: Mimmo Paone** (one of the best monovarietal examples; deep ruby, expresses lovely aromas of fresh herbs, ripe red cherries, and tar, full-bodied and thick-textured on the long smooth finish; the estate also makes a very good, if lighter-styled, Malvasia delle Lipari), Tenuta Gatti**, Cambria** (Mastronicola, just as good as the Mimmo Paone), and Vasari* (good, if simple; made from organic grapes). Enza La Fauci might consider making a monovarietal Nocera wine sometime in the future.

Nosiola

WHERE IT'S FOUND: Trentino, Lombardy, Veneto. NATIONAL REGISTRY CODE NUMBER: 173. COLOR: white.

Nosiola is a versatile grape variety that, like few others, can successfully deliver pleasant dry white wine of crisp, concentrated lemony zip, and when late harvested or air-dried, makes one of the world's greatest sweet wines. For most experts, this variety's name derives from *nocciola* (hazelnut), given both the color of the grapes and their stalks when fully ripe, and the aromas of hazelnut exuded by the wine. Others believe the name comes from the local dialect word *ociolet*, but this is less likely; still others point to origins in the Celtic prefix *nos*, a diminutive of *nostrales*, meaning "local."

For the longest time Nosiola was considered to be identical to Durella (hence it was also called Durel), which Di Rovasenda (1877) long ago showed to be completely different; other synonyms were Gropel Bianc and Noselara. Many authors, including Babo and Mach (1923), mention a Nosiola Spinarola (or Spargelen, in German) characterized by a very loosely packed bunch and few berries, ideal for *vino santo* production. Unfortunately, modern clones have gone in the direction of tightly packed bunches, perhaps ideal for dry white wine production but not for *vino santo*. In 2007, Vouillamoz, Schneider, and Grando showed that Nosiola (and Groppello di Revò) is most likely the offspring of Rèze, an ancient Valais variety (any one of the three could be a parent or offspring, but because Rèze has been described since the fourteenth century, the other two only since the nineteenth, it seems logical that Rèze is the parent and the other two the progenies).

Always considered a worthy table grape, Nosiola was rarely used to make wine on its own but rather was used in blends, though in 1822 Giacomo Sommadossi, cellar master of the Count Wolkenstein estate, made the first ever *vino santo* with Nosiola, apparently because his employers, the noble Wolkenstein family, wished to be surprised by something different upon their return to the family castle at Easter time (D'Agata 2001a). In 1825 he won a diploma of excellence at the Melbourne International Exhibition for this then-groundbreaking wine. The variety's isolated geographic location in small, mountaintop vineyards means it wasn't uprooted in favor of international varieties and has been linked to Trentino since at least the fifteenth century. Interestingly, the archbishop of Trento decreed in 1930 that Nosiola wines be used to celebrate the Holy Mass, rather than red wines, which risked irremediably staining the white religious vestments.

Nosiola has medium-sized berries and bunches; the latter are elongated, winged, and loosely packed. It's resistant to most diseases and inclement weather, but spring frosts are a risk, for it buds early, and desiccation of the spine is also common. It does best in well-ventilated sites because it is susceptible to sour rot. An irregular producer, in flatland vineyards it produces copious amounts of large flavorless berries. There are three clones: SMA 74 is best for *vino santo* production, as it's less compact than the other two.

Nosiola grows mainly in Trentino but is also found in Lombardy and Veneto close to the shores of Lake Garda. Already in the 1800s, the best production areas were considered to be Trentino's Valle del Sarca and near Lavis. Today, the most important production zone is in the postcard-perfect setting of the Valle dei Laghi, around the towns of Calavino, Cavedine, Lasino, Padergnone, and Lezzano, which is where the best *vino santo* is made (though it can also be made around Arco, Drena, Dro, Nago-Torbole, Riva del Garda, and Tenno). The area of the Valle dei Laghi benefits from the drying effect of the Ora del Garda, a breeze moving northward from Lake Garda that creates a specific microclimate ideal for air-drying grapes in which noble rot thrives.

Which Wines to Choose and Why

Nosiola is used to make both a light, refreshing white wine and the unctuously sweet *vino santo* (made in Trentino only and hence called Trentino Vino Santo). The former is deliciously crisp; the latter is one of Italy's ten best wines, red, white, or sweet, but unfortunately is not very well known. The grapes used for *vino santo* production are air-dried for up to five to six months and lose roughly 50 percent of their weight. The best wine to try is the DOC Trentino Nosiola or the Trentino Vino Santo: the latter is a truly unique, mesmerizingly good sweet wine. Note that the *vino santo* of Trentino is spelled differently than the better-known Tuscan or Umbrian *vin santo* (that's *vin* instead of *vino*); it also tastes very different, much sweeter and creamier.

Dry white nosiola exudes delicate hazelnut and white flower and citrus aromas and flavors, and has a pleasant freshness due to a noteworthy saline element that lasts and lasts on the palate. The *vino santo*s are rich, complex, very sweet, and crammed with ripe peach, almond paste, lime, candied pineapple, tropical fruit jelly aromas and flavors. The variety's archetypal high acidity lifts the rich flavors and extends them at the back.

WINES TO TRY: For Nosiola (dry), try: Cantina Toblino*** (L'Ora), Pojer & Sandri***, Cesconi**, Giuseppe Fanti** (a very rich mouthfeel), Gino Pedrotti**, Riccardo Battistotti*, Bolognani*, Giovanni Poli* (Goccia d'Oro), Enrico Spagnolli*, and Zeni* (Maso Nero; a little too herbal and sauvignony to me). For *vino santo,* try: Gino Pedrotti***, Pisoni***, Francesco Poli***, and Giovanni Poli*** (all of these are outstanding).

Nuragus

WHERE IT'S FOUND: Sardinia. NATIONAL REGISTRY CODE NUMBER: 175. COLOR: white.

Every time I hear someone make the blanket statement that Italy's native varieties aren't all that interesting or capable of high-quality wines, I think of Nuragus. For the longest time, wines made from Nuragus were unimpressive, usually flabby and insipid. Trouble was that yields were always too high, and many local synonyms for Nuragus tell the story: Abbondosa (abundant, as in a copious producer), Preni Tineddus (grab the buckets), or Axina Scacciadeppidus (grape that clears debts). Perhaps even more worrisome was it being listed as Trebbiana in a *Bollettino ampelografico.* In reality, Bruni (1964) describes two Nuragus biotypes, one of them less productive. High yields plagued many Italian native grapes for centuries, and so these were consequently unable to prove their worth, a fate that befell Nuragus too. However, with Nuragus matters didn't improve in modern times when yields were reduced. This is because so little was known about the variety that in trying to make the best wines possible, serious producers applied viticultural techniques such as heavy pruning and aggressive deleafing. Unfortunately, Nuragus drops its acidity quickly and needs canopy production to avoid yielding flabby, low-acid wines. So only after years of observation and trials did the true quality of the variety become evident: today we know it is a very interesting white grape indeed.

Interestingly, Nuragus had always been highly thought of, if for no other reason than because of its extreme resistance to drought (important on Sardinia). Documents from the eighteenth century relate it to the famous wine Moscadeddu de Nuragus. Later, at the end of the nineteenth century, it was the most cultivated grape variety grown near Cagliari and in the Campidano. As recently as 1990 it was still the most abundant variety grown on Sardinia.

Genetic characterization at twelve SSR loci has determined that Nuragus is distinct from all other Sardinian varieties, though it is closely related to Semidano, another native Sardinian white grape, with which it shares ten alleles in the twelve loci studied (these results were published by Nieddu in 2011 in a book on Sardinian varieties). According to De Mattia, Imazio, Grassi, Lovicu, Tardaguila, Failla, et al. (2007), there are two other extremely rare, distinct varieties sharing the Nuragus name: Nuragus Moscadeddu, also known as Nuragus Moscatello or Nuragus Rosso Rompizolla, and Nuragus Arrubiu, currently not being cultivated. As I first wrote in 2003 in the *Gambero Rosso* guide to Italy's native grapes the name Nuragus likely derives from the Phoenician prefix *nur,* meaning "fire" (D'Agata, Sabellico, Aiello, Arru, Buffa, Di Cintio, et al. 2003); others believe it stems from *nuraghi,* Neolithic stone dwellings of the Phoenicians in the Alta Marmilla area near Nuoro. In any case, given the surge of interest in Nuragus and its wines, and with the increasing number of monovarietal bottlings available, you can say this variety is on fire.

Though cultivation of Nuragus was declining in the last decades of the twentieth century, there are now close to three thousand hectares under vine on Sardinia and plantings are on the upswing. Grown everywhere on the island but found mainly in the countryside around Cagliari, Nuoro, and Oristano, it does very well on the marly-clay-calcareous soils northeast of Cagliari: Serdiana, Dolianova, Soleminis, Maracalagonis, Ussana, Donori, and Senorbì are all potential *premier crus* for this variety. Parteolla and Sibiola (in the townships of Dolianova and Serdiana) and Selegas (in the township of Trexenta) are potentially *grand crus*. Also good are Villasimius and Costa Rey (though here the Sette Fratelli mountains provide a sheltered habitat and create a different microclimate). These hillside vineyards (roughly 150–250 meters above sea level) are on heavily drained soils and water shortage is common (this area has the lowest precipitation rates on the island); consequently, vines located in the foothills are subjected to considerable stress, which greatly reduces yields.

Nuragus has medium-large to large (more than 550 grams!), stocky, conical-cylindrical, winged, compact bunches, with medium-large round berries that turn golden-amber if exposed to full sunlight. There is one clone, CFC-26. It's very vigorous, guaranteeing abundant yields, as it's resistant to diseases and drought (rootstocks such as 779R and 140 Ruggeri are best) and it adapts well to just about any kind of soil. However, it tends to overproduce in the presence of too much water. Blessed by a long vegetative cycle with an early budbreak and late harvest, Nuragus can potentially deliver complex, very interesting wines.

Which Wines to Choose and Why

The best wines and the only potentially monovarietal versions are DOC Nuragus di Cagliari, which can be made in *frizzante* (sparkling) and *amabile* (off-dry) styles as well. The maximum allowable yield of two hundred quintals per hectare is a joke, however. Still, that number is positively restrained compared to the three hundred quintals per hectare of centuries past, so I guess legislators were only thinking of tradition when they created the laughable production guidelines. In fairness, one of the trump cards up this variety's sleeve is that it is capable of delivering fresh wines full of charm despite low concentrations of alcohol and aromas and flavors. Still, Nuragus has a high polyphenol concentration in its skins, and care must be taken not to overextract during vinification, lest the resulting wines become bitter and astringent. For this reason, the choice of new oak for aging is not an intelligent one; also, Nuragus is a nonaromatic variety blessed with delicate aromas, so in my view, oak really isn't helpful. However, Mariano Murru of Argiolas, who certainly knows more about this than I do, has been experimenting with gentle oak aging and feels this might be a route by which to make even more interesting, complex Nuragus wines.

WINES TO TRY: Pala*** (I Fiori; the estate has cultivated Nuragus since the mid-nineteenth century and owns two top vineyards, S'Acquasassa near Serdiana and the Is Crabilis near Ussana), Argiolas** (the excellent s'Elegas), Cantina Trexenta*, Cantina Sociale di Monserrato*, and Dolianova* (Perlas).

Olivella Nera

WHERE IT'S FOUND: Campania, Lazio. NATIONAL REGISTRY CODE NUMBER: 176. COLOR: red

Olivella Nera is one of many grapes in Italy named for their olive shape (or *oliva*). There are therefore many *Olivelle* in Italy (or *Livelle* or *Ulivelle*, the latter a term first used by Semmola in 1848), all of which descend, in name at least, from Pliny the Elder's *Vitis oleaginea*. But the main, or true, Olivella cultivar is typical of Lazio and Campania. In the latter region, Olivella Nera (more commonly called Livella in the past) was, and is, always confused with another variety, Sciascinoso; and while Gasparrini reported in 1844 that at least since the nineteenth century Livella and Sciascinoso were considered distinct, Bordignon (1965) confused the two, including Olivella Nera under the Sciascinoso heading. For what it's worth, I believe the two varieties are most likely distinct (from a morphological perspective; I can vouch that while bunches and berries of the two look similar, the leaves are very different). Simply put, it seems logical to me that, given that grapes called Olivella (or Livella) were myriad, it is highly unlikely that these varieties are all identical to Sciascinoso. One maybe, two, but not all.

A very interesting and extremely useful study by Costantini, Monaco, Vouillamoz, Forlani, and Grando (2005) best addressed this issue. The study analyzed 114 accessions putatively corresponding to sixty-nine local cultivars of Campania with eight microsatellite markers, evaluating degrees of genetic relationships. The researchers concluded that Sciascinoso is identical to Livella di Battipaglia, but not to Livella d'Ischia or to Livella di Mirabella, the latter two said to be no longer cultivated. Actually, reading the study carefully, I failed to find evidence of Livella di Battipaglia's identity as Sciascinoso, as the tabulation of the allele sizes at the eight loci for the two varieties (which should read the same) is not listed in the paper. The study refers the reader to table 1, but this table does not describe the allele sizes; it just lists the grape varieties studied. So I'm not sure what to think. In any case, the study results clearly determine that Sciascinoso is not identical to every *Olivella* out there, as two of the Livella varieties are said to be distinct. I would add to these considerations that the Olivella Nera of Ischia differs from the others in that it has round berries, a feature that to my way of thinking would seem to exclude it automatically from the *Olivella* group of cultivars (Migliaccio, Monaco, Ferranti, Nasi, De Gennaro, Granato, et al. 2008). Yet both Froio (1878) and Nesbitt (1884) described an Olivella variety of Ischia but failed to report a Livella there with olive-shaped berries. This might indicate that in the nineteenth century, even the *Olivelle* and *Livelle* were viewed as two different groups of grapes, though I have no hard proof of this. After all this, be warned that books, websites, and locals continue to refer to the Olivella Nera and the Sciascinoso varieties interchangeably.

I view written ampelographic descriptions of Olivella Nera (that is, what you'll read in wine books other than this one) with skepticism, as most get the variety confused with Sciascinoso, so you don't know exactly which grape is being described. Based on my own observations of the Olivella Nera grown in Lazio vineyards, it has small, conical-pyramidal, loosely packed, winged bunches and small dark berries covered with bloom. It's sensitive to peronospora and is extremely vigorous, but most of the vigor is directed to the leaves and the shoots, rather than the grapes, and so productivity is low. In my experience, the Sciascinoso of Campania has compact bunches and is more prone to botrytis bunch rot than to peronospora.

Olivella Nera seems to have fallen on hard times in Campania, where it has been relegated to a secondary role. Not so in Lazio, where Paolo Perinelli, owner of Casale della Ioria (Lazio's best producer of Cesanese del Piglio), has bet that Olivella Nera has a future. Years ago, Perinelli was flabbergasted by an excellent Olivella Nera wine made by a farmer near Esperia, a small town in the province of Frosinone where Olivella Nera was never abandoned. He proceeded to ask around and ultimately selected old vines for propagation. Olivella Nera grows only in Lazio and Campania, and there are no official clones available.

Which Wines to Choose and Why

Much less common than Sciascinoso in Campania, the National Registry makes it clear that Olivella Nera is a distinct variety from Sciascinoso, as Olivella Nera is allowed only in Lazio IGT wines such as Colli Cimini, Frusinate, Civitella d'Agliano, and Lazio. I believe that there are certainly some *Olivelle* growing in Campania too, and they are probably used unknowingly in the area of Vesuvius (in the DOC Lacryma Christi blends), Ischia (DOC Ischia Rosso), and along the Sorrento coast (DOC Penisola Sorrentina), but more often than not, it's Sciascinoso they are using there. The wine has a deeply colored must that adds considerable depth of hue to any wines it is blended with. It's fresh and fruity, with bright red berry and delicate herbal flavors and a saline twist at the back. This wine's sine qua non, though, is lots of fruit, with only medium alcohol and tannin levels. In fact, this is a red wine that can be slightly chilled and matched with grilled salmon steaks and similar fatty fish.

WINES TO TRY: Casale della Ioria*** (the benchmark monovarietal by which all others will be measured).

Ortrugo

WHERE IT'S FOUND: Emilia-Romagna, Lombardy. NATIONAL REGISTRY CODE NUMBER: 177. COLOR: white.

Ortrugo had been relegated to the status of a blending grape until the mid-1970s, when the Mossi family began to select old vines and make monovarietal wine. The University of Piacenza also got involved, creating two clones now commercially available, and consequently, new Ortrugo vineyards have sprung up, right next to old ones full of gnarly old vines resulting from massal selections. Chiara Azzali, owner of Tenuta Pernice, one of the best producers of Ortrugo wines, recalls planting the variety for the first time in 1980. "We liked what we saw, or drank," she smiles, "and so we kept on planting it, in 1989, 2002, and again in 2005. The most interesting aspect about Ortrugo is its great intravarietal variability: the vines planted in 1980 from massal selections all look very different, while clonal selections planted in 2005 are identical to each other." There are three currently available Ortrugo clones, PC ORT 80, PC ORT 81, and VCR 245.

Generally speaking, Ortrugo has large cylindrical-conical compact bunches and medium round berries. It does much better in poorly fertile soils on hillsides, where its natural vigor is reduced. It performs less well in soils that are magnesium deficient, is prone to desiccation of the spine and is susceptible to the European grapevine moth.

Luigi Mossi is called the father of Ortrugo: it's thanks to him that we have Ortrugo and its wines to talk about. "I can't really take that much credit," he objects modestly. "In the early 1970s, all we made and drank here was Malvasia wine, and nobody knew what Ortrugo wine might taste like since everyone blended it with their Malvasia. I had a small parcel of Ortrugo vines planted in a hard-to-work spot, and so they survived essentially on their own. When I decided to replant that site too, curiosity pushed me to see what a wine made only with Ortrugo would taste like before I uprooted everything. I remember just how surprised we all were; the wine was great and different from that made with the Malvasia and so I decided to select the best grapevines and propagate them."

Mossi's choice proved to be a good one, because in the 1980s Malvasia wine sales slumped badly, and producers were left scampering for an alternative to offer consumers. While others chose to try Chardonnay and Pinot Bianco (a big mistake), Mossi went with Ortrugo "because I thought it important to offer people a wine made locally from grapes of local importance."

Simply analyzing the origin of the name Ortrugo confirms Mossi's recollections. Ortrugo was originally called Altruga, as in "other grape" (from *altro*), considered less important than the other varieties it was blended with. The name we know the variety by today was first used by Toni (1927): he described Ortrugo as one of the best white varieties in the province of Piacenza. So this really is a case of one century's dog, another century's star. Which helps you understand what native grapes have had to put up with in their lifetimes.

Ortrugo is especially abundant around Piacenza, in the d'Ardia, Nure, Tidone, and Trebbia valleys, but it is also found in Lombardy in the Oltrepò Pavese area (and I'm not surprised, given how much sparkling wine is made there).

Which Wines to Choose and Why

The best pure examples of Ortrugo can be had in the DOC wine Colli Piacentini Ortrugo. IGT wines that may be up to 100 percent Ortrugo are Bianco di Castelfranco Emilia, dell'Emilia, Forlì, Ravenna, and Rubicone. It is also used in small percentages in the Vin Santo di Vigoleno blend. Even a well-made Ortrugo will never win your nose over with unbelievably intense aromas or your palate with a magically mouthcoating texture, but the wines are always fresh, clean, and crisp. Sparkling Ortrugo wines are not unlike a good Prosecco (but are usually less fruity and more mineral) while still Ortrugo wines have a nice lemony, green apple, delicately herbal, and minerally personality. The better ones will remind you of apricot kernels and white peach. I'm not sure I have ever tasted an Ortrugo wine that qualified as complex, but for early appeal and simple, easygoing sipping on hot summer days, the wine is hard to beat.

WINES TO TRY: Barattieri San Pietro**, La Torretta**, Marco Cordani** (Frizzante), Mossi** (both the still Ortrugo and the Ortrugo Brut, a sparkling wine), Tenuta Pernice**, Cantina Valtidone* (Frizzante). Pusteria's offering also contains 15 percent Trebbiano Romagnolo.

Oseleta

WHERE IT'S FOUND: Veneto. NATIONAL REGISTRY CODE NUMBER: 358. COLOR: red.

One of the many *uve uccelline* (bird grapes) of Italy, varieties so called because birds loved to eat the sweet berries, Oseleta is a true native grape success story. A miserly producer, it had been abandoned by growers in Valpolicella (where it wasn't documented much before the twentieth century anyway). It's not a grape with a long and distinguished history. In part that's because there was more than one *Oseleta* described in the past, when the grape was more commonly referred to as Uva Oselina or Oselina. The first important description was by sixteenth-century humanist scholar Onofrio Panvinio. The ampelographic commissions of 1880 and 1883 listed four red-berried *uve oseline* in the Monti Lessini area of Veneto, and one with white berries: Oselina Rossa, Oselina di Montagna, Oselina Mora, Oselina Nera, and Oselina Biancara. All were characterized by very jagged, intensely green leaves and small bunches and very small and tart berries (Oselina Mora's were the smallest berries of all). Acerbi mentions an Uva Ozilina, but it is unclear if this is today's Oseleta; I have read his description carefully, but I don't find there is enough information to conclusively say the two are the same, despite what you may read elsewhere. Zava (1901) noted the presence of the *Oselinas* around Verona and Treviso. Oseleta has surged back in the last twenty years, mainly thanks to the Boscaini family at the Masi estate. At Masi, they replanted Oseleta in 1985, including it in their wine blend called Toar beginning in 1990 and then creating Osar, which Oseleta gets to play solo. The use of Oseleta on a larger or routine scale, such as in small percentages in Valpolicella and Amarone blends is only very recent, dating back to the late nineties (Tosi and Bletzo 2000). The rebirth of Oseleta happened by chance. Sandro Boscaini, the owner of Masi, was visiting his brother one day and tasted a remarkably tannic and dark Valpolicella. The wine didn't remind Boscaini of any Valpolicella he knew, so he asked to see the vines that had been used, and those didn't remind him of Corvina or any other cultivar commonly used to make Valpolicella. So he had the grapevine analyzed and learned it was Oseleta. Impressed, Boscaini never looked back, and he set up parcels of Oseleta vines on his own estate. Riccardo Tedeschi points out that Oseleta is a highly adaptable grape: it grows well more or less anywhere. "It's also extremely resistant," Tedeschi says, "allowing you to make wine in those weather-challenged vintages such as 2011 in which all the other varieties have to be literally thrown out. It also builds up sugars much faster than other varieties, so the air-drying process doesn't need to last as long, which saves us both time and money." Given Oseleta's very small berries and lack of juice even when not air-dried, this is probably just as well. These last two characteristics explain why, in the beginning, Oseleta's arrival on Veneto's winemaking scene didn't excite or interest the majority of growers: many simply didn't think the grape was suitable for air-drying (D'Agata 2003a).

In fact, Oseleta is characterized by very small bunches (average weight 130 grams) that are cylindrical-pyramidal in shape and extremely compact. Berries are small, round but not uniformly so, and blue-black with thick skins. They contain at least three pips to the two of most other varieties, and the grape is a very resistant, almost rustic variety. For example, even though its bunch is very tightly packed, Oseleta rarely has problems with botrytis. The best sites for Oseleta are characterized by good drainage, but at least some capacity for water retention, and plenty of gravel and sand. Due to Oseleta's morphologic appearance and rustic behavior, experts have postulated that it is a descendant of wild grapevines that were domesticated over time, but there is no definitive evidence of this.

Currently, Oseleta grows only in Valpolicella to the north and northeast of Verona, where there are an estimated twenty-five hectares planted to it (based on 2010 data).

Which Wines to Choose and Why

Pure Oseleta wines are rare because the grape does not yield much juice, due to the extremely small berry, thick skin, and three relatively large pips. It is used to make IGT wines (no DOC wines are yet possible) such as Delle Venezie, Vallagarina, and Rosso Veronese. Air-drying grapes further reduces must available from the berries, which is another reason that large volumes of monovarietal Oseleta wines are unlikely. However, Oseleta had plenty to say, with wines of uncommon power and tannic structure. More important, it is a native alternative to using Cabernet Sauvignon and Merlot as a blending agent for Valpolicella and Amarone; like Molinara, it matches better with Corvina and Corvinone than the two internationals (though because of Oseleta's limited yields, we will likely never see Amarone made with large percentages of the variety). Oseleta's suitability is probably because, like other native grapes, it has lived in a specific area for centuries and is better adapted to the local habitats than recently planted international varieties. Wines made from local grapes invariably show aroma and flavor profiles unique to the production area and more interesting than the predominant coffee-cedar-chocolate-violet of many internationals.

Specifically, I find that Oseleta provides Valpolicella and Amarone with a different tannic texture than Cabernet Sauvignon does, as well as a herbaceousness that is also very different. With a little patience and dedication, it is easy to detect whether a *Cabernet* variety or Oseleta has been added to Amarone. Furthermore, you can guess fairly accurately, given Oseleta's powerful signature, if 5, 10, or 20 percent has been added. According to Raffaele Boscaini, "adding as little as 5 percent of Oseleta will change a wine completely, while it takes at least a 15 percent addition of Rondinella to do the same. Curiously, it's a particularly horrible grape to eat: in the vineyards you just want to spit it out, for it's so tannic." Boscaini loves to add a little of this variety in air-dried form to his wines: "Unlike the *Cabernets*, which tend to produce a large number of bitter substances when air-dried, Oseleta does not, and it really adds a different, better texture to the wine." In my experience, wines that are all or mainly Oseleta have dark hues, exude grapey and violet aromas, and are massively tannic but offer delicate herbal and blackberry flavors, complicated by nuances of tar, leather, fresh herbs, and cinnamon.

Not all Oseleta wines I have tried over the years in Veneto cellars have struck me as successful: some really are too astringent and green, and producers never release those batches of wine as monovarietal examples, preferring to blend small percentages of their oseleta with their other wines to supply backbone and acid nerve. However, Celestino Gaspari, who makes the best Oseleta wine of all and was one of the first to believe in the variety, manages to produce a version that is always marked by very bright red and black fruit flavors and, though typically tannic, is never green or excessively astringent. So it just goes to show that if and when native grapes find someone who believes in them, and dedicates himself or herself to figuring out what works best (given there is very little prior experience with most of these grapes), good things are very likely to happen.

WINES TO TRY: Masi*** (Osar; first made with 85 percent Oseleta in 1995, wholly monovarietal since 2000) and Zymé*** (Oz). La Cappuccina's Carmenos is an interesting but tannic sweet red wine, made with Carmenère and 50 percent Oseleta (hence its name); a very good wine, but that combination ensures tannins not for the faint of heart.

Pampanuto

WHERE IT'S FOUND: Puglia. NATIONAL REGISTRY CODE NUMBER: 179. COLOR: white.

For a while, Pampanuto seemed to be included in just about every white wine from northern and central Puglia. Pampanuto was everyone's favorite party animal, and finding it on its own proved a difficult task indeed. Finally, about ten years ago, for the first time (and after much searching) I found a five-liter demijohn of Pampanuto delle Murge on sale, proving to me that monovarietal Pampanuto wines did exist. And though I wouldn't bet the house that that demijohn really was all Pampanuto (how likely is it that an almost-bulk wine sold in a demijohn is everything the label says it is?), I recall finding the wine delicate and enjoyable and was happy to see that Pampanuto had not gone the way of the dodo.

Also known as Pampanino and Rizzulo (wouldn't you know it, there's an apparently unrelated but similarly named Pampanaro variety in Lazio that needs more study), Pampanuto is now found mainly in northern and central Puglia. Given that Pampanuto is a low-acid variety, it's not surprising that in the Castel del Monte DOC it's usually blended with Bombino Bianco, a variety with no shortage of acidity. According to Count Spagnoletti Zeuli, of the northern Puglia estate of the same name, Pampanuto was always much appreciated, for it builds up plenty of sugar and provides high alcohol levels: "Everyone liked this in the old days, poorer times when wine was a source of calories and a food. Today, people are less thrilled, plus the variety's compact bunch and tendency to rot easily don't do anything for its reputation either."

Not much is known about Pampanuto's history or origins, though Di Rovasenda described it in Puglia in 1877. Pampanuto's relationships to other cultivars are also unknown. A recent study found Pampanuto and Verdeca to be identical varieties, on the basis of ampelographic research consisting of three years' observation of accessions of the Basile Caramia research and experiment station in Locorotondo, in Bari, as well as microsatellite testing (Pirolo, La Notte, Pastore, Torello Marinoni, Giannini, Venerito, et al. 2009). However, these results have not been confirmed by anybody else, and I for one believe the two varieties are not identical. The wines also taste nothing alike. Luigi Moio, university professor and consultant winemaker, one of Italy's acknowledged grape variety experts, who worked in northern Puglia for years, feels the same way: "I worked with Pampanuto at Tenuta Cocevola in Puglia, where we used to make a monovarietal wine, and I never once thought it had anything to do with Verdeca. Plus, the two cultivars are grown in completely different and well-separated areas, with little overlap, perhaps only in a few small areas of central Puglia, so that in itself is indicative." The supposed Pampanuto accessions studied by the researchers were likely Verdeca, but this doesn't mean that every Pampanuto vine out there is Verdeca. Not at all.

Pampanuto is characterized by medium-sized bunches and berries; the bunches are usually conical and the berries round, so it can look like Verdeca at times, which makes confusing the two easier. In my experience, Pampanuto's berries are always paler in color than those of Verdeca, which, as the name implies, are really quite green, though this may also be affected by higher or lower yields. Pampanuto is a good and dependable producer, with copious production of juice that is however usually characterized by low acid and sugar concentrations. There is only one clone available, UBA 20/A.

Which Wines to Choose and Why

In past centuries, Pampanuto was used mainly as a blending agent, as it produces copious quantities of essentially neutral wines that can be easily blended into more important and well-known wines, thereby increasing their production volumes. However, Pampanuto wines tend to oxidize and so they need to be consumed quickly, which has soured some on it, leading to a reduction in total hectares planted and consequently the likelihood of finding monovarietal wines made with the variety. This is a shame, since it can produce a lovely, delicate white wine that deserves more attention.

So, although monovarietal bottlings are extremely rare (only local farmers might have one for you to try), Pampanuto is still used in blends with Bombino Bianco in the excellent DOC Castel del Monte wines and other IGT wines including Daunia, Murgia, Puglia, and Valle d'Itria. Pampanuto has always been known to give light, delicate wines that don't age well (perhaps too delicate, in times when most consumers longed for big, rich white wines). Pre-fermentative techniques may increase the wine's texture, depth of aromas and flavors, and ageworthiness (Chieppa, Lovino, Savino, Limosani, Suriano, Ceci, and Scazzariello 2008). Juice hyperoxygenation, cold soaking (or maceration), and crushed-grape enzymatic treatment processing techniques were applied to Pampanuto grapes that were also treated with traditional vinification techniques (the experimental control). The most promising results were obtained by cold maceration and juice hyperoxygenation, with wines sporting deeper colors and greater texture due to higher polyphenol concentrations. Interestingly, while wines made with hyperoxygenation were characterized by herbal aromas and flavors (sage and basil, with green apple notes), wine made via cold soaking of the grapes was marked by ripe tropical-fruit flavors (mango, banana, guava).

WINES TO TRY: Tenuta Cocevola/Maria Marmo**, CRIFO** (both the dry and the Lame di Sole; at 11 percent alcohol and roughly 5.3 grams per liter total acidity, these are the ultimate uncomplicated aperitif wines), and Santa Lucia.

Pascale

WHERE IT'S FOUND: Sardinia. NATIONAL REGISTRY CODE NUMBER: 180. COLOR: red.

If Rubens had painted grapes rather than people, Pascale might have been a model to his liking. Opulent, excessive, with big fat round berries that make you hungry just looking at them, Pascale is one healthy-looking grape—though with bunches that can reach one kilogram in weight, perhaps it ought to see the grape cardiologist. That said, Alessandro Dettori of the famous Dettori estate points out that there are two biotypes of Pascale found on the island, one with large grapes and berries (the one producing the almost-one-kilogram bunches) and a second that has small bunches and small berries.

Though Pascale is an excellent table grape, today we know that wine made with it is better than what was believed possible centuries ago. We still don't know what the grape was named for or where it came from. Some experts maintain that it is yet another Sardinian variety of Spanish provenance, but I have found no hard evidence of this. First mentioned by Manca dell'Arca (1780), and also called Santu Pascali and Pascansalò, Pascale has been likened by past experts to Monica and Nieddu Mannu; Bruni (1962) even mentioned synonyms such as Giacomino, the name of a local Tuscan variety (which resembled the better-known Tuscan Bonamico), and Barberone, leading others to hypothesize that all these grapes might be related. The truth is, Pascale is not related to Barbera, so the synonym of Barberone is best avoided. De Mattia, Imazio, Grassi, Lovicu, Tardaguila, Failla, et al. (2007) showed Pascale to be identical to Nieddu Mannu, Nieddu Pedra Serra, Falso Gregu, Primitivo Nieddu, and others still. By contrast, a more recent study featuring genetic characterization at twelve SSR loci has shown Pascale to be distinct from all the major Sardinian varieties and to be a relative of little-known locals such as Passale, Vertura, and especially Gregu Nieddu (Nieddu 2011) but apparently distinct from Nieddu Mannu.

Apparently, Pascale has sixteen alleles in common with Gregu Nieddu, on nine of the twelve loci analyzed thus far.

Pascale is characterized by medium-large bunches and berries; the former are either conical or pyramidal, the latter round. It is a very vigorous variety and a dependable producer, though it is sensitive to oidium.

Which Wines to Choose and Why

Despite its other commonly used name of Pascale di Cagliari, this variety is more common in other parts of the island and represents 20 percent of the vines planted in the province of Sassari. Currently, there are more than 1,250 hectares under vine to Pascale, so it's not that rare. It seems to do best in dry granitic-calcareous soils. There are no 100 percent Pascale DOC wines, and it has always been used in blends with Cannonao, to which it confers freshness and grace. Tonino Arcadu, the passionate, talented owner and winemaker of the high-quality Gostolai estate, has also made experimental lots of Pascale wine that is fresh and easygoing, but he hasn't yet decided to bottle it commercially.

WINES TO TRY: Dettori*** (the first to make an excellent pure IGT bottling, Ottomarzo, that shouldn't be missed).

Passerina

WHERE IT'S FOUND: Abruzzo, Marche, Lazio.
NATIONAL REGISTRY CODE NUMBER: 181. Color: white.

Passerina is another complicated population of grape varieties, with members that aren't related at all. For example, I believe the Passerina of southeastern Lazio is radically different from the Passerina of the Marche and Abruzzo, and I'm not alone in this conviction. However, all these grapes share at least some features in common, such as a general hardiness, disease resistance, and reliable productivity. With those characteristics, it follows that farmers liked having Passerina around, which explain its many synonyms, erroneous and correct. Some decided to refer to it as another of the many *Trebbiano*s (Trebbiano Scenciato near Chieti, Trebbiano Dorato near Pescara, Trebbiano Camplese around Teramo and L'Aquila), while others chose names illustrating its tendency to produce large quantities of grapes (and hence wine) by which farmers could pay off their debts (Cacciadebito, Scacciadebito, Pagadebito, the latter not to be confused with the similarly named variety of Emilia-Romagna, Pagadebit). Another synonym, Uva d'Oro, also refers to Passerina's golden *(d'oro)* penchant for helping farmers make ends meet. Rarer synonyms include Camplese and Uva Fermana, while the synonym Caccione is best avoided, as it engenders confusion with Cacchione, a distinct variety grown in Lazio. Of course, it may also be that many of these differently named grapes may in fact be distinct varieties, unrelated to Passerina, but we have no way of knowing until SSR profiling and accurate ampelographic tests are performed. This can be difficult because often these old varieties are limited to very few old vines growing haphazardly in vineyards dotting the countryside, and because many a "Passerina" vine is in fact something else.

Some believe the name Passerina derives from the small dimension of this cultivar's berries and that it was also one of the so-called *uve uzeline* (bird grapes) of northern Italy, those sweet grapes particularly sought after by gluttonous birds. However, the Cocci Grifoni sisters, who arguably make the best Passerina wine in all of the Marche, do not agree at all. Paola is especially decisive when she states, "No, I have never, ever, heard that before." Strange, as it seems to make sense to me, but I defer to her experience on the subject.

Passerina displays quite a bit of intravarietal variability. Abruzzo's Passerina is characterized by more intensely colored yellow grapes, which are dotted, than those of Lazio and the Marche. In southwestern Lazio, Pina Terenzi of the Terenzi estate near Frosinone, points out that their Passerina appears to be a closer relative of Trebbiano Giallo than Trebbiano Toscano. In fact, the Lazio variety looks quite different than these other two, with a bifid cluster and very small berries. Terenzi feels very strongly that the Passerina of Lazio is not at all the same variety as the so-named grape of Abruzzo and the Marche, and I agree. To complicate matters further, there is an aromatic Passerina described in Lazio, but I refuse to consider this possibility: I have always been told that Passerina is a nonaromatic variety, and therefore the rare aromatic Passerina found sporadically in Lazio (where in fact Passerina is also nonaromatic) must be viewed as a different variety altogether (as yet unidentified). Of course local producers don't share my opinion, and no less an expert than Professor Nicotina of the Poggio alla Meta estate believes that Passerina has the ability to release high concentrations of terpenes, depending on soils and how the wine is made. Maybe, but I'm not convinced, though a mutation expressing a *musqué* or aromatic trait is always possible, much like Chardonnay or Chasselas. There are four officially recognized clones of Passerina: VCR 5, UBA RA-PA 6, TGC 2 ISV, and VCR 450.

In the Marche, there exist three recognized biotypes of Passerina: the most common has a leaf with five lobes, a conical, small, and sparse bunch, with a pale small berry. The second most-common biotype instead has a large and compact bunch, and the leaf always has only three lobes. The berry is also bigger and oval in shape. The least common biotype is similar to the second but easily differentiated from it because it always sports at least one or two wings. It's not clear to me yet if there is a practical difference between these biotypes, that is, better wines being made from one or the other. As is often the case with native grapes, time will tell. An extremely underrated grape, Passerina is a resistant variety that can produce copious quantities of very good wine: and with appropriate reduction of its yields, the wine can be quite special indeed. Currently, it grows mainly in Marche, Abruzzo, Molise, and Lazio.

Which Wines to Choose and Why

The best examples of Passerina wines are those of the DOCG Offida (Marche), DOC Controguerra Passerina (Abruzzo), and the IGT Passerina del Frusinate (Lazio), but many producers make excellent monovarietal wines and Passerina can be included in as many as nineteen different IGT blends. The wines can be still, dry, sparkling, or even sweet, made by late harvesting or air-drying. Wines made with this variety in Abruzzo and the Marche tend to be mineral, almost steely, and high in acid, while those of Lazio's Frusinate area are generally much softer and creamier, marked by herbal notes. However, all Passerina wines tend to have strong notes of ripe citrus and tropical fruit. Professor Leonardo Seghetti clarifies my point when he says that "in Abruzzo, the variety is characterized by a slow accumulation of sugars that is not matched by a proportional reduction of acidity." In other words, this variety tends to maintain high total acidity and that is why it has been used successfully to make sparkling wines. In Lazio, this would be unthinkable, since that local Passerina variety is instead a low-acid cultivar (which further leads me to believe that Lazio's is a distinct cultivar from the one grown in the Marche and Abruzzo: certainly the wines taste very different, even when made using the same viticultural and enological methods). Furthermore, Pina Terenzi has told me time and again that "the real problem with our Passerina is that we have to time the harvest perfectly, for it drops its acidity practically overnight right on the vine"—the risk being that the wine can go from potentially very interesting and good to flat and boring. According to Domenico Pasetti, in Abruzzo harvesting at exactly the right moment is a big concern too, lest the grapes don't reach optimal maturity and thereby produce bitter wines. In conclusion, talking about Passerina as a single grape variety and wine is next to impossible, at least at the current state of knowledge. It is very likely that the name Passerina refers to distinct grape varieties, or at the very least, that one region's Passerina grape is most likely a variety distinct from that of other regions.

WINES TO TRY: From the Marche, try: Cocci Grifoni*** (Adamantea), San Giovanni** (Offida Passerina), Saputi** (they believe Passerina's future is in sparkling wines and plan to produce a sparkler soon), Castello Fageto* (Letizia), Centanni*, and Le Caniette* (Lucrezia and Vino Santo). Villa Pigna's Majia bottling contains 15 percent Sauvignon Blanc and Chardonnay, so, though good, it's not my idea of a Passerina wine worth recommending to see what the variety is about. From Abruzzo, try: Lidia e Amato** (Elena), Barone di Valforte**, Faraone** (Trebbiano d'Abruzzo; though their wine is so-labeled because the grapes were originally thought to be Trebbiano Abruzzese, but are actually Passerina), Agri-Verde* (Riseis), Anfra*, Camillo Montori* (Trend), Cioti* (Pathernus), and San Lorenzo Vini*. From Lazio, try: Terenzi*** (Villa Santa) and Casale della Ioria** (Collebianco).

Pecorello Bianco

WHERE IT'S FOUND: Calabria. NATIONAL REGISTRY CODE NUMBER: 183. COLOR: white.

Pecorello Bianco is another of the many grapes in Italy whose name is linked to sheep: either because the sheep liked to eat the grapes, or more likely because the ripe grapes were fodder for sheepherders who walked their grazing herds from valley to valley for weeks on end. Interestingly, this variety is often just called Pecorello (and that's still the name used in the National Registry), but this leads to considerable confusion. In fact, Pecorello is a red variety previously listed in the National Registry, while the variety described here is a white grape and was not originally included. This has been rectified: this white grape is now listed instead of the red one. In any event, Pecorello Bianco is also called Pecorello di Rogliano and, unfortunately, Pecorino, which is instead a distinct and by now famous variety from Abruzzo and the Marche. Even worse, around the town of Rogliano Calabro, Pecorello Bianco is called Greco Bianco, and the last thing needed is more confusion regarding that variety. In reality, Pecorello Bianco has only recently begun to resurface: a good thing, as it will hopefully get more producers to stop mindlessly planting Sauvignon Blanc or Pinot Bianco in ultrahot regions of Italy's deep south.

Not much has been written about Pecorello Bianco, but Marchi and Lanati (2008) have studied the grape and wine constituents. Pecorello Bianco is characterized by good total acidity yet has high pH values. The aromatic components in the grapes are mainly of benzenoid origin, such as 2-phenylethanol, benzylic acid, and 4-vinylguiacole; and even though Pecorello Bianco is a nonaromatic variety, it has relatively high concentrations of terpenes, which makes for an interesting monovarietal wine. Its ampelographic description is difficult because different growers called distinct varieties by the same name; even the National Registry's very short description refers to blue-colored berries, in reference to the grape that was previously listed by this name. It follows that until more research is done we won't know exactly what Pecorello is all about. Apparently, Pecorello Bianco is very common in Calabria, particularly in the Valle del Savuto and in the provinces of Catanzaro and Cosenza, especially in the latter.

Which Wines to Choose and Why

The variety has always been blended with other local grapes to make light, easygoing white wines and is usually present in significant percentages in the wines of the DOC Donnici. I don't remember having tried many wines said to be made with this grape and so I cannot characterize the wines made with it. Perhaps in the near future more Pecorello Bianco wines will be made, giving us all a chance to learn more about the grape and wine.

WINES TO TRY: Ceraudo** (owner Roberto Ceraudo wanted to see what the grape could offer all on its own; this wine is made with organic grapes, is fresh and uncomplicated, with simple but bright white flower and green apple aromas and flavors, a great aperitif or paired with simple vegetable and fish dishes).

Pecorino

WHERE IT'S FOUND: Marche, Abruzzo, Lazio, Tuscany, Umbria. NATIONAL REGISTRY CODE NUMBER: 184. COLOR: white.

No, this is not the sheep cheese: this variety's curious name refers to sheepherders who ate the grapes while accompanying their flocks up and down the valleys in search of food. For this reason, it was once also called Uva delle Pecore or Uva Pecorina, as well as Pecorina Arquatanella or Arquatana, in reference to the Arquata area in the Marche where Pecorino has always been cultivated.

Pecorino is not just a great grape variety; it is also one of Italy's biggest wine success stories of the twenty-first century. Whereas I would have had trouble writing about monovarietal pecorino only fifteen years ago, today there are more than twenty such wines of variable quality. If Pecorino has managed such a striking comeback, the merit goes to Guido Cocci Grifoni of the Cocci Grifoni estate in the Marche and Luigi Cataldi Madonna of the Cataldi Madonna estate in Abruzzo. These two men set the stage by example and created a whole new wine. In fact, Pecorino, while always one of the more common varieties in the Marche (the variety was grown in the province of Ancona in 1876), fell by the wayside in the twentieth century, replaced by more productive varieties. But Cocci Grifoni, who was unhappy with local *Trebbiano*s and *Malvasia*s, wanted better. In the early 1980s he set out to rediscover old native varieties: having heard of an eighty-year-old farmer from Aquata del Tronto who owned a largely abandoned vineyard at about one thousand meters above sea level that was planted with a forgotten variety called Pecorino, he went to take a look. Cocci Grifoni met with the vineyard's owner, a Mr. Cafini, in September 1982, and after looking over the vines, he marked those he liked best with colored tape. The following February he returned and brought the select grapevines back to his own estate, setting up the first vineyard of Pecorino mother plants. Cocci Grifoni's first official Pecorino wine (which he called simply "Colle Vecchio") was made with the 1990 vintage. For ten years he was the sole producer to commercialize this wine, but its peculiarities, coupled with its commercial success, induced other producers (in both Abruzzo and the Marche) to plant the variety and start bottling their own versions.

Over in Abruzzo, Pecorino always lagged behind Trebbiano d'Abruzzo in importance. It was only with a series of award-winning wines by Cataldi Madonna, a philosophy professor and passionate winemaker (and the first in Italy to label a wine as Pecorino), that other producers took note and began producing their own Pecorino wines. Everyone credits Cataldi Madonna, or one of his wines, with pushing them to try Pecorino themselves. Perhaps the best compliment of all came from Domenico Pasetti of the Pasetti estate, who after trying Cataldi Madonna's first ever pecorino, immediately thought, "This is my wine," and decided to start producing it as well. Pasetti remembers planting his Pecorino vines in 1996; at that time the international varieties were all the rage, and so in order to avoid needless arguments in the family, he lied to his parents, telling them he was planting Chardonnay. His risk paid off handsomely: in 2000, he produced only 1,200 bottles, while in 2011 he sold 250,000—50 percent of the entire Pasetti wine production. One may wonder at such an increase in bottle production in such a short time span, but the wine has undoubtedly met with huge success. Lorenzo Landi, who is the consultant winemaker at Cataldi Madonna, marvels at the passion and dedication of Cataldi Madonna, who "has basically tried to make every wine possible with the variety, from sparkling to sweet."

Different clones of Pecorino exist, as do different biotypes. Available clones include UBA-

RA PE 19 (much bigger bunch and yields more structured wines that can stand up to oak), 1 ISV (low production, ideal for sparkling wines), and VCR 417 (for fresh wines that can also be made as sparklers). There are three main biotypes. One has a five-lobed leaf, a medium-sized, winged, and loosely packed cylindrical bunch. A second biotype has leaves with only three lobes and much smaller compact bunches and berries. The rarest biotype has a three-lobed leaf, like the second biotype, but features a large compact bunch; and the berries are large too, but always perfectly round and thick skinned. What I find perhaps most characteristic of Pecorino is its leaf: small and round, with very few indentations, making it very easy to spot this grapevine in vineyards. It's a very resistant, rustic variety but prefers cooler microclimates to warm ones and prefers clay-rich soils that are not too strong in lime content. Due to its sterile basal bud, long pruning systems are best, such as Guyot or the classic *pergola abbruzzese,* while the best rootstocks push vigor and are actively lime resistant (for example, Berlandieri × Riparia Kober 5 BB or Berlandieri × Rupestris 1103 P). Its low productivity is why Pecorino was abandoned decades ago.

Today, Pecorino is grown mainly in the Marche and Abruzzo, though it is also found in Lazio, Umbria, and Tuscany, where it was called Dolcipappola. Vineyards devoted to it have been increasing steadily every year over the last decade; 2011 data shows 326 total hectares of Pecorino, an almost fourfold increase since 2000, when there were only 87 hectares planted in Italy.

Which Wines to Choose and Why
The best pure examples are the DOC Offida Pecorino wines or one of the many Abruzzo IGT bottlings, such as Terre di Chieti or Colline Pescaresi. Other possibilities include DOC wines such as Falerio dei Colli Ascolani, Colli Maceratesi, and Controguerra (where it is made as a sparkler). In these DOCs, Pecorino is part of a blend, so though good, these wines don't speak much of the variety on its own.

For example, according to the informative book sponsored by the Cocci Grifoni estate in collaboration with the Università Politecnica delle Marche, the Pecorino by Cocci Grifoni (representative of the wines of the Offida area in the Marche) is characterized by significantly high levels of β-phenyl-ethylalcohol (which smells of roses), isoamyl acetate (banana), ethyl-octanoate (citrus), and ethyl-hexanoate (apple). As the wine ages, it shows increased levels of the diethyl ester of butanedioic acid, which produces a milky or delicately cheesy smell recognizable in both the 1997 and 2002 Pecorino Cocci Grifoni. Furthermore, these wines are always characterized by relatively high dry extracts (greater than twenty-four grams per liter) and very high acidities (average pH 3 and total acidity eight grams per liter). While high acidity is a sine qua non of Pecorino wines (the variety is especially rich in malic acid), the high extract of Pecorino wines from the Marche are usually a reflection of the winemaking techniques employed, such as extended maceration of the must on the skins. In Abruzzo, Pecorino is instead not usually macerated, and the wines are therefore lighter and fresher. In general, Pecorino wines are usually delicately herbal (sage, thyme, mint), with balsamic nuances to the crisp apple and pear aromas and flavors, and they are usually medium bodied. Due to generally low productivity, the wines can be quite concentrated and high in alcohol: 14 percent is common, but even at 14.5 percent, well-made Pecorino wines manage to stay balanced and crisp.

Recent winemaking advances, such as hyper-reductive techniques and the use of special selected yeasts, have created some Pecorino wines that smell and taste of Sauvignon Blanc. Picking grapes that had been exposed to sunlight at length, and allowing the must to come into contact with too much oxygen, had kept the wine from showing off the lemony, figgy, and herbal qualities that are now very apparent. Cataldi Madonna, whose Pecorino wines are one of the most like Sauvignon Blanc (after starting off early in life as one of Italy's most overoaked wines), always likes to say, half-jokingly, "It's not that Pecorino is Sauvignonesque, but rather that Sauvignon is Pecorinoesque." They'll be glad to learn that in the Loire and in New Zealand. All kidding aside, his 2008 and 2010 Pecorino wines made from old vines are among the hundred best white wines Italy has ever made. Cristiana Tiberio, of the up-and-coming Tiberio estate and recognized Pecorino expert (her wine has won numerous awards and accolades for the last two years), loves the variety, finding it "a remarkable combination of rusticity and refinement." I couldn't have said it better myself.

WINES TO TRY: From the Marche, try: Cocci Grifoni*** (Colle Vecchio), Aurora** (Fiobbo), Le Caniette* (Io Sono Gaia), Poderi San Lazzaro* (Pistillo), and San Savino* (Ciprea). From Abruzzo, try: Cataldi Madonna***, Tiberio***, Il Feuduccio di Santa Maria d'Orni*, Pasetti* (Colle Civetta), Strappelli* (Soprano), Torre dei Beati* (Giocheremo con i Fiori), and Torre Zambra* (Colle Maggio). Note that Pecorino has become a hot commodity and many estates are churning out their versions of the wine, not all of them memorable.

Pelaverga Grosso

WHERE IT'S FOUND: Piedmont. NATIONAL REGISTRY CODE NUMBER: 309. COLOR: red.

Pelaverga Grosso, also called Pelaverga Comune, is differentiated from the Pelaverga Piccolo by its larger-sized cluster and berries (especially). It was first cultivated by friars at a convent near Pagno in Val Bronda, so it is also called Pelaverga di Pagno. Another Piedmontese variety, Peilavert, appears to be genetically distinct from the two *Pelavergas*, despite the very similar names.

The first to mention Pelaverga Grosso was Giovanni Battista Croce in 1606. He referred to it as Cario (Cari remains a commonly used synonym for this cultivar), and noted the "delicate, sweet, and good wines made from" it. I'm not too sure about the "sweet" part, since Pelaverga wines have always been, and are, classically dry. Nevertheless, Croce is an interesting figure in the history of Italian wine: an architect and a jeweler by trade who worked for the Duke Emanuele Filiberto, he owned a vineyard on the hillsides of Torino, to which he devoted much attention, being also an expert on gardens and orchards. Besides his day job, he managed to write quite a bit on Italian native grape varieties.

Pelaverga Grosso grows only in Piedmont. It is typical of the countryside around Saluzzo and Chieri (near Turin), where it is also called Cari, and is a reliable, copious producer. However, it ripens late in the year (the first two weeks of November is common) which can be a problem in Piedmont's cool and wet autumns, and because it is both very vigorous and fertile, it tends not to ripen evenly when overcropped. Reducing yields and planting it in well-exposed, sunny sites appears to be the best choice in order to nudge the berries to optimal maturity. Pelaverga Piccolo, on the other hand, is typical of Verduno in the Langhe, while Peilavert is grown in the Canavese portion of Piedmont close to the Saluzzo area.

Which Wines to Choose and Why

The wines are the DOCs Colline Torinesi and Colline Saluzzesi. Though the grape can be blended with Nebbiolo and/or Barbera, these two DOCs also allow monovarietal wines. As the latter area never produced white wines of note, a few producers have taken to using Pelaverga Grosso to make a *rosato* as well, not a bad idea given the variety's naturally high acidity (and the large day-night temperature differentials in the area). A good Pelaverga wine should smell and taste of peppery strawberries and violets and should not be too dark in color (though the grapes are dark red-blue, the skins release pigments with difficulty). "But we can neither macerate the skins for more than six to seven days nor use too high temperatures during maceration and fermentation," explains Andrea Occelli of Produttori Pelaverga di Castellar, "because the skins start breaking apart and then the wine picks up unpleasant off odors. Racking and air contact are all-important with Pelaverga." It's an interesting problem, for Pelaverga Grosso is blessed with thick skins that can stand up to inclement weather: "True, so I'm not sure why we have this problem. I remember my grandfather always used to say that if it rains one day during the harvest it wasn't a big deal," says Occelli.

WINES TO TRY: Produttori Pelaverga di Castellar** (Petalo, their excellent *rosato;* also a very good red Pelaverga), Casetta*, Maiero*, and Terre dei Santi* (Cari).

Pelaverga Piccolo

WHERE IT'S FOUND: Piedmont. NATIONAL REGISTRY CODE NUMBER: 330. COLOR: red.

A sign of the difficulties facing Italian native grapes, or anyone wanting to learn about them, is that even bona fide experts have trouble knowing all the rare natives the country boasts. For example, in books on Italy's wines, the two Pelaverga varieties are often not mentioned, which is not surprising given that until recently making wines with these varieties was mainly a local phenomenon. Unlike Pelaverga Grosso, which is still very much a grape and wine of only local importance, Pelaverga Piccolo is becoming better known, at least in Italian wine circles. The variety known as Pelaverga Piccolo is also called Pelaverga di Verduno, as it's grown almost exclusively around the town of Verduno, more famous for its Barolo production. Legend has it that Piccolo was brought to the area from Saluzzo by a friar, Sebastiano Valfré, in the eighteenth century. It's not without interest that Valfré hailed from that area, home to Pelaverga Grosso. The two *Pelaverga*s are actually completely unrelated, but locals historically had no way of knowing this: it's not illogical that they assumed the good friar was importing the *Pelaverga* variety from his neck of the woods.

Verduno Pelaverga makes an excellent wine, and credit goes to the local producers who believed enough in the variety to attempt monovarietal bottlings rather than blends with Barbera or Nebbiolo, as was customary. Since the 1980s, the small production of Pelaverga wines has met with both critical and consumer acclaim. Consequently, the only three hectares planted to Pelaverga Piccolo in 1987 have increased to the twelve of today, a fourfold increase. This success has led some producers to experiment further with the variety; Castello di Verduno has started production of a white wine from Pelaverga Piccolo grapes by removing the must off the skins immediately. Only time will tell if other producers will follow suit, though I find the red so good, why make a white wine with this grape?

The name Pelaverga derives from the combination of *pela* and *verga*, which mean, respectively, "to peel" and "branch," so it is thought that *pelaverga* refers to some old vine-training technique ("branch-peeler").

Which Wines to Choose and Why

Pelaverga Piccolo is found only in Piedmont, in the DOC Verduno Pelaverga, mainly around the towns of Verduno and Roddi. A good Pelaverga Piccolo wine is bright red, with small redberry and herbal aromas and flavors. The redberry notes border on syrup in hotter years, but the wine is always blessed with fine acidity, so never causes palate fatigue. The best wines are remarkably balanced midweights that offer completely different aromas and flavors than do wines made with Barbera or Dolcetto. In fact, a Pelaverga Piccolo wine is not unlike a good Schiava, and like that variety, it is characterized by a lack of strong tannins. Pelaverga Piccolo is remarkably versatile; excellent sparkling and both light- and full-bodied red wines are possible. The only difficulties in production are the wine's tendency to form reductive off odors and the necessity of leaching out as much color from the skins without also releasing bitter tannins.

WINES TO TRY: Castello di Verduno*** (Basadone), Fratelli Alessandria***, G. B. Burlotto***, Ascheri** (Do ut Des), and Bel Colle** (Le Masche).

Perricone

WHERE IT'S FOUND: Sicily. NATIONAL REGISTRY CODE NUMBER: 185. COLOR: red.

Every time I see a Perricone grape bunch, I think my apartment needs sweeping. This seemingly odd association is actually brought on by Perricone's extremely long grape cluster, indeed one of the longest among all Italian grape varieties: you really could sweep floors with it! Actually, Perricone has many endearing features, not least its delicious, midweight, and highly perfumed wines. Perricone used to be more common than it is today, especially in the provinces of Palermo and Trapani on the western side of Sicily, where it was mainly blended with white grapes to make *ambrato* wine, a sort of rustic *rosato*. However, Perricone was also used to make full-bodied wines that could keep: in the second half of the nineteenth century, it was used to make the important and much sought after Zucco Rosso wine by the Duke d'Aumale (in reality Henry d'Orleans, the son of the then king of France), who owned six thousand hectares near Palermo and made both white and red wines. According to Will Stigand, then the British consul, in 1889 the Palermo countryside was mainly planted to Perricone (which he called Pignatello), and a producer of the time, Salvatore Salvia, had great success in exporting his Perricone wine to northern Italy, France, and Germany. Most important, Perricone has always been used (and still is today) to make ruby Marsala.

Alas, Perricone is yet another variety almost crippled by phylloxera. Abundant all over Sicily in the nineteenth century, the cultivar is now planted mostly around the cities of Trapani and Marsala, in just 328 hectares (based on 2010 data). It is only the twentieth most commonly planted variety on the island, and it is hard to find monovarietal wines. With its original acreage devastated by the arrival of the infernal louse, Perricone has had trouble returning to its former glory, mainly because farmers in the post-phylloxera period opted for more resistant and productive varieties.

Synonyms include Niuri, Pignatello, Pirricuni, and Tuccarino (rarely used nowadays). There are at least two biotypes, but they don't seem that different, both ampelographically and enologically. Though malvin is the most common pigment, up to 30 percent of the anthocyanin profile is constituted by peonin and delphin: this, and acylated anthocyanin concentrations (less than 10 percent), explains the light and unstable color of the wines. Over the centuries, Perricone was always appreciated for its tannic structure and was much in vogue as a blending agent or for the production of concentrated grape must.

Ampelographically, Perricone has medium-sized bunches with medium-large round dark-blue berries; the variety especially characterized by its extremely long (even thirty-three centimeters!), cylindrical-conical or conical-pyramidal bunch. It is irregularly yielding, with productivity varying greatly from year to year, and green harvests are necessary to achieve vegetative equilibrium between foliage and fruit production. It usually ripens in mid- to late September, later than many other Sicilian varieties, on average about two weeks later than the *Cataratto*s. Timing the harvest correctly is all-important with Perricone, since acidity drops quickly as sugars rise, and the risk, especially with low-lying vineyards, is that the wines will be high in alcohol but flabby. At higher altitudes, grapes can be late harvested, but this exposes the mid- to late-ripening Perricone to the vagaries of inclement fall weather.

Which Wines to Choose and Why

Monovarietal examples are rare, but the DOC wines Contea di Sclafani, Delia Nivolelli, Eloro, and Monreale can be 100 percent Perricone. One reason why monovarietal Perricone is not common is that the variety's role has always been, much like Canaiolo Nero with Sangiovese or the *Malvasia Nera*s with Negro Amaro, to soften Nero d'Avola wine; but differently from Canaiolo Nero and those *Malvasia*s, Perricone's high polyphenol content also helps increase Nero d'Avola's textural presence. In general, wines made in southeastern Sicily to me seem less intensely colored and less astringent, even though this grape's high polyphenol content ensures a very tactile, and at times coarse, mouthfeel. Producers outside Perricone's classic production zone in western Sicily believe theirs is a different biotype, accounting for the different characteristics of their wines. I believe Perricone is underrated and deserves to be followed with interest.

WINES TO TRY: Tamburello** (Pietragavina; the family deserves credit for rescuing a native grape at risk of being forgotten; their first vintage was 2003 and met with enough success to inspire other producers), Barraco*, Castellucci Miano* (Maravita), Caruso & Minini* (in their I Sicani lineup of wines, the Sachia, a non-oaked Perricone), and Feotto dello Jatto* (Vigna Curria).

Petit Rouge

WHERE IT'S FOUND: Valle d'Aosta. NATIONAL REGISTRY CODE NUMBER: 186. COLOR: red.

Petit Rouge is one of the oldest and most important cultivars of the Valle d'Aosta: while other native red grapes risked extinction only twenty years ago, this was never true of Petit Rouge. Characterized by great intravarietal variability, reflected in a large number of biotypes, it is the senior member of the ancient *Oriou* family of grapes, named after a hamlet near Saint-Vincent, which included such *Oriou* biotypes as Oriou Curaré, Oriou Voirard, Oriou Gris, Oriou Lombard, Oriou Gros, and more. Recent DNA analysis by Vouillamoz and Moriondo (2011) demonstrated Petit Rouge to be, with Mayolet, one of the two parents of Rouge du Pays (also known as Rouge du Valais, typical of Switzerland's Valais region), and likely of Vien de Nus as well (but the other parent is unknown). Furthermore, its family tree shows that it's a brother of Fumin and that it has second-degree relationships (grandfather-grandson, uncle-nephew, or half brothers) with most of the other red grapes of the Valle d'Aosta, especially Cornalin, Roussin, and Neyret de Saint-Vincent. Due to the intricate ramifications of this family tree, some have postulated that the *Oriou*s are best viewed as members of a variety-population rather than as wholly distinct varieties, but the concept of variety-populations is not accepted by most modern ampelologists.

Petit Rouge, then called Picciourouzo, was first mentioned by Gatta in 1838, but Vouillamoz and Moriondo (2011) recently located what they estimated to be a two-hundred- to three-hundred-year-old vine of Petit Rouge near Chambave. Actually, Gatta described two very different-looking Petit Rouge vines, which he differentiated by the numbers 12 and 21–25 (of these, the real Petit Rouge was number 21–25). Nevertheless, Petit Rouge is still fourth in line in order of historical citation among the Valle d'Aosta natives, after Prié (1691), Fumin (1785), and Mayolet (1787). Today, there are roughly thirty hectares of Petit Rouge, mainly planted in the middle valley, from Saint-Vincent to Arvier, especially around Aymaville, Saint-Pierre, and Villeneuve, where it is a very important red variety.

Which Wines to Choose and Why

There are some wonderful monovarietal Petit Rouge wines made today, which can be particularly fruity midweight wines. However, the most famous wine is a blend, the DOC Torrette, where Petit Rouge is the main variety (70 percent at least), with small percentages of Mayolet, Fumin, Vuillermin, and other local varieties (none can exceed 10 percent of the total). Torrette is a *cru* where Petit Rouge seems to produce wines of particular finesse and depth. Though an important and high-quality variety, I am not sure that Petit Rouge is one of the region's most exciting grapes: my preferences go to Mayolet and Vuillermin. But Petit Rouge has a versatility and dependability that explains its great success. Its name may mean, when literally translated, "little red one," but there's nothing little about Petit Rouge. Given its diffusion, the number of different wines made by a slew of producers, and its long history, it's a real giant among Valle d'Aosta's native grapes.

WINES TO TRY: Anselmet*** (full of red-berried fruity charm and mouthwatering acidity; you'll have trouble putting the glass back down; their Torrette is excellent too), L'Atouéyo** (Torrette Supérieur), Didier Gerbelle**, Elio Ottin** (Torrette Supérieur), Feudo di San Maurizio** (Torrette Supérieur), Les Crêtes** (Torrette), Di Barrò* (Torrette Supérieur Vigne de Torrette, in which the effects of air-drying grapes are evident, perhaps too much, with a creamy, residual sugar-like finish), Chateau Feuillet*, and La Source*.

Picolit

WHERE IT'S FOUND: FVG. NATIONAL REGISTRY CODE NUMBER: 188. COLOR: white.

Luigi Veronelli, Italy's greatest wine writer, called picolit Italy's noblest wine: not Barolo, not Brunello, but picolit. I agree, with caveats. Dare I say it? Along with Nebbiolo, Picolit is my favorite Italian grape. Friulian on the maternal side, I spent many summers in what Joyce would have defined as my salad days, walking the *ponca*, the marly-arenaceous soil typical of the Colli Orientali del Friuli (COF) where Picolit thrives. And it thrives only there. Whereas Picolit wines are now being produced in Collio and other DOCs of Friuli Venezia Giulia, the wine has really always been associated with COF, though experimentally minded producers tried their hand at it in Veneto, Lombardy, Emilia-Romagna, and Tuscany. It is one of Italy's oldest native varieties, with official documentation dating to the twelfth century, though the most common reference is the 1682 wedding banquet of Alvise Contarini, doge of Venice, where picolit was one of the wines served. This brightly golden sweet wine has always been lauded with hyperbole and praise, both among lay people (the few who could afford it)

and in the royal courts of Europe, where the wine was a huge success. Picolit was so important and highly thought of that fakes were common already in the eighteenth century (Bergamini and Novajra 2000), a problem also present in later centuries. Above all, Picolit is one of the few truly Italian wines to have a noble history, something not true even of Brunello or Amarone.

Two people were especially important for Picolit's rise to fame, as they did much to further the cause of both grape and wine. In the late eighteenth and early nineteenth centuries, Count Fabio Asquini from Fagagna was a Picolit PR machine, bottling his production in handblown Murano glass bottles and selling all over Europe in personally owned wine shops. As a result, Picolit wine became a major competitor to the famous Hungarian Tokaj. Made from air-dried grapes (late harvesting on the vine is a risky proposition in Friuli Venezia Giulia's cool, northern, and especially rainy climate) and variously affected by noble rot depending on the vintage, Picolit shares more than a few similarities with the Hungarian sweet wine, and it therefore appealed to much of the same noble Euro crowd. Cultivation of Picolit declined in the nineteenth century because the female flowers led to unreliable fruit set; plus, the unpredictable development of noble rot diminished grower enthusiasm. It was only in the 1950s that another count, Gaetano Perusini, brought the grape and wine successfully back to life. Beginning in the 1930s, with only a few sporadic vines still alive, Perusini set out in the hillside vineyards of his family's Rocca Bernarda castle to find the healthiest-looking Picolit vines, which he then selected and propagated. It's fair to say that if Picolit is being talked about today, Perusini deserves most of the credit; without his efforts, there may not have been any Picolit to talk about.

With Picolit, the name tells the story. It's a deformation of *piccolitto*, meaning "small," and one look at the grape cluster tells you why: it's downright scrawny, with very few berries (a normal grape bunch has one hundred to two hundred berries; a classic Picolit has fifteen or less). This condition is the result of floral abortion, due to partial sterility of the male pollen, resulting in incomplete fecundation of the flower. Few berries are formed, and so sorry-looking grape bunches are the variety's distinguishing morphologic feature. Of course, others in Italy have different opinions (don't they always), believing that Picolit does not mean small, but instead evolved from *pecol*, then to *peculita,* and finally to *piculit,* all meaning "summit of a hill"; this is reasonable enough, since Picolit is a variety that craves sunlight and performs best in slightly warmer microclimates. That the imagination of grape historians and ampelographers knows no bounds (perhaps fueled by too much study of the matter) is illustrated by the hypothesis that Picolit's name descends from the French grape Piquepoul, which later evolved in the Picpul and finally Piculi grapes (the two are completely unrelated). Though the exact origins of Picolit are unknown, its male sterility suggests that it may derive from domestication of local wild vines (there is no proof of this). As there is no documentation to the best of my knowledge of a similar variety grown outside Friuli Venezia Giulia prior to records of its appearance in Italy, this hypothesis is not illogical. There is little doubt that Picolit is a true native grape of Italy.

I think Picolit is a really pretty grape: ampelographically, it has very small, conical-cylindrical, loosely packed bunches and small, round-oval, bright yellow berries, so translucent you can see through them and count the pips. However, as Picolit is an extremely ancient variety, it has much intravarietal variability that has gone largely unnoticed, probably due to the variety once being extremely scarce. There are *Picolit*s with a green stalk and bright yellow berries, a red stalk and smaller berries, or with a blood-red stalk, all described by Pietro di Maniago in 1823. According to Andrea Felluga of the Livio Felluga winery, the best of these is the red-stalked biotype, while the big-bunched biotypes are more recent arrivals, specifically selected in the 1980s when Picolit grappa was all the rage (and a lot of pomace was needed). Paolo Rodaro makes his Picolit wine using a local biotype selected from 150-year-old ungrafted vines. In Slovenia, two different *Picolit*s are described—Pikolit Vienna and Pikolit Italia—but Štajner, Korosec-Koruzam, Ruzjan, and Javornik (2008) showed them to be identical. Clones available in Italy include ISV Conegliano 1, ISV-F4, and ISV-F6, but their quality is suspect, having been created mainly with increased productivity in mind (which explains the Picolit grapevines with bunches reminiscent more of fat turkeys than the original Picolit). Picolit is unrelated to Piculit Neri, another similarly named Friuli Venezia Giulia variety (the two are not color mutations, and the spelling of the cultivar names is also different). Picolit is characterized by strong vigor but unfortunately pushes vegetative growth (shoots especially) rather than grape production, which is extremely low. It's very sensitive to peronospora and even more to oidium. And though Picolit craves sunlight, it doesn't perform well in excessively hot areas that lack ventilation.

Picolit is grown mainly, if not only, in the countryside around Udine and Gorizia in Friuli Venezia Giulia. It is also grown in small amounts in Slovenia (where it's called Pikolit) and even Australia (in King Valley, where Pizzini makes wines from it, and in Mudgee, where di Lusso makes the only other monovarietal Australian Picolit). Curiously, though I know of no Picolit grown or made in the United States, there is a street named Picolit Court in Fairfield, Connecticut.

Which Wines to Choose and Why

Picolit wines are all labeled DOCG Picolit. It is a delicately sweet wine, though the variety is also used in dry white wine blends such as Collio Bianco and Rosazzo Bianco to increase the sweetness and honeyed texture of those wines. The majority of Picolit wines are made from air-dried grapes (late-harvest wines were once more common, though the vagaries of Friuli Venezia Giulia weather always posed a risk), but there is no consensus on the amount of air-drying required and consequently little consistency of style. Hence Picolit wines can range from light and delicately sweet (rare nowadays) to super thick and sweet (the unfortunate majority). Unfortunately, that's not the wine's only problem.

For a variety of reasons, there has always been too much Picolit wine sold that wasn't worth its high price, ultimately damaging the wine's reputation. This is a real shame, for Picolit is an ugly duckling meant to fly like a wild swan; it's potentially one of the world's best sweet wines. I say *potentially* because there are a number of obstacles on the road to reaching this goal. First, it's virtually impossible to make large quantities of wine from Picolit vines. Yet, human nature being what it is, everybody tries. Only a few estates produce up to four thousand half bottles a year; and even La Roncaia, the biggest Picolit wine producer, does not exceed annual productions of six thousand 375-milliliter bottles. Most other producers make far less than a thousand half bottles a year. Given the high prices the wine can fetch, it's not surprising that increasing volume has been a goal; and since clonal selections haven't been the answer, modifying the legal production guidelines has been another strategy. New legislation was passed in 2006 (modified in 2010), turning Picolit into Friuli Venezia Giulia's second DOCG wine, decreeing that DOCG Picolit could be made using a minimum of 85 percent Picolit.

Let me be blunt: the only reason for this change is to allow more Picolit wine to be produced. Since the implementation of this legislation, I have been chagrined time and again in tasting wines that have more in common with Sauvignon Blanc or Chardonnay than true Picolit, an utter travesty. Unless something is done, this will inevitably lead to people shying away from an expensive sweet wine that offers neither unique redeeming features nor a sense of place. This is something that they are only too aware of in Chianti and many other Italian DOCs and DOCGs, but I guess the failure to learn from others' mistakes is a human trait.

Historically it was always a risk to buy Picolit wines, because unscrupulous producers cut them with copious amounts of Verduzzo and other cheaper sweet wines (nevertheless selling their artful "creations" at stellar Picolit prices). The sad irony is that the recent DOCG legislation has effectively done little more than legalize a practice that had always taken place.

There is another toxic by-product of the new DOCG legislation: the elimination of subzones. This is an utterly nonsensical move, as Picolit is one of the few Italian native cultivars that has been clearly associated over the centuries with at least three *crus* of specific quality: Rosazzo (a particularly warm microclimate); Rocca Bernarda (where the eponymous castle sits atop the hill; art lovers and history buffs will know it was designed by Giovanni da Udine, famous for the Raphael rooms in the Vatican); and Cialla, a much cooler microclimate, where Picolit produces a wine of a lightness of being that would make Milan Kundera proud (D'Agata 2007). Thanks to active lobbying by the Rapuzzi family (no fools they) of the outstanding Ronchi di Cialla estate, Cialla is the one subzone that still remains. Furthermore, Cialla has a much stricter and more quality-oriented legislation, as its wine is monovarietal by law. I think a fourth Friuli Venezia Giulia subzone must be considered a *grand cru* for Picolit: Savorgnano del Torre, where Picolit often has the charm of Cialla and the sweetness and power of Rosazzo. Certainly, some of the greatest Picolit wines I have ever tasted have been made by local farmers from the Savorgnano area.

That producers years ago failed to understand the problems they were getting themselves into is demonstrated by the following story. In 2006, an official presentation celebrating the new Picolit DOCG was organized in Cividale del Friuli by the Consortium of the Colli Orientali del Friuli, with many tastings and dinners and a conference. It was a truly wonderful, well-organized weekend-long event, with foreign journalists, local experts, star-quality chefs, producers, and government officials. I was invited to be the official moderator and one of the guest speakers at the conference, which I still view today as one of the greatest honors to have come my way in a lifetime dedicated to wine. However, at the end of my very positive and uplifting presentation on Picolit, one well-known producer took me aside to bitterly complain that I had cast Cialla in a favorable light while making all other DOCG Picolit wines seem of lesser quality. Publicly a staunch supporter of a regionwide Picolit DOCG, he knew in private that the product had been turned into a lesser one. Rather than do something about it, which he didn't (and still doesn't) want to do, his solution was to gloss over the issue. Last but not least, another problem for Picolit is that not all producers are blessed with crystalline winemaking talent (something hampering Verduzzo's chance to shine as well), and unbalanced wines with off odors, hints of grey rot, or poor use of oak are not uncommon.

Lest it seem that I am something of a Picolit basher, let me be clear: I love Picolit. I spent the better part of my university days in the 1980s hunting down every bottled example, scavenging for forgotten vintages on dusty wineshop shelves and hitting every local fair to try the artisanally made Picolit bottlings meant for family consumption. My mother remembers the last part all too well, for she used to drive me around to all those fairs (she never complained once: while I conducted my Picolit taste tests, she did the same with grilled sausage sandwiches of every ilk). I believe that when producers get picolit right, it's a mesmerizing drinking experience, not easily forgotten. Unlike wines made with varieties such as, for example, Moscato Bianco, Moscato di Alessandria, Moscato Ottonel, or Welschriesling, Picolit wines are characterized by a refinement and grace uncommon in most sweet wines (this hamstrings picolit in poorly run blind tastings where it gets sandwiched between supersweet, alcoholic, vanilla-laden behemoths). A great picolit is first and foremost a wine of wonderful delicacy, not just sweet and velvety, with the texture, sweetness, and acidity worthy of a high-wire act.

Wine color varies from bright yellow to amber-gold (depending on how ripe and air-dried the grapes are). Aromas are captivating and complex (orange blossoms, acacia honey, tangerine, yellow peach, poached quince, spiced pear, dried apricot, ginger) and flavors range from delicate and refined to rich and thick. The variety can at times be low in acidity; the best wines are those that have fragrant, vibrant aromas and flavors thanks to lively acids. If there is one weakness to my "picolit is one of the world's great wines" axiom, it's that, in my extensive experience, the wine does not age particularly well and is best drunk within five years of the harvest. It may last longer, but it rarely improves. I have bought and cellared as many as ten different wines of every vintage from 1979 to today, and I have yet to find one that improves much after five years postharvest. So in that light, if a wine's greatness is measured by its ageworthiness, then picolit falls a little short.

In Australia, a number of wineries are trying their hand at Picolit, either as a monovarietal or in blends (Pizzini, Di Lusso). In Canada, Donald Ziraldo has decided to honor his roots (he is from Fagagna in Friuli Venezia Giulia, an area indelibly linked to picolit production) and has made a "Canadian" picolit from grapes culled in the Fagagna area.

WINES TO TRY: Aquila del Torre*** (a very good example of Savorgnano Picolit), Livio Felluga*** (from the hotter Rosazzo subzone), Ronchi di Cialla*** (from the cooler Cialla subzone), Vigna Petrussa***, Ermacora**, Girolamo Dorigo**, I Comelli**, Paolo Rodaro**, Marco Sara** (another wine from Savorgnano), La Roncaia*, Rocca Bernarda*, and Torre Rosazza*.

Piculit Neri

WHERE IT'S FOUND: FVG, Veneto. NATIONAL REGISTRY CODE NUMBER: 322. COLOR: red.

Once believed to be synonymous with Refosco Gentile or di Rauscedo, Piculit Neri was later thought to be a close relative of Refosco Nostrano or even del Peduncolo Rosso. Or, later still, some thought it might even be a biotype of either Refosco Nostrano or Refosco del Peduncolo Rosso. Other synonyms include Terrano Piccoletto or Piccolit Nero; Di Rovasenda (1877) called it Piccolit Rosso. Certainly, Manlio Collavini of his family's Friuli Venezia Giulia estate believes that Piculit Neri is a biotype of Refosco Nostrano, while Emilio Bulfon, who has long championed the variety, thinks it is completely distinct from all *Refoscos*. Carlo Petrussi, one of Friuli's leading viticultural experts, told me that he adamantly believes the variety is unrelated to any other *Refosco*, intelligently pointing out that, in more than fifty years of walking Friuli's vineyards, he has never met anyone who referred to Piculit Neri with a Refosco name: "At most, I have heard some people call it the French grape, though I don't know why, as there is no documentation of it having been brought over from France." In the past, other experts believed that Piculit Neri was identical to Refosco degli Uccelli (or Refoschin), and given the small size of the grape bunch and berries, I'd be inclined to agree if Petrussi hadn't recently told me that Refoschin is genetically identical to Refosco del Peduncolo Rosso (Refoschin's scrawny appearance is a result of Refosco del Peduncolo Rosso being planted in poor, nutrient-deficient soils). Certainly, given the inaccuracies possible in poorly conducted ampelographic studies (Petrussi's experience with Friuli native grapes being unimpeachable) and the fallacy of genetic testing conducted on vegetative material, in the absence of clear-cut genetic results from other suitably cultured researchers, the jury's out. However, you couldn't be blamed for thinking that the "Refoschin" diminutive makes sense given Piculit Neri's small-sized bunch and berries (that are very blue-black and have little bloom). What has been established is that Piculit Neri is completely unrelated to Picolit: one is not a mutation of the other.

Thanks to Claudio Fabbro, we know that Piculit Neri was on show at the grapevine fair organized by the Friulian Agrarian Association of Udine in 1863 and 1921 and was considered typical of the area around Castelnovo. This cultivar is also cited in the *Vocabulary of the Friuli Language* written by Pirona (1871–1935). Historically, it has always been cultivated on the right bank of the Tagliamento River around the town of San Vito near Friuli Venezia Giulia's western border with Veneto, and even as far as Schio (Vicenza) in Veneto. Documents show it was grown at the beginning of the twentieth century by the Conti Zoppola and the Luchini estates. Candussio published a complete ampelographic study of the variety in 1977. A vigorous variety, farmers appreciated its dependable, abundant production and disease resistance (but it's sensitive to botrytis bunch rot, despite its thick-skinned berries); the wines were likewise held in high esteem due to their finesse.

Which Wines to Choose and Why

Piculit Neri wines can be excellent and, in my experience, are considerably better than those made with *Refoscos*, if for no other reason than the more refined tannins of the Piculit Neri wines (I've had almost every Bulfon vintage numerous times and also many examples from other producers in each vintage). Only Refosco Nostrano wines can match piculit neri's silky tannins, but I find the latter usually has deeper, richer black fruit flavors. Usually pale to medium ruby, Piculit Neri wines have intense aromas and flavors of underbrush, red currant, and chestnuts, all complicated by sweet spice notes. Again, its winning hand is a graceful mouthfeel, with balanced tannins and acids and a midweight frame.

WINES TO TRY: Bulfon** (two different versions, one aged in small oak barrels; unfortunately some recent vintages seemed to contain notable levels of residual sugar, which is a shame), Ronco Cliona*, and Florutis*.

Piedirosso

WHERE IT'S FOUND: Campania, Puglia. NATIONAL REGISTRY CODE NUMBER: 189. COLOR: red.

Piedirosso is one of the most ancient of Italy's grapes, and some historians trace its roots far back, to an ancestor called Colombina, a grape Pliny the Elder wrote about at length in his *Naturalis historia*. Piedirosso, a name coined by Carlucci (1909), refers to the typical red stalks of the variety's grape bunches, akin to the red color of pigeon claws (*piedirosso* means red foot). Piedirosso was also called Palombina Nera, Per e Palummo, Palummina, Piede Palombo, and Piede di Colombo, all of which refer to the color red or pigeon feet.

Piedirosso exhibits a great deal of intravarietal variability, and this explains the many phenotypic expressions observed in vineyards and the wildly different wines made from Piedirosso's many biotypes. It also accounts for past errors in ampelographic identification: for example, Gasparrini (1844) mistakenly believed Piedirosso to be identical to Piedmont's Dolcetto. In all honesty, the extent of biodiversity among *Piedirosso* populations is startling: on the island of Ischia, in the vineyards I have been visiting annually for the past decade or so, one common biotype is called Streppa Verde, but it lacks the red stalk even when grapes have attained full ripeness. To me, this simple fact provides more than enough grounds to exclude it from the *Piedirosso* group (after all, the variety's name is related to its red-colored stalks), but most other experts do not see it this way. This being Italy, you won't be surprised that there is also a Streppa Rossa, yet another synonym of Piedirosso; but you'll no doubt be relieved upon hearing that this biotype at least isn't red-stalk challenged.

Of the many other *Piedirosso*s you may encounter around Campania (in my experience, seemingly everywhere), we now know that Piedirosso Beneventano and Piedirosso Napoletano are identical and essentially toponyms (they're the same variety, each named after its province of cultivation, and so their correct name is Piedirosso). In contrast, Piedirosso Avellinese grown, logically enough, in the province of Avellino differs both in leaf and cluster shape from the standard Piedirosso variety and is a distinct variety, closely related to the rare, currently noncultivated Uva Strone (Costantini, Monaco, Vouillamoz, Forlani, and Grando 2005). The same studies suggest that Piedirosso has close genetic ties to Caprettone, which is not surprising, given that both have lived for centuries in close contact on the slopes of Vesuvius.

Which Wines to Choose and Why

After Aglianico, Piedirosso is the second most-planted red grape of Campania (the most common in the province of Naples) and so is part of an infinite number of IGT, DOC, and DOCG wines. Most of the time it's used in blends, usually with Aglianico, which it helps soften (much like Canaiolo Nero with Sangiovese), but many monovarietal wines exist too. An only partial list of DOC wines includes Ischia (both in the Ischia Rosso blend and the pure Ischia Per e Palummo), Campi Flegrei, Lacryma Christi, Penisola Sorrentina Rosso, Taburno Piedirosso, Sannio Piedirosso, and Sant'Agata dei Goti Piedirosso. In the last three especially, wines can be 100 percent Piedirosso.

Piedirosso is not particularly easy in the cellar. The main difficulty lies in its poor anthocyanin content, and all producers worry about extracting color to the fullest degree without risking bitterness. Massimo Di Renzo, winemaker at the world-famous Mastroberardino estate says, "We do pre-macerations for three days at about 8°C, nothing lower than that for we'd never extract any color; then in fermentation we quickly bring the temperature to 24°C to leech out tannins fast in order to help stabilize the anthocyanins. Our perennial concern is to both extract pigments and not lose them." For the same reason, at Mastroberardino they micro-oxygenate the must to create oxygen bonds between pigment molecules and tannins, which is another method by which to stabilize color. "The oxygen is an absolute necessity, for at that stage the yeasts are still alive and very active, and most of the available oxygen gets used up by them," summarizes Di Renzo. Piedirosso wines are characterized by lower acidity and softer tannins than Aglianico wines, but they almost always show a green or herbal streak that in my opinion rarely goes missing even with very ripe grapes. In bad wines, the green note is very apparent and frankly weedy or vegetal: to my palate, unbearable. However, when Piedirosso ripens properly it yields a remarkably satisfying wine characterized by bright red-berry and floral aromas and flavors, complicated by obvious tar and herbal notes and a saline tang. It's the floral element (geranium, lavender, and with age, violet) that sets the good wines apart from the bad ones (which aren't floral, but vegetal). In fact, I find Piedirosso a good candidate for carbonic maceration techniques, for its effusively fruity and floral aromas can be downright charming. Piedirosso Nouveau, er Novello, anyone?

WINES TO TRY: La Rivolta***, D'Ambra** (Per' e Palummo), Cantine Federiciane Monteleone**, Masseria del Borro**, Sorrentino** (Versacrum), Varchetta**, Contrada Salandra*, and La Sibilla (Piedirosa).

Pignola

WHERE IT'S FOUND: Lombardy. NATIONAL REGISTRY CODE NUMBER: 191. COLOR: red.

Distinct from Friuli Venezia Giulia's more famous Pignolo, Pignola shares with it and many other similarly named cultivars a very compact grape cluster, which resembles a small closed fist or pinecone *(pigna)*. Though many refer to this variety as Pignola Nera, the official name in the National Registry is Pignola and so that's the one I shall use here. Once common in Piedmont, the region it is believed to be a native of, Pignola nowadays grows practically only in Lombardy, where Pier de' Crescenzi first described it in 1495. A little more than three centuries later, Acerbi (1825) described two different *Pignolas*, Croattino Piccolo and Neretto di Monte Segale. Molon (1906) wrote that the Pignolo Spano of Novara and the Pignola Spanna of the Vercellese were identical varieties (Novara and Vercelli are very close to one another), and Schneider, Carrà, Akkak, This, Laucou, and Botta (2001) proved that Pignola and Pignola Spano are identical. Further research showed that Pignola is likely a cousin of Nebbiolo (Schneider, Boccacci, Torello Marinoni, Botta, Akkak, and Vouillamoz 2004), and that the *Pignolas* from Lombardy's Valtellina and Friuli Venezia Giulia are different from those of Lombardy's Bergamo and the Oltrepò Pavese winemaking zones (Fossati, Labra, Castiglione, Scienza, and Failla 2001). In fact, Cancellier, Giannetto, and Crespan (2009) showed Pignola to be identical to Groppello di Breganze, a very rare *Groppello* that from the start struck most observers as fairly different from the main *Groppello* varieties known (save for some morphologic features resembling those of Groppello di Revò). Characteristically, Pignola heals quickly from hail damage and is resistant to even very cold temperatures, all-important qualities in alpine vineyards; though sensitive to oidium and botrytis bunch rot (especially in very rainy autumns), it's resistant to peronospora. Today, Pignola Nera is essentially found only in Lombardy, in the provinces of Bergamo, Brescia, and Pavia.

Which Wines to Choose and Why

Pignola is most typically associated with the Oltrepò Pavese and Valtellina production zones, and it is usually found in blends with other local varieties in IGT wines such as Terrazze Retiche di Sondrio. Pignola had been reduced to a blending agent, and it is only thanks to recent efforts and dedication from the esteemed Triacca estate in Valtellina that we can hope to see more monovarietal Pignola wines on the market. Since Groppello di Breganze and Pignola are supposedly identical, wines made with this variety can be found around Vicenza in Veneto.

The Triacca estate has made as many as three different wines from Pignola: Their white wine is called La Contea (blended with Sauvignon Blanc). A second very interesting version was a sparkling wine made by secondary fermentation in the bottle; the 2002 vintage was all sold in Switzerland or used as an aperitif for those visiting the estate of La Gatta near Bianzone. The third version is Pinea, made as an IGT Terrazze Retiche di Sondrio, a classically dry red wine that has very mineral aromas and flavors of raspberry, white truffle, gunflint, and black pepper, fresh and vibrant, with youthfully chewy tannins, which I find are not as harsh as those of other varieties with *pigna*-related names (such as Pignolo, for example).

Firmino Miotti makes the only monovarietal Groppello di Breganze I know of. Interestingly, the Cantina Col Dovigo produces a wine they name Groppello, though they don't specify which *Groppello* variety is used. The wine is an IGT, but the word Breganze is printed in small lettering on the label below the words Indicazione Geografica Tipica. The wine is made with Groppello di Breganze.

WINES TO TRY: For Pignola Nera, try: Triacca** (Pinea). For Groppello di Breganze, try: Firmino Miotti***, Col Dovigo.

Pignoletto

WHERE IT'S FOUND: Emilia-Romagna, Umbria, Lazio, Marche. NATIONAL REGISTRY CODE NUMBER: 300. COLOR: white.

Many Italian native grape varieties are plagued by myriad erroneous names and synonyms, and Pignoletto is no slouch in this department. It is called Grechetto di Todi in Umbria, where it is an important part of the Orvieto wine blend. In Emilia-Romagna it is called Rèbola, but the two are identical. In the past it has been called Pignolo (a distinct red variety of Friuli Venezia Giulia), Pulcinculo (most often a synonym of *Grechetto*s in Umbria), and Ribolla (both a white and red variety of Friuli Venezia Giulia), as well as confused with Pinot Bianco and Riesling Italico or Welschriesling. Clones of Pignoletto include CAB 3, CAB 5, and VCR 3, but as mentioned in the Grechetto entry two of these were previously thought to be Grechetto di Todi clones. It would be interesting to know if these clones, selected from mother plants that had probably long inhabited the specific *terroirs* of two different regions (Umbria and Emilia-Romagna), thereby adapting over time to different living conditions, yield exactly the same wine. My experience is that, though the varieties may be genetically identical, the ensuing wines may not be, even if the exact same agricultural and vinification techniques are employed. Also, the Grechetto clone G5 ICA PG is in fact identical to Pignoletto CAB 5, while Grechetto clone VCR 2 is identical to Pignoletto VCR 3, yet these are all included in the National Registry's Grechetto entry. Grechetto clone R3 biotype Ribolla is not related to Ribolla Gialla at all, and so allowing this name for the clone only led to more confusion. In any case, the ICA PG clone is especially resistant to oidium and botrytis, though it drops acidity quickly when overripe (notably tartaric acid), especially in hot, humid years (Borgo, Cartechini, Lovat, and Moretti 2004).

Rèbola is the name for Grechetto di Todi or Pignoletto in the Romagna section of Emilia-Romagna, where it was also called Ribolla (erroneously, since Ribolla Gialla is a native of Friuli Venezia Giulia) and Pignulèt. It was first described in this part of Italy by De Bosis in 1876 (in the *Bollettini ampelografici provinciali*) as a variety commonly found in the countryside of Rimini.

The Grechetto di Todi variety, which is in fact Pignoletto, is instead more abundant around Todi as well as in the whole province of Perugia, and of course in Emilia-Romagna. In fact, though Pignoletto is generally considered a variety native to Emilia-Romagna, it is most typically found on the hills around Bologna in the Emilia portion of the region (though in the past it was also grown in Romagna, where it is uncommon today). It also has a limited extension in the Marche.

Which Wines to Choose and Why

Good to great Pignoletto DOC wines of Emilia-Romagna are Colli Bolognesi and Colli di Rimini. The latter are often made with what is called Rèbola there. Though the excellent wines of Colli Martani are labeled as Grechetto, in my experience they are most often made with Grechetto di Todi, or Pignoletto. The best wines to try are the DOC Colli Bolognesi Pignoletto; historically the wines of the San Pietro area were considered best, and they set the prices for all others. The wines of the DOC Reno Pignoletto can also be 100 percent Pignoletto. Pignoletto makes uncomplicated, light, lemony wines that are easygoing, with hints of white flowers, aniseed, chamomile, and Golden Delicious apples and high acidity and delicate textures. Thanks to high natural acidity, the variety can yield pleasant sparkling wines as well; when harvested late, it can give concentrated wines of real depth. At high yields, though, the wines are tart and neutral, with little in the way of redeeming qualities. Interestingly, though, the variety has highly tannic skins, meaning that if they are pressed lightly, the wine will still have a chewy, pleasant mouthfeel. In Romagna, there are some very interesting, though now rare, sweet wines made from air-dried grapes.

WINES TO TRY: Vallona*** (Primedizioni Cuvée and Amestesso, which are simply exceptional wines, and a very good late-harvest Permartina), Isola** (Frizzante Cuvée Picri), Corte d'Aibo* (Montefreddo), Tenuta Bonzara* (Frizzante Vigna Antica), and Tizzano* (Spumante Brut, Frizzante, and Superiore). For Rèbola, try: Podere Vecciano*** (Vigna La Ginestra).

Pignolo

WHERE IT'S FOUND: FVG. NATIONAL REGISTRY CODE NUMBER: 285. COLOR: red.

If it hadn't been for the Abbazia di Rosazzo (the ancient *monasterium rosaceum*) and the intelligence, passion, and foresight of at least three different men, I would not be writing about Pignolo. Nor would anybody else, for that matter. Pignolo is one of many Italian varieties named for its very small and compact bunch, reminiscent of a pine cone *(pigna)*, but it was practically an extinct variety as recently as the 1950s. Almost no one knew anything about the variety or grew it, despite what people might tell you today. Pignolo's story is different than other Friuli Venezia Giulia native varieties such as Schioppettino or Ucelut, which for most of the twentieth century were little known and not made into monovarietals; but this was a choice, for estates preferred to use them in blends. Pignolo was different: simply put, nobody owned vines in any commercially significant number. The cultivar's plight began in the early twentieth century, when most experts recommended against its cultivation (not the only example in Italy's history of so-called luminaries wreaking havoc on the country's viticulture). Others were more hopeful (for example, Poggi 1939), which only seems logical, since documents from the twelfth century show that the city of Udine thought enough of Pignolo wine to use it as a welcoming gift for visiting notables. In the seventeenth century, Abbot Giobatta Micheli lauded Pignolo in the dithyramb "Bacco in Friuli," and Claudio Fabbro, one of Friuli's most knowledgeable grape and wine historians, told me that no less an expert than Dalmasso believed Pignolo could make a wine as good as those made from the *Cabernets* or Merlot and that he had written a very complementary tasting note on a 1930 Pignolo wine.

One of the Pignolo heroes was an Abbazia di Rosazzo vineyard worker called Casasola, who helped preserve the grapevine when it was on the brink of extinction. The other two heroes are Silvano Zamò, now the owner of the Le Vigne di Zamò estate (located close to the abbey), and winemaker Walter Filiputti, who worked together to save the variety and make a monovarietal wine from it again. Thanks to them we know there are at least three different Pignolo biotypes: one with a heavily indented leaf (a scantily productive biotype), one with a lobed leaf, and one with a leaf that shows a degree of indentation in between the other two (and is slightly more productive). All three are sensitive to extreme temperatures but need heat units to ripen completely; due to the very compact bunch, well-ventilated sites such as the top of a hill are always best. These also ensure plenty of sunlight, giving Pignolo a better shot at reaching optimal ripeness.

Pignolo is very sensitive to oidium; in really old vineyards, the vines were apparently ungrafted, a rarity because the variety is very sensitive to phylloxera. Pignolo is unrelated to any of the other main *pigna*-named varieties in Italy, such as Pignoletto or Pignola Nera.

Which Wines to Choose and Why

Pignolo is grown in many parts of Friuli Venezia Giulia but is most abundant around the towns of Albana, Premariacco, Prepotto, and Rosazzo in the Colli Orientali del Friuli (COF), and these DOC wines are labeled COF Pignolo.

According to Silvano Zamò, Pignolo is tough to work with in the cellar: its extreme wealth of polyphenols causes high osmotic pressure in the must, which makes life difficult for yeasts. Therefore, stuck fermentations are always a possibility with Pignolo. The other huge difficulty is Pignolo's brute tannic power. Though the wines can express delicious blackberry and blueberry aromas and flavors, complicated by herbal nuances and a juicy mineral tang, these characteristics become apparent only after six to eight years from the vintage. This is because Pignolo is one of Friuli Venezia Giulia's (and all of Italy's, for that matter) most tannic varieties, and as it has only recently been rediscovered, the best way to manage those tannins is still a matter of conjecture. Producers and winemakers have tried everything from late harvesting the grapes to air-drying them on mats, shortening *cuvaisons*, and decreasing fermentation temperatures. Consequently, today's Pignolo wines exhibit considerable stylistic differences, but all young wines share almost brutal mouth-coating tannins. Think Sagrantino, or a Barolo on steroids. While big, tannic wines are certainly impressive, producers are still learning to tame this tannic bounty, and I'm not sure I've tasted enough Pignolo wines that have achieved a degree of refinement similar to Italy's and the world's greatest wines. Even worse, having tasted numerous Pignolo wines and many with almost a decade of bottle age, I have yet to find one that has developed the nuances of truly noble grape varieties, which makes me think the variety may be limited in what it can really express. Big and brawny always, maybe even with an increased degree of gentleness: but truly noble? I wonder. Undoubtedly, time will tell and plays in Pignolo's favor.

WINES TO TRY: Dorigo***, Valentino Butussi**, Paolino Comelli**, Petrucco**, Torre Rosazza**, Le Vigne di Zamò**, Moschioni** (grapes are gently air-dried on the vine), Castello di Buttrio**, and Ermacora**. The last three are much softer than others, with less obvious tannins, a neat trick given Pignolo's intrinsic characteristics. Alessandra Felluga of Castello di Buttrio told me it's her particular *terroir,* and Dario Ermacora maintains he does not blend any softening agents in such as Merlot. Good for them, as the wines are excellent and give Pignolo lovers hope that the wines will soon reach the considerable potential the variety seems blessed with.

Pinella

WHERE IT'S FOUND: Veneto. NATIONAL REGISTRY CODE NUMBER: 192. COLOR: white.

Pinella is a very old variety, well known along the Adriatic coast in the thirteenth century, mentioned in the statutes of the city of Vicenza in 1264. It was once also common in Friuli Venezia Giulia, described in 1324, but today it is found mainly in Veneto. Many of today's producers choose to call the variety Pinello instead of Pinella. The bunch is medium-small, shaped like a truncated cone, and extremely compact: in fact, the round berries are often deformed by being so tightly squeezed together. There is one clone available, Fedit 7 C.S.G., developed in 1970. Like many other grapes with similarly compact and small bunches, its name derives from *pigna* or *pugno*, meaning "pine cone" or "fist." An abundant and dependable producer, it does best in well-ventilated sites and on marly-clay, fresh soils (due to their clay content, which allows for water retention). The ventilation aspect is obviously key with Pinella, in view of its supertight bunches, and it won't surprise anyone to know that botrytis bunch rot can be a big problem.

Which Wines to Choose and Why

Today you're likely to find very few vines of Pinella, as it only grows in sporadic rows in Veneto around Padova, where it's used as a blending grape for DOCs Colli Euganei Pinella, Colli Euganei Bianco, and Bagnoli di Sopra Bianco wines. However, interest in its fine winemaking potential is considerable and monovarietal wines can be found. There is also a Pinela (or Pinjela) variety in Slovenia, where they also make monovarietal wines with it, but in the absence of accurate ampelographic description or genetic profiling, it is unclear if these two similarly named varieties are identical or distinct. I have never tasted wines made with the non-Italian variety so I can't add anything to that discussion. Pinella wine has a delicately aromatic nose of sweet spices and flowers (jasmine), and it is bright and fresh on the palate with hints of pineapple and apple. The variety's acidity is such that sparkling wines can also be made from it.

WINES TO TRY: Francesca Callegaro** (Antichi Reassi), Le Coste** (Rime Disperse, aged in oak barrels), Cantine dei Colli Tramonte* (Pinello di Pinello Spumante), and Dotto Lidio* (Pinello, a sparkling wine).

Prié

WHERE IT'S FOUND: Valle d'Aosta. NATIONAL REGISTRY CODE NUMBER: 311. COLOR: white.

I'm scared of heights, and getting into a jeep to drive up alpine paths more suited to mountain goats and mules always proves a daunting experience. Unfortunately for my coronaries, Prié only grows in mountaintop vineyards that are, arguably, among the most beautiful in the world. The vines hug the slopes, planted on little terraces stolen from the cliffs and trained with a low canopy, so that you often need to get on all fours and look up to see the beautiful pale green, almost white grapes. In a truly enchanted landscape, first described by Horace Bénédict de Saussure in the eighteenth century, Prié usually thrives on ungrafted vines since phylloxera doesn't survive cold mountain environments, at altitudes (from eight hundred to twelve hundred meters above sea level) that are anathema to most other grape varieties. In fact, Prié grows in the highest vineyards of Europe, though there's a Swiss *vigneron* or two who'll argue that.

Prié is the oldest documented variety of Valle d'Aosta. The earliest mention of the name Prié is found in a manuscript dated January 22, 1691, detailing the sale of specific goods, excluding a parcel of vines of Priés situated in the Clos Morant near Saint-Pierre. Another interesting manuscript contains the 1786–93 cellar records of Louis-Joseph Cunéaz from Gressan, who recorded *vin blanc* and *vin prié*, most likely because these were made with different varieties (the former wine was most likely made from Blanc Comun). Due to its old age, Prié has been shown to be one of the two parents of a slew of other Valle d'Aosta grapes, including Roussin de Morgex, Primetta, Mayolet, and Blanc Comun. Surprisingly, genetic profiling has revealed that it is most likely an offspring of Lugliatica Bianca (known as Lignan Blanc in France), a now rare variety diffuse all over Europe in the sixteenth century. Prié's name probably refers to the wine's use in Sunday Mass by priests (*prier*, in French, or pray); other records show that the church discouraged using red wines for Holy Mass because they were too liable to stain the priest's white garb. Prié is actually better known as Prié Blanc, a more recent name created to differentiate the variety from Prié Rouge (Prëmetta or Primetta). Other synonyms include Blanc de Valdigne (the Valdigne is the northernmost part of the Valle d'Aosta and Prié's natural home) and Agostenga, which is best not used because it has been applied to many other varieties (it refers to early ripening grapes).

Lorenzo Gatta (1838) did a masterful job of describing all of Valle d'Aosta's varieties and left an impressive body of information detailing Prié's presence in the region, telling us almost everything we need to know. Prié was the only vine able to survive the brutally cold conditions of Morgex, La Salle, Valpellin, and Allein, and grapes were harvested either in August (to produce a very fresh, high-acid wine) or at the end of September (for fuller-bodied wines). Outside the Alta Valle, that northernmost third of the Valle d'Aosta region that hugs the French border, Prié was usually consumed locally as a table grape. Mario Vevey of the Albert Vevey estate likes to point out that Prié behaves like a wild vine and if left to its own will grow very long shoots and quickly wrap itself around natural supports such as trees. He thinks the cultivar is a resistant one save for the fact that its thin skins make it easily subject to botrytis. In Valle d'Aosta there are more than twenty-five hectares of Prié, and it grows practically everywhere in the upper third of the valley. According to Vouillamoz and Moriondo (2011), there is also a scant 0.02 hectare in Spain's Castilla y León zone, where the variety is called Legiruela.

Which Wines to Choose and Why

Prié is the source of one of Italy's best light-bodied white wines: the Blanc de Morgex et La Salle, the only wine of any commercial significance in the Alta Valle. The highest-quality grapes come from the vineyards around the towns that give the wine its name. I think that the very best grapes come from the Morgex area, blessed with poor, mineral soils of morainic origin, which yield wines that are steely, floral, and brightly acidic. In Morgex, Vevey believes the very good *cru* is Eicheru, while Nicola Del Negro of the Cave du Vin Blanc thinks that La Piagne vineyard is also a *grand cru*. The wines of La Salle, due to different morainic-alluvial soils, are less steely and softer, and when blended with those of Morgex help round out the final wine by diminishing what are normally enamel-cringing levels of acidity. With a little practice, it's not hard to tell where most of the grapes in a particular wine come from. A great Blanc de Morgex et La Salle is a thing of beauty: fresh and fragrant, with aromas and flavors of thyme, chlorophyll, mint, green apple, and white flowers. In warmer years hints of apricot emerge. There are also sweet and sparkling versions made (not surprising, given the variety's high natural acidities), but the best wines are the dry ones. Blanc de Morgex et La Salle is the ultimate aperitif wine, but one that matches remarkably well with simple fish and vegetables dishes too. There are fewer wines I would rather drink on a hot summer day; but then, I like to drink it in the dead of winter too.

WINES TO TRY: Cave de Morgex et La Salle*** (the entry-level wine and the creamier Rayon; the sparkling wines, made both by the Charmat method and by Champagne's technique of refermentation in the bottle, are also outstanding), Piero Brunet*** (owns some of the best vineyards of all in a *grand cru terroir* for the variety), Albert Vevey***, Marziano Vevey**, and Ermès Pavese*.

Prié Rouge

WHERE IT'S FOUND: Valle d'Aosta. NATIONAL REGISTRY CODE NUMBER: 312. COLOR: red.

Though the official name of this variety in the National Registry is Prié Rouge, everyone in Italy calls it Prëmetta. In 1982 Luigi Veronelli spoke to me enthusiastically about Prëmetta and Fumin, two native varieties of the Valle d'Aosta I had never heard about. That was enough to set me off on a wine-hunting mission in Roman wineshops, where I discovered a slightly dusty bottle of prëmetta. It was love at first sight: I liked the label, and even more I liked the light pinkish liquid that poured from the bottle. The grape itself is lovely to look at: large, pretty, rosy pink berries and opulent clusters spilling out from the vines that make you want to start eating. In fact, Prëmetta was long considered an excellent table grape. Its name derives from the Italian words *prima* or *primaticcia,* meaning "before" or "early," referring to the grape's early ripening (the same applies to Primitivo and other similarly named varieties).

In observance of the guidelines expressed by the International Council for the Nomenclature of Cultivated Plants (Brickell, Baum, Hetterscheid, Leslie, McNeill, Trehane, Vrugtman, and Wiersema 2004), the correct name should be Primetta, for that is how this grape was originally known in the nineteenth century. According to Gatta (1838), it was then grown mainly in north-exposed vineyards and was also called Neblou or Prié Rouzo, the latter becoming Prié Rouge in French. Both Prié Rouge and Prëmetta are in fact twentieth-century creations: Prié Rouge was coined because Primetta is the result of a natural crossing between Prié Blanc and an unknown other parent. Actually, Berget (1904) had already noted the ampelographic similarities between Prié Blanc and Primetta and wrote that the latter was most likely a subvariety of the former (in fact, though related, the two are distinct varieties). As Prié Rouge is also the official name listed in the National Registry for this cultivar, that's an argument for using it in this book too. However, the name you are most likely to come across is Prëmetta, and it's also the name I use for the variety. In the last twelve or thirteen years of annual visits to the Valle d'Aosta, I have yet to meet a producer or local wine lover who has once, and I mean just once, referred to this cultivar as Prié Rouge.

Though rare today, in 1877 Prëmetta represented 40 percent of the grapes grown around Charvensod and Saint-Nicolas and 30 percent of the those around Jovençan. Costantino Charrère, who was the first to believe in Prëmetta and began growing it in 1972, loves the variety, and though he realizes it's not the noblest grape he'll ever work with, he loves its many qualities and is pushing younger wine producers around him to give it a try. Like Charrère, I think Prëmetta is a very pretty grape. The large, pyramidal, winged bunches have medium-sized round berries of a lovely dark pink but with thin skins. Interestingly, it appears that Didier Gerbelle, a talented local *vigneron,* has identified a biotype of this cultivar that yields darker wines and is currently studying it. Today Prëmetta is fairly rare, located in a few hectares mainly around Saint-Pierre, Aymavilles, Saint-Denis, and Quart. It is very productive and mercifully early ripening, given the alpine climate it lives in. Fortunately, it tolerates cold weather well, and vines have been planted as high as eight hundred meters above sea level.

Which Wines to Choose and Why

Valle d'Aosta DOC Prëmetta is the wine to look for; it can be monovarietal, though usually 10 percent is made up of other local varieties. The wine is dark pink with garnet-amber tinges. The scent is intense, with aromas and flavors of roses, red currants, and herbally strawberries, with light tannins. It is a red wine that looks like a rosé and tastes like one too. Costantino Charrère of Les Cretes has recently decided to make a sparkling wine with Primetta: "I always felt that, more than any other of our native varieties, Prëmetta has a very unique aromatic and flavor expression; so I asked the Institut Agricole Régional to help make a sparkling wine by conducting the secondary fermentation in the bottle, much like in Champagne." This is an interesting if strange choice, I might add, given the variety's naturally low acidity. "That's why it's such a pleasantly creamy sparkling wine," explains Charrère. His daughter Eleonora, who is slowly taking over the day-to-day running of the estate, adds, "Like all experiments, we've tinkered with it over the years, harvesting earlier to preserve acidity and adding small percentages of Pinot Nero to obtain a more stable color." Bich (1896) documents that Primetta was used to make *vins de paille* (in which the grapes were air-dried to make luxurious, even sweet wines), though nobody has, until now, thought of resurrecting that technique. Charrère first made a sparkling wine in 2005; personally, I prefer the still version and am sorry he doesn't make it anymore.

WINES TO TRY: Grosjean** and the sparkling version by Les Cretes** (Neblù, made initially as a collaboration between Les Crêtes and IAR). Didier Gerbelle** has resurrected the technique of air-drying Prëmetta and produced a first vintage in 2013.

Primitivo

WHERE IT'S FOUND: Puglia, Campania. NATIONAL REGISTRY CODE NUMBER: 199. COLOR: red.

This variety is called Primitivo in Italy because it ripens very early in the season (and not because of primitive or rustic-tasting wines, a mistaken though understandable assumption given some truly horrible bottlings over the years). The name Primitivo derives from the Latin *primativus* and the Italian *primaticcio* (both meaning first to ripen, or early ripening). In fact, all of this variety's phenological steps, from flowering to color change, are precocious. Hence, it is one of the first grapes to be picked in Italy: in Puglia, its main Italian home, this means August (unless the producer wants to make a late-harvest-style wine).

There have been fewer longer-lasting debates in the world of wine concerning a grapevine's provenance than those involving Primitivo. For the cultivar is a friendly grape doppelgänger, grown in several countries: today, most everyone agrees that Italy's Primitivo, California's Zinfandel, and Croatia's Crljenak Kastelianski (and you thought Italian names were tough to pronounce) or more accurately, Tribidrag, are one and the same. Accepting this hasn't been easy for anyone involved. I remember only too well the anger (I'm not exaggerating in using that word) and unwillingness of some Puglian growers and producers (even famous ones) to accept the Zinfandel name as recently as the late 1990s. Of course, some in the United States have long insisted that Zinfandel is a native American species,

another hilarious viewpoint and a lesson on just how far the concept of "nativeness" can be stretched—and also absolutely impossible, since *Vitis vinifera* isn't native to American soil. Others claimed that Hungarian immigrant Agoston Haraszthy, who planted more than three hundred different grape varieties after arriving in 1837 (and also founded Sonoma's Buena Vista winery in 1857), was the first to plant Zinfandel; but this is unlikely, as New York State nurseries were selling a "zinfendel" already in the 1820s (Zinfandel's final U.S. spelling was decided upon only in the 1860s).

Not to be outdone, Italians unleashed their usual litany of ancient Greek, Roman, and medieval potential grape origins to claim Primitivo as one of their own (undoubtedly, in the world of grapes, there are some clear-cut advantages to having been around for thousands of years). The vexing issue in Italy was really just trying to decide whether Primitivo was first brought to Italy by Phoenician traders or by Illyrian Greek colonists more than two thousand years ago, or if it had been brought to Gioia del Colle in the seventeenth century by Benedictine monks from Burgundy (when it comes to wine, Burgundian ancestry never hurts). The Burgundy hypothesis is a real stretch, given the variety's historical seaside Croatian and Italian homes. The first official documentation of Primitivo in Puglia dates back to the seventeenth century, but it apparently wasn't called Primitivo then. What is sure is that Primitivo rapidly gained a foothold all over Puglia thanks to the work of Don Francesco Filippo Indellicati, who was the first to select vines in old vineyards around Gioia del Colle and helped propagate them elsewhere. A priest and amateur botanist, he was the one who gave the early ripening variety its Latin-derived name; prior to Indellicati the variety was known by other names, for example, Zagarese (a likely reference to Zagreb in Croatia), and other varieties elsewhere in Italy were similarly named. The Primitivo vines arrived in 1799–1800 in Manduria (the cultivar's other famous Puglian home) from Gioia del Colle, thanks to migrant workers but also by way of the dowry of Countess Sabini di Altamura, who married Tommaso Schiavoni Tafuri di Manduria.

So just how did Italians become aware that their Primitivo may have been someone else's Zinfandel? In 1967, Austin Goheen, a plant pathologist from the U.S. Department of Agriculture and professor at University of California, Davis, was the first academic to realize that the grapes there looked very similar to California's Zinfandel, and that the wines tasted the same too. In 1972 he established the close ampelographic similarity between the two grapevines, and in 1976 Wade Wolfe presented isoenzyme pattern data that supported the Zinfandel-Primitivo identity. This led to many studies both at UC Davis and the Istituto Sperimentale per la Viticoltura of Conegliano, culminating in the 1994 work by Carole Meredith and John Bowers proving the two varieties' genetic similarity.

Identifying the Croatian counterpart of this dynamic duo proved even harder, with plenty of false hopes along the way; most famous was the "Zinfandel/Primitivo is Plavac Mali" fiasco, despite isoenzyme studies excluding this. Only in 2001 was the variety's similarity with Crljenak Kastelianski finally determined. This variety was then shown to be the same as Pribidrag; more recently, Malenica, Šimon, Besendorfer, Maletić, Karoglan Kontic, and Pejic (2011) proved it synonymous with Tribidrag, a grape apparently already known in Croatia in the fifteenth century and hence the oldest name used for this variety. The variety is also one of the parents of Plavac Mali. Lacombe, Boursiquote, Laoucou, Dechesne, Varès, and This (2007) demonstrated that a Primitivo/Zinfandel/Tribidrag × Verdeca crossing originated Plavina; and not surprisingly, there is controversy about the latter's Croatian or Puglian heritage too (see VERDECA entry). Presently, it is not clear if Primitivo/Zinfandel/Tribidrag made its way to the United States via Croatia or Italy or if it arrived on American shores by yet another other route; but clearly, Primitivo/Zinfandel/Tribidrag travels well. And given the many high-quality California Zinfandel wines, it is not a stretch to say that Primitivo has lived out the American dream.

Primitivo is known to be difficult in the vineyard and not particularly user-friendly in the cellar, so producers tend to love or hate it. It's certainly not the most resistant variety, as it's susceptible to drought, spring frosts, and floral abortion (in rainy or humid years), and its at times very compact bunch makes it susceptible to vine pests. Actually, the latter is less of a problem in Italy, where Primitivo, in contrast to the Zinfandel biotype, is characterized by looser bunches (and more of them) and smaller berries, so botrytis bunch rot is usually less of a concern than in California. However, it's just as prone in Italy to uneven ripening even within individual bunches; plus, it's an irregular producer, but of usually high-quality grapes, its saving grace. Characteristically, the berries accumulate sugar easily (reaching high alcohol levels has never been a problem for Primitivo, and that explains the wine's long and distinguished career as an alcohol booster for many more famous wines), and they have very good concentrations of anthocyanins. However, the higher levels of cyanin (an unstable anthocyanin) and slightly lower concentrations of malvin (a more stable pigment) mean that the color of Primitivo wines is less stable and, in the long run, less dark than that of wines made with, for example, Cabernet Sauvignon, Merlot, or Aglianico.

There are two main biotypes of Primitivo: Primitivo di Gioia del Colle and Primitivo di Manduria, both also the names of wines. The former is more typical of the province of Bari (its northern portion), while the latter is typical of the province of Taranto. It's likely that Primitivo di Gioia del Colle is the original Primitivo that later made its way to Manduria. Producers always tell me the grapevines look the same and that people only speak of different biotypes because the vine changes morphologically when planted in the very different *terroirs* of Manduria and Gioia del Colle. Therefore, estates in the two production zones appear to be using essentially the same genetic material, and most have planted the same clones, of which 55/A is considered most interesting. As Filippo Cassano of the star-studded Polvanera estate in Gioia del Colle has told me, "I don't even think the clone is important, though I agree 55/A is a good one and we're going to plant more of it; the key with Primitivo is the rootstock, for if the vine is too vigorous it has trouble producing fruit after flowering." Cassano likes to use an old rootstock, the 157/11 Couderc that tames vigor. Marianna Annia of the Pietraventosa estate, a small but up-and-coming operation, told me of experiments done at the Research Center Basile Caramia in Locorotondo: "Having selected three biotypes in the Gioia area, they replanted them in Manduria, obtaining in a short time still different-looking plants, though genetically they were the same." There are also many available clones of Primitivo: UBA 55/A, UBA 47/B, UBA 46/H, UBA 47/A, UNIMI-VITIS-PRI VV 501, UNIMI-VITIS-PRI VV 501, VCR 367, VCR 368, and VCR 369 (the UBA clones are selections from Gioia del Colle).

Puglia is Primitivo's home in Italy, and at 11,133 hectares it is one of the country's ten most-planted red varieties (though Puglia's other famous red variety, Negro Amaro, is still more common). Primitivo is a variety on a roll: in the decade separating the last two Italian agricultural censuses, the surface area devoted to the variety has increased by close to 40 percent. Still, this cultivar more than any other has suffered from EU financial incentives for vine removal. Though the increase in hectarage under vine has improved impressively since 2000 (when total hectares were only 7,951), the total surface area devoted to Primitivo (at 1.7 percent of Italy's surface planted to grapevines) remains much less today than the 17,000+ hectares recorded in 1990. And I won't even begin to talk about the fact that the vines pulled were beautifully old, centenary vines. Besides Puglia, where the vast majority of Primitivo plantings are found, the variety is also grown in northern Campania, and there are sporadic plantings elsewhere, such as in Lazio.

Primitivo of course grows in many other parts of the world. In the United States it has had amazing success as Zinfandel (the 20,377 hectares planted as of 2008 in California alone are more than all the Primitivo in Italy), but it is also grown in Oregon and Washington State. There are small holdings of Primitivo even farther north on the Pacific coast, in Canada's British Columbia, and much farther south, where Mexico's sunny and warm climate makes it a logical choice. Primitivo has met with a little success in other European countries such as Montenegro; far more in Croatia, where it has been all the rage for some time, especially along the Dalmatian coast. There is Primitivo in South Africa as well. Even more successful has been its Australian adventure, with plantings in regions as diverse as Barossa Valley, Clare Valley, Heathcote, Hunter Valley, Langhorne Creek, Margaret River, McLaren Vale, and Rutherglen.

Which Wines to Choose and Why

The most famous Primitivo wines in Italy are Primitivo di Manduria and Gioia del Colle Primitivo. The wine can be dry or more rarely sweet, and even fortified (Liquoroso Secco and Liquoroso Dolce). Falerno del Massico wines near Caserta in Campania are also made with Primitivo. The most famous of all these wines is Primitivo di Manduria, which explains why so much Primitivo is planted in the province of Taranto (Manduria is a town in this province). Insiders know that the Primitivo wine of Sava (another town in this province) was always considered better by the locals, but a lack of quality producers in the Sava area makes this hard to judge nowadays. I do not have any recollection of great Sava Primitivo wines. Conversely, real excitement is being generated by the Gioia del Colle Primitivo, of which there are now many excellent examples.

In theory, the Primitivo di Gioia del Colle is lighter and more graceful than the wine of

Manduria, due to geologic and climate factors (in the late twentieth century, poor winemaking skill in the Gioia del Colle area precluded the possibility of identifying such nuances by any but the wine's most fervent admirers). In Gioia del Colle, the vines are planted in hillside vineyards between 250 and 500 meters above sea level, rather than in the flatland seaside parcels of Manduria and Sava. Therefore, Gioia del Colle has higher altitudes, wider day-night temperature shifts (as much as 20°C in the summer, meaning—in theory—greater aromatic expression in the wines), and lower average yearly temperatures, plus shallow calcareous soils rich in minerals with only a little red clay (while there's more red sand and clay over limestone near Manduria). These factors should contribute to the Primitivo di Goia del Colle wines being more nervy, with higher acidities and more graceful tannic structures and less ultraripe creamy fruit aromas and profiles, but today such differences in the wines are blurred, as all Primitivo wines tend to be high in alcohol. Primitivo di Goia del Colle had virtually disappeared from important commercial marketplaces in the latter half of the twentieth century but has made a resounding comeback in the last five years. A consortium formed in 2000, with only four founding members controlling only 17 percent of the DOC surface under vine, burgeoned by 2002, with thirty-three members counting 94 percent of the total DOC Primitivo di Gioia del Colle area.

When very good, Primitivo is creamy-rich and heady, usually not shy in alcohol (16 percent is common) and awash with aromas and flavors of ripe red cherry, strawberry jam, and plums macerated in alcohol. In some more traditionally made wines there are obvious tobacco and underbrush notes, and the wines can actually be rather herbal and tarry. In fact, had I been writing this book in the late twentieth century I would have said that Italian primitivos differed from California zinfandels because of stronger herbal nuances and less of the ultraripe, almost sweet fruit of some zins; but today some primitivos seem bent on "outzinfandeling" zinfandel. In other words, though many herbal, more restrained wines are still being made in Puglia (and are not to everyone's liking), there's now an ocean of ultraripe, lusciously syrupy, red fruit–crammed primitivo just waiting to greet your taste buds.

Good U.S. Zinfandel wines are too numerous to mention, so I'll just limit myself to an arbitrary choice of three: Ravenswood, Seghesio, and Turley; it's fair to say that the United States makes the best Primitivo wines in the world today. In Australia, Cape Mentelle in Margaret River and Nepenthe in Adelaide Hills were the first to develop good reputations for their Primitivo wines, but there are many other producers of note: Arimia, By Jingo Wines, Cargo Road Wines, Chateau Tanunda (they make a shiraz-primitivo blend), Groom, Rusden, and more. I haven't tried most of them, but those I have tasted seem impressive and to have potential. Zinfandel is the name most used in Australia.

WINES TO TRY: Gianfranco Fino*** (Es; a uniquely rich, decadent version that manages to stay balanced), Racemi*** (Zinfandel Sinfarosa and Dunico), Attanasio***, Feudi di San Marzano** (60 Anni), Zicari** (Patruale and Apulus), Pirro Varone**. For Primitivo Gioia del Colle, try: Nicola Chiaromonte*** (Riserva), Polvanera*** (the wines called 16 and 17, especially), Pietraventosa** (Riserva), and Angiuli Donato**. For Primitivo Dolce Naturale, try: Attanasio**, Masseria Ludovico** (their dry primitivo is also one of the best around), Consorzio Produttori Vino** (Madrigale), and Gianfranco Fino** (Es Più Sole; almost impossible to find, given the small, homeopathic-like quantities made).

Pugnitello

WHERE IT'S FOUND: Tuscany. NATIONAL REGISTRY CODE NUMBER: 371. COLOR: red.

A relative newcomer, Pugnitello has only been around for about ten years on the Italian wine scene but has met with resounding success. The variety's name derives from its small, compact bunch, reminiscent of a closed, small fist (*pugno* means fist; the *-tello* suffix makes it a small fist). Practically nobody had ever heard of Pugnitello until 1981, when it was discovered at Poggio di Sassi, near the Tuscan coastal town of Grosseto. It was then propagated and studied extensively by the San Felice estate in Chianti Classico (the first vines were planted in 1987).

Morphologically, Pugnitello looks a little like Montepulciano, and some experts consider Pugnitello a biotype of Montepulciano, though published DNA profiling results exclude this (Vignani, Scali, Masi, Milanelli, Scalabrelli, Wang, et al. 2008). Winemaker Maurizio Castelli isn't so convinced, saying "It looks and behaves like a Montepulciano." Another winemaker, Gabriella Tani, who at Paterna oversees production of the excellent Pugni Rosso wine, believes the two varieties are sufficiently different that a trained eye should not be easily fooled: "The bunch of Pugnitello is much smaller; you actually have to go looking for them on the vines by moving the leaves around. Undoubtedly there is a resemblance, but with a little care nurseries can avoid pulling a switch on unsuspecting estates."

Producers find Pugnitello interesting due to its small berries, resistant skins, and sparse bunch; plus, it has shown noteworthy ability to accumulate sugars and polyphenols. It has also proven disease resistant and very vigorous, though low fertility and small bunches make for small productions. The only clone available is PU-PA 1. Pugnitello was entered into the National Registry on April 15, 2002. Given its considerable critical and commercial success, this is one grape variety and wine we are likely to hear much more of in the future. For the moment, however, its diffusion is limited to Tuscany, mainly around Grosseto, Florence, Siena, and Arezzo.

Which Wines to Choose and Why

Pugnitello is used in IGT blends such as Costa Toscana and Montecastelli. The San Felice estate planted one thousand vines from which three *barriques* of wine were made in the first vintage, and the estate was the first to produce a pure Pugnitello wine. Today, numerous other bottlings of Pugnitello exist, either as a monovarietal or in blends with other varieties. Winemakers like it because it has many of the qualities of Montepulciano (rich color, fleshy fruit) but is not as reductive and therefore is less work in the cellar, and the wines tend to be more fruity and perfumed. "Sure, it's still a work in progress," says Tani. "For example, I think it needs less oak than Sangiovese; I started out using *barriques* [a roughly 225-liter oak barrel], then moved to *tonneaux* [a 500-liter barrel], and now much bigger oak casks. I think that Pugnitello's greatest calling card is the rich fleshy fruit it can deliver, so maybe oak isn't the answer at all. I am beginning to look at aging it in amphoras." However, oak is not likely to disappear in conjunction with Pugnitello. In fact, Tani cautions that Pugnitello wine requires a lot of oxygen and oak helps to avoid the development of reductive aromas: "It's very rich in anthocyanins and so tends to reduce easily, though not as badly as Montepulciano or Ancellotta, but off odors during the winemaking process can be a problem, so you can't work with steel tanks that allow no oxygenation to take place. Rack and returns and pumping over are also techniques used commonly in an effort to maximize oxygen contact with the must."

A good Pugnitello wine has very rich and thick red-cherry aromas and flavors, complicated by plum jam, burnt almond, leather, and earthy notes. Tani also finds suave, almost decadent aromas and flavors of dark fruit macerated in alcohol and a hint of marzipan. She loves the wine, finding it to be fruitier and richer than those made with Sangiovese: she also believes it to have higher total acidity, which gives it a long cellar life. "If well made," she says, "it's a real fruit bomb, but with plenty of acidity to help it keep from becoming heavy." And pugnitello also ages better than people are inclined to think, adds winemaker Attilio Pagli: "I always find it's much better a few years after the vintage, as it usually picks up a note of refinement that isn't very noticeable in its youth, when the wine's fruity, fleshy exuberance tends to dominate. I think it's a great grape, and I'd like to see what it could do in Abruzzo, instead of always planting Montepulciano there."

WINES TO TRY: San Felice***, Paterna*** (Pugni Rosso; the first vintages, due to limited availability of grapes, were only 80 percent Pugnitello), Le Buche*, Mannucci Droandi*, and Poggio al Gello* (Pugnitello del Piaggione).

Quagliano

WHERE IT'S FOUND: Piedmont. NATIONAL REGISTRY CODE NUMBER: 325. COLOR: red.

Quagliano is the only Italian wine grape listed under the letter "Q" in the National Registry. It will also prove one of the least-known varieties in this book, and yet it is a locally important grape and wine, albeit limited to a very small zone of Italy. Quagliano production was documented in the eighteenth century (it was first cited in 1721 in agricultural documents of the town of Busca, and then in 1749 in those of Costigliole Saluzzo); it was probably already in place in the 1600s, but called Negro Dolce. Some researchers identify Quagliano with the ancient wine *aglieucos*, though there is no definitive proof of this.

Quagliano has always been appreciated for more than just the quality of its wine: considered an excellent table grape, it fetched much higher prices than other grapes of the area. The first accurate description of Quagliano is by Molon (1906), who believed the variety capable of producing delicious wines. The local nobility believed in Quagliano "grape therapy" as well, centuries before modern preparations of antioxidant creams and grape-skin massages became the norm. It seems Quagliano's low sodium concentration lends it diuretic qualities, which might not be what producers of a fine wine want to be known for today, but so be it.

The problem with Quagliano is its extremely thin skin. All it takes is some rain during the harvest period and the berries split open, a mecca for botrytis bunch rot. Otherwise, it's a fairly hardy grape. The variety is pretty to look at, with large pyramidal bunches and large round, pale blue-red berries. The origin of Quagliano's name is unknown: it may be a derivation of the term *caià* (or *cagliato*), in reference to the way the wine was once produced. Recent DNA results suggest that Quagliano is a possible parent of Impigno, a variety typical of Puglia, though this is hard to understand, as to the best of my knowledge neither variety has ever been associated in the literature, nor have the two been described in the other's region (Cipriani, Spadotto, Jurman, Di Gaspero, Crespan, Meneghetti, et al. 2010).

Quagliano is native to the Salluzese area of Piedmont, in the province of Cuneo (not that far from where the much more famous Barolo and Barbaresco are made). Vines grow everywhere around the towns of Pagno, Piasco, Busca, Brondello, Costigliole Saluzzo, Saluzzo, and Verzuolo.

Which Wines to Choose and Why

The wine is the DOC Colline Saluzzesi Quagliano, also available in a sparkling version. It's a delightful, pink-hued, light-bodied sweet wine that will remind you of strawberries and has considerable tannins that will coat your palate. If the grapes aren't fully ripe, then the wine can be green and less than thrilling, however. Quagliano is characterized by low alcohol levels (a minimum of 10 percent and 11 percent for still and sparkling, respectively). There has been a lovely wine festival celebrating Quagliano wines held annually in September since 1928.

WINES TO TRY: Poderi del Palas*, Tomatis*, and Serena Giordanino*.

Rabosos

See RABOSO FAMILY, chapter 3.

Refoscos

See REFOSCO FAMILY, chapter 3.

Ribolla Gialla

WHERE IT'S FOUND: FVG. NATIONAL REGISTRY CODE NUMBER: 208. COLOR: white.

Ribolla Gialla presents a modern Italian wine conundrum. In Italy, the variety grows only in Friuli Venezia Giulia, and even in this region it is limited essentially to two DOC areas, the Colli Orientali del Friuli and the Collio. Grown in flatland vineyards, it produces a prodigious number of grapes unless curbed by ultrarigorous pruning or stress; short of that, the wine is watery, insipid, and mind-bendingly acidic. Furthermore, Ribolla Gialla has become the darling of artistically inclined, experimentally minded producers (who, in my view, must have far too much free time on their hands) and have decided to treat this white grape as if it were a red variety, subjecting it to months of macerations on the skins, often in porous terracotta amphoras. The resulting wines are reddish-amber tinged and often oxidized beyond redemption (what are now called "orange" wines). In fairness, this was a very traditional way of making wine in centuries past (they have been making wines in this manner in Georgia for thousands of years) and so such winemaking methods are intimately linked to single production areas and are part of local history. Last but not least, another set of forward-thinking Friuli producers have, at least this time not illogically, decided that Ribolla Gialla's naturally high acidity makes it a perfect candidate for sparkling wine production, and with Prosecco's economic and popular success dead in their sights, have proceeded to churn out hectoliter after hectoliter of sparkling ribollas of often dubious complexity and interest. After all that, a small percentage of diehards are still treating Ribolla Gialla the way it was meant to be, making a dry white wine. These wines are immensely popular, the ones that people clamor for and actually buy, though the sparkling versions have been gaining in popularity.

The *giallo* (yellow) adjective in the name Ribolla Gialla is important, as there is a lesser quality and common (in Italy) Ribolla Verde (*verde* means green). Di Rovasenda (1877) and Zava (1901) both also mentioned a Ribolla Bianca, but this was most likely another, unrelated variety. Also called Rebolla, Ribuèle, Ràbuele, Ribuèle Zale, Ribolla di Rosazzo, Raibola, Ràbola, and Rèbula, Ribolla Gialla is an extremely ancient cultivar native to the hills of Gorizia but also common in nearby Slovenia's Goriska Brda. In the latter country some call it Rebula, but this is incorrect, for there are distinct *Rebula* varieties and *Rebula* biotypes in Slovenia and Croatia (for example, Rebula, Rebula Briška, and Rebula-Old are homonyms, not synonyms). In any case, relative to the possible relationships and similarities of Italian Ribolla Gialla and Slovenian Rebula (and its many subvarieties), a recent study revealed that Ribolla Gialla and Rebula Briška share an identical SSR profile at eight out of nine loci (Rusjan, Jug, and Štajner 2010). Ribolla Gialla is also distinct from both the similarly named Rèbola of the Romagna portion of Emilia-Romagna, which is identical to Pignoletto, and from Ribolla Spizade, a synonym for Glera Lungo. Recently, Crespan, Giannetto, Meneghetti, Petrussi, Del Zan, and Sivilotti (2011) proved that Ribolla Gialla is completely unrelated to Schioppettino, once called Ribolla Nera.

Ribolla gialla was long considered one of Italy's greatest wines, and in the thirteenth century it was a regular presence on the dining tables of Venice's nobility. The first mention of it is in medieval times, in a 1299 deed of sale written by notary Ermanno di Gemona in *Notariorum joppi* (Filiputti 1983). A legal document from 1376 concerning a land sale near Barbana in the Collio specified that the farmer had been producing *"sex urnas raboli."* Apparently, 1327 was a poor vintage characterized by low wine production, especially of Ribolla wine. The Germans especially loved this wine: so much that when Trieste was annexed to the Hapsburg empire, Duke Leopold III of Austria demanded that "one hundred urns of the best ribolla wine" be delivered to him annually. In the 1800s,

Ribolla wines were the most popular of all wines made in Friuli Venezia Giulia.

Ribolla Gialla has very pyramidal-cylindrical, very small bunches (as little as eighty grams!), with medium-large berries. It tends to do poorly in flatland vineyards, where it becomes overly productive and yields neutral, insipid wines; use of the Kober 5BB rootstock exposes it to risk of drought sensitivity. It's also subject to shot berries (Ribolla Verde suffers less from this but is more prone to botrytis, due to its more compact bunch). There are two clones of note, ERSA-FVG 180 and VCR 100.

Which Wines to Choose and Why

Ribolla Gialla wines are typical of Friuli Venezia Giulia: the best and easiest to find are those labeled Colli Orientali del Friuli (COF) Ribolla or Collio Ribolla, which are also the only two DOCs that contemplate monovarietal ribolla. There are two recognized *grand crus* for the variety, wines that have been famous and sought after throughout history: Rosazzo in the COF and Oslavia in the Collio. Ribolla from Rosazzo, a warm microclimate, is generally deeper and richer than most (though rich is relative with ribolla, which, at its best, is always a fresh, fragrant white wine); ribolla from Oslavia, where vineyards are at higher altitudes and in a cooler microclimate, are mineral, lemony, and higher acid. Both are characterized by the variety's telltale nuance of white pepper, but which is never found when yields are high. Dario Ermacora of the Ermacora estate believes ribolla gialla is best when made from grapes grown in poorly fertile soils rich in mineral salt, such as those of Buttrio, Rocca Bernarda, Spessa, Dolegna del Collio, and San Floriano, near Oslavia. All of these areas save for San Floriano give a softer ribolla, while the cooler San Floriano produces higher-acid wines. Silvano Zamò of Le Vigne di Zamò says that soils ought to be low in clay content and well drained, which helps diminish the cultivar's naturally high vigor.

I love the fresh buttercup, tangerine, and lemony-pepper zing and bracing acidity of a well-made Ribolla Gialla wine. In theory, the wine can be one of Italy's best light-bodied white wines and one of the greatest summertime wines; in practice, it seldom is. In fact, Ribolla Gialla's full potential is rarely achieved, for its versatility and generosity are such that too many different wines are made with it. At last count, it is available in many wine styles, including light-bodied and dry, oak-aged and dry, easygoing sparkling (made with the Charmat method), more complex sparkling (made in the manner of Champagne, with a secondary fermentation in the bottle), an off-dry, sweet, wannabe red (with macerations on the skins lasting up to four months), and oxidized (when aged in terra-cotta amphoras). Many producers are not happy with this army of ribolla styles. Paolo Rodaro has written and spoken often about the folly of a sparkling ribolla, which in his view only "creates confusion in the minds of consumers. It took us twenty years to make people understand that Schioppettino was not a sweet wine; now we are about to create a similar mess with Ribolla."

Ribolla Gialla can show all it's got when grown in ideal hillside vineyards, by limiting yields, and by making the wine like any other white wine, with low fermentation temperatures that help the variety express its delicate aromas. Avoiding oak, which is too dominant for an essentially delicate wine, is also a good idea. Off-dry and sweet versions of ribolla were once a typical local accompaniment to boiled or roasted chestnuts, but they are uncommon nowadays.

In California, there are many interesting ribollas to try: Arnot-Roberts, Forlorn Hope, Grassi, and Ryme Cellars make interesting examples (all made with Ribolla Gialla fruit grown by George Vare, who is passionate about the variety).

WINES TO TRY: Miani*** (the greatest Ribolla wine and, I believe, one of Italy's five or six greatest white wines, made by Enzo Pontoni; it's a four-star wine, if only I had that option in this book), Luisa***, Ronchi di Cialla***,

Ronco delle Betulle*** (Vigna Citronella), Ronco dei Tassi***, Thomas Kitzmüller**, Collavini** (Turian; they were also the first to believe in sparkling ribolla, and theirs is the best), La Sclusa**, La Viarte**, Paolo Rodaro**, Valentino Butussi**, Venica & Venica** (L'Adelchi), Attems**, Borgo Conventi**, Cantarutti**, Isidoro Polencic**, Livio Felluga**, and Villa Russiz**. The only macerated ribollas I recommend are by Damijan Podversic* and Renato Keber* (Extreme).

Rossara

WHERE IT'S FOUND: Trentino. NATIONAL REGISTRY CODE NUMBER: 287. COLOR: red.

Rossara is also called Rossera, Rossar, and Rosa Ciàr (meaning light red). Most people believe that it's the same grape as the *Schiavas* (or one of them, at least), which is not true. Interestingly, the German name for Rossara *(Geshlafene)* recalls the medieval name for Schiava used in Trentino *(sclaf)*, but back then there was a widespread tendency to consider many grapes to be part of the *Schiava* group, such as Cimesara, Zaccola, Rossanella, and Cagnara. Certainly, Cimesara is not identical to the *Schiava* varieties, and neither is Rossara. However, some important Italian researchers still believe that Rossara may be a subvariety of one of the *Schiavas*, as it appears to be genetically related to that family. Others have suggested a relationship with Sgavetta, a variety typical of Emilia-Romagna; but Rossara is unrelated to another Emilia-Romagna variety, the similarly named Rossara or Rossèra cultivar, now practically extinct (Boccacci, Torello Marinoni, Gambino, Botta, and Schneider 2005).

Rossara has always had to share the spotlight with Teroldego, the most important red grape of Trentino, as the two have always been grown side by side in the vineyards of the Piana Rotaliana. This is not by chance, as Rossara is to Teroldego as Canaiolo Nero is to Sangiovese. Rossara provides the somewhat rustic and heavy Teroldego wines with a touch of aromatic spiciness and freshness; plus, it appeals to growers because of its regular, dependable production volume. Rossara is a very vigorous variety that is precocious in all its phenological phases except for ripening, as it's harvested in October.

Rossara is today found exclusively in Trentino, close to the border with Alto Adige. It was once common in the Piana Rotaliana and in the Val di Non as well (where at the end of the 1800s a reported thirty-eight thousand hectoliters of rossara were made).

Which Wines to Choose and Why

Very common in Trentino as recently as thirty years ago, Rossara is now mostly grown only in sporadic rows. There are clearly no DOC wines and few monovarietal wines, as Rossara is almost always blended with Teroldego and/or Negrara Trentina. Thanks however to Roberto Zeni, we now have the opportunity to taste a monovarietal rossara labeled as an IGT Vigneti delle Dolomiti. He initially sourced grapes from an old vineyard near Giare and then selected vines and propagated them on his own estate. The wine has a very pretty, clear, dark-pink hue and exudes aromas of fresh small red berries, lemon apples, plus hints of iris and jasmine. Though I wouldn't say the wine has nostril-piercing aromatic intensity, it's vibrant and uncomplicated, with a definite saline tinge and plenty of acidity, and I quite like it. It's an ideal aperitif and a perfect match with slightly fatty *charcuterie* and white-meat dishes. Zeni's 2011 vintage showed 11.5 percent alcohol, 24 grams per liter extract, and 5.4 grams per liter total acidity, and those numbers are more or less typical for the wine every year, virtually guaranteeing Rossara wines to be refreshing and easygoing. I know of no other monovarietal examples of Rossara commercially for sale, though I have tried some artisanally made potables over the years that still linger in my memory (unfortunately, not always for their high quality).

WINES TO TRY: Zeni***.

Rossese

WHERE IT'S FOUND: Liguria. NATIONAL REGISTRY CODE NUMBER: 213. COLOR: red.

Every time I look at a Rossese vineyard, I get a neck ache. Clinging precipitously to mountainsides plunging down to the marvelous Ligurian sea below, in a fairytale world more suited to chamois and alpine ibex than "I really need to hit the gym" wine writers, Rossese grapes bask in the sunshine while reminding you of the amazing amount of hard work that goes into every glass of wine. In Italy, the list of native grapes that strongly mark the territory they are grown in is almost endless, but few do so to the extent of Rossese. There are no other red varieties of similar relevance in its whole production area, and so for locals Rossese is a family member of sorts. Gianni Guglielmi, one of the better producers of Rossese wines, recalls that his ancestors have been growing Rossese since at least the early 1800s, and that sort of family tradition breeds fierce loyalty toward both the grape variety and wine.

Despite its limited cultivation area (a small section of western Liguria, itself not exactly the biggest of Italian regions), there are a number of different *Rosseses*, the most famous being Rossese di Dolceacqua (also the name of a wine); another red-berried variety is Rossese di Campochiesa, and the two are genetically distinct. There are also at least three completely unrelated white-berried varieties also called Rossese Bianco-Something. One of these, Rossese Bianco di Arcola, is actually Ruzzese (see RUZZESE entry). Of course, Rossese Bianco seems something of an oxymoron (given that *rossese* ought to refer to a red coloration), but as these white-berried varieties were thought to be color mutations of the dark-skinned cultivars, I guess my snickering is out of line. The present discussion is limited to the red-berried *Rosseses*, and today most everyone grows the Dolceacqua variety (or so they all tell you), because Rossese di Campochiesa is viewed as of a lesser quality (its cultivation is on the decline). Actually, the latter was never used to make the Rossese di Dolceacqua wine, which is produced only using its eponymous cultivar. So, generic Rossese wines are different from those sporting the Dolceacqua moniker, and this not just because of different *terroirs* but also because of different cultivars used—yet another example of the importance that grape varieties have always played in Italy's winemaking.

It is unclear if Rossese di Dolceacqua is a true Italian native or if it ought to be considered a traditional variety. A recent study showed that Rossese di Dolceacqua is genetically identical to a French variety called Tibouren (Torello Marinoni, Raimondi, Ruffa, Lacombe, and Schneider 2009). Regarding this identification, it is difficult to say whether Tibouren came to Liguria from Provence first or if Rossese arrived in France from Liguria. According to Ganzin (1901), Tibouren was introduced into the Var (southern France) in the late eighteenth century by a navy captain named Antiboul (hence the French synonym Antiboulen). That a French variety might make its way into Italian countrysides and vice versa was not that uncommon; there are many examples of this throughout the wine-production zones of both countries, which share a long border. In Italy some believe that the grapevine was brought to western Liguria from France by soldiers of the noble Ligurian Doria family, but as is often the case with these historical reconstructions, conclusive evidence is hard to come by. Though I have gone looking, I have been unable to find any convincing evidence of the variety being called either Tibouren or Rossese first, and so I fail to see how anyone could decide that the correct name should be one or the other. Granted, this is probably not the most important dilemma facing mankind, but local growers are fiercely attached to their grapes and they'd like to be sure matters have been carefully looked into, and clearly resolved, before we "steal" a variety away from them. I would humbly submit that we owe them no less.

Rossese di Dolceacqua has medium-large, truncated, conical, winged bunches with medium to medium-small, round, almost oval dark blue-purple berries. In contrast, Rossese di Campochiesa has similarly sized bunches and berries, but the bunch is more compact and cylindrically shaped, with as many as three wings and berries of a lighter reddish-blue hue. It also looks like it has a longer bunch, but various growers don't find this is true, and I defer to them. What helps me distinguish between the two *Rosseses* are the leaves: Dolceacqua's leaf is pentagonal and has seven lobes; Campochiesa's is orbicular (round), with only three lobes.

Of the two, Dolceacqua is especially hard to grow, with both berry shatter and chlorosis as potential problems. Alessandro Anfosso, one of the better local producers, concurs: "It's a very finicky cultivar that seems to do well only in specific *terroirs*. Well-draining soils seem to be most suitable, but things aren't quite so cut and dried. Even in Liguria, when the variety has been planted elsewhere than its home provinces of Imperia and Savona close to the French border, results have been poor at best. So, for reasons that are still unclear, the *Rosseses* seem to do particularly well only in this small section of Liguria." Filippo Rondelli of the high-quality Terre Bianche estate believes that "Rossese di Dolceacqua is an early ripening variety that needs water-retaining, better ventilated hillside vineyard locations in order to reach the best possible equilibrium between sugar buildup, freshness, and potential alcohol. That combination is never achieved, however, if vines are planted too close to the sea." In fact, Rossese di Dolceacqua does best in almost mountainous, subalpine territory, though it has difficulty ripening fully if planted at higher than six hundred meters above sea level. Maurizio Anfosso, another young, up-and-coming producer, cautions that the variety's thin skin is its biggest problem: "From a viticultural perspective, it's easily attacked by botrytis bunch rot and hence I deleaf twice a year to ensure adequate ventilation."

In Italy, *Rossese* diffusion is limited to about 280 hectares, not an altogether small amount given where it grows, but statistics don't distinguish between the two main red-berried *Rossese* varieties. Producers have told me that Rossese di Campochiesa is now much harder to find but is more common in the area around Savona in Liguria, east of Imperia. In France, the variety is grown in Provence, most typically in the Var, where cultivation extends over roughly 420 hectares.

Which Wines to Choose and Why

Rossese wines are labeled in many different ways. Rossese di Dolceacqua is the most famous, but there is also Rossese di Riviera Ligure di Ponente, Rossese di Albenga, and even some bottles simply labeled Rossese. They are all made mainly in western Liguria, toward France, not far from Imperia: specifically, in the countryside around the towns of Dolceacqua, Apricale, Baiardo, Camporosso, Castelvittorio, Isolabona, Perinaldo, Pigna, Rocchetta Nervina, San Biagio della Cima, and Soldano, as well as in part of the townships of Vallecrosia, Ventimiglia, and Vallebona (the latter limited to the right side of the Borghetto stream). For Rossese di Dolceacqua, the *grand cru* areas today are generally considered to be Galeae (near Soldano), Beragna (Soldano), Luvaira (near San Biagio della Cima), Pini (Soldano), Posaù (San Biagio della Cima), and Arcagna (near Dolceacqua). Luigi Veronelli (1995) believed there were other worthy, very specific *crus* for *Rossese* wine production. For example, he also liked Terre Rosse, Terre Bianche, and Tramontina in Camporosso; Addolorata and Rocchini, as well as the previously mentioned Arcagna, in Dolceacqua; Posatoio, Garibaudo, and Abrigheto at San Biagio della Cima; Fulavino at Soldano, besides Pini and Beragna; Curli, Möglie, and Massabò at Perinaldo. He also always repeated that a great *Rossese* wine was *vino di latte*, or "milk wine," a wine produced in the vineyards of Latte, specifically Piemattone, Trinchi, and those of the Marchesi Orengo. I don't think I ever tasted one, twenty or thirty years ago, but then, I don't remember where I parked my car last night.

There are two DOC wines, the Rossese Riviera Ligure di Ponente (RLP) and the Rossese di

Dolceacqua; the latter is the better wine. In theory, Rossese di Campochiesa ought to be used to make the former wine. According to Filippo Rondelli, "The RLP rossese used to be made with Rossese di Campochiesa. It was never made with Rossese di Dolceacqua, and so the two wines were very different. With the modifications to the DOC legislation, now Rossese di Dolceacqua is used by everyone making either wine, but it's a mistake and one that flies in the face of tradition. That said, even by using the same variety, the two wines remain different, mainly because of diverse microclimates and soils. The RLP wine is a more neutral product, lightly fruity and thin; the Dolceacqua version is more intense, salty, spicy and with greater depth of fruit."

Soils are all-important when dealing with *Rossese* varieties, which are very good translators of *terroir* in the glass. In general, they do best on well-drained, clay-calcareous-sandy soils, but in Liguria the geological characteristics of the soils change quickly and substantially even over small distances. The local *sgruttu* soil, a marly-clay mix, is the one that Maurizio Anfosso believes gives the most complex wines. For example, in the Val Verbone the soils tend to be more calcareous clay but with plenty of sand and gravel, and so wines from these *terroirs* tend to be more perfumed and ready to drink sooner. In the Val Nervia, where soils are more loamy clay, the wines tend to be more structured and deeper in hue. The wine is never dark, but always a bright, clear, red hue, with at most ruby tinges; black or ink are not present in the pantheon of rossese colors. Rondelli believes the aromas of the wines are all-important: "Since the wine is light to mid-weight in structure, the nose becomes fundamental for it to have success. After all, we're not going to impress anyone with depth of color." Anfosso agrees, adding that "enologically, the skins break down easily, and the wine can easily have off odors unless the lees are stirred often and energetically, allowing for plenty of oxygen contact. If you don't do that, you risk losing our wine's pretty fragrance."

Rossese di Dolceacqua will remind you of violets, red currants, graphite, and roses, occasionally even strawberries. I believe that the sine qua non of a good wine is the presence of a salty-sour component, more reminiscent of red currant and cranberry than of sour red cherries. Besides a lovely fragrance, the wine is always blessed with vibrant acids and a dry (not drying) mouthfeel. It will always be graceful and charming in its easygoing, light- to medium-bodied delivery. Almost all Rossese di Dolceacqua wines are best drunk within two years of the vintage, though some examples can age remarkably well, easily improving and lasting eight to ten years. In France, few producers are making great amounts of monovarietal Tibouren wines, as locals prefer using it in rosés along with Grenache and Cinsault. Besides Domaine Sainte Marie (their Paparazzi Rosé has 40 percent Tibouren), Clos Cibonne is the French producer that perhaps most believes in Tibouren, as owner André Roux has always loved the cultivar and wine; his descendants make two rosés, the Tibouren (with 10 percent Grenache) and the Tibouren Cuvée Speciale des Vignettes Rosé (made from sixty-year-old Tibouren vines).

WINES TO TRY: Maccario-Dringberg*** (Posau, fresher and fruitier; and Luvaira, more earthy and animal), Ka Manciné*** (Galeae, late harvested; and Beragna), Tenuta Anfosso*** (Poggio Pini Superiore, more balsamic; and Luvaira, fruitier), Terre Bianche*** (the entry-level and the Bricco Arcagna), Lupi**, Massaretti** (Cascina Feipù Rossese di Albenga), Rocche del Gatto** (Rossese di Albenga; made with both Dolceacqua and Campochiesa), Poggi dell'Elmo. For Riviera Ligure di Ponente Rossese (di Campochiesa), try: Durin** (Rossese di Riviera Ligure di Ponente), Rosella Salguato**, Torre Pernice** (RLP; also the excellent Rosa dell'Aleramo, an excellent late-harvest, air-dried combination sweet wine). For a white wine, try: A Maccia** (U Rosau; a rare example of Rossese wine made as a white, avoiding skin contact between must and grape skins).

Rossese Bianco

WHERE IT'S FOUND: Piedmont, Liguria. NATIONAL REGISTRY CODE NUMBER: 374. COLOR: white.

Ironically, Rossese Bianco used to be more common in Italy than the red-berried *Rosseses*, whose wines you're far more likely to taste nowadays. Rossese Bianco was all but forgotten and fell by the wayside, which is a shame. In 1596, Bacci documented a white-berried Rossese Bianco, or Roxeise, known for excellent wines in the sixteenth century. Gallesio also describes the variety in detail in his *Pomona italiana* ([1817] 1839).

Though some believed this grape was a white-berried mutation of a *Rossese* variety, Rossese Bianco is so named for both its white grape and the white wine it produces and also because the whitish berries have a faint red glimmer. So Rossese Bianco may not be such an oxymoron after all. The trouble is, there is more than one grape called Rossese Bianco in Italy, with probably distinct varieties growing in well-defined areas of Piedmont and Liguria (in Piedmont, a Rossese Bianco variety grows near Sinio and Roddino, but it's likely the same as that grows in nearby Monforte; there is no certainty at present). Unfortunately, in the absence of accurate ampelographic descriptions and DNA profiling, the National Registry officially lists only one Rossese Bianco, the Piedmontese one. In fact, it lists Langhe as the only DOC wine the grape can be used in. It is therefore this variety that can lay claim, for now, to the Rossese Bianco name.

Besides the one Piedmontese Rossese Bianco, there are at least two different but similarly named Rossese Bianco grapevines of Liguria: Rossese Bianco di Arcola, which is identical to the variety called Ruzzese (and therefore the latter name should be used); and Rossese Bianco di San Biagio (also known as Rossese Bianco di San Biagio della Cima e Soldano), currently the subject of further studies. Interestingly, the excellent 2009 study on Ligurian native grapes found that several vines believed to be Rossese Bianco were actually Sicily's Grillo (Torello Marinoni, Torello Marinoni, Raimondi, Ruffa, Lacombe, Schneider, et al. 2009). These days, Rossese Bianco di San Biagio is found around San Biagio in Liguria thanks to the hard work of Count Nino Picedi Benettini and Mario Maccario, but it has been planted in both eastern and western Liguria. Rossese Bianco proper is instead limited to the Monforte d'Alba area of Langhe, far more famous for its Barolo.

Which Wines to Choose and Why

Based on my repeated tastings of Giovanni Manzone's wine (every vintage he has ever made, incidentally), I can say that this specific Rossese Bianco will remind you a little of Vermentino, but with more flesh to the delicate fruit aromas and flavors (ripe citrus, nectarine, winter melon) and stronger herbal nuance (chlorophyll, thyme, mint), with less salinity. Manzone is a well-known Barolo producer, but I salute him here for his efforts and passion: if we can drink Rossese Bianco wine today, it's thanks to him.

Rossese Bianco di San Biagio, based on the Anfosso and Maccario bottlings, is leaner and fresher, with more floral and saline nuances.

WINES TO TRY: For Rossese Bianco, try: Giovanni Manzone*** (Rosserto). For Rossese Bianco di San Biagio, try: Tenuta Anfosso** (Bianco, which is a *vino da tavola*) and Maccario**.

Rossetto

WHERE IT'S FOUND: Lazio, Umbria. NATIONAL REGISTRY CODE NUMBER: not registered. COLOR: white.

Though it is a white grape, Rossetto is one of many Italian varieties named for the grape's red skin color (*rossetto* means "little red one"). This variety assumes a pinkish tinge when the golden-yellow berries are fully ripe. In the last twenty years people have taken to using the names Roscetto and Rossetto interchangeably, but some documentation suggests that the two names refer to different varieties; at present, we have no way of elucidating this. One producer, Stefanoni, even decided to call his wine Roscetto. In northeastern Lazio and southwestern Umbria, they call the variety Roscetto, but others there also speak of Rossetto, so I don't know what to think. Prosperi (1939) mentions Rossetto as a synonym for the Castelli Romani's Trebbiano Giallo, probably only adding to the confusion. Stefanoni also considers Trebbiano Giallo a synonym for Rossetto. Growers in the Castelli Romani and Cori areas don't agree at all, however, firmly standing behind their Trebbiano Giallo as the only original one. In the absence of DNA profiling and accurate, believable ampelographic descriptions, your guess is almost as good as mine. Even better, Rossetto is at times called Greco Giallo or Greco di Velletri, though Muganu, Dangl, Aradhya, Frediani, Scossa, and Stover (2009) showed Rossetto to be completely unrelated to Greco or Greco Bianco. In fact, it's almost certainly unrelated to the Greco Giallo I have seen in the Castelli Romani and Cori countryside, as the two have nothing in common, at least morphologically.

Which Wines to Choose and Why

Wines can be made as IGTs and as DOC Colli Etruschi Viterbesi. Historically, a little Rossetto was also added to the Est! Est!! Est!!! di Montefiascone blend (the exclamation marks are not typos: this is the exact spelling of the wine). The irony is that based on Rossetto wine's personality—big, rich, and tannic—it seems to have more in common with the *Greco*s than with the *Trebbiano*s. However, that's not a fair assessment, as we have too few examples to go by, mainly the wines made by the Falesco estate in Umbria. Their version is very rich and textured, with honeyed tropical-fruit flavors reminiscent of a cross of Chardonnay, Petit Manseng, and Sauvignon Blanc. Creamy and delicately oaked, the grapes undergo a flash freeze to help release pigments into the must. Stefanoni's version is much lighter and fresher, with less buttery tropical fruit and more floral and yellow fruit aromas and flavors. Both are good, a case of different strokes for different folks, but I'd be lying to you if, based on these two wines, I told you what a Rossetto wine is really supposed to taste like.

WINES TO TRY: Falesco** (Ferentano) and Stefanoni* (Roscetto).

Roussin de Morgex

WHERE IT'S FOUND: Valle d'Aosta. NATIONAL REGISTRY CODE NUMBER: not registered. COLOR: red.

Once you finally manage to come face-to-face with the rare Roussin de Morgex, you'll feel like you've been on a thrilling safari. Its habitat is high up in the Alps, on slopes so steep that you'll be huffing and puffing during the climb; you may very well find yourself wishing you had gone on an African safari instead. The moment your gaze falls on the Roussin de Morgex, however, all your efforts will be rewarded. You'll immediately recognize the variety, long on the brink of extinction, for this extremely pretty grape has highly characteristic leaves, very jagged, with numerous small indentations, almost as if someone put them through a shredder. My memory of first stumbling on this variety roughly nine years ago is vivid, one of the happiest and most meaningful moments in my many years of walking vineyards all over the world. Clearly, DNA profiling needs to be done on the plants that have been identified, but based on ampelographic examination the grapevines I saw were certainly Roussin de Morgex.

Not much is known about Roussin de Morgex, which has always been a bit of a mystery grape. There exists no documentation of it prior to the latter part of the nineteenth century, when it was first mentioned as Rossano Rosso in the Ampelography Commission's newsletter of 1877. Already back then it was believed to grow only in the vineyards of Morgex, and in very small numbers at that. It is not related to the similarly named Roussin, another rare variety found in Valle d'Aosta and the one officially listed in the National Registry. Recent DNA analysis has revealed that Roussin de Morgex shares a parent-progeny relationship with Prié. The other parent is unknown, so one can only guess which variety is the parent and which the offspring; but as Prié is the oldest-mentioned variety in the Valle d'Aosta, and not even Gatta mentioned the existence of Roussin de Morgex in 1838, it is logical to infer that Prié is the parent. In an effort to safeguard Roussin de Morgex from extinction, since 1998 it has been reared in the experimental plot set up by the Institut Agricole Régional at Hospices, but the winemaking potential of the grape is as yet untested. Gianluca Telolli, past winemaker at the Cave du Vin Blanc, was growing some Roussin de Morgex in 2001 and 2002 but apparently wasn't impressed by its fine wine potential and so didn't pursue the project further. Maybe that will change one day. Lost up high in the alpine clouds for centuries, Roussin de Morgex may have long been relegated to an afterthought, but my hope is that, with my help too, this is one native variety that will be allowed to come in from the cold.

Which Wines to Choose and Why

My love for native grapes, and for this little, near-extinct variety, is such that I have started a unpaid collaboration with the Cave du Vin Blanc in an effort to resurrect the variety and attempt to make the wine again, even if only in small quantities. The goal is to make small batches available for sale, only at the winery at first; hopefully, enough people will like what they taste to make larger volumes a commercially feasible endeavor. All my thanks and admiration go to current Cave du Vin Blanc winemaker Nicola del Negro and the Cave's president, Mauro Jacod, whose willingness to devote time and resources to bringing Roussin de Morgex back from oblivion is nothing but commendable. Roussin de Morgex is therefore currently an experimental project that will hopefully conclude its journey in 2015, when the first wine will be released. Microvinifications of experimental batches of the wine reveal piercingly fragrant aromas of wild strawberry, almond flowers, and fresh mountain herbs. The acidity is almost painful, though, and so I think the variety's potential lies in the realm of sparkling wines, at least given our present and scant state of knowledge.

WINES TO TRY: Cave du Vin Blanc (expected in spring 2014).

Roviello

WHERE IT'S FOUND: Campania. NATIONAL REGISTRY CODE NUMBER: 430. COLOR: white.

Roviello is this variety's oldest and correct name, though Grecomusc' (or Grecomuscio) is the most commonly used name by locals (*musc'* deriving from *moscio,* meaning flaccid, because the short-on-juice berries look just so). The variety is also called Roviello Bianco or Rovello Bianco. It was first described in 1875 as Roviello Bianco (near Mercogliano Roccabascerana and Fontanarosa in the province of Avellino) or simply Roviello (from Altavilla Irpina). In fact, the term Grecomuscio does not appear anywhere in the nineteenth-century ampelographic literature. Roviello is also the name listed in the National Registry: according to DNA studies, Roviello isn't a *Greco* (Francesca, Monaco, Romano, Lonardo, de Simone, and Moschetti 2009).

Roviello was recently rediscovered by producer Sandro Lonardo, owner of the Contrade di Taurasi estate in Campania, with the help of university researchers Antonella Monaco (University of Naples) and Giancarlo Moschetti (University of Palermo). They found old and often ungrafted Roviello vines growing haphazardly in the countryside around Taurasi, Passo di Mirabella, and Bonito: the cultivar has pyramidal, medium-small bunches and medium-small berries with thick skins. Though it seems to thrive on sandy-loamy soils of volcanic origin, as vines are few and far between we can't be sure this is the best soil type for the variety. Most likely, Roviello's fall from grace was due to practically minded farmers not wanting to bother with an earlier-ripening variety than Fiano or Greco, which subjected them to the extra work of two harvests.

Which Wines to Choose and Why

The wine has generated considerable interest lately and so Roviello is increasingly planted. It's a very difficult variety in the cellar, as the thick skins and sparse pulp make for plenty of polyphenols and solids. While these can easily oxidize or make for bitter wines, high polyphenol concentrations also allow for potential age-worthiness (2004 and 2005 vintages tasted in late 2012 were still in excellent shape).

Roviello is an aromatic variety, so the wines are reminiscent of those made with Muscat or Gewürztraminer. But Roviello isn't nearly as aromatic, and there are obvious differences in the aromatic profiles of each wine. Roviello wines have strong flint, almond, grass, and apple aromas and flavors, complicated by aromatic spices, though much depends on how the wine is made. In my opinion, its aromas are more herbal-floral than fruity. In an extremely interesting study, chemical analysis of Roviello wines showed high concentrations of furfural (a molecule that brings toasted almonds to mind), phenylethylalcohol and 3-methyl-tiopropanol (explaining the nuances of rose and spices), and isoamylic acids formed during fermentation and associated with aromas of grass and unripe fruit, with hints of butter (Francesca, Monaco, Romano, Lonardo, de Simone, and Moschetti 2009).

The benchmark for the variety comes from Cantine Lonardo / Contrade di Taurasi. But because winemaker Maurizio De Simone has thus far employed different winemaking techniques, the jury is out on what the exact characteristics of a good roviello might be. From 2004 to 2007, their wines were not monovarietal (they included small percentages of Coda di Volpe, Fiano, and Moscatella); the 2004 spent two to three months in *barriques*, while the 2005–7 wines were aged in *tonneaux*. A new winemaker, Vincenzo Mercurio, has been on board since the 2010 vintage, and it remains to be seen what this passing of the guard might entail.

WINES TO TRY: Cantine Lonardo / Contrade di Taurasi** (Grecomusc'; the 2004 is lovely, with aromas and flavors of candied ginger, saffron, toasted hazelnut, sage, and diesel fuel; but the 2008 and 2009 are better, riesling-like in their fresh citrus, white pepper, and diesel-fuel notes).

Ruché

WHERE IT'S FOUND: Piedmont. NATIONAL REGISTRY CODE NUMBER: 313. COLOR: red.

If there is one Italian grape that wine lovers really ought to know, it is Ruché. A rare example of an aromatic red variety, Ruché makes wines that are impossible to confuse with any other variety, despite superficial resemblance with wines made with Lacrima or Brachetto (when the latter has been fermented dry).

Ruché is probably native to Piedmont, though many hypothesize that it arrived in Piedmont from Burgundy in the eighteenth century. There is no proof of this, and those who point to the French spelling of the name (Rouchet), which is still in use in Piedmont but rarely, forget that Piedmont itself has French roots. The name Ruché is believed to derive from the word *roncet*, a viral degeneration that the grape is far more resistant to than are other local varieties, such as Barbera. Today Ruché is believed to have developed in the hills northwest of Asti. The site, once known as Castagnolis Casalensis, today belongs to the commune of Castagnole Monferrato, where most Ruché wines are made today. Unfortunately, as there is practically no documentary evidence available, the history of Ruché can only be traced via oral traditions that have been handed down from one generation to the next.

Franco Cavallero, co-owner of the Cantina Sant'Agata estate with his brother Claudio, remembers that in the early to mid-twentieth century people weren't quite sure how to use

Ruché, often just adding small amounts to other wines such as barbera or grignolino to make them more perfumed, thanks to Ruché's strongly aromatic personality. For the longest time, people made only sweet wine with the variety; it was the town priest, Don Giacomo Cauda, who first understood the potential of making a dry wine. His wine, the Vigna del Parroco (vineyard of the priest) was the best ruché made for a very long time. That wine is now being made by Francesco Borgognone, who told me, "I think Ruché needs cool sites, and that's why many of us like northern exposures; the goal is never to maximize all of its aromatic potential, by not running the risk of baking the grapes." Interestingly, Borgognone remembers that between 1995 and 1998 university personnel scoured the local vineyards and identified thirty-five biotypes of Ruché, eventually choosing four with the best apparent fine wine–making potential. Ruché is a fairly resistant variety, though oidium can be a problem. It is early ripening.

Typical of Piedmont, wines are produced mainly around the two small towns of Castagnole Monferrato and Scurzolengo (vines are also planted, if in smaller amounts, in nearby Viarigi, Portacomaro, Montemagno, Grana, and Refrancore, in the province of Asti). Ruché does best in calcareous soils that are dry and well exposed, but lighter soils help enhance the wine's natural fragrance.

Which Wines to Choose and Why

Ruché has always been held in high esteem locally; the wines made from it were reserved for special occasions, such as children coming home from abroad, birthdays, or graduations (admittedly, the latter were rare in rural Piedmont for the longest time). The best wine to try is the DOC Ruché di Castagnole Monferrato. The ruchés of Scurzolengo and those of Castagnole Monferrato are very different: the former are more fruity, lighter, and more purple in color; the latter are more floral, bigger, and richer. This is not surprising given, for example, the lighter, white-colored and chalky soils of Scurzolengo.

Annual output of Ruché wine, which in the past was almost entirely consumed by local families, is still modest although steadily expanding. When well made, ruché is a thing of beauty: delicately floral (rose, iris, lavender), spicy (black pepper, mint, coriander, cinnamon, nutmeg), with a red-berry cocktail quality to its aromas and flavors. One taste may remind the inexperienced of Lacrima di Morro d'Alba, but the two wines are recognizably different and should not be confused. Ruché is spicier and less floral, and the red-fruit aromas and flavors are very different from the black ones more typical of lacrima, which is a bigger, creamier wine.

WINES TO TRY: Dacapo*** (Majoli; in good years, so pure and fragrant it can be one of Italy's thirty or so greatest wines), Crivelli***, Cantina Sant'Agata*** (Na'vota), Montalbera*** (La Tradizione), Cascina Tavjin**, and La Miraja** (harder to find but absolutely pure, delicious wines; if you visit, you can drink them at the local restaurant).

Ruggine

WHERE IT'S FOUND: Emilia-Romagna. NATIONAL REGISTRY CODE NUMBER: 431. COLOR: white.

The Ruggine name derives from the fact that, when fully ripe, the berries have a brownish rusty color (*ruggine* means rust). Also called (rarely) Ruginoa or Ruzninteina, Ruggine is a high-quality but until-now forgotten native grape of Emilia-Romagna, single-handedly brought back to life by a restaurant owner (as if we didn't owe these wonderful people enough). Italo Pedroni, who loved the wine and did much to extol its virtues, kept producing the variety for his own joy and that of his clientele. Pedroni found abandoned vines of Ruggine in the flatland vineyards between Manzolino and Bagazzano near Modena (in the direction of Bologna); by the 1970s, the grape had been essentially abandoned. His wine was so famous that scientists of the agriculture and enological research institute in Tebano came calling. In 2000, the Vitigni Minori project was launched, sponsored and financed by the government of the Regione Emilia-Romagna and aimed at characterizing the rare native grapes of Emilia-Romagna and evaluating their fine wine potential. Ruggine was identified and microvinifications greatly impressed local growers, who then took up the challenge and planted the vines and began making Ruggine wine.

There are only a few hectares specifically devoted to the variety, all in Emilia-Romagna near the town of Rubbiara, but the vine can still be found in many old vineyards in the countryside around Modena. Furthermore, the encouraging results obtained with the first few pure bottlings have led many producers to start planting Ruggine and to make the wine. It's safe to say this is one variety that has shaken the rust off.

Which Wines to Choose and Why

A good ruggine has a nose that is honeyed and ripely citrusy, with average acidity and delicate herbal flavors on the palate, complicated by notes of dried apricot and ripe tropical fruit. Some producers tend to oak it, but in my view that can be a risky endeavor, since the wine's delicate aromas and flavors are easily overwhelmed.

WINES TO TRY: Leone Conti*** (Anghingò) and Pedroni** (also an outstanding producer of Aceto Balsamico Tradizionale di Modena, the real, very expensive, great stuff; true balsamic vinegar always has the word *tradizionale* attached—without, it's not the real thing).

Sagrantino

WHERE IT'S FOUND: Umbria. NATIONAL REGISTRY CODE NUMBER: 217. COLOR: red.

Sagrantino is apparently a very ancient variety, possibly the Hirtiola described by Martial and Pliny the Elder as typical of the territory of Mevania (once located in the area between the modern-day towns of Bevagna and Montefalco). In reality the origins of both the grape variety and name are unclear. While local old-timers have sworn to me time and again that the variety has grown in and around Montefalco since the dawn of time, documentation of this seems lacking. In contrast, the existence of a wine called sagrantino has been documented since 1598, and apparently a red wine made by blending Trebbiano Spoletino with Sagrantino won numerous awards in the late nineteenth century. However, much like Amarone, sagrantino was originally most often a sweet wine; in fact, the DOC Montefalco Sagrantino was created in 1977 for the *passito* (sweet wine made from air-dried grapes). Dry sagrantino became a DOC only a few years later. Both wines have since been elevated to DOCG status (in 1992).

The name Sagrantino is believed to derive from *sagra* (feast), since the wine was almost always made sweet and drunk mainly on holidays and other festive occasions. Others theorize that the name derives from "wine of the mass," or *sacrestia,* but not everyone agrees. It seems plausible enough, given that sagrantino's rich endowment of polyphenols guarantees it will keep longer than many other wines, making it ideal for the Holy Mass. The variety looks somewhat like Canaiolo Nero, Sangiovese, some *Colorino*s, and Marzemino but can easily be differentiated from these by careful observation; there are also several clones that look and behave differently. The available clones are 2 ISV-ICA PG, UNIMI-CAPRAI-25 Anni, UNIMI-CAPRAI-Cobra, UNIMI-CAPRAI-Collepiano, and VCR 226. Of these, the 2 ISV-ICA PG clone is ideal for air-drying; and the 25 Anni has a bigger bunch than the Cobra, which is not just small but also cylindrical in shape (its name is an homage to the highly tannic, polyphenol-rich wine produced with it). Both it and the Collepiano are less fertile than the 25 Anni, and the best wines are made by blending the three together. Sagrantino shows above average vigor but is not particularly productive; it needs plenty of sun and heat to ripen properly (at least nineteen hundred growing degree days) and is susceptible to peronospora but not oidium. The underside of its leaf is hairy and so is often the home of damaging spiders; the variety also suffers magnesium deficiency and so can present dissection of the stem, especially with the SO4 rootstock.

Sagrantino's home is Umbria, but given the high quality of its wines, Sagrantino has been planted elsewhere: for example, Alessio Planeta of the famous Sicilian estate of Planeta told me it does very well in some parts of Sicily. Sagrantino has done well on non-Italian soil as well. In Australia it has been planted in areas as diverse as McLaren Vale, Barossa Valley, Eden Valley, King Valley, Adelaide Hills, Murray Darling, and Hunter Valley. In the United States, it is grown in Dry Creek Valley and Central Valley. It has also been planted in Argentina.

Which Wines to Choose and Why

The DOCG wine is called Montefalco Sagrantino. Montefalco Rosso is sagrantino's baby brother but, unlike its sibling, is not 100 percent Sagrantino, containing Sangiovese and other varieties.

Today, the wine is produced in the area around the towns of Montefalco, Bevagna, Gualdo Cattaneo, Giano dell'Umbria, and Castel Ritaldi. Researchers also found biotypes sporadically grown near Macerata (in the Marche). There are clear-cut differences in style between Sagrantino wines made in different areas of the production zone, much as the Bordeaux of Saint-Estèphe are different than those of Margaux. For instance, the Sagrantino wines of Montefalco is more structured yet refined, those of Bevagna more floral, and those of Castel Ritaldi and Gualdo Cattaneo softer and readier to drink. In general, Sagrantino does best on clay-containing soils, though it performs well on loam-rich ones as well.

Despite its fame, dry sagrantino is a relatively young wine; in centuries past, sagrantino was always sweet (the 1898 *L'Italia enologica* listed winners of a national wine fair, with the gold medal won by a sagrantino from Argante Pagliochini from Bevagna in the red and white wine categories, but there is no mention of a dry sagrantino). Though the most famous sagrantino of all is the 25 Anni made by the world-renowned Arnaldo Caprai estate (the Caprai family is to be commended for all they have done for the variety), one of the best and oldest sagrantinos is that of Adanti, whose first real winemaker was a fashion designer. Winemaker Alvaro Palini, an old friend of owner Domenico Adanti, had been a successful fashion designer in Florence, Milan, and Paris. From 1962 to 1974 he worked in Paris with Franklin Shauman, creator of the world-famous Sisley brand (now owned by Benetton), and some of his creations have graced the pages of magazines such as *Vogue*. He loved wine and spent plenty of his free time in Bordeaux and Burgundy, drinking great wines and learning the aspects of modern winemaking. Most of what he needed to know he had already learned during childhood, by observing his grandfather make wine from the family's few Sagrantino vines. One day, Domenico, so fed up with Palini's incessant criticism of the Adanti wine, angrily challenged Palini to do better. Palini never looked back: he lowered yields, enforced parcel-by-parcel harvesting at only optimal ripeness levels, and concentrated on making a dry wine. Results were quick to arrive, and Palini became a much listened to expert winemaker in the area. His 1980 sagrantino was one of the first ever produced and commercially available; on its heels, wines became available from the Cantina Cooperativa di Foligno and the Tardiola estate (the latter does not exist anymore). Arnaldo Caprai bought his estate in 1971 and planted 5.5 hectares in 1973; its successes and example spawned huge interest in Sagrantino and the Montefalco area, and now there are numerous valid producers to choose from.

If the high polyphenol content allows the wine to age well, this tannic wealth is also a hindrance. Sagrantino is Italy's most tannic red wine, by far. All too often the wines are hard and unyielding, and no amount of cellar time will reduce their stubbornly tannic aura.

However the tannins are remarkably polished, according to winemaker Emiliano Falsini. "It's not at all like Nerello Mascalese, where you can macerate on the skins only for ten days at most or risk leaching out very dry, astringent tannins. Despite their wealth of polyphenols, Sagrantino skins can be put through even long macerations because the tannins are usually smooth and polished, though there are a lot of them." When sagrantino is well made by gifted producers, it offers rich, brambly black fruit and aromatic herb aromas and flavors that are persistent and pure.

I have tried interesting sagrantinos made in Australia by Chalmers and Coriole, though there are many others. These wines are usually smoother than their Italian counterparts, not a bad thing in my book.

WINES TO TRY: For Montefalco Sagrantino, try: Antano Milziade*** (Colleallodole), Antonelli*** (Sagrantino Chiusa di Pannone, Sagrantino), Arnaldo Caprai*** (25 Anni and Collepiano), Fratelli Pardi***, Adanti**, Colpètrone**, Di Filippo**, Tabarrini** (these can be some of the most tannic wines around, sometimes painfully so), Paolo Bea** (biodynamically made), Perticaia**, Scacciadiavoli*, and Tenuta Alzatura*. For Montefalco Sagrantino Passito, try: Colpètrone***, Ruggeri***, Antonelli**, and Tabarrini**.

Sanforte

WHERE IT'S FOUND: Tuscany. NATIONAL REGISTRY CODE NUMBER: 412. COLOR: red.

Sangiovese Forte, or Sanforte, first mentioned by Villifranchi in 1773, has a medium-sized, pyramidal, and compact bunch with medium round berries. Its bunch and berries don't weigh much more on average than those of a standard Sangiovese clone, but Sanforte is more fertile and tends to produce more bunches per plant in similar conditions. Most important, it is a much earlier ripener than Sangiovese, not a bad thing in those colder parts of Tuscany such as Chianti. The high-quality Villa Calcinaia estate, among others, has planted vines and is currently evaluating Sanforte. Roberto Bandinelli of the University of Florence told me that the variety's name derives from its ability to pile up sugar in its berries; in fact, it was planted in the Lamole zone of Chianti Classico because of this very trait. Lamole is one of the highest, coolest parts of all of Chianti, and therefore Sanforte was and is ideal to pump up the anemic Sangiovese wines of those temperature-challenged areas.

Currently, Sanforte is found in IGT Costa Toscana wines. I have tried numerous vintages of the Sanforte wine made at Villa Calcinaia, and I find it is a more massive wine than the Sangiovese made at the same estate. The wine is interesting because it retains a large dose of elegance, despite its size (always a relative term with Sangiovese, or in this case Sanforte). There is plenty to like, from the violet and underbrush aromas to the dark red cherry and tarry, almost savory flavors.

Sangiovese

WHERE IT'S FOUND: Tuscany, Emilia-Romagna, Lazio, Marche, Puglia, Sicilia, Umbria. NATIONAL REGISTRY CODE NUMBER: 218 (number 96 as Grechetto Rosso, number 201 as Prugnolo Gentile). COLOR: red.

Italy's most abundant red variety, and probably its most important given the extraordinarily large number of wines made from it, Sangiovese is anything but easy. It's neither easy from a historical viewpoint, with at first scanty and then copious but contrasting documentation, nor from a viticultural or enological perspective, as the variety is one of the more finicky to work with; producing truly great (not just very good), world-class wines seems possible only for a lucky or gifted few. All of that, plus endless confusion about its origin and different family members, makes Sangiovese a fascinating if complex subject.

There are countless synonyms for this variety. It is also called Morellino on the Tuscan coast, Brunello in Montalcino, Prugnolo and

Prugnolo Gentile in Montepulciano, Nielluccio on the French island of Corsica, and Toustain in Algeria. Sangiovese is also correctly but rarely referred to as Sangiogheto, Sangiovese di Lamole, Sangiovese Dolce, Sangiovese Gentile, Sangioveto, Sangioveto Montanino, Sanzoveto, and Uvetta. Sangiovese Grosso and Sangiovese Piccolo are names of the cultivar's two main biotypes, though discussing Sangiovese in terms of this dual classification is antiquated and essentially incorrect.

For such an important cultivar, documentation of Sangiovese's existence is relatively thin and doesn't go that far back. Sangiovese was first mentioned by Soderini in his 1590 treatise on the cultivation of grape varieties; he called it Sangiogheto and described it as a variety always capable of yielding quality wines. At the end of the seventeenth century, it was depicted in a painting, under the name Sangioeto, by Bartolomeo del Bimbo, nicknamed Il Bimbi, artist of the Medici court. Trinci (1726) sang the praises of San Zoveto, known for "grapes of wonderful quality produced in huge quantities every year." Villifranchi also praised the productive dependability of San Gioveto in his *Oenologia toscana* (1773) and was probably the first to begin differentiating between different Sangiovese types, mentioning a San Gioveto Forte (for him, synonymous with Inganna Cane, another variety) and a San Gioveto Romano cultivated in the Marca, in particular in the Faentino region. Very interestingly, Villifranchi mentions that Carmignano, one of the oldest and most famous Sangiovese-based wines, was made by including air-dried grapes of Canaiolo Nero, Aleatico, and Moscadello. Also in 1773, the existence of Sangiovese wines from Romagna are mentioned in a text by Ghini de' Minimi. The Ampelography Commission of Siena (1875–76) listed Sangioveto among the most widespread grapevines in the Chianti region, and similarly, Prugnolo in Montepulciano and Brunello in Montalcino. Interestingly, the commission asked if Sangioveto, Prugnolo, Brunello, and Sangioveto Piccolo might not be identical. Di Rovasenda (1877) mentions a Sangioveto in Tuscany, while he writes of Sangiovese in Romagna. This is an important if seldom-used geographic distinction in nomenclature: because Tuscany's variety is generally viewed as better quality (perhaps not actually true), some modern-day producers and experts would prefer it if everyone took to referring to Tuscany's Sangiovese as Sangioveto, limiting the name Sangiovese to the grapevine grown in Emilia-Romagna and elsewhere. Paolo Panerai of the famous Castellare estate in Castellina in Chianti certainly does; and Badia a Coltibuono, another world-class Chianti Classico producer located in Gaiole in Chianti, has named its top wine Sangioveto.

The existence of different biotypes of Sangiovese became the subject of much study and discussion in the late nineteenth and early twentieth centuries. Molon (1906) wrote that the two most common types of Sangiovese were Sangioveto Grosso (also called Sangioveto Dolce) and the Sangiovese Piccolo (also called Sangioveto Forte, but this is a mistake: we know today Sangiovese Forte, or Sanforte, to be genetically distinct from Sangiovese; see Sanforte entry). A little later, Breviglieri and Casini (1964) agreed with Molon's view but expanded upon it, including still other synonyms: according to them, Sangiovese Grosso was synonymous with Sangiovese Dolce and Sangiovese Gentile, while Sangiovese Piccolo was the same as Sangiovese Forte and Sangiovese Montanino.

At the beginning of the nineteenth century the cultivation of San Gioveto appears to have been limited to Tuscany and Romagna (in the provinces of Forlì and Ravenna), interestingly the opposite slopes of the Apennines that face the province of Florence on one side and that of Forlì on the other. Sangiovese does not appear to have been grown all over Tuscany at that time (unlike today), and there is apparently no mention of its presence in southern Italy, where some recent genetic data suggests the variety might actually be native to (see below). In addition to the province of Florence, where it was most common, Sangiovese was also cultivated in the province of Siena under the names Prugnolo, Brunello, and Morellino. In the Casentino area in the province of Arezzo, it was called Nerino or Sanvicetro (but we now know that Sanvicetro is a distinct cultivar, different from Sangiovese). Even worse, around the city of Arezzo it was known as Calabrese, a synonym for the Sicilian Nero d'Avola, which provides one of Sangiovese's earliest links to the deep south. From the nineteenth century, Sangiovese (or Sangioveto) spread all over central and southern Italy, reaching the Marche, Umbria, Lazio, Campania, Abruzzo, Molise, and Puglia (but only the northern province of Foggia). Also at that, confusion began to reign supreme in relation to Sangiovese and Montepulciano, because the town of Montepulciano in Tuscany exported a great deal of Sangiovese (see MONTEPULCIANO entry).

Differences between the various Sangiovese and/or Sangioveto grapevines grown all over Italy notwithstanding, the origin of the variety's name itself is also unclear. One of the etymological possibilities includes a mythological reference to the blood of Jupiter (*sanguis Jovis*, or blood of Jove), unsurprising given wine's longtime association with myth, symbols, and sacrifices to the gods. Another possibility is that the monks in Santarcangelo di Romagna, at the foot of the Monte Giove near Rimini, chose the name *sanguis Jovis* when forced to call the wine they made by a name other than *vino*. Perhaps the name refers to yoke (*giogo* in Italian, *jugum* in Latin), the top of a hill, or even of a wine "good for blood" (*giovevole al sangue;* but this is a stretch), as postulated by Mainardi (2001). An interesting origin story was suggested by Hohnerleien-Buchinger (1996), who drew attention to the variety's early season budbreak, linking the name Sangiovese to the dialect term *sangiovannina*, which means "early grape." Mainardi, in noting that Sangiovese might be a product of Etruscan times, drew truly fascinating and erudite links to the ancient language of those people: for example, there are assonances between Sangiovese and *thana-chvil* (a votive offer), *tbcms-zusleva* (an offer by someone who presides over a ritual), *thezin-eis* (an offer to the god), and *sani-sva* (meaning father or an offer to the fathers), which is very close to the *romagnolo* dialect word *sanzve* used for Sangiovese. And you thought all the fun was in drinking the wine.

The Origins of Sangiovese, Its Parents and Kin Group, and Controversy

The origins of Sangiovese are unclear. It has always been presumed to be an very old, native cultivar of Tuscany, according to an almost endless list of experts, including Breviglieri and Casini (1964), and Calò, Scienza and Costacurta (2001). Still more experts have postulated it might be of Etruscan heritage (Mainardi 2001). Unfortunately, Sangiovese wasn't written about much prior to the sixteenth century, so tracing its origins is difficult.

Sangiovese has long been thought to have descended, wholly or in part, from domesticated wild grapevine species. In a report presented at the Second International Symposium on Sangiovese held in Florence in 2004, Di Vecchi Staraz, Lacombe, Laucou, Bandinelli, Varès, Boselli, et al. (2006) wrote that Sangiovese "has only a few alleles in common with the wild compartment." Subsequently, Di Vecchi Staraz, Bandinelli, Boselli, This, Boursiquot, Laucou, Lacombe, et al. (2007) rewrote the description, saying that "nor were any genetic relationships with regional wild relatives noted." I trust you will agree that those two statements aren't saying exactly the same thing. However, a closer look at the results of the Di Vecchi Staraz studies is revealing: using twelve microsatellite markers and analyzing twenty-nine cultivars and ten wild grapevine species, they found that all the wild grapevine species had four out of twelve alleles in common with Sangiovese. In particular, three grapevines (Silvestris MT-B2, Silvestris R-E4, and Silvestris T-B1) shared a common allele with Sangiovese in eight of twelve loci, which, in my view, is hardly "no genetic link" or an absence of "any genetic relationship." On the contrary, these results at least suggest some relationship between the cultivar and wild grapevines. Though there may be no link whatsoever between Sangiovese and wild grapevines, further study of Tuscan wild grapevine species is probably required.

Subsequent studies have added to the complexity that is Sangiovese's world. Vouillamoz, Imazio, Stefanini, Scienza, and Grando (2006) and Vouillamoz, Monaco, Costantini, Stefanini, Scienza, and Grando (2007) both describe Sangiovese as a Ciliegiolo × Calabrese Montenuovo crossing (the latter a rare, little-known southern Italian grape). Another recent study also suggests Ciliegiolo as one of the two parents of Sangiovese (Bergamini, Caputo, Gasparro, Perniola, Cardone, and Antonacci 2013). However, while intellectually stimulating, this parentage finding is controversial. Di Vecchi Staraz, Bandinelli, Boselli, This, Boursiquot, Laucou, Lacombe, et al. (2007) published contrasting results (also partly arguable, as I shall explain) detailing the genetic structuring and parentage of a very large database comprising 2,786 unique multilocus genotypes (twenty nuclear SSRs of *Vitis vinifera* ssp. *sativa*), with a special focus on Tuscan cultivars, Sangiovese *in primis*. The authors found that Sangiovese's kin group is composed of a majority of ancient cultivars common to southern Italy, such as Gaglioppo and Nerello Mascalese, allowing for a possible Calabrian or Sicilian origin for Sangiovese. Sangiovese appears to be closely related to ten cultivars, all sharing at least one allele with it: Capibianchi, Catarratto Bianco Faux, Ciliegiolo, Frappato, Gaglioppo, Greco Nero di Cosenza, Marzemino Faux, Nerello Mascalese, Perricone, and Poverina. Nerello Mascalese and Gaglioppo showed the closest genetic ties to Sangiovese, while Capibianchi, Greco Nero di Cosenza, Perricone, and Poverina were the most removed, though still closely related. However, a particularly interesting finding was that Ciliegiolo is an offspring of Sangiovese and Muscat Rouge de Madère, also known as Moscato Violetto. These findings therefore conflict with the notion that Ciliegiolo is a parent of Sangiovese, though all studies agree that Ciliegiolo is a relative of Sangiovese (Crespan, Calò, Costacurta, Milani, Giust, Carraro, and Di Stefano 2002). We are left with two contrasting Sangiovese parentage possibilities: Is Sangiovese an offspring of Ciliegiolo? Or is Sangiovese a parent of Ciliegiolo?

Based on the published data, arguments can be made for and against each position. In favor of Di Vecchi Staraz group are consistent parent and grandparent pairs with high logarithm of odds scores and high cumulative likelihood ratios. Also, their conclusion relative to Ciliegiolo being an offspring of Sangiovese (rather than the other way around) is a logical one, supported by the fact that Sangiovese is cited much earlier in the available literature (Soderini 1590) than Ciliegiolo (Racah 1932), but Soderini also described a Ciregivolo in the 1600s. This makes it highly unlikely that the latter is a parent of the former (though admittedly, Ciliegiolo has always been misidentified and confused with other varieties, so therein lies a possible explanation for its parenting going unnoticed). Last but not least, the Di Vecchi Staraz et al. findings have been apparently duplicated in at least two different studies (Cipriani, Spadotto, Jurman, Di Gaspero, Crespan, Meneghetti, et al. 2010; Lacombe, Boursiquote, Laoucou, Dechesne, Varès, and This 2013), while I am not aware of the Vouillamoz et al. results having been confirmed by any other group. On the other hand, in favor of the work by the Vouillamoz et al. (2007), they used fifty DNA markers instead of only thirty-eight different sites. Also, accepting Muscat Rouge de Madère as a possible parent of Ciliegiolo is admittedly a hard thing to do; Ciliegiolo isn't an aromatic variety, and to the best of my knowledge Muscat Rouge de Madère has been seldom, if ever, cultivated in Italy. Of course, Calabrese Montenuovo isn't exactly a household name either, and it's not listed in Italy's National Registry; again to the best of my knowledge, the only time it has been mentioned in a research paper of note was in Costantini, Monaco, Vouillamoz, Forlani, and Grando (2005). So the exact parentage of Sangiovese remains a contentious issue, one that will require further study.

What recent studies show is that a southern Italian birthplace for Sangiovese is possible: Sicily and Calabria seem to be likely prospects, as we know that since the sixteenth century at least, there were exchanges of cultivars between southern Italian regions and the rest of Italy: for example, according to Basso (1982), Vernaccia di Siracusa (both a black and a white grape), probably originating from Syracuse in Sicily, was cultivated in Tuscany; while varieties such as Inzolia (a Sicilian native) and Trebbiano Toscano are common to both Sicily and Tuscany. Therefore, some experts hypothesize that Sangiovese originated from crossings in southern Italy, rather than from Tuscany or other central Italian regions, and was later transferred north. However, the findings that Sangiovese shares at least a small part of its genetic makeup with local wild Tuscan grapevines, and the lack of clear documentation reporting Sangiovese's presence in southern Italy centuries ago, provide food for thought. Once again, Sangiovese has left us in a quandary.

The Extended "Family" of Sangiovese and Similarly Named Grapes

Sangiovese's high intravarietal diversity has been well documented, and because of this widespread difference in phenotypes among Sangiovese grapevines, these and other experts postulated that Sangiovese is not a single variety but a "variety-population," the result of polyclonal inheritance (Vignani, Scali, Masi, and Cresti 2002; Filippetti, Intrieri, Centinari, Bucchetti, and Pastore 2005). This is a minority hypothesis nowadays, with most experts believing that a single parent pair is at the origin of Sangiovese, as demonstrated for practically all other grape cultivars. Marzotto (1925), Breviglieri and Casini (1965), and many others have confirmed the great variability of Sangiovese grapevines due to the presence of subpopulations more or less easily distinguished, especially by berry dimensions and leaf characteristics. These many biotypes are currently the subject of study, the aim being to identify those individuals that might prove most interesting from a viticultural and enological perspective.

The simplest and best-known classification of Sangiovese biotypes, now hopelessly outdated, divides the cultivar into two main biotypes, Sangiovese Grosso and Sangiovese Piccolo. The former has always been associated with the Sangiovese or Brunello grown in Montalcino, but matters are far more complicated; for instance, there also exists a Sangiovese Piccolo of Montalcino that seemingly few have ever heard of or written about. According to early studies, the majority of Tuscan and Romagna Sangiovese biotypes—including Brunello, Prugnolo Gentile, Sangiovese Grosso di Lamole, Sangiovese Montanino, Sangiovese Romagnolo, Sangiovese Marchigiano, and Nielluccio—are of the Sangiovese Grosso biotype, while Sanvicetro (again, now known to be a variety distinct from Sangiovese), Sangiovese Piccolo di Montalcino, and Morellino are of the Sangiovese Piccolo biotype (Silvestroni and Intrieri 1995; Calò, Costacurta, Paludetti, Crespan, Giusti, Egger, et al. 1995). Except Sanvicetro, all have been confirmed as genetically identical to Sangiovese, though they look and behave slightly differently due to usually minor phenotypic differences, probably because of environmental and human selection pressures exerted over centuries. Hence, as Prugnolo Gentile and Brunello both share a genetic profile with Sangiovese, they must all be considered the same. However, both Prugnolo Gentile and Brunello are still mistakenly described as different cultivars in the National Registry, as well as in books and websites devoted to the subject of Italy's native grapes.

In contrast, not all the *Morellino*s are identical: different *Morellino*s are qualified by suffixes such as Pizzuto, di Pitigliano, del Valdarno, and del Casentino, but Morellino Pizzuto is most likely a distinct cultivar from Sangiovese (Scalabrelli and Grasselli 1985). In 2000, Scalabrelli, Vignani, Scali, Di Pietro, Materazzi, and Triolo suggested that Morellino Pizzuto was a biotype of Sangiovese, one that exhibited both ampelographic and genetic differences that did not appear to be related to a viral infection, suggesting that the two are actually two closely related but distinct varieties. Incredible as it may seem, there are reportedly at least thirty biotypes of *Morellino* in the Scansano area alone; but unlike in other areas, such as Chianti Classico, Montalcino, Montepulciano, or even the Pisan hills, very little work has been done to evaluate the various types of Sangiovese growing there. According to Crespan, Calò, Giannetto, Sparacio, Storchi, and Costacurta (2008), another *Morellino*, Morellino del Valdarno, while identical to Puglia's Negrodolce, has a parent-offspring relationship with Sangiovese.

Other Sangiovese-Something or Sangiovese-named varieties have been identified: Sangiovese Polveroso Bonechi is actually Ciliegiolo, and Brunelletto and Sangiovese Forte have been proven to be distinct. Brunelletto is characterized by medium-small berries, medium-early ripening, and good concentrations of polyphenols. Another biotype of Sangiovese is apparently found in northern Lazio, around the lake of Bolsena near Gradoli, called locally Greghetto Rosso. Over the years I have asked Andrea Occhipinti (of the Occhipinti estate) about Greghetto Rosso, and though he's not convinced about its synonymity with Sangiovese, he admits the two share many features in common. However, his Greghetto Rosso has a large, conical, and compact bunch, and even though it ripens late, like Sangiovese, it rarely falls prey to common grapevine pests, not even botrytis.

Recent research has been looking into still more Sangiovese-named or Sangiovese-Something varieties. The list includes Brunellone (usually thought to be identical to Ciliegiolo, but it appears there actually exists a distinct Brunellone variety), Casentino, Chiantino, Prugnolino Dolce, Prugnolino Medio, and Prugnolino Acerbo.

Revenge of the Clones

Currently, Sangiovese has the highest number of clones registered in the Italian National Registry, with a whopping 102 different ones: many have very different morphological, phenological, and enological characteristics. Ironically, the one that producers believe almost always makes the best wines is T-19 (where T stands for Tebano); but it is a diseased clone, virus-affected, and therefore planting it is not officially allowed. Of course, that doesn't stop anyone in Italy. Even more ironic is that both T-19 and R-24, another worthwhile clone, are of Emilia-Romagna origin, which clashes a tad with those who uphold the superiority of Tuscan Sangioveto. For example, R-24 (also known as Medio Predappio; while clone R-10 is known as Grosso Lamole) is viewed as a very good clonal choice, as its wines are characterized by lovely bright ruby-red hues and floral, earthy aromas and flavors, with plenty of spicy red-berried nuances. T-19 yields even deeper, richer, and more complex wines. My hunch is that if the Sangiovese grapevines from Emilia-Romagna have such a poor reputation today, this has less to do with their intrinsic qualities than with a paucity of truly gifted winemakers in the Sangiovese di Romagna wine-production area. A big problem for all Sangiovese wines has always been that clonal research into the variety began in earnest only toward the end of the twentieth century; prior to 1960, practically nothing had happened. Most clonal selection work had been done by private estates, first by Biondi Santi (one of the first wine families in the world to have a clone named after it, the BBS-11) and later by Col d'Orcia and Isole e Olena. The latter is owned by Paolo De Marchi, one of Italy's greatest winemakers and producers, and his selection of Sangiovese, known as Selezione De Marchi (performed in collaboration with the famed Guillaume nursery of France), is one of the best to this day, and estates line up for the vines.

In 1988, the Chianti Classico Consortium, in collaboration with the Universities of Pisa and Florence, launched the Chianti Classico 2000 project, which, though heavily criticized by some for employing less than accurate methodologies, did have the benefit of providing the new CCL series of clones. These have met with considerable success and are today commonly planted in most Tuscan vineyards. Unfortunately, some other clones, such as the Janus series developed by the famous Italian researcher Attilio Scienza, in collaboration with Montalcino's Banfi estate, yield almost impenetrably dark, massive wines that remind one more of Syrah than of Sangiovese. Personally, I do not view these as especially successful examples of Sangiovese grapevines, though I have nothing but admiration for the energy, passion, and expense that the Mariani family (owners of Banfi) and their talented staff have lavished on their estate and Montalcino in general. Clearly, over the years clonal selection research efforts were mainly directed toward developing Sangiovese clones that would have looser bunches (allowing for better disease control and prevention), be less productive (so as to produce lower yields of more concentrated grapes, enabling estates to do away with costly manual labor tactics like repeated green harvests), and ripen earlier, a problem with a late-ripening variety like Sangiovese that happens to like living in essentially cool microclimate areas (where grapes are still hanging on the vines come late fall, when the likelihood of rain, hail, or both is increased). And given the notoriously light, garnet-tinged color of Sangiovese wines, another objective of clonal research was to develop clones that would guarantee deeper hues, just like the Janus series allows. Of course, getting Sangiovese wines to be pitch black, or even inky-ruby, is another story.

What a Wine Lover Really Needs to Know about Sangiovese

Though newer and better clones have undoubtedly helped Sangiovese, producers need to plant clones that do not change the essential makeup of the wine made with that specific grape variety. The anthocyanin profile of Sangiovese is rich in malvin and cyanin, and there are virtually no acylated anthocyanins (anthocyanin molecules bound to a sugar molecule), those anthocyanin conjugated forms typical of many other varieties such as Merlot and Cabernet Sauvignon (Mangani, Buscioni, Collina, Bocci, and Vincenzini 2011). Donato Lanati, one of Italy's best known winemakers, recommends analyzing anthocyanin ratios to determine if the supposedly monovarietal Sangiovese wine you are drinking really is made with 100 percent Sangiovese, as these ratios are genetically determined and unaffected by winemaking techniques. Actually, because Sangiovese does not have acylated anthocyanins, just finding elevated counts of them indicates that the wine is not a monovarietal Sangiovese. In this respect, the anthocyanin profile acts very much, and can be used as, a fingerprint. The importance of anthocyanins is finally becoming appreciated by many in the wine business, when for the longest time all everyone ever wanted or talked about were the biggest, blackest (and to my way of thinking, meanest) red wines possible. Interestingly, the Brunello consortium in the wake of the Brunellogate scandal of 2008, has sponsored a study analyzing the anthocyanin levels of the wines of Montalcino, in an effort to better understand the spectrum of local Sangiovese color possibilities.

Sangiovese, when done right, can be one of the world's greatest wines. Yet there have been, and still are, countless obstacles in the variety's path to stardom. In the wake of the post-phylloxera reconstruction of vineyard areas, Sangiovese was planted extensively, but unfortunately not always with quality in mind. Poorly chosen vineyard sites were the main problem; at other times, selection of less than stellar clones. As Sangiovese does not grow well just anywhere (in this it is very much like Pinot Nero and Nebbiolo), poor sites have long contributed to limiting expression of Sangiovese's considerable winemaking potential. This led to, among other things, the conviction that it was neither a noble cultivar nor a possible source of world-class wines, unless "helped out" by international varieties such as Merlot or Cabernet Sauvignon. This is but one of the factors that contributed to the birth of "supertuscan" wines in Italy. With the 1990s, the vineyards were renewed, but this time more attention was paid to clonal material, soils, exposures, training systems, and planting densities.

Sangiovese can produce light, juicy wines and big, complex ones. For example, in cool Chianti Classico (where snow is common in the winter) the best results are obtained by planting vines on south- and southwest-facing slopes between 250 and 500 meters of elevation (though vineyards are planted there from 100 to 550 meters above sea level). At least for now, anything more ambitious is asking for trouble, even in these globally warmed times. In Tuscany, Sangiovese ripens better in warmer, more southerly Montalcino than it does in Chianti Classico, and of course even more in the Maremma, where a hotter climate and shorter growing season produce a richer, broader wine, but where too much alcohol and overripe aromas can be problematic (and where paradigmatic Sangiovese finesse is usually nowhere to be found). In the latter coastal areas it can also be subject to damage by late springtime frosts, because Sangiovese buds early in the season; therefore, save for lower Maremma, Sangiovese is not an important player on the Tuscan coast, where international varieties rule instead. The best soils for Sangiovese are not very fertile, well drained, and with minimal water retention: producers will regulary tell you that the friable, poor soils of Chianti's *galestro* are probably the best of all. A touch of limestone is necessary for Sangiovese to express all of its considerable charm and refinement, but soils richer in clay can also deliver intriguing wines. As a general rule, though, heavy clay soil is for Merlot, not Sangiovese.

Cool climates, characterized by large day-night temperature differences, and long growing seasons are essential, but warm summers and falls are just as necessary for Sangiovese to reach optimal ripeness. Planting Sangiovese vines at densities of 5,000–7,000 plants per hectare may be optimal, compared to the traditional 2,700–3,300 in the past, which usually gives wines that lack concentration. In Montalcino, most tests have shown that 5,000 is the right number and yields need to be low (for example, no more than 1.5 kilograms of fruit per plant. Sangiovese can adapt to various training and pruning systems. Maurizio Castelli and Andrea Machetti, who work together at the famous Montalcino estate Mastrojanni, now owned by the Illy family of coffee fame, believe Guyot is the best option. Machetti says, "A double Guyot reduced to three buds per side, that almost looks like a fork, reduces bunches and makes it easier to select the best-looking grapes come harvesttime. On the other hand, the spur cordon system produces wines that I feel age faster, after about fifteen years in the bottle." Castelli adds simply that all the world's greatest wines are made with grapes trained by the Guyot system. Rootstocks vary, but 420A is most commonly used, especially as it keeps Sangiovese's vigor in check. The 775 Paulsen is a good choice of rootstock when Sangiovese is planted on clay, as it reduces the tannic weight of the wines. Rootstocks like SO4 and Kober B5 allow too much vigor. Where there isn't any risk of extended drought, less vigorous rootstocks (161/49, 101–14) are employed, especially with a high-density plantation. The 110R is used where there is the need of higher drought tolerance, while in more difficult conditions use of 1103 Paulsen rootstock is predominant.

At over seventy thousand hectares, Sangiovese is the most important cultivar in Italy, and the sun never seems to set on its popularity. Today, it represents 11 percent of all grape varieties planted in the country, and it is also one of the ten most-planted cultivars in the world. In Italy, Tuscany has the lion's share of the area devoted to Sangiovese, followed by Puglia, Emilia-Romagna, and the Marche, with Umbria, Campania, Basilicata, Abruzzo, Lazio, Sardinia, Calabria, Molise, and Liguria all growing it in commercially significant amounts. In fact, Sangiovese is planted everywhere in Italy save for the northernmost, colder regions. Sangiovese proves popular outside Italy too. Though it is less fashionable in California today than it was in the heady days of "Cal-Ital" varietal wines, there are still close to eight hundred hectares planted (and many excellent wines made by Seghesio, Montevina, and others) in AVAs as different as Napa, Sonoma, Santa Barbara, and others. Sangiovese is also planted in Washington State and New Mexico, as well as to the north (in both the Canadian provinces of Ontario and British Columbia) and to the south (Mexico). Elsewhere, Sangiovese has encountered unbelievable success in Australia, despite less than stellar early results (but by 2009, more than two hundred wineries were trying their hand at a Sangiovese wine, monovarietal or not). Mostly, Sangiovese has been planted in eastern Australia, while it is less common in western Australia, where nursery errors made for lost time (for example, estates thought they were planting Sangiovese only to learn later that it was Carnelian). Sangiovese is also planted in New Zealand, South Africa, Argentina, Chile, and Brazil, among other countries.

Which Wines to Choose and Why

Sangiovese is the fundamental grapevine of Tuscany, being the principal component of the six Tuscan DOCGs, from a minimum of 50 percent up to a 100 percent: Brunello di Montalcino (100 percent monovarietal), Carmignano, Chianti, Chianti Classico, Morellino di Scansano, and Nobile di Montepulciano. It is present, in various percentages, in almost all the main DOCs and IGTs of Tuscany, such as Barco Reale di Carmignano, Capalbio, Colli dell'Etruria Centrale, Colli di Luni, Cortona, Elba, Montecarlo, Montecucco, Monteregio di Massa Marittima, Montescudaio, Orcia, Rosso di Montalcino, Rosso di Montepulciano, Sovana, Val di Cornia, and Valdichiana. Sangiovese is also used to make sweet wines, such as the outstanding Vin Santo Occhio di Pernice. Of course, it is also part of many other DOC and IGT wines in other regions, such as Veneto's Bardolino, Valdadige, and Valpolicella; Sangiovese di Romagna (Emilia-Romagna); Montefalco Rosso (Umbria); Rosso Piceno and Rosso Conero (the Marche); Velletri (Lazio); and Gioia del Colle (Puglia). Being a real jack-of-all-trades, Sangiovese can be used to make a complete range of wines, from *rosato,* to light and refreshing reds, to full-bodied and very ageworthy reds.

When bad, Sangiovese wines can be very pale in color, lack fruit, and still have high tannins and acidity, making for a less than thrilling experience. In the past this led to the (at times illegal) practice of adding various percentages of deeper-colored and fruitier wine from warmer parts of central and southern Italy, such as negro amaro, nero d'avola, or montepulciano. However, in my experience, an attentive, truly knowledgeable wine taster should always be able to recognize when 10 percent of a wine made from another grape variety has been added to sangiovese. A great monovarietal sangiovese will vary considerably in its organoleptic characteristics, depending on climate and soil: for example, those from the hot Tuscan Maremma area are marked by very ripe dark red-cherry, plum, and aromatic herb aromas and flavors; while in cooler areas such as Chianti Classico or Montalcino (though the latter is already warmer than the former, and so the wines differ considerably), notes of sour red cherries, red berries, licorice, violet, and tea leaf dominate. With age, all Sangiovese wines show hints of underbrush, leather, and tobacco. Cooler regions, such as the Chianti Rufina (some areas of which, like those around Dicomano, have more in common with mountain viticulture than sunny Tuscany), produce many very fine wines blessed by lacy acidity and refined texture. These are wines that also age extremely well.

Clearly, the most famous wines made with Sangiovese are Chianti Classico and Brunello di Montalcino, and they offer a whole spectrum of Sangiovese aromas and flavors. Chianti Classico wines from Gaiole, especially in the Monti subzone, are perhaps the most complete of all, but those from Radda can have a magical, unforgettable perfume, though much depends on which complementary grapes have been added to the blend. I find that Sangiovese wines with a little Canaiolo Nero or Malvasia

Nera are always fresher and more perfumed than those featuring additions of Cabernet Sauvignon or Merlot, which while fleshier and richer, rarely have the gracefulness and balance of the best Chianti classicos made with only native grapes. Over in Montalcino, there is a world of difference between Brunellos (and Rossos) made in the northern exposed sites as compared to the much warmer, drier southern ones. Brunello di Montalcino made near the town itself, or just north of it, is usually lithe and refined, with redcurrant and sour red-cherry aromas and flavors to go along with at times mouth-searing acidity. By contrast, wines made from the southeastern and southwestern sectors of the Montalcino production zone (around the towns of Castelnuovo dell'Abate and Sant'Angelo in Colle, respectively) are characterized by riper red-cherry and even dark plum aromas and flavors. These wines have also much fleshier and richer mouthfeels and at times can almost seem like different wines. Such is the ability of Sangiovese to translate even minor differences in microclimates and soils into wine.

Sangiovese di Romagna can also be a very interesting wine, though its reputation has been sullied by too many thin and tart wines of no interest. That said, many of the hilariously dark, award-winning Sangiovese wines made in Tuscany and Emilia-Romagna in the last decade (wines smelling of tar, black pepper, graphite, and other atypical Sangiovese aromas and flavors) are just as bad as the previously described lot. True, Sangiovese from Emilia-Romagna gives wines that are usually slightly darker in hue and richer in body than most Tuscan examples of Sangiovese. Though they rarely share the complexity of the finest 100 percent Sangiovese supertuscans, the best examples are rich and satisfying and are bound to surprise wine lovers who never thought of trying them. The Marche's two best-known dry reds are Rosso Piceno and Rosso Conero, the latter recently subdivided into a Conero DOCG wine and the simpler Rosso Conero. In essence, both Rosso Piceno and Rosso Conero were always Sangiovese-Montepulciano blends, the lighter Rosso Piceno historically containing more Sangiovese. Since Rosso Piceno is the most extensive of all of the Marche DOCs, covering a large and diverse territory, variation in wine styles is to be expected. While many wines are Montepulciano top-heavy, many Rosso Picenos are light and fruity, and locals love to drink them even with fish dishes, such as the hearty soup called *brodetto anconetano*.

Very good California producers of Sangiovese include Dalla Valle, Duxoup, Robert Pepi, Seghesio, and Shafer, while in Washington State, Leonetti comes to mind. Zonin makes an herbal-accented Sangiovese wine in Virginia. Sangiovese is also grown in Canada: Pillitteri in Ontario and D'Angelo in British Columbia are good choices. In Australia good producers include De Bortoli, Mount Langi Ghiram, and Pizzini; in New Zealand, I can think of Heron's Flight. Terre da Capo is a solid South African example.

WINES TO TRY: For Chianti Rufina, try: Selvapiana***, Colognole**, Frascole**, Frescobaldi**, Grignano**, I Veroni**, and Travignoli**. For Chianti Classico, try: Badia a Coltibuono***, Capannelle***, Castellare***, Castello di Ama*** (Vigneto Bellavista), Fontodi*** (also the 100 percent Sangiovese Flaccianello), Isole e Olena (also the 100 percent Sangiovese Cepparello), Monte Vertine (no Chianti Classico made, but the 100 percent Sangiovese Le Pergole Torte is one of Italy's greatest wines), and San Giusto a Rentennano (also the 100 percent Sangiovese Percarlo). For Brunello di Montalcino, try: Poggio di Sotto***, Il Poggione***, Pian dell'Orino***, Salicutti***, Stella di Campalto***, Biondi Santi**, Col d'Orcia, Costanti**, Cupano**, Fuligni**, Il Marroneto**, Le Potazzine**, Lisini**, Mastrojanni**, Piancornello**, and Siro Pacenti**; and there are many more. For Grechetto Rosso, try: Occhipinti** (Caldera).

Schiavas

See SCHIAVA GROUP, chapter 3.

Schioppettino

WHERE IT'S FOUND: FVG. NATIONAL REGISTRY CODE NUMBER: 290. COLOR: red.

I have followed Schioppettino's course from all-but-forgotten to budding superstar for the better part of twenty years. When still a twenty-something and in university, I began buying and collecting Schioppettino wines and never missed a vintage (admittedly, it wasn't that hard an undertaking, since there wasn't much wine being made). Simply put, it's one of my favorite wines of all, and one of the high points of my career in wine was when the newly formed Association of Schioppettino Producers of Prepotto asked me to moderate the first-ever conference dedicated to the variety during their inaugural weekend celebration. To think that all this almost never came to be: for Schioppettino, as recently as 1976, was an outlaw.

An example of the harm politicians can cause is the 1976 law by the Prepotto local government that essentially impeded planting of Schioppettino, a grape historically linked to both the town and nearby Albana. This was a seriously misguided move, as Prepotto and Albana are true *grand crus* for the variety. Had it been for some politicians, yet another part of Friuli Venezia Giulia would be awash with even more *Cabernet*s and Merlot than it already is today. Fortunately, the inhabitants of Prepotto rebelled en masse, led by an understanding mayor who campaigned for years for the rehabilitation of Schioppettino. An emergency town council meeting held in 1977 had a "save Schioppettino" motion as the only order of the day, which effectively set things in motion, leading to the law being repealed and Schioppettino being included in the list of authorized winegrape varieties for the province of Udine (two years later this was further modified to make Schioppettino a recommended variety). However, it's doubtful that matters would have taken the highly positive course they did, or as quickly, if it hadn't been for the dynamic husband and wife duo of Paolo and Dina Rapuzzi, owners of the Ronchi di Cialla estate.

Schioppettino has always thrived in the Colli Orientali del Friuli, where it is also rarely called Pocalza (the variety's Slovenian name) or Ribolla Nera. In fact, historically the latter name was most commonly used to describe both the grape variety and the wine made, while Schioppettino referred specifically to the wine made in and around Prepotto, considered of a higher quality already in the early twentieth century (therefore, it is incorrect to say that Schioppettino was used to refer to any wine made with this grape variety). Schioppettino's name may derive from its crunchy berries, which literally explode *(scoppiettare)* in the mouth; another equally plausible hypothesis is that the explosion referred to the unexpected secondary fermentation that routinely took place in the closed bottles in less enologically savvy times (due to residual sugar left over in unfiltered wines, causing them to referment, with bottles bursting from the resulting carbon dioxide produced within the closed vessels). Many an old-timer has told me that walking into the cellar come springtime was a real nightmare and care had to be taken not to get hurt!

Surprisingly, there is very little historical documentation on Schioppettino. Di Rovasenda (1877) is one of the few ampelographers of the past to have given an accurate description. In 1907, the Consorzio Antifilosserico (Antiphylloxera Consortium) recommended that Schioppettino be used to replant vineyards devastated by the invading louse: in so doing, it effectively confirmed Schioppettino's value and quality potential. It's not surprising, then, that Marinelli wrote in 1912 that Pokalça (the Slovenian spelling of Pocalza, a Schioppettino synonym) was one of the most commonly cultivated varieties around Cividale in the aftermath of phylloxera (along with Verduzzo, Refoscone, Refosco, and Ribolla). We know from a document written in 1282 and published in honor of the Rieppi-Caucig wedding of 1910 that in the thirteenth century the amphitheater of Albana-Prepotto was almost completely under vine, and that Schioppettino represented about 75 percent of the vines planted there. The Rieppi family is a centuries' old dynasty of Albana, and though the estate is no longer in that family's possession (it was bought by a talented and passionate winemaker, Lino Casella), its history is closely linked to Schioppettino. In the 1960s and 1970s, the Rieppi wines were highly thought of, and Maria Rieppi was considered an excellent winemaker. Her brother-in-law, Luigi Rieppi, tried planting Schioppettino near Buttrio but didn't meet with success, in his words a sign that Schioppettino is not a variety that travels particularly well; this was something that Poggi, in his 1939 treatise on Friuli viticulture, had already noticed, writing that at just a few kilometers away from the Prepotto *terroir,* the wine wasn't as interesting. The Rieppi family was therefore intimately linked to Schioppettino and its wines, and in 1979, in recognition of her efforts on behalf of Schioppettino, Maria Rieppi was awarded the prestigious Risit d'Aur, an award created by the Nonino family of worldwide grappa fame as a means to recognize all those who persevered on behalf of the Friuli Venezia Giulia region and its native cultivars. Another recipient of the Risit d'Aur, in fact of the award's first edition in 1976, had done even more for Schioppettino.

Dina and Paolo Rapuzzi arrived in the hamlet of Cialla in 1970 and singlehandedly did more for a specific *terroir,* and later a DOC, than perhaps anybody else anywhere in Italy. Cialla, whose name derives from *cela* (stream, in Slovenian), has a unique microclimate, with fewer sunlight hours and heat units than many other parts of the region, but is temperate nonetheless, so much that even olive trees manage to grow there. Furthermore, Cialla being fairly isolated, it had a long-standing association with the production of quality wines from local native varieties, and its steep slopes had always been dotted by terraced vineyards. Documents from 1496 reveal that the wines of Cialla were appreciated by nobles in Cividale and Venice, and so the Rapuzzis (a new generation is slowly taking over, with sons Piepaolo and Ivan more involved each year) set out to produce wines from Refosco del Peduncolo Rosso, Picolit, Verduzzo, and of course Schioppettino. Paolo Rapuzzi had heard the local old-timers marvel about Schioppettino wine, but there were very few grapevines left. His next step was to scour the countryside of both Friuli Venezia Giulia and Slovenia, ferreting out old vines; he then had about one hundred grafted by the Rauscedo nursery and planted an entire single vineyard to the variety. Thus Schioppettino was reborn: the Rapuzzis' stroke of genius was in recognizing the merits of the variety, that it was good enough to stand on its own rather than be used solely in blends.

The Rapuzzis' initial production of schioppettino in 1977 met with instant success and many awards, as well as much positive press later on. Their estate is considered one of the quality leaders in not just Friuli Venezia Giulia but all of Italy. Even better, others soon followed; by the 1980s, a few estates were once again producing significant quantities of Schioppettino wine. Undoubtedly, it is the Rapuzzis who showed people the way. I state this clearly, to set the record straight, because I have heard far too many times in the last ten years that other producers had rows and rows of Schioppettino and everyone knew of the wine's quality and were believers. That's just not so: and even though I understand that Schioppettino is becoming something of a cult wine, and everyone wants to jump on the bandwagon, I think that credit needs to be given where credit is due (and without forgetting Maria Rieppi, like most everyone does). In the end, what matters most is that success has arrived, and Schioppettino grapevines and wines are back from the dustbin of memory, infusing new life in the economies of Prepotto and Albana (as well as other parts of Friuli Venezia Giulia, all making Schioppettino wines now). In this light, that about twenty local producers have joined forces to form the Association of Prepotto Schioppettino Producers to promote the wine and the production zone is further good news.

Honestly, looking at Schioppettino you couldn't be blamed for wondering what the fuss is all about. The variety hardly gives the impression it could deliver anything liquid worth remembering. Its big, Rubenesque bunch, with one or two large wings and similarly large, round berries is not the prototype of the quality grape variety, as modern thinking is that quality wine grapes have small bunches and berries. Fortunately, Schioppettino manages to prove everybody wrong, as long as the grower and winemaker are equipped with patience. Schioppettino is not particularly resistant, and in rainy, cold springs it suffers from extreme *millerandage* and floral anomalies, so yields are anything but dependable or copious. It has fragile stems and is susceptible to peronospora. It's also a late ripener, something that does not sit well with most farmers in Friuli Venezia Giulia, where cool and rainy autumns are the norm, not the exception. Two clones are available, VCR 412 and ERSA-FVG 430.

Now grown all over Friuli Venezia Giulia but nowhere else in Italy, Schioppettino is most common in the Colli Orientali del Friuli, where more than 90 percent of the vines are located, mainly near Cividale. Although it has almost completely disappeared in Slovenia, Schioppettino has found admirers outside Italy. In California it has been planted in AVAs such as Sonoma County, with examples by the Holdredge MacBryde vineyard.

Which Wines to Choose and Why

There are, in my view, two *grand cru* areas: one is Prepotto and Albana, the other Cialla. In recent years, outstanding Schioppettino wines have also been made near Rosazzo and Premariacco, another good site for the variety. I discuss Prepotto and Albana jointly here, but there are noticeable differences between their wines, partly due to soil differences (more marly in Albana, slightly more alluvial in Prepotto). There is potentially another *grand cru*, that of Centa, but as no wines of note are being produced there, it's hard to prove my point.

Prepotto and Albana are situated at the mouth of the extremely narrow Judrio Valley, which allows for excellent ventilation, with little in the way of fog and stagnant humidity, both potentially devastating to a variety like Schioppettino, which in 1867 Levi characterized as "delicate" (Calò and Costacurta 1991). The warmer days and frankly cold nights also guarantee those day-night temperature variations that allow for aromatic compound precursor buildup and potentially more fragrant wines. Wines made here are usually slightly bigger bodied and richer than those of Cialla, which due to its shady and cool microclimate allows for a unique interpretation of Schioppettino wines, blessed with high natural acidity, usually excellent balance, and a one-of-a-kind refined mouthfeel. Think Margaux, compared to Albana-Prepotto's Saint-Julien. Centa, which is characterized by red-clay soil rich in iron, would produce wines a bit more like Saint-Estephe. Recognizing the various *terroirs* available is important, for Schioppettino is uniquely sensitive to site, and in areas of lesser quality it can fail to ripen properly. When optimal ripeness is not achieved, Schioppettino can show a vegetal streak, leading some producers to partially air-dry grapes, thereby producing creamier, bigger wines. This is why the style of Schioppettino runs the gamut, from velvety Amarone-like behemoths to the refined, almost meager wines of Cialla. Unfortunately, whether the producer air-dries the grapes or not is rarely indicated on the label. Hence you must get to know what each producer likes to do with his or her Schioppettino grapes, in order to know if you'll like it too, or not.

I believe Schioppettino is bound for stardom, as it can give extremely elegant red wines laced with black currant, black cherry, and green peppercorns, with high acidity and smooth tannins. As the wines age they pick up complicating notes of underbrush and tar, but they are especially characterized by a midweight body, sound acidity, and especially that green-peppercorn note. The variety's telltale aroma of green peppercorn is due to high levels of rotundone, a concentration roughly thirty-five times the level needed for the olfactory mucosa to be aware of its presence. You will have understood by now that Schioppettino wines are not the second coming of full-bodied syrahs or cabernets. Schioppettino offers a gentler, less muscular, and perfumed red wine to spend time with, and, I'm sure you'll agree, there are plenty of times when that's just what you need.

WINES TO TRY: Grillo***, La Viarte***, Ronchì di Cialla***, Vigna Petrussa***, Antico Broilo**, Bressan**, Ermacora**, Gigante**, La Tunella**, Lino Casella/Rieppi**, Paolo Rodaro** (about 30–40 percent of the grapes are air-dried, so the wines have a much thicker, creamier appeal), Petrussa**, La Sclusa**, and Moschioni** (grapes are gently air-dried on the vine).

Sciaglin

WHERE IT'S FOUND: FVG. NATIONAL REGISTRY CODE NUMBER: 323. COLOR: white.

The earliest mention of Sciaglin in Italian vineyards dates back to the fourteenth century, when the wine was already considered one of Friuli Venezia Giulia's best and longest lived. Its name, like all the synonyms it is known by (Scjarlin, Schiarlina, Schiglin), derives from *s'ciale*, or "terraces," which tells us that even many centuries ago locals were already aware that Sciaglin does best on high hillside slopes (some experts alternately believe that the name Sciaglin derives from *schiavolino*, or Slavic). At the time of the 1863 Regional Exposition of Grape Varieties organized by the Friuli Agricultural Association, Sciaglin cultivation ranged from Vito d'Asio near Pordenone to Magagna near Udine. Poggi (1935) states that Sciaglin was still very common at the beginning of the new century, as it continued to be only sixty years ago. Sciaglin cultivation was gradually abandoned, though I'm not sure why, since the variety is a regular and dependable producer and is not particularly disease sensitive. It may well be that in the planting craze of the international white varieties following the phylloxera epidemic, Sciaglin simply fell by the wayside, a shame.

Which Wines to Choose and Why

Today, Sciaglin's area of cultivation is still more or less that of 1863, only it is less common within its production zone, reduced to sporadic vines here and there. Only near Pordenone, Maniago, Spilimbergo, Fagagna, and Vito d'Asio in the westernmost part of Friuli Venezia Giulia is there a higher density of grapevines.

The only monovarietal wine I know of is by Bulfon. The wine is pale straw-yellow, delicately floral and fruity (jasmine, buttercups, chlorophyll, aniseed, lemon, tangerine, lime, with a complicating hint of acacia honey), blessed with high acidity and mineral, floral freshness. It is a remarkably delicate wine of real refinement and excellence, so much so that I would dearly love to see other producers try their hand at the variety.

WINES TO TRY: Bulfon*** (bright and refreshing with sneaky concentration).

Sciascinoso

WHERE IT'S FOUND: Campania, Lazio. NATIONAL REGISTRY CODE NUMBER: 225. COLOR: red.

Sciascinoso is one of the many olive-shaped grapes found in Italy—all descendants of the *Vitis oleaginea* described by Pliny the Elder—and has long been confused with Olivella, which is the more ancient of the two varieties. The confusion still reigns today, so caveat emptor when consulting books or websites on Italy's native grapes and wines. The distinction between Sciascinoso and Olivella dates to only a few years: Froio (1875, 1878), who wrote about many Campanian varieties, believed Sciascinoso and Olivella to be distinct. Conversely, a grape variety called both Livella and Sciascinoso has been described by other experts as different varieties since the nineteenth century at least. Carlucci, in his 1909 contribution to Vialà and Vermorel's *Traité général de viticulture*, states that Olivella and Sciascinoso are distinct: "Sciascinoso is very common in the provinces of Avellino and Salerno, less so in that of Naples and immediate surroundings, where Olivella is more common."

Interestingly, most everyone believes today that Livella is Olivella, simply called by its Campanian dialect name. However, Livella and Olivella are names attributed to many different grapes in Italy, and it is not at all likely that they are all one and the same (see OLIVELLA NERA entry). Costantini Monaco, Vouillamoz, Forlani, and Grando (2005) found a genetic identity between Sciascinoso and the Livella grown around Battipaglia, but this was just one of the three different Livella accessions included in the study, so there are other Livella varieties out there in the vineyards of Campania that may be completely distinct grapes or homonyms of others.

Which Wines to Choose and Why

Sciascinoso is rarely produced in pure versions. It is part of blends (usually with wines made from Piedirosso) of DOC wines such as Lacryma Christi del Vesuvio Rosso, Campi Flegrei Rosso, Penisola Sorrentina Rosso, and Costa d'Amalfi Rosso and Rosato. Recently, some producers have started bottling 100 percent Sciascinoso wines, such as those of the DOC Sannio Sciascinoso. The variety also grows in southern Lazio, near Frosinone.

A good sciascinoso is characterized by fruity fragrances (mainly red berries), high acidity, and a midweight frame. The grapes never accumulate high amounts of sugars, so the wine tends to be bright and fresh; it's an ideal blending partner with Piedirosso, as the two varieties ripen at about the same time. Since Piedirosso builds up sugar easily, a small percentage of sciascinoso helps the final wine achieve better balance. Antonio Mastroberardino likens Sciascinoso to a quiet old man sitting on park bench feeding the pigeons: he basically does no harm, creates no problems for anyone, and actually delivers happiness (the pigeons certainly are happy). "It's really an easy variety to deal with," he tells me. "It gives no problems whatsoever, and the wines have a pretty, deep color and very smooth tannins. If I may quibble, I don't think the aromas and flavors are so memorable or intense, but they certainly are easygoing, highly enjoyable, smooth wines."

WINES TO TRY: Capolino Perlingieri** (Sciascì), Dedicato a Marianna**, and Tenuta Vitagliano (also a good sparkling version).

Scimiscia'

WHERE IT'S FOUND: Liguria. NATIONAL REGISTRY CODE NUMBER: 377. COLOR: white.

Unique to a small area of Liguria, Scimiscia' (or Simixaa or Scimisaa or Çimixaa; the National Registry officially lists Scimiscia') was essentially saved from extinction in the 1970s by Marco Bacigalupo, a pastry chef from the town of Cicagna, who collected the remaining, very few vines of the variety and planted them in a single vineyard near Cassottana. At the end of the 1990s, the Comunità Montana della Val Fontanabuona decided to get involved and asked the Cooperativa di San Colombano to clean the by-then abandoned vineyard and identify any healthy vines. Finally, in 1998, the research community got involved and studying Scimiscia' began in earnest.

Studies by Torello Marinoni, Raimondi, Ruffa, Lacombe, and Schneider (2009) proved that the Corsican variety called Genovese, thought in the past to be a distinct cultivar, is in reality Scimiscia'. Scimiscia' is also grown sporadically in the Cinque Terre, where it is also known as Frate Pelato. Names such as Simixaa or Scimixaa refer to the spotted berries, small dots that recall mite or tick bites (the mite in local dialect is called *simixa*). In fact, it is not uncommon to find members of Hemiptera, family Pentatomidae, species *Nezara viridula*, living inside bunches of this variety.

There appear to be at least two biotypes of Scimiscia', one with medium-large, conical bunches and bigger berries, the other with medium-sized, pyramidal bunches and very small berries. Both are winged, but the latter are more compact. Today, Scimiscia' grows in Liguria's Valle del Tigullio, especially around the towns of Cicagna, Leivi, Avegno, Camposasco, and Lorsica, but its presence has been documented even in the Val Graveglia (Campo di Né and Zerli) and in the countryside of Chiavari. It also still grows in Corsica under the name of Genovese.

Which Wines to Choose and Why

A good Scimiscià wine has a bright straw-yellow color with green tinges and an intense nose of ripe pear and even banana, with a nice saline tang and plenty of refreshing acidity, though it is creamier and bigger bodied than many other Ligurian whites, such as albarola. At the current state of my knowledge, I am not confident enough to say that one biotype makes better wine than the other, as only small-batch microvinifications have been made thus far. The wine is a real rarity, and you might taste it only when visiting this beautiful part of Liguria.

WINES TO TRY: La Ricolla** and Cantina Çimixaa**.

Semidano

WHERE IT'S FOUND: Sardinia. NATIONAL REGISTRY CODE NUMBER: 226. COLOR: white.

Semidano is potentially one of Italy's greatest grape varieties, and it's ridiculous that it's so little known and that there are so few wines made with it. In fact, Semidano is the poster child for everything that was wrong with Italian viticulture and winemaking in the post-phylloxera period and in the 1980s heyday of the international oaky whites. Simply put, quality but little-known grapes were all but forgotten, not studied, and even abandoned in favor of overly productive varieties or those that were easiest to work with. This sorry state of affairs has only led to more than one great native grape being pushed to the brink of extinction, and every time I hear about how Italian native grapes aren't so interesting after all, I count to ten and then mention Semidano (or Schioppettino, or Uva di Troia, or . . .).

Also known locally as Laconarzu, Mizu, Migiu, and Semidamu, Semidano is a potentially great grape variety waiting to be rediscovered by more than those few producers who are still working with it. Believed to be one of the many imports to Sardinia by way of the Phoenicians (a claim that's admittedly hard to prove), Semidano has always been co-planted with Nuragus, with which it shares a common past. As Semidano is less resistant than the latter to phylloxera and oidium, it risked extinction because farmers preferred to replant with Nuragus, a much hardier variety. Semidano never endeared itself to farmers not only because is it disease sensitive but also because it has greatly variable yields from year to year.

Recent SSR genetic testing at twelve loci reported by Nieddu (2011) in a book on Sardinian grape varieties (not published in a peer-reviewed journal) demonstrated that Semidano is separate from all other Sardinian grape varieties, though it is closely related to the little-known local variety named Lacconargeddu.

Which Wines to Choose and Why

Unfortunately, Semidano is rare: only fifty hectares are planted, mainly around Cagliari. The DOC wine is Sardegna Semidano, and the Mogoro subzone is the best (wines carrying the Mogoro subdenomination label have to be made from lower yields, 110 quintals per hectare instead of 130). Sardegna Semidano can also be made a *spumante* (sparkling) and *passito* (air-dried and sweet) versions. It is usually blended with Nuragus to add elegance and refinement. As a monovarietal, it's a beautifully graceful, lightly aromatic wine of real refinement, redolent of tangerine, apricot, and strong mineral notes.

WINES TO TRY: Gigi Picciau*** (bone dry with plenty of character, not unlike a dry, saline, fuller-bodied riesling—think Pfalz, not Mosel), Il Nuraghe** (the sparkling Puisteris is my favorite offering by this producer, late harvested, big, bold, and rich without being over the top; also Anastasia, a solidly made dry white wine).

Spergola

WHERE IT'S FOUND: Emilia-Romagna. NATIONAL REGISTRY CODE NUMBER: 364. COLOR: white.

Until recently, Spergola was routinely confused with Sauvignon Blanc, though I have a hard time understanding why, since the two varieties don't look anything alike and ripen at different times. Filipetti, Silvestroni, Thomas, and Intrieri (2001) dispelled that notion, releasing Spergola to fly under its own power. Spergola was highly thought of in the past, with even the fifteenth-century Grand Duchess of Tuscany, Bianca Cappello, reportedly a fan of the wine made with it. Matilde di Canossa reportedly gave a bottle of Spergola wine as a gift to Pope Gregory VII.

The first precise studies detailing Spergola characteristics and viticultural behaviors where those of Tanara in 1644, and at a time when the variety was also called Spergolina or Spargolina (Tanara called it Pomoria or Pellegrina). The Spargolina name, obviously a derivation from the Italian word *spargolo*, seemingly implies that the variety has a loosely packed, or sparse, bunch. Interestingly, and I'm not sure why, this is not the case with the bunches of Spergola I have observed in vineyards of today. In truth, Gallesio ([1817] 1839) described two biotypes of Spargolina: Spargolina Normale, with larger berries and bunches; and Spargolina Molle, characterized by very small, loosely packed bunches. Most of what we know about modern-day Spergola is thanks to Filippetti, Silvestroni, Thomas, and Intrieri (2001), who have documented the basic and standard phenotypic and phenological aspects of the variety, suggesting also genetic ties between it and Pignoletto.

Spergola is rare today, but less so than people think. It's grown around the towns of Scandiano and Albinea near Reggio Emilia in the Emilia-Romagna region; recent estimates show that plantings are on the increase. There are currently two hundred hectares of the variety in Emilia-Romagna.

Which Wines to Choose and Why

The wines are often (but not necessarily) bottled as Colli di Scandiano e Canossa: pale straw-green in hue, with bright aromas of white flowers (acacia, white buttercups, jasmine) and riper citrus and both green- and yellow-apple flavors on a fresh, light, high-acid palate that will remind you a little of apple cider. Given its natural acidity, the wine is also produced as a sparkling and as a sweet, air-dried wine. Recently, five estates (Bertolani, Cantina di Arceto, Cantina Colli di Scandiano, Casali Viticultori, and Tenuta di Aljano) from the area around Scandiano have joined forces to promote the merits of the variety and its wines, creating La Compagnia della Spergola (Association of Spergola).

WINES TO TRY: Tenuta di Aljano** (Brina d'Inverno, a sparkler, but especially La Vigna Ritrovata, an extraordinarily good nonbubbly spergola; the estate has invested heavily in this variety), Casali Viticultori** (Albore and Albore Dolce, two sparkling wines made in the manner of Champagne), Ca' dei Noci (Extra Brut Riserva dei Fratelli, another sparkler, but I much prefer the Querciole bottling, a still wine with just a hint of fizz), and Cantina Sociale di Arceto (in the I Tradizionali line of wines, Bianco Secco and Bianco Dolce, but they make many different versions).

Susumaniello

WHERE IT'S FOUND: Puglia. NATIONAL REGISTRY CODE NUMBER: 229. COLOR: red.

Susumaniello has always been considered a very productive variety and little else, which explains its name, a reference to "loading up the donkey." The vine will indeed produce a huge number of grapes unless curbed by ultra-rigorous pruning or stress. But according to Donato Lazzari, the general director of the Agricole Vallone estate in Puglia, Susumaniello is a generous producer only in the first ten years of life, after which it becomes distinctly less prolific.

The variety was originally thought to be of Dalmatian origin, but this seems much less likely in light of DNA profiling results that show Susumaniello to be a Garganega × Uva Sogra crossing (Di Vecchi Staraz, Bandinelli, Boselli, This, Boursiquot, Laucou, Lacombe, et al. 2007). Due to its relationship to Garganega, one of Italy's oldest and most important cultivars (in that it is related to many other Italian varieties), Susumaniello must be either the grandparent or a half sibling of Albana, Cataratto Bianco, Dorona, Malvasia Bianca di Candia, Marzemina Bianca, Montonico Bianco, Mostosa, and Trebbiano Toscano. Susumaniello is potentially one of the up-and-coming native grapes of Italy, and plantings have been increasing steadily over the last ten years. Other synonyms include Cozzomaniello, Cucciguaniello, Susipaniello, Cuccipaniello, Cozzomaniello, Grismaniello (or Gerismaniello), Somarello, Susumariello, Susumariello Nero, Zingariello, and Zuzumaniello. Of note, the National Registry has recently added a Somarello variety (another reference to donkeys: a *somarello* is a small donkey), which is going to cause confusion among professionals and wine lovers, since Somarello is a commonly used synonym for both Susumaniello and Uva di Troia.

Gregory Perucci and Salvatore Mero of Racemi (formerly Accademia dei Racemi) have devoted the greatest amount of time to studying and working with this variety. "When we started out in 1998," Perucci told me, "we were set on resurrecting ancient local varieties and found both Ottavianello, better known as Cinsault, and Susumaniello, which was the much harder of the two to locate, near Brindisi." Perucci found a seventy-year-old vineyard that the owner's grandfather had planted following the traditions of his time: one-third Negro Amaro for body, one-third Malvasia Nera for perfume, and one-third Susumaniello for color. "Honestly, I don't know of any other Susumaniello vines anywhere in Puglia at that time, and we really went looking long and far," muses Perucci, who wonders about the new monovarietal susumaniello or other wines made with high percentages of a variety nobody had heard of only fifteen years ago. "Anything is possible, I guess," he shrugs, "but I do think it's good for the variety to be out there and talked about."

There are two biotypes of Susumaniello: one has a trilobed leaf and a midsized, compact bunch; the second has a leaf with five lobes and a smaller, loosely packed bunch. Both are characterized by small berries with very large pips. "The really interesting thing is that the pip's tannins aren't bitter, as they are in every other Puglian red variety: this allows us to perform very long, slow extractions," says Mero. Susumaniello is grown mainly in the countryside around Bari and Brindisi; plantings are on the increase (only thirteen hectares in 2006, more than twenty in 2010) and can also be found in the provinces of Taranto and Lecce. It seems to do best in soils that are not too fertile, clay-rich, or humid, for these characteristics all push the variety's naturally high vigor. There is one clone available, CRSA-D86.

Which Wines to Choose and Why

Susumaniello wines are a work in progress, since the variety has only been on people's radars for a decade or so. Perucci believes the wine does not take well to oak and so avoids using it, but not all his colleagues agree. It seems to be generally accepted that though the wine starts out rude and tannic when young, with six to eight years of bottle age it softens and becomes smooth and stylish. Not everyone is as sold on Susumaniello and its star qualities. Donato Lazzari of the Agricole Vallone estate in Puglia's Salento is not so sure the cultivar's tannins will ever be refined or soft enough to give a truly noble wine: "In blends however, I think Susumaniello can be a really great addition, for I find that the texture of wines is greatly improved by its presence." The pure examples I have had so far have always offered a strong but not massive cloak, also plenty of dark-cherry and plum aromas and flavors. I think there's a lot of potential to the "Susie" wine, as it's nicknamed in Anglophile circles.

As Susumaniello has only recently been brought back to life, monovarietal wines are still rare. Agricole Vallone owns some beautiful and extensive Susumaniello vineyards, which I had the pleasure of almost getting lost in one summer day, finding myself immersed in a seemingly never-ending sea of green. As these vines are still young, the must from the grapes is blended with Negro Amaro in the very good Vigna Castello wine. Technical director Donato Lazzari is not sure he'll ever make a pure susumaniello, but as they're just getting to know the variety at the estate, he plans on studying Susumaniello more before making a final decision.

WINES TO TRY: Racemi** (Sum), Cantina Due Palme* (Serre), Lomazzi & Sarli* (Nomas), and Tenute Rubino* (Torre Testa).

Tazzelenghe

WHERE IT'S FOUND: FVG. NATIONAL REGISTRY CODE NUMBER: 293. COLOR: red.

Tazzelenghe is one of Friuli Venezia Giulia's many native red grapes, but the one that in these tougher economic times is at risk of disappearing, as cash-strapped estates look to cut costs everywhere. Unfortunately, the wonderfully crisp and clean high-acid reds made with Tazzelenghe have a hard time competing with softer, high-pH wines that are all about creamy fruit and ripe flavors and usually more sought after by novice or everyday wine drinkers.

The name Tazzelenghe derives from *tàcelenghe*, which in the local dialect means "cuts the tongue," a reference to this variety's amazingly high acidity levels and not-shy tannin concentrations that literally make your palate pucker and the rest of you cringe. It is native to the area around Udine, where it was first documented in 1863, and has always been grown mainly around the towns of Buttrio and Manzano in Friuli Venezia Giulia's Colli Orientali del Friuli. Today it is still only grown in Friuli Venezia Giulia, in the countryside around Buttrio, Manzano, and Cividale near Udine. In the past, Tazzelenghe was considered a member of the *Refosco* family, identified with the variety then called Refosco del Boton. Tazzelenghe has a medium bunch and berry (the latter is sometimes medium-large), and its loosely packed grape bunch has a characteristic truncated cone shape. One clone is available today, ERSA-FVG 435.

Which Wines to Choose and Why

The only DOC wine is Colli Orientali del Friuli Tazzelenghe, otherwise the wine is included in blends. It's a shame that Tazzelenghe is falling out of favor: many producers I have talked to are considering uprooting it and sticking with more popular and better-known varieties. As is all too often the case, it's not the grape variety that doesn't cut it, but the lack of appropriate vineyard and cellar techniques that work against the cultivar. True, the high acidity, strong tannins, and light to medium frame are about as far removed from the chocolaty soft, high-alcohol wine prototype that was all the rage in the last decade of the twentieth century, but mercifully that fad is on its last legs. Furthermore, the chiseled, precise, and light aroma and flavor profile of well-made Tazzelenghe wines makes them ideal sparring partners at the dinner table with most foods.

One encouraging sign is that the wine is still being made by lesser-known producers such as Beltrame in the DOC Aquilea, while Anselmi (Giuseppe and Lino) makes an IGT Tazzelenghe delle Venezie. Another is that some of the monovarietal tazzelenghe producers have agreed, at my urging, to band together to form an association to promote their grape and wine. Unfortunately, the Dorigo estate has fallen on very hard economic times and has had to sell off or rent out its vineyards; I remember an amazing Ronc di Juri 2001 (still spectacular), and hope that the people taking over will give Tazzelenghe a chance.

When properly grown and vinified (some producers purposely harvest it as late as possible in order to naturally decrease acidity levels), Tazzelenghe yields a very elegant red wine that ages extremely well. Its deep purple hue, with intense aromas of violets and fresh blackberries, with more blackberry and black currant on the palate and delicate hints of roses, underbrush, and tar, all make this a complex, very interesting, and unique red. As it ages it smoothes out and picks up a complexity that I have yet to find in Pignolo wines, generally considered the much better variety of the two. It probably is, but I don't think Tazzelenghe is so inferior. I think Tazzelenghe has a future and a role to play, especially if wine lovers take the time to let its wine age for a few years and smooth out.

WINES TO TRY: Lino Casella** (Cassella has taken over the once-famous Rieppi estate in Albana), Gianpaolo Colutta**, D'Attimis Maniago**, Jacuss**, La Viarte**, and Le 2 Torri**.

Teroldego

WHERE IT'S FOUND: Trentino, Tuscany, Sicily.
NATIONAL REGISTRY CODE NUMBER: 232.
COLOR: red.

Teroldego is the most important red grape variety of Trentino, where other good red wines are made—from Pinot Nero to Cabernet Sauvignon to Marzermino—but Teroldego rules. Legend has it that the variety's name derives from *oro* and Tirolo, as this wine was called "the golden one from Tirolo" at the royal court of Vienna and in other European cities, where it was very popular in the eighteenth and nineteenth centuries. Alternatively, the name may be a corruption of Tiroldola (or Teroldola), an ancient native variety grown near Verona. Though first documented by Filippo Re in the 1811 *Annali dell'agricoltura del Regno d'Italia*, there are references to Teroldego wines dating back to the fourteenth century (though which grape they were made of is less clear). Michelangelo Mariani, historian of the Concilio di Trento, documented that Teroldego wine was made in particularly large volumes near the town of Mezzolombardo in 1673.

Recently, the origin of Teroldego has been clarified. DNA parentage analysis showed that Syrah is a cross between Mondeuse Blanche and Dureza, two varieties typical of the Savoie and Ardèche regions of France (Bowers, Siret, and Meredith 2000). In 2006, Vouillamoz and Grando at the Istituto Agrario di San Michele all'Adige showed Dureza to be a sibling of Teroldego. Interestingly, it follows that, since Syrah is a progeny of Dureza, it is therefore a nephew of Teroldego, which makes Teroldego look like a pretty important grape. A second-degree genetic relationship between Pinot Nero and both Dureza and Teroldego was also found in the 2006 study, which means that Pinot Nero might be a close relative of the two. However, since Pinot Nero was known and cultivated in France and in the Tyrol in the fourteenth century, before any documented reference to either Dureza or Teroldego being planted in the region, it is possible that Pinot Nero is their ancestor, most likely either their grandparent or their uncle. However, Roncador (2006) reports the presence of vineyards in Trentino in the fifteenth century that were most likely of Teroldego, so the latter is also a very ancient variety. It also appears likely that Teroldego spontaneously crossed with an unknown and possibly now extinct variety, potentially even a wild grapevine species, to give birth to Lagrein in Trentino or Alto Adige and to Marzemino in Trentino or Lombardy (Vouillamoz and Grando 2006).

Teroldego is one of Italy's ancient and wilder varieties, and training it up high above the ground can keep its vigor under control. Generally speaking, Teroldego has medium bunches and medium-large berries; the bunch is pyramidal, elongated, and compact, with two small wings. The berries detach easily, not a good thing in windy conditions. It's slightly sensitive to oidium and peronospora, and in humid years botrytis bunch rot becomes a problem. Of the five main clones available today, the best two are 145 and 152, developed in 1990 and 1992, respectively (while 146 is too productive and of a lesser quality). While both yield wines with intense aromas, the latter is markedly different phenotypically, earlier ripening and with smaller bunches. However, Elisabetta Foradori, the best producer of Teroldego wines, detests clones and points out she has been working for more than twenty-five years with massal selections.

The variety has been planted all over Italy, but the wine is mainly limited to Trentino, and monovarietal wines are made only there. There's quite a bit of Teroldego in Tuscany and even in Sicily, but mainly used only for blends or on an experimental basis. For example, in Tuscany, Poggio al Cassone has bottled a Teroldego wine under the name La Cattura, and many other estates, including Suvereto's famed Tua Rita, have given it a try, if only in experimental batches. Teroldego has also been planted outside Italy: California, Brazil, and Australia have all given it a try. In Australia, areas as diverse as Margaret River, McLaren Vale, Alpine Valleys, and Langhorne Creek have gotten involved, while in the United States it grows in areas like the Central Valley and Sierra foothills.

Which Wines to Choose and Why

The recognized, historic *grand cru* for Teroldego is the Campo Rotaliano, a sandy-gravelly plain born of the alluvial deposits of the Noce Stream and Adige River, found between San Michele all'Adige, Mezzocorona, and Mezzolombardo at about 230 meters above sea level. Today, this is still the wine's most important production area. Actually, the Campo Rotaliano is one of the very few documented *grand crus* related to a specific grape variety in all of Italy (for example, Cannubi is a *grand cru* for Barolo, but there are surprisingly few such variety-specific site pairs with historical significance). The wine is always darkly colored because of its total anthocyanin concentration (one of the highest of any Italian wine) and the prevalence of malvin, petunin, and delphin in its anthocyanin profile (roughly 65 percent of the total anthocyanin content), while the more easily oxidized cyanin and peonin are present only in small amounts. The wines are always very fruity and softly tannic, so much so that Teroldego makes possibly Italy's best *novello* (or *nouveau*) wines, in which soft tannins and bright fruity aromas are everything. Aroma and flavor profiles resting on ripe red cherry, quinine, ink, tar, and fresh herbs are typical of Teroldego wines, which often maintain a wild, slightly vegetal connotation (downright weedy if the grapes are not perfectly ripe), perhaps a vestige of the variety's descent from a wild grapevine species. Despite Teroldego's noble family tree, only recently has Teroldego been used to make consistently truly important, ageworthy wines. For the longest time the wine was sold off in bulk and used all over Italy to pump up the color and perfume of more anemic wines. Over the last thirty years however, Teroldego production has improved immeasurably and very fine wines are here to stay.

In Australia, Blue Poles Vineyard, Hand Crafted by Geoff Hardy, Michelini, and Zonte's Footstep are the names to look for, while in California, Montoliva, Heringer Estate, Podere dell'Olivos, Terzetto, and Wolff Vineyards have been successful.

WINES TO TRY: Elisabetta Foradori*** (Granato, huge and ageworthy; Vigneto Sgarzon, aged in terra-cotta amphoras, characterized by extremely high acidity), Zeni**, and Barone di Cles*.

Terrano

WHERE IT'S FOUND: FVG. NATIONAL REGISTRY CODE NUMBER: 233. COLOR: red.

Terrano may well be the ancient variety known as Pucinum described by Pliny the Elder, but such assertions are very hard to prove (and some experts disagree, believing instead that Pucinum wine was made with a white variety similar to Glera). Though Terrano is related to Refosco del Peduncolo Rosso and has long been referred to as Refosco del Carso or Refosco d'Istria, recent studies have determined the variety to be distinct. In a sign of just how complicated it is to correctly classify members of the *Refosco* group, differences between Terrano and Refosco del Peduncolo Rosso are unquestionably fewer and smaller than those between it and other members of the *Refosco* family. In fact, Carlo Petrussi, probably Friuli's most respected viticulture expert, has told me numerous times that he believes Terrano to be only a biotype of Refosco del Peduncolo Rosso, one that has adapted over the centuries to its specific Istrian habitat, which would explain their differences in morphology and viticulture behaviors. Poggi (1939) described the sensory profile of wines made with Terrano, and affirmed that it was similar to the *Refoscos*.

Terrano is also called Cagnina, Teran, and Lambrusco dal Peduncolo Rosso (or Lambrusco Pjcol Ros). This last name is limited to a few vineyards around Reggio Emilia, where the variety was long believed to be a biotype of Lambrusco Grasparossa, though we know today that it is not a *Lambrusco* at all. This "Lambrusco" was so named because its stalk is very red (red stalk, or *pjcol rosso* in local dialect); its berries, almost black in hue, are darker than any *Lambrusco*. Others have proved that Terrano, Refosco d'Istria, and the Slovenian Refošk are identical (Maletic, Pejic, Karoglan Kontic, Piljac, Dangl, Vokurka, et al. 1999; Kozjak, Korošek Kozuka, and Javornik 2003).

The name Terrano refers to the wine's very dark color, reminiscent of tar (*ter* in German). According to Dalmasso (1946), Terrano was first mentioned by Francesco da Manzano in the *Annals of Friuli,* which describes a wine called *terrain* that was so highly thought of that the city of Udine used to present visiting notables with a gift bottle. It also grows in Emilia-Romagna, where it is called Terrano Refosco; most likely it arrived in Romagna along with the famous Istria stone used to build many of the palaces and buildings in Ravenna and other cities. The cluster is medium-sized and not that tightly packed, the berries large and very thick skinned.

Terrano is typical of the Carso area of Friuli Venezia Giulia, but in reality, there are two different Carso areas that both produce Terrano wines: the better-known Carso Triestino, a narrow strip of land characterized by extremely rocky, almost barren, iron-rich red soils; and the smaller Carso Goriziano, where the soils are less poor and ferrous. The variety also grows in Emilia-Romagna in the provinces of Forlì and Ravenna. According to Giuseppe Fontana of the La Piccola estate, it seems the best Lambrusco Pjcol Ros grapes are those grown around the town of Montecchio, to the east of the Enza Stream. Terrano is also planted in Slovenia and in Macedonia.

Which Wines to Choose and Why

The wines to buy in Friuli Venezia Giulia are the DOC Carso Terrano; in Emilia-Romagna, the DOC wine is Cagnina di Romagna (an off-dry, slightly sweet red wine), though the Lambrusco Pjcol Ros wines are also made with a locally grown Terrano. In early twentieth-century Friuli Venezia Giulia, young girls were given a small glass of terrano from time to time to ward off anemia, as terrano has always been believed to make "good blood" due to its strong iron content. A good Terrano wine is purple-ruby, with expressive violet, blackberry, and black-currant aromas and flavors, with almost painful acidity and strong minerality. It's a great food wine. Cagnina di Romagna is a light-bodied sweet wine, with fragrant and delicately sweet red-berry aromas and flavors.

WINES TO TRY: For Terrano, try: Zidarich***, Skerk***, Kante***, Castelvecchio***, and Castello di Rubbia** (the latter two from the Carso Goriziano). For Cagnina di Romagna, try: Tenuta Amalia**, Bissoni**, and Celli Vini*. For Lambrusco Pjcol Ross, try: Rinaldini-Moro*** (Pjcol Rosso; rich, complex, and fruity), La Piccola*** (Lambrusco Picol Ross; also rich, complex, and fruity).

Timorasso

WHERE IT'S FOUND: Piedmont. NATIONAL REGISTRY CODE NUMBER: 234. COLOR: red.

Timorasso yields an intellectual wine, not unlike a very dry riesling from the Nahe or the

Rheinhessen. And much like many intellectuals you might know, these are sometimes best taken in small doses. There is no denying the intensely mineral and herbal aromas and flavors of these wines, and the lesser examples can be too much of a good thing and a taste one needs to acquire. Still, the excitement about Timorasso and its wines is palpable, since the best wines really are some of Italy's most unique, interesting white wines. The fact is, Timorasso has only resurfaced to international attention recently, and this thanks to the initial efforts of Walter Massa, a wine producer of the Colli Tortonesi area in southeastern Piedmont who basically brought Timorasso back from oblivion all by himself. The exact measure of just how unknown Timorasso was for most of the twentieth century is that there is no mention of it in Nicholas Belfrage's excellent *Barolo to Valpolicella*, first published in 1999; only Dolcetto, Barbera, and Cortese are mentioned when the Colli Tortonesi is very briefly discussed, but understandably so, as back then Timorasso's time had not yet come.

Found in southern Piedmont and to a small extent in southern Lombardy, Timorasso (or Timuasso, as it is known in the local dialect) was once grown in Liguria, where it was considered a very good table grape. Timorasso was once the most commonly grown white variety of Piedmont, along with Cortese, and was used to produce *torbolino*, a vinous product that was exported to Switzerland and Germany. Legend has it that even Leonardo da Vinci liked Timorasso wines, so much so that his gifts at Isabella di Aragona's wedding were the Montebore, an ancient cheese of the area, and a bottle of white wine, the *timuràs*, which was supposedly the best possible match for that cheese. Past ampelographers, including De Maria and Leardi (1875) and Di Rovasenda (1877), all documented that Timorasso was a noble variety.

Studies have suggested that Timorasso is genetically identical to Carica L'asino, but as the latter is a name given to many varieties all over Italy this identification means little, as there is a true Carica L'asino variety that is distinct from Timorasso. Instead, a recent study using microsatellites to analyze several grapes from Piedmont, all named Lambrusca or Lambrusco, showed first-degree parentage relationships between Lambruschetto and Timorasso, while the *Lambrusco*s from Emilia-Romagna were genetically distant (Torello Marinoni, Raimondi, Boccacci, and Schneider 2006).

Timorasso is very easy to recognize, since it has berries of different sizes within the same bunch, usually also at different stages of ripeness: asynchronous maturation of the berries is one of the reasons this variety is a pain to grow and that making great wine from it is difficult. It also suffers from floral abortion, with many flowers never bearing fruit. The berries also fall off the vine very easily, not a good thing in windy conditions. Furthermore, it is very thin skinned and easily falls prey to grey rot, so it is very important to work in the vineyards to distance the bunches and shoots, and avoiding humid or scarcely ventilated locations is key. When global warming wasn't an issue, the variety also never ripened well, or did so late in the fall season, another no-no in the eyes of farmers. For these reasons, Timorasso cultivation had been abandoned: its production was too irregular and the variety too difficult to grow for farmers to bother in times when wines (some, at least) did not fetch today's high prices.

Which Wines to Choose and Why

Today, Timorasso's acreage is reduced compared to the pre-phylloxera age, when it rivaled Cortese as the most common white variety in Piedmont. Now, Timorasso is associated mainly if not only with the Colli Tortonesi, but more precisely, it is especially abundant in the northern, mountainous part of this DOC (whereas Barbera and Dolcetto are more common in the southern part). The northern Colli Tortonesi area is made up of a series of valleys: Val Curone, Val Grue, Val Ossona, Val Borbera, and Val Spinti are characterized by their unique wine production (it's not only Timorasso that thrives here; another, rarer native, Lambrusca di Alessandria, does too). Viticulture and winemaking are economically important in this area as well, with 638 hectares under vine. The talented Elisa Semino, who runs La Colombera estate with her father and did her enology school thesis on this variety, points out that there are still some centenary, ungrafted vines to be found, especially in the higher part of the Val Curone.

The wine is crisp, high acid, and very mineral; it will remind you of a very dry riesling, with less sweet fruit when it is about five years old or more. Before that, it has aromas and flavors of white flowers, unripe white stone fruit, and bright citrus. High acidity and good aromatic persistence are typical, though some producers have been trying to create creamier versions.

WINES TO TRY: Massa*** (Sterpi and Coste del Vento; the latter more mineral and less creamy), La Colombera*** (Il Montino and Derthona), Mutti*** (Derthona Castagnoli), Claudio Mariotto (Pitasso and Derthona)**, Carlo Daniele Ricci** (San Leto, from late-harvested grapes), Maurizio Bruno**, Boveri Luigi** (Filari di Timorasso), and Clemente Mogni**.

Tintilia

WHERE IT'S FOUND: Molise. NATIONAL REGISTRY CODE NUMBER: 372. COLOR: red.

Tintilia (or Tintiglia; but Tintilia is the official name and spelling) is an important native variety typical of Molise, the little region often lumped in with Abruzzo (as in Abruzzo and Molise, rarely Molise on its own). Quality winemaking has long been nearly nonexistent in the region, and even the better-known wineries have relied on famous consulting winemakers. Time is needed to understand a local variety or to create an identity for a winery, but given Tintilia's recent success, Molise has something to look forward to. Part of the problem is that Tintilia was never a favorite of farmers: though rustic and hardy, it yields very few grapes per bunch, and so more productive varieties were preferred. Thus, the cultivar survived only in a few old and forgotten vineyards in the province of Campobasso. The wine actually had great success at the dawn of the twentieth century: a wine from Molise made with Tintilia won gold at the Paris Wine Exhibition of 1900.

Where exactly Tintilia comes from, or whether it's a true native, has been discussed at length for some time. Some experts believed it was brought to Molise from Spain by viticulturalist Raffaele Pepe in 1810, others that it was identical to Sardinia's Bovale Grande variety. Still others believed Tintilia to be the anciently described Campanian grape called Tintiglia Nera that has since disappeared from its original home in Irpinia. The word *tintiglia* (or *tintilia*) could easily derive from the Spanish *tinto*, meaning red (in Italian, calling something *tinto* means it's colored). In any case, joint credit must go to the politicians of Molise and to the University of Molise, who ten years ago decided together that genetic studies of a local grape, not found much anywhere else, were warranted. Recent research results have helped clarify that Tintilia is very much its own grape. Reale, Pilla, and Angiolillo (2006) analyzed thirteen SSR loci to screen a collection of *Vitis vinifera* cultivars named Tintilia harvested both in southern Italy and in Spain. The thirty-seven accessions were analyzed and showed a perfect genetic match between those named Tintilia from Molise (which differed from Tintilia from other Italian regions) and from Spain. Nieddu (2011) has recently reported similar results in a book on Sardinian grape varieties.

Another word of thanks must go to producer Claudio Cipressi, of the estate Cantine Cipresso, who in 1995 set out to recuperate old vines of Tintilia with the aim of once again making a wine with this variety. Cipressi knew his grandparents had always made a tintilia for local consumption but couldn't find a single bottle anywhere. Therefore, he selected and propagated old vines, recognized courtesy of old local farmers, and planted a seven-hectare vineyard. His winemaker, Goffredo Agostini is learning on the job, for practically nobody knows anything about the variety. "It certainly has a very specific, almost unique aromatic character," he told me, "but it's not very productive at all, and that's why it was abandoned. To make matters worse, the berry is very small and it has three pips (I find most cultivars have two), further reducing the juice in the berries. It also does best at higher altitudes, above four hundred meters above sea level, and this was another drawback limiting its appeal."

Which Wines to Choose and Why

Molise or bust, you might say. The latest data (2010) shows there are only sixty hectares planted to Tintilia (though that number is certain to rise in the next decade), all of which are in Molise. Long used as a blending grape, it is now possible to taste pure Tintilia in wines of the DOC Molise Tintilia (created only in 1998). Tintilia is actually a pretty good wine. Saturated red and pleasantly spicy and floral on the nose, it's full-bodied, with flavors of ripe red fruit, leather, and tobacco and a pleasant saline bent, with very good acidity and noble tannins.

Tintilia is still little known, and so describing what a well-made monovarietal ought to be about is difficult. In fact, when I tasted wines with world-famous winemaker Attilio Pagli, who, to his credit, has devoted himself to making authentic wines from native grapes (his greatest, though not his only, success is with Ciliegiolo), I mentioned that I didn't know much about Tintilia and what it's supposed to taste like. He laughed and told me flat out: "Ian, nobody knows anything about Tintilia and what it's supposed to taste like. We're all just learning."

The few wines I have had thus far, from producers I trust not to throw in a dollop or two of merlot or syrah for added body or creaminess or whatever, are all wines characterized by very deep, almost inky hues, with fruit-forward, creamy personalities but with a nice underbrush and herbal element that keeps them from being just New World chocolaty-vanilla wannabes. Furthermore, Tintilia wines, when well made, are all characterized by sound levels of acidity, so that the less concentrated versions of this wine are midweight and easygoing. The best tintilias I've had are marked by very ripe red-fruit aromas and flavors, with hints of flint and tar that are very enjoyable. I am not yet convinced the variety will be able to give wines of mind-bending complexity, but wonderful to drink wines that are above average in depth and texture, yes.

WINES TO TRY: Cantine Cipressi**, Cianfagna**, Angelo D'Uva*, and Cantina Salvatore*.

Tintore di Tramonti

WHERE IT'S FOUND: Campania. NATIONAL REGISTRY CODE NUMBER: 444. COLOR: red.

Tintore and *Tramonti*, two words that tell you all you need to know. Tintore di Tramonti is yet another *teinturier* grape, varieties so called because their juice is very intensely colored. As a result, throughout history, the *teinturiers* were always used to boost the anemic hues of wines made with other varieties. The French *teinturier* means "to tinge," or "color"; the Italian *tinto* also means "tinged" or "colored," and a *tintore* is he who colors. (As an aside, the famous Venetian painter Tintoretto received that nickname because his father was a dyer: as the son of a Mr. Tintore, he was dubbed Tintoretto, or little Tintore.) There are many such color-endowed *teinturier* varieties in Italy (some are actually American hybrid grapes), and almost all are recognizable because of a colored pulp: a rarity, since almost all grapes used to make fine wine have colorless juice (as an example, wines made with Merlot or Syrah are red only because the grape juice was allowed to sit in contact with the grape skins for a certain number of hours; generalizing somewhat, the longer that skin contact, the darker the red wine).

Tintore di Tramonti is genetically linked to other minor Campanian varieties: Livella Ischia, Mangiaguerra (but not the Magliocco Dolce of Calabria, also at times called Mangiaguerra locally), and a Tintiglia variety different from the much better-known Tintilia of Molise.

In the nineteenth century, ampelographers believed that Tintore di Tramonti was also related to Tintora di Lanzara and Olivella Tingitora, two other local coloring grapes.

Tintore di Tramonti also takes its name from the little town called Tramonti, which offers breathtaking views of the Amalfi coast that are a must-see when you next visit the area. It is also one of the few parts of the coast with serious tracts of vineyard land still available. Tintore di Tramonti remains a rare variety; most of the remaining vines in the area are ungrafted and more than a hundred years old. Tramonti can be a windy and cold place, though: not by chance Tramonti derives from the Latin *triventum*, meaning "three winds," as this part of Campania is often plagued by strong cold winds swirling about. Tintore di Tramonti is not a particularly fertile variety, but local producers have always appreciated it for its deep hue and capacity to accumulate sugars (thereby allowing for the production of strong, alcoholic wines). It's very vigorous, high yielding, and rustic, but sensitive to botrytis bunch rot and berry shatter. It has a deep blue-red-colored pulp.

Which Wines to Choose and Why

Tintore di Tramonti is grown mainly in the beautiful countryside around Tramonti, less in the Valle dell'Irno, near Salerno. The DOC Costa d'Amalfi Rosso, subzone Tramonti (and to a lesser degree, subzones Ravello and Furore), are the wines most likely to contain small percentages of this variety. Here the vines are often close to a hundred years old and are commonly ungrafted.

There have been only ten thousand bottles of monovarietal tintore made thus far, but it's encouraging to see winemakers trying their hand at a local variety that had been forgotten. Besides a deep hue, the wines exude lovely ripe red cherry and almost jammy, spicy aromas and flavors, but with very high levels of acidity, so they never come across as heavy or cloying. As the grapes are often slightly air-dried, the tannins are usually remarkably smooth.

WINES TO TRY: Reale*** (Borgo di Gete), Apicella** (La Scippata), Monte di Grazia**, and Tenuta San Francesco** (È Iss) (all are making pure Tintore di Tramonti wines as well as others in which it plays a major role; these estates' wines are some of the most unique and interesting coming out of Italy, far better than those made with most other coloring varieties).

Tocai Friulano

WHERE IT'S FOUND: FVG. NATIONAL REGISTRY CODE NUMBER: 235. COLOR: white.

Along with Ribolla Gialla, Tocai Friulano is Friuli Venezia Giulia's most emblematic grape variety and the classic *tajut* of wine (the local phrasing for a glass of wine) in every *osteria* or *trattoria* of the region. After decades of squabbles and petitions, people in Friuli Venezia Giulia have come to accept that their wine can no longer be called Tocai (much as in Alsace there is no longer a tokay–pinot gris, but just pinot gris), as the moniker "Tokaj" or "Tokay" is now allowed only for the Hungarian wine made in the eponymous region. Therefore, the wine is now simply called friulano. Interestingly, and in a very Italian twist on the matter, though the Italian wine can no longer be called Tocai, in Italy the grape's name continues to be Tocai Friulano.

Tocai Friulano has a long and distinguished history in Friuli Venezia Giulia. Documents inform us that already in the twelfth century, the Abbott Giacomo Vinciguerra from Collalto owned "a wonderful vineyard of Tokay in San Salvatore"; centuries later Poggi (1939) thought Tokay was one of Friuli Venezia Giulia's best wines. What grapes were used to make those wines is unclear, though of course in Italy everyone believes it was Tocai Friulano. Italians also underscore that King Bela IV planted Friulian grapevines in Hungary in the Tokay production zone (Perusini 1935) and that Count Formentini from Friuli Venezia Giulia also brought Friulian grapevines to Hungary. In a truly clever observation, those who staunchly defend Italy's right to use the Tocai name for the wine point out that Hungary's main wine grape, called Furmint, bears a clear resemblance to the Friuli nobleman's last name.

Tocai Friulano is an interesting variety far beyond its complicated historical roots. In fact, we know today that it is identical to Sauvignon Vert or Sauvignonasse. Once a common variety in France, it is now found mainly in Friuli Venezia Giulia and in Chile (a number of very good Chilean wines labeled Sauvignon taste of Tocai Friulano and not of Sauvignon Blanc at all). There are some plantings of Tocai Friulano in other parts of the world as well, such as California, New York State, and New Zealand, and it is interesting to see that this cultivar is starting to gain a measure of recognition all its own, with estates starting to bottle it with its real varietal name (most usually, the chosen name is Sauvignon Vert or Sauvignonasse, occasionally Tocai Friulano). The variety is a resistant one and has problems only with botrytis in the fall, but as the fungus usually arrives in the vineyards when the grapes are ready to be picked the problem is marginal. One difficult aspect of Tocai Friulano cultivation is its thin skin and susceptibility to autumn rains during harvesttime, when ill-timed showers can wreak havoc quickly. Also, according to producers such as Paolo Rodaro and Giorgio Badin, there appear to be two different biotypes of Tocai Friulano, one with very green berries (even when ripe) and a yellow-berried one. The latter is far more common nowadays, and clonal selections have been propagated from it (clone R14 is an example). However, most producers point out that it is the green-berried biotype that has the more intense aromatics. Recently, viticulture expert Carlo Petrussi has described a red-stalked Tocai Friulano biotype (Petrussi 2013).

Tocai Friulano is grown everywhere in Friuli Venezia Giulia and even in nearby Veneto, where the grape is usually called Tocai Italico. There is some Tocai Friulano also growing in Lombardy, mainly near the border with Veneto. This variety seems to be on the upswing outside Italy: in Chile (especially the Central Valley, especially the subregion of Curicó, in particular Teno, Lontué, Entre-Cordilleras, and Andes, but also in other denominations such as San Antonio and Casablanca); in the United States (Napa County, Mendocino County, Santa Maria Valley, Carneros, Santa Ynez Valley, and Finger Lakes); and also in Argentina and New Zealand (D'Agata 2013).

Which Wines to Choose and Why

You'll find Tocai Friulano wines from every Friuli DOC, while in Veneto DOCs such as Piave, Lison-Pramaggiore, and Garda are your best bets. Lombardy wines to look for are Garda Colli Mantovani.

Badin thinks that friulano wines are muscular on their own and don't need oak and other trappings to show well. He laughs when I mention his good friend Gianfranco Gallo, who makes very rich wines: "I've been telling him for years that friulano doesn't need to be aged in small oak barrels or made with selected yeasts: it's best left alone to do its own thing. Though I'll admit one has to be careful with possible off odors developing because of reduction, something the variety is prone to." A good friulano is a pale straw-green, with delicate aromas of white flowers, sweet almonds, and green apple. It can stand up to a judicious oaking, but can be overwhelmed easily by too much vanillin.

Non-Italian Tocai Friulano wines I have found to be very successful include California's Larkmead, Viansa, Palmina, and Jacuzzi Family; New York State's Millbrook; and New Zealand's Balnarring Vineyard.

WINES TO TRY: Borgo del Tiglio*** (the oakaged Ronco della Chiesa is one of Italy's greatest white wines), Ronco del Gelso*** (Toc Bas), Toros***, Vie di Romans*** (Dolé), Cantarutti**, Doro Princic**, Ermacora**, Scarbolo**, Livio Felluga*, Drius*, Dario Raccaro*, and Tomasella*.

Torbato

WHERE IT'S FOUND: Sardinia. NATIONAL REGISTRY CODE NUMBER: 237. COLOR: white.

Torbato is very much a one-region, one-area, and one-estate grape and wine. It has always been associated only with Sardinia and the Sella & Mosca estate and has been known for fresh, light, simple white wines. Also known as Turbat, Razola, Cuscosedda, Trobadu, and Vitis Iberica in the past, it has been grown since ancient times in the area of Alghero. Genetic analysis at twelve SSR loci has demonstrated a relationship to the Portuguese variety Arinto: the two share seventeen alleles in eleven of the twelve loci examined (Nieddu 2011). Also, Lacombe, Boursiquote, Laucou, Dechesne, Varès and This (2007) relate Torbato to the French Malvoisie de Roussillon, now rare in France too.

Viticulturally, Torbato is a difficult variety to work with because it is a late ripener, its berries have thin skins, it tends not to accumulate much sugar when yields are allowed to run too high, and it's easy prey to viruses. It's also a low-acid variety. There are an estimated 135 hectares planted to Torbato, especially in the countryside around Alghero, in northwestern Sardinia (based on 2010 data), though there are some vines in the countryside around Sassari as well. It likes dry, warm weather and calcareous-clay soils, though it gives its best results on the *terre bianche,* chalk-rich soils of marine origin found in and around Alghero.

Which Wines to Choose and Why

The variety is used to make the DOC wine Alghero Torbato, of which there is a sparkling version as well, but often, acidification is necessary because the pH of Torbato musts tends to run high (3.8–4). It has always been associated with the house of Sella and Mosca, who basically make all of Italy's Torbato, with decent to sometimes excellent results. The wine is light and fresh, with very delicate aromas of yellow plums and pear and hints of thyme and pistachio nuts. One needs to pay attention when sipping, though, or torbato's rather delicate charms might pass you by.

WINES TO TRY: Sella & Mosca**** (Terre Bianche is the best version, though the super premium Cuvée 161 is the most important wine made by the estate).

Trebbianos

See TREBBIANO GROUP, chapter 3.

Turca

WHERE IT'S FOUND: Veneto, Trentino. NATIONAL REGISTRY CODE NUMBER: 246. COLOR: red.

Turca is a rare variety grown only in Veneto and Trentino, mainly around the hamlet of Arsiè, west of Feltre near Belluno and in the Valsugana. It was once much more prevalent than it is today; at the end of the 1800s there were roughly two thousand hectoliters of Turca wine produced annually. Apparently, a nursery worker planted it in 1920 in Trento, and finding the wine to his liking, propagated some of the cuttings in his home province of Belluno. Afterward, it was the owner of a wine-distribution company who kept nurturing Turca wines, of which he was a great fan. Giordano Emo Capodilista tells me that the variety was also present in the countryside around Padova in centuries past and that frescoes in his sixteenth-century villa depict the Turca variety; he also wants to give credit for the recent rebirth of the variety in Veneto to a Signore Girardi, who used to work for Proposta Vini; apparently it was he who selected vines in the Vallagarina of Trentino and brought them back to Veneto.

The name Turca refers not to Turkey but to a word in the Trentino dialect meaning hard or heavy, which are also characteristics of the wine made with Turca (it is a dark wine, and while not too tannic, its naturally high acidity makes it seem more tannic than it really is). This cultivar is not to be confused with Puglia's similarly named Turca, which is a table grape, or with Veneto's Turchetta, a very high-quality but also nearly extinct grape that is being studied and groomed for a return to its winemaking destiny. It has been written that Turca is identical to Douce Noire, which is possible given the intense traffic of grapevines from France directed toward northeastern Italy in the eighteenth and nineteenth centuries. Furthermore, it was believed that Piedmont's Dolcetto and Douce Noire were one and the same (they are not), so a local grower who wished to try planting the French grapevine that had been so successful in Piedmont might well have planted Turca instead. (I can just imagine the conversation between grapevine seller and potential buyer: "You must try this variety here—you know, it's the same one they use in Piedmont to make dolcetto..."). In any case, I know of no peer-reviewed study supporting the identity between Douce Noire and Turca; until one exists, I will consider Turca a separate variety, just as it is listed in the National Registry.

Which Wines to Choose and Why

Turca may be found in IGT blends such as Delle Venezie, Veneto, and Vigneti delle Dolomiti. Conte Emo Capodilista is heavily involved in Turca cultivation and is now bottling a table wine called simply Turca, which is the only monovarietal Turca wine I know. It's not the last word in complexity, but an enjoyable wine and one that will match with simply prepared pasta and meat dishes—despite the *turca* name and it's supposed meaning. Angelo Sabbadin, the sommelier at Italy's three-Michelin-star Le Calandre restaurant, and to whom I owe a public thank-you for informing me about this grape now being bottled as a monovarietal wine for the first time, finds the wine interesting. He believes Turca can add complexity to red-wine blends as well as making a good wine on its own, "though I'm not sure such a light-bodied, fresh wine has much of a commercial future. Of course, I'm hoping to be proven wrong." Amen, wine-loving brother.

WINES TO TRY: Conte Emo Capodilista** (Turca; deep ruby-purple, with grapey, plummy aromas, complicated by ink and balsamic reduction, which turns lighter and high acid on the medium-weight frame).

Ucelut

WHERE IT'S FOUND: FVG. NATIONAL REGISTRY CODE NUMBER: 324. COLOR: white.

Ucelut is a rare grape variety, but I find the wine made from it is one of rare potential greatness. Ucelut is another of the *uve uccelline* (bird grapes), sweet grape varieties left to hang on the vine late into the season and often eaten by gluttonous birds. Not much historical information is available on Ucelut, but we know the variety was presented at the 1863 Udine Exhibition, and the following year cultivation was started at the breeding center of the Stabilimento Agro-orticolo (Agricultural-Garden Establishment), with vines selected in the countryside around the villages of Ramuscello and San Giovanni, supposedly the original production areas for this wine. Ucelut is also named in the *Vocabulary of the Friulian Language*, written by Abbott Jacopo Pirona in 1871, which would tend to mean that the variety was thought to be indigenous to the region.

Ucelut appears to have been cultivated throughout the Friuli Venezia Giulia in the nineteenth century, and its wines were made in both a dry and sweet style (especially the latter), as the variety accumulates sugars very easily. It was also believed to give the best results in hillside vineyards, per existing documents relating to the Friulian Antiphylloxera Consortium fair of 1921, where experts such as Francesco Antonio Sannino and Giovanni Dalmasso were among the speakers. The latter described Ucelut's cultivation zone at that time as limited to the countryside around Valeriano, Castelnovo del Friuli, and Pinzano, in the province of Pordenone. Some have postulated that the variety is the result of the domestication of a native wild grapevine, but there is no proof of this. In Bulfon, Forti, and Zuliani's 1987 book devoted to the grape varieties of the Spilimbergo zone, they report that in the nineteenth century Ucelut was very important for socioeconomic and cultural reasons to the people of San Vito al Tagliamento, Castelnovo del Friuli, and other nearby towns in the Pordenone province.

Clearly, neither I nor anyone else would not be able to write about any wine made from Ucelut had it not been for the passion of one man, Emilio Bulfon, a graduate in agriculture/enology who moved to the Spilimbergo hills near Pordenone in the 1970s and single-handedly retrieved many cultivars that had been completely abandoned. Thanks to his dedication, plus the help of important Friuli men of wine such as Orfeo Salvador, longtime director of the experimental research arm of the government's agriculture division, the indigenous varieties of Spilimbergo and immediately surrounding areas such as Ucelut were admitted to the National Registry in 1991. Years ago, Bulfon told me that if it hadn't been for the disinterested help of people such as Ruggero Forti (then director of the Rauscedo nursery) and Antonio Calò (then head of the Enology School in Conegliano), he would have been unable to succeed in saving Ucelut and other local grapes (D'Agata 2003b).

Ucelut is characterized by medium-large, tightly packed, pyramidal bunches and large round berries that have thick skins. It ripens in late September but more often in early October. There are no official clones available. Ucelut's modern-day production zone is not too different from that of the early twentieth century, as the variety is still found only in the province of Pordenone, close to Friuli Venezia Giulia's western border with Veneto. It has much larger berries than Picolit and Verduzzo, the varieties that give Friuli Venezia Giulia two other great sweet wines.

Which Wines to Choose and Why

Ucelut is rarely used in IGT blends such as Delle Venezia and Venezia Giulia. Good ucelut made from late-harvested grapes is a wonderful dessert wine that is not overly sweet and not too full-bodied, though some estates have turned to air-drying the grapes and making a much richer, sweeter wine. Aromas and flavors of ripe citrus, pineapple, and sweet almonds are common in lighter, fresher wines made in the former style, while sweet almonds, acacia honey, ripe mango, and dried apricot are common in the latter version. The non air-dried version is perfect with shellfish and vegetable or simply prepared fish dishes; both versions are much less sweet than picolit and much less tannic than verduzzo or Ramandolo. Again, it's one of Italy's least-known wines and yet could be one of its best. I really hope more estates will explore producing an ucelut in the years to come. There is no DOC, and so the only wines available are generic *vino da tavola* or IGT. Though production volumes are still small, don't miss out on potentially great wines next time you vacation in Italy.

WINES TO TRY: Florutis** (the only almost dry ucelut listed here), Vicentini Orgnani**, Ronco Cliona** (owned by the Maley family, former expatriates in Hong Kong who moved to northern Italy to devote themselves to local indigenous grape varieties; their first winemaker was none other than Emilio Bulfon), Tenuta Pinni** (in an attractive seventeenth-century villa; grapes are air-dried for six months, making an ucelut that resembles a Ramandolo more than it does the other uceluts here; it's also more alcoholic and thicker), and Bulfon**. There is also apparently a wine labeled ucelut delle Venezie by Vigneti Torre Orientale, of the Pecol Boin winery in Tauriano di Spilimbergo, but I have not yet tasted it.

Uva del Tundè

WHERE IT'S FOUND: Emilia-Romagna. NATIONAL REGISTRY CODE NUMBER: 436. COLOR: red.

The ongoing rediscovery of all but forgotten native Italian grape varieties is exemplified by Uva del Tundè, an extremely rare variety grown in the countryside around Ravenna in Emilia-Romagna. Buoyed by enthusiasm and interest in native Italian grapes (as well as the potential financial returns for both individuals and local economies), roughly thirty years ago the Vitigni Minori project was launched and financed by the Regione Emilia-Romagna, with the objective of identifying and characterizing local native cultivars. The morphologic and genetic studies performed identified many native varieties and in particular, Uva del Tundè (also rarely called Uve del Tondini), now included in the National Registry. The name appears to derive from a farmer named Primo Tondini (del Tundè means "of Tundè," or "of Tondini"), who first selected, or discovered, the variety in his vineyards between 1932 and 1956. His daughter Ines then continued her father's work with passion and energy, continuing to grow the variety on her estate, and today all us wine lovers can only thank them for their efforts. Fontana, Filippetti, Intrieri, and Pastore (2007) proved it to be distinct from other varieties listed at the time in the National Registry based on ampelographic, isoenzymatic, and molecular analysis. Genetic analysis hints that Uva del Tundè may be related to Calabria's Magliocco Canino, with which it appears to share alleles at many loci (thirteen out of twenty examined).

The variety is characterized by a medium-sized, cylindrical-pyramidal bunch and medium to medium-small, round berries. It has very strong vigor and a high basal fertility.

Which Wines to Choose and Why

Currently, the wine is produced only in Romagna and can be used in IGT blends such as Dell'Emilia, Forlì, Ravenna, and Rubicone. The wine is deep ruby-purple and has complex aromas of red berries (strawberry, raspberry) and hints of underbrush, with juicy, fruity flavors and smooth tannins on the midweight finish.

WINES TO TRY: Sbarzaglia** (Silente, the entry-level wine, and Sospiro, the *riserva*). Some wine is also bottled by the Tondini family, at their bed-and-breakfast, Azdora.

Uva di Troia

WHERE IT'S FOUND: Puglia. NATIONAL REGISTRY CODE NUMBER: 247. COLOR: red.

The correct name for this cultivar is Uva di Troia, as listed in the National Registry and as written in the first published guide to Italy's native grapes and wines (D'Agata, Sabellico, Aiello, Arru, Buffa, Di Cintio, et al. 2003), though Nero di Troia has taken hold in the twenty-first century (more often used to indicate the wine). This variety is another sterling example of what the renewed interest in native grapes has meant for wine lovers and producers, with a considerable intellectual, hedonistic, and financial windfall for everyone involved. When I was co-writing the Puglia section of the *Gambero Rosso* annual wine guide at the beginning of the twenty-first century, along with soul and drinking mates Paolo Zaccaria and Marco Sabellico of the Gambero, the rise to prominence of Uva di Troia and its wines was all too obvious. If memory serves, in 2001 there were only about two or three Uva di Troia wines presented in the regional preliminary blind tastings I was co-leading for the guide. In 2002 there were six or seven, and so I suggested we create our first-ever blind tasting series of only Uva di Troia wines, though not all were convinced it was worth the time and energy to do so. However, only one year later, in 2003 the Uva di Troia bottlings sent to us were legion, and Sabellico and Zaccaria were the first in line in creating a section of Uva di Troia wines to be tasted blind!

Uva di Troia is now used to make an ever-increasing number of monovarietal wines or blends of all types, even *rosati* and white wines. Importantly, it adds considerable finesse and freshness to wines containing Primitivo, Montepulciano, or Negro Amaro, one of the reasons it was always viewed as a good blending grape. In the process, Uva di Troia has contributed to economic growth in Puglia's Castel del Monte area, known mainly for its weird yet wonderful octagonal Templar castle built by King Federico II. Today, everyone in Italy associates Castel del Monte with Uva di Troia, a situation analogous to the identification of Sicily with Nero d'Avola. And as an added bonus, the bright lights that have shined on Uva di Troia have also lit up interest in Bombino Bianco and Bombino Nero, two other local natives used to make lovely wines that were, in my view, grossly underestimated prior to Uva di Troia's rise to fame (and in fact, I believe they still are, to an extent).

Legend has it that Uva di Troia got its name, and arrived on Puglia's northern shores, thanks to Diomedes, king of Argo and best friend of Ulysses, who like that well-traveled fellow fought in the Trojan War. Apparently, Diomedes later busied himself with other endeavors, such as traveling with Uva di Troia vines in his suitcase. I'm certainly not going to be the one to downplay that theory, if for no other reason than because some wines made mainly with Uva di Troia (witness Rivera's Il Falcone 1953 or 1955) are pretty legendary in their own right. However, I will point out that it's a bit more likely that the grape's name derived either from the small town of Troia (near Foggia, in northern Puglia) or from Cruja, the small town in Albania just across the sea from Puglia and where the grape may in fact have come from. Another theory is that the variety is an ancient import from Spain's Rioja, though to the best of my knowledge there is no variety resembling Uva di Troia in that famous wine region today.

The earliest official mention of Uva di Troia dates back to 1854, when the Pavoncelli estate opted to plant their lands in northern Puglia with "the indigenous Uva di Troia, robust, drought resistant and fairly productive, that gives strong blending wines" (Antonacci 2004). Blends have always been a way of life for this variety: Trojan horse–like, Uva di Troia has always been used to add an extra something, a surprising touch (usually grace and refinement, and when produced from excessive yields, extra high-acid juice), to add another dimension to wines. Many other famous ampelographers described Uva di Troia as well, from Di Rovasenda (1877) to Vialà and Vermorel (1901–10), all pointing to the quality of the wine made with it and its important role in the blends Rosso Barletta, Rosso Cerignola, and Rosso Canosa, which though less famous nowadays are still being made. For Italians, the grape is apparently also linked to an important historical moment that all children learn about in school, the Disfida di Barletta (or the Barletta Challenge). On February 13, 1503, during a war between France and Spain, thirteen Italian soldiers (fighting at that time for Spain) squared off against thirteen French ones, after the French captain, the nobleman Charles de Torgue, nicknamed Monsieur Guy de la Motte, had unwisely mocked the valor of Italian soldiers in battle at a banquet. Needless to say, in those less bureaucratic times things were resolved on the battlefield, and the Italians soundly defeated their French opponents (and perhaps this is why all of us in Italy get to hear about this event in school); rumor had it that the French defeat was to be ascribed partly to their having spent too much time in a Barletta tavern, overindulging in the merits of Rosso Barletta.

Uva di Troia is known by many synonyms (though only Nero di Troia is used regularly): for example, Barlettana, Somarella, Uva di Barletta, and Uva di Canosa. The clones available are UBA 49/G, UBA 49/M, VCR 1, UBA 52/N, UBA 53/N. More important, there exist two well-recognized biotypes of this variety: the Barletta (also called di Ruvo) and the Canosa. The two are very different, with the former having larger, loosely packed bunches and larger berries, and the latter smaller, cylindrical bunches with smaller berries. The Canosa biotype is now very hard to find, as the former's greater proclivity for large yields made it the preferential choice of farmers when they planted new vineyards. However, recent field selections and clonal research have all looked to the rarer variety, as it gives the better wines. According to Count Onofrio Spagnoletti Zeuli of the Spagnoletti Zeuli estate, the Canosa biotype is still present in many old vineyards around Andria, whereas it has disappeared around Barletta, "where historically they only wanted to make high volumes of wine. I believe that both are useful, and best blended together. The Canosa gives color and structure; the Barletta biotype adds perfume and freshness."

Everyone agrees that Uva di Troia hardly produces a relaxing time in the vineyards. Sebastiano De Corato of the well-respected Rivera estate mentions that "it takes extremely long to ripen properly; while it's the first red variety to turn color, it's the latest to reach optimal ripeness and before it ever gets there, the Barletta or large-berried biotype almost always rots on the vine, so people tend to harvest this biotype early, when it still doesn't always have fully ripe polyphenols. For this reason, many choose to use it for *rosato* production, but it's a mistake, for Uva di Troia is not ideal for *rosato* production, being a low-acid cultivar." Spagnoletti Zeuli is even more harsh: "It's a pain. The fact is that the variety sunburns easily, can't take the hot *favonio* wind typical of our area; it has low acidity and so you can't deleaf much, plus it's extremely sensitive to oidium, plus the different bunches never ripen in unison, so the workers have to pass through the vines time and again, a huge expense. I'll admit, though, that it does give the most elegant red wines in all of Puglia, perhaps all of Italy's south." Leonardo Palumbo, winemaker at Rivera, adds only that "with the new generation of grapevine material, at least the ripening has become a bit more uniform; but it does have markedly hard tannins, and its color isn't the deepest."

Uva di Troia has enjoyed a remarkable ride in the last twenty years: like many stagehands, this native variety has toiled in the background for centuries, but its moment has finally come. No longer relegated to being the surprise additive to red wine blends from Puglia, but now a main actor in its own right, it has forced Primitivo and Negro Amaro, forever blessed with leading roles on the Puglia wine scene, to share the applause with their northern colleague.

Which Wines to Choose and Why

Uva di Troia is grown practically only in Puglia, where it is part of the DOC blends Rosso Canosa (65 percent Uva di Troia minimum), Rosso Barletta (70–100 percent Uva di Troia minimum), Castel del Monte Rosso (a blend of Uva di Troia, Montepulciano, and Aglianico, with a maximum 35 percent other varieties), and other now less common DOC wines such as Cacc' e Mmitte di Lucera, Orta Nova, and Rosso di Cerignola. The latter wine was once very famous, thanks mainly to the Pavoncelli estate of Cerignola: I have been surprised over the years at how fondly locals remember and have spoken to me about it. In fact, the Istituto Tecnico Agrario of Cerignola (where the University of Foggia holds a satellite course in *scienza della produzione e marketing agroalimentare*) was named in the noble family's honor. The institute has a vineyard where they make award-winning wines with local cultivars such as Uva di Troia. *Cru* areas for Uva di Troia are Santa Maria and Tafuri. Of all Uva di Troia wines, only the Castel del Monte is easy to find, even in Italy—unless you're visiting Puglia. At roughly eighteen hundred hectares, Uva di Troia is the third most-planted red grape variety in the region. It also characterizes the red wine production of a specific part of Puglia: just as Negro Amaro is synonymous with the provinces of Lecce and Brindisi in southern Puglia (the Salento), and Primitivo with the province of Taranto in central Puglia, so Uva di Troia typifies the wine offerings of the province of Foggia and the uppermost part of Bari Province in the northern and north-central sections of the region.

A good Uva di Troia wine will remind you of red cherries, red currants, black pepper, tobacco, and underbrush and will strike you for its sleek midweight texture, high but balanced acids, and very refined tannins. The wine is never a blockbuster, but rather an exercise in equilibrium: think Marcello Mastroianni, Cary Grant, or Hugh Grant, not the bodybuilders in your gym. It is very different from the richer, alcoholic primitivos or the at times rustic, leathery Negro Amaro wines made all over the region.

WINES TO TRY: Rivera*** (Puer Apuliae and Il Falcone, the latter a Castel del Monte and so not pure Uva di Troia), D'Alfonso del Sordo*** (Gualdo San Leo), Alberto Longo*** (Le Cruste), Vigne di Rasciatano** (Rasciatano),

Cefalicchio* (Rosso Canosa, also the very good Rosato Ponte della Lama), and Villa Schinosa.

Uvalino

WHERE IT'S FOUND: Piedmont. NATIONAL REGISTRY CODE NUMBER: 370. COLOR: red.

This very rare cultivar is also known as Lambrusca or Lambruschino in the Roero, which is unfortunate, as these varieties are unrelated and distinct, though perhaps reasonable enough in that Uvalino, like the *Lambrusco* varieties, is a very hardy, rustic cultivar. It is also unrelated to Lambrusca di Alessandria, another native variety of Piedmont that is also distinct from the better-known *Lambrusco*s of Emilia-Romagna. In reality, Uvalino is the name used for this variety in the Astigiano, while in the Canavese it is called Curnaiola; and while I find that Uvalino looks a little like Neretto di Marengo (yet another rare Piedmontese variety), the two are also distinct (Uvalino has an obviously much longer bunch, is less loosely packed, and has smaller leaves). A recent study analyzed nuclear microsatellites on several grapes from Piedmont, all named variations on Lambrusca or Lambrusco, including Uvalino (or Lambruschino), Lambrusca di Alessandria, Lambrusca Vittona, and Lambruschetto (Torello Marinoni, Raimondi, Boccacci, and Schneider 2006). Twenty SSR loci were used for DNA typing, and the genetic profiles were compared to those of other grapes from Piedmont and of the well-known *Lambrusco*s from Emilia-Romagna. The results showed first-degree parentage relationships between Uvalino and Neretto di Marengo, but the *Lambrusco*s from Emilia-Romagna were genetically distant.

We have a beautiful and sweet lady to thank for the opportunity to taste and drink an uvalino today. Maria Borio, owner of the Cascina Castlèt in Piedmont, at Costigliole d'Asti, a person for whom time seems to have stood still ("everyone on my mother's side seems to live forever, ninety plus and more," she laughs), began working at the family estate in the 1970s and has gone from one success to another. "It's a nice story," she tells me. "I remember that the Uvalino harvest was always one big party, it was the last grape we picked, around November 11 for the San Martino feast ... there wasn't much of it, but all the local families owned a row or two of it and so we all used to get together and just make a fun day of it." However, Uvalino was far from being an afterthought or a game: everyone considered uvalino a very important and high-quality wine (no doubt in part due to its rarity), and it was added to other wines to supply backbone and power. In an example of how truly enlightened Borio is, her estate still sponsors scholarships for enology graduates who are interested in studying Uvalino. "It's also an extremely resistant variety. We have left it to air-dry well into February, and it never rots," she says.

According to Borio, who has studied Uvalino long and hard, first with the help of Professor Corino (then director of the Istituto Sperimentale Enologia di Asti) and then with other luminaries, Uvalino belongs to a family of grapes once known as *uvari*, or "uve rare" (rare grapes). The name of the grape was actually Uvarino; in the local Astigiano dialect, the *r* is rarely if ever pronounced, and hence Uvalino is the way everyone refers to it, though it's not technically correct. The *-ino* ending, however, is *not* a diminutive, for there is very little *-ino* about this grape. In fact, Uvalino yields high-acid, brutally tannic wines that are quite a mouthful. Unfortunately, Uvalino fell out of favor mainly because of its very late ripening season (as much as twenty or thirty days after all the other local grapes), which made it more difficult to work with: obviously, local farmers preferred working with other grapes that more or less could all be picked at the same time.

Though Borio is the main producer of Uvalino today, she is quick to point out that many other producers have tried their hand at it too; for example, the great, late Renato Ratti planted it at Villa Pattono. "But I don't know what it came to," she wonders. Nevertheless, Borio's faith never wavered. Even though Uvalino wasn't an allowed variety when she started working with it in the 1980s (thus all the wine could be was a lowly *vino da tavola*, much like Sassicaia in its early days), she persisted and completed all the bureaucratic paperwork and met all the viticultural and enological requirements so that the variety was officially included in the National Registry in 2002.

One November evening, many years ago, after a hard day's night of driving nonstop all over the region, tasting Piedmontese reds in cellars dotting the countryside, I suddenly remembered to ask Maria what I'd always wanted to and had managed to forget each time: Why? Why does someone who has experienced so much success with her many other wines get involved in a new venture that took so much time, money, and energy, with a wine that is tough as nails and admittedly not going to be a darling of the majority? Maria flashed me her calm smile and said softly, "I like it; and because in this way I leave memories."

Which Wines to Choose and Why

Uvalino only grows in the Astigiano and mainly around Costigliole d'Asti. The wine is a Monferrato Rosso, and the only producer of note (and whose wine you are most likely to find, as they make about five thousand bottles a year) is Cascina Castlèt. In order for Uvalino to give good results, the grapes have to be air-dried, and at least thirty days are best. Without air-drying it tends to have too light a color and the tannins are really tough. The wine is normally deeply hued, with aromas of sweet spices and blackberries (though I wouldn't say the somewhat neutral nose is this wine's strong suit) and an amazingly high-acid, tannic mouthfeel but with enough bright, small dark-berry fruit so as not to make the experience painful.

WINES TO TRY: Cascina Castlèt** (Uceline).

Uva Longanesi

WHERE IT'S FOUND: Emilia-Romagna. NATIONAL REGISTRY CODE NUMBER: 357. COLOR: red.

Uva Longanesi is one of Italy's most recently discovered varieties, having come to prominence only in 1933, when Aldo Longanesi noted a very gnarly old vine in a field on his property on via Boncellino in Bagnacavallo, unlike any other he had ever seen. In the 1950s, Longanesi decided to try and make a wine from those grapes and was pleasantly surprised by the result—so surprised, that he decided to plant a whole vineyard to the variety, though part of his intent was also to use the intensely colored and alcoholic wine made with Uva Longanesi to spike the other estate wines made at that time, like the one made with Fortana. Nowadays, the grape variety is also called Burson, as this was the nickname of the Longanesi family, to whom credit must be given if we are able to talk about Uva Longanesi, and taste the wines. Though Burson is also included in the name of a local producers' association named Consorzio del Burson di Bagnacavallo, I stress that the officially recognized name of the variety is Uva Longanesi.

Some experts have hypothesized a Spanish origin for Uva Longanesi, but I have seen no hard evidence of this; most believe the variety is the result of the domestication of an ancient wild species or perhaps a natural crossing between a wild grapevine and a cultivated one. Certainly, a look at the grapevine and a taste of the wines lends credence to the ancient wild grapevine theory. The bunch and berries are medium-large; the bunch is conical-pyramidal, and the berries round, with thick skins. There is one clone available, Ampelos DGV 1.

In any case, Uva Longanesi looks similar but is different from Negretto, another rare local red native variety that has recently come under study. Uva Longanesi is grown over roughly two hundred hectares, mainly around Bagnacavallo, Cotignola, Fusignano, Godo, Lugo, and Russi in the Romagna portion of Emilia-Romagna, near the cities of Faenza and Ravenna.

Which Wines to Choose and Why

Uva Longanesi can be used in different IGT blends, including dell'Emilia, Forlì, Ravenna, and Rubicone. The wine is always very full-bodied, strong, and tannic, similar to a barbera or Aglianico but with even more gravitas and weight. Uva Longanesi wines aren't for the faint of heart, as it doesn't have a wealth of fresh fruity aromas but rather plenty of evolved, almost tertiary aromas such as tobacco, underbrush, and tar. The wine needs plenty of time in the cellar, as the hard tannins soften very slowly. Most producers have told me that only after seven years of bottle age do the tannins tend to become more civilized, and even air-drying the grapes doesn't help soften the tactile sensation of a burson much. The tannins risk being green even in the warmest, downright hot years (and the fact that some people blend cabernet sauvignon with burson makes no sense to me whatsoever). The wine does exude very intense black cherry and plum aromas and flavors. For these reasons, the burson association differentiates between a burson *etichetta nera* (black label), made at least partly from late-harvested grapes (at least 50 percent of the grapes have to be air-dried or late harvested, and the wine has to spend a minimum of eighteen months in barrel), and the *etichetta blu* (blue label), which is a fresher, readier to drink style of burson, in which a minimum of 40 percent of the grapes undergo carbonic maceration, much as in the style of Beaujolais Nouveau. The intent to tame burson's naturally overly-tannic tendency is all too obvious.

WINES TO TRY: Daniele Longanesi***, Celti Centurioni**, Tenuta Uccellina**, Francesco Tonini**, Massimo Randi**, and Spinetta**.

Uva Rara

WHERE IT'S FOUND: Piedmont, Lombardy. NATIONAL REGISTRY CODE NUMBER: 248. COLOR: red.

In the never-ending fun provided by Italy's native grapes, Uva Rara is also erroneously called Bonarda Novarese and Croatina, distinct varieties. The name Uva Rara derives from the variety's extremely sparse or loosely packed bunch, which makes this cultivar practically immune to botrytis and ideal for air-drying (Uva Rara literally translates to "rare grape," meaning rare grapes on the bunch). Uva Rara is characterized by bunches of various sizes even on the same grapevine, though they are usually medium-large and pyramidal or conical. A vigorous variety, it is resistant to peronospora and less to oidium, but is unfortunately very subject to *millerandage*, apparently more so in the Oltrepò Pavese area than in the Novara-Vercelli area (Dalmasso, Cacciatore, and Corte 1962). It ripens very late in the season (a November harvest used to be common in less climate change-challenged times); in fact, locals had a habit of eating Uva Rara grapes for Christmas. Its suitability for air-drying is historically why people in Italy would hang the grapes in well-ventilated areas of the house or the stable and then would eat them all winter long, when other fruits were hard to come by. Nowadays, this characteristic is advantageous for making sweet wines. Very interestingly, Christoph Künzli of the high-quality Le Piane estate in Boca, who is not a fan of Uva Rara, says its big round berries make it look like a table grape, which really ought to be its destination, as far as he's concerned.

Uva Rara's presence has been documented in Piedmont and Lombardy since at least the ninth century, but unfortunately even important, knowledgeable ampelographers of the past, such as Di Rovasenda (1877) and Molon (1906), confused Croatina, Bonarda, and Uva Rara, describing one as the other.

Which Wines to Choose and Why

Uva Rara is very abundant in Lombardy, especially in the Oltrepò Pavese area in the province of Pavia (where they even use it to make *rosato* and *novello* wine, the latter Italy's version of *nouveau* wines). It is also especially found in northeastern Piedmont and in smaller amounts in the Astigiano and Alessandrino areas. Therefore, the wines usually are from either the Oltrepò Pavese or Piedmont's Colline Novaresi. In the Oltrepò Pavese, the three highest-quality areas are Rovescala, Buttafuoco, and Casteggio. They differ mainly in soil composition: mainly clay, marl, and sandy-gravel, respectively. The Valle di Recoaro and the Val Maga at Broni, where the famous Barbacarlo is made, can be considered the true *grand cru* of the Oltrepò Pavese for the red wines. These valleys are very tight, stuck down deep between two cliffs, with poorly fertile, rocky soils and very large day-night temperature variations due to nighttime cold air currents that are always sweeping through. This unique microclimate explains the greatness of the wines. Künzli states flatly that Uva Rara is of no interest in Boca (the northeastern portion of Piedmont), as the wine produced is neutral and insipid; though it can be used to make everyday simple wines. Not everyone in the area agrees with this view, however.

The most famous wine in which Uva Rara is used is Ghemme, though Boca and Sizzano are also well thought of. These are most often blends; pure Uva Rara wines are very rare, but not unheard of. There have also always been monovarietal wines, just like with Vespolina, the other main native grape of the areas where Uva Rara grows. Uva Rara has traditionally been used to make a fresh everyday table wine in areas where bigger, full-bodied wines were already available, such as the wines from Gattinara or Boca in Piedmont and the many cabernet-merlots of the Oltrepò. A pure Uva Rara wine is bright dark-ruby in color, but without the purple tinges that are far more typical of wines made solely with Vespolina. The aroma is usually very complex, with hints of red roses, violet, red, almost black cherries, and raspberries and sweet spices. The wine always comes across as very fresh, high acid, and vibrantly tannic, but it never has much power or structure. One limit I find to Uva Rara wines is that they do not have the magical perfume exuded by pure vespolinas, but, in the end, that may just be a matter of personal taste.

WINES TO TRY: Antico Borgo dei Cavalli** (Spumante Curticelli Rosè and Lea, the former a sparkling wine), and Francesco Brigatti**. From the Oltrepò Pavese, try: Frecciarossa** and Podere Il Santo* (Rairon).

Verdea

WHERE IT'S FOUND: Lombardy, Emilia-Romagna, Tuscany. NATIONAL REGISTRY CODE NUMBER: 251. COLOR: white.

A little-known grape, Verdea has plenty to offer wine lovers, though you'd never guess it by some of the neutral, insipid stuff that's bottled. A good Verdea wine will surprise more than one wine expert who may never have heard of it. In 1495 Pier de' Crescenzi referred to it as Verdea, and many expert ampelographers of the past confused this grape with Puglia's Verdeca, Tuscany's Vernaccia di San Gimignano, and still other varieties. Today it is still commonly called San Colombana, Colombana Bianca, or Colombana, especially in Tuscany (in honor of the so-named Irish saint who supposedly introduced the variety into the region), where locals also call it Colombana di Peccioli. However Di Rovasenda (1877) believed that the various *Colombana*s were distinct from the *San Colombana* grapes, and that both were large families of grapes rather than just one grape, though we have no knowledge of that distinction today. In Tuscany and Emilia-Romagna Verdea is better known as a table grape (though it is used in blends to make at times very good wines, especially sweet Vin Santo), while in Lombardy it has always been used to make wines.

Some modern experts, such as Roberto Bandinelli of the University of Florence, believe the Verdea of Lombardy to be distinct from that of Tuscany, and they have plenty of morphological evidence to back up these impressions. There is also a Verdea grown in Emilia-Romagna. It is very similar to the Tuscan Malvasia Bianca Lunga but has a stocky bunch with no wings and remains green even when ripe, while, as its name implies, Malvasia Bianca Lunga has a long bunch and at least one if not two wings. San Colombano has a big bunch and an elongated berry. So, according to Bandinelli, none of these varieties really looks anything like the others, save for the fact they all sport green berries (hence the name Verdea, from *verde,* or green). I am not aware of any definitive genetic studies on the matter, so it looks like we will stay in the dark for a while, until someone gives us a green light ahead. The studies that have thus far addressed Verdea have in fact only muddled the picture further. One found Verdea to be identical to Sangiovese Forte (the name the researchers used; Sanforte is the official name), but this seems strange, at the very least because this would mean that one variety is a color mutation of the other (Di Vecchi Staraz, Bandinelli, Boselli, This, Boursiquot, Laucou, et al. 2007). That genetic profiling is not the answer to all of our grape-related problems is evidenced by the fact that earlier research found that Sangiovese and Sangiovese Forte were identical, which most everyone today believes they are not (Filipetti, Intrieri, Centinari, Bucchetti, and Pastore 2005).

Verdea has a conical-pyramidal, medium-large bunch, with large, oval berries. It ripens late in September or in early October and is very resistant to botrytis. There is one clone, the VCR 115. It is grown mainly in the provinces of Pisa in Tuscany and in Milan, Piacenza, and Pavia in Lombardy.

Which Wines to Choose and Why

The wine to look for is Collina Milanese, an IGT in which up to 15 percent Riesling and Trebbiano Toscano are allowed. Consequently, there are some Verdea bottlings that are amazingly steely and mineral, and I always wonder just how much Riesling found its way into the wine. In fairness, however, Verdea does make for very steely, mineral, and floral dry wines. Do not confuse the variety with the DOC San Colombano al Lambro, which are red wine blends made with large percentages of Croatina. Other IGT blends it is used in are Castelfranco dell'Emilia, Costa Toscana, Ravenna, and Rubicone.

A good dry Verdea wine will remind you of green apples and white flowers. It's a very light, thin wine that serves well as an aperitif or to accompany light vegetable and fish dishes. Excellent wines can be the sweet ones, made by air-drying the grapes: in this case, the wine is a very deep yellow-gold hue, rich in honey, tropical-fruit, and candied-pear flavors, with a thick, rich mouthfeel—usually very sweet and impressive.

WINES TO TRY: From Lombardy, try: Nettare dei Santi** (outstanding Passito di Verdea; also good dry still wine simply labeled Verdea; the La Tonsa, though a good sparkling wine, is made with 15 percent other white grapes), Pietrasanta* (lovely dry sparkling white), and Panizzari*. From Emilia-Romagna, try: La Pergola** (Passito Solis).

Verdeca

WHERE IT'S FOUND: Puglia, Campania. NATIONAL REGISTRY CODE NUMBER: 252. COLOR: white.

Of uncertain origin, Verdeca is one of Italy's many grapes named after the green color of its berries, and many of the variety's synonyms also recall this trait (though many are erroneous and should not be used). A recent study announced that Verdeca is identical to Pampanuto, another well-known variety of northern Puglia (while Verdeca is more typical of central Puglia) (Pirolo, La Notte, Pastore, Torello Marinoni, Giannini, Venerito, et al. 2009). I'm not sure what to think of this, since I don't think the two varieties look at all alike, and the wines couldn't be any more different (see PAMPANUTO entry). I would caution that further testing is needed, also because the paper analyzed only forty-nine OIV ampelographic descriptors (eighty-three is usually the minimum number required); and though nine SSR microsatellite loci were studied, perhaps a few more would help make the identification more certain (in general, closely related varieties require study of more SSR loci, for more precise identification). Another study showed that the Verdeca × Primitivo (Tribidrag) crossing gave us the

Plavina variety (Lacombe, Boursiquot, Laoucou, Dechesne, Varès, and This 2007).

Historically, Verdeca was used in the production of vermouth, a popular aperitif in twentieth-century Italy, and wasn't used to make much wine of note at all. What was turned into vermouth was blended with Bianco d'Alessano to make the Locorotondo white wine—cheap, cheerful, and nothing more. Verdeca has a conical bunch with medium-large, oval berries, and is productive and resistant to most diseases. It is grown especially in central Puglia, in the provinces of Bari and Taranto, and in the countryside around Alberobello, Crispiano, Locorotondo, and Martina Franca.

Which Wines to Choose and Why

In the last few years, Verdeca has been increasingly used to make monovarietal wines of some distinction, and some are promising. I'm not sure that all the wines are 100 percent Verdeca, but they are very enjoyable and bright and have given the variety a new lease on life: if they don't quite grant it entry into the big leagues, at least they get it close. Given enough time, any native variety with some potential can blast back from a nondescript past to possible wine stardom.

Verdeca was, and is, almost always used in blends with Bianco d'Alessano to make the DOC wines Locorotondo and Martina. It can also be part of the blend of the DOC Lacryma Christi of Campania. The wine is fresh and crisp, with delicately herbal and green-apple flavors. Some producers choose to blend it with aromatic varieties such as Minutolo: this is not a good idea in my view, as the delicate Verdeca presence is all but lost.

WINES TO TRY: I Pastini-Lino Carparelli*** (Faraone; dry and taut, with a laser beam of acidity, delicate white fruit, and herbal aromas and flavors), Leone de Castris** (Messapia; excellent and a huge success, with a delicate spiciness reminiscent of Incrocio Manzoni Bianco or even a high-quality Ribolla Gialla wine), Masseria Ludovico** (Occhio di Sole), Li Veli* (Askos), Rosa del Golfo* (Bolina, with 80 percent Verdeca, 20 percent Chardonnay; I'd get rid of the latter, but the wine is crisp fresh, a real success), Feudi di San Marzano* (Sud), and Feudi Salentini (Luporano). These last two are reportedly made with 100 percent Verdeca.

Verdello

WHERE IT'S FOUND: Umbria, Tuscany, Lazio. NATIONAL REGISTRY CODE NUMBER: 253. COLOR: white.

Though Verdello is just one of many grape varieties in Italy so called because of its green berries, it was always believed to be unrelated to other green grapes such as Verdeca, Verdicchio, or Verduzzo. Also rarely called Duropersico, Verdetto has also been used as a synonym for Verdello, but not all I have talked to over the years believe that these two are identical. Its presence is first mentioned around Orvieto in the nineteenth century and then by Molon (1906), and some researchers today hypothesize a similarity, or at least a relationship, to Portugal's Verdelho, but this remains unproven. Recently, Crespan, Armanni, Da Rold, De Nardi, Gardiman, Migliaro, et al. (2012) studied twenty-five accessions of Verdicchio, Verdello, and Verduschia genotyped at eleven SSR markers, and because only one DNA profile was obtained for all twenty-five accessions, they logically concluded that the three varieties are identical. I have no doubt that this is so, but as there are myriad green-named grape varieties in Italy today, I find it hard to extrapolate this to all other varieties with similar names grown in the country. And while Verduschia is rare enough that its shared identity with Verdicchio is easier to accept, the plethora of Verdello-named grapes out there recommends caution, because it may be that there are "Verdello" grapevines that are not Verduschia or Verdicchio. For example, Cartechini and Moretti (1989) do not believe that the Verdicchio of the Marche and Verdello are the same cultivar.

As there are many different-looking Verdello grapevines, I'm afraid that DNA profiling of a very large number of accessions will be necessary to establish definitive identities. Certainly there appear to be at the very least different biotypes of Verdello: one particularly high-quality biotype is found in the area hugging the border between Umbria and Lazio, and another good one grows in Tuscany's lower Maremma region. Two clones are also available: V 27 ICA-PG and VCR 1. Stefano Grilli, of the esteemed La Palazzola estate in Umbria, believes that the grape probably first arrived with some Hungarian monks in the mid-nineteenth century, who were moving to the Franciscan Sant' Urbano monastery near his estate. Verdello's popularity then took off, as it is a dependable and abundant producer and does not succumb easily to disease, though in Umbria it appears to be prone to grey rot. Overall, Verdello is a very late ripening variety (October) and is always blessed with high natural acidity.

On the Tuscan coast, the problem for Verdello is that it has had to fight Vermentino's huge popularity, and so producers there all prefer to make vermentino rather than verdello, since the former will sell much better. Which is not to say that this is as it should be, since a well-made verdello has plenty to offer.

Which Wines to Choose and Why
Verdello grows in Umbria and Tuscany, along the latter's coastline; it appears to grow particularly well in clay-rich soils. Wines to look for are DOC Orvieto, Bianco di Pitigliano, Colli Amerini, Colli del Trasimeno, and Torgiano Bianco; the variety is almost always used in blends, and a pure verdello is rare. This is a shame, for over the years I have tasted some outstanding examples of Verdello wine, and the grape has a lot to say. The wine is less saline than vermentino, with riper, fruitier aromas and flavors (green apple, ripe pear, citrus, white flowers, and a hint of chlorophyll). It is always simple and fresh, but with a lot more character than you might think.

WINES TO TRY: La Palazzola*** and Cantina di Pitigliano** (Duropersico).

Verdicchio

WHERE IT'S FOUND: Marche, Veneto, Lombardy, Lazio. NATIONAL REGISTRY CODE NUMBER: 254. COLOR: white.

Verdicchio is arguably Italy's greatest native white grape variety. That statement may come as a surprise to those who have tried only neutral or watery Verdicchio wines, at times even bottled in improbable amphora-shaped bottles. Paradoxically, these latter wines vividly illustrate Verdicchio's potential, as wine bottled in such a ludicrously shaped vessel has no business being as good as it actually is. Verdicchio is used to produce all kinds of wines, from dry to sweet to sparkling, though the best are dry, some of which can easily age ten or more years. It is also most probably the one Italian native white grape whose wines have the greatest affinity with oak aging; most wines made with Italian native cultivars are overwhelmed by overenthusiastic oak use. The only other white varieties in Italy that can match Verdicchio's versatility and potential for great wines are Veneto's Garganega (with which Soave and Recioto di Soave are made) and Campania's Fiano.

Verdicchio is one of the many Italian varieties named for its color, in this case the very obviously green *(verde)* tinged berries. Other less common synonyms for the variety all hark back to the grape's hue: Verdone, Verzana, Verdetto, and Verzello. Verdicchio has been grown in central Italy at least since the fifteenth century, though some have postulated its presence between Jesi and Matelica in the Marche as early as the eighth century. In Veneto, there is a wealth of documentation detailing the presence of a *Trebbiano* variety since at least the thirteenth century: unfortunately, there is no way of knowing which of the many *Trebbiano* varieties was being discussed. In any case, a locally produced *Trebbiano* (Turbianum, Tribianum, or Terbianum) was well known then, and

Agostino Gallo later ([1595] 1937) wrote of Trebbiane Bianche varieties, which he suggested blending with Vernaccie Nere to make the best wines. Alessandro Peccana (1627) also mentioned a "Trebiano," while Francesco Dalla Negra (1811) wrote that in the western half of the Vicenza area, Turbiana was considered the best of the "delicate" grape varieties (in those times, "delicate" was the greatest of compliments, a sign of refinement); when blended with Marzemina Bianca and Garganega, he said, Turbiana was the basis for a great local wine. Of course, this being Italy, it won't surprise you that the wine was improperly called Piccolit, a completely different grape and wine, typical of Friuli Venezia Giulia. Nevertheless, a Torbiana or Turbiana and a Trebbiano di Soave have been documented in Veneto by numerous other authors well into the twentieth century. These two grapes were believed to be identical and had many synonyms, including Trebbiano di Lugana, Trebbiano di Lonigo, Trebbiano Veronese, Trebbiano Verde, Turbiano, and Turviana. Finally, on the basis of Molon's (1906) distinction between Trebbiano Toscano and Trebbiano di Soave, confirmed by Cosmo and Polsinelli (1965), Trebbiano di Soave was included in the National Registry as a separate variety in 1970.

However, many expert observers had always thought that Verdicchio of the Marche and Trebbiano di Soave had a great deal in common. In 1991, on the basis of ampelographic descriptions and enzyme analysis, Calò, Costacurta, Cancellier, and Forti demonstrated that Trebbiano di Soave is identical to Verdicchio, leading to Trebbiano di Soave being identified as Verdicchio in the National Registry though curiously the two maintain separate headings and their original descriptions (by Bruni 1962 for Verdicchio, and by Cosmo and Polsinelli 1965 for Trebbiano di Soave). These early results were confirmed ten years later with DNA profiling by Labra, Winfield, Ghiani, Grassi, Sala, Scienza, and Failla (2001). Subsequently, Vantini, Tacconi, Gastaldelli, Govoni, Tosi, Malacrinò, Bassi, and Cattivelli (2003) performed DNA profiling not just on Verdicchio and Trebbiano di Soave but also on Trebbiano di Lugana. They studied ten SSR microsatellite loci and confirmed the shared identity between Verdicchio and Trebbiano di Soave (the varieties have identical alleles at all ten loci; the likelihood of that happening and the two varieties *not* being the same is one in eight billion). But the researchers also found an abnormal allele of five hundred nucleotide bases in the VVMD36 locus that allows genetic differentiation between Trebbiano di Soave and Trebbiano di Lugana, which on the basis of these results are probably more correctly viewed as biotypes. Apparently, Ghidoni, Emanuelli, Moreira, Imazio, Grando, and Scienza (2008) confirmed the synonymity between Verdicchio and Trebbiano di Lugana and established a new one between Verdicchio and Trebbiano Valtenesi. A close relationship between Verdicchio and Maceratino has been suggested by Filipetti, Silvestroni, Thomas, and Intrieri (2001), and Di Vecchi Staraz, Bandinelli, Boselli, This, Boursiquot, Laucou, Lacombe, and Varès (2007) have described a pink-berried Verdicchio that is related to Mammolo (I think it is unlikely to be the real Verdicchio, as I am completely unaware of any Verdicchio color mutations). Clearly, further studies are needed.

The fact that Verdicchio is prevalent in the Venetian countryside, under the name Trebbiano di Soave, has led some experts to hypothesize that Verdicchio originates from Veneto and not from the Marche, which is the region the modern-day wine is largely associated with. This is not unlikely, since Venetians were famous traders and merchants responsible for the popularization of many grape varieties all over Italy (and Europe, witness the many different *Malvasia* varieties). Furthermore, documentation shows that previously plague-affected areas of the Marche were repopulated (at the end of the fifteenth century) by farmers from Veneto, who brought animals and plants with them. This is how Verdicchio is believed to have arrived in the Marche. It is also particularly noteworthy that molecular analysis has shown that genetic variability is less in Verdicchio populations than in Veneto varieties, which is in accordance with the process called genetic drift, in which a variety that has moved to another area has reduced genetic variability. Over the centuries, the replanted Trebbiano di Soave vines likely adapted to their new microclimate and soils in the Marche, and this can explain some of the differences in aroma and flavor profiles found in wines made with Trebbiano di Soave or Verdicchio.

Verdicchio has always been a favorite of farmers because it adapts readily to different *terroirs*. Verdicchio's trump cards are its tendency to ripen slowly and evenly (allowing for complex wines) and to always maintain high levels of tartaric acidity, meaning the wines can be both crisp and refreshing as well as very ageworthy. There exist different clones to choose from, generally regarded as being of better quality than the clones of many other varieties available to growers: the R2 is very productive but allows for good everyday table wines; the CSV clones have thicker skins and are ideal for late harvest and sparkling-wine production (though in my experience, wines made with these clones are not particularly ageworthy); the ERPT 155 and CVP 01–162 are clones of Turbiana, and these typically yield wines that are mineral, refined, and ageworthy. Not surprisingly, Verdicchio's great popularity and adaptability have led researchers to try to create new crossings with it: one such variety, simply called Incrocio Bruni 54 (or IB54), was developed in the 1930s and is a Verdicchio × Sauvignon Blanc crossing. The crossing maintains the characteristics of Verdicchio (if attenuated), with a delicate aromatic note typical of Sauvignon Blanc, even when planted in warmer microclimates. Differently from Trebbiano di Soave and Verdicchio, Turbiana shows much greater intravarietal variability. A few years ago, out of an understandable desire to separate themselves and their local cultivar from the large and quality-challenged *Trebbiano* family, growers and producers in Veneto opted to call the variety Turbiana instead of Trebbiano di Soave or Lugana.

Clearly, viewing Trebbiano di Soave and Verdicchio as one variety (and Turbiana as a biotype) means that the cultivation area of this variety in Italy is huge. Verdicchio's main homes are therefore the Marche, Veneto, and Lombardy, though it's grown in numerous other regions, including Umbria, Lazio, Tuscany, Sardinia, and Abruzzo. In Veneto, Verdicchio the Trebbiano di Soave is found mainly in the province of Verona, while Turbiana is more typical of the area around Lake Garda. The latter is grown especially on the eastern shores of that lake, Italy's largest, which neatly separates Veneto from Lombardy.

Which Wines to Choose and Why

In the Marche, Verdicchio is best represented by two different DOCG wines, Verdicchio dei Castelli di Jesi and Verdicchio di Matelica. Much as with Brunello di Montalcino or Vino Nobile di Montepulciano, the names of these two different Verdicchio wines tell you that they are made in or around the towns indicated in the name. As a general rule, differences in microclimate give the Verdicchio di Matelica a higher acidity level and more body and alcohol than wines of Jesi (usually lighter and more floral). Both wines share the telltale varietal note of sweet almond, sometimes with a pleasantly bitter twist. In reality, the characteristics of Verdicchio wines can be wildly different depending on the subzone they come from, as is the case, for example, with Barolos from La Morra versus those from Monforte d'Alba. For example, the Verdicchio dei Castelli di Jesi produced from grapes grown around the charming town of Montecarotto are closer in weight to those of Matelica, while those of Cupramontana are fresher and lighter (in fact, these grapes have long been sought after for the production of sparkling wines). In Veneto, as Trebbiano di Soave, the grape has always been used as a complementary variety to Garganega in the production of wines such as Soave and Gambellara, as Trebbiano di Soave/Verdicchio is rich in malic acid and therefore blends very well with Garganega. Verdicchio therefore plays a role in many DOC wines such as the Colli Berici, Colli Mantovani, Garda, Lugana, and Recioto di Soave. As Trebbiano di Lugana (or Turbiana), it is the main grape variety used to make the DOC Lugana wines. In other regions, Verdicchio can be included in wines as diverse as the Castelli Romani, Colli Albani, Marino of Lazio, and many more in other regions, but these are never monovarietal and as such provide little understanding of what a native variety and its wine are all about.

Young Verdicchio wines are very floral and delicately fruity; older wines have a distinct flintiness, even a note reminiscent of riesling, carricante, or timorasso-like kerosene. This latter note is due to the aromatic molecule precursors formed in carotene metabolic pathways; the resulting concentration is correlated to the amount of sunlight radiating onto the berries in the early phases of the growth cycle (as a general rule, the warmer and brighter the climate, the faster wines made with a few specific varieties will develop hydrocarbon-like aromas and flavors). Both young and old Verdicchio wines always exude a lovely, and very typical, sweet almond note, which veers to marzipan in richer, concentrated, aged examples of the wine. Sweet wines are also made from Verdicchio, as it likes noble rot; unfortunately, even though the high natural acidity guarantees these sweet wines are never cloying, Verdicchio is not an aromatic variety and so dessert wines made with it are of limited interest compared those delivered by Riesling or Moscato Bianco, for example. Come to think of it, this is another point that Verdicchio has in common with Chardonnay, the sweet wines of which are nothing to write home about (despite Austrians trying their best). Instead, the better, and still rare, examples of monovarietal wines made from Trebbiano di Soave are floral and fresh, lightly acidic, and delicate with hints of chlorophyll and unripe apricot. Trebbiano di Lugana wines can be more full-bodied and richer, perhaps due to the warmer microclimate of the growing area. Some of the latter wines can be somewhat overoaked, though.

WINES TO TRY: For Verdicchio dei Castelli di Jesi, try: Sartarelli*** (Balciana, a rare late-harvest example and one of Italy's top-five white wines), Bucci*** (their Riserva is one of Italy's top-ten white wines, and one of the few that can improve with age; it's splendid even ten years out), Garofoli*** (Podium, an amazing wine that shows just how great unoaked verdicchio can be), and Borgo delle Oche** (sometimes a bit oaky). For Verdicchio di Matelica, try: La Monacesca** (Mirum, their reserve wine) and Collestefano*** (outstanding minerality and depth, like a great dry Mosel Riesling). For Trebbiano di Soave, try: Suavia*** (Massi Fitti). For Lugana, try: Cà dei Frati*** (I Frati and especially Brolettino, mercifully now less oaked than in the past), Ottella** (Brut and Le Crete), Zenato** (if you prefer an oaked version), Fratelli Zeni, and Le Morette (owned by Valerio Zenato). For Bianco Veronese IGT, try: Filippi** (Turbiana).

Verdiso

WHERE IT'S FOUND: Veneto. NATIONAL REGISTRY CODE NUMBER: 255. COLOR: white.

Also known as Verdiga and Verdisot, Verdiso is yet another of the many Italian grape varieties named for the green hue of its berries. Verdiso is, however, unrelated to all of them. It is best known today as the complementary grape to Glera in the production of Prosecco, but centuries ago it was Verdiso that was the more important of the two. Its presence in Veneto appears to have been first documented as Verdise by G. B. Barpo (1634), and workers at the Abbey of Follina in 1688 were planting it. However, it was Count Pietro Caronelli in 1788 who first wrote in depth about Verdiso, citing it as locals' chosen variety to replant with following the horrific frost of 1709, when most other less-hardy varieties died. For example, Carpenè and Vianello (1874) documented that by the end of the 1800s, Verdiso was grown in fifty of the ninety-six townships in the province of Treviso; and at twenty-four thousand hectoliters a year, its wine was by far the most abundant in the area. However, Caronelli was not thrilled by the variety's enological potential, mainly because farmers preferred planting higher-yielding, low-quality biotypes known as Verdisone as opposed to the better Verdiso Gentile. According to Caronelli, Verdisone is characterized by greater productivity, much larger bunches and berries, thinner and greener skins, and a more neutral, less sweet pulp and wine.

Molon (1906) later recorded the existence of a Verdisa Grossa (or Verdiso de Campagna) and a Verdise Zentil (or Verdiso Gentile), but we know today that the two are not biotypes but are simply adaptations of Verdiso to different environments. When the cultivar is grown in deep, excessively fertile and wet soils, it tends to grow in size and look and behave like a Verdisone, while if those same vines are brought back to poorer hillside sites the grapevine morphs back to the Verdiso phenotype. This also appears true of another Verdiso biotype that was described by the Conte Pietro di Maniago in 1823, which he called Verdisa Lunga (or Strascalone). According to research, Verdiso is identical to Pedevenda, a variety typically associated with the Colli Euganei (Crespan, Cancellier, Costacurta, Giust, Carraro, Di Stefano, and Santangelo 2003). Verdiso has also been used to two different laboratory crossings, called Italica and Flavis, both Verdiso × Graševina crossings. Graševina is probably better known, and recognized, by the names Riesling Italico or Welschriesling.

Verdiso grows in Veneto, especially in the countrysides of Conegliano, Vittorio Veneto, and Valdobbiadene near Treviso, and also in the Refrontolo hills.

Which Wines to Choose and Why

The main wines are DOCG Conegliano-Valdobbiadene and DOC Colli di Conegliano: the latter wines can often be monovarietal Verdiso. Verdiso is blended with Glera in various Prosecco wines, and also with the sweet Torchiato di Fregona wines, made from air-dried grapes (the latter blend also includes Boschera, now believed to be Verdicchio). Verdiso has always been added to these other varieties for its freshness and acid lift. Pedevenda is associated with the DOC Breganze and is used in small percentages in the Torcolato sweet wine blend.

A very good verdiso is a thing of beauty: mouth-searingly fresh, extremely crisp, a smorgasbord of white flowers and green apples, with hints of ripe apricots in the background. Not particularly complex and not ageworthy, it will prove remarkably successful on any hot day by the pool or on a picnic by the sea or lakeshore; but its lack of almost any complexity whatsoever can turn some tasters off. It can be made both as a still wine or a sparkling one, and though I prefer the still version, both are satisfying, though too many producers limit themselves to churning out a high-acid, high-volume wine. Angelo Sabbadin, the sommelier in Veneto's famous three-Michelin-star Le Calandre restaurant near Padova, says pointedly, "I hate to be negative, but the fact is Verdiso grows well just about anywhere, and the resulting wine is always palatable. This has led many producers to just go with the flow and really not try too hard." Nevertheless, thanks to its high acidity, low alcohol level, and crisp, fresh fragrances and flavors, verdiso is currently enjoying a popularity boom and there are an increasing number of monovarietal bottlings being made.

WINES TO TRY: Gregoletto***, Toffoli***, Il Colle**, and Conte Collalto**.

Verduzzo Friulano

WHERE IT'S FOUND: FVG, Veneto. NATIONAL REGISTRY CODE NUMBER: 256. COLOR: white.

Verduzzo Friulano is, like Picolit and Ribolla Gialla, an emblematic cultivar of Friuli Venezia Giulia. The variety and the wine have been closely linked to the region for centuries, and it likely descends from a domesticated local wild vine. There are two Verduzzo Friulano subvarieties in Friuli Venezia Giulia, Verduzzo Giallo and Verduzzo Verde (a distinction made for the first time by Poggi in 1939 based on the color of the floral cap, not of the berries, as you might read elsewhere); both are distinct from Verduzzo Trevigiano, typical of Veneto, that has very few morphological or phenological aspects in common with Friuli Venezia Giulia's *Verduzzo*s. The Verde is mainly grown in Friuli Venezia Giulia's flatland vineyards to make dry white wines; the Giallo is at home on steep hillsides and is most often used to make a sweet, at times very sweet, wine from air-dried grapes in the Ramandolo DOCG (where some Verde is also found). The Giallo subvariety is believed to be the higher-quality grape of the two, but there are two biotypes of it (Perusini described them in the Ramandolo as early as 1935): the Ross (with a small compact bunch) and the Ras'cie (with a semicompact bunch). Due to its more loosely packed bunch, the latter maybe better suited for late-harvest wine production, where the grapes are left on the vine to dehydrate, though in Friuli Venezia Giulia's fickle autumn weather few producers are willing to risk true late harvests.

Over the years, since everyone thought (or was made to think) that Verduzzo Giallo was the superior of the two *Verduzzo*s, growers in Friuli Venezia Giulia slowly phased the Verde out, so that it is far less common than it used to be. Today, the best-quality Verduzzo Giallo is thought to come from around Nimis, especially the subareas Ramandolo and Torlano. Paolo Rodaro of the Rodaro estate mentions that *Verduzzo* is not a particularly vigorous variety (and using rootstock 3309 further reduces vigor) and that it is rarely attacked by botrytis, noble or not, when the grapes are left hanging on the vine (but it is sensitive to peronospora and botrytis bunch rot during flowering). It needs very well-exposed sites and does not like humid habitats (such as areas close to forests), preferring marly-rocky soils not too rich in clay (since it doesn't like excessive water retention).

Verduzzo Friulano is grown all over Friuli Venezia Giulia; it is most common in the province of Udine, less so in the provinces of Gorizia and Pordenone, and even grows in Veneto. Verduzzo has found a new home in Australia, where it has been planted in diverse regions such as Hunter Valley, King Valley, Mornington Peninsula, and Yarra Valley.

Which Wines to Choose and Why

The most important wines are the DOCG Ramandolo or the various Friuli DOCs' Verduzzo wines. In Veneto, the DOC is Lison-Pramaggiore. When simply labeled Verduzzo, the wine is generally an off-dry, light-bodied white wine; if made mainly with Verduzzo Verde, it is very light, delicately floral and citrusy, while if Verduzzo Giallo predominates then the wine will have richer, riper aromas and flavors, hinting even at acacia honey and apricots. Dry wines are also made, but the high tannic content is such that they risk being bitter. In any verduzzo, there is always a characteristic note of sweet almonds, both on the nose and the palate; this becomes particularly intense, turning to marzipan and burnt caramelized almonds in the very sweet wines.

Another typical characteristic of verduzzo is its tannic finish, due to the grape being a rare tannic white variety (with considerable tannin levels not just in the skins but also in the pulp). Ramandolo is the most famous wine made with Verduzzo Friulano; it can be made only in the specific DOCG zone that covers the townships of Nimis, Faedis, Tarcento, Torlano, and Ramandolo, from which the wine takes its name. The vines grow on very steep slopes located between 250 and 370 meters above sea level in a very cool microclimate, indeed one of the coldest, if not the coldest in all of Friuli Venezia Giulia. However, the vineyards in the town of Ramandolo are protected by Mount Bernadia: its rocky walls shelter the grapes from cold northerly winds while capturing and subsequently reflecting the sunlight onto the grapes, therefore ensuring that this area has a slightly warmer microclimate than neighboring towns. For this reason, many experts such as Perusini in 1935 and Filiputti in more modern times have always insisted that the one true *grand cru* of Ramandolo consists only of the town. Perusini, in what was perhaps an extreme but arguably not incorrect view, didn't think wines made outside the town should be allowed to be called Ramandolo. Nevertheless, all DOCG Ramandolo wines are thick and very sweet, with deep, extremely rich honey, caramelized almond, and ripe tropical-fruit aromas and flavors. Like all wines made with Verduzzo Friulano, they have a considerable tannic mouthfeel. Outside Italy, *Verduzzo* varieties seem to be doing very well in Australia, where to the best of my knowledge at least four different producers are making interesting wines: Bianchet, Lazzar Wines, Pizzini Wines, and Tallavera Grove (from the Carillion vineyard).

WINES TO TRY: I Clivi*** (Vecchia Vigna ai Clivi, a dry/off-dry wine), Lis Neris*** (Tal Luc; sticky sweet and one of Italy's greatest sweet wines, but contains 10 percent Riesling), La Sclusa** (an off-dry wine), Marco Sara** (Verduz, very sweet), Meroi** (very sweet), Paolo Rodaro** (Pra Zenar and Verduzzo, both super sweet), and Scubla** (very sweet, but not 100 percent Verduzzo). For the best in Ramandolo, try: Anna Berra***, Giovanni Dri**, and Toblar*.

Verduzzo Trevigiano

WHERE IT'S FOUND: FVG, Veneto. NATIONAL REGISTRY CODE NUMBER: 257. COLOR: white.

Little is known about Verduzzo Trevigiano, including where it comes from. While most experts currently favor the hypothesis that it is a twentieth-century import into Veneto from Sardinia, I have difficulties with this because, to my knowledge, there is no grapevine even remotely similar to Verduzzo Trevigiano on that island. Cosmo (1959) apparently recommended it as an ideal variety to grow on the Treviso plains.

The grape has pyramidal or cylindrical, medium-sized bunches; the berries are also medium-sized and oval. There is one clone, ISV-SV 5. It is apparently a solid, dependable producer and ripens in early October. Verduzzo Trevigiano is morphologically very dissimilar to Verduzzo Friulano; a hardy, rustic variety, it seems to thrive in both the rocky soils of the upper Piave River basin and the clay-rich soils of the lower basin.

Which Wines to Choose and Why

Grown mainly around Treviso, the DOC wines are Piave, Venezia, and Lison-Pramaggiore, but there are also IGT wines, such as Alto Livenza, Colli Trevigiani, Marca Trevigiana, and Delle Venezie. Clearly, the wine is not a blockbuster, offering a pale-straw, green-tinged, light-bodied wine with delicate aromas and flavors of white flowers and pear, with a twinge of bitterness at the back. Good examples are refreshing and crisp and are enjoyable with simple fish dishes (though there are a variety of wine styles available, including sparkling; the latter are the least interesting).

WINES TO TRY: I Vini delle Baite*, Casa Piave*, and Casa Roma* (Passito, so this is a sweet wine).

Vermentino

WHERE IT'S FOUND: Sardinia, Liguria, Tuscany, Umbria, Abruzzo, Lazio, Sicily. NATIONAL REGISTRY CODE NUMBER: 258 (number 80 as Favorita, number 190 as Pigato; both are errors, as the three are the same variety). COLOR: white.

Vermentino is actually Pigato. Wait a minute: no, Pigato is not Vermentino. After years debating the issue, researchers, wine experts, and producers in Italy (and not just in Italy) all agree to disagree on the subject. The academicians all apparently believe that Pigato and Vermentino are the same; many of Liguria's wine producers do not. Being facetious, you might say that's because the grapes are both Favorita. No, wait: they're all Piccabon (a wrong attribution: we now know Piccabon is identical to Vernaccia di San Gimignano). And so the story goes on. And on.

Throughout history, Vermentino has been called many different things depending on the production zone, and not just in Italy. According to recent genetic testing, however, Piedmont's Favorita and western Liguria's Pigato appear to be biotypes of Vermentino, rather than distinct varieties. Still, many growers who have worked with the varieties for decades (especially Pigato) remain unconvinced. Some insist that Pigato is its own grape, arriving on Ligurian shores from Spain by way of Corsica, though this is also unclear, because existing documentation from the nineteenth century apparently never mentions the name Pigato (reinforcing the notion that Pigato evolved later). The name Pigato derives from the local dialect word *pigau*, meaning "spotted," or from the Latin word *picatum*, meaning "aromatized with bitumen." Apparently, Sardinia's Vermentino di Alghero and Vermentino di Gallura are also just biotypes, distant relatives of a rare local variety called Bianca Antica. And it doesn't get any easier in southern France, where Vermentino is known as Rolle (Nice), Verlantin (Antibe), Malvoise à Gros Grains (Midi), and Malvasia Grossa or Carbesso (Corsica). Of course, this wouldn't be Italy if Rollo, despite its very *Rolle*-like name, ends up being not Vermentino but an ancient local variety known as Bruciapagliao.

In the past, unavailability of genetic testing and the shortcomings of ampelographic recognition made it difficult to differentiate between the three and led to Vermentino, Favorita, and Pigato all being included in the National Registry as separate varieties. Nowadays, most experts agree this was an error. Already in 1990, Schneider and Mannini had identified the latter two as biotypes of the former (on the basis of ampelographic descriptors), results confirmed by other studies; and accurate historical research revealed that, at the turn of the twentieth century, Favorita had been grown in Piedmont (near Alba, Mondovì, and Cuneo) and Pigato in the province of Savona. Subsequent microsatellite analysis has confirmed the three to be synonyms and not distinct entities (Botta, Scott, Eynard, and Thomas 1995). The grape we call Favorita is grown exclusively in Piedmont around the Roero region and is thought to have arrived there more than three hundred years ago via Ligurian oil merchants. It is known for having large berries and has been a popular table grape for many years, which many credit for its name, Favorita. When it was used for wine, historically it was blended with Nebbiolo in an effort to smooth over some of that variety's rough edges. Varietal wines made from Favorita have enjoyed some success recently, but plantings lag well behind those of Arneis and Chardonnay in the Langhe. Many U.S. examples of Favorita wine are slightly spritzy, though I'm not sure how prevalent that style is elsewhere.

With Vermentino, nothing is easy: its origin is also clouded in mystery. Is it a true Italian native, or was it imported from Spain? Or did Vermentino travel in the opposite direction, from Italy to Spain? Still other luminaries are certain that the variety was transported suitcase-style into the Mediterranean basin from the Orient by sailors and merchants. Strangely enough, Vermentino is not mentioned in the 1877 *Bollettino ampelografico* of Sardinian varieties, while Cettolini does mention it less than ten years later.

For all of the uncertainties that surround this variety, on one point all agree: Vermentino is an excellent variety from which great wines can be made, and it is of real economic importance for the many families involved in its cultivation and wine production. In fact, Vermentino has always enjoyed good press: Gallesio ([1817] 1839) (who didn't make it any easier on us by calling it Vernaccia di Corniglia) wrote that the wine was the favorite of Genoa and much sought after in the nineteenth century. This explains why plantings of Vermentino have increased steadily for the last hundred years. For example, whereas it represented just 1 percent of total grape varieties grown on Sardinia early in the twentieth century and covered only 1,366 hectares on Sardinia in the 1960s, today more than 3,300 hectares of Vermentino are planted on the island (or 12 percent of all grape varieties planted there). Growers have fifteen official clones to choose from (selected from populations in Sardinia, Tuscany, Liguria, and Piedmont; for example, the CAPVS series is of Sardinian origin), plus another ten French clones selected from Corsica. It is not without interest that many producers in Italy have planted French clones as well as Italian ones: as I discussed this in chapter three, I won't dissect this here, but I will repeat that I am not in favor of such actions, for they will ultimately lead to a globalization of wine production and harm locally specific biodiversity and plant genetic makeup. That said, viticulture expert Stefano Dini points out that France's ENTAV has done an amazing job with Vermentino clonal selection, and in his opinion many of their clones are better than the ones available in Italy. He especially singles out the older AP series for criticism as not allowing the highest-quality wines to be made; these grapevines are easy to recognize because their berries are quite big and tend to gain a reddish hue as they ripen, and because they are not very crunchy when you bite into them. According to Dini, many Ligurian Vermentino grapevines are characterized by these bigger berries.

Vermentino yields the best results in poorly fertile soils and has good tolerance to salty marine winds and dry climates. Producers will tell you it's a rare variety in that it craves the sun and does best in relatively hot habitats. (Vermentino prefers sunny exposures and poorly fertile soils in general.) It is sensitive to moths and mildew, especially in dense foliage conditions, and is moderately tolerant to oidium. Though unquestionably a citizen of southern Europe, it is cultivated mostly in Italy, with more than 4,000 hectares planted to it: roughly 3,300 hectares in Sardinia, 544 in Tuscany, 250 in Liguria, and 105 in Piedmont (in Sardinia, most is in two provinces: roughly 1,300 hectares at Olbia Tempio and another 1,100 around Sassari). There are an estimated 750 hectares in France (in Provence and especially Corsica, where 80 percent of all French Vermentino is found).

Which Wines to Choose and Why

I'm not the only one who thinks Vermentino makes a great little wine. It is made in bucolic countrysides where the vineyards sometimes seem like a prop for tourist snapshots rather than a source of serious wines, and the first taste is usually enough to prove how wrong first impressions can be. More than fifty differently named white wines are produced in Italy with Vermentino, involving one DOCG and twenty-two DOCs (eleven in Tuscany, six in Liguria, three in Sardinia, and one each in Piedmont and Umbria). As Pigato, it is mainly grown in the western half of Liguria, especially in the Valle Arroscia up to Pieve di Tenco, where the provinces of Savona and Imperia meet. The best wines to try are the DOC Riviera Ligure di Ponente Pigato, though they need be only 95 percent Pigato to earn the label. To my taste, Pigato yields bigger, fatter wines than Vermentino, with similar saline nuances but a creamier texture. The aromas and flavors recall delicate notes of apricot, peach, and ripe Golden Delicious apple but are more typically musky and floral.

Wines can differ greatly based on degree of berry ripeness and use of oak (or not), as well as soil and climate diversity: some Italian estates produce many different Vermentino wines simply by harvesting at different times. Winemaking techniques employed usually involve short pellicular macerations, followed by fermentation in steel, while barrel fermentation is less commonly used in an effort to avoid camouflaging the wine's delicate aromas and flavors. Recently, many winemakers have begun adopting techniques aimed at minimizing air contact, to prevent oxidation and loss of aromas. Greater texture and richness is achieved by aging on the lees, with more or less *bâtonnage* (stirring of the lees) depending on what style of wine the estate is aiming for. Therefore, vermentino can range from light and fresh to structured and alcoholic. Wines offer a large range of aromas and flavors: from citrus to ripe tropical fruit, with floral (acacia) and herbal (rosemary, thyme) notes. Most always, the wine is recognized by a definite saline nuance on the finish.

Vermentino is thriving outside Italy. Very good examples can be had in the United States, such as those by Bailiwick in Sonoma, Tablas Creek in Paso Robles, and Uvaggio in Lodi. In Australia, look for wines by Chalmers, Fox Creek, Brown Brothers, Box Grove Vineyard, and Berton (the wine is called Spotlight). There are many more.

WINES TO TRY: Ottaviano Lambruschi*** (Sarticola is unfortunately no longer made; the Costa Marina is just as good, fruitier and almondy), Giacomelli*** (Boboli), Bisson** (Vigna Erta), Maria Donata Bianchi**, Poggio dei Gorleri** (Vigna Sorì and Vermentino), Laura Aschero*, and Terre Bianche*. For the best pigatos, try: Bruna*** (especially U Bacan, balsamic and rich), Cascina delle Terre Rosse** (Apogeo and Pigato), BioVio** (Bon in da Bon, from slightly late-harvested grapes), Claudio Vio** (U Grottu, late harvested and with lots of *bâtonnage*), Sancio**, Durin*, Laura Aschero*, and La Vecchia Cantina* (Passito; also makes a rare air-dried pigato, unfortunately in homeopathic quantities that you'll likely only be able to try on your next Ligurian vacation).

Vermentino Nero

WHERE IT'S FOUND: Liguria, Tuscany. NATIONAL REGISTRY CODE NUMBER: 259. COLOR: red.

A rare variety, Vermentino Nero was essentially saved from extinction by the Podere Scurtarola estate in the 1980s. Not much is known about the variety, but it appears not to be a mutation of the better known Vermentino and is rather a separate variety. Also, there is no DNA evidence I know of to support synonymity with any other variety. Pierpaolo Lorieri of Podere Scurtarola is certainly the biggest expert on the variety today (his 2000 and 2001 offerings were particularly good). His first vintage was 1989, and he remembers not being too positive or sure about the variety at the time. According to Lorieri, Vermentino Nero originated in the hills surrounding Massa, about halfway up the coast between Livorno in Tuscany and Genoa in Liguria, and was first mentioned in print in 1874, though other sources suggest it was already grown on the Ligurian coast in the sixteenth century. Diego Bosoni, of the Lunae Bosoni estate in La Spezia, believes that "we are really only starting out with this cultivar, and it will take time to understand it fully. We do think that it has amazing potential and that the wines can be remarkably interesting, both as *rosato* and *rosso*. In fact, after our first three vintages of a *rosato*, we plan to come out with a red wine soon too." Looks like the other Vermentino is on the path back from oblivion.

Vermentino Nero has long been confused with Merlot, according to Stefano Dini: "That's why many Vermentino Nero wines were inky, when in fact a wine truly made with Vermentino Nero is not so deeply hued. It's easy to tell the two apart, all you need to do is look at the leaves." Vermentino Nero is also a much later ripener than Merlot, and is usually picked at the end of September or the beginning of October. It is also especially sensitive to oidium: Dini throws his hands up in the air recalling how "one little row of Vermentino Nero was hit by oidium and it spread the stuff to over seven hectares of nearby Chardonnay. If we didn't pull up all the Vermentino Nero on the estate immediately at that time, I guess we never will." In Tuscany, there are roughly seventy hectares of Vermentino Nero grown today, more than half of which are found near Massa Carrara.

Which Wines to Choose and Why

It is used in the DOCs Candia dei Colli Apuane, Colline Pisane, and Colline Lucchesi, while in Liguria it can be included in IGT wines such as Golfo dei Poeti and the DOC Colli di Luni.

The wine is rich in black fruit aromas and flavors, with coffee nuances; some producers, finding the latter too intense, prefer to blend it with other varieties. There are both midweight, fresh wines and bigger, full-bodied ones, depending on what the producer is out to achieve. With acidities ranging around 5.8 grams per liter, extracts of 30 grams per liter, and alcohol levels around 13.5 percent, and not a steel tank anywhere in sight, Podere Scurtarola's Vernero is an oaky wine with some aging potential (best within five to eight years of the vintage, in my mind). Every bottle of vermentino nero I have ever had (and I've had a few) was marked by very high acidity. For this reason too, Lorieri has also tried air-drying the grapes to make sweet versions of the wine.

WINES TO TRY: Podere Scurtarola** (Vernero), Cima***, Terenzuola** (a fresh, midweight example), and Lunae Bosoni** (Mearosa, a *rosato*; owner Diego Bosoni says they plan to be making a monovarietal red vermentino nero in the next few years).

Vernaccias

See VERNACCIA GROUP, chapter 3.

Vespaiola

WHERE IT'S FOUND: Veneto. NATIONAL REGISTRY CODE NUMBER: 263. COLOR: white.

A native of Veneto—where it is or has also been called Bresparola Bianca, Vespaia, Uva Vespera, and Vesparola—Vespaiola is clearly named for the hungry wasps *(vespe)* that target its sweet grapes. Fausto Maculan, of the famous Maculan estate in Veneto, told me that the variety was rarely mentioned prior to the nineteenth century, and that its name first appeared in a 1754 poem, "*Il roccolo*," which lists all of the cultivars grown around Vicenza at that time. Acerbi (1825) was the first to describe in some depth a Vespaiola grown near Bassano, and later Di Rovasenda (1877) wrote of various *Vespaiolas* near Vicenza. Marzotto (1925) believed the many various *Vespaiolas* of Alessandria, Siena, and Vicenza to be the same variety.

Researchers of late have focused mainly on developing better clones to work with. Vespaiola has been on a roll mainly due to the success of Torcolato, one of Italy's very best sweet wines. Maculan thinks the variety is high quality but is just a little too vigorous in its youth and hence has to be trained with long-pruning systems to keep its vigor under control.

Which Wines to Choose and Why

A good monovarietal vespaiola brings to mind acacia blossoms, pear, and ripe citrus; frankly sweet wines also feature ripe tropical fruit and honeyed notes. Clearly, the winemaking has to be on the ball, for any excessive oxidation will cause the wine to lose its bright aromatic flavors. "Its principal characteristics," says Maculan, "are the high tartaric acid concentration and its extremely delicate floral nose. Dry versions match perfectly with dishes such as *baccalà alla vicentina* and with white asparagus. Thanks to this wonderful acidity, it's an even better grape with which to make sweet wines, and in fact a well-made Torcolato is never cloying."

There are many very good wines to choose from, but for monovarietal sweet vespaiola made from air-dried grapes, try the wines called Torcolato (the clusters are bound together with two pieces of twine that are twisted or wound, a method known as *torcolare* in local dialect; the clusters are then suspended over rafters to dry).

WINES TO TRY: Firmino Miotti***, Maculan***, Beato Bartolomeo**, and Villa Angarano** (Torcolato Riserva). For Breganze Vespaiolo (dry wine), try: Contra Saordà*** (Vignasilan), Ca' Biasi***, Villa Angarano* (Angarano Bianco Vespaiolo), and Maculan* (Vespaiolo).

Vespolina

WHERE IT'S FOUND: Piedmont, Lombardy. NATIONAL REGISTRY CODE NUMBER: 264. COLOR: red.

I believe Vespolina to be one of Italy's best native grape varieties: no small praise, considering this is the country of Nebbiolo, Fiano, Sangiovese, and Aglianico. Like all things worthwhile, it can be difficult: according to more than one viticulturist I have spoken with over the years, it's not the easiest cultivar to work with. Nevertheless, I am glad to see that producers are increasingly producing monovarietal wines with it, undoubtedly buoyed by consumer interest in midweight, perfumed red wines: though I caution readers that Vespolina only seems like a medium-bodied wine. In fact, its wines can be characterized by very tough tannins, depending on what producers do in the vineyards and in the cellar; their actions will go a long way in determining how successful they are with this variety. But in the hands of a talented producer, Vespolina can achieve halcyon heights that most other varieties, not just those of Italy, can't remotely aspire to. Perhaps the greatness of Vespolina can be explained by the fact that it is a progeny of Nebbiolo (Schneider, Boccacci, Torello Marinoni, Botta, Akkak, and Vouillamoz 2004), making it a half sibling of other Nebbiolo progenies: Bubbierasco, Brugnola, Freisa, Nebbiolo Rosé, Negretta, Neretto di Bairo, and Rossola Nera.

Vespolina was first described by Acerbi (1825) and then by Gallesio ([1817] 1839), who called it *Vitis vinifera circumpadana,* while today almost the only synonym used is Ughetta, or Uvetta di Canneto in Lombardy. With the advent of phylloxera, Vespolina cultivation declined, for Vespolina is less resistant than other varieties to disease and it adapted poorly to American rootstocks, with irregular grape ripening and production. As it is extremely subject to dissection of the spine, magnesium and potassium soil concentrations are very important and must be monitored closely, and the choice of rootstock is also very important. This also means that the grapes have a tendency to start dehydrating directly on the vine; a welcome event when it happens just before harvest (it concentrates the aromas and flavors of pepper and red cherry), but an absolute nightmare when it occurs in August or so, because the grapes never recover and fail to ripen fully. It's a low-productivity variety, so green harvests aren't especially necessary: a simple deleafing will suffice to help the grapes reach optimal ripeness, but very deep fertile soils are best avoided because they hamper maturation.

Like Uva Rara and Bonarda, Vespolina is one of the many native red grapes of northeastern Piedmont and Lombardy (especially in the provinces of Novara, Vercelli, Varese, and Pavia).

Which Wines to Choose and Why

Vespolina has always been used to make DOCG, DOC, and IGT blends of note. As it is blessed with plenty of polyphenols, monovarietal wines are both dark and tannic, and this explains why producers have always preferred using it as a blending agent rather than trying it solo. In Piedmont it is often blended with Nebbiolo, Croatina, and Uva Rara to make the world-class wines of Boca, Gattinara, Ghemme, and Lessona. Other DOC wines worth hunting down are Bramaterra, Coste della Sesia, Colline Novaresi, Fara, Oltrepò Pavese, and Sizzano. Most monovarietal versions are labeled Coste della Sesia or Colline Novaresi, and they can be mesmerizingly good wines.

While monovarietal versions are uncommon, they can increasingly be found, for Vespolina yields wines that are not only very intensely colored and tannic, but also perfumed and bright. Skin contact is kept short, roughly four to seven days at no more than 28°C (no sense leaching out even more tannin), followed by eighteen to twenty-four months in the barrel or the bottle to help soften the wine. A well-made vespolina is a thing of beauty. There are few red grapes in the world that can make a wine seem like a red-fruit cocktail, and Vespolina is one of them. The best wines have aromas that are reminiscent of those made with Nebbiolo and Pinot Nero, but are usually more spicy. Hence, the wines have lightish red colors, with penetratingly intense and pure sour red-cherry and red-berry aromas, lifted by balsamic notes, roses, violets, and spices (cinnamon, marjoram, and white pepper, especially) on the nose, and mouthwatering acidity and juicy red-berry flavors on the palate that will make you not want to put the glass back down. The pepper note can be extremely strong in vespolina, even bothersome. A recent interesting study showed that Vespolina wines are rich in rotundone, an aromatic molecule that smells of spices such as marjoram and rosemary (in fact, both herbs are rich in rotundone too) (Mattivi, Caputi, Carlin, Lanza, Minozzi, Nanni, et al. 2011). Clearly, as this is a fairly tannic variety (and the tannins can be a problem when the grapes are not perfectly ripe,) the use of new oak in the aging process is contraindicated.

WINES TO TRY: Ioppi*** (Coda Rossa), Rovellotti***, Francesco Brigatti***, Antichi Vigneti di Cantalupo**, and Torraccia del Piantavigna** (Maretta). But any wine you pick will likely prove well made and wonderful.

Vitovska

WHERE IT'S FOUND: FVG. NATIONAL REGISTRY CODE NUMBER: 320. COLOR: white.

Also called Organca, Gargania, Gargana, and Vitouska (and in bordering Slovenia, Vitovska Grganja or Garganja), Vitovska is a white grape that in Italy is grown only in Friuli Venezia Giulia. Even there, it's predominantly found in Friuli Carso, with only a few vines also grown in Friuli Isonzo. Clearly, the name of the grape is of Slovenian origin (Vitovska is common in the Slovenian Carso, or Kras, specifically in the Vipava Valley), probably deriving either from *vitez* (wine of the chevalier) or Vitovlje, a small town located in the Slovenian Brda region. Since Vitovska is a Slovenian name, its correct pronunciation involves accenting both the *i* and the *o* (so, Vìtòvska).

As it is found nowhere else in the Mediterranean and its history is part of local traditions, Vitovska is considered a native variety, though whether that means native to Italy or Slovenia is open to debate. In fact, though opinion is widespread that Vitovska originated in the Carso area, there is little information to support the assertion that this cultivar is strictly localized in the region, and there are no traces of its presence elsewhere. There is precious little historical information of any kind available on Vitovska, a variety that was brought back from limbo in Italy thanks to the passion and commitment of a handful of Carso producers.

However, if little is known about what our ancestors thought of Vitovska, recent research has shed light on the parentage of the variety. Crespan, Crespan, Giannetto, Meneghetto, and Costacurta (2007) compared data from eleven SSRs, and suggested that this variety could be an offspring of Malvasia Bianca Lunga (alias Malvasia del Chianti) and Prosecco Tondo. By extending molecular analysis to thirty-seven nuclear SSR loci, they found further evidence for the origins of Vitovska: the additional data confirmed the two putative parents indicated previously. Interestingly, recent work showed Vitovska Grganja to share only 55 percent of analyzed alleles with Vitovska (Rusjan, Jug, and Štajner 2010); and other researchers showed a first-degree (parent-progeny) relationship (Štajner, Korosec-Koruzam, Ruzjan, and Javornik 2008). This means it is incorrect to refer to Vitovska and Vitovska Grganja interchangeably, for they are not identical varieties. Notably, Vitovska Grganja appears to be identical to another old and little-known Slovenian variety called Racuk; however, the synonymy of Vitovska Grganja and Racuk can't yet be confirmed as we still lack an accurate morphological characterization of Racuk.

I remember extremely well when the first bottles of vitovska arrived on my tasting table in the early 1980s, from a grape nobody (myself included) had ever heard of. Yet, the wines were exceptionally good from day one, and it didn't take the variety long to make waves and snag a market niche for itself. Vitovska's renaissance began in the 1960s, when Luigi Lupinc, a small wine producer in San Pelagio di Prepotto, was the first to perform field selections of Vitovska, grafting it onto American rootstocks, propagating it, and finally bottling a finished wine. Other local estates soon took up Lupinc's example, first and foremost Edi Kante, who soon became the recognized ambassador of Vitovska in Italy and abroad. That it took the Italian bureaucracy until

1996 to allow Vitovska be legally recognized as a cultivar with which to make DOC Carso wine is another matter: obviously, the Carso *contadini* are a patient bunch. In the end, what matters most is that Vitovska is yet another example of an Italian (?) native grape and wine success story: producers who believed in the potential quality of this grape have enabled all of us wine-loving individuals to learn about, and indulge, in yet another new and interesting wine.

Which Wines to Choose and Why

Vitovska is grown only in the Friuli Carso, that barren mass of ferrous-rich red rocks that are nutrient poor and help produce no-frills wines of incredible minerality. Monovarietal vitovska is a wine of delicate, nuanced charms: if your vinous preferences are for Playboy-bunny-type proportions, give vitovska a wide berth, for you are likely to be left nonplussed by its faint lemony, pear, sage, and chlorophyll aromas and flavors. Others will love them, as well as the wine's usual lightweight, high-acid frame, and zippy minerality.

WINES TO TRY: Zidarich**, Kante** (the entry-level wine is just as good as the more expensive, later released Selezione), Skerk**, Skerlj*, and Lupinc*.

Vuillermin

WHERE IT'S FOUND: Valle d'Aosta. NATIONAL REGISTRY CODE NUMBER: 356. COLOR: red.

Seriously at risk of extinction at the beginning of the twentieth century, Vuillermin gained a new lease on life in the twenty-first century, becoming the most recent Valle d'Aosta native grape to be the subject of monovarietal winemaking. Pure vuillermin follows the monovarietal wines made from Primetta, Fumin, Cornalin, and Mayolet, in that chronological order. In some respects, vuillermin may prove the best.

Strangely enough, the Vuillermin variety was never described by Lorenzo Gatta, to whom we are indebted today for whatever knowledge we have about the native varieties of the Valle d'Aosta. The first to document Vuillermin's existence was Louis Napoléon Bich (1890), who wrote that it was a variety resistant to sunburn, always an important feature in high mountain vineyards—an advantage offered by Vuillermin that leads me to think that it must have been present in the region prior to Bich making a note of it, though I'm at a loss to explain why nobody had written about it prior. According to Moriondo (1999), it may be that Vuillermin had been always present but known as Eperon or Spron, a variety that was later thought to have become extinct. Today we know that Vuillermin is an offspring of Fumin (Vouillamoz) and it has second-degree relationships with Rouge du Pays, Rèze (a Valais variety), and even with Trentino's Nosiola, a white variety.

Which Wines to Choose and Why

The wine can be made as a DOC Valle d'Aosta Vuillermin. It's best described, in my view, as a cross between mayolet and cornalin, offering the aromatic fragrance of the former and the powerful structure of the latter; in fact, it's probably better than the sum of its parts, with a lovely floral and spicy nose and fresh but mouth-filling flavors of red berries, mountain herbs, and tar. It's a really lovely midweight wine.

WINES TO TRY: Feudo di San Maurizio*** and IAR** (probably their best wine is made from the recently rediscovered old varieties of the region).

Wildbacher

WHERE IT'S FOUND: Veneto. NATIONAL REGISTRY CODE NUMBER: 303. COLOR: red.

Just like Cannonao can't be considered a native grape to Italy, neither is Wildbacher, which is, at the present state of our knowledge, a native of the Styrian region of Austria. Most likely, Wildbacher was imported into Italy by the Conte Abate Vinciguerra VII di Collalto, born in 1727, who was a famous traveler, gourmet, and in love with agriculture. The original vines died out, and so Wildbacher was replanted in the later half of the nineteenth century by the Conte Ottaviano Antonio, who also built the cellars at the Collalto estate that still today makes one of Italy's best Wildbacher wines. As Italy's version of wildbacher differs considerably from that made in Austria, and as the variety has been on Italian soil for centuries, it is certainly a traditional variety of Italy, just like Cannonao. The name Wildbacher means "wild stream" and derives from the town of Wildbach in western Styria.

Wildbacher is an authorized variety for the province of Treviso but grows only in the countryside around the towns of Pieve di Soligo, Collalto, Breda di Piave, and Vacil di Piave.

Which Wines to Choose and Why

Wildbacher is used to make such wines as the Colli Asolani, Colli di Conegliano-Refrontolo Passito, and Montello. A good wildbacher is rich and alcoholic, with ripe dark cherry and plum aromas and flavors, complicated by a noticeable forest floor and herbal streak. The tannins are actually smooth and polished.

WINES TO TRY: Conti Collalto*** and Col Sandago*** (they also make a sparkling Brut Rosé and a sweet version called Dagoberthus, which at roughly 130 grams per liter of residual sugar and more than 7 grams per liter of acidity, is never a sticky-sweet dessert wine).

FIVE

Little-Known Native and Traditional Grape Varieties

IN MANY BOOKS and articles (both scholarly and not) devoted to the subject of native cultivars, and even in everyday wine tastings and discussions, Italy's "other native grapes" are often referred to as "minor grape varieties." I think this is a shame, but "rare grape varieties" isn't much better. I prefer to refer to these grapes as "little-known" cultivars, in an effort not to stress their scarcity and thereby put them at a disadvantage with respect to better-known varieties. As long as we continue to view cultivars that are not widely grown as "minor," we will inadvertently continue to damage them, by implying that they are children of a lesser grape-god.

In all honesty, given the many lackluster Italian wines made with Chardonnay, I think a good argument can be made that there are few grape varieties in Italy more "minor" than that very famous cultivar. Chardonnay is unquestionably a truly great grape variety in Burgundy and in parts of Sonoma, Napa, Australia, and other countries. But with perhaps two or three exceptions, it is never a truly great grape variety in Italy (before Italian producers start waiting for me outside my home with less than friendly intentions, let me add that I think Italy makes world-class sauvignon blancs and pinot grigios).

At present, grapes and wines made from the likes of Veneto's Spigamonte or Sardinia's Granazza are little known, but this may not be true for long. In fact, among the hundreds of little-known grape varieties already identified, and the many hundreds more that await rediscovery, there are—are bound to be—true gems. This is because the reasons that led to some native grape varieties being abandoned, even risking extinction, are no longer valid today. Modern wine drinkers value wines in different ways than did our wine drinking ancestors. With better characterization of each of these little-known cultivars, it may be that a large number will show unexpected enological potential, and lead in turn to new and interesting monovarietal wines in the bottle. Then again, maybe not—but the trick is to undertake a voyage of discovery.

Over the years, my tastings of essentially unknown varieties such as Ucelut and Vuillermin, and even more obscure ones like Garofanata and Coda di Volpe Rossa, have borne out, time and again, the wonderful fine-winemaking potential of many of these "other" natives. One problem is who evaluates the microvinifications of new varieties and how they are evaluated. I distinctly remember thinking, on my first taste of Coda di Volpe Rossa, what amazing potential it had: yet the researchers had presented it as a grape of no interest, at most worth considering for sparkling wine production. When I mentioned this to Maurizio De Simone, a well-known consulting winemaker in Campania and Lazio, he just shook his head and laughed: "You know what I call that grape variety? Campania's Pinot Nero, so you know just how highly I think of it."

Some of the varieties listed below are not yet officially included in Italy's National Registry of Grape Varieties. I also include a number of cultivars that have not yet been sufficiently studied (and that further research may identify with another, already known cultivar) but that I believe are, at the present state of knowledge, distinct enough to describe in this book. It wasn't so long ago that many now important cultivars such as Pecorino and Uva di Troia were essentially unknown, and practically nobody used to make monovarietal wines with them. In fact, even grapes that have shot to stardom, like Nerello Mascalese, are only recent rediscoveries. Had I written this book in 1995 or 2000 the Nerello Mascalese entry would have been much shorter, as at the time there was only one easy-to-find monovarietal bottling. Many of the little-known varieties in this chapter are in that same condition today: and yet I am confident that, one day, at least some of them will be shown to have previously untapped fine-wine potential. The future will tell which of the following "little-known" grape varieties make the grade and which risk oblivion.

New "old" varieties from which to make wine are springing back to life all the time. The most recent additions to the list include Antinello (number 446) and Somarello Rosso (number 459). Others such as Gradò (number 464) or Serbina (number 433) have not been associated with any quality wines that I know of. For example, Lambruschino di Cavria, or Festasio, has recently been rediscovered. But who knows? We might one day see monovarietal wines made from one, some, or even all of these, and it will be great to say we were there right from the start.

Abbuoto

WHERE IT'S FOUND: Lazio. NATIONAL REGISTRY CODE NUMBER: 1. COLOR: red.

Abbuoto has the honor, given the spelling of its name, to be the first variety listed in Italy's National Registry of Grape Varieties. Is Abbuoto a *numero uno* wine too? Initial enological results seem to indicate so. Abbuoto appears to be a very high-quality variety, allowing for complex, ageworthy red wines. It is also sometimes known as San Giuseppe Nero or Aboto. Winemaker Maurizio De Simone tells me that Abbuoto was used to make cécubo, a wine famous in ancient Rome, and considered a worthy rival to falernum. Pliny thought highly of the abbuoto from Amicle, a small town near Terracina; he believed this wine's superior quality was due to the marshy soils where poplars provided natural supports for the vines.

Nowadays Abbuoto is cultivated mainly in the province of Latina (near the towns of Fondi, Formia, Sperlonga, and Gaeta) along the southeastern coast of Lazio, and in small vineyard plots around the towns of Frosinone and Fiuggi in southwestern Lazio. Recently a few vineyards have been replanted around Spigno Saturnia, Santi Cosma, and Damiano, towns located in the provinces of Latina and Caserta in Campania. Still, plantings remain scarce, and the cultivar has only recently become the subject of renewed interest. Abbuoto is not particularly vigorous and its limited productivity explains why farmers chose to abandon it. In particular, Abbuoto has suffered the competition of Cesanese Comune and Cesanese d'Affile, much better-known and more profitable native red varieties of southern Lazio.

Abbuoto's leaf is large and pentagonal, and its cluster medium-large, cylindrical-conical, often with one or two wings. The berry is medium-large, not perfectly round, thick skinned, and dark violet-black. Biotypes of Abbuoto from Itri in Lazio appear to have smaller bunches and berries. While it is resistant to oidium and (less so) to peronospora as well as to drought, it is very sensitive to spring frosts due to early flowering; the harvest is in mid-September. Curiously, Abbuoto shares its name with a traditional dish typical of the Frosinone area, a slow-cooked stew of lamb intestine, celery, fresh tomato, parsley, white wine, chili pepper, salt, and other ingredients. The wine is bright ruby-red, with fresh red-berry and floral aromas. Full-bodied, with good acidity levels, it has always been known to age, and takes to oak well; its tannins require patience. The examples of pure abbuoto I have tasted over the years have left me suitably impressed. Lazio produces both a sparkling and a sweet version as well, made from air-dried *(passito)* grapes. Top producers include Terra delle Ginestre and Terre Pontine, two small cooperatives that however do not yet bottle 100 percent Abbuoto, though the percentage of Abbuoto in Terra delle Ginestre's Il Generale, now 40 percent, is increasing every year and will soon be 100 percent. Villa Matilde, a well-known Campanian producer, and where De Simone used to work once, is often cited as a source of Abbuoto wines, but they have never produced a monovarietal wine. Wines made with 40 percent Abbuoto or less really do not speak of Abbuoto (or any other variety, for that matter, so it's pointless to use such wines as an example of what a grape variety might deliver).

Acitana

WHERE IT'S FOUND: Sicily. NATIONAL REGISTRY CODE NUMBER: not registered. COLOR: red.

Acitana takes its name from a number of small towns north of Catania in Sicily's northeastern tip all of which begin with Aci: Aci Bonaccorsi, Aci Castello, Aci Catena, Aci San Filippo, Acireale, and more. It is a practically unknown grape variety apparently no longer cultivated (or limited to a few sporadic vines) near Catania and found today only in the Faro red wine production zone, also in the northeastern corner of Sicily. Faro is a blend of the better known grapes Nerello Mascalese and Nerello Cappuccio with relative unknowns such as Acitana, Galatena, and Cor' e Palummo. Like these last two, Acitana is not officially listed in the National Registry and I have no knowledge of any accurate ampelographic descriptions or DNA profiles of it. It remains to be seen whether this is a distinct cultivar or just another name for a grape known elsewhere. Still, locals are convinced of its uniqueness and claim that they include 5–10 percent of it (though I wonder if those percentages are ever reached in any bottled wine) in their Faro blends.

Addoraca

WHERE IT'S FOUND: Calabria. NATIONAL REGISTRY CODE NUMBER: not registered. COLOR: white.

Addoraca is an essentially unknown grape variety used in the Moscato di Saracena blend, a lovely sweet wine that has been brought to everyone's attention in the last ten years by some excellent wines made by the likes of I Feudi di San Severino and Cantine Viola.

Aghedene

WHERE IT'S FOUND: FVG. NATIONAL REGISTRY CODE NUMBER: not registered. COLOR: white.

Rediscovered in 2005 in an old vineyard at Colle Villano near Faedis, Aghedene was well known in the first part of the twentieth century. According to Carlo Petrussi, Friuli Venezia Giulia's most eminent viticultural expert, its wine was never considered noteworthy; in fact the variety's name refers to dilution in the Friuli dialect. Aghedene was always mainly blended in with other grapes, mainly with Ribolla Gialla. Aghedene has a medium-sized, pentagonal leaf, with five to seven lobes. A late-ripening variety offering good productivity, Aghedene also has decent concentrations of benzenoids (38 percent) and norisoprenoids (42 percent) according to microvinifcations performed at the Friuli Venezia Giulia's Agenzia Regionale per lo Sviluppo Rurale (ERSA). The wine is simple, thin, and tart, with decent acidity and floral aromas and flavors.

Albaranzeuli Bianco

WHERE IT'S FOUND: Sardinia. NATIONAL REGISTRY CODE NUMBER: 6. COLOR: white.

Albaranzeuli Bianco is a very interesting variety that may not be a Spanish import (as its name might suggest) but rather the result of a natural crossing between Girò and the Spanish table grape Panse Rosa di Malaga (Cipriani, Spadotto, Jurman, Di Gaspero, Crespan, Meneghetti, et al. 2010). Nieddu (2011) has pointed out that Albaranzeuli Bianco's pink-streaked berries make this possibility look likely. It appears there is a close relationship between Albaranzeuli Bianco and the *Girò* family: in particular, microsatellite SSR testing has shown it to be virtually identical to a local Sardinian variety called Zirone Bianco, and related to a lesser degree to the red-berried varieties Zirone di Spagna and Zirone Alzu (Nieddu 2011). It was once considered identical to Albanello, Albillo, and Albicello (Cettolini 1935) and these synonyms are still included in the National Registry of Grape Varieties, but this appears, at our present state of knowledge, to be an error (Bruni 1962). In particular, Albanello is the name of a distinct Sicilian grape variety. In Sardinian dialect Albaranzeuli Bianco is called Lacconargiu and Lacconarzu.

The bunch is described by experts as medium-large (but at four hundred to five hundred grams it looks larger), conical or cylindrical-conical (sometimes pyramidal), with one to three wings, and not too compact. The berry is spherical and medium-sized, thick skinned and yellow, with pink-golden streaks or blotches when fully ripe, usually by late September. Though I have been shown the grape by eager and patient growers, I haven't tasted any monovarietal wines made with it.

Albaranzeuli Nero

WHERE IT'S FOUND: Sardinia. NATIONAL REGISTRY CODE NUMBER: 7. COLOR: red.

Unrelated to the similarly named Albaranzeuli Bianco, Albaranzeuli Nero might have arrived on the island courtesy of the Spanish during the fourteenth and fifteenth centuries, making it a traditional rather than native variety. Other names for it are Alvarenzelin Nero, Alvarenzeuli Nero, and Albarenzelin Nero. Now almost extinct, it is still grown in a few vineyards around Nuoro. The bunch is medium-sized, cylindrical, winged, and somewhat compact. The berry is spherical, medium-sized, with a thin but fairly resistant skin, pale red-violet in color. The grapes ripen late, and are usually harvested in mid-October. It was always used either to make *rosato* wine or to blend with other varieties, for the wine is usually low in both acidity and alcohol levels. It is very similar in appearance but genetically distinct from Girò, another Sardinian traditional grape. I haven't tasted any monovarietal wines made with it, and have yet to see the grapevine.

Albarola Nera

WHERE IT'S FOUND: Tuscany. NATIONAL REGISTRY CODE NUMBER: not registered. COLOR: red.

This variety was described by Scalabrelli, D'Onofrio, Paolicchi, and Bucelli (2005), but I am not aware of any further work on this particular grape.

Alionza

WHERE IT'S FOUND: Emilia-Romagna. NATIONAL REGISTRY CODE NUMBER: 315. COLOR: white.

Alionza is also known as Aleonza, Glionza, Uva Lonza, Aglionga Bianca, and confusingly, Uva Schiava. It was probably present in the countryside around Modena and Bologna even before Tanara wrote of it in 1674; Trinci and Acerbi also mention it, but it is only thanks to the Commissione Ampelografica Bolognese (Bologna Ampelography Committee) of 1874 that Alionza is described in detail. However, the wine must have had merits since it appears that already in the fifteenth century, Cesare Borgia, after having tasted it, sent two small barrels (under armed escort!) to Pope Alexander VI. Toni (1927) wrote that Alionza was one of the grape varieties that helped improve the quality of wine made around Bologna. All authors seem to concur that the wine made from it was of high quality, a neat trick given the 2001 suggestion by Filippetti, Silvestroni, Thomas, and Intrieri that it might be related to Trebbiano Toscano. Alionza is characterized by a large, long, pyramidal bunch, sparse, with one or two big wings. The round, yellow, thick-skinned berries are large. An early ripener (in the first ten days of September), it was abandoned, like many other varieties, due to poor productivity. There are currently only forty-three hectares under vine to Alionza in Italy, thirteen of which are near Bologna, its original home. The farmers who still apparently have Alionza in their vineyards include Walter Baiesi (1.1 hectares), Fernando Carretti (0.6 hectare), Guglielmo Falchieri (0.8 hectare), Mauro Baroni (1.3 hectares), and Laura Malaguti (1.5 hectares). It is part of the blend of the DOC Reno, and I am not aware of any pure bottling. The few artisanally made wines I have tried are perfumed, fresh, with notes of green apple, herbs, and yellow flowers. I may be wrong, but I think this wine deserves better than its present sorry fate.

Alvarega

WHERE IT'S FOUND: Sardinia. NATIONAL REGISTRY CODE NUMBER: not registered. COLOR: white.

Alvarega is a recently described variety grown in the Logudoro, in central-north Sardinia, around Ozieri. Cara (1909), in his treatise on the grape varieties of Sardinia, refers to large-scale cultivation of this variety and notes that it was much sought after by the local nobility. Thanks to the passion and energy of a group of local wine growers, the Associazione Alvarega di Ozieri, the variety has been brought back to national attention. These devoted volunteers sampled and selected the few Alvarega grapevines remaining back in 2003 and had them propagated. Alvarega is now the subject of ampelographic and genetic studies, with the aim of having it recognized as a distinct cultivar and getting it officially included in the National Registry of Grape Varieties. Microvinifications have been performed in the 2008, 2009, and 2010 vintages. Though I have yet to see the genetic data compiled, early information I have been given suggests that Alvarega is a distinct cultivar, and different from the Alvusignadu (or Arvesiniadu) variety also grown around Ozieri. The jury's out until we know more.

WINES TO TRY: Tonino Arcadu of Cantine Gostolai and Paolo Cardu, winemaker at Cantina di Monserrato, help produce Nobile Tola, the only monovarietal Alvarega wine I know. The wine is bright and fresh, sporting only 13 percent alcohol and reminds me of dried apricots, almonds, and fresh bread. Curiously, the late Giovanni Battista Columbu's excellent Malvasia Planargia is called Alvarega, which might not be a great idea.

Angela

WHERE IT'S FOUND: Emilia-Romagna. NATIONAL REGISTRY CODE NUMBER: not registered. COLOR: white.

Angela was once common in vineyards around Bologna, where in the nineteenth century it was part of the estimated fifty thousand quintals of table grapes produced each year. Today, though it has always been consumed as a table grape as well as used in wine, this variety risks extinction. In 2000 there were only a reported eight hectares of Angela planted in Italy, six of which were in the province of Bologna. This is a shame considering its antiquity: Marescalchi and Dalmasso (1937) report that Francesco Sacchetti wrote of an "Angiolla" grape already in the fourteenth century. There are apparently two biotypes, a Bolognese and a Romagnola, that are different both phenotypically and isoenzymatically, though some believe the latter to be identical to Verdea (also called San Colombano). I don't know of any SSR testing done on the two to determine if they are distinct varieties, but there is evidence suggesting the Romagnola biotype may also be Paradisa, a distinct local variety. Marzotto in 1935 describes Angela as "a magnificent grape and much in vogue on export markets," as it held up well to travel. In effect he was confirming what others, including Soderini (1590) and Di Rovasenda (1877), had written before him. I haven't tasted any monovarietal wines made with it, but have a few local names to visit.

Arilla

WHERE IT'S FOUND: Campania. NATIONAL REGISTRY CODE NUMBER: not registered. COLOR: white.

Arilla is typical of Ischia where it is still commonly used in DOC Ischia Bianco blends. It was first mentioned by D'Ascia (1867) and then by Nesbitt (1884), both of whom called it Agrilla; I find that nowadays most locals call it Uva Rilla. Its large bunch is compact, with medium-sized oval berries. The wine is rich and concentrated, but can develop volatile acidity. In old vineyards around Forio there is also an extremely rare biotype called Arillottola. I have spoken about Arilla many times to local growers on my annual visits to Ischia, and almost everyone on the island, from Andrea d'Ambra to Gino Iacono of Pietratorcia, feels the grape could have a fine-wine future but it is excessively sensitive to oidium, and therefore that goal has never been much pursued. Certainly, curbing Arilla's very generous productive tendencies would be a must for any discernible flavor to become apparent. I have tasted supposedly pure, artisanally made Arilla wines and found them to be tannic and a little neutral, with lowish acidity. However, the value of such a tasting experience was strongly limited by the winemaking talent involved, so I'm not sure what to think of Arilla's potential, or lack thereof. In 2013, I began a project with Giancarlo Carriero, the enlightened owner of the Albergo Regina Isabella at Lacco Ameno in Ischia, in which the hotel will work with small local growers in an effort to help preserve Ischia's viticultural biodiversity. It is everyone's hope that limited little quantities of monovarietal bottlings of arilla and other local cultivars will be successfully produced, and in that case the hotel will buy the bottles and offer local wine producers an opportunity to sell more of their wines. I am doing so free of charge and am impressed by Carriero's enthusiasm and willingness to give this a try; only time will tell how successful the project will be, but it's a start.

Arvesiniadu

WHERE IT'S FOUND: Sardinia. NATIONAL REGISTRY CODE NUMBER: 15. COLOR: white.

A true native of Sardinia rather than a Spanish import, Arvesiniadu is now almost extinct, remaining in only a few scattered plots in the provinces of Sassari and in the Campidano area of Sardinia. However, it may be more abundant than is commonly believed, since it was recently reported that the Vernaccia di Oristano grown around Arguingeniau is actually Arvesiniadu. Arvesiniadu has been described by Manca dell'Arca (1780), who called it Arvu Siniagu, and by Cara (1909), who listed its synonyms as Alvusignadu (Ozieri), Arvisiniadu (Bono), and Arvusiniagu (Sassari). Other synonyms used today include Argu Ingiannau, Alvu, and Arvu Siniadu. The first complete description is by Bruni (1964), who explains that the variety's scarce diffusion was due to a low base fertility rate. Sanna (2000) has since described three different biotypes that are currently the subject of university studies, and are distinguishable by morphologic differences: long-clustered, short-clustered, and double-clustered; in all three the cluster is very large. According to Sanna these three biotypes are genetically separate from any other island variety. All three have a cuneiform-shaped leaf, and small berries with thick golden-yellow skin. Vigorous, but characterized by extremely frail shoots, Arvesiniadu seems to take well to granite-rich soils. In the past, it was usual to make three different wines featuring it: pure 100 percent arvesiniadu, a blend with Vermentino, and an oxidized *Vernaccia*-like wine where the open-top barrels were attacked by flor. The grape is included in a slew of Sardinian wine blends, including Barbagia, Isola dei Nuraghi, Planargia, Romangia, and Valle del Tirso. It is also used as a table grape locally.

The wine was essentially brought back to life in the early 1990s thanks to the efforts of a group of local growers collaborating with experts at the Consorzio Interprovinciale della Frutticoltura di Cagliari and the University of Sassari. The Mulas estate is currently the only producer of monovarietal wines that I know. Founded in 2002 (prior to this it was the Salvatore Cabras estate), Mulas owns three hectares of the variety near Nurcoro (Bono) on the hills of Goceano. The wine I have tried over the years are by only one estate, so it's difficult to draw any conclusions about what the variety is all about. I can say the dry wine is refreshing and easygoing, showing a lovely floral side, with breezy sage and thyme nuances complementing yellow apple and pear flavors. I have yet to taste the sweet version.

WINES TO TRY: Mulas* (Niadu, a dry wine, and Avrè, a delicately sweet one).

Avarengo

WHERE IT'S FOUND: Piedmont. NATIONAL REGISTRY CODE NUMBER: 18. COLOR: red.

Also called Avarenc, Avarena, Mustèr (in the Canavese), and Riundasca (in the Biellese), Avarengo must not be confused with another rare local native typical of the Val Chisone called Avarenchetto, which is apparently a distinct variety. Avarengo was first mentioned by the Marchese Incisa di Rochetta Tanaro in 1852, who described two variants, the more common Avarengo and Ramefessa Avarengo, named for its copious, branch-filled canopy. It was popular in the nineteenth century, at least in Piedmont, and wines were classified as *grosso* (coarse), *fine* (fine), *piccolo* (small), *mezzano* (half), and, somewhat confusingly, *di Piemonte* (of Piedmont). Vouillamoz and Moriondo (2011) reported a close genetic relationship between it and Ner d'Ala, another variety typical of the area and of the Valle d'Aosta. Avarengo's cluster is medium-large, conical-pyramidal, winged, and fairly compact. The berry is medium-large and spherical, with thick, very resistant skin of a deep blue-black hue. It's an early ripener. Avarengo was also used as a table grape, but its small yields (its name stems from *avaro*, miserly) spelled doom for it in the twentieth century. Today it grows mainly in the Pinerolese area of Piedmont, and in the Chisone, Pellice, and Susa valleys; it is used in the Ramié blend with other local grapes such as Avanà. There probably aren't more than 200 or 250 hectoliters of wine made annually, and none, to the best of my knowledge, are 100 percent pure. Locals have told me that the grape produces a lightly hued red wine, with aromas of faded flowers and flavors of fresh red berries.

Baratuciat

WHERE IT'S FOUND: Piedmont. NATIONAL REGISTRY CODE NUMBER: 413. COLOR: white.

A rare native of Piedmont limited to the Val Cenischia and the Valsusa, Baratuciat's name is derived from *baratuciati*, or *bale di cià* in the Piedmontese dialect, meaning "cat's testicles": apparently, the cultivar's long, oval berries are reminiscent of a tomcat's reproductive organs. It prefers rocky soils not rich in clay and is both vigorous and disease resistant, ripening by late

September. In my view, this variety has huge potential; Cesare Zeppa and Luca Rolle of the University of Turin's agriculture department, who have studied its viticultural and enological aspects, agree. However, if we are even able to talk about this variety, the credit must go to Giorgio Falca, a passionate nature lover who unexpectedly passed away in the summer of 2012 (it was his vines of Baratuciat that Zeppa and Rolle studied). Falca singlehandedly brought Baratuciat back to everyone's attention by propagating a century-old pergola-trained Baratuciat vine in a modern vineyard in Almese. Wines I tried by Falca (he made only a few hundred bottles a year) showed pretty white-flower and delicately spicy notes that make it not unlike a very delicate blend of Sauvignon Blanc and Gewürztraminer. I'm holding out hope that Baratuciat will be heard of a lot more in the near future, and that Falca's absence won't mean a loss of interest in this great little variety and wine.

WINES TO TRY: Giorgio Falca. Casa Ronsil owns sixty-, and even eighty-year-old vines, and makes a wine called Maestro that is 60 percent Baratuciat, but no pure version unfortunately.

Barbarossa

WHERE IT'S FOUND: Liguria. NATIONAL REGISTRY CODE NUMBER: not registered. COLOR: white.

Though there are many Barbarossa varieties (Di Rovasenda alone lists thirteen different ones in 1877), the one I describe here is the one historically grown in Liguria and is still found in sporadic rows; other Barbarossa varieties are grown today in Emilia-Romagna and Calabria. Apparently the variety is named after Barbe-Russe, a famous Turkish admiral and corsair whose real name was Khair Ad-Din, who conquered Algiers, Tunis, and Nice in 1543, but this may only be the stuff of legends. For this reason some have hypothesized a Middle Eastern origin for this variety. The Ligurian variety is also known as Barbarossa di Finalborgo, and as Verduna or Verdona in the area around Finale. The bunch is compound and sparse, with oval or irregularly spherical, thin-skinned berries; it changes color late in the season, at the end of August. Galet believed that this Barbarossa was synonymous with the Barbarossa variety grown on the island of Corsica, but there is no real proof of this. Scalabrelli, D'Onofrio, Paolicchi, and Bucelli (2005) studied the genetic and ampelographic characteristics of vines identified in the Lunigiana, and found that Barbarossa ripens well, has moderately loose clusters and low susceptibility to rot, and gives very good-quality wines.

Where the myriad of other grapes called Barbarossa is concerned, there's practically no chance that any of them are related, though in the absence of genetic profiling, I have no way to be sure. In 1955, Mario Pezzi, former owner of Fattoria Paradiso in Bertinoro in Emilia-Romagna discovered a century-old vine of a variety that he also called Barbarossa, but some think it was actually Centesimino. Zulini, Russo, and Peterlunger (2002) mentioned a Puglian Barbarossa, while Costantini, Monaco, Vouillamoz, Forlani, and Grando (2005) reported on a Campanian Barbarossa variety.

WINES TO TRY: I haven't yet tasted any monovarietal wines made with the Lunigiana Barbarossa. The Barbarossa by Fattoria Paradiso in Emilia-Romagna is fruity and thick, with almost red-fruit jam flavors, but with vibrant acids giving it a light palate presence. It's a medium-bodied wine that will match well with simple pasta dishes and pizza; I wouldn't hold on to it for more than a year or two.

Barbera Bianca

WHERE IT'S FOUND: Piedmont, Lombardy. NATIONAL REGISTRY CODE NUMBER: 20. COLOR: white.

Barbera Bianca is an ancient variety originating from the Aqui and Alessandria territories in Piedmont, though a Barbera Bianca, possibly not the same grape, was also grown in the Oltrepò area of Lombardy according to Di Rovasenda (1877) and Molon (1906). Once common, it is now reduced to only a few rows of vines in scattered vineyards of Piedmont, mainly in the countryside around Ovada and Acqui Terme (Cremolino, Morsasco, Strevi). To make a complicated subject matter even more difficult, in these regions it is unfortunately also called Carica L'asino, of which there are countless similarly named grapes in Italy, one of which is synonymous with Barbassese.

Different research teams have shown that Barbera Bianca is unrelated to the more famous red-berried Barbera variety (Sefc, Lefort, Grando, Scott, Steinkellner, and Thomas 2000; Schneider and Mattivi 2006). Barbera Bianca's name derives from its physical resemblance to Barbera and its wine can be just as acidic as that made with its red namesake, but the similarities end there. In fact, both Demaria and Leardi (1855) and Di Rovasenda (1877) found that the two varieties shared slightly similar oval berries and little else. Barbera Bianca has a thick-skinned elliptical berry, ripens neither early nor late, and is very resistant to spring frosts and most diseases. The bunch is cylindrical-conical and medium in size. The wine made from it is apparently fresh and easygoing, not very alcoholic, and delicately perfumed with white-flower aromas. Barbera Bianca is always blended into a generic white wine with other local grape varieties such as Timorasso, Favorita, and even Moscato Bianco (for example in the Colli Tortonesi Bianco DOC).

Barbera del Sannio

WHERE IT'S FOUND: Campania. **NATIONAL REGISTRY CODE NUMBER:** not registered. **COLOR:** red.

Froio was the first to call this variety Barbera del Sannio, for its morphological resemblance to Piedmont's Barbera. In fact, the variety had been previously described first by Gasparrini (1844) and later by Semmola (1848), by the name of Lugliese or Lugliatica. It is not yet officially recognized in the National Registry, though Costantini, Monaco, Vouillamoz, Forlani, and Grando (2005) found it to be a genetically distinct variety possibly related to Catalanesca, Casavecchia, and Summariello. The Summariello in this study was considered synonymous to Uva di Troia (which Sommarello has long been a synonym of), however, many other Somarello-named varieties exist in Italy; one, also from Puglia, has now been officially recognized as Somarello Rosso in the National Registry (number 459). In any case, I think it would be best if Barbera del Sannio's name were changed, since the Barbera tag only adds to confusion. As this is a completely different variety and wine, I think a distinct name might help not just producers, but also the wine-loving public.

The variety has conical-pyramidal bunches and slightly flattened round berries. Growers describe it as not too vigorous but a reliable producer, and susceptible to botrytis. It ripens early in October, and despite its "Barbera-like" name, it is apparently not so rich in acids.

Antica Masseria Venditti has always made a wine called Barbetta that I have followed over the years. Pleasant and easygoing, it has a juicy, savory quality to its red-cherry and delicate herbal flavors. A well-made, medium-bodied red wine, it's ideal with hearty fare. Anna Bosco also makes an impressive, more floral (geranium and rose, with hints of underbrush) version with the usual barbera-like juicy, fresh acidity. The wine also ages very well, and I have had the chance to try bottles going back to 2007 numerous times. Though the 2007 might be beginning to fade, the 2008 is still drinking splendidly, and the 2009 is the best of all thus far.

WINES TO TRY: Antica Masseria Venditti** (Barbetta), Anna Bosco** (Armonico), A' Cancellera.

Barbera Sarda

WHERE IT'S FOUND: Sardinia. **NATIONAL REGISTRY CODE NUMBER:** 21. **COLOR:** red.

Despite its name, Barbera Sarda is completely unrelated to the better-known Barbera of Piedmont, and is a recent island discovery, as it was not listed in official documentation until 1965. It was inserted into the National Registry of Grape Varieties in 1988 and was well described only in 2001. It grows mainly around Cagliari; as of 2002 there were roughly 174 hectares planted. SSR microsatellite testing has shown it to be distinct from but closely related to both Muristellu and Bovale Sardo (Nieddu 2011). Barbera Sarda (or, more precisely, the Barbera Sarda that was sampled in the Parteolla countryside of Sardinia) is genetically unrelated to any other Sardinian variety (Lovicu, Farci, Sedda, Labra, De Mattia, Grassi, and Bacchetta 2010). It is not identical to Carignano, as had been previously thought. The bunch is conical-cylindrical, medium-small (270 grams), with medium-sized, roundish-oval, deep-blue berries. It ripens in September. A few artisanally made wines I have tried over the years were, not surprisingly given its name, characterized by high acidity, but I can't be sure that the wines really were monovarietal, as these grapevines are often interplanted with other cultivars and the farmers usually harvest all the varieties together.

WINES TO TRY: There are no monovarietal Barbera Sarda wines, but the Cantina di Dolianova has started making a wine called Terresicci in which Barbera Sarda is the main player (85 percent), together with Syrah and Montepulciano.

Barbesino

WHERE IT'S FOUND: Emilia-Romagna, Lombardy. NATIONAL REGISTRY CODE NUMBER: not registered. COLOR: white.

Though it's making a comeback of sorts today, Barbesino is another variety that was much thought of by farmers of centuries past and has not made it into modern times in any large numbers, essentially because its wines lack much color. It is also known as Barbesina, Barbesino Bianco, Ortrugo di Rovescala, and Ortrugo di Bobbio, though the latter two are particularly inaccurate terms as they engender confusion with Ortrugo, a completely different variety. It is originally from the Val Trebbia zone of Emilia-Romagna, and is characterized by good vigor and productivity, a cylindrical, small and compact grape bunch, and round, medium-sized, yellow-green berries. It ripens quickly, so it is usually harvested in the first ten days of September. Clearly, this is a different variety from Grignolino (which is red), though Barbesino was long used as a synonym for it.

Bariletta

WHERE IT'S FOUND: Campania. NATIONAL REGISTRY CODE NUMBER: not registered. COLOR: red.

Antonio Di Spirito, a proud southern Italian who has written in some of my wine guides and web sites, discovered Bariletta wine a few years back on one of his forays in the Campanian countryside and quickly let me have a smell and taste. The wine was impressive enough that we presented it at the 2010 Roma Vino Excellence wine fair, when the wine was still in the final stages of production. This was almost surely a first for Bariletta, at least outside Campania. An apparently very old grape variety that was well known to ancient Romans, according to recent DNA analysis Bariletta might be related to the *Primitivo*s. The first commercial vintage was 2010. Loaded with red-cherry and dark-berry fruit, this midweight is marked by a note of licorice and smooth tannins.

WINES TO TRY: Telaro.

Belzamino

WHERE IT'S FOUND: Emilia-Romagna. NATIONAL REGISTRY CODE NUMBER: not registered. COLOR: white.

Very rare, almost extinct variety that survives in only a few sporadic rows near Faenza and Lugo in the province of Ravenna in the

Romagna portion of Emilia-Romagna. It must not be confused with Marzemino, which is also called Berzamino and Balsamina, or with Berverdino, though in the past it was considered to be a biotype of Marzemino. Silvestroni, Marangoni, and Faccioli (1986) describe it as one of the local grapevines of Emilia-Romagna. Apparently, it has medium-large, conical bunches and round berries, and ripens in late September. I have never seen it and have never tasted a wine made with it; but for Belzemino, survival is all that matters right now.

Bertinora

WHERE IT'S FOUND: Emilia-Romagna. NATIONAL REGISTRY CODE NUMBER: not registered. COLOR: white.

Bertinora is another almost-extinct variety that was once more common in the countryside around Cesena and Bertinoro. It was also known as Rossola and numerous writers including Pasqualini and Pasqui (1878) and Bazzocchi (1923) described it as having tightly packed bunches and very large, round berries. Bazzocchi pointed out the existence of a higher-quality biotype characterized by much looser, winged bunches and oval berries. All experts agreed that Bertinora was also an especially good table grape that kept longer than most other grape varieties. Bertinora ripens in the second half of September, but according to Marisa Fontana is now reduced to only a few scattered vines. The grapes are reserved for home consumption and it's not clear to me if anyone is making wine with it.

Bervedino

WHERE IT'S FOUND: Emilia-Romagna. NATIONAL REGISTRY CODE NUMBER: 24. COLOR: white.

Also known as Berverdino and now quite rare, Bervedino is found mainly in the Valle dell'Arda in Emilia-Romagna. Along with other rare varieties such as Melara and Santa Maria, it is used to make Vin Santo di Vigoleno, a Colli Piacentini DOC, and one of Italy's better sweet wines. Historically, it was often confused with Erbaluce though the two varieties are not found in the same regions and have since been determined to be distinct (Cosmo, Sardi, and Calò 1962). A rare description in the literature is by Boselli and Venturi (1993). The bunch is medium in size, pyramidal or conical, usually winged, and compact. The berry is thick skinned and dehydrates very well, explaining its usefulness in late-harvest and air-dried wines. As they ripen, the berries turn an almost amber-gold hue; the harvest usually takes part in the last half of September. Apparently it thrives in poorer soils, and does not like excessive humidity. I've tried artisanal pure dry wines, all blessed with high acidity and delicate floral aromas, but I am unaware of any monovarietal bottling commercially available. Genetic analysis performed on Bervedino accessions by Torello Marinoni, Raimondi, Ruffa, Lacombe, and Schneider (2009) confirmed that it is synonymous with Vernaccia di San Gimignano, but I am unaware of any further studies on the matter. However, the same study apparently misattributes Canaiolo Bianco as synonymous with Vernaccia di San Gimignano (according to Storchi, Armanni, Randellini, Giannetto, Meneghetti, and Crespan 2011), further evidence of how hard it is to draw conclusions from genetic tests if sampling errors occur in the vineyards. As the National Registry lists Bervedino separately, and Marisa Fontana, probably the greatest expert on Emilia-Romagna grape varieties, also considers the variety distinct from others, I will continue to consider it a distinct variety until new research results help us clarify the matter.

Bianca Capriana

WHERE IT'S FOUND: Veneto. NATIONAL REGISTRY CODE NUMBER: not registered. COLOR: white.

Sporadically grown in the province of Verona, Bianca Capriana seems not to have left any believable historic documentation—

though the annals are filled with "Bianco-Something" varieties, and understanding which might be Bianca Capriana is no easy task. It was rediscovered and planted in the experimental vineyard of the Centro per la Sperimentazione in Vitivinicoltura (Center for Study and Experimentation in Viticulture) of the province of Verona in the late 1970s. A nonaromatic variety, it is characterized by a medium-small, cylindrical, usually sparse grape bunch (130 grams on average), and round, thick-skinned, yellow berries. It ripens in September, has good vigor and medium resistance to common pests. The microvinifications I've tasted remind me of dried fruits and ripe, almost stewed apples. The wine is light bodied and fresh, with clean acidity and a saline nuance; it's actually not bad.

Bianchino Faentino

See MONTÙ, chapter 4.

Bianco Antico

WHERE IT'S FOUND: Campania. NATIONAL REGISTRY CODE NUMBER: not registered. COLOR: white.

Also known as Pinot Antico, Bianco Antico is a very rare variety that has genetic profiles similar to those of the *Falanghina*s and Pinot Blanc. It has only recently come back to attention; the first Bianco Antico wines were made in 2009. I have not tasted it, but reportedly the wine tastes of ripe citrus fruit and yellow apple, with a pretty floral nose. As Bianco Antico is high in acidity, it is thought it might make very good sparkling wines. I know of no bottles available for sale.

Bianco Comune

WHERE IT'S FOUND: Valle d'Aosta. NATIONAL REGISTRY CODE NUMBER: not registered. COLOR: white.

This is one of the most recently rediscovered native grape listed in this book. Prior to 2007, the variety was thought extinct, but Vouillamoz and Moriondo located two centenary vines near the Valle d'Aosta cities of Gressan and Aosta, which were subsequently proven to be Bianco Comune or Gros Blanc (or Blanc Comun, as it is called in French Switzerland). The phenotype of the two grapevines reportedly matched with that of Bianco Comune as documented by Gatta in 1838, and DNA testing proved the vines under examination to be of a distinct variety. Bianco Comune was the most common white grape of the middle Valle d'Aosta in the nineteenth century, but only a few years later its cultivation was declining. Clearly, there is no wine yet made from this variety, so all we can do is wait and hope that it will be multiplied and propagated quickly so that we may all taste a sip of history.

Biancone

WHERE IT'S FOUND: Tuscany. NATIONAL REGISTRY CODE NUMBER: 30. COLOR: white.

Limited to the island of Elba, and not produced in any numbers of commercial interest, Biancone's high yields have masked its true potential in recent years. For this reason, it was long confused with the highly productive Trebbiano Toscano. The bunch is short and pyramidal, with two wings, and like those of the *Trebbiano*s, very large (roughly seven hundred grams!). The berries are dark yellow-green and are harvested in September, usually later than Trebbiano Toscano. Biancone appears to grow particularly well on the island of Elba. For wines, search for the estate of Antonio Arrighi, who knows Biancone better than most people and is in love with his local native grapes. He owns fifty-year-old vines but not enough to make a monovarietal bottling, choosing to blend Biancone into his Elba Bianco wine. Arrighi feels that Biancone adds perfume and acidity to *Trebbiano*-based wines, but that it needs well-exposed sites, otherwise it doesn't ripen fully. Biancone has been apparently planted in Australia, though I'm not sure the variety planted there is exactly the same variety grown on Elba, given that Biancone is a name commonly used to describe other varieties in Italy. Furthermore, it's used there to make dessert wines, which is not the case in Italy. It's reportedly grown in South Australia by Angoves Winery, and in Victoria by Lake Moodemere Vineyards, and apparently results are more than satisfying.

Bian Ver

WHERE IT'S FOUND: Piedmont. NATIONAL REGISTRY CODE NUMBER: not registered. COLOR: white.

Bian Ver, also known as Verdesse in France, is also found in the Valais of Switzerland. In Piedmont it is now rare, with sporadic vines located in the Alta Valsusa, in the Val Chisone (Pomaretto and Perosa Argentina) and in the Pinerolese; it's just as rare in France, which some believe it is native to (specifically, the Vallée de Grésivaudan in Isère). It is characterized by a small, cylindrical bunch, with one or two small wings, and medium-small berries. However, the grape has noteworthy winemaking potential according to Piedmontese producers who still own vines, accumulating sugars easily while maintaining very high acidity levels and expressing ripe tropical fruit aromas and flavors in the finished wines. I hope it makes a comeback quickly, and there are some encouraging signs. My glass is ready and waiting.

Bigolona

WHERE IT'S FOUND: Veneto. NATIONAL REGISTRY CODE NUMBER: not registered. COLOR: white.

A very rare variety grown especially around Verona (in the Valpolicella and the Val Illasi), Bigolona is also known as Bigolara, Sampagna, and Smarzirola. It has always been used with other local varieties to make an air-dried sweet wine. The grape cluster is cylindrical, long, compact, and large (432 grams), with round but not uniform berries of golden-yellow hue. It ripens by September and is characterized by high vigor but very poor resistance to grey rot (not surprising, given the compact bunch). I have tasted microvinifications and the wine has a strong citrus note, with hints of sweet spices and white flowers. It struck me as a potentially interesting, nonaromatic variety, but I can't see farmers lining up to plant it, given its botrytis sensitivity.

Blanchet

WHERE IT'S FOUND: Piedmont. NATIONAL REGISTRY CODE NUMBER: not registered. COLOR: white.

One of the many "whitey" or *Bianchetto* varieties of Italy, Blanchet is characterized by early ripening and good sugar accumulation, and by medium-sized, pyramidal bunches and medium-sized, round berries. As it is low in acids, it has historically been blended with another local but high-acid native, Preveiral, to make the wines typical of the Valli Chisone and Germanasca in the Pinerolese, in Turin. The wines are simple and easygoing, ideal as aperitifs or paired with simply prepared fish and vegetable dishes.

The French variety Roussette d'Ayze grown in the Haute-Savoie region is supposedly synonymous to Italy's Blanchet. Which country can lay claim to the grape as their own is still a matter of some conjecture.

Bonamico

WHERE IT'S FOUND: Tuscany. NATIONAL REGISTRY CODE NUMBER: 34. COLOR: red.

Originally from the Pisa area in Tuscany, Bonamico was first documented by Di Rovasenda in 1877, and is also known as Giacomino or Uva di Palaia. However, viticulturalist Stefano Dini believes that Giacomino and Bonamico are two distinct varieties: "Bonamico's leaf has a downy underside, making it resemble Canaiolo Nero, while Giacomino's is hairless—that's a big difference in ampelographic circles." Bonamico was always a favorite with farmers, as it flowers late (and hence does not suffer spring frosts) and because of its abundant productivity; as its name indicates, it was seen as a "good friend" to farmers. Due to its high vigor and potentially copious productivity, it is best planted in poorly fertile soils. "It's a very hardy variety," says Dini. "At the Fattoria del Buonamico, in Montecarlo near Lucca, there are very old Bonamico vines growing near an old dilapidated house. Even completely abandoned, they still manage to produce grapes every year. It just won't take no for an answer, and we're going to start making monovarietal *rosato* with it." Today Bonamico is grown mainly in the viticultural areas around Pisa, Pistoia, and Lucca; Montescudaio DOC wines can contain Bonamico. It tends to produce wines of low alcoholic strength and color, in which optimal polyphenolic ripeness is achieved only by green harvesting with gusto or by draconian yield reductions.

Bonarda Piemontese

WHERE IT'S FOUND: Piedmont. NATIONAL REGISTRY CODE NUMBER: 35. COLOR: red.

Not to be associated with the wine bonarda, which is made mainly with the Croatina grape, Bonarda Piemontese is also known as Bonarda di Chieri and Bonarda del Monferrato. In Northern Italy another cultivar, Uva Rara, is often referred to as Bonarda, further confusing matters. First described by Count Nuvolone in 1799, who was excited about its winemaking qualities, today Bonarda Piemontese is found especially around the towns of Chieri, Castelnuovo Don Bosco, and Albugnano (Asti). Small percentages are used in DOC wines Bramaterra, Coste della Sesia, Collina Torinese, Canavese, and a few others, none very famous. The grape bunch is medium-large, pyramidal, with two or even three wings, and is sparse. The medium-small, spherical or elliptical, deep blue-black berries are harvested in late September or early October. The wine is fresh and floral, lightly acidic, and quite tannic, leaving you with a dry mouthfeel, but unless you vacation locally, it's very hard to find one that is 100 percent pure Bonarda Piemontese. And even then, given the local habit of calling any wine made with various blends of many different grapes "bonarda," I'm not sure how one could be certain about exactly what he or she is drinking.

There is plenty of so-called Bonarda planted in Argentina, but most of it is in fact another variety altogether, Corbeau. Some true Bonarda probably does grow in Argentina, thanks to Italian immigrants who brought it with them during their immigrant travels—though which Bonarda they brought is anybody's guess. While in London recently to do some work, I tasted a Argentinean Sangiovese-Bonarda wine made by the Zuccardo Family ("Vida Organica") and though their Bonarda grapes were reportedly brought over from Italy, I have yet to confirm that.

Bonda

WHERE IT'S FOUND: Val d'Aosta. NATIONAL REGISTRY CODE NUMBER: 348. COLOR: red.

The name of this variety derives from the Bonda or Bondaz family, a very common surname in both Valle d'Aosta and Piedmont, where this variety might have originated; the first to mention the grape Bonda was Gatta in the mid-nineteenth century. Even then Bonda was one of the least common grape varieties of the region. Subsequently in the nineteenth century, Di Rovasenda and Louis Napoléon Bich created confusion by conflating it with Prié Rouzo or Prié Rouge, an altogether different (and far more abundant) grape, better known as Prëmetta or Primetta. DNA testing by Vouillamoz and Moriondo (2011) has proved that Bonda has second-degree relationships with Nosiola from Trentino and with the rare Mossano Nero of Piedmont; the latter is practically no longer cultivated. Today, Bonda is sporadically found in the middle part of the Valle d'Aosta, mainly around the hamlets of Chatillon and Quart, on the right bank of the Dora Baltea River. The bunch is large, pyramidal, winged, and compact. The berry is also large, spherical, thick skinned, and blue-black. It is very resistant to sunburn (an important quality in sun-soaked, high-altitude mountain vineyards) and it is usually harvested in mid-October (clearly, this late-ripening quality is not much appreciated in alpine environments). The wine is ruby-purple in hue with garnet tinges, lightly fruity and vinous on the nose, almost tart and low in alcohol. The Institut Agricole Régional has saved vines and planted them in experimental vineyard collections, so at least the variety will not become extinct while people figure out what winemaking potential it might have, if any.

Boschera

WHERE IT'S FOUND: Veneto. NATIONAL REGISTRY CODE NUMBER: 326. COLOR: white.

Boschera's name derives from *boschi* (woods), since this variety once grew near forests at high altitudes, though it is also called Pevarela, Peverella, Uva del Prete, Balotona, Biancona, and Agresto. It used to be widely planted in the Treviso area where it was appreciated for its resistance to vine diseases. Today it is found in significant quantities only in the production zone of Vittorio Veneto, in the DOC Colli di Conegliano-Torchiato di Fregona. The bunch is medium-sized but heavy (350 grams), pyramidal, winged, and medium compact. The berry is medium-sized and oval in shape, but often has variable shapes. The skin is medium-thick and yellow-green, with small brown spots when fully ripe. It is very vigorous, so lowland vineyards on fertile soils are best avoided. The wine is yellow-green, bright and fresh, with white stone-fruit and fresh flower aromas and flavors. Robinson, Harding, and Vouillamoz (2012) list it as identical to Verdicchio based on unpublished data by Vouillamoz and Grando, but I have failed to find other evidence of this, and none of the local producers I have talked to over the years has ever mentioned that they thought or knew Boschera might be Verdicchio. Of course, this doesn't mean that it isn't Verdicchio, but for now it remains officially listed as a separate variety in the National Registry.

Bracciola Nera

WHERE IT'S FOUND: Tuscany, Liguria. NATIONAL REGISTRY CODE NUMBER: 39. COLOR: red.

Apparently, Bracciola Nera was first described in 1590 by Soderini as growing in northern Tuscany and the eastern viticultural production zone of Liguria (Riviera di Levante), but strangely he listed it as a very good *white* grape. Acerbi described it in the Cinque Terre in 1825 and so did De Astis in 1937. Today it is grown in only 25 hectares in the provinces of Massa Carrara and La Spezia, and can be tasted in the DOC Colli di Luni blends. The variety is easy to recognize thanks to its large, very elongated cylindrical, sparse, winged bunch. The dark-blue berries come in various shapes and are midsized. It ripens late (end of September or early October), and production is usually abundant. It is characterized by high total acidity and fresh floral and fruity flavors.

Bressana

See SCHIAVA GROUP, chapter 3.

Brugnola

WHERE IT'S FOUND: Lombardy. NATIONAL REGISTRY CODE NUMBER: not registered. COLOR: red.

Brugnola's main claim to fame is that it has a parent-offspring relationship with Nebbiolo, which has been cultivated in the same Lombard areas for millennia. Brugnola was once considered a synonym of Emilia-Romagna's Fortana, but this is incorrect as the two are distinct varieties. Brugnola's bunch is medium-large, conical, and long, while the blue-black berry is oval and large. There are two clones: clone 10, with a round leaf and a sparse bunch, and clone 12, which has a pentagonal leaf and a more compact bunch. There is also a biotype that has a red stalk. In Lombardy, Brugnola is grown mainly around Tirano in Valtellina. It is never bottled as a monovarietal wine, but instead is used as a minor blending component of wines which feature Nebbiolo. The best grapes were always thought to be those of Poggioridenti in Inferno or Montagna on the borders of Valtellina.

Brunetta di Rivoli

WHERE IT'S FOUND: Piedmont. NATIONAL REGISTRY CODE NUMBER: not registered. COLOR: red.

Not to be confused with Brunetta (a synonym for Chatus), Brunetta di Rivoli is a very rare variety grown in sporadic vines all over Piedmont, especially in the Val Susa and near Rivoli. Local growers who still make small amounts of wine for family consumption speak highly of its deep colored, soft wines. It can have trouble ripening in cooler years and suffers from berry shot, but is otherwise resistant and productive. The bunch is medium-sized, cylindrical, and winged while berries are round and small.

Bsolla

WHERE IT'S FOUND: Emilia-Romagna. NATIONAL REGISTRY CODE NUMBER: not registered. COLOR: white.

Bsolla is an almost extinct variety that to the best of my knowledge has only been described ampelographically, and has never had any genetic analysis performed on it. According to Baldini (1995), Gallesio was the first to describe the variety in 1839, but Morri also mentions it in 1840 as a "loosely packed, large-berried grape." Bazzocchi (1923) gave the first accurate description of Bsolla, mentioning that it was allowed to run free, and was typically wound around trees for support. It appears that when this type of viticulture was abandoned, so was the variety. Bsolla is characterized by medium-large, conical bunches and round berries, and is very vigorous and a high yielder. Apparently, in centuries past it was used to make a good wine for everyday drinking.

Bubbierasco

WHERE IT'S FOUND: Piedmont. NATIONAL REGISTRY CODE NUMBER: not registered. COLOR: red.

This rare variety is the offspring of Nebbiolo and Bianchetto di Saluzzo and grows typically in the Salluzese area of the region. It is currently the subject of microvinifications to see what winemaking potential it may have.

Bundula

WHERE IT'S FOUND: Piedmont. NATIONAL REGISTRY CODE NUMBER: not registered. COLOR: red.

Bundula is also known as Bondola or Bonda, and should not be confused with the Bonda of Valle d'Aosta (see BONDA entry), which though rare is more common than Bundula. That tells you that Bundula is an almost mythical variety in Italy. By contrast it is common in Switzerland's Ticino region, where it is a true native variety. In Italy it's grown only in the Val d'Ossola. It has a small, conical, winged bunch and medium-sized, oval berries. As it is an early ripener it is sensitive to spring frosts, and it is also sensitive to magnesium deficiency. The perfumed, light- to medium-bodied wine is simple and easygoing, with flavors and aromas of red currant and raspberry. In Ticino it lost out in favor of Merlot, but some producers are looking to bring it back. Frei, Porret, Frei, and Tafner (2006) showed that it is identical to the almost extinct Briegler, a grape that also used to grow in Switzerland.

Buriano

WHERE IT'S FOUND: Tuscany. NATIONAL REGISTRY CODE NUMBER: not registered. COLOR: white.

Buriano is a rare white cultivar found in northern Tuscany near Montecarlo that, though similar to Trebbiano Toscano, has very different leaves and much smaller bunches with pinkish berries when fully ripe. The wine is also very different because of aromas that are smoky and terpenic. The only producer of this wine was Fattoria Michi, under the winemaking consultation of Lorenzo Landi. However the cultivar has not been genetically analyzed, and so while I am listing it separately, we may yet learn that it is a biotype of Trebbiano Toscano or of another variety. The wine is certainly more interesting than any dry white wine made with the lowly Trebbiano Toscano.

WINES TO TRY: Fattoria Michi* (winemaker Lorenzo Landi tells me that this winery has been inactive since 2012).

Cabrusina

WHERE IT'S FOUND: Veneto. NATIONAL REGISTRY CODE NUMBER: not registered. COLOR: red.

Not much is known about Cabrusina, beyond that it is found in Valpolicella, where it is also known as Cambrusina and Montanara. Cosmo, writing in the mid-twentieth century, was so sure it was destined to become extinct that he didn't furnish ampelographic descriptions. In fact, Dalmasso, Cosmo, and Dell'Olio (1939) write that as vineyards were replanted, Cabrusina plantings decreased sharply, because people chose not to replant it in light of the less than stellar wines made with it. The first accurate description is by Cancellier, Costacurta, Angelini, and Segattini in their *Vecchi vitigni veronesi* (1980). The cluster is very large and can weigh up to one kilogram; it's pyramidal and compact, with one or two wings, and has large spherical but not uniform berries. The variety is vigorous and productive, with good disease resistance; the harvest is in late September or early October. The wine, tasted from microvinifications, is light ruby, fairly neutral in its aromas (which can be described as vinous or grapey at best), medium bodied, and tart. I'm not sure it's the Italian native grape with the brightest future.

Cacamosca

WHERE IT'S FOUND: Campania. NATIONAL REGISTRY CODE NUMBER: not registered. COLOR: white.

The curious name of this variety (*cacamosca* means fly excrement) derives from the brown blemishes that appear on the yellow-green berries when the grapes are fully ripe. Found only in Campania, and mainly in the provinces of Naples and Salerno, Cacamosca was believed to be identical to the Riciniello Bianco of Gaeta (Froio 1875). Both Froio and Nesbitt (1884) believed that the variety was especially abundant in the countryside around Naples, along the Amalfi coast near Ravello, and even in Irpinia around Avellino, where it was called Gaglioppo (the same name as the completely unrelated red variety of Calabria). According to Costantini, Monaco, Vouillamoz, Forlani, and Grando (2005) it has close genetic ties to Fenile, a variety typical of the Amalfi coast. Froio believed it to be a very high-quality variety, and according to him the wine made from Cacamosca was highly thought of and popular in nineteenth-century Paris. Today the grapevine is almost extinct. This is not surprising given the variety's low productivity, due to extremely poor vigor, very small cylindrical bunches, and very small spherical grapes. The wine made from it usually has good alcoholic strength and low acidity, so historically it was mainly used in blends.

Cacchione

See BELLONE, chapter 4.

Caddiu

WHERE IT'S FOUND: Sardinia. NATIONAL REGISTRY CODE NUMBER: 44. COLOR: red.

A rare variety currently grown on only twelve hectares in Sardinia (almost all around Oristano, in the lower valley of the Tirso), Caddiu is appreciated as a table grape because of its large, sweet berries. It is distinct from all other Sardinian varieties but is closely related to a little-known local called Paddiu. Most likely a true native of Sardinia, it's a variety with different names depending on which part of the island it is grown: Caddu (Bosa), Caddiu Neddu (Oristano), and Niedda Perda Sarda (Terralba). Very vigorous but not productive, it concentrates its energy into growing foliage. The bunch is medium-large (four hundred grams), cylindrical-pyramidal, and fairly compact. The grapes are medium-small and spherical, with a thick, crunchy skin, blue-black in hue; it ripens in late September or early October. I have yet to taste a pure Caddiu wine, but of course, I'd like to.

Calabrese di Montenuovo

WHERE IT'S FOUND: Sicily. NATIONAL REGISTRY CODE NUMBER: not registered. COLOR: red.

An important study addressing the genetic relationships between Campanian cultivars describes a number of different local *Calabrese* varieties (Costantini, Monaco, Vouillamoz, Forlani, and Grando 2005), of which Calabrese di Montenuovo became the most famous when, in 2007, Vouillamoz et al. concluded it was one of Sangiovese's parents, in a natural cross with Ciliegiolo (Vouillamoz, Monaco, Costantini, Stefanini, Scienza, and Grando 2007). Unfortunately this interpretation has since been contradicted by another couple of fine studies in which Ciliegiolo was determined to be an offspring of Sangiovese (Di Vecchi Staraz, Bandinelli, Boselli, This, Boursiquot, Laucou, et al. 2007; Cipriani, Spadotto, Jurman, Di Gaspero, Crespan, Meneghetti, et al. 2010). Clearly, more research on the matter is required.

Calbanesco

WHERE IT'S FOUND: Emilia-Romagna. NATIONAL REGISTRY CODE NUMBER: not registered. COLOR: white.

Calbanesco is a unique variety that was discovered in the vineyards of the Le Calbane estate in Emilia-Romagna, at Ricò di Meldola, in the valley of the Ridente; owner Cesare Raggi thought he had planted Sangiovese but a part of the vines was so different from the latter variety that studies were undertaken and showed a unique isoenzymatic pattern and SSR profile on ten microsatellite loci. The wine is also called calbanesco and is made by only one estate. It tastes and smells like a very good sangiovese, or perhaps like a richer Brunello.

WINES TO TRY: La Calbane**.

Campolongo

WHERE IT'S FOUND: Lazio. NATIONAL REGISTRY CODE NUMBER: 417. COLOR: white.

In the 1881 ampelographic bulletin drawn up by the Ministry of Agriculture, Industry and Commerce, Campolongo was considered a high-quality wine grape. Today its diffusion is miniscule, limited to the Valle del Comino and the Valle del Liri in southeastern Lazio, near the bustling city of Frosinone. The bunch is medium-sized, cylindrical, often winged, and fairly compact, with what to me look like very large berries (though ampelographic descriptions refer to them as medium-sized), oval and yellow-golden. Microvinifications reveal a very intense nose of flowers, apple, and citrus fruit complicated by richer notes of dried apricot. On the palate it shows balanced but high acids and considerable structure. Biochemical analysis has revealed significant concentrations of phenylethanol in the wine, which smells of roses. A promising variety.

Canaiolo Bianco

WHERE IT'S FOUND: Tuscany. NATIONAL REGISTRY CODE NUMBER: 48. COLOR: white.

Also commonly known as Drupeggio, Canaiolo Bianco is typical of Tuscany, where it was documented in 1817 by Gallesio. It appears also to have been grown in the region of Molise, around the town of Campobasso, where it was called Caciumo or Cacinello, and in Marche near Ascoli Piceno, where it was called Canina or Uva dei Cani (confusingly so, since there are other, unrelated *Canina* varieties in Italy). Today there are believed to be only about 110 hectares of Canaiolo Bianco left in Tuscany, mainly around the cities of Arezzo, Florence, Pisa, Prato, and Siena, though its presence is important in Umbria. There is one clone, ARSIAL-CRA 402. Historically, it was confused with Vernaccia di San Gimignano and only recently has its synonymity with Drupeggio been determined (Storchi, Armanni, Randellini, Giannetto, Meneghetti, and Crespan 2011). The grape cluster is medium-sized, pyramidal, winged, and compact. The grapes are medium-small and round, thick skinned, and whitish-green. The grapes are usually harvested in the first half of September. The wine actually holds promise, with a bigger body and more intense perfume than one would have believed. The main wines in which to catch a whiff of Canaiolo Bianco are Barco Reale di Carmignano, Bianco di Valdinievole in Tuscany, and Orvieto in Umbria.

This variety goes by many names: by Cardìn around Monastero Vasco (near Mondovì), around Montemale (near Dronero), and around Borsé (near Boves); by Montanera in the Saluzzese; by Neirano near Bibiana; by Barbera Dou Ciorniu (or Barbera Del Sordo) in Val di Susa; and by Dousét Vej (or Tadone) in the Canavese. Tadone and Neirano are misnomers, since these two are distinct varieties. It should also not be confused with Montanara, which is a synonym of both Cabrusina and Uva Tosca. Interestingly, a Cardìn described in the 1800s was late ripening, while the one I describe here is very early ripening, so it is likely they are different grapes. Historically Cardìn was also a table grape, and due to its precocious ripening, was used to make *nouveau*-styled, early drinking wines. Characterized by medium-sized berries and bunches, today it is virtually extinct but its early ripening personality is of interest to researchers and producers alike so we may yet hear more about this grape in the future.

Canino

WHERE IT'S FOUND: Emilia-Romagna. NATIONAL REGISTRY CODE NUMBER: not registered. COLOR: white.

First described by De Bosis in the *Bollettini Ampelografici Provinciali* (1879) as common in the countryside around Rimini, Canino is believed to be identical to Canino di Montiano and Canino di Bertinoro. It was not considered to be a source of high-quality wines, but was appreciated as a table grape; all the same, farmers grew it and made wine with it, since the variety is a hardy and dependable producer. It appears to be related to Vernaccina, and though it is also called Riminese, appears to be distinct from Riminese di Santo Rocco, another very little-known variety that is still being studied.

Cardìn

WHERE IT'S FOUND: Piedmont. NATIONAL REGISTRY CODE NUMBER: not registered. COLOR: red.

Cargarello

WHERE IT'S FOUND: Emilia-Romagna. NATIONAL REGISTRY CODE NUMBER: not registered. COLOR: white.

Typical of the area around Rimini, Cargarello is characterized by a very compact, large bunch and medium-large, round, yellow-green berries. It is currently the subject of in-depth studies, as it appears to have considerable fine-winemaking potential. Time will tell.

Caricagiola

WHERE IT'S FOUND: Sardinia. NATIONAL REGISTRY CODE NUMBER: 52. COLOR: red.

Caricagiola is also known as Bonifaccenco, Carcajola, and Garrigadolza; roughly 90 percent of the eighty-five hectares planted to it in Sardinia are in the northwestern Gallura area. Genetic testing has proved its relationship to a little-known native called Nieddu Procco, while it is neither related to the very similarly named Corsican variety Carcajola, as first postulated by Foëx (1909), nor to Mourvèdre. No clones are available yet. Apparently, its name derives from Carcaghjolu Nero ("the black one that gives lots of grapes," in the Corsican dialect). Some experts find it bears a very strong phenotypic resemblance to the Vermentino Nero of Liguria and Tuscany. It has also been suggested that Caricagiola is identical to Spain's Parraleta, since DNA profiling studies have suggested genetic identity between the latter and Tinta Caiada, which is believed to be identical to Corsica's Carcajolo Nero. However, until clearer, and more definitive evidence arrives, I will continue to list the variety separately as does Italy's National Registry.

Caricagiola's bunch is medium-sized, conical or cylindrical, with one or two wings, usually not compact. Grapes are medium-sized, round-oval, blue-black, and thick skinned. It ripens fully between the end of September and the beginning of October. I have tasted caricagiola made by local growers as well as the trial effort kindly sent me from the Convisar consortium; the wine is deeply colored, with very grapey, black- and red-berry aromas, rustic tannins, and mouth-searing acidity despite what you'll read elsewhere. It has promise, if not as a monovarietal wine then as part of blends, where its high acidity will add a measure of lightness to some heavy rich and alcoholic Sardinian reds. I liked what I've tasted so far, and as it's very different from carignanos or cannonaus (it's usually lighter, fruitier, and fresher), there may be a place for it among the island's vinous offerings.

Cascarolo

WHERE IT'S FOUND: Piedmont. NATIONAL REGISTRY CODE NUMBER: not registered. COLOR: white.

Cascarolo is cultivated only sporadically in the provinces of Asti and Turin, but has been well known since the 1600s (Croce 1606). It was once also popular as a table grape, but it does not appear that anyone is using it to make a monovarietal wine today. It is closely related to many French varieties (Vouillamoz, Schneider, and Grando 2006). Cascarolo's bunch is medium-large, long, and sparse. The name refers to berry shot (*cascola* from *cascano*, in reference to the flowers dropping).

Castagnara

WHERE IT'S FOUND: Campania. NATIONAL REGISTRY CODE NUMBER: not registered. COLOR: red.

Castagnara is found today mainly in the northern part of the Sorrento coast, especially on the slopes of the Lattari mountains around the towns of Casola, Gragnano, Lettere, and Sant'Antonio Abate. In the nineteenth century it was common around Naples and even on the slopes of Vesuvius. Today, the wine you are most likely to taste Castagnara in is the DOC Penisola Sorrentina, especially those from Lettere and Gragnano, but just how much Castagnara is included is anybody's guess. Some believe that Castagnara is identical to Sannese and Santamaria, but the three are reportedly phenotypically very different so I wonder. DNA analysis by the University of Portici has not shown any genetic ties to other known Campanian varieties thus far. Farmers have always loved this variety, as it's a very heavy producer. The bunches are medium sized, cylindrical, and winged, while grapes are small, spherical, and intensely blue-black. Harvest occurs in early October. The wine is weak in alcohol, and doesn't seem to have any redeeming features.

Castiglione

WHERE IT'S FOUND: Calabria. NATIONAL REGISTRY CODE NUMBER: 56. COLOR: red.

Grown in the provinces of Reggio Calabria and Cosenza, Castiglione has a medium-sized, pyramidal, winged, and sparse bunch, with large, oval, blue-black grapes; it is disease resistant. Unfortunately in Calabria they also use the name Castiglione for Magliocco Dolce and Nerello Mascalese, leading to confusion in correctly identifying the three. According to Grimaldi (2002), Castiglione was probably imported into Calabria in the 1700s, and was a favorite of farmers due to its productivity. It yields deeply hued wines since the grape skins are rich in malvin and not in easily oxidized pigments.

Catanese Nero

WHERE IT'S FOUND: Sicily. NATIONAL REGISTRY CODE NUMBER: 57. COLOR: red.

Catanese Nero is a little-known and rare grape that has little in common with other local grapes native to the area of the Etna volcano. Though it seems to have originated on the eastern part of the island, today it is cultivated only on the western side, around Palermo, Trapani, and Agrigento. It is mainly used to make simple rosé wines, and no DOC includes it. The bunch is medium-sized and elongated, with one or two wings. The grapes are big and round or at times oval. The skin is thin and blue-black. It is usually harvested in mid-September, and gives very acidic wines so it's best in blends. Famous winemaker Salvo Foti isn't even sure the vine still exists in vineyards anymore.

Cavrara

WHERE IT'S FOUND: Veneto. NATIONAL REGISTRY CODE NUMBER: 405. COLOR: red.

In 1754, Acanti described a wine named cavraio made around Vicenza, so this variety has been hanging around (literally) on Italian soil for quite some time. In 1825, Acerbi called the grape Caprara, but for many centuries there appeared to be more than one Cavrara, so experts spoke of a group of *Cavrara* grapes. For example, the *Bollettino del Comizio Agrario di Vicenza* (1868) listed Cavrara (or Garbiona), Cavrara di Monte, Cavrara del Picciuolo Verde, and Cavrara della Madonna. In 1901, Zava added the synonyms Bassanese and Bassanese del Peduncolo Rosso, and in 1925 Marzotto added Sgarbiona. Whether these were all the same variety or truly distinct cultivars is anybody's guess. Marzotto also mentions that Cavrara is a quality grape, confirming Zava's opinion; by contrast, earlier authors felt that Cavrara, or the *Cavrara* family, was good only for the production of inconsequential, light-bodied wines, though Cavrara del Peduncolo Rosso was the best of the lot. Today most experts believe there is only one Cavrara, generally called Cavrara or Cavrara Nera, while Cavrara Garbini is considered a biotype (Costacurta and Cancellier 1999). In any case, due to uneven and poor productivity, Cavrara was slowly phased out by producers. However, there are still some Cavrara grapevines growing in Veneto's Colli Berici near Vicenza, and in the flatland vineyards around Roncà near Verona.

The grape bunch is medium-large, pyramidal, winged, and neither compact nor sparse with oval, medium-sized, thick-skinned, blue-black berries. It is usually harvested in mid-October, when its leaves turn a deep red. Though it is generally disease resistant (except to peronospora) and fertile, it suffers during cold rainy springs due to its early flowering. The wine is dark purple-red and perfumed (raspberry, blackberry), with good alcohol levels and high acidity, though it tends to lack body. It might have a future for sparkling wine production.

Cellerina

WHERE IT'S FOUND: Piedmont. NATIONAL REGISTRY CODE NUMBER: not registered. COLOR: red.

Sporadically present in the Tortonese, Ovadese, and Astigiano areas on both sides of the Tanaro River, Cellerina seems to grow best on alluvial, iron-rich soils. It has a long, medium-sized, very sparse bunch and long wing, with medium-sized, round berries. Botrytis resistant, it is used mainly in blends to make air-dried or late-harvest sweet wines for local consumption. Cellerina is at times erroneously called Balsamina, a name usually reserved for Uva Rara in Piedmont and for Marzemino elsewhere in Italy.

Cenerente

WHERE IT'S FOUND: Veneto. **NATIONAL REGISTRY CODE NUMBER**: not registered. **COLOR**: red.

Much like Molinara, Cenerente's name is due to its berries, so thickly covered in bloom they look coated by ash (*cenere*). For this reason it was also called, especially in the Soave area, Farinente, from *farina* (flour). Actually, Di Rovasenda describes both varieties in 1877, but Bertani in 1883 reiterates that the two are synonyms. Opinions about its winemaking potential were discordant: while Alberti (1896) thought it magnificent (in particular because of its late budbreak, disease resistance, and high capacity to adapt to different *terroirs*), Zava (1901) was much less positive, criticizing the wines for being deficient in both acid and alcohol. I have not yet been able to taste a microvinification, so the jury's out on this one.

Chiavennasca Bianca

WHERE IT'S FOUND: Lombardy. **NATIONAL REGISTRY CODE NUMBER**: not registered. **COLOR**: white.

Chiavennasca Bianca is found today in the Valtellina area in northern Lombardy, where it is much appreciated for its resistance to cold weather and its vigor. It was once also found in other parts of Lombardy but has since disappeared. First described in 1752 by Ligari as a high-quality variety due to wines high in extract and perfume, its called Chiavennasca Bianca because it resembles the red Chiavennasca, though the two are distinct varieties. The bunch is large, pyramidal/cylindrical, elongated, and compact, with large wings that hang off to the sides. The grapes are medium-small and round or slightly flattened, with a thin yellow-green skin, reddish when very ripe. It is harvested in the latter half of September. The wines are delicately fruity, with surprising structure and a saline finish.

Coda di Cavallo

WHERE IT'S FOUND: Campania. **NATIONAL REGISTRY CODE NUMBER**: not registered. **COLOR**: white.

Also known as Cavalla, Coda di Cavallo takes its name from the resemblance the grape cluster has to the tail of a horse (*coda di cavallo* means horse's tail). Today it is grown mainly in the Campi Flegrei of Campania as well as on the islands of Procida and Ischia. The vines are often ungrafted. It is unclear if the Coda di Cavallo of Vesuvius is the same as those of Ischia and Procida or even that of the Campi Flegrei. Very vigorous and fertile, it has a small, cylindrical bunch, with small, oval berries that are golden-yellow in hue when fully ripe. An early ripener (harvested usually at the end of August), it is not very resistant to grey rot.

Coda di Pecora

WHERE IT'S FOUND: Campania. **NATIONAL REGISTRY CODE NUMBER**: not registered. **COLOR**: white.

Coda di Pecora was long felt to be identical to the much better known and more abundant Coda di Volpe Bianca, but we know today that these two varieties are genetically distinct (and don't look anything like each other, I'd like to add). The cluster's shape resembles the tail of a sheep (*coda di pecora*). Today it grows in the vineyards of Caserta in northern Campania, especially between Roccamonfina and Maggiore, near Concadella Campania, Galluccio, Mignano Monte Lungo, and Piccilli. It may be analogous to ancient varieties called Verdicchio di Caiazzo and Verdone di Puglia. The cluster is compact, large, conical-pyramidal, with two wings and is prone to grey rot. The berries are medium-sized, oval, and yellow-green. Low in acid and sugar levels, Coda di Pecora is used mainly as a blender and can be tasted in the DOC Galluccio Bianco wines; on its own it's too meager, neutral, and flat.

Coglionara

WHERE IT'S FOUND: Campania. NATIONAL REGISTRY CODE NUMBER: not registered. COLOR: white.

Typical of the island of Ischia, where it is still common, Coglionara also grows on the nearby island of Ventotene. It was first described by D'Ascia (1867) and then by Froio (1878) and Nesbitt (1884), who referred to it as Coglionara Grossa. The bunch is medium-sized and cylindrical while the berries are medium-sized and round. It is used to make the DOC Ischia Bianco blend and other local white wines. Compared to other more famous and more frequently planted island varieties such as Biancolella and Forastera, it loses out by a nose, as this is an aromatically challenged grape. However, it has an interesting tactile presence and adds body and savor to the blends it is part of. Coglionara is less susceptible to oidium than are other little-known varieties of Ischia such as Sanlunardo and Arilla, and so may have a future in monovarietal wines. In 2013, I began a project with Giancarlo Carriero, owner of Ischia's Albergo Regina Isabella in Lacco Ameno, aimed at having a local winery make a monovarietal bottling of Coglionara as well as other monovarietal wines from local, almost abandoned grapes. Only time will tell if Coglionara will sing its tune solo or is forever doomed to be part of a chorus.

Colombana Nera

WHERE IT'S FOUND: Tuscany. NATIONAL REGISTRY CODE NUMBER: 66. COLOR: red.

Colombana Nera is a rare grape limited to vineyards around the towns of Livorno, Lucca, Massa Carrara, Pisa, and Pistoia, and especially near the border with Liguria; its name derives from the monastery of San Colombano in Bobbio. Occasionally called Besgano or Besgnano, it's also grown near Piacenza and in the Oltrepò Pavese. It doubles as an excellent table grape, thanks to large bunches and medium-large, oval berries. According to Calò, Scienza, and Costacurta (2001), there appear to be at least three different biotypes: Rustico, Gentile, and Bianco (the last of these better known as San Colombano). Grapes are harvested in the first part of October, and the resulting wines are light colored, and medium-bodied, with good to high alcohol levels due to the sugar-rich berries, and honeyed and floral aromas and flavors.

WINES TO TRY: Podere Poggiarellini** by Bruno Meicci in Terricciola.

Corbina

WHERE IT'S FOUND: Veneto. NATIONAL REGISTRY CODE NUMBER: 406. COLOR: red.

This recently rediscovered variety is generating excitement based on preliminary vinifications. In fact, of all the grapes listed in this chapter, this may turn out to be the one with the brightest future. Corbina, once also called Crovino (not to be confused with the Ligurian variety), appears to always have been highly thought of by both producers and experts. Different from the similar-sounding Corvina, the famous cultivar used to make Valpolicella and Amarone, Corbina belongs to the large family of *Corbina* grapes, which once included Corbinella (now suspected to be just a virus-affected form of Corbina), Corbinone, Corvara, and Crovaja. How many of these were truly different varieties rather than synonyms or biotypes is not known.

The list was actually once much longer: there were nine *Corbina* varieties listed in the 1868 *Bollettino Ampelografico del Comizio Agrario di Vicenza* (Corbina, Corbina Dolce or Marzemina di Spagna, Corbina della Madonna, Corbinella or Pelosa or Pelosetta, Corbinella di Camino, Corbinella Padovana, Corbinella Piccola, Corbinona, and Corbinone di Timonchio). The fourth volume of the *Bollettino Ampelografico* (1884–87) names which grape varieties were most suited to each viticultural area of Veneto; Corbina was thought most appropriate for Vicenza and Padova, Corbinella and Corbinone were thought to perform best around Verona, and Crovaja near Vicenza. It was clear to experts already in the nineteenth and early twentieth centuries that there was much confusion surrounding the *Corbina* grapes, a problem compounded by the fact that everyone mixed them up with the *Corvina* grapes (remember that at that time Corvinone was also thought to be just a biotype of Corvina). It is thanks to Marzotto (1925) that the situation was clarified: he illustrated how the *Corvina* grapes were typical of the area around Verona and Bardolino (where they are still grown today), while the *Corbina* were more typical of the countryside of Minerbe, Legnago, and Treviso. The two groups of grapes are easily differentiated because the *Corvina* grapes have usually oval berries as opposed to the *Corbinas'* generally round ones. Finally, Marzotto also divided the *Corbina* group into two subgroups, the *Corbinas* and the *Corbinones*, the latter characterized by larger grapes. Of course, we might one day learn that Corbina and Corbinone are distinct grapes, much as Corvina and Corvinone are.

In any case, everyone seems to have been in agreement that the *Corbinas* gave remarkably dark-colored wines that were excellent: their only drawback was that they were also extremely tannic, and required at least three years of aging in order to become drinkable. Marzotto quite intelligently suggested that in order to avoid making excessively dark, tannic wines, it was best to remove the stalks from the grapes and to blend in more or less small amounts of white grape must. Wines made with Corbina were presented at many national fairs in the nineteenth century: Riccardo Tedeschi of the famous Tedeschi estate in Valpolicella tells me they met with critical acclaim. Unfortunately, the strong color and tannins typical of Corbina wines were viewed as potentially unappealing to the winebuying public of the mid-twentieth century, and so during the post-phylloxeric period, many local experts suggested that vineyards be replanted with other, gentler varieties such as Merlot and even Barbera.

However, it's hard to keep a good grape down, and recently, Corbina has been well characterized by Cancellier, Coletti, Coletti, Soligo, and Michelet (2007). Today, many producers are looking to Corbina with renewed interest, thanks mainly to work done by Emanuele Tosi of the Centro per la Sperimentazione, Servizio Agricoltura, of the province of Verona. For example, Tedeschi, in collaboration with Tosi, has reserved part of a vineyard for experimental plantings of Corbina and other local rare natives. The grape bunch is medium-sized, pyramidal, and winged and runs the gamut from sparse to compact; berries are medium-sized, round, very thick skinned, and blue-black. Corbina is resistant to common pests; budbreak is late and harvest occurs in late September or early October. The wine (from microvinifications) is deeply hued, the nose balsamic and fruity (blackberry, black cherry), with strong tannins and good acidity levels. I can easily see this grape being used in Valpolicella and Amarone blends along with Rondinella, Oseleta, and Molinara in the course of the next decade. After that, finding someone willing to try bottling it on its own will only be a matter of time.

Cördusël

WHERE IT'S FOUND: Emilia-Romagna. NATIONAL REGISTRY CODE NUMBER: not registered. COLOR: white.

Also called Cör d'Usël, Cördusël is native to the Faenza area; the only one to bottle a monovarietal Cördusël wine today is Paolo Francesconi. He makes it in the modern faddish style of long macerations on the skins (a whopping ninety days), and then—just in case it was still too faint of heart for thrill-seeking modern palates—finishes it off with another twelve months in small oak barrels. Though all that might finish you off too, the nose is interesting, with hints of flint, acacia honey, and aromatic herbs. To the best of my knowledge there has been no genetic testing done on the variety, and so what this grape is or might be is open to question.

Corinto Nero

WHERE IT'S FOUND: Sicily. NATIONAL REGISTRY CODE NUMBER: 68. COLOR: red.

An ancient variety brought over to Sicily by the Greeks, Corinto Nero shares, erroneously, the same name as a variety abundant in Greece and Turkey, from which it differs. Cupani (1696) described three *Corinto* varieties called locally Tuccarino, Tuccarineddu, and Tuccarino cù Cocci. It is unrelated to Corinto Bianco and Corinto Rosa, other local Sicilian natives that are now virtually extinct. It appears that Corinto Nero is a distant relative of Sangiovese, though some experts believe it to be either a seedless mutation or a biotype of the famous Tuscan native, though with a very different phenotype due to being heavily virus-affected over the centuries. I find this possible Sangiovese relationship interesting, for a Puglian variety called Tuccanese (a very similar name to the previously mentioned Tuccarino, Tuccarineddu, and Tuccarino cù Cocci) has been found to be genetically identical to Sangiovese (Zulini, Russo, and Peterlunger 2002). Emilia-Romagna's Termarina Rossa is remarkably similar, ampelographically speaking, to Corinto Nero, but the two are genetically distinct (Boccacci, Torello Marinoni, Gambino, Botta, and Schneider 2005).

It is a poorly vigorous vine (as virus-affected grapevines often are) with a small, short, cylindrical bunch, winged, with very small, round, purple berries. In Italy it grows only in the Messina province of Sicily. Very rarely used in a 100 percent pure red wine, it is part of DOC Lipari Rosso and amounts to 5 percent or less of DOC Malvasia di Lipari.

Cornacchia

WHERE IT'S FOUND: Emilia-Romagna. NATIONAL REGISTRY CODE NUMBER: 447. COLOR: red.

Early budbreak and late ripening (it's harvested in early October) characterize this vigorous and productive variety, which is usually blended with Canina Nera and other local grapes. Cornacchia does not accumulate a lot of sugar, so it has traditionally been used to make light, slightly sweet wines to be drunk during the daytime. It has never been a particularly popular wine grape, and its diminishing presence in the country's vineyards had been noticed already in the late nineteenth century (*Bollettino Ampelografico* 1878) along with other grapes such as Potanèvola, Uva Scruccona, and Raffone di Forlì. Bazzocchi (1923) also confirmed that the variety was disappearing, despite its productivity, because the wine really wasn't very good at all, though I wonder how much of that perceived lack of quality may have been due to overproduction and high yields. A biotype called Cornacchia Donati shares ten alleles out of twenty with Sangiovese. Its high National Registry code number tells you this is one of the more recently listed varieties, added only in 2011. In my view, this is also an encouraging sign that Italy's powers-that-be are not going to stand around idly while the country's grape biodiversity disappears.

Corvino

WHERE IT'S FOUND: Friuli Venezia Giulia. NATIONAL REGISTRY CODE NUMBER: not registered. COLOR: red

Also called Curvin, Corvino is reduced to only a few sporadic vines in old vineyards and ampelographic collections, but is currently being studied by the University of Udine in collaboration with estates such as Ronchi di Cialla. In centuries past Corvino seems to have been the second most cultivated variety after the *Refoscos* in some parts of Friuli Venezia Giulia. Unfortunately, as it requires plenty of sunlight and heat to ripen fully (it has big, seven-lobed, pentagonal leaves), it lost favor with farmers faced with the region's chilly and rainy spring and fall climate. Its name recalls the dark plumage of blackbirds (*corvo*, or raven). Microvinifications of the wine have shown deep color, intense red-berry aromas and flavors, and plenty of tannic structure. According to microvinifications performed at the Agenzia Regionale per lo Sviluppo Rurale (ERSA) of Friuli Venezia Giulia, there are apparently high norisoprenoid concentrations (45 percent) and good benzenoid and terpene levels. Corvino's anthocyanin profile features very high cyanin concentrations, a rarity among grapevines. I have been told by various experts that this is potentially a very good wine grape; however, winemaking friends in Friuli Venezia Giulia caution that it can be very reductive, so needs plenty of oxygen contact during the winemaking process.

Croà

WHERE IT'S FOUND: Lombardy, Piedmont. NATIONAL REGISTRY CODE NUMBER: not registered. COLOR: red.

Once considered one of the more interesting varieties of the Oltrepò Pavese, Croà's glory days are well behind it. It belongs to the same grape family as Moradella and Vermiglio. The grape's name may be due to its dark color (*corvino* or dark) or to its hard crunchy pulp (*corba* or container, as in the grapes are so tough they can be carried long distances in containers). There appear to be at least three biotypes, of which the second is characterized by the smallest and most compact bunch, while the standard bunch is large, compact, and short, with oval, medium-large berries.

I am told the wine is light-bodied and pale red, acidic and tannic, with perfumes of red berries; apparently it benefits from at least a year of cellaring.

Crova

WHERE IT'S FOUND: Emilia-Romagna. NATIONAL REGISTRY CODE NUMBER: not registered. COLOR: red.

Most likely identical to Crovarina, Crova is grown mainly in Emilia-Romagna's Val Tidone and Val Trebbia areas and in Lombardy's Oltrepò Pavese. There are many Crova-like varieties in northern Italy, more or less related to one another. An ancient cultivar grown by Benedictine monks in the Middle Ages, its name derives either from the dark hue of the skins (*crova* is a corruption of *corvo* or raven) or due to the *corba*, the local basket in which the grapes are carried. The cluster is large, pyramidal or conical, and very compact. The berries are medium-sized and oval-round, of dark blue color and not too thick skinned. Crova is usually harvested in mid-September.

Crovassa

WHERE IT'S FOUND: Valle d'Aosta. NATIONAL REGISTRY CODE NUMBER: 349. COLOR: red.

Crovassa is almost extinct, with very few rows left near the towns of Issogne and Donnas. Gatta (1838) described it as rare already in his time, and Louis Napoléon Bich felt it was of limited enological interest. Also called Corassa and Crova Nera, the bunch is large, pyramidal, and compact, with large, spherical, thick-skinned, and deep-blue berries. The harvest is in the last week of October, and the wine has a delicate red hue, fruity, very tart, and light, though I am only reporting the experiences of local farmers. In Valle d'Aosta, neither Costantino Charrère of the world-famous Les Cretes estate nor Nicola Del Negro of the well-respected Cave du Vin Blanc de Morgex et La Salle think highly of it. The name derives from *corvo*, or raven, due to the deep color of the berries.

Crovino

WHERE IT'S FOUND: Liguria. NATIONAL REGISTRY CODE NUMBER: not registered. COLOR: red.

Almost extinct because of its miserly productivity, Crovino was once famous in Ligurian areas around Genova and Finale Ligure. Today only the Punta Crena estate continues to make it (and call it Crovin).

Damaschino

WHERE IT'S FOUND: Sicily. NATIONAL REGISTRY CODE NUMBER: 72. COLOR: white.

Nobody really knows for sure, as documentation is absent, but this variety's name is believed to derive from the Syrian city of

Damascus; some believe the grape may have been imported to Sicilian shores during the Arab domination of the island. However, the first to mention Damaschino was Mendola in 1884. Damaschino was also a much appreciated table grape, and a favorite of wine producers looking to make light white wines. For this reason, Damaschino knew an intense replanting phase in the post-phylloxeric period. Unfortunately, though it is still grown in the provinces of Trapani (where it's used to make Marsala) and Agrigento, Damaschino has since fallen out of favor because of sensitivity to diseases (it's not particularly resistant to grey rot or peronospora) compared to other locals such as the *Catarattos*. The DF 1 is the only clone available to date. A very vigorous vine, with a large, pyramidal, winged grape bunch, it has medium-large, round berries that tend to be pinkish rather than yellow-green when exposed to strong sunlight. The pure damaschino wines I have had (the easiest to find are from the DOC Delia Nivolelli) have all been very light and crisp, with delicate white-flower and lemony aromas and flavors. Based on my limited experience, I think there is potential for damaschino, as some wines are noteworthy; unfortunately there are far too many less interesting ones made. I don't believe it can age much beyond a year, so it's best to consume it young. Unfortunately, there is a wine sold under the commercial name "damaschino," but it is apparently not made with the Damaschino grape.

Denela

WHERE IT'S FOUND: Veneto. NATIONAL REGISTRY CODE NUMBER: not registered. COLOR: red.

Denela was first described in 1980, and historical information on this Veronese native is lacking (Canceller, Costacurta, Angelini, Segattini, and Cabrusina 1980). Sporadic vines have been found in the Valle di Montorio and in the Val Squaranto in the province of Verona. The bunch is medium-sized, almost compound due to a large wing, very compact and stocky. The berries are small and round-oval, thick skinned, and dark blue. Not too vigorous and botrytis sensitive, it ripens in early September. Microvinifications have shown neutral wines that are tannic and quite saline. I doubt that Denela will ever be more than a blending grape, possibly appreciated for its tannic clout.

Durasa

WHERE IT'S FOUND: Piedmont. NATIONAL REGISTRY CODE NUMBER: 76. COLOR: red.

There are apparently Durasa vines in almost every viticultural zone of Piedmont, but in almost thirty years of visiting that region's vineyards I don't remember a single producer even mentioning Durasa grapevines. Durasa is mainly found in the Canavese area (near Turin), as well in the hills near Novara, around Chieri and Asti. The Canavese area is an important one for native grapes, since throughout history this remote region was difficult to reach; consequently, not much genetic contamination of local grapes occurred. Also, farmers continued to grow those varieties that had always been highly thought of locally, rather than turning to more popular varieties. The cluster is sparse, medium or medium-small in size, conical, sometimes truncated and short, with a large wing. The berry is medium-sized, spherical, with a thick, blue-black skin. An excellent table grape, it is very resistant to rot and other diseases, while the wine produced can be a real revelation; medium bodied, smooth, dark-red, and fruity, though low in pH.

Fenile

WHERE IT'S FOUND: Campania. NATIONAL REGISTRY CODE NUMBER: 338. COLOR: white.

A white grape that is grown only along the Amalfi coast, Fenile's name is due to the straw-yellow color of its berries, which recalls hay. Fenile is found mainly in the areas of Furore, Positano, and Amalfi, where it is used to make the excellent DOC blends Costa d'Amalfi Bianco, Furore Bianco, and Ravello Bianco. The vines are really a spectacle, trained in canopies and hugging the incredibly steep rugged shoreline. Fenile ripens early, in late August or early September, and needs to be picked very quickly as its thin skin breaks easily when the grapes are ripe. Given the extremely high quality of wines made with it (usually in association with other local grapes such as Ripoli and Ginestra), I only wish there was more of it to go around. Make no mistake: white wine blends from this part of Italy are some of the country's greatest white wines, so it's a shame there isn't anyone trying to bottle a monovarietal Fenile wine. In fairness, given that the Fenile vines are interplanted with many other varieties in messy hodgepodges of usually gnarly old vines, and that there are no large vineyards in the area, making a monovarietal Fenile (or Ripoli or Ginestra) wine would be a difficult proposition indeed.

Forcella

WHERE IT'S FOUND: Emilia-Romagna. NATIONAL REGISTRY CODE NUMBER: not registered. COLOR: white.

Forcella is a recently discovered ancient variety that was found surviving as a centenary vine in the cloister of the Santa Maria in Regola church, a former Benedictine convent located right in the middle of the busy city of Imola. Forcella was well known in centuries past, and Acerbi described it in his treatise on the grapes of Bologna (1825); Agazzotti (1867) and Cavazza (1904) also describe this variety. Forcella is not to be confused with Albana della Forcella, a biotype of Albana characterized by a bifid cluster.

Forselina

WHERE IT'S FOUND: Veneto. NATIONAL REGISTRY CODE NUMBER: 317. COLOR: red.

Called Forselina because it frequently has forked shoots (most likely a result of viral disease), this variety was first mentioned by Pollini in 1824. Also called Forcellina, Forsellana, and Forsella, it was well studied and described only in the twentieth century, first by Zava (1901) and then by Sormani Moretti (1904). A more detailed and recent ampelographic description is by Cancellier (1980). The bunch is medium-sized, cylindrical, compact, usually not winged; the berries are medium, irregularly elliptical, with a thin but resistant blue skin. Due to these morphologic characteristics, it is not an ideal variety for air-drying, so it's not suitable for Amarone production. Vigorous but sensitive to grey rot, it ripens in September. Forselina is a very interesting variety giving lovely light red wines redolent in strawberry and raspberry aromas and it may have quite the future as a blending agent for Valpolicella and Bardolino. As I happen to love delicious, balanced, light red wines, I wouldn't mind seeing some forward-thinking, risk-taking producer try a hand at a monovarietal bottling, but admittedly, I am in the minority on this one.

Francavidda

WHERE IT'S FOUND: Puglia. NATIONAL REGISTRY CODE NUMBER: 85. COLOR: white.

This variety is also known as Francavilla, after the small town near Brindisi that gives this variety its name (the town's name is actually Francavilla Fontana). The cluster is medium-large, pyramidal-cylindrical, rarely compound, and can at times be very sparse. The berry is also midsized, round, with a thick, green-white skin. Clonal research begun in the 1970s and continued until the 1990s has provided two clones, CRSA-C134 and CRSA-C135, originating from two very old vineyards located in Francavilla Fontana and Ostuni. Clearly, the two have slightly different phenotypes. Francavidda is usually harvested in mid- or late September, but it has fallen out of favor over time because it is too sensitive to spring frosts and to cold weather in general, as well as to diseases. The variety's geographic distribution has not changed much over the centuries, and today it continues to be grown over a total of about ten hectares mainly around the town of Brindisi, near Francavilla, Carovigno, Ostuni, San Michele Salentino, and San Vito dei Normanni. It is usually blended with another rare local variety called Impigno in the DOC wine Ostuni. The wines are very light and fresh, good for uncomplicated drinking and don't age particularly well, but are perfect with light vegetable and fish dishes.

Fruhroter Veltliner

WHERE IT'S FOUND: Trentino. NATIONAL REGISTRY CODE NUMBER: not registered. COLOR: red.

With its German-sounding name, Fruhroter Veltliner certainly comes across as a member of the group of varieties that like Gewürztraminer, Kerner, Riesling, and Sylvaner really cannot be considered native or traditional Italian grapes (at least not yet). However, producer Alfio Nicolodi believes that this variety has been grown in his area of Trentino for centuries at least, and so I'll defer to his experience on the matter, and include the variety in this book, though it is probably most correct to consider Fruhroter Veltliner as a native Austrian variety only traditional to Italy. Apparently, it is a natural crossing of Roter Veltliner and Sylvaner, but is unrelated to Austria's better-known Gruner Veltliner. Alfio Nicolodi is the only producer of a monovarietal Fruhroter Veltliner wine I know of in Italy; bright red, with grapey aromas and flavors of fresh red berries, it is an ideal everyday wine best paired with simply prepared fare.

Fumat

WHERE IT'S FOUND: Friuli Venezia Giulia. NATIONAL REGISTRY CODE NUMBER: not registered. COLOR: red.

Another of Italy's many grapes named after a physical trait, Fumat takes its name either from the smoky-black color of its berries or the slightly smoky aromas and flavors of the wine (most experts favor the latter hypothesis). Once diffusely cultivated between San Daniele and Fagagna right up into the hills of Spilimbergo, today it is found only in the latter production zone. It has medium-sized, triangular leaves with small, conical bunches and one to two wings. It's a very late ripening variety, characterized by good vigor and productivity, but it has small berries, which limits just how much juice can be pressed from the bunches. Its lack of resistance to oidium and peronospora was the main reason it lost favor with local growers. The wine, according to microvinifications made by Friuli Venezia Giulia's Agenzia Regionale per lo Sviluppo Agrario (ERSA), is ruby-purple in hue, with bright aromas of blueberry and blackberry, and a fresh palate full of vibrant blackberry and delicately spicy nuances. The latter notes are what give the wine a "smoky" quality, though the finish does have a flinty edge. There are reportedly high benzenoid concentrations (60 percent), with high concentrations of malvin and acylated anthocyanins, hence wines with a stable, deep color. It has a very good tannic structure that is neither bitter nor astringent, and offers plenty of black fruit aromas and flavors with delicate spicy and licorice nuances. To my way of thinking, in which balance in wine is almost everything, Fumat actually seems like a variety worth insisting on.

Galioppo

WHERE IT'S FOUND: Marche. NATIONAL REGISTRY CODE NUMBER: 122. COLOR: white.

Unfortunately, this variety's name sounds and looks like Gaglioppo, a Calabrian variety that is unrelated to Galioppo. Galioppo is a Sangiovese look-alike that holds court in the Marche, where historically it was long confused with the more famous Tuscan cultivar.

Garofanata

WHERE IT'S FOUND: Marche. NATIONAL REGISTRY CODE NUMBER: 463. COLOR: white.

Garofanata is one of the less obscure varieties in this chapter and in fact you can find monovarietal wines being made from it. Cipriani, Spadotto, Jurman, Di Gaspero, Crespan, Meneghetti, et al. (2010) have demonstrated that Garofanata is an offspring of Trebbiano Toscano (the grape is called Garofana in the paper). Garofanata is characterized by a medium-small, pyramidal bunch and round, golden-green berries. According to Giancarlo Soverchia, a well-respected winemaker working to save local forgotten grapes and trying to make monovarietal wines from them, Garofanata has a delicately aromatic perfume and excellent acidity. Locals believe the variety's name derives from a hint of geranium aroma (*garofano*) in the wine's nose. Soverchia likes the variety and honestly I can see why: the wine is clean and fresh, offering hints of unripe peach, chlorophyll, and white flowers. It's very light bodied but it makes an ideal sipping wine.

WINES TO TRY: Terracruda** (Garofanata, a very good wine).

Ginestra

WHERE IT'S FOUND: Campania. NATIONAL REGISTRY CODE NUMBER: 384. COLOR: white.

This variety's name is thought to derive from the yellow flower of same name (*ginestra* or broom) as both grapes and wines smell intensely like the flower. Ginestra is grown all along the Amalfi coast, especially near Scala, Ravello, Amalfi, Maiori, and Minori. It is called Biancazita around Furore, Tramonti, Corsara, and Positano, and Biancatenera around Scala. It has been known since the early nineteenth century, but for the longest time confusion reigned supreme as it was believed to be distinct from Biancazita and Biancatenera (the three are identical), but synonymous with Falanghina or Biancolella (two varieties distinct from Ginestra). The synonymy between Ginestra and Biancazita was first suspected by Froio (1875), while today Biancatenera seems more likely to be a biotype characterized by particularly soft skin (*tenera*, or soft). Ginestra is a vigorous, productive variety that produces grapes high in sugar and low in acid content; the wine can be thrilling, so this is another variety, like Fenile, that I'd like to see become more present in Campania—in all another wonderful Italian native that deserves rediscovery.

Granè

WHERE IT'S FOUND: Tuscany. NATIONAL REGISTRY CODE NUMBER: not registered. COLOR: red.

Another very rare Tuscan *teinturier* grown mainly around Pisa and Lucca. The bunch is large, pyramidal, winged, and the berry is oval, blue-black, and has a colored pulp. It ripens late, in October.

Granoir

WHERE IT'S FOUND: Tuscany. NATIONAL REGISTRY CODE NUMBER: 352. COLOR: red.

Also known as Grand Noir, Granoir is one of the many coloring grapes or *teinturiers*, with a delicately colored pulp that has been used throughout the centuries to increase the color of more anemic wines. The bunch is small, winged, and pyramidal and the grapes are also small and round, blue-black. It grows mainly in Tuscany, but is not very common. Some believe that there are two distinct Granoir grapes in Tuscany, either of which may also be called Grand Noir; all this engenders confusion with the Granoir of Valle d'Aosta, a crossing of Gamay and Reichensteiner Bianco that was originally called Gastar. The same crossing has given rise to another variety called Gamaret, National Registry code number 351.

Gratena

WHERE IT'S FOUND: Tuscany. NATIONAL REGISTRY CODE NUMBER: not registered. COLOR: red.

We know a little bit about this variety today thanks to Fabio De Ambrogi, owner of the Fattoria di Gratena where roughly eight hundred vines growing in a small parcel called "the vineyard of Beppone" were identified as Gratena. In 2000 six thousand more vines were planted and studies by Attilio Scienza and his team in Milan confirmed the variety to be distinct from all other known varieties. The wine is suave and perfumed, redolent of red berries and herbs.

Grero

WHERE IT'S FOUND: Umbria. NATIONAL REGISTRY CODE NUMBER: 448. COLOR: red.

One of Italy's most recently rediscovered grapes, Grero is typical of Umbria. The bunch is medium-large, long, and usually loosely packed. The berries are round and have thick skins. Grero is resistant to most common grapevine pests but is susceptible to peronospora. According to winemaker Emiliano Falsini, who is probably the biggest expert on this variety (he has been working intensely with it at Tudernum in Umbria), it's a variety that prefers clay-loamy soils with some marl. A monovarietal wine is not planned yet but I've liked what I have tasted so far. The wine is smoothly tannic and full bodied, with dark-berry and underbrush aromas and flavors.

Grisa Nera

WHERE IT'S FOUND: Piedmont. NATIONAL REGISTRY CODE NUMBER: not registered. COLOR: red.

Also known as Grisa di Cumiana (in the Pinerolese) or simply Grisa, in Roero this variety is called Freiza Grossa, which is more properly a synonym of Neretta Cuneese. Rare today, Grisa Nera grows in Pinerolese Orientale, the Bassa Valle di Susa, and, less so, in Cuneo. Everything about this variety is large: large round leaf, large bunch (elongated, conical, winged), and large oval, thick-skinned berries. The latter are purple-blue, but with a greyish tinge that explains the variety's name, *grisa*. A late ripener much like Barbera, it suffers from berry shot. It's believed to be ideal for the production of *rosato*.

Grisa Rousa

WHERE IT'S FOUND: Piedmont. NATIONAL REGISTRY CODE NUMBER: not registered. COLOR: red.

Also known as Ivernasso near Chiomonte, this variety was once simply called Grisa, but its name was changed in order to avoid confusion with Grisa Nera; in France it's named Grec Rouge. Rare today, it grows in Valle di Susa (especially in the high, alpine valley), and a little in Val Chisone (Pinerolese) and the Tortonese. The bunch can be very large and is occasionally winged, while the medium-small, slightly flattened berries have a reddish-pink hue, hence the variety's name. An early ripening variety (akin to Dolcetto), it's mainly a table grape, but can be used to make very light, delicate white and *rosato* wines.

Gruaja

WHERE IT'S FOUND: Veneto. NATIONAL REGISTRY CODE NUMBER: not registered. COLOR: red.

This virtually extinct grape was always associated with very fine wine, but unfortunately its poor productivity made it unpopular with farmers and winemakers of centuries past. This is a shame, since most writings attest that the wine made with Gruaja was of noteworthy finesse: "not unlike a claret" according to Acanti (1754), "one of our best and most cultivated grapes" (*Bollettino Ampelografico* 1868), and "a very refined grape" (da Schio 1905). Not everyone was overwhelmed with what he had tasted: Acerbi (1825) thought the wine was too light and that it didn't keep past the summer following the harvest, but liked Gruaja as a table grape. There were also biotypes of Gruaja described, but little else is known about this grape and wine.

WINES TO TRY: The only monovarietal Gruaja wine I know is called Gruajo, made by Firminio Miotti in Veneto. It smells and tastes of dark cherries and small dark berries, with hints of tar and underbrush.

Guarnaccino

WHERE IT'S FOUND: Basilicata. NATIONAL REGISTRY CODE NUMBER: 122. COLOR: red.

Guarnaccino is a variety I'd never heard of until I read the abstracts of the Thirty-fifth World Congress of Vine and Wine. Apparently it is native to Basilicata, the very small region tucked between Calabria and Puglia. I have no reason to doubt it's a newly discovered native variety, and I await publication of the research results in a reputable peer-reviewed journal so we can all learn more about this grape.

Impigno

WHERE IT'S FOUND: Puglia. NATIONAL REGISTRY CODE NUMBER: 107. COLOR: white.

Impigno is the name of a farmer credited with having brought this variety to Ostuni between 1904 and 1905. A recent study suggests that Impigno is a natural cross between Puglia's Bombino Bianco and Piedmont's Quagliano, which is strange only because neither Quaglaino nor Impigno, to the best of my knowledge, has ever been described in the other region (Cipriani, Spadotto, Jurman, Di Gaspero, Crespan, Meneghetti, et al. 2010). Not that it is unfathomable that an immigrant or two (to either region) might have chosen to travel with their favorite grapevines packed away along with toothbrush and underwear. Today the variety is rare, and over the years I have had real trouble finding anyone who might make a monovarietal wine with it. In all honesty, during my grapevine travels I got the distinct impression that most people I talked to didn't understand why I even bothered with Impigno. However, Impigno still grows in the countryside around Ostuni, Brindisi, Carovigno, San Vito dei Normanni, and a few other towns of the area, where growers hold it in higher esteem than do other Puglian winemakers (all not from that specific area, mind you). The bunch is medium-sized, loosely packed, and winged. The berry is oval, medium-sized, and green. A good producer of DOC Ostuni is Greco (Donna Nina), whose wine is made with 75 percent Impigno and 25 percent Francavidda. Light, crisp, and easygoing, it won't put Montrachet out of business but it's a perfectly acceptable wine for simple summer sipping—if you can find it.

Janese

WHERE IT'S FOUND: Campania. NATIONAL REGISTRY CODE NUMBER: not registered. COLOR: red.

Also called Gaianaese, Janese is an almost extinct variety of Campania, found mainly in old vineyards around Avellino and Baronissi. Froio describes its existence in the nineteenth century but it does not appear that the variety was ever extremely popular. Medium-sized with a compact cluster and small berries, Janese is remarkably resistant to botrytis and other diseases and the wine itself holds promise, though its elevated vigor needs to be tamed. Examples I have tasted made by welcoming farmers attest to the grape's fine-wine potential, not unlike a good quality, slightly less herbal piedirosso, but as Janese is interplanted with Piedirosso and other varieties, there's always quite a bit of Piedirosso in these wines.

Lacrima del Valdarno

WHERE IT'S FOUND: Tuscany. NATIONAL REGISTRY CODE NUMBER: not registered. COLOR: red.

Lacrima del Valdarno is a very rare variety found in some vineyards of Tuscany, where it has been cultivated since the mid-nineteenth century. A small grape with small clusters and berries, Lacrima del Valdarno flowers and ripens late; the latter is hardly an endearing quality to Tuscan farmers of the Valdarno area, where it's cold and rainy in the fall, leading to ripening difficulties. In this variety's defense, it has proven to be very resistant overall, so perhaps farmers can wait to shed tears after all.

Lagarino

WHERE IT'S FOUND: Trentino, Alto Adige. NATIONAL REGISTRY CODE NUMBER: 399. COLOR: white.

A prime candidate for the most unfortunately named Italian grape variety, Lagarino's name derives from the German *lager*, meaning an "area of predetermined dimension" or "circumscribed field"; its local dialect names *chegarèl* and *sghittarella* aren't much better, as they refer to this white grape's laxative properties. All that is a little unfair, as Lagarino produces lovely light white wines that are high in acid and fresh flavors. It is also a very pretty variety, with large clusters and round, voluminous berries. Furthermore, it is very hardy, one of the few that survives at over one thousand meters above sea level, where almost all other varieties succumb to the frigid weather. It's not surprising then that it grows in the northern Italian regions of Trentino (especially in the Val di Sarca and the Val di Cembra) and Alto Adige. At the end of the 1800s it is estimated that over 12,500 hectoliters of lagarino were produced annually. It gives a high-acid juice ideal for sparkling wine production.

Lambrusca di Alessandria

WHERE IT'S FOUND: Piedmont. NATIONAL REGISTRY CODE NUMBER: 113. COLOR: red.

Lambrusca di Alessandria is known by many different synonyms: Crova (in the Pinerolese), Neretto di Alessandria (in Val Chisone), Crovìn (in Roero), Croetto or Moretto (in Alessandrino), Stupèt (in some areas of the Astigiano), and Lambrusca; it is sometimes also confused with Lambruschino, Lambrusca del Roero, Lambruschetto, and Lambruschetta di Castelnuovo Bormida, all of which are distinct varieties. Of course, it has no relationship with the *Lambrusco*s (Torello Marinoni, Raimondi, Boccacci, and Schneider 2006) and is identical to the variety called Brachetto Valsusino. It appears to have been first described by Count Giuseppe Nuvolone, who was the assistant director of Piedmont's agricultural society near the turn of the nineteenth century. Once common in the areas surrounding the towns of Alessandria in Piedmont and Pavia in Lombardy, Lambrusca di Alessandria's cluster is large and conical or pyramidal, with big wings. The berry is small and round, with a thick skin. It's very resistant to all of the most common grapevine diseases. Importantly, budbreak is very late so it's ideal in those areas where cold weather and spring frosts are common. It also ripens very late, even after Barbera. The wine is reportedly deeply colored, reasonably tannic, medium to full bodied and can age, but lacks complexity; however, I have not yet tried a monovarietal wine I can describe confidently. Strange as it may seem, there appears to be a monovarietal Lambrusca di Alessandria wine made in California by Cougar Vineyards in Temecula (and apparently Eusinius Vineyards in San Diego County also grows the grape): it appears the grapevine was originally misidentified as Nebbiolo and the wines garnered considerable critical and commercial success, which in itself suggests that Lambrusca di Alessandria is potentially an outstanding wine grape indeed. I have yet to taste these California wines, but I look forward to doing so, and to visiting the wineries soon. Lambrusca di Alessandria may be the first example of an Italian grape being used to make wine outside the country, while in Italy nobody does currently. In this light, Lambrusca di Alessandria is yet another Italian emigrant that has captured the American Dream.

Lambrusca di Vittona

WHERE IT'S FOUND: Piedmont. NATIONAL REGISTRY CODE NUMBER: not registered. COLOR: red.

Also called Vittona, Lambrusca di Vittona is typical of the Pinerolese, where it was once very common in the countryside around Cumiana, Bricherasio, Santo Secondo, and Prarostino. It is now common only around Barge and in the Valli Chisone and Germanasca, where it is an important part of the blend used to make the wine Ramìe. The bunch is medium-small, the berries midsized with a pale blue hue due to plenty of bloom. Lambrusca di Vittona is curious in that its leaves have different shapes even on the same plant, and walking through the vineyards it's easy to see and recognize. Resistant and fertile, it is however not that productive, due to the small bunches.

Lambruschetta

WHERE IT'S FOUND: Piedmont. NATIONAL REGISTRY CODE NUMBER: not registered. COLOR: red.

Described already in the 1800s and known already then to be distinct from Lambrusca di Alessandria, Lambruschetta was highly valued, though locals erroneously believed that it was related to the *Lambruscos* of Emilia-Romagna. Today it grows only near Castelnuovo Bormida, in the province of Alessandria, but I have yet to see it in vineyards there. It has a medium-sized and pyramidal bunch, with small, round berries, and is fairly resistant. It is currently being studied for its wine potential.

Lecinara

WHERE IT'S FOUND: Lazio. NATIONAL REGISTRY CODE NUMBER: 442. COLOR: red.

In the 1881 Ampelographic Bulletin of the Ministry of Agriculture, Industry and Commerce, Lecinara, also named Lecinaro, was considered a synonym of Zinna di Vacca, Lecina, and Cicirana. Today its diffusion is limited to a very small area in southeastern Lazio, between the Valle del Comino and the Valle del Liri, near Frosinone. The bunch is medium-sized, conical, usually winged, and fairly compact with medium-sized, elliptical, blue-purple berries. Microvinifications reveal a red-purple color, and a delicate nose of rose and violet, with red-berry nuances. On the palate there is high acidity and a very light structure, so this is a grape probably best suited to make light reds. Biochemical analysis has revealed significant concentrations of phenylethanol in the wine, which smells of roses.

Livornese Bianca

WHERE IT'S FOUND: Tuscany. NATIONAL REGISTRY CODE NUMBER: 122. COLOR: white.

Usually used as a blending agent in the DOC Colli di Luni, not much is known about this cultivar except that it actually grows more in the area of Massa Carrara than it does near Livorno. It seems to be resistant to both diseases and climatic adversities.

Maiolica

WHERE IT'S FOUND: Abruzzo. NATIONAL REGISTRY CODE NUMBER: 126. COLOR: red.

Maiolica's origins are unknown, though it seems to have lived in Umbria, Marche, and Abruzzo for centuries; it has been documented in Abruzzo since 1892. Today it is most common in the Abruzzo provinces of Pescara and Chieti, while it is scarce in the Marche. An abundant producer, it is sensitive to cold temperatures. Usually it is blended with Montepulciano; prior to blending, the wine is ruby-violet, with aromas of spices and violets, medium body and structure, and low acidity.

Maligia

WHERE IT'S FOUND: Emilia-Romagna. NATIONAL REGISTRY CODE NUMBER: not registered. COLOR: white.

A white grape variety already known in the Middle Ages according to Pier de' Crescenzi (1305), Maligia has always found its home around the Emilia-Romagna towns between Modena and Forlì, especially around Imola and Faenza. It was once one of the most common varieties planted on the hills of Imola, especially near Dozza (where it was called Malis), but today it also grows in Romagna and Emilia, around Bologna, where they call it Maligia, Malise, or Malisia. It is also referred to as Maligia Omalise, though some believe this may be a biotype; Tanara (1644) believed that it was related to the *Malvasia* family, but we know this not to be the case. Agazzotti (1867) was not a fan at all, writing that it was a grape with which to make wine best used for distillation purposes. In more modern times, Cappucci (1954) was the first to describe the variety in depth, praising it for its rusticity, productivity, and resistance to disease.

The vine is vigorous, with large cylindrical-conical, sparse bunches. The berries are medium-large and spherical, grey-green in color. It ripens late and is usually harvested well into October, when the berries can take on a decidedly golden tinge. The wine is simple, easygoing with good body and alcoholic strength; for this reason it was historically used to beef up weaker wines in blends. It is still found sporadically in old vineyards around Bologna and Ravenna, perhaps Forlì and Faenza.

Marchione

WHERE IT'S FOUND: Puglia. NATIONAL REGISTRY CODE NUMBER: 453. COLOR: white.

Also known as Maricchione, Marchione is a high-quality grape characterized by good total acidity levels and the capacity to give highly perfumed, almost aromatic wines. Furthermore, it also produces copiously and reliably; its Achilles's heel is that it is exquisitely sensitive to most common vine diseases, explaining why it gradually disappeared from vineyards. Characterized by a large, loosely packed bunch and large berries of pinkish hue when fully ripe, it's harvested in September and may have a future for the production of sparkling wines. It is typical of the Valle d'Itria, where it was always grown along with Verdeca and Bianco d'Alessano.

WINES TO TRY: Currently the only wine I know made with this variety is by Santoro*: very pleasant, fresh and delicately aromatic, the wine and the grape deserve to be better known.

Maresco

WHERE IT'S FOUND: Puglia. NATIONAL REGISTRY CODE NUMBER: not registered. COLOR: white.

Believed to be typical of the Valle d'Itria, Maresco used to be called Maruggio, the name of the town in the epicenter of the variety's production zone. As place names are no longer allowed to name grapes in Italy, this variety's name has been changed to Maresco. It's a little-studied variety that ripens in September and is characterized by medium-strong vigor and good productivity of light white wines blessed with very good acidity. For this reason, the variety has been looked at as a source of good sparkling wines.

WINES TO TRY: The only monovarietal maresco I know of is made by Donato Angiuli** (Maccone), who also produces a good Primitivo di Gioia. This sparkling wine sits six months on the lees and offers aromas and flavors of green apple, citrus, and pear.

Marzabino

WHERE IT'S FOUND: Emilia-Romagna. NATIONAL REGISTRY CODE NUMBER: not registered. COLOR: red.

Though their names are similar, Marzabino has nothing in common with Marzemino. De Bosis first described it in 1876 and considered it identical to varieties then known as Marzanino di Ravenna and Balsamina di Forlì. In 1896 Di Rovasenda wrote that Marzabino was identical to the *Refoscos* that at that time were common in the northern part of Italy's Adriatic coast. It gives a very perfumed and intensely colored wine, hence it used to be blended with Sangiovese.

Marzemina Nera

WHERE IT'S FOUND: Veneto. NATIONAL REGISTRY CODE NUMBER: not registered. COLOR: red.

The Marzemina Nera I describe here is just one of many grape varieties called Marzemina Nera in Veneto; it is not yet clear if the others are biotypes or distinct varieties. More than one Marzemina Nera and even more Marzemina-

Something grapes have been described over the centuries. For example, the 1868 *Bollettino Ampelografico* of the Vicenza area listed seven *Marzeminas*: Marzemina, Marzemina Bastarda, Marzemina Gentile, Marzeminone, Marzemina Rossa, Marzemina Groppella, and Marzemina Oseleta. One wonders if some of those *Marzeminas* really weren't other varieties altogether, such as Oseleta or one of the *Groppellos*. Not long thereafter it was determined that Marzeminone was synonymous with Marzemina Grossa, though Marzotto in 1925 distinguished between the former and a Marzemina Grossa that grew only around Brogliano near Vicenza. According to him it had even bigger berries and bunches. He also pointed out that there was a Marzemina Gentile that was identical to the grape called Balsamina di Forlì in Emilia-Romagna. Though most of these grapes were described as early ripening (some were picked as early as mid-August) and productive, not all were so: Marzemina Gentile was described by Marzotto as ripening in late September and even October. Clearly, besides confusing the various *Marzeminas* between themselves and other grapes too, many also confused the *Marzeminas* with Marzemino, though looking at the underside of the leaves helped (hairy in Marzemino, smooth in the *Marzeminas*). In more modern times, some light has finally been shed on this subject, as genetic studies by Salmaso, Dalla Valle, and Lucchin (2008) showed that Marzemina Nera and Marzemina Cenerenta were identical at thirty SSR loci, but different from Marzemina Bianca and Marzemina Nera Bastarda (commonly also called Marzemina Grossa Bastarda). Others have told me there is also a Marzemina Friulana, which appears to be distinct from these *Marzeminas* of Veneto.

Marzemina Nera is the most abundant of the *Marzeminas* that still exist today, but it's still not very common. Once abundant, especially in the area around Padova, Marzemina Nera is present today in sporadic plantings there and in the vineyards around Verona. Though it is no longer common, I have seen it during my vineyard walks, and can guarantee that it is immediately recognizable, with an extremely large, long bunch almost cascading from the vine. It also has very indented leaves, and between its massive look and the indented, jagged leaves, it's like no other red variety commonly found in Valpolicella. The grape cluster is indeed huge (875 grams on average), pyramidal, winged, with reportedly black-blue, round berries. Though I was told the grapevines I visited were Marzemina Nera, I now think it is most likely that what I observed was Marzemina Grossa. The Tedeschi estate in Valpolicella is growing Marzemina Nera (Grossa, most likely) in one of its vineyards: anyone interested in taking a gander can count on Riccardo Tedeschi gladly showing you the vineyard (though I caution the well-fed among us grape watchers and wine lovers that the walk is all uphill!).

Maturano

WHERE IT'S FOUND: Lazio. NATIONAL REGISTRY CODE NUMBER: 424. COLOR: white.

In the 1881 Ampelographic Bulletin from the Ministry of Agriculture, Industry, and Commerce, there were two Maturano varieties described. Maturano Nero di Alvito, a red grape, and Maturano (or Motulano), a white grape. We do not yet know if the two varieties are in fact related or just called by similar names. The latter appears to have been used to make a well-regarded wine, a favorite of writer D. H. Lawrence when he visited Italy. Only this Maturano is found in any significant quantities today, but its diffusion is limited to a very small area in southeastern Lazio, between the Valle del Comino and the Valle del Liri. The bunch is medium-sized, conical, winged, and fairly compact with medium-sized berries characterized by a terminal depression or umbilicus. The wine is yellow-green and not aromatic, with striking green tinges, floral and citrus aromas, and good structure. There are producers in Lazio planning to release a monovarietal bottling soon.

Mazzese

WHERE IT'S FOUND: Tuscany. NATIONAL REGISTRY CODE NUMBER: 145. COLOR: red.

Its existence documented as far back as 1679, Mazzese is one of Tuscany's oldest grape varieties, probably native to the areas around Pisa and Grosseto, where it was known as Vajano; its other names include Rinaldesca and Orzese. It also grows sporadically in old vineyard plots in Sardinia. Recent studies imply that there may be two different biotypes, so much so that the Mazzese of Pisa is also called Mazzese di Parlascio. There are many old vines around Grosseto (the warmer climate of southern Maremma apparently suits this variety better), Pisa, and even in Sardinia. The bunch is large, long, and sparse, with one or two wings. The berries are medium-small, slightly oval, thick skinned, and pink. Early ripening, it's usually picked a month ahead of Sangiovese, in the first week of September. Mazzese is a high-acid variety, and pure Mazzese wines (which I have not yet tasted) have an intense, sour-cherry smell. For this reason, some believe Mazzese to be Ciliegiolo, or a biotype of it.

Melara

WHERE IT'S FOUND: Emilia-Romagna. NATIONAL REGISTRY CODE NUMBER: 399. COLOR: white.

Melara is also known as Merlara, as small blackbirds (*merli*) are fond of the sweet, ripe berries. It has always been grown in the countryside around Piacenza. The bunch is medium and compact, a truncated pyramid in shape, with large, round or almost oval berries, with a thick yellow-green skins. It accumulates sugar easily and is therefore picked early, usually by the last week of August. Due to its very thick skin, historically it has been used most often for the production of sweet wines, such as the DOC Colli Piacentini Vin Santo di Vigoleno, one of the best—and least-known—sweet wines of the country.

Merla

See CANAIOLO NERO, chapter 4.

Merlina

WHERE IT'S FOUND: Lombardy. NATIONAL REGISTRY CODE NUMBER: not registered. COLOR: red.

First described in the eighteenth century in Valtellina, the northern alpine area of Lombardy where it is still (and only) found today, Merlina has always been appreciated for its strong dark wines. Traditionally it was blended with Chiavennasca (the local name for Nebbiolo) which is notoriously light colored. It was also often air-dried, as is the tradition in Valtellina, home of the famous Sfursat wine. The bunch is medium to medium-small, cylindrical or pyramidal, with two wings usually. The berry is round and medium-large, blue-black, and ripens in early October. Your best bet is to visit farmers in the areas of Tirano and Grosotto and taste their homemade wines: your taste buds will be greeted by a thick dark wine that is amazingly fresh and quite tannic, with blueberry and dark plum flavors.

Minnella Bianca

WHERE IT'S FOUND: Sicily. NATIONAL REGISTRY CODE NUMBER: 147. COLOR: white.

Described by Sestini in 1760, Minnella Bianca is now a rare variety grown almost exclusively on the slopes of the Etna volcano and very sporadically in the province of Enna. Its name derives from the Sicilian word for female breast *(minna)*, as this variety's berries have a shape recalling that anatomic part. It is not particularly resistant, neither to spring frosts nor to common vine pests. A low-acid variety, it was historically always used as a blending agent with which to reduce the strong acidity and tannins of most Etnean reds. Salvo Foti believes that due to its low acidity and tendency to oxidize easily it really isn't all that interesting to make wines with it on its own, though for a few vintages, he made some excellent minnellas in the I Monovitigni series of wines from Benanti. Those wines were fresh, herbal and floral, with a soft-bodied texture and a creamy finish reminiscent of unripe apricot and pear. Though Foti obviously didn't think too much of them, I actually thought they were pretty good.

Molinelli

WHERE IT'S FOUND: Emilia-Romagna. NATIONAL REGISTRY CODE NUMBER: not registered. COLOR: white.

Molinelli is a one-family or one-estate variety if you will: the grape was discovered in the 1960s by the Molinelli family (who gave it their name) in their vineyards. Studies performed by the esteemed Fregoni (1969) have shown Molinelli to be a variety distinct from others known to date.

WINES TO TRY: La Celata* is a brand of the Molinelli family, which produces wines under its family name as well. La Celata's Tabula Rasa is bright and fresh, with herbal and winter melon notes complicated by flinty and tropical fruit nuances. It has good length and clarity of flavor: I enjoy it as an aperitif or with lightly prepared fish and vegetable dishes. However, since it is aged five months in small, used oak barrels, it can stand up to more complex fish dishes as well.

Montanera

WHERE IT'S FOUND: Piedmont, Lombardy. NATIONAL REGISTRY CODE NUMBER: not registered. COLOR: red.

The variety I describe here is Montanera di Perosa, an alpine variety, rediscovered only recently in hard-to-reach mountain vineyards of the Val Chisone, Biellese, Val d'Ossola, and Valtellina. It was documented in the 1800s (Provana di Collegno 1883) but should not be confused with the similarly named Montanera del Saluzzese. It appears to have fine-wine potential, with bunches that are neither too compact nor too sparse, and with good sugar accumulation in the berries. I have not yet tried any microvinifications, and I don't know how wines made with it would differ from those made with Montanera del Salluzzese.

Montonico Pinto

WHERE IT'S FOUND: Calabria. NATIONAL REGISTRY CODE NUMBER: not registered. COLOR: white.

Not to be confused with Montonico Bianco, this variety is also known as Montonico Ciarchiarisi and is found in vineyards around Frascineto, Civita, Castrovillari, and Cassano Ionico, in the province of Cosenza. It is not a very resistant variety, and the wine, when one is able to find a monovarietal version, is light and acid with aromas and flavors of white flowers and citrus fruits. The DOC Pollino is where Montonico Pinto is likely to be included.

Moradella

WHERE IT'S FOUND: Lombardy. NATIONAL REGISTRY CODE NUMBER: not registered. COLOR: red.

Moradella was once the most important variety grown in the province of Pavia, where it was cultivated in ninety-six townships. Acerbi (1825) described two biotypes, a Moradella Piccola and a Moradella Grossa. It lost out to Barbera and other hardier cultivars with the arrival of oidium, to which it is very sensitive. In the area of Voghera it is also called Croà, but the two varieties often don't look at all like each other; whether this is just a matter of intravarietal variability or of truly distinct varieties is still unknown. In the past, some experts found a strong resemblance between Moradella and Mourvèdre. The bunch is conical and small, the berries round and very dark blue-black. The best sites are well exposed (both in terms of sunlight and of aeration), on preferably clay-sandy soils with good drainage. Apart from oidium sensitivity, it's fairly disease resistant.

WINES TO TRY: In Lombardy, Fortesi** is making experimental batches of moradella wine on sale at the estate. If you're in the area, stop by, since the wine is not yet available elsewhere.

Morone

WHERE IT'S FOUND: Tuscany. NATIONAL REGISTRY CODE NUMBER: not registered. COLOR: red.

Morone is also known as Moro; there exist three different biotypes, all grown in the Lunigiana area of Tuscany, near the city of Massa-Carrara, on the border with Liguria. The standard biotype has a medium to medium-large bunch with medium-sized, blue-black, round berries that have a strongly colored pulp. It is usually harvested in mid- to late September. This is one cultivar people could look at for future monovarietal bottlings.

Mostarino

WHERE IT'S FOUND: Emilia-Romagna. NATIONAL REGISTRY CODE NUMBER: not registered. COLOR: red.

Called so because it produces copious quantities of must (*mosto*), Mostarino is a variety grown mainly around Piacenza. It has a medium-sized, conical, and compact bunch. The berry is medium-large, round, and blue-black with plenty of juice, but I haven't tried any monovarietal wines.

Mostosa

WHERE IT'S FOUND: Emilia-Romagna. NATIONAL REGISTRY CODE NUMBER: 157. COLOR: white.

This grape lives in what is perhaps Italy's single most confusing grape variety situation, since it has always been mixed up with Bombino Bianco, a distinct variety, among others. Only described at the beginning of the twentieth century by Cavazza, Mostosa's name hints at copious must (*mosto*) production. In fact, as it produces well, it is also known as Scacciadebiti and Empibotte ("get rid of your debts" and "fill the barrels," respectively). Though it may be similar to some of the Passerina varieties found all over central Italy, it is still not completely clear whether it is the same grape as Pagadebit. Certainly, the Pezzi family of the Fattoria Paradiso in Emilia-Romagna thinks the two are different. However, most experts I have talked to over the years believe it is used to make the wine called pagadebit, which has also always been made with Bombino Bianco as well as Mostosa, due to the confusion surrounding the varieties (apparently nurseries, in good faith, sent Bombino Bianco to growers looking to plant Mostosa/Pagadebit). Recently researchers have shown that Mostosa has a parent-offspring relationship with Garganega, thereby making it a half-sibling or grandparent of Albana, Cataratto Bianco, Dorona, Malvasia Bianca di Candia, Marzemina Bianca, Montonico Bianco, Susumaniello, and Trebbiano Toscano (Crespan, Calò, Giannetto, Sparacio, Storchi, Costacurta, et al. 2008). At our present state of knowledge, we can say that Mostosa is Empibotte, but not Bombino Bianco. It is also likely to be Pagadebit.

Some figures show that Mostosa is also grown in Puglia, Marche, and Abruzzo, but I think this results from confusing Mostosa with Bombino Bianco; that larger distribution should be attributed to Bombino Bianco. Over my years of speaking to local growers and producers, the general consensus is that, though Mostosa was common once, today there isn't much anywhere except in the vineyards of Emilia-Romagna, and even there it has been supplanted by plantings of Bombino Bianco.

The bunch is large, pyramidal or conical, compact, and winged. The berry is large too, round, thin skinned, and yellow-green. Harvest is in late September or early October. It is sensitive to strong winds and to peronospora.

Negrat

WHERE IT'S FOUND: Friuli Venezia Giulia. NATIONAL REGISTRY CODE NUMBER: not registered. COLOR: red.

Almost extinct today, Negrat was never grown much and then only in the countryside around Santo Giorgio della Richinvelda, in the province of Pordenone. Its name derives from its dark-hued berries, much like other similarly named but unrelated grapes (Negrara, Negronza, Neyret, and many more). The wine, tasted from microvinifications, is dark-ruby in color, very grapey and fresh in its aromas and flavors (with hints of underbrush and black currant), and medium bodied. It seems a little neutral for it to hold interest as a monovarietal wine.

Negratino

WHERE IT'S FOUND: Tuscany. NATIONAL REGISTRY CODE NUMBER: not registered. COLOR: red.

Medium-sized bunch and berries characterize this rare Tuscan variety, part of the *teinturier* family. It should not be confused with the similarly named Negrottino, a non-*teinturier* variety from Emilia-Romagna.

Negro Amaro Precoce

WHERE IT'S FOUND: Puglia. NATIONAL REGISTRY CODE NUMBER: 361. COLOR: red.

Another Negro Amaro exists, called Negro Amaro Precoce, or less commonly, Negro Amaro Cannellino. In 1994, researchers at the Istituto Sperimentale per la Viticoltura of Conegliano realized that a set of Negro Amaro grapevines were characterized by an earlier budbreak and by berries that turned color sooner in the season (the time period between flowering and *veraison*, or the color change of the berries, was only twenty days). Importantly, they also reached full ripeness earlier (usually two to three weeks sooner).

The variety is now listed under its own heading in the National Registry, though genetic studies by Calò, Costacurta, Cancellier, Crespan, Milani, Carraro, et al. (2000) proved it to be identical to Negro Amaro. It follows that Negro Amaro Precoce is a biotype of the better known Negro Amaro. Like Negro Amaro, Negro Amaro Precoce has a compact, medium-sized bunch, but it's more conical-pyramidal in shape. The berries are much smaller than those of regular Negro Amaro, though just like the latter, they are oval shaped and blue-black. The anthocyanins of Negro Amaro Precoce are much easier to extract from the skins, while the flavans from pips are not, which potentially can lead to darker, smoother wines. Negro Amaro Precoce shows the same degree of disease and drought resistance as its more famous namesake, and as its name implies, it ripens and is harvested much sooner than Negro Amaro, usually in the first ten days of September. To the best of my knowledge, there is no monovarietal Negro Amaro Precoce wine yet on sale.

Negrone

WHERE IT'S FOUND: Trentino. NATIONAL REGISTRY CODE NUMBER: not registered. COLOR: red.

Characterized by bigger berries and bunches than Negrara Trentina, the more common variety in Trentino, it is similar to the latter variety but increases, due to its larger size, both the pros and cons of Negrara Trentina. Negrone was never that common: for example, at the end of the 1800s there were only fifteen hundred hectoliters produced, most in the Vallagarina and near Civezzano in Trentino. Wines made with grapes from the latter area were particularly sought after (Gorfer 1977). I am not aware of anyone who makes monovarietal wines from Negrone today.

Nera dei Baisi

WHERE IT'S FOUND: Trentino. NATIONAL REGISTRY CODE NUMBER: not registered. COLOR: red.

Nera dei Baisi is another extremely rare variety that has been saved thanks to the passion and dedication of Albino Armani, who already deserves credit for having saved Foja Tonda. Not much is known about Nera dei Baisi except that its name may derive from the wealthy merchant family Ecchelli-Baisi, whose stately palace still stands in the town of Brentonico. Nera dei Baisi is a late ripening, hardy variety with considerable winemaking potential and appears to contain American grapevine genes in its DNA. Armani makes about one thousand bottles at present and the wine shows considerable promise. Raspberry and a hint of strawberry on the nose and the palate, complicated by tobacco and spices, low alcohol (12.5 percent usually), and plenty of freshness prove it. Nera dei Baisi may be coming back from the forgotten.

Ner d'Ala

WHERE IT'S FOUND: Valle d'Aosta. NATIONAL REGISTRY CODE NUMBER: 354. COLOR: red.

Ner d'Ala is a grape of many names. It is also known as Gros Vien and Nerdela in Valle d'Aosta; as Vernassa and Neirét dal Picul Rus in Carema; as Barau in Chiaverano; as Durás in Quincinetto; as Provinè or Pruinè in Castagneto Po; as Fiorì in Pinerolese; and as Verdés and Uva di Biella in Piedmont. It is most likely a native of Piedmont, and takes its name from the Val d'Ala, northwest of Turin—though some experts believe the name is due to a prominent grape bunch wing, or *ala*. It should not be confused with Verdese or Verdesse or similarly named varieties; it is identical to the Vernassa or Verdés of Piedmont. Recent work by Vouillamoz and Moriondo (2011) have shown it to have a close genetic link with Piedmont's Avarengo.

Ner d'Ala was well described by Gatta in 1838. Today it is limited to few sporadic rows of vines in both Piedmont and Valle d'Aosta: it is most common in Piedmont's Canavese and Pinerolese. Not surprisingly, in Valle d'Aosta it is found especially in the lower or southern part of the region (which borders Piedmont), near the towns of Arnad and Montjovet. The bunch is medium-large, pyramidal, and winged, with large blue-black and very juicy berries. Ner d'Ala presents high intravarietal variability, and it is not clear yet if this reflects the existence of different biotypes (the Picul Rus has smaller but longer bunches, the Verdés has very large bunches and berries that often fail to become completely dark red-blue, remaining green) or whether there are distinct varieties currently erroneously considered to be Ner d'Ala. It's wind and cold resistant, but in fertile soils can develop a compact bunch that makes it prone to botrytis. It ripens in early October; the wines (tasted from microvinifications only) are vinous, delicately spicy and fresh. Especially pleasant is the light note of white pepper that makes Ner d'Ala a very interesting variety. It is also a very good table grape due to its large, juicy berries.

Nereto

WHERE IT'S FOUND: Tuscany. NATIONAL REGISTRY CODE NUMBER: not registered. COLOR: red.

Nereto is a typical *teinturier* of Tuscany, and very similar to another member of the coloring agent family, Raspo Rosso. Nereto is characterized by a medium-sized, short pyramidal bunch and medium-round, blue-black berries with a delicate colored pulp. It usually ripens before Sangiovese.

Neretta Cuneese

WHERE IT'S FOUND: Piedmont. NATIONAL REGISTRY CODE NUMBER: 166. COLOR: red.

Like all the various and many *Neretto*s, *Neretta*s and *Nero*-Something wines, Neretta Cuneese is plagued by many synonyms, often used to describe varieties that are altogether different. All these names refer to the very dark, practically black (*nero* means black), hue of the berries. First described by Nuvolone in 1799, it is grown today mainly in the Cuneese area of Piedmont around Turin, though vines are found everywhere in the region. Moderately vigorous yet a consistent producer, it makes dark wines that lack complexity but that are balanced and fresh. The bunch is medium-large, cylindrical, and winged; the berry is large, round or oval, thick skinned, and blue-black. It ripens late (usually in the first half of October), but is extremely hardy and endears itself to farmers as it will grow where many other varieties succumb, and is extremely vigorous and productive. It's found in blends of the DOC wine Valsusa.

Neretta di Marengo

WHERE IT'S FOUND: Piedmont. NATIONAL REGISTRY CODE NUMBER: not registered. COLOR: red.

Another of the many *Neretto*s in Piedmont, it used to be grown in the flatland vineyards of Alessandria but is rare nowadays, since it is plagued by extreme vegetative vigor and by berry shatter. Modern microvinifications reveal a lightly hued, delicately scented (red berries), high-acid wine. Though plantings are few and far between, there is some interest in this variety and both university producers and producers are studying it presently.

Neretto Duro

WHERE IT'S FOUND: Piedmont. NATIONAL REGISTRY CODE NUMBER: not registered. COLOR: red.

Yet another one of the many *Neretto*s of Piedmont, Neretto Duro should not be confused with the better known Neretto di Bairo. It is also called, erroneously, Barbera Rotonda or Bonarda Rotonda around Albiano and Roppolo (it is neither a Barbera nor a Bonarda); Dolcetto di Boca in the Novarese (nor is it a Dolcetto); it goes by Peilavert near Dorzano, Salussola, and Cavaglià; it is known as Freisone in the western Tortonese area; and, correctly, Uva 'd Galvan or Galvan in the Pinerolese. In the Novarese area it is also named Durasa, though there are other grapes with that name in other parts of Piedmont. The bunch is medium to medium-small, conical but short, winged, sparse, with round, medium-sized berries, and thick blue-black skin. The wine is a little neutral in its nose, but has lively acidity and delicate red-berry flavors.

The Cantina Sociale di Bricherasio used to produce a pure galvan wine a few years ago, but production stopped, after the social cooperative closed and fused into a new entity called Il Tralcio. Simple and straightforward, with bright dark-berry and saline aromas and flavors, with hints of violet and tar, it made for a good match with light meat dishes.

Neyret

WHERE IT'S FOUND: Valle d'Aosta. NATIONAL REGISTRY CODE NUMBER: 169. COLOR: red.

Recent DNA testing (Moriondo, Sandi, and Vouillamoz 2008) has clarified that there exists a *Neretto* typical of the Valle d'Aosta, distinct from all the other Neretto varieties of Piedmont such as Neretta Cuneese or Chatus; subsequently, this discovery was given the name Neyret (some spell it Neret). Also called Neyret de Saint-Vincent, it has a phenotypic resemblance to the descriptions of nineteenth-century *Neretto*s from Valdostani, first described by Gatta in 1838 (he mentioned three different biotypes that no longer exist). One of its parents is the Swiss variety Rouge du Valais, which means that Petit Rouge, Mayolet, and Fumin are its grandparents. An almost extinct variety limited to a few vineyards between Arnad and Montjovet, it has a medium-sized, cylindrical, long-winged, and compact bunch, with medium-sized, thick-skinned, and blue-black sweet berries. It is a useful blending grape, as its delicate, perfumed wine contributes alcohol, color, and a measure of refinement. Unfortunately the vines are very scarce and it is my hope that an innovative producer will want to look at the good-quality wines that seem possible with this grape.

Nieddu Mannu

WHERE IT'S FOUND: Sardinia. NATIONAL REGISTRY CODE NUMBER: 171. COLOR: red.

In the past Nieddu Mannu was also called Bovale Mannu and Muristellone and was confused with Pascale and Nieddera (though recent SSR microsatellite testing has shown it to be at least related to the latter). Nowadays, Nieddu Mannu is rare, with only an estimated eighty hectares in the provinces of Sassari and Oristano, mainly around the town of Nuoro. The bunch is medium-large, pyramidal, winged, and compact, with large, round, medium-thick-skinned berries of red-violet hue. It is a late-ripening variety, usually picked in October. I have yet to try a monovarietal wine, but this is going to be hard as no single producer owns enough vines to make the wine in economically feasible quantities at present.

Notardomenico

WHERE IT'S FOUND: Puglia. NATIONAL REGISTRY CODE NUMBER: 174. COLOR: red.

Mainly found in Puglia around the towns of Cistenino, Carovigno, Ostuni, and San Vito dei Normanni, Notardomenico is usually used as part of the blend in the DOC Ostuni Ottavianello, typically for *rosato* production. However it can also be found in small percentages in blends such as Murgia, Puglia, Salento, Tarantino, and Valle d'Itria. Apparently it was also once made as a monovarietal *rosato* wine, and it continues to be appreciated as a table grape. The bunch is medium-small and conical; the berry is medium-sized, round but not uniform, thin skinned, and reddish-violet; it is harvested in mid-September. The wines are low in alcohol, high in acids, and delicately flavored.

Occhio di Pernice

WHERE IT'S FOUND: Tuscany. NATIONAL REGISTRY CODE NUMBER: not registered. COLOR: red.

A little-known aromatic variety characterized by red berries of different shades, a feature that is not due to asynchronous maturation of the berries but rather to a strong viral load affecting virtually all grapevines of this variety. Occhio di Pernice has a long, sparse cluster and two large wings so it looks almost compound in shape. The very large round berries caused this variety to be confused with Muscat of Hamburg, also an aromatic variety.

Occhiorosso

WHERE IT'S FOUND: Tuscany. NATIONAL REGISTRY CODE NUMBER: not registered. COLOR: red.

Roberto Bandinelli of the University of Florence, winemaker Federico Staderini, and Sebastiano Capponi, owner of the Villa Calcinaia estate in Greve in Chianti, are working on this rare variety and are making an interesting monovarietal wine. Bandinelli discovered the variety while talking one day to Nunziatina Grassi, an eighty-five-year-old who took him around her vineyards and showed him Occhiorosso; the variety is characterized by a stalk that has a sinuous shape and a very unique sandpapery feel. The minute Bandinelli showed me what to look for in an Occhiorosso grapevine I was immediately able to recognize it without fail in any other vineyard I visited that day with him. The bunches are medium-small and compact, the berry small with a thick, resistant skin. Microvinifications of the wine reveal red-fruit aromas and flavors and spicy tobacco, cedary nuances.

Orpicchio

WHERE IT'S FOUND: Tuscany. NATIONAL REGISTRY CODE NUMBER: 377. COLOR: white.

Grown in Tuscany already in the mid-nineteenth century, Orpicchio has always been associated with the Fattoria di Petrolo estate (its owner, Giorgio Perrin first described the variety in 1854), where the last few vines were found and reproduced by the experimental station of the Unità per Ricerca of Arezzo. The variety has medium vigor, a small, short, cylindrical bunch (though some have looked pyramidal to me), and round, medium-sized, green-yellow, thin-skinned berries that look greyish because of thick bloom. It is harvested in mid-September. No monovarietal wines are being currently produced to the best of my knowledge.

Pampanaro

WHERE IT'S FOUND: Lazio. NATIONAL REGISTRY CODE NUMBER: 426. COLOR: white.

In the 1881 Ampelographic Bulletin from the Ministry of Agriculture, Industry, and Commerce, there were three different white grapes identified as Pampanaro: Pampanaro di Atina (or Mustosa di Alvito), Pampanaro di Arce, and Pampanaro di Fondi. Whether these three were homonyms or perhaps biotypes is not known. The one that is found most commonly today is the first, and it is typical of the Val Comino. However, I have met with growers near the lake of Bolsena in north-central Lazio, and they also mention a Pampanaro in their vineyards, which may in fact be one of the other two previously described. If proper research is ever performed on these separate grapevines, we will know more.

The bunch is medium-sized, conical, winged, not too compact, with medium-sized rather green, elliptical/round berries characterized by a terminal depression or umbilicus. The wine is yellow-green and delicately aromatic, with green tinges and notes of yellow flowers, ripe tropical fruit, and even a hint of basil. Pampanaro may have plenty to offer as a wine grape, but clearly this will only come about with the aid of further studies and of government funding to set up experimental vineyards and mother plants, as at present this grapevine is grown in only small vineyard parcels.

Paolina

WHERE IT'S FOUND: Trentino. NATIONAL REGISTRY CODE NUMBER: 427. COLOR: red.

At the end of the 1800s, there were about three thousand hectoliters of this wine made yearly in Trentino, where the now very rare grape is still grown in the Valle del Sarca and on the shores of the Canzolino lake. It's characterized by an absolutely gigantic cluster and high-acid wines, and it is used as a blending agent. I have not tasted any monovarietal wines and given the very few grapevines present in the vineyards, I doubt there is one being made.

Paradisa

WHERE IT'S FOUND: Emilia-Romagna. NATIONAL REGISTRY CODE NUMBER: not registered. COLOR: red.

Paradisa was grown more or less in the same areas as the Angela variety and was appreciated both as a table grape and a wine grape. On the hills of Savignano near Bologna, an old row of Paradisa has been recently identified. Actually, it seems that Paradisa may be more common than originally believed, as research done on numerous Emilia-Romagna accessions have shown that grapes believed to be Verdea, Cellino, Uva della Madonna and, possibly, Angela Romagnola are all Paradisa instead. A great deal more work is needed on this subject, including an enological evaluation of this variety's exact winemaking potential.

Parporio

WHERE IT'S FOUND: Piedmont. NATIONAL REGISTRY CODE NUMBER: not registered. COLOR: red.

Once grown in the Saluzzese, Parporio was most popular consumed fresh in a *nouveau* style much like the famous Beaujolais Nouveau or Novello wines of today (Di Rovasenda 1877), but its extreme sensitivity to oidium proved to be its downfall. It's characterized by a bunch that has a strong curvature and flattened berries; the leaf is heavily indented. The variety appears to have fine-wine potential according to experimental microvinifications that I have not yet tried.

Pattaresca

WHERE IT'S FOUND: Veneto. NATIONAL REGISTRY CODE NUMBER: not registered. COLOR: red.

First described in an 1868 catalogue published for a local grape fair in Vicenza, Pattaresca is believed to originate in the Padova area of Veneto. Practically no other historical documentation exists. The bunch is medium-sized, pyramidal, and winged; the berry medium-sized and round, with a very thick skin; the variety is fairly resistant to most diseases, but becomes more susceptible to botrytis when yields are allowed to run high. The wine is medium red in color, with delicate red-fruit aromas and is both acidic and tannic. It finishes with a lightly saline touch. It might be worth to study Pattaresca more.

Pavana

WHERE IT'S FOUND: Veneto, Trentino. NATIONAL REGISTRY CODE NUMBER: 182. COLOR: red.

This grape's name derives from Padovana, the area it comes from and is grown in: it reached Trentino by way of the Veneto (in fact German ampelographers such as Goethe in 1887 don't mention it at all). It was once very abundant, with over eighty thousand hectoliters of wine made at the end of the nineteenth century. There's not much Pavana around today: you'll find rows of these vines only in and around Novaledo, Levico, Borgo Valsugana, and northwest of Vicenza. The bunch is medium-sized, pyramidal, and winged, with round, medium-sized, blue-purple berries harvested in October. It is also called Nera Gentile, Nostrana Nera, and Visentina, and is used in IGT blends such as Vallagarina and delle Venezie

Pecorello

WHERE IT'S FOUND: Calabria. NATIONAL REGISTRY CODE NUMBER: not registered. COLOR: red.

Pecorello is yet another headache-inducing native variety of Italy, as it is often called Pecorino by locals, though it has nothing in common with the more famous variety of the same name in Marche. There is also a white-berried Pecorello (at times called Pecorella in Calabria) that is unrelated to this red-berried variety. Today Pecorello grows around Catanzaro and Cosenza in the DOC Savuto. The bunch is medium-sized, conical or cylindrical, winged, and sparse; the berry is medium-small, thick skinned, and blue-black. Harvest is between the end of September and early October. Originally, it was this variety that was listed as a red-berried grape at number 183 in the National Registry of Grape Varieties but this was corrected in 2010, and now the white-berried variety is in its place.

Pedevenda

WHERE IT'S FOUND: Veneto. NATIONAL REGISTRY CODE NUMBER: 334. COLOR: white.

Described by Valerio Canati (more familiar by his pen name, Aureliano Acanti) in 1754 as an important component of the local Torcolato sweet wine, Pedevenda is cultivated today around Breganze, where the DOC Torcolato is located. The bunch is medium-sized, long, and pyramidal with a large wing and medium-sized, oval berries that are thick skinned and yellow-pink. It is a late ripener and resistant to most diseases. Harvest takes place in mid-September, though it is usually late harvested or air-dried for the production of sweet wines, since it doesn't drop its acidity easily. The name refers either to the peppery quality of its wines or to the relatively small size of its berries.

WINES TO TRY: Firmino Miotti (Pedevendo, light bodied and delicately floral, with hints of citrus and unripe apricot).

Pelagòs

WHERE IT'S FOUND: Emilia-Romagna. NATIONAL REGISTRY CODE NUMBER: 456. COLOR: red.

All the Pelagòs in Italy derive from two centenary vines saved by the Bagnari estate of Bagnocavallo, near Ravenna in Emilia-Romagna. Pelagòs is highly fertile and vigorous, an abundant producer. It grows in the area of Bagnocavallo, near Ravenna in Emilia-Romagna. Though it has the same isoenzymatic pattern as Ancellotta and Lambrusco di

Sorbara, DNA analysis has shown these three varieties to be distinct. It is instead related to the Canena Bucci, with which it shares one allele in common on fourteen out of twenty sites (Fontana, Filippetti, Pastore, and Intrieri 2007). It has a small, compact, short bunch with small, round berries. Microvinifications have shown very dark wines of intense perfume (red berries and dark cherries) and abundant tannins, according to Marisa Fontana, who believes that this variety holds promise for fine-wine production.

Pepella

WHERE IT'S FOUND: Campania. NATIONAL REGISTRY CODE NUMBER: 385. COLOR: white.

Pepella is a relatively recent variety, not documented prior to the nineteenth century and scarce after that. It is found on the Amafi coast along with many other rare natives, with which it is blended to make the DOC wine Costa d'Amalfi. The bunch is medium in size, conical-pyramidal, and sparse. The berries are non-uniform in size, and due to flowering issues many berries are so small they resemble pepper grains (hence the variety's name, *pepella* from *pepe*, pepper). Susceptible to botrytis, it is somewhat protected by the sparse bunch and thick skins of the berries. Genetic analysis confirms that it is distinct from all other known Campanian varieties (Manzo and Monaco 2001). Not very fertile and a small producer, it yields lightly alcoholic, high acid, and very floral wines. It grows in limited numbers in the areas around Tramonti, Ravello, and Scala in province of Salerno.

Perera

WHERE IT'S FOUND: Veneto. NATIONAL REGISTRY CODE NUMBER: 331. COLOR: white.

One of the historical varieties of Conegliano-Valdobbiadene, Perera has always been part of the grapes used to make Prosecco but is more commonly air-dried and used to make the sweet wine Torchiato di Fregona. Also known as Pevarise, it is currently risking extinction because it is very sensitive to *flavescence dorée*, a disease caused by the *Scaphoideus titanus* insect. Perera has a medium-large, conical, compact, winged bunch with round, midsized berries and is harvested in mid-October. The name may derive from the upside down pear shape of the berries (Cancellier, Giacobbi, Coletti, Soligo, Michelet, Coletti, and Stocco 2003). In the Vicenza area it used to be called Uva della Madonna.

Perla dei Vivi

WHERE IT'S FOUND: Emilia-Romagna. NATIONAL REGISTRY CODE NUMBER: 394. COLOR: red.

Perla dei Vivi, or Lambrusco dei Vivi is a recently studied and rediscovered variety that despite its *Lambrusco* moniker does not seem to be closely related to them.

Peverella

WHERE IT'S FOUND: Trentino. NATIONAL REGISTRY CODE NUMBER: not registered. COLOR: white.

A very rare variety that is grown in only a few plots in Trentino's beautiful Valle dei Laghi, Peverella was also known in the past as Pevana, Peverenda, and Pevarise. The bunch is medium-sized and stocky with medium-small, green berries that are rarely yellow even when fully ripe. It flowers and ripens early, and so is harvested in early September. The cultivar's name may derive from its piquant, even peppery, acidity or from the fact that it was always grown in vineyards near churches *(pieve)*. Apparently, Vouillamoz and Grando have unpublished data identifying Peverella with Verdicchio, but perhaps it's best to wait for the data to be evaluated and published in a peer-reviewed journal.

Plassa

WHERE IT'S FOUND: Piedmont. NATIONAL REGISTRY CODE NUMBER: 196. COLOR: red.

An extremely rare grapevine grown in Piedmont around the towns of Bricherasio, Cuminana, Camopiglione-Fenile, and Pinerolo, Plassa has a midsized, long, cylindrical bunch, with medium-sized, oval, thick-skinned berries. Its thick skin both explains its name (it derives from *pellaccia,* thick skin) and makes it very resistant to hail. It was also called Scarlattino due to the red hue of its stalk and twigs. Though its wine is not particularly famous, growers have always had a soft spot for it, since it's a very dependable producer and because of its cold-weather resistance.

Pollera Nera

WHERE IT'S FOUND: Liguria. NATIONAL REGISTRY CODE NUMBER: 197. COLOR: red.

Originally grown in Liguria's beautiful Cinque Terre, a Unesco world heritage site, Pollera Nera is also called Corlaga, which is properly the name of one of its two biotypes: Pollera Corlaga and Pollera Nera Comune. It is also grown in the Lunigiana area and it can be found in both Cinque Terre wines as well as those of the Colli di Luni. The bunch is large, cylindrical-pyramidal, long, and winged with medium-large, thick-skinned, blue-black berries. The Corlaga subvariety has a smaller bunch and smaller berries. Diego Bosoni of the Lunae Bosoni estate has been studying it in view of possibly producing a monovarietal wine, and though he admits he's still learning the ropes, he finds the wines have plenty of color, red-fruit and underbrush aromas and flavors, and a good tannic structure.

Pomella

WHERE IT'S FOUND: Veneto. NATIONAL REGISTRY CODE NUMBER: not registered. COLOR: red.

Pomella is a little-known variety with a small, cylindrical, compact bunch and medium-large berries, but low resistance to most common diseases. The grapes have a medium-low content of anthocyanins and polyphenols, and tend to give light-colored, medium-bodied wines with decent balance. According to Raffaele Boscaini of the world-famous Masi estate of Valpolicella and Amarone, it is probably best as a blending grape, but unfortunately, I have not tried any microvinifications, yet.

Preveiral

WHERE IT'S FOUND: Piedmont. NATIONAL REGISTRY CODE NUMBER: not registered. COLOR: white.

Preveiral is also known as Proveiral, Pruverà, or Perveiral in the Pinerolese; as Blancio in Val Maira; as Liseiret in Alta Val Bormida; as Lisöra in the Piacentino area of Emilia-Romagna; as Gouais Blanc in France; and as Weisser Heunisch in central Europe. It is not related to Preveiral Nero, a different red grape that shares a similar name. In Italy, its cultivation is limited today to Piedmont's Val Bormida, Val Maira, and Val di Susa (especially the first of these), where it grows even at high altitudes. Medium-sized and winged, the bunch has medium-sized, round, golden-yellow berries covered with brown dots. It's very fertile and productive, but is very disease sensitive. An early ripening variety (early September), Preveiral is blessed with very high total acidity; it can make for a lovely, delicate white wine exuding aromas of citrus and green apples.

Primaticcio

WHERE IT'S FOUND: Tuscany. NATIONAL REGISTRY CODE NUMBER: not registered. COLOR: white.

Primaticcio is a very rare variety found only around Florence, though there are experimental plots in Maremma and Montescudaio. So called due to the fact it ripens early, it has been known since 1858 when it was common around San Gimignano. Long confused with Canaiolo Bianco (itself always confused with Vernaccia di San Gimignano), it's morphologically quite different, with a large, stocky, compact, cylindrical bunch, and large, round berries. A vigorous variety, it ripens in early September. I know of no monovarietal wines being made with it.

Prunesta

WHERE IT'S FOUND: Calabria. NATIONAL REGISTRY CODE NUMBER: 202. COLOR: red.

Also known as Uva del Soldato and Ruggia, Prunesta probably takes its name from the copious bloom covering the breast-shaped berries; this shape causes others to believe the variety's name stems from the Latin grape Bumastos, which had a berry in the shape of a cow breast. It has a medium-sized, very stocky, pyramidal, winged bunch, with large, oval, blue-black berries. It ripens in mid-September. It is not the same as the similarly named table grape of Puglia.

Quaiara

WHERE IT'S FOUND: Veneto. NATIONAL REGISTRY CODE NUMBER: not registered. COLOR: red.

Sormani-Moretti (1904) is the only historical resource available by which to learn something about this rare variety; he also calls it Quagliara, Cojara, and Guajara. Cancellier in 1980 was the first modern ampelographer to describe it in some detail. The cultivar has a medium-sized bunch (average weight: 370 grams), more or less sparse, long, and winged, with medium-large, elliptical, red-blue berries. The wine is thoroughly uninteresting, reddish-orange in hue, with neutral, vinous aromas and an unpleasant earthy-herbal taste.

Raspo Rosso

WHERE IT'S FOUND: Tuscany. NATIONAL REGISTRY CODE NUMBER: not registered. COLOR: red.

Another of the *teinturier* grapes of Tuscany, which are so plentiful in Tuscany and so rare worldwide, Raspo Rosso is characterized by a medium-sized, conical-cylindrical grape bunch and small, round, blue-black grapes that do not have a colored pulp. The stalk is red, hence the name, which means red stalk.

Recantina

WHERE IT'S FOUND: Veneto. NATIONAL REGISTRY CODE NUMBER: 409. COLOR: red.

The *Recantina* family of grapes have been cultivated at least since the 1600s in the area around Treviso in Veneto, though we do not know if the various *Recantinas* documented were truly different varieties or just biotypes. The best-known among them are Recantina Pecolo Rosso (red-stalked), Recantina Pecolo Scuro (green-stalked), and Recantina Forner (named after the estate where it was found). I have been told by Emanuele Tosi of the University of Verona that it is likely that the main Recantina variety is Recantina Pecolo Rosso.

In any case, this has always been a highly regarded variety: Agostinetti in 1679 and Zambenedetti a century later strongly recommended and pushed for its cultivation; Zambenedetti referred to it as *Recaldine* (Zoccoletto 2001). The grape cluster is medium-large, pyramidal, winged, generally sparse, with round, medium-sized, blue-black berries. It ripens in late September, and is vigorous and resistant to common diseases. I have seen the variety in numerous vineyards in Veneto. Microvinifications have yielded a very perfumed wine (blackberry and an intense note of violet) with good tannic structure and acidity. Not only will *Recantina* almost certainly one day be included in the Valpolicella and Amarone blend, but I can certainly see it standing on its own as well. Given this variety's qualities, it's probably only a matter of time.

Retagliado Bianco

WHERE IT'S FOUND: Sardinia. NATIONAL REGISTRY CODE NUMBER: 207. COLOR: white.

Also known as Arba-Luxi, Arretallau, and Mara Bianca, Retagliado Bianco was apparently mainly used as a table grape in the nineteenth century. Today there are only thirteen hectares cultivated near Sassari and in the Gallura, in the northeast corner of the island. The rare Orrotozau variety is a biotype, and no clones are available. It is unrelated to the Brustiniau of Corsica, as was initially hypothesized by Bruni.

Ripoli

WHERE IT'S FOUND: Campania. NATIONAL REGISTRY CODE NUMBER: 386. COLOR: white.

Ripoli is also called Ripolo or Uva Ripoli; the only description of any kind of this variety until recently was that of Arcuri and Casoria in 1883, though Di Rovasenda mentioned it in 1877. Viala and Vermorel included it in their famous *Ampélographie* of 1901–1909. Though once common around Naples, today it's grown almost exclusively along the Amalfi coast in the idyllic surroundings of Positano, Amalfi, and Furore. The bunch is small and sparse with two conical wings. It suffers from floral sterility, so the berries are not uniform in size, and are generally small, round, and thin skinned. It is most likely to be found in the white DOC Costa d'Amalfi. It is a poor and very irregular producer, but the wine is excellent, and my hope is that more producers will plant it and try their hand at a monovarietal wine. There are some lovely honeyed notes to pure ripoli, but very few producers have enough to harvest and make wine from it alone, so it's usually just lumped together with other local varieties such as Fenile and Ginestra.

Rollo

WHERE IT'S FOUND: Liguria. NATIONAL REGISTRY CODE NUMBER: 211. COLOR: white.

Rollo should not be confused with Rolle, which is typical of southern France and is a synonym of Vermentino; Rollo was long thought to be Vermentino or a biotype of it. It grows on both sides of Liguria: on the western side (in Riviera Ligure di Ponente and around Genoa) it goes by Rollo; on the eastern side (in Riviera Ligure di Levante and the Cinque Terre), it is commonly referred to as Bruciapagliaio. In Corsica they refer to it as Pagadebiti and around Massa Carrara as Livornese Bianca. It is most often found in white wines of the DOC Polcevera. The bunch is large, conical-pyramidal, stocky, and compact. The berry is large and round, slightly elongated, and thick skinned. Harvest is in the first two weeks of October; it's an abundant but irregular producer.

Rondinella

WHERE IT'S FOUND: Veneto. NATIONAL REGISTRY CODE NUMBER: 212. COLOR: red.

Rondinella is another of the many bird-grapes of Italy: its name refers either to the dark color of the berry skin (black as the plumage of the small swallow, *rondine*) or to the fact that these small birds are happy to feast on the ripe grapes. It is somewhat surprising that we have no documentation prior to 1882 about a grape that is so well known today in Veneto, and one that presents few if any problems to farmers and growers. Then again, Rondinella's explosion onto the Italian grape and wine scene occurred after the arrival of phylloxera; it represents an interesting example of how some varieties have been improved by the graft with American rootstocks (while others, like Malbec in France, suffered greatly). So it is quite possible that a grape variety that was once boring and uninteresting has become more interesting and useful. Or perhaps the lack of Rondinella documentation is due to it being only a late arrival to Veneto, where farmers were previously using the Negrara varieties in its place.

This cultivar is very easy to recognize when walking through any vineyard in Valpolicella, not just because of its characteristic leaf but especially because of its small, slightly curved, very compact bunch and round, medium-sized berries. With Rondinella, there are no big disorganized bunches *à la Corvinone,* no scrawny bunches like Corvina, no pink berries like Molinara. Rondinella is loved by farmers for its hardy nature, great resistance to cold and drought and because it's a very consistent, reliable producer and very adaptable to different soils. While some producers claim that Rondinella is an invaluable part of Valpolicella or Amarone as it confers a lovely herbaceous note to the wines, others insist that the variety's greatest and perhaps only real virtue is its reliable and at times very neutral output. Noble rot doesn't hit it as much as it does the other typical grapes of the Valpolicella; according to Boscaini, this is probably because its skin doesn't allow the botrytis hyphae to penetrate through to the flesh.

Rondinella is harvested at the end of September. There are a slew of clones to choose from: R 1, ISV-CV 73, ISV-CV 76, ISV-CV 23, VCR 32, and VCR 38. Rondinella is considered to be indispensable for Recioto, since it accumulates sugars much better than the other varieties used, while it is not appreciated much as a monovarietal dry wine, giving neutral wines that at best can have a pleasant herbal touch. The best way to taste it is in Bardolino and Valpolicella, where it can compose up to 30 percent of the blend. I know of no pure 100 percent rondinella wines. Strange as it may seem, Rondinella has been planted in Australia, where it has met with some success. It is grown in the Hilltops region by Freeman Vineyards, where it is blended with Corvina in an Amarone-style wine; this estate also makes a monovarietal *rosato* called Rondò. I am told that in the Southern Highlands region, Centennial Vineyards also made a limited-release Rondinella wine in the past.

Rosciola

WHERE IT'S FOUND: Lazio. NATIONAL REGISTRY CODE NUMBER: 429. COLOR: red.

In the 1881 Ampelographic Bulletin of the Ministry of Agriculture, Industry, and Commerce, Rosciola is also named Pentellino or Rosaiola. The bunch is medium-sized, cylindrical, and not too compact, with medium-sized, pink-red, round berries characterized by a terminal depression or umbilicus. The wine is also a dark pink or light red, with very complex aromas of red berries, licorice, and black pepper, and a graceful, high-acid, medium-bodied mouthfeel. A grape that grows at relatively high altitudes (six hundred meters), Rosciola might be very interesting to work with, as the wines, at least at this early stage, seem impressive.

Rossetta di Montagna

WHERE IT'S FOUND: Veneto. NATIONAL REGISTRY CODE NUMBER: not registered. COLOR: red.

Rossetta di Montagna was first described by Moroni in 1775 (according to Calò, Paronetto, and Rorato 1996) and later by Sormani-Moretti, who documented its presence around the shores of Lake Garda as well as in Valpantena and Valpolicella. It has a medium-small, short grape bunch with medium-large, irregularly oval berries of a pretty pinkish-red hue. Biting into a ripe berry will reveal a very tannic skin. This is one variety I have not been able to taste the microvinification of, so I am at a loss to pass judgment on its winemaking potential: researchers in Verona tell me they were completely unimpressed by what they tried.

Rossignola

WHERE IT'S FOUND: Veneto. NATIONAL REGISTRY CODE NUMBER: 214. COLOR: red.

Not the darkest or most complex red wine you'll ever taste, Rossignola's tendency to give light, uncomplicated red wines has turned it into essentially a blending grape, used to supply freshness. First described by Moroni in 1775 (according to Calò, Paronetto, and Rorato 1996), then by Pollini in 1824 and Acerbi in 1825, it is most typically found around Verona and on the shores of Lake Garda. It is a dependable producer and adds a nice saline touch (much like Molinara) to wines it is added to. You are most likely to find it in DOCs Bardolino, Breganze Rosso, Garda, Valdadige, and Valpolicella, but at 10 percent or less, Rossignola hardly sticks out. Furthermore, there are very few vines left; it's easiest to find in plots situated at the highest altitudes. Its grape bunch is medium-large, pyramidal, compact, and has a small wing. The berry is medium-sized, oval, thin skinned, and pinkish-violet. There are three clones: ISV-CV 3, ISV-CV 7, and ISV-CV 9. Late ripening, it is harvested in mid-October, and is very sensitive to most diseases. From my tastings of microvinifications, I can say that the wine is light red and has very delicate redcurrant aromas and flavors, with lasting saline finish. I actually like the wine.

Rossola Nera

WHERE IT'S FOUND: Lombardy. NATIONAL REGISTRY CODE NUMBER: 215. COLOR: red.

Also called Rossera, Rossola, or Rossolo, Rossola Nera has been grown in the cold Valtellina region of Lombardy at least since the seventeenth century. Today it continues to be found in this pretty alpine region of Lombardy, though scattered vines of Rossola Nera are found everywhere in the region. The bunch is medium-small, cylindrical or pyramidal, short, and compact, with small wings. The berry is medium-sized and round, but is often compressed due to how compact the bunch is. The skin is reddish-violet and darker if exposed to intense sunlight. It is usually harvested in mid- to late October. Clone 29, developed in 2003, is the only one available and is characterized by less compact bunches.

Roussin

WHERE IT'S FOUND: Valle d'Aosta. NATIONAL REGISTRY CODE NUMBER: 355. COLOR: red.

Also called Roussin Masciou, Gros Roussin, Rouzola, and Roussé, Roussin is distinct from Roussin de Morgex and was never one of the more common varieties of the region; it was found mainly in the area between Arnad—where you are still most likely to find it today—and Verrayes. Lorenzo Gatta (1838) mentions a subvariant called Roussin Picciout or Piciout Roussin. Most researchers have agreed that Roussin was always scarce and was never of the greatest winemaking quality (Bich 1896). The bunch is medium-sized, pyramidal, long, and often winged, with small, round, pink-purple berries. It ripens in October and needs low-lying southern exposures to ripen fully.

Ruzzese

WHERE IT'S FOUND: Liguria. NATIONAL REGISTRY CODE NUMBER: 432. COLOR: white.

Also called Razzese, Ruzzese is the dialect name of the Rossese Bianco di Arcola variety, but officially adopted by the National Registry to avoid confusion with other Rossese Bianco varieties. Limited to the area of La Spezia, it has mid-sized, cylindrical and winged bunches, with medium-small, oval berries with thin skins. Early flowering and ripening, wines have good alcohol levels and lovely floral and citrus aromas and flavors, and are less acid than those made with Rossese Bianco.

Sagrestana

WHERE IT'S FOUND: FVG. NATIONAL REGISTRY CODE NUMBER: not registered. COLOR: white.

Found in 2001 in old vineyards near Clamara di Buttrio, Sagrestana is, according to Carlo Petrussi, a natural crossing between Verduzzo and Picolit. It has a medium-sized circular, leaf with five lobes, and a medium-sized, conical, compact bunch with up to five wings. It is a very late-ripening variety. The wines also appear to have very good structure and aging potential, with complex aromas of honey and ripe citrus fruits.

San Colombano

See COLOMBANA NERA entry.

Sanginella Bianca

WHERE IT'S FOUND: Campania. NATIONAL REGISTRY CODE NUMBER: not registered. COLOR: white.

Also known (depending on where it is grown) as Regina Bianca, Sanginella Grossa, Sanginella di Napoli, Sanginella di Salerno, Sanginella di Eboli, Sanginella Bianca may be a family of grapes rather than just one. University studies are under way to determine if some *Sanginella* varieties are in fact altogether different grapes. A *Sanginella* was first described in 1804 by Nicola Columella Onorati; by 1825 Acerbi listed four different *Sanginellas* (Sanginella, Sanginella Vera, Sanginella Barietà, and Sanginella di Salerno). It is rare today, found only around Salerno and in the Val del Calore, which is strange enough since historically it doubled as a very good table grape as well. The bunch is medium-sized, conical-pyramidal, with a large, oval, yellow-green berry.

San Lunardo

WHERE IT'S FOUND: Campania. NATIONAL REGISTRY CODE NUMBER: 220. COLOR: white.

Most likely, this variety was named after either a place or a person (in fact it is also called Don Lunardo), as was often the case with varieties grown on Ischia. The most common hypotheses refer to a Don Lunardo, former priest on the island, and to Saint Leonard, the patron saint of Panza. On the island of Ventotene, San Lunardo is known as Bianca. Though basal fertility of its buds is low and it is only a medium-vigorous variety, productivity is good and dependable. It is also a variety that despite its compact bunch, has good botrytis resistance. The bunch is pyramidal and the oval berries a very pretty pale green. San Lunardo was first described by D'Ambra in 1962. In 2010 Cipriani proposed that San Lunardo is an Albana Bordini × Biancolella crossing; Albana Bordini is a very rare red-berried variety possibly from Emilia-Romagna (Cipriani, Spadotto, Jurman, Di Gaspero, Crespan, Meneghetti, et al. 2010).

San Pietro

WHERE IT'S FOUND: Campania. NATIONAL REGISTRY CODE NUMBER: not registered. COLOR: white.

San Pietro is a very rare variety that lives only in old vineyards of the Caserta area, between Monte Maggiore and the Roccamonfina volcano. According to Manzo and Monaco (2001) it is genetically distinct from other Campanian grapevines, but little is known about it relative to its fine winemaking potential. The bunch is conical or pyramidal, with two wings, and the berries are round.

Santa Maria

WHERE IT'S FOUND: Emilia-Romagna. NATIONAL REGISTRY CODE NUMBER: 340. COLOR: white.

Excellent when employed as an air-dried grape to make sweet wines, Santa Maria is found today mainly around Piacenza, where it is used along with the similar (but distinct) Melara variety to make the DOC Vin Santo di Vigoleno. The bunch is small, cylindrical or shaped like a truncated cone, and short; the berry is more or less oval, medium-sized, and yellow-green. It ripens early, in the first two weeks of September.

Sant'Antonio

WHERE IT'S FOUND: Campania. NATIONAL REGISTRY CODE NUMBER: not registered. COLOR: white.

Sant'Antonio is a very little-known grape found in the Caserta area, in vineyards of the township of Galluccio. The grape was documented in this area in the early twentieth century, and presents ampelographic traits and genetic data that differentiate it from other known Campanian varieties. It has a large, conical-pyramidal bunch and round berries. It ripens late in September or in the first week of October. Very vigorous, it offers abundant yields and its thick-skinned berries make it resistant to botrytis. However, according to Manzo and Monaco (2001) the grape has trouble building up sugar levels and is low in total acidity, though this may be due to the usually high yields.

Scarsafoglia

WHERE IT'S FOUND: Emilia-Romagna. NATIONAL REGISTRY CODE NUMBER: 458. COLOR: white.

Scarsafoglia was added to the National Registry in 2011, though it was first described in 1839 by Gallesio, who named it as one of the grapes used to make the then-famous wines of Scandiano. Aggazzotti (1867) and Di Rovasenda (1877) also described it, calling it Squarciafoglia Bianca. Some producers believe it to be a biotype of Trebbiano Toscano. The Barbolini estate in Emilia-Romagna makes a wine called Il Civolino, which is mainly Scarsafoglia with small additions of Chardonnay and Pinot Bianco.

Scroccona

WHERE IT'S FOUND: Emilia-Romagna. NATIONAL REGISTRY CODE NUMBER: not registered. COLOR: white.

Described in 1923 by Antonio Bazzocchi in his *Ampelography of Romagnoli Wines*, Scroccona has always been common in the province of Rimini. It has a large bunch and large berries, and so always has doubled as a table grape. It's a productive and resistant variety, with very sweet berries that often never make it to the cellar: since there's not much of it in the rows, harvesters just choose to eat it while picking the other more abundant varieties.

Serpentaria or Uva Serpe

WHERE IT'S FOUND: Campania, Lazio. NATIONAL REGISTRY CODE NUMBER: not registered. COLOR: red.

This variety has long engendered confusion, with various experts considering it to be synonymous with Piedirosso, Streppa Rossa, and Mangiaguerra, varieties historically also grown in the provinces of Naples and Salerno. It also appears to grow in southern Lazio, where it is more commonly called Uva Serpe, though it is unclear if the latter variety is identical to the one grown in Campania, or even if Serpentara and Uva Serpe aren't distinct: DNA studies are lacking to date. It is an extremely ancient variety, apparently mentioned by Columella in the first century C.E. as Dracontion (meaning snake). Apparently it was first brought into Italy by the Spartans, and was later part of the *cecubum* blend. Vigorous and pest-resistant, it has a conical, medium-small bunch and small, blue-black, round berries that stain remarkably permanently with their dark juice. It is used mainly as a blending agent in the wines of the DOC Costa d'Amalfi plus various IGT wines; in Lazio a number of producers, including Terre delle Ginestre, are actively cultivating and studying it. It is likely we shall see a monovarietal wine in the near future; microvinifications seem encouraging enough thus far.

Sgavetta

WHERE IT'S FOUND: Emilia-Romagna. NATIONAL REGISTRY CODE NUMBER: 228. COLOR: red.

Grown today in the vineyards around Modena and Reggio Emilia, Sgavetta is a relatively recent variety first described by Di Rovasenda in 1877 (who thought it was related to the *Schiavas*); Ghetti in 1926 and Toni in 1927 wrote that it was one of the highest quality grapes from which to make wine around the territories of Modena and Reggio Emilia. It appears to be different from Sgavetta a Raspo Rosso (that is, with a red stalk), which is grown in minimal quantities around Modena. The bunch is medium-sized, long, pyramidal, and very sparse. The berries are round, medium-sized, deformed, blue-black, and thick skinned. It is usually harvested in the latter third of September. It supplies color to other, lighter-hued wines. Apparently a small producer called Morsi Franzoni is making experimental batches of a sgavetta wine.

Simesara

WHERE IT'S FOUND: Veneto. NATIONAL REGISTRY CODE NUMBER: not registered. COLOR: red.

Also called Cimesara, not much is known about Simesara, as historical information is scanty at best. Its name probably derives from *simese orcimice* (flea), much like other cultivars named after insects apparently fond of them (for example, the wasps of Vespaiola). It was first mentioned by Acerbi (1825), but its winemaking potential must not have attracted a lot of admirers for neither Montanari and Ceccarelli (1950) nor Cosmo (1962) recommended its cultivation. In the 1970s, the Istituto Sperimentale per la Viticoltura di Conegliano set up two experimental vineyards planted with, among many other native varieties, Simesara, in an effort to preserve the genetic material of this variety (Costacurta, Cancellier, Angelini, Segattini, and Farina 1980). The bunch is large and pyramidal, the berries medium-large and elliptical, and the wine not particularly interesting, with weak, herbal aromas and flavors. It is currently not included in the makeup of any DOC wine, and has been abandoned for the most part due to its irregular and scarce yields.

Sirica

WHERE IT'S FOUND: Campania. NATIONAL REGISTRY CODE NUMBER: not registered. COLOR: red.

One of the oldest-known varieties in Italy, Sirica has recently been rediscovered in the Taurasi area near Avellino: the Feudi di San Gregorio estate found four old vines (from 250 to 280 years of age) on its estate and they are now the subject of university studies by Attilio Scienza and his team in Milan. In 75 B.C.E. Pliny the Elder believed Sirica to be of Greek origin and thought its name derived from *syricum*, a red coloring agent imported from Syria), while Isidoro felt the grape itself was of Syrian origin. Scienza believes that its name derives from the city of Siri in Basilicata, which became an ancient Roman colony after the Second Punic War. Today, we know that Sirica is not related to Syrah, while it is apparently related to Aglianico, of which Sirica may be a parent or ancestor. It is vigorous and late ripening (second half of October), with medium-sized, compact, cylindrical-pyramidal bunches and small, black berries. It makes a very rich, dark red wine with plenty of plum and smoke flavors and great tannic structure.

Suppezza

WHERE IT'S FOUND: Campania. NATIONAL REGISTRY CODE NUMBER: not registered. COLOR: red.

This variety apparently takes its name from an estate on the grounds of which it was discovered. Suppezza is grown only along the Sorrento coast, near Gragnano, Pimonte, Lettere, and Castellamare di Stabia. It has a small, conical-pyramidal bunch and round berries and is very vigorous and productive. It is used in the blends of the DOC Penisola Sorrentina (Lettere and Gragnano).

Tamurro Nero

WHERE IT'S FOUND: Basilicata. NATIONAL REGISTRY CODE NUMBER: not registered. COLOR: red.

A rare grape that was probably introduced into Italy from France under the rule of Duke Filiberto di Savoia, who did not appreciate the high alcohol and structure of aglianico, Tamurro Nero was originally known as Coll d'Tamurr. Today the only estate that bottles a pure monovarietal version is Tenuta Le Querce, though I fail to see why others haven't gotten into the act. It certainly would have helped this cultivar's and wine's notoriety.

Termarina Nera

WHERE IT'S FOUND: Emilia-Romagna. NATIONAL REGISTRY CODE NUMBER: 395. COLOR: red.

This variety has a very small bunch and small berries that are practically seedless, though there are always a few bigger berries that do contain normal-looking pips. Termarina Nera is used to make lovely *rosati* and late-harvest sweet wines of real character and fine taste. Some think Termarina Nera resembles Corinto Rosso, but DNA profiling has disproved this (Boccacci, Torello Marinoni, Gambino, Botta, and Schneider 2005). There is also an unrelated Termarina Bianca.

WINES TO TRY: Podere Pradarolo makes a very interesting wine in a *solera* style, Il Canto del Ciò. Unfortunately, due to this heavily oxidative technique it's hard for me to pinpoint the exact characteristics of a termarina wine, but I do think it's very exciting that an estate has decided to take up making wine from this variety again. We can hope that more will follow suit soon.

Theilly

WHERE IT'S FOUND: Valle d'Aosta. NATIONAL REGISTRY CODE NUMBER: not registered. COLOR: white.

Up until World War II, Theilly, also called Gouais Blanc (I'm not sure how correctly) was diffusely cultivated in the Valle d'Aosta around Perloz, but now is limited to just a few vines in the area around Colleré (at 767 meters above sea level) by Gianluigi Soudaz. It however also grows sporadically in Piedmont (Schneider, Torello Marinoni, Boccacci, and Botta 2006). The variety produces a good, fresh white wine but as it has difficulty ripening in cold weather it was abandoned by ever-practical farmers. Theilly differs from Prié, the most famous and most abundant white variety of the region, as it ripens later in the season, accumulates less sugar, and maintains higher levels of acidity (which, considering Prié's already eyewatering levels of total acids, may not be such a good thing). However locals liked the fact that wines made with Theilly lasted longer. Theilly is also important because it is related to a number of well-known varieties such as Chardonnay, Gamay, Aligoté, l'Auxerrois, Colombard, and Furmint.

Trevisana Nera

WHERE IT'S FOUND: Veneto. NATIONAL REGISTRY CODE NUMBER: 245. COLOR: red.

Trevisana Nera is identical to Refosco di Guarnieri (or Refosco Guarnieri) and to a very obscure grape simply called Borgogna or Gattera from Veneto (Crespan, Calò, Giannetto, Sparacio, Storchi, and Costacurta 2008). Morphologic differences between Refosco Guarnieri and the other *Refoscos* were noticed by ampelographers of the past, who found that the berries of Refosco Guarneri are more oval and more covered in bloom than those of other *Refosco* family members. Wines made with this variety also differ from all other *Refosco* wines, for they are more intensely herbal and less immediately fruity, with higher levels of tartaric acid than, for example, Refosco del Peduncolo Rosso. Rare today (Tazzer was already lamenting its disappearance in 1976), limited to a few vineyards in and around Belluno, very little is known about Refosco Guarnieri; it is used in blends such as IGT Vigneti delle Dolomiti. The bunch is large, pyramidal, and winged with large round-oval, blue-black berries. It flowers early but ripens late, around mid-October.

Tronto

WHERE IT'S FOUND: Campania. NATIONAL REGISTRY CODE NUMBER: 387. COLOR: red.

Also called Aglianico di Napoli but genetically distinct from Aglianico (though the two are related, and look somewhat similar morphologically), Tronto grows on the Amalfi coast, especially around Furore, Positano, and Amalfi, and also around Naples, in the famous vineyard of the Eremo di San Martino. The bunch is compact and conical-pyramidal, the berries medium-sized, round, and blue-black. It is used in the blend of the DOCs Costa d'Amalfi Rosso, Furore, and Ravello. However, as it doesn't accumulate much sugar (hence low alcohol levels) and has low acidity, it is not ideal for monovarietal bottling.

Turchetta

WHERE IT'S FOUND: Veneto. NATIONAL REGISTRY CODE NUMBER: 410. COLOR: red.

In an ampelographic bulletin from 1884–87, there are both a Turchetta and a Calma Turchetta described, the former the more commonly grown of the two. It's hard however to be sure of just how common Turchetta was in the past, as experts often wrote of a grape called Turca, and it's not clear whether they were referring to Turchetta or really to Turca, a distinct variety. The grape bunch is medium-small (average of 250 grams), pyramidal, and winged; the berry is medium-sized, round, very thick skinned, and blue-black. The Tedeschi estate in Valpolicella has planted a few rows of Turchetta vines in a portion of a vineyard devoted to rare native varieties (where they also have Marzemina Nera, Corbina, and Recantina) and Riccardo Tedeschi is very happy about this cultivar's winemaking potential. The microvinifications I have tried are indeed impressive, with wines showing very intense raspberry and blackberry aromas, good acidity, supple tannins, and a saline nuance on the finish. It is a bigger, fuller-bodied wine than the one made with Turca.

Uva del Fantini

WHERE IT'S FOUND: Emilia-Romagna. NATIONAL REGISTRY CODE NUMBER: 435. COLOR: red.

Uva del Fantini is a recently rediscovered variety, as a century-old vine was found by Luigi Fantini, and the variety is named after him. The vine is very vigorous and accumulates lots of sugar, but very little is known about it, save that it does not share genetic profiles with any other known varieties (Fontana, Filippetti, Pastore, and Intrieri 2007). Microvinifications have revealed a ruby-purple wine, with floral and red-berry notes, plus black cherry flavors on a midweight frame.

Uva della Cascina

WHERE IT'S FOUND: Lombardy, Piedmont. NATIONAL REGISTRY CODE NUMBER: not registered. COLOR: red.

Uva della Cascina was recently rediscovered: four estates in Lombardy replanted this variety in the early 1990s, though it also grows sporadically in Piedmont, where it is called Uva della Cassina. The bunch is pyramidal, loosely packed, and medium-large; the berry is medium-large too. Vigorous and disease resistant, it buds early, so spring frosts are a risk. Winemaker Mauro Maffi is working closely with this variety but has yet to produce a monovarietal wine; thus far he blends in about 30 percent of Freisa and Barbera. The wine is lightly aromatic and fresh, and resembles Piedmont's ruché somewhat. I think this variety has real potential.

WINES TO TRY: In Lombardy, Fortesi** is making experimental batches, on sale at the estate. If you're in the area, don't miss it.

Uva Tosca

WHERE IT'S FOUND: Emilia-Romagna. NATIONAL REGISTRY CODE NUMBER: 249. COLOR: red.

Uva Tosca was first described by Tanara in 1644. Very little is known about this variety, though it seems to have been popular with local growers, as it survives well at seven hundred to nine hundred meters above sea level, where the various *Lambrusco* varieties do not. Today it is found mainly around the hamlets of Zocca, Ploinago, Ligonchio, and Carpiteti, and especially in the high Valle del Secchia where it is the only variety that will grow. The bunch is large, pyramidal, and sparse, with two wings and large, thick-skinned, grey-red berries; the variety is prone to berry shot. It is usually ripe by mid-September. Recent genetic work with microsatellite analysis has suggested a parent-offspring relationship between Uva Tosca and Lambrusco Montericco.

Varano Bianco and Varano Rosa

WHERE IT'S FOUND: Emilia-Romagna. NATIONAL REGISTRY CODE NUMBER: not registered. COLOR: white/red.

The *Varano* family of grapes includes white, pink, and red varieties. First described by De Bosis near Rimini (1879), the most abundantly cultivated are Varano Rosa and Varano Bianco. Not much is yet known about these very ancient varieties (Trinci describes a Varano in 1726), though it appears that they grow in Tuscany as well. All the *Varano*s once doubled as table grapes, as they all have large, succulent berries. Varano Bianco has a stocky, compact, medium-large bunch with round berries; Varano Rosa has large, compact, pyramidal bunch with round, pink berries.

Verdealbara

WHERE IT'S FOUND: Trentino. NATIONAL REGISTRY CODE NUMBER: 401. COLOR: white.

Verdealbara is yet another of the many varieties sporting names related to the color green: in Verdealbara's case the green hue of its berries is so pale that it recalls the color of the light at dawn, hence its derivation from *verde* (green) and *alba* (dawn). Grown mainly in the Vallagarina of Trentino (where at the end of the nineteenth century roughly two thousand hectoliters of wine were made from it yearly), it is sometimes confused with even lesser known cultivars such as Wanderbara and Maor. It has a small, compact bunch and is harvested late in October. It is being actively studied by the Istituto di San Michele all'Adige and by the Vallarom estate, which located old vines in the forest growing on its land. I've liked what I have tried so far: experimental microvinifications have shown high-acid, citrusy wines with a future, as far as I am concerned, as light aperitif wines or wines can be paired with simply prepared freshwater fish and vegetable dishes.

Verdetto

WHERE IT'S FOUND: Emilia-Romagna. NATIONAL REGISTRY CODE NUMBER: not registered. COLOR: white.

Another of the many little-known cultivars grown around Rimini and first mentioned by De Bosis (1879), Verdetto is rare in that it never seems to have been grown much even in the nearby areas around Forlì and Cesena. Though it has been suggested that Verdetto is identical to Verdicchio, this is unclear, given the myriad of green-named grape varieties in Italy; it may well be that one accession of Verdetto was in fact Verdicchio, but more studies are necessary. Today there are only sporadic rows grown around San Giovanni in Marignano, but indications are the cultivar makes very good wine and ought to be the subject of more study and propagation.

Verduschia

WHERE IT'S FOUND: Tuscany. NATIONAL REGISTRY CODE NUMBER: not registered. COLOR: white.

One of the many members of the "green family" of grapes, Verduschia is less common than Verdicchio or even Verdello, with which it shares some common traits (though they ripen at different times). Today it's found in the Lunigiana area but as it is not officially recognized by the legislature, clever growers label it Verdello, which is a recognized and allowed variety. The bunch is medium-small, pyramidal, and winged, with medium-small, thick-skinned, round berries. A recent study of twenty-five accessions of Verdicchio, Verdello, and Verduschia at eleven SSR markers concluded that as only one DNA profile was obtained for all twenty-five accessions, the three varieties are identical (Crespan, Armanni, Da Rold, De Nardi, Gardiman, Migliaro, et al. 2012). I have no doubts this is so, but as there are myriad green-named grape varieties in Italy today I find it hard to extrapolate these identities to all other varieties with similar names grown in Italy. And while Verduschia is rare enough that the identity with Vermentino is easier to accept, the plethora of Verdello-named grapes out there suggests a little caution is required.

Verucchiese

WHERE IT'S FOUND: Tuscany, Emilia-Romagna. NATIONAL REGISTRY CODE NUMBER: 438. COLOR: red.

Also called Sangiovese Verucchiese, Verucchiese was originally grown only around the Rocca di Verucchio, usually interplanted with Sangiovese, with which it shares a considerable phenotypic resemblance. In the past, the wine it produced was viewed as very fine, a gentle wine that was easy to drink and uncomplicated. Verucchiese is productive but sensitive to grey rot. It also ripens early, in mid-September, but flowers later than Sangiovese.

Vien de Nus

WHERE IT'S FOUND: Valle d'Aosta. NATIONAL REGISTRY CODE NUMBER: 265. COLOR: red.

Mainly found today in the high part of the region, the Alta Valle on the border with the Alps and France, Vien de Nus is named after the town of Nus, where it was once very abundant. *Vien* in the local *patois* means plant or cultivar, so literally, Vien de Nus is the cultivar of the town of Nus, where it is still grown today and used in red wine blends. There is actually enough of it that a producer could try his or her hand at a monovarietal bottling. Vien de Nus was born from the natural crossing of Petit Rouge and an unknown, probably extinct other parent. The bunch is medium-large, pyramidal, winged, and compact, with big, round, thick-skinned, blue-black berries. It is harvested around mid-October.

Volpola

WHERE IT'S FOUND: Tuscany. NATIONAL REGISTRY CODE NUMBER: not registered. COLOR: white.

People are excited about this Tuscan native that gives a white wine which bears more than a passing resemblance to Sauvignon Blanc, but that is much better adapted to the Tuscan *terroir*. Volpola is characterized by a uniform size of berries, reduced bunch size, and resistance of the skins; the wine has light aromas and flavors reminiscent of sage and citrus skin. It's really an interesting grape and we should hear a lot more about it in the future, especially in terms of bottled wines.

Zanello

WHERE IT'S FOUND: Piedmont. NATIONAL REGISTRY CODE NUMBER: not registered. COLOR: red.

Also known as Zanè, Zanello was abundant in the Monferrato Casalese area in the 1700s, when it was usually planted alongside Grignolino, though it was preferentially used in blends with Dolcetto. Like Grignolino, it is characterized by irregular annual productions and berries that don't always turn red, especially when it is allowed to yield too much. Today Zanello is virtually extinct, found only in occasional lone vines in small family vineyard holdings. Modern microvinifications have not shown Zanello to be capable of producing high-quality wines: they are lightly tannic and orangey in hue, less acidic than grignolinos, but also less alcoholic (and grignolinos are low in alcohol themselves). Zanello lacks some of the aromas of Grignolino too, so I'm not sure how much winemaking potential this native really has.

SIX

Crossings

NOT ALL THE wines we drink are made from naturally occurring *Vitis vinifera* grapevines. Some are born in laboratories thanks to the ingenuity of men and women all over the world who try to create, *ex novo*, varieties that they hope will improve on the original set of parents. A crossing occurs between two varieties of the same species, while a hybrid is obtained by crossing members of different species (in the case of grapevines, this means crossing a *vinifera* with another vine species such as *rupestris* or *riparia*). In nature, hybrids rarely survive and are often sterile, a mechanism by which nature attempts to protect itself from cross-species communions, such as a tiger and a lion hitting it off or a lake trout and brook trout mating. For example, in the latter case, the offspring is called a splake or wendigo, and though it is also a very beautiful trout, it's sterile. Crossing the huge but very slow-growing lake trout with the much smaller but quick-growing brook trout makes sense if the result is a much bigger fish that grows rapidly. Unfortunately, though splake grows fast and can reach relatively big sizes, it has little or no appeal for governments or commercial fisheries, since, being sterile, it's not self-sustainable. There are countless similar examples in the world of wine.

No matter how well intentioned human beings are, it's hard to improve on Mother Nature's work. The simple truth of the matter is that neither wine crossings nor wine hybrids have been extremely successful in creating high-quality wine grapes. There are exceptions, and in general, crossings have been much more successful than hybrids, which are not found in Italy at all. In fact, they're not even officially allowed in Europe, save for some that have been associated historically, or out of necessity, with certain production zones, such as Baco Noir and Armagnac in France. When they are allowed, they can usually only qualify only as "table wines" in those countries, rather than "quality wines." Generally speaking, hybrids today are more abundant in countries with extreme weather conditions where *Vitis vinifera* has trouble surviving (for example, Vidal in Canada, Seyval Blanc in the United Kingdom, and Johanniter in the Netherlands), and in situations where their reduced susceptibility to the various diseases that can affect grapevines is at the forefront. Extreme weather is not a problem in Italy, making the need for hybrids close to null.

I think that at times crossings and hybrids can get an unfair rap, and blanket statements are made about how poor the wines are. This is quite simply wine snobbism at its worst. Even in the case of hybrids, while it's true that some hybrid wines are best forgotten, Canadian Vidal ice wines, Dutch johanniters and British seyval blancs are lovely wines. Unfortunately, though hybrids usually have increased resistance to difficult weather and disease conditions, they may present other problems: for example, Seyval Blanc's thin skin is a problem in Ontario's cold fall and winter weather, making Seyval Blanc late-harvest wines or ice wines hard to produce, at least in Canada. Of course some lovely dry wines can still be made (the grapes are picked sooner in the fall) but the range of possibilities is fatefully limited, making the usefulness of that hybrid in that specific habitat questionable. Seyval Blanc is more popular in the United Kingdom, where ice wine production is not a concern, than it is in Canada, where estates consider the ice wine option when they decide which hybrid to plant.

Relative to fine-wine quality, some crossings have been spectacularly unsuccessful as well: I doubt readers will object to my considering German crossings such as Optima (Sylvaner × Müller-Thurgau) or Ortega (Müller-Thurgau × Siegerrebe) anything but poor. However, many crossings have given much better results. In my view, the same wine snobbery directed toward hybrids is also at work against crossings, since many wines made from crossings are quite acceptable if not downright delicious. In Italy, Müller-Thurgau and Kerner have been very successful crossings; and whereas decades ago many wine experts believed these crossings to be unequivocally poor and best uprooted, opinions regarding them have changed considerably in recent times. Better viticultural practices and winemaking techniques have finally shown us that such crossings can really deliver. Simply planting crossings in more suitable sites and reducing their yields has shown that their wines can be downright memorable; but not surprisingly, hardly the same results are possible when the crossing is planted in lousy flatland vineyards made to pump out grapes and wines in industrial fashion. So it's a matter of fairness. Few true Italian wine experts anywhere would dispute that the Müller-Thurgau wine called Feldmarschall (made by Tiefenbrunner) or that various kerners (those by Kofererhof, Pacherhof, and Manni Nossing spring immediately to mind) are among Italy's best thirty or forty white wines. So I rest my case. As Müller-Thurgau and Kerner are essentially Germanic grapes (created by researchers in countries such as Switzerland or Germany), I won't discuss them in this book. That said, the wine lover in me would do everyone a huge disservice if I didn't at least mention the exceptionally high quality of these wines made in Italy's Alto Adige region.

There are numerous crossings that have proven more or less successful in Italy. The word for crossing in Italian is *incrocio;* all crossings in Italy officially carry the element *incrocio* in their name followed by another descriptor, such as the name of their creator and a code or color (e.g., Incrocio Dalmasso 13.26 or Incrocio Manzoni Bianco). In those cases where the variety begins to have commercial appeal, the name is inevitably (and I would add, mercifully) changed to be better sounding, easier to use, and easier to remember (hence, Albarossa or Manzoni Bianco). In fairness, not a single wine made with these Italian-born crossings can compete with the extraordinary quality of some of the wines made with their Germanic counterparts, but it's also true that the Italian grapes have been studied and planted less, so less is known about them. Some have recently been reevaluated however, and Manzoni Bianco especially is beginning to attract considerable attention. I list here those crossings that I believe are relevant to wine drinkers.

Albarossa

WHERE IT'S FOUND: Piedmont. NATIONAL REGISTRY CODE NUMBER: 267. COLOR: red.

Albarossa is an up-and-coming grape in Piedmont, and is one of the few truly successful crossings in viticulture, at least in relation to wine. Much like Müller-Thurgau and Kerner, Albarossa was created in a laboratory—in this case, that of Giovanni Dalmasso in 1938, who crossed Nebbiolo and Barbera, or so he thought. Like Müller, who wished to obtain a vine that would express the qualities of Riesling and those of a more productive, hardier vine such as Sylvaner, Dalmasso sought to create a new variety that would combine the quality of Nebbiolo with the rusticity and fertility of Barbera. And once again, just as Müller mistakenly crossed Riesling not with Sylvaner but with Madeleine Royale, so recent genetic analysis has shown that one of the two parents of Albarossa is not Nebbiolo, but Chatus (also known as Nebbiolo di Dronero), another native variety (see CHATUS, chapter 4). Similar mistakes are not hard to imagine, given that field recognition of vines is always difficult, and that it was only in the mid-1960s that other researchers, Eynard and Curzel, finally studied Albarossa's ampelological, viticultural, and enological characteristics. Better late than never, you might say. In fact, it was Eynard who renamed this crossing Albarossa; its original name was the much less poetic Incrocio 13.26.

Which Wines to Choose and Why

Albarossa grows only in Piedmont, in the provinces of Alessandria, Asti, and Cuneo: it is most abundant around Acqui and in the northern part of the Asti area. Tenuta Cannona, the Experimental Center of the Piedmont Region, in Carpaneto di Alessandria, planted thirteen different *Incrocio Dalmasso* vines), and of these two performed particularly well: Albarossa and Bussanello (a crossing of Riesling Italico and Furmint). Well-known producer Michele Chiarlo, after tasting wines made with Albarossa, so fell in love that he and Tenuta dei Vallarino (owned by Gancia), Prunotto (owned by Antinori), and Vigne Regali (vini Banfi) sponsored a more complete study of the crossing and had one hectare planted with it, the first in Italy (government permission to cultivate it only arrived in 2001). The goal was to investigate propagating the variety and experimenting with it on their estates. In the Acqui area, the first estate to produce an albarossa was Zunino in 2002.

The wine made with Albarossa is deep ruby-red, with purple tinges that tend to hang around even as the wine ages. The nose is delicately spicy and very fruity (blackberry, strawberry, plum) complicated by a strong note of tobacco that is not for everyone; it has a full body, with good creamy flavors of ripe red fruit. Today, there are a dozen quality producers who are using Albarossa. In 2010, the DOC Piemonte Albarossa was created, which requires a minimum of twelve months of aging before the wine can be put on sale.

WINES TO TRY: Michele Chiarlo*** (Montald), Prunotto*** (Bricco Colma), Castello di Neive***, Cascina Sant'Ubaldo*, Viotti Vini* (they also make a very good albarossa grappa).

Bussanello

WHERE IT'S FOUND: Piedmont. NATIONAL REGISTRY CODE NUMBER: 269. COLOR: white.

Bussanello is another of the many *Incrocio Dalmassos*, a white grape variety created by Dalmasso at the end of the 1930s by crossing Riesling Italico (Welschriesling) and Furmint, with the goal of obtaining a variety more generous in its yields than Furmint, which is subject to berry shot. Today Bussanello is grown mainly around Alessandria, Asti, and Cuneo, though it is found also in Langhe and even in Friuli Venezia Giulia. The bunch is medium-small, cylindrical, often winged, and compact. The berry is medium-sized and spherical, with thick yellow skin. It is harvested at the end of September or early October. The wine is yellow-green (golden if made from very ripe grapes), and has lovely aromas of jasmine, pear, and red apple.

WINES TO TRY: Tenute dei Vallarino** (La Ciò). Be aware that the Emilia-Romagna estate Casa Mora bottles a red wine they call "Bussanello" that has nothing to do with this variety.

Cornarea

WHERE IT'S FOUND: Piedmont. NATIONAL REGISTRY CODE NUMBER: 271. COLOR: red.

Another of the crossings obtained by Dalmasso when he thought he was working with Nebbiolo and Barbera (again, it was not Nebbiolo but Chatus, also called Nebbiolo di Dronero), this is a resistant variety that handles grey rot well even in rainy years. The bunch is medium-sized, pyramidal, and winged, while berries are small and oval. I don't know of any commercially available wines.

Cove'

WHERE IT'S FOUND: Piedmont. NATIONAL REGISTRY CODE NUMBER: 267. COLOR: red.

Cove' is a very little-known grape created by Dalmasso in 1936 that was until recently believed to be a Harslevelu × Malvasia Bianca Lunga crossing (some have named the latter "Malvasia Trevisana," which to the best of my knowledge, doesn't exist). However, recent data (Cipriani, Spadotto, Jurman, Di Gaspero, Crespan, Meneghetti, et al. 2010) shows Cove' to be a selfing of Harslevelu, so in this case it is not a true crossing at all (selflings arise thanks to berries that fall to the ground and grow from seeds that manage to take root). Clearly, more research is needed. In any case, it's a rare grape in Italy, and I have no knowledge of anybody making a wine with it.

Ervi

WHERE IT'S FOUND: Emilia-Romagna. NATIONAL REGISTRY CODE NUMBER: 338. COLOR: red.

Ervi is a crossing of Barbera and Croatina created by Mario Fregoni in 1977, professor at the Università Cattolica di Piacenza, who, as usual, wished to create a variety without the flaws of the two parents. In the Colli Piacentini of Emilia-Romagna, Barbera often fails to ripen properly, yielding very acidic and tannic wines, while Croatina, another locally important grape, is plagued by irregular annual production. Since the main DOC wine of the area is Gutturnio, obtained by blending the two, Fregoni thought it might be better to make Gutturnio with one grape only. Fregoni's goal was to create a loosely packed, small-berried variety, resistant to disease, that resembled Croatina more than it did Barbera (which tends to be overly acidic). Of the initial 649 vines cultivated, researchers finally selected, after eleven years of observation, vine number 108, seemingly the sturdiest and the most regularly productive of the lot. Hence, Ervi's original name was Incrocio Fregoni 108; it was later given the name by which it is known today. The name Ervi was chosen for two reasons: it means wine in Aramaic, and it includes the initials of Ernesto Vigevani, a grower in Rivergaro who was of great help to the university during the early years that Ervi was being studied. Ervi joined the National Registry of Italian varieties in 1999.

Which Wines to Choose and Why

The first estate to try a pure ervi was Alberto Lusignani, who planted nine hundred plants in 2003, after having conducted microvinifications and liking what he saw (and tasted). The wine is characterized by ripe red-fruit and herbal notes not unlike those of negro amaro, with low acidity and soft tannins. The finish is characterized by a sweet almond note. Ervi cannot be used to make Gutturnio on its own, but it could be used as a softening agent in place of at least a percentage of Barbera, which gives the biggest problems in the Colli Piacentini. It would certainly seem a better choice than international varieties such as Merlot, another low-acid variety but not native or typical of this corner of Italy, unlike Ervi, which was born here.

WINES TO TRY: Alberto Lusignani*** and Mossi***.

Fedit 51

WHERE IT'S FOUND: Veneto, Emilia-Romagna, Friuli Venezia Giulia, Lazio. NATIONAL REGISTRY CODE NUMBER: 276. COLOR: white.

Fedit 51 is a crossing of Malvasia Bianca Lunga Toscana and Garganega obtained by the Federazione Italiana dei Consorzi Agrari at the Vivaio di Carrara San Giorgio in 1951 (hence the name, "Fed" + "It" + 51). The variety has a large, long, pyramidal bunch with medium-sized, round, pinkish-yellow berries. All its phenological phases fall late and it is not particularly vigorous when grown on hillsides, but wine quality is far superior to that of grapes grown in the flatlands. It is grown mainly in Veneto (Padua and Vicenza), in Emilia-Romagna (Forlì, Cesena, Bologna, and Ravenna), and sporadically in Lazio and Abruzzo.

WINES TO TRY: Emilia-Romagna's excellent Tenuta Pederzana*** (Rioforeste Raffinata Passione, a sweet wine).

Fubiano

WHERE IT'S FOUND: Piedmont. NATIONAL REGISTRY CODE NUMBER: 275. COLOR: white.

A white grape variety obtained by Dalmasso in 1936 by crossing Furmint with Trebbiano Toscano. It has a medium-sized, compact grape bunch, pyramidal in shape, with one wing and small, thick-skinned, straw-yellow berries. It is used to make a good sparkling wine not unlike Prosecco. I think Fubiano is an interesting variety and one that could have a future.

WINES TO TRY: Piedmont's Tenuta Cannona**, which is the experimental viticulture and winemaking research station of the regional Piedmontese government (Centro Sperimentale Vitivinicolo della Regione Piemonte), where a great deal of experimentation has been performed over the years with this and many other crossings.

Goldtraminer

WHERE IT'S FOUND: Trentino. NATIONAL REGISTRY CODE NUMBER: 368. COLOR: white.

A Trebbiano Toscano × Gewürztraminer crossing obtained by Rebo Rigotti in 1947 and originally listed as Incrocio Rigotti 84–11. Unfortunately many in Italy refer to this as a Trebbiano Toscano × Traminer crossing, but this is incorrect as it is Gewürztraminer, a much more aromatic variety, that was used. The bunch is medium-small and loosely packed, while the berries are medium-sized; both are bigger than those of Gewürztraminer. There is one clone available: ISMA-AVIT 3001. This crossing's name was changed to Goldtraminer due to the intense color of its berries and their characteristic aroma (Roncador, Malossini, Grando, Mattivi, Nicolini, and Versini 2002). It was first planted in an experimental vineyard of the Fondazione Mach (then called Istituto Agario di San Michele all'Adige) in 1951 alongside three hundred different crossings and then selected from these and planted in a vineyard near Becchetti in 1951, and again in a vineyard of the Fondazione De Bellar in 1971.

Roncador, Malossini, Grando, Mattivi, Nicolini, and Versini found that Goldtraminer ripens in late September and is an ideal grape to try late-harvest or air-dried wines with, thanks to thick berry skins that make it resistant both to cold weather and to botrytis. The wine has much higher concentrations of terpenes such as citronellol and geraniol than does Gewürztraminer, so comes across smelling and tasting like an aromatic fruit bomb when late harvested. It can be included in IGT blends such as Delle Venezie, Vallagarina, and Vigneti delle Dolomiti.

WINES TO TRY: Cantina Toblino*** (Goldtraminer, a very good example of an air-dried, luscious, and intensely aromatic wine that will remind you of peach, mango, saffron, and sweet spices).

Gosen

WHERE IT'S FOUND: Trentino. **NATIONAL REGISTRY CODE NUMBER:** 367. **COLOR:** red.

Gosen was believed to be a Cabernet Franc × Marzemino crossing obtained by Rebo Rigotti in 1948 and originally listed as Incrocio Rigotti 123-4. Thanks to modern microsatellite testing, we now know that Gosen is most likely a Carmenère × Teroldego crossing (Roncador, Malossini, Grando, Mattivi, Nicolini, and Versini 2002), two varieties that have had their shares of misidentifications in Italy. Italy's Carmenère was until very recently thought to be Cabernet Franc (in fact, practically all "Cabernet Franc" planted before the 1980s in Italian vineyards is Carmenère). The Marzemino-Teroldego mix-up echoes that endured by Dalmasso, with Chatus (or Nebbiolo di Dronero) being misidentified for the real Nebbiolo; Rigotti's people somehow mixed up Marzemino with Teroldego. The crossing was renamed Gosen in honor of Olimpio Gosen, a collaborator of Rigotti who was also in charge of the experimental station of the Fondazione Mach (previously known as the Istituto Agario di San Michele all'Adige). Gosen was originally planted at the experimental vineyard of the Fondazione Mach in 1953 and then propagated along with a few other of the more promising *incroci* to another vineyard near Pozza in 1964.

Gosen has a medium-sized, relatively loosely packed bunch and is a regular producer; it ripens about a week later than Rebo. The wines, which I have not yet tasted, are said to be very *bordelais* in their makeup, with a refined Cabernet-like aroma and flavor, and a strong herbal note. Gosen is allowed in IGT blends such as Delle Venezie, Vallagarina, and Vigneti delle Dolomiti. Gosen has adapted very well to Sicilian *terroirs* and represents another card the island's producers have to play (Sparacio, Prinzivalli, Genna, Sparla, Capraro, Melia, and Verzera 2010). Gosen ripens in the last week of September in the area around Palermo and though it does not seem to be particularly productive in Sicily, the wines appear to hold considerable promise. A mainly teroldego-cabernet sauvignon blend by Dorigati (called 1858) contains small percentages of Gosen.

Incrocio Bruni 54

WHERE IT'S FOUND: Marche, Emilia-Romagna, Tuscany, Umbria. **NATIONAL REGISTRY CODE NUMBER:** 108. **COLOR:** white.

Created in 1936 by ampelographer Bruno Bruni by crossing Sauvignon Blanc with Verdicchio (it was his fifty-fourth try, hence the number 54 in the variety's name), this is a high-quality white grape that is beginning to make a timid comeback as a source of good, fresh, perfumed white wines. It was also Bruni's most successful crossing as it's the one still being used to make wine today, albeit in small quantities. However, in the 2010 study by Cipriani, Spadotto, Jurman, Di Gaspero, Crespan, Meneghetti, et al., the parentage of Incrocio Bruni 54 (the authors call it Selezione Bruni in their paper) was found to be Aleatico and Lacrima, which seems unlikely to me, if for no other reason that those two are both red varieties. Of course, white grapes can be born from red grapes, and so more research is needed on the parentage of Incrocio Bruni 54.

Incrocio Bruni's bunch is medium-sized, usually loosely packed and pyramid shaped; the berries are medium-large and round. It was abandoned because it doesn't produce many grapes (there are many bunches but few grapes, neatly differentiating it from Sauvignon Blanc) and yields are always naturally low. Consultant winemaker Giancarlo Soverchia knows this variety well and makes wine with it at the Terracruda estate. He recalls selecting old vines roughly ten years ago and propagating them to a vineyard; but once the farmer who tended the vineyard saw just how little grape production there was, he wanted nothing more to do with the variety. It is used to make the DOC wine Colli Maceratesi and IGT blends such as Allerona, Cannara, Costa Toscana, Marche, and Spello, but is grown mainly in the Marche, in the hinterland not far from Ancona. The wine certainly reminds one of sauvignon blanc on the nose (aromas of white flowers, passion fruit, green fig, and winter melon), with a slightly richer mouthfeel and creamier texture more typical of Verdicchio. I have been very impressed with what I have tasted so far.

WINES TO TRY: Terracruda***, Silvano Strologo**, and Viticoltori Finocchi*.

Incrocio Terzi n.1

WHERE IT'S FOUND: Lombardy. NATIONAL REGISTRY CODE NUMBER: 110. COLOR: red.

Terzi, a viticulturalist from Bergamo, crossed Barbera with Cabernet Franc (or what he thought was Cabernet Franc: given that in Italy Carmenère was regularly confused with the former variety, I wonder). In any case, the resulting crossing, which bears his name, proved a success, mainly due to high productivity and the intense hue of the wine. Today Incrocio Terzi n.1 is found in vineyards around the cities of Bergamo and Brescia, and on the shores of Lake Iseo. The variety's cluster is medium-sized, pyramidal, and compact, with one or two smallish wings. The berry is round-oval, medium-sized, and blue-black in hue. It ripens in late September and early October. The wine is deep red, vinous, lightly tannic, and can age. It is generally used as part of the blend in DOC wines such as Cellatica and Capriano del Colle, neither exactly household names.

WINES TO TRY: Ca' del Vènt** near Bergamo, in Lombardy.

MANZONI CROSSINGS

The name *Incrocio Manzoni* (Manzoni crossings) refers to a group of crossings created by Luigi Manzoni in the 1920s and 1930s at the enological and viticultural school of Conegliano. Manzoni attempted many crossings, using both local varieties such as Raboso Piave and Verdiso and internationals such as Riesling and Cabernet Sauvignon, and it is generally felt that many of his crossings are particularly suited to the making of fine wine. Unfortunately, in a clear demonstration of how little attention was paid to grape cultivars in Italy even in academic institutions, Manzoni's experimental vineyard was apparently uprooted after his retirement, and many of the crossings have been lost forever. Unbelievable as it may seem, the same fate befell the experimental vineyard set up by Manzoni's son Gianfranco, then president of the Istituto San Michele all'Adige, another of Italy's finest enological and viticultural schools of the time. Mercifully, today things are functioning more smoothly where crossings are concerned.

Still, two crossings survived, the Incrocio Manzoni 6.0.13 and the Incrocio Manzoni 2.15, and were listed in the National Registry of grape varieties: they are routinely used to make wine in Italy to this day. To their credit, in the 1990s the alumni association of the Conegliano enological school actively set about recovering any other *Incrocio Manzoni* vines that still survived, unidentified, in old local vineyards. In this manner, another five *Incrocio Manzoni* vines were saved, one table grape and four wine grapes. The latter are used to make wine today by a few estates. Recently, in 2010, two more crossings by Manzoni were listed in the National Registry of Grape Varieties: Incrocio 2–14 (a red variety) and Incrocio 2–3 (a white variety).

Manzoni Bianco

WHERE IT'S FOUND: Veneto, Trentino, FVG, Puglia, Sicily. NATIONAL REGISTRY CODE NUMBER: 299. COLOR: white.

The best and most popular of Manzoni's crossings is the arduously named Incrocio Manzoni 6.0.13, now simply called Manzoni Bianco. In fact, like most other crossings, all of the Manzoni cultivars were also originally named by using numbers: in Manzoni's case, these referred to the location coordinates of the newly created varieties in the experimental vineyard. The first number refers to the row number, the second to the crossing's position in the row; to make matters even less easy to grasp and remember, and for reasons still unclear today, some crossings were named with three numbers, the second of which was always a zero. It is hypothesized that the zero was used to identify crossings produced between 1930 and 1935, as opposed to those created in the 1920s, but nobody knows for sure. In any case, with names like 6.0.13 and 2.15 you can tell these wines were born in far less marketing-oriented and media-savvy times.

Nevertheless, Incrocio Manzoni 6.0.13 has proven a remarkable success. Now simply called Manzoni Bianco, it was long believed to be a crossing of Riesling and Pinot Bianco, but recent genetic studies suggest that Chardonnay may have been used instead of the latter. There are two clones available of Manzoni Bianco, both developed in 1992 and very similar: clone ISMA-ISV 237 has slightly smaller berries and is more compact than clone ISMA-ISV 222. It is an extremely high-quality variety, one of the world's few truly successful crossings, and plantings are on the rise in Italy, with an average of thirty new hectares planted in each year of the first decade of the new century.

Manzoni Bianco is not the easiest of varieties, however. Giorgio Cecchetto, best known for his excellent Raboso wines, also makes a very good Manzoni Bianco wine. "It's a pain, really," he says. "We have to harvest it as early as late August or early September; it's hardly vigorous, and it produces scrawny bunches with small and scarce berries. I remember a winemaking colleague who had never seen Manzoni Bianco, asking me one day if the vines were about to die! And wait, it gets better: though they are thick skinned, the berries are easily sunburned, and so deleafing is out." It was only natural that I ask him why he ever bothered to plant Manzoni Bianco in the first place. "Because the wine's good," was the reply.

Which Wines to Choose and Why

Manzoni Bianco is found mainly in Veneto and Trentino. In the former region, DOC Vicenza wines can be 100 percent Manzoni Bianco, but it is most often blended in DOC Colli di Conegliano Bianco, while in the latter there are excellent DOC Trentino wines that are pure Manzoni Bianco. The success of the variety is such that it has also been planted in Friuli Venezia Giulia, and in southern regions such as Puglia and Sicily, though readers ought to know that its presence is often not declared on labels or information from producers. It is used to spark up wines that sport the name of a usually less interesting but better known or more famous local native, adding zippy acidity and a welcome delicate spiciness.

As Manzoni Bianco is a lightly aromatic variety, its wines are fresh and crisp, and exude intense floral and spicy aromas and flavors (white flowers, white peach, green apple, white pepper, lemongrass). In fact, the wine resembles riesling to a startling degree; a lighter riesling perhaps, but riesling nonetheless, which is a lot more than can be said for other crossings in which Riesling was one of the parents. Manzoni Bianco's aromas are only partly due to aromatic terpenes such as geraniol and linalool, as gas chromatographic analysis have revealed their concentrations to be fairly low (they are highest when the variety is grown in warmer sites). Nicolini, Versini, Moser, Carlin, and Malossini (2003) have shown that, like Riesling, with age Manzoni Bianco wines develop kerosene-like notes due to an increase of free 1,1,6-trimethyl-1,2 dihydronaphthalene.

WINES TO TRY: For Trentino, try: Istituto San Michele all'Adige-Fondazione Mach*** (Trentino Incrocio Manzoni) and Elisabetta Foradori*** (Fontanasanta). For Veneto, try: Giorgio Cecchetto** (Marca Trevigiana), Conte Collalto**, Sutto** (Campodipietra), and Ca' Lustra** (Pedevenda; it's unfortunate that this wine's name is also the name of a distinct cultivar). Frassinelli* makes a good sparkling version.

Manzoni Rosso

WHERE IT'S FOUND: Veneto. NATIONAL REGISTRY CODE NUMBER: 109. COLOR: red.

Almost better known as Incrocio Manzoni 2.15, this is another successful crossing, but unlike Manzoni Bianco, is a red variety. Like many other crossings, it was the result of a mistake: the original intent was to create a new white grape by crossing Glera (the grape with which Prosecco is made) with Sauvignon Blanc, but somehow pollen from Cabernet Sauvignon was used instead of the latter. The resulting wine, not surprisingly, is red. However recent data suggests that the red-berried parent is not Cabernet Sauvignon, but rather Cabernet Franc, and the same is true of Incrocio Manzoni 2-14 (Cipriani, Spadotto, Jurman, Di Gaspero, Crespan, Meneghetti, et al. 2010). Though good wines are made with this crossing, it has never reached the quality or the fame of its white sibling. It is a vigorous variety that does well in both hillside and flatland vineyards, but needs hot microclimates to perform best; a high clay percentage in the soil is also helpful.

Which Wines to Choose and Why

Today Incrocio Manzoni 2.15 is found mainly, if not only, in the hills surrounding Treviso in Veneto, especially those outside Conegliano and Montello. It can compose up to 10 percent of the DOC Colli di Conegliano Rosso blends. When pure, a rare find, I have found it to have a medium-dark red hue and aromas that are fruity and vinous, with hints of herbs and raspberry. I have also tasted five- and six-year-old wines that show it can age well.

WINES TO TRY: As usual, an excellent source for these wines is the very competent Conte Collalto estate**.

Manzoni Rosa

WHERE IT'S FOUND: Veneto. NATIONAL REGISTRY CODE NUMBER: 375. COLOR: pink.

Manzoni Rosa, originally named Incrocio Manzoni 1-50, is a crossing of Trebbiano Toscano and Gewürztraminer that, not surprisingly, gives wines characterized by extremely intense floral and spicy aromas. In the words of Manzoni himself, the wine has aromas more intense than those of gewürztraminer, which is quite a result, given that variety's in-your-face aromatic personality. In fact, Manzoni Rosa's aromatics were so powerful that it was ultimately decided it was best suited to make a sweet rosé. When made as a white wine, its color is amber-yellow, with strong aromas of peach, dried apricot, and rose. It's full bodied and velvety, but very hard to find as a wine on its own. It was included in the National Registry of grape varieties in 2003.

WINES TO TRY: Conte Collalto** (Rosabianco).

Manzoni Moscato

WHERE IT'S FOUND: Veneto. NATIONAL REGISTRY CODE NUMBER: 376. COLOR: red.

Manzoni Moscato, originally known as Incrocio Manzoni 13.0.25, is a crossing of Raboso Piave and Moscato d'Amburgo. Like Manzoni Rosa, Manzoni Moscato was first listed in the National Registry in 2003, but unlike it, Manzoni Moscato has had more success with producers and you can find many interesting, good, and inexpensive examples. It is the result of a strange crossing: Manzoni felt that to counterbalance Raboso's innate tendency to produce wines that were both very tannic and acidic, the gentler Moscato d'Amburgo was an ideal candidate. Today it is grown only in small plots in the province of Treviso. Most producers choose to make a sparkling, lightly off-dry pink wine, but thanks to notable acidity, it comes across as relatively dry. The wines are also more complex than those made with Manzoni Rosa, featuring not just red-berry aromas and flavors but also hints of peach, apricot, vanilla bean, and citrus.

WINES TO TRY: Conte Collalto**, Barbaran*, Molon*, Casa Roma*, Tenuta San Giorgio* (Il Bizzarro), and Villa Almè (Petalo Rosa).

Merlese

WHERE IT'S FOUND: Emilia-Romagna. NATIONAL REGISTRY CODE NUMBER: 400. COLOR: red.

A crossing of Sangiovese and Merlot listed at number 400 of the National Registry of Grape Varieties as of 2011, Merlese has been under copyright of the University of Bologna since 1983. Medium vigorous, it ripens in September, before Sangiovese, one of the reasons why the latter was crossed with Merlot. The bunch is medium-sized, pyramidal, winged, and sparse. The berry is medium-sized, blue-black, and round. Microvinifications have shown a deep ruby hue, and aromas and flavors of bell pepper, almond, and dark small berries. One clone is available, CAB 1.

Nebbiera

WHERE IT'S FOUND: Piedmont. NATIONAL REGISTRY CODE NUMBER: 282. COLOR: red.

Also known as Incrocio Dalmasso XV/29, Nebbiera was obtained by Dalmasso in 1938 by crossing what he thought was Nebbiolo (in reality, Chatus) with Barbera. It has a medium-large, pyramidal or cylindrical, compact bunch with small, round, thin-skinned, purple-red berries. It ripens in late September and has medium vigor. Microvinifications show the wine has a medium-red, almost amber-red hue, with aromas and flavors of red cherry and violet. It is tannic and acidic (though less acidic than wines made with Barbera) but lacks the complexity of Nebbiolo wines. I know of no commercially available bottles yet.

Nigra

WHERE IT'S FOUND: Veneto. NATIONAL REGISTRY CODE NUMBER: 283. COLOR: red.

Nigra is a rarely planted Merlot × Barbera crossing developed by Italo Cosmo that still survives in scattered vineyards around Treviso, but I don't believe anybody plans to make monovarietal wines with it any time soon.

Passau

WHERE IT'S FOUND: Piedmont. NATIONAL REGISTRY CODE NUMBER: 284. COLOR: red.

Also known as Incrocio Dalmasso 17/25, Passau is another Chatus × Dolcetto crossing, like San Martino and Valentino Nero. It also grows in Piedmont but I have never tasted or even heard of any varietal wines being for sale.

Rebo

WHERE IT'S FOUND: Trentino. NATIONAL REGISTRY CODE NUMBER: 301. COLOR: red.

Originally named Incrocio 107-A, the variety's name was later changed to honor its creator, Rebo Rigotti. Rigotti, a graduate of San Michele all'Adige who continued to work there as a botanist and researcher, created many different crossings, though for now it appears his greatest success has been this grape that took his name. In 1948, he successfully crossed what he believed at the time were Merlot and Marzemino to create this variety, though recent analysis has shown the latter not to have been Marzemino but Teroldego. Rebo is actually an abundant variety in northern Italy, grown mostly in Trentino around Calavino, Padergnone, San Michele all'Adige, and Volano. It has conical, winged, medium-small bunches, with medium-small, round (but not uniform), thick-skinned, blue-black berries. It ripens in mid- to late September. There are three clones available: Ampelos VCP 3, ISMA-AVIT 583, and ISMA-AVIT 590. The wine is very dark in hue and fresh, brimming with aromas of small red and black fruits, with a hint of fresh herbs. You can find Rebo used in DOC wines such as Trentino and in over fifteen different IGT wines, such as Allerona, Alto Livenza, Benaco Bresciano, Costa Toscana, Marca Trevigiana, Marche, Narni, Terrazze Retiche di Sondrio, Umbria, and Vallagarina. There are therefore scattered plantings of Rebo outside Trentino (Umbria, Tuscany, Veneto), where the crossing is easiest to find. It's not particularly tannic and comes across as bright and refreshing. Though best consumed young, when judiciously oak-aged it can take a few years in the cellar. This is certainly one of Italy's most successful crossings and I encourage you to give the wines a try.

WINES TO TRY: Cantina Isera**, Cantina Toblino**, Dorigati**, Fratelli Pisoni**, Istituto San Michele all'Adige/Fondazione Mach**, Pratella**, Pravis**.

San Martino

WHERE IT'S FOUND: Piedmont. NATIONAL REGISTRY CODE NUMBER: 280. COLOR: red.

Also known as Incrocio Dalmasso 7/21, San Martino is a Chatus × Dolcetto crossing, like Passau and Valentino Nero. It grows in Piedmont but I have no firsthand knowledge of any varietal wines being made.

San Michele

WHERE IT'S FOUND: Piedmont. NATIONAL REGISTRY CODE NUMBER: 288. COLOR: red.

Also known as Incrocio Dalmasso 15/34, San Michele is another Chatus × Barbera crossing, like Albarossa, Cornarea, Nebbiera, and Soperga. It also grows in Piedmont but I have never tasted or even heard of any varietal wines being for sale.

Sennen

WHERE IT'S FOUND: Trentino. NATIONAL REGISTRY CODE NUMBER: 368. COLOR: red.

Originally known as Incrocio Rigotti 107–2, this was originally thought to be a crossing of Merlot and Marzemino. Modern microsatellite analysis has shown this to be a Merlot × Teroldego crossing instead; somehow the Marzemino and Teroldego accessions were mixed up and so Teroldego was used instead. The variety was renamed Sennen in honor of Rebo Rigotti's brother, named Sennen (as Incrocio Rigotti 107–2, Sennen is generally referred to as Rebo's "brother" grapevine, as Rebo was Incrocio Rigotti 107–3). According to Roncador, Malossini, Grando, Mattivi, Nicolini, and Versini (2002), Sennen was initially planted in the main experimental vineyard of the Fondazione Mach (then the Istituto Agrario San Michele all'Adige) in 1951 and then propagated in 1957 to another vineyard near Pozza along with those *incroci* that had most impressed the researchers (such as Rebo and Gosen). It has medium-sized bunches and berries: the latter are slightly oval. It ripens early and is considered extremely promising since it accumulates sugar with greater ease than does Rebo while maintaining more than adequate total acidity levels. As it's not very sensitive to botrytis, a role in the making of air-dried wines has also been postulated. It can be used in IGT blends such as Delle Venezie, Vallagarina, and Vigneti delle Dolomiti. Recently researchers have also found that Sennen has adapted very well to the much warmer Sicilian climate around Palermo (Sparacio, Prinzivalli, Genna, Sparla, Capraro, Melia, and Verzera 2010). I have not tasted any of the wines yet: the dry wines are said to have early accessibility but also the capacity to age five or six years. It is generally believed that Sennen is best used to make lighter-bodied wines of early appeal, while Gosen, another *incrocio* by Rigotti, can be used to make ageworthy, structured wines.

Soperga

WHERE IT'S FOUND: Piedmont. NATIONAL REGISTRY CODE NUMBER: 292. COLOR: red.

Also known as Incrocio Dalmasso IV/31 or Superga, Soperga is another Chatus × Barbera crossing, like Albarossa, Cornarea, Nebbiera, and San Michele. It also grows in Piedmont but I have never tasted or even heard of any varietal wines being for sale.

Valentino Nero

WHERE IT'S FOUND: Piedmont. NATIONAL REGISTRY CODE NUMBER: 295. COLOR: red.

Also known as Incrocio Dalmasso 16/8, Valentino Nero is a Chatus × Dolcetto crossing, like Passau and San Martino. It grows in Piedmont but I have no firsthand knowledge of any varietal wines being made.

APPENDIX

TABLE 1
Total plantings and regional distribution of grape varieties in Italy (in thousands of hectares)

Variety	Total hectares planted	Hectares planted, by region						
Sangiovese	70.3	Tuscany 30.0	Puglia 10.0	Emilia-Romagna 9.2	Marche 3.4	Umbria 3.0	Abruzzo 1.0	Sardinia 2.0
		Campania 1.5	Calabria 1.0	Sicily 1.5	Lazio 1.0	Basilicata 0.1	Molise 0.1	Other regions 6.5
Trebbiano Toscano	38.3	Puglia 15.0	Sicily 6.0	Abruzzo 5.0	Lazio 2.0	Tuscany 2.0	Umbria 2.0	Campania 1.2
		Marche 0.8	Calabria 0.5	Molise 0.2	Basilicata 0.1	Other regions 3.5		
Catarratto	37.8	Sicily 37.8						
Montepulciano	31.1	Abruzzo 15.1	Puglia 7.0	Marche 5.0	Molise 2.0	Campania 0.9	Lazio 0.5	Sardinia 0.6
Merlot	24.1	Veneto 10.3	Tuscany 3.5	FVG 2.5	Lazio 1.0	Trentino-Alto Adige 1.6	Umbria 1.5	Other regions 3.7
Barbera	21.3	Piedmont 12.5	Emilia-Romagna 2.4	Lombardy 2.4	Campania 1.0	Other regions 3.0		
Calabrese	18.4	Sicily 18.3	Calabria 0.1					
Negro Amaro	16.6	Puglia 16.6						
Chardonnay	15.5	Lombardy 4.8	Trentino-Alto Adige 3.5	Veneto 3.0	FVG 1.3	Piedmont 1.0	Emilia-Romagna 0.5	Sicily 1.0

(continued)

TABLE 1 *(continued)*

Variety	Total hectares planted	Hectares planted, by region					
Trebbiano Romagnolo	16.3	Emilia-Romagna 16.3					
Glera	16.2	Veneto 14.8	FVG 1.4				
Cabernet Sauvignon	15.9	Tuscany 2.0	Sicily 2.8	Veneto 1.3	Puglia 1.3	Trentino-Alto Adige 0.7	FVG 0.6
		Umbria 0.5	Marche 0.5	Lazio 0.4	Abruzzo 0.4	Emilia-Romagna 0.3	Sardinia 0.3
Malvasia Bianca di Candia	13.4	Lazio 6.0	Campania 3.0	Puglia 1.0	Abruzzo 0.2	Other regions 3.2	
Moscato Bianco	11.7	Piedmont 11.0	Lombardy 0.5	Puglia 0.2			
Garganega	11.3	Veneto 11.1	Puglia 0.2				
Primitivo	11.1	Puglia 10.0	Other regions 1.1				
Aglianico	10.5	Campania 5.1	Basilicata 3.0	Puglia 0.3	Molise 0.1	Other regions 2.0	
Pinot Grigio	10.1	Veneto 3.5	FVG 2.5	Trentino-Alto Adige 3.0	Lombardy 0.5	Umbria 0.1	Other regions 0.5
Syrah	7.1	Sicily 3.5	Other regions 3.6				
Ansonica	6.8	Sicily 6.6	Tuscany 0.2				
Grillo	6.1	Sicily 6.1					

Corvina/Corvinone	6.1	Veneto 6.1			
Dolcetto	6.0	Piedmont 6.0			
Croatina	5.9	Lombardy 3.7	Emilia-Romagna 2.2		
Trebbiano Abruzzese	5.7	Abruzzo 5.7			
Nebbiolo	5.5	Piedmont 5.0	Lombardy 0.5		
Nerello	5.0	Sicily 5.0			
Lambrusco Salamino	4.7	Emilia-Romagna 4.3	Lombardy 0.4		
Grecanico Dorato	4.6	Sicily 4.6			
Verdicchio	4.5	Marche 3.6	Veneto 0.5	Lombardy 0.4	
Ancellotta	4.3	Emilia-Romagna 4.3			
Cannonau	4.1	Sardinia 3.9	Veneto .2		
Lambrusco Maestri	4.1	Puglia 2.7	Emilia-Romagna 0.6	Lombardy 0.5	Campania 0.3
Pinot Nero	4.1	Lombardy 3.2	Trentino-Alto Adige 0.5	Veneto 0.2	FVG 0.1	Piedmont 0.1
Cabernet Franc/ Carmenère	4.0	Veneto 2.7	FVG 1.1	Trentino-Alto Adige 0.2	

(continued)

TABLE 1 *(continued)*

Variety	Total hectares planted	Hectares planted, by region					
Ciliegiolo	3.4	Puglia 2.0	Tuscany 0.4	Emilia-Romagna 0.3	Campania 0.3	Lazio 0.2	Abruzzo 0.1	Umbria 0.1
Vermentino	3.1	Sardinia 2.1	Liguria 0.5	Tuscany 0.4	Piedmont 0.1			
Malvasia Nera	3.0	Puglia 2.9	Tuscany 0.1					
Cortese	2.8	Piedmont 2.7	Lombardy 0.1					
Falanghina	2.8	Campania 2.7	Molise 0.1					
Pinot Bianco	1.7	Veneto 0.6	FVG 0.6	Trentino-Alto Adige 0.4	Lombardy 0.1			
Rondinella	2.7	Veneto 2.7						
Schiava	2.6	Trentino-Alto Adige 2.6						
Tocai Friulano	2.1	FVG 1.1	Veneto 1.0					
Gaglioppo/Magliocco	2.0	Calabria 2.0						
Lambrusco Grasparossa	2.0	Emilia-Romagna 2.0						
Sauvignon	1.8	FVG 1.0	Veneto 0.4	Trentino-Alto Adige 0.2	Emilia-Romagna 0.1	Tuscany 0.1		
Zibibbo	1.8	Sicily 1.8						

Albana	1.5	Emilia-Romagna	1.5				
Carignano	1.5	Sardinia	1.5				
Grechetto	1.5	Umbria	1.5				
Malvasia Bianca Lunga	1.5	Tuscany	0.6	Lazio	0.4	Umbria	0.1
Fiano	1.4	Campania	1.4				
Lacrima	1.4	Puglia	1.4				
Lambrusco di Sorbara	1.4	Emilia-Romagna	1.4				
Pignoletto	1.4	Emilia-Romagna	1.4				
Riesling Italico	1.4	Lombardy	1.4				
Uva di Troia	1.4	Puglia	1.4				
Bombino Bianco	1.3	Puglia	1.3				
Brachetto	1.3	Piedmont	1.3				
Canaiolo Nero	1.3	Tuscany	1.3				
Greco	1.3	Campania	1.3				
Marzemino	1.3	Trentino-Alto Adige	0.6	Veneto	0.3	Emilia-Romagna	0.2	Lombardy	0.2	Puglia	0.3	Abruzzo	0.1

(continued)

TABLE 1 *(continued)*

Variety	Total hectares planted	Hectares planted, by region		
Lambrusco Marani	1.2	Emilia-Romagna 1.0	Lombardy 0.2	
Müller-Thurgau	1.2	Trentino-Alto Adige 1.1	FVG 0.1	
Cococciola	1.1	Abruzzo 1.1		
Malvasia di Candia Aromatica	1.1	Emilia-Romagna 1.1		
Freisa	1.0	Piedmont 1.0		
Raboso (Piave/Veronese)	1.0	Veneto 1.0		
Sagrantino	1.0	Umbria 1.0		
Arneis	0.9	Piedmont 1.9		
Grignolino	0.9	Piedmont 0.9		
Terrano	0.8	FVG 0.8		
Verduzzo Friulano	0.8	FVG 0.6	Veneto 0.2	
Vernaccia San Gimignano	0.8	Tuscany 0.8		
Cesanese	0.7	Lazio 0.7		

Traminer Aromatico	0.7	Trentino-Alto Adige	0.5	FVG 0.2
Lagrein	0.6	Trentino-Alto Adige	0.6	
Malvasia del Lazio	0.6	Lazio	0.6	
Ortrugo	0.6	Emilia-Romagna	0.6	
Teroldego	0.6	Trentino-Alto Adige	0.6	
Bellone	0.5	Lazio	0.5	
Bonarda	0.5	Piedmont	0.5	
Molinara	0.5	Veneto	0.5	
Montù	0.5	Emilia-Romagna	0.5	
Verdeca	0.5	Marche	0.5	
Verduzzo Trevigiano	0.5	Veneto	0.5	
Manzoni Bianco	0.4	Veneto	0.3	FVG 0.1
Durella	0.3	Veneto	0.3	
Monica	0.3	Sardinia	0.3	

(continued)

TABLE 1 (continued)

Variety	Total hectares planted	Hectares planted, by region	
Riesling	0.3	Trentino-Alto Adige 0.2	FVG 0.1
Aleatico	0.2	Lazio 0.1	Tuscany 0.1
Colorino	0.2	Tuscany 0.2	
Greco Nero	0.2	Calabria 0.2	
Malvasia Istriana	0.2	FVG 0.2	
Nuragus	0.2	Sardinia 0.2	
Uva Rara	0.2	Lombardy 0.2	
Albarola	0.1	Liguria 0.1	
Moscato Giallo	0.1	Veneto 0.1	
Trebbiano Giallo	0.1	Lazio 0.1	

Adapted from: Istituto Nazionale delle Statistiche (2010), Sixth General Census of Agriculture; G. Tempesta and M. Fiorillo (2011), *Patrimonio Varietale*, www.vivaioenotria.com.

TABLE 2
Total plantings of grape varieties in Italy, 1970–2010 (in thousands of hectacres and percentage of total hectacres)

	1970	1982	1990	2000	2010
Sangiovese	86.4 (7.8%)	101.0 (9.2%)	87.4 (9.9%)	69.9 (10.3%)	70.3 (11.9%)
Trebbiano Toscano	61.2 (5.5%)	60.0 (5.5%)	61.6 (7.0%)	44.5 (6.6%)	38.3 (6.5%)
Catarrato	82.5 (7.4%)	82.0 (7.5%)	74.8 (8.5%)	50.8 (7.5%)	37.8 (6.4%)
Montepulciano	25.5 (2.3%)	35.0 (3.2%)	31.0 (3.5%)	29.8 (4.4%)	31.1 (5.2%)
Merlot	53.0 (4.8%)	49.0 (4.5%)	31.9 (3.6%)	25.6 (3.8%)	24.1 (4.1%)
Barbera	78.7 (7.1%)	63.0 (5.7%)	47.2 (5.4%)	28.3 (4.2%)	21.3 (3.6%)
Calabrese	15.3 (1.4%)	20.0 (1.8%)	14.2 (1.6%)	11.4 (1.7%)	18.4 (3.1%)
Negro Amaro	41.0 (3.7%)	39.0 (3.6%)	31.4 (3.6%)	16.8 (2.5%)	16.6 (2.8%)
Chardonnay	2.7 (0.2%)	5.0 (0.5%)	6.2 (0.7%)	11.8 (1.7%)	16.5 (2.8%)
Trebbiano Romagnolo	25.9 (2.3%)	26.0 (2.4%)	21.3 (2.4%)	20.0 (3.0%)	16.3 (2.7%)
Glera	5.8 (0.5%)	6.0 (0.5%)	7.1 (0.8%)	8.1 (1.2%)	16.2 (2.7%)
Cabernet Sauvignon	0.9 (0.1%)	2.0 (0.2%)	3.2 (0.4%)	8.0 (1.2%)	15.9 (2.7%)
Malvasia Bianca di Candia	17.4 (1.6%)	29.0 (2.6%)	23.1 (2.6%)	13.8 (2.0%)	13.4 (2.3%)
Garganega	13.5 (1.2%)	13.0 (1.2%)	13.1 (1.5%)	11.6 (1.7%)	11.3 (1.9%)
Moscato Bianco	10.3 (0.9%)	13.0 (1.2%)	13.4 (1.5%)	13.3 (2.0%)	11.7 (2.0%)
Primitivo	46.0 (4.1%)	32.0 (2.9%)	17.3 (2.0%)	8.0 (1.2%)	11.1 (1.9%)
Aglianico	13.0 (1.2%)	15.0 (1.4%)	13.0 (1.5%)	10.0 (1.5%)	10.5 (1.8%)
Pinot Grigio	1.0 (0.1%)	2.0 (0.2%)	3.1 (0.4%)	6.7 (1.0%)	10.1 (1.7%)
Syrah	0.0 (0%)	0.0 (0%)	0.1 (0%)	1.1 (0.2%)	7.1 (1.2%)
Ansonica	7.5 (0.7%)	14.0 (1.3%)	12.7 (1.4%)	9.5 (1.4%)	6.8 (1.1%)
Corvina/Corvinone	4.0 (0.4%)	5.0 (0.5%)	4.5 (0.5%)	5.0 (0.7%)	6.1 (1.0%)
Grillo	6.0 (0.5%)	3.0 (0.3%)	2.2 (0.2%)	1.8 (0.3%)	6.1 (1.0%)
Dolcetto	14.8 (1.3%)	12.0 (1.1%)	10.0 (1.1%)	7.3 (1.1%)	6.0 (1.0%)
Croatina	5.1 (0.5%)	5.5 (0.5%)	4.5 (0.5%)	3.3 (0.5%)	5.9 (1.0%)
Trebbiano Abruzzese	2.4 (0.2%)	7.0 (0.6%)	12.0 (1.4%)	7.9 (1.2%)	5.7 (1.0%)
Nebbiolo	5.7 (0.5%)	6.0 (0.5%)	5.3 (0.6%)	4.9 (0.7%)	5.5 (0.9%)
Nerello (Mascalese and Cappuccio)	17.0 (1.5%)	20.0 (1.8%)	18.5 (2.1%)	6.0 (0.9%)	5.0 (0.8%)
Lambrusco Salamino	4.1 (0.4%)	6.1 (0.6%)	4.7 (0.5%)	4.3 (0.6%)	4.7 (0.8%)
Grecanico Dorato	2.1 (0.2%)	3.5 (0.3%)	4.5 (0.5%)	5.2 (0.8%)	4.6 (0.8%)
Verdicchio	6.1 (0.5%)	4.0 (0.4%)	4.9 (0.6%)	5.5 (0.8%)	4.5 (0.8%)
Ancellotta	6.0 (0.5%)	5.8 (0.5%)	4.7 (0.5%)	4.5 (0.7%)	4.3 (0.7%)
Cannonau	12.0 (1.1%)	15.0 (1.4%)	12.1 (1.4%)	7.2 (1.1%)	4.1 (0.7%)
Pinot Nero	1.4 (0.1%)	2.0 (0.2%)	3.5 (0.4%)	3.3 (0.5%)	4.1 (0.7%)
Lambrusco Maestri	7.4 (0.7%)	5.1 (0.5%)	3.0 (0.3%)	1.5 (0.2%)	4.1 (0.7%)

(continued)

TABLE 2 *(continued)*

	1970	1982	1990	2000	2010
Cabernet Franc/Carmenere	4.6 (0.4%)	6.0 (0.5%)	5.8 (0.7%)	7.1 (1.0%)	4.0 (0.7%)
Vermentino	4.0 (0.4%)	3.6 (0.3%)	4.0 (0.5%)	3.9 (0.6%)	3.1 (0.5%)
Malvasia Nera	6.4 (0.6%)	9.0 (0.8%)	8.0 (0.9%)	6.4 (0.9%)	3.0 (0.5%)
Falanghina	0.9 (0.1%)	0.5 (0%)	0.7 (0.1%)	1.7 (0.3%)	2.8 (0.5%)
Cortese	1.8 (0.2%)	2.2 (0.2%)	3.0 (0.3%)	3.1 (0.5%)	2.8 (0.5%)
Pinot Bianco	0.0 (0%)	2.0 (0.2%)	4.0 (0.5%)	5.1 (0.8%)	2.7 (0.5%)
Rondinella	2.9 (0.3%)	3.5 (0.3%)	3.0 (0.3%)	2.9 (0.4%)	2.7 (0.5%)
Schiava	8.2 (0.7%)	5.4 (0.5%)	4.0 (0.5%)	3.6 (0.5%)	2.6 (0.4%)
Lambrusco Grasparossa	1.4 (0.1%)	2.1 (0.2%)	2.0 (0.2%)	1.9 (0.3%)	2.0 (0.3%)
Nuragus	17.8 (1.6%)	16.0 (1.5%)	9.0 (1.0%)	3.2 (0.5%)	2.0 (0.3%)
Gaglioppo/Magliocco	9.2 (0.8%)	7.0 (0.6%)	5.1 (0.6%)	4.3 (0.6%)	2.0 (0.3%)
Zibibbo	3.9 (0.4%)	2.0 (0.2%)	1.4 (0.2%)	1.1 (0.2%)	1.8 (0.3%)
Ciliegiolo	3.4 (0.3%)	6.1 (0.6%)	5.0 (0.6%)	3.1 (0.5%)	1.6 (0.3%)
Malvasia Bianca Lunga	15.8 (1.4%)	11.0 (1.0%)	9.3 (1.1%)	4.7 (0.7%)	1.6 (0.3%)
Albana	9.7 (0.9%)	7.1 (0.6%)	4.0 (0.5%)	2.8 (0.4%)	1.5 (0.3%)
Carignano	3.5 (0.3%)	2.0 (0.2%)	3.0 (0.3%)	1.7 (0.3%)	1.5 (0.3%)
Grechetto	1.1 (0.1%)	1.4 (0.1%)	1.0 (0.1%)	1.2 (0.2%)	1.5 (0.3%)
Sauvignon	1.8 (0.2%)	2.4 (0.2%)	3.0 (0.3%)	3.4 (0.5%)	1.5 (0.3%)
Fiano	0.4 (0%)	0.4 (0%)	0.3 (0%)	0.8 (0.1%)	1.4 (0.2%)
Lambrusco di Sorbara	1.8 (0.2%)	2.0 (0.2%)	2.0 (0.2%)	1.5 (0.2%)	1.4 (0.2%)
Pignoletto	0.0 (0%)	0.2 (0%)	0.5 (0.1%)	6.8 (1.0%)	1.4 (0.2%)
Tocai Friulano	7.9 (0.7%)	8.0 (0.7%)	6.9 (0.8%)	4.7 (0.7%)	1.4 (0.2%)
Riesling Italico	1.8 (0.2%)	2.4 (0.2%)	2.0 (0.2%)	2.0 (0.3%)	1.4 (0.2%)
Verdeca	7.9 (0.7%)	6.0 (0.5%)	4.0 (0.5%)	2.3	1.4 (0.2%)
Uva di Troia	9.4 (0.8%)	6.5 (0.6%)	3.0 (0.3%)	1.8 (0.3%)	1.4 (0.2%)
Greco	1.0 (0.1%)	1.0 (0.1%)	1.4 (0.2%)	0.9 (0.1%)	1.3 (0.2%)
Bombino Bianco	7.8 (0.7%)	5.1 (0.5%)	4.0 (0.5%)	3.0 (0.4%)	1.3 (0.2%)
Brachetto	0.2 (0%)	0.2 (0%)	0.3 (0%)	1.6 (0.2%)	1.3 (0.2%)
Canaiolo Nero	6.3 (0.6%)	7.2 (0.7%)	4.0 (0.5%)	2.8 (0.4%)	1.3 (0.2%)
Lambrusco Marani	0.9 (0.1%)	3.0 (0.3%)	2.4 (0.3%)	—	1.2 (0.2%)
Müller-Thurgau	0.2 (0%)	0.8 (0.1%)	1.0 (0.1%)	1.0 (0.1%)	1.2 (0.2%)
Cococciola	1.0 (0.1%)	2.1 (0.2%)	1.4 (0.2%)	0.9 (0.1%)	1.1 (0.2%)
Malvasia Candia Aromatica	0.0 (0%)	1.0 (0.1%)	1.0 (0.1%)	1.8 (0.3%)	1.1 (0.2%)
Freisa	6.8 (0.6%)	4.0 (0.4%)	2.0 (0.2%)	1.5 (0.2%)	1.0 (0.2%)
Raboso	14.1 (1.3%)	2.8 (0.3%)	2.0 (0.2%)	1.7 (0.3%)	1.0 (0.2%)
Trebbiano Giallo	5.8 (0.5%)	4.4 (0.6%)	4.0 (0.5%)	4.3 (0.6%)	1.0 (0.2%)

TABLE 2 *(continued)*

	1970	1982	1990	2000	2010
Sagrantino	0.1 (0%)	0.2 (0%)	0.2 (0%)	0.4 (0.1%)	1.0 (0.2%)
Arneis	0.1 (0%)	0.2 (0%)	0.5 (0.1%)	0.7 (0.1%)	0.9 (0.2%)
Grignolino	0.8 (0.1%)	1.2 (0.1%)	1.4 (0.2%)	1.3 (0.2%)	0.9 (0.1%)
Refosco	0.7 (0.1%)	1.5 (0.1%)	1.0 (0.1%)	1.1 (0.2%)	0.8 (0.1%)
Verduzzo Friulano	1.7 (0.2%)	1.8 (0.2%)	1.8 (0.2%)	1.6 (0.2%)	0.8 (0.1%)
Vernaccia San Gimignano	1.0 (0.1%)	1.0 (0.1%)	1.0 (0.1%)	0.7 (0.1%)	0.8 (0.1%)
Cesanese	5.4 (0.5%)	2.4 (0.2%)	2.2 (0.2%)	1.1 (0.2%)	0.7 (0.1%)
Traminer Aromatico	0.2 (0%)	0.3 (0%)	0.4 (0%)	0.6 (0.1%)	0.7 (0.1%)
Lagrein	1.0 (0.1%)	0.5 (0%)	0.4 (0%)	0.5 (0.1%)	0.6 (0.1%)
Marzemino	1.0 (0.1%)	1.0 (0.1%)	0.9 (0.1%)	1.0 (0.1%)	0.6 (0.1%)
Teroldego	1.0 (0.1%)	0.8 (0.1%)	0.5 (0.1%)	0.5 (0.1%)	0.6 (0.1%)
Malvasia del Lazio	7.5 (0.7%)	4.6 (0.4%)	4.0 (0.5%)	2.6 (0.4%)	0.6 (0.1%)
Ortrugo	0.2 (0%)	0.5 (0%)	0.4 (0%)	0.5 (0.1%)	0.6 (0.1%)
Bellone	10.6	5.5 (0.5%)	3.0 (0.3%)	1.5 (0.2%)	0.5 (0.1%)
Bonarda	4.0 (0.4%)	2.0 (0.2%)	1.9 (0.2%)	2.6 (0.4%)	0.5 (0.1%)
Lacrima	0.0 (0%)	0.2 (0%)	0.8 (0.1%)	0.7 (0.1%)	0.5 (0.1%)
Molinara	2.0 (0.2%)	1.8 (0.2%)	1.6 (0.2%)	1.3 (0.2%)	0.5 (0.1%)
Montu'	3.0 (0.3%)	2.0 (0.2%)	1.2 (0.2%)	1.1 (0.2%)	0.5 (0.1%)
Verduzzo Trevigiano	3.0 (0.3%)	2.5 (0.2%)	2.0 (0.2%)	1.7 (0.3%)	0.5 (0.1%)
Manzoni Bianco	0.0 (0%)	0.1 (0%)	0.1 (0%)	9.5 (1.4%)	0.4 (0.1%)
Durella	1.0 (0.1%)	1.0 (0.1%)	1.0 (0.1%)	0.7 (0.1%)	0.3 (0.1%)
Monica	6.9	6.2	6.0	2.9 (0.4%)	0.3 (0.1%)
Riesling	0.3 (0%)	0.3 (0%)	0.4 (0%)	0.6 (0.1%)	0.3 (0.1%)
Aleatico	2.0 (0.2%)	1.0 (0.1%)	0.6 (0.6%)	0.5 (0.1%)	0.2 (0%)
Colorino	1.1 (0.1%)	1.4 (0.1%)	0.4 (0%)	0.4 (0.1%)	0.2 (0%)
Greco Nero	4.1 (0.4%)	4.0 (0.4%)	3.0 (0.3%)	3.0 (0.3%)	0.2 (0%)
Malvasia Istriana	4.2 (0.4%)	1.5 (0.1%)	0.6 (0.1%)	0.5 (0.1%)	0.2 (0%)
Uva Rara	1.0 (0.1%)	0.6 (0.1%)	0.5 (0.1%)	0.6 (0.1%)	0.2 (0%)
Moscato Giallo	1.2 (0.1%)	1.1 (0.1%)	0.4 (0%)	0.4 (0.1%)	0.1 (0%)
Albarola	2.8	3.0 (0.3%)	4.0 (0.5%)	4.2	0.1 (0%)

Adapted from: Istituto Nazionale delle Statistiche (2010), Sixth General Census of Agriculture; G. Tempesta and M. Fiorillo (2011), *Patrimonio Varietale*, www.vivaioenotria.com.

TABLE 3
Rare Italian native grape varieties (in hectares)

Variety	1970	1990	2000	2010
Abbuoto	50	370	717	37
Aglianicone	–	240	160	25
Albanello	–	150	126	–
Albarenzeuli Bianco	–	30	76	–
Albarenzeuli Nero	–	9	42	–
Albarossa	–	–	9	87
Alionza	–	–	43	14
Arvesiniadu	60	80	156	17
Asprinio	620	230	413	171
Avana	90	70	58	11
Avarengo	30	40	1,679	–
Barbera Bianca	–	240	278	34
Barbera Sarda	–	530	335	17
Barsaglina	270	50	27	–
Bervedino	–	16	85	–
Bianchetta Trevigiana	1,070	190	66	–
Bianco d'Alessano	3,740	1,690	967	456
Biancolella	470	390	412	189
Biancone	780	340	100	–
Bombino Nero	5,158	2,003	1,168	596
Bonamico	1,187	150	106	–
Bosco	710	299	107	104
Bovale	1,620	1,380	600	120
Bracciola Nera	70	20	108	–
Caddiu	80	17	1,101	–
Cagnulari	760	10	318	254
Caloria	–	10	158	–
Canaiolo Nero	415	480	680	60
Canina Nera	940	310	320	16
Caricagìola	740	180	140	–
Carica l'Asino	–	10	301	–
Carricante	–	–	264	146
Castiglione	380	260	89	18
Catanese Nero	–	120	80	–
Clairette	–	20	150	–
Coda di Volpe Bianca	1,290	1,180	1,020	572

TABLE 3 (continued)

Variety	1970	1990	2000	2010
Colombana Nera	140	140	171	–
Cornalin	–	13	1	–
Damaschino	–	273	383	277
Dolciame	–	20	6	–
Doux d'Henry	–	17	27	–
Durasa	–	80	24	–
Empibotte	3,090	–	–	–
Enantio (Lambrusco a Foglia Frastagliata)	2,160	2,180	1,490	172
Erbaluce	240	243	341	287
Fertilia	–	6	14	–
Flavis	–	24	12	–
Foglia Tonda	40	38	42	–
Forastera	810	311	103	74
Fortana	8,530	2,181	1,110	492
Francavidda	550	220	10	–
Franconia	–	209	117	21
Frappato	710	792	785	803
Fumin	180	18	10	14
Gamay	–	159	95	–
Giro	–	551	63	–
Groppello di Mocasina	940	48	54	66
Groppello di Santo Stefano	210	32	10	–
Guarnaccia	460	300	33	30
Impigno	1,080	300	60	15
Invernenga	–	18	33	–
Lambrusca di Alessandria	1,210	203	920	15
Lambrusco Viadanese	1,170	350	456	600
Livornese Bianca	–	50	10	–
Lumassina	–	205	110	38
Maceratino	320	220	140	129
Maiolica	140	145	100	–
Malbec	–	266	38	–
Malbo Gentile	–	–	111	211
Malvasia di Casorzo	170	90	106	66
Malvasia di Lipari	180	121	133	112

(continued)

TABLE 3 *(continued)*

Variety	1970	1990	2000	2010
Malvasia di Schierano	80	95	180	75
Mammolo	1,100	61	147	–
Manzoni Bianco	–	169	322	–
Marsigliana Nera	–	109	210	–
Mayolet	–	25	10	–
Mazzese	350	132	98	–
Minnella Bianca	370	132	86	16
Montonico Bianco	1,490	1,120	810	82
Moscatello Selvatico	–	162	117	62
Moscato di Scanzo	–	138	70	42
Moscato di Terracina	900	260	250	63
Moscato Rosa	–	110	99	27
Nasco	120	170	170	11
Negrara Trentina	920	530	260	–
Negretto	1,200	940	310	71
Neretta Cuneese	1,600	600	410	144
Neretto di Bairo	350	149	59	15
Nero Buono	400	29	122	67
Neyret	40	35	80	–
Nieddera	–	47	59	–
Nieddu Mannu	–	353	41	–
Nocera	420	116	30	25
Nosiola	230	136	190	–
Notardomenico	–	13	10	–
Olivella	–	485	142	16
Ottavianello	2,240	729	280	42
Pagadebito	1,200	–	–	–
Pampanuto	–	817	290	250
Pascale	–	1,273	552	552
Passerina	–	769	695	–
Pavana	1,370	–	97	–
Pecorello	–	21	20	–
Pecorino	760	94	87	936
Pelaverga	–	113	28	–
Perricone	1,580	1,190	620	333
Petite Arvine	–	14	10	–

TABLE 3 *(continued)*

Variety	1970	1990	2000	2010
Petit Rouge	260	200	116	191
Picolit	50	196	90	–
Piculit Neri	–	–	133	–
Piedirosso	1,240	1,330	1,010	1,016
Pignola	140	83	90	–
Pignolo	–	30	20	–
Pinella	320	40	70	–
Plassa	70	22	43	–
Pollera Nera	–	141	73	–
Prié	–	70	–	–
Prie Blanc	–	7	40	45
Prie Rouge	–	30	20	–
Prodest	–	31	10	–
Prunesta Nera	320	150	96	34
Rebo	–	34	39	35
Retagliado Bianco	340	117	28	–
Rollo	70	1	10	–
Rossese	710	340	268	136
Rossignola	260	72	340	–
Rossola Nera	230	186	115	–
Ruché	–	109	46	123
San Giuseppe	–	54	380	–
San Lunare	10	11	20	–
Schioppettino	–	49	100	–
Sciascinoso	1,650	510	169	50
Semidano	–	96	40	–
Sgavetta	170	50	68	15
Susumaniello	610	76	70	58
Sylvaner	280	139	115	–
Tannat	–	–	45	26
Tazzelenghe	–	9	90	–
Timorasso	20	21	20	68
Torbato	10	131	143	136
Trebbiano Modenese	–	667	341	–
Trebbiano Spoletino	150	360	260	109
Trevisana Nera	–	18	36	–

(continued)

TABLE 3 *(continued)*

Variety	1970	1990	2000	2010
Turca	50	73	108	–
Uva Tosca	–	221	115	–
Veltliner	–	123	133	–
Verdea	1,330	–	151	57
Verdello	1,180	860	680	392
Verdisio	1,150	135	81	–
Vermentino Nero	480	189	180	–
Vernaccia di Oristano	2,260	1,210	580	48
Vernaccia Nera	–	262	141	–
Vespaiola	130	119	110	–
Vespolina	310	180	108	55
Viognier	–	–	28	1,262
Vien de Nus	170	76	33	51
Wildbacher	–	11	40	–

Adapted from: Istituto Nazionale delle Statistiche (2010), Sixth General Census of Agriculture; G. Tempesta and M. Fiorillo (2011), *Patrimonio Varietale*, www.vivaioenotria.com.

GLOSSARY

ACCESSION A single grapevine, or the one plant from a collection being examined.

ALLELE The form in which a gene presents itself. The degree of genetic diversity within and between populations depends on the assortment and distribution of alleles.

AMPELOGRAPHY The science that describes grape varieties via the use of drawings and/or photographs.

AMPELOLOGY The term that I, and other experts, believe ought to be used to describe the study of grapevines, instead of the still commonly used term ampelography. As the identification and description of grapevines today is arrived at by more than just drawn or photographic reproductions, but rather by a combination of morphologic, biochemical, cellular, and molecular biology data, ampelology is the more correct term by which to identify this specific branch of science.

ANTHOCYANIN The pigments typically associated with grapes and all higher plants. These are found mainly in grape skins, but can also be found in varying concentrations within the pulp of some grape varieties. Usually, the best wine grapes have colorless pulps. Anthocyanins are derived from molecules called anthocyanidins, which have a molecule of sugar attached that is cleaved to form anthocyanins. There are five major groups of anthocyanins in grapes: cyanins, petunins, peonins, malvins, and delphins. The presence and concentration of each relative to the others contributes to the intensity and tonality of color of both grapes and wines made with those grapes.

AVA (AMERICAN VITICULTURAL AREA) A specific grape-growing and wine production area in the United States, created along the lines of France's Appellation d'Origine Controlée (AOC) and Italy's Denominazione di Origine Controllata (DOC). The AVAs are federally recognized and determined on the basis of geographic characteristics. Unlike European versions, AVAs do not include guidelines or requirements as to types of grapes used or maximum allowed yields of the wines produced there.

BIOTYPE A grapevine that though genetically identical to others, presents enough morphologic and behavioral diversity to be viewed as a separate subvariety of the same family. Unfortunately, in Italy's National Registry, biotypes are not yet officially recognized or described as such, though it appears that this will become a necessary step in the future.

CLONAL SELECTION The process by which farmers and wine producers propagate those individuals in their vineyards that have the desired characteristics. These positive attributes (such as generous yields or disease resistance) change over time: whereas in the nineteenth century it was more important for growers to identify and reproduce high-yielding varieties, today lower-yielding cultivars and biotypes are preferred.

CLONE A cell or individual genetically identical to another, and derived from one cell or individual (plant or animal) without fertilization or by asexual reproduction. All cells or individuals born out of this process are completely identical and indistinguishable, genetically, morphologically, and biochemically from the mother plant.

CULTIVAR A cultivated grape variety; any variety that is grown by human beings.

DOC (DENOMINAZIONDE DI ORIGINE CONTROLLATA) A specific, limited grape growing and wine production area in Italy. In order to make a DOC wine it is not sufficient to just grow grapes within the boundaries of the government-identified geographic area, but also to abide by strict legal requirements addressing grape varieties allowed or not, maximum yields, vinification methods, minimum aging requirements, and more. Those who grow grapes within a DOC but do not follow the other guidelines (for example, a producer may choose to use a *Moscato* variety that is not included in the list of grape varieties allowed in that DOC) may not call the resulting wines a DOC wine.

DOCG (DENOMINAZIONE DI ORIGINE CONTROLLATA E GARANTITA) A step above DOC in Italy's hierarchy of wines. In order for a wine to merit DOCG status, all the requirements of the DOC have to be met; in addition, DOCG wines undergo two different tasting panel assessments by government-named experts such as winemakers and viticulturalists who determine that the wine is true to type. Therefore the "guarantee" in the DOCG name refers to this aspect of conformity to expectations and not to the wine's quality; in fact, there are many DOCG wines made by growing grapes in the right place and by following all the rules that are less than stellar in quality because those who make them are not particularly talented.

ER Emilia-Romagna, one of Italy's twenty regions, located in the central part of the country, just above Tuscany. It is the home of the world-famous *Lambrusco* varieties.

FVG Friuli Venezia Giulia, one of Italy's twenty regions, located in the northeast corner of the country, on the border with Austria, Slovenia, and Croatia. Generally considered to be Italy's best source of white wines made from native and local, non-Germanic grape varieties.

GENE A specific nucleotide sequence of the DNA coding for protein or RNA production.

GENOTYPE The specific genetic material and makeup of an individual.

GERMPLASM The total number of genes and cytoplasmic factors that govern heredity in individuals and species.

GRAND CRU A specific plot of high-quality land, from which better than average wines are made. When the quality of the vineyard spot is less exceptional, it can be referred to as a *premier cru* These terms were born in France, where the classification of wine and vineyard quality was studied centuries ago.

GRAPEVINE FANLEAF VIRUS DISEASE The oldest-known virus disease of grapevines, and also one of the most serious grapevine virus diseases worldwide. The disease brings about deleterious morphologic changes and has detrimental effects on yield, grape quality, and longevity of grapevines.

GRAPE LEAFROLL DISEASE Grapevine disease associated with at least ten different viruses (named GLRaV-1 through GLRaV-10, based on the order of their discovery). Affected grapevines will be less vigorous, and will produce much less than unaffected grapevines.

HECTARES Unit of land measurement used in Europe. One hectare is equivalent to 2.47 acres.

HOMONYMS Different varieties that have been erroneously given the same name.

IGT (INDICAZIONE GEOGRAFICA TIPICA) An important category of wines in Italy that allows producers a bit more freedom than the strict DOC and DOCG requirements. An IGT wine must be made using 85 percent grapes grown within a specific area (areas that are always much larger than those identified as DOC or DOCG), but the other 15 percent can come from just about anywhere. The wine also has to smell and taste of typical wines made in the area, but more leeway is allowed with this category than in the others. Some of Italy's best wines are IGTs. Interestingly, in Valle d'Aosta, which is a bilingual Italian-French region, the term IGT can be replaced by the term *Vin de Pays*, while in the province of Bolzano in Alto Adige, a bilingual Italian-German area, the term *Landweine* can be used in place of IGT.

INTRAVARIETAL VARIABILITY The condition by which the same grape looks different in distinct areas via adaptation to diverse selection pressures, diverse environmental conditions, and viral diseases. Intravarietal variability is responsible for biotypes.

MASSAL SELECTION Selection of mother plants for propagation by choosing the plants that look the best and give desired characteristics.

MICROSATELLITE ANALYSIS Currently the most important method by which grape varieties are identified. Microsatellite analysis recognizes specific areas of a grape variety's genome, usually short, simple repeats of the genome that occur in the same place of the genome within members of the same variety and not others. It is commonly used in studies addressing identification, parentage, and population issues. It has limitations and should always be used in combination with ampelographic methods.

MILLERANDAGE Condition when grape clusters ripen unevenly, with some clusters fully ripe and others very underripe, or when some grapes within a cluster are fully ripe and others underripe.

MONOVARIETAL WINE Wine made with 100 percent of a single variety. For the purposes of this book, monovarietal and "pure" are used interchangeably.

MUTATION A permanent genetic change involving some part of the DNA molecule.

NATIONAL REGISTRY OF GRAPE VARIETIES Italy's official, government-determined list of grape varieties; it includes wine grapes, table grapes, special destination grapes, and those used as a source of rootstocks. It is updated every year by the Ministry of Agriculture (the Ministero per le Politiche Agricole, Alimentari e Forestali) with the academic and practical help of the viticultural research center in Conegliano (Centro Ricerche Agricoltura-Viticoltura, or CRA-VIT). The registry is an official requirement instituted by the European Union in 1968 for each of its member countries: not only do all these registries need to identify and list all the officially recognized grape varieties present in the country, but to also provide precise morphologic, viticultural, and genetic data on each variety. Only those varieties that have been sufficiently studied and proven to be distinct and found in homogenous populations may be listed.

OIDIUM A common grapevine disease also known as powdery mildew. It can cause small, decrepit-looking berries and off-flavors in wine. Powdery mildew also reduces the resistance of table grapes.

OIV (ORGANIZATION INTERNATIONALE DE LA VIGNE ET DU VIN) The International Organization of Vine and Wine, formerly the International Vine and Wine Office, was founded in 2001. It is an intergovernmental association that encourages and supports bench and field research, and promotes grape growing, wine production, and wine marketing in member countries.

PERONOSPORA A common grapevine disease also known as downy mildew. It affects the leaves, fruit, and shoots of grapevines, causing decreased berry production and production of poor-quality wine.

PHENOTYPE What an individual looks like, or the observed characteristics of an organism, which are the result of the interactions between genotype and environment.

PHYLLOXERA An aphid that feeds on the roots of European grapevines and kills them. It arrived in Europe from the United States toward the end of the nineteenth century and destroyed most of the continent's vineyards; only those grapevines planted on very sandy or volcanic soils and in cold, high mountain environments, where the aphid cannot live, managed to survive. European wine production was saved by grafting European grapevines onto American grapevine rootstocks, the roots (but only the roots) of which are immune to the parasite. Previously known as *Phylloxera devastatrix* (an apt name), it was renamed *Viteus vitifoliae;* its current scientific name is *Dactylosphaera vitifolia*. However, use of the phylloxera name is so engrained that the new name is rarely if ever used outside scientific circles. Pre-phylloxera vines are those still with their original European rootstock, but such plants are rare and limited to the specific habitats mentioned previously.

POLYPHENOL Micronutrients found in nature (for example, in vegetables and fruits) that have a positive effect in fighting diseases and the aging processes of cells, organs, and organisms; better known as antioxidants. Though the exact effects of dietary polyphenols are hard to judge for a variety of reasons, it appears that a regular dietary intake of these molecules is linked to lower incidences of many unhealthy conditions, including cardiovascular disease, various cancers, and Alzheimer's disease. The best known polyphenol molecules in grapes and wines are tannins and anthocyanins, but there are many more.

QUINTAL A common unit of mass in Europe, equal to one hundred kilograms.

SSR (SIMPLE SEQUENCE REPEAT) A synonym of microsatellite.

SUBVARIETY Different-looking individuals of the same species: for example, one might say that a black-coated jaguar is a subvariety of jaguar, an animal more commonly associated with a yellow, spotted fur. In the realm of wine grapes, subvarieties are more correctly called biotypes, individuals that are considered to be genetically identical (at the current state of scientific knowledge) but show obvious phenotypic differences.

SYNONYMS Grape varieties with identical genotypes that are known, erroneously, under different names.

TERPENE Unsaturated hydrocarbons (more rarely called isoprenes), commonly found in the plant kingdom. In grapes, it is the alcohol derivatives of terpenes (more correctly called terpenoids) that are most common; they are aromatic molecules responsible for many of the floral and spicy aromas that characterize certain grapes and wines, such as the *Moscato*s.

BIBLIOGRAPHY

Acanti, A. 1754. *Il Roccolo.* Venezia: Stamperia Pezzana.

Acerbi, G. 1825. *Delle viti italiane ossia materiali per servire alla classificazione, monografia e sinonimia, preceduti dal tentativo di una classificazione delle viti.* Milano: G. Silvestri.

Agazzotti, F. 1867. *Catalogo descrittivo delle principali varietà di uve coltivate presso il cav. Avv. Francesco Aggazzotti del Colombaro.* Modena: Tipografia Carlo Vincenzi.

Agostinetti, G. (1679) 1988. *Cento e dieci ricordi che fanno il buon fattor di villa.* Reprint edited by U. Bernardi. Vicenza: Neri Pozza Editore.

Alonso de Herrera, G. (1593) 1790. *Agricultura General.* Madrid: Don Josef de Urrutia.

Angelini, U., A. Costacurta, S. Cancellier, G. Segattini, and C. Farina. 1980. "Vecchi vitigni veronesi." *Rivista di Viticoltura e di Enologia* (Conegliano), supplement Ottobre.

Antonacci, D. 2004. *I vitigni dei vini di Puglia.* Martina Franca: Edizioni Pugliesi.

Aradhya, M.K., G.S. Dangl, B.H. Prins, J.M. Boursiquot, M.A. Walker, C.P. Meredith, and C.J. Simon. 2003. "Genetic structure and differentiation in cultivated grape, *Vitis vinifera* L." *Genetical Research* 81, 179–82.

Arapitsas, P., D Perenzoni, G. Nicolini, and F. Mattivi. 2012. "Study of Sangiovese wines pigment profile by UHPLC-MS/MS." *Journal of Agricultural and Food Chemistry* 60(42): 10461–71.

Arcuri, R., and E. Casoria. 1883. *L'Agricoltura Meridionale* (Portici) 6(22).

Arroyo-García R., L. Ruiz-García, L. Bolling, R. Ocete, M.A. López, C. Arnold, A. Ergul, G. Söylemezoğlu, H.I. Uzun, F. Cabello, J. Ibáñez, M.K. Aradhya, A. Atanassov, I. Atanassov, S. Balint, J.L. Cenis, L. Costantini, S. Goris-Lavets, M.S. Grando, B.Y. Klein, P.E. McGovern, D. Merdinoglu, I. Pejic, F. Pelsy, N. Primikirios, V. Risovannaya, K.A. Roubelakis-Angelakis, H. Snoussi, P. Sotiri, S. Tamhankar, P. This, L. Troshin, J.M. Malpica, F. Lefort, and J.M. Martinez-Zapater. 2006. "Multiple origins of cultivated grapevine (*Vitis vinifera* L. ssp. *sativa*) based on chloroplast DNA polymorphisms." *Molecular Ecology* 15(12): 3707–14.

Avise, J.C. 1994. *Molecular markers, natural history and evolution.* New York: Chapman and Hall.

———. 2000. *Phylogeography: The history and formation of species.* Cambridge: Harvard University Press.

Babo, A.W., and E. Mach. 1923. "Wein Wissenschaft." In *Handbuch des Weinbaues und der Keller-Wirstschaft,* 61–69. Berlin: Paul Parley.

Bachechi, E. 2008. "Contributo alla conoscenza di tre antichi vitigni toscani: Grand Noir, Giacomino, Canina Nera." Tesi di laurea, Università degli Studi di Pisa.

Baldini, E. 1995. *Giorgio Gallesio: I giornali dei viaggi.* Trascrizione, note e commento di Enrico Baldini. Firenze: Nuova Stamperia Parenti.

Bandinelli, R., M. Borselli, E. Masi, A. Materazzi, and E. Triolo. 2004. "Selezione clonale del Mammolo e Vermentino bianco." In *Miglioramento qualitativo delle produzioni vitivinicole e* del materiale di propagazione. Firenze: Quaderno ARSIA 1.

Bandinelli R., M. Di Cesari, L. Ceseri, L. Pieragnoli, and M. Boselli. 2005. "Obbiettivi e risultati della ricerca condotta dall'Università di Firenze per la valorizzazione dei vitigni autoctoni." 2nd Forum Internazionale sugli autoctoni. Vitigni e Vini. Salone del Vino, Torino, 25–30 Ottobre.

Barba, M., G. Di Lernia, G. Chiota, F. Carimi, A. Carra, and L. Abbate. 2008. "Recuperare i vitigni autoctoni grazie al risanamento dai virus." *L'Informatore Agrario, Supplemento Sicilia: Innovazione Agroalimentare* 10: 14.

Barpo, G. B. 1634. *Delizie e frutti dell'agricoltura e della villa, libri tre.* Venezia: Sarzina.

Barresi, S., S. Foti, A. Gabbrielli, E. Iachello, E. Magnano di San Lio, and P. Sessa. 2003. *La Sicilia del Vino.* Catania: Giuseppe Maimone Editore.

Basso, M. 1982. "Uve." In *Agrumi, frutta e uve nella Firenze di Bartolomeo Bimbi pittore mediceo,* 137–57. Firenze: F. & F. Parretti Grafiche.

Bazzocchi, A. 1923. *Ampelografia dei vitigni romagnoli.* Forlì: Premiata Cooperativa Tipografica Forlivese.

Belfrage, N. 1999. *Barolo to Valpolicella: The wines of northern Italy.* London: Faber and Faber.

———. 2001. *Brunello to Zibibbo: The wines of Tuscany, Central and Southern Italy.* London: Faber and Faber.

Benin, M., J. Gasquez, A. Mahfoudi, and R. Bessis. 1988. "Caracterisation biochimique des cepages de Vitis vinifera par electrophoresis d'isoenzymes foliares: Essai de classification des varieties." *Vitis* 27: 157–72.

Bergamini, C., A. R. Caputo, M. Gasparro, R. Perniola, M. F. Cardone, and D. Antonacci. 2013. "Evidences for an alternative genealogy of Sangiovese." *Molecular Biotechnology* 53(3): 278–88.

Bergamini, G., and P. Novajra. 2000. "Picolit, oro del friuli." In *Vino e territorio.* Udine: Regione Friuli Venezia Giulia.

Berger, R. G. 2007. *Flavours and fragrances: Chemistry, bioprocessing and sustainability.* Berlin: Springer-Verlag.

Berget, A. 1904. "Rouge du Valais." In *Ampélographie,* edited by P. Viala and V. Vermorel. Paris: Masson.

Berta, P. S., and G. Mainardi. 1997. *Storia regionale della vite e del vino in Italia: Regione Piemonte.* Milan: Edizione Unione Italiana Vini.

Bertani G. B. 1886. "Lavori eseguiti nella Commissione Ampelografica di Verona: Primi studi ampelografici fatti in quel di Caprino e di Bardolino." *Bollettino Ampelografico* 16: 168.

Biagini, B., ed. 2011. *Origini della viticoltura.* Paper presented at the conference Le Origini della Viticultura. Podere Forte, Castiglione d'Orcia, Italy, April 2–3. Castiglione d'Orcia: Podere Forte.

Bianchi G. 1893. "I vitigni e vini della Basilicata." *Annuario generale per la viticoltura e l'enologia* (Roma) 2: 62–73.

Biasi, R., E. Brunori, I. Ceccariglia, and F. Botti. 2010. "Il sistema vigneto del Lago di Bolsena: Caratterizzazione della produzione della Cannaiola di Marta." In *Proceedings VIII International Terroir Congress,* 165–70. Vol. 2. Conegliano Veneto: CRA-VIT.

Bich, L. N. 1896. *Monographie des cèpages de la Vallée d'Aoste et leurs systèmes de culture.* Aoste: Imprimerie L. Mensio.

Bigliazzi, J., M. Scali, E. Paolucci, M. Cresti, and R. Vignani. 2012. "DNA extracted with optimized protocols can be genotyped to reconstruct the varietal composition of monovarietal wines." *American Journal of Enology and Viticulture* 63: 568–73.

Boccacci, P., D. Torello Marinoni, G. Gambino, R. Botta, and A. Schneider. 2005. "Genetic characterization of endangered grape cultivars of Reggio Emilia Province." *American Journal of Enology and Viticulture* 56(4): 411–16.

Bollettino del Comizio Agrario di Vicenza. (1868a) 2004. "Relazione sommaria sullo stato attuale dell'Agricoltura vicentina." Anno I, fasc. 3. In *Recupero, conservazione e valorizzazione del germoplasma viticolo Veneto.* Legnaro: Azienda Regionale Veneto Agricoltura.

———. (1868b) 2004. "Quali vitigni debbansi preferire per piantare le nostre vigne." Anno I, fasc. 5. In *Recupero, conservazione e valorizzazione del germoplasma viticolo Veneto.* Legnaro: Azienda Regionale Veneto Agricoltura.

———. (1868c) 2004. "Osservazioni sulla sinonimia delle viti vicentine." Anno I, fasc. 9. In *Recupero, conservazione e valorizzazione del germoplasma viticolo Veneto.* Legnaro: Azienda Regionale Veneto Agricoltura.

Bondi, M. 2009. "Caratterizzazione ampelografia, ampelometrica, molecolare e valutazione qualitativa del vitigno Spergola nelle colline di Scandiano." Tesi di laurea, Università degli Studi di Modena e Reggio Emilia.

Bonghi, C., G. Cargnello, F. Ziliotto, F. M. Rizzini, G. Teo, L. Veilleux, G. Cecchetto, E. Serafin, L. Pezza, G. Gallo, and M. Pancot. 2006. "Evoluzione di parametri produttivi, sensoriali, biochimici e molecolari in uve della cv Raboso Piave sottoposte alla doppia maturazione ragionata ed alla vendemmia tardiva." Paper presented at 3rd Convegno Nazionale di Viticoltura (CONAVI), Sessione 1, Biologia, fisiologia, adattamento agli stress biotici ed abiotici. San Michele all'Adige, 5–9 July.

Bordignon S. 1964. "Greco." In *Principali vitigni ad uva da vino coltivati in Italia. Vol. 3*. Roma: Ministero dell'Agricoltura e delle Foreste.

———. 1965. *Principali vitigni ad uva da vino coltivati in Italia, 18*. Vol. 4. Roma: Ministero dell'Agricoltura e delle Foreste. See esp. "Falanghina," "Biancolella," and "Sciascinoso."

Borgo, M., A. Cartechini, L. Lovat, and G. Moretti. 2004. "Nuove selezioni clonali dei vitigni umbri." *Vignevini* 31(5): 73–80.

Borrego J., M. T. Rodriguez, J. P. Martin, J. Chavez, F. Cabello, and J. Ibañez. 2001. "Characterization of the most important Spanish grape varieties through isoenzyme and micro satellite analysis." *Acta Horticulturae* 546: 371–75.

Boselli, M., C. Corso, and A. Monaco. 2000. "Ampelographic characterization of white grape varieties in Campania (Southern Italy) by multivariate analysis." *Acta Horticulturae* 528(1): 75–84.

Boselli, M., C. Iannini, C. Corso, A. Monaco, D. Iannelli, and C. Cottone. 2000. "Analysis of variability in the Aglianico grapevine (Vitis vinifera) in Campania." *Acta Horticulturae* 528(1): 45–50.

Boselli, M., and A. Venturi. 1993. "Descrizione ampelografica di alcune varietà coltivate in Emilia Romagna." *Vignevini* 5: 55–60.

Botta, R., A. Akkak, and A. Schneider. 1999. "Caratterizzazione di Moscati in collezione a Canelli mediante marcatori molecolari: Analisi di sinonimie, omonimie e relazioni di parentela." Paper presented at Convegno Il Moscato alle soglie del 2000, Canelli, I, 6–7 November.

Botta, R., A. Schneider, A. Akkak, N. S. Scott, and M. R. Thomas. 2000. "Within cultivar grapevine variability studied by morphometrical and molecular marker based techniques." *Acta Horticulturae* 528(1): 91–96.

Botta, R., N. S. Scott, I. Eynard, and M. R. Thomas. 1995. "Evaluation of microsatellite sequence-tagged site markers for characterizing Vitis vinifera cultivars." *Vitis* 34(2): 99–102.

Bourdieu, P. 1986. "The forms of capital," translated by Richard Nice, 241–58. In *Handbook of theory for the sociology of education*, edited by J. E. Richardson. Westport, CT: Greenwood Press.

Bowcock, A. M., A. Ruiz-Linares, J. Tomfohrde, E. Minch, J. R. Kidd, and L. L. Cavalli-Sforza. 1994. "High resolution of human evolutionary trees with polymorphic microsatellites." *Nature* 368: 455–57.

Bowers, J. E., G. S. Dangl, and C. P. Meredith. 1999. "Development and characterization of additional microsatellite DNA markers for grape." *American Journal of Enology and Viticulture* 50: 243–46.

Bowers, J. E., G. S. Dangl, R. Vignani, and C. P. Meredith. 1996. "Isolation and characterization of new polymorphic simple sequence repeat loci in grape (*Vitis vinifera* L.)." *Genome* 39(4): 628–33.

Bowers, J. E., and C. P. Meredith. 1997. "The parentage of a classic wine grape, Cabernet Sauvignon." *Nature Genetics* 16: 84–87.

Bowers, J. E., R. Siret, and C. P. Meredith. 2000. "A single pair of parents proposed for a group of grapevine varieties in Northeastern France." *Acta Horticulturae* 528(1): 129–32.

Branzanti, E., L. Brancadoro, A. Scienza, G. Fichera, and G. Raiti. 2010. "Genotypic and phenotypic characterization of *Nerello mascalese* and *Nerello cappuccio*." Paper presented at Third International Congress of Mountain Viticulture, 12–14 May.

Branzanti, E., C. Maitti, A. Scienza, L. Brancadoro, R. Di Lorenzo, G. Fichera, R. Bonsignore, R. Di Giovanni, G. Raiti, and F. Trovato. 2007. "Individuati numerosi biotipi di Nerello Mascalese." Supplemento Sicilia, *Informatore Agrario* 11: 18.

Braudel, F. 1979. *Afterthoughts on material civilization and capitalism*, translated by P. M. Ranum. Baltimore: Johns Hopkins University Press.

Brescia, M. A., V. Caldarola, A. De Gilio, D. Benedetti, F. P. Fanizzi, and A. Sacco. 2002. "Characterization of the geographical origin of Italian red wines based on traditional and nuclear magnetic resonance spectrometric determinations." *Analytica Chimica Acta* 458: 177–86.

Brescia, M. A., M. Monfreda, A. Buccolieri, and C. Carrino. 2005. "Characterization of the geographical origin of buffalo milk and mozzarella cheese by means of analytical and spectroscopic determinations." *Food Chemistry* 89(1): 139–47.

Breviglieri, N., and E. Casini. 1964. "Riordinamento ampelografico in Toscana." In *Vitigni ed uve da vino per i futuri impianti, Accademia Italiana della vite e del vino*, 35–41. Treviso: Atti. Vol. 17.

———. 1965. *Sangiovese*. Treviso: Longo e Coppelli.

Brickell, C. D., B. R. Baum, W. L. A. Hetterscheid, A. C. Leslie, J. McNeill, P. Trehane, F. Vrugtman, and J. H. Wiersema. 2004. "International code for nomenclature of cultivated plants: Code international de nomenclature pour les plantes cultivées." *ISHS Acta Horticulturae* 647.

Bruni, B. 1962. *Principali vitigni da vino coltivati in Italia*. Vol. 2. Roma: Ministero Agricultura e Foreste. See esp. "Albaranzeuli Bianco," "Montepulciano," "Pascale," "Nuragus," "Verdicchio Bianco," and "Vernaccia Nera."

Bruni, B., N. Breviglieri, and E. Casini. 1952–62. "Vernaccia di Oristano." In *Principali vitigni da vino coltivati in Italia*. Vol. 2. Roma: Ministero Agricultura e Foreste. Treviso: Arti Grafiche Longo e Zoppelli.

Bucelli, P., E. Egger, V. Faviere, F. Giannetti, M. Pierucci, A. Piracci, and P. Storchi. 1999. "Valutazione viticola ed enologica di vitigni a bacca bianca di più recente introduzione in Toscana: Incrocio Manzoni 6.0.13, Sauvignon b. e Fiano." *Rivista di Viticoltura e Enologia* 2: 31–39.

Buhner Zaharieva, T., S. Moussaoui, M. Lorente, J. Andreu, R. Nuñez, J. M. Ortiz, and Y. Gorgorcena. 2010. "Preservation and molecular characterization of ancient varieties in Spanish germplasm collections." *American Journal of Viticulture and Enology* 61(4): 557–62.

Bulfon, E., R. Forti, and G. Zuliani. 1987. *Dalle colline spilimberghesi nuove viti e nuovi vini*. Pordenone: Amministrazione Provinciale Pordenone.

Cabezas J. A., M. T. Cervera, R. Arroyo-García, J. Ibáñez, I. Rodríguez-Torres, J. Borrego, F. Cabello, and J. M. Martínez-Zapater. 2003. "Garnacha and Garnacha Tintorera: Genetic relationships and the origin of teinturier varieties cultivated in Spain." *American Journal of Enology and Viticulture* 54: 237–45.

Cain, A. J. 1959. "The post-Linnaean development of Taxonomy." *Proceedings of the Linnean Society of London* 170(3): 234–44.

Calò A., and A. Costacurta. 1991. *Delle viti in Friuli*. Udine: Arti Grafiche Friulane.

Calò, A., A. Costacurta, S. Cancellier, M. Crespan, N. Milani, R. Carraro, M. Giust, E. Sartori, F. Anaclerio, R. Forti, L. Ciprian, R. Di Stefano, R. Pigella, S. Bottero, and N. Gentilini. 2000. *Delle viti Prosecche*. Pordenone: Libra Edizioni.

Calò, A., A. Costacurta, S. Cancellier, and R. Forti. 1991. "Verdicchio bianco, Trebbiano di Soave: Un unico vitigno." *Vignevini* 11: 49–52.

Calò, A., A. Costacurta, R. Carraro, and M. Crespan. 2004. "Identità e caratterizzazione di antichi vitigni italiani: Fiani, aglianici, aglianiconi e ciliegiolo." *L'Enologo* 40(5): 89–94.

Calò, A., A. Costacurta, M. Crespan, N. Milani, L. Aggio, R. Carraro, and R. Di Stefano. 2001. *La caratterizzazione dei Fiani: Fiano e Fiano aromatico*. Conegliano: Acc. Italiana Vite e Vino.

Calò, A., A. Costacurta, G. Paludetti, G. Calò, G. Aruselsekar, and D. Parfitt. 1989. "The use of isoenzymes to characterize grape cultivars." *Rivista di Viticoltura e di Enologia* 1: 15–22.

Calò, A., A. Costacurta, G. Paludetti, M. Crespan, M. Giusti, E. Egger, A. Grasselli, P. Storchi, D. Borsa, and R. Di Stefano. 1995. "Characterization of biotypes of Sangiovese as basis for clonal selection." Paper presented at International Symposium on clonal selection. ASEV, Portland, Oregon, 21–22 June.

Calò, A., Paronetto, L., and G. P. Rorato. 1996. *Storia regionale della vite e del vino in Italia: Veneto*. Milano: Unione Italiana Vini.

Calò, A., A. Scienza, and A. Costacurta. 2001 and 2006. *Vitigni d'Italia*. Bologna: Calderini Edagricole.

Campostrini, F., L. De Micheli, M. Bogoni, and A. Scienza. 1995. "Study of Sangiovese ecotypes as a tool for new strategies for clonal selection." In *Proceedings of the International Symposium on Clonal Selection*, edited by J. M. Rantz. Davis, CA: American Society for Enology and Viticulture.

Cancellier, S., and U. Angelini. 1993. "Corvina Corvinone: Due varietà diverse." *Vignevini* 5: 44–46.

Cancellier S., A. Coletti, M. Coletti, S. Soligo, and E. Michelet. 2007. "Quattro nuovi vitigni per la viticoltura Veneta." *Quaderni di viticoltura ed enologia dell'università di Torino* 29: 5–25.

Cancellier, S., P. Giacobbi, A. Coletti, S. Soligo, E. Michelet, M. Coletti, and A. Stocco. 2003. *Vecchi vitigni del Veneto*. Legnaro: Veneto Agricoltura.

Cancellier, S., S. Giannetto, and M. Crespan. 2009. "Groppello di Breganze e Pignola sono lo stesso vitigno." *Rivista di Viticoltura e Enologia* 62(2/3): 3–9.

Candussio, R. 1977. "Sì, esiste e sopravvive il Picolit nero." *Il Vino* 7(4).

Caparra, P. 1921. "La ricostruzione dei vigneti a Cirò e i criteri da seguire." Tesi di laurea, Regia Scuola Superiore di Agricoltura, Portici.

Capucci, C. 1954. "La vite Maligia (osservazioni e ricerche)." *Rivista di frutticoltura* 16(3): 81–111.

Caputo, A. R., M. L. Brini, M. Gasparro, R. A. Milella, L. R. Forleo, R. Pepe, and D. Antonacci. 2008. "Fiano, fiano minutolo e fiano rosa: Sinonimie e/o varietà diverse?" Paper presented at the 31st Congresso Mondiale OIV 2008, Verona, 15–20 June.

Cara, A. 1909. *Schizzo di vocabolarietto ampelografico comprendente le varietà di vite coltivate in Sardegna*. Cagliari: Serreli.

Carastro, V., J. Cricco, R. Bonsignore, G. Fichera, G. Cappadonna, G. Raiti, P. Di Giovanni, F. Trovato, G. Pulvirenti, F. Lo Presti, P. Scalisi, V. Falco, G. Ansaldi, G. Fici, A. Parrinello, M. Squadrito, F. Amato, G. Marino, M. Perciabosco, A. Drago, L. Pasotti, G. Dimino, A. Scienza, and O. Failla. 2010. "Phenology and ripening profiles of Nerello mascalese and Carricante in Etna DOC area." Paper presented at the Terzo Congresso Internazionale sulla Viticoltura di Montagna (CERVIM), Castiglione di Sicilia, Sicily, Italy, 12–14 May.

Carimi, F., F. Mercati, L. Abbate, and F. Sunseri. 2010. "Microsatellite analyses for evaluation of genetic diversity among Sicilian grapevine cultivars." *Genetic Resources and Crop Evolution* 57(5): 703–19.

Carlucci, M. 1905–9. "Fiano, Greco, Coda di Volpe." In *Traité général de viticulture: Ampelographie*, edited by P. Vialà and V. Vermorel. Paris: Masson et Cie. Vol. 6.

Carpenè, A., and A. Vianello. 1874. *La vite e il vino in Provincia di Treviso*. Roma: Loescher.

Cartechini, A., and G. Moretti. 1989. "Verdello." In *Principali vitigni da vino coltivati in Italia. Nuova serie, Vol. 1*. Conegliano Veneto: Ministero dell'Agricoltura e delle Foreste.

Carusi, D. 1879. "Viti coltivate nella provincia di Benevento." Ministero Agricoltura, Industria e Commercio. *Bullettino Ampelografico* 10.

Caruso, M., F. Galgano, M. A. Castiglione Morelli, L. Viggiani, L. Lencioni, B. Giussani, and F. Favati. 2012. "Chemical profile of white wines produced from 'Greco bianco' grape variety in different Italian areas by nuclear magnetic resonance (NMR) and conventional physicochemical analyses." *Journal of Agricultural and Food Chemistry* 60(1): 7–15.

Catalano, V., A. Cersosimo, and L. Stramaglia. 1989. "Malvasia nera di Basilicata." In *Principali vitigni da vino coltivati in Italia. Nuova serie, Vol. 2*. Conegliano Veneto: Ministero dell'Agricoltura e delle Foreste.

Catalogo ed illustrazione dei prodotti primitivi del suolo e delle industrie della Provincia di Vicenza offerte alla pubblica mostra nel Palazzo del Museo Civico il 25 agosto 1855. Vicenza: Eredi Paroni. http://biodiversita.provincia.vicenza.it/pagstor/h_rossignola.html.

Caudana, A., L. Rolle, and V. Gerbi. 2009. "Nuove tecniche di vinificazione per la valorizzazione del Freisa." *Vino e Tecnica* 3: 24–26.

Cavalli Sforza, L. L., P. Menozzi, and A. Piazza. 1994. *The History and Geography of Human Genes*. Princeton, NJ: Princeton University Press.

Cavazza, D. 1904. "Albana nera." *L'Italia agricola: Giornale di agricoltura*. Milano-Piacenza-Bologna: Marchesotti e Porta.

———. 1914. *Viticoltura*. Torino: Unione Tipografico-Editrice Torinese.

Cercone, F. 2000. *La meravigliosa storia del Montepulciano d'Abruzzo*. Rocca San Giovanni: Amaltea Editore.

Cettolini, S. 1897. *Annuario per gli anni scolastici 1893–94 e 1894–95 della Regia Scuola di Viticoltura ed Enologia di Cagliari*. Vol. 3. Bari: Editore Laterza.

Cettolini, S., and I. Mameli. 1933. *I vini tipici della Sardegna*. Cagliari: Valdes.

Chieppa, G., R. Lovino, M. Savino, P. Limosani, S. Suriano, G. Ceci, and R. Scazzariello. 2008. "Pampanuto: Influenza delle principali tecnologie prefermentative sulla qualità del vino." Paper presented at the 31st Congresse Mondiale OIV, Verona, 15–20 June.

Cinelli, O. 1884. *La cantina sperimentale di Viterbo*. Bologna: Società Tipografica.

Cipriani, G., G. Frazza, E. Peterlunger, and R. Testolin. 1994. "Grapevine fingerprinting using microsatellite repeats." *Vitis* 33: 211–15.

Cipriani, G., A. Spadotto, I. Jurman, G. Di Gaspero, M. Crespan, S. Meneghetti, E. Frare, R. Vignani, M. Cresti, M. Morgante, M. Pezzotti, E. Pe, A. Policriti, and R. Testolin. 2010. "The SSR-based molecular profile of 1005 grapevine (*Vitis vinifera* L.) accessions uncovers new synonymy and parentages, and reveals a large admixture amongst varieties of different geographic origin." *Theoretical and Applied Genetics* 121: 1569–85.

Cirigliano, P. 2012. "The Guarnaccino, an autochthonous grape of Basilicata, Italy." Paper presented at the Thirty-fifth World Congress of Vine and Wine, Izmir, Turkey, 18–22 June.

Coletta, A., M. Crespan, A. Costacurta, A. R. Caputo, C. Taurisano, S. Meneghetti, and D. Antonacci. 2006. "Preliminary investigations on Malvasia nera di Lecce and Malvasia nera di Brindisi varieties." *Rivista di Viticoltura e Enologia* 2/3: 51–56.

Comizio Agrario di Conegliano. (1870) 2008. *Ampelografia Generale della Provincia di Treviso*. Castelfranco Veneto: Verdeservizi.

Comizio Agrario di Forlì. (1877) 2008. *Le macchine e le uve alla mostra ampelografica di Forlì*. Forlì: Febo Gherardi Editore.

Coombe, B. G., and P. G. Iland. 1987. "Grape berry development." In *Proceedings of the Sixth Australian Wine Industry Conference*, 50–54, edited by T. H. Lee. Adelaide: Australian Industrial Publisher.

Cosmo, I. 1959. "Vitigni ad uva da vino per i futuri impianti delle Venezie, Emilia e Lombardia." *Annali Stazione Sperimentale di Viticoltura e Enologia* (Conegliano) 19.

Cosmo, I., and M. Polsinelli. 1960. *Principali vitigni da vino coltivati in Italia*. Vol. 1. Roma: Ministero dell'Agricoltura e delle Foreste. See esp. "Corvina" and "Prosecco."

———. 1962. "Lambrusche." In *I principali vitigni da vino coltivati in Italia*. Vol 2. Roma: Ministero dell'Agricoltura e Foreste.

Cosmo, I., and F. Sardi. 1964. "Groppello Gentile." In *Principali vitigni da vino coltivati in Italia*. Vol. 3. Roma: Ministero dell'Agricoltura e delle Foreste.

———. 1965. *"Tocai rosso."* In *Principali vitigni da vino coltivati in Italia*. Vol. 4. Roma: Ministero dell'Agricoltura e delle Foreste.

Cosmo, I., F. Sardi, and A. Calò. 1962. "Bervedino." In *Principali vitigni da vino coltivati in Italia*. Vol. 2. Roma: Ministero dell'Agricoltura e delle Foreste.

Costacurta A., A. Calò, D. Antonacci, V. Catalano, M. Crespan, R. Carraro, M. Giust, L. Agio, M. Ostan, R. Di Stefano, and D. Borsa. 2004. "La caratterizzazione di Greci e Grechetti a bacca bianca coltivati in Italia." *Rivista di Vitivinicoltura e Enologia* 3: 3–20.

Costacurta, A., A. Calò, R. Carraro, M. Giust, L. Aggio, D. Borsa, R. Di Stefano, F. Of De Zan, A. Fabbro, and M. Crespan. 2005. "L'identificazione e la caratterizzazione dei Refoschi." In *Dei Refoschi*. San Dorligo della Valle: Lloyd.

Costacurta, A., A. Calò, M. Crespan, N. Milani, R. Carraro, L. Aggio, R. Flamini, and A. Marsan. 2001. "Caracterisation morphologique, aromatique, et moléculaire des cépages de Moscato et recherche sur leurs rapports philogénétiques." *Bulletin de L'OIV*: 841–42.

Costacurta, A., and S. Cancellier. 1999. *I vitigni dei Berici*. Vicenza: CCIAA.

Costacurta, A., M. Crespan, N. Milani, R. Carraro, R. Flamini, L. Aggio, P. Ajmonte-Marsan, and A. Calò. 2003. "Morphological, aromatic and molecular characterization of Muscat vines and their phylogenetic relationships (*Vitis vinifera* L.)." *Rivista di Viticoltura e di Enologia* 56(2/3): 13–30.

Costantini, L., A. Monaco, J. F. Vouillamoz, M. Forlani, and M. S. Grando. 2005. "Genetic relationships among local *Vitis vinifera* cultivars from Campania (Italy)." *Vitis* 44(1): 25–34.

Costantini, L., I. Roncador, and M. S. Grand. 2001. "Il caso groppello della Val di Non chiarito con Il DNA." *L'Informatore Agrario* 57(45): 53–56.

Cravero, M.C., F. Bonello, F. Piano, L. Chiusano, D. Borsa, C. Tsolakis, and P. Lale Demoz. 2010. "'Cinque Terre'—vintage 2007: Profilo sensoriale e composizione chimica di vini bianchi 'Albarola' e 'Bosco' delle 'Cinque Terre.'" Paper presented at the Third Annual Congress of Mountain Viticulture, Castiglione di Sicilia, 12–14 May.

Cravero, M. C., and R. Di Stefano. 1992. "The phenolics of some grape varieties grown in Piemont." *Vignevini* 19(5): 47.

Crespan, M. 2003. "The parentage of Muscat of Hamburg." *Vitis* 42(4): 193–97.

———. 2009. "La Malvasia nera in Toscana? E' Tempranillo." *Corriere vinicolo* 82(40): 13.

Crespan, M., A. Armanni, G. Da Rold, B. De Nardi, M. Gardiman, D. Migliaro, S. Soligo, and P. Storchi. 2012. "Verdello, Verdicchio and Verduschia: An example of integrated multidisciplinary study to clarify grapevine cultivar identity." *Advances in Horticultural Science* 26(2): 92–99.

Crespan, M., F. Cabello, S. Giannetto, J. Ibanez, J. Karoglan Kontic, E. Maletic, I. Pejic, I. Rodriguez, and D. Antonacci. 2006a. "Malvasia delle Lipari and its synonyms." *Rivista di Viticoltura e di Enologia* 2–3: 19–27.

———. 2006b. "Malvasia delle Lipari, Malvasia di Sardegna, Greco di Gerace, Malvasìa di Sitges and Malvasia Dubrovačka-synonyms of an old and famous grape cultivar." *Vitis* 45(2): 69–73.

Crespan, M., A. Calò, A. Costacurta, N. Milani, M. Giust, M. Carraro, and R. Di Stefano. 2002. "Ciliegiolo ed Aglianicone: Unico vitigno direttamente imparentato col Sangiovese." *Rivista di Viticoltura ed Enologia* 2/3.

Crespan, M., A. Calò, S. Giannetto, A. Sparacio, P. Storchi, and A. Costacurta. 2008. "Sangiovese and Garganega are two key varieties of the Italian grapevine assortment evolution." *Vitis* 47(2): 97–104.

Crespan, M., S. Cancellier, R. Chies, S. Giannetto, and S. Meneghetti. 2006. "Individuati i genitori del Raboso veronese: Una nuova ipotesi sulla sua origine." *Rivista di Viticoltura e di Enologia* 59(1): 3–12.

Crespan, M., S. Cancellier, R. Chies, S. Giannetto, S. Meneghetti, and A. Costacurta. 2006. "Molecular contribution to the knowledge of two ancient varietal populations: Rabosi and Glere." Paper presented at the Ninth Conference on Grape Genetics and Breeding, Udine, 2–6 July.

———. 2009. "Molecular contribution to the knowledge of two ancient varietal populations: Rabosi and Glere." *Acta Horticulturae* 827: 217–20.

Crespan, M., S. Cancellier, A. Costacurta, M. Giust, M. Carraro, R. Di Stefano, and S. Santangelo. 2003. "Contribution to the clearing up of synonymies in some groups of Italian grapevine cultivars." *Acta Horticulturae* 603: 251–54.

Crespan, M., S. Cancellier, and S. Giannetto. 2004. "Raboso Piave e Raboso Veronese: Padre e figlio?" *Rivista di Viticoltura e di Enologia* 57(1–2): 51–57.

Crespan, M., A. Colleta, P. Crupi, S. Giannetto, and D. Antonacci. 2008. "Malvasia di Brindisi/Lecce grapevine cultivar (*Vitis vinifera* L.) originated from Negro Amaro and Malvasia Bianca Lunga." *Vitis* 47(4): 205–12.

Crespan, M., G. Crespan, M. Giannetto, S. Meneghetto, and A. Costacurta. 2007. "Vitouska is the progeny of Prosecco Tondo and Malvasia Bianca Lunga." *Vitis* 46: 192–94.

Crespan, M., A. Fabbro, S. Giannetto S., S. Meneghetti, C. Petrussi, F. Del Zan, and P. Sivilotti. 2011. "Recognition and genotyping of minor germplasm of Friuli Venezia Giulia revealed high diversity." *Vitis* 50(1): 21–28.

Crespan, M., and M. Gardiman. 2011. "La variabilità dei vecchi vitigni del Friuli." Paper presented at conference Alla scoperta dei vecchi vitigni del Friuli, ERSA, Torreano di Martignacco, 27 January 2011.

Crespan, M., and N. Milani. 2001. "The Muscats: A molecular analysis of synonyms, homonyms, and genetic relationships within a large family of related grapevine cultivars." *Vitis* 40(1): 23–30.

Cristoferi, B. 1967. "Contributo allo studio dei vitigni romagnoli minori." Tesi di laurea, Università di Bologna, Facoltà di Agraria.

Croce, G. B. 1606. *Dalla eccellenza e diversità dei vini che nella montagna di Torino si fanno e del modo di farli*. Torino: Pizzimiglia.

Cupani, F. 1696. *Hortus Catholicus*. Napoli: Benzi.

D'Agata, I. 2001a. "Educazione: Viva l'Italia: Il vitigno autoctono." *Porthos*, 6 June.

———. 2001b. "Educazione: Il vitigno autoctono." *Porthos* 7, September.

———. 2003a. "Quei vini un po' difficili: Speciale vitigni autoctoni rossi." *Gambero Rosso*, October.

———. 2003b. "Saranno famosi: Speciale vitigni autoctoni rossi." *Gambero Rosso*, December.

———. 2004. "Speriamo sia autoctono, parte seconda." *Cucina e Vini* 60.

———. 2005a. "Ian D'Agata on Southern Italy." *International Wine Cellar* 121.

———. 2005b. "Un vino moderno alla ribalta: Il Morellino di Scansano." In *Puer Aeternus*, edited by Cont, M., E. Guariglia. Manciano: Statonia Editrice.

———. 2007a. "Ian D'Agata on Tuscany." *International Wine Cellar* 133.

———. 2007b. "Picolit, un amore antico per un ricordo d'infanzia." In *Colli Orientali del Friuli. Dedicato al Picolit DOCG*. Edited by B. Pucciarelli, M. Paladin, and M. Malison. Cividale del Friuli: Consorzio Tutela Vini DOC Colli Orientali del Friuli.

———. 2008. *The Ecco guide to the best wines of Italy*. New York: Harper Collins.

———. 2011. "The return of the native." *Decanter*, Italy issue, April.

———. 2012a. "Going native." *Decanter*, Italy issue, April.

———. 2012b. "The importance of colour." *Decanter*, August.

———. 2012c. "Tuscany part I: Chianti, Vino Nobile, Vernaccia di San Gimignano and Supertuscans." *International Wine Cellar* 163.

———. 2013. "Tocai friulano: Uno sguardo fuori dall'Europa." In *Tocai e Friulano un racconto di civiltà del vino*. Edited by E. Costantini. Udine: Editrice Universitaria Udinese.

D'Agata, I., M. Sabellico, N. Aiello, G. Arru, P. Buffa, M. Di Cintio, E. Guerini, M. Lanza, G. Lo Sicco, N. Pederzoli, and F. Pensovecchio. 2003. *I vitigni autoctoni del Gambero Rosso 2004*. Roma: Gambero Rosso GRH Spa.

Dalla Negra, F. 1811. "Dell'agricoltura nel Cantone di Arzignano e della parte montuosa della provincia di Vicenza." *Annali Agricoltura Regno d'Italia*, t. 11.

Dalmasso, G. 1946. *Uve da vino: Vitigni rossi*. Roma: Ramo editoriale degli agricoltori stampa.

Dalmasso, G., M. Cacciatore, and A. Corte. 1962. "Uva Rara." In *Principali vitigni da vino coltivati in Italia, Volume 2*. Roma: Ministero dell'Agricoltura e delle Foreste.

Dalmasso, G., I. Cosmo, and G. Dell'Olio. 1939. "I vini pregiati della provincia di Verona." Vol. 35. *Annali della sperimentazione agraria*. Roma: Tipografia Failli.

Dalmasso, G., and G. Dell'Olio. 1936–37. "I vini bianchi tipici dei Colli Trevigiani: Sottozone di Conegliano e Valdobbiadene." *Annali Regia Stazione Sperimentale di Viticoltura e Enologia di Conegliano*, v. 7.

Dalmasso, G., and L. Reggio. 1963. *Principali vitigni da vino coltivati in Italia*. Treviso: Arti Grafiche Longo e Zoppelli.

D'Ambra, S. 1962. "La vite e il vino nell'isola d'Ischia." *Atti dell'Accademia Italiana della Vite e del Vino* 14(37).

Da Schio, G. 1905. *Enologia e viticoltura della provincia di Vicenza*. Vicenza: Stabilimenti Tipografici Fratelli Pastorio.

D'Ascia, G. 1867. *Storia dell'isola d'Ischia.* Napoli: Stabilimento Tipografico Gabriele Argenio.

De Astis, G. 1937. *Rassegna e revisione dei vitigni coltivati in Toscana.* Firenze: Progresso vinicolo di Firenze, Vol. 15.

De Bonis, M. 2002. *Terra d'uve: Vini e vitigni in Calabria dall'antichità all'Ottocento: Notizie, curiosità, immagini.* Cosenza: Edizioni Le Nuvole.

De Bosis, F. 1876. "Lavori eseguiti dalla Commissione Ampelografica della provincia di Ravenna." *Bullettino Ampelografico* 5.

———. 1879. "Lavori eseguiti dalla Commissione Ampelografica della provincia di Ravenna." *Bullettino Ampelografico* 10.

de' Crescenzi, P., and B. De Rossi. 1805. *Trattato della agricoltura di Pietro de' Crescenzi traslato nella favella fiorentina, rivisto dallo 'Nferigno accademico della Crusca.* Milano: Società tipografica de'Classici italiani.

Deidda, P. 1994. "La vite." In *Le vecchie varietà della Sardegna,* 279–308, edited by M. Agabbio. Sassari: Carlo Delfino.

Del Treppo, M. 1967. *I mercati catalani e l'espansione della corona d'Aragona nel secolo XV.* Napoli: L'Arte Tipografica.

De Maria, P. P., and C. Leardi. 1875. *Ampelografia della Provincia di Alessandria.* Turin: Negro.

De Mattia, F., S. Imazio, F. Grassi, G. Lovicu, J. Tardaguila, O. Failla, C. Maitt, A. Scienza, and M. Labra. 2007. "Genetic characterization of Sardinia grapevine cultivars by SSR markers analysis." *Journal International des Sciences de la Vigne et du Vin* 41(4): 175–84.

De Mattia, F., G. Lovicu, J. Tardaguila, F. Grassi, S. Imazio, A. Scienza, and M. Labra. 2009. "Genetic relationships between Sardinian and Spanish viticulture: The case of Cannonau and Garnacha." *Journal of Horticultural Science and Biotechnology* 84(1): 65–71.

De Palma, L., M. De Michele, C. D'Onofrio, A. Schneider, C. Fausto, L. Tarricone, P. Limosani, and V. Novello. 2012. "Identificazione e caratterizzazione di vitigni minori pugliesi ad uva da vino." Paper presented at the IV Convegno Nazionale di Viticoltura (CONAVI.TO), Asti, 10–12 July.

De Palma, L., L. Tarricone, A. Costacurta, P. Carparelli, and V. Novello. 2009. "Studi sul Fiano aromatico di Puglia: Dal DNA al vino." Paper presented at the Il Fiano nelle Puglie conference, Cellino San Marco, 25 September.

De Rosso, M. 2010. "Applicazioni di tecniche avanzate nello studio dei composti chimici dell'uva e del vino conservato in botti di legno: Il caso del Raboso." Dottorato di ricerca in viticoltura, enologia e marketing delle imprese vitivinicole, Università degli Studi di Padova.

Di Rovasenda, G. 1877. *Saggio di una ampelografia universale.* Torino: Loescher.

Di Stefano, R., and L. Corino. 1984. "Terpeni ed antociani di alcune uve aromatiche." *Rivista di Viticoltura e di Enologia* 10: 581–85.

Di Vaio, C., C. Pasquarella, G. Scaglione, M. Boselli, and M. Forlani. 1998. "Effect of bud load and pruning system on quantitative and qualitative aspects of Trebbiano Toscano variety in an environment of Southern Italy." *Annali della facoltà di Agraria dell'Università degli studi di Napoli Federico II* 32.

Di Vecchi Staraz, M., R. Bandinelli, M. Boselli, P. This, J. M. Boursiquot, V. Laucou, T. Lacombe, and D. Varès. 2007. "Genetic structuring and parentage analysis for evolutionary studies in grapevine: Kin group and origin of the cultivar Sangiovese revealed." *Journal of the American Society for Horticultural Science* 132(4): 514–24.

Di Vecchi Staraz, M., T. Lacombe, V. Laucou, R. Bandinelli, D. Varès, M. Boselli, and P. This. 2006. "Studio sulle relazioni genetiche tra viti selvatiche e coltivate in Toscana." In *Proceedings of the II International Symposium on 'Sangiovese.'* Florence: Agenzia Regionale per lo Sviluppo e l'Innovazione in Agricoltura.

Di Vecchi Staraz, M., T. Lacombe, V. Laucou, P. This, and M. Boselli. 2009. "Genetic relationship between cultivated and wild grapevines in Tuscany." Paper presented at the Thirty-first World Congress of Vine and Wine, Sixth general assembly of the OIV, Molecular Biology and Genetics panel, Verona, June 2008; http://www.oiv2008.it/.

Dolcini, A., T. Simoni, and G. F. Fontana. 1967. *La Romagna dei vini.* Bologna: Edizioni Alfa.

D'Onofrio, C., G. De Lorenzis, L. Natali, and G. Scalabrelli. 2008. "I retrotrasposoni: Nuovi metodi di indagine molecolare per la caratterizzazione genotipica e lo studio filogenetico della vite: Il caso delle Malvasie." Paper presented at the Convegno Le Malvasie del bacino del mediterraneo, Salina, 3 October 2007. *Rivista di Viticoltura ed Enologia* 2–4: 167–68.

D'Onofrio, C., G. Scalabrelli, G. De Lorenzis, and C. Palazzi. 2008. "Genotipizzazione di accessioni di Malvasia a bacca nera, rosa e bianca." Atti del Convegno Le Malvasie del bacino del mediterraneo, Salina, 3 October 2007. *Rivista di Viticoltura ed Enologia* 2–4: 371–83.

Dotti, F. 1927. "La viticoltura e l'enologia nell'Agro Lughese." Paper presented at the II Congresso nazionale di frutticoltura, Lugo. *Giornata del vino*. Ravenna: Società tipo-editrice ravennate e mutilati.

Ducci, E., C. Fausto, C. D'Onofrio, G. Ferroni, and G. Scalabrelli. 2012. "Comportamento di alcuni vitigni locali delle Colline Pisane." Paper presented at the IV Convegno Nazionale di Viticoltura (CONAVI.TO), Asti, 10–12 July.

Emanuelli, F., J. Battilana, L. Costantini, L. Le Cunff, J. Boursiquot, and P. This. 2010. "A candidate gene association study on muscat flavor in grapevine (*Vitis vinifera* L.)." *BMC Plant Biology* 9–10(1): 241.

Emanuelli, F., S. Lorenzi, L. Grzeskowiak, V. Catalano, M. Stefanini, M. Troggio, S. Myles, J. M. Martinez-Zapater, E. Zyprian, F. M. Moreira, and M. S. Grando. 2013. "Genetic diversity and population structure assessed by SSR and SNP markers in a large germplasm collection of grape." *BMC Plant Biology* 13(39).

Fabbro, C. 2005. *Il vigneto Friuli: Dai Romani alla partenza del Tocai*. Udine: Ducato dei Vini Friulani.

Failla, O., S. Imazio, L. Brancadoro, P. Bianco, and R. Di Stefano. 2011. "Caratterizzazione e valorizzazione del Moscato di Scanzo, stato di avanzamento dei progetti." Paper presented at the Consorzio Tutela Moscato di Scanzo, Scanzorosciate, 17 November.

Fanizza, G., R. Chaabane, F. Lamaj, L. Ricciardi, and P. Resta. 2003. "AFLP analysis of genetic relationships among aromatic grapevines (*Vitis vinifera*)." *Theoretical and Applied Genetics* 107(6): 1043–47.

Ferrante, C. 2000. "La viticultura e la vinificazione nella Sardegna spagnola, XVI–XVII secolo." In *Storia della vite e del vino in Sardegna*, edited by M. L. Di Felice and A. Mattone. Roma: Laterza.

Ferrante, L. 1927. *Un vitigno di antica nobiltà: Il Greco di Tufo*. Avellino: C. Labruna.

Filippetti, I., C. Intrieri, M. Centinari, B. Bucchetti, and C. Pastore. 2005. "Molecular characterization of officially registered Sangiovese clones and of other Sangiovese-like biotypes in Tuscany, Corsica and Emilia–Romagna." *Vitis* 44: 167–72.

Filippetti, I., C. Intrieri, O. Silvestroni, and M. R. Thomas. 1999. "Diversity assessment of seedlings from self-pollinated Sangiovese grapevines by ampelography and microsatellite DNA analysis." *Vitis* 38: 67–71.

Filippetti, I., S. Ramazzotti, C. Intrieri, O. Silvestroni, and M. R. Thomas. 2002. "Caratterizzazione molecolare e analisi filogenetica di alcuni vitigni da vino coltivati in Italia Centro-Settentrionale." *Rivista di Frutticoltura e Ortofloricultura* 64(1): 57–64.

Filippetti, I., O. Silvestroni, M. R. Thomas, and C. Intrieri. 2001. "Genetic characterization of Italian grape cultivars by micro satellite analysis." *Acta Horticulturae* 546: 395–99.

Filiputti, W. 1983. *Terre, Vigne e Vini del Friuli-Venezia Giulia*. Udine: Angelico Benvenuto Editore.

Fiorito, G. 1954. "Il Falerno dei Campi Flegrei." *Agricoltura Napoletana* 4–6.

Foëx, J. A. 1909. "Biancolella." In *Ampelographie*, edited by P. Viala and V. Vermorel, vol. 6. Paris: Masson et cie.

Fontana, M. 2001. "Presente e futuro del miglioramento genetico." *Agricoltura* (Luglio/Agosto): 56–58.

Fontana, M., and I. Filippetti. 2006. "Le vigne dei padri: Vite and vino biodiversità, turismo e tipicità: Le direttrici di un possibile rilancio." *Il Divulgatore* 2–3: 46–60.

Fontana, M., I. Filippetti, C. Pastore, and C. Intrieri. 2007. "Indagine ampelografia e molecolare sui vitigni locali dell'Emilia Romagna: Primi risultati." *Italus Hortus* 14(3): 49–53.

Fontana, M., I. Filippetti, C. Pastore, G. Vespignani, and C. Intrieri. 2006. "Individuazione e caratterizzazione di alcuni vitigni minori dell'Emilia Romagna." Paper presented at the convegno I vitigni autoctoni minori: Aspetti tecnici, normativi e commerciali. Sessione 2, Problematiche di recupero e caratterizzazione. Torino, 30 November–1 December.

Forni, G. 2011. "La matrice euro mediterranea della nostra viticoltura." In *Origini della viticoltura: Atti del convegno*, edited by B. Biagini. Castiglione d'Orcia: Podere Forte.

Fossati, T., M. Labra, S. Castiglione, A. Scienza, and O. Failla. 2001. "The use of AFLP and SSR molecular markers to decipher homonyms and synonyms in grapevine cultivars: The case of the varietal group known as 'Schiave.'" *Theoretical and Applied Genetics* 102(2–3): 200–205.

Francesca, N., M. Monaco, R. Romano, E. Lonardo, M. de Simone, and G. Moschetti. 2009. "Rovello Bianco, caratterizzazione di un vitigno autoctono campano." *Vigne e vini* 4: 106–11.

Fregoni, M. 1969. "Scheda ampelografica del vitigno piacentino Molinelli." *Agricoltura Piacentina* 11: 2–8.

Fregoni, M. 2005. *Viticoltura di qualità*. Affi: Phytoline.

Fregoni, M., M. Zamboni, and R. Colla. 2002. *Caratterizzazione ampelografica dei vitigni autoctoni piacentini*. Università Cattolica Sacro Cuore Cattedra di Viticoltura. Piacenza: Grafica Lama.

Frei, A., N. A. Porret, J. E. Frei, and J. Tafner. 2006. "Identification and characterization of Swiss grapevine cultivars using microsatellite markers." *Mitteilungen klosteneuburg* 56: 147–56.

Froio, G. 1875. "Primi studi ampelografici del Principato Citeriore e del Principato Ulteriore." Ministero Agricoltura, Industria e Commercio, *Bullettino Ampelografico* 3: 184.

———. (1876) 2004. "Presente e avvenire dei vitigni d'Italia." In *Falanghina,* edited by A. Monaco, A. C. Mustilli, and L. Pignataro. Sorrento: Franco Di Mauro Editore.

———. 1878. "Elenco dei vitigni della provincia di Napoli." Ministero Agricoltura, Industria e Commercio. *Bullettino Ampelografico* 9: 878.

Galet, P. 1990. *L'Ampélographie française: Cépages et Vignobles de France.* Vol 2. Montpellier: C. Dehan.

———. 2000. *Dictionnaire encyclopédique des cépages.* Paris: Hachette.

Gallesio, G. (1817) 1839. *Pomona italiana.* Pisa: Niccolò Capurro.

———. 1995. *I giornali dei viaggi.* Florence: Accademia dei Georgofili.

Gallo, A. (1595) 1937. "Dieci giornate della vera agricoltura." In *Le vicende tecniche ed economiche della viticoltura e dell'enologia in Italia,* edited by G. Dalmasso. Venezia: Arti Grafiche Guadoni.

Gani, M. 2004. "Dei Refoschi. Il vino rosso autoctono friulano." *Notiziario ERSA* 2–4: 14–15.

Ganzin, V. 1901–10. "Tibouren." In *Ampelographie,* 237–43. Vol 2, edited by P. Viala and V. Vermorel. Paris: Masson et Cie.

Garofolo, A., S. Favale, D. Proietti, D. Tiberi, A. Cedron, and P. Pietromarchi. 2007. "Caratterizzazione delle uve e dei vini ottenuti da precloni della c.v. Cesanese d'Affile." *Vignevini* 9: 84–91.

Garoglio, P. G. 1959. *La nuova enologia.* Florence: Florentina Stvdiorum Universitas.

Gasparrini, G. 1844. "Osservazioni su le viti e le vigne del Distretto di Napoli." *Annali Civili del Regno di Napoli* 69 (Maggio e Giugno): 3.

Gasparro, M., A. R. Caputo, M. L. Brini, A. Coletta, M. Crespan, F. Lapenna, and D. Antonacci. 2008. "Caratterizzazione di accessioni di malvasia nera con il metodo dei marcatori molecolari." Paper presented at the 31st Congresse Mondiale OIV, Verona, 15–20 June.

Gatta, L. F. (1838) 1971. *Saggio intorno alle viti e ai vini della Valle d'Aosta.* Aosta: Fratelli Enrico.

Genovese, A., A. Gambuti, P. Piombino, and L. Moio. 2007. "Sensory properties and aroma compounds of sweet Fiano wine." *Food Chemistry* 103(4): 1228–36.

Gerbi, V., L. Rolle, G. Zeppa, S. Guidoni, and A. Schneider. 2005. "Indagine sul profile antocianico di uve autoctone piemontesi." *Industria delle Bevande* 34(2): 23–27.

Geremia, G. 1835. "Vertunno Etneo ovvero Stafulegrafia." *Atti Accademici Gioenia.* Vol. 10. Catania: Tipografia G. Pappalardo.

———. 1839. "Continuazione del Vertunno Etneo ovvero Stafulegrafia." *Atti Accademia Gioenia.* Vol. 14. Catania: Tipografia G. Riggio.

Gerini, C. 1882/1884. "Prospetto dei comuni della provincia, delle diverse specie e varietà di viti che si coltivano." *Bullettino Ampelografico* 17.

Ghetti, G. 1926. *La viticoltura modenese e la fillossera.* Modena: Tipografia E. Bassi & Nipoti.

Ghidoni, F., F. Emanuelli, F. M. Moreira, S. Imazio, M. S. Grando, and A. Scienza. 2008. "Variazioni del genotipo molecolare in Verdicchio, Trebbiano di Soave e Trebbiano di Lugana." Paper presented at the 2nd Convegno nazionale di Viticoltura (CONAVI), Marsala, 14–19 July.

Gianferri, R., M. Maioli, M. Delfini, and E. Brosio. 2007. "A low-resolution and high-resolution nuclear magnetic resonance integrated approach to investigate the physical structure and metabolic profile of Mozzarella di Bufala Campana cheese." *International Dairy Journal* 12: 167–76.

Giannetti, F., A. M. Epifani, R. Perria, and P. Valentini. 2012. "Attitudini viti-vinicole di cloni del caniolo nero nel territorio del Chianti Classico." Paper presented at the 4th Convegno Nazionale di Viticoltura (CONAVI.To), Asti, 10–12 August.

Giavedoni, G., and M. Gily, eds. 2011. *Guida ai vitigni d'Italia. Storia e caratteristiche di 600 varietà autoctone.* Bra: SlowFood.

Gnavi, C. 1973. *Caluso Enoica.* Caluso: Credenza di Caluso.

Goethe, H. 1887. *Hanbuch der Ampelographie.* 2e Anfl. Berlin.

Gorfer, A. 1977. *Le Valli Del Trentino, Trentino Orientale.* Calliano: Manfrini.

Gozzi, R., M. Fontana, and A. Schneider. 2002. "Il Lambrusco Oliva, un vitigno da riscoprire." *Agricoltura* 1: 104–11.

Grando, M. S., and C. Frisinghelli. 1998. "Grape microsatellite markers: Sizing of DNA alleles and genotype analysis of some grapevine cultivars." *Vitis* 37(2): 79–82.

Grando, M. S., C. Frisinghelli, and M. Stefanini. 2000. "Genotyping of local grapevine germplasm." *Acta Horticulturae* 528(1): 183–87.

Grando, S., M. Stefanini, J. Zambanini, and J. Vouillamoz. 2006. "Identità e relazioni genetiche dei vitignìì autoctoni trentini." *Terra Trentina,* 24–27.

Grassi, F., M. Labra, S. Imazio, A. Spada, S. Sgorbati, A. Scienza, and F. Sala. 2003. "Evidence of a secondary domestication centre detected by SSR analysis." *Theoretical and Applied Genetics* 107(7): 1315–20.

Graviano, O., G. Musa, F. Piras, L. Demelas, B. Piga, G. G. M. Aini, and L. Sgarangela. 2012. "Alvarega di Ozieri: Recupero e valorizzazione di un vitigno autoctono della Sardegna centro-settentrionale." Paper presented at Fourth National Congress of Viticulture (CONAVI), Asti, 10–12 July.

Gros, A. 1930. "Le vignoble de Princens." *Travaux de la Societé d'Histoire et d'Archéologie de Maurienne* 7(2).

Hardie, W. J., and S. R. Martin. 1990. "A strategy for vine growth regulation by soil water management." In *Proceedings of the Seventh Australian Wine Industry Technical Conference*, 51–57, edited by P. J. Williams, D. M. Davidson, and T. H. Lee. Adelaide: Winetitles.

Hardie, W. J., T. P. O'Brien, and V. G. Jaudzems. 1996. "Cell biology of grape secondary metabolism—A viticultural perspective." In *Proceedings of the Ninth Australian Wine Industry Technical Conference*, 78–82, edited by C. S. Stockley, A. N. Sas, R. S. Johnstone and T. H. Lee. Adelaide: Winetitles.

Heimoff, S. 2009. "Que sera Sangiovese: Lessons learned from a failed experiment." www.steveheimoff.com, 27 May.

Hohnerleien-Buchinger, T. 1996. *Per un sublessico vitivinicolo*. Tubingen: Max Niemeyer Verlag.

Ibañez, J., M. T. Andres, A. Molino, and J. Borrego. 2003. "Genetic study of key Spanish grapevine varieties using microsatellite analysis." *American Journal of Enology and Viticulture* 54(4): 237–45.

Iland, P. G., R. Gawel, B. G. Coombe, and P. M. Henschke. 1993. "Viticultural parameters for sustaining wine style." In *Proceedings of the Eighth Australian Wine Industry Technical Conference*, 167–69, edited by C. S. Stockley, R. S. Johnstone, P. A. Leske, and T. H. Lee. Adelaide: Winetitles.

Imazio, S., M. Labra, F. Grassi, A. Scienza, and O. Failla. 2006. "Chloroplast microsatellites to investigate the origin of grapevine." *Genetic Resources and Crop Evolution* 53(5): 1003–11.

Incisa, L. (1852) 1974. *Catalogo descrittivo e ragionato della coltivazione di vitigni italiani e stranieri*. Asti: Devecchi. Re-edited by Aldo di Ricaldone, Asti, 1974.

Jackson, D. I., and P. B. Lombard. 1993. "Environmental and management practices affecting grape composition and wine quality: A review." *American Journal of Enology and Viticulture* 44(4): 409–30.

Jeffreys, A., V. Wilson, S. L. Thein. 1985. "Individual-specific 'fingerprints' of human DNA." *Nature* 314: 67–73.

Johnson, H., and J. Robinson. 2007. *World atlas of wine*. London: Mitchell Beazley.

Kozjak, P., Z. Korošek Kozuka, and B. Javornik. 2003. "Characterization of cv. Refosk (Vitis vinifera L.) by SSR markers." *Vitis* 42(2): 83–86.

Krings, U., and R. G. Berger. 1998. "Biotechnological production of flavours and fragrances." *Applied Microbial Biotechnology* 49: 1–8.

Labra, M., O. Failla, T. Fossati, S. Castiglione, A. Scienza, and A. Sala. 1999. "Phylogenetic analysis of grapevine cv. Ansonica growing on the island of Giglio by AFLP and SSR markers." *Vitis* 38(4): 161–66.

Labra, M., S. Imazio, F. Grassi, M. Rossoni, S. Citterio, S. Sgorbati, A. Scienza, and O. Failla. 2003. "Molecular approach to assess the origin of cv. Marzemino." *Vitis* 42(3): 147–50.

Labra, M., M. Winfield, A. Ghiani, F. Grassi, A. Sala, A. Scienza, and O. Failla. 2001. "Genetic studies on Trebbiano and morphologically related varieties by SSR and AFLP testing." *Vitis* 40(4): 187–90.

Lacombe, T. 2002. "I vitigni minori da vino in Francia." Paper presented at the Convegno internazionale Valore e funzione dei vitigni autoctoni e tradizionali. Lastra a Signa, 10 December.

Lacombe, T., J. M. Boursiquot, V. Laoucou, F. Dechesne, D. Varès, and P. This. 2007. "Relationships and genetic diversity within the accessions related to Malvasia held in the Domaine de Vassal grape germplasm repository." *American Journal of Enology and Viticulture* 58(1): 124–31.

Lacombe, T., J. M. Boursiquot, V. Laucou, M. Di Vecchi-Staraz, J. P. Peros, and P. This. 2013. "Large scale parentage analysis in an extended set of grapevine cultivars (*Vitis vinifera* L.)." *Theoretical and Applied Genetics* 126(2): 401–14.

Lando, O. 1553. *Commentario delle cose più notabili e mostruose d'Italia*. Cesano.

Laucou, V., T. Lacombe, F. Dechesne, R. Siret, J. P. Bruno, M. Dessup, T. Dessup, P. Ortigosa, P. Parra, C. Roux, S. Santoni, D. Varès, J. P. Peros, J. M. Boursiquot, and P. This. 20011. "High throughput analysis of grape genetic diversity as a tool for germplasm collection management." *Theoretical Applied Genetics* 122: 1233–45.

Lefort, F., M. Anzidei, K. A. Roubelakis-Angelakis, and G. G. Vendramin. 2000. "Microsatellite profiling of the Greek Muscat cultivars with nuclear and chloroplast SSR markers." *Quaderni* della Scuola di Specializzazione in Scienze Viticole ed Enologiche 23: 57–82.

Lefort, F., and K. A. Roubelakis-Angelakis. 2000. "The Greek Vitis database: A multimedia web-backed genetic database for germplasm management of Vitis resources in Greece." Journal of Wine Research 11: 233–42.

———. 2002. "Assessing the identity of grapevine plants from vineyards from Crete and Samos by DNA profiling." Journal International de la Science de Vigne et du Vin 36: 177–83.

Levadoux. 1951. "La sélection et l'hybridation chez la vigne." Annales de l'Ecole Nationale d'Agriculture de Montpellier 28(3–4): 165–358.

Ligari, P. (1752) 1988. Ragionamenti d'agricoltura. Sondrio: Banca Popolare di Sondrio.

Lijavetszky D., J. A. Cabezas, A. Ibanez, V. Rodriguez, and J. M Martinez-Zapater. 2007. "High throughput SNP discovery and genotyoping in grapevine (Vitis Vinifera L.) by combining a resequencing approach and SNPl technology." BMC Genomics 8: 424.

Lomolino, G., and A. Lante. 2012. "Characterization of esterase activity in the Bianchetta Trevigiana grape under reducing conditions." International Journal of Wine Research 4: 45–51.

Lomolino, G., F. Zocca, P. Spettoli, G. Zanin, and A. Lante. 2010. "A preliminary study on phenolic content during Bianchetta Trevigiana winemaking." Journal of Food Composition and Analysis 23: 575–79.

Lopes, M. S., K. E. Sefc, E. Eiras-Dias, H. Steinkellner, M. Laimer, and A. da Câmara Machado. 1999. "The use of microsatellites for germplasm management in a Portugueuse grapevine collection." Theoretical and Applied Genetics 99: 733–39.

Lovicu, G. 2006. "E' certa l'origine sarda del Cannonau." L'informatore Agrario 49: 54–57.

Lovicu, G., M. Farci, M. Sedda, M. Labra, M. De Mattia, F. Grassi, G. Bacchetta, and M. Orrù. 2010. "Sardegna: Individuati circa 150 vitigni autoctoni." L'Informatore Agrario 34: 401–41.

Macagno, I. 1883. Bollettino Ampelografico. Vol. 16. Roma: Eredi Botta.

Madalozzo, G. (1878) 1983. "La bassa Padovana occidentale: Usura e pellagra." In Contadini e agricoltura: L'inchiesta Jacini nel Veneto, edited by A. Lazzarini. Milano: Franco Angeli.

Mainardi, G. 2001. "Storia di un grande protagonista dell'enologia italiana: Il Sangiovese." Proceedings of the First International Symposium on Sangiovese. Agenzia Regionale per lo Sviluppo e l'Innovazione in Agricoltura, Florence, 15–17 February 2000.

Malenica, N., S. Šimon, V. Besendorfer, A. Maletić, J. Karoglan Kontic, and I. Pejic. 2011. "Whole genome amplification and microsatellite genotyping of herbarium DNA revealed the identity of an ancient grapevine cultivar." Die Naturwissenschaften 98(9): 763–72.

Maletic, E., I. Pejic, J. Karoglan Kontic, J. Piljac, G. S. Dangl, A. Vokurka, T. Lacombe, N. Mirosevic, and C. P. Meredith. 2004. "Zinfandel, Dobricic, and Plavac mali: The genetic relationship among three cultivars of the Dalmatian coast of Croatia." American Journal of Enology and Viticulture 55(2): 174–80.

Maletic, E., K. M. Sefc, H. Steinkellner, J. Karoglan Kontic, and I. Pejic. 1999. "Genetic characterization of Croatian grapevine cultivars and detection of synonymous cultivars in neighbouring regions." Vitis 38: 67–71.

Manca dell'Arca, A. 1780. Agricultura di Sardegna. Napoli: Orsini.

Mancini, C. 1893. "I vítigni e i vini del Lazio." Annuario Generale della Viticoltura e dell'Enologia (Roma) 2: 39.

Mancuso, S. 2001. "Clustering of grapevine (Vitis vinifera L.) genotypes with Kohonen neural networks." Vitis 40(2): 59–63.

Mancuso, S., M. Boselli, and E. Masi. 2001. "Distinction of Sangiovese clones and grapevine varieties using Elliptical Fourier Analysis (EFA), neural networks and fractal analysis." Advances in Horticultural Sciences 15(1–4): 61–65.

Mangani, S., G. Buscioni, L. Collina, E. Bocci, and M. Vincenzini. 2011. "Effects of microbial populations on anthocyanin profile of Sangiovese wines produce in Tuscany, Italy." American Journal of Enology and Viticulture 62: 487–94.

Maniago, P. 1823. Catalogo delle viti del Regno Veneto.

Mannina, L., M. Pattumi, N. Proietti, A. L. Segre. 2001. "Geographical characterization of Tuscan extravirgin oils using high field H-1 NMR spectroscopy." Journal of Agricultural Food Chemistry 49: 2687–96.

Mannini, F., N. Argamante, A. Ferrandino, S. Guidoni, G. Praz, P. Lale-Demoz, and S. Dozio. 2006. "Field performances and wine quality of three clones of Nebbiolo (Vitis vinifera L.) grown in two different environments of Northern Italy: Aosta Valley and Langhe." Compte-rendus du Premier Congrès International sur la viticulture de montagne et en forte pente. Saint-Vincent (AO), 17–18 March.

Mannini, F., L. Cavallo, L. Rolle, A. Ferrandino, and A. Mollo. 2008. "Genetic and sanitary selection of Avanà (Vitis vinifera L.), the main variety of the mountain viticultural area of Susa Valley." Paper presented at the Second International Congress on Mountain and Steep Slope Viticulture. Monforte de Lemos, Spain, 13–15 May.

Mannini, F., A. Schneider, N. Argamante, P. Moggia, and R. Tragni. 2010. "Contribution to the safeguard and the exploitation of local minor grape varieties of Eastern-Liguria." Paper presented at the Third International Congress on Mountain and Steep Slope Viticulture, Castiglione di Sicilia (Catania), 12–14 May.

Mannini, F., A. Schneider, V. Gerbi, and R. Credi. 1989. *Cloni selezionati dal centro di studio per il miglioramento genetico della vite, CNR.* Torino: Grafica Offset.

Mannini, F., A. Schneider, V. Gerbi, L. Rigazio, and R. Avetrani. 1992. "Selezione clonale dei principali vitigni valdostani: Aspetti ampelografici, agronomici ed enologici." *Vignevini* 6: 43–52.

Manzo, M., and A. Monaco. 2001. "Aglianicone." In *La risorsa genetica della vite in Campania*, edited by M. Bianco and M. Forlani for the Settore Sperimentazione, Informazione, Ricerca e Consulenza in Agricoltura, Regione Campania, Assessorato Agricoltura. Napoli: Stampa Orpi.

Marangoni, B., A. Venturi, and M. Fontana. 2000. "Uva Longanesi." *Vignevini* 7/8: 63–67.

Marchi, D., and D. Lanati. 2008. "Schede di valutazione analitica delle uve e dei vini." In *Il gaglioppo e i suoi fratelli*, 151–54, edited by C. Fregoni and O. Nigra. Cirò Marina: Librandispa.

Marescalchi, A., and G. Dalmasso. 1937. *Storia del della vite e del vino in Italia.* 3 vols. Milano: Gualdoni Editore.

Market, C. L., and F. Møller. 1959. "Multiple forms of enzymes: Tissue, ontogenic, and species specific patterns." *Biochemistry* 45(5): 753–63.

Martin, J. P., J. Borrego, F. Cabello, and J. F. Ortiz. 2003. "Characterization of Spanish grapevine cultivar diversity by using sequence tagged microsatellite site markers." *Genome* 46(1): 10–18.

Martínez, L., P. Cavagnaro, J. M. Boursiquot, and C. Aguero. 2008. "Molecular characterization of Bonarda-type grapevine (*Vitis vinifera* L.) cultivars from Argentina, Italy, and France." *American Journal of Enology and Viticulture* 59: 287–91.

Marzotto, N. 1923. *Ampelografia del Friuli, contenente la descrizione di 42 vitigni con notizie sulla loro importanza viticola ed enologica:* Estratto de "*L'Agricoltura Friulana 1923.*" Udine: Tipografia Domenico Del Bianco e Figlio.

———. 1925. *Uva da vino.* Vol 1. Vicenza: Commerciale.

———. 1935. *Uve da mensa: Descrizione di varietà, con speciale studio sull'accertamento, nomenclatura e sinonimie di molti vitigni sino ad ora non bene identificati.* Vicenza: Tipografia commerciale editrice.

Mas, A., and V. Puillat. 1874–79. *Le Vignoble, ou Histoire, culture et description avec planches colorées des vignes à raisins de table et à raisins de cuve les plus généralement connues.* Paris: Masson.

Masi, E., R. Vignani, A. Di Giovannantonio, S. Mancuso, and S. Boselli. 2001. "Ampelographic and cultural characterisation of the Casavecchia variety." *Advances in Horticultural Sciences* 15(1–4): 47–55.

Mattivi, F., L. Caputi, S. Carlin, T. Lanza, M. Minozzi, D. Nanni, L. Valenti, and U. Vrhovsek. 2011. "Effective analysis of rotundone at below-threshold levels in red and white wines using solid-phase microextraction gas chromatography/tandem mass spectrometry." *Rapid Communications in Mass Spectrometry* 25: 483–88.

Mattivi, F., G. Cova, A. Dalla Serra, and S. Soligo. 2004. *Classificazione delle uve a bacca nera del Veneto in base al contenuto in polifenoli: Recupero, conservazione e valorizzazione del germoplasma viticolo veneto.* Legnaro: Veneto Agricoltura.

Mattivi, F., A. Scienza, O. Failla, P. Villa, R. Anzani, G. Tedesco, E. Gianazza, and P. Righetti. 1990. "Vitis vinifera: A chemotaxonomic approach: Anthocyanins in the skin." Paper presented at the 5th International Symposium on Grape Breeding, St. Martin/Pfalz, Germany, 12–16 September 1989. *Vitis*, Special Issue 1990: 119–33.

Mazzei, A., and A. Zappalà. 1964. "'Greco bianco' and 'Nerello Cappuccio.'" In *Principali vitigni da vino coltivati in Italia.* Vol. 3. Roma: Ministero dell'Agricoltura e delle Foreste.

Mazzei, P., and A. Piccolo. 2012. "HRMAS-NMR metabolomic to assess quality and traceability of mozzarella cheese from Campania buffalo milk." *Food Chemisty* 132: 1620–27.

Meglioraldi, S., G. Masini, M. Storchi, and M. Vingione. 2008. "Caratteri ampelografici, agronomici ed enologici di vitigni autoctoni reggiani di recente iscrizione." Paper presented at the 2nd Convegno Nazionale di Viticoltura, Marsala, 14–19 July.

Mendola, A. (1868) 1874. "Catalogo generale della Collezioni di Viti italiane e straniere." *Annali di Viticoltura e di Enologia.* Vol. 2. Favara: Parrino e Carini.

———. 1881. *Bollettino della Commissione ampelografica della provincia di Agrigento Girgenti.* Agrigento: Tipografia L. Carini.

———. 1884. *Annali di Agricultura Siciliana.*

Meneghetti, M., L. Bavaresco, A. Calò, and A. Costacurta. 2013. "Inter- and intra-varietal genetic variability in *Vitis vinifera* L." In *The Mediterranean Genetic Code: Grapevine and Olive*, 73–95, edited by D. Poljuha and B. Sladonja. Intech.

Meneghetti, M., A. Costacurta, E. Frare, D. G. Da Rold, D. Migliaro, G. Morreale, M. Crespan, V. Sotes, and A. Calò. 2011. "Clones identification and genetic characterization of Garnacha grapevine by means of different PCR-derived marker systems." *Molecular Biotechnology* 48(3): 244–54.

Meneghetti, S., L. Bavaresco, and A. Calò. 2012. "A strategy to to investigate the intravarietal genetic variability in Vitis vinifera L. for clones and biotypes identification and to correlate molecular profiles with morphological traits or geographic origins." *Molecular Biotechnology* 52(1): 68–81.

Meneghetti, S., A. Costacurta, G. Morreale, and A. Calò. 2012. "Study of intravarietal genetic variability in grapevine cultivars by PCR-derived molecular markers and correlations with the geographic origin." *Molecular Biotechnology* 50 (1): 72–85.

Meneghetti, S., D. Poljuha, E. Frare, A. Costacurta, G. Morreale, L. Bavaresco, and A. Calò. 2012. "Inter- and intra-varietal genetic variability in Malvasia cultivars." *Molecular Biotechnology* 50: 189–99.

Mengarini, F. 1888. *La viticoltura e l'enologia nel Lazio.* Roma: Accademia dei Lincei.

Meredith, C. 2002. "Science as a window into wine history." American Academy Stated Meeting Report. Napa, 2 November.

Migliaccio, G., F. Scala, A. Monaco, P. Ferranti, A. Nasi, T. De Gennaro, T. Granato, V. Nicolella, M. S. Grando, J. F. Vouillamoz, O. Calice, and M. Matarese. 2008. *Atlante delle varietà di vite dell'isola d'Ischia,* edited by A. Monaco and M. S. Grando. Napoli: Franco Di Mauro.

Ministero Agricoltura e Foreste. 1884–87. *Bollettino Ampelografico,* volume 4. *Lavori eseguiti dalla Commissione Ampelografica di Verona.* Verona.

Ministero Agricoltura, Industria e Commercio. 1876–81. *Bollettino Ampelografico.* Torino: Lit. Fratelli Doyen.

———. 1964. *Principali vitigni da vino coltivati in Italia.* Vol. 3. Roma: Ministero dell'Agricoltura Industria e Commercio.

Ministero d'Agricoltura, Industria e Commercio. 1878. *Bullettino Ampelografico,* fascicolo 9. Roma: Tipografia Eredi Botta.

———. 1879a. *Bullettino Ampelografico,* fascicolo 10. Roma: Tipografia Eredi Botta.

———. 1879b. *Bullettino Ampelografico,* fascicolo 12. Roma: Tipografia Eredi Botta.

———. 1880–83. *Bollettino Ampelografico: Lavori eseguiti dalla Commissione ampelografica di Verona.* Vol. 3. Verona.

———. 1883. *Bollettino Ampelografico,* fascicolo 16. Roma: Regia Tipografia D. Ripamonti.

Moio, L., ed. 2012. *Colori, odori ed enologia del Fiano: Sperimentazione e ricerca enologica in Campania.* Naples: Regione Campania, Assessorato Agricoltura.

Molon, G. 1906. *Ampelografia.* Milano: Hoepli.

Monaco, A., A. Nasi, L. Paparelli, and E. Spada. 2011. "Caratterizzazione aromatica ed enologica di uve e vini della varietà Asprinio: Un confronto analitico e storico per una identità lunga sei secoli. Research results 2009–11." Vinitaly conference, Verona, 9 April.

Montanari, V., and G. Ceccarelli. 1950. *La viticoltura e l'enologia nelle Tre Venezie.* Treviso: Longo e Zoppelli.

Morassut, M., and F. Cecchini. 1995. "Composizione fenolica e caratteristiche enologiche del nero buono di Cori." *L'Enotecnico.*

Moretti, G., L. Tarricone, D. Ceccon, and R. Di Lorenzo. 2009. "Il grillo, un siciliano molto promettente." *Civiltà del Bere,* May.

Moriondo, G. 1999. *Vini e vitigni autoctoni della Valle d'Aosta.* Aosta: Imprimerie E. Duc, Institut Agricole Régional.

———. 2001. "Storia del Cornalin della Valle d'Aosta, una nobile varietà di vite da vino."*Rivista di Viticoltura di Montagna* 13: 51–58.

Moriondo, G., G. Praz, and L. Rigazio. 1998. "Primi risultati della selezione massale dei vitigni autoctoni valdostani a minor diffusione: Fumin, Mayolet, Premetta e Prié." *Vignevini* 5: 76–80.

Moriondo, G., R. Sandi, and J. F. Vouillamoz. 2008. "Identificazione del neret de Saint-Vincent, antico vitigno valdostano." *Millevigne Regioni* 3(3): 111.

Moriondo, G., and J. Vouillamoz. 2007. "Valle d'Aosta: Ritrovate due antiche varietà autoctone, Blanc Comun e Petit Rouge a bacca bianca." *Millevigne* 8.

Moris, G. G. 1837–59. *Flora sardoa seu Historia plantarum in Sardinia et adiacentibus insulis vel sponte nascentium vel ad utilitatem latius excultarum.* 3 volumes, with 114 engraved plates after drawings by M. Lisa and J. C. Heyland, and engraved by S. Botta, L. Fea, H. Mil and A. Nizza. Taurini: Ex Regio Typographeo.

Moro, P. 1810. "Memoria sopra i prodotti del territorio veronese." *Annali di Agricoltura del Regno d'Italia*. Milano: Giovanni Silvestri.

Morri, A. 1840. *Vocabolario romagnolo-italiano*. Faenza: Tipografia di Pietro Conti all'Apollo.

Muganu, M., G. Dangl, M. Aradhya, M. Frediani, A. Scossa, and E. Stover. 2009. "Ampelographic and DNA characterization of local grapevine accessions of the Tuscia area." *American Journal of Enology and Viticulture* 60(1): 110–15.

Mullins, M.G., and C.P. Meredith. 1989. "The nature of clonal variation in winegrapes: A review." In *Proceedings of the Seventh Australian Wine Industry Technical Conference*, 79–82, edited by P.J. Williams, D.M. Davidson, and T.H. Lee. Adelaide: Winetitles.

Myles, S., A.R. Boyko, C.L. Owens, P.J. Brown, F. Grassi, M.K. Aradhya, B. Prins, A. Reynolds, J.M. Chiah, D. Ware, C.D. Buistamante, and E.S. Buckler. 2011. "Genetic structure and domestication history of the grape." *Proceedings of the National Academy of Science* 108(9): 3530–35.

Negrul, A.M. 1938. *Evolution of cultivated forms of grapes*. Paris: Librairie Agricole.

Nesbitt, L. 1884. "Risultati delle analisi dei mosti nella provincia di Napoli." *Bollettino Ampelografico*, 26. Fasc. 17. Roma: Ministero Agricultura, Industria e Commercio.

Nicolini, G., G. Versini, S. Moser, S. Carlin, and U. Malossini. 2003. "Aroma characteristics from the cultivar Manzoni Bianco (White riesling x Pinit Blanc')." *Mitteilungern Klosterburg* 53: 251–57.

Nicollier, J. 1972. *Rapport sur les appellations de vin Chardonnay, Oriou, Cornalin-Landroter*. Chatauneuf: Station cantonale d'essais viticoles.

Nieddu, G. 2011. *Vitigni della Sardegna*. Cagliari: Convisar.

Nieddu, G., M. Arca, L. Mercenaro, A.S. De Oliveira. 2010. "La coltivazione del vitigno Vernaccia nell'Oristanese." In *Proceedings of the Accademia Italiana della Vite e del Vino*, 37–51. Belluno: Tipografia Piave.

Nieddu, G., M. Nieddu, G.F. Cocco, P. Erre, and I. Chessa. 2007. "Morphological and genetic characterization of the Sardinian Bovale cultivars." *Acta Horticulturae* 754: 49–54.

Nigro, G. 2004–10. "Progetto Vitigni Minori: Valutazione di vecchie varietà di vite locali in funzione di una differenziazione e del miglioramento della piattaforma varietale dell'Emilia Romagna." Slide presentation. http://www.caiforli.com/site/vitigni%20minori%20-%20roberto%20nigro.pdf.

Nuvolone, G. (1798) 2002. *Sulla coltivazione delle viti e sul metodo migliore di fare e conservare i vini. Istruzione: Calendario georgico compilato e pubblicato dalla Società Agraria di Torino per l'anno VII e VIII*. Torino: Ristampa Enoteca del Piemonte, Sorì Edizioni.

Odart, A.P. 1874. *Ampélographie universelle ou traité des cepages*. Paris: Librarie Agricole.

Onorati, N.C. 1804. *Delle Cose Rustiche Ovvero dell'agricoltura Teorica*. Napoli: A. Trani.

Osterman, V. 1940. *La vita in Friuli*. 2 vols. Udine: Del Bianco e Figlio.

Palumbo, M. 1853. "Sistema ampelografico per la classificazione dei vitigni siciliani." *Giornale Commissioni Agricultura e Pastorizia per la Sicilia* 2.

Pasqualini, A., and T. Pasqui. (1875) 1889. *Saggi analitici and ampelografici intorno a dieci vitigni Romagnoli*. Forlì: Regia Stazione Agraria di Forlì.

Pastena, B. 1971. "I catarratti bianchi." *Atti Accademia Vite e Vino*, 23.

———. 1973. *Il vitigno Nocera nera di Milazzo*. Palermo: Tipografia Kefa-Lo Giudice.

———. 1976. "L'Albanello vitigno dimenticato." *Rivista di Viticoltura ed Enologia* 11: 22.

———. 1993. "La Malvasia delle Lipari ed i suoi vini." *Sviluppo Agricolo Anno* 27(3): 17–31.

Pastore C., and G. Allegro. 2007. "Alla riscoperta dei vitigni autoctoni." *L'Informatore Agrario* (Gennaio): 74–75.

Peccana, A. 1627. *De' problemi del bever freddo*. Verona: A. Tamo editore.

Pejić, I., E. Maletić, and E. Naslov. 2005. "Malvajia istarska and Malvasia dubrovacka: Croatian or Greek cultivars?" Paper presented at Whose Goblet Is Malmsey, 17th Symposium on History and Art, Monemvasia, 30 May–1 June.

Pellerone, F.I., K.J. Edwards, and M.R. Thomas. 2001. "Grapevine microsatellite repeats: Isolation, characterisation and use for genotyping of grape germplasm from Soutehrn Italy." *Vitis* 40: 179–86.

Pelsy, F., S. Hocquigny, X. Moncada, G. Barbeau, D. Forget, P. Hinrichsen, and D. Merdinoglu. 2010. "An extensive study of the gentic diversity within seven French wine grape variety collections." *Theoretical Applied Genetics* 120: 1219–31.

Pereira, L., H. Guedes-Pinto, and P. Martins-Lopes. 2011. "An enhanced method for *Vitis vinifera* L. DNA extraction from wines." *American Journal of Enology and Viticulture* 62(4): 547–52.

Perez, G.B. 1900. *La provincia di Verona ed i suoi vini*. Verona: Franchini.

Perusini, G. 1935. "Note di viticoltura collinare." *L'Agricoltore Friulano*.

Petrussi, C. 2013. "Tocai giallo e Tocai verde: Due facce della stessa medaglia." In *Tocai e Friulano un racconto di civiltà del vino*, edited by E. Costantini. Udine: Editrice Universitaria Udinese.

Pignataro, L. 2011. "Asprinio di Aversa, il punto sulla ricerca scientifica." www.lucianopignataro.it, 4 May.

Pillon, C. 2005. "Malvasia, l'esercito dei cloni." *Civiltà del Bere*, July.

Pineau, B., J. C. Barbe, C. Van Leeuwen, and D. Dubourdieu. 2007. "Which impact for beta-damascenone on red wines aroma?" *Journal of Agricultural Food Chemistry* 55: 4103–8.

Pirolo, C. S., P. La Notte, F. Pastore, D. Torello Marinoni, P. Giannini, P. Venerito, A. Cagnazzo, and A. Schneider. 2009. "Verdeca e Pampanuto sono la stessa varietà." *L'Informatore Agrario* 65(49): 55–56.

Pirona, J. 1871. *Vocabolario di lingua friulana*. Venezia: Antonelli.

Pisani, P. L. 1986. "Primi risultati di ricerche sul patrimonio varietale viticolo della Toscana." *L'Enotecnico* 10: 1001–5.

Pisani, P. L., R. Bandinelli, and A. Camussi. 1997. "Ricerche sul germoplasma viticolo della Toscana. I vitigni da uva di colore." *Quaderno Arsia* 9: 17.

Pizzi, A. (1891) 1982. "Diagramma indicante il titolo zuccherino e l'acidità dei mosti d'uve della provincia di Reggio nell'Emilia." In *Reggio Emilia la provincia 'Lambrusca,'* edited by U. Bellocchi. Reggio Emilia: Editrice Tecnostampa.

Poggi, G. 1935. *I vini del Friuli*. Udine.

———. 1939a. *Picolit*. Edited by the Consorzio Provinciale tra i Produttori dell'Agricoltura, Sezione Viticoltura Udine. Pordenone: Arti Grafiche Pordenone.

———. 1939b. *Refosco d'Istria*. Edited by the Consorzio Provinciale tra i Produttori dell'Agricoltura, Sezione Viticoltura Udine. Pordenione: Arti Grafiche Pordenone.

Pollini, C. 1818. "Osservazioni agrarie per l'anno 1818." *Memorie dell'Accademia di Agricoltura, Commercio ed Arti di Verona* 10.

Pollini, L. 2006. *Viaggio attraverso i vitigni autoctoni italiani*. Siena: Alsaba Editore.

Porta, I. B. 1584. *7 Vinea*. Vol. 12. Naples: Villae.

Powell, W., M. Morgantet, C. Andre, J. W. McNicol, G. C. Machray, J. J. Doyle, S. V. Tingeyt, and J. A. Rafalski. 1999. "Hypervariable microsatellites provide a general source of polymorphic DNA markers for the chloroplast genome." *Current Biology* 5: 1023–29.

Prosperi, V. 1939. *I vini pregiati dei Castelli Romani*. Roma: R.E.D.A.

Provana di Collegno, L. 1883. "Relazione sulla esposizione ampelografica di Pinerolo (25/9–1/10/1881)." *Bollettino Ampelografico* 16.

Racah, V. 1932. *Pagine di viticoltura vissuta*. Firenze: Giunti.

Raimondi S., A. Schneider, and D. De Santis. 2008. "Greco Nero (di Sibari): Schede ampelografiche e analitiche." In *Il Gaglioppo e i suoi fratelli: I vitigni autoctoni calabresi*, 178–79, edited by C. Fregoni and O. Nigra. Cirò Marina: Librandi Spa.

Raimondi, S., A. Schneider, D. De Santis, and L. Cavallo. 2008. *Il Gaglioppo e i suoi fratelli: I vitigni autoctoni calabresi*. Edited by C. Fregoni and O. Nigra. Cirò Marina: Librandi Spa. See esp. "Livelli di espressione dei principali caratteri ampelografici secondo le codifiche del progetto GENRES 081," "Greco Nero (di Verbicaro): Schede ampelografiche e analitiche," and "Moscatello di Saracena: Schede ampelografiche e analitiche."

Raimondi, S., G. Valota, and A. Schneider. 2006. "Lo studio dei vitigni autoctoni minori nella collezione ampelografica di Grinzane Cavour." *Agricoltura* 62: 20–24.

Rasetti, G. E. 1904. "Il Pallagrello." *L'Italia Agricola*, 204–7.

Raven, P. H., B. Berlin, and D. E. Breedlove. 1971. "The Origins of Taxonomy." *Science* 174 (4015): 1201–13.

Reale, S., F. Pilla, and A. Angiolillo. 2006. "Genetic analysis of the Italian *Vitis vinifera* cultivar Tintilia and related cultivars using SSR markers." *Journal of Horticultural Science and Biotechnology* 81(6): 989–94.

Rézeau, P. 1997. *Dictionnaire des noms de cépages de France*. Paris: Centre National de la Recherche Scientifique.

Riaz, S., K. E. Garrison, G. S. Dangl, J. M. Boursiquot, and C. P. Meredith. 2002. "Genetic divergence and chimerism within ancient asexually propagated grapevine cultivars." *Journal of the American Society for Horticultural Science* 127(4): 508–14.

Rigotti, R. 1932. "Rilievi statistici e considerazioni sulla viticoltura trentina." *Esperienze e Ricerche*. Vol. 1 (1929–30). San Michele all'Adige: Stazione Agraria Sperimentale San Michele all'Adige.

Rinaldi, A., and R. Valli. 1992. "I vecchi vitigni di Reggio Emilia." *Vignevini* 10.

Robinson, J. 2005. *Vines, grapes, and wines: The wine drinker's guide to grape varieties*. London: Mitchell Beazley.

Robinson, J., J. Harding, and J. Vouillamoz. 2012. *Wine grapes*. London: Allen Lane.

Romano, P., A. Capece, V. Serafino, R. Romaniello, and C. Poeta. 2008. "Biodiversity of wild strains of Saccharomyces cerevisiae as tool to complement and optimize wine quality." *World Journal of Microbiology and Biotechnology* 24: 1797–1802.

Roncador, I. 2006. "Il Teroldego Rotaliano, vino principe del Trentino." In *Teroldego: Un autoctono esemplare*, 36–75, edited by the Cantina Rotaliana di Mezzolombardo. Trento: Provincia Autonoma di Trento.

Roncador, I., U. Malossini, M. S. Grando, F. Mattivi, C. Nicolini, and G. Versini. 2002. "Caratteristiche viti-enologiche dei nuovi vitigni Goldtraminer, Sennen e Gosen." *Terre Trentine* 10(2): 28–36.

Rovera, V. 1981. *Una selva, un borgo, e una pieve.* Borgo San Dalmazzo: Bertello Editore.

Rubini, G. F. 1887. "Nome dei vitigni che si coltivano nella provincia di Rovigo." *Bollettino Ampelografico*. Vol. 4. Roma: Ministero Agricoltura e Foreste.

Rusjan, D., T. Jug, and N. Štajner. 2010. "Evaluation of genetic diversity: Which of the varieties can be named 'Rebula' (*Vitis vinifera* L.)?" *Vitis* 49(4): 189–92.

Salmaso, M., R. Dalla Valle, and M. Lucchin. 2008. "Gene pool variation and phylogenetic relationships of an indigenous northeast Italian grapevine collection revealed by nuclear and chloroplast SSRs." *Genome* 51(10): 838–55.

Sanna, G. P. 2000. "La coltivazione del vitigno Arvesionadu nel territorio di Benetutti." Tesi di laurea, Facoltà Agraria di Sassari.

Sannino, F. A. 1907. "Prosecco." *Rivista di Viticoltura e di Enologia di Conegliano* 13: 4.

———. 1913. "Note ampelografiche sulle tribù del Prosecco e del Verdiso." *Rivista di Viticoltura e di Enologia di Conegliano* 19: 5.Unione Italiana Vini. "Sangiovese, il re del vigneto Italia." 2012. *Corriere Vinicolo*. Last modified 30 April. http://www.uiv.it/corriere/sangiovese-il-re-del-vigneto-italia.

Scalabrelli G., and C. D'Onofrio. 2013. "Vernaccia di San Gimignano." In Italian Vitis Database, www.vitisdb.it, ISSN 2282–0062010.

Scalabrelli, G., C. D'Onofrio, G. Ferroni, and R. Vignai. 2009. "Indagini ampelografiche e biomolecolari sul vitigno 'Aleatico.'" *Atti Accademia Italiana della Vite e del Vino*. Gorgonzola: Global print.

Scalabrelli, G., C. D'Onofrio, S. Paolicchi, and P. Bucelli. 2005. *Vitigni ad uva nera*. Vol. 1 of *Il germoplasma viticolo della Toscana*. Firenze: ARSIA. See esp. "Albarola Nera" and "Barbarossa."

Scalabrelli, G., and A. Grasselli. 1985. "Recupero dei vitigni coltivati nella zona Bianco di Pitigliano." *L'Informatore Agrario* 5: 59–66.

Scalabrelli, G., R. Vignani, M. Scali, D. Di Pietro, A. Materazzi, and E. Triolo. 2000. "Il 'Morellino Pizzuto': Un biotipo di 'Sangiovese'?" Paper presented at the Simposio Internazionale Il Sangiovese, Florence, 15–17 February.

Scartezzini, H. 2005. "Geschichtliche Spurensuche zur Rebsorte Lagrein." *Deutsches Weinbau-Jahrbuch* 56: 146–56.

Schneider, A. 2005–6. "Genetic aspects in the knowledge of autochthonous wine grape cultivars." *Quaderni di Viticoltura Enologia dell' Università di Torino* 28: 7–16.

———. 2007. "Recupero e salvaguardia del germoplasma viticolo: Biodiversità, un valore in forte erosione; attività svolta in Liguria." Paper presented at the conference Sviluppo e qualità della viticoltura Ligure, Attività e risultati. Genova, 16 May.

Schneider, A., P. Boccacci, and R. Botta. 2003. "Genetic relationships among grapevine cultivars from North-Western Italy." *Acta Horticulturae* 603: 229–35.

Schneider, A., P. Boccacci, D. Torello Marinoni, R. Botta, A. Akkak, and J. Vouillamoz. 2004. "The genetic variability and unexpected parentage of Nebbiolo." *Proceedings of the First International Conference on Nebbiolo grapes*. www.nebbiolo-grapes.org.

Schneider, A., A. Carrà, A. Akkak, P. This, V. Laucou, and R. Botta. 2001. "Verifying synonymies between grape cultivars from France and Northwestern Italy using molecular markers." *Vitis* 40(4): 197–203.

Schneider, A., G. Mainardi, and S. Raimondi. 2011. *Ampelografia universale storica illustrata*. Savigliano: Artistica Editrice Savigliano.

Schneider, A., and F. Mannini. 1990. "Indagine comparativa su Vermentino, Pigato e Favorita in Piemonte e Liguria." *L'Informatore Agrario* 8: 103–8.

———, eds. 2006. "Vitigni del Piemonte varietà e cloni." *Quaderni della Regione Piemonte*, supp. 50. Turin: Regione Piemonte, Assessorato Agricoltura.

Schneider, A., F. Mannini, and N. Argamante. 1993. *I vini liguri: Orientamenti per la vitivinicoltura ligure*. Servizio per Assistenza Tecnica e Sperimentazione in Agricoltura. Genova: Regione Liguria.

Schneider, A., S. Raimondi, and D. De Santis. 2008. *Il Gaglioppo e i suoi fratelli: I vitigni autoctoni calabresi*. Edited by C. Fregoni and

O. Nigra. Cirò Marina: Librandi Spa. See esp. "Greco Bianco: Schede ampelografiche e analitiche," "Iuvarello: Schede ampelografiche e analitiche," "Magliocco Dolce: Schede ampelografiche e analitiche," and "Mantonico Bianco Italico: Schede ampelografiche e analitiche."

Schneider, A., S. Raimondi, and V. Gerbi. 2005a. "Erbaluce: Erbaluce e Vernacce, sorso di tradizione." *Civiltà del Bere* 11: 128–31.

———. 2005b. "Freisa: Freisa e Raboso Piave antiche stirpi autoctone." *Civiltà del Bere* 9: 72–77.

Schneider, A., S. Raimondi, M. S. Grando, R. Zappia, D. De Santis, D. Torello Marinoni, and N. Librandi. 2008. "Studi per il riordino del germoplasmaviticolo della Calabria." In *Il Gaglioppo e i suoi fratelli I vitigni autoctoni calabresi*, 117–24, edited by C. Fregoni and O. Nigra. Cirò Marina: Librandi Spa.

Schneider, A., M. Soster, and L. Ricci. 1994. "Identificazione dei principali vitigni 'Brachetto' coltivati in Piemonte." *I quaderni Piemonte Agricoltura*, suppl. 3: 1–8.

Schneider, A., and D. Torello Marinoni. 2003. "Analisi con marcatori molecolari microsatelliti di vitigni autoctoni della provincia di Reggio Emilia." Paper presented at the Convegno Recupero e valorizzazione di vitigni autoctoni. Correggio, Italy, 12 December.

Schneider, A., D. Torello Marinoni, P. Boccacci, and R. Botta. 2006. "Relazioni genetiche del vitigno Nebbiolo." *Quaderni di Viticoltura di Enologia dell' Università di Torino* 28: 93–100.

Schneider, A., D. Torello Marinoni, S. Raimondi, P. Boccacci, and G. Gambino. 2009. "Molecular characterization of wild grape populations from northwestern Italy and their genetic relationship with cultivated varieties." *Acta Horticulturae* 827: 211–16.

Scienza, A. 2004. "Il terzo anello: Storia di un viaggio." In *La vite e l'uomo: Dal rompicapo delle origini al salvataggio delle relique*, edited by F. Del Zan, O. Failla, and A. Scienza. Udine: ERSA.

———. 2007. "Origine e storia." In *La vite e il vino*, edited by A. Scienza. Bologna: Art Servizi Editoriali.

———. 2011. "Introduzione." In *Origini della Viticoltura: Atti del convegno*, edited by B. Biagini. Castiglione d'Orcia: Podere Forte.

Scienza, A., and M. Boselli. 2003. *Vini e vitigni della Campania: Tremila anni di storia*. Napoli: Agripromis.

Scienza, A., L. Brancadoro, E. Branzanti, R. Di Lorenzo, R. Di Stefano, F. Gagliano, V. Falco, and G. Ansaldi. 2008. "Vitigni autoctoni siciliani, un valore aggiunto che cresce." *L'informatore Agrario*, suppl. 23: 14.

Scienza, A., O. Failla, R. Anziani, F. Mattivi, P. Villa, E. Giannazza, G. Tedesco, and U. Benetti. 1990. "Le possibili analogie tra il Lambrusco a foglia frastagliata, alcuni vitigni coltivati e le viti selvatiche del basso Trentino." *Vignevini* 17(9): 25–36.

Sefk, K. M., F. Lefort, M. S. Grando, N. S. Scott, H. Steinkellner, and M. R. Thomas. 2001. "Microsatellite markers for grapevine: A state of art." In *Molecular Biology and Biotechnology of Grapevine*, edited by K. A. Roubelakis-Angelakis. Dordrecht: Kluwer Academic Publishers.

Sefk, K. M., M. S. Lopes, F. Lefort, R. Botta, K. A. Roubelakis-Angelakis, J. Ibanez, I. Pejic, H. W. Wagner, J. Glössl, and H. Steinkellner. 2000. "Microsatellite variability in grapevine cultivars from different European regions and evaluation of assignment testing to assess the geographic origin of cultivars." *Theoretical and Applied Genetics* 100(3–4): 498–505.

Semenzi, G. B. A. 1864. *Treviso e la sua provincia*. Bologna: Atesa.

Semmola, V. 1848. *Delle varietà di vitigni del Vesuvio e del Somma*. Napoli: Tipografia del Reale Albergo dei Poveri.

Sensi, E., R. Vignaniz, W. Rohde, and S. Biricolti. 1996. "Characterization of genetic biodiversity with *Vitis vinifera* L. Sangiovese and Colorino genotypes by AFLP and ISTR DNA marker technology." *Vitis* 35(4): 183–88.

Sereni, E. 1965. *Per la storia delle più antiche tecniche e nomenclatura della vite e del vino in Italia*. Firenze: L. S. Olschky.

Sesto, S., and M. Rissone. 1988. *Valutazione delle attuali attitudini enologiche dei vini della DOC Lamezia*. Lamezia Terme: Tipografia La Modernissima.

Silvestroni, O., D. Di Pietro, C. Intrieri, R. Vignani, I. Filippetti, C. Del Casino, M. Scali, and M. Cresti. 1997. "Detection of genetic diversity among clones of cv: Fortana (*Vitis vinfera* L.) by microsatellite DNA polymorphism analysis." *Vitis* 36(3): 147–50.

Silvestroni, O., and C. Intrieri. 1995. "Ampelometric assessment of clonal variability in the Sangiovese vinegrape cultivar." *Proceedings of the International Symposium on Clonal Selection*, 137–42. Portland, 20–21 June.

Silvestroni, O., B. Marangoni, and F. Faccioli. 1986. "Identificazione e conservazione dei vitigni locali (*Vitis vinifera* L.) in Emilia Romagna." Paper presented at the Simposio Internazionale di Genetica della Vite. *Vignevini* suppl. 12.

Sivilotti, P., and M. Stocco. 2013. *Autoctoni Friuli.* Udine: Editore Agenzia Sviluppo Rurale Ersa.

Smart, R., and M. Robinson. 1991. *Sunlight into wine.* Adelaide: Winetitles.

Soderini, G. 1590. *Coltivazione toscana delle viti e d'alcuni alberi.* Firenze: Giunti.

Sormani Moretti, L. 1904. *La Provincia di Verona: Monografia statistica, economica ed amministrativa.* Firenze: Leo Olschky Editore.

Sparacio, A., L. Prinzivalli, G. Genna, S. Sparla, F. Capraro, V. Melia, and A. Verzera. 2010. "Vitigni sennen e Gosen: Opportunità per i vini siciliani." *L'Informatore Agrario* 24: 39–42.

Štajner, N., Z. Korosec-Koruzam, D. Ruzjan, and B. Javornik. 2008. "Microsatellite genotyping of old Slovenian grapevine varieties (Vitis vinifera L.) of the Primorje (coastal) wine growing region." *Vitis* 47(4): 201–4.

Stavrakakis, M., and M. Loukas. 1983. "The between—and within—grape cultivars genetic variation." *Scientia Horticulturae* 19: 321–34.

Storchi, P., A. B. Armanni, M. Crespan, E. Frare, G. De Lorenzis, C. D'Onofrio, and G. Scalabrelli. 2009. "A survey on the identity of Malvasias with black berries cultivated in Tuscany." Paper presented at the Third International Symposium Malvasias, La Palma, Spain, 23–27 May.

Storchi, P., A. B. Armanni, L. Randellini, S. Giannetto, S. Meneghetti, and M. Crespan. 2011. "Investigations on the identity of 'Canaiolo Bianco' and other white grape varieties of Central Italy." *Vitis* 50(2): 59–64.

Strucchi, A., and M. Zecchini. (1895) 1986. *Il Moscato di Canelli.* Turin: UTET. Reprinted Canelli: Casa Editrice Dalmasso.

Tamaro, D. (1902) 1915. *Uve da tavola,* 4th ed. Milano: Hoepli.

Tanara, V. (1644) 1674. *L'economia del cittadino in villa.* Venice: Appresso Steffano Curti.

Tazzer, S. 1976. "La Trevisana Nera è una mosca bianca." *Civiltà del Bere,* no. 2.

Tedeschini, G. 1930. *Il passito di Caluso.* Asti: Scuola Tipografica S. Giuseppe.

Tellini, G. 2007. "Tra vini e vini nella letteratura toscana: Da Dante a Carducci." In *Storia della vite e del vino in Italia: Toscana.* Firenze: Polistampa.

Tempesta, G., and M. Fiorillo. 2011. "Patrimonio Varietale." www.vivaioenotria.com.

This, P., A. Jung, P. Boccacci, J. Borrego, R. Botta, L. Costantini, M. Crespan, G. S. Dangl, C. Eisenheld, F. Ferreira-Monteiro, M. S. Grando, J. Ibanez, T. Lacombe, V. Laucou, R. Magalhaes, C. P. Meredith, N. Milani, E. Peterlunger, F. Regner, L. Zulini, and E. Maul. 2004. "Development of a standard set of microsatellite reference alleles for identification of grape varieties." *Theoretical and Applied Genetics* 109(7): 1448–58.

This, P., T. Lacombe and M. R. Thomas. 2006. "Historical origins and genetic diversity of wine grapes." *Trends in Genetics* 22(9): 511–19.

Thomas, M. R., P. Cain, and N. S. Scott. 1994. "DNA typing of grapevine: A universal methodology and database for describing cultivars and evaluating genetic relatedness." *Plant Molecular Biology* 25(6): 939–49.

Thomas, M. R., and N. S. Scott. 1993. "Microsatellite repeats in grapevine reveal DNA polymorphisms when analyzed as sequence tagged sites (STSs)." *Theoretical and Applied Genetics* 86(8): 985–90.

Tibaldi, T. 1886. *La Vallée d'Aoste au Moyen Age et à la Renaissance.* Turin: J. Tarrizzo Editeur.

Tochon, P. 1868. *Les Cépages du Départment de la Savoie.* Chambéry: Bonne, Conte-Grand.

Toni, G. 1927. "Agricoltura emiliana: Viticoltura ed enologia." *L'Italia Agricola,* no. 4.

Torcia, M. (1793) 1986. *Saggio Itinerario Nazionale pel Paese de' Peligni.* Cerchio: Adelmo Polla Editore.

Torello Marinoni, D., S. Raimondi, P. Boccacci, and A. Schneider. 2006. "Lambruschi from Piedmont: Historical investigations, fingerprinting and genetic relationships with other autochthonous Italian grapes (*Vitis vinifera* L.)." *Italus Hortus,* March-April 13(2): 158–61.

Torello Marinoni, D., S. Raimondi, F. Mannini, and L. Rolle. 2009. "Genetic and phenolic characterization of several intraspecific crosses (*Vitis vinifera* L.) registered in the Italian National Catalogue." *Proceedings of the IX International Conference on Grape Genetics and Breeding,* Udine, 26 June 2006. Edited by E. Peterlunger, G. Di Gaspero, and G. Cipriani. In *Acta Horticulturae* 827: 485–92.

Torello Marinoni, D., S. Raimondi, P. Ruffa, T. Lacombe, and A. Schneider. 2009. "Identification of grape cultivars from Liguria (north-western Italy)." *Vitis* 48(4): 175–83.

Tosi, E., and C. Bletzo. 2000. "Vecchi vitigni per la viticoltura veronese: L'Oseleta." *L'Informatore Agrario,* supplemento 36: 6–7.

Trinci, C. 1726. *L'agricoltura sperimentale, ovvero regole generali sopra l'agricoltura, coltivazione delle viti, degli alberi, ecc.* Lucca: Salvatore e Giandomenico Marescandoli.

Università Politecnica delle Marche, Facoltà di Agraria e Economia, eds. 2009. *La riscoperta del pecorino: Storia di un vitigno e di un vino.* Milano: Tecniche Nuove.

Vantini, F., G. Tacconi, M. Gastaldelli, C. Govoni, E. Tosi, P. Malacrinò, R. Bassi, and L. Cattivelli. 2003.

"Biodiversity of grapevines (*Vitis vinifera* L.) grown in the province of Verona." *Vitis* 42(1): 35–38.

Varanini, G. M. 1988. "Aspetti della produzione e del commercio del vino nel Veneto alla fine del medioevo." In *Il Veneto nel Medioevo*, edited by A. Castagnetti and G. M. Varanini. Verona: Arnoldo Mondadori.

Vavilov, N. I. 1926. *Studies on the origins of cultivated plants*. Leningrad: Institute of Applied Botany and Plant Breeding.

Venturi, A., and M. Fontana. 1998. "Yield and quality of Trebbiano romagnolo and Biancame varieties grafted on different rootstocks." *Vignevini* 25(10): 60–67.

Vermeulen, C., L. Gijs, and S. Collin. 2005. "Sensorial contributions and formation pathways of thiols in foods: A review." *Food Reviews International* 21(5): 69–137.

Veronelli, L. 1961. *I Vini d'Italia*. Roma: Canesi Editore.

———. 1971. *Bere giusto*. Milano: Rizzoli Editore.

———. 1974. *Catalogo Bolaffi dei vini d'Italia*. Torino: Bolaffi Editore.

———, ed. 1989. *Le Cantine di Veronelli 1989*. Milan: Giorgio Mondadori Editore.

———. 1995. *Repertorio Veronelli dei vini italiani*. Bergamo: Veronelli Editore.

Viala, P., and V. Vermorel, eds. 1909. *Ampelographie*. Paris: Masson et Cie Editeurs.

Viggiani, L., and M. A. Castiglione Morelli. 2008. "Characterization of wines by nuclear magnetic resonance: A work study on wines from the Basilicata region in Italy." *Journal of Agricultural and Food Chemistry* 56(18): 8273–79.

Vignani, R., M. Scali, E. Masi, and M. Cresti. 2002. "Genomic variability in *Vitis vinifera* L. Sangiovese assessed by microsatellite and non-radioactive AFLP test." *Electronic Journal of Biotechnology* 5(1): 1–11.

Vignani, R., M. Scali, E. Masi, C. Milanelli, G. Scalabrelli, W. Wang, E. Sensi, E. Paolucci, G. Percoco, and M. Cresti. 2008. "A critical evaluation of SSR analysis applied to Tuscan (Vitis vinifera L.) germplasm." *Advances in Horticultural Science* 22(1): 33–37.

Villa, P. L., O. Milesi, and A. Scienza. 1997. *Vecchi vitigni Bresciani*. Brescia: Queriniana.

Villifranchi, C. G. 1773. *Oenologia Toscana o sia memoria sopra i vini ed in special modo toscani*. Firenze: Ciambiagi.

Violante, C., and S. Bordignon. 1960. "Coda di Volpe Bianca." *Principali vitigni ad uva da vino coltivati in Italia*. Vol. 1. Roma: Ministero Agricultura e Foreste.

Vitagliano, M. 1985. *Storia del vino in Puglia*. Bari: Editore Laterza.

———. 1991. *I vini DOC Irpini*. Avellino: Camera di Commercio, Industria, Artigianato ed Agricoltura, 2nd ed.

Vouillamoz, J. F., and C. Arnold. 2010. "Microsatellite pedigree reconstruction provides evidence that Muller Thurgau is a grandson of Pinot and Schiava grossa." *Vitis* 49(2): 63–69.

Vouillamoz, J. F., and M. S. Grando. 2006. "Genealogy of wine grape cultivars: 'Pinot' is related to 'Syrah.'" *Heredity* 97(2): 102–10.

Vouillamoz, J. F., S. Imazio, M. Stefanini, A. Scienza, and M. S. Grando. 2004. "Relazioni genetiche del Sangiovese." In *Proceedings of the II International Symposium on 'Sangiovese,'* 17–19 November. Florence: Agenzia Regionale per lo Sviluppo e l'Innovazione in Agricoltura.

Vouillamoz, J. F., D. Maigre, and C. P. Meredith. 2003. "Microsatellite analysis of ancient alpine grape cultivars: Pedigree reconstruction of *Vitis vinifera* L. 'Cornalin du Valais.'" *Theoretical and Applied Genetics* 107(3): 448–54.

Vouillamoz, J. F., A. Monaco, L. Costantini, M. Stefanini, A. Scienza, and S. Grando. 2007. "The parentage of Sangiovese the most important Italian wine grape." *Vitis* 46(1): 19–22.

Vouillamoz, J. F., and G. Moriondo. 2011. *Origine des cépages valaisans et valdôtains: L'AND rencontre l'histoire*. Fleurier: Éditions du Belvédère.

Vouillamoz, J. F., A. Schneider, and M. S. Grando. 2007. "Microsatellite analysis of Alpine grape cultivars: Alleged descendants of Pliny the Elder's Raetica are genetically related." *Genetic Resources and Crop Evolution* 54(5): 1095–1104.

Weising, K., and R. Gardner. 1999. "A set of conserved PCR primers for the analysis of simple sequence repeat polymorphism in chloroplast genomes of dicotyledonous angiosperms." *Genome* 42: 9–19.

Williams, P. J., C. R. Strauss, B. Wilson, and R. Massey-Westropp. 1982. "Studies on the hydrolysis of *Vitis vinifera* monoterpene precursor compounds and model monoterpene b-D-glucosides rationalizing the monoterpene composition of grapes." *Journal of Agricultural and Food Chemistry* 30: 1219–23.

Zantedeschi, F. 1862. "Meteorologia italica." *Memorie dell'Accademia Di Agricoltura di Verona* 40.

Zappia, R., G. Gullo, R. Mafrica, and R. Di Lorenzo. 2007. "Mantonico vera e Mantonico pizzutella: Descrizione ampelografica, analisi microsatellite e comportamento bio-agronomico." *Italus hortus* 14: 59–62.

Zava, G. B. 1901. *Elenco descrittivo dei vecchi vitigni coltivati nel Veneto, secondo il nome volgare delle uve.* Treviso: Tipo-Litografia Sociale.

Zecca, G., F. De Mattia, G. Lovicu, M. Labra, F. Sala, and F. Grassi. 2010. "Wild grapevine: Silvestris, hybrids or cultivars escape from vineyards? Morphological and molecular evidence in Sardinia." *Plant Biology* 12(3): 558–62.

Zoccoletto, G. 2001. *L'Accademia Agraria degli Aspiranti di Conegliano.* Conegliano: Unione ex-Allievi Scuola Enologica.

Zulini, L., M. Russo, and E. Peterlunger. 2002. "Genotyping wine and table grape cultivars from Apulia (southern Italy) using microsatellite markers." *Vitis* 41(4): 183–87.

GENERAL INDEX

Please note: This index contains personal names and winery names, but brand and proprietary names and those of vineyards are not indexed. Grape varieties are indexed separately, in the Index of Grape Varieties. Wine names are indexed only when especially pertinent to the subject of native and traditional grapes. When a winery name is identical to the owner's, the winery and personal name are combined and indexed with the personal name preceding the winery name. When not immediately clear, an estate is indicated by the term (*winery*). Names of scientists and researchers who have contributed to advancing knowledge about native grapes are indexed, and then selectively. Geographical and historical references are indexed only when pertinent to the subject of native and traditional grapes. Only the most pertinent biochemical, viticultural, and enological terms are indexed.

Abbazia di Novacella (winery), 118, 325
Abbazia di Rosazzo (winery), 402
ABC clubs, 2
Abruzzo, 43
A' Cancellera (winery), 488
Accornero (winery), 96, 191, 317
aceto Balsamico Tradizionale, 141, 145
Acorn Winery/Alegria Vineyards, 334
Acquabona (winery), 178, 181
Acquacalda (winery), 181
acylated anthocyanins, 124, 220, 294, 328, 329, 367, 369, 432, 508
Adami (winery), 312
Adanti (winery), 426
Adolfo Spada (winery), 185, 186
aglianico del Vulture, 166
Agostini, Goffredo, 449
Agricole Vallone (winery), 366, 442
Agriverde (winery), 387
air-drying, 126
Albanesi, Fausto, 347
Albergo Regina Isabella, 485, 502
Alberice (winery), 133
Alberto Lusignani (winery), 542
Albert Vevey (winery), 405
Alberto Loi (winery), 228, 230
Alberto Longo (winery), 458
Alberto Quaquarini (winery), 156

Albino Armani (winery), 238, 239, 519
Aldegheni (winery), 267
Alfredo Mastropietro (winery), 196
Alessandro Bonsegna (winery), 366
Alessandro Pascolo (winery), 91
Allegrini (winery), 264
Alois (winery), 237
Alle Tre Colline (winery), 97
allochthonous grape variety, 2
Almondo, Giovanni, 182
Altura (winery), 181
Altydgedacht (winery), 191
Alziati Annibale/Tenuta San Francesco (winery), 267
A Maccia (winery), 418
Amadio (winery), 166, 184
Amaro (winery), 133
amarone, 127
Ambra (winery), 150
American Viticultural Areas (AVA), 2
Ampelocissus, 25
ampelography, 15, 16
ampelology, 15, 16
ampelometrics, 16, 17
Ampelopsis, 25
amplified fragment length polymorphism (AFLP), 19
Ancarani (winery), 243, 283, 285
Ancient Peaks Winery (winery), 133
Andrea Franch (winery), 66

593

Andreola (winery), 312
Anelli (winery), 325
Anfosso, Alessandro, 417
Anfosso, Maurizio, 417
Anfra (winery), 387
Angelo d'Uva (winery), 450
Angelucci (winery), 105, 109
Angiuli Donato (winery), 410
Angius, Fabio, 208, 211
Anna Berra (winery), 471
Anna Bosco (winery), 488
Anselmi (FVG), 444
Anselmi (Veneto), 306
Antano Milziade (winery), 426
Anteo (winery), 267
anthocyanidin, 9
anthocyanin, 9, 229, 247
anthocyanin profile, 11, 267, 328, 358
Antica Corte Pallavicina (winery), 293
Antica Masseria Venditti (winery), 488
Antichi Vigneti di Cantalupo (winery), 361, 477
Antico Borgo dei Cavalli (winery), 462
Antico Broilo (winery), 439
Antinori, Piero/Antinori (winery), 3–4
Antonelli-San Marco (winery), 148, 314, 426
Antonini, Alberto, 34
Antonio Arrighi (winery), 491
Antonio Caggiano (winery), 167
Antonio Camilli (winery), 251
Antoniolo (winery), 279, 361
Antonio Mazzella (winery), 202, 291
Apicella (winery), 451
Apollonio (winery), 200
Aquila del Torre (winery), 397
Arbios/Praxis Cellars (winery), 325
Arcadu, Tonino, 229
Argillae (winery), 314
Argiolas (winery), 211, 230, 345, 353, 378
Arimia (winery), 410
Armando Simoncelli (winery), 340
Arnaldo Caprai (winery), 425, 426
aromatic molecule precursor analysis, 16
Ascheri (winery), 392
Associazione Produttori della Torre di Oriolo, 243
Associazione Produttori Schioppettino di Prepotto, 436, 437
Associazione Volontaria Viticoltori del Refosco di Faedis, 135
Asti Spumante, 103, 105
Atlas Peak Winery, 3
Attanasio (winery), 410
Attems (winery), 415
Augusto Zadra (winery), 66
Aurora (winery), 390
autochthonous grape variety, 2
Azzali, Chiara, 380

Babini, Paolo, 171
Back Pocket (winery), 288
Badia a Coltibuono (winery), 221, 427, 435
Badin, Giorgio, 90

Baglio Hopps (winery), 320
Bailiwick (winery), 474
Balbiano (winery), 297
Ballentine (winery), 92
Balnarring Vineyard, 452
Bandinelli, Roberto, 21, 94, 95, 159, 192, 220, 426, 462, 522
Banfi (winery), 108, 432
Banrock Station (winery), 348
Baracco de Baracho (winery), 184
Barattieri di San Pietro (winery), 86, 213, 381
Barba (winery), 143
Barbaran (winery), 127, 128, 546
Barbera (winery), 182
Barberani (winery), 314
Barbolini (winery), 532
Bardolino, 343
Barletta, Alberto, 122, 236
Barolo, 166
Baroncini/Fattoria Sovesta (winery), 150
Barone Beneventano (winery), 109
Barone Cornacchia (winery), 349
Barone de Cles (winery), 446
Barone di Valforte (winery), 387
Barone di Villagrande (winery), 88
Barone La Lumia (winery), 219
Barraco (winery), 393
Barsento (winery), 99
Bartoletti, Francesco, 370
Bartolo Mascarello (winery), 361
Basilicata, 44
Basilisco (winery), 167
Bassham, 219, 288, 348
Battista Columbu (winery), 88, 484
Battistini (winery), 147
Beach Road (winery), 57, 166
Bean, Michele, 294
Beato Bartolomeo (winery), 475
Bellanzi (winery), 167
Bel Colle (winery), 392
BellaGrace (winery), 191
Bella Ridge Estate (winery), 150
Bellussi (winery), 127
Beltrame (winery), 444
Belvino (winery), 325
Benanti (winery), 236, 368, 370, 517
Benini, Carla, 250
benzenoid(s), 18, 328, 335, 387, 483, 508
Bernabei, Franco, 34
Bernasno, Arturo, 212
Berrouet, Jean-Claude, 15
berry shatter, 82, 176, 199, 274, 362, 374, 417, 451, 521
Berton (winery), 474
Bertoni, Diego, 343
β-damascenone, 329
bianchello del Metauro, 197
bianco di Pitigliano, 149
Bianchi San Juan Vineyards, 133
Biletta, 96
biochemical methods of grape variety identification, 16
Biondi-Santi (winery), 435

biotypes, 22, 27
Bio Vio (winery), 474
BioViola (winery), 242
Birichino (winery), 92
Bisol (winery), 312
Bisol, Desiderio, 198
Bisol, Gianluca, 273
Bisson (winery), 174, 175, 251, 474
Bissoni (winery), 447
Blackenbrook Vineyard, 348
Black Mesa (winery), 272
Blue Poles Vineyard, 446
Blue Teal Winery, 108
Boeger (winery), 191
Boffa, Pio, 361
Bolognani (winery), 110
Bolzano Cantina Produttori (winery), 118, 139
Bologna, Giacomo, 188
Bonluigi (winery), 332
Bonny Doon (winery), 92
Bonotto delle Tezze (winery), 127
Boplaas Family Vineyards (winery), 113
Borgo Conventi (winery), 415
Borgo delle Oche (winery), 468
Borgo del Tiglio (winery), 91, 452
Borgo Maragliano (winery), 108
Borio, Maria, 459
Bortolomiol (winery), 312
Boscaini, Raffaele, 526
Boscaini, Sandro, 343, 381,
Botrugno (winery), 99
Botrytis cinerea, 196
Bourdieu, Pierre, 4
Boveri Luigi (winery), 449
Box Grove (winery), 311, 474
Box Stallion (winery), 184, 272
Boynton's Feathertop (winery), 311
Braida (winery), 191, 213, 317
Brash Higgins (winery), 219
Braudel, Fernand, 4
Brennan Vineyards, 219
Bressan (winery), 439
Brezza (winery), 297
Bricco Mondalino (winery), 96, 317
Brigaldara (winery), 267
Brighi, Valerio, 192
Brovia (winery), 363
Brown Brothers (winery), 113, 166, 191, 311, 348, 474
Bruna (winery), 474
Brunello di Montalcino, 8, 166
Brunellogate, 11, 432
Bruno Broglia/La Meirana (winery), 261
Bruno Giacosa (winery), 182, 361
Bruno Grigoletti (winery), 340
Bruno Rocca (winery), 361
Bruno Verdi (winery), 191, 267
Bucci (winery), 468
Buglioni, Mariano, 343
Bulfon (winery), 118, 253, 255, 256, 292, 398, 439, 455
Bulichella (winery), 178
Buttarelli (winery), 246

Buranco (winery), 208
Burggrafler (winery), 110
By Jingo Wines, 348, 365, 410

Caciorgna, Paolo, 236
Ca' dei Frati (winery), 468
Ca' dei Noci (winery), 442
Ca' del Vent (winery), 544
Ca' d' Gal (winery), 108
Ca' du Russ (winery), 184
Ca' du Sindic/Sergio Grimaldi (winery), 108
Caesar, Julius, 251
Caffarella (winery), 88
Calabria, 44
Calcagno (winery), 370
Caldaro Produttori/Kellerei Kaltern (winery), 110
Callaway Vineyard and Winery, 108
Calò, Damiano, 366
Ca' Lustra (winery), 545
Cambria (winery), 375
Camigliano (winery), 108
Camillo Montori (winery), 349, 387
Campania, 43
Ca' Nova (winery), 293
Cantarutti (winery), 415, 452
Cantele (winery), 366
Cantina Aldeno, 138
Cantina Ariano, 205
Cantina Bambinuto, 58
Cantina Barone, 351
Cantina Bergamasca, 140
Cantina Bregante, 175
Cantina Calasetta, 234
Cantina Cicala, 186
Cantina Çimixaa, 441
Cantina Colli Amerini, 251
Cantina del Taburno, 167, 255, 282
Cantina del Vulture, 80
Cantina di Arceto, 76
Cantina di Bova, 320
Cantina di Dolianova, 489
Cantina di Nomi, 340
Cantina di Pitigliano, 465
Cantina di Santa Croce in Carpi, 179
Cantina di Venosa, 32, 80, 167
Cantina Formigine, 141
Cantina Frentana, 254, 350
Cantina Isera, 548
Cantina Novelli, 147
Cantina Paradiso, 205
Cantina Puianello, 180
Cantina Rotaliana, 66
Cantina Salvatore, 450
Cantina Santadi, 230, 234, 345
Cantina Sant'Agata, 423
Cantina Santa Maria La Palma, 216
Cantina Sociale del Locorotondo, 200, 341
Cantina Sociale di Arceto, 442
Cantina Sociale di Avio, 277
Cantina Sociale di Bricherasio, 521
Cantina Sociale di Faenza, 351

Cantina Sociale di Gualtieri, 289
Cantina Sociale di Mendrisio, 180
Cantina Sociale di Monserrato, 378
Cantina Sociale di Oristano, 374
Cantina Sperimentale Bonafus, 247
Cantina Sperimentale di Noto, 173
Cantina Toblino, 376, 542, 548
Cantina Trexenta, 345, 378
Cantina Turina, 66
Cantina Valtidone, 381
Cantina Vignuolo, 207
Cantine Bergamaschi, 293
Cantina Buglioni, 343, 344
Cantine Ceci, 71
Cantine Cipressi, 450
Cantine Claudi, 156
Cantine degli Astroni, 255, 282
Cantine dei Colli Tramonte, 404
Cantine del Notaio, 80, 167
Cantine Federiciane Monteleone, 400
Cantine Gallicchio, 329
Cantine Guerrieri, 119
Cantine Gulino, 174
Cantine Lonardo/Contrade di Taurasi, 422
Cantine Olivella, 221, 240
Cantine Riunite, 72
Cantine Rolfo, 214
Cantine Segesta, 175
Cantine Tora, 167
Cantine Torri, 350
Cantine Viola, 109, 482
Canto delle Vigne (winery), 168
Cantrina (winery), 67
Capanna (winery), 108
Capannelle (winery), 94, 435
Caparone, Dave/Caparone (winery), 164, 166, 360
Cape Mentelle (winery), 410
Cape Wine Cellars, 191
Capezzana (winery), 150
Capinera (winery), 327
Capolino Perlingieri (winery), 440
Cappello (winery), 106
Capponi, Sebastiano, 221, 522
Capraia, 178
Caprili (winery), 108
Caputo (winery), 186
Caravaglio (winery), 88
Caretto Loris (winery), 248
Cargo Road Wines, 410
Carlo Benotto (winery), 303
Carlo Boscaini (winery), 344
Carlo Daniele Ricci (winery), 449
Carpante (winery), 216
Carparelli, Lino/I Pastini-Lino Carparelli (winery), 200, 341, 342, 464
Carpineti, Marco/Marco Carpineti (winery), 59, 145, 195, 196, 196, 372, 373
Carra di Casatico (winery), 71
Carriero, Giancarlo, 485, 502
Carthage, 197
Cartizze, 311

Ca' Rugate (winery), 306
Caruso & Minini (winery), 306, 393
Carussin (winery), 232
Casa Barone (winery), 231
Casabianca (winery), 53
Casa Cecchin (winery), 276
Casadei, Stefano, 211, 223
Casa dell'Orco (winery), 255
Casale Cento Corvi (winery), 307
Casale della Ioria (winery), 246, 379, 387
Casale Pilozzo (winery), 85
Casali Viticultori (winery), 332, 442
Casalnuovo del Duca (winery), 330
Casa Piave (winery), 471
Casa Roma (winery), 338, 471, 546
Casa Ronsil (winery), 187, 192, 193, 487
Casa Setaro (winery), 221
Cascina Castlet (winery), 460
Cascina Chicco (winery), 184, 214
Cascina degli Ulivi (winery), 272
Cascina delle Terre Rosse (winery), 327, 474
Cascina Fonda (winery), 108
Cascina Nirasca (winery), 272
Cascina Praié (winery), 327
Cascina Sant'Ubaldo (winery), 540
Cascina Tavijin (winery), 317, 423
Case Rosse (winery), 272
Casetta (winery), 391
Castel de Paolis (winery), 195
Castellare (winery), 94, 427, 435
Castellari Bergaglio (winery), 261
Castellinaldo, 183
Castelli Maurizio, 34, 50, 98, 220, 221, 249, 250, 290, 332, 347, 411, 433
Castelli Romani, 194, 195
Castelli Winery, 223, 360
Castello della Paneretta (winery), 221, 223
Castello del Trebbio (winery), 223
Castello di Ama (winery), 94, 435
Castello di Brolio (winery), 289
Castello di Buttrio (winery), 403
Castello di Cacchiano (winery), 83
Castello di Luzzano (winery), 191
Castello di Neive (winery), 540
Castello di Rubbia (winery), 91, 447
Castello di Semivicoli (winery), 143
Castello di Tassarolo (winery), 261
Castello di Verduno (winery), 391
Castelloducale (winery), 123
Castello Fageto (winery), 387
Castellucci Miano (winery), 393
Castel Salleg/Schloss Sallegg (winery), 110, 118
Castelvecchio (FVG) (winery), 91, 447
Castelvecchio (Tuscany; winery), 221, 223
Cataldi Madonna, Luigi/Cataldi Madonna (winery), 142, 143, 348, 349, 388, 389, 390
Catalogo Istituzionale delle Varietà di Vite, x
Catherine Vale Vineyard, 184, 282
Caudrina (winery), 108
Cavalier Pepe (winery), 255
Cavallero, Franco, 422

Cavalli Sforza, Luigi Luca, 27
Cavallotto (winery), 297, 317
Cave des Onzes Communes (winery), 341
Cave du Vin Blanc de Morgex et La Salle (winery), 32, 405, 421
Cavicchioli (winery), 69, 73
Cecchetto, Giorgio/Giorgio Cecchetto (winery), 127, 545
Cecilia (winery), 181
Cefalicchio (winery), 459
Celesti (winery), 148
Celli (winery), 147, 447
Celso Vandelli (winery), 146
Celti Centurioni (winery), 461
Cenatiempo (winery), 202, 291
Cennatoio (winery), 334
Centanni (winery), 387
Centennial Vineyards, 529
Centopassi (winery), 242
Centro per la Sperimentazione in Vitivinicoltura della Provincia di Verona, 491
Centro Ricerca e Sperimentazione Agricoltura (CRSA), 119
Centro Ricerca per la Viticultura (CRA-VIT), 16
Centro Ricerche Produzioni Vegetali (CRPV), 41, 224, 242, 283, 364
Cerasuolo di Vittoria, 217
Ceratti (winery), 59, 335, 336
Ceraudo (winery), 387
Ceretto (winery), 361
Ceretto, Alessandro, 182
Ceretto, Federico, 182
Cerri (winery), 115
Cesani (winery), 251
Cesconi (winery), 376
Chain of Ponds (winery), 191
Chalmers (winery), 57, 90, 166, 219, 325, 333, 365, 426, 474
Chambave Moscato, 106
Chambers Rosewood (winery), 107
Charrère, Constantino, 407, 505
Charrère, Eleonora, 340
Chateau Feuillet (winery), 300, 394
Chateau Tanunda (winery), 410
Chateau Thomas (winery), 108
Cherchi, Salvatore, 215
Chessa (winery), 216
Chianti, 87
Chianti Classico 2000 Project, 432
Chiarito Vineyards, 219
Chiarlo, Michele/Chiarlo (winery), 261, 361, 530
chlorotypes, 28
Chrismont (winery), 184, 311
Ciabrelli (winery), 255, 282
Cianfragna (winery), 450
Cicchello (winery), 62
Cieck (winery), 279, 371
Cima (winery), 193
Cincinnato (winery), 60, 195, 196, 246, 373
Cioti (winery), 387
Cipressi, Claudio, 449
Cipresso, Roberto, 273

Cirami Estate, 348
Ciro Picariello (winery), 288
Cissus, 25
citronellol, 77
Civielle (winery), 67
Clai Giorgio (winery), 90
Claudio Mariotto (winery), 449
Claudio Morelli (winery), 197
Claudio Vio (winery), 474
Clavelli, Michele, 168
classification of grape varieties, 2–3
Clemente Magni (winery), 449
Cleto Chiarli (winery), 69, 70
clonal selection, 30, 38, 125, 139, 164, 290, 299, 333, 356, 396, 431, 432, 473, 567
Clondaire Vineyard, 57
clones, 22, 27
Clos Cibonne (winery), 418
Clos Canarelli (winery), 334
Clos Ornasca (winery), 334
Cobaw Ridge (winery), 325
Cocci Grifoni (winery), 385, 387, 388, 389, 390
Code des caractères descriptifs des varieties et éspèces de Vitis, 17
Coffele (winery), 306
Cogno, Elvio/Cogno (winery), 351, 352, 361, 363
Col d'Orcia (winery), 108, 435
Col Dovigo (winery), 65, 401
Collavini (winery), 415
Colle di San Domenico (winery), 58, 282
Colle Sereno (winery), 272
Collestefano (winery), 468
Colli di Lapio/Clelio Romana (winery), 288
Colli di Serrapetrona (winery), 156
Collina d'Oro/Tenuta Baldovino (winery), 303
Colline di Affile (winery), 246
Colognole (winery), 435
Colorado State University, 198
Colpètrone (winery), 426
Col Sandago (winery), 479
Colterenzio Produttori (winery), 118
Colucci, Pietro, 98
Col Vetoraz (winery), 312
Comincioli (winery), 67
Common Agricultural Policy (CAP), 29
Compagnia di Ermes (winery), 205
Comte Abatucci (winery), 334
conjugated anthocyanins, 9
Consorzio Interprovinciale per la Frutticoltura di Cagliari, 345
Consorzio Produttori Vino, 410
Constantia Uitsig Winery, 113
Conte Collalto (winery), 469, 479, 545, 546
Conte Emo Capodilista, 110, 454
Conterno, Aldo, 296
Conte Spagnoletti Zeuli (winery), 383, 457
Conte Vistarino (winery), 267
Conte Zandotti (winery), 85
Conti Bossi Fredrigotti (winery), 340
Conti di Buscareto (winery), 323
Contini (winery), 345, 374

Conti Zecca, 78, 288, 366
Contrada Salandra (winery), 282, 400
Contrada Saordà (winery), 475
Contratto (winery), 108
Convisar, 31, 499
Cooperativa de l'Enfer (winery), 341
Cooperativa Viticoltori Coronata (winery), 327
Coopers Creek (winery), 184
Cooper Vineyards, 191
co-pigmentation, 9
Coriole Vineyards, 191, 288, 312, 361, 426
Coronica Moreno (winery), 90
Cornarea (winery), 184
Corte d'Aibo (winery), 402
Corte Madonnina (winery), 293
Corte Manzini (winery), 70, 146
Corte Moschina (winery), 276
Corte Normanna (winery), 282
Corton, 7
COS (winery), 219, 294
Cosimo Taurino (winery), 366
Costalunga (winery), 230
Costanti (winery), 435
Costaripa (winery), 67
Coste Archi (winery), 180
Coste di Brenta (winery), 254
Coste Ghirlanda (winery), 113
Cotarella, Riccardo, 144
Cottanera (winery), 370
Cougar Vineyards, 184, 213, 348, 365, 512
coulure. See berry shatter
Count Odart, 16
Covey Run (winery), 108
Crespan, Manna, 39, 117, 169, 176, 241
CRIFO (winery), 120, 384
Cristiana Meggiolaro (winery), 306
Crivelli (winery), 317, 423
Croce, 186
cross-pollination, 26
cru, 568
cultivar, 1, 6, 7, 568
cultural capital, 4
Cummo (winery), 369
Cupano (winery), 435
cyanin, 9, 124, 358, 369, 408, 432

Dacapo (winery), 191, 423
Daglio (winery), 116, 272
D'Alfonso del Sordo (winery), 205, 458
Dall'Asta (winery), 71
Dalla Valle (winery), 435
Dal Maso (winery), 230
Dal Pizzol (winery), 170
Dal Zotto Estate, 191, 312
D'Ambra, Salvatore/D'Ambra (winery), 201, 202, 291, 400, 531
Damiano Ciolli (winery), 246
Damijan Podversic (winery), 415
Damonte, Roberto, 182
D'Angelo (winery), 435
Daniela Bruno (winery), 275
Daniele Longanesi (winery), 461
Danieli, Savio, 351, 352
D'Arapri (winery), 203, 205
Dario Raccaro (winery), 91, 452
D'Attimis Maniago (winery), 445
D'Attoma, Luca, 221
Davide Sterza (winery), 264
De Bacco (winery), 199
De Bartoli, Renato, 36, 319
De Bortoli (winery), 435
De Conciliis, Bruno, 43, 168
De Corato, Sebastiano, 203, 458
Decanter (magazine), vii, 122
Dedicato a Marianna (winery), 439
De Grazia, Marc, 367
Del Medico, Emilio, 135
Del Negro, Nicola, 32, 405, 421, 505
delphin, 9, 124
Deltetto (winery), 184
De Lucia (winery), 282
Denominazione di Origine Controllata (DOC), ix
Denominazione di Origine Controllata e Garantita (DOC), 30
deoxyribonucleic acid (DNA), 18, 22; nuclear, mitochondrial, 18
Depero (winery), 272
De Simone, Maurizio, 480, 481, 482
De Terczal (winery), 340
Dettori (winery), 230, 345, 384, 385
Di Barrò (winery), 300, 341, 394
Didier Gerbelle (winery), 394, 406, 407
Di Filippo (winery), 259, 426
Di Lusso Estate (winery), 57, 166, 361, 395
Dini, Stefano, 51, 52, 160, 192, 249, 290, 474, 492
Di Prisco (winery), 58, 167, 288
Di Renzo, Massimo, 399
Dolianova (winery), 378
Doloufakis Nikos (winery), 86
Domaine Antoine Arena, 107
Domaine Day, 306
Domaine de Montahuc, 107
Domaine Sainte Marie, 418
Domenico Cavazza (winery), 306
Donatella Cinelli Colombini (winery), 290, 291
Don Guerino (winery), 180
Don Laurindo (winery), 180
Donnachiara (winery), 167
Donnafugata (winery), 113, 219
Donnardea (winery), 205
Dora Renato (winery), 275
Dorigati (winery), 543, 548
Doro Princic (winery), 91, 452
D'Orta-De Conciliis (winery), 167
Dotto Lidio (winery), 404
Dromana Estate, 184
Drius (winery), 91, 452
Drusian (winery), 312
Duca Carlo Guarini (winery), 99
Duca della Corgna (winery), 230
Duca di Salaparuta (winery), 182
Duchman Family Vineyards, 167, 272, 348

Ducks in a Row (winery), 219, 288
Due Palme (winery), 366
Durin (winery), 327, 418, 474
Duxoup (winery), 3, 271, 435

Einaudi (winery), 272
Elba, 178
Elba Bianco, 149
Eleano (winery), 80
Elena Fucci (winery), 167
Elio Ottin (winery), 300, 394
Elio Perrone (winery), 108
Elisabetta Foradori (winery), 446, 545
ellanico, 163
Elvio Zani (winery), 136
Emidio Pepe (winery), 348, 349
Emilia-Romagna, 41
Enotria (winery), 261
Enrico Spagnolli (winery), 340, 377
Enza La Fauci (winery), 375
Erioli Giorgio/Erioli-Laura Malaguti (winery), 363, 364
Ermacora (winery), 397, 403, 414, 439, 452
Ermès Pavese (winery), 405
Estrella del Norte (winery), 133
Ettore Germano (winery), 189, 352
Eubea (winery), 167
Eugenio Rosi (winery), 340
European Fund for Agricultural Orientation and Guarantee, 29
European Fund for Agricultural Rural Development, 29
European Vitis Database, 19
excessive reductionism, 22
excessive revisionism, 22
Dubini, Giovanni 314

Fabbro, Claudio, 398
Fagiuoli, Elisabetta, 52
Falca Giorgio (winery), 487
falernum, 162
Falesco (winery), 420
Falsini, Emiliano, 53, 510
Faraone (winery), 142
Fatto a Mano (winery), 261
Fattoria del Buonamico (winery), 493
Fattoria di Gratena (winery), 509
Fattoria di Petrolo (winery), 522
Fattoria Forano (winery), 327
Fattoria La Traiana (winery), 51, 162
Fattoria Mancini (winery), 173
Fattoria Michi (winery), 496
Fattoria Moretto (winery), 70
Fattoria Paradiso (winery), 487, 518
Fattoria Selvanova (winery), 124, 237
Fattoria Villa Ligi (winery), 179
Fattoria Zerbina (winery), 171
Fausto Consigli (winery), 109
Favaro-Le Chiusure (winery), 279
Fea (winery), 303
Felline (winery), 366
Felluga, Andrea, 395
Fenech, Francesco/Fenech (winery), 86, 88

Feotto dello Jatto (winery), 393
Ferrandes (winery), 113
Ferrando (winery), 279
Ferrara Benito (winery), 58
Ferruccio Deiana (winery), 230, 345
Fessina (winery), 236, 368
Feudi di San Gregorio (winery), 58
Feudi di San Marzano (winery), 410, 464
Feudi di San Severino (winery), 109, 329, 482
Feudi Salentini (winery), 464
Feudo Arancio (winery), 320
Feudo di San Maurizio (winery), 258, 300, 340, 341, 394, 478
Feudo Montoni (winery), 219, 242, 320
Feudo Rudini (winery), 109
Filippetti, Ilaria, 169, 171, 176, 222, 253
Filippi (winery), 306, 468
Filippo Gallino (winery), 214
Filiputti, Walter, 402
Filomusi Guelfi (winery), 349
Fiorini (winery), 70
Firmino Miotti (winery), 65, 338, 401, 475, 510, 524
First Drop (winery), 348
Flavia De Gaspero (winery), 136
Florutis (winery), 253, 398, 455
Fondazione Edmund Mach, 9, 16, 121
Fondo Europeo Agricolo per lo Sviluppo Rurale (FEASR), 29
Fondo Europeo per l'Orientamento e la Garazia in Agricultura (FEOGA), 29
Fondo San Giuseppe (winery), 171
Fongaro (winery), 276
Fontanacota (winery), 272
Fontana Marisa, 21, 169, 171, 196, 224, 253, 292, 490
Fontanavecchia (winery), 282
Fontodi (winery), 435
Foradori Elisabetta (winery), 446
foreign grape variety, 2
Formiconi (winery), 246
Fortesi (winery), 536
Forteto della Luja (winery), 108, 213
Forti del Vento (winery), 272
Foti, Salvo, 34, 173, 516
Fox Creek (winery), 474
Fox Gordon (winery), 288
Fracchia (winery), 96
Framingham (winery), 348
Francesca Callegaro (winery), 404
Francesco Bellei (winery), 69
Francesco Borgognone (winery), 423
Francesco Boschis (winery), 272, 317
Francesco Brigatti (winery), 462, 477
Francesco Candido (winery), 179, 342, 366
Francesco Poli (winery), 377
Francesco Tonini (winery), 461
Francesco Vezzelli (winery), 69
Franco Di Filippo (winery), 106
Franco Martinetti (winery), 261
Franco Todini (winery), 314
Franz Gojer (winery), 140
Frascati Cannellino, 84, 195

Frascole (winery), 435
Frassinelli (winery), 545
Fratelli Alessandria, 391
Fratelli Barba (winery), 348
Fratelli Berger (winery), 275
Fratelli Bortolin (winery), 312
Fratelli Caprari (winery), 180
Fratelli Collavo (winery), 199
Fratelli Grati (winery), 223
Fratelli Pardi (winery), 426
Fratelli Porcu (winery), 88
Fratelli Rabini (winery), 184
Fratelli Rovero (winery), 213
Fratelli Savigliano (winery), 272
Fratelli Zeni (winery), 468
Frecciarossa (winery), 462
Freeman Vineyards, 264, 529
Fregoni, Mario, 276
Freisa di Chieri, 295
Frescobaldi, Lamberto/Frescobaldi (winery), 220, 435
Friggeri, Villiam, 179
Friuli Venezia Giulia, 39
Frozza (winery), 312
Fuligni (winery), 435
Fuocomorto (winery), 221

Gaierhof (winery), 110, 118, 340
Gaja (winery), 361, 363
Gaja, Angelo, 357, 361
Gaja, Gaia, 191
Galassi (winery), 109
Galet, Pierre, 169, 186
Gallo, Gianfranco, 88
Galvanized Wine Group (winery), 348
Gambero Rosso (magazine), vii, 31, 377
Gambino (winery), 242
Gancia, Carlo, 103
Garofoli (winery), 468
Garuti Elio (winery), 69
Gary Crittenden (winery), 184, 191
Gasmayr, Michael, 323
Gaspari, Celestino, 382
Gavi, 259, 260
Gavi di Gavi, 261
G. B. Burlotto (winery), 391
genetic drift, 27
genetic introgression, 27
Georg Ramoser (winery), 325
geraniol, 18, 77, 117, 287, 328, 349
Germano, Sergio, 189
Giacomelli (winery), 474
Giacomo Conterno (winery), 191, 361
Giacomo Fenocchio (winery), 361
Giacomo Vico (winery), 214
Gianduja, 213
Gianfranco Fino (winery), 410
Giannelli (winery), 288
Gianni Comar (winery), 136
Gianni Voerzio (winery), 297
Gianpaolo Colutta (winery), 445
Gigante (winery), 133, 439

Gigante, Giandomenico, 51, 161
Gigi Picciau (winery), 353, 441
Gigi Rosso (winery), 272
Giglio, 180
Gilli (winery), 97, 297
Gini (winery), 306
Gino Pedrotti (winery), 377
Giona (winery), 88
Giorgio Cantamessa (winery), 96
Giovanna Madonia (winery), 170
Giovanna Tantini (winery), 264
Giovanni Almondo (winery), 184, 214
Giovanni Dri (winery), 471
Giovanni Poli (winery), 377
Giovanni Maria Cherchi (winery), 216
Giovanni Veglio (winery), 272
Girlan (winery), 118, 140
Girolamo Dorigo (winery), 397, 403
Girolamo Russo (winery), 236
Giuseppe Fanti (winery), 376
Giuseppe Mascarello (winery), 361
Giuseppe Rinaldi (winery), 361
Giuseppe Sacone (winery), 327
glucose phosphate isomerase (GPI), 18
Golden Grove Estate, 219
Gondi, Bernardo, 52
Gostolai (winery), 229, 230
Graci (winery), 236
Gradizzolo (winery), 191
Grahm, Randall, 361
Grando, Stella, 16, 137, 138, 338, 444
Grant Burge (winery), 272
Greco (winery), 511
Gregoletto (winery), 469
Greppe del Giglio (winery), 181
Grignano (winery), 435
Grigoletto (winery), 138
Groom (winery), 410
Grosjean (winery), 258, 300, 407
Grotta del Sole (winery), 186, 221, 282
Guerrieri (winery), 197
Guglielmi, Gianni, 416
Guglielmo Winery, 316
Guido Galassi (winery), 292
Gulfi (winery), 219, 236
Gulino, Sebastiano, 173
Guttarola (winery), 288
Gutturnio, 191

Hand Crafted by Jeoff Hardy (winery), 325, 446
Harrington (winery), 360
Hauner, Carlo/Hauner (winery), 86, 88
hectare, 3
Heiss-Tschida (winery), 107
Heitz Cellars, 316
Heringer Estate, 446
Heron's Flight (winery), 272, 435
hexanol, 329
homonyms, 21
Horácio Simões (winery), 113
Husch Cellars, 108

I Balzini Humagne Rouge, 257, 334
I Borboni Humagne Rouge, 257, 186
ice wine, 186
I Clivi Humagne Rouge, 257, 471
I Comelli Humagne Rouge, 257, 397
I Dolomitici, 276, 276
I Girasoli di Sant'Andrea/Carlo Massimiliano Gritti (winery), 99
Il Ciaret (winery), 297
Il Cipresso (winery), 115
Il Colle (winery), 469
Il Conventino (winery), 285
Il Feuduccio di Santa Maria d'Orni (winery), 390
Il Frances (winery), 115
Il Marroneto (winery), 435
Il Mongetto (winery), 317
Il Monte (winery), 146
Il Monticello (winery), 251
Il Mottolo (winery), 110
Il Nuraghe (winery), 441
Il Poggione (winery), 108, 435
Il Tralcio (winery), 521
Inama (winery), 306
Incisa della Rocchetta (winery), 16, 317
indigenous grape variety, 2
Inland Desert Nursery, 108
Institut Agricole Régional (winery), 37, 258, 299, 300, 341, 407, 421, 478, 494
Istituto Basile Caramia, 341
International Board for Plant Genetic Resource (IBPGR), 17
International Code for Nomenclature of Cultivated Plants, ix
International Union for the Protection of New Varieties of Plants (UPOV), 17
International Wine Cellar (magazine), vii, xi,
interregional grape variety, 3
intravarietal variability, 27
Iole Grillo (winery), 133
Ioppi (winery), 477
Isabella, 317
I Selvatici, 83
Isidoro Polencic, 415
isoenzyme, 17–18
isoenzyme analysis, 16, 18
Isola, 402
Isolabella della Croce, 213
Isole e Olena, 435
Istituto Agrario di San Michele all'Adige, 16, 66, 238, 242, 519, 542, 545, 547, 548
Istituto di Stato per l'Agricoltura e l'Ambiente-Persolino, 75, 76, 326, 330, 331, 332
Istituto Regionale del Vino e dell'Olio, 45
Istituto Sperimentale per la Viticoltura di Conegliano Veneto, 16
Italo Cescon (winery), 127
Italo Pietrantonj (winery), 348
Iuli (winery), 191
I Veroni (winery), 435
I Vini delle Baite (winery), 471

Jacob's Creek (winery), 288
Jacod, Mauro, 421
Jacuss (winery), 133, 445
Jacuzzi Family Vineyards, 166, 219, 452
Jeff Rundquist (winery), 191
Jorge Ordoñez (winery), 113
Josephus Mayr (winery), 140, 325
Josto Puddu (winery), 345

Kabola (winery), 90
Ka Manciné (winery), 418
Kante (winery), 91, 447, 478
Karanto Vineyards, 166
Karmère Vineyards and Winery, 360
Kay Bothers Amery (winery), 219
Kenneth Volk (winery), 166
Kettmeier (winery), 118
Kihlgren clone, 174
Kimbolton (winery), 348
Klein Constantia (winery), 107
Kozlević Gianfranco (winery), 90
Kracher (winery), 118
Kunzli, Christoph, 267, 461

La Barbatella (winery), 191
La Belèndesa (winery), 115
La Berta (winery), 147, 191
La Biancara (winery), 306
La Bionda (winery), 115
La Borgarella (winery), 297
La Brugherata (winery), 115
La Busattina (winery), 251
La Canova (winery), 303
La Capetta (winery), 117
La Cappuccina (winery), 382
La Carcaia (winery), 179
La Casaccia (winery), 317
La Celata (winery), 517
La Chiusa (winery), 181
La Clarea (winery), 187
La Colombera (winery), 272, 449
La Colombina (winery), 191
La Compagnia della Spergola, 442
La Crotte de Vegnerons (winery), 300
Lacryma Christi del Vesuvio, 231
La Dama (winery), 344
La Fazenda (winery), 178
La Fontuccia (winery), 181
Laganelli (winery), 109
Lageder (winery), 325
La Girolda (winery), 180
La Giustiniana (winery), 261
Lago di Caldaro, 137
La Granera (winery), 184
Lake Moodemere Vineyards, 492
La Miraja (winery), 423
La Montagnetta (winery), 297
La Montecchia (winery), 127
La Moresca (winery), 294
Lamoretti (winery), 267

La Muròla (winery), 327
Lanati, Donato, 35, 77, 316, 432
Landi, Lorenzo, 34, 51, 221, 496
Lanfranco Quacquarini (winery), 156
Langhorne Creek (winery), 325
La Palazzola (winery), 465
La Pergola (winery), 463
La Piana (winery), 178
La Piccola (winery), 332, 447
La Pinona (winery), 332
La Poderina (winery), 108
La Quercia (winery), 349, 350
La Querciolana (winery), 230
La Raia (winery), 261
Laraneta Vineyards, 199
La Ricolla (winery), 441
La Rivà (winery), 275
La Rivolta (winery), 58, 255, 400
Larkmead (winery), 452
La Rodola (winery), 115
La Romanina (winery), 293
La Roncaia (winery), 397
La Sclusa (winery), 415, 439, 471
La Selva (winery), 251
La Sera (winery), 96
La Sibilla (winery), 400
La Source (winery), 394
La Spinetta (winery), 108
La Stoppa (winery), 86, 191
La Toledana (winery), 262
La Tonsa (winery), 463
La Torretta (winery), 381
La Tunella (winery), 439
L'Atouéyo (winery), 394
Laura Aschero (winery), 474
La Vecchia Cantina (winery), 474
La Viarte (winery), 133, 415, 445
La-Vis (winery), 330
La Visciola (winery), 246
La Vrille (winery), 258, 300
Lavorata (winery), 59
Lazio, 42
Lazzari, Donato, 442
leafroll virus, 357
Le Bertole (winery), 312
Le Calbane (winery), 497
Le Caniette (winery), 387, 390
Le Cantine di Hesperia (winery), 123
Le Case Bianche (winery), 312
Le Chiusure (winery), 67
Le Clocher (winery), 258
Le Coste (winery), 404
Le 2 Torri (winery), 445
Le Favole (winery), 91, 133
Le Marne (winery), 261
Lenora Winery, 113
Lento (winery), 336
Leone Conti (winery), 147, 243, 283, 284
Leone de Castris (winery), 366, 464
Leonetti Cellar, 435
Le Poggiette (winery), 223

Le Potazzine (winery), 435
Le Quinte (winery), 85
Les Crêtes (winery), 300, 394, 407
Les Granges (winery), 258, 300
Le Strette (winery), 352
Letrari (winery), 118, 277, 340
Le Tre Stelle (winery), 161
Le Vigne di San Pietro (winery), 264
Le Vigne di Zamò (winery), 403
Librandi (winery), 30, 329, 336
Lidia e Amato (winery), 387
Liguria, 40
Lillypilly Estate, 113
linalool, 18, 101, 287, 349
Lino Casella/Rieppi (winery), 439, 445
Lippi, Enrico, 51
Lisini (winery), 435
Lis Neris (winery), 471
Li Veli (winery), 464
Livio Felluga (winery), 397, 415, 452
Livio Pretti (winery), 230
local grape variety, 2
Lomazzi & Sarli (winery), 78, 179, 444
Lonardo, Sandro, 421
Lombardy, 38
Lomolino (winery), 199
Longariva (winery), 340
Longview Vineyard, 361
Lorenzo Bongiovanni (winery), 277
Lorenzo Negro (winery), 184
Lorenzo Ramò (winery), 272
Lorieri family, 192
Lost Valley Winery, 260
Lo Triolet/Marco Martin (winery), 300
Lucà, 59
Luca & Lewellen (winery), 296
Luciano Saetti (winery), 73
Luciano Sandrone (winery), 361
Ludovisi Boncompagni (winery), 82
Luigi Bassi (winery), 351
Luigi Brunelli (winery), 264
Luigi Giusti (winery), 323
Luigi Maffini (winery), 282
Luigino Dal Maso (winery), 306
Luigino Molon (winery), 128
Luigi Spertino (winery), 317
Luigi Tacchino (winery), 272
Luigi Tecce (winery), 167
Luisa (winery), 414
Lunae Bosoni (winery), 175, 475, 526
Luna Rossa Winery, 167, 272, 348
Lungarotti (winery), 221
Luni 910 (winery), 180
Lupi (winery), 272, 418
Lupinc (winery), 478
Luretta (winery), 86
Lusenti (winery), 267

Macarico (winery), 167
Maccario-Dringberg (winery), 418
Macchia (winery), 191

Macchialupa (winery), 58
Mac Forbes (winery), 184
Machetti, Andrea 433
Maculan, Fausto/Maculan (winery), 475
Madonia Giovanna (winery), 170
Madrevite (winery), 230
Madrona Estate, 360
Mahoney Vineyards, 348, 360
Maiero (winery), 391
Malabaila di Canale (winery), 214
malvasia di Bosa, 87–88
malvasia di Castelnuovo Don Bosco, 100
malvasia di Sardegna, 87–88
malvin, 9, 124, 220, 267, 294, 328, 329, 367, 408, 432, 508
Malvirà (winery), 184, 214
Mamete Prevostini (winery), 361
Mancini family, 172
Mancini Peppe, 122, 236
Mandola (winery), 167, 272
Mandolina (winery), 296
Manincor (winery), 110
Manucci Droandi (winery), 193, 290, 291, 412
Marabino (winery), 109
Marcarini (winery), 272
Marcato (winery), 276
Marche, 42
Marchesi di Gresy (winery), 108, 181, 361
Marchesi di Montalto (winery), 191
Marchesi Pancrazi (winery), 53
Marco Canato (winery), 317
Marco Cordani (winery), 381
Marco De Bartoli (winery), 113, 320
Marco Fellin (winery), 66
Marco Sara (winery), 397, 471
Marenco (winery), 213, 232
Maria Donati Bianchi (winery), 474
Marina Cvetic (winery), 348, 349
Marinig (winery), 133
Mario Lucchetti (winery), 323
Mario Mosso (winery), 97
Mariotto (winery), 293
Marotti Campi (winery), 323
Marsaglia (winery), 184
Marsala, 240
Martello (winery), 254
Martina (winery), 187, 194
Martinelli (winery), 113
Marulli, Concezio, 346
Marziano Abbona (winery), 272
Marziano Vevey (winery), 405
Masciarelli (winery), 348
Masi (winery), 264, 343, 381, 382
Masi Paolo (winery), 50
Maso Bergamini (winery), 118
Maso Martis (winery), 118
Massa (winery), 449
massal selection, 210, 228, 233, 235, 258, 259, 270, 299, 357, 372, 380, 446, 569
Massaretti (winery), 418
Masseria del Borro (winery), 400
Masseria Piccirillo (winery), 123
Masseria Ludovico (winery), 410, 464
Massimo Randi (winery), 461
Mastroberardino, Antonio/Mastroberardino (winery), 31, 162, 163, 166, 167, 239, 255, 282, 286, 288, 399
Mastrojanni (winery), 435
Mathiasson (winery), 133
Mattarelli (winery), 293
Matteo Correggia (winery), 184
MATURA, 160
Maurizio Bruno (winery), 449
Maurizio Perabò (winery), 136
Mazzoni, Alberto, 177
Mazzorbo, 273
Medici Ermete (winery), 73
Meloni Vini (winery), 88, 308, 353
Merano Produttori (winery), 110, 140
mercaptometyhylpentanone, 319
Meroi (winery), 471
Mero, Salvatore, 443
Merryvale (winery), 108
Mesa (winery), 234
mezzadria, 30
Miani (winery), 133, 414
Michele Taliano (winery), 214
Michelini (winery), 446
microsatellites, 19; chloroplast, nuclear, 19
Migrante (winery), 246
millerandage, 319, 326, 569
Milita, Nazzareno, 195
Millbrook (winery), 452
Mimmo Paone (winery), 88, 375
Mina (massal selelection), 88
Mocine (winery), 192, 291
Moio, Luigi, 43, 123, 236, 240, 249, 287, 383
Moletto (winery), 128
Molise, 43
Monemvasia, 76
monoterpenes, 18
monovarietal labeling, 8
monovarietal wines, x, 8–9
Montalbera (winery), 317, 423
Montalcino, 7, 248
Monte delle Vigne (winery), 71, 86
Monte di Grazia (winery), 451
Monte Fasolo (winery), 110
Montegrande (winery), 128
Montemagno (winery), 96
Montepulciano, 334
Monte Saline (winery), 344
Montesissa (winery), 92
Monteu Roero, 183
Montevecchio (winery), 219
Monte Vertine (winery), 435
Montevina Winery, 360
Monte Volpe (winery), 271
Montoliva (winery), 446
Montoliva Vineyards, 365
Morbelli, Claudio, 156
Morella (winery), 288
Morgassi Superiore (winery), 261

Morini, Alessandro/Poderi Morini (winery), 171, 191, 242, 243, 284
Moriondo Giulio, ix, 186
Morris (winery), 107
moscadello di Montalcino, 103, 106
Moschioni (winery), 133, 403, 439
Mossi (winery), 381, 542
Mossi Luigi (winery), 380
Mount Langi Ghiram (winery), 435
Mount Palomar Winery, 251
Mount Surmon (winery), 361
Mount Towrong (winery), 312
Mr. Rigg's Wine Company (winery), 348
Mulas (winery), 486
Muri-Gries Cantina Convento (winery), 325
Murru, Mariano, 31, 211, 378
Musigny, 7, 8
musqué clones, 101
Mustilli, Leonardo/Mustilli (winery), 280, 281, 282
mutations, 22
Mutti (winery), 449

Nalles Magré Cantina/Nals Margreid (winery), 110, 140
Nardello (winery), 306
national grape variety, 3
National Institute for Statistics (ISTAT), 4
National Registry of Grape Varieties, x, 55, 137
Nederburg (winery), 108
Negro (winery), 184
Negro, Angelo, 23, 183
Negro, Giovanni, 182
Negro Lorenzo (winery), 183
Nepenthe (winery), 410
nerol, 328
Nettare dei Santi (winery), 463
Nicodemi (winery), 349
Nicola Bergaglio (winery), 262
Nicola Chiaromonte (winery), 410
Nicolas Gatti Russo (winery), 375
Nico's Wines, 57
Nieddu, Gianni, 208, 209, 210, 215
Nifo Serrapochiello (winery), 282
Noceto (winery), 3
norisoprenoid(s), 18, 483
Novello (winery), 351
nuclear magnetic radioisotope imaging, 11

Oak Works (winery), 348
Obsidian (winery), 348
Occelli, Andrea, 390
Occhipinti, Andrea/Occhipinti (winery), 177, 179, 431, 435
Occhipinti, Arianna/Arianna Occhipinti (winery), 173, 174, 294
Ocone (winery), 255
Office International de la Vigne et du Vin (OIV), 17
Ognibene Luigi (winery), 364
oidium, 29
Oliver's Taranga (winery), 288
Orazio Candido (winery), 108
Oreana (winery), 133

Orlandi Contucci Ponno/Colle Funaro (winery), 349
Ornella Molon Traverso (winery), 127
Orsolani (winery), 279
Osteria di Rubbiara, 141
Osvaldo Barberis (winery), 272
Ottaviano Lambruschi (winery), 474
Ottella (winery), 468

Pace (winery), 184
Pagli Attilio, 34, 50, 192, 250, 333, 343, 411
Pagliari-Verdieri (winery), 74
Pagnoncelli-Folcieri, 115
Paiagallo, 189
Pala (winery), 208, 378
Palazzone (winery), 314
Pallavicini (winery), 31, 85
Palmieri, Beppe, 141
Palmina (winery), 271, 360, 452
Palumbo, Leonardo, 98, 206
Pandolfa (winery), 191
Panerai, Paolo, 427
Panevino (winery), 308
Panizzari (winery), 463
Pantelleria, 112
Paolino Comelli (winery), 403
Paolo Bea (winery), 426
Paolo Calì (winery), 294
Paolo Francesconi (winery), 243
Paolo Pizzorno Vini (winery), 272
Paolo Rodaro (winery), 397, 415, 439
Paolo Saracco (winery), 104, 108
Paolo Scavino (winery), 361
Paola Sordo (winery), 184
Paradiso, Angelo, 203
Paraparoussis (winery), 107
Parish Hill Wines, 184, 272, 312, 361, 365
Parthenocissus, 25
Pasetti, Domenico/Pasetti (winery), 109, 142, 349, 388, 390
Pasini-La Torre (winery), 66
Pasini-San Giovanni (winery), 67
passito di Pantelleria, 112
Passopisciaro (winery), 370
Paterna (winery), 412
Paternoster (winery), 167, 288
Patritti (winery), 184
Pavoncelli Estate, 458
Pecchennino (winery), 272
Pedroni (winery), 141, 424
peonin, 9, 124, 294, 358, 369
Perillo (winery), 167
peronospora, 29
Pertaringa (winery), 166, 219
Perticaia (winery), 148, 426
Perucci, Gregory, 443
Peterluger, Enrico, 338
Petrucco (winery), 403
Petrussa (winery), 439
Petrussi, Carlo, 129, 131, 134, 398, 447, 482
petunin, 9
Pezzuoli (winery), 73

phenotypic plasticity, 27
Phil Church Vineyards, 108
phosphogluco mutase (PGM), 18
phylloxera, 29
Piancornello (winery), 435
Pian dell'Orino (winery), 435
Piandibugnano (winery), 178
Piedmont, 38
Piero Brunet (winery), 405
Piero Gatti (winery), 213
Pieropan, Leonildo/Pieropan (winery), 262, 306
Piero Pancheri (winery), 66
Pietracupa (winery), 58, 288
Pietrasanta (winery), 463
Pietratorcia (winery), 202, 292
Pietraventosa (winery), 410
Pietro Beconcini (winery), 83
Pillitteri (winery), 435
Pino Gino (winery), 175, 251
Pio Cesare (winery), 317, 361
Pirro Varone (winery), 410
Pisoni (winery), 377, 548
Pizzarotti (winery), 86
Pizzini (winery), 3, 184, 213, 361, 395, 435
Planeta, Alessio/Planeta (winery), 108, 219, 234, 288, 375, 425
Plattner, Wally, 118
Plessi, Claudio, 141
Pliny the Elder, 141, 148, 180, 195, 236, 244, 254, 276, 354, 374, 424
Piovene Porto Godi (winery), 230
Podere dell'Olivos (winery), 446
Podere del Pajoré (winery), 362, 363
Podere del Palas (winery), 248, 412
Podere Il Santo (winery), 462
Podere Lavandaro (winery), 223
Podere Marella (winery), 314
Podere Poggiarellini (winery), 502
Podere Pradarolo (winery), 533
Podere Santa Felicità (winery), 160
Podere Scurtarola (winery), 192, 475
Podere Terenzuola (winery), 223, 475
Podere Vecciano (winery), 402
Poderi Morini. *See* Morini, Alessandro/Poderi Morini (winery)
Poderi Parpinello (winery), 216
Poderi San Lazzaro (winery), 390
Poggi dell'Elmo (winery), 418
Poggio al Cassone (winery), 446
Poggio al Gello (winery), 412
Poggio alla Meta (winery), 386
Poggio Argentiera (winery), 251
Poggio Bertolone (winery), 294
Poggio dei Gorleri (winery), 474
Poggio di Sotto (winery), 435
Poggiopiano (winery), 52
Pojer & Sandri (winery), 376
Politini (winery), 219, 306
Pollini, Ciro, 16, 120, 122
Polvanera (winery), 410
polymerase chain reaction (PCR), 19

Ponte (winery), 167
Ponzi (winery), 184, 271
Port Philip Estate, 184
Possa (winery), 208, 223
Prà (winery), 306
Praesidium (winery), 348, 349
Pratella (winery), 548
Pravis (winery), 66, 121, 138, 548
Precept Wines (winery), 108
primary aromas, 10
primary centers of domestication, 28
primary flavors, 10
Produttori Donnas (winery), 361
Produttori Pelaverga di Castellar (winery), 391
Proietti (winery), 246
Proprietà Sperino (winery), 361
Prunotto (winery), 540
Puglia, 44
Punta Crena (winery), 327, 505
Pupillo (winery), 106, 109
Pusterla (winery), 321

Quarenghi, Giacomo, 114
quintal, 60
Quintarelli (winery), 343, 344
Quinto Chionetti (winery), 272
Quintodecimo (winery), 58, 167, 282, 288

Racemi (winery), 366, 410, 444
Raffaella Bissoni (winery), 171
Rallo, Antonio, 111
Ramandolo, 470
Ramìe, 187, 194, 486
Ramoser (winery), 140
random amplified polymorphic DNA (RAPD), 19, 186
Rapuzzi, Paolo e Dina, 436, 437
Rascioni & Cecconello (winery), 251
Ratti, Pietro, 104, 187
Ravenswood (winery), 410
Reale (winery), 451
Redaelli de Zinis (winery), 66
Reggiana (winery), 332
regional grape variety, 3
Registro Nazionale delle Varietà di Vite, x
Renato Anselmet (winery), 256, 258, 300, 394
Renato Keber (winery), 415
Renato Ratti (winery), 361, 459
Renna (winery), 255
Renwood (winery), 191, 360
restriction fragment length polymorphism (RFLP), 19
ribonucleic acid (RNA), 18, 22
ribosomes, 18
Ricasoli, Bettino, 87, 148
Riccardo Albani (winery), 191
Riccardo Battistotti (winery), 110, 118, 340, 377
Rieppi, Maria, 437
Riffaldini Winery, 348
Rinaldini-Moro (winery), 72, 447
Rigotti, Rebo, 137, 138
Rio Favara (winery), 108
Riparia, 25

Rivera (winery), 167, 203, 205, 207, 458
Rivetto, Enrico/Rivetto (winery), 351, 52
Robert Oatley Vineyards, 191
Roberto Lucarelli (winery), 197
Robert Pepi (winery), 435
Robinson, Jancis, 9
Rocca Bernarda (winery), 397
Roccaccia (winery), 251
Rocca del Principe (winery), 288
Rocca di Castagnoli (winery), 223
Rocca di Montegrossi (winery), 83
Roccafiore (winery), 314
Rocche del Gatto (winery), 418
Rodaro Paolo (winery), 395, 414
Ronc dal Luchis (winery), 136
Ronchi di Cialla (winery), 30, 133, 251, 397, 414, 436, 437
Ronco Cliona (winery), 398, 455
Ronco dei Tassi (winery), 415
Ronco del Gelso (winery), 452
Ronco delle Betulle (winery), 415
Rondelli, Filippo, 417, 418
Rosa del Golfo (winery), 366, 464
Rosa d'Oro Vineyards, 57
Rosalba Vendrame (winery), 205
Rossella Salguato (winery), 418
Rosset (winery), 258
rossissimo, 179
Rovellotti (winery), 279
Rota (winery), 180
rotundone, 66
Route 3 Wines, 57
Rovellotti (winery), 477
Roxanich (winery), 90
Ruggeri (winery), 426
Rugrà (winery), 272
Rupestris, 25
Rusden (winery), 410
Rutherglen Estate, 184, 288
Ryme Wine Cellars, 166

Saccharomyces cerevisiae, 35
Salena Estate, 200
Salicutti (winery), 435
Salina (winery), 88
Saltram (winery), 288
Salvatore Molettieri (winery), 58, 167
Sam Miranda Wines, 312
Samson, Savanna 244
Sancio (winery), 327, 474
Sandhurst Ridge (winery), 361
Sandro Fay (winery), 361
San Felice (winery), 412
San Fereolo (winery), 272
San Giovanni (winery), 387
San Giusto a Rentennano (winery), 435
San Joaquin Valley, 198
San Lazzaro (winery), 223
San Lorenzo Vini (winery), 387
San Michele Appiano Produttori (winery), 139
San Rocca (winery), 314

San Romano (winery), 272
San Savino (winery), 223, 390
Santa Lucia (winery), 384
Santa Lucia Vinery (winery), 284
Santa Maddalena (winery), 118, 137
Santa Maddalena Cantina Produttori/Cantina di Bolzano (winery), 325
Sant'Andrea (winery), 99
Santa Venere (winery), 320, 337
Sant'Erasmo (winery), 273
Santoro (winery), 514
Saputi (winery), 327, 387
Sardinia, 45
Sarmassa, 189
Sartarelli (winery), 468
Sassotondo (winery), 251
Savelli, Mariano, 170
Savoldi (winery), 115
Sbarzaglia (winery), 456
Scacciadiavoli (winery), 426
Scalabrelli, Giancarlo, 51, 93, 94, 116, 176, 224, 290
Scala Federico (winery), 336, 337
Scanzorosciate, 115
Scarbolo (winery), 133
Scaroni Giacomo e Alberto (winery), 74
Scarpa (winery), 297
Schneider, Anna, 1, 104, 111, 117, 174, 186, 188, 193, 199
Schraffl, Harald, 137
Sciacchetrà, 208
Scienza, Attilio, ix, 26, 28, 29, 117, 122, 163, 172, 185, 186, 342, 432, 533
Scienza, Filippo, 340
Scribner's Bend (winery), 288
Scubla (winery), 471
secondary aromas, 10
secondary centers of domestication, 28
secondary flavors, 10
secondary metabolites, 17–18
Secondo Marco (winery), 344
Seghesio (winery), 166, 288, 410, 435
6Mura (winery), 234
self-pollination, 26
Sella & Mosca (winery), 453
Selvapiana (winery), 435
Seppeltsfield (winery), 325
Serego Alighieri (winery), 342, 344
Serena Giordanino (winery), 412
Sereni, Emilio, 67
Sergio Mottura (winery), 314
Serraghia-Gabrio Vini (winery), 113
Serrapetrona, 155
Settesoli (winery), 306
Seven Artisans (winery), 348
Seven Ochres (winery), 288
sfursat, 359
Shafer (winery), 435
Sibille (winery), 187, 194
Sicily, 45
Sierra Ridge Winery, 191
Silvano Follador (winery), 312
Silvano Strologo (winery), 544

Silvio Nardi (winery), 108
single nucleotide polymorphisms (SPNs), 19
single sequence repeats (SSR), 19
Siro Pacenti (winery), 435
Sittella (winery), 113
Sivilotti, Paolo, 129
Skerk (winery), 91, 447, 478
Skerlj (winery), 478
Soini Quinto (winery), 140
Soldera/Case Basse (winery), 435
Solis Winery, 288
Sono Montenidoli (winery), 52, 223
Sorelle Bronca (winery), 312
Sorrentino (winery), 231, 240, 400
Soverchia, Giancarlo, 283, 285, 509, 543
Speziale 1855 (winery), 120
Spinetta (winery), 461
Springton Hills (winery), 348
spungone romagnolo, 170
Staderini, Federico, 34, 159, 160
Staffordshire Lane (winery), 219, 348
Statti (winery), 336
St. Clair (winery), 108
Stefano Mancinelli, 323
Stefano Massone (winery), 261
Stefanoni (winery), 420
Stelitano (winery), 59
Stella di Campalto (winery), 435
Stellar Organic Winery, 113
Ste. Michelle Wine Estates, 108
Strappelli (winery), 390
Sturz, Willi, 118
Suavia (winery), 306, 468
subvarieties, 22
Sutter Creek Vineyard, 166
Sutto (winery), 545
synonyms, 21

Tabarrini (winery), 148, 426
Tablas Creek (winery), 474
Tallavera Grove (winery), 365
Tamburello (winery), 393
Tamellini (winery), 306
Taminick Cellars, 150
Tani, Gabriella, 411
Tasca d'Almerita (winery), 88, 219, 319, 320, 370
Taurasi, 162, 165
Tedeschi, Riccardo, 535
teinturier(s), 10, 159
Telaro (winery), 489
Telolli, Gianluca, 421
Telmo Rodriguez (winery), 113
Tenuta Alzatura, 426
Tenuta Amalia, 447
Tenuta Anfosso, 415,
Tenuta Bonzara, 402
Tenuta Cocevola/Maria Marmo, 384
Tenuta del Fasanella, 168
Tenuta delle Ripalte, 178
Tenuta delle Terre Nere, 370
Tenuta di Aljano, 442

Tenuta di Castel Campagnano, 237
Tenuta di Trinoro, 244
Tenuta Il Corno, 52, 53
Tenuta La Traiana, 52, 162
Tenuta Migliavacca, 317
Tenuta Mossi, 92
Tenuta Pederzana, 70, 542
Tenuta Pernice, 380, 381
Tenuta Pinni, 455
Tenuta San Francesco, 451
Tenuta San Giorgio, 546
Tenuta Santomè, 127
Tenuta Sarno 1860, 288
Tenuta Terre Nobili, 330
Tenuta Uccellina, 225, 284, 326, 461
Tenuta Vitagliano, 439
Tenute Chiaromonte, 342
Tenute dei Vallarino, 541
Tenute Rubino, 444
Tenute Tomasella, 133, 452
Terenzi (winery), 246, 385, 387
Terlano Cantina, 139, 325
terpene(s), 18
Terracruda (winery), 179, 285, 509, 544
Terra delle Ginestre (winery), 109, 196, 482
Terra d'Oro (winery), 167
Terra Felix (winery), 312
Terranostra (winery), 207
Terre Bianche (winery), 418, 474
Terre da Capo (winery), 435
Terre dei Briganti (winery), 282
Terre dei Santi (winery), 97, 297, 391
Terre del Gattopardo (winery), 294
Terre del Granito (winery), 178
Terre del Pinerolese (winery), 275
Terre del Principe (winery), 122, 123, 124, 237
Terredora (winery), 58, 167, 288
Terre Pontine (winery), 482
terroir(s), 7–8,
tertiary aromas, 10
tertiary flavors, 10
Terza Via (winery), 113, 319, 320
Terzetto (winery), 446
Thick as Thieves (winery), 184
thiol(s), 28, 36, 45, 319
Thomas Kitzmuller (winery), 415
Thonet, Frankie, 193, 194
Tiberio, Cristiana/Tiberio (winery), 142, 143, 349, 389, 390
Tizzano (winery), 402
Tobin James (winery), 108, 133
Toblar (winery), 471
Toccata (winery), 361
Toffoli (winery), 469
Tomasone (winery), 202
Tomatis (winery), 248, 412
Tondini (winery), 456
Toppani (rootstock), 132
torchiato di Fregona, 198, 338
torcolato, 338
Torengo (winery), 230

Tormaresca (winery), 167
Torraccia del Piantavigna (winery), 477
Torre dei Beati (winery), 348, 390
Torre del Pagus (winery), 282
Torre Pernice (winery), 418
Torre Rosazza (winery), 397
Torre Zambra (winery), 390
Torzi Matthews (winery), 365
Tosi, Emanuele, 304
total number of Italian grape varieties, 1–2
Trader Joe's, 133
traditional grape variety, 2
Tramin Produttori (winery), 118
Trapan Bruno (winery), 90
Trapletti Enrico (winery), 180
Travignoli (winery), 435
Treatch Cellars, 108, 113
Tre Botti (winery), 179
Tre Monti, 147, 171
Trentino, 38
Triacca (winery), 361, 400, 401
Trinchero Family Estates, 312
Trisorio, Giovanna, 31
Tua Rita (winery), 446
Tudernum (winery), 314, 510
Tura, Eraldo, 331
Turley (winery), 410
Tuscany, 41

Umbria, 42
Union of Winemaking Cooperative of Samos (winery), 107
University of Ancona, 285
University of Bologna, 283
University of California—Davis, 16, 201, 333
University of Florence, 431
University of Milan, 342, 533
University of Naples, 287, 421
University of Palermo, 421
University of Pisa, 431
University of Sassari, 345
University of Udine, 133, 134, 180, 504
University of Verona, 343
Urban Legend Cellars, 361
Urciolo (winery), 167, 288
Uvaggio (winery), 474
Uve Apiane, 101

Vadiaperti (winery), 58, 255, 288
Vajra, Aldo/G. D. Vajra (winery), 104, 108, 272, 297, 361
Valcalepio moscato passito, 115
Valentini (winery), 142, 348
Valentino Butussi (winery), 403, 415
Valentino Fiorini (winery), 197
Valerio Rizzi (winery), 66
Vallarom (winery), 277, 340
Valle d'Aosta, 37
Valle dell'Acate (winery), 219, 294
Valle dell'Asso (winery), 288
Vallis Agri (winery), 340
Vallona (winery), 402
Varchetta (winery), 400
varietal, x
variety, x
variety-population, 26
Vasari (winery), 375
Veglio, Luca, 361
Venâncio da Costa Lima (winery), 113
Veneto, 39
Venica & Venica (winery), 91, 415
Venice, 76, 272, 338
Venissa (winery), 273, 274,
Ventimiglia, Edoardo, 250
Venturelli (winery), 141
Vergnano, Gianni, 96
vernaccia delle Cinque Terre, 151
vernaccia di Cannara, 259
vernaccia di Quiliano, 151
vernaccia di Serra Meccaglie, 151
vernaccia di Serrapetrona, 155
vernaccia di Villasor, 151
vernaculum, 151
Veronelli, Luigi, 113, 151, 161, 173, 242, 317, 406, 417
Versio, Francesco, 361
Vesevo (winery), 282
Vestini Campagnano (winery), 122, 123, 124, 186, 237
Vevey, Mario, 405
Viala and Vermorel, 173, 253
Viansa Winery, 200, 296, 452
Vicari (winery), 323
Vicentini Agostini (winery), 306
Vicentini Orgnani (winery), 455
Vidal, Jean-Louis, 148
Vie di Romans (winery), 91, 452
Vietti (winery), 182, 184, 191
Vigna dei Boschi (winery), 243
Vigna delle Beccacce (winery), 136
Vigna Petrussa (winery), 133, 397
Vigne dei Boschi (winery), 332
Vigne di Rasciatano (winery), 458
Vilàr (winery), 340
Villa Almè (winery), 128, 546
Villa Angarano (winery), 475
Villa Calcinaia (winery), 221, 223, 334, 426, 522
Villa Creek (winery), 166
Villa Diamante (winery), 58
Villa di Corlo (winery), 70
Villa Giada (winery), 303
Villa Gianna (winery), 109
Villa Matilde (winery), 282, 482
Villa Papiano (winery), 171
Villa Russiz (winery), 415
Villa Schinosa (winery), 106, 459
Villa Sparina (winery), 262
Villa Venti (winery), 284
Vinea Marson (winery), 90, 312
vino del ghiaccio, 186
vino santo, 376
vin santo, 150
Viotti Vini (winery), 540

Virgilio Vignato (winery), 306
Viticoltore Moccia/Agnanum (winery), 282
Viticoltori Casavecchia (winery), 237
Viticoltori Finocchi (winery), 544
Viticoltori Ingauni (winery), 327
Vitis labrusca, 25, 67
Vitis vinifera, 25; *ssp. sativa*, 25; *ssp. silvestris*, 25
Vittorio Graziano (winery), 70, 146
Vivác (winery), 272
VJB Vineyards & Cellars, 191, 219
Vouillamoz, José, 138, 186, 338, 429, 444
Vulcano, 88

Waldgries (winery), 118
Wattle Creek Winery, 108
Wenzel (winery), 107
Werth Christian, 324
Westend Estate, 166
Whistling Kite (winery), 348
Wilson Creek Vineyard and Winery, 108
wine aroma, 10
wine authenticity, 11
wine color, 9
wine flavor, 10
wine ratings, xi
wine scores, xi
Witch Creek (winery), 167, 348
Witches Falls Winery, 288
Wolff Vineyards, 446

Yorba (winery), 191

Zaccagnini (winery), 109, 143, 346, 348
Zamò, Silvano, 402, 403, 414
Zanchi (winery), 251
Zanoncelli (winery), 138
Zeni (winery), 118, 377, 415, 446
Zicari (winery), 410
Zidarich, 91, 447, 478
Zironi, Roberto, 180
Zonin (winery), 306, 361, 465
Zonte's Footstep (winery), 446
Zuccardo family (winery), 493
Zuddas, Laura, 347
Zuliani (winery), 67
Zymé (winery), 382

INDEX OF GRAPE VARIETIES

Please note: The proper names of grape varieties are indexed, as are the most common synonyms and variants of each. Little-used or dialectal names are not indexed. International grape varieties are indexed only when pertinent, and then selectively.

Abbuoto, 481–82
Abrostine, 29, 50, 158–60
Abrusco, 50, 51, 158, 160–62, 172
Abrusco del Valdarno, 51. *See also* Abrusco
Acchiappalmento. *See* Bianco d'Alessano
Acitana, 45, 482
Addoraca, 482
Aghedene, 482–83
Aglianichello. *See* Aglianico
Aglianico, 21, 29, 43, 162–67
Aglianico Amaro. *See* Aglianico
Aglianico Bastardo. *See* Aglianicone
Aglianico del Taburno. *See* Aglianico
Aglianico del Vulture. *See* Aglianico
Aglianico di Caiazzo. *See* Aglianicone
Aglianico di Napoli. *See* Tronto
Aglianico di Taurasi. *See* Aglianico
Aglianicone, 20, 21, 43, 167–68
Aglianico Pannarone. *See* Aglianico
Agricola Punica, 234
Albana, 169–71
Albana Bordini, 531
Albana della Bagarona. *See* Albana
Albana della Compadrona. *See* Albana
Albana della Forcella. *See* Albana
Albana della Serra. *See* Albana
Albana Gentile di Bertinoro. *See* Albana
Albana Rossa. *See* Albana
Albana Nera, 171–72, 249
Albana Nera Balducci. *See* Albana Nera
Albana Nera di Vignoli, 172. *See also* Ciliegiolo
Albana Pizzigatti. *See* Albana
Albanella, 172–73
Albanello, 173–74, 483

Albarenzeuli Bianco, 172, 483
Albarenzeuli Nero, 483
Albariño, 172
Albarola, 41, 174–75, 207
Albarola di Lavagna, 174
Albarola Nera, 483
Albarossa, 190, 247, 539, 540
Albicello, 483
Aleatico, 109, 114, 175–79, 248, 543
Alicante. *See* Cannonau
Alicante Bouschet, 50
Alionza, 148, 483–84
Alvarega, 484
Amabile di Genova. *See* Malbo Gentile
Amigne, 186
Ancellotta, 50, 179–80, 225
Ancellotta di Massenzatico.
    See Ancellotta
Angela, 484–85
Ansonica, 180–82
Antinello, 481
Arciprete Bianco Liscio. *See* Bellone
Arciprete Bianco Peloso. *See* Bellone
Arilla, 43, 485
Arillottola, 485
Arinto, 453
Arneis, 37, 182–84
Arvesiniadu, 485–86
Arvino, 328. *See* Magliocco
Asprinio Bianco, 28, 55, 184–86
Avanà, 38, 186–87, 486
Avarenchetto, 486
Avarengo, 38, 186, 187, 371, 486
Axina de Tres Bias, 111, 119

Balsamina, 41, 339
Balsamina Bianca. *See* Biancame
Baratuciat, 486–87
Barbarossa, 487
Barbassese, 232. *See* Carica l'asino
Barbera, 38, 187–91, 247, 356, 488, 541, 544, 547, 548
Barbera Bianca, 188, 487–88
Barbera Ciarla, 188
Barbera d'Davi, 188
Barbera del Sannio, 188, 236, 239, 488
Barbera Dou Ciornou, 188. *See also* Cardìn
Barbera Sarda, 488–89
Barbesino, 188, 489
Barbrassa, 188
Bariletta, 489
Barsaglina, 191–92
Barzamino. *See* Marzemino
Bastardo Nero, 214
Becuèt, 192–93
Bellone (Cacchione), 193–96, 204
Belzamino, 489–90
Berla 'd Crava Cita. *See* Becuet
Bermestia Bianca, 273
Bertinora, 490
Bervedino, 490
Berzemino. *See* Marzemino
Besgano. *See* Colombana Nera
Beverdino, 41. *See also* Bervedino
Bianca. *See* San Lunardo
Bianca Capriana, 490–91
Bianca di Poviglio, 41. *See also* Trebbiano Toscano
Biancame, 142, 148, 196–97
Biancara. *See* Bianchetta Trevigiana
Biancatenera. *See* Ginestra
Biancazita. *See* Ginestra
Bianchello. *See* Biancame
Bianchetta Genovese. *See* Albarola
Bianchetta Gentile. *See* Bianchetta Trevigiana
Bianchetta Trevigiana, 6, 197–98, 275, 311
Bianchetto di Saluzzo, 495
Bianchino. *See* Montù
Bianchino Faentino. *See* Montù
Bianco Antico, 491
Bianco Comune, 491
Bianco D'Alessano, 44, 199–20
Biancolella, 43, 200–202, 531
Biancone, 148, 197, 332, 491–92
Bian Ver, 492
Bigolona, 492
Birbet. *See* Brachettone del Roero
Blanc de Valdigne, 404
Blanchet, 492
Bombino Bianco, 142, 202–5, 511, 518
Bombino Nero, 205–7
Bonamico, 220, 492–93
Bonarda (Argentina), 20
Bonarda di Chieri. *See* Bonarda Piemontese
Bonarda del Monferrato. *See* Bonarda Piemontese
Bonarda di Rovescala. *See* Croatina
Bonarda Piemontese, 265, 493
Bonarda Pignola. *See* Croatina

Bonda, 38, 493–94
Bonvino. *See* Bombino Bianco
Boschera, 494
Bosco, 40, 207–8
Bournin. *See* Chatus
Bovale di Spagna. *See* Bovale Grande
Bovaleddu, 209. *See also* Bovale Sardo
Bovaleddu Antigu, 209
Bovaleddu Mannu, 309. *See also* Bovale Grando
Bovale Grande, 208–9, 232
Bovale Mannu. *See* Bovale Grande
Bovale Sardo, 208, 209–11, 214, 489
Bracciola Nera, 494
Brachet (Braquet), 212, 247
Brachetto, 3, 38, 116, 211–13
Brachetto a Grappolo Grosso. *See* Brachettone del Roero
Brachetto Lungo. *See* Brachettone del Roero
Brachetto Migliardi, 211, 212
Brachetto Valsusino, 212. *See* Lambrusca di Alessandria
Brachettone del Roero, 38, 213–14
Brambana, 198
Bressana, 356. See also *Schiava* entries
Briegler. *See* Bundula
Broblanc, 256, 257. *See also* Cornalin
Brugnola, 293, 356, 476, 494–95
Brunelletto, 431
Brunesta. *See* Invernenga
Brunetta, 495. *See also* Chatus
Brunetta di Rivoli, 495
Bsolla, 495
Bubbierasco, 356, 476, 495
Bundula, 495
Buriano, 34, 495–96
Burson. *See* Uva Longanesi
Bussanello, 540–41
Buzzetto. *See* Lumassina

Cabernet Franc, 8, 543, 544, 546
Cabernet Sauvignon, 5, 9, 229, 311, 330, 356, 383, 432, 546
Cabrusina, 496
Cacaboué, 186
Cacamosca, 496
Cacchione. *See* Bellone
Caddiu, 496–97
Cagnina. *See* Terrano
Cagnulari, 208, 209, 214–16
Calabrese, 28, 45, 216–19
Calabrese di Montenuovo, 249, 329, 429, 497
Calbanesco, 497
Caloria, 332
Carmenère, 543
Campolongo, 43, 497
Canaiolo Bianco, 42, 220, 497–98
Canaiolo Nero, 41, 50, 206, 219–23, 434, 492
Canaiolo Rosa, 221–22
Canena Bucci, 525
Canina Nera, 223–25, 292
Canino, 98, 498

Canino di Bertinoro, 498
Canino di Montiano, 498
Cannaiola. *See* Canaiolo Nero
Cannonao, 35, 45, 225–29
Cannonao Bianco. *See* Cannonao
Capibianchi, 429
Caprettone, 230–31, 255
Carcajola, 498
Cardìn, 498
Carenisca, 344
Cargarello, 498
Cari. *See* Pelaverga Grosso
Carica L'asino, 231–32, 448, 488
Caricagiola, 498–499
Carignano, x, 45, 208, 232–34, 367, 368, 489
Carmenère, 544
Carricante, 45, 234–36, 369
Casavecchia, 236–37, 238, 488
Cascarolo, 499
Casetta, 21, 238–39
Casentino, 431
Castagnara, 499
Castiglione, 61, 328, 336, 499–500
Catalanesca, 43, 239–40, 488
Catanese Nero, 500
Cataratto Bianco Comune, 6, 22, 111
Cataratto Bianco Lucido, 6, 22
Cataratto Bianco Extra-Lucido, 22
*Cataratto*s, 23, 28, 240–42
Cavalla. *See* Coda di Cavallo
Cavrara, 500
Cecubo, 236
Cellerina, 500–501
Cenerente, 501
Cenerina, 38, 139
Centesimino, 242–44
Cesanese, 244–46
Cesanese Comune, 42, 481. *See also* Cesanese
Cesanese D'Affile, 42, 481. *See also* Cesanese
Charbono. *See* Corbeau
Chardonnay, 2, 5, 235, 545
Chasselas, 336, 356
Chatus, 246–48, 355, 540, 541, 547, 548
Chiantino, 431
Chiapparone. *See* Montonico Bianco
Chiavennasca. *See* Nebbiolo
Chiavennasca Bianca, 501
Chiavennaschino, 362. *See also* Grignolino
Cianorie, 252–53
Ciliegiolo, 20, 172, 248–51, 274, 329, 332, 367, 429
Cimesara. *See* Simesara
Cividìn, 31, 251–52
Cocacciara. *See* Cococciola
Cococciola, 42, 203, 253–54
Coda di Cavallo, 148, 501
Coda di Pecora, 43, 254, 501
Coda Di Volpe Bianca, 43, 55, 230, 254–55, 501
Coda Di Volpe di Lapio. *See* Coda Di Volpe Bianca
Coda di Volpe Rossa, 123, 254, 481
Coglionara, 43, 201, 502
Colombana Bianca. *See* Verdea

Colombana Nera, 332, 502
Colorino Americano, 50, 52
Colorino del Valdarno, 42, 50, 51, 53, 160
Colorino di Lucca, 50, 51
Colorino di Pisa, 50, 51
*Colorino*s, 50–53, 159, 220, 306
Corbeau, 20, 267
Corbina, 39, 502–3
Corbinella, 39. *See also* Corvina
Cordenossa, 255–56
Cördusël, 503
Cor' e Palummo, 482
Corinto Bianco, 504
Corinto Nero, 45, 504, 534
Corinto Rosa, 504
Corlaga, 526
Cornacchia, 504
Cornacchia Donati. *See* Cornacchia
Cornalin, 256–58
Cornarea, 190, 541
Cornetta, 258–59
Cortese, 38, 259–62
Corvina, 34, 39, 132, 262–64, 382, 503
Corvina Doppia. *See* Corvina
Corvina Rizza. *See* Corvina
Corvino, 31, 504–5
Corvinone, 39, 262, 264–65, 382
Cove', 541
Crljenak Kastelianski. *See* Primitivo
Croà, 505, 517
Croatina, 38, 265–67, 359, 461, 541
Crova, 505
Crovarina, 505
Crovassa, 38, 505
Crovino, 505. *See also* Corbina
Cuccipannelli, 44
Curvin. *See* Corvino

Damaschino, 505–6
Denela, 506
Dindarella, 267–68
Dindarella Rizza. *See* Dindarella
Dolcetto, 58, 268–71, 356, 547, 548
Dolcetto del Peduncolo Rosso. *See* Dolcetto
Don Lunardo. *See* San Lunardo
Dorona, 272–74
Doux d'Henry, 274–75
Drupeggio. *See* Canaiolo Bianco
Duraguzza, 332
Durasa, 506
Durella, 275–76
Durello. *See* Durella
Dureza, 445
Duropersico. *See* Verdello

Elbling, 172
Empibotte. *See* Mostosa; Trebbiano Abruzzese
Enantio, 21, 38, 276–77
Erbaluce, 277–79
Erbarola, 174
Ervi, 41, 190, 541–42

Etraire, 193
Eyholtzer Rote, 186

Falanghina, 279–82
Falanghina Beneventana. *See* Falanghina
Falanghina Flegrea. *See* Falanghina
Falso Manzesu, 344
Famoso, 282–84
Famoso di Rimini/Pesaro, 284–85
Favorita, 6, 22. *See also* Vermentino
Fenile, 506–7
Fermana Bianca. *See* Montonico Bianco
Festasio, 481
Fianello. *See* Minutolo
Fiano, 37, 43, 56, 58, 285–88
Fiano Aromatico. *See* Minutolo
Flavis, 469
Fogarina, 72, 124, 288–89
Foglia Tonda, 289–91
Foja Tonda, 39, 238. *See also* Casetta
Forastera, 43, 201, 291
Forcella, 41, 169, 507
Forcellina. *See* Forselina
Forgiarin, 291–92
Forselina, 507
Fortana, 26, 224, 292–93, 495
Francavidda, 507–8
Francavilla. *See* Francavidda
Francesa Nera, 39
Frappato, 45, 180, 217, 293–94, 429
Frappelao, 41
Freisa, 295–97, 356, 476
Friularo, 124. *See* Raboso Piave
Fruhroter Veltliner, 508
Fruttana. *See* Fortana
Fubiano, 148, 542
Fumat, 40, 508
Fumin, 37, 297–300, 393
Furmint, 540, 542

Gaglioppo, 45, 176, 300–301, 328, 335, 368, 369, 429
Gaglioppo di Cosenza, 300
Galatena, 482
Galotta, 179
Galliopo, 300, 508
Galvan. *See* Neretto Duro
Gamay Perugino, 226
Gamba di Pernice. *See* Gamba Rossa
Gamba Rossa, 301–303
Garganega, 148, 169, 273, 303–6, 337, 443, 542
Garganega Grossa. *See* Dorona
Garganegona. *See* Dorona
Garofanata, 148, 508–9
Gelber Muskateller, 109. *See also* Moscato Bianco
Gewürztraminer, x, 542, 546
Giacchè, 50, 306–7
Giacomino, 492
Gianniello. *See* Casetta
Ginestra, 230, 509
Girò, 307–8, 483
Girone di Spagna, 307

Giugnettina, 180
Glera, 26, 29, 39, 198, 308–12, 546
Glera Lungo, 39, 312
Goldenmuskateller, 109. *See also* Moscato Giallo
Goldtraminer, 542
Gorgottesco, 42
Gosen, 542
Gouais Blanc, 247
Graciano, 209, 210
Gradò, 481
Granazza, 480
Grand Noir. *See* Granoir
Granè, 509
Granoir, 50, 509
Granè, 509
Grasevina, 469
Gratena, 509–10
Grauvernatsch, 137. *See also* Schiava Grigia
Grecanico Dorato. *See* Garganega
Grechetto, 312–14
Grechetto di Orvieto, 42. *See* Grechetto
Grechetto di Todi, 6, 42. *See* Pignoletto
Grechetto Rosso, 6. *See* Sangiovese
Greco, 43, 54–58, 255
Greco Bianco, 55, 58–59
Greco Bianco del Pollino, 58. *See also* Montonico Bianco
Greco Bianco di Cirò, 58. *See also* Guardavalle
Greco Bianco di Cosenza, 58. *See also* Pecorello Bianco
Greco Bianco di Donnici, 58. *See also* Guardavalle
Greco Bianco di Lamezia Terme, 58. *See also* Guardavalle
Greco Bianco di Rogliano, 58. *See also* Pecorello Bianco
Greco del Pollino, 303. *See also* Montonico Bianco
Greco di Caluso. *See* Erbaluce
Greco di Gerace, 58. *See also* Greco Bianco
Greco Giallo, 59–60, 143, 144
Greco Giallo di Velletri. *See* Trebbiano Giallo
Greco Moro, 60–61
Greco Nero, 61–63
Greco Nero di Cirò. *See* Greco Nero
Greco Nero di Lamezia Terme. *See* Magliocco
Greco Nero di Sibari, 61–62
Greco Nero di Scilla, 61. *See also* Castiglione
Greco Nero di Verbicaro, 61–62
Grecos, 53–54
Greghetto Rosso. *See* Sangiovese
Gregu Nieddu, 384
Grenache, x, 46, 150, 151, 155, 226
Grero, 62, 510
Grignolino, 188, 314–17
Grillo, 28, 36, 45, 180, 317–20
Grisa Nera, 510
Grisa Rousa, 510
Groppello dei Berici, 65
Groppello di Breganze, 65. *See* Pignola
Groppello di Mocasina, 65–66
Groppello di Revò, 66
Groppello Gentile, 66–67
Groppello Molinèr. *See* Groppello di Mocasina
Groppellos, 63–67
Gruaja, 121, 510

Grüner Veltliner, 66
Guardavalle, 320
Guarnaccia Nera, 328
Guarnaccino, 511

Harslevelu, 541
Hibou Rouge, 186
Hibou Noir, 186
Humagne Rouge, 257

Imbrunesta. *See* Invernenga
Impigno, 28, 202, 511
Incrocio 107-A. *See* Rebo
Incrocio Bianco Fedit, 51, 82, 542
Incrocio Bruni 54, 543
Incrocio Dalmasso 2/26 (Vega), 88
Incrocio Dalmasso IV/31. *See* Soperga
Incrocio Dalmasso XV/29. *See* Nebbiera
Incrocio Dalmasso 7/21. *See* San Martino
Incrocio Dalmasso 15/34. *See* San Michele
Incrocio Dalmasso 16/8. *See* Valentino Nero
Incrocio Dalmasso 17/25. *See* Passau
Incrocio Manzoni 2.14, 546
Incrocio Manzoni 2.15, 311. *See also* Manzoni Rosso
Incrocio Manzoni 6.0.13. *See* Manzoni Bianco
Incrocio Manzoni 13.0.25. *See* Manzoni Moscato
Incrocio Rigotti 84-11. *See* Goldtraminer
Incrocio Rigotti 107-2. *See* Sennen
Incrocio Rigotti 123-4. *See* Gosen
Incrocio Terzi 1, 190, 544
Invernenga, 320-21
Inzolia, 45, 180, 319. *See also* Ansonica
Inzolia Imperiale. *See* Ansonica
Inzolia Nera, 180
Italica, 469
Iuvarello. *See* Bianco d'Alessano

Janese, 511

Kerner, 539

Lacconargeddu, 441
Lacconargiu. *See* Albarenzeuli Bianco
Lacconarzu. *See* Albarenzeuli Bianco
Lacrima, 176, 321-23, 543
Lacrima del Valdarno, 511
Lagarino, 512
Lagrein, 131, 132, 323-25, 338
Lagrein Bianco, 324
Lambrusca di Alessandria, 95, 512
Lambrusca di Vittona, 512-513
Lambruschetta, 513
Lambruschetto, 448
Lambruschino. *See* Lambrusco Salamino
Lambruschino di Cavria, 481
Lambrusco a Foglia Frastagliata. *See* Enantio
Lambrusco a Foglia Tonda. *See* Casetta
Lambrusco Barghi, 74
Lambrusco Benetti, 75
Lambrusco dei Vivi. *See* Perla dei Vivi
Lambrusco di Corbelli, 74

Lambrusco di Fiorano, 74
Lambrusco di Rivalta, 74
Lambrusco di Sorbara, 68-69
Lambrusco Galassi. *See* Lambrusco Salamino
Lambrusco Gonzaga, 75
Lambrusco Grasparossa, 68, 69-70
Lambrusco Maestri, 70-71, 72, 224, 292
Lambrusco Marani, 71-72, 289
Lambrusco Montericco, 75, 536
Lambrusco Nobel, 75
Lambrusco Oliva, 75
Lambrusco Pjcol Ross, 75. *See also* Terrano
*Lambrusco*s, 29, 67-68
Lambrusco Salamino, 72-73
Lambrusco Viadanese, 73-74
Lancellotta, 179. *See also* Ancellotta
Lanzesa, 325-26
Lecinara, 43, 513
Lexia, 113
Liatika, 176
Livella di Battipaglia. *See* Sciascinoso
Livella di Mirabella, 379
Livella d'Ischia, 379, 450
Livornese Bianca, 513
Lugliatica Bianca, 404
Lumassina, 326-27

Maceratino, 42, 327, 466
Madea. *See* Bosco
Magliocco, 61, 328-29
Magliocco Canino, 328, 329-30
Magliocco Dolce. *See* Magliocco
Magliocco Ovale. *See* Magliocco Canino
*Magliocco*s, 45, 336
Magliocco Tondo. *See* Magliocco
Maiolica, 513
Maiolo. *See* Negretto
Malagouzia, 318
Malbec, 220, 264, 330-32
Malbo Gentile, 224
Maligia, 513-14
Malvasia Bianca, 78-79
Malvasia Bianca di Basilicata, 31-32, 79-80
Malvasia Bianca di Candia, 81-82, 236
Malvasia Bianca Lunga, 82-83, 88, 148, 203, 311, 542
Malvasia del Lazio, 31, 83-85, 96, 111
Malvasia di Arezzo. *See* Malvasia Bianca di Candia
Malvasia di Brolo. *See* Malvasia Bianca di Candia
Malvasia di Candia Aromatica, 81, 85-86, 92, 284
Malvasia di Casorzo, 81, 95-96, 116
Malvasia di Lipari, 44, 49, 86-88
Malvasia di Manresa. *See* Garganega
Malvasia di San Nicandro. *See* Malvasia Bianca di Candia
Malvasia di Sardegna, 59. *See* Malvasia di Lipari
Malvasia di Schierano, 95, 96-97, 99, 100
Malvasia Istriana, 88-91
Malvasia Montanaccio, 332
Malvasia Moscata, 78, 91-92
Malvasia Nera di Basilicata, 97

Malvasia Nera di Brindisi, 82, 88, 93–94, 97–99, 434, 443
Malvasia Nera Di Lecce, 93–94, 98, 99
Malvasia Nera Lunga, 99–100
Malvasia Puntinata. *See* Malvasia del Lazio
Malvasia Rosa, 41, 92, 96
Malvasia Rossa. *See* Malvasia Bianca di Candia
Malvasias, 18, 29, 76–78, 93–95, 204
Malvasier, 100
Mammolo, 332–34, 371, 466
Mammolone di Lucca. *See* Mammolo
Mangiaguerra, 450, 532
Mantonico Bianco, 334–36, 350, 369
Mantonico Bianco Italico, 58. *See* Montonico Bianco
*Mantonico Nero*s, 335
Mantonico Nero Italico. *See* Greco Nero di Verbicaro
Mantonico Pizzutella. *See* Mantonico Bianco
Mantonico Russeda, 335
Mantonico Viru. *See* Mantonico Bianco
Manzesu, 344
Manzoni Bianco, 539, 544–45
Manzoni Moscato, 124, 546
Manzoni Rosa, 148, 546
Manzoni Rosso, 545–46
Maranela, 238
Marchione, 44, 335, 514
Marcigliana. *See* Marsigliana Nera
Maresco, 514
Maricchione, 44
Marsigliana Nera, 28, 43, 328, 336–37
Maruggio. *See* Maresco
Marzabino, 514
Marzemina Bianca, 127, 337–38
Marzemina Nera, 514–15
Marzemina Nera Bastarda, 515
Marzemina Nera Grossa, 515
Marzemino, 38, 131, 172, 225, 263, 337, 338–40, 490, 543, 548
Marzemino Bianco, 339
Marzemino Gentile Comune. *See* Marzemino
Massaretta. *See* Barsaglina
Mataossu. *See* Lumassina
Maturano, 515
Mayolet, 38, 258, 340–41, 393
Mazuelo, 46, 208
Mazzese, 249, 516
Medrulinu, 344
Melara, 41, 516
Merla. *See* Canaiolo Nero
Merlese, 546–47
Merlina, 516
Merlot, 5, 9, 229, 236, 382, 432, 547, 548
Minnella Bianca, 234, 516–17
Minutolo, 200, 286, 341–42
Molinara, 39, 265, 342–44, 382
Molinara Ciara. *See* Molinara
Molinelli, 517
Monastrell, 210
Mondeuse Noire, 20, 131
Monica, 211, 344–45
Monica Bianca (di Campidano), 344

Monica Bianca (di Marmilla), 344
Monica (di Mandrolisai), 345. *See* Nieddu Mannu
Montanara, 496, 498
Montanera. *See* Montanera di Perosa
Montanera di Perosa, 517
Montepulciano, 345–49
Montonico Bianco, 42, 43, 349–50
Montonico Ciarchiarisi. *See* Montonico Pinto
Montonico Pinto, 517
Montu', 350–51
Montuni. *See* Montu'
Moradella, 266, 517–18
Morellino del Valdarno. *See* Negrodolce
Morellino Pizzuto, 300, 430
Morina. *See* Negretto
Morone, 50, 518
Moscatella, 91, 99. *See* Malvasia Moscata
Moscatello Selvatico, 119–20
Moscato Bianco, 91, 102–9
Moscato d'Amburgo, 84, 116, 546
Moscato di Alessandria, 84, 97, 101. *See also* Zibibbo
Moscato di Barletta. *See* Moscatello Selvatico
Moscato di Novoli. *See* Moscatello Selvatico
Moscato di Scanzo, 99, 102, 109, 113–15, 116
Moscato di Terracina, 42, 99
Moscato Fior d'Arancio, 110
Moscato Giallo, 102, 109–10
Moscato Nero, 99, 212
Moscato Nero di Acqui, 114, 115–17
Moscato Rosa, 39, 103, 117–18
Moscato Rosso di Madera. *See* Moscato Violetto
*Moscato*s, 18, 100–102
Moscato Violetto, 102, 109, 249, 332, 429
Mostarino, 518
Mostosa, 202, 518
Müller-Thurgau, 539
Muristellu, 209, 489. *See also* Bovale Sardo
Muscat à Petit Grains. *See* Moscato Bianco
Muscat Canelli. *See* Moscato Bianco
Muscat of Alexandria. *See* Zibibbo
Muscat Rouge de Madère. *See* Moscato Violetto

Nascetta, 351–52
Nasco, 46, 352–53
Nebbiera, 547
Nebbiolo, 3, 9, 22, 165, 353–61, 400, 494, 495
Nebbiolo di Dronero. *See* Chatus
Nebbiolo di Gattinara. *See* Croatina
Nebbiolo Pairolé. *See* Chatus
Nebbiolo Rosé, 355, 356, 357, 361–63, 476
Negraras, 120
Negrara Trentina, 121, 519
Negrara Veronese, 121–22
Negrat, 518–19
Negratino, 519
Negrera, 356
Negrettino. *See* Negretto
Negretto, 363–64
Negro Amaro, 44, 206, 364–66, 443, 519
Negro Amaro Precoce, 519
Negrodolce, 249

Negrone, 519
Nera dei Baisi, 519–20
Ner d'Ala, 38, 486, 520, 546
Nerello Cappuccio, 45, 366–69
Nerello Mantellato, 367
Nerello Mascalese, 45, 180, 335, 369–70, 429
Nereto, 520
Neretta Cuneese, 186, 247, 520–21
Neretto di Bairo, 38, 371, 476
Neretto di Marengo, 95, 521
Neretto di Salto, 371
Neretto di San Giorgio, 356. *See also* Neretto di Bairo
Neretto Duro, 371, 521
Neretto Gentile, 371
Neretto Nostrano, 371
Nero Buono, 371–73
Nero D'Avola. *See* Calabrese
Neyret, 521
Nibieu. *See* Dolcetto
Nibiò. *See* Dolcetto
Niedda Perda Sarda. *See* Caddiu
Nieddera, 373–74, 521
Nieddu Mannu, 344, 373, 384, 521–22
Nieddu Procco, 498
Nigra, 190, 547
Nocera, 45, 374–75
Nosiola, 38, 375–77
Notardomenico, 522
Nuragus, 46, 377–78

Occhio di Gatto, 40
Occhio di Pernice, 522
Occhiorosso, 522
Olivella Nera, 43, 378–79
Optima, 539
Orious. *See* Petit Rouge
Ormeasco. *See* Dolcetto
Orpicchio, 522
Ortega, 539
Ortrugo, 26, 356, 380–81
Orzese. *See* Mazzese
Oseleta, 26, 29, 122, 267, 381–83
Ottavianello, 44
Ottonese. *See* Bombino Bianco

Pacioccone, 195
Pagadebit, 202, 518. *See* Mostosa
Pallagrello Bianco, 254
Pallagrello Nero, 122, 236, 254
Pallagrellos, 122
Palomba, 256. *See* Piedirosso
Palumbo, 44
Pampanaro, 43, 523
Pampanuto, 44, 383–84, 463
Pansale. *See* Monica Bianca (di Campidano), 344
Panse Rosa di Malaga, 483
Paolina, 523
Paradisa, 523
Parporio, 523
Parraleta, 498
Pascale, 229, 373, 384–85, 521

Passau, 547
Passerina, 42, 142, 385–87, 519
Pattaresca, 523–24
Pavana, 198, 524
Pecorello, 524
Pecorello Bianco, 387–88
Pecorino, 42, 388–90
Pedevenda, 524
Peilavert, 390
Pelagòs, 524–25
Pelara. *See* Dindarella
Pelaverga Grosso, 390–91
Pelaverga Piccolo, 391–92
Pepella, 525
Per e Palummo. *See* Piedirosso
Perera, 525
Pergola. *See* Invernenga
Perla dei Vivi, 525
Perricone, 45, 329, 392–93, 429
Persan. *See* Becuet
Petite Blanche, 201
Petit Rouge, 38, 257, 258, 393–94
Petit Verdot, 50
Peverella, 525
Piccabon, 40. *See* Vernaccia di San Gimignano
Picolit, 29, 40, 394–97, 530
Picotener. *See* Nebbiolo
Piculit Neri, 130, 397–98
Piedirosso, 43, 165, 230, 236, 398–400, 532
Pier Domenico, 44
Pigato, 6, 22. *See* Vermentino
Pignatello. *See* Perricone
Pignola, 38, 356, 400–401
Pignola Spano. *See* Pignola
Pignoletto, 20, 401–2
Pignolo, 402–3
Pinella, 403–4
Pinello. *See* Pinella
Pink Muscat, 118
Pinot Bianco, 22, 545
Pinot Grigio, 5, 22, 77
Pinot Nero, 22, 172
Pinot Noir, ix
Plassa, 525–26
Plavina, 464
Pollera Nera, 332, 526
Pomella, 39, 526
Poverina, 429
Prëmetta. *See* Prie' Rouge
Preverail, 526–27
Prie', 37, 393, 404–5
Prie' Rouge, 38, 404, 405–7, 493
Primaticcio, 526
Primintia, 180
Primitivo, 165, 407–10, 463
Procanico, 42
Prodest, 190
Prosecco. *See* Glera
Prosecco Tondo. *See* Glera
Prugnolino Acerbo, 431
Prugnolino Dolce, 431

Prugnolino Medio, 431
Prugnolo, 6. *See also* Sangiovese
Prunent. *See* Nebbiolo
Prunesta, 527
Pugnet. *See* Nebbiolo
Pugnitello, 410–12
Pulcinculo, 401. *See also* Pignoletto

Quagliano, 412, 511
Quaiara, 527

Rabbiosa. *See* Durella
Raboso Friularo, 124. *See also* Raboso Veronese
Raboso Piave, 124–27, 289, 546
*Raboso*s, 124
Raboso Veronese, 127–28, 337
Rambella. *See* Famoso
Raspo Rosso, 520, 527
Raverusto. *See* Abrusco
Rebo, 547–48
Rèbola. *See* Pignoletto
Recantina, 527
Red Hanepoot. *See* Zibibbo
Refoschin. *See* Refosco del Peduncolo Rosso
Refosco Bianco, 130, 131
Refosco del Boton. *See* Tazzelenghe
Refosco del Peduncolo Rosso, 20, 131–33, 263, 338, 398
Refosco di Faedis. *See* Refosco Nostrano
Refosco di Rauscedo. *See* Refosco Gentile
Refosco di Ronchis. *See* Refosco Nostrano
Refosco Gentile, 133, 256, 397
Refosco Guarneri. *See* Trevisana Nera
Refoscone, 130, 133–34
Refosco Nostrano, 20, 130, 131, 134–36, 398
*Refosco*s, 20, 29, 129–31
Retagliado Bianco, 527–28
Ribolla Gialla, 36, 413–15, 483
Ribolla Piccola. *See* Vernaccina
Ribona, 327
Riesling, 8, 235, 447, 545
Riesling Italico, 540
Riminese, 498
Riminèse, 169
Riminese di San Rocco, 169, 498
Riminese Nero. *See* Ciliegiolo
Rinaldesca. *See* Mazzese
Ripoli, 528
Rizzulo, 383
Rolle, 40, 77
Rollo, 40, 528
Rondinella, 39, 132, 264, 382, 528
Roscetto, 144. *See* Rosseto
Rosciola, 529
Rosenmuskateller. *See* Moscato Rosa
Rossara, 415
Rossese, 416–18
Rossese Bianco, 40, 319, 419
Rossese Bianco (di Arcola). *See* Rossese Bianco
Rossese Bianco (di Monforte). *See* Rossese Bianco
Rossese Bianco (di San Biagio), 419

Rossese Bianco (di San Biagio della Cima e Soldano). *See* Rossese Bianco (di San Biagio)
Rossese Bianco (di Sinio e Roddino), 419
Rossese di Campochiesa. *See* Rossese
Rossese di Dolceacqua. *See* Rossese
Rossetta di Montagna, 267, 529
Rossetto, 143, 144, 419–20. *See also* Trebbiano Giallo
Rossignola, 529–30
Rossola Nera, 38, 356, 476, 530
Rossolino Nero, 356
Rothervernatsch. *See* Schiava Gentile
Rouge du Pays 257, 393, 521
Rouge du Valais, 257, 393, 521
Roussette d'Ayze, 492
Roussin, 530
Roussin de Morgex, 32, 420–21
Roviello, 421–22
Ruche', 422–23
Ruggine, 283, 423–24
Ruzzese. *See* Rossese Bianco

Sagrantino, 42, 424–26
Sagrestana, 40, 530
San Colombana. *See* Verdea
San Colombano. *See* Colombana Nera
Sanforte, 426
Sanginella Bianca, 531
Sangiovese, 3, 9–10, 176, 222, 223, 248, 249, 267, 289, 329, 367, 368, 369, 426–35, 504, 547
Sangiovese di Lamole. *See* Sangiovese
Sangiovese Forte. *See* Sanforte
Sangiovese Polveroso. *See* Ciliegiolo
Sangiovese Polveroso Bonechi, 431. *See also* Ciliegiolo
Sangiovese Veruccese. *See* Verucchiese
Sangiovese Verucchiese. *See* Verucchiese
Sangioveto. *See* Sangiovese
San Lunardo, 43, 201, 531
San Martino, 548
San Michele, 190, 548
Sannese, 499
San Nicola. *See* Biancolella
San Pietro, 531
Santa Maria, 41
Sant'Antonio, 531
Santa Sofia, 286
Sanvicetro, 430
Sauvignon Blanc, 537, 543, 546
Savignôn Rosso. *See* Centesimino
Scarsafoglia, 532
Schiava Gentile, 138
Schiava Grigia, 138–39
Schiava Grossa, 84, 139–40
Schiava Lombarda. *See* Schiava Nera
Schiava Nera, 140
*Schiava*s, 38, 39, 136–38
Schioppettino, 36, 66, 436–39
Sciaccarello. *See* Mammolo
Sciaglin, 439
Sciampagna. *See* Marzemina Bianca
Sciascinoso, 43, 378, 379, 439–40
Scimiscia', 40, 41, 440–41

Scroccona, 532
Semidano, 46, 377, 441
Sennen, 548
Serbina, 481
Sérénèze, 247
Serpentara, 532
Sérénèze, 247
Serprina. See Glera
Seyval Blanc, 539
Sgavetta, 532
Simesara, 533
Siora, 40
Sirica, 533
Smarzirola, 492
Somarello Rosso, 44, 481
Soperga, 190, 548
Spanna. See Nebbiolo
Spanna di Ghemme. See Croatina
Spergola, 442
Spigamonte, 480
Streppa Rossa. See Piedirosso
Streppa Verde, 399
Summariello. See Uva di Troia
Suppezza, 533
Susumaniello, 304, 442–44
Sylvaner, 539
Syrah, 445

Tai. See Cannonau
Tamiarello, 44
Tamurro Nero, 533
Tazzelenghe, 33, 444–45
Tempranillo, 93, 97
Tendòla, 43
Teneddu. See Biancolella
Tenerone, 42
Termarina Nera, 504, 533
Teroldego, 38, 131, 445–46, 543, 548
Terrano, 446–47
Theilly, 534
Tibouren, 416
Timorasso, 38, 447–49
Tintilia, 43, 449–50
Tintore Di Tramonti, 450–51
Tintoretto, 221
Tocai Friulano, 451–52
Tocai Rosso, 35. See Cannonau
Torbato, 452–53
Trebbianella. See Trebbiano Modenese
Trebbianina, 141–42, 144
Trebbiano Abruzzese, 140, 142–43, 202
Trebbiano Comune. See Trebbiano Modenese
Trebbiano della Fiamma. See Trebbiano Romagnolo
Trebbiano di Lugana. See Verdicchio
Trebbiano di Modena. See Trebbiano Modenese
Trebbiano di Soave. See Verdicchio
Trebbiano di Spagna, 144. See Trebbianina
Trebbiano Giallo, 60, 141, 143–45, 386
Trebbiano Giallo di Velletri. See Trebbiano Giallo
Trebbiano Modenese, 145–46
Trebbiano Romagnolo, 146–47

*Trebbiano*s, 140–41
Trebbiano Spoletino, 140, 147–48, 424
Trebbiano Toscano, 6, 83, 143, 148–50, 196, 197, 203, 386, 491, 495, 509, 542, 546
Trebbiano Valtenesi. See Verdicchio
Trebbiano Verde. See Trebbiano Toscano
Trevisana Nera, 534
Tribidrag. See Primitivo
Trollinger. See *Schiava*s
Tronto, 20, 534–35
Trousseau, 214
Tuccanese, 504. See also Sangiovese
Turbiana. See Verdicchio
Turca, 453–54
Turchetta, 535

Ucelut, 40, 454–55
Ugni Blanc. See Trebbiano Toscano
Urban. See *Schiava*s
Uva Attina, 44
Uva del Fantini, 41, 364, 535
Uva della Cascina, 535
Uva della Scala, 44. See also Montonico Bianco
Uva del Tundè, 455–56
Uva di Troia, 44, 456–59, 488
Uva d'Oro. See Fortana
Uva Fogarina, 289
Uvalino, 459–60
Uva Longanesi, 460–61
Uva Micella, 43
Uva Molle, 43
Uva Pane. See Bellone
Uva Rambella. See Famoso
Uva Rara, 38, 265, 359, 461–62
Uva Rilla, 485
Uva Serpe. See Serpentara
Uva Sogra, 304, 443
Uva Tosca, 498, 535, 536

Valentino Nero, 548
Varano Bianco, 536
Varano Rosa, 536
Vartzami. See Marzemino
Verdea, 462–63, 485
Verdealbara, 536
Verdeca, 43, 199, 200, 463–64
Verdello, 21, 42, 464–65, 536
Verdesse, 492
Verdetto, 536. See also Verdello
Verdicchio, 286, 465–68, 494, 536, 543
Verdiso, 311, 468–69
Verduna. See Barbarossa
Verdurino. See Bianco d'Alessano
Verduschia, 464, 536–37
Verduzzo Friulano, 40, 469–71, 530
Verduzzo Giallo. See Verduzzo Friulano
Verduzzo Trevigiano, 471
Verduzzo Verde. See Verduzzo Friulano
Vermentino, 6, 22, 207, 471–74
Vermentino Nero, 474–75
Vermiglia, 371

INDEX OF GRAPE VARIETIES 619

Vernaccia di Oristano, 46, 151–53, 485
Vernaccia di Pergola. *See* Aleatico
Vernaccia di San Gimignano, 41, 153–55
Vernaccia di Teramo. *See* Vernaccia Nera
Vernaccia Nera, 42, 155–56
Vernaccia Nera Grossa, 156
Vernaccia Nera Grossa Cerretana. *See* Vernaccia Nera Grossa
Vernaccia Rossa. *See* Aleatico
*Vernaccia*s, 49, 150–51
Vernaccia Selvatica. *See* Vernaccia Nera
Vernaccia Trentina. *See* Bianchetta Trevigiana
Vernaccina, 151, 156–57, 169
Vernaccina Riminese, 157
Vernassina. *See* Bianchetta Trevigiana
Vernatsch, 137
Verrucchiese, 537
Vertura, 61, 384

Vespaiola, 475
Vesparola. *See* Vespaiola
Vespolina, 66, 356, 359, 462, 475–77
Vidal, 148, 539
Vien de Nus, 38, 393, 537
Vitovska, 82, 311, 477–78
Volpola, 41, 537
Vuillermin, 38, 298, 393, 478

Welshriesling, 540
Wildbacher, 478–79

Zanello, 537
Zibibbo, 84, 97, 101, 109, 111–13
Zinfandel, 37
Zirone. *See* Girò
Zirone Alzu, 483
Zirone Bianco. *See* Albarenzeuli Bianco

TEXT:	9.5/13 Scala
DISPLAY:	Scala and Scala Sans
COMPOSITOR:	IDS Infotech, Ltd.
CARTOGRAPHER:	Bill Nelson
PRINTER AND BINDER:	Maple Press